Adapted Physical Education and Sport

SEVENTH EDITION

Joseph P. Winnick, EdD
The College at Brockport, State University of New York

David L. Porretta, PhD
The Ohio State University

EDITORS

HUMAN KINETICS

Library of Congress Cataloging-in-Publication Data

Names: Winnick, Joseph P., editor. | Porretta, David L., editor.
Title: Adapted physical education and sport / Joseph P. Winnick, David L. Porretta, editors.
Description: Seventh edition. | Champaign, IL : Human Kinetics, Inc., 2022. | Includes bibliographical references and index.
Identifiers: LCCN 2021010220 (print) | LCCN 2021010221 (ebook) | ISBN 9781492598022 (paperback) | ISBN 9781492598039 (epub) | ISBN 9781492598046 (pdf)
Subjects: LCSH: Physical education for people with disabilities. | Sports for people with disabilities.
Classification: LCC GV445 .A3 2017 (print) | LCC GV445 (ebook) | DDC 371.9/04486--dc23
LC record available at https://lccn.loc.gov/2021010220
LC ebook record available at https://lccn.loc.gov/2021010221

ISBN: 978-1-4925-9802-2 (paperback)
ISBN: 978-1-7182-1111-7 (loose-leaf)

Acquisitions Editor: Scott Wikgren; **Managing Editor:** Anne E. Mrozek; **Copyeditor:** Heather Gauen Hutches; **Proofreader:** Pamela Johnson; **Indexer:** Dan Connolly; **Permissions Manager:** Dalene Reeder; **Graphic Designer:** Denise Lowry; **Cover Designer:** Keri Evans; **Cover Design Specialist:** Susan Rothermel Allen; **Photograph (cover):** Image courtesy of University of Wisconsin - La Crosse; **Photographs (interior):** © Human Kinetics, unless otherwise noted; **Photo Asset Manager:** Laura Fitch; **Photo Production Manager:** Jason Allen; **Senior Art Manager:** Kelly Hendren; **Illustrations:** © Human Kinetics, unless otherwise noted; **Printer:** Walsworth

Printed in the United States of America 10 9 8 7 6 5 4 3 2

The paper in this book was manufactured using responsible forestry methods.

Human Kinetics
1607 N. Market Street
Champaign, IL 61820
USA

United States and International
Website: **US.HumanKinetics.com**
Email: info@hkusa.com
Phone: 1-800-747-4457

Canada
Website: **Canada.HumanKinetics.com**
Email: info@hkcanada.com

E8064 (paperback) / E8497 (loose-leaf)

Tell us what you think!
Human Kinetics would love to hear what we can do to improve the customer experience. Use this QR code to take our brief survey.

Joseph P. Winnick, coeditor of this textbook, passed away on July 9, 2019, at the age of 83. This edition is dedicated to Dr. Winnick's lifetime of service to adapted physical education. His advocacy, leadership, and passion made an enormous positive impact on the lives of millions of individuals with disabilities worldwide, and he was an inspiration to all the adapted physical educators who have followed in his footsteps. His lengthy and distinguished record of scholarship, teaching, and service is summarized in the About the Editors section of this book. In this dedication, we would like to highlight his passion, his caring, his support of colleagues, his dedication, and his sense of humor. It is our hope that this textbook can inspire future professionals to continue advancing Joe's work of enhancing the lives of individuals with disabilities through physical activity. He will be missed, but his spirit will carry on.

Contents

Preface

It is with a great deal of satisfaction and confidence that the preface for the seventh edition of *Adapted Physical Education and Sport* is being written. A primary goal since the first edition has been to prepare a book that would benefit individuals with unique physical education and sport needs by providing clear and concise information for the teachers, coaches, and other professionals who work with them. In this seventh edition, the book has been conceptualized, developed, and updated to meet today's trends and practices in adapted physical education and sport.

This book is comprehensive, relevant, and user friendly. It is designed to be both a text and a resource. As a text, this book can be used to prepare students majoring in physical education, coaching, recreation, special education, and related disciplines. As a resource, this book aids teachers, coaches, administrators, and other professionals as they plan and provide services. Although the book can serve many purposes, its primary emphasis is on providing quality services to people with unique physical education needs, differences, and abilities.

This preface identifies and explains major influences on the content and organization of the book, briefly summarizes new and continuing features, provides an overview of the parts of the book, and closes with some comments about the value of adapted physical education and sport in the lives of young people today.

Legislation: A Major Influence on This Book

This book helps schools and agencies to develop and implement physical education and sport programs consistent with federal legislation for students with disabilities, as well as for students with other unique needs. This book is influenced by two landmark laws: Section 504 of the Rehabilitation Act (originally passed in 1973 as PL 93-112), and the original and current versions of the Individuals with Disabilities Education Act (originally signed in 1975 as PL 94-142, the Education for All Handicapped Children Act and updated as the Individuals with Disabilities Education Improvement Act of 2004 [IDEIA]). The current version of the law continues to be commonly referred to as IDEA, including in this seventh edition.

One of the major purposes of IDEA is to ensure that all children with disabilities receive a free and appropriate public education that emphasizes special education and related services to meet their unique needs. IDEA makes it clear that this education includes physical education, which in turn may be specified as adapted physical education. Regulations associated with IDEA define physical education as the development of physical and motor fitness; fundamental motor skills and patterns; and skills in aquatics, dance, and individual and group games and sports (including intramural and lifetime sports). In this book, adapted physical education is defined in a manner consistent with key provisions of the IDEA definition and reflects the scope of physical education for this book. The identification of unique needs, which is part of the IDEA definition of special education, is also emphasized. Numerous ways of adapting physical education to meet individual needs are presented. One of the cornerstones of IDEA is the requirement of individualized education programs designed to meet the unique needs of children. Detailed information is presented about components and strategies for developing individualized education programs (IEPs) and 504 plans in chapter 5, and for individualized family service plans (IFSPs) in chapter 21.

Information related to physical education is presented in this book relative to each of the specific disabilities identified and defined by IDEA for children aged 3 to 21. Because IDEA also defines infants and toddlers (birth to age 2) with disabilities, a chapter on physical education services for this population is presented.

Both IDEA and Section 504 require that education be provided in the most inclusive setting possible. In regard to physical education, this book encourages education in inclusive environments to the extent appropriate and prepares readers for working in these environments, with extensive discussions about inclusion in a number of chapters. Although education in the least restrictive environment is the law of the land, the book also prepares readers to provide services in other settings. In regard to sport, this book provides an orientation to sport that enables and encourages participation in a variety of settings and responds to the requirement of equal opportunity for participation in extracurricular experiences.

This book responds to legislative requirements in many ways. These include compatibility with the definition of special education, the requirement for identification of unique educational needs within the context of a broad program of physical education, the requirement for individualized education programs, education in the least restrictive setting possible, and equal opportunity for curricular and extracurricular experiences. Because of the book's orientation, educators can be confident that they are implementing programs that respond to educational needs.

New Features in This Edition

Since the first edition, many changes affecting adapted physical education and sport have occurred, most notably the inclusion movement and universal design for learning (UDL), which promote successful learning experiences for all children, regardless of ability. All chapters in this edition have been updated or revised to incorporate these changes. Coverage of UDL begins in chapter 2 and is addressed more fully in chapter 7, with strategies and applications provided throughout the remainder of the seventh edition, as appropriate.

Although changes occur in many areas of the field, the changes and advances in adapted sport are particularly noteworthy. Advances in school and interscholastic programs, sport organizations, national governing bodies, and international opportunities are significant. Chapter 3 on adapted sport has been further developed and refined to reflect on progress in the field. The chapter continues to be guided by a unique and contemporary orientation to sport adapted for persons with unique needs. It presents and employs a sport framework for individuals with disabilities as a model for the development and implementation of sport programs. With more persons with disabilities participating in adapted sports, enhanced coverage of sport-specific injuries and prevention is presented in chapter 18. A new chapter devoted entirely to adventure sports and activities has also been developed for the seventh edition to reflect the growing popularity among individuals with disabilities.

This seventh edition includes continuing chapters written by authors new to the book: G. Monique Mokha (chapter 18, Activity and Sports Injuries, Longer-Term Disabilities, and Obesity), Stamatis Agiovlasitis (chapter 23, Health-Related Physical Fitness and Physical Activity), David Lorenzi (chapter 24, Aquatics), and Amaury Samalot-Rivera (chapter 25, Team Sports). In addition, several new coauthors joined returning authors to bring their own unique perspectives to the book. Justin Haegele coauthored two chapters with returning author David Porretta: chapter 14, Cerebral Palsy, Traumatic Brain Injury, and Stroke; and chapter 15, Amputations, Dwarfism, and Les Autres. Brock McMullen collaborated with returning author Manny Felix on chapter 4, Measurement, Assessment, and Program Evaluation, as well as chapter 5, Individualized Education Programs. Linda Hilgenbrinck collaborated with returning author Lauren Cavanaugh on chapter 8, Intellectual Disabilities. Lindsay Ball collaborated with returning author Lauren Lieberman on chapter 12, Visual Impairments. Melissa Bittner partnered with returning author Barry Lavay for chapter 11, Specific Learning Disabilities, and chapter 20, Perceptual–Motor Development. Wesley Wilson partnered with returning author Luke Kelly for chapter 16, Spinal Cord Disabilities and Other Spinal Conditions, as well as chapter 28, Winter Sports and Activities. Byungmo Ku joined returning authors John Ozmun and David Gallahue for chapter 19, Motor Development. Finally, co-editors David Porretta and Joseph Winnick have co-authored chapter 1, Introduction to Adapted Physical Education and Sport, and chapter 2, Program Organization and Management, for the seventh edition. Sue Sutherland has authored an all-new chapter 27, Adventure Sports and Activities, for this edition.

Continuing Features

In this and previous editions, many of the chapters focus on physical education and sport rather than solely on disabilities. Relevant information regarding disabilities is presented so that implications for physical education and sport may be understood. Also, considerable attention continues to be given in several chapters to the revised edition of the Brockport Physical Fitness Test. This health-related, criterion-referenced test of physical fitness, applicable for many youngsters with disabilities, has been adopted by the Presidential Youth Fitness Program.

The seventh edition retains a focus on physical education for people from birth to age 21. No attempt has been made to address the entire age span of people with disabilities, although much information in the book is relevant to older individuals. Although this book focuses on the areas of physical education and sport, it also includes information relevant to allied areas such as recreation and therapeutic recreation. Chapter 27 on adventure sports and activities is one example.

Another feature that has been continued in this edition is a list of print, video, and online resources at the end of each chapter, as well as in the instructor guide. These resources should guide both students and instructors to useful further reading and research.

This seventh edition continues two elements that enhance readers' understanding: The opening vignettes present scenarios that introduce one or more chapter concepts, and Application Example sidebars within chapters provide the opportunity to explore real-life situations and show how the text concepts can be applied to situations to solve the relevant issues.

Ancillary materials have again been developed to accompany this edition. An instructor guide provides objectives, suggestions for learning and enrichment activities (such as thought-provoking discussion and problem-solving questions), and, where relevant, suggested resources for further reading. Because it is so important for college students to be aware of people with disabilities and to teach and interact with them in a positive manner, the instructor guide includes additional ideas to provide these opportunities, as well as ideas for an introductory course related to adapted physical education and sport, as well as a sample course syllabus. Ancillary materials include a presentation package of PowerPoint slides, chapter quizzes, and an electronic bank of test questions that can be used to develop quizzes, exams, or study questions. A web resource for students, now in HK*Propel*, continues to be included with this edition. It includes assignable enrichment activities, selected forms from the book, and access to video clips of adapted physical educators and students demonstrating 26 of the fitness test items from *The Brockport Physical Fitness Test Manual*. See the card at the front of the print book for your unique HK*Propel* access code. For ebook users, reference the HK*Propel* access code instructions on the page immediately following the book cover.

Finally, the seventh edition of the book continues with the coeditorship of Joseph P. Winnick and David L. Porretta.

Parts of the Book

The book is divided into four parts. Part I, Foundational Topics in Adapted Physical Education and Sport, introduces the reader to the area of adapted physical education and sport; discusses program organization and management; addresses measurement, assessment, and program evaluation; prepares readers for development of individualized education programs; introduces the reader to behavior management; and discusses instructional strategies related to the field.

Part II, Individuals With Unique Needs, covers all the disabilities specifically defined in IDEA, as well as an overview of temporary disabilities and special conditions. These chapters provide an understanding of disabilities, how they relate to physical education and sport, and educational implications associated with each disability. As appropriate, particular attention is given in each chapter to inclusion and sport programs.

Part III, Developmental Considerations, includes discussion of motor development, perceptual–motor development, adapted physical education for infants and toddlers, and children in early childhood adapted physical education programs.

Part IV, Activities for Individuals With Unique Needs, presents physical education and sport activities for both school and out-of-school settings. A key aspect of this section is the discussion of specific activity modifications and variations for the populations involved in adapted physical education and sport. This part concludes with a chapter on wheelchair sport performance. Part IV serves as an excellent resource for teachers, coaches, and other service providers long after they have left colleges and universities and are involved in providing quality programs.

The appendixes consist of the latest definitions regarding infants, toddlers, and children with disabilities in IDEA; a list of organizations (and contact information) associated with adapted physical education and sport; information related to the Brockport Physical Fitness Test items; and a rating scale to evaluate adapted physical education programs. Each of these complements information presented in the body of the text. Finally, also closely associated with this book is an online video description of the Brockport Physical Fitness Test in HK*Propel*.

Closing

It is evident that more and more individuals with disabilities are participating in physical education and sport activities worldwide. With greater participation, young people with disabilities, parents, medical professionals, educators, and others are recognizing the tremendous value of physical education and sport and the reality that people with disabilities are unique individuals with exceptional abilities. This recognition extends throughout the world, as clearly demonstrated at international symposia related to adapted physical education and sport, international sport competitions, and literature developed and translated in various languages.

As the field of adapted physical education and sport has advanced, so has its knowledge base. Top authorities who are experts in their fields have been assembled, as previously described, to write chapters in this book, thus further enhancing adapted physical education and sport.

The Editors

Acknowledgments

Stamatis Agiovlasitis—I would like to thank Dr. Francis X. Short for his contributions to earlier versions of chapter 23, which were incorporated into the present version of the chapter.

Lauren K. Cavanaugh and Linda C. Hilgenbrinck—Special thanks to Dr. David Porretta for allowing us to be a part of the seventh edition of the text. It has been our honor to have contributed to a text that has, for so many years, been edited by two incredible leaders of the adapted physical education profession. We have always admired both Dr. David Porretta and the late Dr. Joseph Winnick. Finally, thank you to Tammy (Linda), Sarah (Lauren), and our loved ones for the support extended to us when we commit ourselves to such professional pursuits.

Douglas H. Collier—I would, first of all, like to acknowledge my parents, Martin and Barbara Collier, who through their support and example were instrumental in fostering an appreciation for diversity in me and my siblings. Additionally, I would like to thank Dave Porretta for his strong, positive leadership and for his suggestions with regard to the chapter written for this text. I would be remiss if I didn't thank my wife, Chris, for her unwavering support over these many years.

Ronald W. Davis—My thanks to Dr. David Porretta and the late Joe Winnick for guiding me through this edition of *Adapted Physical Education and Sport*. Of course, I want to acknowledge the support from my wife, Janelle Davis, who has been there for me for the past 38 years. I am grateful to all those who have helped me become a better professional, especially our sons LTC Matthew Lane Davis, USAF, and CPT Timothy Davis, USA, and daughter Mrs. Molly Davis-Himmelberg.

Lauren J. Lieberman and Lindsay Ball—For chapter 12, we would like to acknowledge the administrators, specialists, counselors, and campers from Camp Abilities and the Maine Organization for Blind Athletic and Leadership Education Sports Education Camps for their enthusiasm and for showing the world what individuals who are visually impaired, blind, or deafblind can do in the area of sports and recreation. We would like to recognize the College at Brockport, State University of New York for their support of our work and contributions to the field. We would like to thank our adapted physical education colleagues at SUNY Brockport for their encouragement and dedication to enrich the lives of individuals with sensory impairments. For chapter 13, Lauren Lieberman would also like to acknowledge the students from the Perkins School for the Blind for teaching her much of what she knows about sensory impairments. She would also like to thank Jessica Schultz for her help; her life of experience and advocacy helped shape this chapter's content and resources.

Manny Felix and Brock McMullen—We would like to thank Dave Porretta for inviting us to contribute to this textbook. We dedicate these chapters to our mentors in the field of adapted physical education, notably Drs. Hester Henderson and Garth Tymeson, and recognize all of our current and former students and the adapted physical education teachers mentoring these future professionals, all of whom are making a difference in the lives of students with disabilities every day. Lastly, we express special gratitude to our families (Hayley and Elsie McMullen; Cindy, Lexie, Rebecca, and Michael Felix) for their love and support.

Cathy Houston-Wilson—I am fortunate and thankful to have learned from and worked with Dr. Joseph Winnick for my entire professional career. He instilled in me a fierce sense of advocacy, which guides my actions in everything I do. His impact on APE is immeasurable and his legacy lives on. I would also like to thank my family: my husband Kevin, and my daughters Meaghan, Shannon, and Kiera, for their constant love and support of me and the work I do. Finally, I would like to thank Dr. Dave Porretta, whose kindness and patience is unceasing. Through his efforts, this text remains relevant.

Francis M. Kozub—I would like to thank Mary, Patrick, and Jesse for their patience throughout my career. Specifically, I acknowledge Mary's editorial contributions to this book and many other publications over the years.

Barry W. Lavay and Melissa D. Bittner—We would like to acknowledge Joseph Winnick and the many significant contributions he made to the profession throughout his storied career. We thank David Porretta for his leadership and the opportunity to contribute to the seventh edition of this book. We would like to recognize our students, teachers, and colleagues, who throughout our careers challenged us to learn and grow as professionals. Finally, special thanks to our families for their support and help to make life special.

E. Michael Loovis—I would like to thank Jaana Huovinen of the University of Lapland in Rovaniemi, Finland, for her assistance in acquiring the photograph of ice fishing in chapter 26. Also, I wish to acknowledge the work of Boni Boswell, who wrote the chapter on dance that appeared in previous editions of this textbook. My gratitude is likewise extended to Dave Porretta for his assistance and encouragement with the reconceptualization of chapter 26.

David G. Lorenzi—I would like to thank Dr. David L. Porretta for inviting me to contribute to the aquatics chapter in this new edition. A special thank you to the previous authors, Pamela Arnhold and Monica Lepore. I consider you both to be friends and mentors and I have learned a great deal from both of you. A special thank you to the preprofessional students and clients that I have worked with over the years, it has been a pleasure to serve and learn from you. Finally, I would like to acknowledge the support of my family: my wife Melissa, and my children Marina, Nico, and Ava.

G. Monique Mokha—This chapter was made possible by the outstanding work of previous chapter author Dr. Christine B. Stopka; the current author is very appreciative of the generous and invaluable contributions to this chapter and this textbook as well as the mentoring in disability sport health care.

John C. Ozmun, Byungmo Ku, and David L. Gallahue—Our chapter is dedicated to our spouses, children, and grandchildren for their unwavering love, patience, and support.

David L. Porretta and Justin A. Haegele—David Porretta acknowledges the support and cooperation he has received from all the contributors to the seventh edition. Also, a special thanks to the late Joseph Winnick for inviting me to contribute to the book from its inception, as well as the support received from Human Kinetics. Justin Haegele would like to thank David Porretta for the invitation to coauthor these chapters with him. Justin would also acknowledge that all of his work is dedicated to his family: Jane, Casey, and Emma.

Sue Sutherland—I would like to thank Dave Porretta for including me in this edition of the book. This chapter is dedicated to all of the amazing athletes and volunteers I have had the pleasure of working with in adventure sports over the years. Thanks also to my family for their support in my adventures!

Victoria L. Goosey-Tolfrey and Barry S. Mason—This work extends previous contributions of Colin Higgs and Abu Yilla. Appreciation is given to Ronald W. Davis for the opportunity to contribute to this book and to Joseph Winnick and David L. Porretta for their leadership. We also appreciate the support of the School of Sport, Exercise and Health Sciences at Loughborough University and the Peter Harrison Centre for Disability Sport.

Amaury Samalot-Rivera—I would like to thank David Porretta for giving me this opportunity, for his guidance and support over the years, and for his significant contributions in all earlier editions of this book. Also, I would like to thank María, Amaury Jr., and Julián for their patience, love, and support throughout my career. Special thanks to my colleagues in Puerto Rico and at the College at Brockport for their support and friendship.

Wesley J. Wilson and Luke E. Kelly—We would like to acknowledge the important roles our families have played in our professional lives; their support makes contributions like this possible. We also want to recognize and thank all our colleagues, mentors, and students who have made our work so worthwhile.

Lauriece L. Zittel and So-Yeun Kim—We would like to thank Dave Porretta for providing us with the opportunity to be included in this seventh edition. The content of this chapter was continually supported by the knowledge we gained from working with young children with developmental delays and those at risk for developmental delays. We value our partnership with early childhood teachers and children.

Part I

Foundational Topics in Adapted Physical Education and Sport

Part I, consisting of seven chapters, introduces adapted physical education and sport and presents topics that serve as the book's foundation. Chapter 1 defines adapted physical education and sport and offers a brief orientation concerning its history, legal basis, and professional resources. An overview of programmatic planning, inclusion, and qualities of service providers is also covered. In chapter 2, the focus shifts to program organization and management. Topics include programmatic and curricular planning and guidelines for the organization and implementation of programs. Chapter 3 emphasizes information pertaining to adapted sport, including the status of and issues associated with adapted sport, from local school and community programs to the Paralympic Games. Preparing physical educators to enhance the involvement of people with disabilities in sport is stressed in the chapter. Chapter 4 discusses measurement, assessment, and evaluation, which are vital to the development of adapted physical education programs. This chapter also recommends specific strategies for evaluation in regard to adapted physical education. Chapter 5 contains a detailed presentation of individualized education programs developed for students with unique needs, including Section 504 accommodation plans. Chapter 6 emphasizes basic concepts and approaches to behavior management, especially in instructional settings. Chapter 7 presents various instructional strategies related to those with unique needs.

Part I includes information related to overall program planning, organization, structure and management (chapters 1, 2, and 3); learner assessment and program evaluation (chapter 4); individualized education programming (chapter 5); and instructional strategies (chapter 7). A chapter on behavior management (chapter 6) is included in the foundational area preceding chapter 7 because of both its importance in shaping appropriate social behavior and its influence on learning.

1

Introduction to Adapted Physical Education and Sport

Joseph P. Winnick and David L. Porretta

Adapted physical education and sport fulfill individuals' unique needs and abilities related to physical activity. After introducing the reader to the field of adapted physical education and sport, this chapter draws attention to the contemporary status of the field by presenting the meaning of adapted physical education and sport, briefly reviewing its recent history and current orientation, discussing its constitutional and legislative basis, and introducing the professional basis for this field of study.

People who pursue a career of teaching physical education and coaching sports typically enjoy physical activity and are active participants in physical education and athletics. Often, however, they do not become knowledgeable about adapted physical education and sport until they prepare for their careers. With increased awareness and experience, they will realize that people with a variety of unique needs and a range of abilities are involved in adapted physical education and sport.

If physical education and sport opportunities are offered in educational institutions and other societal entities, they must be made available to all students, including those with disabilities. It is neither desirable nor permissible to discriminate on the basis of disability. Provisions should be made to offer equivalent as well as identical services so that equal opportunity for equal benefits may be pursued. Adapted physical education and sport has evolved as a field to meet the unique physical education and sport needs of participants. This chapter introduces the reader to adapted physical education and sport.

Meaning of Adapted Physical Education

Because of the many different terms in use, it is important to clarify the definition of adapted physical education. **Adapted physical education** is an individualized program that includes physical and motor fitness, fundamental motor skills and patterns, skills in aquatics and dance, and individual and group games and sports designed to meet the unique needs of individuals. Typically, the word *adapted* means "to adjust" or "to fit." In this book, the meaning of *adapted* is consistent with these definitions and includes modifications to meet the needs of students. It encompasses traditional components associated with adapted physical education, including those designed to correct, habilitate, or remediate. As described by Sherrill (2004), the word *adapted*, however, must not be confused or used interchangeably with the word *adaptive*. The word *adaptive* is used to describe a person's behavior. Rather, *adapted* is used to describe the modification of activities, games, sports, equipment, facilities, programs, or service delivery outcomes. Adapted physical education is viewed as a subdiscipline of physical education that provides safe, personally satisfying, and successful experiences for individuals of varying abilities.

Adapted physical education is generally designed to meet **long-term unique needs** (more than 30 days). Those with long-term unique needs include people with disabilities as specified in the Individuals with Disabilities Education Act (IDEA). (The Individuals with Disabilities Education Act [IDEA] may also be cited as the Individuals with Disabilities Education Improvement Act [IDEIA]. In this text, it is referred to as IDEA.) According to IDEA, a **child with a disability** means a child with intellectual disability, hearing impairment including deafness, speech or language impairment, visual impairment including blindness, serious emotional disturbance, orthopedic impairment, autism, traumatic brain injury, learning disability, deafblindness, or multiple disabilities or other health impairments that require special education and related services (Office of Special Education and Rehabilitative Services [OSE/RS], 2006). The term *child with a disability* may also, at the discretion of the state and the local educational agency, include children aged 3 to 9 experiencing developmental delays as defined by the state and as measured by appropriate diagnostic instruments and procedures in one or more of the following areas: physical development, cognitive development, communication development, social or emotional development, or adaptive development. This child, by reason thereof, needs special education and related services (OSE/RS, 2006).

Adapted physical education might also include **infants and toddlers** (children under age 3) who need early intervention services because (1) they are experiencing developmental delays in cognitive development, physical development, communication development, social or emotional development, or adaptive development or (2) they have a diagnosed physical or mental condition that has a high probability of resulting in developmental delay. At the discretion of the state, adapted physical education might also include at-risk infants and toddlers (IDEA, 2004). The term **at-risk infant or toddler** means a child under age 3 who would be at risk of experiencing a substantial developmental delay if early intervention services were not provided (IDEA, 2004).

Adapted physical education may also include individuals with disabilities as encompassed within Section 504 of the Rehabilitation Act of 1973 and its amendments. Section 504 defines a person with a disability as anyone who has a physical or mental impairment that substantially limits one or more major life activities, has a record of such an impairment, or is regarded as having such an impairment. Although every child who is a student with a disability under IDEA is also protected under Section 504, all children covered under 504 are not necessarily students with a disability under IDEA. Students with disabilities who do not need or require services under IDEA are, nonetheless, entitled to accommodations and services that are necessary to enable them to benefit from all programs and activities available to students without disabilities.

Adapted physical education may include students who are not identified by a school district as having a disability under federal legislation but who have unique needs that call for a specially designed program. This group might include students restricted because of injuries or other medical conditions; those with low fitness (including exceptional leanness or obesity), inadequate motor development, or low skill; or those with poor functional posture. These students might require individually designed programming to meet their unique goals and objectives.

According to IDEA, students aged 3 to 21 with disabilities must have an **individualized education program** (IEP) developed by a planning committee. When developing an IEP, physical education must be considered and might include specially designed instruction. Individualized education programs should also consider needs in extracurricular activities, including sport participation. Athletes with disabilities are encouraged to include goals related to sport in an IEP. IDEA also requires the development of an **individualized family service plan** (IFSP) for infants and toddlers with disabilities (OSE/RS, 2006). Although physical education services are not mandated for this age group, they may be offered as part of an IFSP. In accordance with Section 504 of the Rehabilitation Act of 1973 and its amendments, it is recommended that an accommodation plan be developed by a school-based assessment team to provide services and needed accommodations for students with disabilities. Although not covered by federal law, an **individualized physical education program** (IPEP) should also be developed by a planning committee for those who have a unique need but who have not been identified by the school as having a disability. Each school should have policies and procedures to guide the development of all individualized programs. More specific information on the development of programs and plans is presented in chapters 5 (ages 3-21) and 21 (ages 0-2).

Consistent with the least restrictive environment (LRE) concept associated with IDEA, adapted physical education may take place in classes that range from fully **integrated** (i.e., general education environments) to completely **segregated** (i.e., including only students receiving adapted physical education). Although adapted physical education is a *program* rather than a *placement*, it should be understood that a program is directly influenced by placement (the setting in which it is implemented). Whenever appropriate, students receiving an adapted physical education program should participate in general physical education environments with appropriate support as needed. Although an adapted physical education program is individualized, it can be implemented in a group setting and should be geared to each student's needs, limitations, and abilities.

Adapted physical education should emphasize a physically **active** program (figure 1.1) rather than a **sedentary** alternative program. The program should be planned to attain the maximum benefits of physical activity for students who might otherwise be relegated to passive experiences associated with physical education. In establishing adapted physical education programs, educators work with parents, students, teachers, administrators, and professionals in various disciplines. Adapted physical education may employ developmental (bottom-up), community-based, functional (top-down), or other orientations and might employ a variety of teaching styles. Adapted physical education takes place in schools and other agencies responsible for education. Although adapted physical education is educational, it draws on related services (more on related services in chapter 2 and later in this chapter), especially medical services, to help meet goals and instructional objectives.

In this text, adapted physical education and sport are viewed as part of the emerging area of study known as **adapted physical activity**, which encompasses the comprehensive and interdisciplinary study of physical activity for the education, sport participation, and leisure of individuals with unique needs (Porretta et al., 1993). Adapted physical activity encompasses the total life span, whereas **adapted physical education** focuses only on ages 0 to 21. Although adapted physical education may exceed the minimal time required by policies or law, it should not be supplanted by related services (such as physical therapy), intramurals, sport days, athletics, or other experiences that are not primarily instructional.

FIGURE 1.1 Students with disabilities and physical activities: *(a)* wheelchair user in extracurricular track event, *(b)* students with visual disabilities scaling a climbing wall.

Photo *a* courtesy of Joseph Winnick and photo *b* courtesy of Camp Abilities, Emily Gilbert.

Adapted Sport

Adapted sport refers to sport modified or created to meet the unique needs of individuals. Based on this definition, for example, basketball is a general sport and wheelchair basketball is an adapted sport. Goalball—a game created for people with visual impairments in which players attempt to roll a ball that emits a sound across their opponents' goal—is another example of an adapted sport. Individuals with disabilities may participate in general sport or adapted sport conducted in unified, segregated, individualized, and parallel settings. Chapter 3 provides a framework for sport opportunities for individuals with disabilities.

Adapted sport encompasses **disability sport** (e.g., Deaf sport), which typically focuses on segregated participation in general or adapted sport. Although *disability sport* terminology has been used to encompass sport related to individuals with a disability, *adapted sport* terminology is preferred for many reasons: It is consistent with the terms *adapted physical education* and *adapted physical activity*; it focuses on the modification of sport rather than on disability; it encourages participation in the most integrated environment; it is consistent with normalization theory; it promotes the creation of sport opportunities; and it provides an opportunity for the pursuit of excellence in sport throughout a full spectrum of settings for participation. This orientation to adapted sport is consistent with the sport delivery options presented in chapter 3. It is believed that these options will lead to more sport participation by individuals with disabilities as well as to more creative offerings and grouping patterns related to sport at every level of participation. Adapted sport terminology supports the development of excellence in sport while promoting growth in sport participation within many settings.

Adapted sport programs are conducted in diverse environments and organizational patterns for a variety of purposes. Educational programs are generally conducted in schools and may include intramural, extramural, and interscholastic activities. **Intramural** activities are conducted within schools, involve only pupils enrolled in the school, and are organized to serve the entire school population. **Extramural** sport activities involve participation of students from two or more schools, and they are sometimes conducted as play days or sport days. **Interscholastic** sports involve competition between representatives from two or more schools and offer enriched opportunities for more highly skilled students. Adapted sport activity might also be conducted for leisure or recreational purposes within formal, open, or unstructured programs; as a part of the lifestyle of individuals or groups; or for wellness, medical, or therapeutic reasons, such as recreational therapy, corrective therapy, sport therapy, or wellness programs. In general, involvement in sport or adapted sport has several purposes. In this book, the focus is on adapted sport in educational settings and in regional, national, and international competition under the governance of formalized organizations.

Planning: Purposes, Aims, Goals, and Objectives

An important step in providing a good adapted physical education program is planning. A plan provides the direction of the program and includes identifying its purpose, aims, goals, and objectives. The purpose of a program should be consistent with the mission of its organization and with the general physical education or sport program available for students without disabilities. In this book, it is assumed that the purpose of adapted physical education is to promote **self-actualization**, which in turn promotes optimal personal development and contributes to the whole of society. This purpose is consistent with humanism, a philosophy that pertains to helping people become fully human, thereby actualizing their potential for making the world the best possible place for all forms of life (Sherrill, 2004).

There is no universal model or paradigm related to purposes, aims, goals, or objectives in adapted physical education. The basic framework presented in figure 1.2 encompasses the statement of purpose as well as the aims, goals, and content areas of a program. It is consistent with federal legislation and the orientation used in this book and assumes that the adapted physical education program is part of the total school physical education program. In essence, the program strives to develop participants to their maximum potential.

In this orientation, the physical education and sport program aims to produce physically educated people who live active and healthy lifestyles that enhance their progress toward self-actualization. The Society of Health and Physical Educators has developed five standards to reflect what the physically educated person should be able to know and do (see the SHAPE America's National Standards sidebar).

The development of a physically educated person is accomplished through experiences related to psychomotor, cognitive, and affective domains of learning. In this paradigm, program goals are accomplished by education of and development through the psychomotor domain. In figure 1.2, education *of* the psychomotor domain is represented by solid lines connecting content and program goals. Development *through* the psychomotor domain is represented by dotted lines among cognitive, affective, and psychomotor development areas.

Program goals are developed through content areas in the physical education program. Content areas related to psychomotor development may be grouped in many ways. Figure 1.2 shows five content goal areas: physical fitness, motor development, rhythm and dance, aquatics, and games and sports. These content areas are consistent with the definition of physical education associated with IDEA. Each of these content areas includes developmental areas of sport skills. For example,

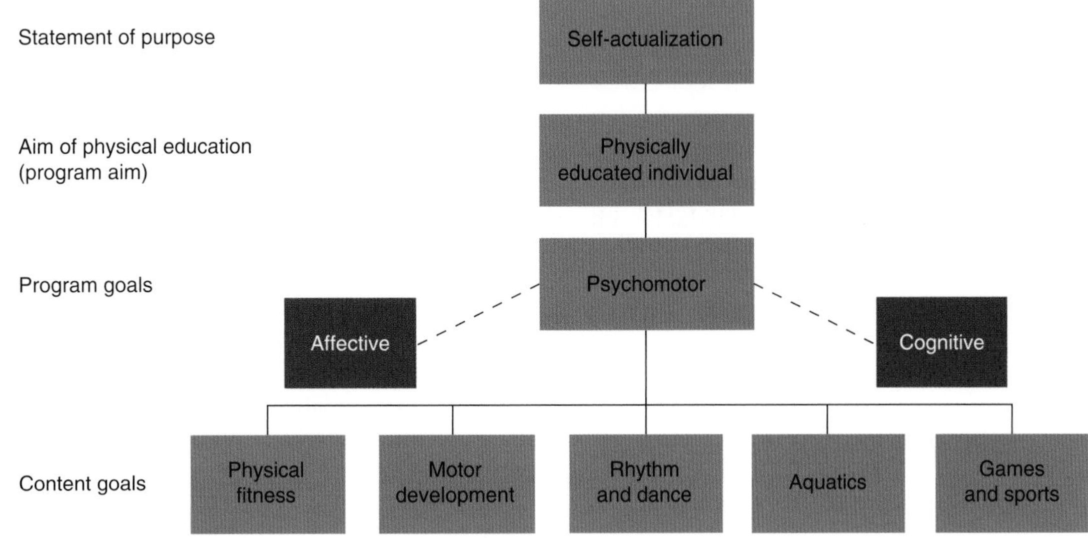

FIGURE 1.2 Aims and goals for an adapted physical education program.

SHAPE America's National Standards

The physically educated person does the following:

Standard 1—The physically literate individual demonstrates competency in a variety of motor skills and movement patterns.

Standard 2—The physically literate individual applies knowledge of concepts, principles, strategies, and tactics related to movement and performance.

Standard 3—The physically literate individual demonstrates the knowledge and skills to achieve and maintain a health-enhancing level of physical activity and fitness.

Standard 4—The physically literate individual exhibits responsible personal and social behavior that respects self and others.

Standard 5—The physically literate individual recognizes the value of physical activity for health, enjoyment, challenge, self-expression, and/or social interaction.

Reprinted from SHAPE America, *National Standards & Grade-Level Outcomes for K-12 Physical Education* (Champaign, IL: Human Kinetics, 2014).

aerobic capacity might be a developmental area under physical fitness, and basketball is a sport within the content area of games and sports.

The content goals shown in figure 1.2, as well as goals in affective and cognitive domains, may serve as annual goals for individualized programs. Specific skills and developmental areas associated with these goals may be used to represent short-term objectives. For example, an annual goal for a student might be to improve physical fitness. A corresponding short-term objective might be to improve health-related flexibility by obtaining a score of 20 centimeters on a sit-and-reach test. Objectives can be expressed on several levels to reflect the specificity desired. The emphasis should be on the student's needs and established objectives should be unique for each student.

In general, the purpose, aims, and program goals are the same for general and adapted physical education. Differences between these programs exist mainly in the content goals, specific objectives, and performance standards and benchmarks. For example, goalball may be a content goal for individuals who are blind, and an objective might relate to throwing and blocking. Teachers may select test items and standards that assess functional as well as physiological health, which relate to health-related physical fitness. Other differences might include the time spent on instructional units or objectives and the scope of the curriculum mastered.

Service Providers

People who provide direct services are the key to ensuring quality experiences related to adapted physical education and sport. These providers include teachers, coaches, therapists, paraeducators, and volunteers. It must be emphasized that adapted physical education and sport is provided not only by educators who specialize in this field but by general physical educators as well. If services were provided only by specialists in adapted physical education, relatively few students would receive services because there are too few specialists.

Teachers of physical education must assume responsibility for all children they teach and must be willing to contribute to the development of each student. This requires a philosophy that looks toward human service and beyond win–loss records as the ultimate contribution within one's professional life. Success for *all* students in physical education requires an instructor who has appropriate professional knowledge, skills, and values, as well as a caring and helping attitude. A good teacher or coach recognizes the importance of positive self-esteem and displays an attitude of acceptance, empathy, friendship, and warmth while ensuring a secure and controlled learning environment. The good teacher or coach of adapted physical education and sport selects and uses teaching approaches and styles beneficial to students, provides individualized and personalized instructions and opportunities, and creates a positive environment in which students can succeed. The good teacher or coach uses an encouraging approach and creates a positive educational environment in which all students are accepted and supported.

People studying to become teachers often have little or no previous experience working with students who have unique physical education needs.

It is important to take advantage of every opportunity to interact with individuals with disabilities, to describe the value of physical activity to them, and to listen to their stories about their experiences in adapted physical education and sport. Being involved in disability awareness activities provide important insights and values to prospective teachers.

Brief History of Adapted Physical Education

Although educational services for individuals with disabilities has made relatively recent progress, the use of physical activity or exercise for medical treatment and therapy is not new. Therapeutic exercise can be traced to 3000 BC in China. It is known that the ancient Greeks and Romans also recognized the medical and therapeutic value of exercise. However, the idea of physical education or physical activity to meet the unique educational needs of individuals with disabilities is a recent phenomenon. Efforts to serve these populations through physical education and sport were given significant attention during the 20th century, although efforts began in the United States in the 19th century.

Beginning of Adapted Physical Activity

In 1838, physical activity began receiving special attention at the Perkins School for students with visual disabilities in Boston. According to Charles E. Buell (1983), a noted physical educator with a visual impairment, this special attention resulted from the fact that Samuel Gridley Howe, the school director, advocated the health benefits of physical activity. For the first eight years, physical education consisted of compulsory recreation in the open air. In 1840, when the school was moved to South Boston, boys participated in gymnastic exercises and swimming. This was the first physical education program in the United States for students who were blind, and, by Buell's account, it was far ahead of the physical education in public schools.

Medical Orientation

Although physical education was provided in the early 1800s to people with visual impairments and other disabilities, medically oriented gymnastics and drills began in the latter part of the century as the forerunner of modern adapted physical education in the United States. Physical education before 1900 was medically oriented and preventive, developmental, or corrective in nature (Sherrill & DePauw, 1997). Its purpose was to prevent illness and promote the health and vigor of the mind and body. Strongly influencing this orientation was a system of medical gymnastics developed in Sweden by Per Henrik Ling and introduced to the United States in 1894. Luther Halsey Gulick, a U.S. physician, was a pioneer in the promotion of medical gymnastics.

Shift to Sport and the Whole Person

From the end of the 19th century into the 1930s, programs began to shift from medically oriented physical training to sport-centered physical education, and concern for the whole child emerged. Compulsory physical education in public schools increased dramatically, and teachers began training specifically in the field of physical education, rather than the medical field (Sherrill & DePauw, 1997). This transition resulted in broad mandatory programs consisting of games, sports, rhythmic activities, and calisthenics that meet the needs of the whole person. Students unable to participate in general activities were provided corrective or remedial physical education. According to Sherrill and DePauw, physical education programs between the 1930s and the 1950s consisted of general or corrective classes for students who today would be described as normal. Sherrill (2004) has succinctly described adapted physical education during this time in the United States:

> Assignment to physical education was based upon a thorough medical examination by a physician who determined whether a student should participate in the regular [general] or corrective program. Corrective classes were composed of limited, restricted, or modified activities related to health, posture, or fitness problems. In many schools, students were excused from physical education. In others, the physical educator typically taught several sections of regular [general] physical education and one section of corrective physical education each day. Leaders in corrective physical education continued to have strong backgrounds in medicine and physical therapy. People preparing to be physical education teachers generally completed one university course in corrective physical education. (p. 18)

Emerging Comprehensive Subdiscipline

During the 1950s, more and more students described as handicapped were being served in public schools, and the outlook toward them was becoming increasingly humanistic. With a greater diversity in pupils came a greater diversity in programs to meet their needs. In 1952, the American Association for Health, Physical Education and Recreation (AAHPER), now known as the Society of Health and Physical Educators (SHAPE), formed a committee to define the subdiscipline and give direction and guidance to professionals. This committee defined adapted physical education as "a diversified program of developmental activities, games, sports, and rhythms suited to the interests, capacities, and limitations of students with disabilities who may not safely or successfully engage in unrestricted participation in the rigorous activities of the regular [general] physical education program" (Committee on Adapted Physical Education, 1952). The definition retained the evolving diversity of physical education and specifically included students with disabilities. In 1954, following the Committee's definition, Arthur Daniels, a professor at the Ohio State University at the time, authored the first textbook entitled *Adapted Physical Education*. *Adapted physical education* still serves today as the comprehensive term for this subdiscipline, although it is not limited to people with classified disabilities.

Recent and Current Status

With the impetus provided by a more humanistic, more informed, and less discriminatory society, major advances continued in the 1960s. Many of these advances were associated with the Joseph P. Kennedy family. In 1965, the Joseph P. Kennedy, Jr. Foundation awarded a grant to the American Alliance for Health, Physical Education, Recreation and Dance (AAHPERD) to launch the Project on Recreation and Fitness for the Mentally Retarded. The project grew to encompass all special populations, and its name was changed in 1968 to the Unit on Programs for the Handicapped and was directed by Dr. Julian U. Stein. The Unit dramatically influenced adapted physical education at every level throughout the United States.

In 1968, the Kennedy Foundation expanded opportunities for individuals with intellectual disabilities by establishing the Special Olympics. Under the leadership of Eunice Kennedy Shriver, this program grew rapidly, with competition held at local, state, national, and international levels in an ever-increasing range of sports. Although its leadership in providing sport opportunities for individuals with intellectual disabilities is well known, this organization has provided much more to adapted physical education and sport. Specifically, Special Olympics, Inc., has played a key role in the attention to physical education in federal legislation for professional preparation, research, and other projects through its advocacy. The organization has provided a worldwide model for the provision of sport opportunities, and its work is acknowledged in several sections of this book.

During the mid-1960s, concern for people with emotional or learning disabilities had a significant effect on adapted physical education in the United States. The importance of physical activity for the well-being of those with emotional problems was explicitly recognized by the National Institute of Mental Health (NIMH) of the U.S. Department of Health and Human Services (DHHS) when it funded the Buttonwood Farms Project. Conducted at Buttonwood Farms, Pennsylvania, this project was valuable for recognizing the importance of physical activity in the lives of individuals with disabilities, bringing the problems of seriously disturbed youths to the attention of educators, and developing curricular materials to prepare professionals in physical education and recreation for work with this population.

During the same era, adapted physical education gained much attention with the use of perceptual–motor activities as a modality for academic and intellectual development, particularly for students with learning disabilities. The contention that movement experiences serve as a basis for intellectual abilities, however, has lost support. Nonetheless, the use of movement experiences, including active games, for the development and reinforcement of academic abilities appears to be regaining popularity and research-based support.

Current direction and emphasis in adapted physical education are heavily associated with the right to a free and appropriate education. Because of litigation and the passage of various federal laws and regulations in the United States, progress has occurred in both adapted physical education and sport. This legal impetus has improved programs in many schools and agencies, extended mandated physical education for individuals aged 3 to 21, stimulated activity programs for infants and toddlers, and resulted in dramatic increases in participation in sport programs for individuals with disabilities. Legislation has also resulted in funds for professional preparation, research, and other special projects relevant to the provision of full educational opportunities for individuals with unique needs. Finally, the impact of federal legislation and a strong belief in the right to and value of an education in the general educational environment have resulted in a significant movement toward inclusion regarding the education of children with disabilities in the United States. Dramatic advocacy and progress have increased relative to the offering of adapted sport opportunities in secondary schools (Frogley & Beaver, 2002; Vaughn, 2007; Winnick, 2007). The elements of modern direction and emphasis mentioned here are covered in detail in several parts of this book, as well as by AAHPERD (2013).

Recent and Current Leaders

As fields of study emerge, evolve, and mature, people always appear who have provided leadership and achieved excellence in the field. These individuals serve as role models for contributions to philosophy, theoretical foundations, research, programs, teaching, and other services to the field. In regard to adapted physical education, the periodical *Palaestra* has identified a number of people who made significant contributions to adapted physical education throughout distinguished careers. Their class of 1991 leaders included David M. Auxter, Slippery Rock University in Pennsylvania; Lawrence Rarick, University of California at Berkeley; Julian U. Stein, AAHPERD and George Mason University; Thomas M. Vodola, Township of Ocean School District in New Jersey; and Janet Wessel, Michigan State University. In 2001, *Palaestra* selected the following nationally and internationally recognized people as leaders in the field of adapted physical education ("Leadership in disability sport," 2000): David Beaver, Western Illinois University; Gudrun Doll-Tepper, Free University of Berlin; John Dunn, Oregon State University; Claudine Sherrill, Texas Woman's University; and Joseph P. Winnick, State University of New York, College at Brockport. In the 2011 group, *Palaestra* selected the following persons for adapted physical education leadership awards ("Leadership in disability sport," 2011): Louis Bowers, University of South Florida; Walter F. Ersing, The Ohio State University; Ronald French, Texas Woman's University; Susan Grosse, F.J. Gaenslen Orthopedic School; and Janet A. Seaman, University of California, Los Angeles, and Texas Woman's University.

The Julian U. Stein Lifetime Achievement Award provided by SHAPE continues to be given to recognize sustained lifetime leadership (25 years or more) in the field of adapted physical education. Holders of this award include leaders such as Julian U. Stein, Claudine Sherrill, Joseph Winnick, David Auxter, Jan Seaman, Janet Wessel, Ron French, Joseph Huber, David Beaver, David Porretta, Dale Ulrich, Martin Block, and Barry Lavay. Although these leaders have been recognized, it is important to realize that they constitute a very small percentage of the people making significant contributions at many levels every day in the field of adapted physical education.

Inclusion Movement

Inclusion means educating students with disabilities in a general educational setting. The movement toward inclusion was encouraged by and is compatible with the LRE provisions associated with IDEA. Education in the LRE requires that children with disabilities be educated alongside children without disabilities to the maximum extent appropriate. However, according to LRE provisions in IDEA, a continuum of alternative environments (including segregated environments) may be used for the education of a student if those are the most appropriate environments. A recommended continuum is presented in figure 2.1 in chapter 2. The inclusion movement has also been given impetus by many who believe that separate education is not an equal education and that the setting of a program provided for a child significantly influences that program. In the United States today, all but a small percentage of students with disabilities attend schools with peers without disabilities, and over 90 percent of children with disabilities spend at least part of their school day in general education classrooms. This is the reality of inclusion and is why appropriately prepared physical educators, coaches, and other professionals are required. Although this book prepares teachers to serve children in all settings, it gives special emphasis to the skills and knowledge needed to optimally educate children with disabilities in general educational environments.

This book provides readers with information on meeting the unique needs of learners. Special attention is given to **universal design for learning** (UDL), which has its roots in the Americans with Disabilities Act of 1990 (Meyer et al., 2014). Following the passage of the ADA, the idea of access to physical environments (then known simply as *universal design*) was eventually applied to the field of education, including facilities, materials, curriculum, instruction, and assessment, resulting in the current term now known as UDL (McGuire et al., 2006). It ensures that *all* students, including those with unique needs, have success in learning, especially in inclusive educational settings. More information on UDL and its implications for physical education and sport for students with unique needs is presented in chapters 2 and 7, as well as in most other chapters of this book.

Litigation

Much has been written about the impact of litigation on the guarantee of full educational opportunity in the United States. The most prominent of cases, which has served as an important precedent for civil litigation, was *Brown v. Board of Education of Topeka* (1954). This case established that the doctrine of separate but equal in public education resulted in segregation that violated the constitutional rights of Black students. Two landmark cases also had a significant impact on the provision of free, appropriate public education for all children with disabilities. The first was the class action suit of *Pennsylvania Association for Retarded Children v. Commonwealth of Pennsylvania* (1972). Equal protection and due process clauses associated with the Fifth and Fourteenth Amendments served as the constitutional basis for the court's rulings and agreements. The following were among the rulings or agreements in the case:

- Labeling a child as mentally retarded [intellectually disabled] or denying public education or placement in a regular [general] setting without due process or hearing violates the rights of the individual.
- All mentally retarded [intellectually disabled] children are capable of benefiting from a program of education and training.
- Mental age may not be used to postpone or in any way deny access to a free public program of education and training.
- Having undertaken to provide a free, appropriate education to all its children, a state may not deny mentally retarded [intellectually disabled] children the same.

A second important case was *Mills v. Board of Education of the District of Columbia* (1972). This action, brought on behalf of seven children, sought to restrain the District of Columbia from excluding children with disabling conditions from public schools or denying them publicly supported education. The district court held that, by failing to provide the seven children and the class they represented with publicly supported specialized education, the district violated controlling statutes, its own regulations, and due process. The District of Columbia was required to provide a publicly supported education, appropriate equitable funding, and procedural due process rights to these children.

From 1972 to 1975, 46 right-to-education cases related to people with disabilities were tried in 28 states. They provided the foundation for much of the legislation to be discussed in the next section.

Laws Important to Adapted Physical Education and Sport

Laws have had a tremendous influence on education programs for students with disabilities. Since 1969, colleges and universities in many states have received federal funds for professional preparation, research, and other projects to promote programs for individuals with disabilities. The government agency most responsible for administering federally funded programs related to adapted physical education and for monitoring educational services for individuals with disabilities is the Office of Special Education and Rehabilitative Services (OSE/RS) within the U.S. Department of Education.

Four laws or parts of laws and their amendments have had significant impact on adapted physical education and adapted sport: IDEA, Section 504 of the Rehabilitation Act of 1973, the Olympic and Amateur Sports Act, and the Americans with Disabilities Act. In December of 2015, PL 114-95, Every Student Succeeds Act (ESSA), was signed into law. It also enhances and supports a fair, equal, and significant high-quality education for individuals with disabilities. Although not specifically designed relative to individuals with disabilities, this legislation enhances funding through state departments of education for the success of all students, including those in well-rounded experiences such as health and physical education. Table 1.1 shows a time line marking important milestones, along with brief statements describing the importance of laws directly related to persons with disabilities.

Individuals With Disabilities Education Act

A continuing major impetus related to the provision of educational services for students with disabili-

TABLE 1.1 Legislative Time Line

Law	Date	Importance
PL 93-112, Rehabilitation Act of 1973	1973	Section 504 of this act was designed to prevent discrimination against and provide equal opportunity for individuals with disabilities in programs or activities receiving federal financial assistance.
PL 94-142, Education for All Handicapped Children Act of 1975 PL 101-476, Individuals with Disabilities Education Act of 1990 (IDEA) PL 108-446, Individuals with Disabilities Education Improvement Act of 2004 (IDEIA)	1975, 1990, 2004	These acts and their amendments are designed to ensure that all children with disabilities have available a free appropriate public education that emphasizes special education (including physical education) and related services designed to meet their unique needs.
PL 95-606, Amateur Sports Act of 1978 PL 105-277, Ted Stevens Olympic and Amateur Sports Act of 1998	1978, 1998	These acts coordinate national efforts concerning amateur activity, including activity associated with the Olympic Games. As a result of this legislation, USOC took over the role and responsibilities of the United States Paralympic Committee.
PL 101-336, Americans with Disabilities Act (ADA)	1990	This act extended civil rights protection for individuals with disabilities to all areas of American life.

ties is PL 108-446, the Individuals with Disabilities Education Improvement Act of 2004. Definitions associated with this law can be found in appendix A. This act expanded on the previous Education for All Handicapped Children Act and amendments. However, IDEA reflects the composite and the most recent version and amendments of these laws (table 1.1). This act was designed to ensure that all children with disabilities have access to a free, appropriate public education that emphasizes **special education** and **related services** designed to meet their unique needs and prepare them for employment and independent living (see the Highlights of the Individuals With Disabilities Education Act sidebar).

In this legislation, the term *special education* is defined to mean specially designed instruction at no cost to parents or guardians to meet the unique needs of a child with disability, including instruction conducted in the classroom, in the home, in hospitals and institutions, in other settings, and in physical education (OSE/RS, 2006). IDEA specifies that the term *related services* means transportation and such developmental, corrective, and other supportive services as are required to help a child with a disability benefit from special education, including speech–language pathology and audiology services, psychological services, physical and occupational therapy, recreation (including therapeutic recreation), early identification and assessment of disabilities, counseling services (including rehabilitation counseling), orientation and mobility services, and medical services for diagnostic and evaluation purposes. Related services also include school health services, social work services in school, and parent counseling and training (OSE/RS, 2006). The act also ensures that the rights of children with disabilities and their parents or guardians are protected and helps states and localities provide education for all individuals with disabilities. In addition, IDEA has established a policy to develop and implement early intervention services for infants and toddlers and their families.

Definition and Requirements of Physical Education in IDEA

Regulations associated with IDEA (OSE/RS, 2006, p. 18) define physical education as the "development of (a) physical and motor fitness, (b) fundamental motor skills and patterns, and (c) skills in aquatics, dance, and individual and group games and sports (including intramural and lifetime sports)." This

Highlights of the Individuals With Disabilities Education Act

IDEA and its rules and regulations stipulate the following:

- A right to a free and appropriate education
- That physical education be made available to children with disabilities
- Equal opportunity for nonacademic and extracurricular activities
- An individualized program designed to meet the needs of children with disabilities
- Programs conducted within the LRE
- Nondiscriminatory testing and objective criteria for placement
- Due process
- Related services to assist in special education

term includes special physical education, adapted physical education, movement education, and motor development. IDEA requires that special education, including physical education, be made available to children with disabilities and that it include physical education specially designed, if necessary, to meet their unique needs. This federal legislation, together with state requirements for physical education, significantly affects physical education in schools. Readers should notice that the definition of adapted physical education used in this book closely parallels the definition of physical education used in IDEA.

Free, Appropriate Public Education Under IDEA

The term *free, appropriate public education* means that special education and related services (1) are provided at public expense, under public supervision and direction, and without charge; (2) meet the standards of the state's educational agency; (3) include preschool, elementary, or secondary school education in the state involved; and (4) are provided in conformity with an IEP (OSE/RS, 2006).

Least Restrictive Environment

IDEA requires that education be conducted in the LRE, meaning that students with disabilities are educated alongside students without disabilities and that special classes, separate schooling, or other removal from the general environment occurs only when the nature or severity of disability is such that education in general classes with the use of supplementary aids and services cannot be achieved in a satisfactory way (OSE/RS, 2006).

Relevant to education in the most appropriate setting is a continuum of instructional placements (see figure 2.1 in chapter 2), which can range from general education to an out-of-school segregated placement. See also the Application Example sidebar.

Focus on Student Needs and Opportunities

IDEA implicitly, if not explicitly, encourages educators to focus on the educational needs of the student instead of clinical or diagnostic labels. For example, as the IEP is developed, concern should focus on present functioning level, objectives, annual goals, and so on. The associated rules and regulations also indicate that children with disabilities must be provided with equal opportunities for participation in nonacademic and extracurricular services and activities, including athletics and recreational activities.

Section 504 of the Rehabilitation Act

The right of equal opportunity also emerges from another legislative milestone that has affected adapted physical education and sport. Section 504 of the Rehabilitation Act provides that no otherwise qualified person with a disability, solely by reason of that disability, be excluded from participation in, denied the benefits of, or subjected to discrimination under any program or activity receiving federal financial assistance (Workforce Investment Act of 1998).

An important intent of Section 504 is to ensure that individuals with a disability receive intended benefits of all educational programs and extracurricular activities. Two conditions are prerequisite to the delivery of services that guarantee benefits to those individuals: Programs must be *equally effective* as those provided to students without disabilities, and they must be conducted in the *most inclusive settings* possible. To be equally effective, a program must offer students with disabilities **equal opportunity** to attain the same results, gain the same benefits, or reach the same levels of achievement as peers without disabilities.

Application Example

Determining Student Placement

SETTING

Individualized program planning committee meeting

STUDENT

A 10-year-old boy with an intellectual disability, inadequate physical fitness (as evidenced by failing to meet adapted fitness zone standards on the Brockport Physical Fitness Test), and below-average motor development (at or below one standard deviation below the mean on a standardized motor development test)

ISSUE

What is the appropriate setting for instruction?

APPLICATION

On the basis of the information available and after a meeting was conducted with the parents and other members of the program planning committee, the following plan was determined:

- The student will receive an adapted physical education program in an integrated setting with support services whenever the student's peer group receives physical education.
- The student will receive an additional class session of physical education each week with two other students who also require adapted physical education.

To illustrate the intent of Section 504, consider a student who is totally blind and enrolled in a course in which all other students in the class are sighted. A written test given at the end of the semester would not provide the student who is blind with an equal opportunity to demonstrate knowledge of the material; thus, this approach would not be equally effective. By contrast, on a test administered orally or in braille, the student who is blind would have an equal opportunity to attain the same results as the other students. By giving an oral or braille exam, the instructor would be giving equivalent, as opposed to identical, services. (Merely identical services, in fact, would be considered discriminatory and not in accord with Section 504.) It is neither necessary nor possible to guarantee equal results; what is important is the equal opportunity to attain those results.

A program is not equally effective if it results in indiscriminate isolation or separation of individuals with disabilities. To the maximum degree possible, individuals with disabilities should participate in the LRE, as represented by a continuum of alternative instructional placements (see chapter 2).

Compliance with Section 504 requires program accessibility. Its rules and regulations prohibit exclusion of individuals with disabilities from federally assisted programs because of architectural or other environmental barriers. Common barriers to accessibility include facilities, finances, and transportation. Money available for athletics within a school district cannot be spent in a way that discriminates on the basis of disability. For example, a recipient of federal funds offering basketball to the general student population must provide wheelchair basketball for students using wheelchairs, if a need exists. If a school district lacks sufficient funds, then it need not offer programs; however, it cannot fund programs in a discriminatory manner.

In accordance with Section 504, children with disabilities who do not require special education or related services (not classified under IDEA) are still entitled to accommodations and services in the general school setting that are necessary to enable them to benefit from all programs and activities available to students without disabilities. Every student with a disability under IDEA is also protected under Section 504, but all students covered under Section 504 are not necessarily students with a disability under IDEA.

Section 504 obligates school districts to identify, evaluate, and extend to every qualified student with a disability (as defined by this act) residing in the district a free and appropriate public education, including modifications, accommodations, and specialized instructions or related aids as deemed necessary to meet their educational needs as adequately as the needs of students without disabilities are being met. School district personnel across the United States develop Section 504 accommodation plans to provide programmatic assistance to students so that they have full access to all activities. For example, a 504 plan related to physical education might seek specialized instruction or equipment, auxiliary aids or services, or program modifications. A sample 504 plan is presented in chapter 5.

The U.S. Government Accountability Office (2010) identified several factors that limit opportunities for students with disabilities to participate in physical education and athletics. In response to this report, in 2011 the U.S. Department of Education provided suggestions for improving opportunities, and in its "Dear Colleague Letter" in 2013, identified and provided guidance on how school districts could improve opportunities for students with disabilities to participate more fully in physical education and extracurricular activities. In response to this letter, the *Journal of Physical Education, Recreation and Dance* (AAHPERD, 2013) published a feature edition providing assistance to general physical educators, adapted physical educators, and school district administrators on how to enhance interscholastic athletics and community sport programming for students with disabilities.

The Rehabilitation Act is complaint-oriented legislation. Violations of Section 504 may be filed with the U.S. Office for Civil Rights (OCR), and under Section 504 parents may request an impartial hearing to challenge a school district's decision regarding their children.

Olympic and Amateur Sports Act

The Amateur Sports Act (ASA) of 1978 (PL 95-606), amended by the Ted Stevens Olympic and Amateur Sports Act of 1998 (PL 105-277), has contributed significantly to the provision of amateur athletic activity in the United States, including competition for athletes with disabilities. This legislation led to the establishment of the United States Olympic Committee (USOC) and gave it exclusive jurisdiction over matters pertaining to U.S. participation and organization of the Olympic Games, the Paralympic Games, and the Pan American Games, including representation of the United States in the Games. Today the United States Olympic and Paralympic Committee encourages and provides assistance to amateur athletic programs and competition for amateur athletes with disabilities, including, where feasible, the expansion of opportunities for meaningful participation in programs of athletic competition for athletes without disabilities. Additional information about the Paralympics is presented in chapter 3.

Americans With Disabilities Act

In 1990, the Americans with Disabilities Act (ADA) (PL 101-336) was passed. Whereas Section 504 focused on educational rights, this legislation extended civil rights protection in all areas of life for individuals with disabilities. Provisions include employment, public accommodation and services, public transportation, and telecommunications. In relation to adapted physical education and sport, this legislation requires that community recreational facilities, including health and fitness facilities, be accessible and, where appropriate, that reasonable accommodations be made for individuals with disabilities. Physical educators must develop and offer programs that allow individuals with disabilities to participate in physical activity and sport experiences within the community.

Every Student Succeeds Act

In December of 2015, the Every Student Succeeds Act (ESSA) (PL 114-95) was passed by Congress and signed into law by President Obama. This federal legislation replaced the Elementary and Secondary Education Act (ESEA) (1965) and the No Child Left Behind (NCLB) Act (2001) as the framework for elementary and secondary education in the United States. ESSA is particularly significant for two reasons: First, it reaffirms the importance of educating children with disabilities consistent with IDEA. Second, health and physical education is included as part of the definition of a "well-rounded education"; the definition of "core academic subject" associated with ESEA did not include health and physical education. This enables school districts to access funding for health and physical education through their state departments of education. Particularly appealing is that funding in connection with Title IV of this act is funding for the Safe and Healthy Students opportunity, including health, physical education, and physical activity. Specifically, after 2016, funding associated with ESSA replaced Physical Education Program (PEP) grant funding. This legislation is designed to encourage the development of 21st-century community learning centers, school and community partnerships, and funds for after-school programs, including nutrition education and physical activity. Health and physical education also can now be supported as a part of professional development. The act requires states to implement high-quality assessments of student progress toward standards that measure the overall performance of students in each public school, as well as the performance of their poor, minority, disabled, and English learner subgroups.

The potential benefit of ESSA to health and physical education is immeasurable. This is particularly true for in-school and out-of-school physical education and physical activity programs. In order to gain these benefits, professionals associated with physical education and sport will need to conceptualize programs, serve as program advocates, and develop relevant needs assessment information for school districts to support projects designed to benefit children and youth with disabilities.

History of Adapted Sport

Deaf athletes were among the first Americans with disabilities to become involved in organized sport at special schools. As reported by Gannon (1981), in the 1870s the Ohio School for the Deaf became the first school for the Deaf to offer baseball, and the state school in Illinois introduced American football in 1885. Football became a major sport in many schools for the Deaf around the turn of the century, and basketball was introduced at the Wisconsin School for the Deaf in 1906. Teams from schools for the Deaf have continued to compete against each other and against athletes in general schools.

Beyond interschool programs, formal international competition was established in 1924, when competitors from nine nations gathered in Paris for the first International Silent Games (now known as the Deaflympics). In 1945, the American Athletic Association of the Deaf (AAAD) was established to provide, sanction, and promote competitive sport opportunities for Americans with hearing impairments.

The earliest formal, recorded athletic competition in the United States for people with visual disabilities was a telegraphic track meet between the Overbrook and Baltimore schools for the blind in 1907. In a telegraphic meet, local results are mailed to a central committee, which makes comparisons to determine winners. From this beginning, athletes with visual disabilities continue to compete against each other and against their sighted peers.

Sir Ludwig Guttmann of Stoke Mandeville, England, is credited with introducing competitive sport as an integral part of the rehabilitation of veterans with disabilities. In the late 1940s, Stoke Mandeville Hospital sponsored the first recognized games for wheelchair athletes. In 1949, the University of Illinois organized the first national wheelchair basketball tournament, which resulted in the formation of the National Wheelchair Basketball Association (NWBA). To expand sport opportunities, Ben Lipton founded the National Wheelchair Athletic Association (NWAA) in the mid-1950s. This organization has sponsored competitive sport at state, regional, and national levels for participants with spinal cord conditions and other conditions requiring wheelchair use. Another advancement was the creation of the National Handicapped Sports and Recreation Association (NHSRA), formed by a small group of Vietnam veterans in the late 1960s and dedicated to providing year-round sport and recreational opportunities for people with orthopedic, spinal cord, neuromuscular, and visual disabilities. The organization was renamed Disabled Sports USA in 1994, then in 2020 merged with another sports organization, Adaptive Sports USA, to form Move United.

Special Olympics—created by the Joseph P. Kennedy, Jr. Foundation to provide and promote athletic competition for individuals with intellectual disabilities—held its first international games at Soldier Field in Chicago in 1968. Special Olympics has served as the model sport organization for individuals with disabilities through its leadership in direct service, research, training, advocacy, education, and organizational leadership. A symbol for the Special Olympics is shown in figure 1.3.

During the last quarter of the 20th century, other national multisport and unisport programs have been formed to provide expanded sport offerings to an increasing number of individuals with disabilities. The latest opportunities have been organized for athletes with visual impairments, cerebral palsy, closed head injury, stroke, dwarfism, and other conditions.

The evolution of sport organizations within the United States has led to greater involvement in international competition. In fact, many U.S. sport organizations participate in international games and have international counterparts (see chapter 3), notably the International Paralympic Committee (IPC). These organizations are multisport programs—that is, several sports are included as a part of these programs. In addition to multisport organizations, several organizations are centered on single sports, such as the NWBA. Sport organizations traditionally offering programs for athletes without disabilities are also beginning to organize

© Joseph Winnick

FIGURE 1.3 This symbol of the Special Olympics was a gift of the former Union of Soviet Socialist Republics on the occasion of the 1979 International Special Olympic Games, hosted by the State University of New York, College at Brockport. The artist is Zurab Tsereteli.

more opportunities and competition for athletes with disabilities, reducing the need for sport organizations focused primarily on types of disability. Several unisport organizations that provide excellent opportunities for athletes with disabilities are identified in other chapters of this book. Many other organizations that promote, advocate, and organize physical education and sport opportunities are identified in appendix B.

In the past few years, much of the impetus for sport for athletes with disabilities has been provided by out-of-school sport organizations. Although developing at a slower rate, other opportunities have begun to surface throughout the United States in connection with public school programs. An important milestone came in 1992, when Minnesota became the first state to welcome athletes with disabilities into its state school association, officially sanctioning interschool sport for junior and senior high school students with disabilities. More recently, a Georgia-based nonprofit organization titled the American Association of Adapted Sports Programs (AAASP) was developed to build interscholastic sport leagues for students with physical disabilities. This group has developed a model for other programs throughout the country to imitate. The AAASP helps states and schools provide equitable school-based sport opportunities for students and has demonstrated that it is possible to add adapted sport programs to existing school district extracurricular offerings without creating an undue administrative burden. More detailed information on these programs is presented by AAHPERD (2013) and in chapter 3.

A few states now organize statewide competition for athletes with disabilities. Some of these are combined with community-based sport programs, and others are provided independently. Finally, sport programs in rehabilitation settings for members of communities are emerging in major cities in the United States. More detailed information on these programs is presented in chapter 3.

Periodicals

The increased knowledge base and greater attention to adapted physical education and sport in recent years have been accompanied by the founding and development of several periodicals devoted to the subject. Among the most relevant of these are *Adapted Physical Activity Quarterly, Palaestra, Sports 'N Spokes*, and the *European Journal of Adapted Physical Activity*. Other periodicals that publish directly relevant information from time to time include *Journal of Physical Education, Recreation and Dance*; *Strategies*; *Research Quarterly for Exercise and Sport*; and *The Physical Educator*.

Organizations

The Society of Health and Physical Educators is an important national organization that makes significant contributions to programs for special populations. The Society of Health and Physical Educators (formerly AAHPERD) has many members whose primary professional concern lies in adapted physical education and sport. Over the years, its many publications, conferences, and conventions have given much attention to adapted physical education and sport—not only on the national level but also within the state, district, and local affiliates of the organization. Its professional conferences and conventions are among the best sources of information on adapted physical education and sport. The organization continues to provide key professional services and leadership.

The National Consortium for Physical Education for Individuals with Disabilities (NCPEID, or the Consortium) was established to promote, stimulate, and encourage professional preparation and research. The organization was started informally in the late 1960s by a small group of college and university directors of federally funded professional preparation or research projects seeking to share information. Its members have extensive backgrounds and interests in adapted physical education and sport. They have provided leadership and input on national issues and concerns, including the development of IDEA and its rules and regulations; federal funding for professional preparation, research, demonstration projects, and other special projects; and monitoring of legislation. The Consortium is recognized for establishing National Standards in Adapted Physical Education as well as a qualifying certification examination. Those who successfully complete the examination are awarded certification in adapted physical education. The organization holds an annual meeting and maintains an active website.

The International Federation for Adapted Physical Activity (IFAPA), which originated in Quebec, has expanded to a worldwide organization with an international charter. Its primary service has been to sponsor a biennial international adapted physical activity symposium. In alternating years, symposia organized by IFAPA are also held in other regions throughout the world. The North American Federation of Adapted Physical Activity (NAFAPA) is the North American affiliate of IFAPA. Other regional affiliates include Africa, Asia, Europe, Middle East, Oceania, and South America. The organization is composed of higher education scholars, practitioners, and students dedicated to promoting adapted physical activity. With its international scope, IFAPA disseminates valuable knowledge throughout the world.

Summary

Over the past few decades, increased attention has been given to adapted physical education and sport. This chapter presented a brief history of this field. Information regarding program direction was presented, and the importance and characteristics of those providing services in this field were recognized. The chapter stressed the importance of litigation, legislation, and the inclusion movement on programs affecting individuals with disabilities. Finally, periodicals and organizations significant to adapted physical education and sport were identified and described.

References

American Alliance for Health, Physical Education, Recreation and Dance (AAHPERD). (2013). Feature edition of helping general physical educators and adapted physical educators address the Office of Civil Rights Dear Colleague guidance letter. *Journal of Physical Education, Recreation and Dance, 84*(8).

Americans with Disabilities Act of 1990, PL 101-336, 2, 104 Stat. 328 (1990).

Brown v. Board of Education of Topeka, 347 U.S. 483 (1954).

Buell, C.E. (1983). *Physical education for blind children.* Charles C Thomas.

Committee on Adapted Physical Education. (1952). Guiding principles for adapted physical education. *Journal of Health, Education and Recreation, 23*(15), 15-28.

Elementary and Secondary Education Act (ESEA), PL 89-10, 79 Stat. (1965).

Every Student Succeeds Act (ESSA), PL 114-95, 129 Stat. (2015).

Frogley, M., & Beaver, D. (2002). Is the time right for interscholastic athletics for student-athletes with disabilities? *Palaestra, 18,* 4-6.

Gannon, J.R. (1981). *Deaf heritage: A narrative history of deaf America.* National Association for the Deaf.

Individuals with Disabilities Education Act Amendments of 2004 (IDEA), PL 108-446, 20 U.S.C. 1400 (2004).

Leadership in disability sport, adapted physical education, and therapeutic recreation. (2000). *Palaestra, 16*(3), 48-52.

Leadership in disability sport, adapted physical education, and therapeutic recreation. (2011). *Palaestra, 25*(4), 22.

McGuire, J., Scott, S., & Shaw, S. (2006). Universal design and its applications to educational environments. *Remedial and Special Education, 27*(3), 166-175.

Meyer, A., Rose, D.H, & Gordon, D. (2014). *Universal design for learning: Theory and practice.* Center for Applied Special Technology (CAST) Professional Publishing.

Mills v. Board of Education of the District of Columbia, 348 F. Supp. 966 (1972).

No Child Left Behind Act of 2001 (NCLB Act), PL 107-110, 115 Stat. 1425 (2001).

Office of Special Education and Rehabilitative Services (OSE/RS), 34 CFR 300 (2006).

Pennsylvania Association for Retarded Children v. Commonwealth of Pennsylvania, U.S. District Court, 343 F. Supp. 279 (1972).

Porretta, D., Nesbitt, J., & Labanowich, S. (1993). Terminology: A case for clarity. *Adapted Physical Activity Quarterly, 10,* 87-96.

Rehabilitation Act of 1973, PL 93-112, 87 Stat. 355 (1973).

SHAPE America. (2014). *National standards & grade-level outcomes for K-12 physical education.* Human Kinetics.

Sherrill, C. (2004). *Adapted physical activity, recreation and sport: Crossdisciplinary and lifespan* (6th ed.). McGraw Higher Education.

Sherrill, C., & DePauw, K. (1997). Adapted physical activity and education. In J.D. Massengale and R.A. Swanson (Eds.), *The history of exercise and sport science* (pp. 39-108). Human Kinetics.

Ted Stevens Olympic and Amateur Sports Act of 1998, U.S.C.A. 220501 *et seq.* (1998).

U.S. Department of Education, Office for Civil Rights. (2013). *Dear colleague letter.* Author.

U.S. Department of Education, Office of Special Education and Rehabilitative Services, Office of Special Education Programs. (2011). *Creating equal opportunities for children and youth with disabilities to participate in physical education and extracurricular athletics.* Author.

U.S. Government Accountability Office. (2010). Students with disabilities: More information could improve opportunities in physical education and athletics. No. GAO-10-519 at 1, 31. www.gao.gov/assets/310/305770.pdf

Vaughn, B. (2007). A response to Joseph P. Winnick [Letters to the Editor]. *Palaestra, 23*(3), 16.

Winnick, J.P. (2007). A framework in interscholastic sports for youngsters with disabilities [Guest Editorial]. *Palaestra, 23*(2), 4, 9.

Workforce Investment Act of 1998, PL 105-220, Sec. 401 *et seq.* (1998).

Print Resources

American Alliance for Health, Physical Education, Recreation and Dance (AAHPERD). (2013). Feature edition of helping general physical educators and adapted physical educators address the Office of Civil Rights Dear Colleague guidance letter. *Journal of Physical Education, Recreation and Dance, 84*(8).

This edition provides general physical educators, adapted physical educators, and school district administrators assistance relative to the Office of Civil Rights Dear Colleague Guidance letter by covering six topics: historical and legal background; what parents need to know and do to ensure extracurricular interscholastic sport opportunities; best practices for practitioners and programs; leading adapted sport groups; extracurricular outdoor pursuits; and professional preparation relative to extracurricular athletic programs.

Meyer, A., Rose, D.H., & Gordon, D. (2014). *Universal design for learning: Theory and practice.* CAST Professional Publishing.

This book details the concept of universal design for learning. It covers re-envisioning education through UDL by describing its scientific rationale, its framework, and its curricular and instructional design.

U.S. Department of Education, Office for Civil Rights. (2013). *Dear colleague letter.* Author.

This letter is a response to the 2010 United States Governmental Accountability Office (GAO) report investigating physical education and extracurricular athletic opportunities in schools. It identifies and provides guidance for four areas in which school districts can improve opportunities for students with disabilities to participate more fully in physical education and extracurricular athletics.

U.S. Department of Education, Office of Special Education and Rehabilitative Services, Office of Special Education Programs. (2011). *Creating equal opportunities for children and youth with disabilities to participate in physical education and extracurricular athletics.* Author.

This document disseminates information on improving opportunities for children and youth to access physical education and athletics. It advances suggestions for improving opportunities based on research and professional opinion for children and youth with disabilities to participate by addressing common barriers to increased access and participation.

U.S. Government Accountability Office. (2010). Students with disabilities: More Information could improve opportunities in physical education and athletics. No. GAO-10-519 at 1, 31. www.gao.gov/assets/310/305770.pdf

This report summarizes an investigation of how physical education and extracurricular athletic opportunities for students with disabilities are provided in schools. It identifies several factors that limit participation in physical education and athletics.

Winnick, J.P., Auxter, D., Jansma, P., Sculli, J., Stein, J., & Weiss, R.A. (1980). Implications of Section 504 of the Rehabilitation Act as related to physical education instructional, personnel preparation, intramural, and interscholastic/intercollegiate sport programs. In J.P. Winnick & F.X. Short (Eds.), *Special athletic opportunities for individuals with handicapping conditions.* SUNY College at Brockport (ERIC Ed210897). Also in *Practical Pointers, 3*(11), 1-20.

This chapter provides a full position paper related to Section 504 of the Rehabilitation Act of 1973.

Online Resources

American Association of Adapted Sports Programs (AAASP): http://adaptedsports.org

AAASP provides an organizational structure and leadership to enable and facilitate statewide competition in school-based adapted sports.

Human Kinetics: www.humankinetics.com

This is the home of *Adapted Physical Activity Quarterly* and other adapted physical education and sport resources, published by Human Kinetics, P.O. Box 5076, Champaign, IL 61825-5076.

Minnesota Adapted Athletics Association (MAAA): www.mnadaptedathletics.org

This organization provides leadership and organizes interscholastic athletic opportunities for students with disabilities in the state of Minnesota.

National Center on Health, Physical Activity and Disability (NCHPAD): www.nchpad.org

NCHPAD provides information and resources to enable people with disabilities to become as physically active as possible.

Sports 'N Spokes: https://sportsnspokes.com

This site is a media source for sports and recreation, especially for those persons with spinal cord injuries, spina bifida, amputations, etc. The source features both national and international news as well as photos and videos. This source also offers an online magazine published by the Paralyzed Veterans of America (PVA).

PE Central: www.pecentral.org

PE Central exists to assist teachers and other adults in helping children become physically active and healthy for a lifetime. It provides up-to-date information on developmentally appropriate programs for school-aged children.

Sagamore journals: www.sagamorepub.com/sagamore-publications-journals and www.palaestra.com

This is the home of *Palaestra*, published by Sagamore Publishing and Applied Health Sciences, 1807 N. Federal Dr., Champaign, IL 61822.

2

Program Organization and Management

Joseph P. Winnick and David L. Porretta

Valeria, an elementary student with cerebral palsy, could definitely benefit from an individualized program to meet her physical education needs. Unfortunately for her, there is a great deal of confusion at her school. Is she eligible for adapted physical education? Should she participate in physical education with her nondisabled classmates? What should she be taught? How much time should she receive in physical education? Should she receive physical therapy? In Valeria's school, these issues are not unusual. Should her school have written guidelines to improve the educational process for her and other students? Yes, written guidelines are needed. This chapter will help you develop such guidelines.

The information in this chapter will help schools organize and manage programs and write guidelines reflecting policies and procedures for implementing adapted physical education programs. The guidelines can be a part of the overall plan for physical education or part of a separate document. In either case, guidelines should reflect current laws, rules and regulations, policies, procedures, and best practices.

Program and Curriculum Planning

An important early step for organizing and managing programs and developing guidelines is to identify the purpose, aims, goals, standards, and objectives for physical education. As part of this step, the similarities and differences between general and adapted physical education should be addressed. This provides a good beginning framework. There is no universal model, so educational entities must establish or adopt their own. A sample framework for adapted physical education is presented in the first chapter of this book (see figure 1.2) and can be adapted for use for a school plan. It also serves as the structure for this book.

Administrative Areas Related to Program Organization and Management

Personnel who administer school programs must develop procedures for organizing and implementing an adapted physical education program. These administrators must ensure that the resources at their disposal adequately meet the needs of the students they serve. They should have procedures in place to identify students who should receive adapted physical education programs, as well as a plan for selecting settings most appropriate for instruction. Because of the current emphasis on inclusion, understanding and promoting inclusion is an important consideration when implementing programs. Administrators must ensure that appropriate class sizes and groupings are provided, schedules are developed to meet student needs, mandated time requirements are met, sport opportunities are provided, and programs are appropriately funded and conducted in accessible facilities. These areas are addressed in more detail in the following sections.

Identifying Students for Adapted Physical Education

It is important to determine at the outset who is eligible for an adapted physical education program. In some instances, the decision is obvious, and an elaborate system of identification is not necessary. In other instances, determination of a unique need can be made only after assessment data are analyzed and compared with the established criteria.

An adapted physical education program is for students with unique needs who require a specially designed program exceeding 30 consecutive calendar days. In selecting candidates for such a program, procedures, criteria, and standards for determining unique needs are important (see chapters 4 and 5). The inability to attain health-related, criterion-referenced physical fitness standards appropriate for the individual is an example of a criterion for establishing a unique need. A unique need is exhibited because individual students are expected to meet standards appropriate for them.

Many procedures are used to identify students who require adapted physical education. These procedures are associated with **Child Find**, a program that tries to determine which children in a school have unique needs, as referred to in the Individuals with Disabilities Education Act (IDEA). The procedures might include screening

- all new school entrants,
- students with disabilities,
- all students annually,
- referrals, or
- students requesting exemption from physical education.

An important Child Find activity is the screening of all new entrants to the school. For transfer students, records should be checked to determine if unique needs in physical education have been previously identified. In the absence of such information, the school, as part of its procedures, might decide to administer a screening test, particularly if a unique physical education need is suspected.

A second Child Find source is a list of enrolled students identified as having a disability in accordance with IDEA. Every student who has been so identified and whose disability is associated with unique physical education needs should be routinely screened. Many children with disabilities have participated in preschool programs, and records from these programs might indicate children with unique physical education needs.

A third activity is the annual screening of all students enrolled in school. Such a screening might involve informal observation as well as formal testing. Conditions that might be detected through informal screening and could warrant in-depth evaluation include disabling conditions, obesity, clumsiness, aversion to physical activity, and postural deviations.

Many students are referred to adapted physical education. School guidelines should permit referrals from

- parents or guardians;
- professional staff members in the school district;
- physicians;
- judicial officers;
- representatives of agencies with responsibility for student welfare, health, or education; and
- students themselves (if they are at least 18 years of age or are emancipated minors).

Referrals for adapted physical education should be received by a specifically designated person in each school.

Medical excuses or requests for exemption from physical education should lead to referrals for adapted physical education. When an excuse or request is made, immediate discussion with the family physician might be necessary to determine how long adaptation might be required. For a period shorter than 30 consecutive days, adjustments can be determined by the general physical education teacher by following established local policies and procedures. If the period is longer than 30 consecutive days, the procedure for identifying students for adapted physical education for a school district should be followed. Typically, these procedures involve a planning committee.

Instructional Placements for Physical Education

Students who are referred or are otherwise identified as possibly requiring a specially designed program should undergo a thorough assessment to determine if a unique need exists. Suggested procedures for assessment appear in chapters 4 and 5. Once it is established that students have unique physical education needs and require an adapted physical education program, they must be placed in appropriate instructional settings. It must be emphasized that adapted physical education may be implemented in a variety of settings. In accordance with IDEA, children with disabilities must be educated in the least restrictive environment (LRE) to the maximum extent appropriate. To comply with the LRE requirement, various authors have proposed options on a continuum of instructional arrangements (figure 2.1). The number of available options is less important than educating students in the environment most conducive to their advancement, and in the general setting to the extent appropriate and possible. The continuum presented in figure 2.1 clearly depicts more possibilities than integrated or segregated placement alone and thus is consistent with IDEA.

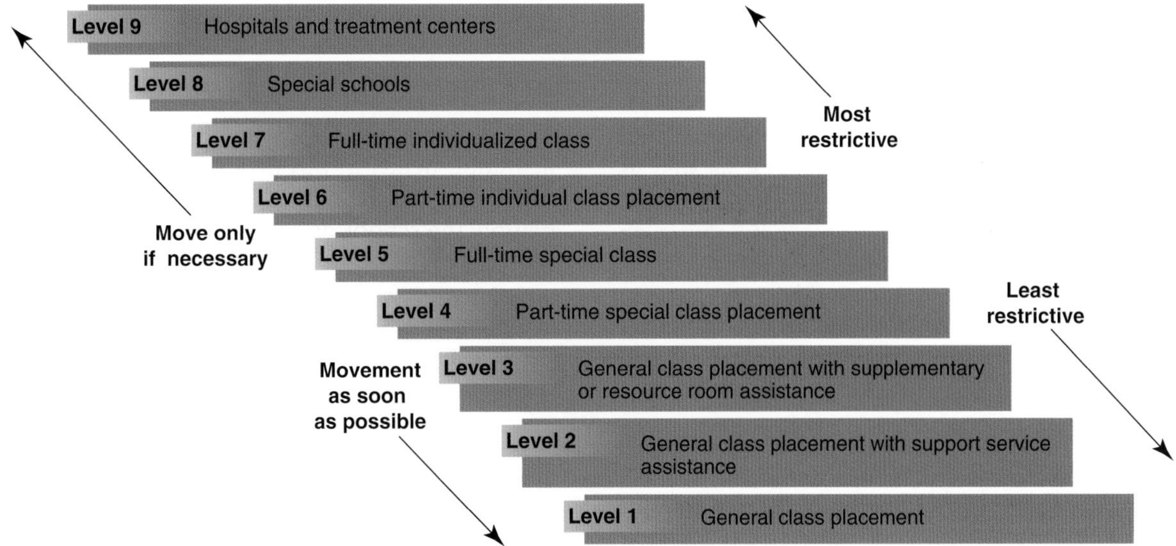

FIGURE 2.1 A continuum of alternative instructional placements in physical education.

The three placements at the base of the continuum occur in a general educational environment, and it is within these levels that the continuum is consistent with education in inclusive environments. Level 1 placement is for students without unique needs or those whose short-term needs are met in the general physical education program. This placement is also appropriate for students with unique needs requiring an adapted education program that can be appropriately implemented in the general physical education setting.

Level 2 is for students whose adapted physical education programs can be met in a general class environment with support services. For example, some students might function well if consultation is available to teachers and parents. In another instance, this level might be warranted if a paraprofessional or an adapted physical education teacher can work with the student with unique needs.

Level 3 is a general class placement with supplementary or resource room assistance. Supplementary services can be provided each day or several times a week as a part of or in addition to the time scheduled for physical education. Where indicated, the student might spend a portion of physical education time supervised in a resource room.

Students who require part-time special class placement represent level 4. Their physical education needs might be met at times in an integrated class and at other times in a segregated class. The choice of setting is determined by the nature of the students' unique needs.

Level 5, full-time placement in a special class, is appropriate for those whose needs cannot be appropriately met in the general physical education setting. Levels 6 and 7 are appropriate when part-time or full-time individual class placement is necessary.

Levels 8 and 9 reflect instructional placement in which needs must be met outside the local school. In level 8, instruction might take place in special schools; in level 9, instruction might occur in hospitals, in treatment centers, or even at a student's home. Students in levels 8 and 9 might be placed outside the school district. In such cases, the local school system is still responsible for ensuring that appropriate education is provided.

Inclusion

Inclusion has been one of the most powerful educational movements over the last 35 years. Although not specifically advocated as a part of IDEA, it is consistent with the requirement that students with disabilities be educated alongside students without disabilities to the maximum extent appropriate. A key foundation of inclusion is the belief that a separate education may not be an equal education.

The overwhelming majority of students with disabilities today are now being educated in general educational environments. For general education settings to be effective, however, they must be welcoming, supportive and respectful of *all* individual differences, and students who are educated in inclusive settings must have appropriate support services. Students not receiving necessary support services to succeed in a general education environment is not consistent with IDEA and the LRE philosophy.

Advocates of the inclusion movement point to many benefits for students. They believe that inclusion is advantageous for several reasons:

- It provides students with a more stimulating and motivating environment.
- It provides increased opportunities for students with disabilities to develop social skills and age-appropriate play skills.
- It promotes the development of friendships among students with and without disabilities.
- It provides a greater sense of acceptance, belonging, and value (Haegele, 2019).
- It provides skilled role models, which fosters the development of skills in all developmental domains.

Those less supportive of inclusion name the following possible problems:

- Students with disabilities might receive less attention and time on task than their classmates do.
- Some teachers are not adequately prepared for successful inclusion and do not possess the interest and motivation to teach in inclusive settings.
- Students without disabilities may be held back in their educational development.
- Inclusion is too expensive if it means providing support services and decreasing class sizes.
- School districts use the inclusion movement as a way of saving money by combining students with and without disabilities but not providing support services for successful educational experiences for all students.

However, these problems can be reduced or eliminated by appropriate program organization and instructional management. Education in the most inclusive setting possible is a legal right in the United States and must be supported.

As discussed in chapter 1, an educational approach now receiving a considerable amount of attention is *universal design for learning* (UDL) (Lieberman et al., 2021; Meyer et al., 2014). As conceptualized, UDL ensures that *all* students have access to and success in learning, especially those with unique educational needs. The UDL framework has particular relevance not only for adapted physical education teachers, but for general physical education teachers as well. UDL encompasses the design of educational facilities, materials, instructional methods, and assessments. To affirm its importance, the Every Student Succeeds Act (ESSA) of 2015 includes reference to UDL, especially as it relates to the design and use of technology to support the learning of all students, including those with disabilities. The overall programmatic framework is conceptualized around nine core tenets as described by McGuire and colleagues (2006) and Block (2016). These include

1. equitable use,
2. flexibility in use,
3. simple and intuitive use,
4. perceptible information,
5. tolerance for error,
6. low physical effort,
7. appropriate size and space,
8. community of learners, and
9. instructional climate.

A key aspect of UDL is for teachers to anticipate student differences and plan for them prior to instruction. However, teachers also need to monitor student progress and be able to implement adjustments along the way as needed.

UDL information relative to individualized instruction is addressed later in this chapter. Given its importance, additional discussion on UDL appears in chapter 7, as well as in many other chapters in this book.

Although this section of the chapter focuses on inclusion for physical education instruction, inclusive practices also have relevance for sport. Schools have a responsibility to provide both curricular and extracurricular experiences in the most inclusive settings possible. This book uses the term *adapted sport* when referring to sport opportunities for individuals with disabilities. A need exists to examine and provide opportunities in sport that include indi-

Participation in an inclusive physical education settng.

viduals both with and without disabilities in general or inclusionary settings. Adapted sport terminology enhances creativity and participation in both segregated and unified sport settings. Chapter 3 presents a model for sport that includes a comprehensive view of sport opportunities for individuals with disabilities. Of course, advocacy for inclusionary sport must not impede the aim for excellence. Athletes with disabilities should be encouraged to develop themselves optimally to participate at the highest level of athletic excellence, no matter the setting.

Functions of Teachers of Adapted Physical Education

This section discusses key functions performed by teachers and others who contribute to successful teaching of adapted physical education. These functions include identifying unique needs, determining appropriate instructional settings and supplementary or support services, selecting strategies for individualizing instruction, and adapting activities. Special consideration is given to individualized instruction and adapting activities within the context of UDL. Finally, preparing students without disabilities for inclusion and preparing support personnel are also discussed.

IDENTIFY UNIQUE NEEDS The first step is to identify the student's unique needs. Once this is accomplished, the most appropriate program content and objectives can be selected. In the absence of unique needs, the appropriate setting is general physical education.

The identification of unique needs is a foundational basis of an individualized education program (IEP). This determination is heavily based on screening and other assessment procedures, which schools will have in place. It is important for physical educators to be involved in determining students' needs in the field of physical education. Sample guidelines for determining unique needs are presented in chapter 4. Several chapters in this book include information to help identify, clarify, and meet unique needs.

DETERMINE APPROPRIATE INSTRUCTIONAL SETTINGS AND SUPPORT SERVICES Once unique needs are determined, settings for instruction and supplementary or support services can be identified. Possible settings are presented in figure 2.1. Settings for instruction depend on the support or supplementary services required. Support services might include team teaching, peer tutoring, teaching assistants, paraprofessionals, or volunteers. In addition to support services, there might be a need to identify and provide Section 504 accommodations to promote interaction, such as interpreters, facilities, equipment or supply modifications, and even rule modifications. Examples of supplementary services include physical, occupational, or recreation therapy as well as orientation and mobility training.

INDIVIDUALIZE INSTRUCTION The ability to individualize instruction is important. Individualization occurs when teachers make modifications in their objectives, methods of assessment, content, instructional materials, teaching styles, and instructional strategies and methods. Examples of individualized cycling activities for students with visual disabilities are presented in figure 2.2.

To enhance individualized instruction, UDL focuses on three overarching principles (Meyer et al., 2014, p. 7):

- *Multiple Means of Engagement.* Utilizing the interests of learners, offering choices of content and tools, and increasing motivation by offering adjustable levels of challenge. Various ways of getting and staying engaged in learning. It is the "why" of learning and results in motivated learners.
- *Multiple Means of Representation.* Giving learners various ways of acquiring information and knowledge by using a variety of methods to present information. Various ways to present and access information, concepts, and ideas. It is the "what" of learning and results in knowledgeable learners.
- *Multiple Means of Action and Expression.* Providing learners alternative ways of demonstrating what they know. Various ways of planning and executing learning tasks or skills. It is the "how" of learning and results in goal directed learners.

Each principle is further organized and expanded upon by guidelines (CAST, 2020). The guidelines for multiple means of engagement provide options for recruiting interest, sustaining effort, and self-regulation. The guidelines for multiple means of representation provide options for enhancing perception, language and symbols, and comprehension. The guidelines for multiple means of action and expression provide options for physical action, expression and communication, and executive functions. Taken collectively, UDL is designed to educate students who are ultimately purposeful and motivated, resourceful and knowledgeable, and strategic and goal-directed. The principles and guidelines are the basis from which appropriate activity variations, modifications, and adaptations (as well as facilities, curriculum, and assessment) in adapted physical education and sport can be used. A number of chapters in the book offer examples of activity variations and modifications. The next section describes possible activity adaptations. Additional ways to facilitate individualized instruction are also discussed elsewhere, including differentiated instruction (chapter 7), cooperative learning (chapter 7), and multisensory teaching (chapter 8).

ADAPT ACTIVITIES In order for individualized instruction within the context of UDL to be successful, teachers must adapt activities. Adapting activities increases the likelihood that students with varying abilities will have the same opportunity to participate and gain equal benefits from participation (see the Application Example sidebar). Of course, not all adaptations are equal, or lead to the same results, or are good. For example, allowing a student using a wheelchair to play in a traditional basketball game involving nine students without disabilities might jeopardize the education and safety of the players and is probably not a good modification strategy. Permitting a double dribble in a basketball game by a student with low cognitive functioning might be considered a good strategy by some teachers and students but be viewed as unfair by others. With this

FIGURE 2.2 Examples of individualized cycling activities for kids with visual disabilities include: *(a)* tandem cycling, *(b)* cooperative cycling, *(c)* group (conference bike) cycling.

Photos courtesy of Camp Abilities, Emily Gilbert.

in mind, it is useful to evaluate adaptations using established criteria. For the purpose of this book, the following criteria are suggested for determining good adaptations in settings that include students receiving adapted physical education. A good adaptation does the following:

- *Promotes interaction and interplay.* Good adaptations enhance interaction, cooperation, competition, and reciprocity to the extent appropriate.
- *Meets the needs of all students in the class.* Good adaptations meet the needs of all students and do not jeopardize the education of any student in class.
- *Improves or maintains self-esteem.* Good adaptations improve or maintain the self-esteem of all students. Adaptations should not embarrass or inappropriately draw attention to students.
- *Provides physical activity.* Good adaptations promote physical activity for all classmates as much as possible (e.g., elimination-type activities would be contraindicated).
- *Provides a safe experience for all.* Good adaptations sustain a safe environment for all participants.

Modifications for physical activities have been directly or indirectly categorized in many ways. Lieberman and Houston-Wilson (2018) suggest four modification areas for adapted activities: equipment, rules, environment, and instruction. Each area involves a change or variation so that students with unique needs might be better able to participate in skills or games. As an example, table 2.1 provides some ways in which the activities associated with softball can be modified using the four categories. The modifications may be applied to most or all physical activities and to one or more individuals participating in the activity. This book provides adaptations for physical education and sport based on these modification areas and others.

Although adapting physical activities via the four modification areas is a useful approach, adaptations can be enhanced in other ways as well. The sidebar Techniques for Promoting Physical Education Participation presents seven helpful techniques for involving students with and without disabilities. These techniques may also be evaluated using the criteria for good adaptations presented earlier. The first suggested technique is to permit the sharing, substitution, or interchange of duties in an activity. This technique is patterned after the idea of a pinch hitter or a courtesy runner in soft-

Application Example

How to Modify a Task to Include a Student With Intellectual Disabilities

SETTING

Seventh-grade physical education class

STUDENT

A 13-year-old student with intellectual disabilities and limitations in motor coordination

UNIT

Basketball

TASK

Dribble the ball around five cones in a weaving manner, return, give the ball to the next person in line, and then sit at the end of the line

APPLICATION

The physical educator might include the following task modifications:

- Permit the use of either the same or alternating hands.
- Permit the skipping of alternating cones or increase the distance between cones.
- Use a different ball size.
- Dribble for a shorter distance around fewer cones.
- Dribble at varying speeds.

Techniques for Promoting Physical Education Participation

- Permit the sharing, substitution, or interchange of duties in activities.
- Select activities in which contact is made and maintained with an opponent, partner, small group, or object.
- Modify some activities in a way that allows students without disabilities to assume disability.
- Modify or avoid elimination-type games and activities.
- Reduce play areas if movement capabilities are limited.
- Modify activities to use abilities rather than disabilities.
- Modify activities by giving handicaps.

TABLE 2.1 Modifications of Softball Activities

Category	Modifications
Equipment	Beep balls, auditory balls, bright balls, foam balls, Wiffle balls, large balls, auditory bases, large bases, tee, large plastic bats, light bats
Rules	Hit off a tee, five-strike rule, no strikeout, three swings and no strikes, running with a partner
Environment	Shorter distance between bases, increased number of players in a game, reduced number of bases, batting cages, smaller field, partner activities
Instruction	Physical assistance, peer tutors, teaching in braille, task analysis, sign language, hand signals, verbal cues, demonstration, auditory cues, one-on-one instruction

Data from Lieberman and Houston-Wilson (2018).

ball. In an inclusive setting, for example, a runner without disabilities might run to first base after a nonambulatory student strikes a softball from a tee, or a runner who is blind might run bases with a sighted partner.

A second helpful technique is to select activities in which contact can be made and maintained with an opponent, partner, small group, or object. Children with auditory or visual impairments might engage successfully in such activities as tug of war, chain tag, square dancing, and wrestling because continual contact is made with partners, team members, or opponents. Children with visual impairments might also use a rail to guide their approach while bowling.

A third helpful technique is to modify activities in such a way that all participants assume an impairment or disability. If not overused, this strategy can be useful in educating all children. Students without disabilities might simulate lower limb impairments during an activity by hopping on one foot; they could also close their eyes or be blindfolded while playing Marco Polo in a pool.

Modifying or avoiding elimination-type games or activities is a technique generally recommended for general physical education. In dodgeball, for example, rather than being eliminated from play when hit by a thrown ball, children might become throwers standing behind their opponents' end line or simply have a point charged against them. In a game of Jump the Shot, the winner could be the one who makes contact with the shot the least number of times rather than the last person remaining in the activity.

Participation is sometimes promoted when play areas are reduced for students with limited movement capabilities. For example, a student with a below-the-knee amputation and a prosthesis might successfully play tennis, badminton, or volleyball in a court that is narrower than standard. Years ago, American football players with vision impairments played on fields 10 yards (9 meters) wide. Reducing the size of play areas might also be advisable to decrease activity intensity for children exhibiting cardiopathic disorders, severe forms of diabetes, or other conditions affected by exercise intensity.

The next technique is to emphasize abilities rather than disabilities. For example, Deaf children or those who have vision impairments might be more successful in activities if auditory or visual cues or goals were used. Instead of running to a line, students with impaired vision might be asked to run toward a bell, horn, whistle, drum, or clapping sound. Students with impaired vision might also shoot baskets, perform archery, or play shuffleboard if an auditory goal locator is placed near the target. Students with severe movement restrictions or using wheelchairs might play a game in which the winner is the one who most closely predicts her time in negotiating 100 yards (91 meters), thus emphasizing cognitive abilities over physical ones.

A final recommended technique, and perhaps the most helpful, involves modifying activities by giving handicaps. This strategy originates from games such as bowling and golf, where handicaps are given to even the playing field. In a running relay, for example, a child with a lower limb impairment may run a shorter distance or be given a head start. In a basketball shooting contest, a student with less ability might participate by standing closer to the basket, using a smaller ball, or shooting at a larger rim. When playing Wiffle ball, students with eye–hand coordination deficits might be permitted to use a much larger plastic bat. In tennis, a player using a wheelchair might be permitted to strike the ball after it has bounced twice. In these instances, the idea is to see who can participate or win under the conditions determined at the outset.

PROMOTE AWARENESS AND ACCEPTANCE OF STUDENTS WITH DISABILITIES A fifth key function is promoting awareness and social acceptance of students with disabilities by general physical education students. It is commonly accepted that positive experiences contribute to overall peer acceptance and healthy social attitudes toward people with disabilities and their involvement in physical education and sport activities. Block (2016) has suggested several activities that general physical education teachers can implement to enhance awareness and acceptance. Examples include the following:

- Inviting guest speakers with disabilities who have had successful experiences in physical education and sport
- Conducting role-playing activities
- Talking about famous people who have disabilities
- Teaching about friendships
- Leading a discussion about disabilities
- Providing ongoing information, encouragement, and support for everyone

Exhibiting positive attitudes and modeling appropriate social behaviors are key factors for successful acceptance by general physical education students. The teacher should clearly convey that students with disabilities are individuals who belong in an inclusive society.

PREPARE SUPPORT PERSONNEL A sixth function of teachers who implement adapted physical education is to prepare support personnel. Successful teaching frequently depends on the provision of appropriate support services. Support services might be quite varied and might involve teaching assistants, paraprofessionals, related service professionals, adapted physical educators, volunteers, students, and others. To optimize the use of support personnel, the teacher needs to be confident that the personnel are prepared to provide their unique contributions. The nature of the preparation will vary according to the role that support personnel provide and the background of each contributor. Readers are referred to the work of Lieberman (2007) for detailed information regarding the preparation of support personnel.

Class Size and Type

Class size is an important variable to consider when placing students in instructional settings. Unfortunately, class sizes for physical education are often excessive. If quality instruction is expected, class sizes should not exceed 30 students in general settings. When students with unique physical education needs participate in the general education environment, the number of students in the class must be adjusted according to the nature of the disability, and supplementary aides and services should be available. Special or separated classes should not exceed 12 students, and this number should be reduced to six or fewer students when extraordinary needs are exhibited. In some rare instances, individualized instruction is warranted. The number of students in classes should be adjusted based on the number of professionals, paraprofessionals, and aides available to provide assistance. Chronological age affects placement as well. Age differences within a class should never exceed three years unless students are 16 or older. School officials should know and comply with their state laws and regulations governing class size and composition. Each school district should specify policies regarding class sizes and support services and apply them equitably to physical education classes and other areas of the school curriculum.

Scheduling

One must consider scheduling when making decisions regarding the setting for instruction. There are many approaches to scheduling that can accommodate various instructional arrangements. One effective method is to schedule supplementary and resource services for adapted physical education at the same time as general physical education. A large school might have four physical education teachers assigned to four general settings during a single period, along with a fifth teacher assigned to provide adapted physical education services. Other instructional arrangements might provide extra class time or alternative class periods to supplement participation in general physical education classes. In one scheduling technique used in elementary schools, a child placed in a special academic class joins an appropriate general physical education class. This arrangement meets the student's need to be integrated in physical education while receiving special support in academic areas. Schools in which students are permitted to select courses or units often have fewer scheduling problems because students may choose activities that fit their schedules and that they can participate in with little or no adjustment needed.

Time Requirements

Requirements for the frequency and duration of adapted physical education must be clearly specified in school plans and should at least equal that of the general physical education program. If state requirements for general physical education instruction are specified for various grade levels, and if adapted physical education students are placed in ungraded programs, the school's guidelines should express equivalent time requirements, using chronological age as the common reference point. A district plan should communicate state and federal requirements for physical education.

Physical education should be required of all students and should be adapted to meet unique needs. In cases of temporary disability, it is important to ascertain how long the student will require an adapted physical education program, and a standard should be set to distinguish temporary and long-term conditions. For this book, a short-term condition (e.g., a sprained ankle) ends within 30 consecutive calendar days and can be accommodated by the general physical education teacher. Participation in physical activity rather than alternative sedentary experiences should be required.

School districts also need to deal with the issue of permitting participation in athletic activities as a substitute for active time in physical education class. Although coordination of instruction and sport participation (general or adapted) is necessary, substitution should not be made unless it is approved in the student's IEP and the practice fits in with the overall physical education plan of the school district. In most cases, the substitution of athletics for physical education is not recommended and should not be permitted.

School districts must also clarify and coordinate instructional time requirements with related services. For instance, time spent in physical therapy must not supplant time in the physical education program. If appropriate guidelines are developed, few, if any, students should be exempt from physical education.

Sport Programs

An adapted physical education plan should include general guidelines on sport participation and its relation to the physical education program. In view of the details involved in implementing a comprehensive extracurricular sport program, a specific operating code should also be developed. The extracurricular sport program should reflect that the sport and adapted physical education programs are interrelated and interdependent. Extracurricular programs, including interscholastic programs, should be educational and build on the basic instructional program in adapted physical education. Students with disabilities should have equal opportunity to attain the same benefits from extracurricular activities as their peers without disabilities.

A sport program should emphasize the well-being of the participants in the context of games and sports. It is also important to ensure participation to the extent possible and reasonable. Health examinations before participation and periodically throughout the season, if necessary, promote safe participation. Athletes with disabilities should receive, at minimum, the same medical safeguards as other athletes.

For an interscholastic program that includes several schools, it is important to have a written statement of the principal educational goals as agreed to by the board of education, the administration, and other relevant individuals or groups. The statement should reflect a concern for student welfare, an interest in the educational aspects of athletic competition, and a commitment to the development of skills that yield health and leisure benefits both during and after the school years.

Over the past few years, increased attention has been given to providing sport opportunities for individuals with disabilities. In response to Section 504 of the Rehabilitation Act of 1973 and IDEA, educational and extracurricular opportunities must be provided in the least restrictive setting possible. Chapter 3 presents a framework to guide decisions on sport participation and stimulate the provision of innovative opportunities. Because interscholastic activities involve individuals and teams in different schools, there is a need for planning, coordination, and implementation at local, regional, county, and state levels. Additional information is presented in chapters 1 and 3.

Facilities

The facilities available for conducting programs in adapted physical education and sport might significantly affect program quality. The school athletic facilities should be operated in a way that makes them readily accessible to students with disabilities; in fact, Section 504 rules and regulations prohibit exclusion of individuals with disabilities from federally assisted programs because of architectural, program, or other environmental barriers. Provision of access may dictate structural changes in existing facilities. All new facilities should be constructed to ensure accessibility and usability.

In planning facilities in which to conduct adapted physical education and sport programs, attention must be given to indoor and outdoor areas, including teaching stations, lockers, and restrooms. Indoor facilities should have adequate activity space clear of hazards or impediments. The environment must have proper lighting, acoustics, and ventilation. Ceiling clearance should permit appropriate play. Floors should have a finish that enables all kinds of ambulation. When necessary, protective padding should be placed on walls. There should be plenty of space for wheelchairs to pass and turn.

Outdoor areas should be equally accessible and properly surfaced. Facilities should be available and marked for activities, including special sports. Walkways leading to and from outdoor facilities should be smooth, firm, free of cracks, and at least 48 inches (122 centimeters) wide. Doorways leading to the facilities should have at least a 36-inch (91-centimeter) clearance and be lightweight enough to be opened without undue effort; when possible, doorways should be automatically activated. Water fountains with both hand and foot controls should be conveniently located for use by individuals with disabilities. Colorful signs and tactile orientation maps of facilities should be posted to assist individuals with visual disabilities.

Participants in both adapted physical education and sport need adequate space for dressing, showering, and drying. Space must be sufficient for peak use periods. The design of locker rooms should facilitate ambulation and the maintenance of safe and clean conditions. Adequate ventilation, lighting, and heating are necessary. The shower room should be readily accessible and provide enough shower heads to accommodate everyone. The facilities should be equipped with grab rails. Locker rooms should include adequate benches, mirrors, and toilets. People with disabilities frequently prefer horizontal lockers and locks that are easy to manipulate. Planning must ensure that lockers are not obstructed by benches and other obstacles. All facilities must be in operable condition. Well-designed restrooms should have adequate space for manipulation of wheelchairs, easily activated foot or hand flush mechanisms, grab rails, and toilets and urinals at heights that meet the needs of the entire school population.

Swimming pools are among the most important facilities. Pool design must provide for safe and quick entry and exit. Water depth and temperature should be adjustable to meet learning, recreational, therapeutic, and competitive needs. Dressing, showering, and toilet facilities must be close by, with easy access to the pool. Additional information about aquatic facilities is included in chapter 24.

Students in adapted physical education and sport programs must have equal opportunity to use integrated facilities. Too often, segregated classes in physical education for students with disabilities are conducted in boiler rooms or hallways. Administrators have the responsibility to make sure that students with disabilities have the opportunity to attain the same benefits from school facilities as students without disabilities. Failure to do so is discriminating and demeaning to both students and school personnel.

Budget

An equitable education for a student with unique needs is more costly than that for a student without unique needs. To supplement local and state funds, the federal government has several programs that provide money for the education of people with unique needs. To facilitate the receipt of federal funds for physical education, physical educators must be sure that they are involved in IEP development.

Funds associated with IDEA are specifically earmarked to help provide for the excess costs of special education (i.e., costs that exceed student expenditure in general education). These funds flow through state education departments (which are permitted to keep a certain percentage) and on to local education agencies. This flow-through money can be used to help cover excess costs already assumed by states. Because physical education involves students both with and without disabilities, it is less discriminatory for schools to employ teachers in physical education, whether general or adapted, from the same local funding source than to rely on federal money. This is justifiable because states are responsible for the education of all their students.

In addition to meeting needs identified in IEPs, funding must support the professional development of teachers to provide quality services for students with disabilities. For example, funds are needed for workshops, clinics, local meetings, professional conferences and conventions, program visitations, and so on. Schools also need funds to maintain up-to-date libraries and reference materials.

Interscholastic teams made up of students with disabilities must receive equitable equipment, supplies, travel expenses, officials, and so on. Although the funding level for curricular and extracurricular activities in a local community is not state dictated, available funds cannot be used in a discriminatory fashion (e.g., available to male students but not female students, or available to students without disabilities but not to students with disabilities).

Human Resources

A quality program in adapted physical education and sport depends to a great extent on quality human resources. People are needed to coordinate and administer services, fulfill technical and advocacy functions, and provide instruction. To provide high-quality services for adapted physical education and sport, involved personnel must work together effectively. In doing so, it is helpful to understand roles and responsibilities and to realize that the concern for students with unique needs is shared by many. This section identifies key personnel and discusses their primary roles and responsibilities. Many perform their responsibilities by serving on committees (identified in chapter 5).

Director of Physical Education and Athletics

Although not a universal practice, it is desirable for all aspects of physical education and sport programs to be under the direction of an administrator certified in physical education. Such centralization enhances coordination and efficiency in regard to personnel, facilities, equipment, budgeting, professional development, and curriculum. The director of physical education and athletics should oversee all aspects of the program, including the work of the coordinator of adapted physical education (if that position exists).

Because adapted physical education and sport is often in the developmental stage and not a well-advocated part of the total program, the physical education director needs to demonstrate genuine concern and commitment to this part of the program. A positive attitude serves as a model for others. With the assistance of other administrative personnel, such as the coordinator of special education services, the director can help the adapted physical education and sport program by ensuring adequate funding, employing qualified teachers, and providing support services. The director must also be knowledgeable about adapted physical education and sport to work effectively with individuals and groups outside the department. The director must work with other directors, coordinators, school principals, superintendents, and school boards and must have positive professional relationships with medical personnel. Other important relationships are those with parents, teachers, students with disabilities, and advocacy groups. For this reason, the director of physical education and sport must stay informed about all students who are identified as having unique needs.

General Physical Educator

Although adapted physical educators are sometimes employed by a school, the general physical educator plays a vital role in implementing quality programs in adapted physical education and sport. Table 2.2 presents several functions that are shared by or are the primary responsibility of general physical educators. General physical educators play an important role in screening and referring students to appropriate committees. They will also implement instructional programs in integrated environments and help implement sport programs. Thus, it is important for general physical education teachers to be knowledgeable and skilled in implementing individualized instruction programs for all students within a UDL framework, regardless of whether students possess a disability.

Adapted Physical Educator or Coordinator

To provide a quality comprehensive school program in adapted physical education and sport, schools are advised to employ a qualified teacher

TABLE 2.2 Primary Responsibility for Functions Relevant to Adapted Physical Education and Sport

	RESPONSIBILITY	
Function	**General physical educator**	**Adapted physical educator or coordinator**
MEASUREMENT, ASSESSMENT, AND EVALUATION		
Student screening	X	X
In-depth testing		X
Student assessment and evaluation		X
Adapted physical education or sport program evaluation		X
TEACHING OR COACHING		
Implementation of instructional programs for students with short-term unique needs	X	
Implementation of instructional programs to meet long-term unique needs in integrated environments	X	X
Implementation of instructional and sport programs with guidance of adapted physical educator	X	
Implementation of adapted sport programs		X
MANAGEMENT AND LEADERSHIP		
Consultation		X
In-service education		X
Advocacy and interpretation		X
Recruitment and preparation of aides and volunteers		X
Chair adapted physical education committee		X
Liaison with health professionals	X	X
Referral and placement	X	X
Organization of adapted sport program		X

of adapted physical education to provide direct teaching responsibilities and program coordination and leadership. In a small school, this might be a part-time position; in larger schools, a full-time adapted physical education teacher or coordinator might be needed. Although most states do not require a special endorsement, credential, or certification to teach adapted physical education, it is best to select someone who has considerable professional experience. If possible, the teacher or coordinator should have completed a recognized specialization or concentration in adapted physical education and, where applicable, should meet the competency requirements for state certification or endorsement. Should the state not have a certification requirement, the district should employ a person who has gained national certification in adapted physical education. The last and least desirable option is to entrust those duties to someone who is a respected physical education professional,

Characteristics of a Good Consultant

- Establishes a positive rapport in the consulting environment
- Is prepared in the field of consultation
- Has a passion for the consulting role
- Encourages others to provide information and share ownership of results
- Works as an equal rather than as an authority
- Asks for feedback during the consultancy (helping) process
- Establishes trust
- Employs empathetic listening
- Plans programs jointly
- Accepts constructive criticism

demonstrates genuine interest in the field, and is willing to enhance their knowledge and skills in teaching children with disabilities.

The role and functions of the teacher or coordinator will depend on the size of the school, the number and types of students with disabilities within the school population, and the number and types of students involved in adapted physical education and sport. Generally, however, the teacher or coordinator needs to assume a leadership role in various functions associated with adapted physical education and sport. The specific functions often differ more in degree than in kind from those performed by general physical educators. Table 2.2 identifies typical functions associated with adapted education and sport and indicates who is responsible for those functions. Functions may overlap or be shared; specific lines of demarcation should be drawn to suit local conditions.

One function that adapted physical educators are increasingly called on to perform is to serve as a consultant for a school or school district. Colleges and universities preparing adapted physical education specialists are increasingly placing more attention on preparing students for this consulting role. Consultants serve as resources to general physical educators and anyone else who affects the quality of services in physical education and sport. They should be able to assess needs, plan and implement programs, and evaluate educational experiences. Consultants might provide information on many topics, including information on disabilities and implications for teaching physical education; ways of adapting methods, activities, and assessment practices and procedures for students with unique needs; strategies for controlling student behavior; information regarding recent legislation affecting students receiving special education; and information on developing individualized education and 504 plans for students with disabilities. (See the Characteristics of a Good Consultant sidebar for more.)

Nurse

The school nurse is an allied health professional with an important part in the successful development and implementation of adapted physical education and sport programs. The nurse must be knowledgeable about the adapted physical education and sport program and, ideally, should serve on the committee on adapted physical education. If time permits, the school nurse can assist the physical education staff in testing students, particularly in the case of postural screening. The nurse can also keep medical records, communicate with physicians, and help parents and students understand the importance of exercise and physical activity. By helping to convey information required for individual education planning, the nurse can be a valuable resource.

Physicians

Physicians have an important relationship with the adapted physical education and sport program. The physician's role is so important that it is often addressed in federal, state, or local laws, rules, and regulations. In some instances, states look to a designated school physician for the final decision on athletics. School physicians also provide and interpret medical information on which school programs are based. The responsibility for interpreting the adapted physical education and sport program for family physicians and other medical personnel also lies with the school physician.

In states where physical education is required of all students, physicians must know and support laws and regulations. They must be confident that if a student is unable to participate without restriction in a general class, adaptations will be made. Physicians should be aware of how physical education and adapted physical education have changed over recent years and should understand their role and responsibilities within the existing programs.

One of a physician's important functions is to administer physical examinations. Examination results are used as a basis for individualized student evaluation, program planning, placement, and determination of eligibility and qualification for athletic participation. It is desirable for students with unique physical education needs to receive an exam every three years, beginning in the first grade. Exams should be annual for those assigned to adapted physical education because of medical referrals. School districts that do not provide physical exams should require adequate examination by the student's family physician. For students covered by IDEA, medical examinations must be given in accordance with state and local policies and procedures. For athletic participation, exams should be administered at least annually.

Coaches

Adapted sport programs should be operated under the direction of qualified school personnel. When an adapted program includes interscholastic athletic teams, standards for coaches must be consistent with those for the general interscholastic athletic program. Teachers certified in physical education should be permitted to coach any sport, including those in which participants have disabilities. Ideally, coaches of teams composed primarily of players with unique needs should have expertise in adapted physical education.

Coaches must follow acceptable professional practices. These include maintaining a positive attitude; insisting on good sportsmanship, respect, and personal control; and continuing to improve professionally through in-service programs, workshops, and clinics.

Related Services Personnel

Under IDEA (Office of Special Education and Rehabilitative Services [OSE/RS], 2006), related services include transportation and other developmental, corrective, and supportive services required to help children with disabilities benefit from special education. Related services include speech–language pathology and audiology services; psychological services; physical and occupational therapy; recreation, including therapeutic recreation; early identification and assessment of disability in children; counseling services, including rehabilitation counseling; orientation and mobility services; and medical services for diagnostic and evaluation purposes. Related services also include school health services, social work services in schools, and parent counseling and training.

Related service providers who significantly influence physical education include occupational and physical therapists. According to the rules and regulations for the implementation of IDEA, occupational therapy includes improving, developing, or restoring functions impaired or lost through illness, injury, or deprivation; improving ability to perform tasks for independent functioning when functions are impaired or lost; and using early intervention to prevent initial or further impairment or loss of functioning. The same rules and regulations define physical therapy as services provided by a qualified physical therapist. These services have traditionally included physical activities and other physical means for rehabilitation prescribed by a physician. The rules and regulations specify that recreation includes assessment of leisure function, therapeutic recreation services, recreation programs in schools and community agencies, and leisure education.

Much has been written about the relation of adapted physical education to physical and occupational therapy. The lines of responsibility among these areas are often blurred; however, it is clear that related services—for example, physical and occupational therapy—must be provided if a student requires them to benefit from physical education or other direct services. IDEA specifies that physical education must be made available to children with disabilities, and states have their own requirements concerning the provision of physical education. Clearly, physical therapy and adapted physical education are not identical, and related services are not to supplant physical education or adapted physical education, which are direct services under IDEA.

Several assumptions about the role of physical education might underlie the decision about who will design programs to improve the physical fitness of students with disabilities. First, it is the physical educator's responsibility to design these programs. Thus, the physical educator is involved with the development of strength, endurance, cardiorespiratory endurance, and flexibility (range of motion); this responsibility concerns both affected and unaffected parts of the body. Physical educators must consult physicians and other medical personnel as they plan and implement programs. Such consultations should be consistent with the adapted physical education program of the school.

Sometimes improvements in physical development cannot be attained by a physical educator using the usual time allotments, methods, or activities associated with physical education. In such cases, physical or occupational therapy can enhance physical fitness development. Activities included in the physical education programs of students with disabilities should be those that are typically within the scope of physical education. These are the kinds of activities subsumed under the definition of physical education in the rules and regulations of IDEA, as described in chapter 1.

The physical educator must offer a broad spectrum of fun and well-liked physical education activities. Children who require exercise lasting an entire physical education period should meet this need in class time added to the regularly scheduled physical education period, or it should be a provided service. This approach would permit involvement in a broad spectrum of activities within the regularly scheduled physical education class. Physical educators should also have the knowledge to help students appropriately use wheelchairs and supportive devices in physical education activities. However, it is not their responsibility to provide functional training in the use of those aids for basic movement or ambulation.

Although much can be written concerning roles and responsibilities, the quality of services provided often depends on the interpersonal relationships of service providers. Successful situations are those in which professionals have discussed their roles and responsibilities and work hard to deliver supportive services to benefit students with unique needs.

Paraeducators

Paraeducators and many other support personnel play a vital role in adapted physical education and sport; therefore it is important that they be appropriately prepared for their roles and responsibilities (Lieberman, 2007). Paraeducators should provide assistance in instructional and extracurricular experiences, which may include assisting teachers with implementing behavior management plans, providing performance feedback, and collecting and documenting student learning, among other responsibilities. Paraeducators should be provided at a ratio that is consistent with the other subject areas according to state laws, rules, regulations, and guidelines. Qualifications should be in accord with appropriate state and local regulations. Ideally, paraeducators will enhance and assist other support personnel, including instructional volunteers, tutors, coaches, or officials who serve to enhance the learning environment. As a result, their efforts should be recognized and valued.

General Program Evaluation

At the beginning of this chapter, the importance of guidelines for program organization and management was stressed. This chapter has presented background information that can be used to develop such guidelines. Once in place, the guidelines can serve as a basis for program direction, implementation, and evaluation. Program evaluation might encompass the total physical education program or just the adapted physical education component. Ideally, the guidelines should be evaluated at five-year intervals and draw on data collected from a variety of relevant sources.

Appendix D presents a sample rating scale to assess six essential areas related to program organization and management: curriculum, required instruction, attendance, personnel, facilities, and administrative procedures. It contains a series of criterion statements that reflect guidelines suggested in this chapter. The entire scale or selected parts may be used to collect data for program evaluation. An instrument for evaluation is best used for self-appraisal and developing a plan to identify and remedy weaknesses and reinforce strengths. The areas of evaluation related to program organization and management in appendix D supplement the instructional and standards-based assessment and evaluation discussed in chapter 4.

Summary

Well-organized and well-managed programs for adapted physical education are built on appropriate policies and procedures, which are enhanced by written guidelines on how to implement them. This chapter has provided information that may be used for the development of programs and program guidelines in the areas of program and curriculum planning, administrative procedures and program implementation, human resources, and general program evaluation.

References

Block, M.E. (2016). *A teacher's guide to adapted physical education: Including students with disabilities in sport and recreation* (4th ed.). Brookes.

Center for Applied Special Technology (CAST). (2020). *Universal design for learning guidelines: Frequently asked questions*. Wakefield, MA: Author. Retrieved from https://udlguidelines.cast.org/more/frequently-asked-questions

Haegele, J. (2019). Inclusion illusion: Questioning the inclusiveness of integrated physical education. *Quest, 71*(4), 387-397. http://doi.org/10.1080/00336297.2019.1602547

Lieberman, L.J. (Ed.). (2007). *Paraeducators in physical education*. Human Kinetics.

Lieberman, L., Grenier, M., Brian, A., & Arndt, K. (2021). *Universal design for learning in physical education*. Human Kinetics.

Lieberman, L., & Houston-Wilson, C. (2018). *Strategies for inclusion: A handbook for physical educators* (3rd ed.). Human Kinetics.

McGuire, J., Scott, S., & Shaw, S. (2006). Universal design and its applications to educational environments. *Remedial and Special Education, 27*(3), 166-175.

Meyer, A., Rose, D., & Gordon, D. (2014). *Universal design for learning: Theory and practice*. CAST Professional Publishing.

Office of Special Education and Rehabilitative Services (OSE/RS), 34 CFR (2006).

Print Resources

Craft, D.H. (Ed.). (1994). Inclusion: Physical education for all. *Journal of Physical Education, Recreation and Dance, 65*(1), 22-56.

This periodical provides a special issue on inclusion, including information on making curricular modifications, promoting equal-status relationships among peers, and teaching collaboratively with others, as well as research on inclusion, ideas on infusion, and experiences implementing inclusion in two schools.

Lieberman, L.J. (Ed.). (2007). *Paraeducators in physical education*. Human Kinetics.

This manual is a training guide on the roles and responsibilities of paraeducators in physical education.

Lieberman, L., Grenier, M., Brian, A., & Arndt, K. (2021). *Universal design for learning in physical education*. Human Kinetics.

This book provides the framework and principles of UDL within the context of physical education. It covers assessment, practical applications, and sample unit plans.

Lieberman, L., & Houston-Wilson, C. (2018). *Strategies for inclusion: A handbook for physical educators* (3rd ed.). Human Kinetics.

This source provides background information and strategies for successful integration of a child with disabilities into a traditional physical education setting and contains teachable units that include assessment tools for curriculum planning as well as a chapter on UDL.

Winnick, J.P. (2014). *Rating scale for adapted physical education*. Unpublished manuscript. The College at Brockport, State University of New York.

This rating scale can be used as a self-assessment instrument on which to base evaluation of an adapted physical education program. The scale presents criterion statements reflecting guidelines implicitly suggested in this chapter. The rating scale can be found in appendix D.

3

Adapted Sport

Ronald W. Davis

Beth is a champion swimmer. She competed in the sport through middle school, high school, and college and at the world-class level. At each stage of her swimming career, Beth had success and setbacks but remained focused on her goal of becoming one of the top swimmers in the world.

Swimming as an athlete for the United States Association of Blind Athletes (USABA) eventually brought Beth an invitation to the Paralympic Trials for the 1996 Atlanta Paralympic Games. The Paralympic Trials not only earned Beth a spot on the U.S. Paralympic team, but also secured her a full scholarship as a collegiate swimmer.

Beth accomplished her goals through a combination of hard work, coaching, and family support, plus the guidance of others through various sport settings empowered by several sport delivery options.

Given the impact and growth of sporting opportunities for individuals with disabilities, it is important to note that various terminology may be used, such as *traditional sport*, *general* or *regular sport*, *disability sport*, or *adapted sport*. This author believes that "sport is sport," rather than getting mired in the issue of which term is correct—however, for consistency, the term *adapted sport* encompasses disability sport as well as sport modified or created to meet the unique needs of individuals.

This chapter discusses opportunities for individuals with disabilities to experience and benefit from extracurricular interscholastic sport as part of their educational journey. It covers the legislative background, a sport framework for individuals with disabilities, and the special education and general physical education services available to address adapted sport. A final section deals with the organizational structure of adapted sport, including the national and international levels and competitions.

© Laura Leonard Fitch

Sport can provide a sense of accomplishment.

Legislative Background

Although this chapter focuses largely on competitive athletic opportunities, physical educators should consider adapted sport in the broadest sense possible, including leisure-time recreational pursuits that enable students with disabilities to practice healthy living outside the school setting. Adapted sport should also be viewed as legitimate, serious sport with competition of highest quality; it should not be seen as only a social experience. A decisive piece of legislation that helped open the doors for the development of sport for individuals with disabilities was the Olympic and Amateur Sports Act of 1998. Additional legislative support for adapted sport and extracurricular activities in schools included the 1973 Rehabilitation Act, with a focus on Section 504, and the guidance document issued by the Office of Civil Rights, housed within the U.S. Department of Education, titled the "Dear Colleague" Letter (Arnhold et al., 2013). This legislation is discussed in more detail in chapter 1.

Olympic and Amateur Sports Act and USOC

The Amateur Sports Act of 1978, amended in 1998 as the Olympic and Amateur Sports Act (within the omnibus appropriations bill), was perhaps the one piece of legislation that provided the catalyst for the expansion of adapted sport. Sponsored by former senator Ted Stevens of Alaska, the Olympic and Amateur Sports Act reorganized the United States Olympic Committee (USOC) and administration of amateur sport in the United States. The amended act strengthened the linkage between the USOC and athletes with disabilities by including the Paralympic Games and amateur athletes with disabilities within its scope and within the USOC. With the available resources and prestige attached to the USOC, sport organizations for people with disabilities had more opportunities to build their sport programs. The USOC's constitution was rewritten to reflect the new commitment to adapted sport and intent of the law:

> To encourage and provide assistance to amateur athletic programs and competition for amateur athletes with disabilities, including, where feasible, the expansion of opportunities for meaningful participation by such amateur athletes in programs of athletic competition for able-bodied amateur athletes. (USOC, 1998)

Formal Name Change by United States Olympic Committee

On June 20, 2019, the United States Olympic Committee (USOC) and the Paralympic Committee (PC) merged to create the U.S. Olympic and Paralympic Committee (USOPC). This was a landmark change by the board of directors that was passed to promote and celebrate these organizations' commitment to providing all individuals the opportunity to engage in competitive sport. This change is not in name and branding only, but helped to clarify that elite athletes from the United States are represented by one organization. This landmark event has also fostered the name change for the U.S. Olympic Hall of Fame to the U.S. Olympic and Paralympic Hall of Fame and will increase monetary awards for U.S. Paralympic medalists to match those earned by Olympic athletes.

Additional Legislation to Support Extracurricular Activities

Section 504 of the Rehabilitation Act of 1973, 29 U.S.C. §794 *et seq.* (Rehabilitation Act, 1973) is the United States' first civil rights law for persons with disabilities. PL 93-112 was passed to guarantee individuals with disabilities inclusion in all aspects of society through equal opportunity. Other civil rights laws such as the Americans with Disabilities Act (ADA) (1990) and the 2004 Individuals with Disabilities Education Act (IDEA) addressed discrimination against persons with disabilities, including segregation, the right to vote or marry, and other exclusions from opportunities such as hiring practices based on disability discrimination (ADA, 1990). The discrimination prohibitions recognized by ADA were also recognized in the Rehabilitation Act of 1973. Within Section 504 of the Rehabilitation Act, students with disabilities were provided the right to access and opportunity with regard to extracurricular activities, including interscholastic sports.

In 2010, the federal government revisited the implementation of PL 93-112 and Section 504 to assess how students with disabilities were being served in physical education and extracurricular sporting activities. As part of the reassessment, Congress charged the Government Accountability Office (GAO) with investigating the status of Section 504 and its impact on extracurricular sport for students with disabilities. The results were shared with Congress in a 2011 GAO report and used as a guide in the writing of the 2013 Dear Colleague Letter from the Office of Civil Rights (OCR). The Dear Colleague Letter was sent to all public school administrators whose programs received federal funding, highlighting four key points of guidance. The GAO suggested that schools

1. address general legal requirements of the Rehabilitation Act—that is, implement a review of the mandates;
2. recognize that school districts cannot rely on generalizations and stereotypes—that is, school districts must use some form of assessment or performance to justify participation in a sport program (i.e., school districts cannot cut a player from a team solely based on disability);
3. ensure equal opportunity for participation—that is, conduct school-sponsored interscholastic teams and, if this is not possible, implement alternative activities such as clubs or intramurals; and
4. offer separate or different athletic opportunities—that is, engage community-based sport programs.

The Dear Colleague Letter offered guidance to ensure that students with disabilities are provided with equal opportunities for sport participation to the maximum extent possible. The letter recognized that creating these opportunities would require adjustments or modifications to rules, playing areas, and equipment that should not change the integrity of the competition and should include reasonable accommodations. Such accommodations may come in the form of rule changes—for example, modifying the two-hand touch in breaststroke for a student with a below-elbow amputation, allowing two bounces in a tennis match for a wheelchair user, or providing for the use of an extension pole to tap swimmers who have a visual impairment on the back as they neared the wall to execute a flip turn. The following sport framework is offered to address the four key points highlighted in the Dear Colleague Letter and to help school, community, and athletic administrators implement sport competition programs for individuals with disabilities.

Support Documents and Agreements Affecting Adapted Sport

In 2015, the following documents became available to assist in the development of school-based and community-based adapted sport. The American Association of Adapted Sports Programs (AAASP), the National Federation of State High School Associations (NFHS), and the National Interscholastic Athletic Administrators Association (NIAAA) submitted guidelines titled "Addressing Best Practices in Education-Based Athletics for Students With Physical Disabilities Through Interscholastic Adapted Team Sports" (AAASP, 2019). The intent of this document was to provide school officials, teachers, and coaches with best practices for including team sports for students with physical disabilities within an existing athletic public school structure.

A second document promoting long-term athlete development was created by the United States Olympic Committee in partnership with the national governing bodies to help Americans realize their full athletic potential and utilize sport as a path toward an active and healthy lifestyle (World Para Winter Sports, 2016). Content pertaining to Paralympic sport is included in the model, which features four key elements: Statement, Visual Model, NGB Programming, and Resources.

Sport Framework for Individuals With Disabilities

This section presents a sport framework for individuals with disabilities that will serve as a reference point for the majority of this chapter. This framework is designed for implementing adapted sport in schools, community, college, and beyond. The framework has two key options: (1) sport settings and (2) sport delivery options. Sport settings are defined as the locations of sport programs, or *where* they occur, whereas sport delivery options are defined as the formats for *how* the sports are delivered.

This framework is designed to be interactive by crossing sport settings with delivery options in a manner that fits students and athletes or other program needs. This combination enables the user to combine delivery options across different settings and not be concerned about a hierarchy or continuum of implementation (see figure 3.1).

Sport Settings

This section discusses the following types of sport settings within the framework: school based, interscholastic, community, college, and open. Each sport setting provides an example of how students with disabilities can excel in sport across settings familiar to all athletes.

School Based

School-based settings are those considered part of the infrastructure of a school campus or building. School-based sport program settings might include intramural programs such as floor hockey or indoor soccer or traditional sports such as basketball, softball, and volleyball. These school-based settings may also include school sport clubs such as outdoor recreation, camping, or hiking.

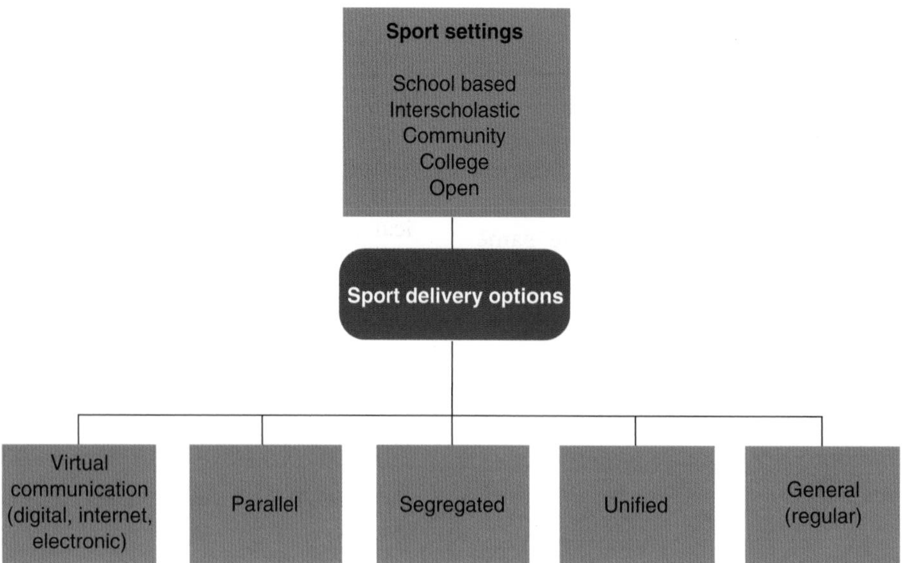

FIGURE 3.1 Sport framework for individuals with disabilities.

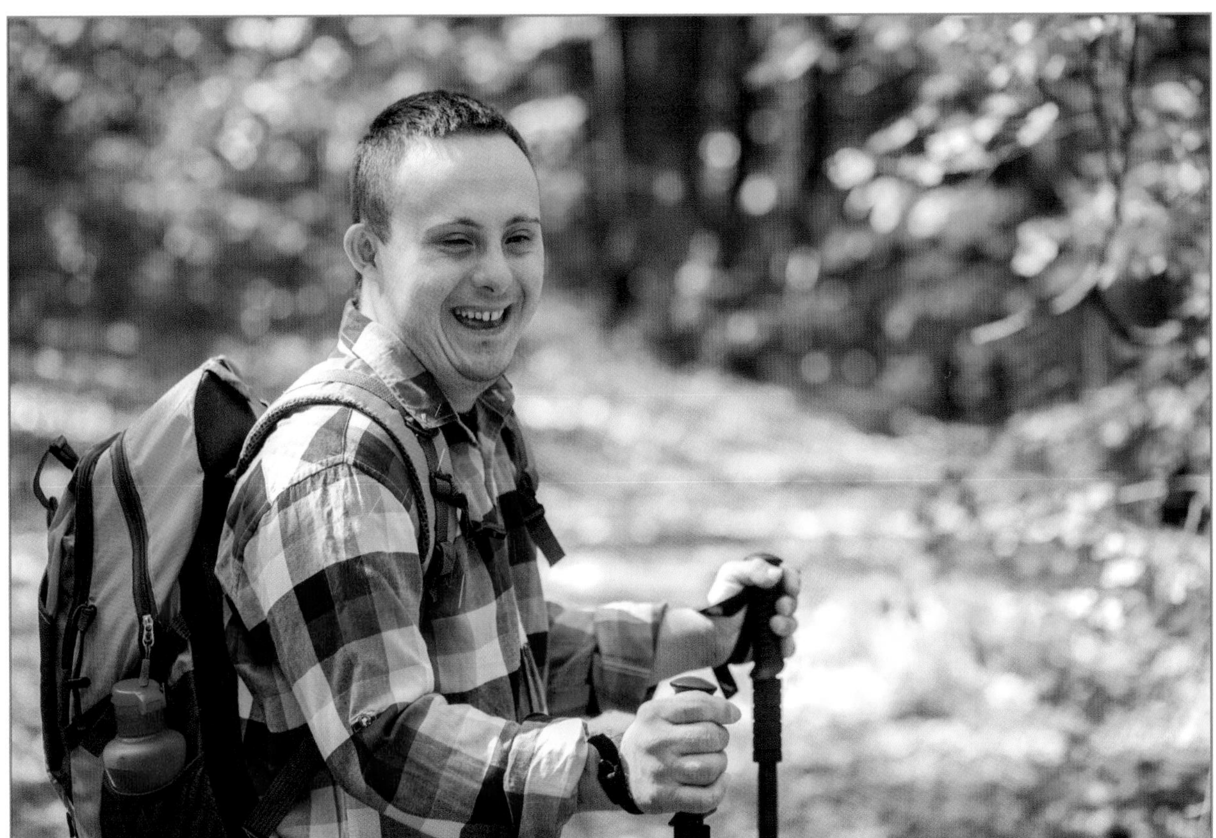

Sladic/E+/Getty Images

Participating in a school-based hiking sport club.

Interscholastic

Similar to school-based settings, interscholastic sport program settings emphasize competition against other schools, usually on a district or conference level, resulting in regional and state championships. Interscholastic sport programs are highly competitive and often offer gateways for athletes to continue competing at the college level via scholarships. Interscholastic sport settings should be offered for individuals with disabilities (as supported by the GAO findings, Section 504, and the Dear Colleague Letter) with the same opportunities, competitions, and rewards.

As mentioned earlier in the chapter, the United States Olympic and Paralympic Committee have formed a new brand. The official acronym is USOPC and it will govern all Olympic and Paralympic athletic competition. Another merger was the creation of the sport organization called Move United Sport. This merger combined the organizations of Adapted Sports USA and Disabled Sports USA. Move United has reported the top 10 states in the nation that offer leading adapted sport programs: Colorado, California, Florida, New Hampshire, Oregon, Maryland, Virginia, Maine, Michigan, and Vermont (Move United, n.d.). The next section provides additional information about Move United.

Community

Community sport settings are programs offered by recreation centers or by sport clubs associated with established disability sport organizations. For example, Paralympic Sport Clubs, associated with the U.S. Paralympics, are community-based programs to involve youth and adults with physical disabilities and visual impairments in sport and physical activity, regardless of skill level. All programs and activities are run by the local organizations. The U.S. Paralympics is committed to working with community organizations across the United States to ensure that Paralympic Sport Clubs are operating in strategic locations in all 50 states. The goal of this community program setting is to expand Paralympic programs across the United States (www.teamusa.org/US-Paralympics/Sports).

Another example of a community sport setting is the BlazeSports America program (www.blazesports.org). The mission of BlazeSports America is to change the lives of children and adults with physical disabilities through sport. BlazeSports America offers a Certified Disability Sports Specialist (CDSS) course, which helps ensure quality program development in the community.

In most communities, the Special Olympics organization—which is nationally and internationally renowned for its contributions to sport for individuals with intellectual disabilities—is another example of a community sport setting. Some school districts link their Special Olympics programs through school infrastructures, which addresses the Dear Colleague Letter's fourth key point encouraging schools to work with community-based sport programs. This might be interpreted as an interscholastic sport setting; however, this is not accurate. Special Olympics conducts athletic competition within a school district, but the competition is not between two school-based Special Olympics programs; it is competition between athletes within a community-based program (i.e., Special Olympics) who attend the schools, but are not sponsored by the schools.

The most recent example of a new community-based program occurred when Adaptive Sport USA and Disability Sport USA, two organizations with similar goals related to the involvement of athletes with disabilities, merged in May 2020 to create Move United (Groth, 2020). Move United's focused goal is to fully include individuals with disabilities using sport, exercise, and recreation as vehicles for change. Move United will seek to unite communities around the United States to enhance the perception of individuals with disabilities and promote health, fitness, and recreation. Move United will offer programs that address sport training (e.g., swimming, track and field, and wheelchair football), inclusive outdoor recreation (e.g., orienteering and hiking), and more. Read more about this newly formed organization at www.moveunitedsport.org.

College

In January 2015, the Eastern College Athletic Conference (ECAC) announced a monumental opportunity for student-athletes with disabilities. The board of directors adopted an inclusive sport strategy that includes new intercollegiate athletic opportunities for student-athletes with disabilities, making the ECAC the first NCAA-sanctioned conference to provide multiple opportunities for athletes with disabilities to engage in intercollegiate varsity athletics in NCAA Divisions I, II, and III (Breaking a Boundary, 2015).

Historically, the National Wheelchair Basketball Association (NWBA) has also recognized seven college or university wheelchair basketball teams with a focus on training, winning, and high performance. Search for current members of the college division of the NWBA at www.nwba.org.

Open

Open sport settings are those that may exist simultaneously with high school interscholastic settings and college or university settings or beyond. These settings are usually sponsored by one of many adapted sport organizations established for a particular disability group (blind, Deaf, amputee) or sport (track and field, basketball, rugby). Many of the athletes competing in this setting have a common interest in becoming a world-class athlete who may one day compete in the Paralympics. Beth, the world-class swimmer mentioned at the beginning of this chapter, is such an athlete.

Sport Delivery Options

Sport delivery options, as previously mentioned, are formats for how sport settings can be delivered. Five delivery options are presented in the sport framework for individuals with disabilities: virtual communication, parallel, segregated, unified (or allied), and general (regular). Sport delivery options are not specific to any single setting, but rather can cross over several settings (table 3.1). It would not be uncommon to experience virtual communication, parallel, and unified deliveries in an interscholastic sport setting. Read through the descriptions of sport delivery options in the following section and see if you can apply more than one sport delivery option to any given sport setting.

Virtual Communication

According to Frogley and Beaver (2002, pp. 4-5), "attempts to conduct state-wide competitions have centered more on accepting certain events within already staged state championships, rather than the adoption of a state-wide program of interscholastic competition for student-athletes with disabilities." To address this concern, Winnick (2007) identifies a virtual delivery option. Historically, this option was patterned after the telegraphic sport conducted in the United States over 100 years ago for athletes in track competition who were visually impaired. Results of the meet were mailed to a central committee that made comparisons to determine winners.

One example of the use of virtual communication is a districtwide competition between schools in a tournament format, resulting in crowning of a

TABLE 3.1 Matrix of Possible Interactions Between Sport Settings and Sport Delivery Options Using the Sport Framework for Individuals With Disabilities

Sport delivery options	SPORT SETTINGS				
	School based	Interscholastic	Community	College	Open
(A) Virtual communication (B) Parallel (C) Segregated (D) Unified (E) General	A, B, C, D	A, B, E	A, B, C, D	A, C, E	A, C

district champion. Such a competition occurred for the Paralympic sport of boccia in a school district in Texas. The tournament was conducted among four middle schools across a large geographic area. Tournament play was held during the general physical education class period, involving students with and without disabilities in these classes. The adapted physical education teachers introduced the sport of boccia as a unit to the general physical education teachers, who served as local coaches. One adapted physical education teacher was the league commissioner, and students without disabilities were coaches and teammates in a unified (allied) setting.

Each school was responsible for keeping score and reporting the results to a centralized Internet spreadsheet that was posted and available to all schools. Teams would submit results and review tournament standings on a daily basis. Points were awarded to determine wins and losses and establish a playoff series. Results from the championship round were once again posted on the virtual database, and champions were recognized at the conclusion of the tournament. The use of virtual communication minimized issues of logistics, travel, and equipment needs.

Within each school district, virtual communication to promote interscholastic sport for individuals with disabilities could be facilitated through social media. An example at the district level is a Facebook page for adapted sport. Such a page could be monitored by coaches or district officials for purposes of posting new information, promoting future competition, and highlighting individual performances. In this example, virtual communication could be used to track progress within a district and create a following by students with and without disabilities across districts. For more rural school districts, Facebook pages or web-based leagues could be established to monitor performances and share highlights, which could be moved on to the dedicated state-supported athletic webpage for athletes with disabilities.

Parallel

The focus of the parallel sport delivery option is to provide an opportunity for the athlete to build skills within the sport environment through training and practice before competing. For example, consider a student with mild-to-moderate ambulatory cerebral palsy who wants to participate on the high school swim team. The student is new to the general sport setting, which includes competitors and teammates who are not disabled, and she is not secure in her starting techniques using pool deck starting blocks and is inexperienced with flip turns approaching the wall. The coach wanted this student-athlete on the team but agreed she was not ready for competition, so he allowed her to spend much of the season practicing in parallel with the team. With this parallel sport delivery, the swimmer would be able to participate in mock meets during practice, receive additional coaching from assistants, and advance her skills at an individualized pace.

Segregated

This sport delivery option is adapted sport designed solely for individuals with disabilities. Perhaps the best model to consider is the Minnesota Adapted Athletics Association (MAAA), incorporated in 1984. The MAAA included only students with physical impairments until 1988, when the Minnesota Special Interscholastic Sports Association was created for students with cognitive impairments. The MAAA later decided to create two divisions within the organization, one for students with physical impairment and one for those with cognitive impairment. Over the next four years, the MAAA approached the Minnesota State High School League to sanction adapted sport, until the league finally approved the MAAA as a sanctioned sport league for individuals with disabilities in 1992 (Doyle, 2013).

In 2001, the American Association of Adapted Sports Programs (AAASP) and the Georgia High School Association (GHSA) formed an alliance to promote the AAASP adapted sport model (along with its sister program, Project Aspire) as a viable component of the overall athletic structure and sport delivery option for the state. The GHSA looks to the AAASP for guidance in adapting sports for students with physical disabilities or visual impairments within high schools and has designated the AAASP as the official sanctioning and governing body for Georgia's interscholastic adapted athletics (AAASP, 2021).

Unified

The unified (also called *allied*) sport delivery option promotes competition between teams composed of athletes both with and without disabilities. The State of Maryland has led the way in delivering sport using a unified option. In spring 2008, Maryland passed the Fitness and Athletics Equity for Students with Disabilities Act, which required schools to allow athletes with disabilities to play wheelchair basketball or tennis, swim, or play other sports either among themselves or side-by-side with students without disabilities (Williams, 2008). The act allowed students with disabilities to try out for teams and to use modifications, accommodations, or assistive devices normally used to play the sport. This made Maryland the first state to require schools to create equal athletic and physical education opportunities for students with disabilities; this preceded guidance provided by the Dear Colleague Letter.

General

The general sport delivery option (reasonable accommodation) focuses on providing students with disabilities the opportunity to participate in the general sport setting with minimal modifications or adaptations. In this form of delivery, the student has high functional ability and needs only rule modifications. An example is allowing a student on the track and field team who is visually impaired to participate in the pole vault event through use of colored markers on the runway to help count steps in the approach run. Another example is allowing an American football player who is Deaf to use hand signals or printed cue cards to communicate plays from the sidelines.

Runners who are blind may be allowed to participate in track and cross country with sighted guides in mixed competition; wrestlers who are blind are allowed to use a touch start. Various accommodations are also being made in recreation programs without fundamentally altering competition. League officials must continue to consider and implement commonsense changes that enable a student with a disability to meet the same eligibility requirements that other team members must meet in the general sport.

Working Through Special Education and General Physical Education Services to Address Sport

Opportunities for students without disabilities to participate in sport and leisure programs within and outside of school are well documented. Most middle and high schools provide a full range of sports for the interested student. Opportunities for students with disabilities, however, are not always apparent or available. Although federal legislation supporting these programs has been in place since 1973, many schools have been slow to respond. Many court cases have documented the rights of students with disabilities to have access to the same quality of programs available to students without disabilities.

Physical educators have the responsibility to provide specific goals and objectives related to sport participation in the individualized education program (IEP). Physicians and parents of children with disabilities can also be enlisted to advocate for sport opportunities (Murphy & Carbone, 2008). One way general physical educators can promote IEP goals and objectives is to offer adapted sport within their general physical education curriculum.

This next section highlights many of the issues associated with implementing sport for students with disabilities. Students with disabilities receiving special education services often receive their physical education in a general physical education setting, which should include exposure to sport. This section presents suggestions to assist general physical educators with this process.

Transition Services

Important goals of general and adapted physical education programs are to provide students with the functional motor skills, knowledge, and opportunities necessary for lifelong, healthy, independent living. Adapted sport programs can play a vital role in assisting with independent living and should be seen as a logical extension of the school-based program. These programs should provide for a clear transition between the school and community living. IDEA mandates that a statement of the student's transition service needs be provided beginning by age 14 but no later than age 16, and when determined appropriate, should include a statement of needed transition services, including interagency responsibilities or needed links between the school and community (see the Application Example sidebar).

Application Example

Using Adapted Sport to Help Transition an Athlete

SETTING

Individualized education planning committee meeting

STUDENT

A 17-year-old student with spina bifida who is a wheelchair user

ISSUE

At the beginning of the meeting, the student's parents ask about an educational program to teach their child about community recreation opportunities.

APPLICATION

Because federal law requires that transition services be included in a student's IEP **by** age 16, the physical educator has already considered the available options. The IEP contains goals and objectives relating to the following information:

- Each week the student and other classmates will leave the school for various community recreation programs. They will attend swimming and fitness classes at the local fitness facility, where they will receive instruction on the use of the equipment.
- The physical educator has also planned trips to the adapted sport program at the local rehabilitation hospital, where the student will participate in the competitive sport programs of sitting volleyball and sailing.
- The physical educator has also collaborated with the special education resource teacher to include instruction on using public transportation to get to recreational programs.
- The IEP also includes goals and objectives related to participation in a recreational activity such as bowling.

Although a transition plan must be provided no later than age 16, transition services in physical education and sport should begin at a much earlier age to foster independence and inclusion in community living. Taking into account the needs and desires of each student, the physical educator should use the IEP to identify and recommend extracurricular programs, including intramurals and general sport. Adapted physical education and sport can provide a vital link to assist the person with a disability to fully integrate into community life (Megginson & Lavay, 2001).

Teaching Adapted Sport in General Physical Education

Davis (2002, 2011) has advocated teaching adapted sport in a general physical education curriculum as a way of promoting inclusive participation and developing a more comprehensive physical education curriculum. Inclusive participation should be defined as participation in activities that elicits a sense of belonging, acceptance, and value within the group for the participating individual (Haegele, 2019). General and adapted sport (e.g., goalball, see chapter 25) can be blended with the help of universal design for learning (UDL) to support inclusive participation, resulting in all students learning about adapted sport while enjoying a sense of belonging. As previously mentioned, according to PL 93-112, Section 504, and the guidance from OCR's Dear Colleague Letter, students with disabilities should engage in meaningful participation, equal opportunities, and participation in activities with peers to the maximum extent possible in sport and education, including physical education. General physical educators can accomplish this by implementing curriculums that include selected adapted sports matching sports from a general sport curriculum. (The term *selected* indicates that most general sports have a counterpart in adapted sport.) It is important to encourage physical educators to communicate actively with all students regarding sport selection. With careful selection and active communication, the general physical educator could teach sports that reach all populations (those with and without disabilities) through UDL and the common ground of sport.

Teaching adapted sport in a general sport curriculum can promote inclusive participation, help develop social networks between students with and without disabilities, and lay the groundwork for students with disabilities to improve their sport and social skills. Improving sport and social skills for students with disabilities within their physical education experience follows a paradigm similar to that for students without disabilities—that is, sport skills learned in general physical education can lead to engagement in intramurals, which could lead to participation in interscholastic sports and beyond, including making new friendships. To support friendship development between students with and without disabilities, teachers must provide opportunities for positive peer interactions, particularly those that are viewed as supportive, consensual, and caring (Goodwin, 2001; Seymour et al., 2009). Units should be proactively planned (a characteristic of UDL) and responsive to students' feedback and perspectives about the selected activities. For the student with a disability, the sport setting would be school based (in the general physical education class) and facilitated through virtual communication, parallel, segregated, and unified delivery options (see table 3.1). Taking this approach would strengthen the UDL guidelines of representation (e.g., using a variety of methods to present information), action and expression (e.g., providing learners with alternative ways to act skillfully and demonstrate what they know), and engagement (e.g., tapping into learners' interests and offering choices). Additional information related to UDL instructional strategies can be found in chapter 7.

For a more specific example, consider a batting activity during a softball unit that includes a student who is visually impaired. To address this student's means of action and expression, this student could strike a softball from a batting tee rather than hitting a pitched ball. After putting the ball into play, this student could run to first base by locating a sound coming from the base (i.e., clapping hands or a drum beating). Over time this student may learn to hit a pitched ball and run to the base to demonstrate what they have learned about this sport (UDL action and expression). Who knows? One day this student may join a beep baseball team.

Implementing Traditional and Adapted Sport in General Physical Education

Physical educators require students with disabilities to learn certain general sport skills by using adaptations or modifications—why not require students without disabilities to learn skills from an adapted sport curriculum, such as overhead set used in sitting volleyball or blocking a goalball? Davis (2011) offers four key steps that will assist in teaching adapted sport in a general sport curriculum.

1. Determine the sport to play; then cross-reference that sport to an adapted sport—for example, volleyball and sitting volleyball or tennis and wheelchair tennis.
2. Learn about similarities and differences between general and adapted sport skills and rules—for example, skills of chest pass and dribble are similar for general and wheelchair basketball.
3. Assess the performance for all students on the skills needed to successfully participate. For example, skill analysis of chest pass in basketball—(a) eyes on target, (b) two hands on ball, (c) flex elbows in preparation, (d) extend elbows, and (e) release and follow through—is the same in general and wheelchair basketball.
4. Implement and teach using general or adapted sport or both (figure 3.2). As you consider combining general and adapted sport in your physical education curriculum, remember that bringing students with and without disabilities together requires careful planning when selecting teaching formats, strategies for instruction, and time available to deliver curriculum (Block, 2016). Stations might be utilized to allow the students (both with and without disabilities) to pick the distance from the net they feel would result in a successful tennis serve. Consider teaching students concepts of rules, continuous play, and social engagement.

Organizational Structure of Adapted Sport: National and International

Sports for elite athletes without disabilities at the Olympic level are governed by the International Olympic Committee (IOC) (www.olympic.org), and sports for athletes with disabilities at the Paralympic level are governed by the International Paralympic Committee (IPC) (www.paralympic.org). The IOC and IPC work in a coordinated manner when planning the Olympic and Paralympic Games. More is discussed later in the chapter about this

© Ronald W. Davis

FIGURE 3.2 Physical educators play a significant role in developing lifelong sport skills for students, such as for boccia.

cooperative venture for conducting world-class competition.

The USOPC, which is represented by the IOC, is governed by a 16-member board of directors and a professional staff headed by a CEO. The USOPC also has three constituent councils to serve as sources of opinion and advice for the board. The three councils are the Athletes' Advisory Council, the National Governing Bodies Council, and the Multi-Sports Organizations Council.

Role of National and International Governing Bodies

National governing bodies and international federations are organizations dedicated to the development and promotion of specific sports. These organizations generally sanction competitions and certify officials, as well as nominate athletes to the U.S. Olympic, Paralympic, Youth Olympic, Pan American, and Parapan American teams. By law, each of the national governing bodies affiliated with the USOPC must allow participation by people with disabilities and assume a greater responsibility for elite athletes with disabilities. National governing bodies and international federations now routinely include information on adapted sport participation through the use of subcommittees, information on specific programming options, or the inclusion of adapted sport rules. For example, the United States Racquetball Association includes wheelchair racquetball rules in its official rulebook. Some sport organizations have merged with others; for example, the National Foundation of Wheelchair Tennis (NFWT) merged with the United States Tennis Association in 1998 to offer expanded programming for athletes with disabilities.

International Organizations of Sport for the Disabled

The International Organization of Sports for the Disabled (IOSD) is an independent organization recognized by the IPC as the sole representative of a specific disability group to the IPC. The IPC currently recognizes four IOSDs: the Cerebral Palsy International Sports and Recreation Association (CPISRA), the International Blind Sports Federation (IBSA), Virtus: World Intellectual Impairment Sport (formerly the International Sports Federation for Persons with Intellectual Disability), and the International Wheelchair and Amputee Sports Federation. See table 3.2 to review adapted sport organizational representation at the national and international levels.

As legislation has led to more inclusion in all aspects of daily living, an explosion has occurred in the number of organizations that provide sport programming for individuals with disabilities. These can be categorized into multisport and unisport organizations.

TABLE 3.2 Relationship Among USOC Disabled Sport Organizations and IOSDs

American sport organization	IOSD	Disability areas
BlazeSports America*	Cerebral Palsy International Sports and Recreation Association (CPISRA)	Cerebral palsy, traumatic brain injury, stroke survivors
Move United*	International Wheelchair and Amputee Sports Federation (IWASF)	Spinal cord injury, amputee, dwarfism, other wheelchair users
Dwarf Athletic Association of America (DAAA)*	IWASF	Spinal cord injury, amputee, dwarfism, other wheelchair users
Special Olympics, Inc. (SOI)***	Virtus: World Intellectual Impairment Sport	Intellectual disabilities
United States Association of Blind Athletes (USABA)*	International Blind Sports Federation (IBSA)	Visual disabilities
USA Deaf Sports Federation (USADSF)**	International Committee of Sports for the Deaf (ICSD)	Deafness

*Paralympic-affiliated organization.

**Non-Paralympic organization (participates in the Deaflympics).

***Special Olympics, in conjunction with the USOC, has assumed the responsibility for athletes with intellectual disabilities participating in the United States.

Community-Based Multisport Organizations

Multisport organizations provide training and athletic competition in sports for individuals with a particular disability. For instance, BlazeSports America provides competition in 10 sports for people who have cerebral palsy, stroke, or traumatic brain injury. These organizations serve in much the same capacity as sport national governing bodies for athletes without disabilities: They oversee the development and conduct of their sports and promote athletic involvement for their members. In addition to the athletic competition involved, athletes have used these organizations as support groups and discussion forums. There are six disabled multisport organizations affiliated with the USOC (now USOPC), including BlazeSports America, Dwarf Athletic Association of America (DAAA), Special Olympics, Inc. (SOI), United States Association of Blind Athletes (USABA), USA Deaf Sports Federation (USADSF), and Move United (formerly Adaptive Sports USA and Disabled Sports USA).

Each organization provides sport opportunities in different ways. Some organizations, such as BlazeSports America, rely on sport technical officers to oversee programs; others, such as USADSF, are divided into sport federations. The USADSF operates outside the IPC. Its athletes compete internationally in the Deaflympics (formerly the Deaf World Games) and do not compete in the Paralympic Games. Each of these sport organizations is affiliated with an international counterpart for world competition (see table 3.2). More information on multisport organizations can be found in the later chapters on specific disabilities.

Unisport Organizations

Unisport organizations promote participation in a single sport, either for a single disability or for several disabilities. For instance, North American Riding for the Handicapped Association offers therapeutic and competitive horseback riding for people regardless of specific disability. The Handicapped Scuba Association offers individual and instructor training programs in a similar manner, whereas Achilles Track Club affiliates offer road-racing opportunities for athletes with disabilities. Examples of unisport organizations for people with disabilities include the United States Quad Rugby Association (see figure 3.3), the United States Sled Hockey Association, and the National Beep Baseball Association, to name a few.

U.S. Paralympic Structure

The Amateur Sports Act influenced the USOC's (now USOPC's) mission to include responsibilities for development and training of athletes with disabilities. In 2001, the U.S. Paralympics organization was created as a division of the USOC (now USOPC). This new alignment has helped provide sport opportunities to more than 21 million Americans with disabilities by operating programs in four areas: community, Paralympic Sport Clubs, the Paralympic Military Program, and elite athlete and team support.

Community and Paralympic Sport Clubs

An earlier section of this chapter discussed the use of Paralympic Sport Clubs to promote adapted sport in the community. The goal is to increase the availability of Paralympic sport programming for Americans. Paralympic Sport Clubs are discussed further in the section Sport Framework for Individuals with Disabilities.

U.S. Paralympics and Department of Veterans Affairs' Partnership

The U.S. Paralympics, in partnership with the U.S. Department of Veterans Affairs (VA), provide postrehabilitation support and mentoring to U.S. servicemen and women who have sustained physical injuries such as traumatic brain injury, spinal cord injury, amputation, visual impairment or blindness, and stroke (figure 3.4). Veterans are introduced to adapted sport techniques and opportunities through clinics and camps and may be connected to Paralympic sport programs in their hometowns (www.teamusa.org/US-Paralympics).

Elite Athlete and Team Support

In the current organizational structure, the U.S. Paralympics has partnered with the VA to work with sport national governing bodies and disabled sport organizations to provide support services to elite athletes with disabilities in training.

Natalie Behring/Getty Images

FIGURE 3.3 The United States Quad Rugby Association is an example of a unisport organization.

FIGURE 3.4 The U.S. Paralympics partners with the VA to offer sport opportunities for injured war veterans.

Competition: Paralympic Games, Warrior Games, and Sports Classification

This section discusses two of the biggest recognized competition events for athletes with disabilities—the Paralympic Games and the Warrior Games—as well as classification in adapted sport and how this system is the foundation of all competitions.

Paralympic Games

The Paralympic Games (*para* meaning "equal to") are the equivalent of the Olympic Games for athletes with physical disabilities or visual impairments. Athletes with intellectual disabilities also compete in the Paralympics; however, individuals with hearing impairments compete in the Deaflympics. The Paralympics began in 1948, when the Stoke Mandeville Games were held in Aylesbury, England—the same year the 14th Olympic Games were held in London.

The first Paralympic Summer Games were held in Rome in 1960 and drew 400 athletes representing 23 countries. Since then, the Olympic and Paralympic Games have led a parallel existence, being held in the same city or same country whenever possible. The 1988 Seoul Games marked the first time the term *Paralympics* was used.

The 1992 Barcelona Paralympics marked the introduction of a joint Olympic and Paralympic Committee. International Olympic Committee then-president Juan Antonio Samaranch decreed that, after 1996, all bids for the Olympic Games must be submitted by joint Olympic and Paralympic Committees. "The Paralympic Games have been as successful as the Olympic Games," said Samaranch, "that is an indication that we must take another look at, and think seriously about the subject of disabled people. It was the same organizing committee and the same volunteers that worked out very well" (Samaranch, 1992).

The host bidding process is deeply influenced by how well the bid proposal addresses the needs of the Paralympic Games (Gold & Gold, 2011). Inclusion in a host proposal has slowed the process of selection when host cities had to identify how they would address transportation, housing, and other forms of access. According to Gold and Gold (2011), cities that declined to include the Paralympics in their proposal, such as Mexico City, forced the Games to be moved to Tel Aviv in 1968 (Enos et al., 2012). Progress occurred in proposal development, and in 1992, Barcelona's bidding committee provided a model for success that has been used since. Competition in the 2012 London Paralympic Games helped close the gap between athletes with and without disabilities in the sports of track and field and swimming.

As the global governing body of the Paralympic Movement, the IPC organizes the Summer and Winter Paralympic Games and serves as the international federation for 12 sports, for which it supervises and coordinates the world championships and other competitions. The governance of 26 sports (20 Paralympic Summer sports, 5 Paralympic Winter Sports, 1 non-Paralympic sport) falls under the responsibility of various bodies. Every country that participates in the Paralympic Games has a national counterpart to these federations.

Warrior Games

In 2010, the Warrior Games were created by the U.S. Paralympics in coordination with the Department of Defense (DOD) and the Veterans Administration (VA). The intent of the Warrior Games was to provide an introduction to Paralympic sports for injured, ill, or wounded service members and veterans. In 2013 the DOD and the VA restructured oversight, management, and operations of the Warrior Games to include regional qualifying competitions, hosted by identified military instillations, and conclude with a national competition, also hosted on a single military installation. Military personnel serving in Warrior Transition Units (WTU) through an Adaptive Sport Reconditioning Program participate in these Games. The global purpose of these WTUs is to support wounded, ill, or injured veterans' transition to civilian life. Each branch established a specific unit; the most commonly recognized comes from the Army's Warrior Transition Command and is called the Army Warrior Transition Unit. The Marine Corps created the Wounded Warrior Regiment, the Navy established the Safe Harbor Program, and the United States Air Force launched the Air Force Warrior and Survivor Care Program (Davis et al., 2013; Legislative Mandate Wounded Warrior Units & Programs [Public Law 111-84, section 724], October 2011). The Warrior Games competition events include archery, cycling, shooting, sitting volleyball, swimming, track and field, and wheelchair basketball. Athletes compete for the Chairman's Cup, which is awarded to the top overall service branch performing at the Warrior Games.

Warrior Games and the Wounded Warrior Project are not the same. Warrior Games provide an introduction to Paralympic sport, whereas the Wounded Warrior Project is more comprehensive and broader in scope (Davis et al., 2013). The Wounded Warrior Project has four programs of emphasis, all created to improve the quality of life for wounded, injured, or ill veterans beyond the entity of sport competition: Mind, Body, Economic Empowerment, and Engagement, each with a specialized interest (www.woundedwarriorproject.org/programs.aspx).

Sport Classification

Perhaps the feature most distinctive to adapted sport is *sport classification*, an assessment process conducted to ensure that competition is equitable and that the athlete's impairment minimizes the impact on the sport performance.

Historically, classification systems were based on impairment location (medical) or performance (functional) (Davis & Ferrara, 1996). Today the classification process has shifted to what is referred to as Code Compliance, which involves evaluating how much the impairment affects the performance of the athlete in the sport. Athletes are then grouped by the impairment's impact, not on impairment type, which often results in cross-disability competitors in the same event—for example, athletes with spinal cord injury competing with athletes who have cerebral palsy (see classification codes at www.paralympic.org/classification-code).

Code Compliance was put into place to minimize the impact of impairments on sport performance and to ensure that the success of an athlete was determined by skill, fitness, power, endurance, tactical ability, and mental focus—in other words, the same factors that account for success in sport for athletes who do not have a disability. The present system groups athletes by sport and is referred to as *sport specific*. As a result, many of the events are considered cross-disability (e.g., the 200-meter wheelchair sprint event includes athletes with a spinal cord injury, cerebral palsy, or an amputation; the focus is on the impairment, not disability type). Because the impairment affects the ability to perform in different sports to different extents, the impact of the impairment must be proven. Results of such assessments could mean that an athlete meets the criteria for one event and not another.

The latest classification system focuses on impairment types as defined by the World Health Organization International Classification of Functioning, Disability and Health (2001), which can present in several different categories of disabilities. The 10 types of impairments deemed eligible for consideration in sports within the Paralympic Movement are (1) impaired muscle power, (2) impaired passive range of movement (ROM), (3) limb deficiency, (4) leg-length difference, (5) short stature, (6) hypertonia, (7) ataxia, (8) athetosis, (9) vision impairment, and (10) intellectual impairment (Busse, 2014, pp. 19-21).

A key application to this new classification system is that a Paralympic sport group must identify the impairment group for whom it provides sporting opportunities. Some sport groups include athletes from all impairments (e.g., athletics, swimming), whereas others focus on one impairment (e.g., goalball). The sports of equestrian and cycling identify a specific selection of impairment groups. Keep in mind that the presence of the impairment allows the athlete only to be eligible for the sport; it is not the sole criterion for entry or acceptance into Paralympic sport. Consideration must be given to qualification times, skill performance, training levels, and format of competition (individual or team).

The process of classification is dynamic. Athletes are classified before, during, and after competitions by teams of trained professionals. The classification process involves three phases: physical evaluation and assessment, technical evaluation and assessment, and observation during competition. Professionals from the medical fields (e.g., medical doctors, physical therapists, or athletic trainers) conduct the physical evaluations. The technical phase of the classification process is conducted by a trained technician familiar with the sport and the mechanics of movement needed to perform—for example, stroke analysis in swimming. Observation during competition is conducted by all sport professionals who participated in the physical and technical evaluations.

Whichever classification system is used, the system should ensure that the training and skill level of the athlete become the deciding factors in success, not the type or level of disability (Paciorek & Jones, 2001). Classifications related to specific disabilities and specific sports are discussed in other chapters of this book.

Summary

Over the past 40 years, many advances have occurred in adapted sport. Federal legislation, the work of advocates and professional sport organizations, increased awareness of health benefits, and involvement with the USOC are some reasons for the growth of adapted sport. Many opportunities exist today for people with disabilities to participate in sport and leisure activities throughout communities and school settings. Opportunities exist at regional, national, and international levels for people interested in elite levels of competition through multi- and unisport organizations. Based on the GAO report to Congress and the OCR response of guidance through the Dear Colleague Letter, state legislatures are recognizing the rights of students with disabilities to participate in extracurricular activities, including interscholastic sport programs. Many models can enhance the development of interscholastic and adapted sport programs for students with disabilities.

Physical educators must use multiple sport settings and delivery options as well as appropriate instructional strategies to teach students with disabilities. They need to be aware of the programs in their communities for students with disabilities in order to take the skills and knowledge they have acquired in adapted physical education and use them to teach all students—those with or without disabilities—in their general physical education curriculum.

References

American Association of Adapted Sports Programs (AAASP). 2019. *Best practices in adapted team sports* (2nd ed.). American Association of Adapted Sports Programs, Inc.

American Association of Adapted Sports Programs (AAASP). (2021). Retrieved from https://adaptedsports.org/aaasp-resource-center/#aaasp-guides

Americans with Disabilities Act of 1990, PL 101-336, 2, 104 Stat. 328 (1990). www.ada.gov/pubs/ada.htm

Arnhold, R., Young, L., & Lakowski, T. (2013). The historical and legal background leading to the Office of Civil Rights "Dear Colleague Letter." *Journal of Physical Education, Recreation and Dance, 84*(8), 20-23.

Block, M.E. (2016). *A teacher's guide to adapted physical education: Including students with disabilities in sport and recreation* (4th ed.). Brookes.

Breaking a boundary: Conference opens doors to athletes with disabilities. (2015, April 18). Retrieved from https://ecacsports.com/news/2015/4/18/4_18_2015_165.aspx?path=gen

Busse, S. (2014). Eligibility and classification in Paralympics Sports. *Palaestra, 28*(2), 19-21.

Davis, R. (2002). *Inclusion through sports.* Human Kinetics.

Davis, R. (2011). *Teaching disability sport: A guide to general physical education.* Human Kinetics.

Davis, R., Enos, M., Jordan, L., & Belanger, J. (2013). The 2013 Warrior Games: More than a competition. *Palaestra, 24*(7), 41-49.

Davis, R., & Ferrara, M. (1996). Athlete classification: An exploration of the process. *Palaestra, 12*(2), 38-44.

Doyle, M. (2013). Minnesota's model sports program to address interscholastic extracurricular athletics and Office of Civil Rights guidance. *Journal of Physical Education, Recreation and Dance, 84*(8), 31-32.

Enos, M., Busse, S., Davis, R., & Megginson, N. (2012). The influence of Paralympic Games proposals on successfully hosting the Olympics. *Palaestra, 26*(3), 53-55.

Frogley, M., & Beaver, D.P. (2002). Editor's corner: Is the time right—interscholastic athletics for student-athletes with disabilities? *Palaestra, 18*(2), 4-5.

Gold, J., & Gold, M. (2011). *City agendas, planning, and the world's games, 1896-2016* (2nd ed.). Routledge.

Goodwin, D.L. (2001). The meaning of help in PE: Perceptions of students with physical disabilities. *Adapted Physical Activity Quarterly, 18,* 189-203.

Groth, J., (2020). The extra point: Making a major move. *Sports 'N Spokes, 46*(4), 14-15.

Haegele, J.A. (2019). Inclusion illusion: Questioning the inclusiveness of integrated physical education. *Quest, 71*(4), 387-397. http://doi.org/10.1080/00336297.2019.1602547

Individuals with Disabilities Education Act Amendments of 2004 (IDEA) PL 108-446, 20 U.S.C. 1400 (2004).

Megginson, N.L., & Lavay, B.W. (2001). Providing disability sport opportunities in adapted physical education. *Palaestra, 17*(2), 20-26.

Move United (n.d.). Top Ten States for Adaptive Sports. Retrieved from www.moveunitedsport.org/top-adaptive-sports-states/.

Murphy, N.A., & Carbone, P.S. (2008). Promoting the participation of children with disabilities in sports, recreation, and physical activities. *Pediatrics, 121*(5), 1057-1061.

Paciorek, M.J., & Jones, J.A. (2001). *Disability sports and recreation resources* (3rd ed.). Cooper.

Rehabilitation Act of 1973, PL 93-112, 87 Stat. 355 (1973).

Samaranch, J.A. Closing Ceremonies, Paralympic Games. Barcelona, Spain, September 14, 1992.

Seymour, H., Reid, G., & Bloom, G. A. (2009). Friendship in inclusive PE. *Adapted Physical Activity Quarterly, 26,* 201-219.

Storms, T. (2007). The wheels of justice turn in adapted interscholastic sport-making progress. *Palaestra, 23*(3), 4-5.

United States Olympic Committee (USOC). (1998). *USOC constitution.* Author.

Williams, J. (2008, August 31). School programs for disabled taking shape. *Baltimore Sun,* A11.

Winnick, J.P. (2007). A framework for interscholastic sports for youngsters with disabilities. *Palaestra, 23*(2), 4, 9.

World Health Assembly. (2001). Resolution WHA 54.21.

World Para Winter Sports. (2016, January 18). *Paralympics launches athlete development model.* www.paralympic.org/news/us-paralympics-launches-athlete-development-model

Print Resources

American Alliance for Health, Physical Education, Recreation and Dance. (2013). Feature edition of helping general physical educators and adapted physical educators address the Office of Civil Rights Dear Colleague guidance letter. *Journal of Physical Education, Recreation and Dance, 84*(8).

This feature provides general physical educators, adapted physical educators, and school district administrators assistance relative to the Office of Civil Rights Dear Colleague guidance letter by covering six topics: historical and legal background; what parents need to know and do to ensure extracurricular interscholastic sport opportunities; best practices for practitioners and programs; leading adapted sport groups; extracurricular outdoor pursuits; and professional preparation relative to extracurricular athletic programs.

Davis, R. (2011). *Teaching disability sport: A guide for physical educators* (2nd ed.). Human Kinetics.

This is an excellent resource for physical education teachers or recreation specialists to help establish a comprehensive physical education program for students with and without disabilities using the medium of sport. The book describes many disability sports and how activities can be modified and taught in physical education settings.

United States Department of Education, Office for Civil Rights. (2013). *Dear colleague letter.* Author.

This letter is a response to the 2010 United States Governmental Accountability Office (GAO) report investigating physical education and extracurricular athletic opportunities in schools. It identifies and provides guidance for four areas in which school districts can improve opportunities for students with disabilities to participate more fully in physical education and extracurricular athletics.

United States Government Accountability Office. (2010). Students with disabilities: More information could improve opportunities in physical education and athletics. No. GAO-10-519 at 1, 31. Retrieved from www.gao.gov/assets/310/305770.pdf

In response to a request by the U.S. Congress in 2008, this report summarizes an investigation of how physical education and extracurricular athletic opportunities for students with disabilities are provided in schools. This GAO report identifies several factors that limit opportunities of a student with disabilities to participate in physical education and athletics.

Online Resources

MOVE United: www.moveunitedsport.org

This site provides information pertaining to the organization, sport offerings, current events, resource library, as well as other pertinent information.

4

Measurement, Assessment, and Program Evaluation

Brock McMullen and Manny Felix

You have just been hired as an adapted physical education teacher by a school district that takes pride in making effective, data-driven decisions. These decisions have allowed the school district to provide a high-quality PK-12 education, attain standards-based, grade-level student outcomes, and show improvement in both academic and nonacademic outcomes for its students, as well as provide individualized and meaningful programs for students who need special education services. The implementation of data collection, evaluation, and assessment is a core practice used by this school district to make important decisions for individual students and many education programs.

The school district administrators, special education teachers, physical education teachers, related service personnel, and parents are relying on your expertise to implement effective data-based assessment practices. What testing policies and procedures would you recommend for determining eligibility, identifying needs, and monitoring progress in adapted physical education? How would these policies and procedures comply with current legislation and best practices? This chapter will help you answer these questions.

Note: The authors sincerely thank Francis X. Short, professor, State University of New York, College at Brockport, and Garth Tymeson, University of Wisconsin – La Crosse, for their contributions to this chapter in earlier editions.

Measurement and assessment serve significant purposes in physical education. One critical purpose—to assist in determining eligibility for adapted physical education—is alluded to in the scenario just presented. The Individuals with Disabilities Education Act (IDEA) requires periodic measurement and assessment throughout the special education process in order to ensure that an appropriate education, including physical education, is provided. This chapter identifies concepts of measurement and assessment as they relate to adapted physical education. Major topics include terminology, test standards and approaches, testing and assessment used in adapted physical education, test instruments, and program evaluation.

Terminology

It is important to distinguish among tests, measurement, evaluation, and assessment. Many of these terms are used synonymously, but this is not the case. **Test** refers to instruments, protocols, or techniques used to measure a quantity or quality of properties or attributes of interest (Lacy & Williams, 2018). For example, a flexibility test may require the use of an instrument (e.g., a sit-and-reach box) and a specific procedure (e.g., seated, one leg at a time) in order to gather measurement data on lower back and hamstring flexibility. **Measurement** is the result of the process of collecting data through testing on the property or attribute of interest (Lacy & Williams, 2018). For instance, body fat can be measured using a skinfold test, which is expressed in millimeters. Of course, there are several ways to test for and measure a desired characteristic. In addition to skinfold measurements, body fat can be measured by other clinical methods such as hydrostatic underwater weighing or bone densitometry, but these methods are not feasible for the physical educator.

Evaluation and **assessment** are synonymous terms that include the process of interpreting the measurement data and making a judgment by comparing results with predetermined criteria or objectives (Lacy & Williams, 2018). For example, a 15-year-old male student with intellectual disability runs the 20-meter PACER test and receives a score of 30 laps. This score can then be compared to a predetermined standard (42 laps with use of the Brockport Physical Fitness Test [BPFT]). Because this student's score does not meet the predetermined standard, it indicates that the student does not have a level of aerobic functioning consistent with good health. Had the student's score been higher than the predetermined standard (at least 42 laps), then the interpretation would have been different (i.e., the performance score would indicate

Evaluation and assessment of scores on tests such as the PACER test facilitate objective educational decisions regarding eligibility, program planning, placement, and performance goals.

adequate levels of aerobic functioning consistent with good health). Evaluation and assessment of scores thus facilitate objective educational decisions regarding eligibility, program planning, placement, and performance goals. In this example, because the student lacks adequate aerobic functioning, it may be decided that his measurable individualized education program (IEP) goals and objectives should address the need to improve cardiorespiratory fitness.

Standards for Assessment

In order to evaluate performance scores and subsequently make appropriate assessment decisions, it is necessary to understand standards of performance. Standards most commonly used to evaluate test scores in physical education may be norm referenced or criterion referenced. Test instruments may use norm or criterion referencing or both for evaluation of student scores.

Norm-Referenced Standards

Norm-referenced standards allow comparison of one student's performance against the performance of others from a particular peer group with similar characteristics (e.g., a 10-year-old girl's score will be compared with other 10-year-old girls' scores). Norm-referenced standards allow for evaluation statements such as, "Lexie's object-control motor area of functioning is above average for girls her age," "Bekki is two years behind her age group in locomotor skill functioning," and "Mike's abdominal curl-up performance score places him at the 21st percentile compared to other boys his age." Examples of norm-referenced standards include percentiles, chronological age norms, T-scores, z-scores, and other test-specific standard scores (Morrow et al., 2016).

Norm-referenced standards are generally established by testing large numbers of individuals from specifically defined population groups. The distribution of these test scores should be consistent with normal curve theory. Through statistical analyses, scores are summarized and percentiles and standard scores are then derived by age and sex. Norm-referenced standards are usually associated with standardized testing approaches discussed later in this chapter.

Criterion-Referenced Standards

Whereas norm-referenced standards allow comparison of individual performance scores with other scores of a comparable group, **criterion-referenced standards** allow comparison of individual scores to some predetermined criterion or absolute level of mastery. This score represents a minimally acceptable level of performance for the test instrument or item. Mastery scores can be determined by expert judgment, research data, logic, experience, or other means (Morrow et al., 2016).

An example of criterion-referenced standards is the running test item (table 4.1) from the Test of Gross Motor Development (TGMD-3). The TGMD-3 is a test instrument commonly used in adapted physical education to measure locomotor and ball skills (object-control functioning) in children 3 to 10 years of age (Ulrich, 2019). When the test item is implemented, the child's performance is compared to the performance criteria listed. Thus, TGMD-3 individual test-item scores are criterion referenced. (However, summative scores on the TGMD-3 are norm referenced.)

In the past, many tests used norm-referenced standards that generated percentile scores. For instance, on a fictitious health-related physical fitness test, a student received a 30 percent body fat measurement, which placed this person at the 50th percentile based on age and sex. Although the 50th percentile is statistically average (most people will score near the average), the score does not necessarily indicate that the student is

TABLE 4.1 Criterion-Referenced Measurement of the Run on the TGMD-3 Sample

Performance criteria	Trial 1	Trial 2	Score
1. Arms move in opposition to legs with elbows bent	0	0	0
2. Brief period where both feet are off the surface	1	1	2
3. Narrow foot placement landing on heel or toes (not flat-footed)	1	1	2
4. Nonsupport leg bent about 90 degrees so foot is close to buttocks	1	1	2
Skill score			6

Scoring: 0 = criterion not exhibited; 1 = criterion exhibited.

healthy. In this case, people might misinterpret that a statistical average of 30 percent body fat is at an adequate level for health. One advantage of using criterion-referenced standards is that a performance score is not compared with others but instead with a mastery level that has been deemed acceptable.

Now, greater attention has been placed on the use of tests with criterion-referenced standards for determination of unique needs and instruction in physical education. FitnessGram (Cooper Institute, 2017) is a good example. FitnessGram test items are shown in table 4.2. Standards associated with the FitnessGram test represent a level of performance that is indicative of good health and lower health risks. For each test item, standards for a Healthy Fitness Zone (HFZ) are provided by sex and age (5 to 17+ years). The HFZ is defined by a lower-end score and an upper-end score. All students are encouraged to achieve at least the lower-end criterion, which would mean that their score is at least at a level associated with good health for a particular area of fitness. A score in the HFZ represents the level of fitness thought to provide some protection from the potential health risks that result from a lack of fitness associated with a particular test item. Little or no emphasis may be placed on going beyond the upper-end criterion, because most health-related objectives can be attained simply by staying within the HFZ. (At times, it may be inappropriate to exceed performance outside health fitness zones, such as exceeding a recommended score on the trunk lift or having extremely low levels of body fat, particularly in females.)

Similar to the FitnessGram, the BPFT (test items shown in table 4.2) uses criterion standards with established HFZs as well as Adapted Fitness Zones (AFZs). However, the standards are uniquely organized not only by age and sex but also by disability, which makes this test very useful in adapted

TABLE 4.2 FitnessGram and BPFT Test Items Arranged by Fitness Components

FitnessGram	BPFT
Aerobic capacity PACER (20 m and 15 m) 1-mile run Walk test	Aerobic functioning PACER (20 m and 15 m) 1-mile run/walk Target aerobic movement test
Muscular strength, endurance, and flexibility Curl-up Trunk lift Push-up Modified pull-up Flexed arm hang Back-saver sit-and-reach Shoulder stretch	Musculoskeletal functioning Reverse curl Seated push-up 40 m push or walk Wheelchair ramp test Push-up Isometric push-up Pull-up Modified pull-up Dumbbell press Bench press Dominant grip strength Flexed arm hang Extended arm hang Trunk lift Curl-up Modified curl-up Target stretch test Shoulder stretch Modified Apley test Modified Thomas test Back-saver sit-and-reach
Body composition Skinfold measurements (triceps and calf skinfolds) Body mass index Bioelectric impedance analysis	Body composition Skinfolds (triceps, subscapular, and calf) Body mass index Bioelectric impedance analysis

physical education programs. As exemplified by these two tests, criterion-referenced standards can be associated with standardized tests, but they can also be found with some of the alternative testing approaches discussed later in this chapter.

Standardized Testing Approaches

Standardized testing involves implementation of previously established test procedures and protocols in controlled environments in order to objectively collect data. In this manner, students are tested in exactly the same way under exactly the same conditions. Through controlling, or standardizing, the environment, validity and reliability (including objectivity) of the test results are maximized. Standardized testing is frequently used to determine if a student is making reasonable progress on skill and fitness development compared with similarly defined students (e.g., by age and sex) or with levels of achievement thought to be appropriate for students with certain characteristics. In doing so, standardized testing is often used for eligibility and placement decisions when school districts use specific objective criteria (e.g., two standard deviations below the mean, below the 20th percentile) to determine eligibility for adapted physical education.

Although standardized testing approaches may be appropriate for the general student population, a physical educator must be careful not to use this approach indiscriminately, because unique physical, cognitive, and behavioral characteristics may reduce the validity of the test result. Some test instruments that have been standardized with the general population in mind are now suggesting test modifications for use with students with disabilities. Also, some tests and procedures, such as the BPFT, have been specifically developed for students with and without disabilities. A few of the many tests of physical fitness, motor development, and sport skills that use standardized testing are described later in the chapter.

Alternative Approaches

Alternative testing refers to the gathering of data through a variety of testing means and environmental conditions. For example, a checklist that identifies presence or absence of key throwing components (e.g., opposition, weight transfer, follow-through) may be used when the student is engaging in throwing practice trials during a lesson activity, during a tee-ball modified activity, or even during a more formal one-on-one testing situation. Alternative testing methods often include the use of observations, checklists, rubrics, task analyses, and portfolios. Some of these techniques are alternative strategies to tests that use standardized approaches.

Authentic testing refers to testing in real-world environments or activities. Because some standardized test items are not natural or authentic and thus are less helpful in identifying appropriate instructional needs, authentic testing can be more efficiently aligned to directly measure the skills that students need for successful participation in physical education. This may be even more appropriate for students with disabilities due to varying abilities and instructional needs. Techniques associated with authentic assessment are discussed next.

Checklists

Checklists indicate the presence or absence of essential behaviors or characteristics in list format. No attempt is made to determine the extent or quality of the characteristic; the list is simply checked to indicate whether the characteristic is exhibited (Lund, 2000). Checklists are particularly helpful for using task analysis. An example of a simple checklist is provided in figure 4.1. A point-system

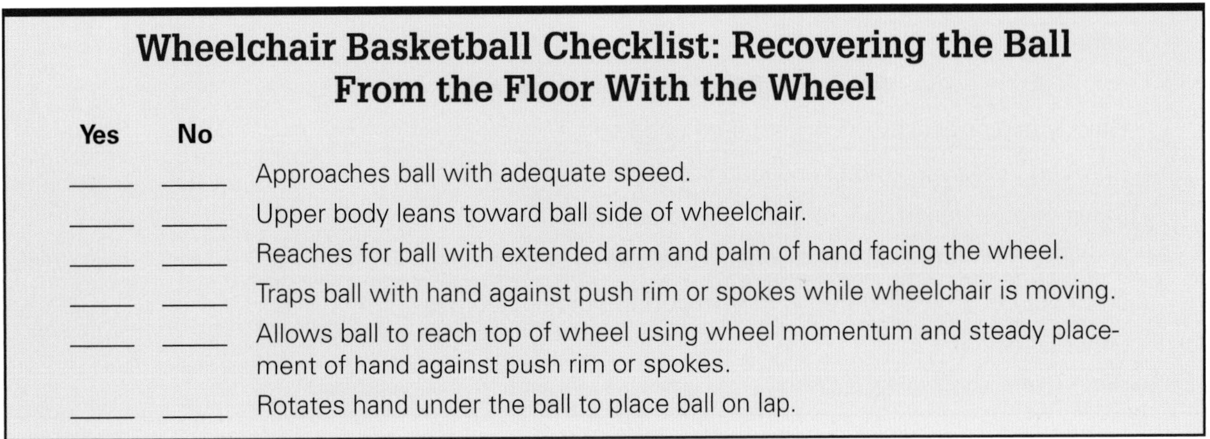

Wheelchair Basketball Checklist: Recovering the Ball From the Floor With the Wheel

Yes	No	
_____	_____	Approaches ball with adequate speed.
_____	_____	Upper body leans toward ball side of wheelchair.
_____	_____	Reaches for ball with extended arm and palm of hand facing the wheel.
_____	_____	Traps ball with hand against push rim or spokes while wheelchair is moving.
_____	_____	Allows ball to reach top of wheel using wheel momentum and steady placement of hand against push rim or spokes.
_____	_____	Rotates hand under the ball to place ball on lap.

FIGURE 4.1 A simple checklist.

checklist is a variation in which points are assigned to behaviors or characteristics. This may be useful for teachers if numerical grades are given. Checklists are appropriate if the intent is to simply tell what students can do; however, if the intent is to determine the quality of performance, then analytic rating scales would be more appropriate. When used in authentic teaching situations, checklists can be a valuable and practical tool to identify instructional needs.

Rubrics

Rubrics are rating scales that distinguish among varying levels of performance or skill through clear performance criteria (SHAPE America, 2019). By using rubrics, teachers can identify the skills a child is able to perform on functionally relevant physical education content and make accurate, consistent, and objective judgments about the quality performance level of that skill. A major advantage of using rubrics (and checklists) is the ease with which curricular-embedded, measurable IEP goals and objectives can be assessed.

An analytic rating scale is one type of rubric that uses ratings such as excellent, good, fair, and poor to distinguish degrees of performance. Rubrics can be either quantitative (numerical) or qualitative. Quantitative rubrics (figure 4.2) use numbers to

Behavioral Rating in Physical Education

Desired behaviors	1	2	3	4	5	NA
Responding to the teacher						
Quietly listens to instruction						
Follows directions in a timely manner for introductory activities						
Follows directions in a timely manner for skill development						
Stops and listens during activity transitions						
Uses positive or neutral language with teacher						
Is willing to accept help when needed						
Other (specify):						
Relating to peers and equipment						
Works cooperatively with a partner when asked						
Works cooperatively with a group (>2) when asked						
Uses positive or neutral comments with peers						
Displays sportsmanship by avoiding conflict with others						
Does not become frustrated with group performance outcomes						
Helps others when appropriate						
Uses equipment appropriately						
Other (specify):						
Effort and self-acceptance						
Quickly begins activity once instructed to do so						
Stays on task during motor-engaged activities						
Stays on task during non–motor-engaged activities						
Is willing to improve own performance; strives to be successful						
Does not become frustrated with own performance outcomes						
Other (specify):						

Scale: 1 = very poor; 2 = poor; 3 = adequate; 4 = good; 5 = very good; NA = not applicable.

FIGURE 4.2 Sample quantitative rubric of desired behaviors in physical education.

distinguish levels of performance, whereas qualitative rubrics (table 4.3) use adjectives or other words to differentiate performance. One of the distinct advantages of testing and evaluating through rubrics is that students and teachers know what performance needs to be exhibited in order to get the best possible score. For instance, in the basic game-play rubric shown in table 4.3, performance is judged to be at one of the four levels of performance for each content area of game play (e.g., positioning, skill mechanics). With this particular rubric, evaluation can be unobtrusive and take place in a natural environment as students play an actual game.

Physical educators may need to make modifications to existing rubrics in order to test students with disabilities on functionally relevant skills and content. For example, a rubric in which a level of performance characteristic is stated as "moves into position quickly" could be modified to read "wheels into position" or "attempts to wheel into position." Another example of a modification might be the substitution of a beach ball for a regulation volleyball with use of a volleyball rubric. These types of modifications may be especially necessary with use of ecological task analysis (ETA) in teaching.

For physical education content that is personalized to the student (e.g., effective wheelchair propulsion and agility, behavior in public physical activity settings), a rubric may need to be created to address the specific area of need. Creating well-written rubrics is worthwhile if the rubric allows for more effective educational decision making and enhanced instruction. For more on developing rubrics, see Lund and Veal (2013).

Task Analysis

Task analysis can be used to identify movement capabilities and limitations as well as consequent instructional needs. The process of task analysis involves breaking down a movement skill into its component parts and determining which tasks were accomplished. Assessment of the student's performance of specific parts of a task allows educators to determinate appropriate instructional content for that student. For more information on the development and use of task analysis, refer to chapter 7.

Portfolios

Portfolios consist of a purposeful, integrated collection of exhibits and performance samples to show an authentic picture of effort, progress, and achievement (Melograno, 2006). In adapted physical education, teachers can identify any number of items that students can choose to include in their physical education portfolio. Examples include test results (including standardized tests), teacher observations, peer evaluations, rating scales, checklists, journals, self-reflections, self-assessments, student projects, activity logs, and digital media. As photo and video capture capabilities have been made easier with technology advances, visually documenting performance of physical education

TABLE 4.3 Sample Qualitative Rubric of Game-Play in Physical Education

Component	Peewee	Rising star	Collegiate	Olympic
Positioning	Frequently flat-footed; waits for play or is not aware of upcoming plays	Occasionally uses correct positioning; often waits for play	Demonstrates correct positioning on offense and defense; anticipates play	Demonstrates use of strategies during game play while maintaining a high level of intensity
Skill mechanics	Avoids using skills	Occasionally exhibits proper skill mechanics	Frequently uses proper skill mechanics	Demonstrates proper skill mechanics consistently
Rules	Does not adhere to rules	Occasionally adheres to rules	Usually adheres to rules	Adheres to rules on a regular basis
Team play	Demonstrates poor sportsmanship or teamwork skills	Shows little tendency toward sportsmanship or teamwork skills	Cooperates with teammates and demonstrates good sportsmanship	Organizes teammates toward a positive common goal

skills has become more prevalent. For example, providing video evidence of physical education performance has been useful for IEP goal monitoring.

Materials, however, are not just dumped into a portfolio. Teachers must establish criteria for what goes in the portfolio and how it will be evaluated. One common way to organize the portfolio is by standard and sample benchmarks (Melograno, 2006). The contents of a portfolio will vary depending on the student's age and cognitive ability as well as the purpose of the portfolio (SHAPE America, 2019). Portfolios should reflect assessments and performances related to all three domains of behavior (cognitive, affective, psychomotor), adapted as necessary for students with disabilities. For instance, a rubric addressing behavioral characteristics might be appropriate to add to a portfolio to demonstrate affective functioning.

Synthesis

The push for alternative or authentic assessment has gained momentum. Authentic testing approaches can assist in aligning planning and assessment. When conducted properly, authentic approaches inform students of their progress and what they need to work on next. Testing and learning become seamless because students learn, in part, from the testing program.

Alternative approaches, however, are not without limitations. Many alternative approaches rely heavily on subjective observation. As Hensley (1997) has noted, such assessment practices "have frequently been criticized on the basis of questionable validity and reliability, being susceptible to personal bias, generosity error (the tendency to overrate), lack of objective scoring, as well as the belief that they are conducted in a haphazard manner with little rigor" (p. 21). Furthermore, both IDEA and the Every Student Succeeds Act (ESSA) require that the unique needs of young people be determined using valid, reliable, objective, and nondiscriminatory instruments, and authentic assessment strategies often do not meet these criteria.

Consequently, it is recommended that measurement and assessment strategies include both standardized and alternative approaches. Because the establishment of appropriate levels of validity and reliability requires controlled circumstances, tests with stronger psychometric qualities (including validity and reliability) tend to have lower authentic qualities. Conversely, those with stronger authentic qualities tend to have weaker psychometric properties. Of course, teachers should attempt to select tests that have acceptable levels of both properties.

Test selection will also be influenced by the purpose of testing. When making important educational decisions based on testing (e.g., eligibility for adapted physical education), the teacher should give preference to tests with stronger psychometric properties. When a student is learning a skill to be used in a particular context (e.g., dribbling a basketball for eventual use in a game situation), the teacher should give preference to tests with stronger authentic properties to monitor student progress. The application of both standardized and alternative assessment strategies in adapted physical education is explored further in the next section.

Testing and Assessment in Adapted Physical Education

There are many reasons for testing and assessment in physical education, including increasing motivation, determining strengths and weaknesses, classifying students, determining degree of achievement, evaluating instruction and programs, predicting future success, and conducting research designed to answer questions and solve problems (Morrow et al., 2016). In adapted physical education, testing and assessment strategies are often employed to assist in the determination of unique need (eligibility for services and subsequent placement) and in providing a basis for instruction. The relation of testing and assessment to these functions is discussed in the following sections.

Determination of Unique Need

Students suspected of having unique physical and motor needs should be referred to appropriate personnel within the school for further testing. Increasingly, more school districts are using response-to-intervention (RTI) strategies before referrals are processed. Response to intervention consists of tiers of intervention strategies that can be employed in the general education classroom to determine if struggling learners require specialized services (Center for Parent Information and Resources, 2012). Thus, the referral process does not mean automatic entry into special education. Referrals must document the reasons why the student should be considered for further testing. Testing and assessment at the referral level, usually called **screening** or **informal assessment**, document the need for an in-depth evaluation to determine if the student has a unique need in physical education.

Determining unique need is critical for two reasons. First, a student must have a unique need to be eligible for adapted physical education. This is true both for students considered to have disabilities under IDEA and for those without disabilities who have unique physical education needs. Second, once a unique need is determined, it serves as the basis for developing measurable IEP goals.

In dealing with the question of eligibility, a distinction must be made between an adapted physical education *program* and the instructional *placement* to which a student is assigned. A student might qualify for an adapted program but receive those services in a general placement. Thus, placement is established after the IEP goals have been determined. When a student is referred for possible adapted physical education services, the school district must first conduct more thorough, formalized assessments to determine if the student is eligible for the adapted physical education program. In the absence of a medical referral, the criteria for entry into the adapted program (in most cases) should be based primarily on psychomotor performance. Usually, measurement and assessment for the purpose of determining program eligibility should focus on standardized testing (i.e., tests with strong psychometric properties and standards for evaluation). Most districts have established eligibility criteria, and teachers are expected to follow those district policies.

Some states and many school districts have developed criteria for adapted physical education services. For instance, in order for a student with a documented disability to be eligible for adapted physical education in the state of Minnesota, the student must either (1) fall one-and-a-half standard deviations below the mean on a standardized psychomotor evaluation or fitness test that is administered individually by an appropriately licensed teacher, (2) have documentation of inadequate development, or (3) exhibit limited achievement and independence in general physical education based on at least two of the following: motor and skill checklists; criterion-referenced measures; parent and staff interviews; informal tests; medical history or reports; systematic observations; social, emotional, and behavioral evaluations; and deficits in achievement related to the defined curriculum (Minnesota Department of Education, 2007).

In states without such criteria, it is recommended that school districts adopt specific criteria for eligibility in adapted physical education. It is also recommended that districts consider one or more of the following criteria for eligibility based on test results that measure aspects of physical education:

1. *Delayed motor development.* The student exhibits a motor delay of at least two years or performance one standard deviation below the mean in motor development.
2. *Low motor skill performance.* The student fails to meet age- or grade-level competencies or criterion-referenced standards or benchmarks in one or more physical education content areas.
3. *Poor health-related physical fitness.* The student does not meet specific or general standards of health-related physical fitness.

Because formal testing often takes place under artificial conditions, districts might consider additional salient criteria. For example, corroboration of standardized test results through observational techniques, authentic test results, or a temporary trial placement might also be required. Also, one may consider behavioral, communication, and assistive technology needs when making professional judgments regarding eligibility. These factors are reflected in criteria used to determine eligibility for adapted physical education in Minnesota. Thus, a variety of relevant professional judgments can supplement eligibility criteria and decision making. Other examples of these considerations include the following:

1. Need for a specially designed physical education program recommended by an individual education planning team
2. Need for safe participation
3. Medical condition or disability that affects participation in physical activity
4. Need for a specially designed program to meet unique needs (strengths) for intramural and interscholastic sport experiences

Once eligibility has been established based on a documented unique need, appropriate goals and objectives are written. Chapter 5 reviews aspects of writing measurable and observable annual goals and short-term objectives. Once goals and objectives are written to address the student's unique needs, the most appropriate educational placement in the least restrictive environment is selected. When possible, teachers should attempt to modify activities and instructional methodologies so that the student's goals can be met in the general class.

Although there is one primary criterion for admission into the program (i.e., performance), there are several considerations in the selection of the appropriate placement. Placement might partly depend on what is being taught in the general class. A student who uses a wheelchair, for instance, could probably meet appropriate goals for individual sports (e.g., swimming, weightlifting, track and field) in a general physical education class, but the same student might be assigned to a more restrictive setting for team sports (e.g., volleyball, soccer, football), although alternative activities also could be offered within the same placement. Another important consideration during placement is the input of students and parents. Whatever placement is selected, the student and parent should be comfortable with it. In some cases, when students are unable to understand concepts or safety considerations being taught in the general class or if there are behavioral or other affective concerns, students might need to be assigned to a more restrictive placement (see the continuum of alternative instructional placements in chapter 2).

Measurement in the Affective Domain

Students with or without unique needs in the psychomotor domain might be placed in more restrictive physical education settings if they have unique needs in the affective domain. The affective (or social–emotional) domain is broad and encompasses elements such as attitudes, interests, values, beliefs, and personality, but social behavior is the element of the affective domain that often gets the greatest attention in schools. The ability (and willingness) to follow directions, take turns, respect others, play fair, and demonstrate sportsmanship, for instance, is important in physical education and community-based physical activity settings.

Although physical educators can certainly make observations about a student's behavior in physical activity settings, it is unlikely that they will administer any standardized tests to help determine a unique need in the affective domain. Such an assessment would most likely be conducted by a school psychologist and might include administration of tests such as the Vineland Social Maturity Scale or the Behavior Assessment System for Children. Physical educators would more likely assess behavior in an authentic context and, as such, would develop their own rubrics, checklists, task analyses, or rating scales to measure behavior. Refer to figure 4.3 for a behavioral rating scale that can be used in physical education.

Physical educators might also be involved with functional behavioral assessment (FBA), which is designed to gradually reduce unwanted behaviors while also increasing more desirable behaviors (PACER Center, 2015). In FBA, data such as frequency of behaviors, response rates, intervals, time sampling, durations, and latency periods are commonly gathered. The collection of behavioral data through the use of rubrics and FBA processes can lead to individualized behavioral intervention plans deemed necessary for the child to achieve educational success. Behavioral intervention plans based on FBA are covered in chapters 6 and 9.

Providing a Basis for Instruction

The student's progress on annual goals should be monitored throughout the year. As suggested earlier, alternative tests can be used for this purpose. For instance, students can work (individually, in pairs, or with the teacher) from task sheets or cards that include rubrics or task analyses for a particular activity. Teachers can help students devise practice regimens that promote learning, as evidenced by scoring at a higher level on the rubric or by demonstrating previously missing techniques on the task analysis. Skills learned in practice situations also need to be transferred to natural environments, such as daily activities, games, and sports.

At the conclusion of the instructional program or unit, the teacher should conduct final testing to determine the student's exit abilities. In some cases, grades are awarded based on this final assessment. Whether the program is graded or not, progress should be evaluated in terms of the written goals and objectives. For nongraded situations, Melograno (2006) suggests a checklist on which teachers can mark "achieved," "needs improvement," or "working to achieve" for each of the student's goals. Summary sheets from portfolios can also be used for evaluating exit abilities. Teachers might choose to give awards to students on the basis of their final test performances.

Meeting District and State Testing Requirements

IDEA requires that students with disabilities be included in state- or districtwide assessment programs (Center for Parent Information and Resources, 2017). These assessment programs include tests that are periodically given to all students in order to measure achievement in academic areas, including physical education. Because IDEA states that students with disabilities should have as much involvement in the general curriculum as possible, a child who is receiving instruction in

Affective Domain Criteria

Etiquette

- Respects others' personal space and boundaries.
- Honors activity dynamics.
- Conforms to standards of conduct of the sport.

Fairness

- Plays fair.
- Accepts defeat and does not complain.
- Accepts victory and does not gloat.

Communication With Peers

- Encourages others.
- Accepts skill levels of others.
- Assists others in reaching personal success.
- Uses active listening, positive words, and body language respectfully.

Communication With Instructor

- Uses active listening, positive words, and body language respectfully.
- Accepts coaching cues in a positive manner.
- Responds to instruction and seeks clarification.
- Remains on task.

Scoring

Each of the four categories is rated on multiple occasions as follows:

A = appropriate = always meets behavioral criteria.

NI = needs improvement = sometimes meets behavioral criteria.

I = inappropriate = never meets behavioral criteria.

FIGURE 4.3 Sample rating scale for the affective domain.

Adapted by permission from A.M. Gallo, "Assessing the Affective Domain," *Journal of Physical Education, Recreation & Dance,* Volume 74, no. 4 (2003): 46.

the general curriculum could take the same standardized test given to children without disabilities. Accordingly, the IEP must indicate how the child is participating in state- or districtwide assessments. Participation in a state- or districtwide test can fall under one of the following three options (Center for Parent Information and Resources, 2017):

1. *Participation in the same standardized test.* The same test and testing methods that are given to peers without disabilities are given to the student with a disability. For example, beginning at the ninth grade, all students, including those who receive special education services, perform the 20-meter PACER test to measure aerobic capacity.

2. *Appropriate accommodations are provided.* In order to enable children with disabilities to participate in such general assessments, appropriate accommodations may be necessary. The IEP team specifies what accommodations a given child will need in order to participate. For instance, instead of the 20-meter PACER test, a student with a disability might be allowed to perform the 15-meter version with the assistance of a peer tutor. This particular test would allow for appropriate evaluation according to disability-specific standards.

3. *An alternative test is given.* The IEP team may determine that the student cannot participate in a particular state- or districtwide test, even with modifications. If this is the case, the team must include a statement in the IEP explaining why the test is not appropriate for the student and what assessment will be used instead. The child is then tested using an alternative method that measures the same content area. In the case of measuring

aerobic capacity (the purpose of the PACER test), bike or arm ergometry, swim tests, or the Target Aerobic Movement Test (as described in the BPFT) may be used instead.

Test Instruments Used in Adapted Physical Education

Many published tests are available to physical educators. Most of these tests are standardized and tend to have established levels of validity and reliability, provide norm-referenced or criterion-referenced standards, and require controlled testing environments. Some of these tests, however, do contain alternative elements such as rubric scoring systems (e.g., TGMD-3) or task-analysis sequences and checklists (e.g., Special Olympics coaching guides).

Available tests in physical education measure a range of traits and abilities. Most, however, fall within five traditional areas of physical and motor development and ability: (1) reflexes and reactions, (2) rudimentary movements, (3) fundamental movements, (4) specialized movements (including sport skills, aquatics, dance, and activities of daily living), and (5) health-related physical fitness. (Note that these categories are somewhat arbitrary and do not encompass all possibilities. In some situations, for instance, teachers might routinely test and assess posture or perceptual–motor abilities.) More recently, a sixth area, physical activity, has gained attention. The rest of this section is devoted to a discussion of tests or measures from these six areas. One instrument from each area is highlighted. The highlighted instruments are representative of a particular content area and are recommended or used by many adapted physical educators. Other tests are available within each area, and teachers always have the option of designing alternative measures to augment or replace published instruments. There are some circumstances when published instruments are inappropriate or discriminatory for a particular student, and teachers must modify or design instruments in accordance with the student's abilities. (Additional tests are listed in the Print Resources section of this chapter.) The Application Example sidebar illustrates how tests can be used.

Measuring Reflexes and Reactions

The measurement and assessment of primitive reflexes and postural reactions is an important consideration for those with developmental delays, particularly in early intervention and childhood programs. As educational services are extended to infants and toddlers, as well as to persons with more severe disabilities (especially those that are neurologically based, such as cerebral palsy), physical educators need to understand the influence of reflexes and reactions on motor development milestones and motor skill learning (see chapter 19).

Because primitive reflexes normally follow a predictable sequence for appearing, maturing, and eventually disappearing, they are particularly helpful in providing information on the maturation of the central nervous system. If a primitive reflex persists beyond schedule, presents an unequal bilateral response (i.e., is present on one side but absent or not as strong on the other), is too strong or too weak, or is completely absent, then neurological problems might be suspected. When primitive reflexes are not inhibited, they will undoubtedly interfere with voluntary movement because muscle tone involuntarily changes when reflexes are elicited.

The adapted physical educator should collaborate closely with a physical therapist to identify the presence of primitive reflexes and postural reactions and further determine an appropriate motor intervention. Most adapted physical education educators seek the expertise of a physical therapist who has specialized training in this area. Many early motor development tests incorporate testing of specific reflexes, but all generally involve manipulation of the body to determine evoked responses and spontaneous behaviors (Blythe, 2017).

Measuring Rudimentary Movements

Rudimentary movements are the first voluntary movements and include reaching, grasping, sitting, crawling, and creeping (see chapter 19). Most instruments that assess rudimentary movements use a developmental approach to testing—that is, motor milestones associated with specific ages are arranged chronologically and tested individually. By determining which milestones the child can perform, the teacher can estimate the child's developmental age and suggest future learning activities (i.e., the behaviors in the sequence that the child cannot currently do). The Peabody Developmental Motor Scales (PDMS-2) is an example of this approach, with some additional enhancements (other instruments are discussed in chapters 21 and 22).

Peabody Developmental Motor Scales

- *Purpose.* The PDMS-2 (Folio & Fewell, 2000) assesses the fine and gross motor development of

Application Example

Determining Whether a Student Should Receive an Adapted Program

SETTING

A new 10-year-old student with mild intellectual disability received special education services, including adapted physical education, at his previous school. As a matter of policy, the district will reevaluate the student before determining proper programs and placements. A physical education teacher is invited to be a member of the IEP team.

ISSUE

How should the physical educator determine if the student should receive adapted services?

APPLICATION

The physical educator might do the following:

- Administer the BPFT to determine if the student's fitness is sufficiently developed. (The student would be expected to achieve at least specific standards for children with intellectual disabilities.)
- Administer the TGMD-3 to determine if fundamental movements are completely developed. (Maximum or near-maximum scores would be expected for a 10-year-old.)
- Compare standardized test results (i.e., BPFT and TGMD-3) with the district guidelines or criteria for adapted physical education.
- Place the student in one or more trial placements and collect authentic assessment data. (Determine, for instance, if rubrics used with general education classes are reasonably appropriate, with or without modification, for the new student.)
- Consider all assessment data when formulating a recommendation for the IEP team.

children from birth to 83 months. Items are subcategorized into the following six areas: reflexes, stationary (balance), locomotion, object manipulation, grasping, and visual–motor integration.

- *Description.* A total of 249 test items (mostly developmental milestones) are arranged chronologically within age levels (e.g., 0-1 month, 6-7 months, 18-23 months), and each is identified as belonging to one of the six categories being assessed. It is recommended that testers begin administering items one level below the child's expected motor age. Items are scored from 0 to 2 according to specified criteria. Testing continues until the ceiling-age level is reached (a level for which a score of 2 is obtained for no more than 1 of the 10 items in that level). Composite scores for gross motor (reflexes, balance, locomotion, and object manipulation), fine motor (grasping and visual–motor integration), and total motor (combination of gross and fine motor subtests) areas of functioning can be determined.
- *Reliability and validity.* Empirical research has established adequate levels of reliability and validity. Evidence information is provided for subgroups as well as for the general population.
- *Comment.* The PDMS-2 appears to have certain advantages over other rudimentary movement tests. First, the large number of test items represents a larger sample of behaviors than exists in many other tests. Second, the six categories help teachers pinpoint deficit areas of gross motor development. Finally, the scoring system and availability of normative data provide the teacher with more information on student performance than many other tests do. Supplementary materials, including a software scoring and reporting system and a motor activity program, are also available in conjunction with PDMS-2.
- *Availability.* Pro-Ed, 8700 Shoal Creek Boulevard, Austin, TX 78757-6897. www.proedinc.com
- *Note.* The PDMS-2 is currently being revised at the time of this writing.

Measuring Fundamental Movements

The critical window of opportunity—the time during which experience has the most influence on developing fundamental motor skills—seems to be the early childhood and early elementary years. Fundamental movement skills can be classified as locomotor (traveling skills such as jumping), nonlocomotor (stationary skills such as one-foot balance), or manipulative (object-control skills such as throwing). Some fundamental movement test instruments measure how far the performance has progressed along a motor continuum, but most use a point system to evaluate either the process of the fundamental movement or its product. Process-oriented approaches generally attempt to break down a movement into its component parts and then evaluate each component individually. This approach assesses the quality of the movement, not its result. Product-oriented approaches are concerned primarily with outcome. Product-oriented assessment is more concerned with the quantity of the movement (e.g., how far, how fast, how many) than with its execution. The TGMD-3 emphasizes a process-oriented approach to the assessment of fundamental movements.

Test of Gross Motor Development-3

- *Purpose.* The TGMD-3 (Ulrich, 2019) uses both norm-referenced and criterion-referenced standards to measure gross motor content frequently taught in preschool and early elementary grades, including special education, with a priority on the gross motor skill process rather than the product of performance. It can be used by various professionals with a minimum amount of training.
- *Description.* The test measures 13 fundamental motor skills, subdivided into two subtests: locomotor and ball skills. The locomotor subtest items include the run, gallop, hop, horizontal jump, skip, and slide. The ball skill subtest items consist of the one-hand strike, two-hand strike, stationary dribble, catch, kick, overhand throw, and underhand throw. For each skill, the tester is provided with criteria used to assess the child's performance. Children are allowed two trials and receive 1 point for meeting each performance criterion. These criterion-based scores can be added and compared to norm-referenced standards in order to make summative evaluations regarding locomotor, object-control, and overall gross motor performance. Percentiles, standard scores, and chronological age equivalents can be determined for assessment purposes.
- *Reliability and validity.* Inter- and intra-rater reliability coefficients are quite high (generally .92 to .96) for total score as well as locomotor and ball skill subtests. Acceptable levels of content-related, criterion-related, and construct-related validity are provided.
- *Comment.* The sound process of test construction should provide the user with a good deal of confidence that children's scores accurately reflect their fundamental movement abilities. Availability of both criterion-referenced and norm-referenced standards (based on 2017 U.S. Census) enhances the capability of the test to support eligibility, placement, IEP planning, and instructional decisions. Test scores allow for easy monitoring of student progress and reporting to parents.
- *Availability.* Pro-Ed, 8700 Shoal Creek Boulevard, Austin, TX 78757. www.proedinc.com

Measuring Specialized Activity Movements

A wide variety of possible physical education and sport activities could be tested under this category. Sport skills tests can take many forms, but often they are criterion referenced and teacher constructed (in fact, many teachers prefer to use authentic techniques to assess game and sport skills). Teachers often develop rubrics to measure learning progress in relatively unique skills taught in physical education (e.g., wheelchair locomotion or functional performance using the treadmill at a local health club). Teachers who work with students who compete in special sport programs, including those offered by multisport organizations (e.g., United States Association of Blind Athletes), are encouraged to develop their own tests specific to the event in which the athlete competes. One example of a sport skills test that can be used for athletes with disabilities comes from the Special Olympics coaching guides.

Sport Skills Program Guides

- *Purpose.* Special Olympics, Inc., provides coaching guides that can complement or supplement existing physical education and recreation programs for people with disabilities (aged 8 and older) in sport skills instruction.
- *Description.* Guides are provided for 38 sports and recreation activities. Although the guides are not test instruments per se, authentic assessment is a critical aspect of the instructional programs recommended in the guides. Assessments consist of both task analyses and checklists. Testers check off task focal points that the student is able to perform. For instance, in athletics there are 16 test items corresponding to track and field events (e.g., "Performs a single-leg takeoff for a running long jump").

• *Reliability and validity.* No information has been reported, but content validity probably could be claimed because the checklists reflect task analyses of sports skills developed by experts in the field.

• *Comment.* A primary advantage of the coaching guides is convenience—a teacher or coach can adopt the existing task-analysis curriculums for many sport activities and further modify for specific students and situations as needed. The well-established Special Olympics program has been used with participants with intellectual disabilities and has been shown to have good utility for that group. Participants can engage in year-round, lifelong physical activity through Special Olympics sports and recreation. A disadvantage is that neither reliability nor validity of the various test instruments has been formally established.

• *Availability.* Special Olympics, Inc., 1133 19th Street NW, Washington, DC 20036-3604. https://resources.specialolympics.org/sports-essentials

Measuring Health-Related Physical Fitness

Because health-related physical fitness is an increasing concern in the health and well-being of young people, it is crucial to use fitness tests that provide meaningful data and allow sound instructional decision making. Over the years, many standardized tests of physical fitness have become available to teachers. The BPFT (Winnick & Short, 2014) is one criterion-referenced test that is recommended to measure and assess the health-related physical fitness of young people with disabilities. Access to the proper techniques for conducting the 27 tests in the BPFT has been included in HK*Propel*.

Brockport Physical Fitness Test

• *Purpose.* The BPFT is a health-related, criterion-referenced physical fitness test appropriate for young people (aged 10-17) with and without disabilities.

• *Description.* The test battery includes 27 test items (refer to table 4.2). Typically, students are tested on four to six test items from three components of fitness: body composition, aerobic functioning, and musculoskeletal functioning (muscular strength, endurance, and flexibility). Although specific test items are recommended for children with intellectual disabilities, cerebral palsy, visual impairments, spinal cord injuries, and congenital anomalies and amputations, teachers are encouraged to personalize testing. Personalization involves identifying the student's health-related concerns, establishing a desired fitness profile, selecting components and subcomponents of fitness to be assessed, selecting test items to measure those components, and selecting health-related, criterion-referenced standards to evaluate fitness. Thus, teachers have the option to modify any of the elements of the testing program as outlined in the test manual. Both general and disability-specific standards are available for assessment and evaluation. A general standard is one appropriate for the general population; a specific standard is one that has been adjusted for the effects of a disability and is available only for selected test items for particular groups of people.

• *Reliability and validity.* The BPFT test items have been shown to be valid and reliable through various studies. Evidence for validity and reliability is provided in a lengthy technical report published in a special issue of *Adapted Physical Activity Quarterly* (Winnick, 2005).

• *Comment.* The BPFT was patterned after FitnessGram, and many of the standards, especially for the general population, were adopted from that test. Thus, teachers in inclusive settings should find it relatively easy to use both tests as necessary. In addition to the test manual, a training guide is also available (Winnick & Short, 1999).

• *Availability.* Human Kinetics, P.O. Box 5076, Champaign, IL 61825. Phone: 800-747-4457. www.humankinetics.com/products/all-products/brockport-physical-fitness-test-manual-2nd-edition-with-web-resource

Measuring Physical Activity

Much research has established the positive relationship between regular physical activity and health, and many physical education programs promote physically active lifestyles as a primary goal. Consequently, it is becoming increasingly important for physical educators to objectively measure physical activity levels in ways that are sensitive enough to document change. At present, four types of activity measures are available to teachers: heart rate monitors, activity monitors (e.g., pedometers, accelerometers, motion sensors), direct observation, and self-report instruments (Welk & Wood, 2000). Despite their accuracy, heart rate monitors have limited applicability in school situations because of the cost and limitations of individually measuring students in large classes. Pedometers are relatively inexpensive and accurate and have good utility for measuring walking activity, but they do not have broad applicability in measuring general physical activity. Coding student activity through direct observation is not expensive, but it can be inefficient and time consuming because only a few children can be monitored at one time by a trained observer. Consequently, these approaches might be more effective in settings with fewer students.

More recently, smartwatch technologies (e.g., Fitbit) and associated software and apps have become increasingly popular as a valid physical activity tracker (Mooses et al., 2018). Although some schools have utilized Fitbit technology in their physical education programs, little has been reported on the current and potential use for school-aged individuals with disabilities. Therefore, Fitbit applications tracking physical activity should be more thoroughly investigated for use in adapted physical education programs.

Self-report instruments are appropriate for measuring physical activity in most school settings. Self-reporting requires students to recall and record their participation in physical activity over a set amount of time (usually from one to seven days). Although many self-report instruments are available (see Welk & Wood, 2000), all seek to quantify the frequency, intensity, and duration of students' physical activity. If students with disabilities have difficulty with self-reporting, teachers or parents might need to provide an estimate of the information instead. ActivityGram is a computer software program that helps students learn more about their physical activity habits through self-reporting.

ActivityGram

- *Purpose.* ActivityGram (Cooper Institute, 2017), a program associated with FitnessGram, records, analyzes, and saves student physical activity data and produces reports based on those data.

- *Description.* ActivityGram prompts participants to recall their physical activities over the previous two or three days in 30-minute time blocks. Students select activities from within six categories: lifestyle activity, active aerobics, active sports, muscle fitness activities, flexibility exercises, and rest and inactivity. Students are provided with personalized information about their general level of physical activity and learn strategies to increase or maintain physical activity, both in and outside of school. Personalized recommendations are based on national guidelines endorsed by the Society of Health and Physical Educators (SHAPE America).

- *Reliability and validity.* Because of the subjective nature of self-report measures, measurement error may reduce validity. Nevertheless, the Previous Day Physical Activity Recall instrument, on which the ActivityGram program is based, has been shown to provide valid and reliable estimates of physical activity and also accurately identifies periods of moderate to vigorous activity (Plowman & Meredith, 2013). Measurement error can be minimized when parents, teachers, and others can verify activity measures.

- *Comment.* Although designed primarily for students without disabilities, ActivityGram can be useful for students receiving adapted physical education. Specific activities will vary (e.g., running vs. pushing a wheelchair), but the six categories of physical activity are appropriate for most students with or without disabilities. Younger children and those with intellectual disabilities, however, might have trouble recalling and entering activity data. Peer tutors, teacher aides, or parents could be prepared to make direct observations and enter the data on behalf of a student who has difficulty using the system.

- *Availability.* Human Kinetics, P.O. Box 5076, Champaign, IL 61825. Phone: 800-747-4457. https://us.humankinetics.com/blogs/excerpt/fitnessgram

Program Evaluation

One of the time-honored purposes of measurement in physical education is program evaluation. As used in this section of the book, the term *program evaluation* relates to the evaluation of instructional programming. (Other aspects of a program, including management and organization, can be evaluated in other ways; see chapter 2 and appendix D.) Program evaluation seeks to answer the question, "Is the physical education program doing what it purports to be doing?" This evaluation is important because if the answer to this question is "no," then changes need to be made in order to improve the program.

Program evaluation can also have a powerful public relations function in schools. Physical education teachers are all too familiar with attacks on their programs by administrators or school boards when fiscal or instructional resources are limited. Unfortunately, physical education has not always been able to successfully defend against these attacks. For instance, low numbers of high school students attend physical education because many schools require only one semester of it, or waive requirements, or allow exemptions due to sport participation (U.S. Department of Health and Human Services [USDHHS], 2014). To remedy these limitations and others like it, physical educators must overcome perceptions that their programs are merely playtime, glorified recess, or open recreation. Physical educators certainly must build good programs, but it is insufficient for them to simply claim the program is effective—they must objectively demonstrate that it is effective.

To conduct program evaluation, program goals must be in place. These goals might be determined locally (in a specific school or school district), statewide, or even nationally. A school district, for instance, might base its program goals or aims on SHAPE America's physical education content standards (2014), which state that the physically literate student meets the following five criteria:

1. Demonstrates competency in a variety of motor skills and movement patterns
2. Applies knowledge of concepts, principles, strategies, and tactics related to movement and performance
3. Demonstrates the knowledge and skills to achieve and maintain a health-enhancing level of physical activity and fitness
4. Exhibits responsible personal and social behavior that respects self and others
5. Recognizes the value of physical activity for health, enjoyment, challenge, self-expression, or social interaction

Although helpful in articulating a direction for a program, these standards in their current form may be too broad to be used for program evaluation. It is up to the local physical education staff to operationalize the standards in ways that can be measured and evaluated. Some states such as Minnesota have developed K-12 academic standards and benchmarks in physical education (Minnesota Department of Education, 2018). These grade-level benchmarks serve as a basis for measuring performance and knowledge across all five state standards and thus provide an objective evaluation of the physical education program.

Examples of benchmarks or student learning outcomes for two of the SHAPE America standards are provided next. These outcomes are example statements and can be used by physical education programs where district or state physical education standards and outcomes are not available.

Standard 1

To evaluate standard 1, the terms *competency* and *variety* must be defined. For instance, a district might choose to define beginning, intermediate, and advanced competencies for the motor skills and movement patterns taught in its curriculum and define variety by the number of activities for which some level of competency is claimed. So, a physical education benchmark indicative of student competency in standard 1 could be as follows:

> By the end of the year, at least 80 percent of all fourth graders will reach target proficiency levels (minimum score of 3 on a four-point rubric) in at least six object-control skills as measured by district fundamental motor skill rubrics.

If staff members can specify beginning, intermediate, and advanced competencies for a variety of sports taught in the curriculum, they can specify levels of accomplishment for each grade. Then, perhaps by graduation the program goal might be for 80 percent of the students to have met beginning-level competencies in at least 10 activities, intermediate in at least 5, and advanced in at least 3. This would contribute to the district's operational definition for documenting evidence of student achievement in SHAPE America's national physical education standard 1. Students and teachers could develop portfolios that follow students through their school years, with teachers helping students acquire additional competencies in various sports as they move toward graduation.

Standard 3

Physical education staff might decide to adopt the Centers for Disease Control and Prevention (CDC) and American College of Sports Medicine (ACSM) joint physical activity guidelines for secondary students, as follows (USDHHS, 2008):

> For grades 7 to 12, 90 percent of all students will perform at least 60 minutes of daily moderate-intensity physical activity during the school year.

The ActivityGram program could be used to monitor progress and encourage accurate self-reporting. Pedometers, accelerometers, and heart rate monitors are relatively inexpensive and are commonly used to gather data on physical activity and further evaluate this standard.

FitnessGram and the BPFT (Fitness Challenge) could be used to evaluate a program goal based on standard 3 as well. Fitness Challenge, for instance, provides a report that summarizes the performance of all class members for all items in the test battery. Physical education staff might operationalize standard 3 as follows:

At least 80 percent of all students aged 10 to 17 will meet either minimal general or specific health-related physical fitness standards for their age, sex, and, as appropriate, disability on at least one measure of aerobic functioning.

Other program goals could be written for other components of fitness and monitored with help from ActivityGram or Fitness Challenge. Because Fitness Challenge includes both general and specific standards, it is useful in inclusive settings.

Program goals that have been operationally defined for a general physical education program might not always be useful in evaluating an adapted physical education program. In the absence of general program goals that might apply to a diverse student body in adapted physical education, teachers could choose to report program evaluation data as a function of success in meeting students' short-term objectives on their IEPs (see chapter 5). Such a program goal might read as follows:

At least 80 percent of all short-term physical education objectives appearing on a student's IEP will be achieved for at least 90 percent of students enrolled in adapted physical education.

These short-term objectives would be based on the alternative or standardized measurement strategies discussed in this chapter.

Related to program evaluation is the extent to which the adapted and general physical education programs are committed to inclusion and universal design for learning (UDL) practices. Because students with disabilities should be receiving physical education services alongside their nondisabled peers to the maximum extent possible, program evaluation components now include the level of effort made by teachers to include children with disabilities in a general physical education environment (Lieberman et al., 2019; Lieberman et al., 2021). The Lieberman-Brian Inclusion Rating Scale for Physical Education (LIRSPE) can measure the extent to which physical education teachers attempt to make their programs more inclusive. Through the use of this rating system, an emphasis on utilizing more UDL practices, especially in inclusive settings, can be used to encourage specific teaching practices that promote positive and successful inclusion of students with disabilities in general physical education. The LIRSPE and associated rubrics for each of the 28 items associated with effective inclusion practices are referenced in the Online Resources section of this chapter.

Summary

Measurement and assessment serve several important functions in adapted physical education. Most significantly, they are a means for determining whether a student has a unique need, and they provide a foundation for structuring learning experiences and monitoring progress. Measurement and assessment strategies range from techniques with stronger psychometric properties conducted in less natural environments (standardized assessment) to those with weaker psychometric properties conducted in more natural environments (authentic assessment). Each of these approaches has strengths and weaknesses and should be selected in accordance with the purposes of the assessment. These approaches are best combined to yield a more accurate picture of the student's level of performance.

Assessment in adapted physical education should focus on physical fitness and motor development and ability (including reflexes, rudimentary movements, fundamental movements, activities of daily living, sport skills, aquatics, and dance, as appropriate). Standardized tests are commercially available for each of these areas and are especially useful for summative purposes, such as determining unique need. Some standardized tests, however, might be inappropriate for students with disabilities and may not provide a basis for instruction and learning. Authentic techniques may be used when standardized tests are inappropriate and are especially useful for formative or instructional purposes such as monitoring student progress. Test data generated from the assessment of individual students can be aggregated to yield information on the effectiveness of the physical education instructional program, as well as to show teachers' efforts to include students with disabilities in general physical education.

References

Blythe, S. (2017). The significance of primitive and postural reflexes. In S. Blythe, L. Bearet, P. Blythe, & V. Scaramella-Nowinki (Eds.), *Attention, balance, and coordination: The A.B.C. of learning success* (2nd ed., pp. 29-63). John Wiley & Sons, Ltd. https://doi.org/10.1002/9781119164746.ch2

Center for Parent Information and Resources. (2012). Response to intervention (RTI). Retrieved from www.parentcenterhub.org/rti/

Center for Parent Information and Resources. (2017). *Supports, modifications, and accommodations for students.* www.parentcenterhub.org/repository/accommodations

Cooper Institute. (2017). *FitnessGram administration manual: The journey to MyHealthyZone* (5th ed.). Human Kinetics.

Folio, M., & Fewell, R. (2000). *Peabody developmental motor scales* (2nd ed.). Pro-Ed.

Hensley, L. (1997). Alternative assessment for physical education. *Journal of Physical Education, Recreation and Dance, 68*(7), 19-24.

Lacy, A., & Williams, S. (2018). *Measurement and evaluation in physical education and exercise science* (8th ed.). Taylor and Francis Group.

Lieberman, L., Grenier, M. & Brian, A. (2019). How inclusive is your physical education class? Introducing the Lieberman/Brian Inclusion Rating Scale for physical education. *Journal of Physical Education, Recreation & Dance, 90*(2), 3-4. https://doi.org/10.1080/07303084.2019.1548179

Lieberman, L., Grenier, M., Brian, A., & Arndt, K. (2021). *Universal design for learning in physical education.* Human Kinetics.

Lund, J. (2000). *Creating rubrics for physical education.* NASPE.

Lund, J., & Veal, M. (2013). *Assessment-driven instruction in physical education.* Human Kinetics.

Melograno, V. (2006). *Professional and student portfolios for physical education* (2nd ed.). Human Kinetics.

Minnesota Department of Education. (2007). *Developmental adapted physical education.* www.revisor.mn.gov/rules/3525.1352/

Minnesota Department of Education. (2018). *Minnesota K-12 academic standards: Physical education.* https://education.mn.gov/mdeprod/groups/educ/documents/basic/bwrl/mdcz/~edisp/mde073333.pdf

Mooses, K., Oja, M., Reisberg, S., Vilo, J., & Kull, M. (2018). Validating Fitbit Zip for monitoring physical activity of children in school: A cross-sectional study. *BMC Public Health 18*, 858. https://doi.org/10.1186/s12889-018-5752-7

Morrow, J., Mood, D., Disch, J., & Kang, M. (2016). *Measurement and evaluation in human performance.* Human Kinetics.

PACER Center. (2015). *What is a functional behavioral assessment and how is it used? An overview for parents.* www.pacer.org/parent/php/php-c215a.pdf

Plowman, S.A., & Meredith, M.D. (Eds.). (2013). *FitnessGram/ActivityGram reference guide* (4th ed.). The Cooper Institute. www.cooperinstitute.org/vault/2440/web/files/662.pdf

SHAPE America. (2014). *National standards & grade-level outcomes for K-12 physical education.* Human Kinetics.

SHAPE America. (2019). *PE metrics* (3rd ed.). Human Kinetics.

Ulrich, D. (2019). *Test of gross motor development* (3rd ed.). Pro-Ed.

U.S. Department of Health and Human Services (USDHHS). (2008). *Physical activity guidelines for Americans.* DHHS, CDC, National Center for Chronic Disease Prevention and Health Promotion (NCCDPHP).

U.S. Department of Health and Human Services (USDHHS). (2014). *Physical education profiles, 2012: Physical education and physical activity practices and policies among secondary schools at select US sites.* DHHS, CDC, NCCDPHP.

Welk, G., & Wood, K. (2000). Physical activity assessment: A practical review of instruments and their use in the curriculum. *Journal of Physical Education, Recreation and Dance, 71*(1), 30-40.

Winnick, J. (Ed.). (2005). Introduction to the Brockport physical fitness technical manual [Special Issue]. *Adapted Physical Activity Quarterly, 22*(4). https://doi.org/10.1123/apaq.22.4.315

Winnick, J., & Short, F. (1999). *The Brockport physical fitness training guide.* Human Kinetics.

Winnick, J., & Short, F. (2014). *The Brockport physical fitness test manual* (2nd ed.). Human Kinetics.

Print Resources

Brockport Physical Fitness Test Manual (2nd ed.). (2014). Human Kinetics, P.O. Box 5076, Champaign, IL 61825-5076. www.humankinetics.com

This test tool measures health-related physical fitness among youngsters with a variety of disabilities. It can be used alongside FitnessGram to facilitate a comprehensive fitness program for any physical education program. It includes online resources for test demonstration for specific disabilities, data summary, and report generation.

Hawaii Early Learning Profile 3-6. (2010). Vort Corporation, P.O. Box G, Menlo Park, CA 94026. www.vort.com/home.php?cat=2

This curriculum-based assessment tool measures developmental skills in the age 3 to 6 range in areas of cognitive, language, gross motor, fine motor, social–emotional, and self-help functioning. Additional assessments are available for ages 0 to 3 and 0 to 14.

Video Resources

Universal Design for Learning in P.E.—How Inclusive Are Your Classes?: https://ifapa.net/lieberman-brian-scale/

This video offers a brief tutorial on how to assess various components of your classroom (e.g., support, equipment options, assessment strategies, and classroom management protocols) and the level to which they are inclusive of all students, including those with disabilities.

Online Resources

Determining Eligibility for Adapted Physical Education: www.wrightslaw.com/info/ape.la.elig.crit.pdf

This developmental assessment tool distinguishes children who have average motor skills from those who have significantly below-average motor skills. Movement profiles summarize areas of strengths and weaknesses among children in six different grade levels. For more, contact the Louisiana Department of Education, Division of Educational Improvement and Assistance, P.O. Box 94064, Baton Rouge, LA 70804.

FitnessGram and ActivityGram: www.fitnessgram.net

This tool is used to assess the health-related physical fitness of children. In conjunction with online FitnessGram software, individual and group reporting for various educational purposes can be generated. Moreover, ActivityGram is used to provide fitness education through hands-on learning experiences. For more, contact the Cooper Institute for Aerobics Research, 12330 Preston Road, Dallas, TX 75230.

Lieberman-Brian Inclusion Rating Scale for Physical Education (LIRSPE): www.nchpad.org/1702/6814/Universal~Design~for~Learning~in~Physical~Education

The full Lieberman-Brian Inclusion Rating Scale for Physical Education (LIRSPE), including rubrics, can be found at the National Center on Health, Physical Activity and Disability website. For more, contact the National Center on Health, Physical Activity and Disability, 4000 Ridgeway Drive, Birmingham, AL 35209.

Presidential Youth Fitness Program: https://pyfp.org

This online-based fitness education and assessment program is available to teach fitness concepts, assess fitness and understand results, plan for improvement or maintenance of fitness levels, and empower students to be fit and active for life. For more, contact the National Fitness Foundation, P.O. Box 4849, Silver Spring, MD 20914-4849.

5

Individualized Education Programs

Brock McMullen and Manny Felix

Hayley Griswold, a high school physical education teacher, was at school reviewing materials for an IEP meeting later in the day. She asked her student teacher, Elsie, to accompany her to the meeting.

"Good morning, Elsie! Don't forget we have our IEP meeting for Jerry this afternoon. I would like you to come along so you understand what is required when you have your own students."

"Sounds good. I know we revised Jerry's physical education IEP a couple of weeks ago. What else do we to do need to be prepared?" Elsie asked.

"I like to come prepared with a copy of his current goals, assessment results, and notes on his annual physical fitness, sport skills, and swimming goals. Since there will be an entire team present—Jerry's special education teacher, the principal, the school psychologist, the physical therapist, and his parents—I need to be able to speak to any progress he's made in PE this year. Jerry often attends his own IEP meetings, too. With everyone in the room, we can collaborate and address Jerry's strengths and weaknesses as a student in each of our subject areas. We meet at least once a year to develop, monitor, and revise his IEP."

"I see. It looks like there is a lot of information in the IEP; what is the most important part for me to understand as his teacher?" asked Elsie.

"You will need to know the student's measurable standards-based annual goals and the resources that the student needs to work toward achieving those goals. We use this information to track his progress so the information can be used on quarterly progress reports that are sent home," said Hayley.

"It's great that there is so much support for students with disabilities!" said Elsie.

"It takes time, but it's important to develop an individualized program for students with unique needs in physical education. Besides, an IEP is required by law for eligible students with disabilities. I wish all kids could have this type of individualized program so their personal instructional needs were addressed."

"So, what happens if Jerry doesn't achieve his IEP goals? Can we get in trouble, since it's required by law?"

"You can relax," Hayley laughed. "We won't get fired if Jerry only does one curl-up or can't run a four-minute mile! I review his goals regularly and make teaching adjustments to best provide experiences that meet his needs in physical education."

Note: The authors sincerely thank Francis X. Short, professor, State University of New York, College at Brockport, and Garth Tymeson, University of Wisconsin – La Crosse, for their contributions to this chapter in earlier editions.

United States education laws require that eligible students with disabilities receive individualized programs to meet their unique needs. Depending on age and other factors, a student's individualized program might be developed in the form of an individualized education program (IEP) or a Section 504 accommodation plan. Further, students who are not disabled but who have unique needs in physical education might also need individualized programs. Such programs, though not required by federal law, are recommended in this text and are called *individualized physical education programs* (IPEPs). This chapter provides an overview of these programs and discusses in detail the requirements and procedures for developing IEPs, Section 504 plans, and IPEPs.

Overview of Individualized Programs

The foundation of special education services required by the Individuals with Disabilities Education Act (IDEA) is the provision of an IEP. Often called the heart of IDEA, an IEP is a comprehensive written document used to describe the process of providing services and the details of what those services will include (Morrow, 2017). The most recent amendments to IDEA in 2004 reaffirmed the importance of IEPs for providing free, appropriate public educational services for students with disabilities in the least restrictive environment (U.S. Department of Education, 2006). An IEP describes the student's present levels of academic achievement and functional performance, identifies measurable annual goals, and lists the types, frequencies, and durations of educational services necessary to meet those goals. IDEA requires that educational teams develop IEPs for all eligible students with disabilities between the ages of 3 and 21 (see appendix A for an overview of disabilities defined in IDEA).

IDEA also has provisions for addressing the developmental needs of infants and toddlers with disabilities. In accord with state discretion, local agencies may provide these early intervention services as detailed in an individualized family service plan (IFSP). Early intervention services and the development of an IFSP are described in chapter 21.

Some students with disabilities, however, might not meet the eligibility criteria to qualify for federally mandated special education services provided by IDEA. Students with conditions such as HIV (human immunodeficiency virus) or AIDS (acquired immune deficiency syndrome), asthma, seizure disorder, diabetes, attention deficit/hyperactivity disorder (ADHD), or mild physical or learning disabilities may not be eligible for special education IEPs, but they might be entitled to appropriate accommodations and services tailored to meet their needs as provided in a Section 504 disability accommodation plan (see chapter 1 for a description of Section 504 of the Rehabilitation Act). These 504 plans often include accommodations for physical education and extracurricular participation needs.

In physical education there might be a third group of students (in addition to those covered by IDEA and Section 504) who require individualized programs. These students do not qualify as having a disability that affects their education as defined under federal law, but they do have unique needs in physical education. Students who are recuperating from injuries, are recovering from noncommunicable diseases, are obese, have low skill levels, or have deficient levels of physical fitness might fall into this category based on district criteria. Although this group of students is not covered by federal law, it is recommended that school districts develop IPEPs to document programs modified to meet students' unique physical education needs.

Whether or not a student is deemed to have a disability under the provisions of IDEA or Section 504, physical education teachers should provide an individualized program if the student has a unique need. A unique need is apparent when a student cannot safely or successfully participate in the general physical education program. Figure 5.1 summarizes the individualized programs that are either required or recommended for students with disabilities and other unique needs in physical education.

Students With Disabilities: The IEP Document

An IEP is a comprehensive written document that is developed, implemented, reviewed, and revised in a meeting to describe the free, appropriate public education for an eligible child with a disability as defined by IDEA (U.S. Department of Education, 2006). School districts may develop their own IEP document format; thus it is not unusual for neighboring districts to use different IEP forms. Although formats vary, each IEP must include cer-

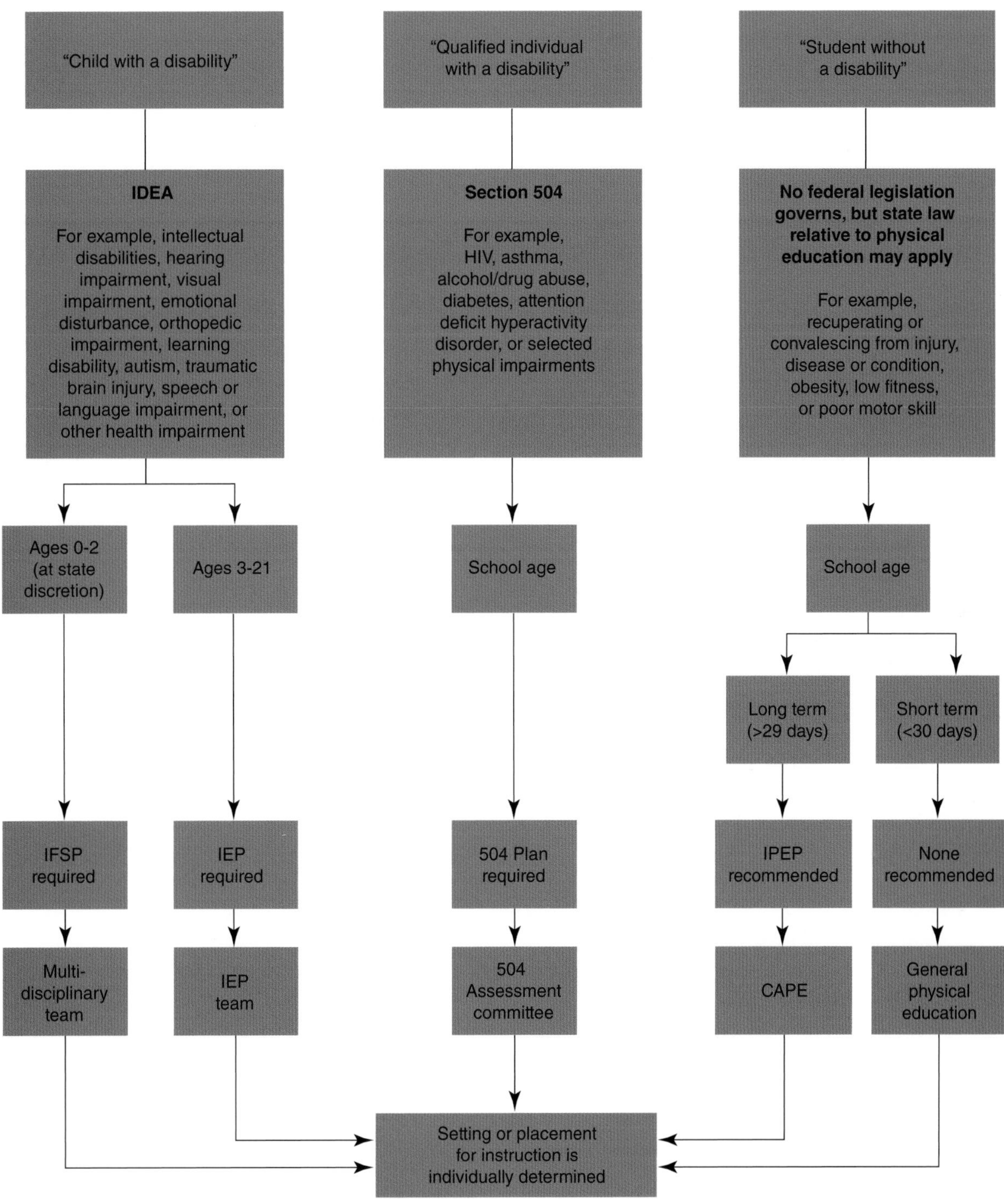

FIGURE 5.1 Individualized programs for students with unique needs in physical education.

tain components. Refer to the U.S. Department of Education website (www2.ed.gov/parents/needs/speced/iepguide) for a model IEP form.

The IEP contains information about the entire instructional program for a student. Physical education, if determined to be part of the IEP, is only one of many content areas of this comprehensive document. To efficiently manage these documents, many school districts use secure Internet-based IEP management programs that allow teachers and other school personnel to develop, monitor, revise, and complete IEPs electronically. See the Skyward item in the Online Resources at the end of this chapter.

Components of the IEP

Although school district IEP forms might include additional information and vary in format, IDEA requires that an IEP contain several specific components (Yell et al., 2013). Each of these required components is discussed here, and sample physical education information that might be included in an IEP is discussed and shown in figure 5.2. Many other subjects and services besides physical education are on most IEPs.

Individualized Education Program (Physical Education Content)

Student's name: Kyle Hernandez (student with Down syndrome; moderate cognitive disability)

Age: 16

Present Levels of Performance

1. Completes 28 laps on the 20 m PACER test (Brockport Physical Fitness Test [BPFT] adapted fitness zone standard is 34 to 46 laps and the healthy fitness zone standard is >47 laps). Kyle demonstrates a well-coordinated, mature running pattern but needs a peer buddy to run with him during the test to motivate him and keep him from stopping and sitting when reaching end lines.
2. Performs 20 modified curl-ups (exceeds the BPFT specific standard but does not meet the minimal general standard of 24). Demonstrates very good form for curl-ups.
3. Successfully performs the trunk lift at 12 in. (30 cm; BPFT general standard is 9-12 in., or 23-30 cm).
4. Back-saver sit-and-reach score for both right and left sides is 8 in. (20 cm; BPFT general standard is 8 in.).
5. Averages 4,700 steps per day on a pedometer. General recommendation is about 10,000 per day.
6. Scores 1 (out of a possible 3) on the overhand throwing rubric. (Characteristics: Ball is brought behind the head in preparation and release is high over the shoulder, steps forward with the leg on the same side as the throwing arm, trunk rotation is limited in preparation and during throw, trunk flexes slightly in follow-through.)
7. Throws a baseball a distance of 30 ft (9 m) (average of five trials) using an overhand pattern.
8. Scores 3 (out of a possible 10) on the overhand throwing accuracy test (target is 4 ft by 4 ft [1.2 m by 1.2 m] with the bottom line 2 ft [0.6 m] from the floor; student stands 30 ft [9 m] away and attempts to throw an indoor baseball to the wall target 10 times, earning 1 point for each successful throw).
9. Averages three inappropriate social behaviors or physical provocations (hitting, pushing others) per physical education class.
10. Swims 25 m in 45 seconds using the front crawl stroke with inconsistent rhythmic breathing (typically holds breath and lifts head to breathe; when prompted to breathe to the side, he can do so but usually reverts to holding breath and lifting the head after the first stroke); arm strokes barely break surface of water, with irregular flutter kick often characterized by bicycle kicking; body position is less than horizontal due to lifting the head out of the water and inadequate flutter kicking; overall stroke technique appears to be inefficient and counterproductive to forward propulsion; endurance is good; does not fatigue or stop while swimming 25 m. He is very motivated and cooperative in the aquatic setting, and he has excellent water adjustment skills.

Effect of disability on involvement and progress in the general education curriculum: Kyle has Down syndrome with moderate cognitive disability. His disability generally contributes to lower performance in physical fitness and sport activities because he has difficulty understanding rules, concepts, and strategies of many curricular units, which at times makes it difficult to interact with his peers without disabilities. His muscle tone is poor (very hypotonic), he is overweight, and he tires easily. Kyle sometimes requires physical assistance or prompting when participating in physical education and is

FIGURE 5.2 Sample physical education information for an IEP.

occasionally physically aggressive toward other students. With assistance, he can participate in several general physical education units (mostly those focused on individual sports; he demonstrates little positive participation or interactions in team-oriented units).

Measurable Annual Goals and Short-Term Objectives

Note: IEP goals 1 and 2 are written in the traditional format that includes related short-term instructional objectives; goals 3 through 6 are written in the multielement format discussed in this chapter and do not have accompanying objectives or benchmarks.

Goal 1. Kyle will improve his aerobic functioning.

Short-Term Objectives

1.1 With a peer buddy running side by side, Kyle will run 30 laps of the 20 m PACER without sitting between laps during three consecutive class days.

1.2 Kyle will run 35 laps of the 20 m PACER with a peer buddy during three consecutive class days.

1.3 Kyle will independently run 40 laps of the 20 m PACER during three consecutive class days.

Goal 2. Kyle will improve his overhand throwing ability as demonstrated by scoring a 3 on the throwing technique rubric during three consecutive class days.

Short-Term Objectives

2.1 Kyle will score a 3 on the overhand throwing rubric. (Characteristics: Arm is swung backward rather than upward, ball is above the throwing elbow, throwing elbow moves horizontally during throw, thumb points down in follow-through, trunk rotates in preparation, throwing shoulder drops slightly in preparation, foot opposite the throwing arm steps forward with weight transfer from back foot to front.)

2.2 Kyle will throw a baseball overhand 50 ft (15 m) 8 out of 10 trials during three consecutive class days.

2.3 Kyle will score 7 out of 10 on the throwing accuracy test from 30 ft (9 m) during three consecutive classes.

Goal 3. By June 2022, following verbal instructions, Kyle will demonstrate improved abdominal muscular strength and endurance by achieving minimal general standards on the BPFT (will perform at least 24 modified curl-ups) when assessed by his adapted physical education teacher.

Goal 4. By December 2022, when provided with daily verbal reminders based on his behavior intervention plan at the start of class, Kyle will decrease his inappropriate behaviors in physical education as demonstrated by having two or fewer physical provocations with peers per 45-minute class for three consecutive class periods.

Goal 5. By June 2022, when assisted by a family member or friend, Kyle will increase his daily out-of-school physical activity by achieving an average of 7,000 steps for five consecutive days as measured by a pedometer (measurements taken at home by parents at night and reported to adapted physical education teacher via email).

Goal 6. By May 2022, following verbal instructions, Kyle will swim 25 m in less than 40 seconds using the front crawl, demonstrating at least 10 consecutive correct rhythmic breathing sequences to the same side, with both arms emerging fully out of the water with each stroke while continuously performing proper straight-legged flutter kick during three consecutive classes, as assessed by the adapted physical education teacher.

Procedures for Measuring and Reporting Child's Progress to Parents

Criteria for evaluation of progress are contained in the measurable goals and short-term objectives. Progress on the goals and objectives will be monitored monthly or during the appropriate curriculum unit. A written report describing Kyle's progress on his goals and objectives will be sent to the parents at

FIGURE 5.2 *(continued)*

least quarterly (or at the same time as report cards for students without disabilities). A final summative assessment will be conducted during the week of June 1. The BPFT, pedometer readings, swimming skills rubric, and three throwing tests will be used for this evaluation. The teacher will maintain a daily record of Kyle's physical provocations to determine a three-day analysis of inappropriate behaviors.

Statement of Services and Supplementary Aids

Kyle will receive adapted physical education services with his intact special education class three times during the six-day high school class cycle for 35 minutes each class period (except when participating in general physical education units). In addition, Kyle will participate in the general physical education class (45 minutes per class period) during personal fitness, softball, swimming, and adventure education units. No special equipment or aids are required, but a trained peer tutor will be assigned to Kyle during the units in the general physical education class. It is important for Kyle to be in general physical education class during these units so he can observe socially appropriate behaviors.

Statement of Participation in General Education Settings

To best meet Kyle's needs, he will be placed in a combination of adapted physical education and general physical education for participation with other students without disabilities. During the personal fitness, softball, swimming, and adventure education curriculum units, Kyle will receive 100 percent of his physical education program in a placement with peers without disabilities (the general education setting).

Assessment Accommodations

The BPFT includes appropriate accommodations for health-related fitness assessment in accord with the FitnessGram test that is administered at the high schools in the district (e.g., the curl-up to measure abdominal strength is modified so that the hands slide along the thighs to the knee rather than sliding across a strip placed on the floor). The swimming skills rubric is used by all students in high school. The three overhand throwing tests (technique, distance, accuracy) are modified from those ordinarily administered at the elementary level but were deemed appropriate for Kyle given his interest in baseball. Kyle currently cannot score on the baseball skills test routinely given at the secondary level.

Schedule of Services

Kyle will have adapted physical education from 9:30 to 10:05 a.m. every other day during the six-day cycle. During the personal fitness, softball, swimming, and adventure education units, he will attend the general physical education class from 1:15 to 2:00 p.m. on three days during the six-day class cycle.

Transition Services

Kyle loves baseball, frequently attends games with his family, plays baseball video games, and watches games on television. In the spring and summer, Kyle will participate in the community-based Challengers baseball program for the first time. Development of baseball skills, with an emphasis on throwing, will take place in his adapted physical education class. Rules of the game will be reinforced both in physical education and at home. Mr. Hernandez (Kyle's father) will spend additional time each weekend working on batting skills (off a tee and underhand pitch). During the winter Kyle will accompany his older brother to the Snap Fitness Center at least two days a week after school (for strength and aerobic activities). This will provide needed exposure to community physical activity facilities for Kyle's future use. Mrs. Hernandez will take Kyle for walks around the community after dinner at least three times per week. It is also recommended that Kyle's parents consider enrolling him in Special Olympics swimming and other activities where he could compete and continue to increase his physical activity in community-based settings.

FIGURE 5.2 *(continued)*

Statement of Child's Present Levels of Academic Achievement and Functional Performance

Every IEP must include a statement of the child's present levels of academic achievement and functional performance, including how the child's disability affects involvement and progress in the general education curriculum or, for preschool children, how the disability affects participation in age-appropriate activities (U.S. Department of Education, 2006). The present level of performance (PLP) component is used to establish the student's baseline educational abilities and is where all relevant evaluation and background information is presented. This evaluation information has two purposes: (1) to determine if a child has a disability (this is especially critical during the student's initial evaluation and formal reevaluations, which must take place at least once every three years) and (2) to determine the educational needs of the child.

The PLP is the cornerstone of the IEP. Information presented in all subsequent IEP components is related to the PLP content. If the PLP is not properly determined or is incomplete, the student's specially designed instructional program may not be appropriate. Statements in the PLP should be data based, objective, observable, and measurable (Capizzi, 2008). Ordinarily, this component consists primarily of test results, which can come from standardized tests with performance criteria, or from less formal tests, including authentic assessments like rubrics or checklists.

Both standardized and authentic assessment results have roles to play in the IEP. When the purpose of the evaluation is to determine if the student qualifies as a child with a disability according to IDEA (especially during the initial evaluation and any triennial reevaluations), the assessment instruments must be technically sound, validated for the purposes for which they are used, and given by qualified personnel knowledgeable in the content area—therefore, standardized assessments are best. On the other hand, authentic, teacher-constructed tests can be helpful in clarifying the PLP and educational needs of the child in many content areas. In fact, IDEA requires current classroom-based assessments and observations as part of the evaluation of any student under consideration for special educational services.

The PLP information should be presented in a way that places the student on a continuum of achievement—that is, the test results shown should discriminate among levels of ability. For this reason, tests on which students can attain only minimum or maximum scores are not very helpful in determining PLP (although some criterion-referenced tests might simply have pass–fail standards). This performance continuum should note what the student *can* do, not just what he cannot do. It is important to provide positive performance information, including behavioral aspects of participation, to parents and other IEP team members. Finally, PLP information should be presented in a way that is immediately understandable; it should not require additional explanation from the teacher. When standardized test results are included, it is helpful when percentiles, criterion-referenced standards, or other references are presented as well as the raw scores; teacher-constructed tests should be adequately described so the conditions can be replicated at a later date. Short video clips of student assessments and actual physical education class participation are very useful and commonly shown at IEP and other parent–teacher meetings. (See chapter 4 for information on measurement and assessment in adapted physical education.)

Statement of Measurable Academic and Functional Annual Goals

Every IEP requires a statement of measurable goals that describe what a student is expected to achieve in a specific content area in a given year. These goals are designed to enable the child to be involved in and make progress in the general education curriculum (U.S. Department of Education, 2006). Additionally, to ensure students are being sufficiently challenged, the IEP goals should be standards based and aligned with the grade-level academic content standards for their particular state of residence.

Some professionals write IEP goals as general statements that give direction to instructional programs, followed by several more specific and measurable short-term objectives or benchmarks related to the goal. Examples of these general goal statements are "To improve physical fitness," "To develop a front crawl stroke," or "To increase gross motor skill performance." This traditional practice of writing general goals is changing as a result of reauthorized federal legislation (IDEA, 2004) that does not mandate short-term objectives for IEP goals, as well as more stringent accountability practices in special education (Morrow, 2017). Annual IEP goals are now often written in a much more measurable and specific format, sometimes without objectives or benchmarks. These are referred to as *multielement annual goals* (Kosnitsky, 2018). However, states still may require school districts to include short-term objectives or benchmarks for IEP goals. In addition, school districts may opt to include short-term objectives, or parents may request that they be included, to more easily monitor student learning and progress toward a goal. This chapter will discuss both specific, multielement IEP goals that do not include short-term objectives as well as traditional IEP goals (general or broad statements) that are accompanied by short-term objectives or benchmarks. Figure 5.2 provides examples of traditional and multielement annual IEP goals.

Writing Traditional Annual IEP Goals

When IEP goals are accompanied by related short-term objectives or benchmarks, the goals are written in a more general format compared to the specific, measurable goals presented in the multielement format. For example, IEP goals written in a more traditional or general format might look like this:

- Marissa will improve her fundamental movement patterns.
- Ryan will increase his level of physical activity in out-of-school settings.
- Maggie will improve her striking skills for application during individual sports.

These broad goals must be supplemented with measurable and specific benchmarks used to assess progress toward the annual goal. As with all IEP goals, they should give guidance to the instructional program, be based on the child's unique need as identified in the PLP data, and relate to a goal content area that is agreed upon by the IEP team, including parents.

Although IDEA no longer requires short-term objectives or benchmarks for annual goals unless the child takes alternative assessments aligned with alternate achievement standards, many professionals and school districts encourage their use to assist with measuring student progress (Bateman & Herr, 2006; Jung, 2007). In addition, parents may request short-term objectives or benchmarks on an IEP. Teachers should follow school district policies and format when writing goals, short-term objectives, and benchmarks for their students' IEPs.

Though similar in concept, there is a difference between short-term objectives and benchmarks in IEPs. Both must be measurable and are used to determine how well the student is progressing toward an annual goal. Short-term objectives break down skills described in the annual goal into discrete and progressively more challenging steps toward the goal. Benchmarks indicate the amount of progress the child is expected to make within a specified part of the year (Lignugaris-Kraft et al., 2001). Benchmarks and short-term objectives focus on the same skills, but the criterion, or level of proficiency, will change to measure progress toward goal attainment (Downing, 2008). For example, a short-term objective related to improving the overhand throw may be written as "When given a verbal prompt and handed a 12-inch (30-centimeter) softball, Marissa will throw overhand with arm–leg opposition using her right (dominant) hand as characterized by across-the-body follow-through 8 out of 10 times as measured by the adapted physical education teacher." All short-term objectives must clearly describe the action, conditions, and criterion in order to be measurable. These three aspects relate to information presented in the six-element format discussed in the following section (will do what, under what conditions, and at what level of proficiency).

Benchmarks related to the same goal for overhand throwing may include statements regarding how far and how accurate student throws will be at the end of each month (time period):

- By October 1, Marissa will throw a tennis ball overhand 10 feet (3 meters) and hit a 3-foot (0.9-meter) diameter hula hoop taped to a wall 6 feet (1.8 meters) off the ground, 5 out of 10 trials as measured by the adapted physical education teacher.
- By December 1, Marissa will throw a tennis ball overhand 20 feet (6 meters) and hit a 3-foot (0.9-meter) diameter hula hoop taped to a wall 6 feet (1.8 meters) off the ground, 7 out of 10 trials as measured by the adapted physical education teacher.
- By March 1, Marissa will throw a tennis ball overhand 30 feet (9 meters) and hit a 3-foot (0.9-meter) diameter hula hoop taped to a wall 6 feet (1.8 meters) off the ground, 9 out of 10 trials as measured by the adapted physical education teacher.

Just as an annual goal must relate to PLP information, short-term objectives and benchmarks must relate to the IEP goal. If an annual goal stresses the content area of eye–hand coordination, the short-term objectives or benchmarks must include eye–hand coordination skills such as dribbling, catching, and striking. The student's baseline (pretest) ability must also appear in the

IEP as part of the PLP component. For example, a short-term objective might specify that a student will be expected to do 15 curl-ups in less than 60 seconds at some future date, but this statement has little meaning unless it is specified how many curl-ups the student can do now. An easy way to write a short-term objective is to take a well-written multielement IEP goal statement (see next section), copy the information from elements 3 and 4 (what action or skill and under what conditions), and make a reasonable change in the criterion or proficiency. The teacher must use professional judgment based on experience and knowledge of the student to determine what constitutes a reasonable expectation for improvement. It should be noted that although goals, short-term objectives, and benchmarks are helpful in identifying activities to be conducted in class, they are primarily used to prioritize content and measure student progress, not to replace carefully designed daily lesson plans.

Writing Multielement Annual IEP Goals

Well-written, measurable goals are one of the most critical aspects of an IEP and should contain specific, meaningful information. For writing annual IEP goals that will not have related short-term objectives, the following six elements are recommended by Kosnitsky (2018):

1. By when
2. Who
3. Will do what
4. Under what conditions
5. At what level of proficiency
6. As measured by whom or what

The following information describes each of these elements as used when writing measurable annual IEP goals.

By when: This can be written as a date or length of time for intervention. For example, a goal may state "By May 2022" or "In 24 weeks." Because goals must be written annually, school districts often use a time period aligned with yearly IEP reviews or meetings. The time period could also coincide with when the school district needs to report academic progress to parents, or it could align with the length of the instructional intervention within a curriculum unit. School districts usually have a recommended format for this time period and other IEP annual goal elements.

Who: An IEP goal is written to describe what a specific student will be expected to accomplish in one school year. The IEP document will likely contain information about others who provide supports and services for the student, but goals must be written for individual students (not a class of students).

Will do what: This element states the skills or behaviors that can be changed, observed, and measured, based on areas of need inferred from the PLP. Teachers writing this element of measurable goals may ask themselves, "What will I see if the student meets the goal?" (Kosnitsky, 2018). Areas of need in physical education can include health-related fitness components, aquatic skills, fundamental motor patterns, team and individual sport skills, community-based physical activity participation, and outdoor pursuits, among others.

Under what conditions: This element of the goal specifies what conditions must be present for the student to perform the targeted skill or behavior at the desired level. The teacher determines and provides these conditions for testing. The condition often describes the environmental arrangements or degree of assistance needed by the student (e.g., "given a verbal prompt and visual demonstration," "when given a tennis racket and verbal instructions"). Conditions could also include the assessment circumstances (e.g., "while participating in a game of five-on-five soccer with peers," "given a plastic baseball bat," "while in a prone position with a flotation device around the waist in water that is 5 feet [1.5 meters] deep"). Learning conditions are often taken for granted, but changes in the conditions can have a major impact on the difficulty, and therefore achievement, of the desired task. If the conditions are not precisely specified, it is difficult to determine how the student is to perform the task and what the student's real ability is for that task. These specifics therefore need to be part of a measurable IEP goal in order to objectively document student progress or learning.

At what level of proficiency: Often called the *performance criteria*, this element determines the change that the IEP team expects the student will attain based on the instruction during the IEP cycle. There are no strict guidelines or standards for establishing criteria. Critical factors used to set the level of proficiency or criteria include the student's baseline or PLP; frequency, duration, and intensity of instruction or intervention; appropriate and attainable criterion- or norm-referenced standards; type of task or behavior being taught; support services and assistance available; and meaningful and realistic circumstances regarding the area of need.

As measured by whom or what: Measurability requires information such as how progress is assessed, who will collect data, where and when data are obtained, and what method will be used to gather data. Some school districts use IEP forms that allow for this information to be placed in other sections and not directly in the goal statement. The following sample goals contain this information, but it can be removed if a district uses another format or if it is included in another section of the IEP document.

These sample measurable annual IEP goals are written in the multielement format:

- By June 2022, given a plastic baseball bat and verbal prompts, Ryan will properly hold the bat, position himself next to home plate, and strike a 12-inch (30-centimeter) stationary plastic ball off a tee 8 of 10 times for a distance of at least 25 feet (7.5 meters), demonstrating weight shift and shoulder and hip rotation, when assessed by his physical education teacher with a rubric during a team sport unit.
- By October 2022, while wearing goggles and participating in an aquatics unit in general physical education, Marissa will swim underwater in water that is at least 5 feet (1.5 meters) deep, retrieve five diving sticks (one at a time) from an area 10 feet by 10 feet (3 meters by 3 meters) in less than 1 minute, and swim to the surface and side of the pool when assessed by a paraprofessional using an aquatic skills rubric.
- By November 2022, while lying on a mat with knees bent approximately 140 degrees, Michael will improve his abdominal strength as demonstrated by independently completing at least 20 modified curl-ups according to the Brockport Physical Fitness Test (BPFT) protocol (cadence of 1 curl-up per 3 seconds; hands sliding along thighs until fingertips reach the knees; tester's hands on knees for target reach).

In contrast to these measurable IEP goals, the following goal statements are not measurable or appropriate because they are vague and arbitrary.

- Lexi will practice cardiorespiratory endurance this year.
- Steve will participate in a team sport to enhance his self-esteem.
- Cindy will continue a fitness program to improve abdominal strength.
- Juan will work on his striking skills for community-based sport participation.

IEP Progress Monitoring

An advantage to writing measurable, observable, and specific IEP goals (and, if necessary, short-term objectives or benchmarks) is the information they can provide when reporting student progress at planned intervals. This progress documentation must be shown to parents and should be reported in objective terms and measures (as opposed to subjective or vague statements). In most cases, progress is determined by testing the multistep IEP goals or short-term objectives or benchmarks. The evaluation should indicate the student's progress toward achieving the final goals by the end of the year (or designated period). Evaluation can be scheduled to occur at any time within 12 months from the time the IEP takes effect (the entire IEP must be reviewed at least annually and student disability status must be reviewed at least every three years).

School district IEP forms contain a section where teachers record how and when progress toward a goal will be measured. In addition, the IEP states how often and when progress is to be reported to parents, as determined by state or school district requirements. Although IDEA does not require report cards or quarterly reports, progress reporting generally takes place at the same time for all students, with or without special education needs (Morrow, 2017). Parental notification of the progress of a student with a disability should occur at least as often as parents are informed of the progress of a student without disabilities (e.g., the frequency of general education report cards).

Statement of Special Education and Related Services and Supplementary Aids and Services

Another required component of the IEP is a statement of the specific special education and related services, supplementary aids and services, and program modifications or supports for school personnel that will be provided for (or on behalf of) the student. These services, aids, and supports should be based on peer-reviewed research (to the extent practicable) and enable the student to make progress toward the annual IEP goals, be involved in the general education curriculum, participate in extracurricular and nonacademic activities, and be educated with other students with and without disabilities (U.S. Department of Education, 2006).

Once the PLP is determined and measurable annual goals are written, decisions must be made regarding the student's educational placement, any additional services to be provided, and the use of special instructional media and materials. The agreed-upon placement should be the least restrictive environment for the student.

In addition to appropriate placement, other direct special education and related services might be prescribed. A **special education service** refers to instruction designed to meet the unique needs of a student with a disability that directly affects educational goals, such as physical education. Provisions for this service must be specified in this component of the IEP. Most school district IEP forms have a section or boxes to check that indicate the type of physical education program in which the student will participate. For some students, both general and adapted or specially designed physical education may be provided based on skill level, units of instruction, age, and other factors. A **related service** is designed to help the student with a disability benefit from special education. Examples include physical therapy, counseling, occupational therapy, psychological services, and speech therapy. Not all special education students need or qualify for related services. However, physical education is a direct special education service (part of a required free and appropriate public education), not a related service, and should be addressed on the IEP when appropriate (see the sidebar An Important Question: When Is Physical Education Included in the IEP?).

In some cases, modified physical education equipment (e.g., beep baseball, audible goal locator, snap-handle bowling ball, bowling ramp) and support personnel (e.g., teacher assistants, paraprofessionals, peer tutors, volunteers) are required for the education of students with disabilities. These should also be listed in this IEP component.

Statement of Participation in General Education Settings and Activities

It is required that the student participate in the general education program with peers without disabilities to the maximum extent possible. The IEP must contain an explanation of the extent, if any, to which the child will not participate with children without disabilities in the general education class (U.S. Department of Education, 2006). If a child is removed from the general physical education setting to participate in an adapted or specially designed physical education program or class, for instance, it must be noted in this component of the IEP. Usually this explanation includes a percentage of time the student is excluded from (or included in) the general educational setting and for what kinds of activities or curricular units. It must be remembered that an adapted physical education program may be provided in a variety of settings, including an inclusive or general education setting.

Statement of Alternate Assessment Accommodations

Another required IEP component is a statement of any accommodations that are necessary for the child to appropriately participate in state- and districtwide assessments of student achievement. If it is determined that the child will not participate in a particular assessment, the IEP must state why the child cannot participate in the general assessment and why the selected alternative assessment is appropriate for the child (U.S. Department of Education, 2006). Thus, if a school district routinely administers physical education tests (physical fitness, fundamental motor skills, sport skills, aquatics, and so on) to its students, the appropriateness of those tests for a student with a disability must be considered. In this case, accommodations or alternative test items must be explained as necessary and noted on the IEP (refer to chapter 4 for more details about alternative assessments and test accommodations).

Schedule of Services and Modifications

The IEP must include the projected date for the beginning of the special education and related services and modifications listed earlier in the IEP, as well as the anticipated frequency, location, and duration of those services and modifications (U.S. Department of Education, 2006). This component would include details of the specially designed physical education schedule for the student. The number of minutes per week (or other agreed-upon time frame) of physical education instruction should be listed in this IEP component.

Transition Services

The IEP also requires the following to be in effect when the child turns 16 (or younger, if determined appropriate by the IEP team) and updated annually thereafter: (1) measurable postsecondary goals based on age-appropriate transition assessments related to training, education, employment, and,

An Important Question: When Is Physical Education Included in the IEP?

When must physical education be described or referred to in the IEP? The answer depends on the type of program the student is in (U.S. Department of Education, 1998).

- *General physical education.* When a student with a disability participates fully in the general physical education program without any special modifications to compensate for that student's disability, it is not necessary to describe or refer to physical education in the IEP. On the other hand, if some modifications to the general physical education program are necessary for the student to be able to participate, those modifications must be described in the IEP.
- *Specially designed physical education.* If a student with a disability needs a specially designed physical education program, that program must be addressed in all applicable areas of the IEP (e.g., present levels of educational performance, goals, objectives, services to be provided).
- *Physical education in separate facilities.* If a student with a disability is educated in a separate facility, the physical education program for that student must be described or referred to in the IEP. However, the kind and amount of information to be included in the IEP depend on the physical motor needs of the student and the type of physical education program to be provided. For example, if a child at a residential school for students who are Deaf is able to participate in that school's general physical education program (as determined by the most recent evaluation), then the IEP need only note such participation. On the other hand, if special modifications are required for the student to participate, those modifications must be described in the IEP. Moreover, if the student needs an individually designed physical education program, that program must be addressed under all applicable parts of the IEP.

Support personnel play an important role in learning.

where appropriate, independent living skills; and (2) a statement of transition services, including courses of study, needed to assist the student in reaching those goals (U.S. Department of Education, 2006). This component includes services and actions to help the student transition successfully from the school-based educational program to a community-based option no later than age 22. Many students, for instance, might eventually be enrolled in vocational training programs, some might go on to college, and others might enter alternative adult service programs (e.g., group homes, supported employment settings). School personnel should attempt to prepare students for the most appropriate option once they age out of school.

For physical education teachers, secondary transition programs include preparing students to extend opportunities for physical activity into community settings. Examples of IEP goals during this important transition phase could include participation in community-based adapted sport, extracurricular and other nonacademic activities, outdoor recreation, or leisure programs designed to enhance physical fitness, motor ability, sport skills, social skills, or community adjustment. Adapted physical educators, along with families, community agencies, and other school-based professionals planning for transition should conduct student interviews or administer surveys to determine the sport, recreation, or leisure interests of

Application Example

Determining Physical Education Transition Services

STUDENT

A 16-year-old female student with a disability

ISSUE

What strategies might the physical education teacher consider for transitioning the student to community-based physical activity programs?

APPLICATION

The teacher might consider the following steps:

- Interview the student to determine her physical activity preferences, experiences, and abilities (including those related to sport, physical recreation, and physical activity–related leisure).
- Contact her family, friends, and teachers to determine their physical activity interests and current and future expectations for the student relative to community-based physical activity, sport, recreation, and leisure.
- Contact representatives from relevant community agencies to determine the feasibility of having the student participate in their physical activity programs, including the identification of necessary supports and accommodations (e.g., equipment or procedural modifications, human assistance such as a peer mentor). Are there physical activity programs in place for students with disabilities?
- Write a physical activity–based ITP that includes meaningful, realistic, and measurable goals (e.g., participate appropriately at least two days per week in the open swim program), activities to meet the goals (e.g., transportation, checking in, locker room use, swimming skills, pool rules and etiquette), and identification of the people responsible for supporting each activity, including evaluating the student's progress in the activity (e.g., physical education teacher, special education teacher and paraprofessionals, community service provider, family members, peer mentors, transition coordinator).
- Design a school-based physical education curriculum unit that teaches the necessary skills to support transition goals (e.g., swimming skills, pool rules, fitness center behaviors, etiquette).
- Teach those skills in the community-based setting whenever possible (e.g., at the pool of the local recreation center rather than at the school pool).
- Evaluate progress on the transition goals regularly, as stated in the student's IEP. Use authentic rubrics for these community-based skills.

their students; take student field trips to community facilities and programs; compile an inventory of community facilities and programs that can be matched with student interests, abilities, and resources; and work with community-based service providers to expand the possibilities for people with disabilities (Modell & Megginson, 2001; Roth & Columna, 2011).

Although IDEA requires only that transition services be included in the IEP (either as a separate component, as described here, or embedded in other components of the IEP), some authorities (e.g., Roth & Columna, 2011) have suggested the development of an individualized transition plan (ITP) to address this important element of a student's physical education. An ITP might list community transition goals for young adults, list the necessary steps for achieving those goals, and identify the people responsible for each of the transition activities (see the Application Example sidebar on the previous page). Planning for lifetime physical activity as part of secondary transition services is important for students with disabilities, and it should be part of the required IEP document.

Transfer of Rights at Age of Majority

The final required component of an IEP is a statement that the child has been informed of his rights under IDEA, if any, that will transfer to him on reaching the age of majority (age 18 in most states). This statement must be included beginning no later than one year before the child reaches the age of majority under state law. This aspect of the IEP deals with legal rights of students, and school districts have a process in place to monitor this requirement.

Development of the IEP

Procedures for developing an IEP vary slightly from state to state and even among school districts within a state; however, they should all be developed in a collaborative manner with relevant special education and service personnel. Generally, the process involves two steps: (1) determining if the student is eligible for special education services, and (2) developing the most appropriate program, including establishing measurable annual goals and determining appropriate placement (Wright et al., 2010). The IEP development process usually begins with a referral. Any professional staff member at a school who suspects that a child might possess a unique educational need can refer the child for an evaluation to determine eligibility for special education. A physical education referral should outline the reasons a disability is suspected, including test results, records, observations, or reports; attempts to remedy the student's performance; and the extent of parental contact before the referral. Parents might also refer their own children for evaluation, and the district may ask the parents of newly enrolled children about the possibility of special education needs. Physicians, human services staff, and judicial officers sometimes make referrals as well. A sample referral form is shown in figure 5.3.

IDEA requires an IEP team, consisting of one or both of the student's parents, at least one general education teacher, at least one special education teacher, a representative of the school district qualified to provide or supervise the provision of special education, someone who can interpret the instructional implications of evaluation results (this may be one of the other school team members), the child with a disability (whenever appropriate), and other appropriate individuals at the discretion of either the parents or the school who have knowledge or special expertise regarding the child, including related service personnel (U.S. Department of Education, 2006). The title of the IEP team or committee varies from state to state; examples include *committee on special education*, *multidisciplinary team*, or *admission, review, and dismissal committee*.

In many cases the IEP team determines unique needs by assessing the results of standardized tests. But before reaching a final decision, the team also considers other information, such as samples of current academic work and functional performance; the role of behavior, language, and communication skills on academic performance; the amount of previous instruction; and anecdotal accounts, including parental input. Based on the information gathered and the ensuing discussion, the IEP team decides if the student has a disability and thus is qualified for special education; if so, the team recommends a program and a placement based on all available relevant student information.

The IEP document represents collaborative efforts—both the school and the parents have input into its development and must agree on its contents before it is signed and implemented. In the event that the two parties cannot agree on the IEP content, IDEA provides procedures for resolving the disagreement. These **due process** procedures

WWW

Department of Physical Education Referral Form

This form should be used by teachers or administrators of physical education and others to refer students with unique needs to chairpersons of APEC, CSE, CPSE, or the school building administrator.* Referrals should be processed through the office of the adapted physical education coordinator to the director of physical education or special education, who shall forward the referral to the appropriate people. Referrals may be made to change the program or placement of the student or for any other action within the jurisdiction of the APEC, CSE, or CPSE.

Faculty member making referral: ______________________ Date: ________________

Student referred: ______________________ Age: ____ Gender: ________________

Present physical education placement/class: ______________________

Student's primary or homeroom teacher: ______________________

A unique physical education need has been identified for the student:

By the CSE? Yes No

By the CPSE? Yes No

By the APEC? Yes No

If no, give reasons for believing a unique physical education need exists. ______________________

____

Give test results, observations, records, or reports upon which a referral is based. ______________

____

Describe previous attempts to remediate student's performance. ______________________

____

Has parental contact been made? Yes No

If yes, describe: ____

If a recommendation for placement or other action is included as a part of this referral, indicate the recommendation: ____

Referral processed by: ______________________ Referral initiated by: ______________________

(Director of physical education): ______________________ (Staff member): ______________________

*Legend: APEC, Adapted Physical Education Committee

CSE, Committee on Special Education

CPSE, Committee on Preschool Education

FIGURE 5.3 A sample referral form for adapted physical education.

are designed to protect the rights of the child, the parents, and the school district as well as to ensure fairness to all parties involved (figure 5.4). The IEP requires the school to provide a free, appropriate public education, including special education, physical education, related services, and supplementary aids and services listed in the IEP, but it does not guarantee achievement of the goals. A recent U.S. Supreme Court ruling specified that, even with the child's specific disability taken into consideration, the educational program of a child with a disability must be "appropriately ambitious" and should encourage students to meet challenging objectives (*Endrew F. v. Douglas County School District,* 2017). Therefore, it is the responsibility of the district to ensure all involved personnel make good faith efforts to assist the student in achieving IEP goals (Morrow, 2017).

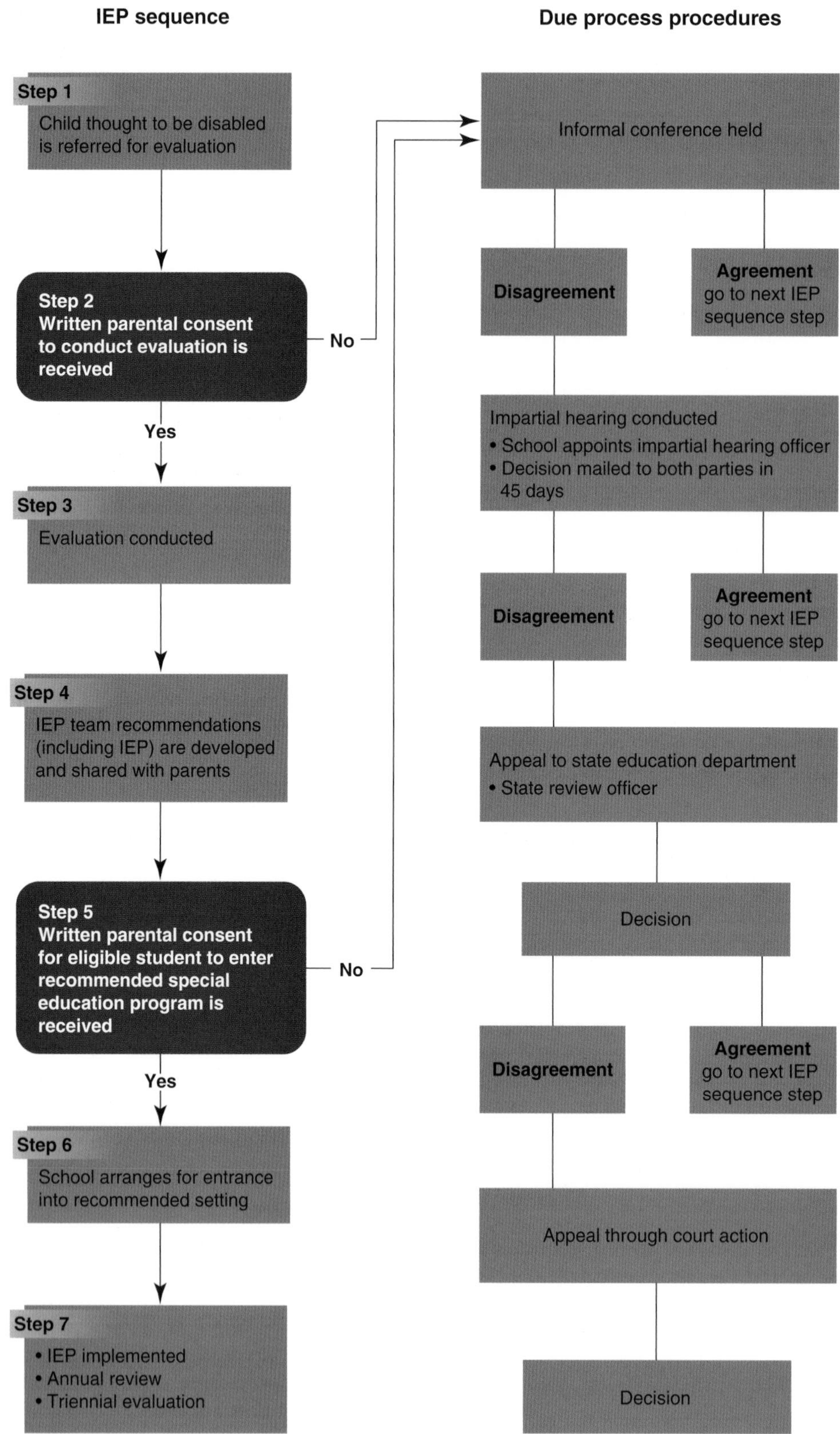

FIGURE 5.4 Sample IEP sequence and due process procedures.

Section 504 and the Accommodation Plan

Although Section 504 of the Rehabilitation Act of 1973 was enacted many years ago, its implications and requirements are still important in physical education and sport (Kowalski et al., 2005). Because the definition of a qualified individual with a disability in Section 504 is broader than the definition of a student with a disability in IDEA, some students with disabilities will not have IEPs (under IDEA) but nevertheless might require appropriate accommodations and services (U.S. Department of Education, 2005). These accommodations and services must be individually determined and documented in a Section 504 accommodation plan. These plans are common in schools.

Unlike the IEP, 504 plans do not have mandated components and, consequently, school districts usually develop their own format. A sample 504 plan is presented in figure 5.5. A 504 plan template for a student with diabetes can be found at http://main.diabetes.org/dorg/PDFs/Advocacy/Discrimination/504-plan.pdf. The plan is developed by a committee consisting of at least two school professionals who are familiar with the student (e.g., teachers, nurses, counselors, administrators), as well as the school district's 504 officer, who is required to monitor the implementation of the plan in school districts with more than 15 employees (Kowalski et al., 2005). Technically, students with unique needs under Section 504 do not require a full evaluation by a multidisciplinary diagnostic team, but an individualized assessment should focus on areas of student need that might necessitate the expertise of more than one professional.

The elements of the 504 plan found in figure 5.5 are self-explanatory, but note that item 5 ("Does the disability affect a major life activity?") is particularly important. To meet the definition of a qualified person with a disability under Section 504, the student must have a physical or mental impairment that substantially limits one or more major life activities (Kline, 2018). The accommodations listed in the plan (see item 6 in figure 5.5) are usually selected to help the student benefit from instruction in the general education classroom. More restrictive educational placements, although possible, require explanation just as they do on an IEP.

Students Without Disabilities Who Have Unique Needs

As mentioned at the beginning of this chapter, students without disabilities who have unique

WWW

Section 504 Accommodation Plan

Name: ______________ Date of birth: ______________ Grade: ________

School: ______________ Date of meeting: ______________

1. Describe the nature of the problem or student need.
2. List evaluations completed, including dates of each evaluation.
3. List the basis for determining that the child has a disability (if any).
4. Describe the nature of the child's disability.
5. Does the disability affect a major life activity? If so, explain how.
6. List the accommodations (e.g., specialized instruction or equipment, auxiliary aids or services, program modifications, and so on) the team recommends as necessary to ensure the child's equal access to all district programs.

Review and reassessment date: ______________ (must be completed)

Participants (name and title): ______________________________

cc: Student's cumulative file

Attachment: Information regarding Section 504 of the Rehabilitation Act of 1973 due process notice

Date: ______________

FIGURE 5.5 Sample Section 504 accommodation plan.

needs in physical education are not covered by IDEA or Section 504. School districts, however, still must provide an appropriate education for these students.

It is recommended that school districts establish an **Adapted Physical Education Committee (APEC)** to address unique needs of students without disabilities in physical education. This committee should consist of at least three members: the director of physical education or designee, the special education teacher, and the teacher of adapted physical education. When possible, the student's general physical education teacher should also be a member of the committee, and a school administrator should be available for consultation. This committee can provide guidance for district policies such as (1) establishing eligibility criteria and evaluation mechanisms for adapted physical education services; (2) defining the nature of that program, including placement options; and (3) evaluating and assessing the district program. A recommended procedure is outlined in figure 5.6 and discussed in the following seven steps. These may be modified as necessary to meet the needs of the school district.

- *Step 1.* Referrals are made to the chairperson of the APEC by a physical educator, family physician, parent, or even the student when it is felt that the student has a unique need in physical education. The committee should consider only those referrals in which needs are believed to be long term (more than 30 days).
- *Step 2.* When the APEC receives a referral form from a source other than the parents, the committee should notify the student's parents and indicate that an adapted program will be considered. The notification should point out that physical education is a required subject area under state law (where applicable) and that blanket excuses, waivers, or substitutions are not appropriate options; that development of an adapted program would not mean that the district considers the student to have a disability under IDEA or Section 504; and that any change in program will be reviewed regularly (at least annually). Parents should also be invited to submit their own concerns or goals for their child's physical education program.
- *Step 3.* In the case of a medical excuse or referral, the APEC should contact the family physician to determine the nature of the condition or disease and the impact on physical education. The APEC should also consult the student's general physical education teacher to determine the student's performance level and any difficulties the student experiences in the current program. It might also be necessary to conduct additional testing to better understand the student's strengths and weaknesses.
- *Step 4.* After considering all the information collected in step 3, the APEC must decide if an adapted program is appropriate. If the student does not have a unique need, the parents are informed, and the process is over. If, however, the student is eligible for an adapted program, the committee must develop an IPEP for the student. The IPEP is similar to the IEP and should include program goals, PLP (including any medical limitations), short-term objectives, placement and schedule of services, and a schedule for review. Again, parents and the student should be consulted for input on goals and activities for the IPEP.
- *Step 5.* Parents are notified of the APEC's decision. If the student is eligible, parents should receive an explanation of the adapted program and a copy of the IPEP. It is also recommended that the general physical education teacher and, in the case of a medically initiated referral, the family physician receive copies of the IPEP as well. (The district should have due process procedures comparable to those depicted in figure 5.4 in case the parents do not agree with the committee's decision or with the program outlined in the IPEP.)
- *Step 6.* The adapted program described in the IPEP is implemented. Most IPEPs can be implemented in an integrated placement (general physical education). In cases in which a one-to-one or segregated placement is recommended, however, school districts must obtain parental permission before changing the placement, unless the board of education has other procedures in place that are appropriate.
- *Step 7.* The IPEP will be in effect for the time specified under the schedule for review section. At the conclusion of this time, the APEC evaluates the student's progress and decides whether to continue or discontinue the program.

Formation of an APEC is solely at the discretion of the school district and is not required by law. Districts must recognize, however, that a student need not be classified as having a disability to possess a unique need in physical education. It is incumbent on districts to develop procedures to ensure that all students receive an appropriate education. Given the mounting prevalence of obesity and secondary conditions in the United States, for instance, the IPEP provides an option for schools

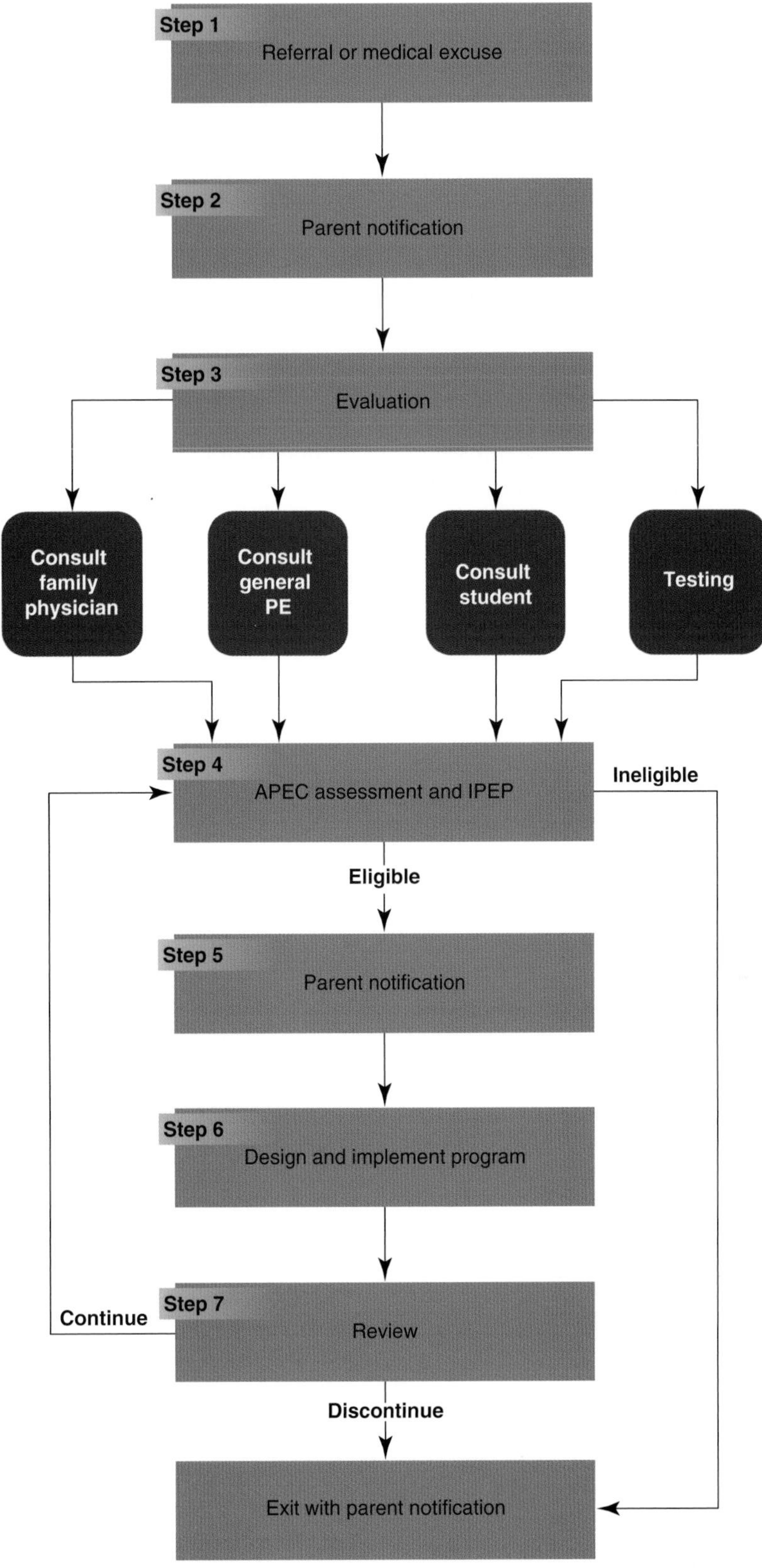

FIGURE 5.6 A recommended procedure for evaluating the need for adapted physical education services for students without disabilities.

looking to help all students address serious health and physical activity–related problems.

Summary

Students might be eligible for adapted physical education if they exhibit a unique physical education need. IDEA and Section 504 of the Rehabilitation Act of 1973 provide procedures for modifying and offering specially designed educational programs for students with disabilities. Infants and toddlers (birth to age 2) who meet the criteria established by IDEA may receive early intervention services under the act, which must be documented in an IFSP (see chapter 21).

Similarly, individualized programs for qualified children (aged 3-21) are required by IDEA. This program and the details of services provided for eligible students with disabilities, including physical education services, must be described in written IEPs. Physical education teachers are often IEP team members. Not all students with disabilities qualify for services under IDEA, but they might still be entitled to special accommodations or services under Section 504. These modified programs must be described in a Section 504 accommodation plan. Finally, there might be students without disabilities in a school district who have unique needs in physical education. These students would not qualify for services under either IDEA or Section 504 but might still require a modified physical education program. Although not required by law, it is suggested that districts develop written IPEPs to document the adapted physical education program.

References

Bateman, B., & Herr, C. (2006). *Writing measurable IEP goals and objectives* (2nd ed.). Attainment Company.

Capizzi, A. (2008). From assessment to annual goal: Engaging in a decision-making process in writing measurable IEPs. *Teaching Exceptional Children, 41*(1), 18-25. https://doi.org/10.1177/004005990804100102

Downing, J. (2008). *Including students with severe and multiple disabilities in typical classrooms* (3rd ed.). Brookes.

Endrew F. v. Douglas County School District, 580 U.S. 15-827 (2017).

Individuals with Disabilities Education Act Amendments of 2004 (IDEA) PL 108-446, 20 U.S.C. 1400 (2004).

Jung, A. (2007). Writing S.M.A.R.T. objectives and strategies that fit the R.O.U.T.I.N.E. *Teaching Exceptional Children, 39*(4), 54-58. https://doi.org/10.1177/004005990703900406

Kline, J.J. (2018). *Extended school year services under the IDEA and Section 504: Legal standards and case law.* LRP.

Kosnitsky, C. (2018). *IEP goals that make a difference: An administrator's guide to improving the process* (2nd ed.). LRP.

Kowalski, E., Pucci, G., Lieberman, L., & Mulawka, C. (2005). Implementing IEP or 504 goals and objectives into general physical education. *Journal of Physical Education, Recreation & Dance, 76*(7), 33-37. https://doi.org/10.1080/07303084.2005.10609310

Lignugaris-Kraft, B., Marchand-Martella, N., & Martella, R.C. (2001). Writing better goals and short-term objectives or benchmarks. *Teaching Exceptional Children, 34*(1), 52-59. https://doi.org/10.1177/004005990103400107

Modell, S., & Megginson, N. (2001). Life after school: A transition model for adapted physical educators. *Journal of Physical Education, Recreation and Dance, 72*(2), 45-48, 53. https://doi.org/10.1080/07303084.2001.10605835

Morrow, E.A. (2017). *What do I do when: The answer book on individualized education programs* (4th ed.). LRP.

Roth, K., & Columna, L. (2011). Collaborative strategies during transition for students with disabilities. *Journal of Physical Education, Recreation and Dance, 82*(5), 50-55. https://doi.org/10.1080/07303084.2011.10598629

U.S. Department of Education. (1998). *Federal Register,* 34 CFR Ch. III, July 1, 1998.

U.S. Department of Education. (2005). *Protecting students with disabilities: Frequently asked questions about Section 504 and the education of children with disabilities.* Retrieved from www.ed.gov/about/offices/list/ocr/504faq.html

U.S. Department of Education. (2006). *Federal Register,* Part II, 34 CFR Parts 300 and 301. Final regulations for IDEA 2004—Individuals with Disabilities Education Improvement Act of 2004—PL 108-446. Retrieved from https://sites.ed.gov/idea/files/finalregulations.pdf

Wright, P., Wright, P., & O'Connor, S. (2010). *All about IEPs: Answers to frequently asked questions about IEPs.* Harbor House Law Press.

Yell, M., Katsiyannis, A., Ennis, R., & Losinski, M. (2013). Avoiding procedural errors in IEP development. *Teaching Exceptional Children, 46*(1), 56-64. https://doi.org/10.1177/004005991304600107

Print Resources

Bateman, D., & Bateman, C. (2014). *A principal's guide to special education* (3rd ed.). Council for Exceptional Children.

This resource provides guidance to teachers and administrators seeking to meet the needs of students with disabilities, including a chapter on the IEP process.

Kowalski, E., & Lieberman, L. (Eds.). (2011). *Assessment for everyone: Modifying NASPE assessments to include all elementary school children*. National Association for Sport and Physical Education.

This booklet provides numerous examples for assessing physical education content areas among students with disabilities in general and adapted physical education to establish present levels of performance for use on IEPs.

Kowalski, E., Lieberman, L., & Daggett, S. (2006). Getting involved in the IEP process. *Journal of Physical Education, Recreation and Dance, 77*(7), 35-39. https://doi.org/10.1080/07303084.2006.10597905

This article discusses numerous strategies for the general physical educator to become more knowledgeable and active in IEP development, implementation, and revision.

National Association of State Directors of Special Education. (2006). *The Individuals with Disabilities Education Act: Comparison of IDEA regulations (August 3, 2006) to IDEA regulations (March 12, 1999)*. Retrieved from www.nasdse.org. Author.

This document provides a detailed side-by-side comparison of the implementation of federal regulations for the two most recent reauthorizations of IDEA. The comparison allows for easy identification of changes.

Ferreri, F. (2019). *What to do when: The answer book on Section 504* (5th ed.). LRP.

This resource addresses issues related to Section 504 and the education of students with disabilities in an easy-to-use question-and-answer format. Additional information is included on extracurricular activities, interscholastic sport, field trips, and other noneducational services.

Online Resources

Center for Parent Information and Resources. (2017). *All about the IEP*. Retrieved from www.parentcenterhub.org/repository/iep/

This resource describes the special educational services that a child with an IEP will receive.

Council for Exceptional Children (CEC): www.cec.sped.org

This site provides a catalog of books and resources related to the special education process and IEP development.

IDEA Partnership: www.ideapartnership.org

This site contains extensive materials on all aspects of educating students with disabilities, including development of individualized education programs, model IEP forms by the U.S. Department of Education, IEP requirements and practices, and instructional resources.

Individuals with Disabilities Education Act: https://sites.ed.gov/idea/

This is the official U.S. Department of Education's Individuals with Disabilities Education Act (IDEA) website. It contains numerous resources on IDEA, including instructional videos, frequently asked questions and answers, and learning modules.

IRIS Center (IDEA 2004 and Research for Inclusive Settings): http://iris.peabody.vanderbilt.edu

This site presents materials for faculty and professional development providers for the preparation of current and future school personnel who work with students with disabilities in inclusive settings.

National Center for Learning Disabilities (2008). *Understanding the standards-based Individualized Education Program (IEP)*. Advocacy Brief. www.advocacyinstitute.org/resources/UnderstandingStandards-basedIEPs.pdf

This document provides guidance for the development of IEPs for students with learning disabilities.

National Center on Health, Physical Activity and Disability (NCHPAD): www.nchpad.org/1748/6899/IEP~Road map~for~Physical~Education

This site includes an IEP Roadmap for physical education providing parents and other special education professionals with an interactive guide to the IEP process.

Skyward: www.skyward.com

This resource is an electronic database management system for schoolwide tracking and recordkeeping. Included are many special education applications designed to streamline procedures that require careful recordkeeping, such as referrals, evaluations, IEP meeting information, teacher caseloads, and report templates for parents and meetings.

Special Education Electronic Data System (SEEDS): www.cesa6.org/services/seeds/

This is another commercial product for special education electronic recordkeeping.

U.S. Department of Education. (2020). *Protecting students with disabilities: Frequently asked questions about Section 504 and the education of children with disabilities*. www.ed.gov/about/offices/list/ocr/504faq.html.

This site expands on Section 504 and provides guidance for eligibility and Section 504 plan development.

6

Behavior Management

E. Michael Loovis

Mr. Adams has a young man in his ninth-grade physical education class who is on the autism spectrum. John, the student, enjoys vigorously bouncing a medium-sized playground ball, to the exclusion of other teacher-selected activity. In fact, John will engage in this bouncing activity every time he is provided with the playground ball. Mr. Adams believes John's desire to bounce the ball qualifies as a preferred activity, but John is unlikely to want to engage in catching activities (his least preferred activity). Mr. Adams knows that one of John's IEP objectives involves eye–hand coordination, including the ability to track and catch a projectile. Therefore, Mr. Adams presents John with the following contingency: If John engages in catching the playground ball, he will be permitted to bounce the ball a predetermined number of times. Mr. Adams begins with one catch, leading to the chance to bounce the ball 10 times. This quickly increases to 10 consecutive catches for the opportunity to bounce the ball 10 times. Now that he knows how to control John's attention and motivation, Mr. Adams is able to determine that John has reasonably good eye–hand coordination and can program more challenging catching activities.

For years, educators have used a host of behavior management practices, in worst cases including corporal punishment, suspension, and expulsion for misbehavior. In most cases, these practices are **reactive**—that is, a method is applied only after a particular misbehavior has occurred. However, many of the behavior problems that educators face on a daily basis could be prevented if the educators took a more **proactive** approach by discontinuing ineffective practices and making a staunch commitment to promoting a positive school and classroom climate (Council for Exceptional Children, 2008; Schweig et al., 2019). For example, it is difficult for a physical educator to establish an appropriate instructional climate in a self-contained class for students with behavior disabilities when several students persist in being verbally and physically abusive toward the teacher and other class members.

From another perspective, behavior management interventions include "all those actions (and conscious inactions) teachers . . . engage in to enhance the probability that children, individually and in groups, will develop effective behaviors that are personally fulfilling, productive, and socially acceptable" (Shea & Bauer, 2012, p. 6). For example, a behavior management approach can help a physical educator determine the appropriate level at which to begin golf instruction for students with intellectual disabilities and to maintain the students' enthusiasm for learning the activity over time. Behavior management has also been used to teach social behaviors considered essential to performance in school, at home, and in the community. This chapter offers several proactive approaches to help teachers and coaches achieve the goals and objectives of their programs in a positive learning environment. Physical educators are likely to use an eclectic or pragmatic approach to behavior management, depending on what works best in a given situation. This chapter will mainly focus on the applied behavior analysis approach, with a brief discussion of the psychoeducational, ecological, biogenic, and humanistic approaches.

© Laura Leonard Fitch

A high-five is a positive reinforcer.

Applied Behavior Analysis

According to Cooper and colleagues (2020), applied behavior analysis (ABA) is a "scientific approach for discovering environmental variables that reliably influence socially significant behavior and for developing a technology of behavior change that takes practical advantage of those discoveries" (p. 3). More specifically, ABA is the application of reinforcement learning theory derived from operant psychology. Applied behavior analysis includes such procedures as **respondent conditioning** (the automatic control of behavior by antecedent stimuli), **operant conditioning** (the control of behavior by regulating the consequences that follow a behavior), **contingency management** (the relation between a behavior and the events that follow it), and **behavioral modeling**, also called **observational learning** (learning through observing another person engaged in a behavior).

All of these procedures have one thing in common: the planned systematic arrangement of consequences to alter a person's response (or at least the frequency of that response). As it relates to an individualized education program (IEP) designed to improve physical fitness, this arrangement could involve the use of rewards to encourage students with intellectual disabilities to engage in sustained exercise behavior, or establishing a contract with a student who has cerebral palsy to define a number of tasks to be completed in a unit on throwing and catching skills.

To understand ABA, one must understand basic terminology. The first step toward understanding the management of human behavior is to define the stimuli that influence people's behavior. A measurable event that might have an influence on behavior is referred to as a **stimulus**.

Reinforcement is a stimulus event that increases or maintains the frequency of a response. In physical education, reinforcement is feedback provided directly or indirectly by the teacher or coach. **Positive reinforcement**, one of the principles of operant conditioning described in this section, includes rewards or stimuli that students perceive as good—that is, as something they want. These can be physical, verbal, visual, edible, or active, such as a pat on the back (physical), an approving comment such as "Good job!" (verbal), a smile (visual), a piece of candy (edible), or a chance to bounce on a trampoline (active). If a response occurs and it is positively reinforced, the likelihood of the response recurring under similar circumstances is maintained or increased. For example, a teacher might praise a student who demonstrates appropriate behavior during instruction in the gym. If praise is positively reinforcing to that student, the chances of the student's attending to instruction in the future are strengthened. Certainly, positive reinforcement is the preferred strategy in adapted physical education; to the extent possible, the entire instructional experience should be positive. Figure 6.1 illustrates this principle as well as the others examined in this chapter.

The presence of an aversive stimulus—something students want to avoid—is commonly called **negative reinforcement**. If a response occurs and it successfully averts a negative stimulus, the likelihood of the desired response recurring under similar circumstances is maintained or increased.

Because positive and negative reinforcement are intended to produce similar results, (i.e., they both increase the desired behavior), the distinction between them is not always readily apparent. An example might clarify the difference: Suppose that a student has been talking to a friend and distracting the teacher and the rest of the class while the teacher is explaining a lesson. If the teacher warns that continued talking will result in after-school detention (possible aversive stimuli), and if the student perceives that stimuli as something to avoid, then the likelihood that the student will attend to instructions will increase. By listening in class, the student will avoid staying after school. This is an example of negative reinforcement because the stimulus increases the likelihood of a desired behavior through the avoidance of an aversive consequence rather than the presentation of a positive one.

Just as teachers and coaches seek to maintain or increase the frequency of some behaviors, they might want to decrease the occurrence of others. When the consequence of a certain behavior has the effect of decreasing its frequency, the consequence is called **punishment**. Punishment can be either the presentation of an aversive stimulus (type I punishment) or the removal of a positive stimulus (type II punishment). The intention of punishment is to weaken or eliminate a behavior. The following scenario illustrates the effect of type

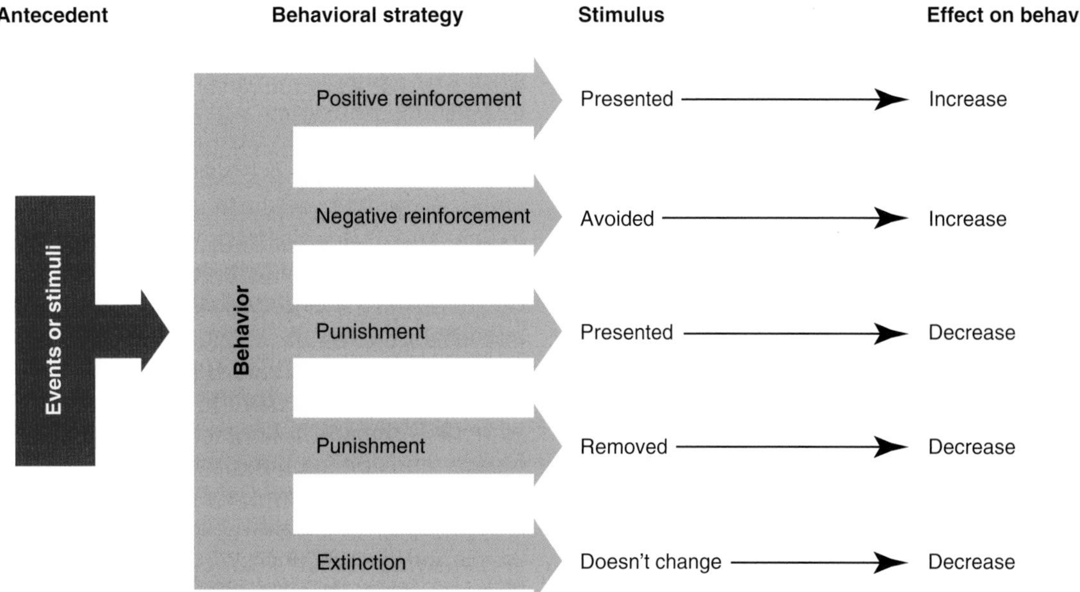

FIGURE 6.1 Principles of operant conditioning.

I punishment on the student from the previous example: The teacher has warned the student that continued talking during instructional time will result in detention. The student ignores the warning and continues to talk. The consequence for talking when she is supposed to be listening will be the presentation of the aversive stimuli.

A slightly different scenario illustrates the notion of punishment as the removal of a positive stimulus. Our student, still talking after the teacher's warning, is punished by being barred from a five-minute free-time activity at the end of class—an activity perceived as a positive stimulus. The removal of this highly desirable activity fits the definition of type II punishment and weakens or eliminates the disruptive behavior in future instructional episodes.

In contrast to punishment, withholding of reinforcement after a response that has previously been reinforced results in **extinction** or cessation of a behavior. Extinction differs from punishment in that no consequence follows the response; a stimulus (aversive or positive event) is neither presented nor taken away. For example, teachers or coaches who pay attention to students when they clown around might be reinforcing the very behavior they would like to see eliminated. If they ignore (i.e., stop reinforcing) the undesired behavior, the behavior will probably decrease in frequency.

Applied behavior analysts emphasize the importance of **antecedent events** or **stimuli** in controlling human behavior. These events or stimuli occur before the behavior of interest and signal an opportunity for a consequence (see figure 6.1). This recognition of the importance of antecedent events has led applied behavior analysts to think in terms of a behavioral paradigm or sequence that recognizes the three-term contingency of antecedent–behavior–consequence (ABC).

Antecedent events that stimulate the occurrence of a certain behavior consist of actions such as questioning, prompting, or cueing techniques employed by the teacher (opportunities to respond to academic requests, or OTRs); demonstrations of appropriate behavioral responses before students engage in practice; or announcements from the teacher about the appropriate manner for transitioning from one activity to another. For example, a teacher asks a student to identify one of the two types of serves in badminton (antecedent), the student responds with the correct answer (behavior), and the teacher tells the student that the answer is correct and says, "Nice job!" (consequence). (Note that antecedents in the ABA context are not to be confused with intrapsychic causes for aberrant behavior, which are prevalent in psychoanalytic theories.)

In addition, behavioral outcomes that are functionally related to antecedent events can involve changing the environment in ways that stimulate behavior to occur. For example, before the initiation of a lesson, a teacher could partner a student who is known to be disruptive with a peer who has had a calming influence on the student while engaged in physical activity in the past (antecedent). The student with the disruptive behavior participates in relative calm and finishes the lesson without being disruptive (behavior), and the teacher rewards the student with five minutes of free time at the end of class (consequence).

With the reauthorizations of the Individuals with Disabilities Education Act (IDEA) in 1997 and again in 2004, emphasis has been placed on one of the most powerful tools of ABA, functional behavioral assessment (FBA). IDEA 2004 mandates "a functional behavioral assessment, behavior intervention services and modifications, that are designed to address the behavior violation so that it does not recur" (Section 615 (k) (1) (F) (i)). Chapter 9 provides an explanation and illustration of FBA.

Antecedent events have gained greater clarity in light of the Positive Behavioral Interventions and Supports (PBIS) movement. The PBIS movement and ABA parallel each other in the sense that they start with an examination of the three-term contingency (ABC) and conclude with a behavioral intervention plan designed to either promote more positive behaviors or eliminate problematic behaviors. Later in the chapter the relationship between PBIS and ABA is discussed in greater detail.

Table 6.1 summarizes the basic strategies of ABA. The examples provided illustrate the range of learning principles available to teachers and coaches who want to change student behaviors. No one principle is the best choice all the time; which to apply depends on the specifics of the situation. Each principle has a specific purpose, and application of the principles requires that teachers or coaches analyze behaviors carefully before attempting to change them. Later in this chapter (and again in chapter 9), recommendations are provided that originated from *A Data-Based Gymnasium* by Dunn and colleagues (1980). Although no longer available commercially, its basic principles are illustrated in Dunn and Leitschuh (2014). After reading the section on the rule of thumb (chapter 9), readers are encouraged to review table 6.1 to better understand the role of selected learning principles in ABA strategies.

TABLE 6.1 Behavior: Consequence, Classification, and Probable Effect

Behavior	Consequence	Classification	Effect
Susan engages effectively in drills.	Teacher praises Susan.	Positive reinforcement	Susan will continue to do well in drills.
Juan forgets to wear his gym uniform.	Teacher suggests that next time he will lose 5 points.	Negative reinforcement	Juan will wear his gym uniform next time.
Tenora forgets her tennis shoes for the second day in a row.	Teacher deducts 5 points from her grade.	Punishment (type I)	Tenora will not forget her shoes again.
Bill makes aggravating noises during class.	Teacher ignores Bill's noises.	Extinction	Bill will stop making noises during class.
Chris is overly aggressive during game play in class.	Teacher withdraws opportunity to participate in free time at end of class.	Punishment (type II)	Chris will tone down his aggressiveness during game play.

Types of Reinforcers

Several types of reinforcers can be used in ABA, including primary (unconditioned), secondary (conditioned), and vicarious reinforcers. The use of highly preferred activities to control the occurrence of less preferred responses, known as the Premack principle, is another reinforcer.

- *Primary reinforcers.* **Primary (or unconditioned) reinforcers** are stimuli necessary for survival. Examples include food, water, and other phenomena that satisfy biological requirements such as the need for sleep and warmth. A physical educator who reinforces a successful trial of kicking with a food treat is using a primary reinforcer.
- *Secondary reinforcers.* **Secondary (or conditioned) reinforcers** acquire their reinforcing properties through learning. A few examples are praise, grades, money, and completion of a task. Because secondary reinforcers must be learned, stimuli or events must often be paired repeatedly with other primary or secondary events before they will become reinforcers in their own right. For example, a student earns a good grade after a successful free throw trial, and the student works to be successful in subsequent trials in hopes of earning another good grade.
- *Vicarious reinforcers.* **Vicarious reinforcement** occurs while observing the reinforcing or punishing consequences of another person's behavior. As a result of vicarious reinforcement, the observer will either engage in the behavior to receive the same positive reinforcement or avoid the behavior to avert punishment. An example of vicarious reinforcement entails a student observing a peer receiving praise for completing an obstacle course and immediately emulating a similar successful attempt in the hope of also receiving praise.
- *Premack principle.* According to the **Premack principle** (Cooper et al., 2020), activities that have a high probability of occurrence can be used to elicit low-probability behaviors. To state this another way, activities that an individual or group prefer can be used as positive reinforcers for activities that are not especially favored. For example, a student performs a catching activity (least preferred), knowing that success will earn him the opportunity to shoot baskets (highly preferred). This principle was illustrated in the chapter-opening vignette.

Schedules of Reinforcement

When using the ABA approach, the instructor must understand when to deliver a reinforcer to attain an optimal response. During the early stages of skill acquisition or behavior change, it is best to provide reinforcement after every occurrence of an appropriate response. This is called **continuous reinforcement**. After a behavior has been acquired, continuous reinforcement is no longer desirable or necessary. Behavior is best maintained not through a process of continuous reinforcement but through a schedule of intermittent or partial reinforcement. Several types of intermittent schedules exist, but the two most common are ratio and interval schedules.

In **ratio schedules**, reinforcement is applied after a specified number of defined responses have occurred. **Interval schedules**, on the other hand, provide reinforcement when a specified time has elapsed since the previous reinforcement. Associated with each of these major schedule types are two subtypes: (reinforcement occurring after a specific number of responses or elapsed time) and **variable** (reinforcement occurring after an average number of responses or elapsed time). When these types and subtypes are combined, four alternatives for dispensing reinforcement are available. Both fixed and variable ratio schedules of reinforcement (e.g., providing praise after every third successful throw or after every second successful throw on average, respectively) produce high response rates. In the case of interval reinforcement, a fixed schedule (e.g., praising the first successful throw at the end of each three-minute interval) produces a high response rate just before the time for the next reinforcement, but there is a cessation of response after reinforcement. Variable intervals of reinforcement, on the other hand, produce consistent response rates because the person cannot predict exactly when the reinforcer will be dispensed (e.g., praising the first successful throw after intervals of one minute, five minutes, and three minutes, for an average three-minute interval).

Procedures for Increasing Behavior

Once it is determined that a behavior not currently in a student's repertoire is desired or that the frequency of a behavior needs to be altered, the targeted response must be defined in measurable and observable terms. After clear identification has been made, behavioral intervention can begin. The following discussion highlights several popular strategies for increasing desirable behavior, including shaping, chaining, prompting, fading, modeling, token economy, contingency management, and discrete trial training.

- *Shaping.* The strategy of **shaping** involves administering reinforcement contingent on the learning and performance of sequential steps leading to development of the desired behavior. Shaping is most often employed in the teaching of a new skill. Once the desired behavior has been learned, it is no longer necessary to perform all steps in the progression. For example, the use of shaping to teach a dive from a 1-meter diving board might include the following progression: kneeling dive from a 30-centimeter elevation, squat dive from a 30-centimeter elevation, standing modified dive from a 30-centimeter elevation, squat dive from the 1-meter diving board, and standing modified forward dive from the diving board. Once the dive from the 1-meter board has been learned, there is no longer any reason to perform the steps in the progression.

- *Chaining.* Unlike shaping, which consists of reinforcing approximations of a new behavior, **chaining** develops a series of discrete portions or links that, when tied together, lead to enhanced performance of a behavior. Chaining is distinct from shaping in that the steps necessary to achieve the desired behavior are still performed each time the response is emitted.

There are two types of chaining: forward and backward. In forward chaining, the initial step in the behavioral sequence occurs first, followed by the next step, and so forth until the entire sequence has been mastered (see the Application Example sidebar). A student learning to execute a layup from three steps away from the basket would take a step with the left foot, take a step with the left foot while dribbling once with the right hand, repeat the previous step and add a step with the right foot, repeat the previous step with an additional step with the left foot, and finally repeat the previous step with a jump off the left foot up to the basket for the layup attempt. In some cases a student's repertoire is limited, or the last step in the sequence is associated with a potent reinforcer. Under these circumstances, it might be necessary to teach the last step in a behavioral sequence first, followed by the next-to-last step, and so on until the entire sequence is learned. This is called *backward chaining.*

- *Prompting.* Events that help initiate a response are called **prompts**. These are cues, instructions, gestures, directions, examples, and models that act as antecedent events and trigger a desired response. In this way the frequency of responses and thus the chances of receiving reinforcement are increased. Prompting is crucial in shaping and chaining procedures. Prompts can be thought of as a continuum of cues. They are arranged in ascending order of intrusiveness, from verbal to visual to physical assistance. The objective is to encourage a response by using the least intrusive or direct cue; for example, a student who requires a visual prompt from a teacher is receiving a less intrusive prompt than one who requires physical assistance to perform the same behavior. Another form of prompting commonly used with individuals with intellectual disability and autism is redirection. The purpose of a redirect is to engage the learner's attention on the task at hand. The redirect can be in the form of a physical or gestural cue, including pointing, touching materials, or touching the person's hand (if touching can be tolerated). Visual schedules are also commonly used prompts. These can illustrate an entire day's activities or communicate the intent of a single physical activity lesson.

- *Fading.* The ultimate goal of reinforcement is for the desired response to occur without the need for a prompt or reinforcer. The best way to reach this goal is by gradually **fading** the prompts and reinforcers over time so that the student must perform more trials or demonstrate significantly better response quality in order to receive reinforcement. For example, a student who has been receiving positive reinforcement for each successful basket must now make two baskets, then three baskets, and so on before reinforcement is provided. Prompts can also be faded this way—for example, if footprints are used to teach the correct stepping pattern in a throwing task, then the footprint can be systematically reduced in size until only a small dot remains on the floor.

- *Modeling.* The strategy of **modeling** is a visual demonstration of a behavior that students are expected to perform. From a behavioral perspective, modeling is similar to vicarious reinforcement, in which a person learns by watching someone else respond to a situation in a way that produces reinforcement or punishment. As technology continues to expand in educational applications, the use of video modeling using smartphones and tablets has proven instrumental in improving social communication, functional skills, and behavioral functioning with populations of students who have autism spectrum disorder and developmental disability (Goodwyn et al., 2013).

- *Token economy.* Using tokens (e.g., poker chips or checkmarks on a response tally sheet) as secondary reinforcers that are earned, collected, and subsequently redeemed for a backup reinforcer (e.g., consumables, privileges, or activities) is called a **token economy**. Establishment of a token economy includes a concise description of the targeted behavior along with a detailed accounting of the tokens administered for performance of the behavior. For example, students might earn checkmarks on their task sheets for every successful attempt at a long serve in badminton. At the end of the lesson, provided the predetermined number of checks have been achieved, students can redeem their completed task sheet for a reward, such as free time in the gymnasium.

- *Contingency management.* When teachers change a behavior by providing a stimulus contingent on the occurrence of a desired response, they are practicing **contingency management** (Shea & Bauer, 2012). The most sophisticated form of contingency management is the behavior contract. The contract (which is an extension of the token economy) specifies the relation between behaviors and their consequences. The well-developed contract contains five elements: (1) a detailed statement of what each party (i.e., student and teacher) expects to happen; (2) a targeted behavior that is readily observable; (3) a statement of sanctions for failure to meet the terms of the contract; (4) a bonus clause, if desirable, to reinforce consistent compliance with the contract; and (5) a monitoring system to keep track of the rate of positive reinforcement given (Kazdin, 2013). An example of a behavior contract appears in chapter 9.

- *Discrete trial training (DTT).* An extension of ABC, **discrete trial training** is a step-by-step instructional method with application to teaching gross motor as well as recreational skills. This method relies on four components: the teacher's instructions or cues, the student's response to the antecedent event, the consequence resulting from the student's response, and the process by which prompts are faded or completely eliminated. Unlike other instructional methods, DTT incorporates short, brief, and precise instructions; rapidly executed massed trials; and regimented use of prompting and corrective procedures. All these are designed to produce mastery of a single skill or skill component (Lovaas, 2003). For example, the instructor directs the student to "step and throw the ball overhand at the target." The student then makes 25 throws in rapid succession, with correct throws being immediately reinforced and obvious errors being prohibited from occurring (e.g., an underhand throw is immediately stopped and corrected, another trial is initiated, and, if correct, is reinforced).

Application Example

How to Use a Variety of Strategies to Improve Throwing Skills

SETTING

An elementary physical education class

STUDENT

A nine-year-old student with high-functioning autism with delays in throwing and catching

UNIT

Fundamental motor skills and patterns

TASK

Throwing with a mature, functional throw—at the very least, stepping with the leg opposite the throwing arm

APPLICATION

The physical educator might do any of the following:

- Use forward chaining of the throwing mechanics.
- Use a visual prompt, such as a footprint, to aid in the stepping action.
- Use continuous reinforcement until correct throwing is well established.
- Use discrete trial training to promote skill acquisition.

Procedures for Decreasing Behavior

On occasion, an undesirable behavior needs to be decreased. Traditionally, decreasing the frequency of behavior has been accomplished using extinction, punishment, reinforcement of alternative responses, and time out from reinforcement. In this section, positive management techniques are stressed because they have been successful in reducing or eliminating a wide range of undesirable behaviors. Moreover, these techniques model socially appropriate ways of dealing with troublesome behaviors and are free of the undesirable side effects of punishment. It is important to note that reinforcement is ordinarily viewed as a process to increase, rather than decrease, behavior; consequently, extinction and punishment are most often mentioned as methods for decreasing behaviors. However, in this section, the use of reinforcement techniques to decrease unwanted behavior (Cooper et al., 2020) is emphasized. These techniques either deliver or withhold reinforcement based on whether a predetermined frequency or quality of behavior has been achieved.

- *Reinforcement of other behavior.* Reinforcing a student for engaging in any behavior other than the targeted behavior is known as **differential reinforcement of other behavior**. The reinforcer is delivered as long as the targeted behavior (e.g., inappropriate running during the gym class) is not performed. Thus, the student receives reinforcement for sitting on the floor and listening to instructions, standing quietly and listening to instructions, sitting on the bleachers and listening to instructions—anything other than inappropriate running during class. This reinforcement has the effect of decreasing the targeted response.
- *Reinforcement of incompatible behavior.* This technique reinforces behaviors that are directly incompatible with the targeted response. For example, if a student has a difficult time engaging cooperatively in games during physical education class, reinforcing cooperation during game play eliminates the uncooperative response. Unlike reinforcement of other behavior, this strategy defines diametrically opposed behaviors—playing uncooperatively versus playing cooperatively—and reinforces instances of positive behavior only.
- *Reinforcement of low response rates.* With a technique known as **differential reinforcement of low rates of responding**, a student is reinforced for gradually reducing the frequency of an undesirable behavior or for increasing the amount of time during which the behavior does not occur. For instance, a student who swears an average of five

times per day would be reinforced for swearing only four times. This schedule would be followed until swearing is eliminated completely.

These three techniques use positive reinforcement to decrease the frequency of undesirable behavior. Research does suggest, however, that acceptable levels of behavior might not be achieved without a punishment component (Lerman & Vorndran, 2002). For example, in cases in which the factors that maintain behavior cannot be identified or controlled or in which rapid behavior suppression is necessary to prevent physical harm, punishment might be part of the behavior management strategy. In recognition of the breadth and diversity of ABA techniques, more traditional methods of decreasing inappropriate behaviors are described next.

- *Punishment.* Normally, punishment is thought of as the presentation of an aversive consequence contingent on the occurrence of an undesirable behavior (type I). In the Skinnerian (or operant psychology) tradition, punishment also includes the removal of a positively reinforcing stimulus or event (type II), which is referred to as **response cost**. In either case, a punishment is a consequence that is not pleasing or deprivation of something that is pleasing. For instance, a student who is kept after school for being disobedient or who has lost some hard-earned tokens that buy free time in the gym is experiencing punishment. Response cost is most effective when used in combination with systematic reinforcement of appropriate behavior (Thibadeau, 1998). In each case the effect is to reduce the frequency of the undesirable behavior.

Shea and Bauer (2012) detail the advantages and disadvantages of using punishment. One advantage is the immediacy of its effect; usually, an immediate reduction occurs in the response rate. Punishment can also be effective when a disruptive behavior occurs with such frequency that reinforcement of an incompatible behavior is not possible and when a behavior must be temporarily suppressed while another behavior is reinforced. The disadvantages of punishment are numerous, including undesirable emotional reactions, avoidance of the environment or person producing the punishment, aggression toward the punishing person, modeling of punishing techniques by the person who is punished, and reinforcement for the person who is delivering the punishment. Additionally, physical punishment might result in physical abuse, although that may not have been the intent. For these reasons positive reinforcement is strongly encouraged in physical education for all students, including those with disabilities. Emphasis should always be on creating positive instructional environments that promote successful experiences.

- *Time out.* Time out (from reinforcement) is an extension of the punishment concept, which often involves the removal of a positive event. The **time-out** procedure is based on the assumption that some positive reinforcer in the immediate environment is maintaining the undesirable behavior. In an effort to control the situation, the student is physically removed from the environment and consequently deprived of all positive reinforcement for a specified time. The three types of time out are observational, exclusion, and seclusion (Lavay et al., 2016). In observational time out, the student is removed from an activity but is permitted to watch as classmates engage in the lesson. Exclusion time out, on the other hand, isolates the student within the physical education setting without the opportunity to observe what is going on in the lesson, e.g., sitting in the physical education office. Finally, seclusion time out completely isolates the student by removing him from the physical education setting, e.g., being sent to the principal's office or to a crisis-intervention room. In the case of exclusion and seclusion procedures, serious consideration must be given to the "Position Summary on Physical Restraint & Seclusion Procedures in School Settings" from the Council for Children with Behavioral Disorders (2009), which states the following:

> CCBD calls for any school that employs . . . seclusion procedures to have a written positive behavior support plan specific to that program, pre-established emergency procedures, specific procedures and training related to the use of . . . seclusion, and data to support the implementation of the principles of positive behavior supports in that environment as well as data regarding the specific uses of . . . seclusion. (p. 40)

Uses of Applied Behavior Analysis in Physical Education and Sport

Most people use some form of ABA in their daily lives. In ordinary situations, however, this use of ABA might not be thorough and deliberate. On the other hand, the purposeful application of reinforcement learning principles in an attempt to change behavior is a systematic, step-by-step procedure (see the Example of Applied Behavior Analysis sidebar at the end of this section). According to Block (2016), evidence supports the use of ABA in both segregated and inclusive programs for students with special needs. A classic example of using ABA in adapted physical education is the data-based gymnasium (DBG) for teaching students with severe disabilities (Dunn & Leitschuh, 2014). Successful implementation of the DBG depends on systematic use of behavioral principles to teach skills and change social behaviors. These include the use of naturally occurring reinforcers such as social praise or extinction (i.e., ignoring a behavior). Tangible reinforcers such as food, toys, or desirable activities, which are earned as part of a token economy, are not instituted until it has been demonstrated that the consistent use of social reinforcement or extinction is ineffective.

In skill-acquisition programs, task-analytic phases and steps are individually determined, and students move through the sequence at a rate commensurate with their ability. For example, a **phase** for kicking with the toe of the preferred foot consists of having students swing the preferred kicking leg backward and then forward to contact the ball with the toes of the foot, causing the ball to roll toward the target. **Steps** represent distances, times, or numbers of repetitions that might further subdivide a particular phase (e.g., kicking the ball with the toe of the preferred foot a distance of 10, 15, or 20 feet [3, 4.6, or 6 meters]). Decisions about program modifications or changes in the use of behavioral strategies are made on an individual basis after each student's progress is reviewed. Further discussion of the DBG and managing inappropriate behavior in physical education with students with severe disabilities is presented in chapter 9.

Advantages of ABA include the following:

- It considers only behaviors that are precisely defined and capable of being seen.
- It assumes that knowing the intrapsychic cause of a particular behavior is not a prerequisite for changing it; however, this in no way diminishes the importance of understanding the antecedents that may cause the behavior.
- It encourages a thorough analysis of the environmental conditions and factors that might influence the behavior in question—that is, the antecedents.
- It facilitates functional independence by employing a system of least prompts—that is, a prompt hierarchy from least to most intrusive (see chapter 7).
- It requires precise measurement to demonstrate a cause-and-effect relation between the behavioral intervention and the behavior being changed.

Disadvantages of ABA that one should consider before implementing such a program include the following:

- The actual use of behavioral principles in a consistent and systematic manner is not as simple as it might seem.
- Behavioral techniques might fail when what is thought to be the controlling stimulus is not so in reality (e.g., a Premack reinforcer constructed on the incorrect assumption that a student prefers a particular activity is destined to be unsuccessful).
- Behavioral techniques might not work initially, requiring more thorough analysis by the teacher to determine if additional techniques would be useful; this can entail implementing a new approach immediately, if necessary.

Positive Behavioral Interventions and Supports (PBIS)

According to the Office of Special Education Program's Technical Assistance Center, School-Wide Positive Behavior Support "refers to a systems change process for an entire school or district. The underlying theme is teaching behavioral expectations in the same manner as any core curriculum subject" (www.pbis.org). When engaging the topic of PBIS for the first time, it is important to define its parameters. Positive Behavioral Interventions and Supports is "a framework or approach (some even suggest an applied science [Carr et al., 2002]) for assisting school personnel in adapting and organizing evidence-based behavioral interventions into an integrated continuum that enhances academic and social behavior outcomes for all students" (U.S. Department of Education, Office of Special Education Programs Technical Assistance Center, 2016). Therefore, any discussion of PBIS must address school and classroom climate and recognize a number of its distinct characteristics—namely, safety, engagement or the quality of human interaction, and environmental factors that foster

Example of Applied Behavior Analysis

The process for implementing a behavioral system, ABA, requires reasonably strict adherence to several well-defined steps. The following example illustrates the teaching of a skill using the three-term contingency (ABC) and a limited number of behavioral principles. A similar process is outlined in chapter 9 using FBA and a behavioral intervention plan to remediate an aberrant social behavior.

Identifying the Behavior

Standing long jump

Establishing the Baseline

In a pretest condition, the student is observed on three occasions performing the long jump with faulty mechanics, most notably in the takeoff and landing portions of the jump.

Objective

When requested to perform a standing long jump, the student jumps a minimum of 3 feet (1 meter), demonstrating appropriate form on takeoff, in the air, and on landing.

Choosing the Reinforcer

The teacher determines that social reinforcement (verbal praise) is effective.

Scheduling the Reinforcer

The teacher decides to use continuous reinforcement initially and then switch to a variable ratio as learning and performance increase.

Prompt

Using the system of least prompts, the instructor employs prompts in order from least to most intrusive: (1) "Please stand behind this line and do a standing long jump" (verbal prompt); (2) "Please stand behind this line, bend your knees, swing your arms backward and forward like this, and jump as far as possible" (verbal plus visual prompt); and (3) "Please stand behind this line, bend your knees, feel how I'm moving your arms so they swing back and forth like this, and jump as far as possible" (physical guidance prompt). In this example, prompts serve as antecedent events that cause the behavior to occur.

Behavior

The student acknowledges the prompts, assumes the correct position, and executes the long jump as intended.

Reinforcement

The teacher says, "Good job!" (verbal reinforcement).

Subsequent Behavior

The student likely maintains or improves performance.

a positive milieu for all students (Schweig et al., 2019). Failure to incorporate these characteristics within the framework of PBIS certainly will make it more difficult to achieve its stated purpose.

PBIS is an overarching model that incorporates a plethora of behavioral strategies and instructional techniques to prevent problem behaviors from occurring and ameliorating their impact once they do occur. PBIS is not a curriculum, intervention, or instructional practice. It was originally established as part of the reauthorization of IDEA in 1997 for the express purpose of implementing evidence-based interventions with students with emotional disturbance. Its focus more recently has shifted to all students and is referenced as School-Wide Positive Behavior Support (Horner & Sugai, 2015; Sugai & Horner, 2009).

PBIS has its roots in three major sources: ABA, normalization and inclusion, and person-centered values (Carr et al., 2002). The emphasis of PBIS is on improving the quality of life not only for the students with disabilities but also for those who engage with and support them. PBIS is not synonymous with ABA, but relies substantially on the science of ABA and therefore shares a close relationship with its principles and techniques. PBIS notes that challenging behaviors do occur; however, a central principle of PBIS is to recognize when those behaviors are not occurring. It emphasizes positive support techniques rather than the traditional use of aversive or negative procedures to control challenging behaviors. The way to accomplish this goal is to teach desirable behaviors by altering or redesigning environments to support appropriate behavior and encouraging and facilitating informed choice making. It means providing appropriate role models, including peers, teachers, and coaches.

Lastly, PBIS recognizes the need to respond to and manage crisis situations. For example, when challenging behaviors become extreme, teachers and coaches need to know their options for helping students while being sensitive to students' rights. According to Johnston and colleagues (2006), "It is clear that PBIS emphasizes certain values in its approach to services. These values include commitments to respect for the individual, meaningful outcomes, social validation, dignity, normalization, inclusion, person-centered planning, self-determination, and stakeholder participation, among others" (p. 52).

PBIS is required when students' behaviors impede their ability to learn or interfere with others' learning and are caused by or related to their disability. School personnel should consider and address these individual needs by altering environments and explicitly teaching new skills to students with challenging behaviors so that they genuinely appreciate positive behavior. One way to achieve this objective is to implement a major tenet of PBIS—the three-tier model of supports and interventions. Beginning with tier 1, designed to promote an overall understanding of the rules and behavioral expectations for all students in a school or classroom, and terminating with tier 3, which focuses specifically on a small fraction of students who have the most severe and intense behavior challenges, this model provides school personnel with strategies and interventions to prevent problem behaviors from occurring and manage more effectively when they do occur (see table 6.2 for a description of each tier and associated interventions).

TABLE 6.2 Three-Tier Model of PBIS

Tier	Description	Interventions
1	**Primary** level involves all students in a school, with emphasis on general comportment and reduction of potential behavioral difficulties.	School-Wide Positive Behavior Support (SWPBS) Behavioral expectations are 1. defined, 2. taught, and 3. encouraged. Hellison's personal and social responsibility model works well here.
2	**Secondary** level targets those at risk; problem behaviors demonstrated by a relatively small percentage of students (≈15 percent).	Check In Check Out Activity schedules Group contingencies Social skills training
3	**Tertiary** level targets students who demonstrate high-risk behaviors; intensive interventions are designed to reduce the severity and intensity of current behavioral challenges on the part of few students (≈5 percent).	Behavioral contracts Behavioral intervention plan Functional behavior assessment Response to intervention Self-monitoring Conflict resolution Structured time out Social stories Reward systems Seclusion and restraint

Other Approaches

There are a variety of theoretical and philosophical views on behavior management. No fewer than five major approaches have been postulated to remediate problems associated with maladaptive behavior. Two models (either singly or in combination) guide most educational programs today (Hallahan et al., 2015): the behavioral and psychoeducational approaches. The behavioral approach, ABA, has already been discussed. The psychoeducational approach is discussed next, along with a brief overview of the ecological, biogenic, and humanistic approaches. Resources are suggested at the end of the chapter for those who wish to further explore a particular intervention and its primary proponents.

Psychoeducational Approach

The psychoeducational approach views inappropriate behavior as students' maladaptive attempts to cope with their environment; it assumes that academic failure and misbehavior can be directly remediated if students are taught how to achieve and behave effectively. This approach emphasizes the education of the student's whole self, balancing the educational and psychological perspectives. It focuses on the affective and cognitive factors associated with the development of appropriate social and academic skills useful at home, at school, and in the community.

Proponents of psychoeducation recognize that some students do not understand why they behave as they do when their basic instincts, drives, and needs are not satisfied; however, psychoeducation is only concerned with the here and now. Although it acknowledges the influence of past events on a student's behavior and psyche, it is less concerned with explanations for this behavior; identifying the student's potential and emphasizing his abilities are more important functions of this approach. Diagnostic procedures include observational data, measures of achievement, performance in situations requiring particular skills, case histories, and measures of general abilities.

The psychoeducational approach focuses on strengthening the student's self-esteem and relationships with teachers. This is accomplished through compensatory educational programs that encourage students to acknowledge that what they are doing is a problem, understand their motivations for behaving in a certain way, observe the consequences of their behavior, and plan alternative ways of behaving in similar circumstances.

The psychoeducational approach assumes that making students aware of their feelings and having them talk about the nature of their responses will give them insight into their behavior and help them develop control. This approach emphasizes the realistic demands of daily functioning in school and at home as they relate to improving inappropriate behaviors. Among several strategies teachers can use to implement the psychoeducational approach are self-instruction, modeling and rehearsal, self-determination of goals and reinforcement standards, and self-reward.

Teachers are in an advantageous position to encourage students to use self-instructional strategies. This means helping students reflect on the steps of good decision making when it is time to learn something new, solve a problem, or retain a concept. The process involves teaching students to listen to their private speech, whether speaking aloud or mentally to themselves. An example of private speech would be when a person makes a faulty ceiling shot in racquetball and says, "Come on, reach out and hit the ball ahead of the body!" Self-instruction can be as simple as a checklist of questions for students to ask themselves when a decision is required: What is my problem? How can I do it? Am I using my plan? How did I do? These are the types of questions asked within the self-instructional process.

In the modeling and rehearsal strategy, students who have a difficult time controlling their behavior watch others who have learned to deal with similar problems. Beyond merely observing the behavior, the students can see how the models respond in a constructive manner to a problematic situation. Modeling could include the use of relaxation techniques and self-instruction. Students can also learn appropriate ways of responding when time is provided to mentally rehearse or practice successful management techniques. Much of the modeling and rehearsal strategy is steeped in Bandura's work on social learning theory (Engler, 2014) and Goldstein's cognitive–behavioral procedures known as *skillstreaming* (McGinnis et al., 2011).

Another strategy that has proven effective in helping students control their behavior works by including them in the establishment of goals, reinforcement contingencies, or standards. An example of this process occurs when a group of adolescents with behavior disabilities determines which prosocial behaviors each member needs to concentrate on during an overnight camping trip. Likewise, the group establishes the limits of inappropriate behavior and decides what the consequences will be if anyone exceeds these limits.

A final strategy used in the psychoeducational approach is self-reward, which involves preparing students to reward themselves with some preestablished reinforcer. For example, a student who completes the prescribed tasks at a practice station might immediately place a check on a recording sheet posted at that station. The student is thus instrumental not only in seeing that the goal of the lesson is achieved, but also in efficiently implementing the reinforcement process.

Ecological Approach

The ecological approach assumes that behavioral problems are caused by a disturbance in the student's environment or ecosystem (i.e., some characteristic of the student disturbs the ecosystem, and the ecosystem responds in a way that causes the student to further agitate it). "The problem arises because the social interactions and transactions between the child and the social environment are inappropriate—both the behavior and the responses to it are problematic" (Hallahan et al., 2015, p. 182). Said another way, a student's problems are affected by the environment; the student is not the only one causing the problems. For example, a student who cannot get to class on time and thus is in conflict with teachers might be reflecting a cultural disregard for punctuality rather than disrespect for the teacher or the school schedule.

Evaluative procedures for assessing the causes of disturbed behavior are difficult at best. Educators have purported to use a five-phase process for collecting ecological data: describing the environment, identifying expectations, organizing behavioral data, summarizing the data, and establishing goals. This corresponds to the two-stage process of functional behavior assessment and behavior intervention planning that will be discussed in greater detail in chapter 9.

The goal of the ecological approach is not simply to stop a disturbed or unwanted behavior but to change an environment, such as the home, in substantive ways. This is important if the environment is to continue supporting desirable behavior once the intervention is withdrawn. Generally speaking, the focus of intervention within the ecological approach is on one or more environments; however, interventions that focus on only one environment are frequently unsuccessful given that the behavior likely occurs in more than just one location (Cullinan, 2007). For example, if a student is experiencing the same problems at home and in school, intervention must address how the behavior will be handled in both places. This is a particularly difficult issue because students are often permitted to behave in one way at home only to find that the behavior is not tolerated in school. This could create a conflict between the school and the family that could necessitate working with family members as well as the student.

Educational applications of the ecological approach are designed to make environments accommodate students rather than helping students fit into environments. In a classroom, this might require physical and psychological adaptations, such as individual or small-group work areas, time-out areas, or reinforcement centers. This approach entails having teachers create environments in which students succeed rather than anticipate failure. Changes in the home ecosystem might require parental involvement (e.g., talking with parents), respite care, or family therapy. At times, changes in several ecosystems are required (e.g., home, school, and community).

Of interest are present-day attempts to establish ecologically based programs. PBIS is one option that is influenced by a confluence of approaches, in this case the ecological approach and ABA. To develop an effective behavioral intervention, educators must engage in a three-step process: Perform a functional assessment of the student's behavior, determine and implement intervention strategies, and evaluate the results. Assessing the student's behavior includes observing and recording behavior patterns in several settings (e.g., classroom, playground, cafeteria, gym) with the intention of profiling the student's conduct. Establishing a baseline helps teachers understand why a student is behaving in a certain way or who is controlling or reinforcing a student's behavior.

After completing the functional assessment, the teacher develops and implements an intervention. The intervention should set realistic goals, including the temporary acceptance of behaviors that would ordinarily not be appropriate. For example, a student who fights with a certain teammate each time she misses a shot during a basketball drill might realistically be permitted to shout or curse at that teammate as long as she does not physically assault her. After a while, shouting and cursing would be similarly faded. As many people as possible who work with the student should develop the intervention plan, including the student herself. Behavioral interventions must be team based so that the student experiences consistency.

In the final step, teachers assess how effective the intervention plan is and if modifications are necessary. Most experts agree that evaluation should occur monthly, if not weekly. An in-depth explanation and illustration of PBIS, including the articulation with ABA, is presented in chapter 9.

Biogenic Approach

The central focus of the biogenic approach is neurophysiological dysfunction. Closely associated with the medical model, this approach relies on diagnostic techniques that explore signs and symptoms. Physicians attempt to localize problems using neurological soft signs (e.g., the results of gait and postural assessments); timed, repetitive movements; and visual–motor sequencing tasks. Lack of definitive results from lesser diagnostics might prompt the use of electroencephalography (EEG), computed tomography (CT), or magnetic resonance imaging (MRI) scans. Identification of students with disabilities in this realm is made on the basis of general behavioral characteristics (e.g., hyperactivity, distractibility, impulsiveness, emotional lability) and specific functional deficits (e.g., disorders in perception, language, motor ability, and concept formation and reasoning) that are attributable to injury or damage to the central nervous system.

The biogenic approach places considerable importance on etiological factors. The integrity of the central nervous system is assessed on the basis of performance in selected activities or tests, such as walking a line with eyes closed, touching a finger to the nose, or reacting to stimuli such as pain, cold, and light. Additionally, a neurological examination, including an EEG, is often part of the diagnosis. Following diagnosis, treatment might include drug therapy, surgical procedures (e.g., removal of a tumor), physical therapy, sensory integrative therapy, or developmental training.

A major strategy associated with the biogenic approach is drug therapy (though the use of drugs to control or modify behavior cuts across several behavioral approaches). Students may be medicated for the management of such challenges as short attention span, distractibility, impulsiveness, hyperactivity, visual–motor impairments, and large motor coordination problems. At the present time, the medical field believes that psychotropic drugs are overprescribed for children and adolescents, especially for those with disabilities. It is likewise thought that these drugs are being used in far too many cases as the only treatment. Currently, the best recommendation is that drug therapy should work hand-in-hand with evidence-based behavioral interventions (McLaren & Lichtenstein, 2018). Psychotropic drugs represent the major category of substances used to control emotional, behavioral, and cognitive changes of people with disabilities. These drugs include medications typically classified as antianxiety, antidepressant, antimanic, stimulant, sedative-hypnotic, or antipsychotic, including atypical antipsychotics such as risperidone, which is used to treat irritability in patients with autism disorder (Mullin, 2012). The most common categories of psychotropic drugs for the purpose of this discussion are stimulants, neuroleptics, and antidepressants.

- *Stimulants.* Stimulants are administered primarily for the management of attention deficit/hyperactivity disorder (ADHD). ADHD is the only condition other than obesity and narcolepsy for which there is Food and Drug Administration (FDA) approval for the use of stimulants. The most frequently prescribed family of stimulants is the methylphenidate hydrochlorides. These include Ritalin (the most commonly prescribed), Concerta (a long-acting form prescribed for children under six years of age), Metadate CD, Metadate ER, Focalin, and Methylin ER (Elbe et al., 2018). All of these drugs are adjunctive therapy and are used with students who experience moderate to severe hyperactivity, short attention span, distractibility, emotional lability, and impulsiveness. Although it seems contraindicated to treat an overactive child with stimulants, these drugs increase concentrations of dopamine, norepinephrine, and serotonin, which improve cognition, memory, and attention (Sullivan & Sadeh, 2015). Possible side effects include loss of appetite, weight loss, stomachache, headache, irritability, anxiety, and insomnia. These effects are more profound in individuals with intellectual disabilities (Moncrieff et al., 2013).
- *Neuroleptics.* These drugs, also called *tranquilizers*, remain the most widely prescribed class of psychotropic medications for individuals with intellectual disabilities. They are also used to control bizarre behavior in psychotic adults. In children they are used to control hyperactivity, aggression, self-injury, and stereotypic behavior. Tranquilizers are classified as either major or minor. Major tranquilizers, also called *antipsychotics*, include such drugs as Mellaril (thioridazine hydrochloride), Thorazine (chlorpromazine hydrochloride), and Haldol (haloperidol), all of which are prescribed for the management of psychotic disorders, including severe behavior disorders marked by aggressiveness and combativeness (Elbe et al., 2018). Possible

side effects of the major and minor tranquilizers include dizziness, drowsiness, vertigo, fatigue, diminished mental alertness (which could impair performance in physical activities), tardive dyskinesia (involuntary movements of the tongue and facial muscles), and movement disorders, referred to as the *extrapyramidal effect.*

- *Antidepressants.* Antidepressants are prescribed to adults to alleviate depression. In children they have a more diverse function, including not only the management of obsessive–compulsive disorder (OCD), affective disorders, and ADHD but also the treatment of nocturnal enuresis and, to a lesser extent, ritualistic behavior, self-injurious behavior, and aggression. Because of the documented side effects of antidepressants—ataxia, muscle weakness, drowsiness, anxiety, sleep disruption, decreased appetite, increased blood pressure, and mental dullness (Sullivan & Sadeh, 2015)—physical educators and coaches should know when students are receiving such medication. Commonly prescribed antidepressants include Anafranil (clomipramine) and Tofranil (imipramine), which is used for ADHD when patients show excessive side effects or fail to respond favorably to stimulants.

Humanistic Approach

Based on the work of Maslow (Engler, 2014), the humanistic approach uses the self-actualization theory as its foundation. Five primary human needs are identified in ascending order, including physiological needs, safety, belonging and love, esteem, and self-actualization. According to this theory of motivation, humans seek to meet unsatisfied needs at progressively higher levels as lower needs are met. For example, someone lacking food, safety, love, and esteem would probably hunger for food more strongly than for anything else. But when the need for food is satisfied, the other needs become stronger. In this hierarchy, self-actualization is the fulfillment of one's highest potential. Maslow considered the following to be attributes of self-actualized people: accepting, spontaneous, realistic, autonomous, appreciating, ethical, sympathetic, affectionate, helpful, intimate, democratic, creative, and sure about right and wrong.

Self-actualization is the process of becoming all that one is fully capable of becoming. Most often, people without disabilities develop self-actualization naturally. People with disabilities, on the other hand, might not achieve the same relative status of self-actualization because they sometimes lack the intrinsic motivation and external assistance to become all they are capable of becoming. The desire to move people with disabilities toward self-actualization is supplied, at least initially, by those who care about them as individuals first and foremost and as individuals with disabilities to a secondary degree.

In the sixth revision of her text on adapted physical education, Sherrill (2004) continued to draw extensively on Maslow's self-actualization theory, noted psychotherapist Carl Rogers' concept of the fully functioning self, and newer sources in attitude theory and disability studies to develop a humanistic orientation to adapted physical education in general and to affective development in particular. Sherrill is not only the spokesperson for the humanistic philosophy—she works to apply its concepts in the gym and on the field. In an effort to demonstrate how the humanistic philosophy can be translated into action, Sherrill and her colleagues suggest that teachers and coaches of students with disabilities do the following:

- To the degree possible, use a teaching style that fosters self-determination and encourages learners to make some of the major decisions during the learning process. This implies that students should be taught with the least restrictive teaching style or one that most closely matches their preferred learning styles.
- Use assessment and instruction that are success oriented. If tasks are sufficiently broken down (i.e., task analyzed), positive reinforcement and success will characterize the learning environment. No matter where students score in terms of the normal curve, they have worth as human beings and must be accepted as such.
- Listen to and communicate with students in an effort to encourage them to take control of their lives and make personal decisions affecting their physical well-being. Counseling students to become healthy, fit, and self-actualized requires the skills of active listening, acceptance, empathy, and cooperative goal setting. Such interaction helps people with disabilities reinforce their internal locus of control.
- Use teaching practices that enhance self-concept. Show students that someone genuinely cares for them as human beings, teach students to care about each other by modeling caring behavior in daily interactions, emphasize social interaction by using cooperative rather than competitive activities, and build success into the instructional plan through the careful use of task and activity analysis.

Hellison (2011) is another physical educator who has been instrumental in disseminating the humanistic viewpoint. He has developed a set of alternative goals or levels for physical education that focus on human needs and values rather than specifically on fitness and sport skill development. The levels are developmental in nature and reflect a loosely constructed progression of attitudes and behaviors, including self-control and respect for the rights and feelings of others, participation and effort, self-direction, and caring and helping. Hellison applied this model in a basketball unit described in chapter 9.

Summary

Lack of discipline has been identified as one of the most significant problems confronting public school teachers. An equally significant problem is how to replace old, worn-out thinking about how discipline should be delivered in favor of effective, proactive practices. A number of behavior management systems are available that can significantly affect skill acquisition, enhance social behavior, and reduce the need to discipline students. One potential solution is the advent of Positive Behavioral Interventions and Supports (PBIS), which uses a three-tier model to ameliorate challenging behavior.

As students with behavior disabilities are integrated into a general physical education class and demonstrate persistent disruptive behavior, a behavior management program might include any of the following: ABA using functional behavior analysis and a behavior intervention plan; a psychoeducational approach using modeling and rehearsal strategies; an ecological approach using a behavior intervention plan that includes the school as well as the student's home and community environment; a biogenic approach using medication; a humanistic approach using self-actualization, self-concept, and attitude theory; or a mixture of these approaches, which is the more common scenario in adapted physical education. Physical educators use mainly ABA, humanistic, and psychoeducational approaches, depending on the setting.

References

Block, M.E. (2016). *A teacher's guide to adapted physical education: Including students with disabilities in sport and recreation* (4th ed.). Brookes.

Carr, E.G., Dunlap, G., Horner, R.H., Koegel, R.L., Turnbull, A.P., Sailor, W., Anderson, J.L., Albin, R.W., Koegel, L.K., & Fox, L. (2002). Positive behavior support: Evolution of an applied science. *Journal of Positive Behavior Interventions, 4,* 4-16. http://dx.doi.org/10.1177/109830070200400102

Cooper, J.O., Heron, T.E., & Heward, W.L. (2020). *Applied behavior analysis* (3rd ed.). Pearson Education.

Council for Children with Behavioral Disorders. (2009). Physical restraint and seclusion procedures in school settings. *Beyond Behavior, 19*(1), 40-41.

Council for Exceptional Children. (2008). *Policy on safe and positive school climate.* Retrieved from https://exceptionalchildren.org/policy-and-advocacy/policy-agenda

Cullinan, D. (2007). *Students with emotional and behavioral disorders* (2nd ed.). Pearson Education.

Dunn, J.M., & Leitschuh, C. (2014). *Special physical education* (10th ed.). Kendall/Hunt.

Dunn, J.M., Morehouse, J.W., Anderson, R.B., Fredericks, H.D.B., Baldwin, V.L., Blair, F.L., & Moore, W. (1980). *A data-based gymnasium.* Instructional Development Corporation.

Elbe, D., Black, T.R., McGrane, I.R., & Procyshyn, R.M. (2018). *Clinical handbook of psychotropic drugs for children and adolescents* (4th ed.). Hogrefe Publishing.

Engler, B. (2014). *Personality theories: An introduction* (9th ed.). Wadsworth.

Goodwyn, F.D., Hatton, H.L., Vannest, K.J., & Ganz, J.B. (2013). Video modeling and video feedback intervention for students with emotional and behavioral disorders. *Beyond Behavior, 22*(2), 1-5. https://doi.org/10.1177/107429561302200204

Hallahan, D.P., Kauffman, J.M., & Pullen, P.C. (2015). *Exceptional learners: Introduction to special education* (13th ed.). Pearson.

Hellison, D.R. (2011). *Teaching responsibility through physical activity* (3rd ed.). Human Kinetics.

Horner, R.H., & Sugai, G. (2015). Schoolwide PBIS: An example of applied behavior analysis implemented at a scale of social importance. *Behavior Analysis in Practice, 8*(1), 80-85. https://doi.org/10.1007/s40617-015-0045-4

Individuals with Disabilities Education Act Amendments of 2004 (IDEA), PL 108-446, 20 U.S.C. 1400 (2004).

Johnston, J.M., Foxx, R.M., Jacobson, J.W., Green, G., & Mulick, J.A. (2006). Positive behavior support and applied behavior analysis. *Behavior Analyst, 29,* 51-74. https://doi.org/10.1007/bf03392117

Kazdin, A.E. (2013). *Behavior modification in applied settings* (7th ed.). Waveland Press.

Lavay, B.W., French, R., & Henderson, H.L. (2016). *Positive behavior management in physical activity settings* (3rd ed.). Human Kinetics.

Lerman, D.C., & Vorndran, C.M. (2002). On the status of knowledge for using punishment: Implications for treating behavior disorders. *Journal of Applied Behavior Analysis, 35,* 431-464. https://doi.org/10.1901/jaba.2002.35-431

Lovaas, O.I. (2003). *Teaching individuals with developmental delays.* Pro-Ed.

McGinnis, E., Sprafkin, R.P., Gershaw, N.J., & Klein, P. (2011). *Skillstreaming the adolescent: A guide for teaching prosocial skills* (3rd ed.). Research Press.

McLaren, L.L., & Lichtenstein, J.D. (2019). The pursuit of the magic pill: The overuse of psychotropic medications in children with intellectual and developmental disabilities in the USA. *Epidemiology and Psychiatric Sciences, 28,* 365-368. https://doi.org/10.1017/S2045796018000604

Moncrieff, J., Cohen, D., & Porter, S. (2013). The psychoactive effects of psychiatric medication: The elephant in the room. *Journal of Psychoactive Drugs, 45*(5), 409-415. https://doi.org/10.1080/02791072.2013.845328

Mullin, S. (2012). Use of antipsychotics and psychostimulants for challenging behavior in the intellectually disabled. *Mental Health Clinician, 2*(3), 64-66. https://doi.org/10.9740/mhc.n115492

Schweig, J., Hamilton, L.S., & Baker, G. (2019). *School and classroom climate measures.* Rand Corporation. https://doi.org/10.7249/RR4259

Shea, T.M., & Bauer, A.M. (2012). *Behavior management: A practical approach for educators* (10th ed.). Pearson.

Sherrill, C. (2004). *Adapted physical education, recreation, and sport: Crossdisciplinary and lifespan* (6th ed.). McGraw-Hill.

Sugai, G., & Horner, R.H. (2009). Responsiveness-to-intervention and school-wide positive behavior supports: Integration of multi-tiered approaches. *Exceptionality, 17,* 223-237. https://doi.org/10.1080/09362830903235375

Sullivan, A.L., & Sadeh, S. (2015). Psychopharmacological treatment among adolescents with disabilities: Prevalence and predictors in a nationally representative sample. *School Psychology Quarterly, 30*(3), 443-455. http://dx.doi.org/10.1037/spq0000105

Thibadeau, S.F. (1998). *How to use response cost.* Pro-Ed.

U.S. Department of Education, Office of Special Education Programs Technical Assistance Center. (2016). *SWPBIS for beginners.* www.pbis.org

Print Resources

Hulac, D.M., & Briesch, A.M. (2017). *Evidence-based strategies for effective classroom management.* Guilford Press.

This text presents strategies for preventing challenging behaviors and promoting expected behaviors within the framework of PBIS, with emphasis on strategies that have a strong evidential basis.

Lavay, B.W., French, R., & Henderson, H.L. (2016). *Positive behavior management in physical activity settings* (3rd ed.). Human Kinetics.

This manual describes in greater detail many of the approaches suggested in this chapter. It likewise provides many practical examples of how to manage behavior in physical education settings.

Video Resources

Western Michigan University, Department of Psychology (2015). *Differential reinforcement procedures in applied behavior analysis* [Video]. http://wmich.edu/autism

This video explains and demonstrates the variety of differential reinforcement strategies that are discussed in this chapter.

National Professional Development Center on Autism Spectrum Disorder. (n.d.). *Discrete trial training* [Video]. http://autismpdc.fpg.unc.edu

Several videos are embedded in the instructional module "Discrete Trial Training (DTT)". Once logged in, cycle through to the sixth and seventh steps of DTT and watch the videos demonstrating massed trials, prompt fading, reinforcement selection, and error correction.

Heward, W. (2012, February 29). *Applied behavior analysis* [Video]. University of Western Ontario, Autism Center of Excellence. www.youtube.com/watch?v=vT73KEwVAx0.

This presentation by acclaimed author William Heward addresses applied behavior analysis, explains what it is and is not, and provides examples of specific teaching techniques.

Maslow's Hierarchy of Needs [DVD]. 2007. Insight Media, Inc., 350 7th Ave., Ste. 1100, New York, NY 10001.

Basic needs such as food, shelter, security, recognition, and achievement are reviewed in light of Maslow's hierarchy of needs; their meaning for motivation in organizational settings is analyzed and illustrated using dramatized incidents. Running time is approximately 16 minutes.

U.S. Department of Education. (2020, January 9). *Students with disabilities and the use of restraint and seclusion in K-12 public schools* [Video]. YouTube. www.youtube.com/watch?v=EZ9Yx0LC8TI&feature=youtu.be

This webinar describes how the Office of Civil Rights and the Office of Special Education and Rehabilitative Services of the U.S. Department of Education collaborated to provide technical assistance to K-12 public schools relative to how federal laws apply to the use of seclusion and physical restraint.

Online Resources

Medline Plus Drugs, Herbs and Supplements: www.nlm.nih.gov/medlineplus/druginformation.html

This site allows practitioners to search for information on psychotropic drugs, including brand names, descriptions, proper use, precautions, and side effects.

National Professional Development Center on Autism Spectrum Disorder: http://autismpdc.fpg.unc.edu

This site provides a series of detailed briefs designed to instruct practitioners about evidence-based instructional methods, many of which are based on applied behavior analysis—antecedent-based interventions and discrete trial training, to name just two.

PsychoEducation Behavior Advisor: www.behavioradvisor.com/PsychoEdModel.html

This site provides information about psychoeducation. It is oriented toward educators of moderately and severely emotionally disturbed students. Child care workers and mental health professionals might also find this information helpful. Psychoeducational approaches helpful for troubled children and youth are presented.

Touch Autism Preference & Reinforcement Assessor App: http://touchautism.com/app/preference-reinforcer-assessment/

This app allows the user to run a reinforcer preference assessment to determine a child's or client's most preferred reinforcer. It is designed for both iPhone and iPad. The app costs $9.99 on iTunes.

7

Instructional Strategies

Douglas H. Collier

Mr. Ellis, the newly hired physical education teacher, was discouraged. "Whenever Peter and Jasmine come to physical education, I just get this tight feeling across my chest. Yes, I know I should be able to accommodate them, and I'd like to be able to, but I just don't feel qualified, so I get nervous. Peter has been diagnosed with Asperger syndrome and Jasmine has Down syndrome. That's as much as I know. What am I supposed to do with that information? Oh, yes—I get an aide when they come to the gym with their 30 classmates. On the one hand, I'm glad they're in the class with their buddies. On the other hand, I wish I had better ideas of how to work with them. Do I change my approach? My curriculum? What if the other students get angry or bored? What if I don't have time for all of the others? Boy, with all the different skill levels and learning styles, I wish that I'd been a little better prepared."

Teaching physical education effectively and efficiently so that students learn and retain meaningful content is a challenging undertaking, made even more so by the increasing diversity of the student body. Although multiple physical education environments exist for students with identifiable disabilities, these students are frequently being included in the general education environment alongside their peers without disabilities (Block, 2016; Dunn & Leitschuh, 2014). Thus, planning and presenting appropriate physical education content require more attention to individual differences than ever.

This type of planning does not mean coming up with a laundry list of instructional modifications based on perceived characteristics of a particular disability. For example, it would be inappropriate to say, "If she's been diagnosed with autism, I'd better avoid physical prompts" or "Given that he has Down syndrome, I'll expect oppositional behavior." Instructional decisions are not based only on a student's medical or behavioral diagnosis, but also on the learning style, strengths, and shortcomings of the individual student as well as the objectives of the class. For example, some students with autism learn more effectively through a command style of teaching, whereas other students with the same diagnosis learn more effectively when given options on how to perform a given skill. Effective physical educators have long known that all students come to physical education with different strengths, learning styles, and rates of learning and take these differences into account when planning, delivering, and assessing content. Having preconceived ideas based on a student's diagnosis is extremely ill-conceived.

Teaching quality physical education classes to typically developing students is a demanding undertaking that requires motivation, an extensive knowledge base, lots of practice, and appropriate feedback from skilled observers. When the classes include students with unique needs—whether the setting is inclusive or not—the challenge to teach effectively is increased. Siedentop and Tannehill (2000) have noted that a committed and competent physical education teacher has extensive skills in the areas of conceiving and planning the curricula, managing behavior and teaching content, optimizing the program through appropriate administration, and creatively linking the school program to community opportunities. Physical education teachers who work with students with unique needs require these skills to an even greater degree as they face additional challenges that have not been traditionally emphasized in teacher preparation programs. These challenges include writing goals and objectives for individualized education programs (IEPs) or individualized family service plans (IFSPs), adapting activities, performing task analysis, providing the appropriate level of prompting, training and managing volunteers, working with parents and allied professionals as part of an interdisciplinary team, and effectively managing idiosyncratic or challenging behavior.

This chapter provides information that will assist teachers in structuring a physical education environment that optimizes learning for students with unique needs.

Philosophical Approaches to Adapted Physical Education and Sport

Teachers of adapted physical education who implement effective individualized physical education programs believe in each participant's inherent worth and are dedicated to the development of their students' full potential. These general characteristics are present in two primary orientations that have influenced adapted physical education over the past few decades—**humanism** and **applied behavior analysis** (ABA), discussed in chapter 6. Although humanism and ABA (also called *behavior therapy* or *behaviorism*) have different traditions and emphases and often use different empirical tools, they share a commitment to providing ethical and high-quality instruction for people with and without disabilities. Both traditions, along with other approaches in this text (discussed in chapter 6), emphasize nonaversive, affirming teaching strategies in terms of both skill acquisition and the management of challenging behaviors. When teaching adapted physical education and sport, the practitioner must remain open-minded and, when appropriate, take the best elements of each tradition.

Teachers who embrace these approaches use instructional methodologies that best allow people to be productive and move toward self-reliance while maintaining individual dignity. Although choosing humanism or applied behavior analysis is often cast as an either–or proposition, the thoughtful practitioner is able to embrace the best of each tradition without hypocrisy. Indeed, from an ethical and strategic perspective, these traditions have much in common. Both orientations, as noted already, stress the importance of human dignity.

Practitioners from both the humanistic and ABA perspectives stand together in creating appropriate environments where people with unique needs can live full, positive, and valued lives.

Systematic Teaching: How to Facilitate Motor Learning

Experts in the development and teaching of movement skills have stressed the importance of examining variables that relate to the learner, the task, and the environment when designing learning opportunities for students with unique needs (Haibach et al., 2017; Haywood & Getchell, 2018; Newell, 1986). These variables are not independent of one another; rather, they interact in sometimes complex ways. Variables that relate to the learner include age, body build, sex, socioeconomic class, culture, attitudes, actual and perceived competence, creativity, motivations, disability, and ability. Some of these variables might change over the course of a unit or even a lesson, depending on the situation. For example, Zaria, a student with Down syndrome, might be excited about taking part in a jump rope activity, but after 10 minutes of doing the same thing with little success, her motivation level, as well as her perceived competence in jumping rope, might diminish considerably. On the other hand, Va, a student with cerebral palsy, might come into the gym feeling nervous about taking part in line dancing, but given an excellent breakdown of the skill; some thoughtful, unobtrusive peer tutoring; and great music, his motivation to participate could increase dramatically.

When examining environmental variables, educators must think beyond the physical. Although the indoor or outdoor setting, facilities, equipment, space, floor surfaces, lighting, and temperature must be considered, it is also imperative that teachers of adapted physical education carefully consider the emotional environment. Do activities take place in a positive, affirming environment in which individual differences are embraced? Is there mutual respect? Are all students treated with dignity? Along with making sure the physical environment is universally designed (see chapter 2 and later discussion in this chapter), safe, and appropriate, effective teachers must also monitor the environment for emotional safety (Sherrill, 2004).

The third variable—the task—gets at the curriculum and the task at hand. Are the movement skills of interest and use to the students? Do instructors teach skills because *they* enjoy the activity or because it's "just the way it's always been done"? Or, much more appropriately, are skills taught because they are valued by the student and will be useful now, in the next educational placement, or at home or in the community? Additionally, the task variable includes the rules that govern the activity and the equipment used. Shooting at a 7-foot (2.1-meter) basket instead of a 10-foot (3-meter) basket could certainly have a positive effect on the form—and the success—of an athlete with poorly developed upper body strength. Beyond scaling equipment or playing surfaces, we must ask ourselves: Just how important are the rules? Although some may be immutable, other rules can and should be modified; maybe for a little while and maybe for a longer period of time.

Research in the disciplines of motor learning, motor development, motor control, biomechanics, physiology, special education, and pedagogy has uncovered certain principles that can help significantly in the teaching and learning of movement skills. Keeping in mind the interaction of variables related to the learner, the environment, and the task to be accomplished, Dunn (1997) has compiled a list of motor skill tenets. A partial list follows.

- *Growth and maturation influence the ability to learn a movement skill.* It is detrimental to the physical and emotional well-being of students to pressure them to take part in tasks that they are not ready to accomplish physically, cognitively, or socially—that is, tasks that are developmentally inappropriate. Although teachers should organize learning environments in which students can explore their movement potential, they must carefully consider cognitive, affective, and physical strengths and limitations.
- *Mechanical and physiological principles of movement dictate the best way to perform a given skill.* The laws of stability and motion, along with clearly established physiological principles of exercise, apply to all people regardless of functional level or disability. For example, the principle of stability posits that balance is enhanced when the center of gravity falls within the base of support. This principle should be considered when, for example, students with amputations are asked to perform movement skills in a gym or pool.
- *Reinforcement and repetition are needed when learning a new skill.* As discussed earlier in this chapter and in other chapters in this book, it is imperative to identify consequences that will increase the likelihood that a response will take place. Although being intrinsically motivated to

take part in an activity is preferred, this is often not the case, especially regarding students with affective or intellectual disabilities. Thus, it is necessary to find extrinsic reinforcers that are effective and applied with an eye toward systematic fading. Reinforcers must be individualized, chosen carefully, and provided effectively. Too often, educators assume that a consequence is reinforcing to a given learner when, actually, it is punishing. Conversely, educators may attempt to reduce behavior using what they believe to be aversive or punishing consequences when these consequences are reinforcing, thus having the opposite effect on the learner. (For example: "Okay, Mikey, you've been warned about talking out of turn. So, instead of dancing for the next five minutes, I want you to sit on the blue bench and think about what you could do differently." With a smile, Mikey heads on over to the blue bench, getting exactly what he was hoping for. The teacher shouldn't be too surprised when, moving forward, Mikey talks out of turn even more.) In terms of repetition, students with unique needs must have multiple opportunities to perform a given movement skill. Too often, a student does not get enough opportunities to practice, making it unlikely the skill will be established. The teaching situation must allow for plenty of "perfect practice" (practicing a skill accurately). Practice sessions must be structured so that students have the opportunity not only to repeat a given skill several times but also to repeat it in a stimulating, exciting activity during which their attention is focused on the relevant cues.

When considering these tenets, note that much of the research has been conducted with children who are developing typically, as opposed to those with identifiable disabilities. Although students with unique needs are more similar to their typically developing peers than not and thus these findings will largely apply, additional research with a wider range of subjects will significantly increase the knowledge base.

Meeting Individual Differences

A major focus of this text is to help the reader address individual differences in a way that leads to significant educational gains for students with unique needs. In the context of this chapter, the word *unique* applies not only to a student's needs but to *all* of the student's attributes. As previously mentioned, teachers must focus on a learner's distinct learning style, strengths, and limitations. Although a thorough understanding of the etiology and characteristics of a given disability (e.g., autism or cerebral palsy) is important—and extensively covered in this text—an excellent understanding of the person standing in the gym is more important still. To borrow a phrase from research, as teachers, our unit of analysis is one—we look at students as individuals first and foremost.

A number of philosophical and practical initiatives in the area of special education inform what and how educators teach students. These approaches are as critical to learning in the gymnasium as they are to learning in the classroom.

Accountable and Accessible Instruction

For all students to reach their academic potential, it is clear that what educators teach and how they teach it must be of the highest quality. To ensure that this is the case, physical educators must not only use state-of-the-art approaches as identified by best practices in the field and empirical research, but also carefully assess the progress of their students. As wonderful as the gymnasium might look and as imaginative as the activities might be, the proof of an excellent program is whether the students are learning meaningful content. To this end, carefully designed formative and summative assessments must be administered regularly and with fidelity. If adequate progress is not being made, the assessments will demonstrate this, and modifications to curricula and the educational approach can be made. Given the range of learners with unique needs taking part in physical education, it is imperative that practitioners develop the skills to identify the appropriate assessments and make the necessary modifications to obtain meaningful information regarding their students' progress (Collier, 2016; Smith et al., 2008).

Universal Design for Learning

Universal design for learning (UDL) is a philosophical and practical approach to effectively educating *all* students, in their multifaceted, interesting complexity. For much of the 20th century, teachers at all educational levels and in all disciplines have generally taught to that mythical, nonexistent "average" student. Although this illusory student was rarely, if ever, observed, these days she is even less likely to be found given the appropriate push toward inclusive education (Meyer et al., 2014). With the greater heterogeneity of the student body within physical education programs (Collier, 2016) and the aforementioned inclusion of students with identifiable disabilities in these programs, it is even more important that we design our physical and instructional environments to maximize the learning of all students. Physical educators have too often come from the perspective that learners with unique needs should either fit in—if they are included at all—or receive a specially designed curriculum with individualized accommodations and modifications, as necessary (Friend, 2008; Smith et al., 2008). Although this differentiated approach to curricular design and pedagogy was in accord with the principles of inclusion, UDL turned this paradigm on its head. Instead of modifying the educational offerings for each individual student, in all their often-changing complexity, UDL intentionally modifies the learning environment so that all students can be successful.

As discussed in chapter 2, UDL offers students a wide variety of ways to be involved in their learning (multiple means of engagement); a variety of methods to learn information (multiple means of representation); and, a variety of ways to express themselves and demonstrate what they've learned (multiple means of action and expression). These principles focus on making the learning environment responsive, flexible, and appropriate for a wide variety of learners who are not static in their abilities and requirements (CAST, 2020). When developing the framework for universal design for learning, CAST grounded their work in not only the best practices in the fields of education and special education, but in powerful historic and current research in the fields of neuroscience, developmental and cognitive psychology, and the learning sciences. Indeed, the seminal theoretical and applied works of such noted educational researchers as Lev Vygotsky, Jerome Bruner, Benjamin Bloom, and Jean Piaget inform CAST's worldview.

Ultimately, the overarching goal of UDL is to develop "expert learners" who, irrespective of their skills and shortcomings, can become more "resourceful and knowledgeable, strategic and goal-directed, purposeful and motivated" (Bray, 2019, para. 5). Thus, expertise is less a destination and more a process of continuous improvement. For more information about UDL, the reader is referred to *Universal Design for Learning: Theory and Practice* (Meyer et al., 2014) as well as *Universal Design for Learning in Physical Education* (Lieberman et al., 2021).

Major Considerations for UDL

Educators need to be aware of a number of major considerations as they implement UDL. The following have been adapted from work initially done by Connell and colleagues (1997) and Scott and colleagues (2001).

EQUITABLE USE Instruction is designed to be useful to and accessible by students with diverse abilities and to be used similarly by all students whenever possible (with equivalent accommodations when not). Therefore, physical educators should do the following:

- Avoid segregating or stigmatizing any users.
- Make provisions for privacy, security, and safety equally available to all users.
- Make the design appealing to all users.

FLEXIBILITY IN USE Instruction is designed to accommodate a wide range of individual abilities and provide choice in methods of use. Therefore, physical educators should do the following:

- Accommodate right- or left-handed access and use.
- Facilitate the user's accuracy and precision.
- Provide adaptability to the user's pace.

SIMPLE AND INTUITIVE USE Instruction is designed in a straightforward and predictable manner, regardless of the student's experience, knowledge, language skills, or current concentration level. Unnecessary complexity is eliminated. Therefore, physical educators should do the following:

- Be consistent with user expectations and intuition.
- Accommodate a wide range of literacy and language skills.
- Provide effective prompting and feedback during and after task completion.

PERCEPTIBLE INFORMATION Instruction is designed so that necessary information is communicated effectively to the student, regardless of ambient conditions or the student's sensory abilities. Therefore, physical educators should do the following:

- Use multiple modes of presentation for essential information (pictorial, verbal, tactile).
- Provide adequate contrast between essential information and its surroundings.

- Maximize legibility of essential information.
- Give clear, simple instructions.

TOLERANCE FOR ERROR Instruction is designed for a variation in individual student learning pace and prerequisite skills. Therefore, physical educators should do the following:

- Anticipate variation in individual student learning pace and prerequisite skills.
- Arrange elements to minimize hazards and errors—most used elements should be most accessible; hazardous elements should be eliminated, isolated, or shielded.
- Provide fail-safe features.

LOW PHYSICAL EFFORT Instruction is designed to minimize nonessential physical effort in order to allow maximum attention to learning. (Note: This principle does not apply when physical effort is integral to essential requirements of a course.) Therefore, physical educators should do the following:

- Allow the student to maintain a neutral body position when resting.
- Choose activities that use reasonable operating forces.
- Minimize unnecessary repetitive actions.

SIZE AND SPACE FOR APPROACH AND USE Instruction is designed with consideration for appropriate size and space for approach, reach, manipulations, and use, regardless of a student's body size, posture, mobility, and communication needs. Therefore, physical educators should do the following:

- Provide a clear line of sight to important elements for any seated, standing, or moving user.
- Make all components easy to reach for any seated, standing, or moving user.
- Accommodate variations in hand and grip size.

A COMMUNITY OF LEARNERS The instructional environment promotes interaction and communication among students and between students and teachers. Therefore, when choosing groups, physical educators should carefully consider the following:

- The purpose of the activity
- The movement skills of individuals
- The behavioral challenges of individuals

INSTRUCTIONAL CLIMATE Instruction is designed to be welcoming and inclusive. High expectations are espoused for all students. Therefore, physical educators should do the following:

- Provide clarity regarding the need for class members to respect diversity.
- Encourage students to discuss any special learning needs with the teacher.
- Match the instructional approach to the skills of the learners and the goals of the activity.

Principles for UDL

The following is an overview of the three underlying principles of UDL: engagement, representation, and action and expression. As you read about these principles, keep in mind that within the framework of UDL, an individual is constantly moving toward autonomy and self-direction, progressively requiring less external support.

PROVIDE MULTIPLE MEANS OF ENGAGEMENT A crucial first step for all learners is that they become excited about the enterprise—that is, they become fired up and ready to go. To do this well, educators must get learners interested in the first place, sustain that interest, and, finally, help them develop personal coping skills and strategies, self-assess, and reflect on their performance. Consistent with the underlying principle of UDL is the recognition that learners differ significantly in terms of how they can be motivated to learn. Given differences in culture, background knowledge, socioeconomic level, and neurology, what works well for one student may have the opposite effect on another. For example, whereas some learners appreciate spontaneity and novelty, others find this approach to be upsetting, preferring a set schedule and consistent routines. It is imperative that when we develop avenues of engagement, we look at students individually, as opposed to lumping them together based on a diagnosis. Offering an array of options for engendering and maintaining engagement is imperative; no one approach works for everyone.

PROVIDE MULTIPLE MEANS OF REPRESENTATION As with effectively becoming—and remaining—engaged with a particular activity or unit of instruction, the UDL approach recognizes and embraces the fact that individual learners perceive and comprehend information in different ways. Cultural differences, prior experiences (or lack thereof), and, of course, sensory disabilities (e.g., deafness or blindness) strongly influence the ways students understand instruction. Of course, irrespective of a student's culture or sensory capabilities, one means of representation simply might be more effective than another. Giselle might respond well to being physically guided while being told which racket to pick up, whereas the same approach could be counterproductive for Charisse, who becomes agitated and loses concentration when touched. Although a student might not react negatively to information being presented through a certain modality (e.g., a photograph of a badminton racket being shown to the student), another means of representation (holding the actual racket where the student can see it) may allow the information to be grasped more efficiently or more quickly.

Given the widespread use of computerized devices (including tablets and smartphones), there are many options available to learners. When using computerized aids, an educator can vary the size, contrast, color, font, and layout of visual materials. Additionally, if auditory information is being presented, the volume, rate of speech, and complexity of the language can be modified (of course, this applies to actual live teaching done by the physical educator as well). However, despite the availability of these options, they are not always appropriately used. It is important that the teacher and the student work together, when possible, to identify the best options for a given learner.

PROVIDE MULTIPLE MEANS OF ACTION AND EXPRESSION UDL recognizes that learners are very different one from the other and thus require options that allow them the best opportunity for growth and learning. Multiple means of action and expression give students an array of different ways to demonstrate that they have mastered course content, ranging from high-tech to low-tech to "no-tech." For example, Martha, who has limited strength and coordination, would benefit from playing tennis with a lighter racket and heavier tennis balls that have less bounce. Charisse, who behaves impulsively and struggles with the strategic and organizational requirements of an activity (say, developing a gymnastics floor routine), could use a graphic organizer to sketch out the routine. Although these tools could be particularly useful for a group of learners, the environmental modifications work for everyone. Options should be presented in such a way that individuals aren't singled out and potentially embarrassed. Importantly, UDL recognizes that learners' abilities aren't static; change, whether for the short or long term, is the rule rather than the exception. For example, although a low-bouncing, slower tennis ball was the best choice for Martha during Thursday's class, by the following class, she had mastered her backswing and was now motivated to use a tennis ball that matched her improved skill.

Another example of providing multiple means of action and expression involves John, who wants to begin an individualized exercise program by joining a health club located seven miles away from his house. However, traveling to the health club requires taking two different buses, the cost of the club is prohibitive, and the level of staff training is minimal. Although John's teacher could point out these potential barriers to John, the UDL approach would advocate for teaching him how to recognize these barriers on his own. If John felt that, despite these challenges, he really wanted to pursue joining this club, his teacher would work with him to plan to reach his goal. Some practical strategies include providing checklists, project planning templates, or guides in order to break the long-term goal into manageable short-term objectives. For all learners, but especially those who struggle with their learning, having accessible, timely, informative, and explicit feedback is imperative to know whether the path they're taking toward fitness is working—and if so, to what degree?

Differentiated Instruction

For optimal learning to take place, teachers must differentiate their approach based on the unique skills and deficits a student presents. The skilled educator keeps in mind the learner's abilities and makes changes in the instruction on an individual (that is, differentiated) basis. Many aspects of the learning process can be modified to enhance instruction (Tomlinson & McTighe, 2006). For example, when Juan comes up to bat in a softball game, his inability to clearly see the pitched ball while standing at the plate makes it tough for him to drive the ball, even though his timing and eye–hand coordination are excellent. It makes sense at this time to use a slightly larger ball with red seams so that Juan can see it clearly—that's all he needs to be successful in the game.

Although the educational philosophies of UDL and differentiated instruction share much in common, there are some differences. Novak (2017) thoughtfully explains these differences with an analogy of preparing two meals: With UDL, you prepare a buffet for *all* of your students, with a variety of options available to everyone. Transferred to our gymnasium, every student may have the option of hitting a ball off a tee, pitched by a classmate, or pitched by the teacher. Students can also choose to hit an oversized softball, a regulation softball, or a baseball. What is critical to recognize is that the individual student (with guidance, as necessary) has a choice regarding how they will best learn, making them more creative and self-directed in their learning. Conversely, differentiated instruction would have the cook (the physical education teacher) preparing 30 different meals. You manage the options and decide which adaptation is most appropriate for a given student, removing autonomy and moving away from self-direction—not to mention, it is exhausting to prepare 30 different meals!

Evidence-Based Practices

As discussed earlier in this chapter, it is essential that physical educators teach in a fashion that allows learners to achieve their potential. To do so, the Individuals with Disabilities Education Act (IDEA) encourages the use of evidence-based practice, which means carefully gathering data to help decide what to teach and how that teaching should take place, as well as using programs and strategies that have demonstrated effectiveness. Over the past three or four decades, many educational interventions have been proposed that do not have strong support with regard to their effectiveness. By definition, students with unique needs are at greater risk than the general population and, thus, teachers must be thoughtful and rigorous when deciding which approaches they adopt.

Response to Intervention

Because of a need to identify students who may be at educational risk, a framework referred to as **response to intervention** (RTI) has been advocated. Consistent with an emphasis on individualized, evidenced-based instruction, RTI carefully integrates assessment and intervention in such a way that student learning is maximized and behavior problems are minimized from an early age. When appropriately implemented, RTI has the potential to improve the educational experiences and learning of all students and to identify those learners who are at risk for failure at a much earlier point. This relatively recent option is in accordance with the 2004 reauthorization of IDEA.

Although much about RTI is appealing for the general physical educator as well as the adapted physical education specialist, a major selling point is the early use of valid and reliable curriculum-based assessments that inform specific interventions. Equally important, the RTI approach requires ongoing monitoring to ensure that teaching is resulting in improvements and that interventions are implemented appropriately. This has been referred to by RTI adherents as *continuous progress monitoring*. If adequate progress is not being demonstrated (and the interventions have been carried out appropriately), modifications to either the instructional approach or the goals must be made. These points are, of course, in accord with evidence-based practice, as previously discussed in this chapter.

An ancillary benefit of the RTI model is that, along with a much earlier identification of students at risk, learning deficits will be effectively addressed within a general education placement—that is, in an inclusive classroom setting along with typically developing peers. If there is a need for a more intensive educational approach, often involving a lower student-to-teacher ratio, it is provided within the RTI framework. Generally, needs are addressed within a three-tiered intervention approach (Friend, 2008; Mellard & Johnson, 2007) wherein more intensive and structured interventions are provided based on well-thought-out assessment data. This important component of RTI is outlined in figure 7.1. With respect to physical education, the three-tiered intervention approach would work in the following way:

1. All students in the school would be given valid and reliable movement evaluations. Based on this initial screening, a subset of at-risk students would be identified. These students would receive personalized movement instruction within the general physical education setting (tier 1), with their progress on deficient areas being monitored weekly for five to eight weeks. If progress is low after this period of research-based instruction, the student will enter tier 2. Between 75 and 85 percent of students are in tier 1.

2. Within tier 2, students receive extensive small-group instruction, along with the instruction previously given within tier 1. This small-group instruction will take place for 10 to 20 weeks, with progress assessed weekly. If progress is strong, the student will once again be provided with tier 1 services. If students are not maintaining an appropriate rate of improvement in tier 1, they will be provided with tier 2 services again.

3. If a student's response to tier 2 intervention is not adequate—as demonstrated by a lack of

improvement on valid and reliable weekly assessments—the student then receives a comprehensive evaluation involving a multidisciplinary team. The result of this evaluation may indicate a need for tier 3 instruction. Within tier 3, a more intensive instructional program is put into place, often involving one-to-one interventions outside of the general education setting in accord with an IEP. In many cases, tier 3 interventions are done in addition to the instruction given within the general education setting (tier 1).

As pointed out by Winnick (personal communication, August 20, 2009), these principles may sound familiar to physical educators who have for many years thoughtfully applied a systematic, problem-solving approach to teaching adapted physical education. This approach involves screening to determine if there is a problem, defining and analyzing the problem, developing an intervention plan, and regularly evaluating whether the plan has been effective. What the RTI approach offers is a clear framework to work within.

It is evident from the literature associated with special education that RTI has predominantly addressed academic performance and social behavior. However, the principles apply equally to the physical education setting, and physical educators must be familiar with RTI as behavioral intervention plans are involved in physical education. Although RTI has largely not been emphasized in physical education, its principles may be employed in the development of movement skills.

Historically, physical educators have been involved in universal assessment and screening within the general physical education setting. The evolving practices associated with RTI, developed to more appropriately meet the needs of students, deserve serious consideration and study on the part of physical educators.

Assistive Technology

It has been observed that, although the explosive growth in assistive technology over the course of the 21st century has made things for people without disabilities significantly *easier*, it has made things for people with disabilities *possible*. Although this may sound somewhat overstated, educators—including those working in adapted physical education—have begun to recognize how these nascent technologies enable students to more easily capitalize on their strengths and minimize their shortcomings, thus allowing for significantly increased learning and functional independence within increasingly inclusive environments. Indeed, the appropriate use of technology is now

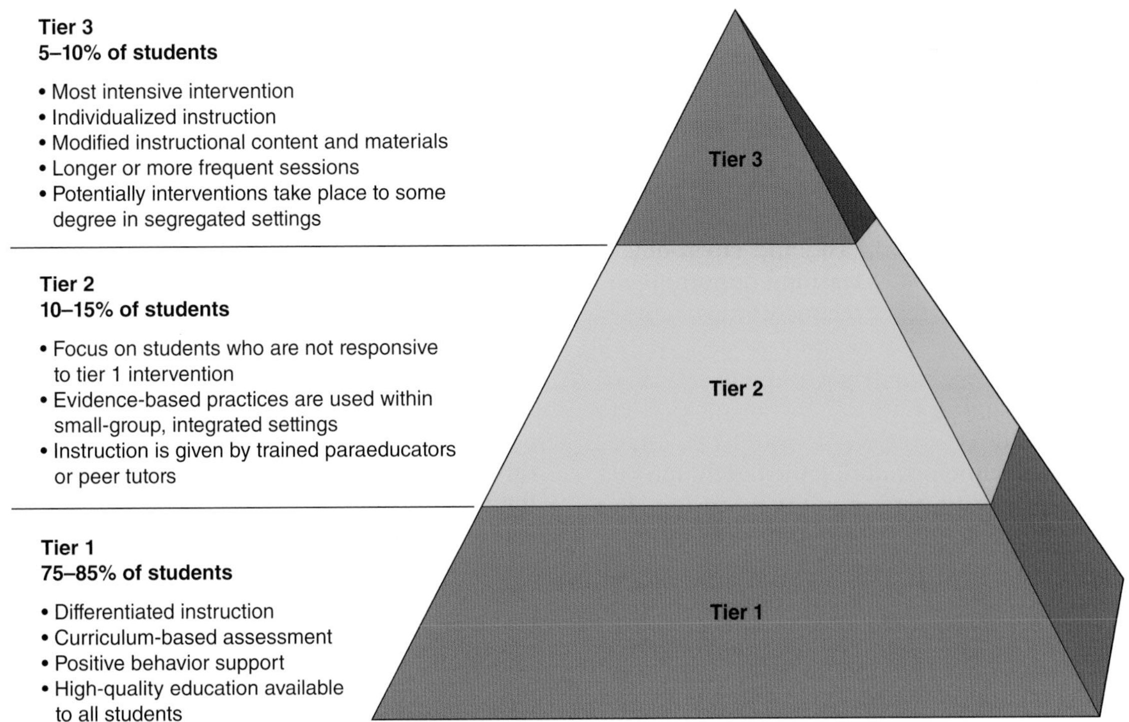

Tier 3
5–10% of students
• Most intensive intervention
• Individualized instruction
• Modified instructional content and materials
• Longer or more frequent sessions
• Potentially interventions take place to some degree in segregated settings
Tier 2
10–15% of students
• Focus on students who are not responsive to tier 1 intervention
• Evidence-based practices are used within small-group, integrated settings
• Instruction is given by trained paraeducators or peer tutors
Tier 1
75–85% of students
• Differentiated instruction
• Curriculum-based assessment
• Positive behavior support
• High-quality education available to all students
Tier 3
Tier 2
Tier 1

FIGURE 7.1 The three-tiered approach of the RTI model.

considered an important component within a system of individualized supports for students with identifiable disabilities. Broadly defined, **assistive technology** refers to any equipment, device, or system, whether acquired commercially, modified, or customized, that is used to maintain or improve the functional abilities of individuals with disabilities as well as the training of individuals to effectively use this equipment.

Although the proliferation of powerful mobile computing devices such as smartphones and computer tablets might have one believe that these are the only assistive technology devices to consider, this is not the case. Indeed, there is an assistive technology continuum that runs the gamut from "low-tech" solutions (e.g., Velcro softball mitts or beep baseballs) to "medium-tech" solutions (e.g., relatively complicated mechanical items such as racing wheelchairs) to the aforementioned "high-tech" devices (e.g., smartphones, tablets, or interactive Smart Boards). Some in the educational field believe that the appropriate approach is to employ assistive technology on an as-needed basis, beginning at the low-tech end of the scale and moving up the continuum only as needed. Others, however, see the advances in computerized devices as tremendously valuable tools in the teaching of motor, affective, and cognitive skills to learners with and without identifiable disabilities (Baert & Feith, 2014; Roth, 2013).

Regardless of the tech level or specific type of assistive technology being contemplated, for it to be used effectively, the dynamic interaction among the individual, the task, the environment, and the technology itself must be carefully examined (Raskind & Bryant, 2002). This perspective aligns closely to that of Newell (1986), who stressed the importance of individual, task, and environment variables when designing learning opportunities. Individualizing the use of technology, as in other areas of teaching, is of paramount importance. In order to assess whether a particular type of technology is appropriate for a given student, it is imperative to directly observe the student interacting with the technology during the task of interest (e.g., using a heart rate monitor to ensure that work was being done within a safe and health-promoting zone) in a real-world context (during physical education class, on the indoor track). As the student is introduced to and experiments with the technology (in our example, the heart rate monitor), one should observe (1) the interest and comfort level demonstrated; (2) the degree of ease in learning about and using the technology; (3) the degree to which this technology aligns with the student's strengths, and (4) the extent to which the student can use this technology independently. If a student doesn't show aptitude (or interest) in the technology but the teacher believes that using it is in the student's best interest, all is not lost. Here is where—as in other pedagogical areas—progressive and appropriate learning experiences should be designed and implemented (Baert & Feith, 2014).

Although assistive technologies are intuitively appealing and hold great promise, for them to be effectively used in the physical education setting, a number of factors must be carefully examined (Alper & Raharinirina, 2006). These factors include the following:

1. *Setting.* Studies regarding the effective use of assistive technology have focused on their use in the general education classroom, with less research on any other settings, including the home, community, and gymnasium.
2. *Skills addressed.* The vast majority of studies have focused on the learning of academic subjects, such as math, reading, or writing, with significantly less emphasis on movement skills, communication, and social skills. In a related vein, skill maintenance and skill generalization require more investigation.
3. *Individual assessment.* In their review of the assistive technology literature, Alper and Raharinirina (2006) noted that individualized preassessment was seldom done before the selection and introduction of a particular device. This is particularly troublesome given that a lack of assessment was linked to abandonment of devices and created an obstacle to the effective use of technology.
4. *Family involvement.* It is imperative that families be supported by professionals and involved in the ongoing use of technology by their child. Too frequently, family members report a lack of respect for their contributions and concerns.

It should be noted that practitioners, as well as those teaching in higher education, have embraced the potential power of assistive technology. Applications (apps) designed specifically for effectively educating people with identifiable disabilities have proliferated, with new programs being developed on an almost daily basis. These apps address such important pedagogical areas as (1) making teaching more efficient, (2) enhancing instruction, (3) engaging learners, (4) monitoring and reinforcing behavior, and (5) professional development.

Curricular Options: What to Teach?

Along with a thorough understanding of *how* to effectively teach students with disabilities come the equally important decisions regarding *what* should be taught. One way to address individual differences, briefly discussed in chapter 2, is to individualize and formalize objectives and activities.

Given that a significant number of students with disabilities are taught with their typically developing peers in inclusive physical education settings, curricular modifications are often appropriate. Four categories have been suggested (after Block, 2016) that allow for the meaningful integration of students with unique needs: (1) the same curriculum, (2) multilevel curriculum, (3) overlapped curriculum, and (4) different curriculum. The *same curriculum* suggests that students with disabilities follow a curriculum identical to that of their typically developing peers, although their objectives might be different from those of the other students. Within the *multilevel curriculum* option, the student with a disability follows the general physical education curriculum with activity modifications made as necessary (e.g., if a student with Down syndrome is playing a small-sided game of volleyball, she might serve from a distance closer to the net than regulation). Master teachers generally have activity modifications or options available for all students, thus appropriately challenging them at their own developmental level. In this way, everyone in the class is accommodated without anyone being singled out.

An *overlapped curriculum* is used, often, for students with more severe disabilities whose unique IEP goals don't match up precisely with what is being taught in the general education curriculum. When using an overlapped curriculum, the students with identifiable disabilities work on their own related objectives, as detailed in their IEP. Nevertheless, for ethical and pedagogical reasons, having *all* students in the same physical space is strongly recommended. For example, Peter, a sixth-grade student with cerebral palsy, is working on the grasp and release of a tennis ball to knock down three bowling pins, whereas the other students are rolling plastic bowling balls down a 15-foot (4.6-meter) alley to knock down 10 bowling pins. In this example, Peter's unique IEP objective (working on grasp and release) overlaps with bowling, a functional, age-appropriate leisure skill that is part of the general sixth-grade physical education curriculum. The activity Peter is doing is different but related to what the other students are doing—that is, all students are working on bowling tasks.

When a student's unique physical education needs cannot be safely and meaningfully overlapped with the general physical education curriculum, work on IEP objectives might have to take place separately from the main physical education activity. In this case, the student with a disability works on a *different curriculum* than the one pursued by other students in the class. For example, while classmates are playing small-sided games of ultimate Frisbee, the student with a disability is working on upper body strength through an individualized weight training program. This is not necessarily an all-or-nothing proposition; alternative activities might be necessary for part of the curriculum but not for others. Block (2016) has suggested that students without disabilities rotate away from their activities and take part in the alternative activity (e.g., weight training) for a set amount of time. In this way, all students receive the benefit of interacting with their peers while working on meaningful activities. As always, teachers must carefully examine task, environmental, and performer variables when deciding which curricular approach is the most appropriate for a given student at a given time.

A fundamental question related to curriculum concerns whether specific functional, age-appropriate movement skills should be the focus of instruction (a **top-down approach** to teaching) or whether it is more appropriate to follow a developmentally focused curriculum (a **bottom-up approach**). Adapted physical education researchers and practitioners advocating the top-down approach target the movement skills a person needs to learn in order to independently enjoy community recreation. The curricular emphasis is on teaching age-appropriate leisure skills valued by the person, the person's family, and the community at large. The learner's abilities and shortcomings with regard to the skill being taught are carefully examined, and educational experiences are designed to achieve the end result. For example, if a valued leisure skill for Shannon is playing two-on-two basketball on the driveway with her dad, mom, and sister, all the subskills needed to play (e.g., dribble, pass, shoot, rebound, and defend) will be carefully examined in relation to Shannon's demonstrated abilities. If Shannon needs to work on passing the ball accurately, this skill will be directly taught. Teaching age-appropriate and valued leisure skills in real-world contexts is a hallmark of the top-down approach.

Those who advocate a bottom-up perspective (also called a **developmental approach**) also believe that the ultimate goal of adapted physical education is to prepare students to independently engage in recreational and sport skills. Graham and colleagues (2012), among others, view the bottom-up approach as providing students with a broad foundation of fundamental movement skills during the elementary years. These foundational skills are then combined into games, dance, and athletics during the middle and high school years. Although the focus is on providing instruction in many developmentally appropriate movement skills, if a student is considered at risk, a physical education teacher using the bottom-up approach will intervene earlier rather than later in order to identify the building blocks (neurological, reflexive, or motor) that are lacking and select activities to remedy the observed shortcomings; this will enable participation in chronologically and developmentally appropriate activities. To return to the earlier example, the teacher using a bottom-up approach must be sure that Shannon has mastered the locomotor and object-control abilities important for success in basketball before she plays a two-on-two game.

As is often the case when teaching adapted physical education, an open-minded and eclectic approach is recommended. If the student is very young and the disability (or delay) is minimal, the bottom-up approach might be best. Conversely, if a student has significant physical or intellectual deficits, spending extensive time on the fundamental building blocks likely means the student will not be taking part in meaningful, socially valued activities with typically developing peers. When making decisions about what to teach, always keep in mind individual characteristics and values as well as the unique ecology surrounding the learner.

Activity Modifications

When deciding on the most appropriate curricular approach and activities to meet the student's learning goals, it might become apparent that modifications are necessary for the student to participate successfully. Lieberman and Houston-Wilson (2017) have suggested that **activity modifications** can be broken down into four categories: equipment, rules, environment, and instruction. The game of softball provides examples of activity modifications for students with various disabilities. If a student has below-average intellectual abilities, the rules might be simplified, whereas for those with visual impairments, the base paths could have a different texture than the field, and the ball and bases might include auditory devices. If a student struggles with muscular strength, the bat or ball could be lighter; for students who have decreased coordination or cardiorespiratory fitness, reducing the distance between bases could help; and modified rules for making outs might help players with limited mobility to compete at their highest level of ability.

Modifications do not have to affect every component of an activity; they should be limited to those necessary to meet individual needs. Modifications to equipment, rules, or activity parameters must be made cautiously and carefully, keeping in mind the educational experiences of both the students for whom the modifications are being made and their classmates. When modifying an activity, the educator should try to stay as close to the traditional activity as possible. The Application Example sidebar describes an activity modification for a student with a visual impairment in an archery class.

Teaching Style

As used in this chapter, the term *teaching style* refers to how the teacher organizes and delivers instruction to learners. There is no one best style; rather, effective instructors adapt their instruction to variables that include personal skills and preferences, the nature of the content, the characteristics of the learners, and the teaching context. As Siedentop and Tannehill (2000) point out, teachers perform better when they are comfortable with and believe in the style being used. For example, if instructors feel pressured to use a more student-directed approach but are not convinced of its efficacy, teaching results will likely suffer. This is not to suggest that teachers should not become familiar and skilled with teaching styles with which they are less comfortable. On the contrary, being limited to a narrow range of style options (generally, the more directive, teacher-mediated approaches) may hinder a learner's development of important skills. However, experimentation and practice in this area should be the result of professional development and reflection, not an administrative directive.

An array of student and teacher variables, curricular considerations, and environmental factors can affect the teaching and learning enterprise. Given this reality, it is important that teachers not only have the pedagogical skills to effectively deal with this complexity but have a continuum of carefully considered options regarding teaching styles and formats. Indeed, a continuum of options has been developed, refined, and used extensively for

Application Example

Modifying an Activity to Include a Student With a Visual Impairment

SETTING

High school physical education class

STUDENT

A 17-year-old who is legally blind, with a visual acuity of 20/200

ISSUE

Modifications for safe and successful inclusion of a student with a visual impairment into an indoor archery unit

APPLICATION

After discussion among the physical education teacher, the student with the visual impairment, and class members, the following policies are instituted:

- Arrows for the student with visual impairment will be identified with braille tape by the arrow notch.
- A special target face with textured scoring areas will be used.
- A raised rope will be used by all students as the shooting line.
- The archer with visual impairment will use an *L*-shaped wood template to align his feet and the target.
- A tape recorder will be attached to the back of the target to give auditory direction for the archer.
- A rope will be attached to the target and foot templates will be placed on the ground to allow independent movement between the target and the shooting line.
- No one will go past the shooting line until an audible signal to retrieve arrows is given.
- Classmates will assist with scoring and finding stray arrows when asked by the student with visual impairment.

more than 50 years. Referred to as the *spectrum of teaching styles*, this model was developed by Muska Mosston in 1966 and has been subsequently revised and refined by Mosston and Ashworth, most recently in 2004 (Goldberger et al., 2012). In their retrospective analysis of Mosston's work, Goldberger and colleagues (2012) noted that the spectrum of teaching styles provides

> . . . a comprehensive array of alternative teaching approaches, or as we call them teaching styles, from which to select. No teaching style is inherently better or worse than another. Rather each, because of the unique learning conditions it fosters, is either more or less appropriate given the purposes, the context in which it is presented, and the learners involved. (p. 268)

There are 11 distinct teaching styles within the spectrum model (see table 7.1) on a continuum from more directed, teacher-mediated instructional formats (command, practice or task, reciprocal, self-check, and inclusion or invitation) to student-mediated instructional formats (guided discovery, convergent discovery, divergent discovery, learner designed, learner initiated, and self-teaching). In the teacher-mediated formats (also referred to as *reproductive styles*), the student "reproduces" knowledge or actions taught by the teacher, who makes most, if not all, of the pedagogical decisions in terms of what, when, where, and how a skill will be done. Conversely, in the student-mediated formats (also called *productive styles*), the student has a much more active role in deciding what will be done, along with when, where, and how the activities will be done. Within the productive formats, "the students discover and create new knowledge and play increasingly active roles with regard to aspects of decision making" (Jaakkola & Watt, 2011, p. 214)

Within the spectrum model, it is evident that certain content and objectives are more effectively taught via one teaching style than another. If, for example, a goal is to teach students how to throw a Frisbee using a backhand motion and a forehand motion (the flick), a command style would probably be the most appropriate approach. If, later in the unit, the objective is to decide which defensive play is most appropriate, a convergent discovery style might be most effective. Clearly, teaching basic movement skills for a given activity is a different proposition than teaching higher-level strategies (Siedentop & Tannehill, 2000).

However, there is not a single correct way to solve a movement task. Although a teacher could tell the student approaching the tennis net that she should use a backhand slice, keeping the ball low (a teacher-mediated, command approach), it has been suggested that students who learn through active experimentation are potentially more invested in their learning and retain the learning longer. Posing a "movement problem" to the student (a student-mediated, convergent inquiry approach) might be more effective. However, the skill and motivational level of the learner must be considered. Additionally, the domain (cognitive, affective, or psychomotor) that is being emphasized must be considered. If, for example, students are working together to solve a movement task, a student-directed style, such as learner designed, might be most appropriate.

Another important consideration when choosing a particular teaching style is the learner's unique characteristics, particularly when learners have identifiable disabilities. If inattention or inappropriate behavior is an issue, a teacher-mediated instructional format might be the best approach. Conversely, students who have a physical disability might benefit more from a student-mediated instructional format that allows them to discover effective solutions themselves (with support, as needed). However, teachers should take care not to jump to conclusions. An intellectual disability, for example, is not a sufficient reason to rule out a more student-centered teaching style.

Ultimately, when it comes to choosing a teaching style, teacher attributes, comfort level, lesson goals, and learner attributes all must be considered. Although it can be challenging, using multiple styles within a given class is frequently the most effective approach. For example, while the majority of the class might be exploring how angling a Frisbee alters how it flies through the air (convergent discovery), a student with an intellectual disability might be receiving direct instruction (command style) on a backhand throw. As a second example, while most of the class is learning how to serve a tennis ball (command style), one student in a wheelchair, a second with cerebral palsy, and a third whose injured back does not allow a turn of the shoulders might be encouraged to discover unique patterns that allow for fast and accurate serves (divergent discovery). Although, as mentioned previously, we generalize at our peril, in general, the more severe the intellectual disability, the more direct the teaching style.

The effectiveness of a teaching style ultimately depends on the learner and learning outcomes. Is there a considerable amount of academic learning time? Do students demonstrate a willingness to take part in the activities? Are goals of the unit being met? Ongoing program assessment regarding these questions aids in choosing the best styles of teaching.

Along with teaching style, the instructional and managerial tone of the physical education class must also be carefully considered. The tone is independent of both style and format and can range from punitive to positive. Some teachers of adapted physical education would be considered upbeat and excited, whereas others would be best described as relaxed. Teachers might be extremely demanding or laid back. Their tone might even vary within and between classes, depending on the context or personal events that have taken place outside of the gymnasium.

The tone of a given class might be described using terms such as *businesslike*, *demanding*, *aloof*, *warm*, or *caring*. It is, of course, possible to be effective using a businesslike demeanor. It is also possible to be caring and nurturing and equally effective. Physical educators working with students with unique needs must ensure that the tone in the classroom, as well as in small-group settings and individual interactions, is accurately recognized. Furthermore, they should be aware of the effect—both positive and negative—that tone has on the students. If a particular tone is ineffective for a given student, the teacher should be prepared to modify it. For example, a teacher might accurately perceive himself as nurturing and caring. However, a laid-back approach might result in some students being off task because they perceive (mistakenly) that it's okay to goof around because Mr. C doesn't mind. To state this simply, the tone affects student achievement and overall class climate, as well as students' desire to spend time in physical education.

TABLE 7.1 Teaching Styles

Teacher-mediated instructional formats (reproductive styles)	Student-mediated instructional formats (productive styles)
Command Teacher sets up class in orderly manner, makes all decisions, and uses direct instructions (e.g., location, start and stop time, pace, demonstration) Learner responds to instructions Teacher circulates to give feedback	**Guided discovery** Teacher guides students through a series of problems in which students make decisions to arrive at solutions Each step is based on the response to previous step Teacher waits for learner's response and offers frequent feedback or clues
Practice or task Learner performs tasks prescribed by teacher, but learner determines pace, rhythm, start, stop, interval Teacher circulates to give individual feedback Designed for individual practice	**Convergent discovery** Teacher frames a question that has a number of solutions Learner controls the process of learning by using trial and error and logic Learner discovers alternative answers to the posed question
Reciprocal Class is organized in pairs or trios Learners use task cards or criteria sheets designed by teacher Student observer gives feedback, other student performs the skill, observer, if necessary, feeds object to performer Teacher communicates with observers only	**Divergent discovery** Learner is engaged in cooperative learning to discover a number of solutions to a problem Teacher encourages responses, does not make judgments
Self-check Learners assess themselves in comparison to teacher-established criteria sheets (e.g., individual skills, target games, fitness results) Teacher provides feedback at end of class	**Learner designed** Teacher identifies a broad problem or issue Learners construct a plan of action to solve the problem, including the performance criteria
Inclusion or invitation Multiple levels of performance of the same task allow for success of all learners and accommodate individual skill differences Student chooses the level of performance based on perceived ability Student performs self-assessment Teacher provides feedback regarding the decision-making process, not chosen level	**Learner initiated** Learner identifies the focus area Learner designs own learning program Learner meets occasionally with the teacher to discuss progress
	Self-teaching Program developed by the learner based on physical and cognitive abilities Highly individualistic, not suited to all learners Learner designs the questions and the solutions Teacher observes, guides, and provides individual conferences

Adapted from Mosston and Ashworth (2002).

Class Format

Class format is an important instructional consideration related to teaching style (Block, 2016; Graham et al., 2012). This section presents nine formats that have been effectively used in teaching adapted physical education.

ONE-TO-ONE INSTRUCTION To promote acquisition, maintenance, and generalization of skills, students receiving adapted physical education sometimes require a one-to-one student-to-teacher ratio. This format allows for a highly individualized teaching session as well as multiple opportunities for the learner to respond. An approach to one-to-one instruction that is extremely successful in teaching students with more severe disabilities is discrete trial training (DTT) (Sturmey & Fitzer, 2007). Later in this chapter, this approach is presented in considerable depth. In physical education settings, one-to-one instruction can be implemented by the physical education teacher, a trained teaching assistant, a parent, or a trained peer tutor. In order to generalize the learning to other situations, materials, and individuals, DTT is frequently combined with naturalistic approaches such as incidental learning (Lovaas, 2003).

SMALL-GROUP INSTRUCTION Within a small-group instruction format, 2 to 10 students generally work with one teacher or teaching assistant. This format allows for more independent work and the opportunity to teach students how to interact appropriately with their peers.

LARGE-GROUP INSTRUCTION In this format, the entire class participates at the same time under the direction of one or more teachers or teaching assistants. Clearly, it is of great importance to monitor a given student's progress within a large-group format in order to offer the appropriate amount and type of individualized support.

MIXED-GROUP INSTRUCTION Within a mixed-group approach, a variety of formats are used during the same class session. This format is particularly effective when students demonstrate different learning characteristics or are working toward different instructional objectives.

PEER TEACHING OR TUTORING When peer teaching or tutoring takes place, students are taught by their more highly skilled classmates or those from other classes. A second approach—classwide peer tutoring or reciprocal teaching—uses all students in the class as both tutors and tutees.

SELF-PACED INDEPENDENT WORK As the name of this format suggests, self-paced independent work involves students working on their personal goals mostly by themselves. Often, task cards or input from the teacher or teaching assistant helps keep the students focused and on task. In conjunction with task cards, communication boards and visual schedules are particularly effective for students with autism. These approaches are discussed in more depth in chapter 10.

COOPERATIVE LEARNING When students use cooperative learning, subsets of students within a given class work together to accomplish shared goals. This format can be particularly effective when the instructional objectives are affective or when they target the development of social skills.

REVERSE MAINSTREAMING In reverse mainstreaming, students without disabilities join their peers with unique needs in the self-contained class, taking part in movement activities along with them. Although not a substitute for meaningfully integrating students with unique needs into the general education setting, it is important that students with unique needs interact with their typically developing peers because these interactions benefit all students.

LEARNING STATIONS (TASK TEACHING) Learning stations allow a class of students to divide up to work on more than one task at the same time. Students are placed into small groups and assigned to a given station. On the teacher's command, or when students have completed specified activities, each group rotates to the next station. Learning stations are particularly effective when teaching a class of diverse learners at different stages of skill development, because stations can be designed to challenge students at their developmental level.

Generally, three or more stations are set up throughout the gym. Stations might involve related skills, such as the tasks involved in playing hockey (e.g., shooting, passing, stick handling, and goaltending), or they may involve unrelated skills, such as a station devoted to throwing and catching activities and another to jumping rope. Stations can be organized in a hierarchical, progressive fashion; as students progress in skill level, they move to a station requiring more ability for the given task. Conversely, the next station might not require any prerequisite skill. Regardless of the task setup, each station should accommodate students of varying skill levels by including individualized opportunities for learning through multiple challenges. For example, if juggling is the task at a station, there should be an opportunity to juggle one ball, two balls, or scarves. If serving a tennis ball is the task, students should have the opportunity to serve from 8 feet (2.4 meters) from the net, the service line, and the baseline. With multiple levels of performance, students have the opportunity to select their own entry level. There should also be multiple choices of implements (e.g., tennis racket vs. pickleball racket), target size (both service boxes or just one), and numbers of required repetitions. Well-designed stations provide options for students that relate to skill progressions and physical performance criteria. Opportunities to custom design individual stations—that is, offer multiple ways to accomplish a given task—make this approach particularly useful for learners with disabilities.

To let students know what is expected at a given station, effective teachers often supplement verbal descriptions with simple task cards or posters. These cards or posters might use words, pictures, or a combination of the two. (Of course, the developmental level of students in the class must be considered when these cards or posters are designed.) Figure 7.2 provides an example of a task poster.

Siedentop and Tannehill (2000) have also noted that under certain conditions, task teaching might occur without using multiple stations. For example, a single station, such as a climbing wall, could accommodate the entire class at one time. In this case, small groups might work on a set of related tasks, all occurring on the wall. Climbing stations might include a cargo net, climbing wall, and horizontal bouldering wall.

Discrete Trial Training With an Emphasis on Prompting

As noted earlier, when working with students with unique needs, teaching must be structured carefully, particularly for individual student interactions. Discrete trial training (DTT) lends itself well to carefully and appropriately individualizing instruction (Lovaas, 2003).

The discrete trial approach is based on principles of learning derived from ABA and, although used most extensively with children who have autism, it is effectively used with a range of students to teach language skills, social skills, and fundamental movement skills. A discrete trial is a structured method that usually involves teaching

FIGURE 7.2 Task poster for jumping.

in a one-on-one situation. Movement tasks are presented to the student in a series of separate, brief sessions. A trial can be repeated several times in a row, several times a day, or for several days until the skill at hand is mastered. An important benefit of a discrete trial is the precision and care with which each trial is conducted without sacrificing the important affective component. Specifically, the components of a discrete trial are (1) an instruction or environmental cue, (2) an optional prompt, (3) the learner's response, (4) consequences, and (5) an intertrial interval (see table 7.2 for an outline).

Effectively prompting learners is a "must have" skill for physical educators and will be presented here in some depth. Somewhat confusingly, the terms *cue* and *prompt* have been used interchangeably in the literature on special education and adapted physical education. In this chapter, we will use *prompts* to refer to environmental information—often verbal, visual, or physical—that is added to the student's environment to ensure a proper response. Frequently used in special education and adapted physical education to teach a range of skills, prompts are a crucial tool presented at the same time as or immediately following either instruction or the teacher's consequences. For example, telling the student "Serve the shuttlecock" during a badminton lesson would be a cue. If the instructor followed this cue with further verbal information ("Keep your arm and wrist very loose when you serve"), this would be a verbal prompt. After the student served, the teacher might show her the proper technique, thus providing a visual prompt.

A prompting system proven effective with many learners is the **system of least prompts** (Lieberman & Houston-Wilson, 2017). In this system, only as much verbal, visual, or physical assistance is given as is necessary for a task to be completed successfully. A system of least prompts is particularly effective in systematically reducing assistance when each of the major prompting levels (physical, visual, verbal, and no prompts) is further subdivided. For example, at the level of the physical prompt there are three degrees of physical assistance. This precision allows for the careful withdrawal (i.e., fading) of assistance, leading to more autonomous performance on the part of the learner, with the final objective of skilled **independent performance**. Following is an example of an effective system of least prompts (after Watkinson & Wall, 1982) in which prompts are broken down into four categories: physical, visual, verbal, and no prompts. At any of these levels, the competent teacher will give more or less assistance to a learner depending on the learner's skill level.

- *Physical prompts.* When using physical prompts, the teacher touches the student to provide physical assistance. For example, the teacher holds the student's wrist as a pendulum swing is used to roll a bowling ball, assisting the student's arm through the full range of motion. A reduced level of physical prompting might involve moving the student's arm only during the backswing. A further reduction might involve merely touching the student's wrist and applying slight pressure to indicate the direction of the backswing.

- *Visual prompts.* Visual prompts often involve a complete demonstration of the skill in question. In the bowling example, if the skill were rolling the bowling ball from a stationary position, the

TABLE 7.2 Components of a Discrete Trial

Elements	Characteristics to keep in mind
1. Instruction or environmental cue	• Salient, easy to discriminate • Appropriate to the task • Presented when the student is attending
2. Optional prompt	• Presented subsequent to or concurrent with instruction or with the teacher's consequences • Presented with an eye to fading
3. Learner's response	• Either correct, incorrect, or no response • Must be in response to the instruction or environmental cue
4. Consequences	• Applied consistently • Applied unambiguously • Easy to discriminate
5. Intertrial interval	3-5 seconds

teacher would demonstrate the complete skill, including the initial body position, backswing, follow-through, and release of the ball. As the learner's skill increased, less visual information would be given; for example, the teacher might demonstrate only the follow-through. Still less visual information might involve just pointing to the student's knees as a reminder to get into a deeper crouch.

- *Verbal prompts.* Verbal prompts include a sound, word, or instruction to focus the student's attention on the key features of the movements required to complete a skill. As with physical and visual prompts, the physical education teacher might give more or less verbal information, depending on the skill level of the learner. In the bowling example, a high degree of verbal prompting would involve a complete description of how to bowl: "Peter, I want you to bend your knees and then smoothly swing your arm backward and then forward." A reduced level of verbal prompt might involve merely a reference to the skill to be performed: "Peter, it's your turn to bowl." A further reduction of verbal prompts would be a more general indication that it's Peter's turn to bowl or a motivating phrase: "Peter, what do you do now?" or "One, two, three, go!"
- *No prompts.* At this level, the teacher doesn't use a physical, visual, or verbal prompt to help the student perform the skill; rather, the environment is set up to elicit the targeted skill. One way of eliciting the skill is to place an object in the environment that indirectly encourages performance of the skill. For instance, the student enters the bowling alley from a direction that brings him alongside the bowling ball rack, prompting him to pick up the ball and move to the correct lane. Another example would be having the student watch a peer correctly perform the skill before performing it himself.

These prompting categories are not mutually exclusive. Often, verbal prompts are paired with demonstrations or with physical prompts. Similarly, physical and visual prompts can be paired. In any case, the teacher must remember that that assistance should be systematically reduced—skilled independent performance is the goal.

To prompt a student effectively, the following guidelines should be kept in mind.

1. Use prompts that are meaningful to the student. Consider the learner's characteristics (skill level, preferred modality, specific disability). For example, if a student is more receptive to visual prompts than to physical prompts, focus on effectively using visual prompts. If a student is Deaf or hard of hearing, the emphasis might be on visual or physical prompts.
2. Be careful not to underprompt, which might lead to errors on the part of the learner.
3. Do not overprompt, because students might become reliant on prompts, thus hindering the development of an independently skilled performance. If assistance is not needed, do not give it.
4. Focus the learner's attention on the task. Some learners attend to the prompt being given instead of the task.
5. Make sure the prompt is effective. An ineffective prompt might delay or block learning.
6. Assess a student carefully before deciding on prompts—some students might need less assistance than first assumed.
7. Fade physical proximity. The distance between the student and teacher is an important variable influencing the effectiveness of a prompt and the independence of the learner. As the student becomes more independent, move progressively farther away.
8. Couple appropriate verbal prompting with other prompts. This way, when the physical or visual prompt is reduced or eliminated, the student still responds to the verbal command.
9. Fade verbal prompts. Although learners should eventually respond only to verbal instructions, true independence means performing activities without even verbal help.

Although not always needed within a discrete trial, the ability to effectively prompt and fade prompts is essential for effective teaching.

Task Analysis

Although people perform many activities of daily living without thinking about them much, in reality these are often quite complex, comprising many subtasks. Students with good cognitive, affective, and movement skills are usually able to learn these tasks from their daily interactions with the environment, especially when the environment is varied and thoughtfully arranged, but students with unique needs often require more systematic and planned learning experiences. When combined with effective prompting and reinforcement, task analysis is a powerful strategy to improve the learning of students with unique needs.

Although task analysis involves the careful examination of the factors or skills involved in the performance of a task, the term *task analysis* can be confusing because authors, researchers, and theorists have used it to refer to somewhat different processes. Whereas a traditional task analysis involves identifying components of an activity and then ordering the components from easiest to most difficult (Dunn & Leitschuh, 2014), Herkowitz (1978) uses the term *developmental task analysis* to examine the variety of task and environmental factors that influence motor performance. Short (2005) uses the term *biomechanical task analysis* to refer to the focal points of a continuous task, such as a long jump or overhand throw, and Broadhead (2007) uses the term *ecological task analysis* (ETA) to describe a system that, along with recognizing the importance of the task to be completed and the environment, gives equal weighting to the attributes of the learner. The following sections discuss traditional task analysis, biomechanical task analysis, developmental task analysis, and ecological task analysis.

Traditional Task Analysis

An effective approach to **traditional task analysis** involves separating the main task into several related subtasks (figure 7.3). These tasks are arranged into a sequence from easy to difficult, with short-term outcomes determined for each task and subtask. Once all the components of a subtask have been mastered, the learner then moves to the first component of the next subtask. provides a traditional task–subtask analysis for jumping rope.

In writing a traditional task analysis, the teacher must clearly identify the main skill and terminal objective as well as any prerequisite skills. All potential steps should be described in observable behavioral terms, thus aiding in the development of

Traditional Task Analysis for Jumping Rope

Main task: For Mary to jump rope for a full (overhead) turn four times without verbal cues

Prerequisite skills: Ability to jump, ability to stand erect

1. Jump over painted line (over and back) once without verbal cue.
   a. Walk line down and back heel-to-toe with verbal cue.
   b. Face line with toes and jump over once with verbal cue.
   c. Stand parallel with line and jump over and back without verbal cue.
2. Jump over still rope (over and back) twice without verbal cue.
   a. Face rope with toes, jump over once with verbal cue.
   b. Stand parallel with rope and jump over and back with verbal cue.
   c. Stand parallel with rope and jump over and back twice without verbal cue.
3. Jump over wiggly (snake) rope (over and back) 2 inches (5 cm) off ground without verbal cue.
   a. Jump over wiggly rope on ground once with verbal cue.
   b. Jump over wiggly rope 1 inch (2.5 cm) off ground over and back with verbal cue.
   c. Jump over wiggly rope 2 inches (5 cm) off ground over and back without verbal cue.
4. Jump over half-turned rope without verbal cue four times.
   a. Stand and jump on the back swing twice with verbal cue.
   b. Stand and jump on the forward and back swing twice with verbal cue.
   c. Stand and jump on the forward and back swing four times without verbal cue.
5. Jump rope a full turn overhead four times without verbal cue.
   a. Stand and jump once as the rope makes a full turn with verbal cue.
   b. Stand and jump twice as the rope makes a full turn with verbal cue.
   c. Stand and jump four times as the rope makes a full turn without verbal cue.

FIGURE 7.3 Traditional task analysis for jumping rope. Tasks are broken down into related subtasks.

appropriate IEPs and in the assessment of learning. The specificity provided by the task analysis allows for clarity and thus improved communication among IEP team members (e.g., adapted physical education consultant, general physical education teacher, and paraeducators).

There are many benefits to the traditional task analysis, particularly for students who struggle cognitively. First, there is clear recognition of progress by both student and teacher. With meaningful progress comes avoidance of frustration, reduction in off-task behavior, and maintenance of interest in the task on the part of the teacher and the student. As discussed earlier in this chapter, the maintenance of self-esteem is of considerable importance. From a teaching perspective, traditional task analysis allows teachers to see that they have more options than they originally believed, leading to a can-do perspective. Traditional task analysis allows the fading of prompts more quickly, thus increasing independence. Progress can be visually charted, aiding communication with parents and other team members and clearly demonstrating educational gains, in turn allowing for sound educational decisions. For example, have inappropriate objectives (e.g., given the amount of time available) been pursued? Is the order of components appropriate? Are more steps needed? Fewer steps? Increased level of prompting?

Although an extremely effective educational tool, especially for students with more severe disabilities, the traditional approach to task analysis has been criticized (Dunn & Leitschuh, 2014; Rich, 2000) because it might overemphasize the task while deemphasizing characteristics of the performer and the environment. Although it helps to look at an already available task analysis, it is important to come back to the idea of **individualized** teaching. Students will likely differ from one another in terms of the type of breakdown needed, the number of components (and their order) that works best for them, and the most effective manner in which the material is presented. Teachers must look at student strengths, shortcomings, and learning styles, and then be thoughtful and imaginative. The traditional approach to task analysis allows for the aforementioned individualization.

Biomechanical Task Analysis

Biomechanical task analysis has been described by Short (2005) as involving "the biomechanical components or 'focal points' of the task (usually in chronological sequence) so that an 'idealized performance' is described" (p. 59). A biomechanical task analysis for the one-handed backhand stroke in tennis might include the following focal points: (a) Watches ball throughout the skill; (b) moves quickly to ball using proper footwork; (c) brings racket back early in the sequence (early racket preparation); (d) positions body with hips and shoulders perpendicular to the net; (e) transfers weight to front foot at ball contact with rotation of hips and shoulders; (f) makes contact with ball ahead of hips; (g) keeps wrist firm; (h) holds opposite arm away from body for balance; and (i) follows through with hand finishing at or above the shoulder.

Using this analysis, the student would learn which aspects of the backhand he needs to work on. Assessment and instruction can take place in either a naturalistic environment (while playing or rallying) or in a more controlled environment (the ball being carefully fed to the student).

Although frequently used (and discussed in many books on adapted physical education and special education), both traditional task analysis and biomechanical task analysis have been criticized for two reasons. First, although traditional task analysis and biomechanical task analysis generally describe the components of the task accurately, they often do not take into account the capabilities and limitations of the learner. Second, the traditional approach to task analysis is primarily teacher directed, whereby the teacher specifies how a given skill is to be performed. Taylor and colleagues (2007) and others have championed an approach to task analysis in which individuals have more say with regard to how a given task is accomplished.

Developmental Task Analysis

Herkowitz (1978) has pointed out that a number of task and environmental factors can influence motor performance, which the adapted physical education teacher may modify to make the activity easier or more challenging for a student. **Developmental task analysis** has two components: **general task analysis** (GTA) and **specific task analysis** (STA). General task analysis (table 7.3) outlines all of the task and environmental factors that influence the performance of students in the general movement categories (e.g., throw, strike, jump). Under each of these factors, modifications are given from the most simple to the most difficult.

Once teachers of adapted physical education have a good understanding of how task and environmental factors can influence movement proficiency through GTA, they can develop an STA to look at

TABLE 7.3 Factors for General Task Analysis (Throwing)

Factors, simple to complex	Size of object being thrown	Distance object must be thrown	Weight of object being thrown	Accuracy required	Speed of target	Acceleration or deceleration of target	Direction in which target is moving
	Small	Short	Moderately light	None	Stationary	No movement	No movement
							Left to right
	Medium	Medium	Moderately heavy	Little	Slow	Steady speed	Right to left
				Moderate	Moderate	Decelerating	Toward thrower
	Large	Long	Light or heavy	Much	Fast	Accelerating	Away from thrower

Adapted from Herkowitz (1978).

how specific factors influence movement skill. For example, if an instructor decides that it would be beneficial to examine the effect of object size on the learner's throwing performance, the information presented with the STA will be much more precise than information provided by a GTA. Instead of referring generally to ball size (small, medium, large), the instructor precisely manipulates the size (6 inches [15 centimeters], 8 inches [20 centimeters], or 12 inches [30 centimeters]). Of course, other variables (e.g., weight) may also be manipulated. Through the careful identification and manipulation of important variables, it is possible to break down and sequence tasks that are appropriate for given students regardless of their functional level.

Ecological Task Analysis

Whereas Herkowitz's developmental task analysis attends to important task and environmental factors, **ecological task analysis** (ETA) takes the consideration of interacting factors one step further by carefully examining the learner's characteristics (also referred to as *intrinsic dynamics*) and how these characteristics affect the strategies and skills used to solve a particular movement task. A practical and theoretical underpinning of ETA is the belief that "motor skills, the movement form, and performance outcomes are results of the dynamic interaction (constraints) between the task goal and conditions, the environmental situation, and the capabilities and intent of the performer" (Balan & Davis, 1993, p. 54).

First introduced by Davis and Burton (1991), ETA comes from the tradition of dynamic systems (Haibach et al., 2018) and ecological psychology (Adolph & Berger, 2005), in which the characteristics of the performer, task, and environment are believed to interact in important ways and must be taken into account when designing movement tasks.

Significantly departing from more traditional approaches to adapted physical education, practitioners and researchers who embrace ETA posit that learners benefit significantly by initially manipulating variables and choosing the manner in which they will solve a given task goal. This element of choice and the process of discovery involved are thought to have multiple benefits in terms of learning movement skills, maintaining on-task behavior, increasing self-determination, and behaving appropriately (Taylor et al., 2007). Instead of being given an optimal solution to a movement problem, the learner is presented with an array of choices within a well-designed, stimulating environment and is given considerable choice as to how to proceed. For example, for a striking task, all students may choose from balls of various colors, sizes, and textures; bats of various lengths, widths, and weights; and tees or suspended balls. How Pilar hits the ball is up to her in terms of both the implements used and the movement form chosen. Ecological task analysis is a less directive, more student-centered approach to teaching movement skills, one that gives over some control to the student in terms of increased choice. As a result, ETA requires considerable ingenuity and creativity on the part of the teacher to organize an enticing and rewarding environment.

As both a method of assessment and a method of instruction, ETA has four steps (Balan & Davis, 1993):

1. *Identification of the functional movement task goals to be accomplished.* These must be

meaningful to the students and their families and may be written as behavioral objectives or goals. Student input regarding the goals can have a tremendous effect on student interest, thereby positively influencing activity levels and behavior. The emphasis of the ETA approach is on providing rich, responsive, and inviting physical and social environments. Within this environment, students are encouraged to practice clearly defined movement tasks in a manner of their choosing, given their unique abilities. This includes the movement pattern, implement used, and environment (e.g., small group, individual). When structuring the environment, Balan and Davis (1993) have outlined a number of critical considerations. To begin with, the task goal must be clear and student participation invited. There must be enough equipment for all students in the class, and it must allow for student choice (e.g., a variety of dimensions and colors). At this time, students practice the task, determining which patterns and implements work the best for them. As an illustration, let us assume that the task is for an athlete in a wheelchair to put a shot for distance.

2. *Choice.* Choice includes the skill to be accomplished, movement pattern, environment, and implement. During this step, the student practices the skill to be learned and determines which methods work best given the environmental conditions. To use the shot put illustration, the athlete is putting the shot while training for a regional high school track and field competition. She is experimenting with seating arrangements (a standard wheelchair, a racing wheelchair, and an individually designed throwing chair), positions from which she will put the shot (facing the target area vs. with her back to the throwing area), and throwing motions (her arm straight or bent at the elbow upon release). Because the meet in which she'll be competing requires all athletes to use an 8.8-pound (4-kilogram) shot, she is practicing with this specific weight.

3. *Manipulation.* During manipulation, the teacher modifies relevant task variables (including the environment, task, and even occasionally student characteristics) in order to provide challenge and promote success (Balan & Davis, 1993). At the same time, the teacher is also qualitatively and quantitatively observing and measuring student performance in order to determine under which conditions the athlete performs the best. For example, having observed the athlete's various attempts, the teacher decides that she is most successful when she uses the standard wheelchair and puts the shot backward using a straight arm.

4. *Instruction.* Direct instruction should be provided after students understand the task, experiment with movement solutions, and choose the movements that best accomplish the goals. At this point, the athlete's coach gives her direct instruction (based on best teaching and coaching practices) to prepare her for competition. Table 7.4 provides an example of the ETA process, applied to swimming.

When compared with traditional task analysis and biomechanical task analysis, ETA emphasizes the specific needs and abilities of the student when selecting goals, movement choices, and the ways by which success is determined. Ecological task analysis encourages teachers to modify variables by establishing direct links among the task, the constraints of the performer, and the environment (Burton & Miller, 1998). Importantly, ETA provides

TABLE 7.4 Example of ETA Process: Swimming

Selection and presentation of task	Student with a right-arm amputation at the shoulder will independently swim the width of the pool (20 ft [6 m]). Locomotion in water by front float and whip kick, sidestroke, or dolphin kick
Choice	Qualitative criteria for successful completion of the task: efficiency and accuracy of the stroke chosen Quantitative criteria for successful completion of the task: velocity, distance covered, spatial accuracy, and temporal accuracy
Manipulation of relevant variables	Task variables: use of flotation devices, distance to be covered, time constraints in covering the distance, consistency with regard to staying in a given pathway (lane) Environmental variables: water depth, lane width, number of peers present
Instruction	Direct instruction with individualized prompts, reinforcement, and corrective feedback as required

students with opportunities to explore and discover their own abilities.

Different approaches to task analysis are not necessarily discrete. Short (2005) has put forward a biomechanical task-analytic model where significant attention is paid to both environmental and individual (student) factors. This hybrid model combines important elements of both the biomechanical and ecological approaches to task analysis. An example of this model is provided in figure 7.4.

WWW

Student's name: John **Date of observation:** October 5

Observed: ☐ During game ☐ During skills test ☑ During practice

Skill: Forehand stroke in tennis

Performer adjustments necessary? ☐ No ☑ Yes (as indicated next)

☑ Eyes are on the ball throughout the skill.

☑ Moves quickly to the ball using proper footwork.

Self-propels wheelchair; thumb of racket hand is on top of rim or wheel.

☑ Positions body with hips and shoulders perpendicular to the net; knees are bent.

Positions wheelchair at 45-degree angle relative to the net.

☐ Racket is brought back to waist level and parallel with the ground.

Backswing is low to the ground and straight back from rear axle.

☐ Leg drives off rear foot; weight transfers at contact; rotation of hips and shoulders occurs.

Body leans into the shot (toward the net).

☑ Ball is ahead of hips at contact.

Ball is at or slightly ahead of front foot at contact.

☐ Wrist is firm at contact.

☑ Opposite arm is away from body for balance.

Opposite hand is placed on ipsilateral knee or rim for support or balance.

☐ Follow-through is high (hand finishes at or above opposite shoulder).

Environmental factors and modifications:

Court size: ☐ Full court ☑ Half-court ☐ ____________

Racket type: ☐ Standard ☑ Junior ☐ Racquetball ☐ Badminton

Ball type: ☑ Tennis ☐ Foam ☐ ____________

Ball mode: ☐ Hit by opponent ☐ Hit by facilitator

☐ Tossed by facilitator ☑ Hit from tee

______________________: ☐ ______________________ ☐ ______________________

(Others)

FIGURE 7.4 A biomechanical task analysis that considers the task, the individual, and the environment.

Activity Analysis

Activity analysis is a technique for determining the basic requirements for optimal student success in performing an activity. By breaking an activity into its components, the teacher can better understand the value of the activity and modify it to fit a student's needs. Once the needs have been determined, the teacher can use activity analysis to assess whether a given activity can meet these needs.

Activity analysis facilitates the selection of program content based on the teacher's stated objectives. In making the analysis, the teacher must determine the physical, cognitive, social, and administrative requirements for performing the activity. When analyzing an activity from a physiological or biomechanical perspective, the teacher should examine such factors as body positions required, body parts used, actions performed, fundamental movement patterns incorporated, required levels of coordination and fitness, and sensory systems used. Cognitive factors that should be examined include the number and complexity of rules and the need for memorization, concentration, strategies, and perceptual and academic skills. Social factors to consider in activity analysis include the amount and type of interaction and communication required and whether the activity is cooperative or competitive. Such administrative demands as time, equipment, facility needs, and safety factors must also be determined. Table 7.5 shows an activity analysis for table tennis.

TABLE 7.5 Activity Analysis for Table Tennis

Activity demands	Activity	Table tennis
Physical demands	1. Primary body position required 2. Movement skills required 3. Amount of fitness required a. Strength b. Endurance c. Speed d. Flexibility e. Agility 4. Amount of coordination required 5. Amount of energy required	1. Standing 2. Bending 3. Minimal fitness level a. Low (ability to hold paddle) b. Low cardiorespiratory requirements c. Quickness desirable d. Moderate e. High level desirable 4. Important, especially eye–hand coordination 5. Little
Social demands	1. Number of participants required 2. Types of interaction 3. Type of communication 4. Type of leadership 5. Competitive or cooperative activity 6. Amount of physical contact required 7. Noise level	1. Two for singles, four for doubles 2. Little; one to one 3. Little verbal; opportunity for nonverbal 4. None 5. Competitive mainly; cooperative if doubles 6. None in singles; much in doubles 7. Minimal
Cognitive demands	1. Complexity of rules 2. Level of strategy 3. Concentration level 4. Academic skills needed 5. Verbal skills needed 6. Directional concepts needed 7. Complexity of scoring system 8. Memory required	1. Moderate 2. Moderate 3. Moderate 4. Ability to count to 21 and to add 5. None 6. All concepts 7. Simple 8. Little
Administrative demands	1. Time required 2. Equipment needed 3. Special facilities required 4. Type of leadership required 5. Safety factors to be considered	1. Can be controlled by score or time 2. Paddles, balls, tables with nets 3. Area large enough to accommodate tables 4. Ability to instruct small group 5. Space between tables

Using Support Services

To teach physical education skills to students with identifiable disabilities, coteachers, support personnel, aides, volunteers, and peers are needed. The following section outlines their effective use.

TEAM TEACHING If students with unique needs are in an inclusive physical education class, it is often best for two or more teachers to instruct the class together so that learner differences can be accommodated. This approach, called **team teaching**, is especially important in settings in which educators are not well prepared to work with students who have unique needs. Team teaching is often used in inclusive settings in which teachers of physical education work with children with unique needs to allow them to participate with their peers, perhaps with the help of aides.

SUPPORTIVE TEACHING When students with disabilities are included in general physical education classes, it is often necessary for an aide or a volunteer assistant to help the student. The assistant supports the physical education teacher's efforts to include the child fully in the activity of the general class and promotes successful participation. The supportive teaching approach is particularly valuable for students just beginning the integration process.

PEER AND CROSS-AGE TUTORING Peer tutoring involves same-age students helping with instruction. Cross-age tutoring programs enlist older students (such as high school juniors or seniors) to work with younger children receiving adapted physical education, resulting in the development of positive relationships across learners (Lieberman & Houston-Wilson, 2017). The tutor also develops leadership abilities and improved learning of the skill being taught, while the tutee receives individualized instruction, increased practice, and reinforcement of learning and behavior. However, it is imperative is that both same-age and cross-age tutors be well trained. Without appropriate training, the benefits will be greatly diminished.

Summary

Many factors affect teaching for physical education and sport. Educators who can thoughtfully and imaginatively use many approaches and match them to the needs of learners are likely to have success. Master educators are always accountable and differentiate their instruction in order to effectively reach all of their students. Keeping in mind principles of UDL, they teach meaningful content in ways that make sense for their students; this allows them to more fully adapt their teaching to meet individual needs.

In this chapter, the two major approaches to instruction in adapted physical education and sport—humanism and ABA—were presented. Both approaches inform teaching in a valuable, and often compatible, fashion. Important principles of motor learning that apply to students with unique needs were also discussed. The majority of the chapter examined how to meet the challenge of different learners and the power of addressing this heterogeneity through UDL. Curricular options, activity modifications, teaching styles, and class formats were also discussed, along with several powerful educational tools, such as discrete trial training (with an emphasis on prompting), task analysis, and activity analysis. Also discussed was the importance of using support services, especially with increased teacher–student ratios and a diverse student body.

References

Adolph, K.E., & Berger, S.E. (2005). Physical and motor development. In M.H. Bornstein & M.E. Lamb (Eds.), *Developmental science: An advanced textbook* (5th ed., pp. 223-281). Psychology Press.

Alper, S., & Raharinirina, S. (2006). Assistive technology for individuals with disabilities: A review and synthesis of the literature. *Journal of Special Education Technology, 21*(2), 47-64. https://doi.org/10.1177/016264340602100204

Baert, H., & Feith, J. (2014). Resources for teaching the standards & outcomes. In SHAPE America, *National standards & grade-level outcomes for K-12 physical education* (pp. 105-111). Human Kinetics.

Balan, C.M., & Davis, W.E. (1993). Ecological task analysis approach to instruction in physical education. *Journal of Physical Education, Recreation and Dance, 64*(9), 54-62. https://doi.org/10.1080/07303084.1993.10607352

Block, M. (2016). *A teacher's guide to adapted physical education: Including students with disabilities in sports and recreation* (4th ed.). Brookes.

Bray, B. (2019, August 10). *Universal design for learning (udl) starts with why.* Rethinking Learning. https://barbarabray.net/2019/08/10/universal-design-for-learning-udl-starts-with-why/

Broadhead, G. (2007). Enhancing instruction using ecological task analysis. In W.E. Davis & G.D. Broadhead

(Eds.), *Ecological task analysis and movement* (pp. 115-120). Human Kinetics.

Burton, A., & Miller, D.E. (1998). *Movement skill assessment.* Human Kinetics.

CAST. (2020). *The UDL guidelines.* Retrieved from http://udlguidelines.cast.org/

Collier, D. (2016). Instructional strategies for adapted physical education. In J.P. Winnick & D. Porretta (Eds.), *Adapted physical education and sport* (6th ed., pp. 121-150). Human Kinetics.

Connell, B.R., Jones, M., Mace, R., Mueller, J., Mullick, A., Ostroff, E., Sanford, J., Steinfeld, E., Story, M., & Vanderheiden, G. (1997). *Principles of universal design.* North Carolina State University, Center for Universal Design.

Davis, W., & Burton, A.W. (1991). Ecological task analysis: Translating movement behavior theory into practice. *Adapted Physical Activity Quarterly, 8,* 154-177. https://doi.org/10.1123/apaq.8.2.154

Dunn, J.M. (1997). *Special physical education: Adapted, individualized, developmental.* Madison, WI: Brown & Benchmark.

Dunn, J.M., & Leitschuh, C.A. (2014). *Special physical education* (10th ed.). Kendall/Hunt.

Friend, M. (2008). *Special education: Contemporary perspectives for school professionals* (2nd ed.). Allyn & Bacon.

Goldberger, M., Ashworth, S., & Byra, M. (2012). Spectrum of teaching styles retrospective 2012. *Quest, 64,* 268-282.

Graham, G., Holt/Hale, S.A., & Parker, M. (2012). *Children moving: A reflective approach to teaching physical education* (9th ed.). McGraw-Hill.

Haibach, P., Reid, G., & Collier, D. (2017). *Motor learning and development* (2nd ed.). Human Kinetics.

Haywood, K.M., & Getchell, N. (2019). *Life span motor development* (7th ed.). Human Kinetics.

Herkowitz, J. (1978). Developmental task analysis: The design of movement experiences and evaluation of motor development status. In M. Ridenour (Ed.), *Motor development: Issues and applications* (pp. 139-164). Princeton Book Co.

Jaakkola, T, & Watt, A. (2011). Finnish physical education teachers' self-reported use and perceptions of Mosston and Ashworth's teaching styles. *Journal of Teaching in Physical Education, 30*(3), 248-262.

Lieberman, L.J., Grenier, M., Brian, A., & Arndt, K. (2021). *Universal design for learning in physical education.* Human Kinetics.

Lieberman, L.J., & Houston-Wilson, C. (2017). *Strategies for inclusion: A handbook for physical educators* (3rd ed.). Human Kinetics.

Lovaas, O.I. (2003). *Teaching individuals with developmental delays: Basic intervention techniques.* Pro-Ed.

Mellard, D., & Johnson, E. (2007). *RTI: A practitioner's guide to implementing response to intervention.* Corwin Press.

Meyer, A., Rose, D., & Gordon, D. (2014). *Universal design for learning: Theory and practice.* CAST Professional Publishing.

Mosston, M., & Ashworth, S. (2002). *Teaching physical education* (5th ed.). Benjamin Cummings.

Newell, K.M. (1986). Constraints on the development of coordination. In M.G. Wade & H.T. Whiting (Eds.), *Motor development in children: Aspects of coordination and control* (pp. 341-360). Nijhoff.

Novak, K. (2017, January 24). *What is UDL* [Video]. YouTube. www.youtube.com/watch?v=iY9PecIWcWE

Raskind, M.H., & Bryant, B.R. (2002). *Functional evaluation for assistive technology: Manual.* Psycho-Educational Services.

Rich, S.M. (2000). Instructional strategies for adapted physical education. In J.P. Winnick (Ed.), *Adapted physical education and sport* (3rd ed., pp. 75-91). Human Kinetics.

Roth, K. (2013). Adapt with apps. *Journal of Physical Education, Recreation and Dance, 84*(2), 4-6. https://doi.org/10.1080/07303084.2013.757168

Scott, S.S., McGuire, J.M., & Shaw, S.F. (2001). *Principles of universal design for instruction.* University of Connecticut, Center on Postsecondary Education and Disability.

Sherrill, C. (2004). *Adapted physical activity, recreation and sport: Crossdisciplinary and lifespan* (5th ed.). WCB/McGraw-Hill.

Short, F. (2005). Measurement, assessment and program evaluation. In J.P. Winnick (Ed.), *Adapted physical education and sport* (4th ed., pp. 55-76). Human Kinetics.

Siedentop, D., & Tannehill, D. (2000). *Developing teaching skills in physical education* (4th ed.). Mayfield.

Smith, T., Polloway, E., Patton, J., & Dowdy, C. (2008). *Teaching students with special needs in inclusive settings* (5th ed.). Pearson Education Canada.

Sturmey, P., & Fitzer, A. (2007). *Autistic spectrum disorders: Applied behavior analysis, evidence and practice.* Pro-Ed.

Taylor, J., Goodwin, D.L., & Groeneveld, H. (2007). Providing decision-making opportunities for learners with disabilities. In W.E. Davis & G.D. Broadhead (Eds.), *Ecological task analysis and movement* (pp. 197-218). Human Kinetics.

Tomlinson, C.A., & McTighe, J. (2006). *Integrating differentiated instruction and instruction by design: Connecting content and kids.* Association for Supervision and Curriculum Development.

Watkinson, E.J., & Wall, A.E. (1982). *PREP: Play skill manual.* CAHPER.

Print Resources

Canales, L.K., & Lytle, R.K. (2011). *Physical activity for young people with severe disabilities.* Human Kinetics.

This textbook provides excellent physical education activities for students with a wide range of orthopedic impairment, including cerebral palsy and spina bifida. Along with meaningful activities, the authors discuss assessment and teaching strategies.

Donnelly, F.C., Mueller, S., & Gallahue, D. (2016). *Developmental physical education for all children* (5th ed.). Human Kinetics.

This source examines the developmental process from the prenatal period through age 12, including a discussion of psychomotor, cognitive, and affective factors influencing the motor development of children. Also described are teaching behaviors and styles that promote effective teaching of students with special needs. A helpful resource in working with children who have developmental delays.

Hall, T.E., Meyer, A., & Rose, D. (2014). *Universal design for learning in the classroom: Practical applications (what works for special-needs learners).* Guilford.

This book shows how to apply the principles of universal design for learning (UDL) across all subject areas and grade levels. Practical ways to develop goals, assessments, and materials as well as methods that use UDL to meet the needs of all learners are presented.

Online Resources

PE Central: www.pecentral.org

PE Central is a frequently used online resource for general physical educators and for teachers who work with students with unique needs. It includes curricular and lesson planning ideas and teaching suggestions.

Physical and Health Education America: www.pheamerica.org

This site has a vast amount of up-to-date information (as well as links) about technology in physical education and adapted physical education, as well as coaching and sports, elementary physical education, health and nutrition, fitness, and interdisciplinary secondary physical education.

Part II

Individuals With Unique Needs

Part II is composed of 11 chapters relating to individuals with unique needs in physical education. Chapters 8 through 17 address individuals who are categorized in accordance with the Individuals with Disabilities Education Act (IDEA), whereas chapter 18 addresses children with longer-term unique physical education needs who have not been traditionally classified as having disabilities under IDEA.

The disabilities discussed in the first 10 chapters include intellectual disabilities (chapter 8); behavioral disabilities (chapter 9); autism spectrum and social communication disorders (chapter 10); specific learning disabilities (chapter 11); visual impairments (chapter 12); hard of hearing, deafness, or deafblindness (chapter 13); cerebral palsy, traumatic brain injury, and stroke (chapter 14); amputations, dwarfism, and les autres conditions (chapter 15); spinal cord disabilities and other spinal conditions (chapter 16); and other health impairments (chapter 17). These chapters examine the etiology and characteristics of the disabilities covered, with particular attention given to implications for physical education and sport programs. Chapter 18 focuses on other longer-term disabilities not covered by IDEA, activity and sport-related injuries, and a final section on obesity. These chapters are critical for giving service providers the background and understanding they need about the individuals with unique needs they are preparing to serve.

8

Intellectual Disabilities

Lauren K. Cavanaugh and Linda C. Hilgenbrinck

At the front of the gym, a raised platform is readied and a sound system is checked and rechecked. Nearly 200 students with disabilities and their adapted physical education specialists, dance teachers, general physical education partners, classroom teachers and staff, invited district employees, and parents have been ushered to the gym to patiently listen to the introduction of the invited guest dancer. Very few of those present are aware that the loud, pulsating, up-tempo Latin music will soon beckon all to get up and dance. The invited guest here—the first ever Ability Awareness Event, held at Ryan High School in Denton, Texas, in 2016—is Yulissa Arescurenaga, the first certified, licensed Zumba instructor with Down syndrome in the United States. Here is her story.

Yulissa was born in Lima, Peru, on August 9, 1991. Within minutes of her birth, she was diagnosed with Down syndrome. From an early age, she had a strong affinity for music and dance. When she and her family moved to San Francisco, California, in 2003, Yulissa learned to speak English and started using her mantra: "I can." With that mindset, she's accomplished so much, especially as an athlete in sports like soccer, basketball, baseball, swimming, and roller-skating. But it was when Yulissa took her first Zumba class in 2008 that she discovered her true passion. Four years later, she earned her license to teach Zumba, and even got to dance alongside the program's creator, Beto Perez. Yulissa tells us about her experience as an instructor: "When I got to dance on stage alongside Beto for the first time in 2012, it made me feel totally happy and it was a dream come true. I feel like I have a valuable job that has given me more confidence and more friends. My favorite thing is to share my passion. I love to see people smile and dance with me. It makes me feel happy to help other people. I love being able to say that I am a Zumba instructor, and I want to show everybody that yes, we can!"

Yulissa leads Zumba classes at Physique Magnifique Fitness Center, in a program for young people with disabilities called Ability Path, and in different schools around the San Francisco Bay Area. Yulissa travels around the United States making presentations at family congresses, inspirational events, and health events, where she promotes the inclusion of people with different abilities. She has been interviewed on national television and by several newspapers and magazines throughout the United States.

In 2016, Yulissa received the First Trailblazer Award for Zumba at the National Zumba Instructors' Convention in Orlando, Florida. She has been featured in online media outlets of Love What Matters, Woman's Day, Today.com, and Sharing Is Caring. In March 2019, Yulissa was recognized by the website The Mighty as one of their "20 Women With Down Syndrome You Should Know About."

The authors thank Patricia L. Fegan, former President and CEO of Special Olympics, Maryland, for her contributions to this chapter in earlier editions.

Definition, Classification, and Incidence

Although there are several definitions and classification systems for intellectual disability based on various criteria (e.g., medical condition, IQ score, needed supports), this chapter uses the 2010 definition and classification system developed by the American Association on Intellectual and Developmental Disabilities (AAIDD).

Definition

Intellectual disabilities are characterized by cognitive limitations as well as functional limitations in such areas as daily living skills, social skills, and communication, which can present a substantial disadvantage to functioning in society. However, individuals with intellectual disabilities have diverse abilities and potential, and educators must be prepared to accept this diversity. Over the years, the AAIDD definition of and criteria for classification of intellectual disabilities have changed dramatically, affecting the incidence of intellectual disabilities.

Until **Rosa's Law** was signed into law by President Obama in October 2010, the Individuals with Disabilities Education Act (IDEA) used the term "mental retardation" instead of "intellectual disability." Although the law changed the term, the definition did not change. IDEA defines intellectual disability as "significantly subaverage general intellectual functioning, existing concurrently with deficits in adaptive behavior and manifested during the developmental period, that adversely affects a child's educational performance" (IDEA, 2004). This definition is similar to the 2010 AAIDD definition of intellectual disability, which states, "Intellectual disability is characterized by significant limitations both in intellectual functioning and in adaptive behavior as expressed in conceptual, social, and practical adaptive skills. The disability originates before age 18" (Schalock et al., 2010, p. 3).

Thus, three criteria must be met in order for someone to have an intellectual disability. The first, significant limitations in intellectual functioning, refers to a person scoring two or more standard deviations below the mean for the individual's age group on a standardized intelligence test that is normed on the general population, including individuals with and without disabilities. Some of the intelligence tests used include the Stanford-Binet Intelligence Scale, the Wechsler Intelligence Scale for Children (WISC-III), and the Woodcock-Johnson Test of Cognitive Ability.

The second criterion, limitations in adaptive behavior, affects performance in daily life and the ability to respond to changes in daily life and the environment. Significant limitations in adaptive functioning as expressed in conceptual, social, and practical adaptive skills refers to a score that is two or more standard deviations below the mean for the individual's age and cultural group on a standardized assessment measuring one of the three adaptive skill areas, or on an overall score measuring all three of the following adaptive skill areas:

1. **Conceptual skills** include language, reading and writing, money concepts, and self-direction.
2. **Social skills** include interpersonal skills, responsibility, self-esteem, naïveté, obeying of rules and laws, and avoidance of victimization.
3. **Practical skills** include activities of daily living, occupational skills, and maintenance of safe environments.

Adaptive functioning tests used could include the Vineland Adaptive Behavior Scales (VABS), the Adaptive Behavior Assessment System (ABAS), the Inventory for Client and Agency Planning (ICAP), and the Scales of Independent Behavior (SIB) (Texas Health and Human Services, 2018).

The third criterion is that the disability originates before the age of 18. Conception through 18 years of age is considered the developmental period; it is during this time that various developmental processes are being achieved. Adverse influences occurring during this time of brain growth and development may negatively affect these developmental processes. However, as long as the potential for continued growth exists (until about age 18), compensatory actions may occur to counteract these adverse influences and improve the ultimate structure and function of the brain. Thus, an individual with normal intellectual functioning who sustains a brain injury or trauma in adulthood (after 18 years of age), rendering deficiencies in both intellectual and adaptive behavior, is not considered to have an intellectual disability.

Classification and Description

Many systems exist for classifying intellectual disabilities, including intelligence quotient (IQ), intensity of needed supports, behavioral systems, and etiological systems. The International Classification of Diseases (ICD) of the World Health Organization

(WHO, 2001) and the American Psychiatric Association's *Diagnostic and Statistical Manual of Mental Disorders, Fifth Edition (DSM-5)* (APA, 2013) use intelligence test scores to determine the severity of intellectual disabilities (table 8.1).

Although classification systems are necessary for service reimbursement, research parameters, service provision, and communication about selected characteristics, they also stigmatize individuals by assigning labels that tend to trigger behavioral expectations and negative emotional reactions on the part of others. Labels are also erroneously used as a global summary about individuals with intellectual disabilities, when in reality they reflect little about the person and thus have little application for developing support needs based on individual strengths and limitations.

The 2010 AAIDD classification system is multidimensional. It is based on five dimensions of human functioning and the patterns and intensity of supports that enable individuals to participate in home and community life, along with medical and behavioral support needs (Schalock et al., 2010). **Supports** are the resources and strategies that promote development, education, interests, and well-being as well as enhance individual functioning. Thus, once the diagnosis of intellectual disability has been made, an assessment in each of the five dimensions influencing functioning is performed. These five dimensions are

1. intellectual ability (includes reasoning, planning, problem solving, abstract thinking, comprehending complex ideas, learning quickly, and learning from experience),
2. adaptive behavior (includes the collection of conceptual, social, and practical skills),
3. health (includes physical, mental, and social well-being),
4. participation (refers to roles and interactions in the areas of home living, work, education, leisure, and spiritual and cultural activities), and
5. context (the interrelated conditions within which individuals live their everyday lives) (Wehmeyer et al., 2008).

Lastly, AAIDD's Supports Intensity Scale-Children's Version (SIS-C) measures the support needs of children between the ages of 5 and 16 (AAIDD, 2020). The SIS-C has two sections: Exceptional Medical and Behavioral Needs and the Support Needs Scale. More specifically, part 2 identifies and includes activities for Home Living, Community and Neighborhood, School Participation, School Learning, Health and Safety, Social Activities, and Advocacy.

The percentile measures and standard scores derived from the SIS-C are also used for AAIDD's multidimensional classification system. This shift from an IQ-based classification system to one incorporating patterns and intensity of support needs reflects the shift in focus from students with extraordinary support needs to students with mild deficits to successful functioning in physical education and the general curriculum.

This chapter uses AAMR's 1992 classification of intensity of support needs when describing students with intellectual disabilities. These four intensity categories are determined by the type of support needed, how long and how often support is needed, the settings in which the support is needed, the resources required to provide the support, and the degree of intrusiveness in one's life caused by the support. These four support intensities include the following:

1. **Intermittent supports** are episodic and short-term; most are provided on an as-needed basis. These are usually supports required during a job loss, medical emergency, or other life crisis.
2. **Limited supports** are more consistent over time but are still time limited. They require few staff members and minimal cost, such as time-limited employment training or transition support from school to adulthood.

TABLE 8.1 Classification of an Intellectual Disability Based on IQ Scores

Intellectual disability level	IQ score
Mild intellectual disability (MID)	IQ 50-55 to 70-75
Moderate intellectual disability (MOID)	IQ 35-40 to 50-55
Severe intellectual disability (SID)	IQ 20-25 to 35-40
Profound intellectual disability (PID)	IQ below 20-25

3. **Extensive supports** are not time limited and are characterized by regular (daily) involvement in some (though usually not all) environments. Examples are long-term home-living support, ongoing special education classes, and employment in special centers.
4. **Pervasive supports** are constant, highly intense, and potentially life sustaining; they are provided across all environments. Pervasive supports involve several individuals, significant costs, and significant intrusiveness in the person's life.

It is important to note, however, that there are instances in this chapter when classification by IQ level is used because it was the classification system used in the reported research.

Incidence

There are as many as 200 million people worldwide who have an intellectual disability, making up approximately 1 to 3 percent of the global population. In the United States, there are over 6.5 million people living with intellectual disabilities (Special Olympics, 2020d). However, the actual number of children and adults with intellectual disabilities receiving services through educational or governmental systems is often much less than 3 percent of the population. This is because most individuals with intellectual disabilities do not need special services and thus are not on any lists identifying them. For example, during the 2017-2018 school year, states reported serving about 436,000 students with intellectual disabilities, or 0.98 percent of the total student enrollment (National Center for Education Statistics [NCES], 2020).

Causes of Intellectual Disabilities

There are many causes of intellectual disabilities that are reflected in the complex interactions among genetic disorders and genetic predisposition, developmental vulnerabilities, environmental events, traumatic experiences, and personal behaviors. Disorders causing intellectual disabilities are generally categorized according to when they occur—prenatally, perinatally, or postnatally. There are more than 750 genetic disorders associated with intellectual disabilities that fall into three types of genetic disorders: single-gene disorders, chromosomal disorders, and multifactorial inheritance (inheritance of genetic and nongenetic factors), each of which is thought to contribute a small amount toward intellectual disability (Harris, 2010). Intellectual disabilities may also be caused by prenatal environmental factors such as maternal malnutrition; maternal drug misuse and abuse; viral, metabolic, and genetic diseases; and X-radiation (Harris, 2010). Perinatal causes of intellectual disabilities include placental insufficiency, abnormal labor and delivery, obstetrical trauma, neonatal seizures, infections, head trauma at birth, metabolic disorders, and nutritional disorders. Disease, traumatic head injuries, lead and mercury poisoning, near drowning, infections, degenerative disorders, seizure disorders, malnutrition, and environment deprivation are postnatal causes of intellectual disabilities. Although there are obviously many causes, the exact cause of a child's intellectual disability cannot be established in 40 to 60 percent of individuals (Harris, 2010).

Sophisticated genetic mapping research has determined that **X-linked disorders** are the most prevalent inherited disorders leading to intellectual disabilities. Fragile X syndrome (FXS) is caused by excessive repetitions of three DNA nucleotides on the long arm of the X chromosome, one of the pair of chromosomes that determines sex. Fragile X syndrome affects both males and females, with females often having milder symptoms than males (Keysor & Mazzocco, 2002). Although the exact number is unknown, it is estimated that about 1.4 per 10,000 males and 0.9 per 10,000 females have the disorder (Hunter et al., 2014). Not everyone with a fragile X premutation has fragile X syndrome. Some might have noticeable symptoms, whereas others will not. It is estimated that between 1 in 148 and 1 in 291 females and between 1 in 290 and 1 in 855 males in the United States are affected by this premutation (CDC, 2020a). Other co-occurring conditions and characteristics often affect those with FXS (Bailey et al., 2008). These can be seen in table 8.2.

Cognitive Development

The 2010 AAIDD definition of intellectual disabilities is functionally and contextually oriented. Although this orientation is useful for determining individual strengths and limitations in present functioning, it is limited for understanding the dynamic nature of intellectual functioning and how it changes throughout the developmental process. Such a developmental orientation toward intelligence is necessary to promote effective instruction and programming.

TABLE 8.2 Fragile X Co-Occurring Conditions and Characteristics

Co-occurring conditions (as reported by parents)	Males	Females
Developmental delay or intellectual disability	96 percent	64 percent
Attention problems	84 percent	67 percent
Anxiety	70 percent	56 percent
Hyperactivity	66 percent	30 percent
Autism	46 percent	16 percent
Self-injury	41 percent	10 percent
Aggressiveness	38 percent	14 percent
Seizures	18 percent	7 percent
Depression	12 percent	22 percent

To establish developmental orientation, it is necessary to draw on the extensive work of Piaget, who proposed that children move through four stages of cognitive and intellectual development: **sensorimotor**, **preoperational thought**, **concrete operational**, and **formal operational** (Goodway et al., 2021). Some children may progress through the stages at different ages and might also show characteristics of more than one stage at a time. Each of Piaget's stages are marked by new intellectual abilities and cognitive development that follows the sequence depicted in in table 8.3.

Sensorimotor Stage

The sensorimotor stage is the first of Piaget's four stages of development, occurring from birth to approximately 18 to 24 months. During this period of rapid cognitive growth, infants develop an understanding of their world through their senses and actions using trial and error in their immediate surroundings. The main focus is on what they see and do while learning how things react. Infants experiment by shaking or throwing things and putting things in their mouths.

During the sensorimotor stage, children develop, use, and modify their first schemata—forms of knowing that develop, change, expand, and adapt. A schema might be a simple response to a stimulus, an overt action, a means to an end, an end in itself, an internalized thought process, or a combination of overt actions and internalized thought processes. Examples of schemata include tossing a ball, grasping, and sucking. During the sensorimotor stage, for example, a child develops the schema of grasping, which can be used in grasping the mother's finger, picking up various objects, or picking up an object from various angles. A schema often functions in combination

TABLE 8.3 Stages of Cognitive and Play Development

Age range (years)	Cognitive developmental phases	Type of play	Play group
Birth to age 2	Sensorimotor	Practice play and ritualization	Individual
Ages 2 to 7	Preoperational thought	Symbolic	Egocentrism and parallel play Reciprocal play (progressive reciprocity in dyads, triads, and the like)
Ages 7 to 11	Concrete operational	Simple games with rules	Small group games Lead-up games and activities
Age 11 to adulthood	Formal operational	Complex games with rules	Larger group play Team sports

or in sequence with other schemata, such as when a child throws a ball, an action that combines the schemata of grasping and releasing.

To a great extent, the sensorimotor phase is when children learn to differentiate themselves from objects and others. A great deal of attention is given to physically manipulating and acting on objects and observing the effects of such actions. Through exploration, manipulation, and problem solving, children gain information about the properties of objects, such as texture, size, weight, and resiliency, as they drop, thrust, pull, push, bend, twist, punch, squeeze, or lift objects that have various properties. Between seven and nine months, infants develop object permanence (i.e., realize that objects exist, even if they can no longer see them). At this stage, children's functioning is largely sensorimotor, with only rudimentary ability to manipulate reality through symbolic thinking. Children functioning at the sensorimotor stage prefer solitary play and benefit from activities that allow them to explore ways to move their body and manipulate objects. Lastly, near the end of this stage, language development is reached.

Preoperational Stage

The preoperational stage is the second in Piaget's theory of cognitive development. This stage includes the preconceptual subphase, which lasts to about the age of 4, and the subphase of intuitive thought, which spans ages 4 to 7. Toward the end of the sensorimotor stage, the child begins to develop the ability to symbolically represent actions before acting them out; however, this representation is primitive and limited to schemata associated with one's own actions. During the preoperational stage, the child becomes able to represent objects through language and to use language in thinking. The child can now think about objects and activities and manipulate them verbally and symbolically. In this stage of development, children are egocentric and unable to view situations from others' perspectives. Play serves as an important means of assimilation and occupies most of the child's waking hours. Children functioning at the early preoperational stage prefer parallel and associative play and enjoy activities that employ rhythms, dance, and make-believe experiences. The child also begins to exhibit interest in relationships between people. Language games can help stimulate language development at this stage. Rhythmic dance and low-organization games facilitate cooperative play at the later preoperational stage.

Concrete Operational Stage

During the concrete operational stage, occurring from ages 7 to 11, children achieve operational thought, which enables them to develop mental representations of the physical world and manipulate these representations in their minds (operations). The fact that the child is able to develop and manipulate mental representations of the physical world distinguishes this phase from earlier stages. The fact that operations are limited to those of action, to the concrete, or to those that depend on perception distinguishes this phase from the later formal operational stage. In this stage, the child is able to mentally carry through a logical idea. The physical actions that predominated in earlier phases can now be internalized and manipulated as mental actions.

During the concrete operational stage, children's thinking becomes more consistent, stabilized, and organized and increased sophistication is present in the use of language and other signs. In the preoperational stage, the child developed word definitions without full understanding of what the words meant. In the concrete operational stage, language becomes a vehicle for the thinking process as well as a tool for verbal exchange. In this stage, children can analyze situations from perspectives other than their own. This decentering permits thinking to become more logical and the conception of the environment to be more coherently organized.

Although children are able to perform the more complex operations just described, they are generally incapable of sustaining them when they cease to manipulate objects or when the operations are not tied to physical actions. Children in this stage use play to understand their physical and social world. Rules and regulations of play are also of interest to the child at this stage. Children functioning at this stage of development enjoy lead-up sports and individual and dual activities such as dodgeball, kickball, tag, Simon Says, and hide and seek.

Formal Operational Stage

Children functioning at the stage of formal operations (ages 11 to adulthood) are now able to think in terms of the hypothetical and use abstractions to solve problems. They enter the world of ideas and can rely on pure symbolism instead of operating solely from physical reality. They are able to isolate the elements of a problem, understand the effects of a variable on a problem, and systematically explore possible solutions. Whereas children at the concrete operational stage tend to deal largely with the present, those functioning at the formal operational stage are concerned with the future, the remote, and the hypothetical. They can establish assumptions and hypotheses, test hypotheses, and formulate principles, theories, and laws. They can not only think but also think about what they are thinking and why they are thinking it. During this stage, children are able to use systems of formal logic in their thinking, understand and execute complex game strategies of team sport, and create movement sequences that interpret a theme, feeling, or event.

Application of Cognitive Development to Teaching

Cognitive theory has many implications for teaching. Cognitive theory also serves as a basis for some of the organizational and instructional methods suggested later in the chapter. Because of space considerations, only a few examples are presented here. First, the student's language development should be considered. For example, it is often helpful to emphasize action words and simple sentences rather than multiple complex sentences when communicating instructions. Feedback on the quality of performance should be short and specific. Because language is more abstract than concrete examples, teachers may need to reduce verbalization of instructions and emphasize tactile, kinesthetic, visual, and other more concrete forms of instruction. Demonstrations and physical assistance will facilitate the instructional process.

Children who cannot readily transfer learning or apply past experiences to new situations need more gradual task progressions in smaller sequential steps and need to learn and practice skills in the environments in which they are used. It is also important to consider the level of cognitive development when teaching rules and game strategies. As cognition develops, more complex rules and strategies can be introduced.

Knowing the type of play and play groups associated with developmental stages can also influence successful participation in games (table 8.3). Individuals at the developmental age of 6 or younger respond with greater enthusiasm for make-believe games played in small groups.

Characteristics of Individuals With Intellectual Disabilities

Intellectual disabilities are multidimensional; they affect all aspects of an individual's life. The following are characteristics typically manifested in individuals with intellectual disabilities.

Capacity and Rate of Learning

The area in which individuals with intellectual disabilities differ most from others is in cognitive behavior. The greater the degree of intellectual disability, the lower the cognitive level at which the person functions. Other characteristics affecting learning are a limited ability to generalize information, short attention span, and inability to understand abstract concepts.

Although the learning process and stages of learning are the same for those with and without disabilities, children with intellectual disabilities learn at a slower rate than children without intellectual disabilities and thus achieve less academically. The learning rate of children with intellectual disabilities needing intermittent or limited support is usually 40 to 70 percent that of children without intellectual disabilities. They may be limited to simpler forms of formal operations, may not be able to progress beyond the level of concrete operations, or may be incapable of surpassing the preoperational thought subphase. Children needing extensive or pervasive support often function at the sensorimotor stage and may not benefit from traditional schooling. Although self-contained classes and separate schools for children needing extensive or pervasive support exist in most school systems, the primary educational objectives for these children involve mastery of basic life skills and communication skills needed for their care. Adults needing extensive supports might learn to dress and feed themselves and care for their own hygiene and might even benefit from work activities, but they will most likely need close supervision and care throughout their lives.

Social and Emotional Responses

Although children with intellectual disabilities exhibit the same ranges of social behavior and emotion as other children, they more frequently demonstrate inappropriate responses to social and emotional situations. Because they have difficulty generalizing information or learning from past experiences at the same rate or capacity as children without intellectual disabilities, they are likely to be unprepared to handle novel situations. Children with intellectual disabilities often do not fully understand what is expected of them, and they might respond inappropriately because they have misinterpreted the situation rather than because they lack appropriate responses.

Educational programs for children with intellectual disabilities should always include experiences to help them determine social behaviors and emotional responses for everyday situations. Personal acceptance and development of healthy social relationships are critical to independence. The reason that most individuals needing intermittent or limited support lose jobs is inadequacy of social skills, such as poor work habits, and an inability to get along with coworkers. On the other hand, when they develop basic social and emotional skills, they are happier and more accepting—and they are a joy to teach in physical activity settings.

Physical and Motor Development

Children with intellectual disabilities differ least from children without intellectual disabilities in their physical and motor characteristics. Although most children with intellectual disabilities display developmental motor delays, these are often related more to limited attention and comprehension than to physiological or motor control deficits.

Generally, the greater the intellectual disability, the greater the delay in attaining major developmental milestones. As a group, children with intellectual disabilities typically walk and talk later, are slightly shorter, and are more susceptible to physical problems and illnesses compared with other children. In comparative studies, children with intellectual disabilities consistently score lower than children without intellectual disabilities on measures of strength, endurance, agility, balance, running speed, flexibility, and reaction time. Although many students with intellectual disabilities can successfully compete with their peers without intellectual disabilities, those students needing extensive or pervasive support score, on

Players develop social skills while they practice catching.

average, an equivalent to four or more years behind their peers without intellectual disabilities on tests of physical fitness and motor performance.

The fitness and motor performance of children without intellectual disabilities usually exceeds that of children with intellectual disabilities needing intermittent or limited support, who in turn perform better than children needing extensive or pervasive supports (Gillespie, 2003; Pitetti et al., 2000). The performance of boys generally exceeds that of girls, with the differences between the sexes increasing as the intensity of needed supports increases (Eichstaedt et al., 1991; Londeree & Johnson, 1974). Boys with intellectual disabilities also show greater flexibility and balance than girls with intellectual disabilities, in contrast to boys without intellectual disabilities, who do not score as well on these measures as girls without intellectual disabilities. Also, children with Down syndrome exhibit more flexibility than other children with intellectual disabilities (Eichstaedt et al., 1991; Rarick et al., 1976; Rarick & McQuillan, 1977). This is because children with Down syndrome tend to have hypotonic musculature and hypermobility of the joints, which permits them greater than normal flexibility, and, because of weak ligaments and muscles, places them at greater risk of injury.

Winnick and Short (2014) recommend that children aged 10 to 17 with intellectual disabilities needing intermittent or limited support should achieve levels of aerobic capacity, body composition, flexibility, abdominal strength, upper body strength, and endurance (necessary for positive health, independent living, and participation in physical activities) approaching the performance levels of their peers without disabilities. Winnick and Short (1999) also offer activity guidelines for developing these functional and physiological fitness levels in children with intellectual and other disabilities.

Many children with intellectual disabilities are hypotonic and overweight, posing many problems with body mechanics and balance. Activities done on uneven surfaces or requiring rapid change of direction can cause anxiety and pose greater risk of injury and failure. Clubhands and clubfeet, postural deviations, and cerebral palsy are all prevalent among children with intellectual disabilities, and physical educators must consider these factors when planning each child's program (figure 8.1). Intellectual disabilities often coexist with other disabilities, and the number of coexisting conditions increases with increased severity of intellectual disabilities (Harris, 2010; Murphy et al., 1998), as shown in table 8.4.

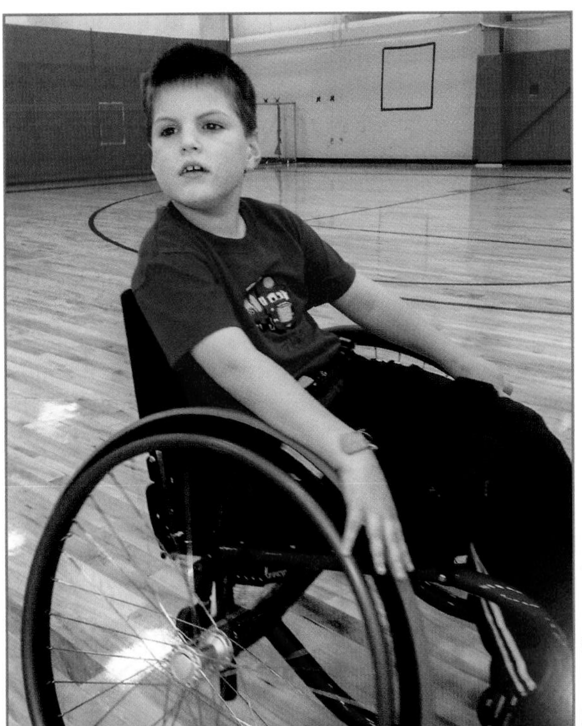

FIGURE 8.1 Many children with intellectual disabilities have other disabilities as well.

Down Syndrome

Down syndrome is the most recognizable genetic condition associated with intellectual disabilities. Because of its prevalence and unique implications for physical education and sport, it is discussed at length here. One in 700 children are born with

TABLE 8.4 Coexistence of Intellectual Disabilities With Other Disabilities

Coexisting disability	With mild intellectual disabilities	With severe intellectual disabilities
Autism	9 percent	20 percent
Epilepsy	3-18 percent	30-50 percent
Cerebral palsy	6-8 percent	30-60 percent
Sensory deficits	10 percent	17 percent

Down syndrome, with approximately 6,000 babies with Down syndrome born each year (NDSS, 2020b). Down syndrome occurs in individuals of all races and economic levels. However, older women have an increased risk of having a child with Down syndrome because older eggs have a greater risk of improper chromosome division. Women over the age of 35 present a high risk (1 in 350) of having a child with Down syndrome; at 40 years of age, the risk increases to 1 in 100, and at 45 years of age, the risk is 1 in 30. However, 80 percent of children with Down syndrome are born to women under the age of 35, simply because there are more births among younger mothers. The likelihood of having a second child with Down syndrome after having a baby with trisomy 21 is 1 in 100 up until the age of 40 (NDSS, 2020b).

Causes

Down syndrome results from one of three chromosomal abnormalities: trisomy 21 (nondisjunction), translocation, and mosaicism. The most common cause, accounting for 95 percent of cases, is trisomy 21, so named because of the presence of an extra 21st chromosome. This results in a total of 47 chromosomes, instead of the normal 46 (23 chromosomes received from each parent). A second cause of Down syndrome is translocation, accounting for about 3 percent of all cases; this occurs when part of chromosome 21 breaks off during cell division and attaches to another chromosome. The characteristics of Down syndrome are a result of the presence of an extra part of chromosome 21. A third cause of Down syndrome is mosaicism, accounting for 2 percent of all cases; this occurs when nondisjunction of chromosome 21 takes place in one of the initial cell divisions after fertilization. People with this type of Down syndrome might display fewer characteristics of Down syndrome compared to the other two types (CDC, 2020b).

Characteristics

Although over 80 clinical characteristics are associated with Down syndrome, the most common physical characteristics are the following (CDC, 2020b):

- Short stature with short legs and arms in relation to torso
- Poor muscle tone or loose joints
- Flattened facial profile and nose
- Small head, ears, and mouth
- A tongue that tends to stick out of the mouth
- Eyes slanted upward and outward
- Tiny white spots on the iris of the eye
- Short neck
- Mild to moderate obesity
- Underdeveloped respiratory and cardiovascular systems
- Small or broad hands and feet with short fingers and toes and a single crease in the palm of the hand (palmar crease)
- Small pinky fingers that sometimes curve toward the thumb
- Poor balance
- Perceptual difficulties
- Poor vision and hearing loss

Many of these characteristics can be seen in figure 8.2.

FIGURE 8.2 Special Olympics athlete displaying some of the many physical and facial features associated with individuals with Down syndrome.

Many individuals with Down syndrome also have an increased risk of certain medical problems such as congenital heart defects, respiratory and hearing problems, Alzheimer's disease, and thyroid conditions. People with Down syndrome are 10 to 15 times more likely to develop leukemia and 62 times more likely to develop pneumonia than the general population. Bowel defects requiring surgery and respiratory infections are also common (Eunice Kennedy Shriver National Institute of Child Health and Human Development, 2014). Individuals with Down syndrome age more rapidly, and, although estimates vary, around 30 percent of individuals with Down syndrome over age 50 have Alzheimer's disease. By their 60s, this increases to 50 percent (NDSS, 2020a). Because of these medical conditions, the life span of individuals with intellectual disabilities tends to be 10 years shorter than that of the general population (Harris, 2010). In the United States, a shocking racial disparity exists in the median life spans of individuals with Down syndrome (Yang et al., 2002). A 15-year study of 34,000 individuals with Down syndrome revealed that the median age at death for Caucasians with Down syndrome is 50 years, whereas it is 25 years for African Americans and 11 years for individuals of other races.

Although some degree of slow development and learning difficulties is always associated with Down syndrome, attainment and functional ability are much higher than previously thought possible. As a result, individuals with Down syndrome are becoming increasingly integrated into society and its institutions, including schools, health care systems, community living, and the workforce.

Physical Education Programming

The many medical problems of children with Down syndrome require medical clearance for activity participation and careful planning of the physical education program. Aerobic activities and activities requiring maximal muscular contraction must be adapted and carefully monitored. Muscle hypotonia (low muscle tone) and hypermobility (above-normal mobility) of the joints often cause postural and orthopedic impairments, such as lordosis, ptosis, dislocated hips, kyphosis, atlantoaxial instability, flat pronated feet, and forward head. Exercises and activities that cause hyperflexion are contraindicated because they put undue stress on the body that could result in hernias, dislocations, strains, or sprains. Instead, exercises and activities that strengthen and stabilize muscles around the joints should be encouraged. Poor eyesight and hearing in children with Down syndrome may require teachers to employ adapted equipment and teaching strategies typical for those with sensory impairments.

Assessment

Assessment is necessary to determine the status and needs of students with intellectual disabilities. Children with intellectual disabilities who need only intermittent or limited support can often take the same tests as children without intellectual disabilities. In some instances, standardized tests might require modification, or standardized tests designed specifically for students with intellectual disabilities might need to be implemented. However, children needing extensive or pervasive support often lack the physical fitness, motor ability, motivation, and understanding required to perform standardized test items. Winnick and Short (2014) recommend using task analysis or other measures of physical activity (e.g., pedometers) as an alternative to standardized tests to measure the physical fitness of those with such support needs. Alternative assessments incorporating teacher-developed or adapted rubrics, analytic rating scales, and checklists are also appropriate to measure the physical abilities of this population.

There are a variety of test options to measure physical fitness for those with intellectual disabilities. The Brockport Physical Fitness Test (BPFT) is designed to measure health-related physical fitness in students with mild limitations aged 10 to 17 (Winnick & Short, 2014). The Test of Gross Motor Development (TGMD-3) is a norm-referenced test used to identify gross motor deficits (Ulrich, 2019). Additional information on testing appears in chapter 4.

Instructional Methods

Certain instructional methods have proven particularly successful in aiding the learning and inclusion of students with intellectual disabilities. These methods ensure positive experiences for students with intellectual disabilities in a physical education class where maximum participation takes place in a controlled environment. These instructional methods are covered in more detail in chapter 7.

How information is presented to students with intellectual disabilities often makes the difference between success and failure. In general, learning is enhanced if it is fun, ensures success, and keeps the student active. Because students with intellectual disabilities need more time and opportunities to learn new skills, good teachers plan an active class and provide many opportunities for students to practice targeted skills. They also carefully select instructional methods to match the students' level of cognitive development. The following instructional strategies have proven successful for students with intellectual disabilities.

Learning Stations

Learning stations divide the gymnasium or play area into smaller areas for small groups or individual students to learn or practice a specific skill or sport. Students may be assigned to a single learning station for the entire activity period or might rotate from station to station after a set amount of time or after a learning goal has been achieved. Stations might focus on a theme (e.g., physical fitness, dance, sport-specific skills like tennis or basketball, motor skills) or form an obstacle course (students perform one skill repetition at each station with a goal of completing all the stations in the shortest amount of time). Learning stations promote full integration, accommodate large numbers of students, permit flexibility for students to progress at their own pace, and provide a safe and successful learning experience for all students.

Differentiated Instruction

Differentiated instruction encourages inclusion by allowing for diverse learning styles and abilities among students. The goals and content are the same for all students, but the teacher employs a variety of teaching methods such that all students in the class are able to learn based on their individual abilities. Student practice and evaluation are also differentiated, allowing for variations in student learning styles, cognitive ability, and motor limitations. Individualized adaptations to the environment, materials, equipment, and rules according to each student's skill level are encouraged.

Universal Design for Learning

Another specific teaching model for the physical education setting is universal design for learning (UDL). UDL specifies that the gymnasium setting must be accessible and effective and that teachers must methodically plan purposeful engagement for learners of all types and all abilities. This requires the teacher to offer a variety of instructional strategies while actively addressing necessary instructional needs, supports, and equipment (specialized or traditional), as well as behavior management and assessment processes and protocols. There are multiple resources to assist physical education teachers and adapted physical education specialists to adopt the UDL framework in their programs and lessons. Lieberman, Grenier, Brian, and Arndt authored the textbook *Universal Design for Learning in Physical Education* (2021), as well as a video, *Design for Learning in Physical Education, How Inclusive are Your Classes?* The latter is combined with the Lieberman-Brian Inclusion Rating Scale for Physical Education (LIRSPE) and a corresponding rubric to support educators in utilizing UDL. The LIRSPE rating scale offers educators an effective tool to evaluate their classes for inclusion. More information about the UDL framework can be located in chapters 2 and 7, as well as throughout the book.

Peer Instruction and Cross-Age Tutoring

One of the most exciting developments in teaching is the use of peers (other students with or without disabilities) to help children with unique needs. Cross-age tutoring is an excellent way of providing children with intellectual disabilities role models whom they can imitate, especially because it is common for young children to rely on slightly older peers as role models. Peer instruction and cross-age tutoring increase personalized instruction time for students with intellectual disabilities.

Community-Based Instruction

Because students with intellectual disabilities who need extensive or pervasive support do not generalize well from one environment to another, teaching skills in the environment where the skills will ultimately be used is preferable to artificial environments such as the classroom or gym. One of the critical steps in teaching skills in natural environments is identifying and prioritizing environments in which the skills will actually be used. This top-down approach to teaching starts with the end result (for example, bowling at the local bowling center) and works backward to identify all the cognitive, social, physical, and environmental components that need to be taught. This would include, for example, traveling to the bowling center, paying for and obtaining the correct-sized shoes and most appropriate bowling ball, keeping score, following bowling rules and etiquette, returning the shoes and ball at the conclusion of the game, and getting home. Each of these components may be task analyzed and used for initial assessment, the basis of instruction, and final assessment. The top-down approach to teaching can and should be applied to all sports (Block, 2016).

Partial Participation

If a student with intellectual disabilities can acquire only some of the skills needed to participate in an activity, he can be accommodated by physical assistance, equipment modifications, or rule changes. For example, a student with an intellectual disability along with cerebral palsy who uses a motorized wheelchair can be assigned a specially lined area of the soccer field. If the soccer ball enters this lined area, a peer tutor stops the ball. The student then has five seconds to maneuver his wheelchair to touch the ball. If the student is successful, the peer tutor then kicks the ball to a member of the student's team. If the student is unsuccessful, the peer tutor kicks the ball to a member of the opposing team.

Concrete Experiences

Because children with intellectual disabilities are slower in cognitive development, concrete tasks and information are more easily learned and performed than their abstract counterparts. Instruction should emphasize only the most important task cues. Verbal instructions and cues should be short and simple (no longer than 30 seconds) and focus on action words; for instance, instead of saying, "Go," say "Run," "Walk," or "Hop." Because verbalization is more abstract, demonstration, modeling, or physical prompting should accompany verbal instruction. It is vital that demonstrations and modeling be performed correctly so that students do not copy incorrect ways of performing the skill.

Data-Based Teaching

Data-based instruction involves monitoring how such factors as environmental arrangement, equipment, task analysis, time of day, levels of reinforcement, and cueing techniques affect a student's progress. By cooperatively charting progress, teachers and students can often determine when an objective will be accomplished (e.g., complete two laps around the gymnasium). This can provide motivation and direction to help a student estimate how long it will take to accomplish any new task, set personal objectives to accomplish a task within a reasonable margin of error, and identify practice techniques for reaching the objectives.

Ecological Task Analysis

Because children with intellectual disabilities are generally unable to attend to as many task cues or pieces of information as children without intellectual disabilities, instructors should use ecological task analysis (ETA) to break skills down into sequential tasks, either chronologically or from simple to complex. The teacher must also account for the child's limitations (e.g., intellectual disability, limited range of motion) as well as any environmental factors (e.g., size of ball, speed of ball, length of bat, distance to target) that may influence performance of the task or skill. The tasks selected, the number and variety of choices the learner has, the opportunity to explore and manipulate environmental variables, and the teaching methods selected are all important components of ETA. Planned programs discussed later in the chapter employ task analysis. More information on ETA can be found in chapter 7.

Behavior Management

Applying behavior management principles such as cueing, reinforcing, and correcting is critical to the success of task analyzing skills and teaching all the behaviors that enable a student to learn and perform the skill. Behaviors to be influenced must be pinpointed and behavioral principles must be systematically employed to promote change in the identified behaviors. Substantial evidence indicates that the shorter the time lapse between student performance and feedback, the more learning is facilitated, especially for individuals with intellectual disabilities who need extensive or pervasive supports. Behavior management principles are discussed in chapter 6.

Moving From Familiar to Unfamiliar

Because students with intellectual disabilities have difficulty applying past experience and previously learned information to new tasks, even similar ones, they are more likely to view each new task as a novel one. Thus, the progression from familiar to unfamiliar must occur gradually and be strongly reinforced. Teachers should begin to teach well within the range of student skill and comprehension. Tasks should be divided into small, meaningful steps; presented and learned sequentially; and rehearsed in total with as little change in order as possible.

A word of caution: Although progression to new tasks should be gradual, children with intellectual disabilities often have short attention spans, so teachers should plan many activities to keep the student's attention. For example, if the lesson is practicing the fundamental motor skill of hopping, the teacher might need to plan several separate hopping activities in a 20-minute lesson. The use of music and make-believe often improves attention span and involvement, especially in younger children. Music may also be used as a reward when a student achieves an objective or goal.

Consistency and Predictability

Consistency of teacher behavior helps establish and maintain a sound working relationship between teacher and students. When students know what to expect, they can plan their behaviors knowing what the consequences will be. Children with intellectual disabilities are often less flexible in accepting or adapting to new routines. Thus, day-to-day consistency in class structure, teacher behavior, and expectations helps promote learning. Teacher behavior should be kind yet firm, patient, and always positive when reinforcing desired behaviors and providing feedback on the execution of a skill.

Choice Making

Because activities for children with intellectual disabilities are often provided without consideration of individual preferences, choice making allows students with little control of their body and environment to regain some control of their activity program. It can consist of allowing students to choose which activity they want to play, which ball they prefer, how they would like to be positioned, who they would like to assist them, when they need to stop and rest, and so on. Giving students choices sometimes makes the difference in whether they truly engage in an activity or just go through the motions. It also stimulates language development in students with minimal verbal skills and is a key feature of ETA.

Activity Modifications

When challenging skills or activities are modified as necessary, students with intellectual disabilities can often participate successfully in physical education and sport alongside peers without disabilities. This is particularly true for children with intellectual disabilities who have associated health or physical impairments or who need extensive or pervasive supports. The following are some of the ways in which activities can be modified.

- Make the rules simpler or clearer based on the learner's level of comprehension. Students sometimes break the rules because they do not understand them.
- Work as a class to create new rules, thus creating a greater chance that students will understand them.
- Break tasks into simpler, smaller steps, reducing the risk of the student becoming overwhelmed.
- Substitute fundamental motor skills and patterns for more highly developed sport skills.
- Allow students to sit, hold on to a bar, or hold a peer's hand for support.
- Use softer, lighter, larger, or slower balls for striking, catching, and kicking.
- Use shorter, lighter, or broader implements for striking.
- Swap stationary or suspended balls for moving balls.
- Enlarge the target or goal area.
- Use distinct boundaries, such as cones, poly spots, and ropes.
- Avoid games with a lot of wait time, which can be difficult and distracting to some students.
- Reduce the number of players per team.
- Narrow and shorten the field of play.
- Create safety zones or special zones within the field of play.
- Decrease the speed of skill execution or the force required to execute a skill.
- Lessen the distance required for skill execution.
- Include many opportunities for positive reinforcement and feedback.
- Keep routines consistent; that is, use similar warm-ups and cool-downs (Rouse, 2010).

Activities

When selecting activities for students with intellectual disabilities, physical educators should be aware of the games, activities, and sports enjoyed by children in the community. These activities are good choices for the physical education class and are consistent with the current emphasis on UDL. Cooperative programming with local recreation agencies can promote successful inclusion of students with intellectual disabilities in structured community-based play groups. Activities should be challenging yet fun—activities are not fun when they are beyond the understanding and skill of the participants. Music and make-believe help stimulate interest and involvement in games when working with younger children.

Activities According to Chronological Age

Instructors should base the activities and skills they teach on a student's chronological age and on activities that the student's similarly aged peers enjoy. However, one must consider students' functional abilities and cognitive development when determining what teaching methods to employ and how to present skills and activities. Teaching age-appropriate and functional skills frequently used by all students in natural environments minimizes the stigmatizing discrepancies between students with and without disabilities. Conversely, selecting activities based on mental age often involves keeping students who need extensive or pervasive supports at the lower end of the developmental continuum, working on prerequisite skills that are often nonfunctional and unlikely to be used in daily living or in community recreation and sport programs. For example, Duck, Duck, Goose is not an activity for high school students. Rhythm and dance, lifelong sport skills, and fitness activities are age appropriate and can be used in community programs. Individuals with intellectual disabilities particularly need to focus on developing the motor skills and physical fitness levels required for optimal vocational training and use of leisure time.

Activities for Students Needing Intermittent or Limited Supports

Teachers should select activities that stimulate language development and problem-solving skills for young children with intellectual disabilities needing intermittent or limited supports. Fun activities that involve make-believe, singing, dancing, and verbalization (e.g., Simon Says) can help keep their attention, therefore stimulating and reinforcing cognitive development. Verbal rehearsal of cues and prompts also stimulates language development. Older students with intellectual disabilities needing intermittent or limited supports often excel in sport; in fact, sport might be their primary avenue for success and self-esteem. Their physical and motor needs are generally similar to those of students without intellectual disabilities, so they are more likely to be included in physical education classes than in any other subject and their physical education activities can often be the same or similar.

Although students needing intermittent or limited supports often excel in physical education and sport, concepts of team play, strategy, and rules can be difficult for them to learn. Highly skilled students with intellectual disabilities can learn strategy and rules through concrete teaching strategies. Skill and sport activities such as those fostered by Special Olympics are enjoyable for students with intellectual disabilities needing intermittent or limited supports; basketball, soccer, hockey, baseball, and dancing are often popular among these adolescents.

Activities for Students Needing Extensive or Pervasive Supports

Students needing extensive or pervasive supports have not traditionally been placed into inclusive public school classes, but rather into special classes, schools, or institutions. Their level of intellectual and motor functioning is basic and activity is generally characterized by little student interaction (i.e., parallel play), with most interactions occurring between teacher and student. However, more and more of these students are functioning successfully in inclusive classroom settings, particularly when appropriate support systems are in place. Children needing extensive or pervasive supports generally need an educational program that includes sensorimotor skills, fundamental skills, movement patterns, and physical and motor fitness development (see the Application Example sidebar).

Sensorimotor programs involve stimulating the senses to develop sensory channels to receive information from the environment. Functional senses then permit the child to respond to the environment through movement and manipulation. In these programs, children are taught the normal infant motor progression of head control, crawling, grasping, releasing, sitting, creeping, and standing. Many students with these needs do not walk before age 9, and many never become ambulatory. Children needing pervasive supports might not readily respond to their environment and might exhibit little or none of the curiosity that would motivate them to explore the environment and learn. Even the most rudimentary skills must be taught. However, through partial participation and activity modification, many students needing extensive supports can participate in physical education classes alongside peers without disabilities. Many of them enjoy and can benefit from participating in lower-ability Special Olympics events or the Special Olympics **Motor Activity Training Program (MATP)** (Special Olympics, 2020b), a comprehensive training program designed for individuals who do not possess the physical or behavioral skills necessary to complete in official Special Olympics sports. Athletes participate in mobility, striking, throwing, kicking, and manual and electric wheelchair activities. MATP athletes participate in activities to perform their own physical best. Coaching training guides provide information on the types of athletes who would benefit, the program's purpose and benefits, and sport activities, as well as ways to promote community involvement.

Another program with particular relevance for students needing extensive or pervasive supports is the data-based gymnasium (DBG), discussed in chapter 6 and again in chapter 9. This program is an instructional model for teaching students with extensive and pervasive support needs that analyzes behavioral principles for the socialization of behaviors. Skills within the curriculum are broken

Application Example

Inclusion of Student With Intellectual Disabilities Needing Extensive Supports

SETTING

Secondary partner physical education class

STUDENT

A 15-year-old student with intellectual disability needing pervasive supports who is ambulatory but needs support by two peer partners in physical education class

UNIT

Volleyball

ISSUE

How to meaningfully include the student and peer partners in the volleyball game alongside the other players

APPLICATION

After consultation with the adapted physical education specialist, the physical educator uses partial participation with peer assistance as follows:

- Supported by peer partners standing on either side, the student assumes a position on the volleyball court with a standard height net and trainer volleyball.
- If the volleyball enters the designated area, the peer partners give the volleyball to the student. The student is assisted to use one or both hands to grasp and hold the volleyball for three counts. The student may grasp and release the volleyball to the peer partners or grasp and throw the volleyball over the net. One point is awarded for each ball held and then released with assistance. Two points are awarded for each ball thrown over the net with assistance.
- Peer partners may offer assistance with hand-over-hand support for the student to perform a one-arm underhand pass or forearm pass (bump), one-hand overhand hit, or one-handed tip. If the student is unsuccessful, the peer partners, with the student watching, send the ball over the net using their choice of volleyball skills and the game resumes.

The following suggestions would also work:

- Volleyball net set at a shorter height (4 to 5 feet)
- Large balloon, punch ball balloon, floater ball, or midsize cage ball used as the game volleyball
- Depending on ability level, student may or may not have to move in rotation
- Student is given two attempts to get ball in air or over the net; point awarded for each ball hit in the air; two points awarded for each ball hit over the net

down into tasks that are sequenced as phases representing shaping behaviors. Students are reinforced for successfully completing tasks that approximate the targeted behavior. The DBG includes a clipboard instructional and management system that helps identify present status, objectives, and progress on skill development, and it includes a game, exercise, and leisure sport curriculum. Although the original text on the DBG is no longer in print, many of the materials and ideas are incorporated in a text by Dunn and Leitschuh (2014).

Mobility Opportunities Via Education/Experience, or MOVE (MOVE International, 2013), is a top-down, activity-based curriculum for students who need extensive and pervasive support to acquire the motor skills for increased independence. It combines natural body mechanics with the instructional process by having participants practice the motor skills necessary to sit, stand, and walk while engaging in other educational or leisure activities. The motor skills sequence is age appropriate and based on a top-down model of needs rather than a developmental sequence of skill acquisition. The motor skills are usable into adulthood and range from levels of no self-management to independent self-management.

Most students needing pervasive supports are unable to independently perform age-appropriate functional skills. However, the addition of physical assistance, adapted equipment (e.g., bowling ramp, lowered basketball net), and computer technology enables many such students to participate in chronologically age-appropriate functional activities in natural environments.

Strategies for Inclusion

Physical education teachers face the task of providing successful, enjoyable, and challenging learning experiences for all students in inclusive classes. Their teaching strategies must ensure that students with intellectual disabilities will comprehend instructions and achieve success in the inclusive gymnasium. They must also ensure that classmates accept and respect their peers with intellectual disabilities and understand how they can best support and communicate with them. Teachers are highly encouraged to promote inclusion by using UDL to maximize participation and learning.

Many students and adults with intellectual disabilities participate in general school and recreational sport programs. Whether participating in general sport programs or in Special Olympics sport programs, all athletes should be able to earn sport athletic letters, letter jackets, and certificates; wear team uniforms; ride team buses to competitions; participate and be recognized in school and recreation award ceremonies; and represent their schools or agencies in local, regional, county, and state competitions.

I Can Do It (ICDI) is another inclusion program, created by the U.S. Department of Health and Human Services (2019) in partnership with the U.S. Department of Education. It is a voluntary, evidence-based, school-based physical activity program designed to encourage youth with disabilities to be physically active for 60 minutes a day. The daily requirement can be achieved through engagement in general physical education, adapted physical education, recess, classroom physical activity breaks, active transport to and from school (walking, jogging, bicycling), and extracurricular activities (clubs, sports, and community-based activities). The program's focus also includes educating students to practice healthy nutritional habits. The year-long program culminates with an end-of-year awards ceremony, where students who fulfill the requirements of the program receive the Presidential Activity Lifestyle Award (PALA). ICDI can be administered by a physical education teacher, adapted physical education teacher, special education teacher, or any school staff member who works with the students during the school day. Materials are available online and include the newest edition manual, *Mentoring Children and Youth with Disabilities to Lead Healthy, Active Lifestyles*. The program is easily implemented in any K-12 education setting and offers an inclusive program of physical education, physical activity, and training in healthy nutrition habits for all students. This program also complements other inclusion offerings (e.g., Special Olympics, NFL Play 60).

Special Olympics

The mission of Special Olympics is to provide year-round sport training and athletic competition in Olympic sports for children and adults with intellectual disabilities. Founded in 1968 by Eunice Kennedy Shriver and the Joseph P. Kennedy Jr. Foundation, Special Olympics has served 5.5 million athletes with intellectual disabilities and over 920,000 Unified Sports partners. Of these athletes, 86 percent live in countries outside of North America. The majority of athletes (58 percent) are between the ages of 8 and 21, 33 percent of athletes are older than 22, and 9 percent are between the ages of 2 and 7 (Special Olympics, 2020a). In

2018, there were 106,300 Special Olympics competitions worldwide—an average of 291 per day, or 12 competitions per hour! Between 2017 and 2020 there was an 8 percent increase in the amount of Unified Sports competitions, with a total of 26,388 (Special Olympics, 2020a).

Special Olympics offers more than 30 individual and team sports. Information on rules, quick start guides, and coaching guides can be found at the Special Olympics website (www.specialolympics.org) for the following sports: alpine skiing, athletics, badminton, basketball, bocce, bowling, competitive cheer, cricket, cross-country skiing, cycling, dance sport, equestrian, figure skating, floorball, floor hockey, football, golf, gymnastics (artistic and rhythmic), handball, judo, kayaking, motor activity training program, netball, open water swimming, powerlifting, roller skating, sailing, short track speed skating, snowboarding, snowshoeing, softball, swimming, table tennis, tennis, triathlon, and volleyball.

To provide consistency in training, Special Olympics uses the rules of each sport's international sports federation (given the responsibility by the International Olympic Committee [IOC] for handling the technical aspects of Olympic Games), except when those rules conflict with the official Special Olympics sport rules (Special Olympics, 2020c).

Official Special Olympics Summer and Winter Games are held annually as national, program (state or province), sectional, area (county), and local competitions (figure 8.3). The World Summer Special Olympics Games, which take place every four years, began in 1975; the World Winter Special Olympics Games, also held every four years, began in 1977. Additional Special Olympics competitions that include two or more sports are defined as tournaments. To advance to higher levels of competition (i.e., from local through area and sectional to program competition), an athlete must have trained in an organized program for that sport; athletes are randomly drawn from among all the division winners at the lower level of competition in the sport.

Local Special Olympics training programs and competitions are available for children aged 8 and older. Before the age of 8, children with intellectual disabilities aged 2 through 7 may participate in the

FIGURE 8.3 The National Summer Games in New Jersey, USA. Each year National Games are hosted at a different location.

Special Olympics **Young Athletes (YA)** program (Special Olympics, 2020e). Young Athletes is a unique program designed to develop motor skills, eye–hand coordination, and basic sport skills for children with and without disabilities. Children in YA engage in developmentally appropriate play activities designed to foster physical, cognitive, and social development through games and activities designed for their individual skill and activity levels. Using basic equipment and the YA Activity Guide, the Special Olympics Young Athletes program can be implemented at home, in schools, or in the community. Activity guides, activity videos, resources for coaches and parents, and so much more can be found on the Special Olympics YA website (https://resources.specialolympics.org/sports-essentials/young-athletes).

Officially launched in 1997, the Special Olympics program **Healthy Athletes** addresses health disparities and offers health services to athletes with intellectual disabilities around the world. So far, Healthy Athletes has offered more than 2.1 million free health examinations in more than 140 countries in the areas of podiatry, vision, audiology, dentistry, physical therapy, sports physicals, emotional well-being, and overall health promotion. In 2018 alone, there were over 175,000 screenings worldwide.

Special Olympics has developed a series of programs to help integrate its athletes into existing community and after-school sports programs. **Special Olympics Unified Champion Schools** empower youth and educators to lead change through social inclusion. Within the program, students with disabilities are welcomed and included in all activities, opportunities, and functions. Its three-component model offers a unique combination of activities, equipping students with the tools and training to create climates of acceptance in sport, in the classroom, and throughout the school. Unified Champion Schools implement inclusive youth leadership opportunities and whole-school engagement policies.

In higher education, Special Olympics College Clubs are official clubs on campus where college students and individuals with intellectual disabilities are connected through sport to lead the social justice movement and to build friendships. In order to transform school campuses into communities of acceptance and respect, three core elements must be included: Unified Sports, Youth Leadership, and opportunities for Full Campus Engagement.

Through Unified Sports, people with and without intellectual disabilities compete on the same team. Approximately 1.4 million people take part in Unified Sports worldwide, with teams made up of people of similar age and ability levels. It is funded through the U.S. Department of Education's Office of Special Education Programs in order to build inclusion and tolerance in schools. There are over 4,500 elementary, middle, and high schools in the United States participating in Unified Sports and over 215 colleges and universities with Special Olympics College Clubs on their campuses. Unified Sports are also supported by various major sports organizations, such as the National Basketball Association (NBA), Major League Soccer (MLS), the National Collegiate Athletic Association (NCAA), and the National Federation of High Schools (NFHS), among others.

Special Olympics creates opportunities for athletes to develop and demonstrate their abilities in various leadership roles. Through Youth Leadership, Special Olympics athletes contribute in ways beyond the sports field. As leaders, these youth can promote inclusive communities where everyone's gifts are valued. Youth Leaders can serve on boards of directors, become coaches or officials, and are even employed by Special Olympics organizations around the world.

Through Whole Campus Engagement, a variety of campaigns throughout the school year, as well as "fans in the stands" can bring college communities together. Some of these opportunities include events like Spread the Word and rallies to engage the entire student body. Opportunities for whole school engagement allow for a better understanding of the Special Olympics movement by enrolled college students, faculty, and staff.

Paralympic Games for Individuals With Intellectual Disabilities

The Paralympic Games are equivalent to the Olympic Games for the world's top athletes with disabilities. They include athletes with spinal cord injuries, amputations, blindness, deafness, cerebral palsy, intellectual disabilities, and les autres (athletes with a physical disability that does not fall under one of the other categories). The Paralympic Games are conducted every four years, following the Olympic Games at the same venues.

In 1986, professionals in the Netherlands who wanted to promote sport participation for those with disabilities founded the International Association of Sports for People with Mental Handicap (INAS-

FMH). These executives later became members of the International Coordinating Committee (ICC), which in 1992 became the International Paralympic Committee (Virtus, 2020). In 1989, the 1st World Games for Athletes with an Intellectual Disability were held in Sweden; in 1991, 70 nations competed in the first Paralympic Games in Madrid (Virtus, 2020). At the 1996 Paralympic Games in Atlanta, 56 elite athletes with intellectual disabilities competed in swimming and athletics. During the 2000 Paralympic Games in Sydney, 244 elite athletes with intellectual disabilities competed in athletics, basketball, swimming, and table tennis. Following these Games, the International Paralympic Committee (IPC) suspended INAS from membership because some athletes did not meet the criteria for intellectual disability. In 2010, athletes with intellectual impairments were voted to be reincluded into the Paralympic Games in three sports: track and field, swimming, and table tennis. To qualify, an intellectual impairment is described as "a limitation in intellectual functioning and adapted behavior as expressed in conceptual, social and practical adaptive skills, which originates before the age of 18" (International Paralympic Committee, 2020). In 2019, INAS was reformed and rebranded as Virtus: World Intellectual Impairment Sport. More information on the organization can be found by referring to the Online Resources section at the end of this chapter.

Safe Participation

If the physical educator plans activities appropriate to the academic, physical, motor, social, and emotional levels of children with intellectual disabilities, there are few restrictions or contraindications for activity. Special Olympics has prohibited training and competition in the following high-risk sports, which could have lifelong deleterious effect: pole vaulting, boxing, platform diving, fencing, shooting, contact football, rugby, wrestling, karate, Nordic jumping, trampolining, most martial arts, and the javelin, discus, and hammer throw. Students with intellectual disabilities may participate in these activities as part of their general school program.

As mentioned earlier, most individuals with Down syndrome have some increased flexibility of joints. **Atlantoaxial instability** is an increased flexibility between the first and second cervical vertebrae of the neck, which could place the spinal cord at risk for injury if an affected individual were to participate in activities that hyperextend or radically flex the neck or upper spine. About 6.8 to 27 percent of individuals with Down syndrome show evidence of instability that is asymptomatic and only discovered through X-ray (Mysliwiec et al., 2015). Only 1 to 2 percent of individuals with Down syndrome have symptoms that require treatment; these symptoms might include neck pain or persistent head tilt, intermittent or progressive weakness, changes in gait pattern or loss of motor skill, loss of bowel or bladder control, increased muscle tone in the legs, and changes in sensation in the hands and feet. Physical education teachers are encouraged to follow the lead of Special Olympics in restricting students who have atlantoaxial instability from participating in activities that result in hyperextension, radical flexion, or direct pressure on the neck and upper spine. Such activities include certain gymnastics activities, the butterfly stroke, starting block dives, diving or jumping into the water, pentathlon, horseback riding, the high jump, heading a soccer ball, football, barbell squat in powerlifting, alpine skiing, and any warm-up exercises that place stress on the head and neck.

Because many children with intellectual disabilities, particularly those with Down syndrome, are cardiopathic, students should receive activity clearance from a physician. Appropriate activities within the limitations specified by the physician should then be planned.

Another common condition of individuals with intellectual disabilities is muscular hypotonia (low muscle tone). Infants with this condition are often called *floppy babies*. Although hypotonia decreases with age, it never disappears; hernias, postural deviations, and poor body mechanics are prevalent because of insufficient musculature. Again, physical educators must refrain from planning exercises and activities that are beyond the capabilities of students with muscular hypotonia, because they can lead to severe injury. Abdominal and lower back exercises must be selected with care, and daily foot-strengthening exercises are recommended.

Summary

Intellectual disability is among the most prevalent of disabilities and can have many causes, resulting in varied characteristics and affecting success and participation in physical education and sport. This chapter suggested teaching methods, tests, and activities appropriate for this population and briefly reviewed selected sport programs relevant to students with intellectual disabilities. With the right program and the right accommodations, individuals with intellectual disabilities can experience success in physical education and sport.

References

American Association on Intellectual and Developmental Disabilities (AAIDD). (2020). *Supports Intensity Scale-Children's Version (SIS-C).* www.aaidd.org/sis/sis-c

American Psychiatric Association (APA). (2013). *Diagnostic and statistical manual of mental disorders (DSM-5)* (5th ed.). Author.

Bailey, D.B., Raspa, M., Olmstead, M., & Holiday, D.B. (2008). Co-occurring conditions associated with FMR1 gene variations: Findings from a national parent survey. *American Journal of Medical Genetics Part A, 15,* 2060-2069. https://doi.org/10.1002/ajmg.a.32439

Block, M.E. (2016). *A teacher's guide to adapted physical education: Including students with disabilities in sport and recreation* (4th ed.). Brookes.

Centers for Disease Control and Prevention (CDC). (2020a, February 14). *Data and statistics on fragile X syndrome.* www.cdc.gov/ncbddd/fxs/data.html

Centers for Disease Control and Prevention (CDC). (2020b, February 14). *Facts about Down syndrome.* www.cdc.gov/ncbddd/birthdefects/downsyndrome.html

Dunn, J.M., & Leitschuh, C. (2014). *Special physical education* (10th ed.). Kendall/Hunt.

Eichstaedt, C.B., Wang, P.Y., Polacek, J.J., & Dohrmann, P.F. (1991). *Physical fitness and motor skill levels of individuals with mental retardation: Mild, moderate, and individuals with Down syndrome: Ages 6 to 21.* Illinois State University Printing Services.

Eunice Kennedy Shriver National Institute of Child Health and Human Development. (2014). *What conditions or disorders are commonly associated with Down syndrome?* www.nichd.nih.gov/health/topics/down/conditioninfo/Pages/associated.aspx

Gillespie, M. (2003). Cardiovascular fitness of young Canadian children with and without mental retardation. *Education and Training in Developmental Disabilities, 38,* 296-301.

Goodway, J.D., Ozmun, J.C, & Gallahue, D.L. (2021). *Understanding motor development: Infants, children, adolescents, adults* (8th ed.). Jones & Bartlett.

Harris, J.C. (2010). *Intellectual disability: A guide for families and professionals.* Oxford University Press.

Hunter, J., Rivero-Arias, O., Angelov, A., Kim, E., Fotheringham, I., & Leal, J. (2014). Epidemiology of Fragile X syndrome: A systematic review and meta-analysis. *American Journal of Medical Genetics Part A, 7,* 1648-1658. https://doi.org/10.1002/ajmg.a.36511

Individuals with Disabilities Education Improvement Act (IDEA) of 2004, PL 108-446, 118 Stat. 2647 (2004).

International Paralympic Committee. (2020). *IPC classification—Paralympic categories and classifications.* Retrieved from www.paralympic.org/classification

Keysor, C. S., & Mazzocco, M. M. M. (2002). A developmental approach to understanding fragile X syndrome in females. *Microscopy Research and Technique, 57*(3), 179-186.

Londeree, B.R., & Johnson, L.E. (1974). Motor fitness of TMR vs. EMR and normal children. *Medicine Science and Sport, 6,* 247-252.

MOVE International. (2013). *MOVE overview/information.* Retrieved November 12, 2014, from www.move-international.org

Murphy, C.C., Boyle, C., Schendel, D., Decoufle, P., & Yeargen-Allsopp, M. (1998). Epidemiology of mental retardation in children. *Mental Retardation and Developmental Disabilities Research Reviews, 4*(1).

Mysliwiec, A., Posluzny, A., Saulicz, E., Doroniewicz, I., Linek, P., Wolny, T., Knapik, A., Rottermund, J., Zmijewski, P., & Cieszczyk, P. (2015). Atlanto-axial instability in people with Down's syndrome and its impact on the ability to perform sports activities: A review. *Journal of Human Kinetics, 48,* 17-24. https://doi.org/10.1515/hukin-2015-0087

National Down Syndrome Society (NDSS). (2020a, February 14). *Alzheimer's disease and Down syndrome.* Retrieved from www.ndss.org/resources/alzheimers/

National Down Syndrome Society (NDSS). (2020b, February 14). *Down syndrome facts.* Retrieved from www.ndss.org/about-down-syndrome/down-syndrome-facts/

Pitetti, K., Millar, A., & Fernhall, B. (2000). Reliability of a peak performance treadmill test for children and adolescents with and without mental retardation. *Adapted Physical Activity Quarterly, 17,* 322-332. https://doi.org/10.1123/apaq.17.3.322

Rarick, G.L., Dobbins, D.A., & Broadhead, G.D. (1976). *The motor domain and its correlates in educationally handicapped children.* Prentice-Hall.

Rarick, G.L., & McQuillan, J.P. (1977). *The factor structure of motor abilities of trainable mentally retarded children: Implications for curriculum development.* (DHEW Project No H23-2544). Department of Physical Education, University of California, Berkley.

Rouse, P. (2010). *Inclusion in physical education.* Human Kinetics.

Schalock, R., Borthwick-Duffy, S., Bradley, V., Buntinx, W., Coulter, D., Craig, E., Gomez, S.C., Lachapelle, Y., Luckasson, R., Reeve, A., Shogren, K.A., Snell, M.E., Spreat, S., Tasse, M.J., Thompson, J.R., Verdugo-Alonso, M.A., Wehmeyer, M.L., & Yeager, M.H. (2010). *Intellectual disability: Definition, classification, and systems of support* (11th ed.). American Association on Intellectual and Developmental Disabilities.

Special Olympics. (2020a, May 29). *About.* Retrieved from www.specialolympics.org/about

Special Olympics. (2020b, February 14). *Motor activity training program proves sports are for everyone.* Retrieved from www.specialolympics.org/stories/news/motor-activity-training-program-proves-sports-are-for-everyone

Special Olympics. (2020c, February 14). *Sports.* Retrieved from www.specialolympics.org/our-work/sports/sports-offered

Special Olympics. (2020d, February 14). *What is intellectual disability?* Retrieved from www.specialolympics.org/about/intellectual-disabilities/what-is-intellectual-disability

Special Olympics. (2020e, February 14). *Young athletes.* Retrieved from www.specialolympics.org/our-work/young-athletes

Texas Health and Human Resources. (2018). *Determination of intellectual disability: Best practice guidelines.* Retrieved from https://hhs.texas.gov/doing-business-hhs/provider-portals/long-termcare-providers/local-intellectual-developmental-disability-authoritylidda/did-best-practice-guidelines

Ulrich, D.A. (2019). *Test of gross motor development* (3rd ed.). Pro-Ed. www.kines.umich.edu/tgmd3

U.S. Department of Health and Human Services. (2019). *I can do it! Mentoring children and youth with disabilities to lead healthy, active lifestyles program manual.* Author. https://acl.gov/sites/default/files/programs/2019-02/ICDIProgramManual2019.pdf

Virtus: World International Impairment Sport. (2020, August 14). *History of Virtus.* Retrieved from www.virtus.sport

Wehmeyer, M., Buntinx, W., Lachapelle, Y., Luckasson, R., Shalock, R., & Verdugo, M. (2008). The intellectual disability construct and its relation to human functioning. *Intellectual and Developmental Disabilities, 46,* 311-318. https://doi.org/10.1352/1934-9556(2008)46[311:tidcai]2.0.co;2

Winnick, J.P., & Short, F.X. (Eds.). (1999). *The Brockport physical fitness training guide.* Human Kinetics.

Winnick, J.P., & Short, F.X. (2014). *The Brockport physical fitness test manual* (2nd ed.) Human Kinetics.

World Health Organization (WHO). (2001). *International classification of functioning, disability and health (ICF).* Author.

Yang, Q., Rasmussen, S.A., & Friedman, J.M. (2002). Mortality associated with Down syndrome in the USA from 1983 to 1997: A population-based study. *Lancet, 359,* 1019-1025. https://doi.org/10.1016/s0140-6736(02)08092-3.

Print Resources

Special Olympics. (2020). *Sports.* www.specialolympics.org/sports.aspx

This resource includes a series of sport-specific instructional manuals. Each manual includes long-term goals, short-term objectives, skill assessments, task analyses, teaching suggestions, progression charts, and related information.

Video Resources

The National Center for Health and Physical Activity and Disability (NCHPAD). www.nchpad.org/351/2037/Exercise~Video~List

The NCHPAD website offers a list of disability-specific videos.

Online Resources

Athletes Without Limits: www.athleteswithoutlimits.org

This website is a volunteer-run nonprofit supporting athletes with intellectual disabilities and Olympic dreams. Athletes Without Limits offers opportunities for athletes to compete in Virtus (formerly known as INAS), Paralympic, and other events in the United States and abroad. This website provides information on athlete bios, teams, sports and events, and eligibility information.

Virtus: World International Impairment Sport: www.virtus.sport

This is the website of the international sports federation for elite athletes with intellectual disabilities. The site provides information on eligibility for competition, member organizations, records and rankings of top competitors, upcoming competitions, and athlete registration.

Special Olympics, Inc.: www.specialolympics.org

This website provides information on Special Olympics worldwide programs, upcoming games and competitions, individual athlete profiles, links to national Special Olympics programs, and information about how to get involved. It also includes coaching guides and instructional videos in each sport and the official sport rules, which can be downloaded free of charge.

9

Behavioral Disabilities

E. Michael Loovis

Robert is a ninth-grade student attending Mrs. Lewis' third-period physical education class. Robert is prone to vulgar outbursts accompanied by physical attacks against any peers who happen to be in the immediate vicinity. Mrs. Lewis has used a variety of interventions with Robert, including conflict resolution (CR), but to no avail—they have only exacerbated the situation, causing Robert to be even more verbally aggressive and hostile toward members of the class. Feeling like she has no other alternative, she now sends for the school's security officer to escort Robert from the gymnasium when these episodes occur. However, Mrs. Lewis is beginning to recognize that removal is also not working, because when Robert returns to class he is still inattentive to her instruction, antagonistic toward his peers, and generally a danger to himself and others. Now the school principal has told Mrs. Lewis that he no longer wishes for Robert to be sent to his office. What are Mrs. Lewis' options?

According to the Office of Special Education and Rehabilitative Services (U.S. Department of Education, 2020a), the number of students with emotional disturbance (ED) decreased from 392,181 in 2014 to 324,494 in 2018. Likewise, the relative percentage when compared with the number of students aged 6 to 21 served under IDEA (2004) decreased from approximately 5.85 percent to its current 5.45 percent, making emotional disturbance one of the smallest disability categories (U.S. Department of Education, 2020b). Nonetheless, only one student with emotional disturbance can significantly disrupt the learning of others.

In the past, these students have been referred to as *emotionally disturbed*, *socially maladjusted*, *behavior disordered*, *conduct disordered*, and *emotionally handicapped*. In this chapter, the terms **emotional disturbance** and **behavioral disorder** (BD) are used synonymously. Although they share certain characteristics, not all children with this condition exhibit the same behaviors. Generally speaking, they tend to demonstrate behavior that is labeled hyperactive, distractive, or impulsive. Some students might exhibit aggression beyond what is considered normal or socially acceptable. Some lie, set fires, steal, or abuse alcohol or drugs. Some might behave in a manner that is considered withdrawn; they might act immature or behave in ways that tend to demonstrate feelings of inadequacy.

Another segment of this population might demonstrate negative behavior directed against society; these youth who are involved with the juvenile justice system are commonly referred to as *juvenile delinquents*. According to the National Center for Education Statistics (Diliberti et al., 2019), there were an estimated 962,300 violent incidents in public schools perpetrated by individuals who, by one definition or another, fit into the category of BD. Increasingly, others fit the category called *at risk*. These young people are mired in an incompatibility between themselves and school, resulting in low academic achievement and high dropout rates (Sagor & Cox, 2004).

According to IDEA, emotional disturbance (ED) is defined as follows (Assistance to States for the Education of Children with Disabilities, 2006, p. 15):

> The term means a condition exhibiting one or more of the following characteristics over a long period of time and to a marked degree that adversely affects a child's educational performance:
>
> - An inability to learn that cannot be explained by intellectual, sensory, or health factors
> - An inability to build or maintain satisfactory interpersonal relationships with peers and teachers
> - Inappropriate types of behavior or feelings under normal circumstances
> - A general pervasive mood of unhappiness or depression
> - A tendency to develop physical symptoms or fears associated with personal or school problems

Identification of students with ED is perhaps the most perplexing problem facing school and mental health professionals. In addition, consideration is given to the ever-expanding number of young people who are at risk. Thus, it is beneficial to understand the three qualifiers that appear in the first paragraph of the federal definition—namely, duration, degree, and adverse effects on educational performance.

- *Long period of time.* This qualifier includes behavioral patterns that are chronic, such as a persistent pattern of physical or verbal attacks on a classmate. It excludes behaviors that could be construed as ED but that are situational in nature and thus are understandable or expected. For example, a death in the family, a divorce, or another crisis situation could alter a student's behavior in a way that makes it appear aberrant.
- *Marked degree.* Under consideration here are the magnitude and duration of a behavior. Intensity of behavioral displays, such as an altercation with a classmate, is considered. For example, a violent physical and verbal attack on a fellow student that requires extensive crisis intervention from teachers and counselors—in contrast to some pushing and shoving—would qualify under this criterion. Also noted is the amount of time a student engages in a particular behavior—for example, if the attacks occur frequently.
- *Adversely affects educational performance.* There must be a demonstrable cause-and-effect relation between a student's behavior and decreased academic performance. This requires, at the very least, determining if students are performing at or near the level they would be expected to attain without a behavioral disorder.

The National Mental Health and Special Education Coalition has proposed an alternative definition for ED (Forness & Knitzer, 1992). Although it has not been able to persuade Congress to change the existing definition, Kauffman and Landrum (2018) suggest that the proposed definition at the very least addresses a major difficulty with the existing definition—that is, the underestimation of students with emotional and behavioral disorders. Given the recent relative decrease in number and percentage of students identified with ED, they appear to have a reasonable objection.

Kauffman and Landrum (2018) provide a more practical framework for understanding the many and varied conditions that are subsumed under the umbrella term *emotional and behavioral disorders*, including attention and activity disorders (e.g., attention deficit/hyperactivity disorder [ADHD]), conduct disorder, problem behaviors of adolescence (e.g., delinquency, substance abuse, and promiscuity), anxiety and related disorders, depression and suicidal behavior, mood disorders, and schizophrenia and other severe disorders. These include many potentially underserved children and youth.

Nature of Emotional and Behavioral Disorders

Studies have shown that several dimensions of behavior disorders (i.e., conduct disorder, anxiety–withdrawal, immaturity, and socialized aggression) are consistently found in special education classes for students who are emotionally disturbed. Quay (1986) conducted the seminal work in dimensional classification. When endeavoring to understand students with a mild or moderate behavioral disorder (the group most likely to be found in an integrated classroom setting), a behavioral classification is the most useful.

An extension of Quay's work included the identification of two primary dimensions of disordered behavior: externalizing and internalizing (Achenbach et al., 1991). Externalizing behavior involves attacks against others, which parallels Quay and Peterson's (1987) original definition of conduct disorder and socialized aggression. Internalizing behavior, on the other hand, involves mental or emotional conflict such as depression and anxiety, which approximates Quay and Peterson's anxiety–withdrawal and immaturity dimensions.

Conduct disorders may be classified as either overt or covert (Kauffman & Landrum, 2018) or undersocialized or socialized (Quay, 1986). Undersocialized (overt) behavior—especially behavior that is aggressive—is associated with violence. According to the American Academy of Experts in Traumatic Stress (2003), students who are at risk for violent behavior typically demonstrate behaviors such as the following:

- Expressing self-destructive ideas
- Talking about specific plans to harm oneself or others
- Having difficulty controlling impulses
- Blaming other people and events for their problems
- Engaging in substance abuse

The *Diagnostic and Statistical Manual of Mental Disorders, Fifth Edition (DSM-5)* (American Psychiatric Association [APA], 2013, p. 469) defines conduct disorder as "a repetitive and persistent pattern of behavior in which the basic rights of others or major age-appropriate societal norms or rules are violated, as manifested by the presence of at least three of . . . 15 criteria in the past 12 months . . . with at least one criterion in the past 6 months." It categorizes conduct disorders under four broad headings representing 15 characteristics. A person has a mild conduct disorder if at least three symptoms from the list of 15 are present (table 9.1). Four or more symptoms indicate a moderate to severe conduct disorder. Of interest is the relation between oppositional defiant disorder (ODD) and conduct disorder. A significant percentage of children and adolescents who develop conduct disorders also show signs of ODD (not to mention ADHD) in early and middle childhood. According to the *DSM-5* (p. 462), ODD is "a pattern of angry/irritable mood, argumentative/defiant behavior, or vindictiveness lasting 6 months as evidenced by at least four symptoms and exhibited during interaction with at least one individual who is not a sibling" (see listing in table 9.1).

Psychiatric disorders are another area of concern for teachers in public schools. These disorders are likely to be more disabling and might require special therapeutic and medical treatments. Included in this category are anxiety disorders (e.g., obsessive–compulsive disorder [OCD] and posttraumatic stress disorder [PTSD]), depression and other mood disorders (e.g., bipolar or manic depressive disorder), and schizophrenic and other psychotic disorders (Forness et al., 2003). Combinations of psychopharmacology and behavioral intervention (see chapter 6) are usually employed in the treatment of these disorders.

TABLE 9.1 *DSM-5* Diagnostic Criteria for Oppositional Defiant Disorder (ODD) and Conduct Disorder

Oppositional defiant disorder	Conduct disorder
Often loses temper Often argues with authority figures or, for children and adolescents, with adults Often actively defies or refuses to comply with requests from authority figures or with rules Often deliberately annoys others Often blames others for mistakes or misbehavior Often touchy or easily annoyed Often angry and resentful Has been spiteful or vindictive at least twice within the past six months	Often bullies, threatens, or intimidates others Often initiates physical fights Has used a weapon that can cause serious physical harm (e.g., a bat, brick, broken bottle, knife, gun) Has been physically cruel to people Has been physically cruel to animals Has stolen while confronting a victim (e.g., mugging, purse snatching, extortion, armed robbery) Has forced someone into sexual activity Has deliberately engaged in fire setting with the intention of causing serious damage Has deliberately destroyed others' property (other than by fire) Has broken into someone else's house, building, or car Often lies to obtain goods or favors or to avoid obligations (i.e., "cons" others) Has stolen items of nontrivial value without confronting the victim (e.g., shoplifting, but without breaking and entering; forgery) Often stays out at night despite parental prohibitions, beginning before age 13 Has run away from home overnight at least twice while living in the parental or parental surrogate home, or once without returning for a lengthy period Is often truant from school, beginning before age 13

Causes of Behavioral Disorders

Several factors conceivably having a causal relationship to behavioral disorders have been identified, including biological, family, school, and cultural factors. These factors may place children at greater risk of developing a behavior disorder. Although space here does not permit a detailed discussion of all the factors that place students at risk, broad societal factors have also been shown to correlate with poor educational performance. These factors include poverty, minority racial or ethnic group identity, non-English or limited English language background, and specific family configuration (e.g., living in a single-parent household, limited education) (Sagor & Cox, 2004).

Biological Factors

According to Kauffman and Landrum (2018), several biological aberrations might contribute to the etiology of behavioral disorders. These include genetic anomalies, difficult temperament, brain injury or dysfunction, nutritional deficiencies and allergies, physical illness or disability, and psychophysiological disorders. With these factors identified, it is important to reiterate Kauffman and Landrum's (2018) contention, "Although biological processes have a pervasive influence on behavior, they affect behavior only in interaction with environmental factors" (p. 99). On the other hand, Cullinan (2007) suggests that research supports the proposition that brain disorders can contribute to emotional and behavioral disorders through hereditary and physical influences.

Family Factors

Pathological family relationships are a major contributory factor in the etiology of behavioral disorders. Broken homes, divorce, chaotic or hostile family relationships (including cases of severe discipline, emotional abuse, and inadequate supervision), child abuse, and parental absence or separation might produce situations in which children are at risk to develop behavioral disorders. Poverty is another factor statistically correlated with risk of disability (Chen et al., 2011). However, it is clear that there is not a one-to-one relation between disruptive family relations and behavioral disorders. Many children find parental discord more injurious than separation from one or both parents. Research also points to a multiplier effect: When two or more factors are present simultaneously, an increased probability exists that a behavioral disorder will develop. Family factors do not cause children's disordered behavior, except in complex interactions with other variables.

School Factors

It has become increasingly clear that, besides the family, school is the most significant socializing factor for a child. For this reason, the school must shoulder some of the responsibility for causing behavioral disorders. According to Kauffman and Landrum (2018), schools contribute to the development of behavior disorders in several ways:

- Insensitivity to students' individuality
- Inappropriate expectations for students
- Inconsistent management of behavior
- Instruction in nonfunctional and irrelevant skills
- Ineffective instruction in skills necessary for school success
- Destructive contingencies of reinforcement
- Undesirable models of school conduct

Cultural Factors

Frequently, there exists a discrepancy between the values and expectations that are embraced by the child, the family, and the school. A lack of multicultural perspective means that teachers find it difficult to eliminate bias and discrimination when evaluating a student's behavior. Consequently, there is an increased probability that the student will violate dominant cultural norms and be labeled as deviant, when in actuality it is only at school that their behavior is considered inappropriate (Kauffman & Landrum, 2018). Thus, educators should intervene only when behaviors are inconsistent with achievement of core educational goals, not simply because they do not conform to educators' cultural mores. In the latter case, disciplining a student would be considered inappropriate.

Part of the problem centers on conflicted cultural values and standards that society has engendered. For example, popular culture has elevated many "heroes" whose behavior is every bit as violent as that of the villains; however, students who engage in similar behaviors are told that their choices are incompatible with society's expectations.

Other cultural factors influencing behavior include the student's peer group, neighborhood, urbanization, ethnicity, and social class. These factors are not significant predictors of disordered behavior by themselves; however, within the context of economic deprivation and family conflict, they can have an adverse effect on behavior (Kauffman & Landrum, 2018).

A significant sociocultural factor linked to the spiraling incidence of behavioral disabilities is substance abuse. Prenatal exposure to drugs and alcohol affects children in two ways. First, there is an increased incidence of neurological impairment because both drugs and alcohol can cross the placenta and reach the fetus, causing chemical dependency, congenital aberrations, neurobehavioral abnormalities, and intrauterine growth retardation. Second, these children are exposed to family situations that are, at best, chaotic and often find themselves in the social service system bouncing from one substitute care situation to another. Sinclair (1998) reported that prenatally drug-exposed children in Head Start programs were more likely to be classified as emotionally or behaviorally disordered and placed in special education upon entrance into kindergarten.

General Implications for Physical Education and Sport

Conceptual models for managing classroom behavior and educating students with disabilities are discussed comprehensively in chapters 6 and 7. These include the psychoeducational, ecological, biogenic, humanistic, and behavioral approaches. What follows is a discussion of the instructional and managerial strategies that can be used effectively in adapted physical education with students who present mild and severe behavior disorders. See also the Application Example sidebar.

Instructional and Management Considerations

Research confirms that students with ED and behavioral difficulties learn best in well-managed environments characterized by effective instruction. In this section, emphasis is placed on instructional and managerial strategies that work for physical educators in both inclusive and noninclusive settings when teaching students with mild to severe

Application Example

How to Handle a Student With Behavioral Disabilities

SETTING

High school physical education class

STUDENT

A tenth grader with ODD who is frequently verbally and physically abusive to his peers and constantly challenges the authority of the physical educator

ISSUE

What are some strategies for handling this situation?

APPLICATION

The physical educator could try

- employing the conflict resolution process,
- examining events or conditions that spark the episodes of abusive behavior,
- praising instances of appropriate behavior,
- and implementing Hellison's responsibility model (described in chapter 6 and later in this chapter).

behavior problems. These strategies include response to intervention, universal design for learning, differentiated instruction, praise, precision requests, and conflict resolution.

Response to Intervention

Being able to adjust the instructional approach based on whether students are achieving their goals is referred to as response to intervention (RTI) (see chapter 7). Teachers can routinely alter the following nine factors to enhance their instruction (Harlacher et al., 2010):

1. Amount of instructional time
2. Grouping patterns
3. Redundant trials to promote success
4. Amount of review time
5. Use of different instructors or facilitators
6. Lesson pacing
7. Ratio of praise to corrective feedback
8. Cueing so the correct response is more easily identified
9. Feedback that makes it easier to identify errors

Universal Design for Learning

A corresponding approach to providing inclusive educational experiences with special emphasis on students with unique needs is universal design for learning (UDL). As discussed in previous chapters, UDL emphasizes three principles: multiple means of representation (different inputs), multiple means of action and expression (different skill sets), and multiple means of engagement (different forms of participation). Each of these could be employed individually or in combination. Hunt (2017) suggests that, when working with students with ED, teachers employ the principle of engagement more easily and more frequently than the other two principles. For example, a student with ED who experiences high levels of frustration and aggression when placed in a competitive situation might benefit from engaging in tennis using Nintendo Wii technology. In this way the student benefits from all three principles: tennis is introduced in a fun, less threatening manner; the student's action is controlled via the use of technology; and the use of a video game serves to shape participatory behavior that may ultimately lead to engagement in the actual game of tennis with peers in physical education. Additional information on UDL can be found in chapter 7, as well as in the Lieberman and colleagues (2021) book titled *Universal Design for Learning in Physical Education*.

Differentiated Instruction

Differentiated instruction became the hallmark of special education in the earliest years of the 21st century. Defined as the "planning of curriculum and instruction using strategies that address student strengths, interests, skills, and readiness in flexible learning environments" (Gartin et al., 2002,

p. 8), differentiated instruction acknowledges that there is no one correct way of instructing children, including those with behavioral disabilities. Effective teachers tailor their instructional techniques according to a student's type of behavioral disorder.

In physical education, differentiated instruction should include consideration of the learning environment. Specifically, physical educators should attend to the organization of the gym (e.g., well-established routines, clearly posted rules, and the establishment of a positive instructional climate, including confirmed behavioral expectations). Additionally, arrangement of the environment includes flexible grouping. Students might benefit from large-group instruction, or they might be served better by small-group instruction, peer teaching, independent study, one-on-one instruction, or cooperative learning groups. Another way to differentiate is to use multilevel instruction, which consists of engaging students in the same curriculum but with different goals and levels of difficulty. Curricular overlapping (Block, 2016) is another modification wherein a student who

In a basketball unit related to learning and performing the jump shot, the physical educator might employ peer teaching, alter the distance from the basket, and reduce the criteria for achievement. This photo shows a peer tutor ready to assist if needed.

is unable to participate in the general physical education curriculum works on unique IEP goals but is accommodated in the general physical education class.

Praise

Praise has been documented to have a positive effect on both academic and behavioral outcomes with students with behavioral disorders. However, Sutherland (2000) found that although students complied with teacher requests 80 percent of the time, teachers provided praise for compliance only 2 percent of the time. There is also a potential relation between how much praise is given and whether the praise is given effectively (i.e., conveyed in a tone that is earnest and reinforcing). However, praise can also be overdone—if delivered continuously, then praise will satiate and lose its reinforcing effect.

Precision Requests

Special educators have devised programs such as **precision requests**, which have proven effective with students who have serious ED and which could easily be used in physical education. Musser and colleagues (2001) described the following steps for precision requests:

Step 1: Make an initial request for compliance by saying, "Please." If the student complies, reinforcement is provided. If there is no compliance, step 2 is implemented.

Step 2: Make a second request with the phrase, "You need to ____." If the student complies, reinforcement is provided. If there is no compliance, the final step of the program is implemented.

Step 3: Noncompliance causes the use of consequences such as a time out.

Conflict Resolution

When teaching students with behavioral disorders, there is an above-average risk of using confrontation to resolve conflict. This does not imply that interpersonal confrontation need be punitive or destructive. On the contrary, a healthy use of confrontation provides the opportunity to examine behaviors in relation to expectations and perceptions as well as to establish rules. This is especially crucial during the *agitation* and *acceleration* phases of the acting-out behavior cycle described by Colvin and Scott (2014) and illustrated later in the chapter. It is here that conflict resolution will produce its sought-after benefit.

The goal of confrontation is resolution of conflicts through constructive behavior change. Several steps are necessary in reaching this desired goal: making an assertive, confrontational statement (one that expresses honestly and directly how the speaker feels about another's behavior); being aware of common reactions to confrontation; and knowing how to deal effectively with these reactions.

Although assertive confrontation can be an effective means of resolving conflicts, it requires skillful use of each step in the process. Without question, the most crucial component of the conflict resolution process is the formulation of an effective confrontational statement. There are three main components: a nonjudgmental description of the behavior causing the problem, a concrete effect that the behavior is having on the person sending the message, and an expression of the feelings produced from the concrete effect of the behavior. Together, these components form an **I-message**. When combined with active listening, which involves attending, listening, and responding to the person, and verbal mediation, which involves students verbalizing the association between their behavior and the consequences of that behavior, the conflict resolution process can be an excellent means to avoid major confrontations, as exemplified in the following conversation:

Teacher: "Robert, your disruptive behavior during class is causing me a problem. When you argue and fight with the other students in class, I have to stop teaching. It's distracting to me, and I'm frustrated." (I-message)

Student: "I get that stuff at home. I don't need it here."

Teacher: "I see. Lately, you're having some problems at home with your parents." (active listening)

Student: "My dad and I have been fighting all week."

Teacher: "You're really upset about the problem you're having with your father." (active listening)

Student: "Yeah! I don't know how much longer I can put up with his bulls—t."

Teacher: "So you're angry because of the situation at home, and it's carrying over into school." (active listening)

Student: "Yeah! I know you're upset about me fighting and not getting along in class. You know I've tried to get along."

Teacher: "You're a little surprised that it's such a problem for me even though the incidents are not always all that extreme." (active listening)

Student: "Well, not really. I see what you're saying. You have to stop teaching and stuff. Mostly I'm taking my anger out on the guys in class. I'll just have to remember that it's not their fault that my dad and me aren't getting along. I'll try harder not to get angry and fight with the guys, okay?" (verbal mediation)

Teacher: "That would sure help me. Thanks, Robert."

In this example, the teacher has used an I-message and the techniques of active listening and verbal mediation to defuse a situation that could have erupted into a major confrontation between teacher and student.

Teacher Behavior and Communication

To many instructors, what is most notable about children and youth with behavioral issues is their inability to respond to directives from adults (Bullock & Menendez, 2001). With this in mind, it is incumbent upon teachers and coaches to recognize how their own behavior (both physical and verbal) can influence the behavior of students leading up to, during, and immediately after a crisis situation. This is referred to as the *escalation cycle* (addressed in more detail toward the end of this section). It should be fairly obvious that working with this population of students will include conflict and confrontations. Note that confrontations are neither good nor bad; they can have positive outcomes if the instructor knows how to handle the situation in a professional manner. In this section we will explore things to do and not to do when engaged in confrontation with a student who demonstrates challenging behavior. Many of these techniques, called "Houdini techniques" (Frank et al. 1998), have become commonplace when intervening with students with challenging behaviors.

Things to Do

There are several ways that teachers and coaches can defuse a confrontational situation while maintaining a supportive and safe environment:

- Monitor body language—avoid the appearance of being upset.
- Monitor tone of voice—keep the tone positive and choose words wisely.
- Provide appropriate options (often referred to as "redirecting").
- Repeat the request while staying calm and allowing time for the student to comply.
- Walk away after making a request that the student do something.

These behaviors have implications across the entire spectrum of acting out, sometimes referred to as the *escalation cycle* (Colvin & Scott, 2014): calm, trigger, agitation, acceleration, peak, de-escalation, and recovery. Most, if not all, of this list will be useful during the most critical phases of the escalation cycle—namely, the trigger, agitation, acceleration, and peak phases. It is during these times that a confrontation can be prevented from turning into a real crisis and channeled into a positive outcome.

Things Not to Do

There are several things that teachers or coaches do that exacerbate the confrontation and produce a heightened crisis situation. Be sure to avoid

- appearing angry and frustrated,
- emotional responses,
- making threats or promises you cannot keep, or
- becoming embroiled in a counter-control narrative.

Counter-control narratives arise when instructors and students get caught in an aversive cycle, most often verbal one-upmanship, until the situation reaches a crisis point and spirals out of control. What follows is an example of verbal counter-control that could just as easily have spiraled into a physical confrontation with potential serious consequences:

Teacher: "Please take your seat."

Student: "Don't start bossin' me around!"

Teacher: "I believe you know the rules."

Student: "I never heard of this d— rule before."

Teacher: "How many times do I have to deal with your attitude? And watch your language."

Student: "I don't have no attitude. You are the one with the attitude."

Teacher: "Pull it together right now or get out!"

Student: "You b—! I don't want to be here anyway."

Situations such as this spiral out of control unless the adult sees fit to intervene using well-established techniques that defuse the situation and restore some semblance of order (Carey & Bourbon, 2004).

Behavioral Contracting

As discussed in chapter 6, contingency management is especially helpful with students who experience behavioral difficulties. One helpful system is the **behavior contract**, a written document that specifies the relation between behaviors and their consequences. An example of a behavior contract is shown in figure 9.1.

Additional Evidence-Based Practices

Other positive practices that have proven effective in shaping behavior for students with ED include choice-making strategies that empower students to determine the order in which instructional tasks will be completed as well as differential reinforcement procedures and high-probability requests using the Premack principle, both discussed in chapter 6 (Lane et al., 2011). Additionally, Farley and colleagues (2012) suggest that peer-assisted learning and self-management are two efficacious strategies that teachers can easily implement.

Physical Restraint and Seclusion

The Children's Health Act of 2000 (PL 106-310) clarified the legality of using physical restraint and seclusion as a tool for managing the behavior of children with behavioral or mental health difficulties in schools and health care settings. According to Van Haren and Fiedler (2004), "Physical restraint is defined as restriction imposed by a person that immobilizes or reduces the ability of a pupil to move his or her arms, legs, or head freely" (p. 18). Van Haren and Fiedler also noted that seclusion should be used as a form of restraint only if it is outlined in the student's IEP.

State education agencies such as the Massachusetts Department of Education have codified the regulatory requirements of PL 106-310 for use by school districts. School personnel receive training annually, including the development of knowledge and skills as they relate to school restraint policies, methods of control without physical restraint, types of restraint employed and concomitant safety considerations, administration of restraint based on individual needs and limitations, and documentation and reporting of incidents.

As recently as 2012, the U.S. Department of Education established the following guideline for the use of restraint and seclusion:

> Restraint and seclusion should not be used as routine school safety measures; that is, they should not be implemented except in situations where a child's behavior poses imminent danger of serious physical harm to self or others and not as a routine strategy implemented to address instructional problems or inappropriate behavior (e.g., disrespect, noncompliance, insubordination, out of seat), as a means of coercion or retaliation, or as a convenience. (p. 3)

Assessment and Activities

According to Steinberg and colleagues (1992), effective physical education programs for students

Physical Education Behavior Contract

The terms of this contract are as follows:

The student will earn 1 point for every positive statement or action made to or about an opponent during participation in the class basketball unit. The student must earn 10 points to qualify for free time in the gym on Friday afternoons.

The teacher will record every demonstration of the student's positive interactions as evidenced by the chart publicly displayed in the gym. The teacher will award points during class and supervise free time in the gym on Friday afternoons if the student earns the prescribed number of points.

This agreement is between [student's name] and [teacher's name]. The contract begins on [specify date] and ends on [specify date]. It will be reviewed on [specify date].

Student's signature ______________________ Date ____________

Teacher's signature ______________________ Date ____________

FIGURE 9.1 A behavior contract in physical education is a written document that specifies the relation between behaviors and their consequences.

with emotional and behavioral disturbances are the exception rather than the rule. These authors suggest that this is especially perplexing in light of increased academic performance and decreased student absenteeism when students are involved in vigorous and systematic exercise programs. Poor motor performance in students with behavioral disorders is often attributed to indirect factors—attention deficits, poor work habits, impulsivity, hyperactivity, feelings of inadequacy, and demonstration of aggressive behavior—rather than to an innate inability to move well.

The approved policies and procedures of a local educational agency should be followed when assessing students with behavioral disorders for the purpose of establishing an IEP. Valid and reliable tests should be used to assess physical fitness and gross motor skills. Instruments such as the Test of Gross Motor Development (TGMD-3) and the Brockport Physical Fitness Test (BPFT) should be used when appropriate. Additionally, ecological or functional assessment techniques (see chapter 4) might be used when standardized testing protocols are inappropriate.

Exercise programs have been shown to exert a positive influence on disruptive behavior (Kantomaa et al., 2008). As little as 10 or 15 minutes of daily jogging has produced a significant reduction in the disruptive behavior of children (Yell, 1988). Elliot and colleagues (1994) reported a reduction in maladaptive and stereotypic behaviors in adults with autism and intellectual disabilities following vigorous aerobic exercise. Using functional analysis, Roane and Kelley (2008) developed an intervention for decreasing problem behavior during a walking program with a 16-year-old female with developmental and physical disabilities, including self-injurious behaviors. Bowling and colleagues (2017) developed a seven-week aerobically progressive physical education curriculum using cybercycling (virtual-reality stationary bicycles) that had significant effects on behavioral self-regulation and classroom functioning with students who had a variety of behavioral health disorders.

Depending on students' developmental abilities and behavioral characteristics, they should be placed in a class that can meet their needs. Regardless of placement, the type of programming chosen and the degree of peer interaction are two variables of considerable importance. The first area of concern is the program itself. Because some students with behavioral disabilities might demonstrate a lag in physical and motor abilities, the physical educator must provide them with appropriate developmental activities. The emphasis should be on physical conditioning, balance, and basic movement. In this regard, Bar-Eli and colleagues (1994) determined that establishing short- and long-term goals produced the greatest increase in performance of a fitness task with a group of adolescent male and female subjects with behavioral disorders. The development of fundamental locomotor and nonlocomotor movements also requires attention. In addition, it might be necessary to emphasize perceptual–motor activities because students with behavioral disabilities often demonstrate inadequacies in this area.

Relaxation is another program component that deserves a special place in the normal movement routine of many students with behavioral disorders. Making the transition from gym to classroom can be difficult for students with hyperactive behavior. This difficulty is not a reason to eliminate vigorous activity from these students' programs; rather, it is a reason to provide additional buffer time during which students can use the relaxation techniques they have been taught. Steiner and colleagues (2013) extended the idea of relaxation to include yoga, which was found to have some benefits for a sample of elementary school children with ED in an urban environment.

The ability to play effectively is crucial to success in physical education. Because games are a part of the physical education program for most students with behavioral disorders, it is essential for teachers to be aware of the relation between the type of activity chosen and the degree to which inappropriate behavior is likely to occur. The type of programming chosen directly relates to the amount of aggression demonstrated by students during activity. Reduced body contact, simplified rules, and fewer skill requirements are some of the variables that seem to control aggression. Not to be overlooked are the efforts of Project Adventure (Aubry, 2008; Rohnke, 2009), which has a cooperative rather than competitive orientation and which works well in therapeutic settings. In light of the problems surrounding self-concept and the antisocial behavior exhibited by some students with behavioral disorders, the least desirable situation is one that prescribes winners and losers or that rewards overly aggressive behavior.

Nontraditional activities such as initiatives and low-ropes challenges also have a place in physical education curricula for students with behavioral disorders. Initiatives are games or other problem-solving activities that foster trust and respect between group members; they provide opportunities to create leadership and team-building skills. Cluphf (2003) describes the use of these activities as a helpful tool in developing physical skills as well as the value of teamwork and personal persistence in the face of failure. Harwood and colleagues (2017) employed a meta-analysis and determined that a program of martial arts was moderately effective in reducing aggression toward peers in children and youth ages 6 to 18.

Specific Approaches for Physical Education and Sport

This section provides two examples of specific approaches used in physical education and sport for students with behavioral disorders. The humanistic orientation can be used with all students, including those who have milder forms of behavioral disorders; educators working with students who have more severe behavioral difficulties employ the behavioral approach.

Humanistic Approach

In physical education, students with behavior disabilities ranging from mild to severe can be taught through the humanistic approach. In this context, humanism is applied to skill acquisition and the management of social behaviors. Generally speaking, some techniques suggested by Sherrill (2004) for improving self-concept are singularly applicable with this population; for example, teachers should strive to do the following (p. 234):

- Conceptualize individual and small-group counseling as an integral part of physical education.
- Teach students to care about each other and show that they care.
- Emphasize cooperation and social interaction rather than individual performance.
- Stress the importance of genuineness and honesty in praise.
- Increase perceived competence in relation to motor skill and fitness.
- Convey that they like and respect students as human beings, not just for their motor skills and fitness.

More specifically, the personal responsibility approach outlined by Hellison (2011) has immediate relevance for practitioners confronted with students who are usually high functioning but who lack self-control and consequently present management problems. The main purpose of Hellison's approach is to develop social responsibility. Hellison has developed a set of alternative goals or levels for physical education that focus on human needs and values rather than on fitness and sport skill development exclusively. The goals are developmental and reflect a loosely constructed level-by-level progression of attitudes and behaviors. They include self-control and respect for the rights and feelings of others, participation and effort, self-direction, and caring and helping.

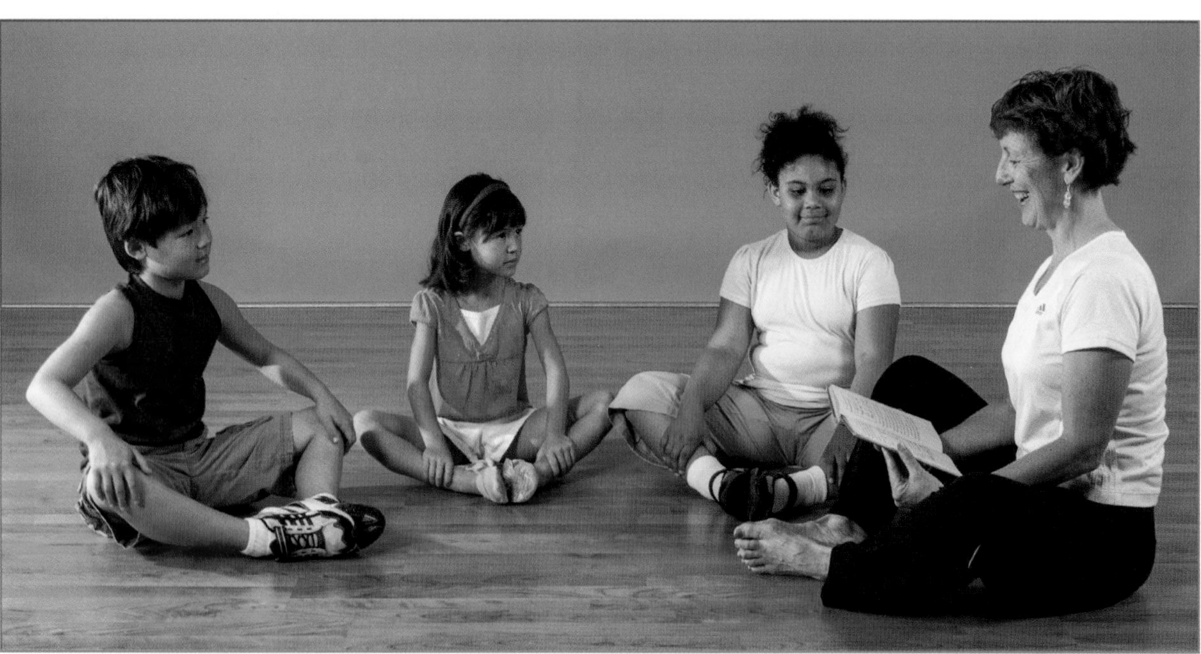

Yoga promotes relaxation and helps in transitioning to the next activity.

Level 0: Irresponsibility. At this level, students fail to take responsibility for either their actions or inactions; they blame others for their behavior and typically make excuses.

Level I: Respecting the rights and feelings of others. Level I deals with the need for control of one's own behavior. Self-control should be the first goal, according to Hellison, because effective learning cannot take place if one cannot control impulses to harm others physically and verbally.

Level II: Participation and effort. Level II focuses on the need for physical activity and offers students a medium for personal stability through experiences in which they can engage on a daily basis. Participation involves getting uninterested students to at least go through the motions, expend various degrees of effort to determine if effort leads to improvement, and redefine success as a personal accomplishment.

Level III: Self-direction. Level III emphasizes the need for students to take more responsibility for their choices and to link these choices with their own identities. Students at this level can work independently in class and take responsibility for their intentions and actions. At this level, students begin to assume responsibility for the direction of their lives and explore options in developing a strong and integrated personal identity. This level includes developing a knowledge base that will enhance achievement of their goals, developing a plan to accomplish their goals, and evaluating their plan to determine their success.

Level IV: Caring and helping. Level IV is the most difficult for students; it is also not a requirement for successful participation in the responsibility model. At this level, students reach out to others and commit themselves to genuinely caring about other people. Students are motivated to give support, cooperate, show concern, and help. Generally speaking, the goal of level IV is the improvement of the entire group's welfare.

Level V: Outside the gym. Level V promotes the opportunity to transfer many of the lessons learned in the gym to other areas of life. It also implies being a role model.

Hellison recognized that these goals provide only a framework and that strategies must be employed to help students demonstrate self-control and respect for others, participate and show effort, be self-directed, and demonstrate caring behavior on a regular basis. He suggests five interaction strategies to help reach the goals:

1. Awareness talks (post goals on gym wall and refer to them frequently)
2. Physical activity lesson (teach students to solve conflict during a game)
3. Group meetings (have students discuss issues of low motivation or difficulty in self-direction)
4. Individual decision making (students determine if their activity selection is the best choice for achieving their goals)
5. Reflection time (have students record in a journal or discuss how they did during class in relation to the goals they had established)
6. Counseling time (have students discuss their patterns of abusive behavior and possibly their underlying motives for such behavior)

This last strategy in particular gives students the opportunity to talk with the teacher about problems preventing them from achieving their goals within specified levels of the responsibility model. These strategies are "processes for helping students to become aware of, experience, make decisions about, and reflect on the model's goals" (Hellison & Templin, 1991, p. 108). See table 9.2 for a brief examination of the relationship between the levels and strategies in Hellison's model.

Many physical education programs use games to accomplish goals and objectives. Because students with behavioral disorders often lack fundamental skills, they frequently are incapable of demonstrating even minimal levels of competence in these games. As a result, they have an increased tendency to act out—perhaps with verbal or physical aggression—or to withdraw, which further excludes them from an opportunity to develop skills.

In an effort to promote a positive learning environment, Hellison (2011) developed a nontraditional approach to working with at-risk students, using basketball as the primary vehicle for empowering students to learn personal and social values. Employing Hellison's responsibility model as the philosophical underpinning, the coaching club is a before-school program in Chicago's inner city. It offers students the opportunity to explore movement through a progression of five levels: (I) self-control (control of one's body and temper), (II) teamwork (full participation by all team members), (III) self-coaching, (IV) coaching another team member, and (V) applying skills learned in the program at

TABLE 9.2 Hellison's Personal and Social Responsibility Model

Strategies	Levels	Examples in physical education and activity settings
Awareness talks	I-V	• Verbally remind students during an activity about the levels of responsibility. • Model attitudes and behaviors associated with levels during an activity. • Conduct student sharing sessions before, during, or after the activity.
Physical activity lesson	I-IV	• Students are encouraged to play in a cooperative game. • Students are taught how to solve conflict during a game. • Students who have been successful in an activity help those who have not been successful.
Individual decision making	I-V	• Students who are abusive can choose to sit out of an activity or modify their behavior. • A student who chooses to participate in a game of table tennis with friends needs to decide if table tennis is the best way to achieve the goal of increased aerobic capacity.
Group meetings	I and IV primarily II and III potentially	• Students discuss what constitutes self-control and the consequences for violating the rules established for participating in the activity. • Students verbally evaluate what they thought of the activity that was just completed and the role of the instructor during class.
Reflection time	I-V	• Students journal about what occurred during class. • Students use a checklist to evaluate the degree to which they were successful in achieving personal goals.
Counseling time	I-V	• Teacher and student discuss the student's pattern of aggressive behavior during that day's activity. • Teacher and student discuss the amount of effort expended by the student during that day's activity and how it related to the student's personal program goals.

school, home, and in the neighborhood. Playing ability is not a prerequisite; the program's purpose is to promote social responsibility. Likewise, extrinsic rewards are unnecessary because students are motivated to reach level IV (Hellison & Georgiadis, 1992, p. 7). Level IV consists of the following:

- Has good attendance
- Is coachable and on task at practice
- Does not abuse others or interrupt practice
- Is able to set personal goals and work independently on these goals
- Possesses good helping skills (such as giving cues, observing, and giving positive feedback as well as general praise)
- Encourages teamwork and passing the ball
- Listens to other players; is sensitive to their feelings and needs
- Puts the welfare of other players above own needs (such as the need to win or look good)
- Understands that exhibiting these characteristics is the key to being a good coach, regardless of personal basketball ability

Behavioral Approach

Students with severe behavior disorders require intense programming efforts. This group includes students who are self-indulgent, aggressive, noncompliant, and self-stimulatory or self-destructive. Using the basic steps of behavioral programming discussed in chapter 6, Dunn and Morehouse developed the data-based gymnasium (DBG). This program incorporates the systematic use of behavioral principles to produce procedural consistency and to bring student behavior under the control of naturally occurring reinforcers. To the latter end, instructors use natural reinforcers available in the environment, such as praising a desirable behavior to strengthen it or ignoring an undesirable behavior to bring about its extinction. Tangible reinforcers such as token economies are introduced only after it has been demonstrated that the consistent use of natural reinforcers will not achieve the desired outcome.

In an effort to equip teachers with consistent behavioral procedures, the DBG uses a variety of strategies, including rules of thumb, to apply to inappropriate behavior. For each area of inappropriate behavior (e.g., self-indulgent behavior), there exists a generally accepted way of responding (a "rule of thumb"). The intent of these rules is to make the development and implementation of a formal behavioral program unnecessary. Although the DBG is no longer available commercially, its basic principles are illustrated in Dunn and Leitschuh (2014), as outlined below.

- *Self-indulgent behavior.* Behaviors in this category include crying, screaming, throwing tantrums, and performing repetitive, irritating activities or making noises. The rule of thumb for handling students who engage in self-indulgent behaviors is to ignore them until the behavior is discontinued and then socially reinforce the first occurrence of an appropriate behavior. For example, one would ignore children's tantrums when they cannot control a play situation with classmates but praise their initial attempts to play cooperatively.
- *Noncompliant behavior.* Noncompliant behaviors include instances when students decline to comply when instructed to do something as well as forgetting or failing to do something they have been asked to do. Noncompliance also includes doing what is requested but in a less than acceptable way. The rule of thumb is that teachers should ignore noncompliant verbalizations, lead students physically through the task, or prevent students from participating in an activity until they follow through on the initial request. Compliance with any request is immediately reinforced socially. For example, one would physically restrict aggressive play and praise a child's positive engagement with a classmate or group.
- *Aggressive behavior.* Verbal or physical abuse directed toward an object or a person is considered aggressive behavior. Examples of aggressive acts include hitting, fighting, pinching, biting, pushing, or deliberately destroying someone's property. The rule of thumb for aggressive behavior is that it is punished immediately with a verbal reprimand and the offending student is removed from the activity. Social reinforcement is given when students demonstrate appropriate interaction with other people or objects. For example, a student who strikes another student is immediately reprimanded verbally (conflict resolution) and is eliminated from the activity (given a time out; see chapter 6).
- *Self-stimulatory behavior.* This category includes behaviors that interfere with learning because students become engrossed in the perseverative nature of the activities. Examples include head banging, hand flapping, body rocking, and eye gouging. As a rule of thumb, Dunn and Leitschuh (2014) recommend a formal behavioral program to deal with this type of behavior. An in-depth discussion of formal principles and programs for behavior modification is presented in chapter 6.

PBIS: Secondary and Tertiary Interventions and Supports

As described in chapter 6, PBIS (Positive Behavioral Interventions and Supports) is a three-tiered model that uses a collection of interventions and support strategies to prevent challenging behaviors from occurring as well as effectively manage episodes of challenging behaviors should they occur. For students with more severe, intense, or even extreme behavioral challenges, teachers and administrators can enlist interventions and supports from the secondary and tertiary levels (see table 6.2 in chapter 6).

Before we discuss and consider these interventions, a brief discussion of IDEA's critical rules and regulations for disciplining students with disabilities is necessary. In these cases, the IEP team must determine if the student's misbehavior was a function of a disability (i.e., was the student's ability to understand the consequences of the behavior or to control the behavior impaired?). This process is called *manifestation determination*. Establishing the standard for manifestation determination is another concept that is crucial to understanding the role of the IEP team.

Discipline

The reauthorization of IDEA in 2004 introduced new standards, provisions, and definitions and considerably changed the rules and regulations for disciplining students with disabilities. The standards for discipline (IDEA, 2004) are detailed here.

- School personnel have the authority to determine on a case-by-case basis the necessity for ordering a change in placement for a student with a disability who violates the student code of conduct.
- School personnel can remove a student with a disability who violates a student conduct code from an existing placement to an interim alternative education placement, another setting, or suspension for not more than 10 consecutive school days, to the extent that such alternatives are applied to students without disabilities.
- Within 10 school days of any decision to change the placement of a student with a disability, the IEP team must determine if the misconduct was a manifestation of (i.e., caused by or related to) the student's disability.

Table 9.3 illustrates the existing standard for manifestation determination.

If the IEP team determines that misconduct was a manifestation of the student's disability, then the team will conduct a **functional behavior assessment** (FBA) and develop a **behavioral intervention plan** (BIP). If a BIP has already been developed, the IEP team will review the plan and make modifications where necessary. If the student has been removed from the original placement, the student will be returned to that placement unless the parent and local education agency agree otherwise.

If students with disabilities violate the school conduct code, they can be suspended for up to 10 days in a school year. Regardless of whether the behavior is determined to be a manifestation of the student's disability, a student can be removed to an interim alternative educational setting (IAES) for up to 45 days for the following: carrying or possessing a weapon; possessing, using, selling, or soliciting illegal drugs; or inflicting serious bodily injury on another person while at school, on school premises, or at a school function. If the student's behavior is determined to be related to the disability, the student is subject to IDEA disciplinary procedures. Implementing a two-stage process—namely, conducting an FBA and designing a BIP—accomplishes this task.

TABLE 9.3 Standard for Manifestation Determination

PL 108-446
Was the conduct caused by or did it have a direct and substantial relationship to the student's disability?
Was the conduct a direct result of failure by the local education agency to implement the IEP?

Functional Behavioral Assessment

Students with disabilities (particularly behavioral disorders) who exhibit dangerous or unruly behavior are not exonerated from responsibility for behavior that is considered extreme. The 1997 and 2004 reauthorizations of IDEA created and extended due process policies to ensure that students with disabilities who violate school conduct codes will continue to receive an appropriate education as specified in their IEP. Additionally, the IEP must specify an appropriate intervention plan to ameliorate the student's challenging behavior.

IDEA requires that before expulsion, alternative school placement, or suspension for more than 10 days, a student with a disability must have an FBA, "a systematic method of gathering information about behavior and its relationship with the environment in which it occurs; its goal is to identify the function or purpose that behavior serves for the student under specific environmental conditions" (Payne et al., 2007, p.158). Functional behavioral assessments can be as simple as a questionnaire completed by the teacher or as involved as direct observation for 20 or more hours with experimental manipulation of variables to promote behavioral control.

Cunningham and O'Neill (2007) demonstrated that rating scales, questionnaires, and teacher and student interviews are significantly less effective in functionally analyzing behavior than are direct observation and informal ABC evaluation (i.e., antecedent–behavior–consequence). For example, a member of the IEP team could observe a student during physical education class and record the frequency of an undesirable behavior, such as physical or verbal abuse during competitive team activities. Additionally, the observer would attempt to identify antecedent events, such as occasions when the student is in a one-on-one situation with a particular classmate. After identifying the student's behavioral difficulty, the IEP team is legally responsible for developing the BIP. Note that IDEA does not specify what components should be detailed in the plan, merely that the plan must be developed (Maag & Katsiyannis, 2006). Figure 9.2 shows an example of an FBA form.

Functional Behavioral Assessment

Student name: Seth Zion **ID: DOB:** 3/9/2008 **Case manager:** Mrs. Loovis

Data sources: ☑ Observation ☑ Student interview ☑ Teacher interview ☐ Parent interview ☑ Rating scales ☐ Normative testing

Description of behavior:

Student physically and verbally abuses classmates during physical education class.

Settings in which behavior occurs:

Abusive behavior typically occurs during competitive situations (e.g., during a basketball game).

Frequency:

Behaviors occur, on average, at least three times per class period.

Intensity (consequences of problem behavior on student, peers, and instructional environment):

Behavior has resulted in physical injury to several students and a general reluctance on the part of most students to want to compete against Seth.

Duration:

Episodes can be as brief as 10 or 15 seconds, in the case of verbal abuse to lengthier confrontations lasting 1 or 2 minutes during physical confrontations.

Previous interventions:

Parent conferences, in-school suspension, and student conference

Educational impact:

Disrupting other peers and failure to make adequate educational progress in physical education

Function of behavior: Specify hypothesized function for each area checked in this section.

☑ ***Affective regulation/emotional reactivity (Identify emotional factors, such as anxiety, depression, anger, and poor self-concept, that play a role in organizing or directing problem behavior):***
Case of verbal abuse, to lengthier confrontations lasting 1 or 2 minutes during physical confrontations.
Student is embarrassed when making mistakes that classmates think are silly.

☐ ***Cognitive distortion (Identify distorted thoughts, such as inaccurate attributions, negative self-statements, and erroneous interpretations of events, that play a role in organizing or directing problem behavior):***

☑ ***Reinforcement (Identify environmental triggers and payoffs that play a role in organizing and directing problem behavior):***

Antecedents: Engaging in team sports such as basketball.

Consequences: Student uses physical and verbal attacks against classmates to deflect attention away from his fundamentally inadequate motor skills.

☐ ***Modeling (Identify the degree to which the behavior is copied, who is the student copying the behavior from, and why the student is copying the behavior):***

Not an issue

☐ ***Family issues (Identify family issues that play a part in organizing and directing problem behavior):***

☐ ***Physiological/constitutional issues (Identify physiological and personality characteristics, such as developmental disabilities and temperament, that play a part in organizing and directing problem behavior):***

☑ ***Communicate need (Identify what the student is trying to say through the problem behavior):***

Student is communicating his embarrassment about his inability to perform basic motor skills.

☑ ***Curriculum/instruction (Identify how instruction, curriculum, or educational environment play a part in organizing and directing problem behavior):***

Abusive behavior occurs when instructional expectations exceed his physical and motor abilities.

FIGURE 9.2 Sample functional behavioral assessment.

Courtesy of Jeffrey A. Miller at Duquesne University; http://mfba.net/forms.html.

Behavioral Intervention Plan

Once the behaviors in question are understood, intervention is designed and implemented. Behavioral intervention plans address students' motives for misbehaving, their likes and dislikes, and the effectiveness of various positive (and negative) reinforcers. Behavioral intervention plans are intended to emphasize positive interactions and behaviors. They should not be designed to punish the student or to catch the student misbehaving. As many people as possible who have interactions with a particular student should be involved in development of the BIP. It is for this reason that physical educators must understand the purpose and design of the BIP and participate in its implementation.

Scott and Nelson (1999) proposed a process that links FBAs and BIPs. This process involves 10 steps:

1. Determining the function of the undesirable behavior
2. Determining an appropriate alternative behavior
3. Determining how frequently the alternative behavior should occur
4. Developing a teaching sequence
5. Manipulating the environmental context to increase the probability of success
6. Altering the environment to decrease the probability of failure
7. Determining how positive responses will be reinforced
8. Determining consequences for problem behavior
9. Developing a data collection system
10. Developing goals and objectives in behavioral and measurable terms

In many respects, development and implementation of the 10-step FBA and BIP process parallel the applied behavior analysis approach outlined in chapter 6. Figure 9.3 is an example of a BIP that has been constructed with consideration of this 10-step process.

Strategies for Inclusion

Based on data collected through 2017 (U.S. Department of Education, 2020), students with behavioral disorders are receiving their education in greater and greater numbers in the general education classroom: 48 percent of students with behavioral disorders spend more than 80 percent of the school day in general classrooms, another 17.4 percent spend between 40 and 79 percent of the school day in the general classroom, and 18 percent spend less than 40 percent of the day in the general classroom. The remaining 16.6 percent receive their education in other placements, including separate facilities, residential facilities, and at home or in hospitals. These data indicate that physical educators are likely to have students with behavioral disorders in their general physical education classes.

The inclusion of students with behavioral disorders into the general class should be based primarily on the frequency, intensity, and duration of behavioral episodes. For those with mild behavioral profiles, the general class is easily the placement of choice. The decision becomes more difficult if the student's behaviors are significantly more severe, even with a management plan in effect.

In terms of students with behavioral disorders, inclusion is facilitated much of the time through development and implementation of a BIP. As discussed previously, these plans detail student expectations and consequences if behavioral expectations are not achieved. Students who have severe behavior disorders such that they are either disruptive and interfere with the operation of the general class or are harmful to themselves or others might require a segregated approach.

Summary

Behavioral conditions correspond to the categories of behavior disorders and emotional disturbance as defined in IDEA. This chapter provided ideas for teaching and managing students with identified behavioral disorders in physical education classes. Effective interpersonal communication was discussed—specifically, active listening, verbal mediation, and conflict resolution. Hellison's social responsibility model and the procedures outlined in the DBG (Dunn & Leitschuh, 2014) were cited as effective approaches in physical education and sport for students with behavioral disorders and students considered at risk.

Physical educators are called on to promote PBIS (Safran & Oswald, 2003). They are asked to not only provide sound and consistent discipline policies, but also address the need for positive behavioral instruction. These models (ERIC/OSEP Special Project, 1997) share several features:

- Total staff commitment to managing behavior, whatever approach is taken

Behavioral Intervention Plan

Name: Seth Zion **Grade:** 7 **Age:** 13 **School:** ABC Middle School **Date written:** 1/15/2021

Strength of Student

- Wants to be in the general physical education class and generally wants to do the same work as his peers.
- Usually responds well to teachers.
- Enjoys praise and positive, social reinforcement.
- Participates in physical education most days.

Individualized Information About the Student

- Some behaviors associated with conduct disorder are apparent. These include bullying and intimidation, initiating fights, and being physically cruel to classmates.
- Often works and moves more slowly than peers.
- Has difficulty with tasks necessitating age-appropriate motor skills.

Previously Implemented Interventions

Negative reinforcement, response cost, and positive reinforcement with tangibles. These interventions were not effective.

Problematic Behaviors: Physical and Verbal Abuse Toward Classmates

Baseline: Average of at least three episodes per day for the last three weeks

Function of Behavior

Student uses physical and verbal attacks against classmates to deflect attention away from his fundamentally inadequate motor skills.

Replacement Behavior

Student will use compliments and positive physical gestures that show respect for classmates.

Interventions

A. Student will learn personal responsibility by participating in and progressing through Hellison's model using appropriate levels and strategies.

B. Student will be teamed with peers who understand his challenging behavior and who have volunteered to prompt appropriate behavior.

C. Student is placed in instructional situations that require fewer skills, thus reducing the likelihood of embarrassing mistakes that typically precipitate abusive episodes.

D. Student will receive social praise from the teacher and classmates for each occurrence of desirable behavior.

E. Student's verbal abuse will be ignored; physical attacks will result in a time out.

Documentation

- Teacher will record the frequency of physical and verbal abuse during scheduled class time.
- Results will be shared with student in an effort to communicate the frequency and perhaps the severity of instances of abuse.
- Teacher will document particular situations or combinations of students that act as antecedents to episodes of abusive behavior.

Amount of Improvement Expected

- No more than one episode of verbal abuse per class session.
- Zero instances of physical abuse.

FIGURE 9.3 Sample behavioral intervention plan constructed with consideration of the 10-step process.

- Clearly defined and communicated expectations and rules
- Consequences and clearly stated procedures for correcting rule-breaking behaviors
- An instructional component for teaching self-control and social skill strategies
- A support plan to address the needs of students with chronic, challenging behaviors

References

Achenbach, T.M., Howell, C.T., Quay, H.C., & Conners, C.K. (1991). National survey of problems and competencies among 4- to 16-year-olds: Parents' reports for normative and clinical samples. *Monographs of the Society for Research in Child Development, 56*(3), serial no. 225.

American Academy of Experts in Traumatic Stress. (2003). *A practical guide for crisis response in our schools.* Author.

American Psychiatric Association (APA). (2013). *Diagnostic and statistical manual of mental disorders (DSM-5)* (5th ed.). Author.

Assistance to States for the Education of Children with Disabilities, 34 C.F.R. 300.530 (2006).

Aubry, P. (2008). *Stepping stones: A therapeutic adventure activity guide.* Project Adventure.

Bar-Eli, M., Hartman, I., & Levy-Kolker, N. (1994). Using goal setting to improve physical performance of adolescents with behavior disorders: The effect of goal proximity. *Adapted Physical Activity Quarterly, 11,* 86-97. https://doi.org/10.1123/apaq.11.1.86

Block, M.E. (2016). *A teacher's guide to adapted physical education: Including students with disabilities in sport and recreation* (4th ed.). Brookes.

Bowling, A., Slavet, J., Miller, D., Hanuese, S., Beardsley, W., & Davison, K.K. (2017). Cybercycling effects on classroom behavior in children with behavioral health disorders: An RCT. *Pediatrics, 139*(2): e20161985.

Bullock, L.M., & Menendez, A.L. (2001). Meeting the needs of children and youth with challenging behavior; module 17: The role of student support teams in meeting the needs of children and youth with challenging behaviors. *Reaching Today's Youth, 5*(2), 46-52.

Carey, T.A., & Bourbon, W.T. (2004). Countercontrol: A new look at some old problems. *Intervention in School and Clinic, 40*(1), 3-9. https://doi.org/10.1177/10534512040400010101

Chen, C-C., Symons, F.J., & Reynolds, A.J. (2011). Prospective analyses of childhood factors and antisocial behavior for students with high-incidence disabilities. *Behavior Disorders, 37,* 5-18. https://doi.org/10.1177/019874291103700102

Cluphf, D. (2003). A low-ropes initiative unit for at-risk students. *Strategies, 17,* 13-16.

Colvin, G.T., & Scott, T.M. (2014). *Managing the cycle of acting-out behavior in the classroom* (2nd ed.). Corwin.

Cullinan, D. (2007). *Students with emotional and behavioral disorders* (2nd ed.). Pearson.

Cunningham, E.M., & O'Neill, R.E. (2007). Agreement of functional behavioral assessment and analysis methods with students with EBD. *Behavioral Disorders, 32,* 211-221. https://doi.org/10.1177/019874290703200305

Diliberti, M., Jackson, M., Correa, S., & Padgett, Z. (2019). *Crime, violence, discipline, and safety in U.S. public schools: Findings from the school survey on crime and safety: 2017-2018* (NCES 2019-061). U.S. Department of Education, National Center for Education Statistics. http://nces.ed.gov/pubsearch

Dunn, J.M., & Leitschuh, C. (2014). *Special physical education* (10th ed.). Kendall/Hunt.

Elliot, R.O., Dobbin, A.R., Rose, G.D., & Soper, H.V. (1994). Vigorous, aerobic exercise versus general motor training activities: Effects on maladaptive and stereotypic behaviors of adults with both autism and mental retardation. *Journal of Autism and Developmental Disorders, 24,* 565-576. https://doi.org/10.1007/bf02172138

ERIC/OSEP Special Project. (1997). *Research connections in special education.* ERIC Clearinghouse on Disabilities and Gifted Education/Council for Exceptional Children.

Farley, C., Torres, C., Wailehua, C.-T.T., & Cook, L. (2012). Evidence-based practices for students with emotional and behavioral disorders: Improving academic achievement. *Beyond Behavior, 21*(2), 37-43.

Forness, S.R., & Knitzer, J. (1992). A new proposed definition and terminology to replace "serious emotional disturbance" in Individuals with Disabilities Education Act. *School Psychology Review, 21,* 12-20.

Forness, S.R., Walker, H.M., & Kavale, K.A. (2003). Psychiatric disorders and treatments: A primer for teachers. *Teaching Exceptional Children, 36,* 42-49. https://doi.org/10.1177/004005990303600206

Frank, K., Paget, M., Bowman, B., & Wilde, J. (1998). *Creative strategies for working with ODD children and adolescents.* Youthlight.

Gartin, B.C., Murdick, N.L., Imbeau, M., & Perner, D.E. (2002). *How to use differentiated instruction with students with developmental disabilities in the general education classroom.* Council for Exceptional Children.

Harlacher, J.E., Nelson Walker, N.J., & Sanford, A.K. (2010). The "I" in RTI: Research-based factors for intensifying instruction. *Teaching Exceptional Children, 42*(6), 30-38. https://doi.org/10.1177/004005991004200604

Harwood, A., Lavidor, M., & Rassovsky, Y. (2017). Reducing aggression with martial arts: A meta-analysis of child and youth studies. *Aggression and Violent*

Behavior, 34, 96-101. http://dx.doi.org/10.1016/j.avb.2017.03.00

Hellison, D.R. (2011). *Teaching personal and social responsibility through physical activity* (3rd ed.). Human Kinetics.

Hellison, D.R., & Georgiadis, N. (1992). Teaching values through basketball. *Strategies, 5,* 5-8.

Hellison, D.R., & Templin, T.J. (1991). *A reflective approach to teaching physical education.* Human Kinetics.

Hunt, C.L. (2017). Universal design for learning and academic interventions for students with emotional and behavioral disorders. In J.E. Gardner & D. Hardin (Eds.), 4th Annual Summit Proceedings [Poster presentation]. Universal Design for Learning—Implementation Research Network: Learning Designed for Everyone (pp. 36-40). UDL-ILN.

Individuals with Disabilities Education Act Amendments of 2004 (IDEA), PL 108-446, 20 U.S.C. 1400 (2004).

Kantomaa, M.T., Tammelin, T.H., Ebeling, H.E., & Taanila, A. (2008). Emotional and behavioral problems in relation to physical activity in youth. *Medicine & Science in Sports & Exercise, 40*(10), 1749-1756. https://doi.org/10.1249/MSS.0b013e31817b8e82

Kauffman, J.M., & Landrum, T.J. (2018). *Characteristics of emotional and behavioral disorders of children and youth* (11th ed.). Pearson.

Lane, K., Falk, K., & Wehby, J. (2011). Classroom management in special education classrooms and resource rooms. In C. Evertson & C.S. Weinstein (Eds.), *Handbook of classroom management: Research, practice, and contemporary issues* (pp. 439-460). Routledge.

Lieberman, L.J., Grenier, M., Brian, A., & Arndt, K. (2021). *Universal design for learning in physical education.* Human Kinetics.

Maag, J.W., & Katsiyannis, A. (2006). Behavior intervention plans: Legal and practical considerations for students with emotional and behavioral disorders. *Behavioral Disorders, 31,* 348-362. https://doi.org/10.1177/019874290603100403

Musser, E.H., Bray, M.A., Kehle, T.J., & Jenson, W.R. (2001). Reducing disruptive behaviors in students with serious emotional disturbance. *School Psychology Review, 30,* 294-304.

Payne, L.D., Scott, T.M., & Conroy, M. (2007). A school-based examination of the efficacy of function-based intervention. *Behavioral Disorders, 32,* 158-174. https://doi.org/10.1177/019874290703200302

Quay, H.C. (1986). Classification. In H.C. Quay & J.S. Werry (Eds.), *Psychopathological disorders of childhood* (3rd ed., pp. 1-34). Wiley.

Quay, H.C., & Peterson, D.R. (1987). *Manual for the revised behavior problem checklist.* Authors.

Roane, H.S., & Kelley, M.E. (2008). Decreasing problem behavior associated with a walking program for an individual with developmental and physical disabilities. *Journal of Applied Behavior Analysis, 41,* 423-428. https://doi.org/10.1901/jaba.2008.41-423

Rohnke, K. (2009). *Silver bullets: A revised guide to initiative problems, adventure games, and trust activities* (2nd ed.). Kendall/Hunt.

Safran, S.P., & Oswald, K. (2003). Positive behavior supports: Can schools reshape disciplinary practices? *Exceptional Child, 69,* 361-373. https://doi.org/10.1177/001440290306900307

Sagor, R., & Cox, J. (2004). *At-risk students: Reaching and teaching them* (2nd ed.). Eye on Education.

Scott, T.M., & Nelson, C.M. (1999). Using functional behavioral assessment to develop effective behavioral intervention plans: A practical classroom application. *Journal of Positive Behavior Interventions, 1,* 242-251. https://doi.org/10.1177/109830079900100408

Sherrill, C. (2004). *Adapted physical activity, recreation and sport: Crossdisciplinary and lifespan* (6th ed.). Brown & Benchmark.

Sinclair, E. (1998). Head Start children at risk: Relationship of prenatal drug exposure to identification of special needs and subsequent special education kindergarten placement. *Behavioral Disorders, 23,* 125-133. https://doi.org/10.1177/019874299802300205

Steinberg, Z., Knitzer, J., & Zabel, R. (1992). Classrooms for emotionally and behaviorally disturbed students: Facing the challenge. *Behavioral Disorders, 17,* 145-156. https://doi.org/10.1177/019874299201700208

Steiner, N.J., Sidhu, T.K., Pop, P.G., Frenette, E.C., & Perrin, E.C. (2013). Yoga in an urban school for children with emotional and behavioral disorders: A feasibility study. *Journal of Child and Family Studies, 22,* 815-826. https://doi.org/10.1007/s10826-012-9636-7

Sutherland, K.S. (2000). Promoting positive interactions between teachers and students with emotional/behavioral disorders. *Preventing School Failure, 44,* 110-115. https://doi.org/10.1080/10459880009599792

U.S. Department of Education. (2012). *Restraint and seclusion: Resource document.* Author.

U.S. Department of Education. (2020a). *41st annual report to Congress on the implementation of the Individuals with Disabilities Education Act, 2019.* Author.

U.S. Department of Education. (2020b). OSEP fast facts: Children identified with emotional disturbance, (2020). Author.

Van Haren, B.A., & Fiedler, C. (2004). Physical restraint and seclusion of students with disabilities. *Beyond Behavior, 13*(3), 17-19.

Walker, H.M., Colvin, G., & Ramsey, E. (1995). *Antisocial behavior in schools: Strategies and best practices.* Brooks/Cole.

Yell, M.L. (1988). The effects of jogging on the rates of selected target behaviors of behaviorally disordered students. *Behavioral Disorders, 13,* 273-279. https://doi.org/10.1177/019874298801300408

Print Resources

Kauffman, J.M., & Landrum, T.J. (2012). *Cases in emotional and behavioral disorders of children and youth* (3rd ed.). Pearson Education.

This is an adjunct resource that accompanies Kauffman and Landrum's popular textbook on the same subject matter. Real-life case studies are presented along with questions that can be discussed in class.

Lane, K.L., Menzies, H.M., Bruhn, A.L., & Crnobori, M. (2011). *Managing challenging behaviors in schools.* Guilford.

This book provides updated evidence-based strategies for preventing problem behaviors and appropriate means for responding to problem behaviors. These strategies have a documented research base and translate effectively into daily practice with students who present with challenging behaviors.

McGinnis, E., Sprafkin, R.P., Gershaw, N.J., & Klein, P. (2011). *Skillstreaming the adolescent: A guide for teaching prosocial skills* (3rd ed.). Research Press.

This innovative program is designed to help adolescents develop competence in dealing with interpersonal conflicts, increase self-esteem, and contribute to a positive classroom atmosphere.

Wood, M.M., & Long, N.J. (1991). *Life-space intervention: Talking with children and youth in crisis.* Pro-Ed.

This is an updated version of the pioneering work of Fritz Redl with emphasis on the intervention. Talking strategies are presented and applied to particular types of problems.

Video Resources

The Behavior Education Program [DVD]. (2006). Guilford Publications, 72 Spring St., New York, NY 10012.

This DVD demonstrates the Check In Check Out intervention that is designated as a tier 2 strategy for students at risk. Several scenarios illustrate the use of this intervention in classrooms and other school and home settings.

Understanding the Defiant Child [DVD]. (2006). Guilford Publications, 72 Spring St., New York, NY 10012.

Dr. Russell Barkley presents a clear and easily understood resource for clinicians, teachers, and parents who must deal with children who have ODD. Using real-life scenes of family interaction and parental commentary, Dr. Barkley helps viewers distinguish ODD from milder forms of misbehavior. The video likewise addresses long-term outcomes for defiant children and the correlation between ODD and ADHD.

U.S. Department of Education. (2020, January 9). *Students with disabilities and the use of restraint and seclusion in K-12 public schools* [Video]. YouTube. www.youtube.com/watch?v=EZ9Yx0LC8TI&feature=youtu.be

This webinar describes how the Office of Civil Rights and the Office of Special Education and Rehabilitative Services of the U.S. Department of Education collaborated to provide technical assistance to K-12 public schools relative to how federal laws apply to the use of seclusion and physical restraint.

Online Resources

Center on Positive Behavioral Interventions and Supports: www.pbis.org

This site is the home of the Center on Positive Behavioral Interventions and Supports. It is housed at the University of Oregon but has four partners: the University of Kansas, University of Kentucky, University of South Florida, and University of Missouri. The center disseminates information to schools and families and communicates information regarding the technology of School-Wide Positive Behavior Support, demonstrating that PBIS is feasible and effective.

Kansas Technical Assistance System Network: www.ksdetasn.org

This site houses the Kansas Technical Assistance System Network. One section provides numerous resources for emergency safety intervention. Included is a description of the acting-out behavior cycle, along with strategies to prevent challenging behavior and techniques to either de-escalate or restore order after a conflict has occurred.

PBISWorld: www.pbisworld.com

This site provides a compendium of challenging behaviors with a query that permits identification of extant characteristics; it then provides a menu of interventions for each behavior depending on tier level.

Wrightslaw: www.wrightslaw.com

This site, created and administered by attorneys Pam and Pete Wright, is the consummate source of information on IDEA. Topics such as behavior and discipline are covered from the standpoint of what professionals, parents, and advocates should know about special education law. Many useful resources are highlighted, including blogs, training programs, e-learning opportunities, and written publications.

10

Autism Spectrum and Social Communication Disorders

Cathy Houston-Wilson

Dylan is an 11-year-old boy who enjoys hiking and climbing, running, and swimming. He is generally happy and easygoing; however, Dylan also likes things to remain relatively the same. He does well with routines and structure. He keeps his room arranged in a certain way and will not go to bed until everything is back in place. Dylan sometimes struggles to express his feelings, wants, and needs, as he does not use language in the conventional manner. He can utter sounds that reflect his feelings (happy, sad, angry) but mostly uses pictures or apps on his iPad to communicate.

Marcia, on the other hand, is talkative. Although she is only 12, her vocabulary resembles that of a sophisticated adult. She began talking at an early age, and by age 3 she had taught herself to read. Instead of playing with typical childhood toys, Marcia was more interested in art and artists. She can look at any art history book and tell you the artist of any picture and the history of the artist. Marcia has a tendency to continue talking about her favorite subject for some time, without regard to her listener's loss of interest, and misses cues of disinterest. As a result, her peers become frustrated with her and have a tendency to ignore her, and Marcia has few friends. Marcia does not seem to be bothered by that.

Dylan and Marcia both have a condition known as autism spectrum disorder and exhibit behaviors that deviate from typical childhood development. The *DSM-5* (American Psychiatric Association [APA], 2013) redefined autism and established two conditions that account for an array of developmental disabilities: **autism spectrum disorder** (ASD) and **social communication disorder** (SCD). Table 10.1 provides an overview of these two conditions. Although they appear to be similar, only children

TABLE 10.1 Summary of the *DSM-5* Diagnostic Criteria for Autism Spectrum and Social Communication Disorder (2013)

Condition	Criteria
Autism spectrum disorder	**A. Persistent deficits in social communication and social interaction across multiple contexts with deficits in the following:** 1. Social–emotional reciprocity 2. Nonverbal communicative behaviors used for social interaction 3. Developing, maintaining, and understanding relationships **B. Restricted, repetitive patterns of behavior, interests, or activities, as manifested by at least two of the following:** 1. Stereotyped or repetitive motor movements, use of objects, or speech 2. Insistence on sameness, inflexible adherence to routines, or ritualized patterns of verbal and nonverbal behavior 3. Highly restricted, fixated interests that are abnormal in intensity or focus 4. Hyper- or hyporeactivity to sensory input or unusual interests in sensory aspects of the environment **C. Symptoms must be present in the early developmental period.** **D. Symptoms cause clinically significant impairment in social, occupational, or other important areas of current functioning.** **E. These disturbances are not better explained by intellectual disability or global developmental delay.**
Social communication disorder	**A. Persistent difficulties in the social use of verbal and nonverbal communication as manifested by all of the following:** 1. Deficits in using communication for social purposes, such as greeting and sharing information in a manner that is appropriate for the social context 2. Impairment of the ability to change communication to match context or the needs of the listener, such as speaking differently in a classroom than on the playground, talking differently to a child than to an adult, and avoiding use of overly formal language 3. Difficulties following rules for conversation and storytelling, such as taking turns in conversation, rephrasing when misunderstood, and knowing how to use verbal and nonverbal signals to regulate interaction 4. Difficulties understanding what is not explicitly stated (e.g., making inferences) and nonliteral or ambiguous meanings of language (e.g., idioms, humor, metaphors, multiple meanings that depend on the context for interpretation) **B. The deficits result in functional limitations in effective communication, social participation, social relationships, academic achievement, or occupational performance, individually or in combination.** **C. The onset of the symptoms is in the early developmental period.** **D. The symptoms are not attributable to another medical or neurological condition or to low abilities in the domains of word structure and grammar, and are not better explained by autism spectrum disorder, intellectual disability, global developmental delay, or another mental disorder.**

who exhibit repetitive behaviors or restricted interests (or both) are classified as having ASD.

Because the *DSM-5* significantly changes the definition and categorization of autism, the following note was added to the manual:

> *Note:* Individuals with a well-established DSM-IV diagnosis of autistic disorder, Asperger's disorder, or pervasive developmental disorder not otherwise specified should be given the diagnosis of autism spectrum disorder. Individuals who have marked deficits in social communication, but whose symptoms do not otherwise meet criteria for autism spectrum disorder, should be evaluated for social (pragmatic) communication disorder.

In addition, the strategies and approaches presented in this chapter are suitable for students diagnosed with either ASD or SCD.

History of Autism Spectrum Disorder

Although autism has been evident for quite some time, it was not until 1943 that Dr. Leo Kanner, a child psychiatrist at The Johns Hopkins University School of Medicine, described the common characteristics of 11 children he had studied between 1938 and 1943. These children were withdrawn and engaged in isolated activities. They did not relate well to people (including their own parents); they insisted on routines; and they displayed unusual body movements, such as hand flapping. Many of the children could talk—saying the alphabet, for example, or reciting whole books—but they rarely used speech to communicate with others. Dr. Kanner borrowed the term *autism* from a Swiss psychiatrist who had coined the term to refer to adults with a certain form of schizophrenia. Because the children Dr. Kanner studied were young, he identified them as having *early infantile autism*.

For many years, only those children who exhibited the same behavior patterns that Dr. Kanner noted were diagnosed with autism, and autism was treated as a form of mental illness (Ozonoff et al., 2014). At around the same time Dr. Kanner first described autism, Dr. Hans Asperger, an Austrian pediatrician, wrote a paper (published in 1944) describing a condition that came to be known as Asperger syndrome. The children described by Dr. Asperger were between the ages of 6 and 11; these children, despite typical communication and cognitive skills, had significant problems with social interactions. However, the paper remained virtually unknown in the United States and other non-German-speaking countries until 1981, when Dr. Lorna Wing, a prominent British researcher, discovered the paper, summarized it, and noted the similarities between Asperger syndrome and autism (Ozonoff et al., 2014).

For many years, not much else was known about autism, and children in America were rarely identified as having Asperger syndrome. However, in 1964, Dr. Bernard Rimland published a book challenging the long-held theory that autism was a form of mental illness and instead considered the condition a biological neurodevelopmental disorder. Rimland, himself a parent of a child with autism, established the Autism Society of America as well as the Autism Research Institute. Through his efforts and those of countless others, the way in which children with ASD are diagnosed and treated has dramatically changed for the better. Today, Asperger syndrome is now considered part of the autism spectrum (Hardy et al., 2014).

Autism

Although the *DSM-5* has redefined autism to be known as ASD, the Individuals with Disabilities Education Act (2004) identifies autism as a specific disability and defines it as

> a developmental disability significantly affecting verbal and nonverbal communication and social interaction, generally evident before age 3, that adversely affects a student's educational performance. Other characteristics often associated with autism are engagement in repetitive activities and stereotyped movements, resistance to environmental change or change in daily routines, and unusual responses to sensory experiences. In addition, individuals with ASD may have a strong interest or affinity to a particular object or activity which can lead to perseverative behavior. The term does not apply if a student's educational performance is adversely affected primarily because the student has an emotional disturbance.

Children may also be diagnosed with autism after age 3 if they meet these criteria. The following sections briefly describe each of these characteristics.

Communication

According to Friend (2018), about 50 percent of children with autism do not speak at all, and others have echolalic speech (*echolalic* meaning "echo"). For example, if a physical education teacher says, "Ryan, throw the ball," Ryan might repeat "Ryan, throw the ball" without comprehending what is being asked of him. This response is known as *immediate echolalia*. In other cases, the echolalia might not occur immediately but instead occurs at odd times; this is known as *delayed echolalia*. A child might recall a TV commercial he saw that morning and begin singing a jingle in the middle of class. In other people with autism who have language skills, the sound of their speech might be flat or monotonous, with no apparent control over pitch or volume. In addition to having speech pattern problems, some people with autism might not comprehend the social norms of communication and might continue to talk about a preferred topic long after the conversation should have ended. Similarly, a person might stand too close to another person when speaking or might say inappropriate things without realizing the statement will offend others (Friend, 2018).

Social Interaction

One of the most noticeable characteristics of people with autism is their inability to develop typical social relationships. Social interaction requires reciprocity; because individuals with autism may struggle with this connection, it is sometimes difficult for them to be socially interactive. Often they prefer to be alone and engaged in isolated activities. They may fail to respond to their name and may avoid eye contact. They may also appear to show few signs of attachment; however, this does not mean they are incapable of making such connections (Sicile-Kira, 2014). Often the problem lies with their inability to understand how to do so. Another problem with the establishment of social relationships is that individuals with autism often do not understand the norms of nonverbal communication (APA, 2013). For example, perhaps they have a strong interest in trains. After speaking for quite some time on the topic, they may not understand the listener's nonverbal signals expressing a desire to end the conversation. Rather than appear rude, the listener may avoid future conversations with the individual, and thus an opportunity for a social relationship has been lost.

Repetitive Activities and Stereotyped Movements

Repetitive activities such as rocking back and forth, twirling, and hand flapping may be seen in children with autism. It is unclear why these movements occur, but it is believed that difficulty in processing sensory information may cause some of these reactions (Sicile-Kira, 2014). For example, fast flailing movements of the hands could signal agitation or an inability to comprehend what is being asked. Rocking back and forth can be viewed as a calming behavior used to filter out the surrounding environment. Some children also engage in self-abusive behavior such as biting or head banging. They also tend to have a high tolerance for pain and may derive some form of physical pleasure or self-stimulation from the behavior. Professionals believe that stimulation of pain reactors releases a rush of endorphins, perpetuating the behavior. Others speculate that self-injurious behavior is a mechanism used to escape an undesirable activity (Sicile-Kira, 2014).

Resistance to Change

Resistance to change is often evident in children with autism. They may become agitated if the bus takes a different route to school or if the daily schedule is changed to accommodate a school assembly. Similarly, they may want play objects to be placed in a pattern that only they understand and become agitated if the placement of an object is disrupted. Objects might also be played with in a peculiar manner. For example, children might spin their toys over and over or look at the toys for hours from various directions. This need for sameness results from the child's inability to interpret and predict daily occurrences, leading to undue anxiety. In addition, the insistence on sameness often disrupts daily activities and interferes with everyday living (APA, 2013).

Sensory Responses

People with autism have difficulty screening out irrelevant information within the environment. Their senses allow them to overattend to some stimuli and underattend to others, making it difficult for them to determine the most important part of a task (Ozonoff et al., 2014). In addition, they may crave physical pressure; it is thought that this tight sensation provides relief from stress. People with autism have been known to lie under couch cushions so that someone can sit on them and squeeze them. Dr. Temple Grandin, a scholar with autism, created a squeeze box, also known as a hug box, that provides pressure on the body. The person crawls inside the box and is able to self-regulate the amount of pressure given to create a calming reaction (Grandin, 2014). Students may also wear weighted jackets to help reduce sensory stimuli. Again, the pressure of the weight tends to produce a calming effect and reduce sensory overload. However, other people with autism may not want to be touched at all. They may also find tactile stimulation disturbing and may resist being cuddled or hugged. All this demonstrates the variety among people with autism. Though all have some form of difficulty with sensory stimuli, the degree varies from person to person.

Children with autism may also be abnormally sensitive to sound or other sensory stimulation. For example, a child with autism may become agitated at the sound of a fire alarm or school announcements. Planning for these activities by providing the child with earmuffs or a warning that it will soon be announcement time may help to alleviate the stress.

In addition, some children with autism experience swift changes in mood, limited food preferences, gastrointestinal problems, sleep disturbances, lack of danger awareness, depression, and in some cases seizures and intellectual disability (Sicile-Kira, 2014).

Etiology

No definitive answer has been reached regarding why some children develop ASD and others do not. According to the National Institutes of Health (NIH), autism is a neurodevelopmental disorder attributed to both genetics and the environment (2018).

Genetic Link

The majority of ASD cases have genetic causes. The most common genetic link is fragile X syndrome (FXS), a condition that affects both boys and girls but most severely affects boys and causes intellectual disability. The NIH (2018) estimates that around one in three children who have FXS also meet the diagnostic criteria for ASD. There is also evidence suggesting that autism might be inherited. Twin studies have revealed that if one twin has ASD, the other twin has a 90 percent chance of also having ASD. Similarly, in families in which one child has ASD, the risk of having another child with ASD is approximately 5 percent, or 1 in 20. This is greater than the risk for the general population. Finally, there is evidence to suggest that in some cases, parents of children with ASD also show mild impairments in social and communicative skills or engage in repetitive behaviors (NIH, 2018).

Neurological Link

Researchers have also hypothesized that children with ASD have problems with serotonin levels, whereby messages from the brain are not transmitted properly and have difficulty reaching their destination (NIH, 2018). In addition, children with ASD have structural brain differences compared to those without ASD. Scientists have discovered that children with ASD tend to have smaller heads at birth but then experience rapid growth within the first year. This rapid growth makes learning difficult because the fast pace creates abnormal neural connections, making it difficult to take in information and use it effectively (Autism Speaks, 2018).

Environmental Link

Scientists use the broad term "environmental factors" to study anything outside of the body that can affect health. This includes such things as the air we breathe, the water we drink and bathe in, the food we eat, and the medicines we take. Other environmental factors such as parental age at conception, maternal nutrition, infection during pregnancy, and prematurity have also been examined to determine links between the environment and ASD (NIH, 2018). Most scientists agree that environmental factors alone do not generally cause ASD, but rather that certain environmental factors appear to influence the risk of developing ASD in those genetically predisposed to the disorder (Autism Speaks, 2020). However, much more research related to the environment and ASD is needed before any conclusions can be drawn.

Vaccination Link

Although some parents in the ASD community continue to voice concern over the connection between vaccinations and ASD, the medical community remains steadfast in its assertion that there is no link between vaccinations and ASD (NIH, 2014). In fact, not vaccinating children poses a greater health risk, as diseases that were once virtually eradicated, such as measles and mumps, are on the rise.

Incidence

The Centers for Disease Control and Prevention (CDC) (2020) has estimated that about 1 in 54 children are identified with ASD, and that males are four times more likely to have ASD than females. Autism spectrum disorder is considered a high-incidence disability. Researchers attribute the rise in ASD to changes in the criteria used to diagnose children, along with early detection and identification.

Physical and Motor Characteristics

Because ASD encompasses a wide range of individuals along the spectrum from mild to severe, physical and motor characteristics vary greatly. Although children generally progress in a typical manner, delays in attaining motor milestones may be evident in some. For example, studies have indicated that hypotonia (low muscle tone) presents in some infants with ASD, hindering their ability to reach the typical milestone for walking. There also appear to be distinct differences in movement in some children with ASD. For example, approximately 20 percent of individuals walk on their toes and take short steps (Ming et al., 2007). Fundamental motor skills also appear to be delayed, which could be attributed to motor apraxia (an inability to make movements or to use objects for their intended purpose) (Ming et al., 2007). However, differences vary greatly depending on the individual. It is also important to note that motor delays as measured on motor assessments could be attributed to lack of motivation to perform the skill rather than some physiological factor. Basically, the overall physical and motor characteristics of those with ASD can vary widely.

General Educational Approaches

Over the years, many educational approaches have been implemented to aid in the development of people with ASD. Some have been around for some time, whereas others have been only recently introduced. Both parents and professionals continue to search for the best possible approach to help people with ASD live their lives to the fullest and with a degree of normalcy. By far the most popular approaches have been applied behavior analysis (ABA) and the TEACCH (Treatment and Education of Autistic and Related Communication Handicapped Children) program. More recently, the Developmental, Individual-difference, Relationship-based (DIR) model, also known as the Floortime approach, and the subsequent Affect-Based Language Curriculum have shown promising results as an early intervention strategy. In addition, Carol Gray's social stories and comic strip conversations are being used to effectively communicate with children with ASD. In recent years there has been a proliferation of downloadable apps to aid in communication and interaction for individuals with ASD. These programs are reviewed in the following sections.

Applied Behavior Analysis

Applied behavior analysis is one of the most widely used forms of intervention for students with ASD and is endorsed by the American Medical Association, the American Academy of Pediatrics, and the U.S. Surgeon General. Applied behavior analysis is used to help students with ASD acquire new skills, such as learning to speak and play, and to reduce and eliminate undesirable behaviors through the use of positive reinforcement and rewards. The premise behind this model is that when an appropriate behavior is followed by positive reinforcement, the appropriate behavior will be repeated. The process involves a trained therapist who conducts a detailed assessment of the child and collaborates with the family to determine goals. The therapist instructs the child in both an age- and developmentally appropriate manner. Skills that are selected are those that will allow the child the greatest level of independence, such as self-care, play skills, motor development, and academic skills. Each skill is broken down into manageable steps from simplest to most complex. Data are documented to note progress, discuss with parents, and make adjustments as needed. Because ABA training requires between 25 and 40 hours per week for changes in behavior to occur, family members are generally trained in the intervention strategy, and the child's day is structured to provide both planned and naturally occurring situations to practice skills. In the past, ABA was adult directed, but today, child-initiated behaviors are also encouraged. The goal of this intervention is to provide an abundance of positive reinforcement for demonstrating useful and socially appropriate skills while ignoring inappropriate behavior (Autism Speaks, 2020).

An important aspect of ABA is noting the antecedent of a behavior or skill performance and the subsequent consequence. This is also known as the ABC model (antecedent–behavior–consequence). Manipulating either the antecedent or the consequence generally brings about desired changes in behavior.

Another intervention strategy that has been used effectively with students with ASD is discrete trial training (DTT), developed by Dr. O. Ivar Lovaas in 1987. Discrete trial training is a method of teaching in simplified and structured steps. Instead of teaching an entire skill at one time, the skill is broken down into steps and built upon using discrete trials. For each trial, the child is either rewarded for completing the task as requested or completing an approximation of the task. If the child makes an incorrect response, she is either corrected or encouraged to try again. Over repeated trials of various tasks, the child is able to more fully engage in the environment (Smith, 2001). Forms of this intervention are more fully discussed in chapter 7. Although DTT is one way to employ ABA, the reality is that ABA is in essence the application of behavioral interventions on a regular basis to increase or decrease targeted behaviors. Additional information on ABA is presented in chapter 6.

TEACCH Program

Another popular program used to assist children with ASD is the North Carolina statewide program known as TEACCH, developed by Drs. Eric Schopler and Robert Reichler in the 1960s. The TEACCH program is teaching based on the culture of autism—that is, teaching based on the needs, interests, and learning style of individuals with ASD. Information is presented visually and in a highly structured and organized manner. The principles of structured teaching—a term synonymous with the TEACCH program—include understanding the culture of autism, developing an individualized and family plan for each client, organizing and structuring the physical environment, and using visual supports such as daily schedules to help make tasks and sequences predictable and understandable (Mesibov et al., 2004).

The TEACCH program also uses sensory integration therapy to determine the cause of inappropriate behaviors or lack of skill acquisition. It is theorized that sensory overload is often the cause of inappropriate behaviors of people with ASD. For example, if a child is overstimulated in an environment, he might experience undue stress. Rather than making the child tolerate the environment, he is removed from the environment or the environment is modified. Thus, a hallmark of TEACCH is an emphasis on modifying the environment and building on the learner's strengths to enhance learning, rather than forcing the learner to conform to traditional environments and socially accepted norms of behavior (Mesibov et al., 2004).

The Greenspan Floortime Approach and Affect-Based Language Curriculum

An exciting intervention for children with ASD is the DIR (Developmental, Individual-difference, Relationship-based) approach, also called Floortime, developed by Dr. Stanley Greenspan in 1998. Floortime is a method whereby children and caregivers interact on the floor to develop and foster connections. Designed to meet children where they are, Floortime builds on their strengths and abilities by creating warm and positive relationships. Floortime is used to inspire interest in activities, facilitate connections, and encourage creative and spontaneous behaviors that aid in intellectual and emotional development. The process involves three steps (Davis et al., 2014):

1. Follow the child's lead (enter the child's world and join in the emotional flow).
2. Create challenges for creative and spontaneous behaviors.
3. Expand the behaviors and interactions to include all or most of the senses, motor skills, and emotions.

The program requires child-directed, interactive experiences in a low-stimulus environment. Using a child-directed versus adult-directed approach encourages the child to want to relate to the outside world. Time required varies from two to five hours a day. Greenspan advocates that the program begin as soon as possible. He contends that the longer the child is allowed to remain uncommunicative and the more parents lose their sense of their child's attachment, the more deeply the child will withdraw and become perseverative and self-stimulatory. The goal of the program is to transform perseveration into interaction. Once this occurs, children become more purposeful in their interactions and can imitate gestures and sounds and engage in play (Davis et al., 2014).

Greenspan and Lewis (2002) have expanded the Floortime program with the Affect-Based Language Curriculum (ABLC). They contend that "affect is more critical for many elements of language acquisition and use than has been traditionally realized" (p. 3). The more the interaction includes affective gesturing, such as pointing, and complex gestures, such as placing a napkin on a plate after finishing eating, the better it will be for the child to understand the connection when words and sentences appear. Greenspan and Lewis recommend using affect and engagement in pleasurable back-and-forth interactions as the foundation for the development of imitation, pragmatics (use of language), and receptive and expressive language.

Gray's Social Stories and Comic Strip Conversations

Carol Gray is credited with introducing the concept of social stories. A **social story** is written according to specific guidelines to describe a situation in terms of the event or activity, using the student's perspective to make sure that the student has all the necessary social information (Gray, 2010). The stories are written in a positive and accessible manner and include information on what may happen and why. Social stories are intended for children with ASD who function in the middle to high range of abilities. Comic strips can accompany a social story. Comic strips are visual representations such as drawings, symbols, stick figures, and color that are used to illustrate ongoing communication between parties (Gray, 1994). Social stories can be created for a variety of situations, including developing social relationships, developing self-help skills, coping with change, providing feedback, and managing behavior. Social stories and comic strips can also be created for physical education to introduce a new skill or activity. Figure 10.1 depicts a social story and comic strip for encouraging a child with ASD to go swimming.

Communication and Interactive Apps

With the increased popularity of smartphones and tablets has come a proliferation of downloadable apps that can be used to aid in the communication and social interaction of students with ASD. The following are some examples of these apps.

- *Boardmaker.* Developed by Mayer and Johnson, Boardmaker (https://goboardmaker.com) is one of the most commonly used apps in schools today. It is an extensive collection of pictures and text that can be combined and used to create visual schedules, communication books, interactive activities, and speech output boards. It is most helpful in supporting students' language and literacy goals through differentiated instruction while providing students with motivational pictures and text.
- *Proloquo2Go.* Proloquo2Go (www.assistiveware.com/product/proloquo2go) is a symbol-supported communication app developed by AssistiveWare to give a voice to people who cannot speak. When letters, phrases, or pictures are tapped, a voice relays the message. The voice can be tailored to a male or female student or adult voice.
- *First Then.* First Then (www.goodkarmaapplications.com/first-then-visual-schedule.html), developed by Good Karma Applications, is a scheduling app that provides an audiovisual representation of a routine, activity, sequence, or transition in order to increase independence and reduce anxiety. It can be viewed on screen with a full view, split view, or list view. First Then provides for customization by allowing for voiceovers so that students can both see and hear the task that needs to be completed and allows for an optional checkmark after each task is completed. In addition to the preloaded pictures in the app, First Then also allows the user to upload pictures from a photo library or the Internet. Schedules can also easily be uploaded to a computer and printed out.
- *iReward.* Developed by Grembe Inc., iReward (www.grembe.com/ireward) allows the instructor to create a star chart or token board to help reinforce positive behavior. iReward comes with custom color backgrounds and tokens that include gold and red stars, smiley faces, check boxes, and gold coins that students work to achieve by completing various tasks. Preloaded pictures enhance motivation for students, or pictures can be uploaded from a photo library or the Internet. Upon completion of a task, preloaded animations appear, and the app also allows for customization by letting users add their own audio to the pictures.

Implications for Physical Education

The following section provides an overview of implications for teaching physical education to children with ASD—specifically, assessment, activity selection, and instructional and management techniques.

Assessment

One method that has been proven helpful in assessing students with ASD is ecological task analysis (Carson et al., 2007). Within this model, the instructor examines the interaction of three factors: the student, the environment, and the task. To derive a good understanding of the student, the assessor should seek information from several sources, including parents, teachers, therapists, and aides. One should fully understand reinforcers and modes of communication before attempting to assess the child. The assessor should also spend time devel-

It's time for PE.
In PE we are going to go swimming in the pool. First, we have to go to the locker room and change into our swimsuits.
In the locker room we need to place our dry clothes in the locker, use the bathroom, and rinse off in the shower.
Then we enter the pool. We can practice our diving to get into the pool.
When we hear the whistle, it is time to get out of the pool.
When we leave the pool area, we walk back into the locker room and rinse off in the shower.
Now we go to our lockers and change back into our dry clothes.
We put our wet clothes in a plastic bag and leave the locker room with our class.

FIGURE 10.1 This social story and comic strip provide specific guidelines to encourage children with ASD to go swimming.

oping a rapport with the child before assessment. When beginning the assessment, it is important to start with activities the child understands and is able to perform and then move on to more difficult tasks. It is also important to understand qualities that inhibit or enhance performance. This approach allows for early success and better compliance throughout the assessment.

The second factor that needs to be considered is the task. To determine if the task being assessed is appropriate, consider the following questions: Is it age appropriate? Is it functional? Will the information gained assist in the development of individualized education program (IEP) goals and objectives? Will the information be used for program development and instruction? If the answer to these questions is yes, then the task is appropriate. To assess the task, the assessor might use a task-analysis approach in which requisite skills are identified and either further broken down or assessed as a whole. For example, when assessing soccer skills, the assessor would determine the requisite skills for soccer (e.g., dribbling, passing, trapping, shooting). Each of these skills could be further broken down and assessed separately, or each skill could be assessed as a whole. Once the assessment is complete, the information gleaned can be used to develop goals and objectives based on unique needs, serve as a basis for instruction, and aid in activity selection.

Finally, the instructor needs to consider the environment. Keeping in mind that children with ASD might be hypersensitive to environmental stimuli, the instructor should provide an environment with limited distractions and focus on one task at a time. In the soccer example, the instructor can provide different-sized balls, different-sized goals, and different surfaces for performing the task. After considering the individual student, the task, and the environmental parameters involved, the instructor observes the student's behavior and preferences and documents his choices. These choices serve as a springboard upon which to build an instructional plan. Ecological task analysis is discussed further in chapter 7.

Activity Selection

When selecting activities for children with ASD, the most important consideration is the needs and interests of the learners and their families. In addition, the functional value of the activity should be taken into account. Activities that have a high probability of success for children with ASD are generally more individual, such as swimming, running, and bowling. However, no one should assume that children with ASD cannot participate in and enjoy team sports. Team sports might need modifications to enhance success, but all children should have the opportunity to explore a range of physical education activities.

The learner's age must also be taken into account. Both developmental appropriateness and age appropriateness should always be considered when selecting activities. Although elementary-aged children spend a great deal of time learning and improving their fundamental motor skills, it would be inappropriate to focus on such skills at the middle school or high school level. When selecting activities, instructors should also consider family and community interests. Does the child come from a family that enjoys hiking or skiing? Or is the family more involved in soccer or softball? Considering these factors helps shape the activity selection so that the child with ASD can more fully integrate within the family and community.

One form of movement, known as *sensorimotor activities*, can be especially beneficial to students with ASD. These activities are designed to stimulate the senses with a focus on kinesthetic awareness, tactile stimulation, auditory processing, and visual–motor coordination. Kinesthetic awareness deals with the relationship of the body to space. Examples of kinesthetic activities include jumping on a trampoline, crawling through tunnels, jumping over a rope, and rolling down an incline mat. Tactile stimulation can be enhanced by having the child interact with objects, such as balls with various sizes, shapes, and textures. Auditory processing can be enhanced through the use of music and songs that instruct the child in a sequence of movements.

Experiencing kinesthetic awareness

Finally, visual–motor coordination can be strengthened by playing games that require tracking, such as kickball, softball, soccer, or lacrosse.

One way to help with physical activity selection and participation is to utilize what Block and colleagues (2020) term the *affinity-based approach*. Because children with ASD often exhibit a strong interest in certain objects or things, the instructor can use that interest to enhance physical activity. Although often viewed as a negative behavior, the affinity-based approach views strong interests as a way to enhance communication as well as skills (e.g., motor skills, physical activities). A more detailed description and specific physical activity examples can be found in the Block and colleagues article.

Instructional and Management Techniques

Teaching students with ASD is not unlike teaching other children. Teachers need to establish rapport with students, develop trust, relay information in a clear and concise manner, and provide reinforcement and feedback to help shape appropriate motor and social behavior. Specific strategies that prove helpful in instructing and managing students with ASD include the use of picture and communication boards, the consistent use of structure and routines, and the use of natural cues in the environment to facilitate the acquisition and execution of skills. Other methods include the correction procedure rule and parallel talk. In addition, teaching to the strengths of learners by considering their preferred learning modality will also prove helpful in teaching students with ASD. Finally, the value of using support staff and peer tutors should not be underestimated in teaching students with ASD. Each of these strategies is more fully explained next.

Picture and Communication Boards

One of the most common and successful methods used to teach children with ASD is the use of picture and communication boards. Pictures can include photographs, lifelike drawings, and symbolic drawings. Some children may not yet understand pictures and may need objects to represent them, such as dollhouse furniture or small figures of objects. When pictures are used, it is best to have only one item in the picture because children with ASD have a tendency toward overselectivity, meaning that they are not able to screen out irrelevant information. For example, if a child is working on basketball skills, it may be preferable to use a picture of a basketball rather than a picture of a basketball court with students playing on it. Pictures can also be arranged to create a daily, weekly, or monthly schedule. Boardmaker, as described earlier, is one of many commercial software programs that can help create picture boards using universally accepted symbols to depict events and actions.

Routines and Structure

Establishing routines and structure aids in managing and instructing students with ASD. Children with ASD often demonstrate inappropriate behavioral responses when new or incongruent information is presented in a random or haphazard manner. Routines with set beginning and end points allow for more predictability and help to reduce sensory overload. Routines are also useful in introducing new information or behaviors. Keeping some information familiar and gradually introducing new information helps students respond appropriately. Routines also help to reduce the need for verbal directions and allow children to work independently.

The following scenario illustrates a typical routine that incorporates pictures and can be useful in physical education. Before Justin goes to physical education class, a classroom teacher gives him a picture of the physical education teacher and says, "Justin, it is time for PE." The picture of the physical education teacher allows Justin to understand what is going to happen next. When the class enters the gym, Justin gives the picture card to the physical education teacher. The physical education teacher then uses a communication board to show Justin the lesson from start to finish. For example, a picture of a child stretching could indicate the warm-up, a picture of a child doing curl-ups could indicate the fitness portion of the lesson, a picture of a soccer ball could identify the lesson focus, and a picture of goalposts can be used to indicate the game activity. Figure 10.2 presents a sample schedule for a physical education lesson. The components of the schedule can remain the same, but the actual activities can be manipulated to prepare the child for the daily lesson. When using words instead of pictures, the words can be erased after the task is completed. This system allows students to understand that the activity has ended and the next activity will soon begin.

When entering a new environment, such as a gym, the atmosphere may create extreme sensory overload for some students with ASD. Structure helps alleviate this stress by creating environments that are easily understood and manageable. In physical education, teachers can structure their

FIGURE 10.2 Physical education sample pictorial schedule. The pictures allow the student to understand what is going to happen in the lesson from start to finish.

space so that the environment is predictable. First, the teacher needs to identify for the child where activities are done (in the gym, on the field, on a mat), where things are located (balls in bin, ropes on hangers, rackets on hooks), and how to move from one place to another (rotating stations, rotating positions, moving from inside to outside). Labels can help organize space—for example, equipment boxes should be clearly labeled so that the child can easily retrieve and put away equipment. Second, the teacher needs to establish concrete boundaries. For example, if a child is to remain on one-half of the field, cones indicating the halfway point should be in place.

At the conclusion of the lesson, the physical education teacher should have a consistent cue to transition the child back to the classroom. This could be a picture of the classroom teacher or a desk. Forewarning is another effective way to transition a child back to the classroom. For example, the teacher might say, "Justin, in three minutes PE will be over." This helps the child better understand time and prepare for the change in routine. A second warning might be given at two minutes and a third at one minute. Through proper preparation, anxiety levels are reduced because the child understands that a change will occur. When he arrives back in the classroom, physical education can be crossed off his daily schedule and he can begin the next activity on the schedule.

The implementation of routines and structure might at first seem time consuming for the teacher. However, once these systems are in place, dramatic improvements in behavior and participation usually occur, making the extra time and effort worthwhile.

Natural Environmental Cues and Task Analysis

In teaching new skills to children with ASD, instructors are urged to use natural cues within the environment and to minimize verbal cues. If the goal is for the child to kick a soccer ball into a goal, the natural cues would be a soccer ball and a goal. To achieve the desired objective, the instructor might need to break the task down into smaller steps; for example: (1) Line the child up at the shooting line; (2) place the ball on the shooting line; and (3) prompt the child to take a shot. One may break the skill down further by placing a poly spot in front of the child to initiate a stepping action with the opposite kicking foot and prompting the child with either a verbal cue or physical assist to use the kicking foot to make contact with the ball. The degree to which skills should be task analyzed depends on the task and the learner. Additional information on task analysis is found in chapter 7.

Demonstrations also prove helpful in the acquisition of new skills. For example, the teacher might teach the child how to stop a ball being passed to the shooting line. If the child is unsuccessful in shooting the ball toward the goal, the teacher could use physical assistance to help her gain a better understanding of what the task requires, allowing her to repeat the task until no physical assistance is needed. Once the child has performed the task correctly, the teacher would move on to the rest of the lesson. Figure 10.3 depicts a child working on soccer skills with assistance.

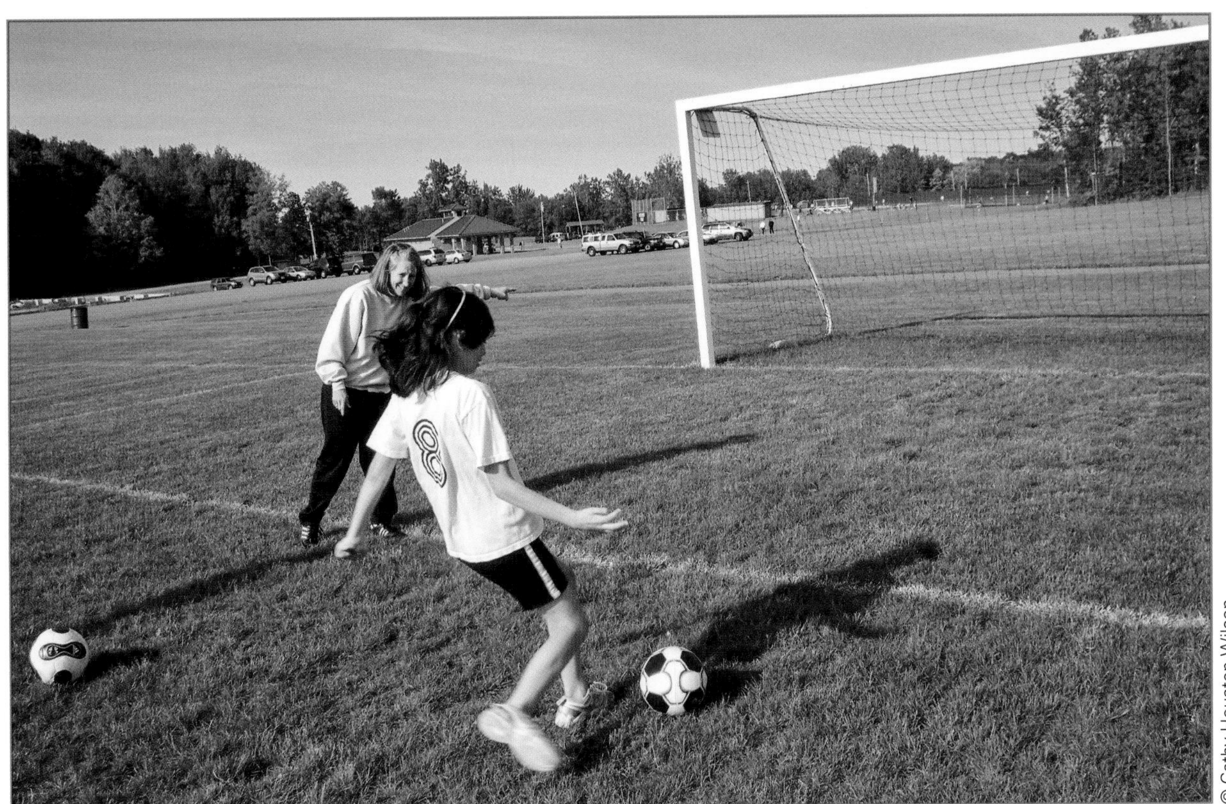

FIGURE 10.3 Shooting a soccer ball into a goal can be broken down into steps. Here the child is on step 3, with the assistant prompting the child to take a shot.

Correction Procedure Rule

Another effective technique in instructing children with ASD is the correction procedure rule, a system used when inappropriate skills or social behaviors occur. Here, the instructor takes the child back to the last task that was done correctly in an effort to redirect the inappropriate behavior. For example, say a child maintains a proper batting stance and properly swings the bat at the ball but then runs to first base with the bat. In this case, the instructor returns the child to the last correct response before the incorrect response by asking the child to repeat the swing, then assisting her in placing the bat on the ground before running to first. The Application Example sidebar shows another scenario in which the correction procedure rule can be used.

Parallel Talk

To promote language and skill acquisition, instructors are encouraged to embed language throughout

Application Example

Importance of Visual Cues in Learning a New Task

SETTING

A physical education class that is working on a tee ball unit

STUDENT

Kiera, a seven-year-old girl with autism in elementary physical education class

TASK

Learning how to hit a ball off the tee and run to first base

ISSUE

Kiera's physical education teacher, Mr. Greer, has been teaching her how to play tee ball. They have practiced swinging the bat at the ball (in a hand-over-hand manner), making contact with the ball, putting the bat down, and running to first base. It appeared that Kiera had the hang of the skill, so Mr. Greer allowed her to bat independently. Kiera stood in the ready position; Mr. Greer placed the ball on the tee and took a step back. Just then a gust of wind came, and the ball fell off the tee. Kiera immediately placed the bat on the ground and began running to first base even though she did not make contact with the ball. This showed that Kiera still did not understand the purpose of the game, which was to contact the ball with the bat before running.

APPLICATION

Mr. Greer used visual cues to create a positive learning environment by doing the following:

- Mr. Greer demonstrated to Kiera what to do if the ball fell off the tee. Mr. Greer put the ball on the tee loosely so that it would fall off. When the ball fell off, he picked up the ball, replaced it on the tee, and struck it with the bat.
- Mr. Greer then signaled to Kiera to try. Again he placed the ball loosely on the tee and gave the bat to Kiera.
- The ball fell off the tee and Kiera picked up the ball and replaced it on the tee. She then struck the ball and ran to first base.

This example illustrates the need for students with autism to see and understand a task. In no way was Kiera being uncooperative or off task. She simply did not understand the task. When she understood the task, she was able to participate in the game independently.

Kiera practices her swing in tee ball.

the lesson. One way to accomplish this is by using parallel talk, in which the teacher talks through the actions that are occurring to aid in the understanding and purpose of these actions. For example, if Marci is rolling a red ball to the teacher, the teacher would say, "Marci is rolling the red ball." Parallel talk can also help children associate certain skills with their verbal meaning, such as spatial concepts (e.g., in, out, under, over) and motor skills (e.g., dribbling, shooting, striking). Another way to foster language acquisition is to create print-rich physical education environments. Pictures, posters, and action words should be displayed prominently around the gym. Labeling the action as it is being performed helps students acquire both receptive and expressive language skills and attach meaning to actions.

Learning Modalities

Learning modalities, or learning styles, refer to the way in which students learn best. The three common categories of learning include auditory, motor, and visual. Auditory learners tend to learn by following verbal commands or prompts and may be easily distracted by background noise. Children who are motor or kinesthetic learners tend to learn by doing rather than watching; they are active learners who enjoy hands-on projects. Children who are visual learners tend to learn by watching and looking at pictures, and they can be easily distracted by surrounding activities and noise. Research indicates that students with ASD tend to be visual learners (Sicile-Kira, 2014), although all learning modalities should be employed from time to time. As indicated previously, the use of pictures and communication boards is by far the most effective teaching strategy used to communicate with and teach students with ASD.

Support Personnel

Teachers should take advantage of support personnel to assist them in implementing programs. Teaching assistants, paraprofessionals, and peer tutors are all valuable resources that can help in providing individualized physical education instruction to students with ASD. Teachers can request support personnel through the child's IEP as a necessary component to support learning.

Managing Behavior

This section presents behavior management techniques that can be useful when teaching children with ASD in order to reduce the occurrence of inappropriate behaviors, such as verbal outburst or self-injury, or to promote appropriate behaviors, such as on-task behavior and motor and language skill acquisition.

Positive Behavioral Interventions and Supports

Positive Behavioral Interventions and Supports (PBIS) (see chapter 6), is an effective model used to manage student behavior. This model is based on the premise that preventing inappropriate behaviors is much more desirable then punishing undesirable behaviors. When inappropriate behaviors are absent, then teaching and learning are more likely to occur. The underlying theme is to teach students positive and acceptable behaviors in a regular and consistent manner. When inappropriate behaviors are displayed, a functional behavioral assessment (FBA) (as discussed in chapter 9) is conducted to determine why a behavior may be occurring. By understanding what triggers the behavior, one can create a behavioral intervention plan (BIP) to minimize or distinguish inappropriate behaviors. Rather than giving consequences or punishment for each infraction, one manipulates the environment to create a positive learning environment.

Token Economy and Premack Principle

The token economy system and the Premack principle, described in chapter 6, are also effective behavior management strategies to use with students with ASD. A token economy is a system in which the student is rewarded with a reinforcer that can be redeemed for a desirable object or privilege. For example, if Justin enjoyed ice-skating, he would need to collect a certain number of coins or tokens in order to be permitted to skate. Similarly, the Premack principle encourages the student to participate in a less preferred activity before the preferred activity. Once again, using Justin's preferred activity of ice-skating, he would be required to participate in other physical education activities before he could skate. However, extreme caution is warranted with the Premack principle, because if it is misused, a desirable object, privilege, or preferred activity may soon become undesirable. If Justin is constantly forced to do things he does not enjoy in order to skate, skating may quickly become a nonpreferred activity.

Finally, instructors should be aware that students with ASD may experience meltdowns. Despite best efforts, structure, and routines, there will be times when students with ASD find it difficult to participate in any activity. Allowing the child to sit it out or go to a quiet space and regain composure may be the best option. When the episode has subsided, the child would be positively reinforced and encouraged to participate in the planned activity.

Strategies for Inclusion

The techniques described in this chapter are useful for helping educators include children with ASD in physical education. Keeping in mind that adapted physical education is a program, not a placement, these ideas are easy to incorporate in an inclusive setting. Using resources within the IEP, physical educators can request support personnel to help provide any one-on-one teaching that might be necessary. In addition, supplemental aids and equipment that might be required to more successfully include the child should also be identified in the IEP. Goals and objectives developed for children with ASD should parallel the physical education curriculum. Due to the wide variability in students identified with ASD, there will be instances when students may not need any form of modification or an IEP in physical education to be successfully included in the class. Determining whether to include students with ASD in general physical education must be based on the individual needs of the learner. In some instances, inclusion is most appropriate; in others, it is not. Responding to the unique needs of the learner is the best approach.

One approach that fosters inclusion is that of universal design for learning (UDL). When considering UDL for your physical education classes, there are many strategies you can employ. The first is to create a welcoming environment for all learners and avoid grouping or isolating students with ASD with a teacher assistant. It is important that all students have opportunities to interact with one another through group games, station work, and group demonstrations. Second, be sure the environment is free of any barriers that would prevent access. This means that all information should be presented verbally and visually as well as kinesthetically (physically) to accommodate a variety of learning modalities. As mentioned previously, students with ASD are frequently visual learners, therefore demonstrations, posters, videos, hands-on activities, and multisensory approaches address the learning needs of students with ASD as well as other students in the class. It is also essential to have a variety of equipment available to complete desired objectives of the lesson—for example, implements of varied colors and textures and equipment with light or sound should be readily available in every lesson and activity.

Finally, it is important to allow and encourage different ways to meet the same objective. For example, when teaching a student with autism to play basketball, a standard basketball may not be conducive to yielding the desired result of dribbling, shooting and passing. Allowing the student to choose from a variety of balls, such as playground balls or bell balls with different sizes (small, medium and large) and textures (smooth, grated), can result in longer engagement.

UDL requires preplanning and a systematic approach; however, the outcome yields higher levels of participation and success for all learners. Readers are referred to the Lieberman and colleagues (2021) book *Universal Design for Learning in Physical Education* for more information on UDL and physical education.

Summary

This chapter provided an overview of autism spectrum disorder (ASD) and its implications for physical education. The cause of ASD has been attributed to genetic, neurological, and environmental factors. Physical and motor characteristics of students with ASD varies depending on the level of severity of the condition. Although the incidence of ASD continues to increase, making ASD the fastest-growing disability in the country, many attribute this increase to better screening and detection.

This chapter reviewed many treatment approaches that have been used to help students with ASD live more productive lives, including ABA, the TEACCH program, the DIR/Floortime approach and its counterpart ABLC, social stories and comic strips, and downloadable apps that can aid in communication and social interaction. These approaches all have merit, and each has led to significant gains in learning, communication, and engagement. Specific information on teaching physical education to students with ASD, as well as strategies for managing behavior, was also presented. It is hoped that this information will assist physical educators to provide appropriate learning experiences for students with ASD.

References

American Psychiatric Association (APA). (2013). *Diagnostic and statistical manual of mental disorders (DSM-5)* (5th ed.). Author.

Autism Speaks. (2018). *Brain study finds evidence that autism involves too many synapses*. Author.

Autism Speaks. (2020). *Applied behavior analysis*. Author.

Block, M.E., Nichols, C., & Bishop, J. (2020). An affinity-based approach to physical activity for children with autism spectrum disorder. *Palaestra, 34*(2), 32-36.

Carson, L.M., Bulger, S.M., & Townsend, J.S. (2007). Enhancing responsible student decision making in physical activity. In W. Davis & G. Broadhead (Eds.), *Ecological task analysis and movement* (pp. 141-157). Human Kinetics.

Centers for Disease Control and Prevention (CDC). (2020). *Autism Information Center frequently asked questions: Prevalence*. Author.

Davis, A., Isaacson, L., & Harwell, M. (2014). *Floortime strategies to promote development in children and teens: A user's guide to the DIR model*. Brookes.

Friend, M. (2018). *Special education: Contemporary perspectives for school*. Pearson.

Grandin, T. (2014). *The way I see it*. Future Horizons.

Gray, C. (1994). *Comic strip conversations*. Future Horizons.

Gray, C. (2010). *The new social story book*. Future Horizons.

Greenspan, S., & Lewis, D. (2002). *Affect-based language curriculum (ABLC): An intensive program for families, therapists and teachers*. ICDL.

Hardy, P.M., Naviaux, R.K., Edelson, S.M., Miller, L.J., Pangborn, J., Auyeung, B., Sullivan, J., Baron-Cohen, S., Lombardo, M., & Goodwin, M. (2014). *Infantile autism: The syndrome and its implications for a neural theory of behavior by Bernard Rimland, Ph.D.* Jessica Kingsley Publishers.

Individuals with Disabilities Education Improvement Act of 2004 (IDEA), 20 U.S.C. 1400 (2004).

Lieberman, L., Grenier, M., Brian, A., & Arndt, K. (2021). *Universal design for learning in physical education*. Human Kinetics.

Mesibov, G.B., Shea, V., & Schopler, E. (2004). *The TEACCH approach to autism spectrum disorders*. Kluwer Academic/Plenum.

Ming, X., Brimacombe, M., & Wagner, G. (2007). Prevalence of motor impairment in autism spectrum disorders. *Brain & Development, 29*, 565-570. https://doi.org/10.1016/j.braindev.2007.03.002

National Institutes of Health (NIH). (2018). *Autism fact sheet*. Author.

Ozonoff, S., Dawson, G., & McPartland, J. (2014). *A parent's guide to Asperger syndrome and high-functioning autism*. Guilford Press.

Sicile-Kira, C. (2014). *Autism spectrum disorder: The complete guide to understanding autism*. The Penguin Group.

Smith, T. (2001). Discrete trial training in the treatment of autism. *Focus on Autism and Other Developmental Disabilities, 16*, 86-92. https://doi.org/10.1177/108835760101600204

Print Resources

Greenspan, S.I., & Wieder, S. (2006). *Engaging autism: Using the floortime approach to help children relate, communicate, and think*. Da Capo Lifelong Books.

This instructional resource includes information on neuroscience research on the effects of the Floortime approach for children with ASD. Unlike approaches that focus on changing specific behavior, Greenspan's program promotes the building blocks of healthy emotional and behavioral development.

Kluth, P. (2010). *You're going to love this kid! Teaching students with autism in the inclusive classroom*. Brookes.

This guidebook for including students with autism in both primary and secondary school classrooms provides first-person accounts that give readers insight into the experience of having autism. This book shows educators how to adapt their environments to support student participation in classwork, school routines, social activities, and more.

Koegel, R.L., & Koegel, L.K. (2006). *Pivotal response treatments for autism communication, social, and academic development*. Brookes.

This resource describes pivotal response treatment, which uses natural learning opportunities to target and modify key behaviors in children with autism, leading to widespread positive effects on communication, behavior, and social skills.

Neisworth, J.T., & Wolfe, P.S. (Eds.). (2004). *The autism encyclopedia*. Brookes.

This A-to-Z reference source on ASD and PDD includes more than 500 terms, alphabetically listed and clearly described, on such topics as causes, incidence and prevalence, interventions, behavior, education, and many more.

Shapiro, B.K., Pasquale, J., & Accardo, P.J. (Eds.). (2008). *Autism frontiers: Clinical issues and innovations*. Brookes.

With cutting-edge information on ASD based on applied research, this resource includes information on early diagnosis and intervention, language and social reciprocity, overlapping syndromes, complementary and alternative medicine, autism and epilepsy, parent advocacy, and a new screening protocol for detecting autism.

Video Resources

Autism and Applied Behavioral Analysis [DVD]. (2001). Films for the Humanities & Sciences, P.O. Box 2053, Princeton, NJ 08543.

This video provides an overview of two children with autism who participate in ABA DTT. Although the degree of improvement attributable to ABA varies from child to child, the gains noted appear to be of great value to the children and their families. Running time is approximately 22 minutes.

Autism: Challenging Behavior [DVD]. (2013). Films for the Humanities & Sciences, P.O. Box 2053, Princeton, NJ 08543.

This video presents the pros and cons of implementing ABA to modify behaviors of children with autism. Running time is 60 minutes.

Autism Spectrum Disorder [DVD]. (2008). Films for the Humanities & Sciences, P.O. Box 2053, Princeton, NJ 08543.

This three-part series presents the diagnosis evolution of autism, describes diagnostic mechanisms, and discusses specific treatment modalities. Running time is 20 to 24 minutes each.

Breakthrough: New Instructional Approaches to Autism [DVD and curriculum manual]. (2002). Child Development Media, Inc., 5632 Van Nuys Blvd., Ste. 286, Van Nuys, CA 91401.

Through a rigorous program of high expectations, physical prompting, modeling, and attending to task, a featured child makes significant progress. Running time is approximately 26 minutes.

The Child Who Couldn't Play [DVD]. (1996). Films for the Humanities & Sciences, P.O. Box 2053, Princeton, NJ 08543.

Filmed at the Princeton Child Development Institute, this is a comprehensive overview of autism and depicts the Institute's highly successful scientific approach to teaching children with autism. Running time is approximately 46 minutes.

On the Spectrum: Children and Autism [DVD]. (2002). First Signs, Inc., P.O. Box 358, Merrimac, MA 01860.

This video assists professionals in recognizing the early warning signs of ASD and understanding the impact of early intervention. It outlines the diagnostic criteria for ASD, provides guidelines for conducting a developmental screening, and describes how to relay developmental concerns to parents. Differences in development are demonstrated through filmed examples of typical and atypical behavior in children from 4 to 36 months of age. Running time is approximately 24 minutes.

Online Resources

Autism Society: www.autism-society.org

The Autism Society is the leading grassroots autism organization in the United States. Its goal is to increase public awareness about the day-to-day issues faced by people on the spectrum; advocate for appropriate services across the life span; provide the latest information regarding treatment, education, research, and advocacy; and improve the lives of all affected by autism. The Autism Society is the leading source of trusted and reliable information about autism and was instrumental in the passage of the 2006 Combating Autism Act, the first federal autism-specific law in the United States.

Autism Speaks: www.autismspeaks.org

Autism Speaks is dedicated to funding global biomedical research into the causes, prevention, treatments, and cure for autism; raising public awareness about autism and its effects on individuals, families, and society; and bringing hope to all who deal with the hardships of this disorder.

National Autism Association: www.nationalautismassociation.org

The National Autism Association was created to empower families affected by autism and other neurological disorders. Its mission is to educate society that autism is not a lifelong, incurable genetic disorder, but one that is biomedically definable and treatable.

11

Specific Learning Disabilities

Barry W. Lavay and Melissa D. Bittner

Calvin is 13 years old and has been receiving special education services since second grade, when he was first diagnosed with a specific learning disability and attention deficit/hyperactivity disorder. This year, Calvin is attending seventh grade at Lexington Middle School. The first two periods of the school day are spent working on math and reading in a special education resource room; during the remaining five periods, Calvin is included in general education classes with his peers without disabilities, including general physical education.

Calvin struggles with physical education class; the acoustics and the noise level make it difficult to concentrate and understand class instructions. Calvin also finds the large gym space with the different floor markings a distraction. Every three weeks after a sport unit is completed, Mr. Santos gives the class a 15-minute test on written rules that Calvin has difficulty reading and completing in such a short amount of time. Recently, two of the more skilled boys whose team he played on in a basketball unit began to bully Calvin and taunted him each time he dropped the ball. When Mr. Santos comes over to help Calvin, he gets nervous and drops the ball even more. He doesn't want Mr. Santos to find out that he has a learning disability and ADHD and is different from the other kids.

As the adapted physical education specialist assigned to Lexington Middle School, how can you assist Calvin and Mr. Santos? You can start by identifying each of the unique behaviors and specific challenges that Calvin faces in class. Next, consider appropriate educational approaches and accommodations to assist Mr. Santos in helping Calvin have a more positive physical education learning experience.

As you read this chapter, think about Calvin and other children with a specific learning disability, attention deficit/hyperactivity disorder (ADHD), or delayed motor skills and consider the challenges each one faces. No two children with a specific learning disability are alike; a wide range of characteristics exists. Skill levels for children with a specific learning disability can vary along a spectrum from highly skilled, such as the star athlete, to unskilled or clumsy. Regardless of skill, these children are often included in general physical education classes, and the information in this chapter will help you provide a more successful learning experience. Topics in this chapter include definitions, causes, and incident rates of specific learning disabilities; common behavioral characteristics; general educational approaches; and specific recommendations for teaching physical education and sport.

What Is a Specific Learning Disability?

No other disability has been more misunderstood or has caused more confusion among professionals and parents than the condition identified as *learning disability*. Too often the general public considers a learning disability a mild condition and therefore assumes that these individuals need only minimal assistance and support. These assumptions, however, are unfounded and can be harmful if intervention is withheld or delayed (Smith et al., 2018).

In the past, terms commonly used to identify this population have been *perceptually handicapped*, *brain injured*, *minimal brain dysfunction*, *dyslexic*, and *developmentally aphasic*. In 1963, Sam Kirk of the University of Illinois, who is considered the father of the field of learning disabilities, coined the term *learning disability* to refer to children who had learning problems but showed no signs of intellectual disabilities or emotional disturbance. Parents quickly adopted the term as a more appropriate label than those used at the time (Dunn & Leitschuh, 2014; Hallahan et al., 2019).

Learning Disability Defined

Professionals are unable to agree on one specific definition of learning disability (Buttner & Hasselhorn, 2011; Hallahan et al., 2019; Kavale & Forness, 2000; Smith et al., 2018). What experts do agree on is that this group has trouble learning for a variety of reasons. Many believe that children with a learning disability have a **neurological disorder** that results in problems with storing, processing, making associations with, and producing information in the central nervous system, thus causing a difficulty in understanding spoken or written words.

A learning disability can manifest itself in a diminished ability to listen, think, speak, read, write, spell, do mathematical calculations, or carry out motor planning. Other possible indications are difficulty in remembering newly learned information, expressing thoughts orally or in writing, understanding information presented, following directions and routines, or moving in space from one activity to the next. More specific difficulties include reversal of letters or words, difficulty with the steps necessary to complete a math problem, or trouble with spatial awareness (e.g., bumping into objects).

Since the mid-1970s, the following Individuals with Disabilities Education Act (IDEA) definition has been used to determine if a child with a learning disability qualifies for special education services in public schools (Assistance to States for the Education of Children with Disabilities, 2006):

> "Specific learning disability" means a disorder in one or more of the basic psychological processes involved in understanding or in using language, spoken or written, that may manifest itself in an imperfect ability to listen, think, speak, read, write, spell, or do mathematical calculations. The term includes such conditions as perceptual disabilities, brain injury, minimal brain dysfunction, dyslexia, and developmental aphasia. The term does not apply to children who have learning problems that are primarily the result of visual, hearing, or motor disabilities; of mental retardation; or of environmental, cultural, or economic disadvantage.

The IDEA definition of a specific learning disability has undergone little change since being introduced in 1975 and still includes such terms as *minimal brain dysfunction*, *dyslexia*, and *developmental aphasia*. Many professionals believe that this definition is difficult to operationalize and fails to provide significant insight into the true nature of a condition (Buttner & Hasselhorn, 2011; Hallahan et al., 2019; Kavale & Forness, 2000). Despite this controversy, the IDEA definition continues to be used in public schools to determine if a child qualifies for special education services.

Learning Disabilities Are Specific

The term **specific** was added to *learning disabilities* by the federal government to underscore that these children have learning difficulties only in specific areas (e.g., reading, speaking, calculating) and that there are other areas of learning in which they are at least of average ability or even gifted. To some degree, most children have difficulty in some areas at one time or another. But when these behaviors occur in more than one setting, persist over an extended period of time, and interfere with learning, they need special attention. In addition, learning disabilities vary among children; one child may have trouble in math only, whereas another child may have difficulty in both reading and writing.

Unexpected Underachievement

A defining characteristic of a learning disability is that an identified **educationally significant discrepancy** exists between measured intellectual potential and actual academic achievement. Educationally significant discrepancy in this context refers to unexpected underachievement in such academic areas as math, reading, and written language that is not attributed to other disabilities. A learning disability cannot be explained by cultural differences, lack of educational opportunities, poverty, or other such conditions. Although the majority of students with a learning disability possess normal intelligence, their academic performance lags behind that of their peers, and they do not perform at grade level. This population has difficulty learning in traditional ways—however, a learning disability affects *how* people learn, not *how well* they learn (Hallahan et al., 2019; Kavale & Forness, 2000; Smith et al., 2018).

Response to Intervention

Although intelligence quotient (IQ) testing has been the traditional approach to specific learning disability identification since the 1970s, there has been a growing dissatisfaction with this method of evaluation, because many children identified as learning disabled do not meet the operational criteria of an IQ–achievement discrepancy. The Individuals with Disabilities Education Act (IDEA) (2004) now allows states and school districts to use the prereferral step in the individualized education program (IEP) process in order to use the most information available to identify students with learning disabilities. Thus, **response to intervention** (RTI), a multitiered method of increasing instruction for students who are identified as struggling with learning or students with specific learning disabilities, is becoming the preferred identification approach (Buttner & Hasselhorn, 2011; Hallahan et al., 2019; National Center on Response to Intervention, 2019; Smith et al., 2018). More information on RTI is provided later in this chapter and in other parts of the book.

The Hidden Disability

A specific learning disability is not always easily recognized or accepted. When a person is missing a limb or using a wheelchair, for instance, the disability is easily visible. However, when a person's disability has no outwardly identifiable signs, it is considered a hidden disability (Bodey, 2010). Many people with a specific learning disability exhibit deficits in receiving, storing, and retrieving information, also known as the perceptual–motor process (Waugh & Sherrill, 2004). Chapter 20 includes an overview of information processing and the tactile, kinesthetic, visual, and auditory sensory systems.

Because they are often hidden, specific learning disabilities are frequently misunderstood; sometimes the main problem is in educating people who do not have the disability. Recognition is made even more difficult because many people with a specific learning disability spend much of their time and energy hiding their disability (Smith et al., 2018). Individuals with a specific learning disability might not feel comfortable reading in public, for example, or might shy away from activities on the playground. Parents might be in denial about their child's disability and feel that it will go away or can be quickly fixed. The truth is that a learning disability presents lifelong challenges to children and their families. However, with modifications, accommodations, and the right type of intervention, many children with specific learning disabilities go on to be productive members of society. For example, Ben Franklin, Woodrow Wilson, Albert Einstein, and Winston Churchill did not perform well in school and are believed to have had some type of learning disability.

Today we better recognize **neurodiversity**, the idea that neurological differences are the result of normal, natural variation in the human genome that should be recognized and respected as any other human variation (National Symposium on Neurodiversity, 2014). This social movement advocates for viewing neurological differences as variations of human wiring, rather than as a disease. Neurodiversity can include those with dyspraxia, dyslexia, dyscalculia, ADHD, autism spectrum disorder (ASD), and Tourette syndrome, among others.

Specific Learning Disabilities and Coexisting Disabilities

Specific learning disability does not occur as a result of other conditions, but it can coexist with other conditions, such as ADHD and developmental coordination disorder (DCD). More than 50 percent of children with specific learning disabilities display **comorbidity** with ADHD or DCD, making it important to discuss these two conditions in this chapter. However, ADHD and DCD are not recognized as a distinct disability category under IDEA, and children with these disabilities do not automatically qualify for special education services.

Children with ADHD who do qualify for services must have, as their primary disability, one of the 14 disabilities identified in IDEA. The primary disability category is usually a specific learning disability or a behavioral disability (see chapter 9). Some children with ADHD can qualify under the category of other health impairments (see chapter 17) if it can be shown that the child's condition causes heightened alertness to environmental stimuli that limits attention to the educational environment and adversely affects educational performance (Smith et al., 2018). Although IDEA does not recognize motor disabilities alone as a diagnosis for a specific learning disability, most authorities believe that a higher-than-average percentage of children with learning disabilities have perceptual–motor and movement-related difficulties that require intensive intervention (Bishop et al., 2018; Hallahan et al., 2019; Harvey & Reid, 2003; Harvey et al., 2009; Nielson et al., 2018; Sherrill, 2004; Whitall & Clark, 2011).

Because IDEA does not clearly identify and recognize ADHD and DCD as distinct conditions, identifying and programming for students with specific learning disabilities and the coexisting conditions of ADHD and DCD have become problematic (Beyer, 1999; Mulrine & Flores-Marti, 2014; Smith et al., 2018; Waugh & Sherrill, 2004; Whitall & Clark, 2011). For example, some believe that the high degree of overlap between DCD and other childhood disorders appears to de-emphasize its acceptance as a distinct syndrome (Cacola, 2016; Henderson & Henderson, 2002). However, other professionals feel it is not important what labels children wear as long as they receive services designed to meet their unique educational needs. In this chapter, the terms *specific learning disability*, *ADHD*, and *DCD* denote that the information provided applies to students with one or more of these conditions.

What Is Attention Deficit/Hyperactivity Disorder?

Attention deficit/hyperactivity disorder is an official clinical label clearly defined and recognized by the American Psychiatric Association (APA). The diagnostic criteria to determine that a person has ADHD are shown in the Diagnostic Criteria sidebar (APA, 2013). No single test to determine ADHD exists, and a comprehensive battery of assessment tests administered by a qualified professional, such as a school psychologist, is necessary for diagnosis. Though ADHD affects many individuals, it does not mean they cannot be successful. Two of the most decorated Olympic champions of all time, Simone Biles and Michael Phelps, both have ADHD.

Attention deficit/hyperactivity disorder is divided into three subtypes: **combined type**, **predominantly inattentive type**, and **predominantly hyperactive–impulsive type** (see Diagnostic Criteria sidebar). The defining features of ADHD are inattention and hyperactivity–impulsivity. Based on the criteria used to diagnose this condition, ADHD is defined as a persistent pattern of inattention or hyperactivity with impulsive behaviors that are more inappropriate, excessive, frequent, and severe than are observed in children of comparable development (criterion A). Some hyperactive–impulsive or inattention symptoms must be present before the age of 12 (criterion B), exhibited in two or more settings, such as the home, school, and or social settings (criterion C), and not be explained by another disorder (criterion E). Children with ADHD are easily distracted by irrelevant stimuli and frequently shift from one incomplete activity to the next. Inattention occurs in academic, occupational, or social situations and is more difficult to observe than hyperactivity (APA, 2013). Children who exhibit inattention without hyperactivity may even be hypoactive. Everyone can exhibit inattention, hyperactivity, and impulsive behaviors from time to time; however, with ADHD these types of behaviors are chronic (six months or longer) and adversely affect academic, social, and life skills (Smith et al., 2018).

Diagnostic Criteria for Attention Deficit/Hyperactivity Disorder

A. Meets either 1 or 2:

1. Six or more of the following symptoms of inattention for children up to 16 years of age, or five or more for adolescents/adults 17 years and older. Symptoms of inattention have been present for at least six months and are inappropriate for the person's developmental level:

Inattention

a. Often fails to give close attention to details or makes careless mistakes in schoolwork, work, or other activities.
b. Often has trouble holding attention in tasks or play activities.
c. Often does not seem to listen when spoken to directly.
d. Often does not follow through on instructions and fails to finish schoolwork, chores, or duties in the workplace (not due to oppositional behavior or failure to understand instructions).
e. Often has difficulty organizing tasks and activities.
f. Often avoids, dislikes, or is reluctant to engage in tasks that require sustained mental effort (such as schoolwork or homework).
g. Often loses things necessary for tasks or activities (e.g., toys, school assignments, pencils, books, or tools).
h. Is often easily distracted by extraneous stimuli.
i. Is often forgetful in daily activities.

2. Six or more of the following symptoms of hyperactivity–impulsivity for children up to 16 years of age, or five or more for adolescents/adults 17 years and older. Symptoms of hyperactivity–impulsivity have been present for at least six months and are inappropriate for the person's developmental level:

Hyperactivity

a. Often fidgets with hands or feet, or squirms in seat.
b. Often leaves seat in classroom or in other situations in which remaining seated is expected.
c. Often runs about or climbs excessively in situations in which it is inappropriate (in adolescents or adults, may be limited to subjective feelings of restlessness).
d. Often has difficulty playing or engaging in leisure activities quietly.
e. Often on the go or acts as if driven by a motor.
f. Often talks excessively.

Impulsivity

a. Often blurts out answers before questions have been completed.
b. Often has difficulty awaiting turn.
c. Often interrupts or intrudes on others (e.g., butts into conversations or games).

B. Some hyperactive–impulsive or inattentive symptoms that caused impairment were present before age 12.
C. Some impairment for the symptoms is present in two or more settings (e.g., at school and at home).
D. There is clear evidence of clinically significant impairment in social, academic, or occupational functioning.
E. The symptoms do not occur exclusively during the course of pervasive development disorder (PDD), schizophrenia, or other psychotic disorders and are not better accounted for by another mental disorder (e.g., mood disorder, anxiety disorder, dissociative disorder, personality disorder).

Code Based on Type

- ADHD, combined type: If both criteria A1 and A2 are met for the past six months
- ADHD, predominantly inattentive type: If criterion A1 is met but criterion A2 is not met for the past six months
- ADHD, predominantly hyperactive–impulsive type: If criterion A2 is met but criterion A1 is not met for the past six months
- Coding note: For people (especially adolescents and adults) who currently have symptoms that no longer meet full criteria, *in partial remission* should be specified.

From American Psychiatric Association (2013).

What Is Developmental Coordination Disorder?

Since 1987, DCD has been officially recognized as an independent neurodevelopmental disorder by the APA, which identifies four diagnostic criteria (APA, 2013; Cacola, 2016; Henderson & Henderson, 2002; Whitall & Clark, 2011):

1. Performance in daily activities must be substantially below expected for a person's age and intelligence.
2. The motor deficiency must interfere with academic achievement or activities of daily living.
3. The motor deficiency cannot be caused by a known general medical condition, such as cerebral palsy, muscular dystrophy, or PDD. For example, children with ADHD might fall and bump into things, but this is usually a result of distractibility or impulsiveness.
4. If an intellectual disability is present, the motor difficulties must be in excess of those associated with the disability alone.

Developmental coordination disorder is operationally defined as performing two standard deviations below age norms on a standardized motor test. In general, children with DCD demonstrate a marked delay in meeting motor developmental milestones, such as walking, and they appear clumsy; exhibit poor handwriting, balance, and spatial ability; and perform behind age-level peers in sport (Cacola, 2016; Cacola & Romero, 2015). Children with DCD often do not exhibit the classic neurological signs of clumsiness, but they lack the motor competence required to cope with the everyday demands of living (Henderson & Henderson, 2002). Approximately 50 percent of children with DCD also have ADHD and do not grow out of their motor difficulties; thus, DCD can be a lifelong challenge (Cacola, 2016; Clark et al., 2005; Whitall & Clark, 2011).

Suspected Causes of Specific Learning Disability, ADHD, and DCD

The cause of learning disability is often unknown. A specific learning disability is complex and multidimensional and possibly the culmination of many causes. Presently, the most common theory is that a learning disability is a neurological condition, such as **central nervous system dysfunction**, meaning that brain or neurological damage is present that impedes motor or learning abilities. Other possible general causes of learning disabilities may be due to brain damage from an accident; lack of oxygen before, during, or after birth; genetic factors; or toxins (Hallahan et al., 2019; Kavale & Forness, 2000). However, teachers must recognize the uncertainty about what causes learning disabilities and not make assumptions without physical evidence or an actual medical diagnosis. Using labels such as *brain injured* might lead educators and parents to presume that educational difficulties cannot be overcome, and consequently student expectations might be set too low.

As is the case with specific learning disabilities, the exact cause of ADHD is unclear and controversial, though experts agree it is a multidimensional disability caused by an interaction of neurological, genetic, and psychosocial factors. Several studies support the theory that the condition is biological, because certain regions of the brain such as the frontal lobe and prefrontal cortex are associated with ADHD. In addition, there is a high probability that the condition can be inherited and is genetic, as it frequently runs in families (Children and Adults with Attention Deficit/Hyperactivity Disorder [CHADD], 2019a). Physical educators must be aware of the probable biological basis for the lack of social control and the inability to self-regulate behaviors that students with ADHD might exhibit. These behaviors can become more erratic in environments with decreasing amounts of social support (CHADD, 2019a; Harvey & Reid, 2003; Harvey et al., 2009; Mulrine & Flores-Marti, 2014).

Incident Rates of Specific Learning Disability, ADHD, and DCD

In 2017 and 2018, 7 million students ages 3 to 21 received special education services under IDEA, or 14 percent of all public school students. Among students receiving special education services, 34 percent were identified as having a specific learning disability. Although the number of students categorized as having a specific learning disability in recent years has begun to slightly decrease, this is still easily the largest category served and almost double the next largest group, speech or language impairments (National Center for Educational Statistics [NCES], 2019). This is because the definition of this disability is exceptionally broad—children who are not succeeding in general education classes are often incorrectly identified as having a specific learning disability, and it is also frequently used to qualify children with other disabilities, such as ADHD, for special education placement (Hallahan et al., 2019; Smith et al., 2018).

Although estimates vary greatly, a high percentage of children with learning disabilities (25 to 50 percent) also display ADHD (CHADD, 2019a; Hallahan et al., 2019). The symptoms of this condition are more likely to occur in a group setting, such as a playground or classroom, than in an individualized setting. This fact has important implications for physical education, in which most activities occur in large-group settings. Because there is no national registry or required reporting system and because IDEA doesn't recognize ADHD as a separate category, there is no definitive number as to how many students with learning disabilities have ADHD. The prevalence of ADHD in school-aged children is 7.2 percent, or approximately 129 million children worldwide (CHADD, 2019a). Within this group, approximately 50 percent do not qualify for special education services. It has long been believed that boys with ADHD outnumber girls 2 to 1. However, many experts speculate that girls with ADHD are underidentified (Hallahan et al., 2019).

Although DCD is highly comorbid with other developmental disorders, it is most commonly associated with ADHD. The incident rate of children aged 6 to 11 identified with DCD has been estimated to be as high as 7 percent, or one child in every class of 30 children (APA, 2013; Cacola, 2016; Cacola & Romero, 2015; Whitall & Clark, 2011).

Behaviors Present Unique Challenges

The movement behaviors or motor competency of people with specific learning disabilities, ADHD, or DCD can vary. Some might be skilled movers and exceptional athletes, but most are at risk for developmental delays compared to peers without disabilities (Bishop & Block, 2012; Bishop et al., 2018; Harvey & Reid, 2003; Nielson et al., 2018). In general, this population exhibits a wide range of physical, cognitive, and social behaviors that affect the ability to move (Beyer, 1999; Bishop et al., 2018; Grosshans & Kiger, 2004; Milne et al., 1991; Mulrine & Flores-Marti, 2014). Some self-regulating behaviors, such as a short attention span, are not specific motor problems but can make it difficult to attend to directions, which consequently affects movement competency and outcomes (Horvat et al., 2019).

Critical to effective instruction is for teachers to have a thorough understanding of their students. Table 11.1 describes unique physical, cognitive, and social behaviors that students with a specific learning disability, ADHD, or DCD may display that can affect movement. Teachers need to be aware of these behaviors because they can interfere with the student's ability to learn. (Other perceptual–motor and sensory behaviors are discussed later in this chapter and more specifically in chapter 20.) In order to provide students with a safe and positive learning experience, the physical educator must carefully consider all of these behaviors and their relationships when designing and teaching activities. For example, if a student is struggling with a skill, the physical educator might notice "difficulty with skill sequencing" in the physical behavior section and ask, "Can I use chunking or task analyze the skill into manageable parts to help the student learn and be successful? Perhaps this child would learn best with a visual model?" Many other teaching strategies to help offset these physical, cognitive, and social behaviors, as well as manage environmental factors and support student learning, are presented throughout the remainder of the chapter.

Figure 11.1 is a flowchart that includes a general list of the possible behavioral and environmental factors that can affect children's movement, the most widely used educational approaches in schools today, and the specific physical education methods and activities that have been effective when teaching children with learning disabilities, ADHD, or DCD. This chart serves as an overview and should help the reader better understand the information provided in this chapter.

General Educational Approaches

Because students with learning disabilities, ADHD, and DCD are a heterogeneous group, it follows that physical educators will use various educational approaches to meet these students' needs. General educational approaches used by educators in other disciplines should also be used by physical educators in order to collaborate effectively. Currently, no one educational approach is universally supported; rather, several approaches have been

TABLE 11.1 Physical, Cognitive, and Social Behaviors That May Affect Movement for People With a Specific Learning Disability, ADHD, or DCD

Behavior	Characteristics
Physical (developmental delay)	**Marked developmental delay:** Lag behind their same-age peers in fundamental gross motor skills such as running, throwing, and catching. **Difficulty with motor planning and an inability to control movements:** Rush to complete the activity and do not perform at a pace or speed needed to successfully perform the task. **Difficulty with skill sequencing:** Unable to initiate a movement that puts the correct parts into a proper sequence, such as breaking down or analyzing the movements needed to successfully plan and perform a skill. **Extraneous movements that are not performed in a smooth and efficient manner:** Require extra movements and the use of unnecessary body parts to perform skills. Movements appear clumsy or uncoordinated and there is difficulty moving one body part independently from others. **Inconsistency in skill performance:** Skill levels vary from practice session to practice session and even within the same session. Skill retention is difficult.
Cognitive (average or above-average intellectual ability)	**Processing information:** Need more time to take in, organize, and produce instructional information. Take in too much extraneous information or too many stimuli at one time and have difficulty remaining focused on the specific instruction or task. Have difficulty taking in more than one given direction at a time. **Perceptual and sensory difficulties:** Difficulties with tactile, proprioception, kinesthetic, visual, and auditory systems; may be hyper- or hyporesponsive to sensory stimuli. **Language/thinking delays:** Delays in expressive, receptive, retention, or sequencing. **Uneven academic achievement:** There is uneven development among educational subject areas. **Difficulty completing tasks and problem solving in allotted time:** Avoid or fail to stay on tasks that require a sustained mental effort. Overall, have difficulty organizing, planning, and solving tasks. **Inability to pay attention to details:** Complete or finish tasks quickly; make careless mistakes in order to move on to the next task. **Perseveration:** Unable to shift easily from one activity to the next (the opposite of distractibility).
Social (lack of social expectations and low self-esteem)	**Low self-concept:** Easily frustrated and have a low perceived competence level. **Impulsive:** Act before thinking and do not consider the consequences of actions. Often interrupt others. Show little inhibition before speaking or acting in front of others. **Hyperactive, easily distracted, and short attention span:** Demonstrate excess energy that is difficult to control, leading to difficulty staying on task, taking turns, or remaining focused.

These common behavioral characteristics can affect movement and vary from person to person.

Adapted from Bishop and Beyer (1995); Milne, Haubenstricker, and Seefelt (1991); Mulrine & Flores-Marti, (2014); Sherrill (2004); Waugh and Sherrill (2004).

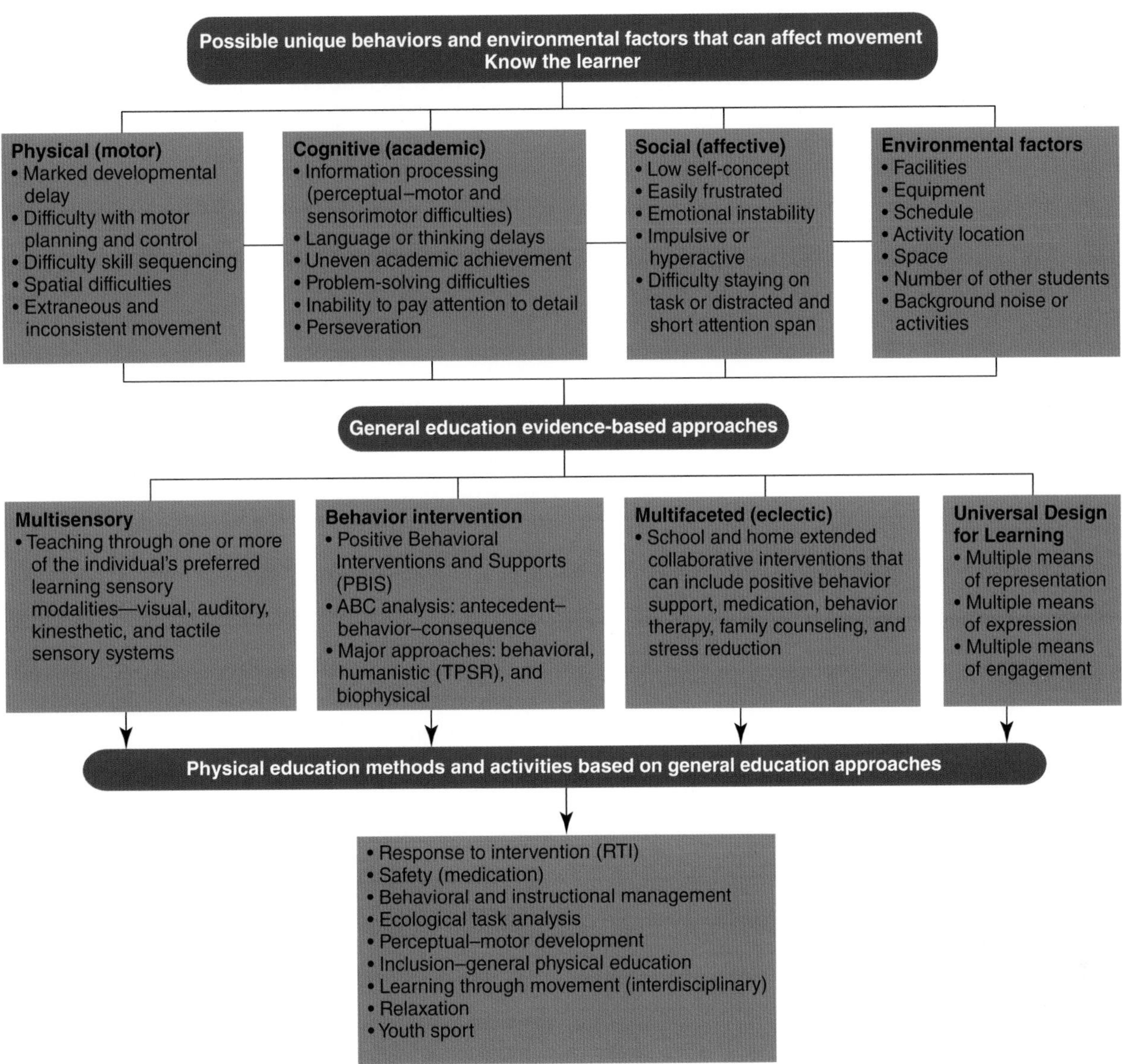

FIGURE 11.1 Unique behaviors and environmental factors that can affect movement when teaching physical education to children with a specific learning disability, ADHD, or DCD.

successful with students with learning disabilities, ADHD, and DCD. Four widely used evidence-based educational approaches—multisensory, Positive Behavioral Interventions and Supports, multifaceted, and universal design for learning (UDL)—are described briefly here. For consistency and when practical, the physical educator might want to follow the same approach in the physical education setting that is used in the student's classroom or home. More than one approach may be used simultaneously. More specific methods and activities for teaching physical education and sport are included later in this chapter.

Multisensory Approach

A child's sensory system has a direct effect on his ability to learn. Children with learning disabilities, ADHD, or DCD can have deficits related to their sensory systems, including poor spatial orientation, difficulty with body awareness, immature body image, poor visual–motor coordination, clumsiness or awkwardness, coordination deficits, or poor balance. (See table 11.1 for more possible sensory deficits under the physical and cognitive categories.) Because of these deficits, effective instruction needs to include a multisensory teaching approach with an understanding of the sensory systems and the perceptual–motor development process (as described in greater detail in chapter 20).

Many students with a specific learning disability, ADHD, or DCD have difficulty learning in traditional ways. To increase each student's opportunity to learn, it is important to determine the student's preferred learning style. The **multisensory approach** emphasizes teaching by combining one or more of the sensory systems through which the child learns best. The Visual, Auditory, Kinesthetic, Tactile (VAKT) model is one such method (Smith et al., 2018). For example, the student can look at a picture or watch a demonstration of a movement (visual), listen to the teacher describe the movement (auditory), and be physically manipulated by the teacher and feel the movement (kinesthetic and tactile). In another example, a student might learn alphabet letters by looking at printed letters (visual), hearing the sounds of the letters (auditory), moving the entire body to form the letters (kinesthetic), and feeling the shapes by tracing the letters (tactile).

Positive Behavioral Interventions and Supports

The foundation of effective instruction is managing student behavior. **Positive Behavioral Interventions and Supports (PBIS)** is a schoolwide system of support that includes proactive strategies for defining, teaching, and supporting appropriate student behaviors to create positive school environments (U.S. Department of Education, Office of Special Education Programs, 2019). There is an emphasis on maintaining and increasing appropriate behaviors and preventing or redirecting inappropriate behaviors in children with learning disabilities, ADHD, or DCD (see figure 11.1). For example, in PBIS, the schoolwide support team analyzes behaviors by focusing on the actions occurring before the behavior (i.e., antecedents) and the consequences occurring after the behavior. This ABC analysis (antecedents–behaviors–consequences) helps the teacher evaluate the student or class and make appropriate interventions, usually with regard to the teaching environment.

Major approaches to behavior management used either separately or collectively are applied behavior analysis, psychoeducational, ecological, biogenic, and humanistic (Lavay, 2019; Lavay et al., 2007; Lavay et al., 2016). A more detailed discussion of these approaches and effective behavior management strategies is presented in chapter 6. The Recommendations for Teaching Physical Education and Sport section later in this chapter also presents strategies for organizing the physical education setting to effectively manage behaviors of students with learning disabilities, ADHD, or DCD.

Multifaceted Approach

Students with specific learning disabilities, ADHD, or DCD often have difficulty learning in traditional ways, requiring an eclectic approach that offers a combination of program services based on what is best for each student. Such a **multifaceted approach** needs to be long-term, consistent, and systematic. In many cases, a team approach involving school personnel and other appropriate individuals (e.g., the special education classroom teacher and the child's family) works best; this can require educational (e.g., PBIS), medical (see Medication: What the Physical Educator Needs to Know sidebar), and behavioral and psychological (e.g., behavioral therapy, family counseling, relaxation techniques) interventions (Hallahan et al., 2019; Lavay et al., 2016; Smith et al., 2018).

Universal Design for Learning (UDL)

Universal design for learning (UDL) is a scientifically valid framework guiding educational practice (Higher Education Opportunity Act, 2008). The UDL framework assists educators with proactively "designing barrier-free, instructionally rich learning environments and lessons" (Meyer et al., 2014, p. 2). Drawing from evidence-based practices and strategies from multiple fields, UDL provides for (a) multiple means of representation (various ways of acquiring information and knowledge); (b) multiple means of expression (various ways to demonstrate learning); and (c) multiple means of engagement (various ways to become engaged in learning) (CAST, 2020). UDL ensures that course materials, notes, and other information resources are engaging, flexible, and accessible for all students (CAST, 2020). To that end, general and adapted physical education teachers can use technology as part of their UDL efforts to improve learning outcomes for students with disabilities. See chapters 2 and 7 for more information on UDL.

Recommendations for Teaching Physical Education and Sport

For many students with a specific learning disability, ADHD, or DCD, physical education can be a series of marked failures, such as repeatedly being the last student picked for teams or dropping a fly ball in front of peers (Bishop et al., 2018). Physical education is unique to other disciplines in that peers can see the end result—if a student fails a math test, those results are personal, but if a student "air balls" a shot, others see. For physical education to be a positive and successful experience, the teacher must create effective programming based on the many factors that can affect student learning.

The next sections provide evidence-based recommendations and best teaching practices that have proven effective in physical education and sport for students with a specific learning disability, ADHD, or DCD. These sections include information, methods, and activities regarding response to intervention (RTI), safety, medication, behavioral and instructional management, task analysis, perceptual–motor development, inclusion, interdisciplinary teaching, relaxation, and youth sport (see figure 11.1). All of these teaching practices work best when accompanied by the principles of UDL and differentiated instruction. In UDL, the teacher designs the curriculum and facilities to be accessible for all by providing multiple options for rules, equipment, and instruction delivered using multiple approaches (CAST, 2020; Columna et al., 2014; Gilbert, 2019; Mulrine & Flores-Marti, 2014). Differentiated instruction, a strategy within the UDL framework, means that students all learn identical content, but students may use different approaches to achieve the common outcome or goal dependent on their diverse needs (Ellis et al., 2009) (see chapter 7). As stated earlier, because of the heterogeneity of students with learning disabilities, ADHD, or DCD, there is no method or activity that will work best. Physical educators must be willing to effectively implement the various practices that follow.

Response to Intervention

In recent years, many schools have implemented the tiered **response to intervention** (RTI) model to improve the early identification process and provide additional levels of support for students who demonstrate difficulty with learning (Lavay et al., 2016; Mulrine & Flores-Marti, 2014; National Center on Response to Intervention, 2019). In Chapter 7, a general three-tier RTI approach was explained. Some school districts may use a four-tier model with IEP services as the fourth tier. This model includes tier 1, general physical education class with group interventions (proactive screening); tier 2, targeted instructional interventions (small group within class, task analysis of skill learning); tier 3, intensive interventions and comprehensive evaluation (one-to-one peer tutoring); and tier 4, IEP individualized special education services (Intervention Central, 2019; Stephens et al., 2010). The physical educator can work closely with the special education support team to identify those students with a specific learning disability, ADHD, or DCD who need support in their classes.

Safety

Always keeping student safety in mind first and foremost, physical educators must be aware of any potentially harmful activities and regularly check all facilities and equipment for potential hazards. Equipment needs to be developmentally appropriate for the student's age, body type, and skill level. Unstructured physical activity designed to blow off steam is contraindicated because it may overstimulate students, especially those with ADHD, allowing them to get out of control and become confused and frustrated. Instead of unstructured activities, provide students with opportunities to perform skills slowly and with control, allowing time to motor plan before performing the activity. Physical educators must also be aware that some students may be taking medication to help manage behavior and learning (see Medication: What the Physical Educator Needs to Know sidebar).

Physical educators need to protect students from both physical and psychological harm. Many students with a learning disability, ADHD, or DCD have low self-esteem consequent to being bullied, which reduces their willingness to engage in physical activity (Kwan et al., 2013; Lavay et al., 2016; Waugh & Sherrill, 2004); this can happen during school activities if educators are not watchful. Bullying must never be tolerated, and discussions should be held in class about respecting individual differences. Instructors must design their programs to promote cooperation and positive interactions among students (Healy, 2014). When possible, a buddy or teammate may be assigned to socialize

Medication: What the Physical Educator Needs to Know

Ritalin (methylphenidate), Dexedrine (dextroamphetamine), Adderall (amphetamine), and Cylert (pemoline) are the most common medications taken by children identified as hyperactive or those who have attention difficulties. These medications increase the student's attention and ability to focus on learning by stimulating the parts of the brain that are not filtering out distractions (CHADD, 2019b; Lavay et al., 2016). Over the past 40 years, Ritalin, the medication most often prescribed by physicians, has been safely and successfully used in the treatment of millions of children with ADHD (CHADD, 2019b; Huber & Duhuis, 2002). Research conducted on medication and its positive effects on behavior and learning is well documented; however, the majority of the work has focused on the classroom and not on motor performance in physical education settings (Beyer, 1999).

Medication must never be viewed as an educational panacea or an easy fix, but rather as part of the student's entire treatment package that includes classroom interventions and support. Professionals caution against the quick prescription of any medications and believe they should be prescribed only after other interventions have been explored. Medications such as Ritalin are short-term, fast-acting stimulants not to be taken by children age 6 and younger (CHADD, 2019b).

Physical educators need to consider a number of factors regarding medication and students with a specific learning disability, ADHD, or DCD (Lavay et al., 2016). First, they need to identify those students who are on medication by getting a list from the school nurse, asking the student's special education teacher, checking school files, or sending a note home to the student's parents asking them to provide general information about their child (Lytle et al., 2010). Physical educators must never recommend that a child be put on medication; this decision is made by the child's parents and physician. Though physical educators will not be required to dispense medication, it is still important to be aware of medication type, dosage, schedule, and possible side effects, which may include poor motor performance and an elevated heart rate. Students on medication may also exhibit drowsiness, fatigue, headaches, loss of sleep, dizziness, blurred vision, irritability, and mood swings (CHADD, 2019b). There is also the possibility of a rebound effect, causing irritability and mood swings when the medication wears off. Physical educators must insist on being informed of those students who are taking medication and their schedule, such as any drug holidays when the student is taken off the medication or transitional periods while dosage is adjusted.

with a student with a learning disability, ADHD, or DCD. Strategies for inclusion and activities that involve cooperation are described throughout this book.

Behavioral and Instructional Management

A supportive and proactive approach to behavior management is important to student success. Being proactive means spending time before class designing an instructional setting consisting of clear class expectations, consistent routines, smooth transitions with signals for changing activities, and reinforcement methods that motivate students to participate. During instruction, these methods are consistently implemented and practiced so that students clearly understand and follow class expectations. For example, during instruction, use phrases to begin a new activity such as "look, think, and act" or "focus, plan, and move." Have students look at the visual picture schedule, give students time to process the first activity on the schedule, then allow students to perform the activity. Organizing the environment and using instructional strategies that are supportive of students with learning disabilities, ADHD, or DCD is an effective way for the teacher to emphasize student success and provide a positive experience.

The section that follows provides behavior management strategies to promote class structure and organization. For other effective methods to increase appropriate behaviors and redirect inappropriate behaviors, see chapter 6.

Class Structure

A structured class format is recommended for students with a learning disability, ADHD, or DCD. It is important to design clear, concise rules and routines that are posted and followed consistently during each class session. Students must know where to go when entering and exiting the gym.

Starting class the same way each time allows students to feel comfortable with the program (Lavay, 2019; Lavay et al., 2007). For example, class can start with an exercise warm-up and certain activities each student knows and feels comfortable with before new activities are introduced. To help alleviate apprehension, the instructor should briefly explain or list the schedule, using a visual with the activities of the day.

Provide clear transitions, using signals to alert students about changing activities or to move from one activity area to the next. Consistent transitions and routines help students stay comfortable in class and learn what is expected of them. Examples of possible transition signals include clapping hands, tossing a scarf into the air, playing music, or counting down. After the transition signal, students freeze and listen for the next set of instructions. It might be helpful to establish an area, such as a big circle in the middle of the gym, where students know to go. For students who struggle with transition, consider giving a verbal warning a few minutes before a transition takes place; provide a one-on-one cue or a secret signal so that the student isn't singled out.

Class Organization

Effective class organization helps students stay active and on task, cuts down on wait time, and reduces behavior problems. Shortening lines, providing each student with a piece of equipment, and individualizing instruction can also increase skill-learning opportunities. Consider using one-on-one instruction (self-paced), partner work, small groups, and multiple learning stations with visuals such as a tablet, picture cards, or task sheets. When teaching students with learning disabilities or ADHD, it is important to eliminate irrelevant stimuli that might cause distractions.

Learning stations provide choices, allow students to perform activities alone or in small groups at their own pace and ability level, and free instructors to work with students who need extra time for instruction. Remember to minimize distractions and reduce irrelevant stimuli at learning stations by using a task card with instructions at marked cones, chalking the area, or creating barriers by positioning folding gymnastic mats vertically (Bishop & Beyer, 1995; Mulrine & Flores-Marti, 2014). Learning stations can also be positioned away from the center of the gym with students' backs toward the extraneous stimuli or in a quiet area with reduced background noise to minimize distraction. For more information, see the section on learning stations in chapter 7.

Many educators are aware that it is important to improve classroom acoustics when teaching students with hearing difficulties; however, many students without hearing disabilities, including students with learning disabilities and those with auditory processing difficulties, can benefit from better acoustics (Acoustical Society of America, 2019). Poor room acoustics and increased noise levels can make it difficult to concentrate and understand instructions. When listening conditions are difficult, physical educators can have the student stand closer in proximity to the instructor and use teaching prompts or cues.

Teaching Prompts or Cues

Students with learning disabilities, ADHD, or DCD may have difficulty attending to the relevant aspects of the learning task. As discussed in Chapter 7, **prompt** or **cue** terminology is often used interchangeably in the literature and is defined as letting the learner know what is expected of them. It can be a verbal, physical, or environmental cue or signal to help the student remember to perform a task. The teacher can help students focus on only the most relevant tasks by keeping directions simple and not providing too much information. This is especially important for students with a limited attention span. During instruction, it may also be helpful to position the student directly in front of the instructor. The Application Example sidebar provides the reader with a variety of **verbal**, **physical**, **visual**, and **environmental** prompting and cueing strategies for a student with a short attention span who demonstrates difficulty staying on task.

Positive Feedback

It is reinforcing for students for the teacher to provide positive feedback, especially students who do not effectively hear instructions or who have difficulty staying on task. When possible, catch students being good. Trocki-Ables and colleagues (2001) reported that boys with ADHD stayed on task and performed better when verbal praise and tokens were used to reinforce their mile-run fitness performance. **Nonverbal positive feedback** can be a high five, thumbs-up, or fist bump. Verbal positive feedback should be specific and provided for student effort and staying on task. For example, say, "Nicole, that's great—you remembered to step with your opposite foot when throwing the ball!" Provide positive feedback to students who are accurate and move under control rather than those who demonstrate speed or how quickly they can complete an activity. Consider spending a shorter

Application Example

Prompting and Cueing Strategies

SETTING

Elementary to high school physical education class

STUDENT

Students with specific learning disabilities, ADHD, and DCD who have short attention spans

ISSUE

What are some possible strategies for getting and keeping student attention during instruction?

APPLICATION

The following prompting and cueing strategies are recommended:

- Have the students make eye contact and listen, and do not let them begin the activity until the directions are completed.
- Give one set of directions at a time, and provide time for the students to take in the information and respond to the directions. Have students repeat the instructions before performing the task in order to check for understanding.
- Encourage verbal mediation or self-talk in which students plan ahead and state aloud the task to be conducted; this strategy will help them get organized.
- Provide verbal reference points. For example, to teach a soccer throw-in, the teacher can say, "Danielle, hold the ball above your head in both hands with your thumbs together."
- Determine the form of instruction or teaching cue that works best for each student, including demonstration, visual aids (such as a poly spot or footprint, picture chart, or tablet), hand signals, verbal instruction (such as specific feedback), or physical guidance.
- Use as few prompts or cues as possible. Start by providing verbal instructions, followed by a visual picture, demonstration, or model, followed by physical guidance. For example, the teacher might say, "Calvin, turn your body to the side before you throw the ball." Give Calvin time to respond to the directions. If he's unsuccessful, say, "Watch me," and then demonstrate the throw. An alternative is to show Calvin a picture or video clip of someone throwing a ball correctly. Again, provide time for Calvin to respond. If he is still having difficulty, then physically assist him: "Let me help you turn your body to the side." Be careful not to overassist. Many students with learning disabilities feel more comfortable watching peers before starting the activity.
- Provide visual or environmental cues such as cones, footprints, poly spots, pictures, or arrows that mark where and when to move. This will make the directions more concrete, gain students' attention, and help students who have difficulty listening and reading directions.

amount of time on an activity than you might with same-age peers. Frequently changing the activity and adding incentives adds variety, keeping students on task and motivated.

Task Analysis

Task analysis, described in chapter 7, is a useful teaching approach for students with a learning disability, ADHD, or DCD that requires breaking down the skill being taught into components (i.e., chunking). When using ecological task analysis (ETA), teachers must also consider the student's strengths and needs and make modifications to the environment, including equipment and facilities. For example, provide enough equipment to accommodate task changes and various skill levels, such as several types and sizes of striking implements (e.g., bats, rackets) and balls (e.g., balloons, beach balls).

Perceptual–Motor Development

As discussed earlier, people with a specific learning disability, ADHD, or DCD may exhibit a variety of perceptual and sensory challenges (see table 11.1) that can affect their movement and consequently their success in physical education (Cacola, 2016; Cacola & Romero, 2015; Nielson et al., 2018; Waugh & Sherrill, 2004; Whitall & Clark, 2011). However, perceptual difficulties can be managed and sometimes overcome by a physical educator who teaches fun and positive movement activities that help develop the tactile, kinesthetic, visual, and auditory sensory systems. See chapter 20 for activities that contribute to development in these areas.

Inclusion in General Physical Education

The majority of students with a specific learning disability, ADHD, or DCD are taught in a general physical education class alongside their peers without disabilities (Block, 2016). Based on the least restrictive environment mandate of IDEA, schools need to avoid placing a large group of students with learning disabilities, ADHD, or DCD in the same general physical education class based on schedule convenience; instead, they should assign students across a range of classes. Further, if inclusion is to be successful, the general physical education placement should be made with a plan that includes school, administrative, and teacher support (Block, 2016; Lieberman et al., 2019; Rizzo & Lavay, 2000; Tripp et al., 2007).

Peer tutor programs are among the most effective methods to promote inclusion. A major benefit is that the student with a specific learning disability, ADHD, or DCD receives increased instruction, practice, reinforcement, and feedback on a continual, individual basis from the tutor (Block, 2016; Lieberman & Houston-Wilson, 2017). However, peer tutors must never overassist or treat a student with a disability in any way other than as a member of the class. Like paraprofessionals, it is essential that peer tutors are trained in order to be effective. When possible, **reciprocal peer tutoring** can be an especially effective method. For example, one student performs the activity while the other tutors and provides feedback, then the partners switch roles. This is an effective way to provide tutoring and show sensitivity by not bringing attention to the student's needs. In addition, Mach (2000) believes that providing students with a specific learning disability, ADHD, or DCD the opportunity to be a peer tutor to classmates or younger students can improve self-esteem and motivation.

Cooperative learning and team building activities are another effective way to promote inclusion and develop effective peer relationships between students with a specific learning disability, ADHD, or DCD and their nondisabled peers (Anderson et al., 2020). In cooperative activities, students are required to work together and trust each other, with all efforts accepted and everyone involved to reach a common goal in a fun, positive way (Orlick, 2006). For example, in a study by Andre and colleagues (2011), sixth-grade students with learning disabilities were more accepted by their peers in cooperative learning physical education classes when compared to a traditional physical education class. These results seem to indicate that cooperative learning settings can create more positive social environments in physical education, translating into a more effective inclusion experience for all involved (Healy, 2014).

To help ensure the success of all students in inclusion settings, the teacher needs proper training to successfully implement teaching practices based on the principles of UDL (CAST, 2020; Gilbert, 2019; Lieberman et al., 2021). It is important to be patient and provide students with a specific learning disability, ADHD, or DCD more time to complete certain tasks, including plenty of repetition and practice. Break skills down into simple, manageable parts and progress from one step to the next in a well-planned, sequential order from simple to complex. For example, have students kick a stationary ball before progressing to a moving ball, or strike a ball off a tee before trying to hit a pitched ball.

Interdisciplinary Teaching

Interdisciplinary teaching is an educational process in which two or more subject areas are integrated to promote learning in each subject area (Cone et al., 2009). Interdisciplinary teaching lends itself well to the multisensory approach because many children with a specific learning disability, ADHD, or DCD learn best through movement. Abstract conceptual information is presented in a concrete manner to actively engage student learning.

Recently there has been a resurgence of interdisciplinary teaching in physical education, which blends subject learning with movement. Movement or motor activities taught in physical education (i.e., perceptual–motor activities) can be integrated with other subject areas throughout the school curriculum. Advantages of using the movement medium include the following (Cone et al., 2009; Pangrazi & Beighle, 2020; Ratey & Hagerman, 2008):

- Helps students learn abstract concepts
- Promotes active rather than passive involvement in learning

- Is effective for students who are kinesthetic learners (see the previous section on the multisensory approach)
- Stimulates expression and communication
- Reinforces learning in a fun and meaningful way
- Helps promote collaboration among professionals (e.g., physical educators and classroom teachers)

This approach must never be viewed as a substitute for a sound, well-rounded physical education curriculum, and it is certainly not a panacea to overcome all the academic difficulties of students with specific learning disabilities, ADHD, or DCD. Rather, it should be understood as a fun, multisensory strategy that will motivate students and enhance movement and learning.

Initially, physical educators can start simple and integrate the motor, cognitive, and affective learning domains into a lesson. For example, the teacher might ask a young child with language delays who is striking a balloon (motor domain) to tell her the color of the balloon (cognitive domain). Young students with a specific learning disability, ADHD, or DCD can work with a peer tutor or in a small group (affective domain) to shape their bodies (motor domain) in various ways to form letters or words (cognitive domain) (figure 11.2).

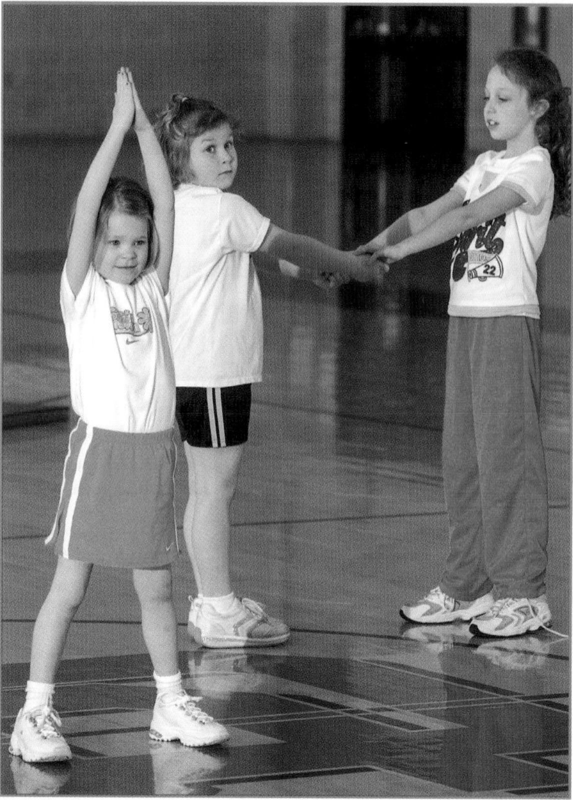

FIGURE 11.2 Having students shape their bodies to form letters is an example of learning language through movement.

The physical educator and classroom teacher can collaborate on a thematic approach and present such themes as the human body, animals at the zoo, transportation, holidays, seasons, the Olympics, and cultures from around the world. For example, students can move as if they were animals at the zoo or on a farm, or as if they were a plane, car, boat, or train. Another approach is to link to a subject area such as math—for example, the teacher can ask students to take a certain number of jumps, or students can add numbers on two dice and complete that number of repetitions for a designated fitness skill. To supplement spelling, the teacher can have the student hop on a letter grid and spell out words.

Relaxation

Relaxation is a socially appropriate way for all students to control their emotions when upset, handle anxiety, and reduce stress. It can be an essential teaching tool when working with students with a specific learning disability, ADHD, or DCD, who may have difficulty attending to tasks and moving under control (Mulrine & Flores-Marti, 2014). Relaxing unneeded muscle groups conserves energy, makes for smoother and more coordinated movements, and helps students solve problems and motor plan. When students lose focus, become too excited, or encounter stressful situations, the physical educator can immediately begin relaxation methods, such as having the student take a few slow, deep breaths. Ending with a relaxing cool-down or closure activity might help calm students before heading to the next scheduled class. Surprisingly, relaxation in physical education is often overlooked as a way of helping students focus their attention.

Relaxation methods used in physical education might include progressive relaxation, yoga, tai chi, static stretching, imagery, and impulse-control games (Lavay et al., 2016). The teacher can introduce a **progressive relaxation activity**, in which muscle groups are tightened for 5 to 10 seconds and then relaxed for 15 seconds. In a quiet setting with the lights dimmed to reduce stimuli, students lie in a comfortable position and take slow, deep, rhythmic breaths, inhaling through the nose and exhaling through the mouth. Soft background music can be played to help students relax.

Physical educators should consider setting aside a few minutes of the class to teach students to move slowly and apply proper force to movements. For example, at the elementary school level, impulse-control games can be introduced by having students pretend to walk on the moon, move in a sea of gelatin, or be a slowly melting ice cream cone on a hot summer day. Teachers can also use **visual imagery** to have students imagine a pleasant scene, such as walking in a forest along a stream, sitting by a campfire, or watching a sunset, which is especially helpful for students with learning disabilities, ADHD, and DCD, who often think in pictures (Waugh & Sherrill, 2004). Edwards and Hofmeier (1991) believe it is important for the instructor to use descriptive terms when teaching relaxation. For example, a relaxed muscle is loose and soft, like a sock, and a tense muscle is hard and tight, like a stick. Instructors can develop relaxation training scripts, asking students to make their arms loose like a noodle or to pretend they have a wet sponge or washcloth in their hands and they must squeeze all the water out as hard as they can (Ballinger & Heine, 1991).

Youth Sport

Students with a specific learning disability, ADHD, or DCD can enjoy the same benefits of youth sport participation as their peers without disabilities. However, difficulty with movement skills or the inability to socially interact with others often creates barriers that inhibit successful sport participation (Bodey, 2010; Flores et al., 2012; SHAPE America, 2012 ; Vargas et al., 2018). Vargas and colleagues (2018) offer a variety of tips that utilize the principles of UDL to effectively coach all athletes, including athletes with hidden disabilities. These coaching tips, many of which are discussed throughout the book and this chapter, include considering behavioral expectations and management, physical arrangement of practice with directions, evaluating skill progress, and parental involvement.

Moreover, physical educators can help students overcome these barriers by teaching skills that are required in youth sport programs. Physical educators can also be resources for students and their parents or guardians by connecting them with community youth sport programs (Lavay & Seamark, 2001). An individual sport that a student enjoys, such as dance, karate, tennis, or swimming, might be a better choice than a team sport because the student will receive more individual attention, and the complexities of working with teammates are minimized. Many individual sports can become lifelong leisure activities.

Proper coach selection is important for students with a specific learning disability, ADHD, or DCD (Flores et al., 2012; Vargas et al., 2018). Parents can assist by giving the coach relevant information on the child's unique behaviors, strategies for overcoming these behaviors, reinforcements that motivate, and learning strategies that have worked well with the child. Many of these are described throughout this chapter. See the Online Resources section for more ideas to assist coaches, parents, and researchers to better meet the needs of athletes with hidden disabilities in youth sport.

Summary

For many students with a specific learning disability, ADHD, or DCD, physical education might be the one area in which they can experience success during the school day. When this is the case, physical educators can showcase these students' movement skills. For others whose movement performances need maturing, physical education can still be an enjoyable experience when conducted in a manner that provides support and does not dwell on the student's deficits. This chapter has examined the importance of being sensitive to the behaviors and unique needs of students with a specific learning disability, ADHD, or DCD when designing a program to promote student success.

When preparing to support and teach students with a specific learning disability, ADHD, or DCD, physical educators can ask the following questions: What are the student's strengths, needs, or present level of performance? How does this student best learn? How can I as the teacher prepare or change the environment and the task to help this student learn? How can I evaluate the program to determine if the child is learning? What approaches and programs are already in place for this student at school and at home? What support systems will I need, and how will I work to get them? And, finally, how can I collaborate with others to ensure this student's success?

To help answer these questions, this chapter has examined the most effective educational approaches used in schools today, including the multisensory, PBIS, multifaceted, and UDL approaches. Also included are specific recommendations and activities based on students' unique behavior needs and environmental factors for physical education and sport, including response to intervention, safety, behavioral and instructional management (e.g., class structure and organization, teaching prompts or cues, positive feedback), task analysis, perceptual–motor development, inclusion in general physical education, interdisciplinary teaching, relaxation, and youth sport. Most importantly, positive movement experiences can translate into a healthy lifestyle and a lifetime of quality physical activity for students with a specific learning disability, ADHD, or DCD.

References

Acoustical Society of America. (2019, December). *Classroom acoustics*. https://acousticalsociety.org/classroom-acoustics/

American Psychiatric Association (APA). (2013). *Diagnostic and statistical manual of mental disorders (DSM-5)* (5th ed.). Author.

Anderson, L., Midura, D.W., & Glover, D.R. (2020). *Team building through physical challenges: A complete toolkit* (2nd ed.). Human Kinetics.

Andre, A., Deneuve, P., & Louvet, B. (2011). Cooperative learning in physical education and acceptance of students with learning disabilities. *Journal of Applied Sport Psychology, 23*(1), 474-485. https://doi.org/10.1080/10413200.2011.580826

Assistance to States for the Education of Children with Disabilities. 34 C.F.R. 300.530 (2006).

Ballinger, D.A., & Heine, P.L. (1991). Relaxation training for children—a script. *Journal of Physical Education, Recreation and Dance, 62*(2), 67-69.

Beyer, R. (1999). Motor proficiency of boys with attention deficit/hyperactivity disorder and boys with learning disabilities. *Adapted Physical Activity Quarterly, 16*, 403-414. https://doi.org/10.1123/apaq.16.4.403

Bishop, J.C., & Block, M.E. (2012). Positive illusionary bias in children with ADHD in physical education. *Journal of Physical Education, Recreation and Dance, 83*(9), 43-48.

Bishop, J., Kelly, L.E., & Hull, M. (2018). Motor domain positive illusionary bias and sources of competence of children with attention-deficit hyperactivity Disorder. *Palaestra, 33*(4), 29-35.

Bishop, P., & Beyer, R. (1995). Attention deficit/hyperactivity disorder (ADHD): Implications for physical educators. *Palaestra, 11*(4), 39-46.

Block, M.E. (2016). *A teacher's guide to adapted physical education: Including students with disabilities in sports and recreation* (4th ed.). Brookes.

Bodey, K.J. (2010). Hidden disabilities in youth sport. *Journal of Physical Education, Recreation and Dance, 81*(8), 5-8. https://doi.org/10.1080/07303084.2010.10598514

Buttner, G., & Hasselhorn, M. (2011). Learning disabilities: Debates on definitions, causes, subtypes, and responses. *International Journal of Disability, Development and Education, 58*(1), 75-87. https://doi.org/10.1080/1034912X.2011.548476

Cacola, P. (2016). Physical and mental health of children with developmental coordination disorder. *Frontiers in Public Health, 24*. https://doi.org/10.3389/fpubh.2016.00224

Cacola, P., & Romero, M. (2015). Strategies to accommodate children with developmental coordination disorder in physical education lessons. *Journal of Physical Education, Recreation and Dance, 86*(9), 21-25. https://doi.org/10.1080/07303084.2015.1085341

CAST. (2020, January). *Universal design for learning*. www.cast.org

Children and Adults with Attention Deficit/Hyperactivity Disorder (CHADD). (2019a, December). *ADHD fact sheets & infographics*. https://chadd.org/understanding-adhd/adhd-fact-sheets/

Children and Adults with Attention Deficit/Hyperactivity Disorder (CHADD). (2019b, December). *Managing medication*. https://chadd.org/for-parents/managing-medication/

Clark, J.E., Getchell, N., Smiley-Owen, A.L., & Whitall, J. (2005). Developmental coordination disorder: Issues, identification, and intervention. *Journal of Physical Education, Recreation and Dance, 76*(4), 49-53.

Columna, L., Lieberman, L.J., Lytle, R., & Arnt, K. (2014). Special education terminology every physical education teacher should know. *Journal of Physical Education, Recreation and Dance, 85*(5), 38-45. https://doi.org/10.1080/07303084.2014.897659

Cone, T.P., Werner, P., & Cone, S.L. (2009). *Interdisciplinary elementary physical education* (2nd ed.). Human Kinetics.

Dunn, J.M., & Leitschuh, C.L. (2014). *Special physical education: Adapted, individualized, developmental* (10th ed.). Kendall/Hunt.

Edwards, V.D., & Hofmeier, J. (1991). A stress management program for elementary and special populations children. *Journal of Physical Education, Recreation and Dance, 62*(2), 61-64.

Ellis, K., Lieberman, L., & LeRoux, D. (2009). Using differentiated instruction in physical education. *Palaestra, 24*(4), 19-23.

Flores, M.M., Beyer, R., & Vargas, T.M. (2012). Attitudes toward preparing youth sport coaches to work with athletes with hidden disabilities. *Palaestra, 26*(1), 5-7.

Gilbert, E.N. (2019). Designing inclusive physical education with universal design for learning. *Journal of Physical Education, Recreation and Dance, 90*(7), 15-21. https://doi.org/10.1080/07303084.2019.1637305

Grosshans, J., & Kiger, M. (2004). Identifying and teaching children with learning disabilities in general physical education. *Journal of Physical Education, Recreation and Dance, 75*(6), 18-20, 58.

Hallahan, D.P., Kauffman, J.M., & Page, C.P. (2019). *Exceptional learners: An introduction to special education* (14th ed.). Pearson.

Harvey, W.J., & Reid, G. (2003). Attention-deficit/hyperactivity disorder: A review of research on movement skill performance and physical fitness. *Adapted Physical Activity Quarterly, 20,* 1-25.

Harvey, W.J., Reid, G., Bloom, G.A., Staples, K., Grizenko, N., Mbekou, V., Ter-Stepanian, M., & Joober, R. (2009). Physical activity experiences of boys with and without ADHD. *Adapted Physical Activity Quarterly, 26,* 131-150.

Healy, S. (2014). Preventing bullying in inclusive physical education: Practical strategies for teachers. *Palaestra, 28*(2), 42-46.

Henderson, S.E., & Henderson, L. (2002). Toward an understanding of developmental coordination disorder. *Adapted Physical Activity Quarterly, 19,* 11-31. https://doi.org/10.1123/apaq.19.1.11

Higher Education Opportunity Act (HEOA), P.L. 110-315 (2008).

Horvat, M., Croce, R.V., Pesce, C., & Fallaize, A.E. (2019). *Developmental and adapted physical education: Making ability count* (6th ed.). Routledge Taylor and Francis Group.

Huber, J., & Duhuis, P. (2002). Ritalin and ADHD—recent developments. *Palaestra, 18*(3), 12.

Intervention Central. (2019, November). *Response to intervention—RTI resources.* Retrieved from www.interventioncentral.org

Kavale, K.A., & Forness, S.R. (2000). What definitions of learning disability say and don't say: A critical analysis. *Journal of Learning Disabilities, 33*(3), 239-256. https://doi.org/10.1177/002221940003300303

Kwan, M., Cairney, J., Hay, J.A., & Faught, B.E. (2013). Understanding physical activity and motivations for children with developmental coordination disorder: An investigation using the theory of planned behavior. *Research in Developmental Disabilities, 34,* 3691-3698.

Lavay, B. (2019). Behavior management: What I have learned. *Journal for Physical Education, Recreation and Dance, 90*(3), 5-9. https://doi.org/10.1080/07303084.2019.1559646

Lavay, B., French, R., & Henderson, H. (2007). A practical plan for managing the behavior of students with disabilities in general physical education. *Journal of Physical Education, Recreation and Dance, 78*(2), 41-48. https://doi.org/10.1080/17408989.2010.548063

Lavay, B., French, R., & Henderson, H. (2016). *Positive behavior management in physical activity settings* (3rd ed.). Human Kinetics.

Lavay, B., & Seamark, C. (2001). Everyone plays: Inclusion of special needs children into youth sport programs. *Palaestra, 14*(4), 40-43.

Lieberman, L.J., Grenier, M., & Brian, A. (2019). How inclusive is your physical education class? Introducing the Lieberman/Brian inclusion rating scale for physical education. *Journal of Physical Education, Recreation and Dance, 90*(2), 3-4. https://doi.org/10.1080/07303084.2019.1548179

Lieberman, L.J., Grenier, M., Brian, A., & Arndt, K. (2021). *Universal design for learning in physical education.* Human Kinetics.

Lieberman, L.J., & Houston-Wilson, C. (2017). *Strategies for inclusion: A handbook for physical educators* (3rd ed.). Human Kinetics.

Lytle, R., Lavay, B., & Rizzo, T. (2010). What is a highly qualified adapted physical education teacher? *Journal of Physical Education, Recreation and Dance, 81*(2), 40-44, 50.

Mach, M.M. (2000). Teaching and coaching students with learning disabilities and attentional deficits. *Strategies, 13*(4), 12, 29-31.

Meyer, A., Rose, D.H., & Gordon, D. (2014). *Universal design for learning: Theory and practice.* CAST Professional Publishing.

Milne, D.C., Haubenstricker, J.L., & Seefelt, V. (1991). Remedial motor education: Some practical suggestions. *Strategies, 4*(4), 15-18.

Mulrine, C., & Flores-Marti, I. (2014). Practical strategies for teaching students with attention-deficit hyperactive disorder in general physical education classrooms. *Strategies, 27*(1), 26-31. https://doi.org/10.1080/08924562.2014.859004

National Center for Educational Statistics (NCES). (2019). *Fast facts: Students with disabilities.* http://nces.ed.gov/fastfacts/display.asp?id=64

National Center on Response to Intervention. (2019, November). *The essential components of RTI.* Retrieved from www.rti4success.org

National Symposium on Neurodiversity. (2014). *What is neurodiversity?* https://neurodiversitysymposium.wordpress.com/what-is-neurodiversity/

Nielson, K., Henderson, S., Barnett, A.L., Abott, R.D., & Berninger, V. (2018). Movement issues identified in Movement ABC2 checklist parent ratings for students with persisting dysgraphia, dyslexia, and OWL LD and typical literacy learners. *Learning Disabilities, 23*(1), 10-23. https://doi.org/10.18666/LDMJ-2018-V23-I1-8449.

Orlick, T. (2006). *Cooperative games and sport: Joyful activities for everyone* (2nd ed.). Human Kinetics.

Pangrazi, R.P., & Beighle, A. (2020). *Dynamic physical education for elementary school children* (19th ed.). Human Kinetics.

Ratey, J.J., & Hagerman, E. (2008). *Spark: The revolutionary new science of exercise and the brain.* Little, Brown.

Rizzo, T., & Lavay, B. (2000). Inclusion: Why the confusion? *Journal of Physical Education, Recreation and Dance, 71*(4), 32-36. https://doi.org/10.1080/07303084.2000.10605127

Sherrill, C. (2004). *Adapted physical activity, recreation and sport: Crossdisciplinary and lifespan* (6th ed.). McGraw-Hill.

Smith, D.D., Tyler, N.C., & Skow, K.G. (2018). *Introduction to contemporary special education: New horizons* (2nd ed.). Pearson.

Society for Health and Physical Education (SHAPE America). (2012, December). *Coaching athletes with a hidden disability.* www.shapeamerica.org//publications/resources/teachingtools/coachtoolbox/upload/Coaching-Athletes-with-Hidden-Disabilities.pdf

Stephens, T.L., Silliman-French, L., Kinnison, L., & French, R. (2010). Implementation of response-to-intervention in general physical education. *Journal of Physical Education, Recreation and Dance, 8*(9), 47-51.

Tripp, A., Rizzo, T.L., & Webbert, L. (2007). Inclusion in physical education: Changing the culture. *Journal of Physical Education, Recreation and Dance, 78*(2), 32-36, 48. https://doi.org/10.1080/07303084.2007.10597971

Trocki-Ables, P., French, R., & O'Connor, J. (2001). Use of primary and secondary reinforcers after performance of a 1-mile walk/run by boys with attention deficit/hyperactivity disorder. *Perceptual and Motor Skills, 93,* 461-464. https://doi.org/10.2466/pms.2001.93.2.461

U.S. Department of Education, Office of Special Education Programs. (2019, November). Positive behavioral interventions and supports (PBIS). www.pbis.org

Vargas, T.M., Beyer, R., & Flores, M.M. (2018). Coaching athletes with hidden disabilities: Using universal design for learning to effectively coach all athletes. *International Sport Coaching Journal, 5*(2), 176-182.

Waugh, L.M., & Sherrill, C. (2004). Dyslexia: Implications for physical educators and coaches. *Palaestra, 20*(3), 20-25, 47.

Whitall, J., & Clark, J.E. (2011). Should we care that Johnny can't catch and Susie can't skip? What should we do about it? *Strategies, 2*(6), 33-35.

Print Resources

Mulrine, C., & Flores-Marti, I. (2014). Practical strategies for teaching students with attention-deficit hyperactive disorder in general physical education classrooms. *Strategies, 27*(1), 26-31.

This resource provides a variety of effective teaching practices and strategies for the inclusion of all students in physical education, including those with ADHD.

Hallahan, D.P., Kauffman, J.M., & Page, C.P. (2019*). Exceptional learners: An introduction to special education* (14th ed). Pearson.

This resource includes a comprehensive chapter on learning disability and another on ADHD in the classroom, with definitions, identification types, history, incidence rates, causes and prevention, learning characteristics, and general educational interventions.

Lieberman, L.J., Grenier, M., Brian A., & Arndt, K. (2020). *Universal design for learning in physical education.* Human Kinetics.

This text provides information regarding universal design and physical education and offers physical educators a systematic guide to create, administer, manage, assess, and apply universal design for learning (UDL).

Online Resources

Children with Attention Deficit Disorders (CHADD): www.chadd.org

This organization's website provides great deal of information for parents or guardians, educators, and other professionals. The site offers a series of fact sheets and information on conferences, legislation, news releases, local chapters, and research studies.

The Council for Exceptional Children (CEC): www.cec.sped.org and Division for Learning Disabilities (DLD): www.teachingld.org

The CEC is the largest international professional organization dedicated to improving educational outcomes for students with exceptionalities, students with disabilities, and the gifted. One of their special interest groups, the DLD, offers an electronic newsletter that provides trustworthy and up-to-date professional resources and information about teaching students with learning disabilities.

Hidden Disabilities in Sport: www.facebook.com/HiddenDisabilitiesInSport

This interactive page assists coaches, parents, and researchers to better meet the needs of athletes with hidden disabilities in youth sport. Focus is on the inclusion of athletes with hidden disabilities, including LD and ADHD, in sport and recreational activities, as well as how to best train professionals to meet this population's needs. Included is a forum for questions and answers.

Learning Differences and Special Needs Guide: www.commonsensemedia.org/guide/special-needs

This page tests and recommends the best apps to help students with learning disabilities address skills such as organization, communication, social interaction, and more.

National Center for Learning Disabilities (NCLD): www.ncld.org

Since 1977 this organization has provided essential information to parents, professionals, and individuals with learning disabilities; it promotes research and programs to foster effective learning and advocates for policies to protect and strengthen educational rights and opportunities.

12

Visual Impairments

Lauren J. Lieberman and Lindsay Ball

Mrs. Treadwell teaches ninth-grade physical education class at Hilton High School. She has a new student, Ruthie, who has retinopathy of prematurity. Ruthie has some usable vision and has been fully included in physical education. Mrs. Treadwell had a student with albinism before, as well as one with a prosthetic eye, but never one with the amount of vision Ruthie has. Ruthie loves sports and plays a variety of sports with her brother and neighbors. She participated in Girls on the Run in seventh and eighth grade and has decreased her 5K time by five minutes!

Mrs. Treadwell immediately thought to call Ruthie's previous physical education teachers to see how they included her in middle school. Ms. Fromm was happy to share her successes with Mrs. Treadwell. Before each unit began, Ruthie was taught the boundaries of the court or field using a tactile board (bought from American Printing House for the Blind) and every aspect of the game, from the positions to the scoring to equipment, specific skills for the given unit, and strategies used during class. She played volleyball using a beach ball with bells, bells on the net, and a peer to help her catch the ball and throw it over the net. The rules were modified for anyone who wanted to use them. Some had no problem allowing the ball to bounce once and then hit it over the net. The game went on for several minutes!

For tennis, Ruthie and her peers served the ball to specific areas for points and did a bounce and hit to specific areas for points using both backhand and forehand, and their tennis skills improved. Ms. Fromm also infused the Paralympic sport of goalball into their curriculum using boundaries made with thin rope and tape. The students loved the challenge of being blindfolded and wanted to add a week to the unit. Ruthie also fully participated in track and field using a shoelace or "tether" to run with a peer. Friends took turns being her guide.

Ms. Fromm also shared her documentation of Ruthie's modifications with Mrs. Treadwell. Lastly, and most importantly, Ms. Fromm told Mrs. Treadwell about American Printing House for the Blind, which is a government-funded program in which she can order necessary equipment such as beeping balls, sound boxes, running kits, and curriculums designed specifically for children with visual impairments. Mrs. Treadwell wanted to schedule a meeting with Ruthie to make sure everything was provided for her, because starting in tenth grade, students choose an activity track, such as outdoor adventure, fitness, or individual or team sports.

Just like people with sight, people with visual impairments want to be accepted and respected as individuals; their visual impairment is just one of many personal characteristics, not their defining characteristic. Educators should keep in mind this quote inspired by athlete Tim Willis: "Tim Willis lost his sight, but he never lost his vision." Just because a student has a vision loss does not mean she cannot participate in sports and games with her sighted peers—in fact, a vigorous physical education program is important. The challenge for physical educators like Mrs. Treadwell is planning and teaching so that students with visual impairments can actively participate in physical education, recreation, and sport in school and throughout life.

However, sometimes the accommodations to minimize visual impairments are the least of the teacher's concerns. Often it is the emotional and social issues resulting from how others treat those who are blind that present the greater challenge. Further, *learned helplessness* results when family members and others are overprotective of the person with visual impairment. Well-intended acts can undermine independence and overall personal development when a child is never allowed to experience personal choice. Much of this chapter suggests ideas for accommodating the child and promoting **self-determination**. The task for the physical educator is to make the activity adaptations as needed but also to expect students with visual impairments to be independent, active members of the class and community (Lieberman et al., 2019).

Definition of Visual Impairment

What is a visual impairment? Who is blind? The educational definition from the Individuals with Disabilities Education Act (IDEA) is as follows:

> Visual impairment, including blindness, means an impairment in vision that, even when corrected, adversely affects a child's educational performance. The term includes both partial sight and blindness. (Assistance to States for the Education of Children with Disabilities, 2006)

Most people with visual impairments still have some usable sight. Perhaps one in four people with visual impairment is blind. Among students with visual losses, about half became blind before or at birth.

Causes of Vision Loss

There are multiple causes of vision loss. Though most causes are associated with aging, occasionally loss of vision occurs before or at birth (**congenital**) or in childhood or later (**adventitious**). Some causes of blindness are as follows.

Before Birth

- *Albinism.* A total or partial lack of pigment causing abnormal optic nerve development, albinism may or may not affect skin color. People with albinism may have one or more of the following conditions: decreased visual acuity, photophobia (sensitivity to light), high refraction error (the shape of the eye does not refract light properly so the image seen is blurred), astigmatism (blurred vision), nystagmus (uncontrollable eye movements that are involuntary, rapid, and repetitive), central scotomas (a blind or partially blind area in the visual field), and strabismus (the inability of one or both eyes to look directly at an object at the same time).
- *Leber's congenital amaurosis (LCA).* Affecting around 1 in 80,000 of the population, this inherited eye disease appears at birth or in the first few months of life. The term *congenital* refers to a condition present from birth (not acquired), and *amaurosis* refers to a loss of vision not associated with a lesion. Leber's congenital amaurosis is typically characterized by nystagmus, sluggish or no pupillary responses, and severe vision loss or blindness.
- *Retinoblastoma.* This malignancy of the retina in early childhood usually requires removal of the eye and can occur in one or both eyes.
- *Retinopathy of prematurity (ROP).* Occurring in some infants who are born prematurely, this condition results in reduced acuity or total blindness. Retinopathy of prematurity occurs when abnormal blood vessels grow and spread throughout the retina, the tissue that lines the back of the eye. These abnormal blood vessels are fragile and can leak, scarring the retina and pulling it out of position. This causes a retinal detachment, the main cause of visual impairment and blindness in ROP.
- *Septo-optic dysplasia.* This disorder of early brain development can affect growth and

development and affects each child differently. The results of this condition can affect either one or both eyes and the effect on a child's vision can vary greatly, although most children have a serious visual impairment.

After Birth or Progressive

- *Cataracts.* Opacity of the lens restricts the passage of light and reduces acuity, resulting in blurred vision, poor color vision, photophobia, and sometimes nystagmus. Visual ability fluctuates according to light (figure 12.1*a*).
- *Cortical visual impairment (CVI).* Caused by a brain problem rather than an eye problem, CVI results in variable vision; visual ability can change day to day and minute to minute. One eye may perform significantly worse than the other, and depth perception can be very limited. The field of view may also be severely limited, and visual processing can take a lot of effort.
- *Glaucoma.* Increased pressure in the eye is caused by blockage in the normal flow of the aqueous humor. Visual loss may be gradual, sudden, or present at birth. People with glaucoma may also have an increased sensitivity to light and glare.
- *Macular degeneration.* Progressive degeneration of the macula, which governs central vision, results in photophobia, poor color vision, and normal peripheral vision (figure 12.1*b*). The inherited form of macular degeneration seen in children is called Stargardt disease.
- *Retinitis pigmentosa.* Retinitis pigmentosa is caused by a variety of inherited retinal defects, all of which affect the ability of the retina to sense light. It is a progressive disorder that causes loss of peripheral vision, night blindness, tunnel vision, decreased acuity and depth perception, spotty vision because of retinal scarring, and photophobia (figure 12.1*c*).

FIGURE 12.1 What a person with a visual impairment might see. *(a)* In cataracts, clouding of the lens causes reduced ability to see detail. *(b)* In macular degeneration or Stargardt disease, central vision is impaired, making it difficult to read or do close work. *(c)* In retinitis pigmentosa, night blindness develops, and tunnel vision is another frequent result.

General Characteristics of People With Visual Impairments

There is tremendous diversity among people with visual impairments, but many share certain characteristics. Remember that the following are only generalities and are not true of all people with visual impairments.

Affective and Social Characteristics

Habits such as rocking, hand waving or finger flicking, and digging the fingers into the eyes are examples of repetitive movements that some people with visual loss or multiple disabilities develop. These repetitive movements are also known as **blindisms** or **self-stimulation**. If the movements are not affecting the child's education or that of others, then some self-stimulating behaviors may be best overlooked (McHugh & Lieberman, 2003).

Fearfulness and dependence may characterize some people with visual losses, whether the loss is due to congenital or adventitious blindness. These characteristics may develop not as a result of the lack of vision but rather as a result of overprotection. Overprotection usually leads to reduced opportunities for students to freely explore their environments, thus creating possible delays in perceptual, motor, and cognitive development (Haibach et al., 2014). Children with visual impairments are born with the same potential in motor development and physical activity as their peers and should be provided the same opportunities and expectations (Haibach, et al., 2014).

Socialization Opportunities

A visual impairment in itself does not affect the social functioning of a child; however, the lack of experiences, expectations, and information may affect children's knowledge of typical customs in their environment. All visual information must be explained explicitly. For example, if a child is not told to put a napkin on her lap, she may not know this is a custom. Also, if a child is not provided an explanation of a high five or a fist bump and when these are typically used, the child is missing out on typical social experiences occurring in most sporting environments.

All information that is available in print must also be simultaneously available in braille if the child is expected to keep up with cognitive and social information. If the physical education teacher distributes a handout on the history of basketball, for example, the printed information must be given to the teacher of the visually impaired (TVI) ahead of time so it can be brailled. The TVI is the person who teaches the child with visual impairment braille, independence, and social skills. Every child who is visually impaired or blind has a TVI who can be contacted by the classroom teacher. Many are itinerant and may come in only once a week or once a month, depending on the needs of the child. Children who are blind or have very low vision will also have an orientation and mobility instructor, sometimes called a Certified Orientation and Mobility Specialist (COMS). This teacher is responsible for cane skills and independent mobility for children who are blind, whether from the classroom to the bathroom or even public transportation.

Socialization opportunities must be nurtured, and self-advocacy must be taught. For example, when a teacher has students partner up, the child with the visual impairment can choose a partner. In addition, **disability awareness** must be taught so the child's classmates know what the child can see and what modifications are made and why. An excellent book to increase understanding for upper-elementary students is *Everybody Plays* (Aillaud & Lieberman, 2013). If paraeducators or aides are used, they must be taught when to step out of the way to encourage social opportunities, because they can inhibit such opportunities if they are not aware.

Implications for Teaching Physical Education

Several possible motor, physical, and fitness characteristics of children with visual impairments have implications for the physical education curriculum. Children with visual impairments demonstrate less-developed motor skills than their sighted peers (Houwen et al., 2008, 2009; O'Connell et al., 2006; Wagner et al., 2013). For this population, motor skill proficiency is as important for daily living and sport activities as it is for any child, but visual impairments may act as a constraint, slowing down motor skill acquisition (Houwen et al., 2010). However, if children with visual impairment have adequate levels of physical activity participation, they will likely have higher motor skill proficiency; positive relationships have been found between motor skills and physical activity in children (Houwen et al., 2009). Figure 12.2 shows a child learning how to do the locomotor skill of sliding.

Photo courtesy of Chris Smoker.

FIGURE 12.2 Student is being taught the slide using a guide wire and physical guidance of the instructor.

Students with visual losses must be encouraged to move in a safe environment to minimize the development of motor delays (Samalot et al., 2015). Enthusiastically encourage and positively reinforce movements by physically demonstrating or prompting and verbally encouraging students that it is safe to move. Motor delays are not usually observed among people who are blind but were previously sighted for years.

Body image and balance may also be delayed among students who are blind (Casselbrant et al., 2007; Haibach et al., 2011). This may be due to decreased opportunities for regular physical activity through which balance and posture are refined, as well as a lack of sight to use as a reference point for aiding stability. Participation in activities such as dance, yoga, movement education, and any age-appropriate activity that promotes lifting the head can be an excellent means of developing body posture and balance.

Physical activity levels of children with visual impairments tend to be low and have been found to be lower than those of their sighted peers (Augestad & Jiang, 2015; Haegele et al., 2017; Haegele & Zhu, 2019; Houwen et al., 2009, 2010; Lieberman et al., 2010). Health-related fitness levels of people who are blind have the potential to match those of their sighted peers, but lack of opportunity to train, difficulty arranging for sighted guides for running, and limited access to facilities can be obstacles to developing fitness. It is important for physical educators to develop fitness programs for students with visual impairments and to work with families in finding fitness activities that students can pursue at home and in the community; examples include jumping rope, weight training, aerobics, bicycling (single in a clear area or tandem), hiking, and walking.

In summary, the missing component in the development of functional movement and fitness abilities among students with visual impairments is not ability, but opportunity. The physical educator must encourage students to feel safe and good about their movements. This can be accomplished both through instruction in physical education and through collaboration with paraeducators, parents, caregivers, and other influential people in the child's life. The following section offers suggestions for helping students with visual impairments enjoy physical activity.

Teaching Students With Visual Impairments in Inclusive Physical Education

Children with visual impairments deserve to be treated with dignity and respect. However, many of the most important strategies to ensure this happens are not intuitive. It is extremely important that you and your students understand the etiquette when it comes to treatment of your students with visual impairments. The following list will help you understand how to create a welcoming and inclusive environment.

Etiquette for interacting with children with visual impairments include the following:

- Say your name first so the person knows who you are right away—never make the student guess who they are talking to.
- Ensure there is a narrative of the game or activity going on at all times.
- Do not change words like "see" or "watch"; these are commonly used, even by people with visual impairments.
- Ask the student if they need assistance—do not assume help is required.
- Ask questions to get an understanding of the student's vision, such as "Can you describe to me what you see?" Do not ask them how many fingers you are holding up.

In the field of visual impairment education, a curricular approach called the **Expanded Core Curriculum** (ECC) has been instituted to ensure that children with visual impairments are receiving the support they need in addition to the core curriculum in order to be independent and successful adults. Like SHAPE America's national physical education standards, the goal of the ECC is for students to receive a holistic learning experience. For children with visual impairments in physical education, components of the ECC can be infused along with cognitive, affective, and psychomotor domains throughout the curriculum (Haegele et al., 2014; Lieberman et al., 2014; Lieberman, Ericson, et al., 2021). Table 12.1 describes these components and provides several examples of how to infuse them into physical education.

TABLE 12.1 Strategies to Infuse the Expanded Core Curriculum (ECC) Into Physical Education

ECC component	Strategies for infusion
Compensatory or functional academic skills, including communication modes	• Provide instructions to activities in braille.[B] • Teach students a variety of guide-running technique options.[B] • Include movement games and activities using sound sources as signals.[E] • Provide a tactile map of floor seating.[E] • Teach all students sports and use a sound source when necessary, such as a beep behind a basketball hoop or a beeper at the end of a pool.[S] • Provide access to rules of sports or activities using braille or computers instead of handouts.[B] • Teach strategies to access control panel of workout equipment including treadmills or ellipticals.[S]
Orientation and mobility	• Preteach the physical activity area and games before class begins.[B] • Collaborate with O & M instructor to provide simulated environments for travel practice.[B] • Create an obstacle course that may allow all students to participate in activities to practice fundamental movement patterns (e.g., walk, run, gallop).[E] • Teach the dimensions of courts and fields.[S] • Teach the process of traveling to and from the pool.[B] • Promote body and spatial awareness with physical activities such as yoga or stretching.[B]

ECC component	Strategies for infusion
Social interaction skills	• Teach physical activities in which sighted peers can play with children with visual impairments by making simple modifications such as adding bells to a ball.[B] • Train peer tutors and paraeducators to facilitate social interactions during class.[B] • Teach team sports and highlight the importance of teamwork to achieve.[S] • Include team-building games and adventure-based learning units to facilitate positive communication among all students.[B] • Encourage students to participate in sport camps or recreational activities designed for individuals with visual impairments outside of school.[B] • Rotate roles (leader, team member) between all students within a group.[B]
Independent living skills	• Emphasize health topics during classes (appropriate sport attire, healthy snacks, bathing after participating in physical activities).[B] • Teach dressing skills for activities such as swimming, bowling, or ice-skating.[B] • Teach functional skills for community involvement such as learning the layout and mechanics of bowling alleys, layout and navigation for health clubs, and ways to navigate skating rinks to promote independence.[B] • Discuss accommodations needed during fitness units.[S] • If possible, take field trips to community recreation facilities to practice navigating and using various environments.[S]
Recreation and leisure skills	• Preteach sport skills in the classroom and facilitate participation in the community by contacting sport clubs or recreational facilities that students can visit.[S] • Teach how to navigate trails and bicycle paths in parks.[S] • Teach fundamental skills for all lifelong leisure activities.[S]
Career education	• Introduce guest speakers who are visually impaired to talk about their career opportunities.[B] • Connect with individuals who are visually impaired and have careers in sport and recreation in person or via phone, e-mail, or Skype.[E] • Perform Internet searches for individuals with visual impairment who are athletes or coaches or are involved in sport or recreation.[B] • Use the sport education model so students learn about careers in sport (coach, announcer, journalist, and statistician).[S] • Discuss how a higher level of physical fitness may increase an individual's marketability during job searching.[S]
Use of assistive technology	• Teach the use of exercise technology such as talking pedometers and talking heart rate monitors.[B] • Incorporate modified Wii or other exergames into the curriculum.[B] • Help children navigate the web for assignments on blind sport, role models, or the history of a sport.[B] • Use sound sources or sound balls in common physical education activities.[B] • Navigate the Internet with students to find sport-related opportunities such as camps for individuals with visual impairments (e.g., Camp Abilities) or sport organizations (e.g., USABA).[B]
Sensory efficiency skills	• Use music, sound, and other modalities that indicate the beginning or ending of an activity.[B] • Infuse games like goalball and beep baseball, with each player blindfolded, to promote the use of hearing to play the game.[B] • For students with low vision, use brightly colored or neon tape to outline boundaries.[B] • For target sports (such as archery), place a sound source behind the target to assist in localization.[B] • In movement activities such as sprinting, sound can be the target toward which the student moves.[B]

(continued)

TABLE 12.1 *(continued)*

ECC component	Strategies for infusion
Self-determination	• Prepare students to be successful in different activities using sport as a medium.[B] • Teach the same sports and units as to peers so students with visual impairment will have choices in the future.[B] • Provide a variety of choices of sports that may allow students to develop a sense of autonomy and competence and at the same time allow them to relate to their peers and family members.[B] • Include students in the process of making accommodations or modifications of activities.[B] • Allow students to make choices as to what accommodations they need to participate; do not assume based on previous students.[B] • Keep track of personal bests and athletic goals. Beating these records can lead to higher self-confidence in sport and activity.[B] • Teach lifelong activities that students can choose to participate in after graduation, including what modifications students may need in order to participate.[S]

[E] An appropriate strategy for an elementary physical education program.

[S] An appropriate strategy for a secondary physical education program.

[B] An appropriate strategy for both elementary and secondary physical education programs.

Reprinted by permission from J.A. Haegele, L.J. Lieberman, L. Columna, and M. Runyan, "Infusing the Expanded Core Curriculum Into Physical Education for Children With Visual Impairments," *Palaestra* 28 (2014): 44-50.

When teaching students with visual impairments in physical education, keep in mind that the universal design for learning (UDL) approach works best. When the teacher universally designs lessons, the variations to instruction, equipment, rules, and the environment are made ahead of time in order for each child to be included from the start (Lieberman & Houston-Wilson, 2018; Lieberman, Grenier, et al., 2021). Thoughtful modifications, such as changing the ball color to one that contrasts sharply with the background, modifying rules, and playing engaging music can all help with inclusion. In addition, working with a paraeducator, adapted physical education specialist, or TVI can help a student with visual impairment learn in physical education (Conroy, 2012; Lieberman & Conroy, 2013; Perkins et al., 2013; Van Munster et al., 2015). The student with the visual impairment and other students in the class are also excellent sources of ideas for inclusion strategies and adaptations. Teachers have had much success in developing accommodations through class efforts.

Children with visual impairments and blindness need more instruction and practice time in order to learn new concepts and movements (Lieberman et al., 2013; Perkins et al., 2013). The teacher must meet the child where she is and begin to build the background knowledge related to the new sport or skill unit. Sapp and Hatlen (2010) suggest that children with visual impairments need preteaching, teaching, and reteaching in order to obtain ECC skills. This teaching cycle is important for learning skills and concepts related to physical education. **Preteaching** must be done before a new unit of instruction. The child must learn the perimeter of the court or field, which can be accomplished with a tactile board. The child must also learn the names of the positions or players, objective of the game, rules, scoring, equipment used, and the various levels of competition (Conroy, 2016). Once these concepts are understood, the pace of the class and the concepts will be easier to acquire, and the student will be more successful. Preteaching can be done before school, after school, during orientation and mobility class, or at home with the help of the physical education teacher, the orientation and mobility instructor, the TVI, the paraeducator, the parent or guardian, or a peer or sibling. It is important that the physical education teacher provide specific preteaching goals and unit objectives to the person who will deliver the preteaching (Conroy, 2016).

The curriculum and programming for students with visual impairments should include a mix of open and closed sports. **Open sports** are those that have variables that change often; for example, tennis, volleyball, American football, soccer, and lacrosse. In other words, the game is unpredictable, and the speed, angle, and direction of the ball and defenders change often and without notice. **Closed sports** are consistent and predictable. Examples of closed sports are archery, bowling, the shot put and discus, and boccia. Students with visual impairments should be introduced to all sports, games, and activities that their peers learn. Enjoyment and skill can be developed through active participation in physical education. Lifetime activities such as tandem biking, running, goalball, swimming, wrestling, judo, kayaking, stand-up paddleboard, and bowling should be explored as well.

The following sections present ideas for adapting instruction for students with visual impairments based on building student's abilities, fostering the student's independence, exploring options for instructional modifications, and obtaining educational items for physical education. See the Application Example sidebar, Including a Student With a Visual Impairment.

Application Example

Including a Student With a Visual Impairment

SETTING

Middle school physical education class

STUDENT

Andrea is an active sixth-grade student who enjoys biking, swimming, in-line skating, and studying judo after school and on weekends. She has retinopathy of prematurity (ROP), resulting in a visual impairment and the risk of a retinal detachment. She has some residual vision and uses her remaining vision for mobility purposes.

ISSUE

Andrea's individualized education program states that she must be fully included in her two 45-minute physical education classes each week, but her teacher believes that her blindness limits her abilities and is concerned about her detached retina. He has her exercising on a stationary bike and walking the perimeter of the gym while her classmates are involved in physical activities and games. Although Andrea does want to be careful about her retinal detachment, she wants to learn all of the units her peers are learning. She has that right as a student who is self-determined. Andrea is becoming more and more frustrated, and this is affecting her performance in other subject areas.

APPLICATION

The following were determined as a result of a meeting with the school administrator, the TVI, her parents, and the physical educator:

- Andrea will participate in all physical education activities with her peers.
- To help him adapt games, sports, and activities, the physical educator will purchase books about accommodations. These books and resources are found in the resources at the end of this chapter.
- The physical educator will search the Internet for information and adaptations to assist him in supporting Andrea in an inclusive setting (see Online Resources).
- The school will buy brightly colored balls and auditory balls and set up a guide-wire system in the gym and outside on the track.
- The curriculum will include a variety of games and activities conducive to Andrea's participation, such as weight training, aerobics, goalball, and cross-country skiing. Three of Andrea's friends will be trained as peer tutors to assist her in class. Andrea can be fully included with the appropriate modifications and by educating her peers in the class (see Pennington & Webb, 2020).
- An additional physical education class with supplemental instruction will be offered during her study hall by one of the other physical education teachers. In this supplemental class, the instructor will preteach the upcoming units so Andrea can choose her equipment, rule modifications, and positioning. This class will include her peer tutors, so they all have an understanding of the instructional approaches to keep Andrea safe and involved.

Adapting Instruction Based on Students' Abilities

An important step in the instructional planning process is to determine each student's present level of performance. Generally, students with visual impairments are capable of taking the same formal assessments and attaining the same standards as students with sight. In case of mobility limitations due to blindness, teachers can modify standards for mobility test items, use assistive devices, or use sighted guides based on suggestions throughout this chapter. For example, auditory cues may be added so students know where to throw and how far to skip or run. The Test of Gross Motor Development (TGMD-3) (Ulrich, 2019) is validated for use with children with visual impairments 6 to 12 years of age with modifications (Brian et al., 2017). The Brockport Physical Fitness Test (BPFT) (Winnick & Short, 2014) assesses the health-related fitness of young people who are blind. Refer to chapter 4 for additional information on measurement and evaluation.

The teacher may seek answers to the following six questions in addition to assessing current performance:

1. *What can the student see?* Ask the student, "What can you see?" rather than "How much can you see?" Ask the same question of others familiar with the student's vision, including the student's previous teachers, parents, caregiver, and TVI. Read the student's educational file for further information regarding what the student can see. Use this important information when teaching.

2. *When (at what age) was the loss of vision experienced, and over what period of time did it progress? Is it still progressing?* Ask the student when the vision loss was experienced. Certain skills are acquired before the ages of 8 to 10 in sighted children, so a student who lost vision after these developmental ages may require less time preparing for specific activities (e.g., hitting a sound-emitting softball and running to a sound-emitting base) than a student who is congenitally blind. A student with congenital blindness may also need detailed explanations that do not depend on analogies for which the student has no basis of understanding. For example, the teaching cue "Jump like a bunny" may not be useful to a child who does not have any visual reference for rabbits jumping.

3. *How can the instructor maximize use of existent sight?* Learn from the students what helps them see best. For most types of visual impairments, bright lighting maximizes vision. For some conditions, such as glaucoma and albinism, however, glare is a problem. Teach these students in lighting free of glare to maximize vision. When outside, these students may need tinted glasses or hats to reduce glare.

4. *Are there any contraindicated physical activities?* To determine if there are any contraindicated (not recommended) physical activities, seek medical consultation. There are few contraindications for people with total blindness, since there is no sight to preserve. For people with partial sight, there might be activity restrictions imposed in an effort to preserve the remaining sight. For example, jarring movements that could cause further detachment are usually contraindicated with retinal detachment. Contact sports, as well as diving and swimming underwater, may need to be modified for safety. Inverted positions and swimming underwater are also often contraindicated with glaucoma because of increased pressure in the eye.

5. *What are the student's favorite scholastic, social, and physical activities?* It is important to learn about the opportunities that exist for the child to participate in physical activities with family and friends as well as in the community. The opportunity to try all the options is important because students may not know their preferences until they have had repeated opportunities to try each one. Students may also be asked what adaptations they prefer. For example, how do they like to run? With a sighted guide? Using a guide wire? Independently on a clearly lined track? These activities and adaptations can be incorporated into the child's physical education program.

6. *What instructional approach does the child prefer?* A child with limited vision will need some physical support to learn new skills. It is important to ask children if they prefer a particular teaching approach, such as physical guidance or tactile modeling. Some students prefer not to be touched at all (Cieslak et al., 2015; O'Connell et al., 2006); in this case, clear explanations may work best.

Fostering Independence

To be independent, students must have the skills, socialization, stamina, and strength to complete everyday tasks. Students with visual impairments can acquire these through physical activity. Consider the following suggestions for teaching.

- *Have a positive attitude about all students.* The teacher's attitude is the determining factor in the classroom. If the teacher is truly interested in teaching all students and provides accommodations and makes adaptations to meet the diverse needs of all students without a fuss, then the students in the class will pick up on this attitude and be more likely to accept classmates with visual impairments or other differences.

- *Use parents as resources.* Most parents are their child's biggest advocates. However, parents can have a negative impact on physical activity if their fears about their child's safety lead to overprotectiveness. If caregivers dwell on what the child can't do rather than on what she can do, the child will rarely have the opportunity at home to try new things, play games that sighted children play, or take risks. Physical educators can collaborate with parents about their children's capabilities by sending home assessment data, personal notes, newsletters with descriptions of the student's accomplishments, photographs of the student doing activities, and lists of the student's favorite physical activities. By learning about their child's current performance and abilities, parents may better understand their child's potential and allow more opportunities for physical activity at home and in the community (Columna et al., 2018; Perkins et al., 2013).

- *Challenge students with visual impairments so they can be successful.* To help improve self-esteem and motivate students to work on their goals, reward and recognize their accomplishments. Using realistic tests that include assessments of process, product, and level of independence will assist the student in observing improvement. The teacher should work with the student to set realistic goals and recognize achievements. Bulletin boards, student newspapers, progress reports, and announcements are all ways to recognize student achievement. In addition, students with visual impairments must be taught how to advocate for their right to play sport and engage in recreation. Self-advocacy must be intentionally taught (for a sample self-advocacy curriculum, see Lieberman and Childs, 2020).

- *Expect the student to move as independently as possible during physical education.* At the beginning of the school year and at the start of each unit, the student with a visual impairment should be oriented to playing fields, gymnasiums, locker rooms, and equipment to increase independence and feelings of security. Landmarks that can help students orient themselves (e.g., mats along the walls at either end of the gymnasium to contrast the paneling along the side walls) can be identified. Students may be encouraged to walk around and touch everything as often as needed in order to create the mental map that will enable them to negotiate the area with confidence. Equipment should be kept in the same position in the gymnasium as much as possible, and students should have extra time before class to orient themselves to any new configuration of equipment. In the locker room, the locker should be in an easily accessible location, and a lock that opens with a key or push-button number rather than a combination should be provided. Accessible locks can be purchased through the American Printing House for the Blind (www.aph.org). A trained peer tutor may be most helpful with mobility, skill acquisition, and feedback for children who are totally blind. Training the peer tutor is imperative to ensure safety, improved skill acquisition, and communication. In addition to the initial training, it is advantageous to meet with the student and peer tutor a few minutes before each class to introduce the student to the concepts and movements to be taught that day (Wiskochil et al., 2007). The sidebar Considerations When Teaching Students Who Are Blind or Visually Impaired offers more suggestions. These suggestions must be shared with the peer tutor.

Exploring Options for Instructional Modification

Incidental learning is the unplanned or "accidental" learning that occurs through observations of events within the natural environment. Knowledge and skills acquired by sighted children through incidental learning must be explicitly taught to children with visual impairments, because they have limited ability to pick up environmental cues and nuances. For example, the social skills needed for daily life in school, at home, and in the community must be strategically taught and integrated into all aspects of their education (Arndt et al., 2014).

Students with visual impairments learn with various levels of prompting and instructional techniques. Some students need a physical demonstration for certain skills and others learn through verbal instruction. In some cases, the complexity of the activity will drive the level of instruction. This varied level of instruction is often referred to as the *system of least prompts.* The following system of least prompts provides examples specific to teaching children with visual impairments. Note that the instructor may use one or more of these teaching strategies to help the student perform the skill. Instructors should know that physical guidance and tactile modeling have both been shown to improve self-efficacy in novel tasks for children with visual impairments (O'Connell et al., 2006), as well as improving swimming skills (Cieslak et al., 2015).

Considerations When Teaching Students Who Are Blind or Visually Impaired

- Narrate during a game or appoint a student narrator so the student can understand what everyone is doing. Remember that what seem like ordinary, everyday happenings might need to be explained.
- Some experiences are not part of every student's direct experience. For instance, tell the child about the martial art of judo and allow the child to experience it.
- Students might need help putting parts together to form a whole concept. Allow time before class for children to feel the entire playground set, the entire gym space, and so on.
- Make a raised tactile map of the playing area that the child can feel to understand the boundaries of the game (see figure 12.3). Boundaries in soccer, basketball, volleyball, goalball, or the pool can be more easily understood with use of this technique. Pipe cleaners, twine, or felt glued on cardboard or on the back of a clipboard are all that is needed. Ask the TVI or orientation and mobility instructor for help if necessary.
- Physically guide or use tactile modeling through movements rather than demonstrating them.
- Verbal or auditory feedback is needed because students cannot always tell how they are doing. Tell students where they threw the ball, or even better, use a beeping ball.

Courtesy of American Printing House for the Blind.

FIGURE 12.3 Tactile print layout of a tennis court.

Verbal Explanations by the Instructor

- In simple terms, explain what the child is to do.
- Use the child's preferred mode of communication.
- If the child does not understand the first time, repeat in a different way.
- If the child has any usable vision, demonstrate to increase understanding.
- Give precise, unambiguous feedback. A statement such as "Hold the racket three to four inches above your left shoulder" provides more feedback than "Hold the racket like this." Precise language benefits all students, with or without visual impairments.
- Include students with visual impairments by assigning a student announcer to describe the action of events, much as a radio announcer describes a ball game. Select an announcer with a lively sense of humor to make the event more fun for everyone.

Demonstrations by the Instructor or Peer

- Show the child the desired skill or movement.
- Demonstrate within the child's field of vision.
- Ask someone close to the student's size and ability to model.
- Use whole–part–whole teaching* when possible. Demonstrate the whole skill, then the parts (based on task analysis), and then the whole task again.

*It is important to note that in order for the student to understand the parts, the whole must be taught first. This is referred to as *whole–part–whole instruction* (Lieberman & Haibach, 2016). For example, the entire game of volleyball must be explained and experienced before it can be broken down into the serve, bump, and set.

Physical Assistance or Guidance From the Instructor or Peer

- Assist the student physically through the movement with either partial physical assistance (e.g., touching the elbow for the crawl stroke) or total physical assistance (e.g., moving the student's arms through the motion of batting).
- Forewarn the student before giving physical assistance in order to avoid startling the student.
- Fade assistance to minimal physical prompts as soon as possible (Cieslak et al., 2015).
- Record which skills require physical assistance, including how much and where on the student's body the assistance was modeled. If asked for legal purposes, the teacher can explain when, where, and why he touched a student.

Tactile Modeling by the Instructor or Peer

- Allow the student to feel a peer or the instructor execute a skill or movement that was difficult to learn using the three other approaches.
- Tell the student where and when to feel you or a peer executing a skill.
- Repeat tactile modeling as many times as necessary to ensure understanding.
- Combine tactile modeling with the other teaching methods to increase understanding.
- Document how much assistance was given, when and where the student felt you or a peer, and why (for legal purposes).

Addition of Sound Devices

- Use beeper balls and bases (available for purchase at www.aph.org), or have a base coach call continuously to direct the batter to the base.
- Tie bells onto net goals so everyone can hear the jingling sound when a goal is scored.
- Make a basket audible by tying a can with rocks to the rim and having a peer jiggle it with a string to emit sound. You can also use a child's cane, a broom, or a hockey stick and tap the rim of the basket to give an auditory signal. Lastly, you can use a doorbell at the back of the rim to emit a sound.

Enhancement of Visual Cues

- Most people with visual impairments have some residual vision. Evaluate each activity to decide what types of visual cues are needed and how to highlight them. Color, contrast, and lighting are important. Be sure to ask students what enhances their vision. For example, a student may not be able to distinguish between a blue and a red pinny but can see a yellow pinny clearly.
- For children who cannot tell you what they can see, assess body language, reactions, and expressions to determine what is seen best and within what range they can see.
- Use colored tape to increase the contrast of equipment with the background, such as high jump standards and poles or the edges of a balance beam. Use rope with tape over it to delineate the end of a balance beam or the center of a trampoline.
- Use brightly colored balls, mats, field markers, and goals that contrast with the background for most students with visual impairments. Remember that students with albinism and glaucoma, however, may need solid-colored objects under nonglare lights.
- Make the gymnasium lighting brighter (or darker for students who have difficulty with glare or who tend to self-stimulate with bright lights).

Obtaining Educational Items

Educating children with visual impairments requires additional funding for items such as electronic equipment, educational materials, and other products necessary for specific instruction. As discussed in the scenario at the beginning of the chapter, **American Printing House for the Blind** (APH) is a government-funded agency that provides equipment and materials to educate children with visual impairments at no cost. These products are on what is called **quota funds**. Educational materials from APH are free for children with visual impairments up to a certain amount of money each year. Products available for physical education can be found at www.aph.org/physical-education/products. In order to access these products, contact your TVI or the orientation and mobility instructor of the children in your classes. Every product comes in large print, audio, and braille versions, depending on the child's needs.

Sports for Athletes With Visual Impairments

There are three major organizations for athletes who have visual impairments: the United States Association for Blind Athletes, the National Beep Baseball Association, and Camp Abilities. The goal of these organizations is to promote instructional and competitive sport opportunities for athletes with visual impairments throughout the United States, as well as to change attitudes toward people with visual impairments.

United States Association of Blind Athletes (USABA)

The United States Association of Blind Athletes is the major sport organization in the United States for athletes 14 years of age and older who have a visual impairment. Organized in 1976, USABA provides competitive sport opportunities at the local, state, regional, national, and international levels. People with visual impairments may choose to participate in integrated sport with their sighted peers, in sport exclusively for people with visual impairments, or both. Many people with visual impairments participate in sport for those who are blind because of the opportunity to meet and compete with others who are also blind. Physical educators are encouraged to contact USABA (www.usaba.org) to connect their students with the location of the nearest sport organization. USABA can also provide the teacher with local role models who will come and speak to the school about competing in international sports against others with visual impairments.

Although recognition of and opportunities for elite athletes who are blind are increasing, there remain few programs designed to bring young people with visual impairments into sport. Physical educators can help by reviewing their physical education curriculum and noting the sports offered that are also USABA sports. While teaching those sports, physical educators are encouraged to make an extra effort to promote them among any students with visual impairments and to assist students in learning how to pursue them through USABA.

USABA offers competition in several sports. Some of the common high school sports are discussed in the following paragraphs, including appropriate modifications to ensure equal competition.

- Cycling
- Blind soccer
- Distance running
- Goalball
- Hockey
- Powerlifting
- Skiing/Biathlon
- Swimming
- Track and field
- Triathlon

USABA athletes who reach an elite athletic level may compete in the World Blind Championships and in the Paralympics. USABA classification for competition is based on residual vision and is explained on its website (USABA.org). Rules for each sport are modified slightly from those established by the national sport organizations. For example, track and field follows most National Collegiate Athletic Association (NCAA) rules, except that guide wires are used in sprints, sighted guides may be used on distance runs, hurdles are eliminated, and jumpers who are totally blind touch the high bar and then back off and use a one- or two-step approach. The use of guides depends entirely on the athlete's visual classification and the particular event. Guides facilitate the activity by running alongside the athlete, with both runners holding on to a tether. Alternatively, stationary guides are positioned around the track to call directional signals to the runner. The following list provides descriptions of various guiding techniques for running.

- *Human guide.* The runner grasps the guide's elbow, shoulder, or hand, depending on what is most comfortable for the runner and guide (figure 12.4*a*).
- *Tether.* The runner and guide grasp a tether (e.g., short string, towel, shoelace). This allows the runner full range of motion of the arms while remaining in close proximity to the sighted runner (figure 12.4*b*).
- *Guide wire.* The runner holds on to a guide wire and runs independently for time or distance. A guide wire is a rope or wire pulled tightly across a gymnasium or track. A rope loop, metal ring, or metal handle ensures that the runner will not receive a rope burn and allows for optimal performance. The runner holds on to the sliding device and runs independently for as long as desired. Guide wires can be set up permanently or temporarily (figure 12.4*c*).
- *Sound source.* The guide rings a bell or shakes a noisemaker for the runner to hear

while running side-by-side. This works best in areas with limited background noise.

- *Sound source from a distance.* The runner runs toward a sound source such as a clap or a bell. This can be done as a one-time sprint or continued for a distance run.
- *Circular running.* In a large, clear, grassy area, a 20- to 25-foot (6- to 8-meter) rope is tied to a stake. The student takes the end of the rope, pulls it taut, and runs in circles. The circumference of the circle can be measured to determine the distance, or the athlete can run for time. A beeper or radio can be placed at the starting point to mark the number of laps completed.
- *Sighted guide.* The runner with partial vision runs behind a guide with a bright shirt or other clear marking. Ask the runner what color she can see best to ensure maximum vision. This must be done in areas that are not too crowded.
- *Independent running.* A runner with usable vision runs independently on a track marked with thick white lines.

FIGURE 12.4 Running using *(a)* a human guide, *(b)* a tether, and *(c)* a guide wire.

- *Treadmill.* Running on a treadmill provides a controlled and safe environment. Select a treadmill with the safety feature of an emergency stop.
- *Wheelchair racing.* A person who is blind and uses a wheelchair can implement any of the aforementioned adaptations as needed. Aerobic conditioning results from pushing over long distances, whether around a track, on neighborhood sidewalks, or along a paved path.

Running is fundamental to many sports and activities. It is crucial to allow students opportunities to experience each technique and decide which technique they prefer. Students may even prefer one technique for speed and another for distance.

Wrestling rules are modified slightly to require that opponents maintain constant physical contact throughout the match. Wrestlers with visual impairments have a long history of victories and state championships against sighted opponents (Buell, 1966).

Swimming follows NCAA rules. Athletes commonly count their strokes so that they can anticipate the end of the pool. Coaches may also tap a swimmer on the shoulder using a pool noodle or long pole with a tennis ball at the end to signal the upcoming end of the pool. Water can be sprayed on the surface of the pool to designate the end of the lane, either for one swimmer or across the end of all lanes. This can be accomplished with a regular backyard sprinkler. When necessary, a spotter may use a kickboard to keep a swimmer's head from hitting the wall at the end of the lane.

Goalball is a sport specifically designed for athletes with visual impairments. The object of the game is to roll a ball that contains bells past the opposing team's end line (figure 12.5).

National Beep Baseball Association (NBBA)

Beep baseball, a popular modification of baseball, is governed by the National Beep Baseball Association (NBBA). Competition culminates with the NBBA World Series. Further details on beep baseball are provided in chapter 25.

Camp Abilities

Camp Abilities is an educational sports camp program for children who are visually impaired, blind, or deafblind. Camps span from a weekend to a whole week. Each participant has a one-on-one coach and is taught after-school sports, Paralympic sports, and various recreational activities. There are Camp Abilities programs all over the United States and in other countries. For more information about Camp Abilities, see www.campabilities.org.

FIGURE 12.5 Physical educators might introduce goalball in an integrated class as a challenge to students who are sighted.

Summary

This chapter has focused on physical education for students with visual impairments. Whether the students are in an inclusive physical education setting or in a self-contained class, it is important to know their abilities and focus on what they can do. It is up to the physical education teacher to make the modifications necessary to ensure a quality experience that will prepare the student for experiences in physical activity throughout the lifetime.

References

Aillaud, C., & Lieberman, L.J. (2013). *Everybody plays: How children with visual impairments play sports.* American Printing House for the Blind.

Arndt, K., Lieberman, L.J., & James, A. (2014). Perceptions of socialization of adolescents who are blind and their parents. *Clearing House, 87,* 69-74.

Assistance to States for the Education of Children with Disabilities. 34 C.F.R. 300.8 (2006).

Augestad, L.B., & Jiang, L. (2015). Physical activity, physical fitness, and body composition among children and young adults with visual impairments: A systematic review. *The British Journal of Visual Impairment, 33*(3), 167-182. https://doi.org/10.1177/0264619615599813

Brian, A., Taunton, S., Lieberman, L., Haibach-Beach, P., Foley, J., & Santarossa, S. (2017). Validity and reliability of the Test of Gross Motor Development-3 for children with visual impairments. *Adapted Physical Activity Quarterly, 35,* 145-158. http://doi.org/10.1123/apaq2017-0061

Buell, C.E. (1966). *Physical education for blind children.* Charles C Thomas.

Casselbrant, M.L., Mandel, E.M., Sparto, P.J., Redfern, M.S., & Furman, J.M. (2007). Contribution of vision to balance in children four to eight years of age. *Journal of Ontology, Rhinology & Laryngology, 116*(9), 653-657. https://doi.org/10.1177/000348940711600905

Cieslak, F., Lieberman, L.J., Haibach, P., & Houston-Wilson, C. (2015). Instructional preferences of children who are blind during swimming. *Brazilian Journal of Adapted Physical Activity (Revista da Sobama, Marília), 16,* 9-14. Retrieved from http://digitalcommons.brockport.edu/pes_theses/12

Columna, L., Norris, M., Rocco Dillon, S., & Barreira, T.V. (2018). Parents' beliefs about physical activity for their children with visual impairments. *Adapted Physical Activity Quarterly, 35,* 361-380. https://doi.org/10.1123/apaq.2017-0084

Conroy, P. (2012). Supporting students with visual impairments in physical education. *Insight: Research & Practice in Visual Impairment & Blindness, 5,* 3-7.

Conroy, P. (2016). Building background knowledge: Pre-teaching physical education concepts to students with visual impairments. *Journal of Blindness Innovation and Research, 6*(2). https://doi.org/10.5241/6-80

Haegele, J.A., Lieberman, L.J., Columna, L., & Runyan, M. (2014). Infusing the Expanded Core Curriculum into physical education for children with visual impairments. *Palaestra, 28,* 44-50. Retrieved from http://researchgate.net

Haegele, J.A., Famelia, R., Lee, J. (2017). Health-related quality of life, physical activity, and sedentary behavior of adults with visual impairments. *Disability Rehabilitation, 39,* 2269-2276. https://doi.org/10.1080/09638288.2016.1225825

Haegele, J.A., & Zhu, X. (2019). Physical activity, self-efficacy and health-related quality of life among adults with visual impairments, *Disability and Rehabilitation, 43*(4), 530-536. https://doi.org/10.1080/09638288.2019.1631397

Haibach, P., Lieberman, L.J., & Pritchett, J. (2011). Balance in adolescents with and without visual impairments. *Insight Journal, 4,* 112-121.

Haibach, P., Wagner, M., & Lieberman, L.J. (2014). Determinants of gross motor skill performance in children with visual impairments. *Research in Developmental Disabilities, 35,* 2577-2584. https://doi.org/10.1016/j.ridd.2014.05.030

Houwen, S., Hartman, E., Jonker, L., & Visscher, C. (2010). Reliability and validity of the TGMD-2 in primary-school-age children with visual impairments. *Adapted Physical Activity Quarterly, 27,* 143-159. https://doi.org/10.1123/apaq.27.2.143

Houwen, S., Hartman, E., & Visscher, C. (2009). Physical activity and motor skills in children with and without visual impairments. *Medicine and Science in Sports and Exercise, 41*(1), 103-109. http://doi.org/10.1249/MSS.0b013e318183389d

Houwen, S., Visscher, C., Lemmink, K.A.P.M., & Hartman, E. (2008). Motor skill performance of school-age children with visual impairments. *Developmental Medicine & Child Neurology, 50*(2), 139-145. https://doi.org/10.1111/j.1469-8749.2007.02016.x

Lieberman, L.J., Byrne, H., Mattern, C., Watt, C., & Fernandez-Vivo, M. (2010). Health related fitness in youth with visual impairments. *Journal of Visual Impairment and Blindness, 104,* 349-359. https://doi.org/10.1177/0145482X1010400605

Lieberman, L.J. & Childs, R. (2020). Steps to success: A sport-focused self-advocacy program for children with visual impairments. *Journal of Visual Impairments and Blindness, 114*(6), 531-537.

Lieberman, L.J., Columna, L., Haegele, J., & Conroy, P. (2014). How students with visual impairments can learn components of the expanded core curriculum through physical education. *Journal of Visual*

Impairment and Blindness, 108, 239-248. https://doi.org/10/1177/0145482X1410800307

Lieberman, L.J., & Conroy, P. (2013). Paraeducator training for physical education for children with visual impairments. *Journal of Visual Impairment and Blindness, 107,* 17-28. https://doi.org/10.1177/0145482X1310700102

Lieberman, L.J., Ericson, K., Lepore-Stevens, M., & Wolffe, K. (2021). Expanded core curriculum during Camp Abilities: A qualitative study. *Journal of Visual Impairment and Blindness, 115*(1), 28-41.

Lieberman, L.J., Grenier, M., Brian, A., & Arndt, K. (2021). *Universal design for learning in physical education.* Human Kinetics.

Lieberman, L.J., & Haibach, P. (2016). *Motor development for children with visual impairments.* American Printing House for the Blind.

Lieberman, L.J., & Houston-Wilson, C. (2018). *Strategies for inclusion: Physical education for everyone* (3rd ed.). Human Kinetics.

Lieberman, L.J., Lepore, M., Lepore-Stevens, M., & Ball, L. (2019). Physical education for children with visual impairments. *Journal of Physical Education, Recreation and Dance, 90,* 30-38. https://doi.org/10.1080/07303084.2018.1535340

Lieberman, L.J., Ponchillia, P., & Ponchillia, S. (2013). *Physical education and sport for individuals who are visually impaired or deafblind: Foundations of instruction.* American Federation of the Blind Press.

McHugh, B.E., & Lieberman, L.J. (2003). The impact of developmental factors on incidence of stereotypic rocking among children with visual impairments. *Journal of Visual Impairment and Blindness, 97*(8), 453-474. https://doi.org/10.1177/0145482X0309700802

O'Connell, M., Lieberman, L., & Petersen, S. (2006). The use of tactile modeling and physical guidance as instructional strategies in physical activity for children who are blind. *Journal of Visual Impairment and Blindness, 100*(8), 471-477. https://doi.org/10.1177/0145482X0610000804

Pennington, C.G., & Webb, L. (2020). Enhancing physical education for students with vision impairment and preventing retinal detachment. *Journal of Physical Education, Recreation, & Dance, 91,* 53-54. https://doi.org/10.1080/07303084.2019.1705134

Perkins, K., Columna, L., Lieberman, L.J., & Bailey, J. (2013). Parental perceptions toward physical activity for their children with visual impairments and blindness. *Journal of Visual Impairment and Blindness, 107,* 131-142. http://doi.org/10.1177/0145482X1310700206

Samalot, A., Haibach, P., & Lieberman, L.J. (2015). Teaching two critical locomotor skills to children who are blind or have low vision. *Journal of Visual Impairment and Blindness, 109,* 148-152. http://doi.org/10.1177/0145482X1510900211

Sapp, W., & Hatlen, P. (2010). The expanded core curriculum: Where we have been, where we are going, and how we can get there. *Journal of Visual Impairment and Blindness, 104*(6), 338-348. http://doi.org/10.1177/0145482X1010400604

Ulrich, D. (2019). *Test of gross motor development* (3rd ed.). Pro-Ed.

Van Munster, M., Weaver, E., Lieberman, L.J., & Arndt, K. (2015). Visual impairment and physical education: Steps to success. *Journal of Visual Impairment and Blindness, 109,* 231-237.

Wagner, M., Haibach, P.S., & Lieberman, L.J. (2013). Gross motor skill performance in children with and without visual impairments—research to practice. *Research in Developmental Disabilities, 34,* 3246-3252. https://doi.org/10.1016/j.ridd.2013.06.030

Winnick, J., & Short, F. (2014). *The Brockport physical fitness test manual.* Human Kinetics.

Wiskochil, B., Lieberman, L.J., Houston-Wilson, C., & Petersen, S. (2007). The effects of trained peer tutors on academic learning time-physical education on four children who are visually impaired or blind. *Journal of Visual Impairment and Blindness, 101,* 339-350. http://doi.org/10.1177/0145482X0710100604

Print Resources

Liebs, A. (2013). *The encyclopedia of sports and recreation for people with visual impairments.* Information Age.

Liebs provides a history of sport, from archery to wrestling, involving people with visual impairments, as well as modifications that can be used and websites from which to order equipment.

Video Resources

Staff Training for Physical Education [Video]. www.perkinselearning.org/earn-credits/self-paced/staff-training-physical-education-children-visual-impairments

This video is a wonderful resource for the physical educator and the paraeducator.

Online Resources

American Blind Bowlers Association: www.abba1951.org

This website provides a description of bowling for people who are blind as well as equipment resources, leagues, and places to join blind bowling teams.

American Foundation for the Blind (AFB): www.afb.org

The American Foundation for the Blind (AFB) website provides information about their advocacy, resources, programs, and publications.

American Printing House for the Blind (APH): www.aph.org/physical-education

The American Printing House for the Blind (APH) is a national organization that publishes braille material as well as accessible curricular material for children who are blind. They also offer physical education equipment free for children with visual impairments and videos featuring sports played by kids who are visually impaired or blind.

Beep Kickball Association: www.beepkickball.com

This site provides a history of beep kickball, the rules and variations that can be used in inclusive settings, and a list of beep kickball leagues throughout the United States. Equipment can also be ordered through the site.

Camp Abilities: www.campabilities.org

Camp Abilities is an educational sport camp for children who are visually impaired, blind, or deafblind. This website also includes instructional materials such as videos (swimming, soccer, tennis, cross-country running, track and field, volleyball, basketball, beep baseball, beep kickball, and wrestling) as well as books, PowerPoints, tip sheets, handouts, assessments, and checklists, among others.

National Beep Baseball Association (NBBA): www.nbba.org

The National Beep Baseball Association (NBBA) website offers information about NBBA competitions and how to play beep baseball.

Perkins School for the Blind: www.perkins.org

Perkins has a variety of educational books for teachers, as well as an e-learning network with a variety of free videos, webinars, and courses to learn about how to teach children with visual impairments.

13

Deaf, Hard of Hearing, or Deafblind

Lauren J. Lieberman

Many teachers with children who are Deaf, hard of hearing (D/HOH), or deafblind in their classes may not understand their students' full potential (Haegele et al., 2018). The following is an example of just how far a student can go when given the opportunity.

Derrick Coleman, a Seattle Seahawk fullback, experienced repeated bullying as a child and went undrafted as a football player out of college. However, his confidence and determination led him to trying out for and making the Seattle team that won the 2014 Super Bowl. Coleman was featured in a Duracell advertisement that quoted him this way:

> They told me it couldn't be done, that I was a lost cause. I was picked on and picked last. Coaches didn't know how to talk to me. They gave up on me. Told me I should just quit. They didn't call my name. Told me it was over. But I've been Deaf since I was three, so I did not listen to these coaches.

This quote contains some excellent advice for physical educators who have D/HOH students in their classroom. It is important that D/HOH students feel as though they are equal members of the class, do not feel left out or like an outcast, are given every opportunity to succeed, and are in a comfortable environment where communication barriers do not exist. In addition, they are being taught by an educator who not only believes in them, but shows this through her actions by encouraging a student's growth and adapting her teaching to match the learning needs and style of the D/HOH student (Ellis & Lieberman, 2016).

There are a number of professionals who have and continue to advance knowledge, understanding, and acceptance of D/HOH people. One such person who devoted her life to that cause was Dr. Marjorie Kathleen Ellis. Therefore, this chapter is dedicated to Dr. Kat Ellis (1967-2020), a champion of Deaf Sport and an advocate for the education, rights, and opportunities for students with disabilities in physical education, recreation, aquatics, and sports. As a proud Deaf woman, she and her family fought for her personal inclusion and access to education. Following her PhD studies in kinesiology and Deaf studies at Michigan State University, Dr. Ellis began her career in adapted physical education professional preparation at the University of Rhode Island, followed by a move to West Chester University of Pennsylvania (WCU). In addition to providing scholarly opportunities in adapted physical activity, Dr. Ellis created the inaugural Deaf studies program at WCU. Her collaboration with Dr. David Stewart, an internationally recognized scholar in Deaf sport, was one of the highlights of her career. Kat's students held her in high esteem, and she prepared them well to continue her legacy of advocacy and activism for equity for persons with disabilities and those who are Deaf.

Teaching children who are D/HOH can be difficult if the instructor does not plan instruction appropriately. This chapter discusses the definitions of hearing loss, types of hearing loss, general characteristics of Deaf students and students who are hard of hearing, considerations for teaching, cochlear implants and physical education, inclusion strategies (including how to use interpreters), and sport opportunities for the Deaf community. Also covered is information on teaching children who are deafblind, including types of deafblindness, general characteristics of children who are deafblind, and adaptations for teaching students who are deafblind.

Definitions of Hearing Loss

Today, about 11.5 million Americans, or 3.6 percent of the U.S. population, have some sort of hearing loss, ranging from difficulty in hearing conversation to total hearing loss (U.S. Census Bureau, 2020). **Hard of hearing** (HOH) refers to a hearing loss that makes understanding audible speech difficult but not impossible. Those with this type of loss may lip read or use amplification with a hearing aid or other remedial help in communication skills. IDEA defines *hard of hearing* as having a hearing loss that might be permanent or fluctuating and that adversely affects the student's educational achievement or performance (IDEA, 2004).

Deaf refers to a severe or profound hearing loss in which hearing is insufficient for comprehension of auditory information, with or without the use of a hearing aid. The Individuals with Disabilities Education Act (IDEA) defines *Deaf* as having a hearing loss so severe that the person is unable to process language through hearing, with or without the use of an amplification device. The loss must be severe enough to adversely affect the student's educational performance (IDEA, 2004).

For this group, do not use the terms *the* hearing impaired, *the* Deaf, or *the* hard of hearing, because this "impairment" is considered a medical term (Reich & Lavay, 2009). One of the reasons Deaf people do not like the term *hearing impaired* is that they feel nothing needs to be fixed; thus, nothing is impaired. Padden and Humphries (1988) suggest using the words *Deaf* and *hard of hearing* to refer to all people with hearing loss. Unlike members of most populations with disabilities, most who are Deaf do not want person-first terminology used to describe them; they prefer to be called a *Deaf person* rather than a *person who is Deaf*. The use of the uppercase *D* in the word *Deaf* is a succinct proclamation by the Deaf community that they share more than a medical condition; they share a culture and a language—sign language. Understanding that many Deaf people do not consider themselves disabled, but rather members of a cultural and linguistic minority, will make teaching more effective.

Most people with hearing losses are hard of hearing, not totally Deaf. Although most of these students "are not culturally Deaf, the majority of hearing loss services and accommodations often go to this group" (Reich, 2007b). It is also important to note that two students might have the same degree of hearing loss but use their residual hearing differently because of age differences when the hearing loss occurred, the age when they received their first amplification device, or the amplification device itself. Motivation, intelligence, presence of disabilities, environmental stimulation, and response to a training program might also affect the degree to which residual hearing is used.

Degree of hearing loss and residual hearing are described in terms of decibel (dB) levels. The ability to detect sounds in the 0- to 15-dB range is considered normal for children. Ordinary conversation occurs in the 40- to 50-dB range, whereas noises in the 120- to 140-dB range are painfully loud. Degrees of hearing loss are presented in table 13.1.

TABLE 13.1 Degrees of Hearing Loss

Hearing threshold	Degrees of hearing loss	Example levels of loudness
27-40 dB	Mild	Faint or quiet speech
41-55 dB	Moderate	Normal speech
56-70 dB	Moderate-severe	City traffic
71-90 dB	Severe	Vacuum cleaner
Greater than 90 dB	Profound	Drums, power saw, airplane

Children with hearing loss may use several communication modes depending on parental influence, educational background, speech therapy, and technological enhancements (such as hearing aids or cochlear implants). The range of communication includes using residual hearing and speech; using Signed Exact English (SEE) with speech (also known as *total communication*); using cued speech, a combination of speaking and signs around the mouth to represent specific sounds; using Pidgin Signed English (PSE), a combination of SEE and American Sign Language (ASL); and strictly using ASL. Some children use more than one of these methods depending on audience, experience, and comfort level. They may even have some of their own "home" signs they use with family and close friends.

Types and Causes of Hearing Loss

The three major types of hearing loss are (1) conductive, (2) sensorineural, and (3) mixed. With a **conductive loss**, sound is not transmitted well to the inner ear—there is no distortion, but words are faint (analogous to a radio with the volume on low). Because a conductive loss is a mechanical problem in which nerves remain undamaged, it can often be corrected with the use of hearing aids, which effectively increase volume. A frequently observed condition is serous otitis media, or middle ear effusion, which often is treated by placement of a plastic tube through the eardrum for several months to allow fluid to drain from sound-conducting inner ear bones. Most children with conductive loss have intelligible speech.

According to the American Speech-Language-Hearing Association (ASHA, n.d.), a **sensorineural hearing loss** occurs when there is damage to the inner ear (cochlea) or to the nerve pathways from the inner ear (retrocochlear) to the brain. Sensorineural hearing loss not only involves a reduction in sound level, or the ability to hear faint sounds, but also affects fidelity, or the ability to hear clearly (analogous to a radio that is not well tuned). Even if words are loud, they may be distorted and garbled. It might help for speakers to raise their voice or for the listener to use a hearing aid, but the listener still may not understand the words. In comparison to a conductive loss, sensorineural loss can be more severe and is more likely to be permanent. Children with a sensorineural loss often have more difficulties with speech than those with a conductive loss do.

It is important that physical educators understand and meet the unique needs of D/HOH students, like this boy with a cochlear implant.

Students with a severe to profound sensorineural loss will likely use sign language, are less likely to use speech, and might have balance difficulties as a consequence of damage to the semicircular canal. A **mixed loss** is a combination of conductive and sensorineural losses. Today, many children with a sensorineural hearing loss undergo surgery for a cochlear implant. However, this practice is controversial—cochlear implants are not accepted in Deaf culture, as Deaf people do not consider Deafness a disability. This will be discussed later in the chapter.

Among Deaf students, approximately two-thirds have congenital deafness (present at birth) and one-third have acquired deafness (developed some time after birth). Medical advances have enabled more severely premature babies and children with meningitis and encephalitis to survive. These survivors might have multiple disabilities, including hearing loss. Other conditions, including injuries, autoimmune conditions, genetic conditions, allergies to drugs, repeated exposure to loud sounds, and infections such as herpes viruses and toxoplasmosis can all result in hearing loss.

Characteristics of Students With Hearing Loss

People who are classified as hard of hearing (HOH) typically can hear speech from up close but still need accommodations to hear from far away (see the sidebar Considerations When Communicating With a Deaf Person). This may be particularly necessary in physical education conducted in outdoor playing areas or noisy gymnasiums. Their hearing losses from slight to moderate might not present major obstacles to speech. Also, most Deaf people have unique characteristics caused by the need to communicate through a means other than spoken language. These characteristics are the focus of the following section.

Language and Cultural Characteristics

American Sign Language (ASL) is the preferred means of communication within Deaf culture in the United States. This shared language is the basis of the shared identity in Deaf culture. Just like English, ASL is a language with its own grammar and structure to convey subtleties of abstractions in addition to describing concrete objects. Most hearing people see only the signs that name objects and directions (figure 13.1) and are unaware of the unique concepts of ASL. Because many prelingually Deaf children do not develop intelligible speech despite speech training and cochlear implants (especially if they do not receive implants until several years after loss is diagnosed), communication between hearing and Deaf people remains a major problem until more hearing people learn ASL. Many Deaf children will learn ASL as their first language. Courtesies to aid communication between hearing and Deaf people are presented in the sidebar Considerations When Communicating With a Deaf Person.

Deaf students and students who are hard of hearing in the hearing community have fewer

Considerations When Communicating With a Deaf Person

- Get the person's attention before attempting to talk.
- Stay in the person's field of vision as much as possible. Also, note that only 20 to 30 percent of speech is visible on the lips even to the best lip readers.
- Speak in a normal voice.
- Establish the gist of what you are going to talk about through gestures, text, pictures, or video.
- Make eye contact throughout communication.
- Use gestures and visual cues.
- Be polite.
- Learn as much sign language as possible (Barboza et al., 2019).
- Ensure having signs for each sport taught (Frydrych, 2012).

Adapted from Columna and Lieberman (2011).

opportunities for *incidental learning* than hearing students do because they cannot overhear conversations. Rarely do hearing parents, teachers, and friends sign or ensure understanding when not directly addressing the child with hearing loss. Thus, there is little opportunity to take in environmental information, and continuity with life events is often missing. This is where the use of sign language becomes important in the socialization and language development of children who are Deaf or HOH (Barboza et al., 2019).

Behavioral and Affective Characteristics

Sometimes students with hearing loss are regarded as slow learners or as having behavior problems when their actions are actually a result of an undetected

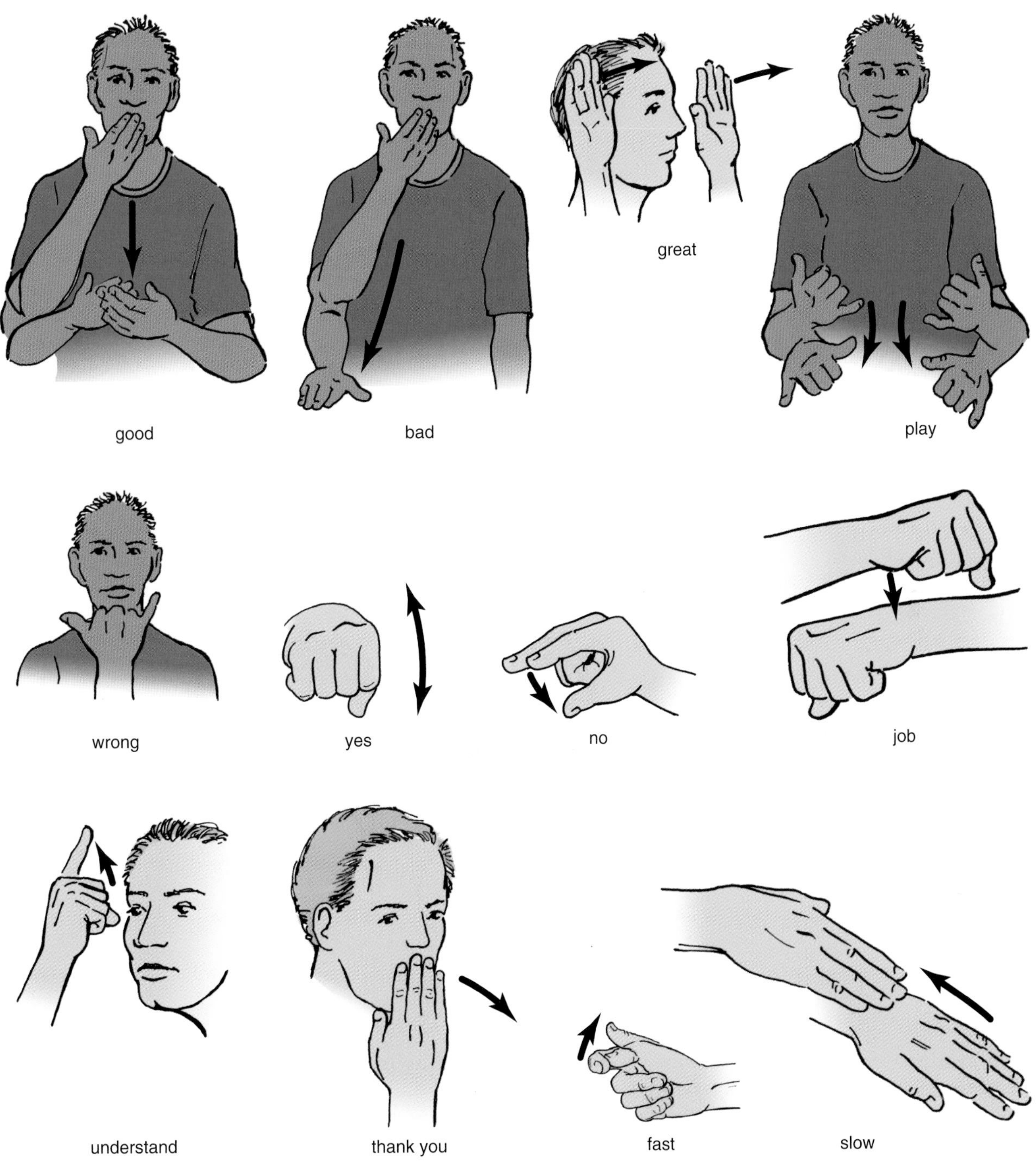

FIGURE 13.1 Signs for physical education.

(continued)

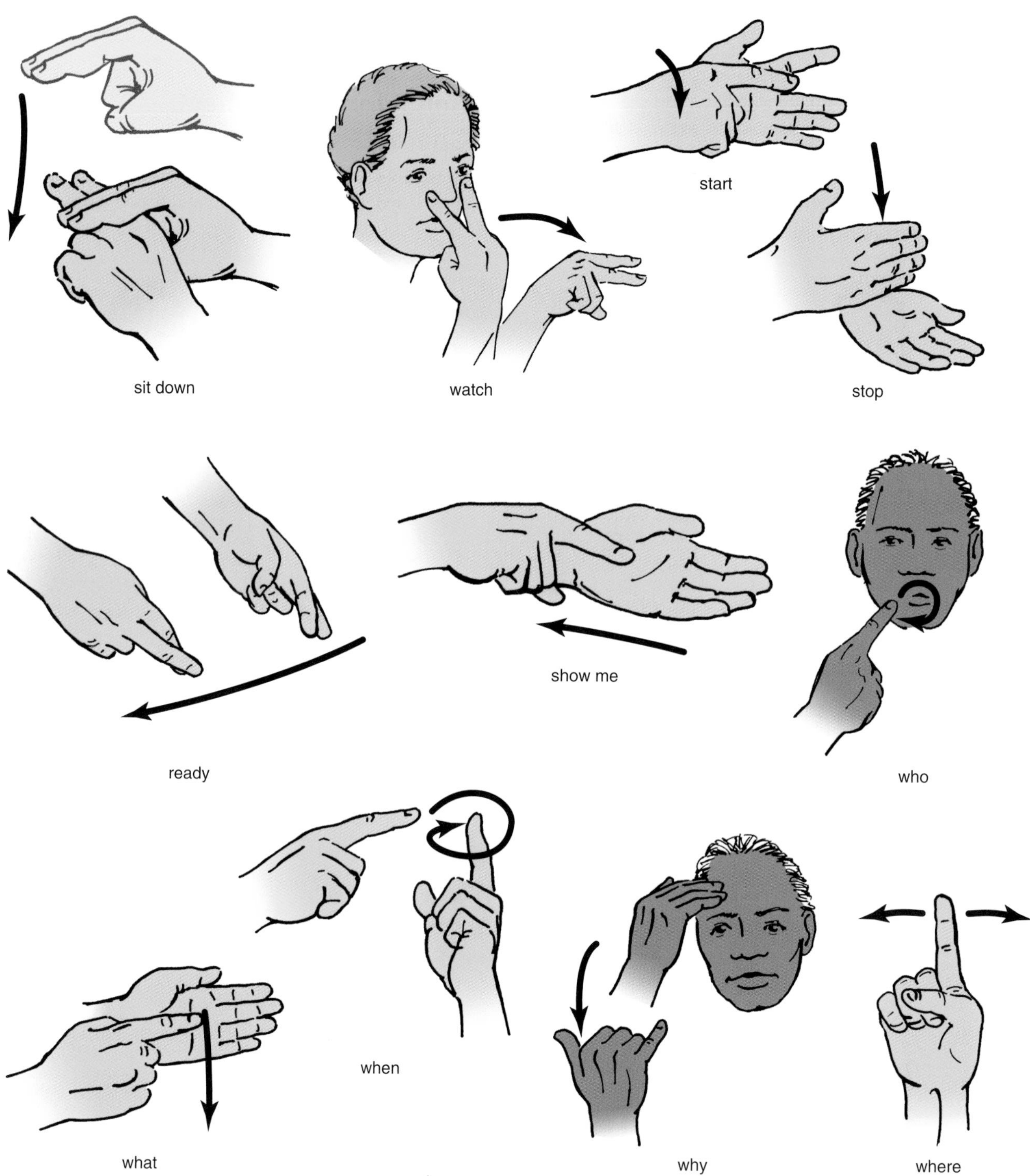

FIGURE 13.1 *(continued)*

mild hearing loss. Perceived impulsivity seems to be greater among students with hearing loss than among hearing students, possibly because these students learn visually and want to examine their surroundings more frequently. Some behavioral problems may be a direct result of frustrations caused by a lack of understanding when adults in the student's world cannot communicate with him in his primary language.

Motor Characteristics

If the semicircular canals of the inner ear are damaged as a part of the hearing loss, as in sensorineural deafness, balance problems may be likely. These balance problems—which occur as a result of vestibular damage, not deafness—can in turn cause developmental and motor ability delays. Hartman and colleagues (2011) found that Deaf children had deficits in motor performance when compared to hearing peers. This outcome was supported by studies showing that delays in sequence processing among Deaf children may result in deficits in motor learning, which in turn may lead to deficits in overall motor development (Khairi et al., 2014; Levesque et al., 2014). This deficit in motor skills may also contribute to the deficits in physical activity in children who are hard of hearing (Lobenius-Palmer et al., 2018).

However, a study by Simon and Koku (2017) found that Deaf children showed deficits in balance and coordination, but not in speed. Majlesi and colleagues (2014) evaluated the effects of interventional proprioceptive training and determined that the exercise program improved somatosensory ability and increased balance in Deaf children. Given equal opportunity to learn movements and participate in physical activity, Deaf children should equal their same-age peers in motor skills (Lieberman et al., 2004). If these children are not afforded equal opportunity, they might lag behind in motor skills.

Hartman and colleagues (2007) found that Deaf children from the Netherlands were physically less fit than hearing children. But when the results of fitness testing of young people with hearing losses were compared against standardized norms, the outcome was drastically different, with Deaf children showing acceptable fitness levels (Ellis, 2001; Ellis et al., 2005). The only reason some fitness scores were low was because of higher body mass index (BMI) scores among some Deaf children (Dair et al., 2006; Stough et al., 2016). Studies found that two primary factors influenced the physical fitness of Deaf children: physical activity participation (just as with hearing children) and parental influence (Dair et al., 2006; Ellis, 2001; Engel-Yeger & Hamed-Daher, 2013; Li et al., 2018). It was also discovered that Deaf children with Deaf parents received greater encouragement and had greater activity participation than Deaf children with hearing parents (Ellis, 2001; Ellis et al., 2013). Recent research has shown that Deaf children who are active have higher self-esteem than children who are sedentary (Nemcek, 2017).

General Considerations for Teaching Physical Education to Students With Hearing Loss

One of the most useful instructional strategies for heterogeneous classes that include children who are hard of hearing or Deaf is universal design for learning. Using this approach, the instructor provides multiple means of engagement, multiple means of representation, and multiple means of action and expression (Lieberman et al., 2020). Engage the student by motivating them with a variety of equipment they like and a stimulating environment with clear directions and rewards for accomplishing short-term goals. In order to promote multiple means of representation, present the lesson a variety of ways, such as videos, demonstrations, posters, or stations with clear directions. Lastly, ensure multiple means of action and expression by allowing each child to show you what they know in a variety of ways, such as by physically doing the activity, showing you on a computer, or writing or signing a description to you. Each variation or equipment modification should be available to every child in the class (Lieberman et al., 2020).

Deaf students need to see demonstrations and modeling in order to understand the skills and activities being taught. Visual aids such as videos, posters, Smart Boards, and computer tablets are some of the best ways of conveying information and instruction to Deaf students (Schultz et al., 2013) (see the Visual Aids to Students Who Are Deaf or Hard of Hearing sidebar). It is also important for the teacher to use plenty of demonstrations for students who are hard of hearing. It is recommended that students with hearing loss demonstrate recently learned skills in order to increase involvement and understanding. It is unlikely that subtle sport strategy and rule concepts could be completely conveyed without demonstration, video with text, or signed information. One of the factors that most compromises the learning process of Deaf students is the lack of knowledge of a sign language by many teachers (Barboza et al., 2019; Tanure Alves et al., 2021). Even Certified Deaf Interpreters (CDIs) seldom have the sport-specific ASL vocabulary with which to explain subtle movement or sport concepts. Barboza and colleagues (2015) searched for the signs of 33 Olympic sports in LIBRAS (LIBRAS is the Brazilian equivalent of ALS)

Visual Aids to Students Who Are Deaf or Hard of Hearing

- Posters presenting instructions and pictures
- Blackboards, whiteboards, or Smart Boards showing explanations, field diagrams, and placement of players
- Demonstrations
- Written announcements
- Videos with captions or English subtitles
- Handouts
- Facial expressions, gestures, and other body language

Schultz et al. (2013).

and found only 10 signs available online. Among these, incorrect and inaccurate signs were also observed. This may also compromise the teaching of physical education to these students.

Deaf students in general schools often experience isolation, social deprivation, and ridicule from peers because they lack a common language with their hearing classmates (Edwards & Crocker, 2008; Graziadei, 1998; Tanure Alves et al., 2021). Deaf and hard of hearing students experience bullying at rates two to three times higher than those reported by hearing students (Weiner et al., 2013). If a Deaf student is placed in an inclusive classroom, a peer tutor should be made available. Trained peer tutors have been shown to improve physical activity in inclusive physical education classes (Lieberman, et al., 2000). As peer tutors learn more signs, new opportunities for appropriate socialization among peers emerge. Additional information on peer tutor programs can be found in Lieberman and Houston-Wilson (2018).

Teaching Considerations for Students With Cochlear Implants

Cochlear implantation is a surgical procedure that implants a device into the inner ear to electrically stimulate the auditory nerve and bypass the damaged cochlea of the inner ear, paired with an external speech processor that communicates with the implant. The goal of the implant is to improve recognition of speech and acoustic information over that with a hearing aid (see figure 13.2). Receiving cochlear implantation early in life can result in good verbal development and improve motor abilities (Schlumberger et al., 2004). Although the National Association of the Deaf (NAD) does not promote cochlear implants, they are becoming more common in children with sensorineural hearing loss.

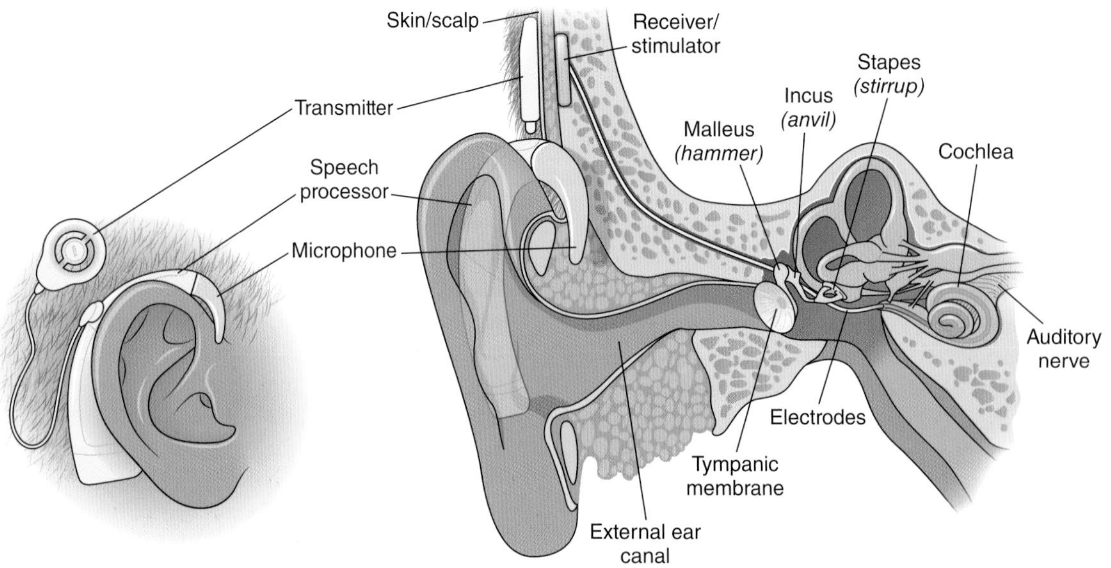

FIGURE 13.2 The device connects the outer ear to the cochlea in the inner ear so the child can hear.

Students with cochlear implants have unique needs when it comes to physical education. The following are teaching considerations for students with cochlear implants, according to Hilgenbrinck and colleagues (2004):

- Avoid sports that might result in serious blows to the head, such as American football, hockey, lacrosse, soccer, wrestling, tumbling, and other contact sports (FDA, 2018). These activities can be enjoyed with adaptations to eliminate contact.
- Avoid activities that increase the risk of falls or blows to the head, such as in-line skating, skateboarding, riding a scooter, and wall climbing (FDA, 2018). With proper instruction, removal of the implant device, and use of helmets, these activities might be enjoyed.
- Use caution when participating in winter activities, such as skiing, snowboarding, sledding, and ice-skating. These situations might create uncomfortable sensations around the head and neck.
- Excessive sweating creates moisture inside the device. This might cause unwanted and unnecessary noise. Students should either take the device off before vigorous activity or wear a headband or hat to keep the device dry.
- At the time of implant, the device is calibrated by an audiologist to custom fit the recipient. This is called *mapping* the device. The interference of static electricity might demap the device, rendering it unusable. Avoid static electricity (balloons, rubber, dry mats, plastic slides) to reduce the risk of demapping the device.

Current technology allows children with cochlear implants to swim with the implant. The Nucleus Aqua Accessory is a single-use plastic enclosure that completely seals in the processing unit, cable, and coil. No wires or upgrades are required; one slips the Aqua Accessory over the Nucleus 5 or 6 processor. This device is designed to be used with rechargeable batteries.

If the student chooses to remove the device during water activities to avoid damage or for other safety reasons, the parts should be placed in watertight containers. Remember, however, that this will leave the student with no usable hearing. If the student does not sign or have an interpreter, it will be necessary to teach him signs related to the activities being taught. It is better to teach the student ASL rather than self-created signs so the signs can be generalized to other situations. Be sure to follow specific teaching techniques for Deaf students when the student does not have the device connected.

Inclusion Strategies for Teaching Students With Hearing Loss

When teaching students with hearing loss, it is important to review the student's individualized education program (IEP) and ask questions of the parents, guardians, or caregivers; educational audiologist; Deaf educator; and educational interpreter (if there is one). In-service education sessions led by the educational audiologist for all students with audiology needs may help answer questions. Most importantly, the students themselves should be asked the following questions:

- What hearing situations are most difficult (Reich, 2007a; Reich & Lavay, 2009)?
- What is the student's preferred mode of communication? How can the teacher maximize communication with the student?
- Are there any contraindications or activities that should be avoided? How can these activities be modified?
- Does the student wear hearing aids? Excessive noise and reverberation caused by substandard room acoustics interfere with speech intelligibility, especially in children with hearing aids or cochlear implants (Reich & Lavay, 2009).

Most students with hearing loss have no restrictions on participation in physical education. Children with frequent ear infections might have tubes placed in their ears, so they might need to wear earplugs when swimming. Not all students with hearing loss have balance problems; however, if there are balance issues, it is necessary to work on tasks to improve balance within the general curriculum (Barboza et al., 2019).

Students with hearing loss might benefit from the use of an interpreter. The role of an educational interpreter is to facilitate communication between D/HOH students and others, such as teachers, service providers, and peers within the educational environment. In inclusive physical education classes, the following suggestions are designed to improve success, communication, and socialization:

- Give lesson plans to the interpreter days in advance so both the interpreter and student can review and understand the lesson before it begins. Include a list of any specialized vocabulary.
- Meet with the interpreter before beginning each unit to clarify sport terminology, instructional cues, and idioms that are likely to be used.
- Teach sport-specific signs at the beginning of each new unit (Columna & Lieberman, 2011).
- Pair each Deaf student with a hearing peer, not the interpreter.
- Encourage the interpreter to stand next to the teacher.
- Face the student (not the interpreter) when addressing the student.
- Use the interpreter to communicate with Deaf students. Ensure the interpreter asks students what type of sign language they prefer.
- Do not ask students to speak if they do not feel comfortable using their voice; allow them to use their interpreter to communicate.
- Include the Deaf student in information taught during teachable moments.
- Understand that the interpreter's role does not include reprimanding a student, working with other students, or assisting with small jobs.
- Remember that the interpreter is not a teacher's assistant and should not be expected to take attendance or distribute and collect equipment.

For students with enough residual hearing to hear background noises, Graziadei (1998) makes these suggestions:

- Minimize background noise—turn off any music (Reich & Lavay, 2009), and expect silence when others are speaking.
- Encourage the student to remove the hearing aid or adjust the volume if there is excessive unavoidable background noise.

The following are general considerations for teaching or coaching students with hearing loss in either integrated or segregated settings:

- Use visual cues when teaching activities that are easily understood.
- Give students with hearing loss copies of lessons modified to their reading levels.
- Use stations with cue cards providing written explanations and illustrations.
- Use clear signals for starting and stopping activities, such as waving arms, flags, lights, or signs.
- Use demonstrations liberally (Barboza et al., 2019).
- Use a scoreboard and a visual timer for games.
- Use highly recognizable and easily visible signals for communication at a distance.
- Make sure there is eye contact before passing a ball.
- When possible, stand near the student with hearing loss and tap the student on the shoulder to gain attention.
- Face the student so that lips and facial expressions are fully visible.
- Avoid chewing gum or covering the mouth; consider shaving a beard or mustache.
- Position the student directly in front of the teacher.
- When outdoors, take care that the student does not face into the sun. Ensure that the teacher is not standing directly in front of the sun or a bright light.
- When indoors, provide adequate lighting (behind the student).
- Assess the distance at which the student can hear your speech. The distance will change in different rooms and situations (Reich, 2007a; Reich & Lavay, 2009). Preference is within six feet (two meters) even in a quiet room.
- Check for understanding. Ask all students if they understand the activity before beginning. Help hearing students appreciate that if the students with hearing loss do not follow the rules, it might be because they do not understand them and not because they intend to cheat or seek unfair advantage (Fiorini & Manzini, 2018).
- Promote leadership skills among students with hearing loss, such as being team captains, group leaders, and referees. Allowing these students to do demonstrations, set out and clean up equipment, or be squad leaders also promotes leadership (Lieberman et al., 2007).
- Ensure that any movie or instructional video is captioned (Reich & Lavay, 2009). Videos on YouTube have a closed captioning option or English subtitles.

- Give students choices and honor them.
- Have students with hearing loss help hearing students and vice versa.
- Provide clear instructions so students with hearing loss do not need to wait and watch others before participating.
- Repeat questions or comments from other students or incorporate students' comments into the answer.

The following recommendations are specifically for Deaf students:

- If teaching students who sign, learn as much sign language as possible (Columna & Lieberman, 2011). A hearing person is encouraged to practice and learn sign language, which takes as much effort as learning any other language (Barboza et al., 2019).

Application Example

Including a Student With Hearing Loss

SETTING

Elementary school physical education class

STUDENT

Samuel is a fourth grader who is HOH and benefits from sign language and speech. Samuel has been going to his elementary school since kindergarten and has many friends. When he was in second grade, Samuel's parents asked for an ASL interpreter to assist him in his academic subjects. Ms. Bowie has been his ASL interpreter for two years, and Samuel likes her a lot. Unfortunately, Ms. Bowie takes her break during physical education class. The administrators made this decision because they felt there was no need for an ASL interpreter in physical education. Many of Samuel's friends know the signs he teaches them and a few they have picked up from the ASL interpreter in passing, and they use it on the bus and in classes. They also understand his speech when they are not in a noisy environment.

ISSUE

Samuel loves physical activity but is reserved in physical education because he does not always understand the directions. He always waits a minute or two at the start of each activity to be sure he knows what the activity involves before starting. Mr. Wineberg, the physical education teacher, has noticed Samuel's reservations and is concerned. Samuel misses at least six minutes of activity during each class watching his peers participate because he is afraid of doing the wrong thing. Mr. Wineberg does not know enough sign language to ask Samuel what is wrong, so he requested an appointment with the school administrator, the Deaf education consultant, the educational audiologist, the ASL interpreter, and Samuel and his parents.

APPLICATION

The following was determined as a result of a meeting with the school administrator, the Deaf education consultant, the educational audiologist, the ASL interpreter, Samuel and his parents, and Mr. Wineberg:

- Samuel will continue to participate in physical education with his peers.
- The ASL interpreter, Ms. Bowie, will take short breaks at reading time, lunch, and recess instead of during physical education.
- Mr. Wineberg will meet with Ms. Bowie before each unit and learn the necessary signs so he can start to communicate with Samuel himself during class. Ms. Bowie will also teach Samuel's peers the signs commonly needed for each unit so they can communicate with him during class.
- Mr. Wineberg and Ms. Bowie will create an appropriate list of modifications to activities, such as using start and stop signals, having students sit in a semicircle instead of rows, and facing Samuel when instructing students.
- Mr. Wineberg will start a peer tutor program so that if Samuel is playing a game and he cannot see the ASL interpreter, the peer tutor can relay important information to him using speech and signs. This will also increase Samuel's self-confidence, the number of peers he can communicate with, and his depth of conversation.
- An additional class with supplemental physical education instruction will be offered should Samuel need more time to grasp a skill or activity, such as dancing or in-line skating.

- Include Deaf students in information taught during teachable moments. These moments often occur in the middle of a game, when an interpreter is on the sidelines and the Deaf student is down the field. Two options are to review the teachable moments at the end of the lesson, or to pause and gather all students along with the interpreter together on the field.
- Dance and rhythms can be especially important for Deaf students. To help students better feel the vibrations of music, place speakers facedown on a wooden floor, turn up the bass and the drums, and dance in bare feet. Strobe lights that flash in rhythm with the music also provide visual cues. Balloons can be used so students can feel the music through their hands by feeling the vibrations through the rubber of the balloon.
- Allow Deaf students the option of taking written tests with an interpreter to clarify and sign test questions. In this way, physical education knowledge is tested, not the Deaf students' knowledge of English, a second language (Graziadei, 1998). Refer also to the Application Example sidebar, Including a Student with Hearing Loss.
- Teach signs to the entire class so there is clear communication among students.
- Schedule Deaf students into the same physical education class and encourage them to work together during class so they can help each other understand the lesson.
- Hold the same expectations for hearing and Deaf students regarding motor performance, fitness, and behavior and clearly communicate these expectations to all students. Educators who offer excessive assistance when students are not prepared for class teach Deaf students that they can rely on others rather than accept responsibility for their own actions.
- Encourage students to become involved in Deaf sport through the USA Deaf Sports Federation (USADSF, www.usdeafsports.org).

Most physical fitness and motor tests can be administered to Deaf students, provided that visual cues are substituted for auditory cues (e.g., dropping the arm in addition to shouting "Go!", banging a large drum, or using strobe lights or cable lights as starting signals). Deaf children whose native language is ASL perform better on motor tests when the test is administered in ASL instead of English. Note that ASL is not semantically similar to English, so care must be taken when signing instructions. The person giving instructions should be skilled in signing and able to give signed instructions that are semantically identical to spoken instructions.

The strategies described apply to individualized, segregated, and integrated settings for students with hearing loss. In addition to a quality physical education program, Deaf students need quality sport opportunities in hearing and Deaf sport.

Deafblindness

People who are deafblind do not have effective use of either of the distance senses (vision and hearing). Although the term *deafblind* suggests that these people can neither hear nor see, this is rarely the literal truth. Most people who are deafblind receive some visual and auditory input, but information received through these sensory channels is usually distorted. Therefore, it is frequently more accurate to say that these people are both hard of hearing and partially sighted. Only in rare instances, such as with Helen Keller, is a person totally blind and profoundly Deaf. Each person with the label *deafblind* has a unique history, and it is important to gather information from the team to understand what the student is able to see and hear. See the sidebar Considerations When Teaching Students With Deafblindness.

Deafblindness has many causes. Understanding the cause might give an indication of the age of onset and whether remaining vision and hearing are likely. Usher syndrome, the major cause of adult-onset deafblindness in the United States, is a congenital disability characterized by hearing loss present at birth or shortly thereafter and the progressive loss of peripheral vision. Usher syndrome type I is congenital deafness and progressive retinitis pigmentosa, whereas type II is adventitious deafness and progressive retinitis pigmentosa. Type III is progressive hearing loss, progressive vision loss, and loss of vestibular function. When teaching students with Usher syndrome, it is important to ascertain the amount of hearing and vision they currently have.

The leading cause of child-onset deafblindness is CHARGE syndrome. An evaluation for possible CHARGE syndrome should be made by a medical geneticist who is familiar with the syndrome. Major features in children with CHARGE include vision problems, swallowing and nasal issues, hearing difficulties, and growth delays. Because children

Considerations When Teaching Students With Deafblindness

- Offer activities that are common with peers and that promote movement.
- Use multiple teaching modes, such as explanation, demonstration, tactile modeling, and physical assistance (Lieberman et al., 2013).
- Set up the environment to accommodate the student's strengths and encourage choice making, such as choice of activity and equipment (Imel et al., 2020). For example, if the student will be batting, offer bats and balls in a variety of sizes, colors, and textures as well as several ways to deliver the ball, such as on a string, on a tee, or from a pitch.
- Be flexible, patient, and creative.
- Facilitate socialization, because students who are deafblind often experience isolation and loneliness (Imel et al., 2020; Lieberman & MacVicar, 2003). Ways to do this include implementing a peer tutor program, teaching the student's mode of communication to classmates, and encouraging the student who is deafblind to become involved in after-school programs and community activities (Imel et al., 2020).
- Provide all incidental information.
- Link movement to language. Teach the word for each skill learned and explain the purpose of each sport and activity.
- Learn the student's form of communication, including gestures and body language.
- Help students find activities in their homes to engage in, with and without siblings and peers.

Lieberman and Pecorella (2006).

with CHARGE experience medical complications such as feeding tubes, tracheotomies, and heart issues, they spend large amounts of time in the hospital, often resulting in delayed gross motor and balance skills (Haibach-Beach et al., 2019, 2020). Therefore, it is imperative that they be taught to their functional ability (Lieberman et al., 2012). As they get stronger and experience fewer visits to the hospital, the instructor can increase the length, duration, and intensity of activities offered.

Deafblindness can also be associated with meningitis, prematurity, parental use of drugs, sexually transmitted diseases (STDs), other syndromes, and unknown causes. People who have both vision and hearing loss often have additional disabilities. These disabilities may include cerebral palsy, intellectual disability, autism, or a combination of several disabilities. No matter what disabilities are present, it is most important to focus on the student's functional ability and communication—for example, providing demonstrations at close distances with plenty of explanation, physical assistance, and feedback. For many children, this level of instruction would necessitate a one-on-one teaching situation.

Characteristics of Children with Deafblindness

Though there is often a tendency for caregivers to focus on the medical aspects of deafblindness, physical educators can help parents begin to focus on their child's quality of life (Lieberman & Haegele, 2019). Physical educators can work to introduce students who are deafblind to enjoyable activities rather than focus only on activities of daily living. Teaching students who are deafblind is a unique experience that requires hands-on work; it is a topic that is difficult to cover comprehensively in the limited time allotted in professional preparation courses (Lieberman et al., 2013; Lirgg et al., 2017). Camp Abilities, an educational sport camp for young people with visual impairments and deafblindness, is held for one week each summer at State University of New York (SUNY) at Brockport and in other locations throughout the United States. This camp is an excellent opportunity for students to learn how to teach young people who are deafblind. For more information on Camp Abilities, see www.campabilities.org. See also the Print Resources at the end of this chapter for more great sources for education and activities for students who are deafblind.

A major consideration for students with deafblindness is isolation (Hersh, 2013). Some people who are deafblind attend camps or move to communities where there are several others who are deafblind. Physical education and sport can provide opportunities to reduce this isolation and introduce the person who is deafblind to activities such as in-line skating, swimming, biking, and gymnastics to increase socialization (Lieberman et al., 2013).

As discussed with both vision and hearing loss, deafblindness presents limited opportunities for *incidental learning*. It is becoming more common to use an intervenor—a person who works one-on-one with the student—to sign exactly what is happening in the environment (Lieberman & Haegele, 2019). For example, the intervenor signs when a child is on the swings, when a certain classmate has recently entered the room, or who is saying what in a discussion. The range of communication methods is similar to the range for children who have only hearing loss; however, signing may need to be done in the child's limited field of vision. This may be close up to the child's face, far away from the child, or in a limited space. If there is no vision, signing may be done tactually in the child's hand, which is called *tactile communication* (Hersh, 2013). ProTactile communication for people who are deafblind is another strategy of signing that enhances tactile cues with the hands, fingers, back, legs, and arms (Berkowitz & Jonas, 2014; Granda & Nuccio, 2018). This strategy may help increase knowledge and understanding of the activity and the environment surrounding the child during the activity. No matter the communication mode, you must work with the intervener to ensure that clear and accurate instruction and feedback are given to the student on a consistent basis (Lieberman & Haegele, 2019).

Communication During Physical Activity

Communication during physical activity with a child who is deafblind can be difficult unless it is planned and discussed ahead of time. Research by Arndt and colleagues (2004) helped create the following steps for setting up clear, planned communication during activity with children who are deafblind:

- Allow the child to explore the equipment and environment to gain a better understanding of the upcoming activity. This will require time for preteaching (discussed in chapter 12). Exploration time will help the child understand the environment and equipment before beginning to learn skills or an activity. The tactile exploration needs to be accompanied by clear terminology regarding what is being felt. For instance, a bike would open up the concepts of wheels, chain, handlebars, seat, and frame.
- It is important to listen to the experts, including the child, paraeducator, and intervenor or interpreter. When children have a question or concern, or if they are apprehensive about a new activity, their feelings and communication must be addressed. For example, if a child is swimming in the shallow end of the pool with a life vest and he points to the deep end, it is likely that he has experienced swimming and is skilled enough to swim in the deep end. Ask questions and explore what the child's communication is conveying.
- Make sure that continuous activities are made discrete until the child feels comfortable. Continuous activities are those that do not have a clear beginning or ending, such as biking, running, rock climbing, swimming, and in-line skating. Discrete activities include those that have a definite beginning and ending (e.g., shot put, rolling a bowling ball, or shooting a free throw in basketball). When children who are deafblind engage in a continuous activity for the first time, it may be scary and they may not know when they can stop, when they will have a chance to communicate what they need, or when they will get feedback. Making a continuous activity discrete and planning ahead of time when communication will happen will minimize fears and allow the child to get more feedback as well as increase opportunities for communication. For example, if a child is swimming in the deep end and is afraid, she can swim for five strokes and then stop and get feedback, rest, or ask a question.
- Make sure the child has the opportunity to receive and express communication clearly with others throughout each activity (Brady et al., 2016). This will take careful planning, discussion, and often positioning before the activity, but it is vital to success (Imel et al., 2020). For example, if the physical education teacher plans for the child to pull himself prone on a scooter and he uses tactile signing, the teacher, intervenor (interpreter), and child need to plan time for instruction, activity, and feedback before the child starts moving (Cavanaugh et al., 2020).

Adaptations for Teaching

Many students who are deafblind need modifications to successfully participate in general activities. The teaching tips for children with visual impairments and for Deaf children also apply to students who are deafblind (Lieberman et al., 2012). Refer to the Considerations When Teaching Students With Deafblindness sidebar for additional points. Keep in mind that a multisensory approach is preferred for teaching these students. Modifications might include changing the rules, equipment, instruction, or environment, as described in chapter 2.

Students with deafblindness uncomplicated by additional disabilities can participate in most sports at both the competitive and recreational levels. As with students who are visually impaired, it is important to teach a combination of open and closed skills. Deafblind athletes wishing to compete might choose to compete in sports for people who are blind or deaf (e.g., via the United States Association of Blind Athletes or USADSF).

Sport Opportunities

Physical educators have the important role of introducing Deaf students to both hearing and Deaf sports, which have shown to increase self-esteem in Deaf children (Uchida et al., 2015). The greatest sport opportunities for most Deaf students usually come from after-school and community sport programs. For many Deaf students attending public schools, the majority of their exposure to Deaf culture is through Deaf sport. One such opportunity is through the USA Deaf Sports Federation (USADSF), originally established as the American Athletic Association for the Deaf (AAAD) in Ohio in 1945. People with moderate or severe hearing loss (55 dB or greater in the better ear) are eligible for USADSF competition. No hearing aids or cochlear implants are permitted during USADSF competition. Involving young people in Deaf sport is an important objective of USADSF. Refer to the Online Resources for this chapter to learn more about student involvement in Deaf sport and to share this information with Deaf students.

The USADSF includes the following sports for men and women:

Badminton
Baseball
Basketball
Bowling
Curling
Cycling
Golf
Hockey
Martial arts
Orienteering
Shooting
Skiing and snowboarding
Soccer
Swimming
Table tennis
Tennis
Team handball
Track and field
Triathlon volleyball
Water polo
Wrestling

The worldwide counterpart of USADSF is the International Committee of Sports for the Deaf (ICSD). Currently, ICSD is not a member of the International Paralympic Committee (IPC). Instead of participating in the Paralympic Games, Deaf sport holds its own Summer and Winter Deaflympics every four years. Winter events include alpine and Nordic skiing, speed skating, and ice hockey.

The rules followed by the USADSF and ICSD are nearly identical to those used in national and international competitions for hearing athletes. To equalize competition, athletes are not allowed to wear hearing aids. A few changes have been made to use visual rather than auditory cues. For example, in team sports, a whistle is blown and a flag is waved to stop play. Strobe lights are used at the starting blocks for swimming events. In track, lighting systems placed 50 meters in front of the starting blocks and to the side of the track are used to signal the start of a race. The NCAA has also approved the use of lights at sporting events where there are Deaf athletes.

The sport skills of Deaf athletes span the range found in the hearing population, from unskilled to highly skilled. Deaf athletes are capable of competing as equals with hearing athletes, and some do so with significant success. For example, Tamika Catchings is a retired basketball star born with a hearing loss who completed 15 seasons in the WNBA, earning WBNA Finals MVP honors as well as the Reynolds Society Achievement Award. You can read more in her book *Catch a Star: Shining Through Adversity to Become a Champion* (Catchings & Petersen, 2016).

Even as far back as 1883, Deaf athletes were competing in professional sport in the United States. William "Dummy" Hoy was a Major League Baseball (MLB) player from 1888 to 1902 and set numerous records throughout his career. The huddle is also said to have been first used by the Gallaudet University Football team to prevent competing Deaf teams from eavesdropping on their plays.

Summary

This chapter reviews types of deafness, characteristics of Deaf individuals, strategies for teaching students who are Deaf or hard of hearing, issues related to cochlear implants, deafblindness, and Deaf sport. Children with sensory impairments are born with the same potential as their hearing and sighted peers. Early intervention and exposure to a variety of sports and physical activities increase fitness and skill level and help maintain a high quality of life. Physical educators are key to instilling movement confidence in students who are Deaf, hard of hearing (HOH), or deafblind.

References

American Speech-Language-Hearing Association. (n.d.). *Causes of hearing loss in children*. www.asha.org/public/hearing/causes-of-hearing-loss/

Arndt, K.L., Lieberman, L.J., & Pucci, G. (2004). Communication during physical activity for youth who are deafblind. *Teaching Exceptional Children Plus, 1*(2), Article 1.

Barboza, C.F.S., Campello, A.R., & Castro, H.C. (2015). Sports, physical education, Olympic games and Brazil: The Deafness that still should be listened. *Creative Education, 6,* 1386-1390. https://doi.org/10.4236/ce.2015.612138

Barboza, C.F.S., Ramos, A.S.L., Abreu, P.A., & Castro, H.C. (2019). Physical education: Adaptations and benefits for deaf students. *Creative Education, 10,* 714-725. https://doi.org/10.4236/ce.2019.104053

Berkowitz, M.C., & Jonas, J.A. (2014). *Deaf and hearing siblings in conversation*. McFarland & Company, Inc.

Brady, N.C., Bruce, S., Goldman, A., Erickson, K., Mineo, B., Ogletree, B.T., Paul, D., Romski, M., Sevcik, R., Siegel, E., Schoonover, J., Snell, M., Sylvester, L., & Wilkinson, K. (2016). Communication services and supports for individuals with severe disabilities: Guidance for assessment and intervention. *American Journal on Intellectual and Developmental Disabilities, 121*(2), 121-138. https://doi.org/10.1352/1944-7558-121.2.121

Catchings, T., & Petersen, K. (2016). *Catch a star: Shining through adversity to become a champion*. Baker Publishing Group.

Cavanaugh, L.K., Hilgenbrinck, L., & Lieberman, L.J. (2020). Physical gross motor assessment and placement in physical education of five students with CHARGE syndrome. *Palaestra, 34*(3).

Columna, L., & Lieberman, L. (Eds.). (2011). *Overcoming language barriers through physical education: Using sign language and Spanish to engage everyone!* Human Kinetics.

Dair, J., Ellis, M.K., & Lieberman, L.J. (2006). Prevalence of overweight among deaf children. *American Annals of the Deaf, 151*(3), 318-326. https://doi.org/10.1353/aad.2006.0034

Edwards, L., & Crocker, L. (2008). *Psychological processes of Deaf children with complex needs*. Jessica Kingsley Publishers.

Ellis, M.K. (2001). Influences of parents and school on sports participation and fitness levels of deaf children. *Palaestra, 17*(1), 44-49.

Ellis, M.K., & Lieberman, L.J. (2016). Deafness or hard of hearing. In M.E. Block (Ed.), *A teacher's guide to adapted physical education: Including students with disabilities in sport and recreation* (4th ed., pp. 217-230). Brookes.

Ellis, M.K., Lieberman, L.J., & Dummer, G.M. (2013). Parent influences on physical activity and physical fitness of deaf children. *Journal of Deaf Studies and Deaf Education, 19,* 270-281. https://doi.org/10.1093/deafed/ent033

Ellis, M.K., Lieberman, L.J., Fittipauldi-Wert, J., & Dummer, G. (2005). Passing rates of deaf children on health-related fitness: How do they measure up? *Palaestra, 21*(3), 36-43.

Engel-Yeger, B., & Hamed-Daher, S. (2013). Comparing participation in out of school activities between children with visual impairments, children with hearing impairments and typical peers. *Research in Developmental Disabilities, 34,* 3124-3132. https://doi.org/10.1016/j.ridd.2013.05.049

Food and Drug Administration (FDA). (2018). *Benefits and risks of cochlear implants*. www.fda.gov/MedicalDevices/ProductsandMedicalProcedures/ImplantsandProsthetics/CochlearImplants/ucm062843.htm

Fiorini, M.L.S., & Manzini, E.J. (2018). Strategies of physical education teachers to promote the participation of students with hearing impairment in classrooms. *Revista Brasileira de Educação Especial, 24,* 183-198. https://doi.org/10.1590/s1413-65382418000200003

Frydrych, L.A.K. (2012). Revisiting the concepts of arbitrariness and iconicity: Implications for the linguistic status of sign languages. *ReVEL, 10,* 282-294.

Granda, A., & Nuccio, J. (2018). *ProTactile principles*. Tactile Communications.

Graziadei, A. (1998). *Learning outcomes of deaf and hard of hearing students in mainstreamed physical education classes* [Unpublished doctoral dissertation]. University of Maryland, College Park.

Haegele, J., Hodge, S., & Filho, P. (2018). Brazilian physical education teachers' attitudes toward inclusion before and after participation in a professional development workshop. *European Physical Education Review, 24,* 21-38.

Haibach-Beach, P.S., Perreault, M, Lieberman, L., & Foster, E. (2019). Gross motor skill performance in children with CHARGE Syndrome: Research to practice. *Research in Developmental Disabilities, 91,* 103423. https://doi.org/10.1016/j.ridd.2019.05.002

Haibach-Beach, P., Perreault, M., Lieberman, L., & Foster, E. (2020). Independent walking and balance in children with CHARGE Syndrome. *British Journal of Visual Impairment.* https://doi.org/10.1177/0264619620946068

Hartman, E., Houwen, S., & Visscher, C. (2011). Motor skill performance and sports participation in deaf elementary school children. *Adapted Physical Activity Quarterly, 28,* 132-145. https://doi.org/10.1123/apaq.28.2.132

Hartman, E., Visscher, C., & Houwen, S. (2007). The effect of age on physical fitness of Deaf elementary school children. *Pediatric Exercise Science, 19,* 267-278. https://doi.org/10.1123/pes.19.3.267

Hersh, M. (2013). Deafblind people, communication, independence, and isolation. *Journal of Deaf Studies and Deaf Education, 18,* 446-463. https://doi.org/10.1093/deafed/ent022

Hilgenbrinck, L., Pyfer, J., & Castle, N. (2004). Students with cochlear implants: Teaching considerations for physical educators. *Journal of Physical Education, Recreation and Dance, 75*(4), 28-33.

Imel, G., Hartshorne, T.S., Slavin, L.J., & Kanouse, S.K. (2020). Participation in and barriers to recreation in CHARGE Syndrome. *Palaestra, 34,* 38-43.

Individuals with Disabilities Education Act Amendments of 2004 (IDEA) PL 108-446, 20 U.S.C. 1400 (2004).

Khairi, Z., Choon, L.D.K., Tan, A.R. (2014). Gross motor development of Malaysian hearing impaired male pre- and early school children. *International Education Studies,* 7(13), 242-252. https://doi.org/10.5539/ies.v7n13p242

Levesque, J., Theoret, H., & Champoux, F. (2014). Reduced procedural motor learning in deaf individuals. *Frontiers in Human Neuroscience, 8,* 1-6. https://doi.org/10.3389/fnhum.2014.00343

Li, C., Haegele, J.A., & Wu, L. (2018). Comparing physical activity and sedentary behavior levels between deaf and hearing adolescents. *Disability and Health Journal, 12,* 514-518. https//doi.org/10.1016/j.dhjo.2018.12.002

Lieberman, L.J., Arndt, K.L., & Daggett, S. (2007). Promoting leadership in physical education and recreation. *Journal of Physical Education, Recreation and Dance, 78,* 46-50.

Lieberman, L.J., Dunn, J.M., van der Mars, H., & McCubbin, J.A. (2000). Peer tutors' effects on activity levels of deaf students in inclusive elementary physical education. *Adapted Physical Activity Quarterly, 17*(1), 20-39. https://doi.org/10.1123/apaq.17.1.20

Lieberman, L.J., Grenier, M., Brian, A., & Arndt, K. (2020). *Universal design for learning in physical education.* Human Kinetics.

Lieberman, L.J., Haibach, P., & Schedlin, H. (2012). Physical education and children with CHARGE Syndrome: Research to practice. *Journal of Visual Impairment and Blindness, 106*(2), 106-119. https://doi.org/10.1177/0145482x1210600205

Lieberman, L.J., & Haegele, J.A. (2019). Teaching children who are deafblind in physical education, physical activity and recreation. In J. Ravenscroft (Ed.), *The Routledge handbook of visual impairment.* Routledge.

Lieberman, L.J., & Houston-Wilson, C. (2018). *Strategies for inclusion: A handbook for physical educators* (3rd ed.). Human Kinetics.

Lieberman, L.J., & MacVicar, J. (2003). Play and recreation habits of youth who are deaf-blind. *Journal of Visual Impairment and Blindness, 97*(12), 755-768. https://doi.org/10.1177/0145482x0309701203

Lieberman, L.J., & Pecorella, M. (2006). Activity at home for children and youth who are deafblind. *Deaf-Blind Perspectives, 14,* 3-7.

Lieberman, L.J., Ponchillia, P., & Ponchillia, S. (2013). *Physical education and sport for individuals who are visually impaired or deafblind: Foundations of instruction.* American Foundation of the Blind Press.

Lieberman, L.J., Volding, L., & Winnick, J.P. (2004). Comparing motor development of Deaf children of Deaf parents and hearing parents. *American Annals for the Deaf, 149*(3), 281-289. https://doi.org/10.1353/aad.2004.0027

Lirgg, C.D., Gorman, D.R., Merrie, M.D., & Shewmake, C. (2017). Exploring challenges in teaching physical education to students with disabilities. *Palaestra, 31,* 13-18

Lobenius-Palmer, K., Sjoqvist, B., Hurtig-Wennlof, A., & Lundqvist, L.O. (2018). Accelerometer-assessed physical activity and sedentary time in youth with disabilities. *Adapted Physical Activity Quarterly, 35,* 1-19. https://doi.org/10.1123/apaq.2015-0065

Majlesi, M., Farahpour, N., Azadian, E., & Amini, M. (2014). The effect of interventional proprioceptive training on static balance and gait in deaf children. *Research in Developmental Disabilities, 35,* 3562-3567. https://doi.org/10.1016/j.ridd.2014.09.001

Nemcek, D. (2017). Self-esteem analysis in people who are deaf or hard of hearing: A comparison between active and inactive individuals. *Physical Activity Review, 5,* 95-104. http://dx.doi.org/10.16926/par.2017.05.14

Padden, C., & Humphries, T. (1988). *Deaf in America: Voices from a culture.* Harvard University Press.

Reich, L. (2007a). *Accommodating the unique needs of individuals who are specifically hard of hearing during physical education, sport, and exercise training* [Thesis project dissertation]. California State University, Long Beach.

Reich, L. (2007b). *Hard of hearing or deaf vs. culturally deaf person: Who receives the services?* Retrieved October 2009 from www.lorireich.com/hoh/index_files/Page633.htm

Reich, L., & Lavay, B. (2009). Physical education and sport adaptations for students who are specifically hard of hearing. *Journal of Physical Education, Recreation and Dance, 80*(3), 1-60.

Schlumberger, E., Narbona, J., & Manrique, M. (2004). Non-verbal development of children with deafness with and without cochlear implants. *Developmental Medicine & Child Neurology, 45,* 599-606. https://doi.org/10.1017/s001216220400101x

Schultz, J., Lieberman, L.J., Ellis, M., & Hilgenbrinck, L.C. (2013). Ensuring success of Deaf students in inclusive physical education. *Journal of Physical Education, Recreation and Dance, 84,* 51-56.

Simon, K.D., & Koku, A.M. (2017). A comparative study of motor skill performance levels of students with hearing-impairment and students without hearing-impairment in Hohoe municipality. *International Journal of Physical Education, Sports and Health, 4*(6), 216-225.

Stough, C.O., Cordts, K.P., Delaney, M., & Davis, A. (2016). Overweight and obesity among children who are deaf: Quantitative and qualitative findings. *Children's Health Care, 45*(1), 109-125. http://doi.org/10.1080/02739615.2015.1038678

Tanure Alves, M.L., de Souza, J., Grenier, M., & Lieberman, L.J. (2021). The invisible student in physical education classes: voices from Deaf and hard of hearing students on inclusion. *International Journal of Inclusive Education*, DOI:10.1080/13603116.2021.1931718

Uchida, W., Marsh. H., & Hashimoto, K. (2015). Predictors and correlates of Deaf athletes. *European Journal of Adapted Physical Activity, 8*(1), 21-30.

U.S. Census Bureau. (2020). *Deaf history month.* Retrieved from www.census.gov/library/audio/profile-america/profileodd/profile-odd-15.html

Weiner, M., Day, S.J., & Galvin, D. (2013). Deaf and hard of hearing students' perspectives on bullying and school climate. *American Annals for the Deaf, 158*(3), 334-343.

Print Resources

Girma, H. (2019). *Haben: The Deafblind woman who conquered Harvard Law.* Twelve Hachette Book Group.

This is the story of a wonderful journey of Haben Girma, a deafblind woman who graduated from Harvard Law School.

Smith, T. (2002). *Guidelines: Practical tips for working and socializing with deafblind people.* Sign Media.

This resource offers a step-by-step guide to working and socializing with people who are deafblind.

Video Resources

Children With CHARGE Syndrome and Motor Skills: www.youtube.com/watch?v=UmI2j7Tl2YU

Eddie, a 15-year-old student with deafblindness, illustrates the importance of not placing limits on expectations by learning to ride the unicycle independently (see a video of the process at www.youtube.com/watch?v=lLYp4b_p_wg). Teaching students who are deafblind challenges physical educators to make appropriate adaptations to enable these students to learn.

Online Resources

American Academy of Audiology: www.audiology.org

As the world's largest professional organization of audiologists, the American Academy of Audiology provides the highest quality of hearing health care service to children and adults.

American Printing House for the Blind: www.aph.org/recreational-wins-for-people-with-deafblindess/

This URL offers an online book titled *Possibilities: Recreational Experiences of Individuals Who Are Deafblind.*

National Center on Deafblindness (NCDB): www.nationaldb.org

The NCDB is a national technical assistance and dissemination center for young people who are deafblind. Funded by the U.S. Department of Education's Office of Special Education Programs (OSEP). This is enough information here.

USA Deaf Sports Federation (USADSF): www.usdeafsports.org

The USA Deaf Sports Federation website provides information about USADSF competition, events, calendar, history of the organization, and news.

14

Cerebral Palsy, Traumatic Brain Injury, and Stroke

David L. Porretta and Justin A. Haegele

Eric Hacker ran in the track and cross-country state championships in his sophomore and junior years in high school, and he is hoping to continue competing in college. However, Eric did not start as a gifted runner. When Eric, who has cerebral palsy, began running in middle school, he wore lower leg braces. Following discussion with his parents and doctors, he eliminated his braces and hasn't worn them since middle school. Nonetheless, Eric needs to continually stretch his hip and leg muscles and work on improving his overall balance. With the help of physical education teachers, coaches, allied health professionals, and physicians, people like Eric can enjoy physical education and sport in settings that are safe and beneficial to health.

Cerebral palsy and other conditions that cause damage to the brain, such as traumatic brain injury (TBI) and stroke, are covered in this chapter. Although CP, TBI, and stroke have their own causes, damage to the brain can result in common motor, cognitive, and behavioral characteristics discussed in this chapter. People with CP, stroke, or TBI at one time were restricted from physical activity for fear that it would aggravate their conditions; however, they are now encouraged to participate in a wide range of physical activities because of the health benefits obtained. Physical education teachers and coaches need to be aware of the difficulties associated with these conditions and how they affect learning and performance in order to provide a successful learning experience.

Cerebral Palsy

Cerebral palsy (CP) refers to a group of permanent disabling symptoms resulting from damage to the motor control areas of the brain (the term *cerebral* refers to the brain and *palsy* to disordered movement or posture). It is a nonprogressive condition that might originate before, during, or shortly after birth, and it manifests itself in a loss or impairment of control over voluntary musculature. Depending on the location and the amount of damage to the brain, symptoms vary widely, ranging from severe (total inability to control bodily movements) to mild (only a slight speech impairment). Damage to the brain contributes to abnormal reflex development in most people with CP, resulting in difficulty coordinating and integrating basic movement patterns. It is rare for damage to be isolated to a small portion of the brain. For this reason, persons with CP may exhibit many other impairments, including seizures, speech and language disorders, sensory impairments (especially those involving visual–motor control), abnormal sensation and perception, and intellectual disability. Seizures are the most common co-occurring condition. People with CP also commonly exhibit secondary medical complications, such as impaired bone growth, joint abnormalities, respiratory conditions, and accelerated cardiovascular disease. Cerebral palsy is the most common motor disorder in children.

Cerebral palsy can result from a myriad of prenatal, natal, or postnatal causes. Some of the more common causes are rubella, Rh incompatibility, prematurity, birth trauma, anoxia, brain hemorrhages or tumors, and other forms of brain injury caused by accidents or abuse. Many medical professionals now believe that CP results from a number of factors rather than any single one. Of all children with CP, about 60 percent are born at term.

Incidence

According to the Cerebral Palsy Foundation (2020a), over 17 million people worldwide have CP. In the United States, there are over 500,000 children and adults who have the condition, including one in approximately 350 children. It is also more common in males than females. Data from eight European countries suggest that their figures are similar to those of the United States (Johnson, 2002).

Classifications

People with CP typically exhibit a variety of observable symptoms, depending on the degree and location of brain damage. Current classifications categorize CP according to **topographical** (anatomical site), **neuromotor** (medical), and **functional**. Of the three, the functional classification is the most recent and most commonly used by therapists and educators.

Topographical Classification

The topographical classification is based on the body segments affected and is typically used by the medical community. Classes include the following:

- Monoplegia: Any one body part involved
- Diplegia: Major involvement of both lower limbs and minor involvement of both upper limbs
- Hemiplegia: Involvement of one complete side of the body (arm and leg)
- Paraplegia: Involvement of both lower limbs only
- Triplegia: Any three limbs involved (a rare occurrence)
- Quadriplegia: Total body involvement (all four limbs, head, neck, and trunk)

Neuromotor Classification

The American Academy for Cerebral Palsy and Developmental Medicine (AACPDM) uses a neuromotor classification system to describe CP. This classification has undergone revisions over the years. Three main types of CP are commonly described: (1) spasticity, (2) dyskinesia, and (3) ataxia (Cerebral Palsy Foundation, 2020b). The characteristics described under each type might overlap; they are not as distinct as one might assume. The most common overlapping types are spastic and dyskinetic movements.

SPASTICITY **Spasticity**, the most common type of CP, results from damage to motor areas of the cerebrum and is characterized by increased muscle tone (hypertonicity), primarily of the flexors and internal rotators, which might lead to permanent contractures and bone deformities. Strong, exaggerated muscle contractions are common, and in some cases muscles continue to contract repetitively. Spasticity is associated with a hyperactive stretch reflex. The hyperactive reflex can be elicited, for example, when muscles of the anterior forearm (flexors) are quickly stretched in order to extend the wrist. When this happens, receptors that control tone in the stretched muscles overreact, causing the stretched muscles to contract. This results in inaccurate and jerky movement, with the wrist assuming a flexed position as opposed to an extended or middle position. If muscles of the upper limb are prone to spasticity, the shoulder will be adducted, the arm will be carried toward the midline of the body, and the forearm will be flexed and pronated. The wrist will be hyperflexed, and the hand will be fisted.

Lower limb involvement results in hip flexion, with the thigh pulling toward the midline, causing the leg to cross during ambulation. Lower limb involvement causes flexion at the knee joint because of tight hamstring muscles. Increased tone in both the gastrocnemius and soleus muscles, along with a shortened Achilles tendon, contributes to excessive plantar flexion of the foot. A scissoring gait characterized by flexion of the hip, knee, and ankle along with rotation of the leg toward the midline is exhibited (figure 14.1). With this narrow base of support, people with a scissoring gait typically have problems with balance and locomotor activities. Because of increased muscle contraction and limited range of motion, they might have difficulty running, jumping, and throwing. Intellectual disability, seizures, and perceptual disorders are more common among persons with spastic CP than in any other type.

FIGURE 14.1 Person exhibiting spastic cerebral palsy.

DYSKINESIA Damage to the basal ganglia (masses of gray matter composed of neurons deep within the cerebral hemispheres of the brain) results in an overflow of motor impulses to the muscles, a condition known as **dyskinesia**. This type is much less common than spasticity. Severe difficulty in head control is usually exhibited, with the head drawn back and positioned to one side. Facial grimacing, a protruding tongue, and trouble controlling salivation are common. The person has difficulty eating, drinking, and speaking. Three movement disorders are commonly exhibited and can exist together in different combinations in persons with dyskinetic CP. *Dystonia* is characterized by twisting and repetitive as well as unplanned and involuntary movements. *Athetosis* is characterized by slow, writhing movements with extreme fluctuations causing difficulty with posture. *Chorea* is characterized by abrupt, fidgety, and unpredictable movements that are uncoordinated and clumsy. Because lack of head control affects visual pursuit, people with dyskinesia might have difficulty tracking thrown balls or responding to quick movements made by others. They will have difficulty performing movements that require accuracy, such as throwing a ball to a target or kicking a moving ball. A lordotic standing posture in which the lumbar spine assumes an abnormal anterior curve is common. In compensation, the arms and shoulders are placed in a forward position.

ATAXIA Damage to the cerebellum, which normally regulates balance and muscle coordination (see figure 14.2), results in a condition known as **ataxia**. It is a rare form of CP that is usually not diagnosed until the child begins to show developmental delays. Muscles show abnormal degrees of hypotonicity, and the person is extremely

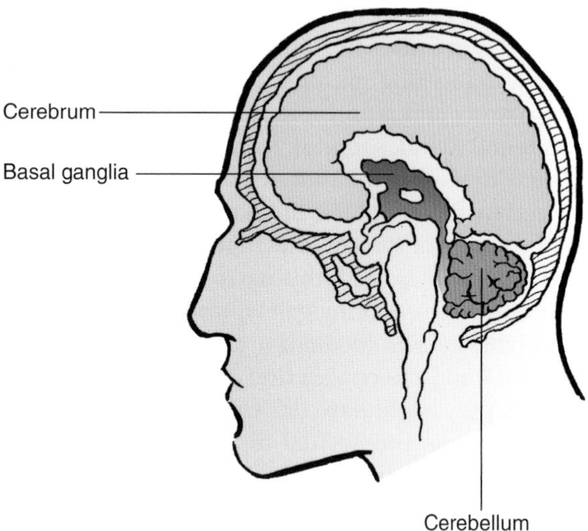

FIGURE 14.2 Areas of the brain involved in major neuromotor types of cerebral palsy.

unsteady because of balance difficulties and lack of coordination necessary for proper arm and leg movement when walking. A wide-based gait is typically exhibited. Visual depth perception is affected, and children have difficulty following objects with the eyes. People with mild forms of ataxia are often considered clumsy or awkward. They have difficulty with basic motor skills and patterns, especially locomotor activities such as running, jumping, and skipping.

Functional Classifications

A number of **functional classification** schemes are commonly used to categorize CP today. One example, developed by the CanChild Research Centre at McMaster University, is referred to as the Gross Motor Function Classification System Expanded and Revised (GMFCS—E&R) (see table 14.1). It is a five-level classification system designed for children aged 0 to 18, where level I describes the most amount of function and level V the least amount of function.

- Level I: Walks without limitations
- Level II: Walks with limitations
- Level III: Walks using handheld mobility device
- Level IV: Self-mobility with limitations, may use powered mobility
- Level V: Transported by others in manual wheelchair

For additional information on the GMFCS—E&R, readers can visit the Research Centre website (www.canchild.ca).

General Educational Considerations

Because CP is not a disease, most medical professionals agree that CP is not treated, but rather managed. Management is aimed at alleviating symptoms caused by damage to the brain and managing motor dysfunction to help the person achieve maximum growth and development. Managing motor dysfunction usually entails developing voluntary muscle control, emphasizing muscle relaxation, and increasing functional motor skills.

TABLE 14.1 Gross Motor Function Classification System Expanded and Revised (GMFCS—E&R) Levels and Age Brackets

Age brackets	Level I	Level II	Level III	Level IV	Level V
Ages 0-2	Can sit, crawl, pull to stand; hold onto or "cruise" long furniture; holds objects with both hands; can walk between 18 months and 2 years of age without assistance	Still requires use of hands for balance while sitting upright on floor; can crawl on hands and knees or move forward while lying on stomach	Needs continuous lower back support and assistance in order to sit up; able to roll and push forward while on stomach	Can control head and can roll back and forth independently; needs adult assistance to sit up because trunk control is lacking	Voluntary control of limbs is limited; assistance required for sitting up, rolling over, and holding head upright

Age brackets	Level I	Level II	Level III	Level IV	Level V
Ages 2-4	Can sit easily while holding objects in both hands without assistance; can walk as preferred method of mobility	Can move in and out of sitting position without assistance; prefers to crawl on hands and knees, cruise along furniture, and walk with a mobility device	Crawling generally preferred method of moving about; typically uses hands and knees to crawl; can sit up unsupported but will sit in "W" position with knees bent and rotated outward and legs facing backward; can pull to stand and cruise short distances; brief periods of walking can be done with walker with assistance needed for turning	Can sit up alone but needs to use hands for support to maintain position; needs adaptive equipment for sitting and standing; crawling is preferred method of moving about	Extremely limited mobility continues; needs assistance in all areas of movement; adaptive equipment cannot fully compensate for limitations, although wheelchair with extreme adaptations may be used
Ages 4-6	Can sit and stand without support; can sit on floor and get up without assistance; climbs stairs; beginning to run and jump	Can sit in a chair or on floor and use hands freely; can move to a stand without much need for stable object to hold or push; can walk for short distances without assistance; can climb stairs holding onto a railing; cannot run, jump, or skip	Can sit in chair but needs trunk support to use hands; can push to stand and climb stairs while holding onto something sturdy; requires assistance walking alone from adult or mobility device	Can walk short distances with walker but should be monitored because of balance and coordination issues; trunk support needed while sitting	No increase in function from previous level; assistance in all areas of mobility required

(continued)

TABLE 14.1 *(continued)*

Age brackets	Level I	Level II	Level III	Level IV	Level V
Ages 6-12	Can run, jump, climb stairs, and walk without any assistance; speed, balance, and coordination somewhat limited	Can walk indoors and outdoors with little or no assistance; still requires assistance for distances; running and jumping are minimal; needs help when carrying objects, climbing steps, and walking on floor or inclined surfaces	Able to walk indoors and outdoors with assistance of handheld device; can climb stairs using railings or adult assistance; cannot walk long distances and requires a wheelchair or physical transport by adult; needs seat belt support when seated	Mobility generally remains same as in previous age level; will need mobility devices such as a wheelchair when starting school	Mobility still extremely limited; power wheelchair may be used independently, or may still be dependent on others for movement and need extensive adaptations to maintain head and body alignment
Ages 12-18	Can walk on all surfaces both indoors and outdoors; can run and jump, but balance, speed and coordination still somewhat limited; can participate in any physical activity based on abilities	Can walk in most settings with mobility aids based on personal preferences; will likely need handheld mobility device for school or work and wheelchair for longer distances; can walk upstairs with a railing; adaptations may be needed for sport participation	Can walk upstairs with railing as long as assistance is provided; will need help with transfers and seat belt for support and balance while sitting; handheld device facilitates walking, but at school powered or self-propelled wheelchair is used	Self-propelled wheeled mobility required in most settings along with seating adaptations; help from adult(s) needed with transfers but will be able to support own weight to assist with standing transfer; adaptations and physical assistance needed for sport and other physical activities	Manual wheelchair with assistance required for mobility, although self-mobility may be attained with extensive adaptations for control and stable seating; maintaining head alignment and arm and leg movements difficult to control; may require mechanical lift for transfers along with physical assistance by one or two persons

Adapted in part from www.cerebralpalsyguidance.com/cerebral-palsy/gross-motor-classification-system/

In some instances, braces and orthotic devices are used to help prevent permanent contractures or to support affected muscle groups.

There are a number of treatments for cerebral palsy. The most common include the traditional therapies such as physical therapy, occupational therapy, and speech therapy. Additional treatments include, among others, oral medications to relax stiff muscles for mild CP or periodic Botox (Botulinum toxin) injections to reduce muscle spasms. A more invasive option is a surgical procedure known as selective dorsal rhizotomy (SDR), in which sensory fibers in the back (dorsal part) of the spinal column are cut, thus reducing the amount of sensory stimulation coming from the brain and therefore reducing the amount of muscle contraction or spasticity. In rare instances, brain surgery can be performed to alleviate extreme hypertonicity as well. Additional research advances such as new neuroimaging techniques, better understanding of the neurobiology of early central nervous system damage, and mechanisms of neural repair such as brain plasticity (recruiting other areas of the brain to perform functions that have been lost) are now being employed. Implantation of stem cells into selected areas of the brain is also now being studied for potential improved brain function.

Treatment emphasis should be directed toward performing and refining motor tasks through active self-control. Functional motor skills such as walking, running, and throwing should be developed and attained. Damiano (2004) suggests five aims when working with people with CP: (1) reducing musculoskeletal impairments to improve function and quality of life, (2) enabling children to function optimally given their existing impairments, (3) preventing or limiting development of secondary impairments, (4) altering the natural course of the disorder, and (5) promoting wellness and fitness over the life span.

Attention must also be given to the psychological and social development of people with CP. Because of the negative reactions that other people might have to their disability, students with CP might face isolation or ostracization. As a result, guidance from psychologists or professional counselors should be sought for both parents and children when emotional conflicts arise.

The primary concern should be for the total person. From an educational perspective, a team approach in which medical and educational personnel work together with the parents and, when appropriate, with the student is strongly recommended.

Traumatic Brain Injury

Traumatic brain injury (TBI) refers to an injury to the brain that might produce a diminished or altered state of consciousness and result in impairment of physical, cognitive, social, behavioral, and emotional functioning. Possible physical impairments include lack of coordination, difficulty planning and sequencing movements, muscle spasticity, headaches, speech disorders, paralysis, and seizures, as well as a variety of sensory impairments, including vision and hearing problems. Physical impairments often cause varying degrees of orthopedic involvement that require the use of crutches or wheelchairs. Even when people exhibit no loss of coordination, motor function deficits, or sensation, apraxia might be evident.

Cognitive impairments many times result in short- or long-term memory deficits, poor attention and concentration, altered perception, communication disorders in such skills as reading and writing, slowness in planning and sequencing, and poor judgment. Social, emotional, and behavioral impairments might include mood swings, lack of motivation, lowered self-esteem, self-centeredness, inability to self-monitor, difficulty with impulse control, perseveration, depression, sexual dysfunction, excessive laughing or crying, and difficulty relating to others. These impairments can range from mild to severe and vary greatly depending on the extent and location of damage to the brain and the success of the rehabilitation process. However, with immediate and ongoing therapy, impairments may decrease in severity. Because of the developmental nature of the central nervous system, children with TBI recover motor and verbal skills faster than adults. However, children's head injuries tend to be more diffuse than focal. A diffuse injury might affect the entire range of academic achievement and thus have significant educational implications for the child.

Traumatic brain injury is often referred to as the silent epidemic because impairments can occur even if no visible signs are present on or around the head. Traumatic brain injury can result from motor vehicle or sport and recreation accidents, child abuse, assaults and violence, and accidental falls. In addition, TBI can be caused by lack of oxygen (anoxia), cardiac arrest, or near drowning. Motor vehicle accidents, violence, and falls are the leading causes of TBI. For active-duty military personnel in war zones, blasts are the leading cause of TBI. As a subgroup, children are especially at risk for brain injury. Head injuries in children and adolescents are commonly caused by the following:

- Traffic accidents (e.g., pedestrian, passenger, cyclist)
- Falls from buildings, play equipment, or trees
- Injuries from objects (e.g., firearms)
- Child abuse
- Sport-related injuries
- Seizures and other causes of lost consciousness

With a greater number of children and adolescents participating in sport, the number of brain injuries is increasing. These injuries are most common in contact sports such as American football, soccer, basketball, lacrosse, and ice hockey. However, only a few first-time direct blows to the head result in severe head trauma. The majority of brain injuries in such sports result from repeated blows to the head that result in various degrees of concussion, or what some authorities term *mild traumatic brain injury* (Brain Injury Association of America, 2020). Repeated brain trauma can most likely result in a condition known as *chronic traumatic encephalopathy* (CTE), a progressive neurodegenerative condition characterized by a buildup of a protein in the brain. CTE is receiving increased attention as a result of being associated with contact sports such as American football.

Because TBI is so common, it is now identified as a separate condition in the Individuals with Disabilities Education Act (IDEA). Given the importance of TBI, Congress passed the Traumatic Brain Injury Program Reauthorization Act (PL 115-377) in 2018, authorizing the CDC to implement a National Concussion Surveillance System to accurately determine the number and causes of concussions each year.

Incidence

Traumatic brain injury is the leading killer and cause of disability in children and young adults in the United States. According to the Centers for Disease Control and Prevention (CDC, 2020b), about 2.8 million emergency department visits, hospitalizations, and deaths related to TBI occur annually in the United States. Of the 2.8 million, about 800,000 are children. It is estimated that 283,000 children visit emergency departments each year for a sports or recreation-related injury—and of these, over 20,000 are 5- to 18-year-olds who participate in American football programs. In the United States, TBI contributes to the death of nearly 57,000 people annually, including nearly 2,600 deaths of children, and results in more deaths than any other sport-related injury. Males are more likely than females to sustain a TBI.

Classification

There are two classifications of head injury: **open head injury** and **closed head injury**. An open head injury might result from an accident, gunshot wound, or blow to the head by an object, leading to a visible injury. A closed head injury might be caused by severe shaking, anoxia, and cranial hemorrhages, among other causes. If the head injury is closed, damage to the brain is usually diffuse, but if the head injury is open, damage is usually more limited. Traumatic brain injury can range from mild to severe. Severe brain injury is characterized by a prolonged state in which the person is unconscious (comatose) and several functional limitations remain following rehabilitation. An injury to the brain can be considered minor when no formal rehabilitation program is prescribed and the person is sent directly home from the hospital. However, minor brain injury should never be treated as unimportant.

The Rancho Los Amigos Scale describes eight levels of cognitive functioning and is typically used in the first few weeks or months following injury. These levels consist of the following:

Level 1, no response. Deep sleep or coma

Level 2, generalized response. Inconsistent and nonspecific response to stimuli

Level 3, localized response. Might follow simple commands in an inconsistent and delayed manner; vague awareness of self

Level 4, confused or agitated response. Severely decreased ability to process information; poor discrimination and attention span

Level 5, confused and inappropriate response. Consistent reaction to simple commands; highly distractible; in need of frequent redirection

Level 6, confused and appropriate response. Responses might be incorrect because of memory loss but are appropriate to the situation; retention of tasks relearned; inconsistently oriented

Level 7, automatic and appropriate. Oriented and appropriate behavior but lacks insight; poor judgment and problem solving; requires minimal supervision

Level 8, purposeful and appropriate. Ability to integrate recent and past events; requires no supervision once new activities are learned

This scale should not be used in the years following the injury as a gauge for improved function.

General Educational Considerations

Many people with TBI need an individualized rehabilitative program. People with severe injury typically need intense rehabilitation as soon as they are medically stable. An interdisciplinary team of medical professionals (e.g., physicians, nurses, speech and occupational therapists) provides such a therapy program, which usually lasts three to four months, depending on the injury. For people of school age, the rehabilitative program takes precedence over educational considerations.

Some people with severe injuries require extended therapy programs following long-term care. These programs might last from 6 to 12 months following injury and usually emphasize cognitive skills, speech therapy, activities of daily living, relearning of social skills, recreation therapy, and, when appropriate, prevocational and vocational training. Individualized educational programming continues in this environment. Only after patients have attained the maximum benefit of the rehabilitation programs will they reenter their local educational environment. According to Patrick and colleagues (2006), school and community reentry planning is critical to the child's recovery. They suggest that successful transitions from hospital to school consist of the following steps: involving special educators with the rehabilitation team, planning for short- and long-term support services, and continuing follow-up by rehabilitation professionals once the child has transitioned to school and community. A number of rehabilitation hospitals now employ school reentry programs that merge educational and medical services.

Educators play a key role in the rehabilitation and educational process. Because of the uniqueness of each injury, no one reentry program fits

Application Example

Developing a Transition Plan for a Student With a TBI

SETTING

High School Physical Education

STUDENT

Carlos is a 16-year-old male with TBI who now uses a wheelchair. Before his injury, Carlos enjoyed participating in interscholastic athletics. However, he has lost many of the sport skills he learned before his injury.

ISSUE

How to teach functional sport, recreation, and leisure skills so that Carlos can successfully maintain a healthy, active lifestyle during his high school years and through adulthood

APPLICATION

Skills and activities once deemed important in general secondary physical education might now need to be reevaluated relative to Carlos' functional needs. To determine the functional sport, recreation, and leisure skills and activities to be learned, the physical education teacher needs to do the following:

- Meet with the rest of Carlos' individualized education program (IEP) team
- Consult with therapists and other educators
- Talk with Carlos' parents about their hopes and expectations for him during high school and after graduation
- Consult with school officials to include Carlos to the maximum extent possible should he be interested in continuing participation in interscholastic athletics
- Seek Carlos' input about his interest in sport and leisure activities
- Identify, contact, and visit community resource centers (e.g., the local YMCA, recreation and adult fitness centers) that can provide services to Carlos after graduation
- Implement Carlos' physical education program in at least one site (when feasible) to aid him in the transitional process

every student with TBI. Rather, educators should recognize that each student presents unique cognitive, behavioral, and psychosocial challenges. Assessments should be functional, collaborative, and contextualized, and supports (e.g., teacher's aide) need to be systematically reduced when appropriate. Educators need to work closely with the student's family to ensure the best reentry program possible. Therefore, building effective parent–professional partnerships is essential.

Educators are encouraged to follow a transitional approach to functional skills. The development and implementation of transitional plans for high school students with TBI is of particular importance. Transitional skills related to physical education include recreation and leisure activities such as bowling, cycling, or swimming, as well as accessing community recreation facilities. For more detailed strategies for functional transitional planning, see Wehman and colleagues (2013). Regardless of the transitional outcomes agreed on, educators must plan appropriate school experiences and establish links with community and postschool resources (e.g., vocational or technical schools). See the Application Example sidebar on the previous page for more information.

Several instructional strategies pertinent to TBI are recommended for teachers and coaches. These include using frequent reminders regarding tasks to be completed, providing additional time for review, rewriting or reteaching complex directions in simple steps, using cooperative learning activities so that the student is not required to complete an entire task alone, having the student use a diary or datebook to help organize information, breaking up a task into distinct sequential parts so that they can be put together meaningfully at the end, and color coding materials for each class or activity. Ideally, multiple means of representation, a guiding principle of universal design for learning, will be provided, where students with TBI are offered a diverse variety (e.g., visual, verbal) of content delivery options.

Stroke

Stroke, or **cerebrovascular accident** (CVA), refers to damage to brain tissue resulting from faulty blood circulation. Cerebrovascular accident can result in serious damage to areas of the brain that control vital functions, including motor ability and control, sensation and perception, communication, emotions, and consciousness, among others. In certain cases, CVA results in death. People who survive CVA have varying degrees of disability, ranging from minimal loss of function to total dependency. Because of the nature of the cerebral arterial system, CVA commonly causes partial or total paralysis on either the left or the right side of the body. This might be one limb (monoplegia) or body segment or one entire side (hemiplegia). People with right-sided hemiplegia are likely to have problems with speech and language; they tend to be slow, cautious, and disorganized when approaching new or unfamiliar problems. People with left-sided hemiplegia are likely to have difficulty with spatial–perceptual tasks (e.g., ability to judge distance, size, position, rate of movement, form, and how parts relate to the whole) and tend to overestimate their abilities. This trait has significant safety implications for those performing in physical education, leisure, and sport settings, because the individual may attempt to do things they cannot do.

According to the American Stroke Association (2020), neonatal (birth through the first month of life) CVA is now an increasingly recognized condition. The peak age for CVA is the first year of life, in which one-third of all cases are reported. In such cases there might be no detectable neurological signs at onset. Rather, neurological signs might appear during the first year after CVA as motor skills develop, and those who survive typically have hemiparesis (partial paralysis to one entire side of the body). Children who have had CVAs tend to exhibit significant long-term disabilities, including cognitive and sensory impairments, CP, and epilepsy.

In adults, several factors contribute to the occurrence of CVA, including uncontrolled hypertension (high blood pressure), smoking, diabetes mellitus, diet, drug (such as heroin and cocaine) and alcohol abuse, and obesity, among others. Many of these risk factors can be controlled through lifestyle changes. The past few years have seen a substantial increase in knowledge regarding CVA and its treatment and prevention, especially regarding the promotion of healthful behaviors such as regular physical activity. As a result of better education and treatment, more people are living who otherwise might have died because of CVA.

Depending on the location of the damage, symptoms of CVA mirror those of CP and TBI. However, people with TBI and CVA can expect varying degrees of improvement following their injury, whereas those with CP cannot. People who have had CVA might exhibit cognitive or perceptual deficits, motor deficits, seizure disorders, and communication problems, which is why a collaborative approach to rehabilitation is necessary. Children show more improvement following brain trauma than do adults.

Incidence

Cerebrovascular accident is a leading cause of long-term disability not only in the United States, but globally as well. About 795,000 Americans experience CVA each year; of these, about 600,000 are first attacks and 185,000 are recurrent attacks (CDC, 2020a). Cerebrovascular accident is the second largest cause of death in the world, and the fifth leading cause of death in the United States, killing about 140,000 Americans per year. Recent statistics also indicate that more than half of all people experiencing their first CVA will survive, although only about 10 percent completely recover. Males have a higher incidence rate than females at younger ages, but not at older ages, and females generally account for about 60 percent of all CVA fatalities. African Americans are also more prone to CVA than Caucasians. Typically, CVA affects older segments of the population and is a common form of adult disability. Although cerebrovascular accident occurring in infants, children, and adolescents is relatively rare (occurring in about 1 out of every 3,500 live births), it is one of the top 10 causes of death for children between the ages of 1 and 19 (American Stroke Association, 2020), and about 30 percent of infants who experience CVA do not survive. Therefore, it has significant implications for educators.

Classification

Although there are many types, CVA can generally be divided into two categories: **hemorrhagic** and **ischemic**. Hemorrhage within the brain is a result of an artery that loses its elasticity and ruptures, resulting in blood flowing into and around brain tissue. This type of hemorrhage is commonly called *cerebral hemorrhage* and is the most serious form of CVA. Ischemia, the most common type of CVA, occurs when a blocked artery leading to or within the brain itself results in the lack of an appropriate blood supply to brain tissue. Typically, the blockage results from a progressive narrowing of the artery or from an embolism (a blood clot or piece of fat deposit that lodges in small arteries). An insufficient or absent blood supply means that oxygen, vital for brain functioning, is absent or diminished. This interruption might be permanent or brief. If the attack is very brief, it is a transient ischemic attack (TIA). About 10 percent of all CVAs are preceded by a TIA, which might occur days, weeks, or months before a major CVA. This type of ischemia results in full recovery but might indicate a future attack that is more severe. Aside from a TIA, when a person experiences a hemorrhagic or ischemic CVA, brain tissue dies, which results in long-term reduced brain function or death. In addition to medications designed to dissolve clots, medical treatment includes the insertion of a catheter into a leg artery and physically removing the clot.

General Educational Considerations

Although CVA may strike without warning, there may also be warning signs. Teachers coaches, and parents should be aware of common warning signs, including sudden weakness or numbness of the face or an arm and leg on one side of the body, sudden dimness or loss of vision in only one eye, sudden loss of speech or trouble understanding speech, sudden severe headache with no apparent cause, and unexplained dizziness, unsteadiness, or sudden falls, especially with any of the previous symptoms. Should any of these symptoms be exhibited, medical attention should be sought immediately. If a student showing one or more symptoms has heart or circulatory problems or has experienced a previous CVA or brain injury, consider the situation an emergency.

Immediately following CVA, survivors need to be placed on a planned, systematic, and individualized rehabilitation program. The intensity and duration of the rehabilitation program will depend on the degree of disability. Someone who exhibits weakness or paralysis in one limb and retains normal voluntary movement for the remainder of the body will need little in the form of therapy, whereas someone who exhibits complete paralysis of all four limbs will need intense, long-term therapy. From an educational standpoint, students will follow a school reentry program similar to that followed by students with TBI, as described in the previous section.

Program Implications

All people with CP, TBI, or CVA can benefit from physical education and sport activities. The type and degree of physical disability, motor educability, interest level, and overall educational goals determine the modifications and adaptations required. Taking these factors into account, an IEP can be planned and implemented.

General Guidelines

Several guidelines apply to programs for students with CP, TBI, or CVA. The guidelines that follow pertain to safety considerations, physical fitness, motor development, psychosocial development, and implications for sport.

Safety Considerations

All programs should be conducted in a safe, secure environment in which students are free to explore the capabilities of their own bodies and to interact with surroundings that nurture their physical and motor development. Teachers and coaches should closely monitor games and activities, especially for students who are prone to seizures or who lack good judgment (e.g., those with TBI). Many take antiseizure medication, and as a result, side effects (e.g., irritability, hyperactivity, slowed physiological responses to exercise) might affect the person's performance in physical education and sport.

Students with severe impairments need special equipment, such as crutches, bolsters (to support the upper body while in the prone position), standing platforms (to assist in maintaining a standing posture), orthotic devices, or seating systems, to help them perform certain motor tasks or in athletic events (figure 14.3). Most students with mild impairments require no specialized equipment. Because many people with physical disabilities have difficulty maintaining an erect posture for extended amounts of time, some activities are best done in a prone, supine, or seated position. Students with physical limitations should be encouraged to experience as many postures as possible not only in physical education classes but also throughout the school day. This is particularly important for those in wheelchairs. Finally, individuals who have balance and seizure problems should always wear headgear to protect against accidental falls.

Because of abnormal muscle tone and reduced range of motion, many people with neuromotor involvement have difficulty moving voluntarily. The teacher might need to assist by getting a student into and out of activity positions, physically supporting her during activity, or helping her perform a skill or exercise. The teacher might also need to position students by applying pressure to key points of the body, such as the head, neck, spine, shoulders, elbows, hips, pelvis, knees, or ankles. An example is applying both hands symmetrically to both elbows in order to reduce flexion at the elbow joints. However, these techniques should be performed only after instruction by a therapist or physician.

The ultimate aim of handling, positioning, and lifting people with CP is to encourage them to move as independently as possible. This is accomplished

Photo courtesy of Challenge Publications, Ltd./Palaestra Magazine.

FIGURE 14.3 Athletes with cerebral palsy using crutches to assist in running.

by gradually reducing the amount of support to key points of the body over time. When possible, teachers should consult with therapists in an effort to coordinate these procedures, especially for students possessing severe physical disabilities. Bower (2009) provides excellent information on appropriate ways to handle children with CP, especially during leisure and fitness activities. In addition, teachers should closely monitor the physical assistance that a student with a disability might receive from trained peers. Peer assistance should be discouraged if it poses a safety risk.

Because the conditions described in this chapter are of medical origin, it is important that physical educators and coaches consult medical professionals when establishing programs to meet unique needs. This is especially important for students with TBI or those receiving physical or occupational therapy, such as students with CP and CVA.

Physical Fitness

Appropriate levels of health-related physical fitness are necessary to assist people with disabilities in performing activities of daily living, recreation, and leisure activities, which in turn promote a healthy lifestyle. Although the health-related physical fitness needs of people with CP, TBI, or CVA are similar to the needs of people without disabilities, some aspects of fitness are particularly important. Reduced muscular strength, flexibility, and cardiorespiratory endurance are common in people with CP, TBI, or CVA and might lead to the inability to maintain balance, independently transfer or move one's body, perform activities of daily living, or participate in functional leisure activities.

Because restricted movement is common, it is vital that strength and flexibility be developed to the maximum extent possible. If unattended, weak musculature and limited range of motion will lead to permanent joint contractures, resulting in significant loss of movement capability. For example, people with more severe forms of spastic CP might have significant range of motion and flexibility needs. People who have experienced TBI or CVA might need to develop and sustain an adequate level of aerobic activity, especially if the trauma is recent. Whatever health-related profiles people with CP, TBI, or CVA exhibit, a personalized approach to enhancing health-related fitness is recommended.

The **Brockport Physical Fitness Test** (BPFT) (Winnick & Short, 2014) is the most current fitness assessment instrument used for youngsters with CP, TBI, or CVA and includes test items, modifications for disabilities, and criterion-referenced standards for achieving fitness. The test includes components of aerobic functioning, body composition, and musculoskeletal functioning (flexibility, muscular strength, and endurance) vital for achieving health-related physical fitness. Various test items may be selected within each of the three components, depending on the student's desired profile (e.g., Target Aerobic Movement Test, upper arm skinfold measures for body composition, modified Apley test for flexibility, seated push-ups for muscular strength and endurance). The BPFT uses a classification system that identifies the person's functional level in order to select specific test items. Detailed information regarding this test can be found in chapter 4.

As is true for anyone who has a low health-related fitness level, certain precautions might need to be taken as programs are established for students with CP, TBI, or CVA. It is especially important that the teacher be sensitive to the frequency, intensity, duration, and mode of exercises and activities. Fatigue might cause the person to become frustrated, which could adversely affect performance. The instructor should permit rest breaks and player substitutions when endurance-related activities such as soccer and basketball are offered. It might be beneficial for those with reduced fitness levels to perform exercises and activities more frequently but with less intensity and duration. Exercises and activities should be selected that the student finds enjoyable, which increases the likelihood that health-related fitness will be maintained over a lifetime.

Motor Development

Cerebral palsy, TBI, and CVA restrict the typical functional movement patterns essential to motor development. As a result, delays in motor control and development are common. People with CP typically exhibit motor delays because they have fewer opportunities to move, lack movement ability, or have difficulty controlling movements. People with varying degrees of TBI or CVA might have difficulty planning and performing movements because of damage to the motor control–related areas of the cerebrum.

Physical education programs should encourage the sequential development of fundamental motor patterns and skills essential for participation in games, sports, and leisure activities. Authentic assessment, which emphasizes the evaluation of functional skills, should be used in physical education programs. When attempting to enhance motor development, the physical educator should be concerned primarily with the manner in which a movement is performed rather than with its outcome. One means of enhancing motor development is the use of ecological task analysis (ETA), which accounts for task requirements, environmental contexts, and learner constraints (see chapter 7 for more on ETA). The goal of every physical education program should be to encourage students to achieve maximum motor control and development related to functional activities (e.g., recreation and daily living activities). Standardized motor development tests recommended for use with younger students include the Denver Developmental Screening Test and the Peabody Developmental Motor Scales (PDMS-2).

Psychosocial Development

Many people with CP, TBI, or CVA lack self-confidence, have low motivational levels, and exhibit problems with body image. An appropriately designed physical education program can provide successful movement experiences that motivate students and help them gain self-confidence, which is vital for emotional well-being. A positive self-image can be developed when the physical education teacher does not expect students to perform skills and activities perfectly—the teacher should promote the attitude that failing is a natural part of the learning process. It is far more important that the student perform the activity as independently as possible with a specified degree of competence. Physical activities perceived as fun rather than hard work can motivate students to perform to their maximum potential.

Implications for Sport

Physical education teachers are encouraged to integrate many of the activities described in the Adapted Sport section of this chapter into their programs. For example, the club throw, an official Paralympic track and field event, can be incorporated into a physical education program as a means of developing strength and a possible opportunity for sport competition. The athlete grasps the club (similar to a thin wooden bowling pin) and throws it in the air as far as possible. Other activity options, such as bowling, cycling, and boccia, make excellent lifelong leisure activities. Team games and sports might include volleyball, basketball, and soccer.

Individual and dual activities may include tennis, table tennis, archery, badminton, horseback riding, billiards, and track and field events. Winter activities, including ice hockey, ice skating, downhill and cross-country skiing, tobogganing, and sledding, are also popular in colder regions. All of these games and sports can be offered with a view toward future competition or leisure activity.

Disability-Specific Guidelines

The previous section describes general program guidelines applicable to CP, TBI, and CVA. However, there are also several guidelines specific to each condition. These guidelines focus chiefly on health-related physical fitness and motor ability.

Cerebral Palsy

According to Winnick and Short (2014), people with CP should be able to sustain moderate physical activity (aerobic functioning), have body composition consistent with positive health, and possess musculoskeletal function (muscular strength and endurance, flexibility) such that participation in a variety of sport and leisure activities is possible. Sustaining moderate physical activity (70 percent of maximum predicted heart rate) for 15 minutes represents the general aerobic standard for young people with CP and has positive implications for sport and leisure activities. General standards are also presented for body composition and musculoskeletal functioning.

Inappropriate reflexive behavior in people with CP contributes to reduced aerobic activity and imbalances in muscle functioning and flexibility throughout the body. Inappropriate reflexive behavior can also contribute to difficulties with motor coordination and equilibrium, which can compromise the ability to attain acceptable health-related fitness and to learn and perform certain motor skills, especially those needed to perform recreation and leisure activities. Because of either restricted or extraneous movements, a person with CP can exert more energy than a person without an impairment to accomplish the same task. The greater the motor deficit, the greater the reduction in work capacity. Maltais (2016) describes this as a downward cycle of *disuse syndrome*. In essence, when physical activity is difficult due to motor impairment, one fatigues easily and then physical activity becomes increasingly harder, thus resulting in an ever downward cycle of disuse.

When a child is receiving therapy for inappropriate reflexive behavior, it is important for the physical educator to work in conjunction with therapists to foster the facilitation of righting and equilibrium reactions. Although many physical education activities help in the development of righting and equilibrium reactions, others might elicit abnormal reflexes. Some of the more common reflexes affecting the performance of physical education and sport skills are the asymmetrical tonic neck reflex (ATNR), the symmetrical tonic neck reflex (STNR), the crossed extension reflex, and the positive supporting reflex. The ATNR can prevent the effective use of implements such as bats, rackets, and hockey sticks. Children exhibiting the ATNR typically jump asymmetrically and may roll to one side when performing a forward roll. When present, the STNR can affect the ability to perform scooter-board activities in the prone position or other activities requiring the chin to be tucked toward the chest (e.g., looking down to control a soccer ball or catch a ground ball). Children exhibiting the STNR can have difficulty swinging on a swing. Difficulty in kicking from a standing position can be affected by the crossed extension and positive supporting reflexes.

As students age, inappropriate reflexes are not inhibited even with therapy. Thus, professionals responsible for physical education programs must pursue attainment of functional skills, such as creeping, walking, running, and throwing, which are important to future skill development. Asking students with CP to repetitively perform activities that elicit unwanted reflexes will not aggravate their condition beyond age 7 or 8. The following sections address components of strength, flexibility, speed, motor coordination, and perceptual–motor disorders as they pertain to physical education and sport.

STRENGTH In addressing strength development, it is important to note that muscle tone imbalances between flexor and extensor muscle groups are common in people with CP. For those with spastic tendencies, flexor muscles might be disproportionately stronger than extensors. This being the case, one should not continue to develop the flexors; strength development should focus on the extensor muscles. The goal is to develop and maintain a balance between flexor and extensor muscles throughout the body. When muscular strength imbalances are present, handheld weights or flexible tubing is now commonly used so that the appropriate resistance can be applied to a particular body part or region.

Strength training does not increase spasticity. However, some people with CP might temporarily exhibit increased spasticity in the involved limb or segment of the body when a contralateral nonspastic limb is involved in a resistance exercise. It is now known that increased spasticity is a temporary phenomenon and that the increased spasticity should subside soon after the session. Strength building exercises may be performed at a moderate speed rather than a fast speed to reduce the spasticity. In any case, spastic muscles should not be subjected to workloads above 60 percent of maximum (DiRocco, 1999).

People with CP can benefit from rigorous strength training programs that include increases in walking speed, walking efficiency, and overall motor activity. Isokinetic resistance exercises are particularly useful for developing strength, because they provide constant tension through the full range of motion and help inhibit jerky movements that are extraneous and uncontrolled. Moving limbs in diagonal patterns (e.g., moving the entire arm across the body in a diagonal plane) encourages muscle groups to work in harmony. A variety of gross motor activities such as throwing, striking, and kicking can elicit such movements.

FLEXIBILITY Tight muscles in both the upper and lower limbs and the hip region contribute to reduced flexibility, especially for those with spastic CP. If left unattended, restricted range of motion leads to contractures and bone deformities. Thus, flexibility exercises and activities should be a regular part of physical education and sport programs. People with spastic CP benefit from an extended period (15 to 20 minutes) of static flexibility exercises (DiRocco, 1999), which should be done both before and after strength and endurance activities (Surburg, 1999). If a student is participating in a ballistic type of activity such as a club throw, ballistic stretching can be used, but static stretching should precede it. Stretching exercises for more severely affected body parts exhibiting spasticity should be done on a regular basis. When flexibility exercises are done, it is recommended that fewer repetitions and longer periods of stretching be performed. The instructor might want to begin a flexibility session by helping students relax target muscle groups.

When possible, students should perform stretching exercises with no assistance (active range of motion). Should the teacher or coach need to assist a student with spasticity in performing flexibility exercises (active–assistive range of motion), the hand should be placed on the extensor muscle, not the flexor (spastic) muscle. For students who cannot voluntarily move a body part because of severe spasticity or limited motor control, passive range of motion (movement performed entirely by the teacher or coach without assistance from the student) can be performed under general medical supervision.

SPEED Many persons with CP have difficulty with games and sport skills that include a speed component because quick movements tend to activate the stretch reflex. However, an appropriate program can permit those with CP to increase their movement speed. Speed development activities for those with CP differ little from those for persons without impairments except that such activities should be conducted more frequently for those with CP (daily activities are recommended). Students should be encouraged to perform movements as quickly as possible but in a controlled, accurate, and purposeful manner. Activities with a speed component include throwing and kicking for distance, running, and jumping. Initially, the student should concentrate on the pattern of the movement while gradually increasing the speed of execution. To develop arm and leg speed, one can throw or kick a ball gently to a target; gradually, the throw or kick can increase in speed.

MOTOR COORDINATION Varying degrees of incoordination (dyspraxia) are common in people with CP and contribute to delayed motor control and development. People with CP often have difficulty controlling balance and body coordination due to abnormal movements and posture. Those who are significantly uncoordinated might have problems ambulating independently or with mobility aids and might need to wear protective headgear. Because they frequently fall, they should be taught to fall in a protective manner. Obstacle courses, horseback riding, bicycling and tricycling, and balance beam and stability board activities can assist in controlling movements.

Difficulties with motor control notwithstanding, people with CP (as well as those with TBI and CVA) can learn to become more accurate in their performance. Because people with CP can have difficulty planning movements involving accuracy, they should be allowed sufficient time to plan the movement before executing it. The use of a weighted ball, bat, or other implement can help reduce exaggerated stretch reflexes, decreasing abnormal flailing or tremor movements and adding control. People with CP possessing deficiencies in motor control resulting from dyskinetic, tremor, or ataxic tendencies can be expected to throw or kick for better distance and to exhibit freer running patterns than people with CP who have limited range of motion because of spastic or rigid tendencies.

Loud noises and stressful situations tend to increase abnormal and extraneous movements, which make motor activities difficult to perform. People exhibiting spastic tendencies tend to relax more when encouraged to make slow, repetitive movements that have a purpose, whereas those with dyskinetic tendencies perform better when encouraged to relax before moving. Highly competitive situations that promote winning at all costs might increase abnormal movements and should therefore be introduced gradually. Relaxation techniques, which involve consciously reducing abnormal muscle tone and preparing for activity and competition, can be beneficial. Another way to help those with CP improve general motor control and coordination is **mental imagery,** in which the person constructs a mental picture of the skill or activity prior to performance to help integrate thoughts with actions.

In motor skill development, activities that help develop basic fundamental motor skills and patterns, such as walking, running, jumping, throwing, and catching, should be taught. Skills should be broken down into components and taught sequentially. This method is particularly useful for uncoordinated persons seeking to learn more complex motor skills. Because of the general lack of coordination, activities should initially focus on simple repetitive movements rather than on complicated ones requiring many directional changes.

PERCEPTUAL–MOTOR DISORDERS Perceptual–motor disorders also contribute to poor motor performance. Because of these disorders, many children with CP exhibit short attention spans and are easily distracted by objects and people in the immediate environment. Activities might need to be conducted in an environment as free from distractions as possible, especially during early skill development.

Visual perceptual–motor disorders are common and can adversely affect activities and events that involve spatial relations. These might include player positioning in team sports such as soccer, remaining in lanes during track events, and determining distances between objects such as boccia balls. Accuracy and aiming tasks, such as throwing, tossing, or kicking an object to a specified target, as well as with activities involving fine motor coordination, such as fishing or billiards, may be difficult to perform.

Traumatic Brain Injury and Stroke

Before their brain trauma, people with TBI once learned and performed physical education and sport skills in the same way as people without disabilities. Depending on the age at the time of trauma, some skills might have already been mastered (e.g., running, throwing, catching), whereas other skills might not yet have been acquired (e.g., specific sport skills). Although some people with TBI or CVA might fully recover the motor skills lost, others with more significant and permanent injury might never regain them. Learning motor skills requires varying amounts of cognition, depending on the level of difficulty. Skills once thought to be quite simple to learn require constant practice and planning by the person with TBI or CVA. For those with TBI and CVA to regain skills to their maximum potential, physical education and sport programs need to be individualized and offered regularly.

Because of the nature of the disability, students with TBI or CVA commonly exhibit weak muscles and balance difficulties. Thus, exercises and activities are necessary to regain functional balance, walking, manipulation, and strength. Inadequate balance hinders the performance of many physical education and sport activities. Readers interested in exercise testing and programming for people with CVA and head injury should consult the work of Macko (2016). The following sections address physical fitness and motor control as they pertain to physical education and sport.

PHYSICAL FITNESS Acquiring and maintaining an adequate level of health-related physical fitness is important. This is especially true for people with severe TBI and those who have been immobile for long periods of time after CVA. Their health-related fitness needs can be considered similar to those of people with CP. As such, people with TBI or CVA need to develop and sustain at least moderate levels of aerobic activity to maintain body composition consistent with good health, as well as musculoskeletal functioning sufficient to participate in sport and leisure activities. Thus, depending on individual need, the physical education program should allow for activities to develop and maintain these health-related components. The BPFT (Winnick & Short, 2014) highlights items and standards that can be used in the assessment of health-related fitness for people with disabilities. A personalized process might be used to design a test for students with TBI and CVA.

Many students with these conditions fatigue easily, especially as they begin their reentry into school. Thus, fitness exercises and activities should be introduced gradually, and sufficient rest should occur between activities, especially if physical education is near the end of the school day. For those who are immobilized for large amounts of time, aerobic activities should be preceded by progressive muscular strength and endurance activities.

The neurological deficits associated with head injury often affect the ability to move efficiently, requiring a significant amount of energy that would otherwise not be used. According to Macko (2016), fitness activities can improve brain function as well as cardiorespiratory endurance and muscle strength. Regular activity raises energy levels and allows locomotor activities (e.g., sport, leisure, activities of daily living) to be performed in a more efficient manner. Raising functional health-related fitness levels enhances the performance of activities of daily living (ADL), thus increasing the chance of living a more fulfilling and productive life.

Some who exhibit spasticity (similar to CP) should focus on relaxation and flexibility exercises, whereas those who exhibit partial paralysis need to maintain residual functioning through muscular strength and endurance exercises. Weight training and flexibility activities will not be new to the person recovering from TBI or CVA because physical and occupational therapy rehabilitation programs typically focus on these areas. In addition to describing a number of rehabilitation programs, Petrofsky and colleagues (2004) provide detailed information on flexibility and strength development.

Universal gym equipment is convenient and safe to use to develop strength and endurance. Except for the bench press, students can stay seated in wheelchairs if necessary (although getting out of the wheelchair is important and should be encouraged). Isokinetic equipment can also be beneficial for exercises performed without a wheelchair. Because muscle weakness on one side of the body might prevent the use of weight machines that require the use of both arms or legs at once, free weights should also be made available. If free weights are not available, stretch bands are an economical way to conduct resistance training.

Because people with more severe brain injury are more likely to be sedentary, aerobic activities, which develop cardiorespiratory endurance, should be performed regularly. These might take the form of low-impact aerobics for those who can ambulate or a recumbent bicycle for those with balance difficulties. Aerobic activities can be done from a sitting position for those using wheelchairs. Students who can perform activities from a standing position but who have limited endurance should have a stationary object available for rest or support as needed. Aquatic activities are especially good for developing physical fitness. People with TBI and CVA should participate in physical fitness programs that address all areas of fitness. The *Brockport Physical Fitness Training Guide* (Winnick & Short, 1999) includes additional exercise and activity suggestions for promoting health-related fitness.

MOTOR CONTROL Depending on the location and severity of injury, people with TBI or CVA can have difficulty planning, initiating, and controlling gross and fine motor movements and typically need to relearn movements and movement patterns they could easily perform before the injury. This has important implications for physical education and sport activities, especially when combinations of separate skills need to be linked together in succession. To assist in this process, more complex skills should be broken down into simpler subskills, which should be practiced sequentially. Because these students typically have problems processing information, allow enough time for them to plan movements before executing them.

As is true for people with CP, visual perception might also be affected in people with TBI or CVA. Thus, they might exhibit difficulty with activities involving spatial relationships and those requiring object control, such as catching, kicking, and striking. Of course, activities incorporating object control need to be individualized. Adolescents with TBI or CVA should be given choices about the type of sport and leisure activities they will learn in physical education classes to enhance interest and motivation. The adolescent may then acquire the needed sense of independence and self-control, contributing to a smooth transition from school to community.

Strategies for Inclusion

Unless otherwise decided by IEP team members, students with CP, TBI, or CVA should participate in general physical education classes. Students with mild to moderate degrees of impairment can safely and effectively participate in general physical education settings. Most students with CP, TBI, or CVA understand verbal and written directions as well as rules and strategies for games and sports. In certain cases, teachers might need to structure activities to suit participants' abilities. For example, students with CP affecting the lower limbs could play goalie in soccer or floor hockey and could pitch or play first base in softball. In addition, athletes with mild degrees of CP can easily compete on their interscholastic track and field team.

Universal design for learning (UDL) is a framework that can be used to proactively design goals, assessments, methods, and materials to enhance the learning of not only the individuals with disabilities described in this chapter, but of all students. More information on UDL can be found in chapters 2 and 7 as well as in the book *Universal Design for Learning in Physical Education* (Lieberman et al., 2021). Physical education teachers can use the tenets of UDL to include multiple means of engagement, multiple means of representation, and multiple means of expression to maximize learning for all students. In addition, providing appropriate inclusive environments using the UDL framework gives these students opportunities for enhancing social and emotional development.

Adapted Sport

At almost all ages, people with CP, TBI, or CVA have the opportunity to become involved in a number of summer and winter sports at local, regional, national, and international levels. Sports include archery, biathlon, boccia, cross-country skiing,

Photo courtesy of Challenge Publications, Ltd./Palaestra Magazine.

FIGURE 14.4 Athlete with cerebral palsy performing the distance kick, a CPISRA-sanctioned event.

curling, sled hockey, slalom, swimming, track and field (athletics), Frame Running (formerly known as RaceRunning), powerlifting, fencing, and soccer, among others. Today, BlazeSports America, a national organization created as a result of the 1996 Paralympics in Atlanta, assists local community sport and recreation programs in providing training and competitive sport opportunities for those with CP, TBI, or CVA, as well as other disabilities. Cerebral Palsy International Sports and Recreation Association (CPISRA) is an official partner of BlazeSports America.

Athletes are eligible to participate in international competition governed by CPISRA and the U.S. Paralympics as long as they meet classification standards and qualify for events. Athletes can participate in a number of competitions, culminating in the CPISRA World Championships (see figure 14.4). Qualifying athletes may also participate in the Paralympic Games.

Each competitive sport has its own specific functional classification. For example, CPISRA classifies athletes for the event of Frame Running, an event for those with high support needs. Internationally, two classes are recognized for Frame Running (more impaired and less impaired). Athletes are assessed by at least one trained medical classifier and one trained technical classifier approved by the governing body for that particular sport. The medical classifier assesses movement, coordination, and function, whereas the technical classifier assesses performance during training or competition for that particular sport.

In addition to each sport's functional classification, CPISRA (2021) supports the GMFCS—E&R system (see table 14.2). CPISRA matches the five levels of the GMFCS-E&R to the specific sports it offers. It is important to note, however, that the GMFCS-E&R and CPISRA sports matching is intended to act as a guide and does not replace formal classification systems.

Readers are referred to the CPISRA (www.cpisra.org) and the IPC (www.paralympic.org) websites for a complete list of sports as well as their descriptions. The BlazeSports America website (www.blazesports.org) can also be accessed for a list of local and regional sport programs.

TABLE 14.2 CPISRA- and Paralympics-Sanctioned Sports for Athletes With CP, TBI, and CVA

Sport	CPISRA	Paralympics
Alpine skiing	✔	✔
Archery		✔
Biathlon		✔
Boccia	✔	✔
Canoe		✔
Cross-country skiing	✔	✔
Curling	✔	✔
Cycling		✔
Equestrian		✔
Fencing		✔
Frame Running	✔	
Powerlifting		✔
Rowing		✔
Sailing		✔
Shooting		✔
Slalom	✔	
Sled hockey	✔	✔
Soccer (seven-a-side)	✔	✔
Swimming		✔
Table cricket	✔	
Table tennis		✔
Track and field	✔	✔

Summary

This chapter described the conditions of CP, TBI, and CVA as they relate to physical education and sport. In addition, physical and motor needs were described and suggestions for programs and activities were presented. Because of the medical nature of these conditions, teachers and coaches are encouraged to plan activities with the input of physicians and allied health professionals.

References

American Stroke Association. (2020). *Knowing no bounds: Stroke in infants, children and youth*. www.strokeassociation.org/idc/groups/heart-public/@wcm/@adv/documents/downloadable/ucm_302255.pdf

Bower, E. (Ed.). (2009). *Finnie's handling the young child with cerebral palsy at home* (4th ed.). Butterworth-Heinemann.

Brain Injury Association of America. (2020). *Injury severity*. Retrieved February 15, 2020, from www.biausa.org/brain-injury/about-brain-injury/basics/injury-severity

Centers for Disease Control and Prevention (CDC). (2020a). *Stroke fact sheet*. Retrieved February 15, 2020, from www.cdc.gov/dhdsp/data_statistics/fact_sheets/fs_stroke.htm

Centers for Disease Control and Prevention (CDC). (2020b). *TBI: Get the facts*. Retrieved from www.cdc.gov/traumaticbraininjury/get_the_facts.html

Cerebral Palsy Foundation. (2020a). *Key facts*. Retrieved June 1, 2021, from www.yourcpf.org/statistics/

Cerebral Palsy Foundation. (2020b). *Types of CP*. Retrieved March 1, 2020, from www.yourcpf.org/types-of-cp/

Cerebral Palsy International Sport and Recreation Association (2021). What sports can I do? Retrieved June 3, 2021, from www.cpisra.org/athletics/

Damiano, D. (2004). Physiotherapy management in cerebral palsy: Moving beyond philosophies. In D. Scrutton, D. Damiano, & M. Mayston (Eds.), *Management of the motor disorders of children with cerebral palsy* (2nd ed., pp. 161-169). MacKeith Press.

DiRocco, P.J. (1999). Muscular strength and endurance. In J.P. Winnick & F.X. Short (Eds.), *The Brockport physical fitness training guide* (pp. 39-73). Human Kinetics.

Johnson, A. (2002). Prevalence and characteristics of children with cerebral palsy in Europe. *Developmental Medicine & Child Neurology, 45,* 633-640. http://doi.org/10.1017/s0012162201002675

Lieberman, L., Grenier, M., Brian, A., & Arndt, K. (2021). *Universal design for learning in physical education*. Human Kinetics.

Macko, R. (2016). Stroke, brain trauma, and spinal cord injuries. In G.E. Moore, J.L. Durstine, & P.L. Painter (Eds.), *ACSM's exercise management for persons with chronic diseases and disabilities* (4th ed., pp. 237-248). Human Kinetics.

Maltais, D. (2016). Cerebral palsy. In G.E. Moore, J.L. Durstine, & P.L. Painter (Eds.), *ACSM's exercise management for persons with chronic diseases and disabilities* (4th ed., pp. 259-266). Human Kinetics.

Patrick, P., Patrick, S., & Duncan, E. (2006). Neuropsychological recovery in children and adolescents following traumatic brain injury. In J. Leon-Carrion, K. von Wild, & G. Zitnay (Eds.), *Brain injury treatment: Theories and practices* (pp. 401-440). Taylor & Francis.

Petrofsky, J., Petrofsky, A., & Bweir, S. (2004). Stroke: Present therapy and treatment, part 2. *Palaestra, 20*(3), 35-43.

Surburg, P.R. (1999). Flexibility/range of motion. In J.P. Winnick & F.X. Short (Eds.), *The Brockport physical fitness training guide* (pp. 75-119). Human Kinetics.

Wehman, P., West, M., Targett, P., & Dillard, C. (2013). Applications for youth with traumatic brain injury and other health impairments. In P. Wehman (Ed.), *Life beyond the classroom: Transition strategies for young people with disabilities* (5th ed., pp. 473-499). Brookes.

Winnick, J.P., & Short, F.X. (Eds.). (1999). *The Brockport physical fitness training guide*. Human Kinetics.

Winnick, J.P., & Short, F.X. (2014). *The Brockport physical fitness test manual* (2nd ed.). Human Kinetics.

Print Resources

Martin, S. (2006). *Teaching motor skills to children with cerebral palsy and similar movement disorders: A guide for parents and professionals*. Woodbine House.

This book is designed to help parents (as well as professionals without a movement background) teach fundamental motor skills through various exercises and activities that can be conducted in the home or other nontherapy settings. The book has a number of excellent illustrations to show how to teach the various movements.

Verschuren, O., Darrah, J., Novak, I., Ketelaar, M., & Wiart, L. (2014). Health-enhancing physical activity in children with cerebral palsy: More of the same is not enough. *Physical Therapy, 92,* 297-303. https://doi.org/10.2522/ptj.20130214

This article provides a summary of evidence related to physical activity in children and adolescents with CP and provides research directions to enhance knowledge and understanding in this area.

Video Resources

Thomas, M. (2012, January 13). *Anybody can do anything* [Video]. http://journal.crossfit.com/2012/01/maddy cerebralpalsy.tpl

This 10-minute video features Maddy, a high school student with CP who participates in an integrated CrossFit program at her school.

University of Oregon School of Journalism. (2018, January 17). *Justin Gallegos: Stronger every mile* [Video]. YouTube. www.youtube.com/watch?v=Mp5SPZyeyps

This 12-minute video highlights the story of Justin Gallegos, an athlete with CP, and his cross-country running experiences from high school to college.

Online Resources

Brain Injury Association of America: www.biausa.org

The Brain Injury Association of America is the national clearinghouse for information related to brain injury. The organization promotes awareness, understanding, and prevention of brain injury through education, advocacy, and research.

HitCheck (app for iOS): https://apps.apple.com/us/app/hitcheck-concussion-test/id1061769052

App uses latest science to measure brain function impacted by concussions in 5-10 minutes. It helps trainers, physicians, coaches, and teachers track brain health over time. App is free.

15

Amputations, Dwarfism, and Les Autres

Justin A. Haegele and David L. Porretta

After completing his four-year collegiate football career as a linebacker for Central Florida University, Shaquem Griffin was among the 336 players to be invited to participate in the 2018 NFL combine. His performance was impressive, including a 4.38 second 40-yard dash, better than any linebacker in the previous 10 years. His performance during his collegiate career and at the combine contributed to him being selected by the Seattle Seahawks in the fifth round of the 2018 NFL draft. Griffin is also the only NFL player with one hand, having lost his left hand at the age of four due to a rare congenital condition known as amniotic band syndrome (ABS), in which strands of the amniotic sac separate and entangle digits, limbs or other fetal parts. Griffin uses a variety of modifications and adaptations to equipment, such as a prosthetic hand to grip a barbell while bench pressing, to succeed on the football field.

People with amputations, dwarfism, and les autres (a French term meaning "the others") impairments were at one time restricted from physical activity for fear that it would aggravate their conditions. Today, they are encouraged to participate in many physical education and sport activities, and they are now approaching many of the national records set by athletes without disabilities. An overview of amputations, dwarfism, and les autres impairments within a physical education and sport context is presented in this chapter, including specific information relating to program and activity perspectives.

Amputations

Amputations are the loss of an entire limb or a limb segment and are categorized as either acquired or congenital. Acquired amputations can result from diabetes, tumor, or trauma, whereas congenital amputations result from failure of the fetus to properly develop during the first three months of gestation. Generally, there are two types of congenital deformities. In one type, a middle segment of a limb is absent, but the proximal and distal portions are intact; this is known as **phocomelia**. In phocomelia, the hand or foot is attached directly to the shoulder or hip without the remaining anatomical structures present. The second type of deficiency is similar to surgical amputation, in which no normal structures, such as hands or fingers, are present below the missing segment. In many cases, however, fingerlike buds are present; this deficiency is usually below the elbow and is unilateral. In most cases, the cause of partial and total congenital limb absence is unknown.

Incidence

It is estimated that approximately 2 million people in the United States are amputees (National Limb Loss Information Center, 2020), with about 185,000 amputations occurring annually. Across all age groups, the leading cause of limb loss is some form of cancer or vascular disease, with below-the-knee amputations being most common. The second leading cause of limb loss is trauma. Over two-thirds of trauma-related amputations involve the upper limb. Congenital limb loss accounts for about 60 percent of all amputations in children.

Classification

Amputations can be classified either according to the site and level of limb absence, or from a **functional** point of view. Sites and levels generally consist of above the knee (AK), below the knee (BK), above the elbow (AE), and below the elbow (BE). In addition, the limb absence can be unilateral (one side), bilateral (both sides) or some combination of both (e.g., bilateral BK and unilateral AE). Functional classifications, on the other hand, are used by sport organizations like the International Paralympic Committee (IPC) for competitive purposes. Generally, those with lower limb amputations compete against each other and those with upper limb amputations compete against each other, although each sport has its own specific classifications. More information regarding functional classifications and sport competition is presented in the Adapted Sport section later in the chapter.

General Educational Considerations

In nearly all cases, a **prosthetic device** is prescribed for the amputee by a team of medical specialists. The prosthetic device is designed to compensate, as much as possible, for the functional loss of the limb and is fit according to the size of the person and the area and extent of limb absence. It is important that lower limb prostheses be fit properly because if they are not, amputees are at risk for secondary conditions such as osteoarthritis, osteoporosis, and back pain. Most experts recommend introducing a prosthetic device as soon as possible following the loss of the limb because the device tends to be more easily incorporated into the person's normal body actions the earlier it is introduced. Learning to use a prosthetic takes time and effort, and some people with more extensive lower limb amputations need training with canes or crutches. However, children with limb deficiencies tend to adapt better than adults to prostheses. Special consideration within the educational environment is needed for students with prosthetic devices. For example, classroom teachers can assist therapists in helping students acquire and maintain important fine motor skills (e.g., cutting, pasting, drawing), whereas physical education teachers can assist with important gross motor skills (e.g., catching, throwing, handling implements such as bats and rackets).

With recent technology, amputees can be fit individually with the assistance of computer-generated designs and advanced prosthetic devices are now commonly seen in educational and sport settings. New types of lower limb prosthetics, made of carbon fiber, can store and release energy, simulating the function of a normal foot. They respond smoothly, gradually, and proportionally to pressure applied by the user. As such, many athletes with both BK and AK amputations use these prostheses for competitive purposes in sports such as soccer, basketball, American football, and sprint and distance running (figure 15.1). Cosmetic prosthetic covers are also available that simulate the form and look of the natural foot. Of course, the use of these cosmetic devices is a personal choice.

People with limb deficiencies often have additional educational needs in the psychosocial domain. Many feel shame, inferiority, and anxiety when in social and educational settings—feelings that might result from stares or comments from their peers. Counseling by a psychologist or professional therapist might be necessary to promote healthy emotional functioning. Cosmetic covers might also be of help, especially if students are self-conscious about their prosthetic devices. To address the social stigma associated with limb loss, the Amputee Coalition of America has created a school-based curriculum titled the Limb Loss Education and Awareness Program (LLEAP). Through multisensory activities, children are taught to recognize and appreciate differences in themselves and others. The Amputee Coalition of America also sponsors Kicking for Kids Who Can't (KFKWC), an annual fundraising event to raise awareness about children with limb loss and to support sending kids to its summer youth camp, the Paddy Rossbach Youth Camp.

Dwarfism

Dwarfism is an umbrella term that describes several hundred conditions resulting in short stature that often have associated hormonal, intrauterine,

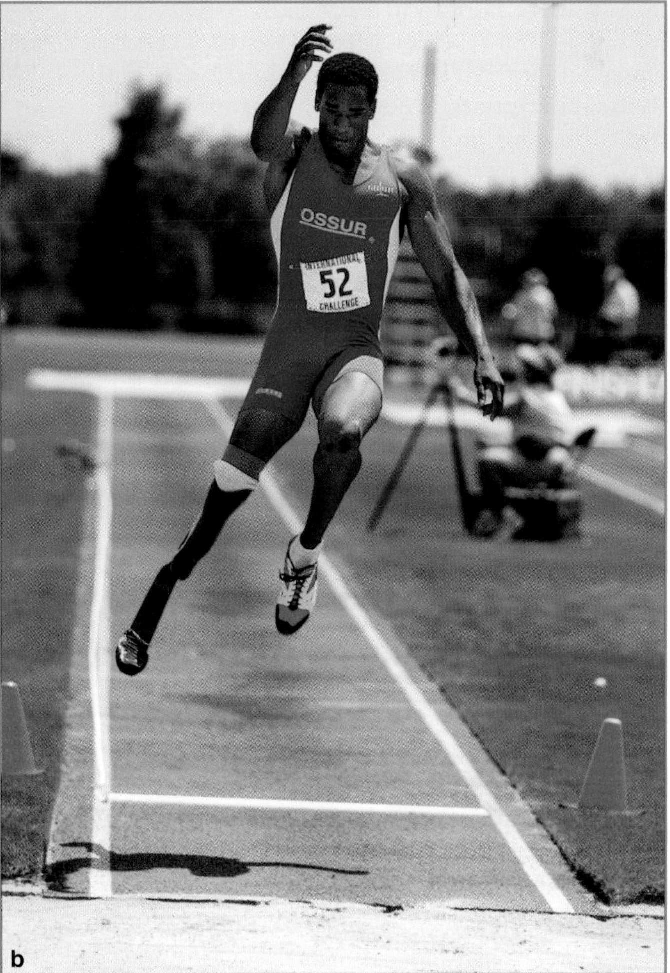

Images courtesy of Ossur, Inc.

FIGURE 15.1 *(a)* Kelly Bruno and *(b)* Roderick Green, two elite athletes performing with state-of-the-art prosthetic devices.

nutritional, and psychosocial differences (Adelson, 2005). The largest organization developed for people of short stature, Little People of America (LPA, 2020), defines dwarfism as an adult height of 4 feet 10 inches or under that is a result of a medical or genetic condition. When compared with the general population, people with dwarfism are shorter than 98 percent of all other people. Generally, dwarfism results from either the failure of cartilage to form into bone as the person grows or from a pituitary irregularity. According to LPA, terms such as *dwarf*, *little person*, *LP*, or *person of short stature* are acceptable when describing individuals with dwarfism—however, most people would rather be referred to by their name than by a label.

Incidence and Classification

One in about every 200,000 people is affected by dwarfism. More than 80 percent of people with dwarfism are born to average-sized parents with no family history of dwarfism. Dwarfism can be classified into two categories: **proportionate** and **disproportionate**. People with proportionate dwarfism have proportionate body parts but are very short. This type of dwarfism results from a deficiency in the pituitary gland, which regulates growth.

Disproportionate dwarfism, on the other hand, is characterized by short arms and legs with a normal torso and a large head. This type of dwarfism, which is the most prevalent, can be caused by a faulty gene that results in failure of the bones to fully develop. **Achondroplasia,** the absence of normal cartilage formation and growth, is the most common type of disproportionate dwarfism and accounts for about 70 percent of all cases of dwarfism (LPA, 2020). This type of dwarfism can manifest itself in a waddling gait, lordosis, limited range of motion, and bowed legs. Additional anatomical features include a large head and flattened face. Many people with achondroplasia are overweight or obese. Because of the abnormal stature, additional weight is carried in the buttocks, hips, and legs. The average height of an adult with achondroplasia is about 4 feet (122 centimeters). In more severe cases in which spinal involvement and additional bone deformities are present, people with achondroplasia might require ambulation devices such as crutches. Lumbosacral spinal stenosis, a structural abnormality of the spine in which the canal that houses the spinal cord is too small, can also occur, causing muscle weakness, pain, and loss of sensation. In severe cases, spinal surgery can alleviate the condition.

Some people with dwarfism who do not have achondroplasia might have cervical vertebrae abnormalities, similar to atlantoaxial instability seen in those with Down syndrome, which might lead to serious neck injury. Thus, the Dwarf Athletic Association of America (DAAA) requires a medical screening for all nonachondroplasic athletes before participation in running, jumping, or swimming events.

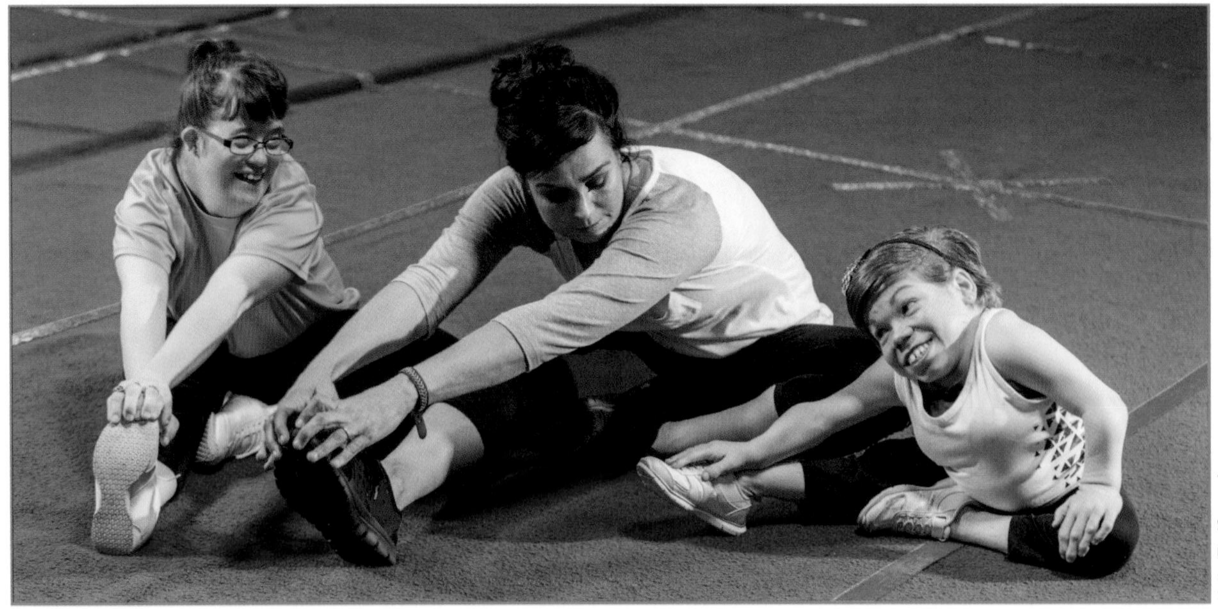

In general, a physical education program for people with dwarfism should follow the same guidelines as a program developed for people without disabilities.

General Educational Considerations

In general, a physical education program for people with dwarfism should follow the same guidelines as a program developed for people without disabilities. Students with dwarfism do not function any differently from students without dwarfism with regard to cognitive ability and academic achievement. Because of the psychosocial implications for children with dwarfism (Adelson, 2005), these students should have the opportunity to develop a positive self-image in a psychologically safe educational environment. Many times, students with obvious physical differences and limitations are subject to ridicule. It is the responsibility of the teacher to maintain an environment that encourages positive interactions and social contact among all students.

Physical education teachers and coaches need to be aware of certain factors associated with physical education and sport activities for people with dwarfism. Because delayed motor milestones and otitis media are common in children with achondroplasia, elementary physical education programs should focus on the attainment of fundamental motor skills and patterns before the performance of more advanced activities. In addition, because of limited stature and disproportionate body segments, people with dwarfism might have a disadvantage in certain activities, such as track and field, tennis, baseball, softball, and basketball. From a safety perspective, because of joint defects, certain activities that place stress on joints (e.g., gymnastics, acrobatics, contact sports) should be modified.

Les Autres

The term *les autres* is used in this chapter as a categorization for several disabilities. These include muscular dystrophy, juvenile idiopathic arthritis, osteogenesis imperfecta, arthrogryposis, multiple sclerosis, Friedreich's ataxia, myasthenia gravis, and Guillain-Barré syndrome.

Muscular Dystrophy

Muscular dystrophy is a group of inherited diseases characterized by progressive, diffuse weakness of various muscle groups. Muscle cells within the belly of the muscle degenerate and are replaced by adipose and connective tissue. The dystrophy itself is not fatal, but secondary complications of muscle weakness predispose the person to potentially fatal respiratory disorders and heart problems. Disease symptoms might appear any time between birth and middle age, but most cases affect children and young people.

There are various types of muscular dystrophy, including the myotonic, facioscapulohumeral, limb–girdle, and Duchenne types. **Myotonic muscular dystrophy**, or Steinert's disease, manifests itself through muscle weakness and affects the central nervous system, heart, eyes, and endocrine glands. It is a slowly progressing disease generally occurring between the ages of 20 and 40. Congenital myotonic dystrophy is rare, occurring almost exclusively in infants of mothers with the adult form. With appropriate care, their condition often improves; however, delayed motor development and intellectual disabilities in late infancy and early childhood are common. **Facioscapulohumeral muscular dystrophy** initially affects muscles of the shoulders and face and, in some instances, the hip and thigh. Facioscapulohumeral dystrophy manifests itself during adolescence or adulthood; life expectancy is usually normal because this type of dystrophy may arrest itself at any time. In **limb–girdle muscular dystrophy**, degeneration might begin in either the shoulder or the hip girdle, with eventual involvement of both. Unlike the facioscapulohumeral type, degeneration continues at a slow rate. The limb–girdle type might be exhibited at any time from late childhood on, though it usually occurs during the teenage years. Males and females are equally affected by both facioscapulohumeral and limb–girdle dystrophy.

Duchenne muscular dystrophy (DMD) is the most common and severe childhood form of the disease. It affects boys more often and more severely than girls, and symptoms can occur as early as three years of age. The Duchenne type is commonly referred to as **pseudohypertrophic muscular dystrophy**. A pseudohypertrophic appearance, especially of the calf and forearm muscles, results from an excessive accumulation of adipose and connective tissues within the interstitial spaces between degenerated muscle cells. Duchenne muscular dystrophy manifests itself in atrophy and weakness of the thigh, hip, back, shoulder girdle, and respiratory muscles. The lower leg becomes extremely weak, resulting in a drop foot, meaning that the foot remains angled downward, making the person prone to falling. Steady and rapid progression of the disease usually leads to the inability to walk within 10 years of onset. The child exhibits characteristics that include a waddling gait, difficulty climbing stairs, a tendency to fall, and difficulty rising from a recumbent position. An almost identical form of DMD is called

Becker muscular dystrophy; however, it is much less severe, and onset is typically between 2 and 16 years of age. Often, Becker muscular dystrophy is not diagnosed until an adolescent or young adult cannot fully participate in physical education or recreational activities.

Those with DMD frequently develop **lordosis** from weakness of the trunk musculature (figure 15.2). As the disease progresses, the child eventually needs to use orthopedic devices (e.g., leg braces, walker) in order to continue walking. However, even with these devices and continued physical therapy, the child is likely to eventually use a wheelchair and grow obese. Stiff joints (contractures) might form at the ankle, knee, and hip, and muscle atrophy is extensive. Soon after the child begins using a wheelchair, scoliosis (lateral curvature of the spine) also develops. Although weakness of the arms is present in the early stages of the disease, it is unlikely to cause real problems until the person begins using a wheelchair. At that time, progressive loss of strength in these muscles continues until it becomes impossible to lift objects or even lift the hands to the mouth.

Survival into the third decade of life is becoming more common in those with DMD. With continued research, a cure might be forthcoming. However, at present, no treatment exists to stop muscle atrophy; any treatment given is for relief of symptoms only. A major treatment goal is to maintain ambulation as long as possible through daily exercise and activity.

Cognitive difficulties are present in about one-third of boys with DMD, but others may exhibit above-average intelligence. Sometimes slowness of movement and limitations in physical abilities are misinterpreted as cognitive difficulties. Should a child have cognitive difficulties, these are stable and do not worsen as the disease progresses.

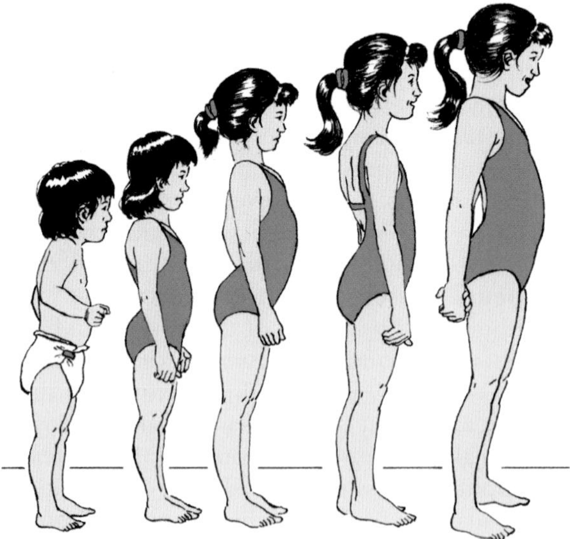

FIGURE 15.2 The developmental posture sequence of a child with DMD. Notice the increased lordosis as the child gets older.

Physical education can play an important role in managing muscular dystrophy, especially when exercises and activities are performed during the initial stage of the disease. Regular muscular strength and endurance activities can have a positive effect on muscular development and help counteract muscular atrophy. Particular attention should be given to the development of the lower leg, hip, abdomen, and thigh because muscles of these areas are used for locomotion. For people with weak respiratory muscles, especially those who use wheelchairs, breathing exercises and activities should be performed on a daily basis in order to slow the loss of vital capacity and forced expiratory flow rate (see the Application Example sidebar for more information). Strength and endurance can be developed through aquatic activities, which can keep muscles toned without undue stress. Performed regularly, flexibility activities help to develop or maintain range of motion so that permanent joint contractures do not develop; dance movements are particularly helpful for improving flexibility and cardiorespiratory efficiency while maintaining students' interest. Low-intensity aerobic activities are also helpful in managing obesity, which is common in people with muscular dystrophy. Arm and upper body movements for students who use wheelchairs can be performed to music. Postural exercises and activities help reduce postural deviations and give the student an opportunity to perform out of the wheelchair.

Juvenile Idiopathic Arthritis

There are various terms to describe arthritis seen in children (e.g., juvenile arthritis, juvenile rheumatoid arthritis). However, **juvenile idiopathic arthritis** (JIA) is most commonly used by specialists in pediatric rheumatology. JIA manifests itself in childhood and is one of several forms of juvenile arthritis. As with adult rheumatoid arthritis, the cause of JIA is unknown (the term *idiopathic* means "of unknown origin"). Depending on the degree of involvement, JIA affects joint movement. Joints become inflamed, resulting in reduced range of motion. In some cases, permanent joint contractures develop, and muscle atrophy is pronounced. Some experts suggest that inflammation of the joints results from abnormal antibodies of unknown origin that circulate in the blood and destroy the body's normal

Application Example

Using Breathing Activities to Improve Capacity for a Child With Muscular Dystrophy

STUDENT

Jarome, an eight-year-old boy with muscular dystrophy who is beginning to exhibit weak respiratory muscles

ISSUE

Jarome's parents have asked the adapted physical education teacher to suggest breathing activities that can be done at home so that he can maintain appropriate function of his respiratory muscles.

APPLICATION

The adapted physical education teacher recommends that Jarome perform the following two activities with a friend, sibling, or parent on a daily basis:

- Jarome and a partner face each other about a yard (1 meter) apart and try to keep a balloon in the air as long as possible by blowing it to each other without letting it touch the ground.
- While facing each other across a table, seated about a yard (1 meter) apart, Jarome and his partner attempt to blow a table tennis ball across each other's goal (end of table).

structures. The disease is not inherited, nor does it seem to be a result of climate, diet, or patterns of living.

JIA is characterized by a series of remissions and exacerbations (attacks). One cannot predict how long affected children will remain ill or how long they will be symptom free. Generally, the prognosis for JIA is encouraging—only about 15 percent of children with JIA will have moderate to severe functional disability in adulthood. The highest frequency of onset is between 6 months and 16 years of age. According to the Arthritis Foundation (2020), about 300,000 infants, children, and teenagers possess some form of arthritis, of which JIA is the most common. Although there are at least nine types of JIA, the three most common are pauciarticular (oligoarthritis), polyarticular, and systemic. **Pauciarticular (oligoarthritis) JIA** affects four or fewer joints, which can include knees, ankles, and elbows. Children with pauciarticular JIA have the highest probability for developing uveitis (chronic eye inflammation), which is seen most frequently in girls. Pauciarticular JIA typically affects one side of the body, particularly the knee. About 40 percent of all children with JIA exhibit the pauciarticular type.

Polyarticular JIA affects five or more joints, which might include hand and finger joints as well as the knees, hips, ankles, feet, neck, and jaw. It affects more girls than boys. The same joints on both sides of the body are typically affected. Malformation of the temporomandibular joint can result in slower jaw growth; other symptoms could include a low-grade fever and anemia. About 25 percent of all children with JIA exhibit polyarthritis.

Systemic JIA affects the entire body, including joints and internal organs. It is the least common form of JIA and affects boys and girls equally. In addition to joint inflammation, symptoms include a high-spiking fever lasting for weeks or months and a body rash. In some instances, there is inflammation of the heart and lungs, along with enlarged liver or spleen. In most cases, the high-spiking fever and inflammation of the internal organs will disappear completely; however, joint inflammation will be chronic. Systemic JIA occurs in about 10 percent of all JIA cases.

At present, there is no cure for juvenile arthritis. Treatment for severe periods of exacerbation consists of controlling joint inflammation, which is accomplished through medicine, rest, appropriately designed exercises, and possibly surgery. During acute stages, complete bed rest is strongly recommended, and excessive weight bearing by inflamed joints should be avoided. In some instances, surgery is performed to remove damaged tissue from the joint to prevent greater deterioration of bone and cartilage. Total hip replacements are now performed in some cases with great success.

Even during acute stages of JIA, joints should be exercised at least once or twice a day so that full range of motion can be maintained. For people who are unable to exercise independently, teachers or therapists can provide partial or total assistance.

The physical education program should stress exercises and activities that help increase or maintain range of motion (e.g., swimming, bike riding) so that permanent contractures do not develop and normal bone density is maintained. Muscular strength and endurance activities should also be offered to decrease muscle atrophy. Isometric activities, such as hooking the fingers of the two hands together and trying to pull them apart, or placing the palms together and pushing, may be particularly helpful to encourage the development of the hand muscles. Another hand exercise involves squeezing objects of various sizes and shapes. Hand exercises are most important in order to maintain and enhance manipulative skills. Most people with severe joint limitation or deterioration should refrain from activities that twist, jar, or place undue stress on the joints; activities such as basketball, volleyball, and tennis might need to be modified accordingly.

Osteogenesis Imperfecta

Osteogenesis imperfecta (OI), also known as *brittle bone disease*, is an inherited condition in which bones are easily broken, and when healed, take on a shortened, bowed appearance.. A defect in the protein matrix of collagen fibers reduces the amount of calcium and phosphorus, which in turn weakens bone structure. According to the Osteogenesis Imperfecta Foundation (2017), up to 50,000 people in the United States may be affected with OI. The disease occurs with equal frequency among males and females as well as in all racial and ethnic groups.

There are eight types of OI, which vary in characteristics and severity. The four original types are I, II, III, and IV; the newly determined types are V through VIII. The types do not progress in sequential order from mild to severe. The mildest and most common form of OI is type I, in which the bones are easily susceptible to fractures. People with type I have normal collagen fibers, but only about half the normal amount. They experience most fractures before puberty, and bone deformity is minimal or nonexistent. People with type I attain normal stature, but they have a tendency toward spinal curvature and a triangular-shaped face. Abnormal joint elasticity and low muscle tone are present. In addition, people with type I exhibit a thinning sclera (white portion of the eye) that takes on a blue, purple, or gray tint. About 50 percent of people with type I OI acquire a hearing loss in early adulthood. Many people with type I do not exhibit all the characteristics described here.

The most severe and least common form of OI is type II, which results in death at or shortly after birth. In type II, the child is born with multiple severe deformities and fractures, is of small stature, and has underdeveloped lungs. In type II, collagen fibers are improperly formed.

Children with type III OI have fractures present at birth, and bone deformity is often severe. They have poor muscle development and abnormal joint elasticity. They are short of stature and exhibit a barrel-shaped chest, a triangular-shaped face, and spinal curvatures. As in type I, eye sclera is abnormal in color, and hearing loss is possible. In type III, collagen fibers are improperly formed.

Type IV is between types I and III in severity. People with type IV have easily fractured bones, which usually occur before puberty. The children tend to be shorter than average and have moderate bone deformity, a barrel-shaped chest, a tendency for spinal curvature, and a triangular-shaped face. Similar to those with types II and III, people with type IV have collagen fibers that are improperly formed. As with types I and III, hearing loss is possible, but in contrast to types I and III, eye sclera is normal in color.

The most distinguishing feature of types V and VI is their similarity to type IV, with moderate severity, fractures, and skeletal deformities. However, type VI is extremely rare and is characterized by a mineral defect. Types VII and VIII are both recessively inherited, with type VII resembling types II and IV and type VIII resembling type III, except for white sclerae.

Students with severe fractures and deformities might require the use of wheelchairs. Multiple fractures over a prolonged time can result in limb deformities and significant lower limb limitations. People with milder types of OI can ambulate independently, whereas those with more moderate degrees of impairment need to use canes or crutches. There is no cure for the disease. At the present time, surgery, which consists of reinforcing the bone by inserting a steel rod lengthwise through its shaft, is the most effective treatment.

Physical activities such as swimming, bowling (with the use of a ball ramp), and the use of beach balls for striking and catching are safe because they do not place undue stress on the joints or bones. Because of abnormal joint elasticity, strength building exercises and activities, which can increase joint stability, should be encouraged. This might be best accomplished with water activities because buoyancy promotes movement without risk of new fractures. Most people with the disorder should not play power volleyball, basketball, or American football unless the games are modified appropriately.

Arthrogryposis

Arthrogryposis, or multiple congenital contractures, is a nonprogressive congenital disease of unknown origin. About 500 infants in the United States are born with arthrogryposis each year. The severity of the condition varies; a person might be in a wheelchair or only minimally affected. The condition affects some or all of the joints and is characterized by stiff joints and weak muscles. Instead of normal muscle tissue surrounding the joints, fatty and connective tissue is present, causing joints to appear large. Affected limbs are usually small in circumference, commonly exhibit deformities, and can be fixed in almost any position. Surgery, casting, and bracing are usually recommended for people with deformities. Most typically, upper limb involvement includes turned-in shoulders, extended and straightened elbows, pronated forearms, and flexed wrists and fingers; trunk and lower limb involvement includes flexion and outward rotation of the hip, bent or straightened knees, and feet turned in and down. People with arthrogryposis typically have partially or completely dislocated hips. Other conditions associated with arthrogryposis include congenital heart defects, respiratory problems, and facial abnormalities. People with arthrogryposis almost always possess normal intelligence and speech.

Because people with arthrogryposis have restricted range of motion, physical and occupational therapies may include stretching, casting, strengthening, mobility training, and fine motor development. Their physical education program should focus on exercises and activities that also increase flexibility and strength. In addition, they should be taught games and sports that make effective use of leisure time. In most cases, exercises and activities appropriate for students with arthritis are also acceptable for those with arthrogryposis and OI. Swimming, an excellent leisure activity, encourages the development of flexibility and strengthens weak muscles surrounding joints. Other activities, modified as needed, include cycling, miniature golf, bowling, shuffleboard, boccia, and table tennis.

Multiple Sclerosis

Multiple sclerosis (MS) is one of the most common central nervous system diseases among young adults. A study in 2017, supported by the National MS Society, estimated that nearly 1 million adults were living with MS in the United States (Wallin et al., 2019)—more than twice the previously reported number in 1975. It is a slowly progressive neurological disorder characterized by changes in the white-matter covering (myelin sheath) of nerve fibers at various locations on the brain and spinal cord. Over time, the myelin sheath, which helps transmit signals, is destroyed and replaced by scar tissue; a lesion might vary from the size of a pinpoint to about 1 or 2 centimeters in diameter. The cause of MS is unknown, but most scientists believe that the disease involves a genetic susceptibility of the brain and spinal cord nerves to losing the ability to transmit electrical signals in combination with an immune response to viral infection. About two-thirds of all those afflicted with the disease experience onset between the ages of 20 and 40, and the disorder affects more women than men. The disease may manifest itself in young children or people who are elderly as well, but this is rare.

People with MS exhibit various symptoms depending on the location of the lesions. The most common symptoms are extreme fatigue, heat intolerance, hand tremors, loss of coordination, numbness, general weakness, double vision, slurred speech, staggering gait, and partial or complete paralysis. According to current estimates, about 75 percent of people with MS experience extreme fatigue. The early stage of the disease is characterized by periods of exacerbation followed by periods of remission. As scar tissue continues to replace healthy tissue, symptoms tend to continue uninterrupted.

Because most people acquire MS in the most productive and enjoyable years of life, many have difficulty coping emotionally with the disease. Additional stress results from the fact that there is no established cure; the main treatment is to maintain the person's functional ability as long as possible. Treatment should be directed toward preventing loss of range of motion (which would result in permanent contractures) and preserving strength and endurance. Many times, the disease progresses to a point at which the person needs braces or a wheelchair. Intensive therapy or physical conditioning during acute phases of MS might cause general body fatigue. An electrical stimulation device (strapped just below the knee) is now available to assist those who exhibit loss of balance and lower body coordination (Patterson & Seale, 2016).

Recent evidence suggests that moderate physical activity, judiciously programmed on a regular basis, significantly reduces non–activity-related fatigue, which a vast majority of people with MS experience. In addition to the physiological effects, regular physical activity provides psychological benefits as well. Mild forms of physical activity that emphasize strength and endurance should be performed for short amounts of time. However, the duration and intensity of the activity should be programmed according to the person's level of exercise tolerance. Activities such as bowling, miniature golf, and table tennis are acceptable if regular rest breaks are provided. Stretching exercises and activities are also recommended to maintain range of motion. Activities incorporating balance and agility might prove to be helpful for those exhibiting a staggering gait or varying degrees of paralysis. Many of these activities can be done in water. However, because of heat intolerance in many people with MS, water temperature must remain in the 80s (27-32 degrees Celsius).

Friedreich's Ataxia

An inherited neurological disease, **Friedreich's ataxia** usually manifests itself in childhood and early adolescence (ages 10-15), but it can occur as late as the age of 20. Early onset is usually associated with a more serious course of the disease. Worldwide, Friedreich's ataxia affects about 1 in every 50,000 people, making it the most common in a group of hereditary ataxias (Muscular Dystrophy Association [MDA], 2020a). The disease was first identified in the 1860s by German neurologist Nikolaus Friedreich, who described the disease as a gradual loss of motor coordination and progressive nerve degeneration. The sensory nerves of the limbs and trunk (peripheral nerves) are affected and tendon reflexes are lost; the disease may progress either slowly or rapidly. When the disease progresses quickly, the person is likely to become a wheelchair user by the late teens to early 20s.

Early symptoms include poor balance and lack of limb and trunk coordination, resulting in a clumsy, awkward, wide gait almost indistinguishable from the gait of ataxic cerebral palsy (CP). This is caused by the inability of the brain to regulate the body's posture and the coordination of its muscle movements. Fine motor control of the upper limbs tends to be impaired because tremors might be present. Atrophy is common in muscles of the distal limbs. People with the disease typically exhibit slurred speech and are prone to seizures. Most develop foot deformities such as clubfoot, high arches, and hammertoes, a condition in which the toes are curled because of tight flexor tendons of the second and third toes. As the disease progresses, spinal deformities, such as kyphosis and scoliosis, are common. Most people exhibit heart problems, such as heart murmur, enlarged heart, and constriction of the aorta and pulmonary arteries, making heart failure a leading cause of death in Friedreich's ataxia. Diabetes develops in 10 to 40 percent of people with Friedreich's ataxia. Visual abnormalities include nystagmus and poor visual tracking.

There is no known cure at this time, but therapy consists of managing foot and spinal deformities and cardiac conditions. Medication might be prescribed to control diabetes as well as cardiac, tremor, and seizure disorders. Certain experimental drugs have shown great promise for slowing and even reversing the fundamental cardiac abnormalities of the disease.

Physical education activities should be planned to promote muscle strength and endurance and body coordination. Activities that develop muscles of the distal limbs such as the wrist, forearm, foot, and lower leg are recommended. The development of grip strength is essential for activities requiring implements, such as rackets and bats. Students exhibiting poor balance and lack of coordination are in need of balance training and activities that encourage development of fundamental locomotor movements. For those who have difficulties with fine motor control, activities might take the form of billiards or archery. Remedial exercises are recommended for people with foot and spinal deviations. Games, exercises, and activities should be programmed according to individual tolerance levels of people with cardiac conditions; those who are prone to seizures should be closely monitored.

Myasthenia Gravis

Myasthenia gravis (MG), meaning "grave muscular weakness," is a neuromuscular disease characterized by a reduction in muscular strength ranging from minimal to severe. The person may perform activities, but often this demands maximum or near-maximum effort. Myasthenia gravis may be easily confused with muscular dystrophy because it is a neurological disease in which muscle weakness affects the back, lower extremities, and intercostal muscles. In Western countries, MG affects about 14 out of every 10,000 people (MDA, 2020b), and affects more females than males. Women often develop MG in their late teens and early 20s, whereas men usually acquire it after the age of 60. The disease is not progressive; it might appear gradually or suddenly. It commonly goes into remission for weeks, months, or years. Thus, those who are affected live in fear of recurrent attacks.

Although the exact cause is unknown, nerve impulses are prevented from reaching muscle fibers because the immune system produces destructive antibodies that block the muscle receptors at the neuromuscular junctions (points at which nerve endings meet muscle cells). Myasthenia gravis is commonly treated with drugs that help strengthen the neuromotor transmission or suppress the immune system. However, these drugs have serious side effects when taken over a prolonged time. Most recently, a blood-flow exchange is now being used that removes antibodies from the blood that might interfere with the transmission of nerve impulses.

One of the main symptoms of MG is abnormal fatigue. Muscles generally appear normal except for some disuse atrophy. Weakness of the extraocular and lid muscles of the eye occurs in about half of all cases; this results in drooping of the eyelid (ptosis) and double vision (strabismus). Fatigue of facial, jaw, and tongue muscles might cause problems with chewing and speaking. Weakness of the neck muscles might prevent holding the head erect. Back musculature might also be weakened, which leads to misalignment of the spinal column, which can further restrict movement. Muscle weakness makes the execution of daily activities difficult and contributes to low levels of cardiorespiratory efficiency. When properly treated, most people can remain physically active.

Physical activities should focus on the development of physical fitness. Because people with MG fatigue easily, their activities should be programmed in a progressive manner and according to individual tolerance levels that take into account the duration, intensity, and frequency of the activity. When the respiratory muscles are weakened, breathing activities are strongly recommended. It is important to strengthen weak neck muscles, especially when the program includes such activities as heading a soccer ball or hitting a volleyball. Fitness levels can be maintained during acute stages via swimming activities. Poor body mechanics resulting from weak musculature will ultimately affect locomotor skills; thus, remedial posture exercises and activities should be offered.

Guillain-Barré Syndrome

Guillain-Barré syndrome (GBS), also known as *infectious polyneuritis*, is a neurological disorder characterized by ascending paralysis of the peripheral nerves. Although rare, GBS occurs worldwide, affecting all ages, races, and sexes equally. The National Institute of Neurological Diseases and Strokes (2020) reports that the syndrome affects about 1 person per 100,000. Initially, the lower extremities become easily fatigued, and numbness, tingling, and symmetrical weakness are present. When initially affected, people involved in locomotor activities of an endurance nature, such as distance running, typically find themselves stumbling or falling as muscles of the feet and lower legs fatigue prematurely. Paralysis, which usually originates in the feet and lower legs, progresses to the upper leg, continues to the trunk and upper extremities, and finally affects the facial muscles. When muscles necessary for breathing cannot be used, the condition is considered a medical emergency. Symptoms usually peak within a few weeks, then stabilize for a number of days, weeks, or months; recovery may be as short as a few weeks or as long as a few years. About one-third of those affected will have some weakness after three years. Most individuals, however, recover completely or with minimal paralysis, and most walk unassisted.

Some authorities believe that the syndrome is an autoimmune disease. However, the condition is frequently preceded by a respiratory or gastrointestinal infection, which suggests that a viral or bacterial infection might be the cause. In recent years, some countries worldwide have reported an increased incidence of GBS following the spread of Zika virus. Neurologists, immunologists, and virologists are cooperatively investigating the syndrome.

Acute-stage treatment includes passive range of motion, exercise, and rest. For people who have made a complete recovery, no restrictions in physical activities are needed. However, those who do not completely recover exhibit weakness in limb and respiratory muscles. Their activities can focus on maintaining or improving cardiorespiratory endurance and strength and endurance of unaffected muscles. When significant weakness remains in the lower extremities, activities might need to be modified accordingly.

Program Implications

All people with amputations, dwarfism, or les autres conditions can benefit from physical education and sport. Should modifications or adaptations be needed, the type and degree of physical involvement, motor educability, interest level, and overall educational goals will determine them. Especially for people with unique physical and motor needs, physical education instruction needs to be individualized and personalized.

General Guidelines

Several guidelines can be applied to programs for people with amputations, dwarfism, and les autres conditions. The guidelines that follow pertain to safety considerations, physical fitness, motor skills, and implications for sports.

Safety Considerations

The physical impairments presented in this chapter are of a medical origin, and accordingly, the physical education teacher or coach needs to be aware of key safety considerations. Students with physical limitations should be encouraged to experience as many postures as possible so that contractures do not develop, thus leading to decubitus ulcers (bedsores) that might require hospitalization. This is especially true for students who use wheelchairs. Before getting a student into or out of a wheelchair or positioning a student who has obvious physical limitations, it is important to consult the student's physical or occupational therapist (should the student be receiving such services). Safe handling of students is of the utmost concern, especially for those who are medically fragile. For example, it is especially important to never pull, push, or twist the limbs of children with arthritis, OI, or arthrogryposis.

Students with the disabilities described in this chapter might tire easily, especially when performing large-muscle activities for an extended time. Fatigue exhibited in MS and DMD, for example, might cause students to become frustrated, which in turn adversely affects performance. The instructor should permit rest breaks and player substitutions when endurance activities such as soccer and basketball are being played. Should teachers fail to take this fatigue into account, the risk of medical problems is high, especially for students with cardiopathic conditions (e.g., children with DMD).

It is important to consult medical professionals before establishing physical education and sport programs to meet unique needs. It is especially important that the teacher be sensitive to the frequency, intensity, duration, and mode of exercises and activities, particularly for students currently under the care of a physician and those receiving physical or occupational therapy. Teachers should also be in direct contact with the school nurse. Typically, the school nurse understands the student's medical condition and knows whether the student is taking any medications. The nurse should also have direct contact with the child's parents and personal physician should medical problems arise during the school day. Lindsley and colleagues (2016) provide more information on the health care needs of students with rheumatic diseases, including community-based care, therapy programs, medication compliance, common school difficulties and strategies to overcome them, counseling, and nutrition, among others.

Physical Fitness

Because restricted movement is common in people whose conditions are described in this chapter, it is important that strength and flexibility be developed to appropriate levels of physical fitness. Range of motion is basic to overall fitness. Maximizing range of motion allows the student to perform physical education and sport skills as well as activities of daily living in the most efficient and effective manner possible. Weak musculature and limited range of motion, if unattended, lead to permanent joint contractures that result in significant loss of movement capability, which in turn reduces the level of health-related fitness. Surburg (1999) provides flexibility and range of motion guidelines and exercise and activity examples that can be applied to people with physical conditions such as amputations, MS, DMD, and JIA.

Motor Development

Many times, amputations and les autres impairments (and to a lesser extent dwarfism) prevent people from experiencing movement patterns essential to normal motor development. As a result, delays in the development of motor skills and patterns are common. Lack of ability to control movements contributes to the performance of inappropriate motor skills and patterns. For example, children born with the absence of an upper limb or with multiple limb deficiencies may have motor delays due to the inability to use their arms to crawl, pull to a stand, or manipulate objects (e.g., toys, balls), whereas children born with the absence of a lower limb might be delayed in acquiring locomotor patterns such as walking and running. Muscle atrophy or weakness prevents people from developing the strength and endurance levels needed to perform fundamental movements vital to overall health.

Physical education programs should encourage the sequential development of fundamental motor patterns and skills essential for participation in games, sport, and leisure activities. When attempting to enhance motor development, physical educators should be concerned primarily with the mechanics of the student's movement, rather than its outcome. The goal of every physical education and sport program should be to encourage students to achieve maximum motor control and development within their ability levels. The motor development of young people with disabilities covered in this chapter might be assessed using standardized tests as well as less formal procedures, like checklists or rubrics. Readers are encouraged to consult chapter 4 for information on assessment of motor development and skills.

Implications for Teaching Sport in Physical Education

Physical education teachers are encouraged to integrate many of the sport activities described in the Adapted Sport section of this chapter into their physical education programs. For example, sitting volleyball, a Move United sport, can be incorporated into a physical education program as a means of developing eye–hand coordination as well as offering an opportunity for sport competition. Other sports offered by organizations such as the Dwarf Athletic Association of America (DAAA), including bowling, archery, cycling, and boccia, can be taught. By incorporating adapted sports into general physical education curricula, physical educators are following several critical tenets of universal design for learning (UDL), including ensuring activities are done as a whole class, rather than segregating students, and making modifications to the games, rather than to individuals, to allow success for all students (Lieberman et al., 2008).

Amputations

In general, a physical education program for students with amputations can follow the same guidelines as those for students without disabilities. Aside from missing limbs, people with amputations are considered nondisabled. However, the location and extent of the amputations might require modifications in some activities.

Students with amputations typically use prosthetic devices in physical education activities. A person with unilateral lower limb amputation usually continues to use the device for participation in American football, basketball, volleyball, and most leisure activities—as previously stated, newer prosthetics are often more mechanically efficient for sports. In some situations, a unilateral BE, AE, or shoulder amputee might consider the device a hindrance to successful performance and discard it during participation; this is common in baseball or softball. Such was the case with Jim Abbott, a former Major League Baseball pitcher who did not wear a prosthetic device for his BE congenital amputation. Currently, the National Federation of State High School Associations (NFHS) allows participating athletes to wear prosthetic devices for interscholastic sports such as American football, basketball, gymnastics, soccer, baseball, and field and ice hockey. However, a device cannot be used if it is more dangerous to other players than a corresponding human limb or if it gives the user an advantage over an opponent (NFHS, 2019). Although some individuals use special prosthetic devices for recreation or leisure swimming, prosthetic devices are not allowed for Paralympic competition swimming events.

Participation in physical education and sport requires some adaptations depending on the location and extent of the amputation and the type of activity. Table 15.1 provides some general participation guidelines for people with amputations.

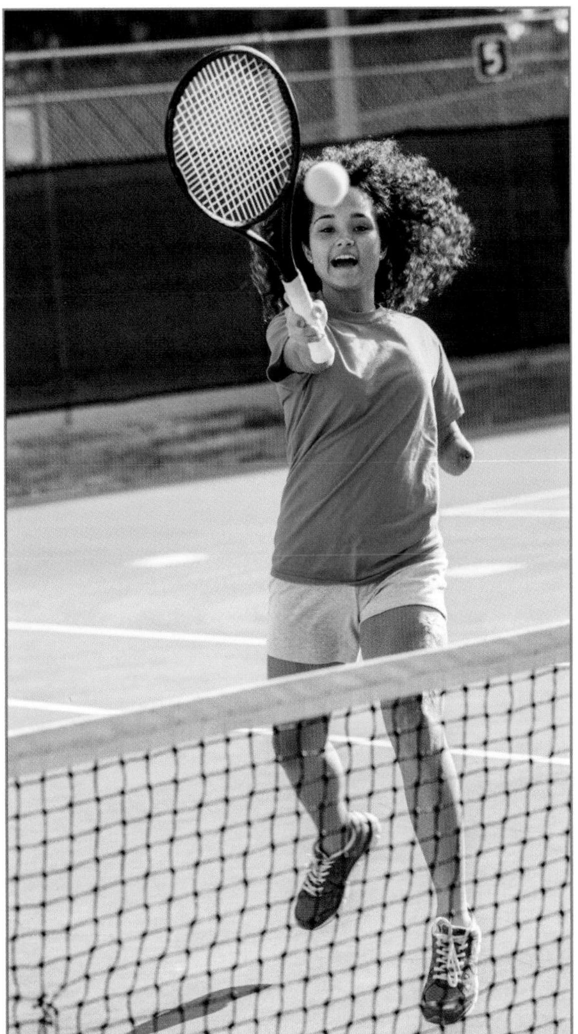

kali9/E+/Getty Images

Regardless of ability, finding an actvity that's enjoyable increases the chances of students adopting lifelong active lifestyles.

TABLE 15.1 Participation Guide for Students With Amputations in Selected Activities

Activity	Upper extremity	Lower extremity (BK)	Lower extremity (AK)
Archery	R A	R	R
Baseball or softball	R	R	R A
Basketball	R	R	WC A
Bicycling	R	R	R
Bowling	R	R	R
Field hockey	R	I	WC A
American football	R	R	I
Golf	R A	R	R
Rifle shooting	R A	R	R
Skiing (downhill)	R	R	R A
Cross-country skiing	R	R	R A
Soccer	R	R	I
Swimming	R	R	R
Table tennis	R	R	R
Tennis	R	R	I
Track	R	R	WC A
Volleyball	R	R	WC A

A = adapted; R = recommended; I = individualized; WC = wheelchair.

Adapted from Adams and McCubbin (1991).

Physical Fitness

Evidence suggests that appropriate levels of health-related physical fitness contribute to the overall wellness of people with amputations. Winnick and Short (2014) recommend that young people with amputations and congenital anomalies (those with fully or partially deformed extremities at birth) achieve physical fitness standards consistent with positive health. This level of functioning includes appropriate fitness levels to adequately perform activities of daily living, including physical education and sport activities. The Brockport Physical Fitness Test (BPFT) (Winnick & Short, 2014) provides selected test items as well as standards for the evaluation of aerobic functioning, body composition, and musculoskeletal functioning (flexibility, muscular strength, and endurance).

For example, a person with a unilateral AK amputation would perform the Target Aerobic Movement Test (TAMT) to assess aerobic functioning. A physical activity should be chosen that is of sufficient intensity to reach a target heart rate; sustaining that level of moderate physical activity for at least 15 minutes would be a minimal general standard for young people with amputations and congenital anomalies. Other BPFT items for a student with a unilateral AK amputation are triceps and subscapular skinfold measures (body composition) and a bench press (muscular strength and endurance).

According to Winnick and Short (2014), those with congenital anomalies or amputations may experience a number of fitness-related concerns, which can restrict their ability to lift and transfer the body independently, overcome architectural barriers, and propel a wheelchair efficiently. Students with bilateral BK or AK amputations often have lower levels of aerobic functioning than upper limb amputees because their locomotor activities might be severely restricted. With low fitness levels, it is recommended that intermittent training be used, especially for students who fatigue easily. Activities performed with greater frequency and with less intensity and duration are recommended.

For long-term aerobic training programs, proper limb care is essential because prosthetic sockets prevent air from circulating around the limb, which can cause eventual skin breakdown. Suggested aerobic activities include swimming, using an arm-propelled tricycle, or using arm, rowing, and cycle ergometers. To further encourage aerobic development, the physical educator could offer activities in which a wheelchair can be used, such as marathon racing or slalom events.

Muscular strength and endurance and flexibility should be developed for all parts of the body, even at the site of the amputation or anomaly. The remaining muscles surrounding the site also need to develop so that they remain in balance with the unaffected side. For a person with only a partial limb amputation, such as an ankle or wrist disarticulation, exercises and activities should be programmed to encourage the most normal possible use of the remaining limb segment.

Because absence of a limb can affect balance and leverage during performance of resistance activities, some strength activities are better and more safely performed with the use of a prosthetic device. This is the case for Shaquem Griffin, who uses a specially made prosthetic device during upper body resistance training exercises. According to DiRocco (1999), if a force of resistance runs through the shaft of the prosthetic device, then it would be acceptable to wear it for that particular exercise—for example, when performing the bench press, the weight is distributed through the shaft of the prosthesis.

Both unilateral and bilateral AK amputees have a tendency to be obese and thus should be encouraged to follow a weight reduction diet if necessary, along with a program of regular, vigorous physical activity. Short and colleagues (1999) describe several desirable characteristics of a weight loss physical activity program for people with disabilities. Some of these characteristics include raising daily total energy expenditure, deemphasizing activity intensity and emphasizing activity duration, exercising daily, participating with partners or small groups, and doing well-liked activities. Exercises and activities that are enjoyable will tend to be continued over time, which increases the chances of these students adopting lifelong active lifestyles.

Motor Skills

Deficiency of an upper or lower limb can affect a person's level of motor skills. For example, acquired amputations of a dominant limb can initially result in awkward or clumsy performance of motor skills, particularly for adolescents and adults who have already mastered motor skills with their dominant limbs (e.g., overarm throwing, kicking a ball). The absence of a limb most often affects the center of gravity, resulting in difficulty with activities requiring balance. Developing static and dynamic balance is crucial to the performance of locomotor skills such as walking, running, or hopping, as well as sitting in a wheelchair. Activities that foster the development of balance and proper body alignment should be encouraged; these might include traversing an obstacle course, performing on a mini-trampoline, or walking a balance beam. Speed and agility might also be adversely affected, especially in people with lower limb deficiencies. People with lower limb amputations are most affected and might have difficulty in locomotor activities that require quick changes of direction, such as basketball, American football, soccer, and tennis.

Although unilateral BE amputees can participate effectively in physical education and competitive sport, others will have activity restrictions. Bilateral upper limb amputees can successfully engage in activities that involve the lower extremities to a significant degree—for example, skating, soccer, and jogging. Unilateral AK amputees can effectively participate in activities such as swimming, waterskiing, snow skiing, weightlifting, and certain field events that do not emphasize locomotion and agility (e.g., shot put and javelin). Bilateral BK and AK amputees are much more restricted in their activities, usually relying on a wheelchair part-time and crutches at other times; activities such as archery and badminton are appropriate.

Dwarfism

Students with dwarfism should be encouraged to perform general physical education and sport activities. The development of health-related physical fitness and motor skills is an important aspect of any physical education program, and students with dwarfism should have the same opportunities to develop these as other students. This is especially true because many people with achondroplasia are overweight or obese. However, certain considerations need to be addressed in programs for developing physical fitness and motor skills.

Physical Fitness

Restricted range of motion, obesity, and joint defects might predispose those with dwarfism to dislocations and joint trauma, and this is especially true for people with achondroplasia. Thus, maintaining flexibility, especially at the elbow joint, is important. Exercises and activities that place undue stress on weight-bearing joints should be avoided or modified. For example, jogging can be replaced with walking or riding a bicycle, and volleyball can be performed with a lighter ball. Swimming, which promotes flexibility and cardiorespiratory endurance, is another excellent activity that does not place undue stress on the joints.

Motor Skills

Because of shorter limbs, movement quality might be affected in some activities, including ball throwing and catching, striking, and locomotor skills such as running, jumping, and hopping. In alignment with principles of UDL, implements such as golf clubs, rackets, and hockey sticks can be adjusted according to the size of the student to ensure successful engagement. Failure to use appropriately sized implements results in inappropriate or inefficient execution of motor skills.

Les Autres

Atrophied or weak muscles, reduced range of motion, and balance and coordination problems may hinder students with les autres conditions in performing physical activities. Many of the conditions presented in this chapter are progressive (e.g., DMD, Friedreich's ataxia, MS); that is, muscles become weaker regardless of the amount of exercise or activity performed. As a result, it is important to maintain current levels of muscular strength and endurance as long as possible. DiRocco (1999) suggests that students with progressive muscular disorders not go beyond 50 percent of their maximum resistance weight when performing muscular strength activities; the exercise intensity is too great if functional strength does not return within 12 hours of exercise. This should be monitored closely by the teacher or coach. De Groot and Bartels (2016) suggest that for children with DMD, light intensity activity incorporating both arms and legs be performed for a maximum of 30 minutes, three to four days per week. Higher intensity activities should only be performed if there are no cardiac risks.

Activities should align with the child's interests and abilities. Exercises that are fun increase the likelihood that students will perform them regularly. For young children, activities should be short and might include rhythmic activities, active lead-up games, and obstacle courses. For adolescents, emphasis should be on lifelong activities such as racket sports, cycling, hiking, and swimming. Students who use wheelchairs can participate in activities such as sled hockey, rugby, seated aerobics, and wheelchair tennis.

Because the limitations presented in this chapter prevent extended periods of activity, low aerobic fitness levels are common. For example, people with MS typically exhibit general body fatigue (not related to exercise), which reduces their capacity to perform physical activity over an extended length of time. Inactivity makes people with amputations and les autres conditions prone to obesity and ultimately places them at greater risk for coronary heart disease and other associated conditions. For students with moderate degrees of orthopedic impairments, low-impact aerobics, cycling, swimming, and brisk walking can achieve aerobic gains. Maintaining a satisfactory level of health-related fitness reduces the risk of associated debilitating conditions, such as osteoporosis.

Severe limitations in strength and flexibility can also hinder people with les autres conditions from acquiring the motor skills they need to become successful in sport and leisure activities. The inability to perform these skills reduces the chances of being physically active and thus places these students at greater risk of reduced health.

Whether physical activity is performed for purposes of fitness or enhanced motor skills, proper warm-up and cool-down activities that emphasize flexibility are needed. This is especially true for people with conditions that limit joint flexibility, such as JIA, OI, and other conditions that might elicit spasticity. Daily range of motion exercises are recommended for those who have joint-limiting conditions such as JIA, arthrogryposis, and GBS. Surburg (1999) offers several excellent recommendations for the development of flexibility and range of motion for people with disabilities.

Strategies for Inclusion

As is true for other disabilities, students with amputations, dwarfism, and les autres conditions must be encouraged to participate in general physical education classes unless the individualized education program (IEP) team decides otherwise. Most students with these conditions can safely and effectively participate in general physical education activities when provided needed support. Even students experiencing severe physical impairments can succeed in general physical education settings as long as appropriate activities are performed and support services are provided.

UDL, as well as differentiated instruction, can be used to foster feelings of inclusion in physical education. UDL is a strategy that eliminates barriers to learning by focusing on equipment that can be modified and used by all students regardless of ability; similarly, differentiated instruction uses various instructional techniques to maximize learning for all students regardless of learning styles. Both concepts are a priori strategies, which consider students' unique needs prior to engagement in the courses, rather than making adaptations as reactions to students' participation in classes. In all cases, decisions about educational placement must be made on an individual basis in consultation with the student's IEP team. The impairments described in this chapter affect physical functioning, not intellectual functioning, so students will clearly understand verbal and written directions as well as rules and strategies for games and sports. In certain cases, teachers might need to structure activities to suit the participants' abilities.

Most students described in this chapter can easily participate in general classroom activities with appropriate accommodations. For example, students with amputations or other lower limb deficiencies could play goalie in soccer or floor hockey and could pitch or play first base in softball. They could also be provided the option of riding a stationary bike when students without disabilities are required to run over a long distance. Students with dwarfism can safely and effectively participate in general physical education classes as long as the proper-sized equipment is offered, including shorter and lighter implements such as bats, rackets, and hockey sticks.

Students with reduced muscular strength and aerobic capacity (e.g., muscular dystrophy, MS, Friedreich's ataxia) can also safely and effectively participate in general physical education classes as long as activities are modified or activity options are provided. For example, when the class performs push-ups and chins-ups for the development of arm and shoulder strength, students with reduced strength can perform modified push-ups (with knees touching the floor) or chin-ups (performed from a supine position on the floor). Activities to enhance aerobic capacity can be modified for students with joint limitations or deficiencies, such as those with JIA, arthrogryposis, and OI. For example, these students can swim or participate in low-impact aerobics while students without disabilities participate in more traditional forms of rope jumping, jogging or running over distance, and bench stepping.

Adapted Sport

At almost all age levels, people with amputations, dwarfism, and les autres conditions now have the opportunity to become involved in competitive sport. Organizations such as Move United, Dwarf Athletic Association of America (DAAA), and BlazeSports America offer a variety of sports to assist athletes in reaching their maximum potential. Athletes participate and compete in these events on the basis of their functional abilities.

Amputations

Move United sponsors organized competition for athletes with amputations, as well as many other conditions, in sports such as archery, basketball, boccia, canoeing, cross-country skiing, curling, equestrian, golf, martial arts, swimming, sitting volleyball, and wheelchair racing. The reader is referred to the Move United website (www.moveunitedsport.org) for a complete list and explanation of each sport.

The U.S. Olympic and Paralympic Committee (USOPC) also offers elite competition for athletes with amputations in sports such as alpine skiing, track and field, badminton, Nordic skiing, judo, powerlifting, soccer, sitting volleyball, wheelchair fencing, and wheelchair tennis; see www.teamusa.org/us-paralympics for a complete list. Those with a lower limb amputation who require the use of a wheelchair are also eligible to compete in events sponsored by Adaptive Sports USA (formerly Wheelchair and Ambulatory Sports USA) and the National Wheelchair Basketball Association (NWBA). Regardless of the organization, classifications for athletes with amputations differ by sport and are governed by the International Federation for that specific sport. The reader is referred to the IPC website (www.paralympics.org) for a complete description of the classifications for each sport.

Dwarfism

The DAAA was established in 1985 for the purpose of providing organized sport competition to people with dwarfism. Sports include track (15-, 20-, 40-, 60-, 100-, and 200-meter runs and relays of 4 × 60 and 4 × 100 meters), field (shot put, tennis and softball throw, flippy flyer throw, discus, and javelin), swimming (freestyle, backstroke, breaststroke, butterfly, individual medley, freestyle relay, lifejacket swim, and kickboard swim), basketball, boccia (individual and team), soccer, flag football, volleyball, table tennis, and powerlifting. Separate competition is offered for men and women except for basketball, volleyball, and team boccia, which is mixed-gender but separated by age division.

Athletes are classified for open division (ages 16-39) track, field, table tennis, swimming, and basketball. There are three classes for track, which are based on a ratio of standing height to sitting height, and three classes for field and swimming, which are based on the ratio of arm span to biacromial breadth. This system is used only for national DAAA events. For international events, the IPC functional classification systems are used.

To be eligible for competition, people with disproportionate dwarfism must be equal to or less than 5 feet (152 centimeters) in height, whereas people with proportionate dwarfism must be equal to or less than 4 feet, 10 inches (147 centimeters) in height. Athletes participate in one of four age divisions (futures, junior, open, and master). Junior events (ages 7-15) emphasize achieving one's personal best. The futures division, for children younger than age 7, offers a limited number of events on a noncompetitive basis. The DAAA also offers clinics and developmental events. The organization sponsors the U.S. National Dwarf Games, as well as coordinates and sponsors a U.S. team every four years at the World Dwarf Games. Athletes who qualify participate in the Paralympic Games.

Les Autres

BlazeSports, Move United, and the Cerebral Palsy International Sports and Recreation Association (CPISRA) serve les autres athletes. Athletes are eligible to participate in the Paralympic Games as long as they can be placed into one of IPC's 10 disability categories and also meet qualifying standards for a particular sport. Typically, athletes such as those with Friedreich's ataxia, MS, MG, and GBS might be placed into one of the four IPC disability categories of (1) impaired muscle power, (2) hypertonia, (3) ataxia, or (4) athetosis. In their classification rules, each Paralympic sport governing body identifies which disability categories are eligible for competition.

Summary

This chapter has described the conditions of amputations, dwarfism, and les autres as they relate to physical education and sport. Physical and motor needs were described and program and activity suggestions presented. Recognizing the medical nature of these conditions, teachers and coaches are encouraged to plan activities in consultation with allied medical professionals and the student's personal physician.

References

Adams, R.C., & McCubbin, J.A. (1991). *Games, sports, and exercises for physically disabled* (4th ed.). Lippincott, Williams, and Wilkins.

Adelson, B. (2005). *Dwarfism: Medical and psychosocial aspects of profound short stature.* Johns Hopkins University Press.

Arthritis Foundation. (2020). *Juvenile arthritis.* Retrieved March 3, 2020, from https://arthritis.org/diseases/juvenile-arthritis

De Groot, J., & Bartels, B. (2016). Muscular dystrophy. In G.E. Moore, J.L. Durstine, & P.L. Painter (Eds.), *ACSM's exercise management for persons with chronic diseases and disabilities* (4th ed., pp. 281-284). Human Kinetics.

DiRocco, P. (1999). Muscular strength and endurance. In J.P. Winnick & F.X. Short (Eds.), *The Brockport physical fitness training guide* (pp. 39-73). Human Kinetics.

Lieberman, L.J., Lytle, R.K., & Clarcq, J.A. (2008). Getting it right from the start: Employing the universal design for learning approach to your curriculum. *Journal of Physical Education, Recreation, & Dance, 79*(2), 32-39. http://doi.org/10.1080/07303084.2008.10598132

Lindsley, C., Russo, R., & Scott, C. (2016). Managing children with rheumatic diseases. In R. Petty, R. Laxer, C. Lindsley, & L. Wedderburn (Eds.), *Textbook of pediatric rheumatology* (7th ed., pp. 129-139). Elsevier, Inc. http://doi.org/10.1016/b978-0-323-24145-8.00011-9

Little People of America (LPA). (2020). *Frequently asked questions.* Retrieved from www.lpaonline.org/faq-

Muscular Dystrophy Association (MDA). (2020a). *About Friedreich's ataxia (FA).* Retrieved from www.mda.org/disease/friedreichs-ataxia

Muscular Dystrophy Association (MDA). (2020b). *About myasthenia gravis.* Retrieved from www.mda.org/disease/myasthenia-gravis

National Federation of State High School Associations (NFHS). (2014). *2014-15 Football rules book.* Author.

National Institute of Neurological Diseases and Strokes. (2020). *Guillain-Barré syndrome fact sheet.* Retrieved February 5, 2020, from www.ninds.nih.gov/Disorders/Patient-Caregiver-Education/Fact-Sheets/Guillain-Barr%C3%A9-Syndrome-Fact-Sheet#3139_1

National Limb Loss Information Center. (2020). *Limb loss statistics.* Retrieved February 5, 2020, from www.amputee-coalition.org/resources/limb-loss-statistics/

Osteogenesis Imperfecta Foundation. (2017). *Fast facts on osteogenesis imperfecta.* www.oif.org/wp-content/uploads/2019/08/Fast_Facts_About_OI.pdf

Patterson, T., & Seale, J. (2016). Multiple sclerosis. In G.E. Moore, J.L. Durstine, and P.L. Painter (Eds.), *ACSM's exercise management for persons with chronic diseases and disabilities* (4th ed., pp. 267-272). Human Kinetics.

Short, F.X., McCubbin, J., & Frey, G. (1999). Cardiorespiratory endurance and body composition. In J.P. Winnick & F.X. Short (Eds.), *The Brockport physical fitness training guide* (pp. 13-37). Human Kinetics.

Surburg, P. (1999). Flexibility/range of motion. In J.P. Winnick & F.X. Short (Eds.), *The Brockport physical fitness test training guide* (pp. 75-119). Human Kinetics.

Wallin, M.T., Culpepper, W.J., Campbell, J.D., Nelson, L.M., Langer-Gould, A., Marrie, R.A., Cutter, G.R., Kaye, W.E., Wagner, L., Tremlett, H., & Buka, S.L. (2019). The prevalence of MS in the United States. *Neurology, 92*(10), e1029-21040. http://doi.org/10.1212/WNL.0000000000007035

Winnick, J.P., & Short, F.X. (2014). *The Brockport physical fitness test manual* (2nd ed.). Human Kinetics.

Print Resources

Bragaru, M., Dekker, R., Geertzen, J., & Dijkstra, P. (2011). Amputees and sports: A systematic review. *Sports Medicine, 41*(9), 721-740. http://doi.org/10.2165/11590420-000000000-00000

This article provides a review of the literature about individuals with limb loss and sport participation. It includes topics such as biomechanical aspects and performance, quality of life, sport participation and physical functioning, and sport injuries.

inMotion magazine, 9303 Center St., Ste. 100, Manassas, VA 20110. www.amputee-coalition.org

This is a bimonthly publication of the Amputee Coalition of America for amputees, caregivers, and health care professionals. It can be obtained in either print or online formats.

Wagner, T., & Sandt, D. (2012). Physical education programming for students with achondroplasia. *Palaestra, 26*(2), 35-39.

This article provides information regarding the characteristics of achondroplasia, physical activity, and health-related fitness, as well as physical education programming.

Video Resources

Zion (2018). Country of Origin, USA. Production Company: The Bindery. Release date: 8/10/2018. Director: Floyd Russ.

This 11-minute documentary short by Netflix chronicles the story of Zion Clark, a young man born without legs and raised in foster care who eventually found and pursued competitive wrestling. The film was an entry in the 2018 Sundance Film Festival. The film is currently available on Netflix.

Online Resources

Challenged Athletes Foundation: www.challengedathletes.org

Because of the high cost of sports equipment and lack of resources, this organization helps those with physical challenges gain access to adapted sports. It has helped over 26,000 individuals across 50 states and 42 countries.

Dwarf Athletic Association of America: www.daaa.org

This site provides information about the organization, its sports, sport rules, competitive venues, and athletes, among other information.

16

Spinal Cord Disabilities and Other Spinal Conditions

Wesley J. Wilson and Luke E. Kelly

High school junior Jasmine pulls even with her friend, Lindsey, around the final turn of their 400-meter race. It is practice, but Jasmine does not want to give her friend the satisfaction of beating her. They jockey for the lead on the final stretch, back and forth. "Yeah!" Jasmine exclaims as she crosses the finish line just before Lindsey.

"You are lucky that my left wheel got loose around that fourth turn," Lindsey says as she takes her gloves off.

"Right, I am sure that *that* was the only reason you lost," Jasmine quips as she points to her friend's racing wheelchair. Both Jasmine and Lindsey are athletes who compete in track and field. Several years ago, Jasmine was involved in a car accident, which resulted in a lower spinal cord injury. Her friend Lindsey, who had been involved in wheelchair sports for years, convinced her to join the track and field team after her rehab. They participate together in the 100-, 200-, and 400-meter events.

The focus of this chapter is to review common spinal cord disabilities, as well as other spinal conditions, and their implications for physical education. Spinal cord disabilities are conditions that result from injury to, or disease of, the vertebrae or the nerves of the spinal column. These conditions are almost always associated with some degree of paralysis caused by damage to the spinal cord. The degree of the paralysis is a function of the location of the injury on the spinal column and the number of neural fibers subsequently destroyed. This chapter will examine traumatic injuries to the spine resulting in tetraplegia and paraplegia, as well as spina bifida. This chapter also reviews several common spinal column postural deviations that can adversely affect body mechanics and predispose the spine to injury. Finally, this chapter covers orthotic devices commonly associated with spinal cord disabilities, as well as physical education and sport implications. After reading this chapter, teachers should be able to modify their programs or develop appropriate alternative programs to accommodate the needs of students with spinal cord disabilities.

Classifications

The physical education teacher should be aware of the systems for categorizing spinal cord disabilities. Medical classifications are based on the segment of the spinal cord that is impaired, whereas sport organizations classify people by their functional abilities in order to match similarly able athletes for competition.

Medical Classifications

As illustrated in figure 16.1, spinal cord injuries are medically labeled or classified according to the segment of the spinal column (i.e., cervical,

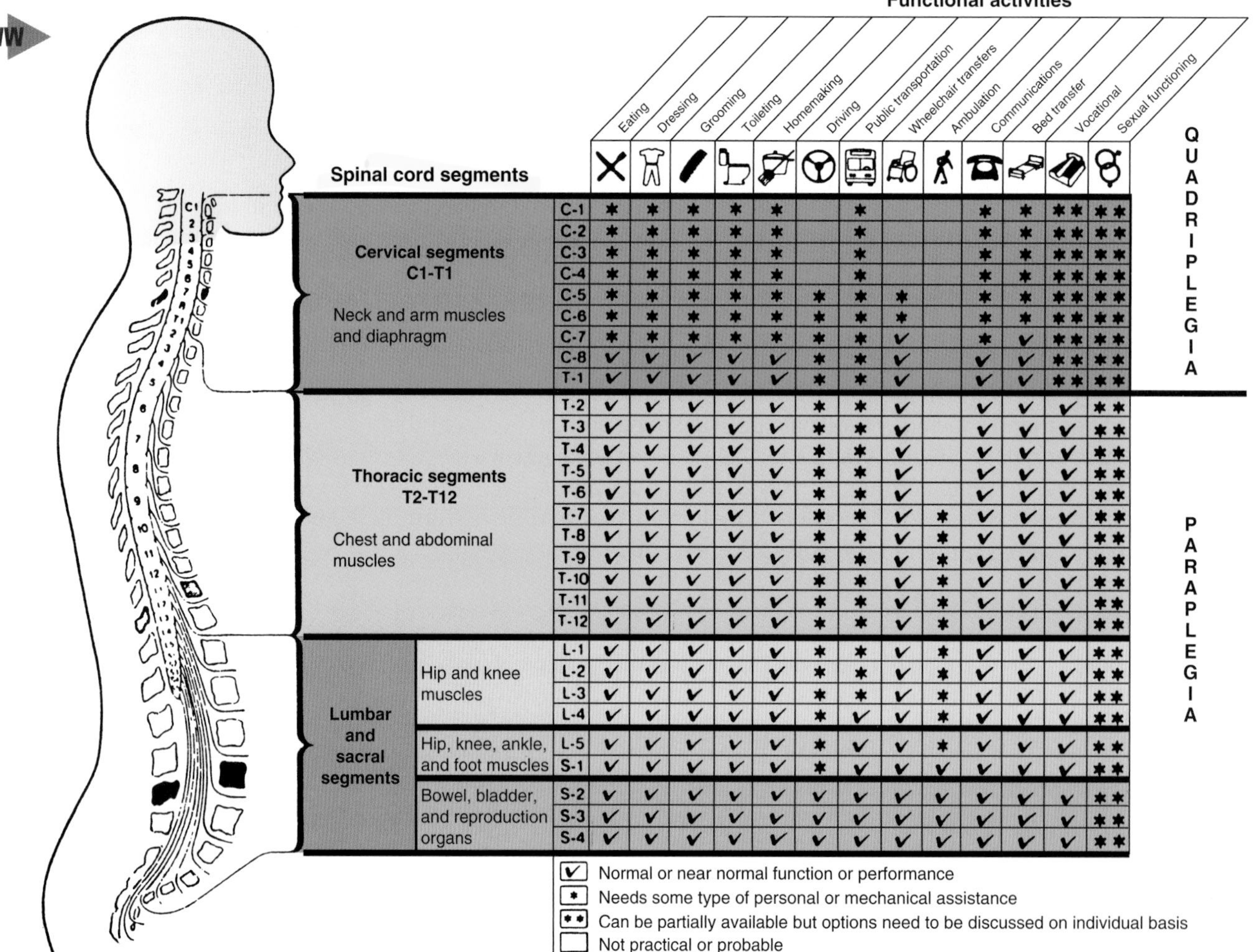

Functional activities

Spinal cord segments		Eating	Dressing	Grooming	Toileting	Homemaking	Driving	Public transportation	Wheelchair transfers	Ambulation	Communications	Bed transfer	Vocational	Sexual functioning	
Cervical segments C1-T1 Neck and arm muscles and diaphragm	C-1	*	*	*	*	*		*			*	*	**	**	QUADRIPLEGIA
	C-2	*	*	*	*	*		*			*	*	**	**	
	C-3	*	*	*	*	*		*			*	*	**	**	
	C-4	*	*	*	*	*		*			*	*	**	**	
	C-5	*	*	*	*	*	*	*	*		*	*	**	**	
	C-6	*	*	*	*	*	*	*	*		*	*	**	**	
	C-7	*	*	*	*	*	*	*	✓		*	✓	**	**	
	C-8	✓	✓	✓	✓	✓	*	*	✓		✓	✓	**	**	
	T-1	✓	✓	✓	✓	✓	*	*	✓		✓	✓	**	**	
Thoracic segments T2-T12 Chest and abdominal muscles	T-2	✓	✓	✓	✓	✓	*	*	✓		✓	✓	✓	**	PARAPLEGIA
	T-3	✓	✓	✓	✓	✓	*	*	✓		✓	✓	✓	**	
	T-4	✓	✓	✓	✓	✓	*	*	✓		✓	✓	✓	**	
	T-5	✓	✓	✓	✓	✓	*	*	✓		✓	✓	✓	**	
	T-6	✓	✓	✓	✓	✓	*	*	✓		✓	✓	✓	**	
	T-7	✓	✓	✓	✓	✓	*	*	✓	*	✓	✓	✓	**	
	T-8	✓	✓	✓	✓	✓	*	*	✓	*	✓	✓	✓	**	
	T-9	✓	✓	✓	✓	✓	*	*	✓	*	✓	✓	✓	**	
	T-10	✓	✓	✓	✓	✓	*	*	✓	*	✓	✓	✓	**	
	T-11	✓	✓	✓	✓	✓	*	*	✓	*	✓	✓	✓	**	
	T-12	✓	✓	✓	✓	✓	*	*	✓	*	✓	✓	✓	**	
Lumbar and sacral segments Hip and knee muscles	L-1	✓	✓	✓	✓	✓	*	*	✓	*	✓	✓	✓	**	
	L-2	✓	✓	✓	✓	✓	*	*	✓	*	✓	✓	✓	**	
	L-3	✓	✓	✓	✓	✓	*	*	✓	*	✓	✓	✓	**	
	L-4	✓	✓	✓	✓	✓	*	✓	✓	*	✓	✓	✓	**	
Hip, knee, ankle, and foot muscles	L-5	✓	✓	✓	✓	✓	*	✓	✓	*	✓	✓	✓	**	
	S-1	✓	✓	✓	✓	✓	*	✓	✓	✓	✓	✓	✓	**	
Bowel, bladder, and reproduction organs	S-2	✓	✓	✓	✓	✓	✓	✓	✓	✓	✓	✓	✓	**	
	S-3	✓	✓	✓	✓	✓	✓	✓	✓	✓	✓	✓	✓	**	
	S-4	✓	✓	✓	✓	✓	✓	✓	✓	✓	✓	✓	✓	**	

✓ Normal or near normal function or performance
* Needs some type of personal or mechanical assistance
** Can be partially available but options need to be discussed on individual basis
(blank) Not practical or probable

FIGURE 16.1 Functional activity for spinal cord injuries.
Courtesy of Healthsouth Harmarville Rehabilitation Hospital, Pittsburgh, PA 15238.

thoracic, lumbar, or sacral) and the number of the vertebra at or below which the injury occurred. For example, a person classified as a C6 complete has a fracture between the sixth and seventh cervical vertebrae that completely severs the spinal cord. The location of the injury is important because it determines which functions are affected. The extent of the spinal cord lesion is ascertained through muscle, reflex, and sensation testing.

The actual effect of a spinal cord injury is best understood in terms of what muscles can still be used, how strong these muscles are, and what can functionally be done with the muscles in the context of activities of daily living (eating, dressing, grooming), movement (wheelchair, ambulation, transfers, bed), vocational skills, and physical education skills.

Table 16.1 provides a summary of the major muscle groups innervated at several key locations along the spinal column, with implications for the movements, functional abilities, and physical education activities that might be possible with lesions at these locations. The functional abilities remaining are cumulative as one progresses down the spinal column. For example, someone with a lesion at or below Tl would have all the muscles and abilities shown at and above that level.

TABLE 16.1 Potential Functional Abilities by Select Lesion Locations

Lesion locations	Key muscles innervated	Potential movements	Associated functional abilities	Sample physical education activities
C4	Neck, diaphragm	Head control, limited respiratory endurance	Can control an electronic wheelchair and other computer electronic devices that can be controlled by a mouth-operated joystick	Bowling
C5	Partial shoulder, biceps	Abduction of the arms, flexion of the arms	Can propel a wheelchair with modified rims, can assist in transfers, can perform some functional arm movements using elbow flexion and gravity to extend the arm	Swimming
C6	Major shoulder, wrist extensors	Abduction and flexion of the arms, wrist extension, possibly a weak grasp	Can roll over in bed; might be able to transfer from wheelchair to bed; improved ability to propel wheelchair independently; partial independence in eating, grooming, and dressing using special assistive devices	Billiards, putting
C7	Triceps, finger extensions, finger flexions	Stabilization and extension of the arm at the elbow, improved grasp and release but still weak	Independent in wheelchair locomotion, bed, sitting up, and in many cases, transferring from bed to wheelchair; increased independence in eating, grooming, and dressing	Archery, crossbow, table tennis
T1	All upper extremity muscles	All upper body lacks trunk stability and respiratory endurance	Independent in wheelchair and bed transfers, eating, grooming, dressing, and toileting; can ambulate with assistance using long leg braces, pelvic band, and crutches	Any activities from a wheelchair

(continued)

TABLE 16.1 *(continued)*

Lesion locations	Key muscles innervated	Potential movements	Associated functional abilities	Sample physical education activities
T6	Upper trunk muscles	Trunk stability, improved respiratory endurance	Can lift heavier objects because of improved stability, can independently put own braces on, can ambulate with low spinal attachment, pelvic band, long leg braces, and crutches using a swing gait but still depends on wheelchair as primary means of locomotion	Track and field, bowling, weightlifting
T12	Abdominal muscles and thoracic back muscles	Increased trunk stability, all muscles needed for respiratory endurance	Can independently ambulate with long leg braces including stairs and curbs, uses a wheelchair only for convenience	Competitive swimming, marathon racing
L4	Lower back, hip flexors, quadriceps	Total trunk stability, ability to flex the hip and lift the leg	Can walk independently with short leg braces and bilateral canes or crutches	Some standing activities
S1	Hamstring and peroneal muscles	Ability to bend the knee, lift the foot up	Can walk independently without crutches, might require ankle braces or orthotic shoes	General physical education

Sport Classifications

Sport organizations that sponsor athletic events for people with spinal cord disabilities use different classification systems to equate athletes for competition. Table 16.2 shows the functional classification system used by the National Wheelchair Basketball Association (NWBA, 2019). In this system, players are classified into one of eight classes. The higher the classification number, the greater the degree of function. To equate competition, the sum of the classifications of the five players on the court cannot equal more than 15.

Move United (2020a) manages competition in many different adapted sports (specific sports are highlighted later in the chapter). Athletes for these sports are classified by functional ability into one of several classes based on the sporting event, degree of **muscular functioning**, and actual performance during competition. Muscular functioning includes such actions as arm function, hand function, trunk function, trunk stability, and pelvic stability in relation to their importance in performing in a given sporting event. These classification systems provide efficient ways of equating competition among a diverse group of athletes with varying types of spinal cord disabilities. For more information on these classification systems, consult the Move United link listed in the Online Resources at the end of this chapter.

Spinal Cord Injuries

Damage to the spinal cord can occur as a result of disease or a variety of genetic and environmental causes. This section describes the common causes of spinal cord disabilities and the implications for planning and delivering physical education.

Traumatic Tetraplegia and Paraplegia

Traumatic tetraplegia and paraplegia refer to spinal cord injuries that result in the loss of movement and sensation. **Tetraplegia**, or quadriplegia, is used to describe the more severe form, in which all four limbs are affected. **Paraplegia** refers to

TABLE 16.2 National Wheelchair Basketball Association Functional Classification System

Class	Description
1.0	No active movement of the trunk in the vertical, forward, or sideways plane.
1.5	Has characteristics of Class 1.0, but able to move partially out into forward plane; able to rotate upper trunk; able to transition from catching to passing or shooting faster than Class 1.0; more stable upon contact than Class 1.0; and more at ease with ball within cylinder of movement.
2.0	Has active use of upper trunk in the vertical and forward planes; able to rotate the upper trunk while upright in both directions; able to hold the ball forward with both arms extended; able to lean the trunk into the forward plane about 45 degrees with control and return to the upright sitting position; able to actively bring upper trunk off the backrest of the chair; and uses hands to return to upright of trunk if no thighs—unless knees are significantly higher than the hips.
2.5	Has characteristics of Class 1.0, but able to lean forward 90 degrees and return to upright sitting position without proper upper extremity assist with knees higher than hips; able to lean forward and rotate the upper trunk simultaneously; active movement of both the upper and lower trunk but not coordinated or as one unit; lower trunk is not against the backrest at all times; may have a lordosis (curve in low back) to assist in returning to upright; and more stable than a Class 2.0 player but still has loss of stability in trunk.
3.0	Displays active use of the upper and lower trunk in the forward and vertical planes; can lean forward 90 degrees, place chest on thighs, and return to upright with ease without knees significantly higher than hips; can hold the ball with both hands outstretched in front of face without loss of stability; can rotate upper and lower trunk as a unit not supported by wheelchair backrest; rotation of the trunk occurs at the level of the pelvis, not the waist; unable to maintain stability leaning sideways; and works within a "cylinder."
3.5	Has characteristics of a Class 3.0, but able to move partially out into the sideways plane and return to upright sitting; able to remain upright in hard contact situations forward; able to sit with hips higher than knees; often raises and lowers trunk with each push; able to generate some power in legs with pushing; able to retrieve a ball with two hands on the floor slightly to the side and return to upright position; can lean to the side but remains within base of support; plays within a wider cylinder than a Class 3.0 player; does not have full volume of action to either side.
4.0	Displays the ability to move the trunk maximally in all planes of movement with weakness to one side; has one strong side and one weaker side; able to lean strongly to one side; usually able to lean to weak side slightly; can hold the ball with outstretched hands in front or overhead without loss of stability even in contact situations; no need to counterbalance even in contact situations unless contact is forceful and directed into the weaker side.
4.5	Displays the ability to move the trunk maximally in all planes of movement with no significant weakness in any direction; full volume of action in all planes; displays ability to lean to either side during shooting, passing, contesting a shot, or trying to intercept a pass.

the condition in which primarily the lower limbs are affected.

The amount of paralysis or loss of sensation associated with tetraplegia and paraplegia is related to the location of the injury (how high on the spine) and the amount of neural damage (the degree of the lesion). Figure 16.1 shows a side view of the spinal column, accompanied by a description of the functional abilities associated with various levels of injury. The functional abilities indicated for each level should be viewed cautiously because the neural damage to the spinal cord at the site of the injury might be complete or partial. If the cord is severed completely, the person will have no motor control or sensation in the parts of the body innervated below that point. This loss will be permanent because the

First Aid for Suspected Neck Injury

The American Medical Association (2009) recommends the following procedures whenever a neck injury is suspected:

> A neck injury should be suspected if a head injury has occurred. *Never* move a victim with a suspected neck injury without trained medical assistance unless the victim is in imminent danger of death (from fire, explosion, or a collapsing building, for example). WARNING: Any movement of the head (forward, backward, or side to side) can result in paralysis or death. (pp. 191-192)

Immediate Treatment If the Victim Must Be Moved

Do not wait and hope someone else will know what to do in this situation. Do the following:

1. Immobilize the neck with a rolled towel or newspaper about 4 inches (10 centimeters) wide wrapped around the neck and tied loosely in place. (Do not allow the tie to interfere with the victim's breathing.) If the victim is being rescued from an automobile or from water, place a reasonably short, wide board behind the victim's head and back. The board should extend to the victim's buttocks. If possible, tie the board to the victim's body around the forehead and under the armpits. Move the victim very slowly and gently. Do *not* let the body bend or twist.
2. If the victim is not breathing or is having difficulty breathing, tilt the head slightly back to provide and maintain an open airway.
3. Restore breathing and circulation if necessary.
4. Summon paramedics or trained ambulance personnel immediately.
5. After moving the victim, place folded towels, blankets, clothing, sandbags, or other suitable objects around the head, neck, and shoulders to keep the head and neck from moving. Place bricks or stones next to the blankets for additional support.
6. Keep the victim comfortably warm.

spinal cord cannot regenerate itself. In many cases, however, damage to the spinal cord is only partial, resulting in retention of some sensation and motor control below the site of the injury. In a case involving partial lesion, the person might experience a gradual return of some muscle control and sensation over several months following the injury. This is a result not of regeneration of damaged nerves, but rather the alleviation of pressure on nerves at the injury site caused by bruising or swelling. Although damage to the spinal cord currently results in a permanent loss of function, promising research results have been found in animals using innovative drug therapies, reactivating dormant nerve cells, and using embryonic transplant therapy.

Incidence

The National Spinal Cord Injury Statistical Center (NSCISC, 2019) estimates that about 17,730 people acquire spinal cord injuries each year in the United States. Among the major causes are automobile accidents (39.3 percent), falls (31.8 percent), acts of violence (13.5 percent), athletic injuries (8.0 percent), and other accidents (7.4 percent). Unfortunately, a large percentage of these injuries happen to students of high school age, with the incidence being greater among males (78.0 percent) than females (22.0 percent). When spinal cord injury is suspected, proper handling of the patient immediately after the injury can play a major role in minimizing additional damage to the spinal cord (see First Aid for Suspected Neck Injury sidebar).

Treatment and Educational Considerations

The treatment of people with spinal cord injuries usually involves three phases:

1. Hospitalization
2. Rehabilitation
3. Return to the home environment

Although the three phases are presented as separate, there is considerable overlap between the treatments provided within each phase. During the **hospital phase**, the acute medical aspects of the injury are addressed, and therapy is initiated. Although length of stay in the hospital is dependent on the severity of the injury, the median hospital stay is 11 days (NSCISC, 2019). Many people with spinal cord injuries are then transferred from the hospital to a rehabilitation center. As indicated by its name, the **rehabilitation phase** centers on adjustment to the injury and mastery of basic living skills (e.g., toileting, dressing, transfers, and wheelchair use) with the functional abilities still available. The median stay in the rehabilitation phase is 31 days (NSCISC, 2019). Near the end of the rehabilitation phase, a transition is begun to move the person back into the home environment. In the case of a student, the transition involves working with parents and school personnel to make sure that they have the appropriate skills and understanding of the student's condition and needs and know what environmental modifications will be required to accommodate those needs.

One of the major secondary problems associated with spinal cord injuries is psychological acceptance of the limitations imposed by the injury and the loss of former abilities. Counseling is usually a major component of the treatment plan during rehabilitation. The rate of adjustment and the degree to which people learn to cope with their disabilities vary tremendously. To achieve their full abilities, people with spinal injuries must realize that their condition is permanent, not be hindered by any secondary health problems, and be highly motivated to rehabilitate.

People with spinal cord injuries are susceptible to a number of secondary health conditions. One of their most common health problems is pressure sores or **decubitus ulcers**. These are caused by the lack of innervation and reduced blood flow to the skin, and they most commonly occur at pressure points where a bony prominence is close to the skin (buttocks, pelvis, and ankles). Because of poor blood circulation, these sores can easily become infected and are extremely slow to heal. The prevention of pressure sores involves regular inspection of the skin, the use of additional padding in troubled areas, and regular changes in position to alleviate pressure (i.e., pressure releases). Individually designed seat cushions are often used to help better distribute pressure and avoid sores. Keeping the skin dry is also important because the skin is more susceptible to sores when it is wet from urine or perspiration.

A problem closely related to pressure sores is bruising. Because no sensation is felt in the limbs that are not innervated, it is not uncommon for them to be bruised or irritated from hitting or rubbing against other surfaces. Because these bruises are not felt, they can go unnoticed and may eventually become infected. Injuries of this nature are common in wheelchair activities such as basketball if appropriate precautions are not taken.

Another health problem commonly encountered by people with spinal cord injuries is urinary tract infections. Because urination is controlled by some form of catheterization on an established schedule, infections can occur when urine is retained in the bladder and backs up into the kidneys. Urinary tract infections can be severe and usually keep the patient bedridden for a prolonged time, which is counterproductive for attitude, rehabilitation, and skill development. Bowel movements must also be carefully monitored to prevent constipation and incontinence; these are usually controlled by a combination of diet and mild laxatives. In cases where bowel movements cannot be controlled by diet, a tube is surgically inserted into the intestine and exits through a small opening in the side of the body to a bag that collects the fecal excretions.

Two other problems closely associated with spinal cord injuries are spasticity and contractures. **Spasticity** is an increase in muscle tone in muscles that are no longer innervated because of the injury, which can nullify the use of still-innervated muscles. A sudden spasm can be of sufficient force to launch someone out of a wheelchair. The best treatment for spastic muscles is to stretch them regularly, particularly before and after rigorous activity. **Contractures** can frequently occur in the joints of the lower limbs if they are not passively moved through the full range of motion at regular intervals. A high degree of spasticity in various muscle groups can also limit the range of motion and contribute to contractures.

The final problem commonly associated with spinal cord injuries is a tendency toward obesity. Estimates of overweight and obesity in this population range from 66 percent to nearly 78 percent (Pelletier et al., 2016; Rajan et al., 2008). The loss of function in the large-muscle groups in the lower limbs severely reduces the calorie-burning capacity of people with spinal cord injuries. However, a corresponding loss in appetite does not also occur. Many people with spinal cord injuries tend to resume their habitual caloric intake or even increase it because of their sedentary condition. Weight and diet should be carefully monitored to prevent obesity and the secondary health hazards associated with it, because once weight is gained, it is extremely difficult to lose.

A major key to rehabilitation success is motivation. Many people with spinal cord disabilities initially have great difficulty accepting the loss of previous abilities and are subsequently reluctant to work hard during the tedious and often painful therapy. Recreational and sport activities are commonly used in both counseling and physical therapy to motivate and serve as positive distractions. However, a physical educator should be sensitive to the motivational needs of a student returning to a program with a spinal cord disability. Although sport can be a motivator for many, it can also highlight the loss of previous skills and abilities.

The physical education teacher should anticipate needs in the areas of body image, upper body strength, range of motion, endurance, and wheelchair tolerance. These needs, together with the student's functional abilities, should be analyzed to determine what lifetime sport skills and wheelchair sports are most viable for future participation. These activities can then become the basis for instructional goals for the physical education program.

Although a student with a newly acquired spinal cord injury may still be learning to deal with the injury, the physical educator and other school personnel (e.g., physical therapist) can assist by anticipating the student's needs and planning ahead (see the Application Example sidebar). This might involve reminding the student to perform pressure releases at regular intervals (shifting the sitting position or lifting the weight off the seat of the chair by pressing on the arm supports) or bringing towels to class to absorb extra moisture in the chair. Because spasticity and spasms are common, stretching at the beginning of class and regularly during the class is recommended. Finally, pads should be provided to prevent bruising in active wheelchair activities. As the student becomes accustomed to the condition, most of these precautions will become automatic habits. A student who has an external bag should be reminded to empty and clean it before physical education class. In contact activities, care should be taken to protect the bag from contact. For swimming, the bag should be removed and the opening in the side covered with a watertight bandage.

Application Example

How to Determine Student Placement and Transitioning After Complete T6 Spinal Cord Lesion

SETTING

Individualized education program (IEP) committee meeting

STUDENT

Fran is 16 years old and returning to school after having a complete T6 spinal cord lesion as a result of a motorcycle accident. Before the accident, Fran was an excellent athlete. During rehab Fran was cooperative and worked hard, but she has expressed concerns about returning to school, particularly physical education class.

ISSUE

What is the best way to transition Fran back into physical education? What would be the most appropriate physical education placement?

APPLICATION

On the basis of the previous information and a meeting with Fran, her parents, and the rehab staff, the following is decided:

- Fran will receive an adapted physical education program, which will include an individually designed strength training and endurance program.
- The program will be initiated in a weight training unit in an inclusive setting with support services as needed.
- Before participating, the physical education staff will work with Fran on learning how to safely perform the exercises in her routine.
- Special arrangements will be worked out with Fran to address any concerns she has related to changing clothes for physical education.
- As Fran's strength and endurance improve, she will begin to train for the school's 5K race that is held each spring.

Spina Bifida

Spina bifida is a congenital birth defect in which the neural tube fails to close completely during the first four weeks of fetal development. Subsequently, the posterior arch of one or more vertebrae fails to develop properly, leaving an opening in the spinal column. Spina bifida can be detected before birth, usually during the 16th to 18th weeks, by a combination of blood tests, amniocentesis, and sonograms. Although the cause of many cases of spina bifida is unknown, there is an established link between spina bifida and folic acid deficiencies in mothers. As a result of this link, the Food and Drug Administration mandated that folic acid be added to all grain products in the United States in 1998. This intervention resulted in a 31 percent reduction in the number of cases of spina bifida in the United States by 2002—from 5.22 per 10,000 births to 3.62 (Williams et al., 2002). More recently, the Centers for Disease Control and Prevention (CDC, 2015) have estimated the prevalence of spina bifida at 3.70 per 10,000 births. If the condition is detected during pregnancy, there are two treatment options. The traditional option has been to deliver the infant by Cesarean section during the 37th week and surgically return the neural matter into the spinal column, then close the opening. The newest option is to perform prenatal repair on the fetus during the 23rd to 25th week of gestation to close the opening in the neural tube (Children's Hospital of Philadelphia, 2020). Although the prenatal repair procedure is still relatively new and presents significant risks to both the mother and fetus, preliminary research has revealed positive results related to improving the motor function of these children (Adzick et al., 2011; Pedreira et al., 2016). In fact, a follow-up study showed that 44.8 percent of children who received prenatal surgery were more likely to walk independently, compared to only 23.9 percent of children who received postnatal treatment (Farmer et al., 2018).

There are three classifications of spina bifida, based on which structures, if any, protrude through the opening in the spine.

Myelomeningocele is the most severe form of spina bifida. In this condition the covering of the spinal cord (meninges), cerebrospinal fluid, and part of the spinal cord protrude through the opening and form a visible sac on the back (see figure 16.2*a*). Some degree of neurological damage and subsequent loss of motor function are always associated with this form. Spina bifida **meningocele** is similar to the myelomeningocele form, except that only the spinal cord covering and cerebrospinal fluid protrude into the sac (see figure 16.2*b*). This form rarely has any neurological damage associated with it. **Occulta** is the mildest and the most common form of spina bifida, as an estimated 10% to 20% of healthy people live with it (Spina Bifida Association, 2021). In this condition, the defect is present in the posterior arch of the vertebra, but nothing protrudes through the opening (see figure 16.2*c*). No neurological damage is associated with this type of spina bifida.

Once detected and surgically corrected, the meningocele and occulta forms of spina bifida have no adverse ramifications. The greatest threat in these conditions is from infection before surgery.

Incidence

Because some degree of neurological damage is always associated with the myelomeningocele type of spina bifida, this is the form discussed in the remainder of this section. It is estimated that this form may affect up to 1 in 4,000 births (National Institutes of Health, 2019). The degree of neurological damage depends on the location of the deformity and the amount of damage done to the spinal cord. Fortunately, spina bifida occurs most commonly in the lumbar vertebrae, sparing motor function in the upper limbs and limiting the disability primarily to the lower limbs. Bowel and bladder control are almost always lost. The muscle functions and abilities presented in table 16.1 for spinal cord lesions in the lumbar region can also be used to ascertain what functional abilities a child with spina bifida will have.

In addition to the neurological disabilities associated with damage to the spinal cord, myelomeningocele is almost always accompanied by three other conditions: hydrocephalus, Chiari II malformation, and tethering of the spinal cord. **Hydrocephalus** is a condition in which circulation of the cerebrospinal fluid is obstructed in one of the ventricles, or cavities, of the brain. If the obstruction is not removed or circumvented, the ventricle begins to enlarge, putting pressure on the brain and enlarging the head. If not treated, this condition can lead to brain damage, intellectual disabilities, and ultimately death. Today, hydrocephalus is suspected early in children with spina bifida and is usually treated surgically by insertion of a shunt during the first few weeks after birth (see figure 16.3*a-c*). The shunt, a plastic tube equipped with a pressure valve, is inserted into a ventricle and drains off the excess cerebrospinal fluid. The fluid is usually drained into either the heart (ventriculoatrial shunt) or the abdomen (ventriculoperitoneal shunt) to be reabsorbed by the body. Additional information

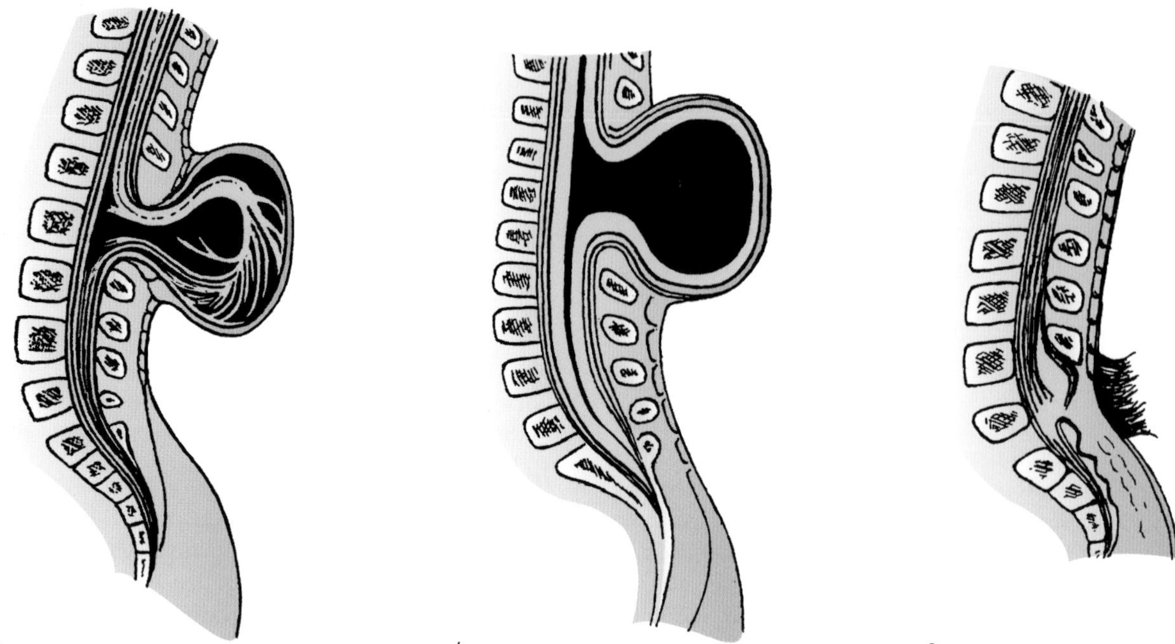

FIGURE 16.2 Diagram of the three types of spina bifida: *(a)* myelomeningocele, *(b)* meningocele, and *(c)* occulta.

Reprinted from *Yearbook of Physical Medicine and Rehabilitation,* G.G. Deaver, D. Buck, and J. McCarthy, Spina Bifida, pg. 10, Copyright 1952, with permission from Elsevier.

regarding shunts can be found in the Online Resources section at the end of the chapter.

Chiari II malformation, or Arnold-Chiari malformation (ACM), refers to a condition in which the cerebellum and lower brain stem are stretched and pulled through the base of the skull and into the top of the spinal column. This condition is always present in children with myelomeningocele. In mild cases the condition does not cause any problems and is left untreated. In more severe cases, where the functions controlled by the brain stem and cerebellum are compromised, surgery is performed to decompress the brain stem by widening the opening at the base of the skull and at the top of the spinal column.

The spinal cord should float in the spinal canal, allowing it to move up and down as the child grows. **Tethering of the spinal cord** refers to anchoring of the cord within the spinal canal at the site where the spina bifida was surgically closed. All children with myelomeningocele have tethered cords; the issue is whether this results in stretching of the cord and loss of function caused by reduced circulation. Common symptoms include loss of muscular strength and tone, reductions in gait quality, and further loss of bowel and bladder functions. Tethering usually does not present problems until the adolescent growth spurt. When tethering prob-

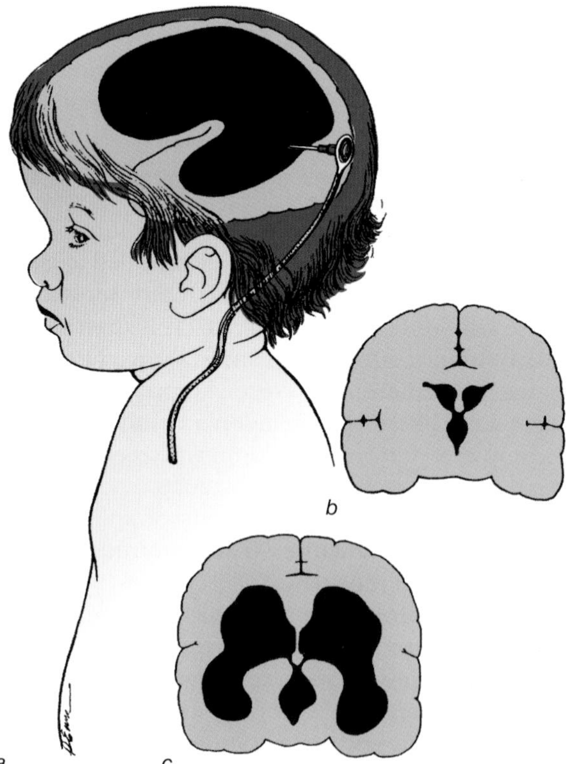

FIGURE 16.3 Shunt being used to relieve hydrocephalus: *(a)* the shunt in place, *(b)* normal ventricles, and *(c)* enlarged ventricles.

lems are diagnosed, the problem can be treated by surgically untethering the cord. It is estimated that approximately 60 percent of all people with myelomeningocele experience tethering symptoms that could benefit from surgical treatment.

Treatment and Educational Considerations

As mentioned earlier, all forms of spina bifida are diagnosed and surgically treated before or soon after birth. The major treatment beyond the immediate medical procedures involves physical and occupational therapy for children, as well as counseling and training for the parents. Assistive devices are used to position children so that they parallel the normal developmental positions (e.g., sitting, crawling, standing), thus maintaining full range of motion and stimulating circulation in the lower limbs. In conjunction with therapy, children with spina bifida are fitted with braces and encouraged to ambulate. Even if functional walking skills are not developed, it is important to perform weight-bearing activities to stimulate bone growth and circulation in the lower limbs. Parents are counseled to provide their children with as many normal and appropriate stimuli as possible. It is important not to overprotect and confine children, which results in further developmental delays.

There are several important similarities and differences in the treatment of spina bifida and the treatment of acute spinal cord injuries. The conditions share similarities in muscle and sensation loss, as well as associated bone deformities, bruising, postural deviations, pressure sores, urinary tract infections, and obesity.

However, different circumstances result in different emotional and developmental ramifications for these conditions. Because the condition is congenital and they have not suffered the loss of any former abilities, children with spina bifida generally have fewer emotional problems related to their condition than do children with acquired spinal cord disabilities. However, this is not to imply that they do not become frustrated when other children can perform skills and participate in activities that they cannot.

A major ramification of the early onset of spina bifida is its effect on growth and development. The lack of innervation and subsequent use and stimulation of the affected limbs slows physical growth, resulting in a greater incidence of bone deformities and contractures in the lower limbs and a greater need for orthotics to assist in providing functional support. A concurrent problem is related to sensory deprivation during the early years of development because of restricted mobility. This deprivation is frequently compounded by overprotective parents and medical problems that confine the child to bed for long periods of time.

Children with spina bifida are vulnerable to infections from pressure sores and bruises. Pressure sores are most common in those who use wheelchairs, whereas bruising and skin irritation are particular concerns for children who use crutches and leg braces. These children have a tendency to fall during physical activities and are susceptible to skin irritation if braces are not put on properly. About 7 out of 10 children with spina bifida have also been found to have an allergy to latex, which can be found in rubber balls and other materials frequently used in physical education such as balloons. If an allergy is suspected, physical educators must diligently check all equipment and materials used in physical education to ensure they do not contain latex.

Bowel and bladder control present significant social problems for the child with spina bifida during the early elementary school years. Bowel movements are controlled by diet and medication, and urination is commonly controlled by a regular schedule of catheterization with assistance by the school nurse or an aide. This dependence on others for help with personal functions and the inevitable occasional accident in class can have negative social implications for children with spina bifida and their classmates.

Finally, approximately 50 percent of children with spina bifida are obese (Spina Bifida Association, 2020). As with spinal cord injuries, the loss of the caloric expenditure typically made by the large-muscle groups in the lower limbs limits the number of calories that can be burned. Caloric expenditure is often further limited by the sedentary environment of these children and their limited mobility during the early years. Control of caloric intake is essential to avoid obesity. Unfortunately, food is frequently used as a primary reinforcer by indulgent parents and caregivers due to issues such as social isolation, restricted mobility, and diet restrictions for bowel control.

Children with spina bifida will most likely be placed in some combination of adapted and general physical education settings during the early elementary years and then be fully integrated into general physical education settings by the end of the elementary years. It is important not to remove these children unnecessarily from inclusive physical education settings; they have the same play and social needs as other children. However, the development of physical and motor skills should not be sacrificed purely for social objectives. If these needs cannot be met in an inclusive setting, the student should receive appropriate support or supplemental adapted physical education to meet these needs in a more restricted setting, such as in self-contained group or one-on-one settings.

Although there has been little systematic and experimentally controlled research on the learning attributes of children with spina bifida, a growing body of literature demonstrates that many children with spina bifida display what is being labeled as nonverbal learning disorders (NVLD) (Fletcher et al., 2008). Individuals with NVLD may demonstrate strong verbal skills but have a range of problems involving attention, memory, and organization (Learning Disabilities Association of America, 2020; Russell, 2004). Although each child's needs should be individually assessed and addressed, physical educators should be aware of potential problems in these areas and modify their instruction accordingly to accommodate these needs.

In summary, although their objectives might be different, children with spina bifida need to pursue the same physical education goals targeted for other students. Modifications might be needed to accommodate their modes of locomotion (crutches or wheelchair) and to emphasize their upper body development, but emphasis should be placed on physical fitness and the development of lifetime sport skills.

Spinal Column Deviations

Mild postural deviations are quite common and can often be remedied through proper instruction and practice in physical education. Although less common generally, the prevalence of serious postural deviations is much greater among students with disabilities than those without.

Poor posture can result from any one or a combination of factors, such as environmental conditions, genetics, physical or growth abnormalities, or psychological conditions. In many cases children are unaware that they have poor posture because they do not know what correct posture is and how theirs differs. In other cases, postural deviations can be traced to simple environmental factors, such as poorly fitting shoes. In students with disabilities, poor posture can be caused by conditions affecting balance (e.g., visual impairments), neuromuscular conditions (e.g., spina bifida and cerebral palsy), or congenital defects (e.g., bone deformities and amputations).

Physical educators play an important role in the identification and remediation of postural deviations in all students (Horvat et al., 2019). Several excellent posture screening tests are available that can be used easily by physical educators and involve minimal preparation and equipment to administer. Two examples, included in the Print Resources list at the end of this chapter, are the Posture Grid (Adams & McCubbin, 1991) and the New York State Posture Rating Test (see figure 16.4) (New York State Education Department, 1966). Posture screening should be an annual procedure in all physical education programs. Particular attention should be paid to children with disabilities because of their generally higher incidence of postural deviation. The educator can address most mild postural deviations within the general physical education program by educating children about proper body mechanics and prescribing exercises that can be performed both in and out of class. Sample exercises are described later in the chapter.

Viewed from the back, the spinal column should be straight with no lateral (sideways) curves. Any lateral curvature in the back is abnormal and is referred to as **scoliosis**. Viewed from the side, the spinal column has two mild curves. The first natural curve occurs in the thoracic region, where the vertebrae are **concave** (curving slightly in a posterior or outward direction). An extreme curvature in this region is abnormal and is known as **kyphosis**. The second natural curve occurs in the lumbar section, where there is mild **convexity** (inward curvature) of the spine. An extreme curvature in this region is also abnormal and is called **lordosis**. An exaggerated lumbar curve in younger elementary children is natural but should disappear by the age of 8.

Scoliosis

Lateral deviations in the spinal column are classified according to whether the deviation is structural or nonstructural. **Nonstructural**, or functional, deviations are those in which the vertebrae can be realigned through positioning or removal of the primary cause—such as ignorance or muscle weaknesses—and remedied with practice and exercise. **Structural deviations** are generally related to orthopedic impairments and are permanent or fixed changes in the alignment of the vertebrae that cannot be altered through simple physical manipulation, positioning, or exercise. Structural scoliosis is also frequently classified according to the cause of the condition. Although scoliosis has many possible causes, the two most common are

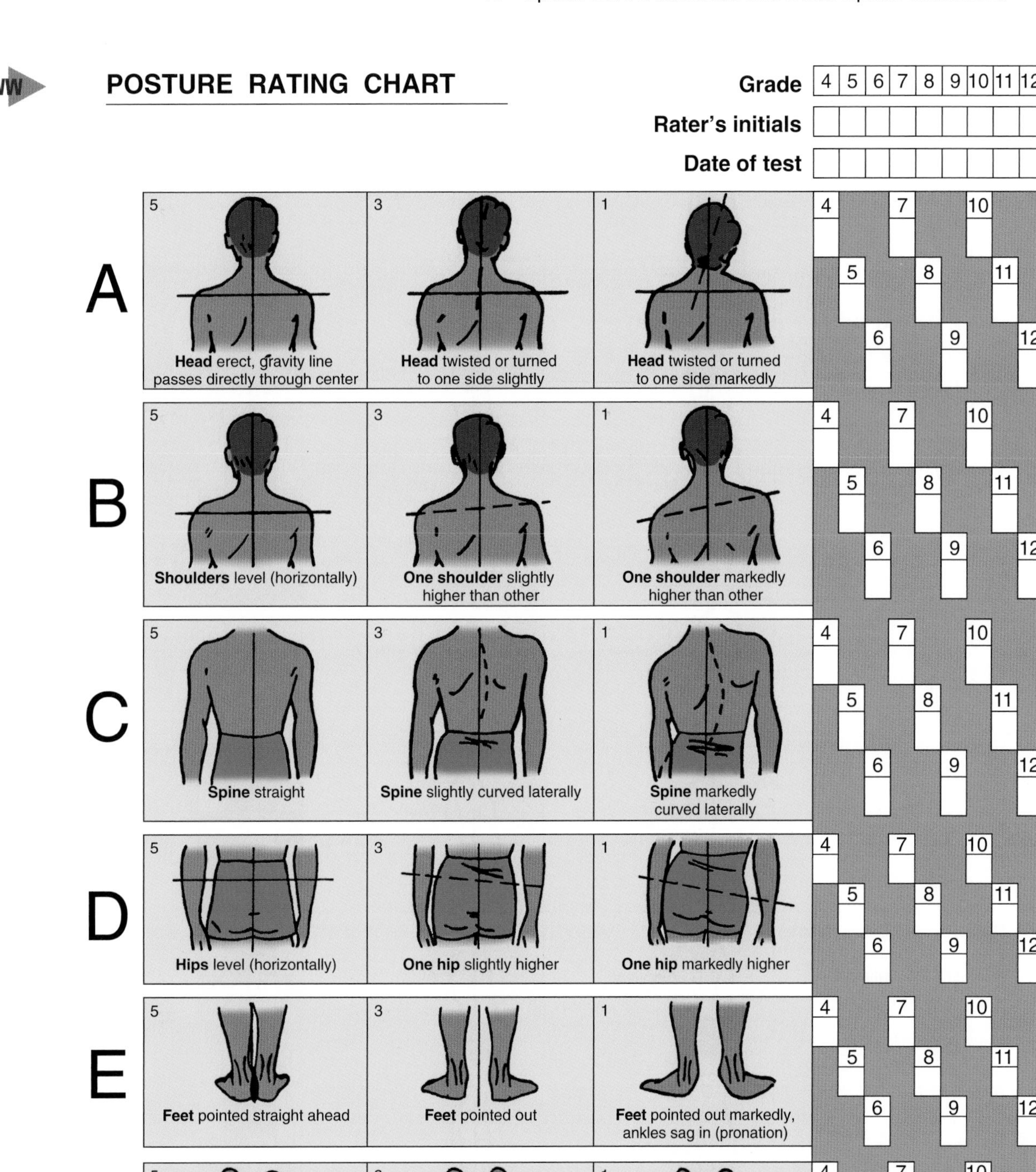

FIGURE 16.4 New York State Posture Rating Chart.

Reprinted by permission from New York State Education Department, *New York State Physical Fitness Test for Boys and Girls 4-12* (New York: New York State Education Department, 1966).

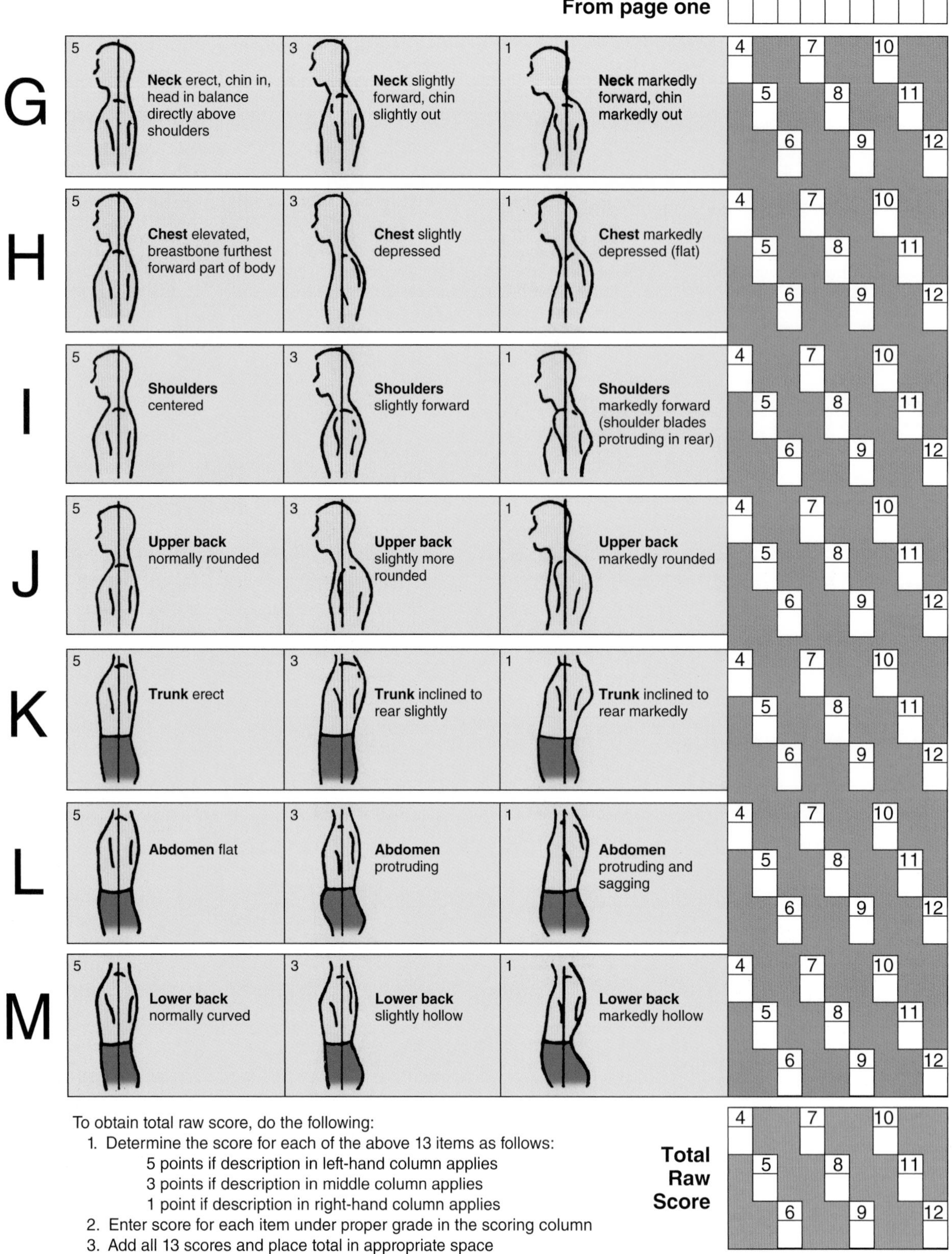

FIGURE 16.4 *(continued)*

idiopathic (e.g., unknown) and **neuromuscular** (e.g., the result of nerve or muscle problems).

Structural idiopathic scoliosis occurs in about 0.5 to 5.2 percent of all schoolchildren (Konieczny et al., 2013). The onset of scoliosis usually occurs during the early adolescent years, when children undergo a rapid growth spurt. This form of scoliosis is characterized by an *S*-shaped curve, usually composed of a major curve and one or two minor curves. The major curve causes the deformity, whereas the minor curves, sometimes called *secondary* or *compensatory curves*, usually occur above or below the major curve and are the result of the body's attempt to adjust for the major curve. Although both sexes appear to be equally affected by this condition, five times as many females have the progressive form that becomes more severe if not treated. The cause of this progressive form of scoliosis is unknown, but there is some evidence that suggests a possible genetic link in females.

Neuromuscular structural scoliosis is more commonly found in children with severe disabilities. This form of scoliosis is usually characterized by a *C*-shaped curve. In severe cases, this form of scoliosis can lead to balance difficulties, pressure on internal organs, and seating problems (pressure sores) for students who use wheelchairs (see the Application Example sidebar).

Nonstructural scoliosis can be characterized by either an *S*-curve or a *C*-curve and broadly classified as either skeletal or muscular in cause. For example, a curve may result because one leg is shorter than the other (skeletal) or because the muscles on one side of the back have become stronger than the muscles on the other side and pulled the spinal column out of line (muscular). Fortunately, nonstructural scoliosis can usually be treated by identification and correction of the cause—for example, inserting a lift in the child's shoe to equalize the length of the legs or strengthening and stretching the appropriate muscle groups in the back.

Assessment of Scoliosis

Early identification is extremely important for both structural and nonstructural scoliosis so that help can begin and the severity of the curve can be reduced. Scoliosis screening should be conducted annually for all children, particularly from the 3rd through the 10th grades, when the condition is most likely to occur. If a child is suspected of having scoliosis or other spinal column deviations, the parents or guardians should be notified, and further

Application Example

Teaching a Student With a Postural Deviation

STUDENT

A 14-year-old girl with cerebral palsy will soon be joining physical education class. This student also has a notable case of neuromuscular structural scoliosis, which presents itself as a *C*-shaped curve. She enjoys recreational activities such as bowling, where she can sit and push the bowling ball down a ramp. She can ambulate, but her spinal column condition makes it difficult for her to balance, which prevented her successful participation in physical education activities at her previous school. The student's guardians are concerned with her fitness and ask that the physical educator design a program that will allow her to exercise despite the fixed curvature of her spine.

APPLICATION

On the basis of the information presented here, the physical educator takes the following actions:

- Contacts the student's guardians to learn more about her past experiences in physical education and discovers that she suffered a serious fall last year during class
- Develops a series of aquatic-based exercises, such as aquatic jogging, which will allow the student to move without fear of losing her balance and falling
- Meets with the student to explain that she will be participating in a variety of exercises in the shallow end of the pool and that the water's buoyancy will keep her upright
- Demonstrates the exercises and has the student perform them a few times to ensure they are done correctly
- Develops a progress chart that he and the student can use to monitor her fitness improvement
- Gives the student a copy of this chart each month to share with her parents

evaluation conducted. Students suspected of having scoliosis should be monitored by appropriate medical professionals approximately every three months to ascertain if the condition is progressing. A scoliosis assessment, which can be performed in less than a minute, involves observing the student shirtless. The assessments should be done individually and by an assessor of the same sex.

To perform a scoliosis assessment, check the symmetry of the child's back while the child is standing and then when the child is bent forward. First, with the child standing erect, observe from a posterior view any differences between the two sides of the back, which follows rows A-D from figure 16.4.

Next, ask the child to bend forward at the waist to about 90 degrees, called Adam's position (figure 16.5). Examine the back from both a posterior and an anterior view for any noticeable differences in symmetry, such as curvature of the spine or one side of the back being higher or lower than the other, particularly in the thoracic and lumbar regions.

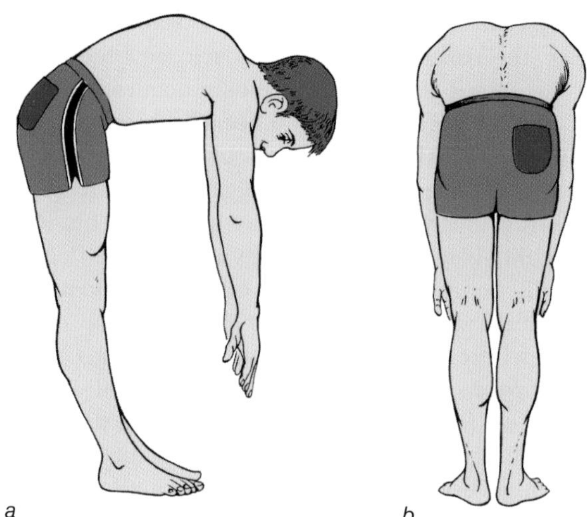

FIGURE 16.5 Adam's position showing normal spinal symmetry: *(a)* side view and *(b)* back view.

Treatment of Scoliosis

The treatment of scoliosis depends on the type and degree of curvature. As mentioned earlier, nonstructural scoliosis can frequently be corrected when the cause is identified and the condition remedied through a program of specific exercises and body awareness. With structural scoliosis, the treatment varies according to the degree of curvature. Children with mild curvatures (less than 20 degrees) are usually given exercise programs to keep the spine flexible and are monitored on a regular basis to make sure the curves are not becoming more severe.

Children with more severe curves (20-40 degrees) are usually treated with braces or orthotics, which force the spine into better alignment to prevent it from deviating further. The bracing is not meant to correct the condition but to keep it from becoming worse. Historically, the Milwaukee brace has been reported as the most effective; however, the visible cervical collar has resulted in lower rates of compliance. Today, most scoliosis braces are made of molded Orthoplast and custom fitted to the individual. These braces, also known as low-profile braces, TLSO (thoracic lumber sacral orthosis) braces, or underarm braces, have been found to be effective in treating mild and moderate curves (see figure 16.6). One of the major advantages of the Orthoplast brace is that it is less conspicuous and therefore tends to be worn more consistently. These braces must be worn continuously until the child reaches skeletal maturity—in many cases, for four to five years. The brace can be removed for short periods for activities such as

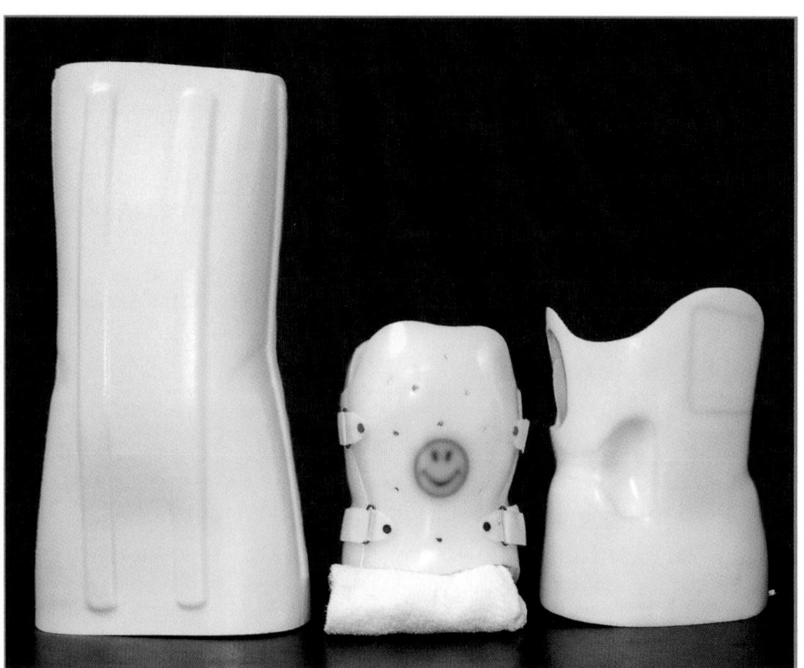

FIGURE 16.6 Sample TLSO braces used in the treatment of scoliosis.

swimming and bathing. The treatment of scoliosis in people who use wheelchairs might also involve modifying the chair to improve alignment and to equalize seating pressures. For the latest information on braces used to treat scoliosis, check the Online Resources listed for this chapter.

Typically, for spinal column deviations in which the curve is greater than 40 to 45 degrees or does not respond to bracing, surgery is employed (Choudhry et al., 2016; Reamy & Slakey, 2001). The surgical treatment usually involves fusing together the vertebrae in the affected region of the spine by means of bone grafts and the implantation of a metal rod. Following surgery, a brace is typically worn for about a year until the fusion has solidified.

Kyphosis and Lordosis

Abnormal concavity (backward curve) in the thoracic region (kyphosis) and abnormal convexity (forward curve) in the lumbar region (lordosis) are usually nonstructural and the result of poor posture (see figure 16.4, rows G-M). These deformities are routinely remedied by exercise programs designed to tighten specific muscle groups and stretch opposing muscle groups, as well as through education designed to make students aware of proper posture and body mechanics. The physical educator can assess kyphosis and lordosis by observing children from the side view under the conditions described previously for scoliosis screening.

Structural kyphosis, sometimes called *Scheuermann's disease* or *juvenile kyphosis*, is similar in appearance during the early stages to the nonstructural form described earlier, but it is the result of a deformity in the shape of the vertebrae in the thoracic region. Although the cause of this vertebral deformity is unknown, it can be diagnosed by X-ray. This form of kyphosis is frequently accompanied by a compensatory lordotic curve. The prevalence of this deformity is not known, but it appears to affect the sexes equally during adolescence.

Early detection and treatment of structural kyphosis can result in effective remediation of the condition. The treatment typically involves wearing a brace continuously for one to two years until the vertebrae reshape themselves. A variety of braces and orthotic jackets have been developed for the treatment of this condition. The Milwaukee brace, also used for the treatment of scoliosis, is considered one of the more effective braces for treating this form of kyphosis. This brace supports the body in an upright position using a pelvic corset connected by metal bars to a neck ring to help prevent and remediate further curvature.

Working With Students With Spinal Column Deviations

Children identified as having mild, nonstructural postural problems should receive special instruction and exercises. Following are several guidelines that should be considered whenever a physical educator is designing, implementing, or monitoring an exercise program to correct postural deviations.

- Establish and follow policies and procedures for working with students suspected of having structural or serious postural deviations of the spinal column.
- In an exercise program to remediate a postural deviation, the objective is to strengthen the muscles used to pull the spinal column back into correct alignment and to stretch or lengthen the muscles that are pulling the spinal column out of alignment. The stretching program should be performed at least twice a day, and muscle-strengthening exercises should be performed at least every other day.
- All exercise and activity programs should begin and end with stretching exercises, with the greatest emphasis on static stretching. Stretches should each be performed five times and held for a count of 15 seconds.
- The exercise program should begin with mild, low-intensity exercises that can be easily performed by the student. The intensity of the exercises should be gradually increased as the student's strength and endurance increase.
- When implementing an individualized exercise program, first explain to the student the nature of the postural deviation being addressed, the reasons why good posture is desirable, and the ways in which the exercises will help. The exercises should then be taught and monitored until the child clearly understands how to perform them correctly. The importance of making the student aware of the difference between the present posture and the desired posture cannot be overemphasized. Mirrors and videotapes are useful for giving students feedback on posture. Feedback may be enhanced by new technology (e.g., iPosture, Upright posture device) provided in the Online Resources at the end of the chapter.
- Children should follow their exercise programs at home on the days they do not have physical education. Some form of monitoring system, such as a log or progress chart, should be used.
- Exercises that make the body symmetrical are recommended. The use of asymmetric exercises,

especially for children being treated for scoliosis, should be used only following medical consultation.

- When selecting exercises to remediate one curve (e.g., the major curve), take care to ensure that the exercise does not foster the development of another curve (e.g., the minor curve).
- Students wearing braces such as the Milwaukee brace can exercise and participate in physical education, although activities that cause trauma to the spine (e.g., jumping and gymnastics) might be contraindicated. As a general rule, the brace is self-limiting.

Recommended Exercises

The following section includes sample exercises for the upper and lower back that can be used in the remediation of the three major spinal column deviations discussed in this chapter. These exercises are only examples and are far from a complete list. Several resources that provide additional exercises and more detailed descriptions of their performance are listed at the end of this chapter. Using the guidelines from this chapter and drawing on an understanding of the muscles involved in a spinal column deviation, a physical educator should be able to select appropriate exercises and activities.

Sample Upper Back Exercises

The following sample exercises can be used to remediate nonstructural deviations in the upper spine.

- Symmetrical swimming strokes such as the backstroke and the breaststroke. If a pool is not available, the arm patterns of these strokes can be performed on a bench covered with a mat. Hand weights or pulley weights can be used to control the resistance.
- Rowing using either a rowboat or a rowing machine. The rowing action can also be performed with hand weights or pulley weights.
- Hanging from a bar; this is a good stretching exercise.

Sample Lower Back Exercises

The following sample exercises can be used to remediate nonstructural deviations in the lower back.

- Any type of correctly performed sit-ups commensurate with the student's ability. Emphasis should be placed on keeping the lower back flat and performing the sit-ups in a slow, continuous action, as opposed to performing a large number of repetitions. Raising the hips and sudden jerky movements should not be allowed.
- Doing a bicycling action with the legs from a supine position on a mat.
- Any variation of leg lifts, as long as the lower back is kept flat and pressed against the floor.

Orthotic Devices

Because of the neuromuscular limitations imposed by spinal cord disabilities, many people with these disabilities use orthotics to enhance their functional abilities. **Orthotic devices** are splints and braces designed to provide support, improve positioning, correct or prevent deformities, and reduce or alleviate pain. As noted earlier, the use of orthotic devices is not limited to people with spinal cord disabilities—for example, the Milwaukee brace is commonly used to treat scoliosis and kyphosis, which can occur in any adolescent. Orthotic devices are prescribed by physicians and fitted by occupational therapists, who also instruct users in wearing and caring for the devices. Examples of the more common orthotics are shown in figure 16.7. They are used both by people who are ambulatory to provide better stability and by people who use wheelchairs to prevent deformities. These devices are commonly referred to by abbreviations that describe the joints they cover: AFO (ankle–foot orthotics), KAFO (knee–ankle–foot orthotics), and HKAFO (hip–knee–ankle–foot orthotics). Additional information on orthotics can be found in the Online Resources at the end of the chapter.

Many newer plastic orthotics can be worn inside regular shoes and under clothing. Under normal circumstances, orthotics should be worn in all physical education activities with the exception of swimming. During vigorous activities, physical educators should periodically check that the straps are secure and that no abrasion or skin irritation is occurring.

Orthotics can also be used to improve positioning to maximize sensory input. Figure 16.8 shows a series of assistive devices often used to help children with spina bifida view and interact with the environment from the developmental vertical postures that they cannot attain and maintain on their own. The last device is a parapodium, or standing table, which frees the individual from the burden of balancing or bearing weight (or

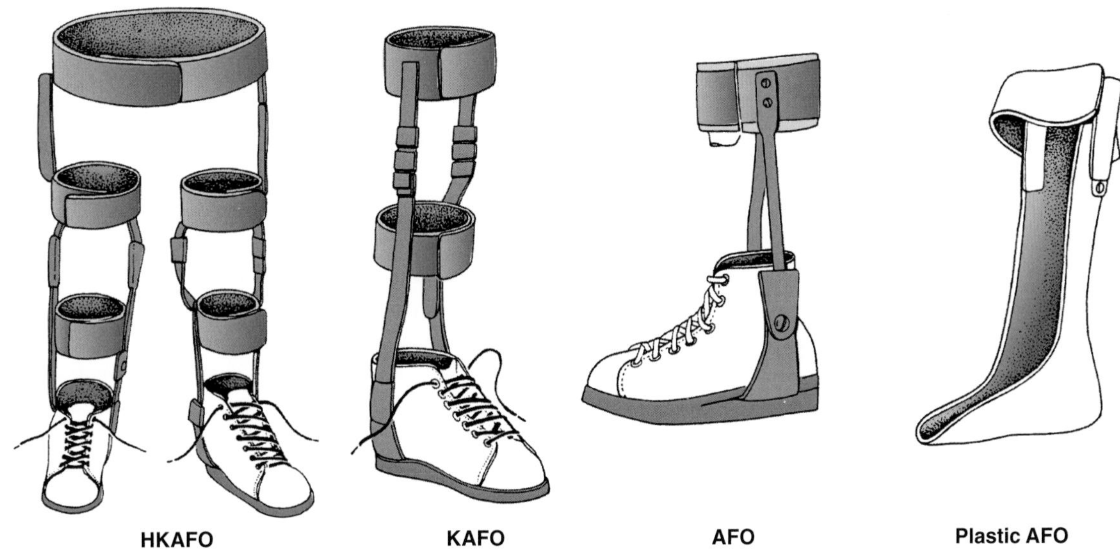

FIGURE 16.7 Common orthotic devices worn by people with spinal cord disabilities.

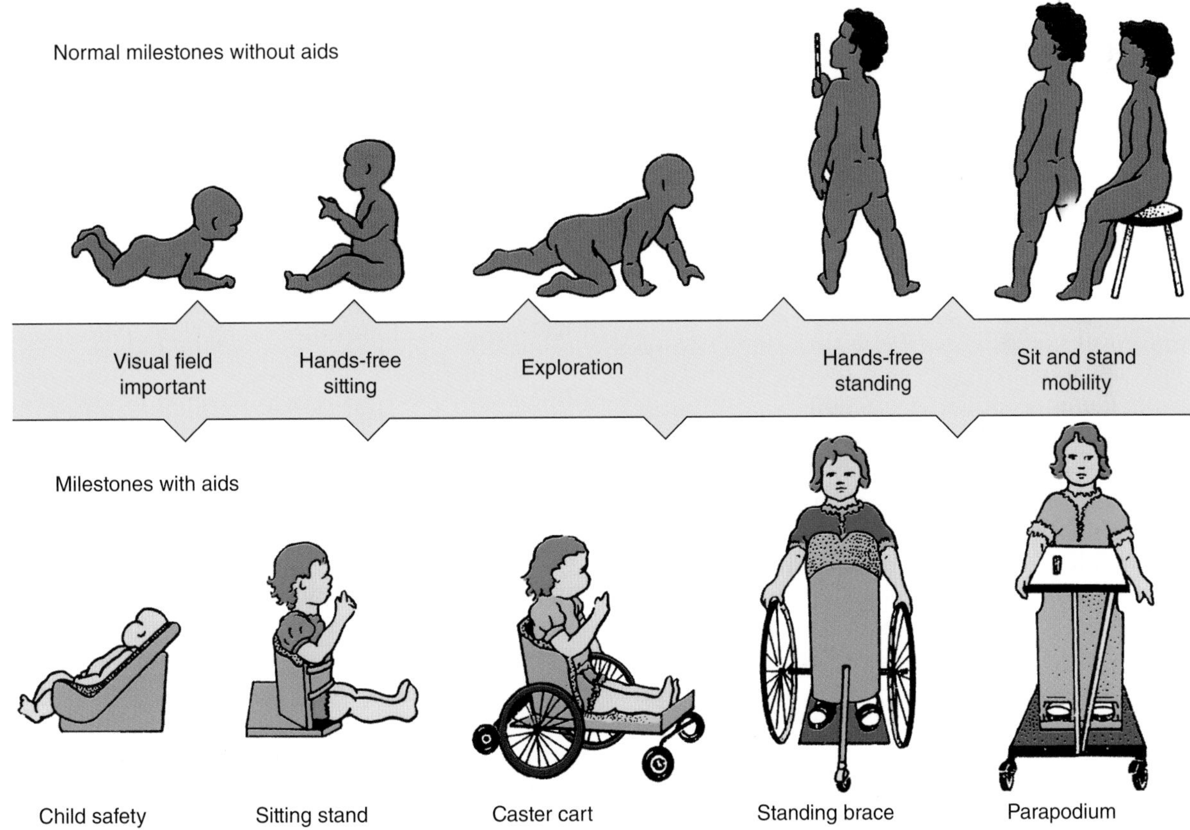

FIGURE 16.8 Orthotic devices help children with spina bifida attain normal developmental postures.

the inability to do so) and also affords complete use of the arms and hands. The parapodium can be used effectively in physical education to teach skills such as table tennis. In recent years, several companies have devised ingenious modifications of the parapodium so that the table can be easily adjusted to many vertical and horizontal positions.

A secondary category of orthotic devices includes canes and walkers used as assistive devices for ambulation. The **Lofstrand** or **Canadian**

crutches are most commonly used by people with spina bifida and spinal cord disabilities who ambulate with leg braces and crutches. Physical educators should be aware that a person using only one cane or crutch employs it on the strong side, thus immobilizing the better arm. Appropriate modifications (e.g., to maintain balance) should be considered for skills in which use of the dominant arm is desired.

Implications for Physical Education

Assessment is the key to successfully addressing the physical education needs of students with spinal cord disabilities. The goal of assessment is to obtain the most accurate and complete data possible so that the most appropriate placement and instruction can be provided (Kelly, 2011; Kelly & Melograno, 2014; Kelly et al., 2010). Because of the uniqueness of each spinal cord disability or condition, physical educators must be willing to devote the time and effort to develop their own authentic assessment tools and scoring rubrics to evaluate and teach functional motor skills to help their students reach their maximum potential in physical education (Horvat et al., 2019). Additional information on assessment is presented in chapter 4; additional information on motor development is presented in chapter 19.

Physical educators must be involved in team-based collaboration to obtain the data they need to provide appropriate instruction. By consulting with each other, the physical educator and the physical or occupational therapist can share essential information and mutually develop goals and objectives for each student. The physical therapist can provide pertinent information about existing muscle strength and prognosis for further development, the range of motion at the various joints, and the presence or absence of sensation in the limbs, as well as useful information about adapted appliances (e.g., a device to hold a racket when a grip is not possible), practical guidance about putting on and removing braces, lifting and handling the student, and adjusting and positioning the wheelchair.

The physical educator must be able to assess the physical fitness and motor skills of students with spinal cord disabilities. The Brockport Physical Fitness Test (BPFT) is currently the only health-related, criterion-referenced physical fitness test that is designed to accommodate people with spinal cord disabilities and provides appropriate standards for the evaluation of physical fitness for this population (Winnick & Short, 2014). The BPFT recommends that people with spinal cord injuries be evaluated in the areas of aerobic functioning, body composition, and musculoskeletal function. Criterion-referenced test items are provided for each area, with modifications for levels of functioning based on the level of the spinal cord injury. For example, the following test items would be recommended for a student who is a paraplegic and uses a wheelchair: for aerobic functioning, the 15-minute Target Aerobic Movement Test; for body composition, the sum of the triceps and subscapular skinfold test; and for musculoskeletal function, the seated push-up, dominant grip strength, and modified Apley tests.

In general, students with spinal cord disabilities score significantly lower than students without disabilities at the same age level on physical fitness measures and in motor skill development. Winnick and Short (1985), for example, have reported that 52 to 72 percent of people with spinal cord disabilities in their Project UNIQUE study had skinfold measures greater than the median value for same-age subjects who were not impaired, and that only about 19 percent of the girls and 36 percent of the boys with spinal cord disabilities scored above the nonimpaired median on grip strength. Winnick and Short (1984) have also reported that young people with paraplegic spinal neuromuscular conditions have generally lower fitness levels than their peers without disabilities of the same age and sex—and that they do not demonstrate significant improvement with age or show significant sex differences as do their peers without disabilities. Research has also revealed that obesity is a significant problem for individuals with spinal cord injuries (Chen et al., 2011). These results, however, should not be misinterpreted to mean that people with spinal cord disabilities or other spinal conditions cannot develop better levels of physical fitness. On the contrary, research has shown that participation in physical activity improves physical fitness and quality of life (Tomasone et al., 2013; Warburton et al., 2007). The key is appropriate instruction and practice designed to address individual needs.

Fitness programs for students with spinal cord disabilities should focus on the development of all components of physical fitness. Although flexibility in all joints should be a goal, particular emphasis should be placed on preventing or reducing contractures in joints in which muscles are no longer innervated. A regular routine of stretching should move these joints through the full range of motion.

Strength training should focus on restoring or maximizing the strength in the unaffected muscles. Care must be taken not to create muscle imbalances by over strengthening muscle groups when the antagonist muscles are affected. Most common progressive resistance exercises are suitable for people with spinal cord disabilities with little or no modification. Posture and correct body mechanics should be stressed during all strength training activities.

One of the most challenging fitness areas for people with spinal cord disabilities is cardiorespiratory endurance. Work in this area is frequently complicated by the loss of the large-muscle groups of the legs, which makes cardiorespiratory training more difficult. Research has shown that people with paraplegia typically have about only half the cardiac output of people without spinal cord injuries, and people with tetraplegia tend to have about only a third the cardiac output of people with paraplegia (American College of Sports Medicine [ACSM], 2016). In these cases, the principles of intensity, frequency, and duration must be applied to less traditional aerobic activities that use the smaller muscle groups of the arms and shoulders. A number of wheelchair ergometers and hand-driven bicycle ergometers have been designed specifically to address the cardiorespiratory needs of people with spinal cord disabilities. Although it is more difficult to attain the benefits of cardiorespiratory training using the smaller muscle groups of the arms and shoulders, it is not impossible. There are several highly conditioned wheelchair marathoners who clearly demonstrate that high levels of aerobic fitness can be attained.

When working with people with spinal cord injuries, safety must be a major concern. People with spinal cord injuries, particularly those with injuries above T6, are subject to a number of problems, such as hypotension, problems of thermoregulation, and limits on their maximal exercise heart rates. **Hypotension** (low blood pressure) is caused by a disruption of the sympathetic nervous system. During aerobic exercise, the body depends on the large muscles in the legs to contract and assist in pumping blood back to the heart. When the legs are not involved, blood can pool in the legs, reducing the amount of blood returned to the heart and, subsequently, the stroke volume of the heart. Some precautions that can be taken to reduce hypotension are exercising in a reclined position and including appropriate warm-ups and cool-downs as part of the workout so the body can gradually adapt to the increased workload.

Thermoregulation refers to the ability of the body to regulate its internal temperature in response to the outside temperature. The higher the injury on the spine, the greater the problems with thermal regulation. When thermal regulation is an issue, care should be taken to avoid exercising in extremely cold or hot environments. Physical educators should also keep cool compresses available to help students cool down after aerobic workouts.

People with spinal cord injuries above T6 are also subject to autonomic dysreflexia and limitations in their maximal exercise heart rates. **Autonomic dysreflexia** refers to a rapid increase in heart rate and blood pressure to dangerous levels. Several factors, including bowel or bladder distension, restrictive clothing, or skin irritation, can trigger a reflex to constrict blood vessels and increase blood pressure. Normally, another set of reflexes should also be triggered that monitors and subsequently relaxes these blood vessels. In people with T6 and higher lesions, however, the second set of reflexes is not triggered, possibly resulting in dangerously high blood pressure levels. Care should be taken to ensure that the bowel and bladder are emptied before exercise and that heart rate and blood pressure are monitored before and during exercise. If not monitored and treated in a timely fashion, this can be a life-threatening condition. Disruption to the integration of the parasympathetic and the sympathetic nervous systems also limits the maximum heart rate in people with injuries above T6 to approximately 120 beats per minute, which limits the aerobic training effects that can be achieved.

Several excellent resources are available to assist physical educators in planning and implementing safe fitness programs for individuals with spinal cord injuries (e.g., ACSM, 2016; Frontera et al., 2006; Winnick & Short, 1999). An online exercise program called Every Body Fitness (2020) is another resource that focuses on strengthening, cardiovascular fitness, and weight loss for a variety of special populations, including individuals with spinal cord disabilities. The ACSM, in collaboration with the National Center on Physical Activity and Disability (NCPAD), has also created a fitness certification, the Certified Inclusive Fitness Trainer, for fitness professionals who work with people with disabilities.

In addition to physical fitness and motor skills, physical educators should concentrate on posture and body mechanics. People with spinal cord disabilities frequently have poor body mechanics as a result of muscle imbalances and contractures.

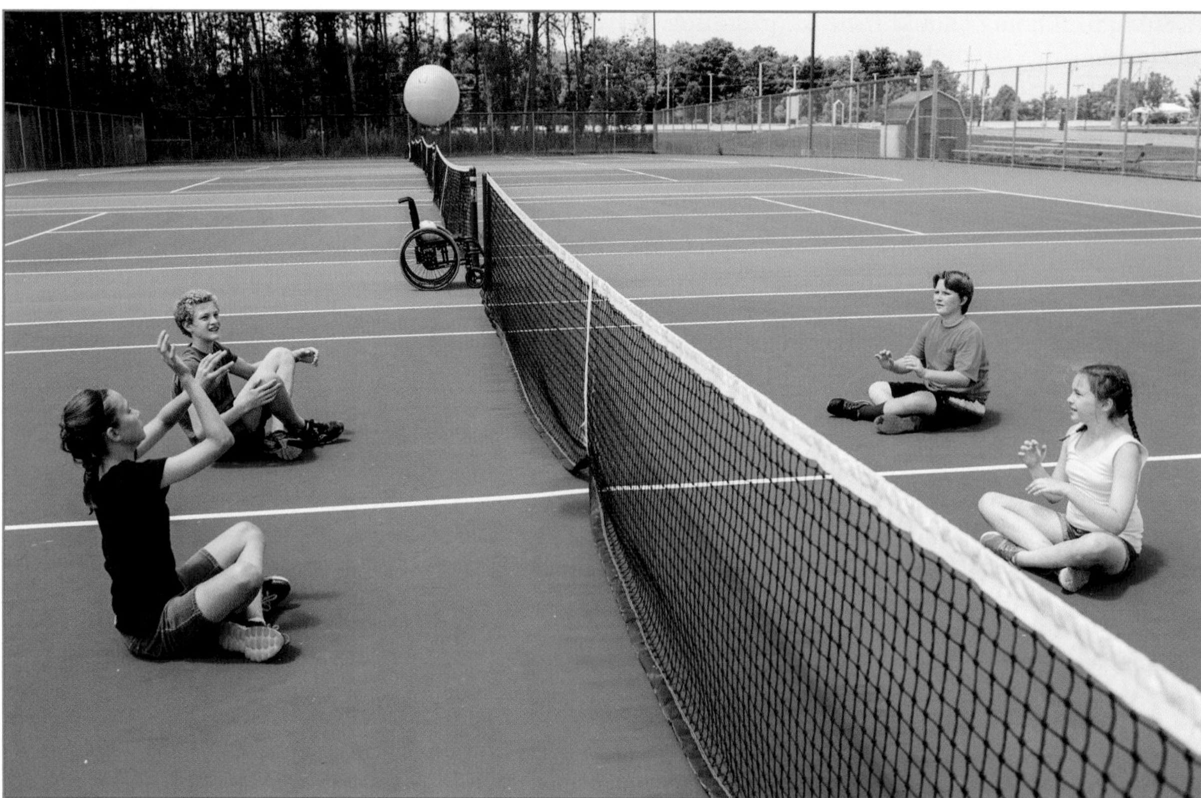

FIGURE 16.9 Sports such as volleyball can be modified to allow for participation by people with disabilities.

Exercises and activities that contribute to body awareness and alignment should thus be stressed.

In terms of sport skills, the most valuable activities are those with the greatest carryover potential for lifetime participation. The selection of activities should provide a balance between warm- and cold-weather sports as well as indoor and outdoor sports. Preference should be given to sports that promote physical fitness and for which there are organized opportunities for participation in the community. Just about any sport (e.g., softball, golf, tennis, swimming, skiing) can be adapted or modified so that people with spinal cord disabilities can participate. Figure 16.9 shows several people playing a game of sitting volleyball on an outdoor court.

Strategies for Inclusion

Once assessment has been completed and goals and objectives are established for a student with a spinal cord disability, the next challenge is providing them with instruction to achieve these goals in the most inclusive physical education setting possible. The teacher must create a learning space that allows students with spinal cord disabilities to feel included—to feel a sense of value, belonging, and acceptance (Stainback & Stainback, 1996). To this end, physical educators should adopt a universal design for learning (UDL) approach for their instruction (discussed in more detail in chapters 2 and 7). Using this approach, a physical educator will proactively and intentionally design the learning space to meet the diverse range of all their students' needs, thus creating an inclusive environment that will not single out any particular student (Burgstahler, 2015). For example, a teacher should offer a variety of equipment that is accessible and usable by all students. Because all students are at different levels of fitness, it is common to develop individual routines based on the students' assessed needs and then use a circuit approach to have students work on their programs. In an individualized setting like this, it is easy to accommodate the unique needs of students with spinal cord disabilities without singling them out.

Other physical education content, such as working on sport skills (e.g., the volleyball serve), can initially appear more difficult to modify because such skills are traditionally taught to the class as a whole, and then used in activities and games.

For example, how do you maximize participation of a student with a spinal cord injury who uses a wheelchair in a volleyball game if the student cannot hit the ball hard enough to serve over the net and cannot move quickly enough to defend part of the court? What are some possible modifications? The student could use a lightweight ball. The student could be allowed to serve closer to the net. The student could be given a smaller zone to defend on the court after the ball is served. More students could be assigned to each side to reduce the amount of space needing to be defended. Such modifications could also be beneficial for students without disabilities who are beginners or low-skilled; thus universal design that provides these opportunities for success for all students is important. These modifications also allow for differentiated instruction and learning, whereby students are able to work on the same content, but in a manner consistent with their diverse learning styles and multisensory needs (Ellis et al., 2009).

Although the physical educator is responsible for creating an inclusive setting in which the needs of all students are addressed, it is also important that students with spinal cord disabilities be taught how to advocate for themselves. This form of self-advocacy involves students being able to analyze new games and activities and then offer suggestions on how the activities could be modified so that they can successfully participate. This is a critical skill for all students with disabilities because the physical educator will not be there to implement a UDL approach in physical activities outside of school. A common transition step from teacher-directed accommodations to those that are student-directed is to have the class help to develop modifications and accommodations. This process also sensitizes the other students to the value of making activities appropriate for *all* participants, not just those with disabilities. The key components of making appropriate modifications are: (1) the activity must still serve its original purpose, and (b) people with disabilities must be working on the same skills or similar skills modified to meet their unique needs. Assigning students with spinal cord disabilities to roles such as scorekeeper is not appropriate integration because they are not developing the skills they need to live and maintain an active healthy lifestyle. Further, this practice is likely not to feel inclusive to the students themselves; being relegated to the sidelines does not promote a sense of value, belonging, or acceptance. In the long term, inclusive physical education settings are beneficial for everyone and require that instruction be assessment based and universally designed. It also requires successful participation of all students in the planned drills, games, and activities, which should result in positive learning outcomes for all students.

Adapted Sport

Today, many organizations sponsor athletic programs and sporting events for people with spinal cord disabilities. Move United plays a major role in organizing and sponsoring both competitive and noncompetitive sport activities for people with disabilities, including those with spinal cord injuries and spina bifida. Its mission is to "provide national leadership and opportunities for individuals with disabilities to develop independence, confidence, and fitness through participation in community sports, competition, recreation, high performance sport and educational programs" (Move United, 2020a). It sponsors a variety of events such as alpine skiing, snowboarding, sled hockey, snowshoeing, Nordic skiing, handcycling, surfing, golf, cycling, kayaking, canoeing, water skiing, sailing, fishing, scuba, climbing, hiking, track, triathlon, and equestrian (Move United, 2020b). This organization is a leader in the development and dissemination of recreation and fitness and training materials related to sport and recreation for people with disabilities. Move United also serves as the official governing body for sport competitions for people with amputations.

Several organizations also sponsor athletic competitions in a specific sport for individuals with disabilities. For example, the National Wheelchair Basketball Association (NWBA) was formed in 1949 and sponsors competition for men, women, and youth. As discussed earlier in the chapter, the NWBA uses its own classification system for play, with each player assigned to one of eight classes based on motor control and functional movement ability. Teams are equated for competition through limiting the sum of the five player classifications to 15 or less (see table 16.2). This classification system provides an excellent model; a similar classification system based on students' skill levels could also be designed and used in integrated physical education classes that include students with spinal cord disabilities.

Over the past decade, wheelchair sports have evolved from primarily recreational activities into highly sophisticated and competitive events, largely as a result of technical advances in wheelchair design and research related to the postural and body mechanics of wheelchair propulsion (see chapter 29 for more on wheelchair sport performance). Several additional resources are available to help physical educators and coaches design and implement training and conditioning programs for their wheelchair athletes (Davis, 2011; Goosey-Tolfrey, 2010).

Adapted sport programs provide students with spinal cord disabilities equal opportunities to gain the benefits, experiences, and motivations that all athletes derive from sport. These activities give participants an opportunity to meet and interact socially with others who have similar characteristics, interests, and needs. Finally, these sport experiences expose students with spinal cord disabilities to positive role models who demonstrate the difference between having a disability and being handicapped. To maximize the probability that students with disabilities will succeed in sport, physical educators must ensure that the physical education curriculum provides instruction in fundamental sport skills and the appropriate transition from skill development to skill application in actual sport situations.

Summary

People with spinal cord disabilities or other spinal conditions need to pursue the same physical education goals as other students. Physical educators must have a thorough understanding of the nature of the disabilities and the functional abilities that can be attained to determine the most appropriate placement and instructional programming for each student. Particular emphasis should be placed on body awareness and proper body mechanics to minimize the negative impact of spinal column deviations. In addition, special attention should be given to physical fitness. Many people with spinal cord disabilities are predisposed to obesity and have imposed constraints on how they can train because of their disability. All programs should be designed so that individuals leave the program with functional lifetime sport skills that can be used to maintain their health and fitness. Adapted sport that uses functional ability classification systems provides excellent opportunities for people with spinal cord disabilities to apply and practice the skills learned in physical education.

References

Adams, R.C., & McCubbin, J.A. (1991). *Games, sports, and exercises for the physically disabled* (4th ed.). Lea & Febiger.

Adzick, N.S., Thom, E.A., Spong, C.Y., Brock III, J.W., Burrows, P.K., Johnson, M.P., Howell, L.J., Farrell, J.A., Dabrowiak, M.E., Sutton, L.N., Gupta, N., Tulipan, N.B., D'Alton, M.E., & Farmer, D.L. (2011). A randomized trial of prenatal versus postnatal repair of myelomeningocele. *New England Journal of Medicine, 364*(11), 993-1003. https://doi.org/10.1056/NEJMoa1014379

American College of Sports Medicine (ACSM). (2016). *ACSM's exercise management for persons with chronic diseases and disabilities* (4th ed.). Human Kinetics.

American Medical Association (AMA). (2009). *Handbook of first aid and emergency care.* Random House.

Burgstahler, S.E. (2015). *Universal design in higher education: From principles to practice* (2nd ed.). Harvard Education Press.

Centers for Disease Control and Prevention (CDC). (2015). Updated estimates of neural tube defects prevent by mandatory folic acid fortification—United States, 1995-2011. *Morbidity and Mortality Weekly Report (MMWR).* www.cdc.gov/mmwr/preview/mmwrhtml/mm6401a2.htm

Chen, Y., Cao, Y., Allen, V., & Richards, J.S. (2011). Weight matters: Physical and psychosocial well being of persons with spinal cord injury in relation to body mass index. *Archives of Physical Medicine and Rehabilitation, 92*(3), 391-398. https://doi.org/10.1016/j.apmr.2010.06.030

Children's Hospital of Philadelphia. (2020). *About fetal surgery for spina bifida (myelomeningocele).* www.chop.edu/treatments/fetal-surgery-spina-bifida/about

Choudhry, M.N., Ahmad, Z., & Verma, R. (2016). Adolescent idiopathic scoliosis. *Open Orthopaedics Journal, 10,* 143-154. https://doi.org/10.2174/1874325001610010143

Davis, R.W. (2011). *Teaching disability sport: A guide for physical educators.* Human Kinetics.

Ellis, K., Lieberman, L., & LeRoux, D. (2009). Using differentiated instruction in physical education. *Palaestra, 24*(4), 19-23.

Every Body Fitness. (2020). *Welcome to every body fitness: Fitness for every body!* Retrieved from www.scitotalfitness.com

Farmer, D.L., Thom, E.A., Brock, J.W., Burrows, P.K., Johnson, M.P., Howell, L.J., Farrell, J.A., Gupta, N., & Adzick, N.S. (2018). The management of myelomeningocele study: Full cohort 30-month pediatric outcomes. *American Journal of Obstetrics & Gynecology, 218*(2), 256.e1-256.e13.

Fletcher, J.M., Ostermaier, K.K., Cirino, P.T., & Dennis, M. (2008). Neurobehavioral outcomes in spina bifida: Processes versus outcomes. *Journal of Pediatric Rehabilitation Medicine, 1*(4), 311-324.

Frontera, W.R., Slovik, D.M., & Dawson, D.M. (2006). *Exercise in rehabilitation medicine* (2nd ed.). Human Kinetics.

Goosey-Tolfrey, V. (Ed.). (2010). *Wheelchair sport: A complete guide for athletes, coaches, and teachers.* Human Kinetics.

Horvat, M., Kelly, L.E., Block, M.E., & Croce, R. (2019). *Developmental and adapted physical activity assessment* (2nd ed.). Human Kinetics.

Kelly, L.E. (2011). *Designing and implementing effective adapted physical education programs.* Sagamore.

Kelly, L.E., & Melograno, V.J. (2014). *Developing the physical education curriculum: An achievement-based approach.* Waveland Press.

Kelly, L.E., Wessel, J.A., Dummer, G., & Sampson, T. (2010). *Everyone CAN: Elementary physical education curriculum and teaching resources.* Human Kinetics.

Konieczny, M.R., Senyurt, H., & Krauspe, R. (2013). Epidemiology of adolescent idiopathic scoliosis. *Journal of Children's Orthopaedics, 7*(1), 3-9. https://doi.org/10.1007/s11832-012-0457-4

Learning Disabilities Association of America (LDAA). (2020). *Non-verbal learning disabilities.* Retrieved from https://ldaamerica.org/types-of-learning-disabilities/non-verbal-learning-disabilities/

Move United. (2020a). Our mission. Retrieved from www.moveunitedsport.org/about/our-mission/

Move United. (2020b). *Adaptive sports.* Retrieved from www.moveunitedsport.org/sports/adaptive-sports/

National Spinal Cord Injury Statistical Center (NSCISC). (2019). *Spinal cord injury facts and figures at a glance.* www.nscisc.uab.edu/Public/Facts%20and%20Figures%202019%20-%20Final.pdf

National Wheelchair Basketball Association (NWBA). (2019). *National wheelchair basketball association official rules book 2019-2020.* www.nwba.org/officialsresources

National Institutes of Health. (2019). *Myelomeningocele.* https://medlineplus.gov/ency/article/001558.htm

New York State Education Department. (1966). *New York State physical fitness test for boys and girls grades 4-12.* Author.

Pedreira, D.A.L., Reece, E.A., Chmait, R.H., Kontopoulos, E.V., & Quintero, R.A. (2016). Fetoscopic repair of spina bifida: Safer and better? *Ultrasound in Obstetrics & Gynecology, 48*(2), 141-147. https://doi.org/10.1002/uog.15987

Pelletier, C.A., Miyatani, M., Giangregorio, L., & Craven, B.C. (2016). Sarcopenic obesity in adults with spinal cord injury: A cross-sectional study. *Archives of Physical Medicine and Rehabilitation, 97*(11), 1931-1937. https://doi.org/10.1016/j.apmr.2016.04.026

Rajan, S., McNeely, M.J., Warms, C., & Goldstein, B. (2008). Clinical assessment and management of obesity in individuals with spinal cord injuries. *Journal of Spinal Cord Injuries, 31*(4), 361-372. https://doi.org/10.1080/10790268.2008.11760738

Reamy, B.V., & Slakey, J.S. (2001). Adolescent idiopathic scoliosis: Review and current concepts. *American Family Physician, 64*(1), 111-117.

Russell, C.L. (2004). Understanding nonverbal learning disorders in children with spina bifida. *Teaching Exceptional Children, 36*(4), 8-13. https://doi.org/10.1177/004005990403600401

Spina Bifida Association (SBA). (2020). *Resource: Obesity.* www.spinabifidaassociation.org/resource/obesity/#special-concerns-for-individuals-who-have-spina-bifida

Spina Bifida Association (SBA). (2021). *Spina bifida occulta: A mild form of spina bifida.* https://www.spinabifidaassociation.org/wp-content/uploads/Spina-Bifida-Occulta1.pdf

Stainback, W., & Stainback, S. (1996). Collaboration, support network and community construction. In S. Stainback & W. Stainback (Eds.), *Inclusion: A guide for educators* (pp. 223-232). Paul H. Brookes Publishing Co.

Tomasone, J.R., Wesch, N.N., Martin Ginis, K.A., & Noreau, L. (2013). Spinal cord injury, physical activity, and quality of life: A systematic review. *Kinesiology Review, 2,* 113-129. http://doi.org/10.1123/krj.2.2.113

Warburton, D.E., Eng, J.J., Krassioukov, A., & Sproule, S. (2007). Cardiovascular health and exercise rehabilitation in spinal cord injury. *Topics in Spinal Cord Injury Rehabilitation, 13*(1), 98-122. https://doi.org/10.1310/sci1301-98

Williams, L.J., Mai, C.T., Edmonds, L.D., Shaw, G.M., Kirby, R.S., Hobbs, C.A., Sever, L.E., Miller, L.A., Meaney, F.J., & Levitt, M. (2002). Prevalence of spina bifida and anencephaly during the transition to mandatory folic acid fortification in the United States. *Teratology, 66*(1), 33-39. https://doi.org/10.1002/tera.10060

Winnick, J.P., & Short, F.X. (1984). The physical fitness of youngsters with spinal neuromuscular conditions. *Adapted Physical Activity Quarterly, 1,* 37-51.

Winnick, J.P., & Short, F.X. (1985). *Physical fitness testing of the disabled.* Human Kinetics.

Winnick, J.P., & Short, F.X. (Eds.). (1999). *The Brockport physical fitness training guide.* Human Kinetics.

Winnick, J.P., & Short, F.X. (2014). *The Brockport physical fitness test manual.* Human Kinetics.

Print Resources

American College of Sports Medicine (ACSM). (2016). *ACSM's exercise management of persons with chronic diseases and disabilities* (4th ed.). Human Kinetics.

This book provides guidelines for exercise testing and programming for people with spinal cord injuries. Excellent recommendations are provided regarding safety and precautions that should be taken to reduce risks during exercise.

Ferrara, M.S., & Davis, R.W. (1990). Injuries to wheelchair athletes. *Paraplegia, 28,* 335-341.

This article is an excellent resource for understanding common injuries that occur in wheelchair athletes and the treatment protocols for these injuries.

New York State Posture Rating Test. (1966). In *New York State physical fitness test for boys and girls grades 4-12.* New York State Education Department.

This is an easy-to-use and comprehensive screening test for upper and lower back postural deviations.

Posture Grid. (1991). In R.C. Adams & J.A. McCubbin (Eds.), *Games, sports and exercises for the physically disabled* (4th ed., pp. 155-162). Lea & Febiger.

This source describes how to make your own posture grid, which can then be used to evaluate postural deviations of the head, spine, legs, and feet.

Rimmer, J. (1994). *Fitness and rehabilitation programs for special populations.* WCB Brown & Benchmark.

This book outlines the physical fitness needs of individuals with various disabilities and provides programming recommendations on how to address these needs.

Wells, C.L., & Hooker, S.P. (1990). The spinal injured athlete. *Adapted Physical Activity Quarterly, 7,* 265-285.

This article highlights the unique fitness and training needs of athletes with spinal cord injuries and how to address these needs.

Video Resources

AbleData, 103 W. Broad St., Ste. 400, Falls Church, VA 22046; phone: 800-277-0216. https://abledata.acl.gov

AbleData provides consumer information for people with disabilities about assistive technology products and rehabilitation resources, both domestic and international. Among these materials are over 20 videotapes designed for people with various physical disabilities, from infants to senior citizens. Examples include exercise ball workouts for individuals with neurological, balance, lower extremity, and extremity disabilities, as well as Exertube workouts for people with upper extremity disabilities.

National Center on Health, Physical Activity and Disability (NCHPAD), 4000 Ridgeway Dr., Birmingham, AL 35209; phone: 800-900-8086. www.nchpad.org/videos/

Funded by a grant from the CDC, NCHPAD offers a number of videos that address the physical and recreation needs of individuals with disabilities. Two examples are the following:

- *Exercise Program for Individuals with Spinal Cord Injuries: Paraplegia* [video, Quick Series Booklet].
- *Exercise Program for Individuals with Spinal Cord Injuries: Tetraplegia* [video, Quick Series Booklet].

National Scoliosis Foundation, 5 Cabot Pl., Stoughton, MA 02072; phone: 800-673-6922; e-mail: NSF@scoliosis.org. www.scoliosis.org

This is an excellent source for videos on the history, nature, and treatment of scoliosis. Videos range in length from 8 to 60 minutes and cost $10 to $50.

Online Resources

Christopher and Dana Reeve Foundation: www.christopherreeve.org/living-with-paralysis

The Christopher and Dana Reeve Foundation paralysis resource center lists a variety of resources in the areas of health travel, rehabilitation, equipment, and more.

Move United: www.moveunitedsport.org

This website includes the official rule books and classifications for many adaptive sports such as archery, basketball, downhill skiing, handcycling, powerlifting, shooting, swimming, tennis, and track and field.

National Scoliosis Foundation: www.scoliosis.org

This website provides links to educational and informational resources on the treatment of scoliosis.

Spina Bifida Association (SBA): http://spinabifidaassociation.org

This site contains the latest information on the treatment of spina bifida.

Tecla: https://gettecla.com/blogs/news/13884757-4-ways-quadriplegics-can-use-an-ipad-or-iphone

This article describes iPad and iPhone adaptations for users who are quadriplegics.

United Spinal Association: www.spinalcord.org

This site provides extensive coverage of the current treatment and latest research developments related to spinal cord injuries.

Other Resources

iPosture: www.iposture.com

This small digital sensor is worn on your shoulder and alerts you when your posture is out of alignment.

Upright: www.uprightpose.com

This small wearable electronic device vibrates to provide feedback on your posture. The device also comes with an app that can record and track your performance.

17

Other Health Impairment Conditions

Francis M. Kozub

William is a 17-year-old boy who has been diagnosed with leukemia. He is starting chemotherapy and his parents are concerned that he should avoid physical education class until treatment is done. William's physical educator is also concerned but has heard that proper physical activity can actually help reduce side effects in children with leukemia. What is proper physical activity programming for William? Should this be discussed at the IEP meeting or left up to the doctors to prescribe?

This chapter provides information to program planners about other health impairment (OHI) conditions covered by the most recent reauthorization of the Individuals with Disabilities Education Act (IDEA). *Other health impairment* refers to

> having limited strength, vitality, or alertness, including a heightened alertness to environmental stimuli, that results in limited alertness with respect to the educational environment, that (i) Is due to chronic or acute health problems such as asthma, attention deficit disorder or attention deficit hyperactivity disorder, diabetes, epilepsy, a heart condition, hemophilia, lead poisoning, leukemia, nephritis, rheumatic fever, and sickle cell anemia, and Tourette syndrome; and (ii) Adversely affects a child's educational performance (National Dissemination Center for Children with Disabilities, 2012).

However, these are only examples of possible conditions that may fall under this category. Others may apply, such as AIDS (acquired immunodeficiency syndrome), neurological disorders, or other types of cancers. In fact, a wide range of conditions may fall under this category, and recent statistics by the U.S. Department of Education indicate that 1.4 percent of the public school-age population are identified as having OHI, demonstrating a substantial increase over prior statistics (U.S. Department of Education Institute of Educational Sciences, 2018). For these students, an IEP committee should discuss potential physical education program modifications consistent with IDEA (National Dissemination Center for Children with Disabilities, 2012).

Other health impairment is defined in school-aged children based on the impact that chronic or acute health problems have on educational programs. This chapter focuses on the most common conditions specified in the IDEA definition, including diabetes, seizures, asthma, cancer, cardiovascular disease, anemia, AIDS, and Tourette syndrome. Many of these conditions require regular medications that may also influence behavior and motor performance. These side effects may be negligible and require no program modification; however, it is important that physical educators and coaches consider this issue when providing physical activity programming for a child with OHI. The physical education implications and a checklist for successful inclusion of children with OHI are provided for each condition in the section on inclusion.

Diabetes Mellitus

Diabetes mellitus is a condition affecting the body's ability to process, store, and use glucose. The incidence of type 1 and type 2 diabetes is 0.18 percent of children in the United States, or 132,000 people under the age of 18 (Centers for Disease Control and Prevention, 2017). **Type 1 diabetes** is the more serious form and affects more children than type 2. There are about 18,000 children diagnosed annually with this more serious form of diabetes, with the highest rate of new cases coming from Hispanic youth. **Type 2 diabetes** results in an additional 5,300 cases annually, again disproportionately affecting minority children between the ages 10 and 19 compared to white peers (Centers for Disease Control and Prevention, 2017).

The human body must maintain adequate blood glucose levels. In this process, the pancreas secretes insulin, which is needed to break down glucose and store it in the liver. Without insulin, glucose is not broken down into glycogen and stored in the liver, resulting in **hyperglycemia** (i.e., high blood sugar), which can cause damage to other parts of the body such as the kidneys, eyes, heart, and blood vessels. Alternatively, when too much insulin is present in the bloodstream due to improper management of injections, food intake, or exercise (which can facilitate the production of insulin in people with type 1 diabetes), a serious condition known as **hypoglycemia** (i.e., low blood sugar) can result. If left untreated, hypoglycemia can result in sudden coma. See the sidebar Symptoms and Treatment of Insulin Shock and Diabetic Coma.

Physical Education and Students With Diabetes

Many factors such as diet, growth, stress, and insulin injection levels are not directly controllable by physical educators, and therefore cooperation by educational team members is necessary. In this team, parents are the first line of defense, along with teachers and other school support staff. Without a collaborative effort, younger children in particular run the risk of repeated problems with blood sugar levels, risking complications later in life. To avoid low blood sugar, regular monitoring of glucose levels is encouraged. This has historically involved using a pinprick to draw a small sample of blood that is then placed on a strip and tested by a device; the blood sugar level is either compared with a chart or recorded by a monitor. In 2016,

Symptoms and Treatment of Insulin Shock and Diabetic Coma

Insulin shock results from excessive insulin in the bloodstream (hypoglycemia). Diabetic coma results from too much glucose and not enough insulin (hyperglycemia).

Insulin Shock (Hypoglycemia)

Symptoms
Rapidly occurring symptoms such as fast pulse, dizziness, weakness, irritability, and eventual loss of consciousness occur with insulin shock.

Treatment
If the person is conscious, provide some fast-acting sugar, such as honey, juice, or regular (nondiet) soda.

Diabetic Coma (Hyperglycemia)

Symptoms
Slower-acting symptoms occur, developing more gradually than with insulin shock. They include thirst and frequent urination over a number of days coupled with nausea and other signs of distress, such as irregular breathing and abdominal pain.

Treatment
Take the person to an emergency room immediately. This is a serious medical situation, and you may not have adequate knowledge on how much or what type of insulin to inject. A person who is in a diabetic coma needs prompt medical care.

The symptoms for these diabetic conditions are similar, and it is helpful to talk with the affected person (if possible) before deciding whether to treat symptoms as hypoglycemia or hyperglycemia. However, insulin shock can occur quickly, and if a person loses consciousness, seek medical attention immediately.

The American Red Cross (2020).

the U.S. Food and Drug Administration approved a mobile continuous glucose monitoring system that replaces the need for fingerstick testing in children older than age 2 (U.S. Food & Drug Administration, 2016). These estimates of blood sugar can be used to adjust food or insulin intake.

When people with diabetes are about to exercise, proper attention to food intake, insulin levels, and exercise amount is critical. Balancing these factors also requires attention to the type of physical activity anticipated. In people with diabetes, insulin and blood sugar levels vary depending on the physical activity, sometimes making it difficult to estimate nutritional needs. For example, Colberg and colleagues (2016) highlighted research showing that intense exercise such as lifting weights can actually cause blood sugar to rise due to increases in counterregulatory hormones, a condition known as **exercise-induced hyperglycemia**. Conversely, **exercise-induced hypoglycemia** occurs when lower-intensity exercise increases insulin sensitivity. These and other factors, such as stress, temperature, and growth spurts, make it important to regularly monitor blood sugar levels and estimate energy expenditure.

Research by Pan and colleagues (2018) demonstrates that various low- to moderate-intensity aerobic and anerobic exercise is effective at lowering glycated hemoglobin (HbA1c). This is important because high levels of HbA1c are responsible for the diabetes-related complications mentioned earlier. In general, exercise has positive effects, but blood glucose should be monitored. Proper eating before exercise and insulin injections are used to prevent hypoglycemia, and monitoring blood glucose levels prior to exercise is important to avoid complications associated with diabetes. Children and adults with diabetes have to learn to regulate their insulin intake to account for the decrease in insulin requirements during exercise (see Application Example sidebar). In physical activity settings, coordinating nutrition, the student's response to exercise, insulin, and curricular offerings is important.

Methods for insulin delivery in children with type 1 and type 2 diabetes vary and require additional attention by physical activity providers. These include syringes, pens, inhalers, and **insulin pumps** (figure 17.1). Insulin pumps, which connect to the abdomen with a small needle to inject insulin

Application Example

Regulating Insulin During Exercise

SETTING

Ms. Jones is a middle school physical educator in a large school district who has decided to start the school year with an aerobic exercise unit to help her students with fitness and give them options to do at home. Her hopes are to increase fitness by the end of the year and also incorporate aerobic homework after the unit concludes.

STUDENT

Carol is a 13-year-old middle schooler who has type 1 diabetes. She is active at home but does not play sports or engage in any other structured physical activities. She has been having trouble with low blood sugar since her most recent growth spurt. Although she is aware of her needs and completely independent in monitoring her blood sugar, she is worried about the upcoming aerobic activities unit; the class runs for over an hour, and her past physical activity experiences have been half-hour classes.

APPLICATION

After consulting her parents and the school nurse, the team has decided that it might be a good idea to have Carol check her blood sugar at the beginning, middle, and end of the class to ensure that she is not experiencing low blood sugar as a result of the increased physical activity. This will relieve Carol's anxiety about having low blood sugar around her new peers. The following points are also important to consider:

- Carol's growth spurt is probably due to puberty, which can affect energy requirements during the day as well as result in the normal self-consciousness that many children experience as their bodies change. Further, the insulin dosage for this child may need to be altered depending on exercise intensity.
- Because Carol is not an experienced exerciser, how her body responds to low- to moderate-intensity physical activity may vary and require monitoring (see earlier explanation of exercise-induced hyperglycemia versus exercise-induced hypoglycemia).

Photo courtesy of Francis Kozub.

FIGURE 17.1 Insulin pumps can now be connected to Bluetooth technology and provide easier access to blood sugar levels in children.

in the fatty tissue under the skin, have become the preferred method of delivery (Maas et al., 2010). For youths, the insulin pump has some advantages, including a reduced risk of hypoglycemia during and following exercise. However, if the pump fails to deliver insulin during exercise, the risk of life-threatening hyperglycemia is increased due to the lack of insulin and the heightened physical activity. Further, temperature is a concern because high or low temperatures degrade the insulin in the pump (Colberg et al., 2016). Instructors responsible for students who use insulin pumps must be aware of the importance of maintaining the pump as well as the integrity of the infusion site.

Exercise in general has significant advantages and is only contraindicated if there is a risk for elevated blood pressure due to poor management of blood sugar levels. Further, individuals with diabetic neuropathy should avoid contact sports (Tran & Galassetti, 2014). Neuropathy is a condition in which nerves in the hands and feet are damaged, resulting in tingling and numbness. Physical educators must be aware of circulation problems and neuropathy in children with diabetes, which can affect foot health and general skin care. It is not recommended that people with diabetes participate in physical activity while barefoot. Socks, water slippers, and other types of appropriate footwear should be available for use during physical activity to avoid the risk of cuts, blisters, and other foot injuries.

Seizure Disorders

Seizures in children and adults are the most common neurological disorder globally, and many people with seizure disorders are advised to avoid regular physical activity because of concerns over safety (Brna et al., 2017). Misunderstandings about seizures and potential contraindications with physical activity are important concerns for physical educators. First, the nature of seizures must be understood. Seizures result when abnormal electrical activity occurs in the brain, causing involuntary movements; varied sensations, perception, and behavior; and altered levels of consciousness. Although seizures are common, the Centers for Disease Control place the prevalence at 1.2 percent of the U.S. population (CDC, 2019b). **Epilepsy**, a condition in which seizures occur with relative frequency, occurs in about 1 percent of children. Uncontrolled and prolonged seizures have the potential to result in serious long-term and even fatal consequences. For this reason, proper attention to help reduce seizures as well as monitor the frequency and duration of episodes is necessary.

Types of Seizures

There are multiple systems used for categorizing seizures. In the system commonly used in educational settings, seizures are classified as either generalized or partial seizures. **Generalized seizures** can be **tonic–clonic (grand mal)** and result in jerking movements and a loss of consciousness, or they may produce a sudden change in muscle tone, with the child perhaps falling. Seizures that result from disturbance in a single portion of the brain, thus affecting one area of control or mental activity, are categorized as **partial** or **complex partial**, depending on whether the person remains conscious. Children are less frequently affected by partial seizures than adults. More common in children are generalized tonic–clonic or grand mal seizures, or the noticeable loss of consciousness followed by thrashing movements, foaming at the mouth, and loss of bladder control. It is important to note that an **aura** or warning precedes many seizures. Many seizures can also be stimulated by a trigger or common factor, such as flashing lights, intense pain, psychological stress, and even fatigue.

First Aid for Tonic–Clonic (Grand Mal) Seizures in Physical Education

1. In many situations, children who have experienced repeated seizures have an aura or warning sign that a seizure is about to happen. In this case, help the child to the floor and be sure to cushion the head.
2. If the child wears glasses, remove them. If the child has some type of mouth guard or prosthetic dental work, remove it if possible so the airway remains open. Turning the head to the side allows saliva to drain and keeps the airway open. Do not attempt to restrain or put any object in the child's mouth.
3. Make sure the area is clear of objects the child may bump into during the seizure.
4. Make sure to note the length of the seizure—a prolonged loss of consciousness or convulsive part of the seizure is a medical emergency. For seizures lasting more than a few minutes, first-time seizures, or seizures occurring in the water, the American Red Cross recommends calling emergency medical personnel.
5. If emergency medical personnel are not needed, let the child rest, if needed. Be sure to inform the child of what happened and discuss missed events or information with the child.

The American Red Cross (2020).

Medications are a common treatment for seizures. Each person with epilepsy is different; some may have a lifetime need for medication, whereas others may be able to discontinue use if seizure activity ceases with age. However, seizures can occur despite consistent efforts to avoid triggers. First aid is an important aspect of helping children to manage seizures. Basic first aid information for educators is included in the First Aid for Tonic–Clonic (Grand Mal) Seizures in Physical Education sidebar. Care must be taken to maintain the dignity of the student when urination or other embarrassing situations occur. Having the rest of the class go to another area, away from the child who is having a seizure, may help maintain control to avoid further injury and preserve the dignity of the child.

Physical Education and Students With Seizure Disorders

Exercise is an important part of the routine necessary for children to normalize the electrical function of the brain (Colson Bloomquist, 2003). Regular exercise has a positive impact on brain activity and has the potential to reduce the likelihood of convulsions and irregular brain activity associated with seizures (Brna et al., 2017). Specifically, the findings of Souza and colleagues (2009) show that a regular swimming program has the potential to reduce seizures. However, these findings do not generalize to all types of seizures, and the nature of the trigger may influence the buffering effect of physical activity for each individual. Fatigue and hyperventilation in intense and stressful competitive sport could be a potential catalyst in persons with seizure disorders; this topic requires further study. Further, some types of seizures are prone to occur in children who are physically active during high humidity and excessive temperatures. High-risk activities such as swimming and climbing, and other activities where risk of falling is a concern, require close monitoring for children with seizures. If a child's seizures are under control, the risks with most forms of physical activity are minimal (Brna et al., 2017). For specific recommendations for aquatic activities, see chapter 24.

Asthma

Asthma is both a common childhood condition and a life-threatening illness affecting 1 in 10 children (U.S. Department of Education Institute of Educational Sciences, 2018). It is a chronic inability to breathe accompanied by wheezing, coughing, and swelling in the bronchial tubes. Asthma is attributed to **extrinsic** allergens or **intrinsic** factors in which the cause of asthma attacks is not readily apparent. As is the case with seizure disorders, different people have different triggers for asthma attacks. Exercise, upper respiratory infections, and other factors can trigger attacks in people who otherwise experience no breathing difficulties.

Symptoms and Treatment of Asthma

Exacerbation of asthma in susceptible students is first observed in an inability to breathe or a persistent cough. Physical educators should be aware of children in their class who have a documented pattern of asthma and should have access to fast-acting inhalers. Some children do not use inhalers but might require medication administration via nebulizer; these may require an electrical outlet and up to 20 minutes to administer. Knowledge about each child's triggers, rate of decline, and treatment is important for helping children engage in structured physical activity. In addition to time needed for a child to return to normal breathing after the use of an inhaler, keep in mind that these medications typically have a stimulant effect, which raises the heart rate and can affect behavior.

Physical Education and Students With Asthma

As a condition affecting physical activity, asthma is most notable when exercise itself is the trigger. This occurs in a large percentage of people with asthma and is referred to as **exercise-induced asthma** (EIA) or **exercise-induced bronchospasm** (EIB). Whether exercise induced or activated by other triggers, asthma presents a challenge to physical activity programmers, particularly when children are overweight (Mitchell et al., 2013). Young children or developmentally immature learners might not be able to regulate hourly dosages or even be able to remember when they last took their medicine; furthermore, physical educators might not always be told when inhalers were last used. For this reason, parents and educators should come up with a system of documenting and communicating when inhalers are used so that the child is not overmedicated. Additional recommendations for dealing with children with asthma include the following:

- Be sensitive to times when children might not be functioning at their best. Prolonged intense physical activity during asthmatic episodes is not recommended.

- Children with EIA might need to avoid physical activity in conditions such as high humidity.
- If fitness levels are low, gradual increases in exercise intensity might help the child with EIA tolerate higher levels of physical activity.
- Children with asthma are prone to having a higher body mass index (BMI) than children without asthma (Wang, Mark, & DeWan, 2015), so attention should be given to all health-related fitness variables.

Cancer

Although often perceived as a single disease, cancer involves many conditions and symptoms that can influence short- and long-term well-being. Over 11,000 cases of cancer occur annually in children between the ages of 1 and 14, with approximately 12 percent of these children dying from the disease. Older children ages 15 to 19 differ in types of cancer; however, the incidence remains high, with the rate increasing annually since 1975 and with cancer remaining as the second leading cause of death in children behind accidents (Siegel et al., 2018). **Leukemia** is the most common form of cancer in younger children, occurring in 28 percent of cases. Tumors in the brain and nervous system are second, affecting one-quarter of children who have cancer (Siegel et al., 2018). **Bone tumors** also affect adolescents at a higher rate than adults. Although the incidences of cancer are on the rise, the death rate from the disease has declined due to improvements in both early diagnosis and treatment—making it more likely that children will survive cancer and require physical activity programming in the schools. Thus, it is very possible that educators in the public schools will have students who are facing this potentially disabling condition. Physical activity plays a vital role in helping children recover and adjust to any permanent outcomes of the disease.

Types of Cancer

Cancer is categorized based on the tissue affected. In cancer, cells grow at an abnormal rate and replace healthy tissue. The mechanism of cell growth and division is not clearly understood, but any body cells can be attacked. Treatment varies and may include surgery to remove abnormal growths, radiation to destroy or reduce tumor mass, and chemotherapy, which involves drugs that retard growth in cancerous cells. Prolonged hospital stays and the side effects from chemotherapy might affect normal development in children. Children may experience pain, anemia, hair loss, and other side effects from treatment, which may create extra program considerations in physical education.

Physical Education and Students With Cancer

All children, including those diagnosed with cancer, can develop fitness. Physical activity plays an important role in recovering from the physical effects of treatments (San Juan et al., 2007). However, when prescribing exercise for children with cancer, caution is warranted based on the lack of research specific to children. A general recommendation is to provide programs that influence multiple systems in the child. Obesity and osteoporosis are major problems in long-term cancer survivors (Warner, 2008). Awareness of these trends and links to inactivity is important to help children with cancer combat obesity and avoid fractures during the various phases of the disease. Side effects related to chemotherapy are also important concerns for program providers; these may range from fatigue and nausea to other, more serious side effects. Although research related to the benefits of physical activity in children is limited, appropriate physical activity during chemotherapy is beneficial (American Cancer Society, 2014). Children should be encouraged to move during chemotherapy to help the body metabolize the medicine and improve posttreatment outcomes related to proper bone and muscle development, as well as to recover from any surgeries. For children, the goal is to keep exercise, play, and fitness activities fun, provide opportunities for interaction with peers, and support emotional well-being (American Cancer Society, 2014).

Cardiovascular Disorders

Cardiovascular disorders include diseases affecting the heart, veins, or lymphatic system. A child can either have a **congenital defect** or acquire the condition from some other illness. Congenital defects occur in approximately 1 percent of newborns each year, and it is estimated that over 100,000 cardiovascular procedures are performed annually on children aged 15 and younger (Centers for Disease Control and Prevention, 2019a). Depending on the nature of the cardiovascular disorder, some exercise prescription may or may not be warranted at the time of acute symptoms. However, in the long term, all children need physical education, and even children with serious heart conditions benefit from appropriate levels of exercise.

Rheumatic Heart Disease

Rheumatic heart disease is a condition resulting from a streptococcal infection that then progresses to **rheumatic fever** and may eventually result in permanent damage to the heart (in about half of all cases). More often than not, mild cardiac effects occur in children with streptococcal infections. This occurs without obvious symptoms in about 15 to 20 percent of children (Kaplan, 2004). However, in some people the cardiac problems associated with rheumatic fever result in heart murmurs, cardiomegaly (enlarged heart caused by additional stress on the muscle itself), **pericarditis** (swelling around the lining of the heart), and congestive heart failure. Symptoms of rheumatic heart disease include shortness of breath, weight gain, dizziness, edema, and palpitations (Kaplan, 2004). Treatment for streptococcal infection includes antibiotics. When damage to the heart valves results, treatment can include surgery to repair or replace the heart valve.

The potential damage to the heart from rheumatic fever varies in individuals. Valvular disorders caused by rheumatic fever can result in breathing difficulties, low energy levels, and heart palpitations (Swank & Sharp, 2018). Based on the severity of the disease, these issues warrant considerations in exercise prescription, particularly exercise intensity, frequency, and duration (Swank & Sharp, 2018). Mode of activity is also an important consideration when working with children who have cardiovascular disorders. Large-muscle activities such as walking, jogging, and cycling are appropriate and longer periods of warm-up are recommended. Lower intensity physical activity is recommended; teachers should determine what intensity is appropriate for each individual child through assessment and consultation with medical providers (Swank & Sharp, 2018).

Prevention is important, and educators who find students with severe sore throats should refer them to the school nurse given the high prevalence of streptococcal infections in school-aged children. An important concern is that rheumatic heart disease is associated with low socioeconomic status and is found in places where there is a lack of community education on symptoms of streptococcal infections (Kaplan, 2004).

Physical Education and Children With Cardiovascular Disorders

Factors that need to be considered when planning physical education experiences for children with cardiovascular disorders include the nature of the disorder and the treatment, specifically any medications being used and the accompanying side effects. Program providers should consult physicians to learn about potential interactive effects between medications and physical activity. In general, basic weight-bearing and large-muscle movements help the recovery process for people with cardiovascular disorders.

Intensity, frequency, and duration of exercise may vary depending on the physician's recommendations. Consultation with medical personnel should be done before programming to ensure that students with cardiovascular disorders exercise for both recovery and health-related fitness. People with cardiovascular disease should never engage in vigorous or high-intensity resistance training without first spending time training at more moderate levels (Williams et al., 2007). Progression of exercise intensity is checked using heart rate monitors or other objective measures. Depending on physician recommendations, it may be appropriate to have children engage in light (35 to 54 percent of maximal heart rate), moderate (55 to 69 percent of maximal heart rate), or vigorous exercise (>70 percent of maximal heart rate).

Anemia

Anemia has many causes, including poor diet and heredity. In anemia, there is a marked reduction in red blood cells or general change in quality of **hemoglobin**. This in turn affects the oxygen-carrying capabilities of the blood, forcing the heart to increase output to compensate for the needs of cells in the body. The most common form of anemia is iron deficiency, which can result in shortness of breath, lack of energy, dizziness, and digestive problems. Also considered part of OHI is sickle cell anemia, a genetic condition most frequently found in African Americans.

Sickle-shaped cells resulting from defective hemoglobin occur in about 10 percent of African Americans carrying the abnormal gene. Sickle cell anemia affects approximately 1 in 500 births in the United States and about 1 in 12 African American families. This condition can also affect families with lineage from South or Central America, the Caribbean islands, Turkey, Greece, Italy, India, and Saudi

Arabia (National Institutes of Health, 2019). There are many general and specific considerations for working with children who have sickle cell anemia.

These considerations include the following recommendations provided by the American College of Sports Medicine (2014) specifically for sickle cell trait that also apply to the broader condition of anemia. First, it is important that physical activity providers be aware of potential issues associated with sickle cell trait—for example, that physical activity participation can result in fatigue, bone and joint pain, and leg ulcers (Gaspard, 2009). However, it should also be noted that in most cases activity restrictions are not necessary for older children with this condition, particularly if the child tests positive for the trait but has not been displaying symptoms. In general, it is important for individuals with sickle cell anemia to avoid dehydration, observe caution in heat and humidity (particularly if not acclimated to the conditions), exercise in ways that build up to vigorous activities, and avoid heavy exercise during the acute phase of the condition (particularly when fever is present) (American College of Sports Medicine, 2014).

Physical Education and Students With Anemia

Addressing the symptoms of anemia in children requires close communication among educators, parents, physicians, and the children themselves. In general, children with all types of anemia should be encouraged to exercise and even engage in individual sport. However, caution is warranted in competitive and high-impact activities for children who lack experience and may not understand their potential physical limitations. This includes higher heart rates resulting from lower oxygen in the blood during aerobic exercise, joint inflammation, and heart problems associated with anemia that may go unnoticed (Moheeb et al., 2007). In general, limited research exists on the effects of exercise on children with sickle cell anemia; however, it is important to note that exercise capacity is lower in children and young adults with the disease. There is an increased risk of issues with circulation and heart function in relation to recovery from exercise, resulting in reduced capacity for exercise in general (Melrose et al., 2018).

AIDS and HIV

Children can contract acquired immunodeficiency syndrome (AIDS) or human immunodeficiency virus (HIV) at any age. Further, there is an increased risk of HIV in children based on race and health disparities. Regardless of age, sexual contact continues to be the leading cause of HIV infection in adolescents (Kann et al., 2018). Most important is for educators to be aware that being **HIV positive** is not the same as having AIDS—only some who are HIV positive develop AIDS symptoms. From a disease control standpoint, those who are HIV positive are carriers of the virus and thus able to infect others. This is perhaps the issue that most alarms communities and creates resistance to the notion that children with HIV or AIDS can integrate into schools without putting peers and teachers at risk.

Facts About HIV and AIDS

It has long been known that HIV, the virus that causes AIDS, is present in the bodily fluids of those who are infected. However, the disease spreads only through direct contact from an open wound, sexual intercourse, or shared needles—not airborne exposure or general casual contact. The CDC monitors the spread of the disease to ensure that children and adults are not put at undue risk, and the reported number of AIDS cases has declined over the last two decades. New drugs (increasing life expectancy and decreasing viral load) and a more informed public have opened the doors for children with HIV to lead normal lives, and it is likely that these children will attend public schools.

Physical Education and Students With HIV or AIDS

Physical education modifications for children with AIDS depend on the presence of secondary opportunistic illnesses. Once acute symptoms such as open sores, cough, or diarrhea begin to show up, the student might need program modifications, depending on the extent of the symptoms. In general, these are conditions that might be present in any child, and notification of appropriate school personnel about medical and hygiene issues is important. Children with AIDS should be treated in a manner consistent with the way all students are treated when blood, vomit, or other biohazards are present. In general, all institutions should have a plan or follow universal precautions for handling biohazards, whether children with AIDS or HIV are present or not.

Knowledge about the effects of exercise on children with AIDS has primarily been generalized from adult studies. The positive effects of exercise are noted in light of many side effects of the medications used to treat the disease—specifically, the redistribution of fat and general weight gain linked to many medications. From the standpoint of health-related fitness, children with AIDS or HIV can benefit both mentally and physically from exercise without further complications (Chow et al., 2006). Resistance training has also had positive effects on strength and lean body mass (Melrose et al., 2018). However, there is some evidence to suggest that adults with HIV or AIDS are prone to fatigue and decreased muscular performance during anaerobic activities (Melrose et al., 2018). Most importantly, addressing the social issues related to children who are HIV positive or have AIDS is more of a concern than potential physical limitations.

Tourette Syndrome

Tourette syndrome is a neurological disease that affects the ability to control movement and in some cases speech. This condition is present in about 1 in 1,000 people in the United States (Berardelli et al., 2003). The involuntary actions and vocalizations are called **tics** and are typically noticed during early childhood between ages 3 and 8 (Copur et al., 2007). Tics can range from mild throat clearing or eye movements to more noticeable rapid movements or sounds repeated over and over. Tourette syndrome varies over the life span, with the worst symptoms usually occurring during the teen years (Hendren, 2002). Medications used in some cases can have side effects such as increased BMI, school phobia, depression, and damage to the liver (Copur et al., 2007).

Physical Education and Students With Tourette Syndrome

There are many examples of athletes with Tourette syndrome, including baseball pitcher Jim Eisenreich and soccer goalie Tim Howard, who are able to participate at high levels. Aside from the medical side effects noted earlier and the social stigma associated with this condition, necessary physical education modifications are few. Physical educators and peers of children with Tourette syndrome should be aware that tics are involuntary, may occur in bouts, and can be absent for long periods of time (Hendren, 2002).

Tourette syndrome can coexist with other conditions such as obsessive–compulsive disorder, behavior problems, attention deficits, and issues with visual–motor integration (Freeman et al., 2000). These situations can interact with physical activity programming if a child with Tourette syndrome is placed in an integrated setting where competitive and social situations are part of the curriculum. Care should be taken to determine if the child with Tourette syndrome has **triggers** for tics. Stress and anxiety can influence the frequency of tics in some children (Hendren, 2002). However, regular physical activity has been found to reduce symptom severity related to vocal tics in children (Doja et al., 2018). For this reason, physical education is important for children with Tourette syndrome, and educators should share information with the entire class to avoid misinformation. Further, children with Tourette syndrome may benefit from programming that is low in stress and high in physical activity. Children with Tourette syndrome need an opportunity to engage socially with peers so that physical activity skills are present later in life, when symptoms are likely to diminish or disappear altogether.

Strategies for Inclusion

Inclusion for children with OHI presents a challenge to educational teams because of the need for case-by-case modifications based on unique learner needs. Medical needs identified throughout this chapter are important for a teacher to consider when deciding on the nature of modifications to an activity. In many cases, successful inclusion can be accomplished with minimal modifications if teachers adopt the practices of universal design for learning (UDL) (Grenier et al., 2017). In some cases, different activities are warranted without undermining the important social aspects of learning. For example, a child with cancer may not be able to swim due to a weakened immune system; however, a modification such as passing to a teammate from the deck while playing water polo allows the child to remain with peers rather than being separated at a time when the child can draw support from classmates. This fits in with what Grenier and colleagues (2017) term as "separate/alternate" within their identified inclusion spectrum and generalizes to the group. Because water polo is a game in which passing strategies are key to successful play, the child's strategic decision making should be the focus for learning. A simple change of focus in learning objectives (from swimming to tactics) allows for inclusion of this child and follows UDL (Grenier et al., 2017). The participation need not be identical to peers—only high expectations are important for this child (Grenier et al., 2017).

This example highlights how lesson focus can be modified to accommodate a learner without a major shift in curricular offering. Table 17.1 outlines some of the considerations related to medical conditions discussed in this chapter. This checklist is recommended when the disability warrants concern about involvement in physical activity. Physical educators are encouraged to address each of these points at a student's individualized education program (IEP) meeting to ensure that appropriate activities are selected, attention is paid to medical aspects of the disability, the child's social needs are addressed, parents understand implications for home programming, and appropriate placement occurs.

Summary

Other health impairment is a broad category that includes many conditions that potentially affect the educational outcomes of children with disabilities. Changes to this category include the addition of Tourette syndrome to the IDEA classification in 2004; other medical conditions may come under the heading of OHI in future reauthorizations. This chapter included information to help promote educational, healthful, and safe involvement in physical education for students with OHI conditions. What separates OHI from other disabilities is the presence of chronic or acute medical conditions that are associated with diseases that potentially affect learning in children.

TABLE 17.1 Inclusion Checklist for Children With Other Health Impairments

	Diabetes	Seizures	Asthma	Cancer	Cardiovascular disorders	Anemia	AIDS and HIV	Tourette syndrome
Exercise intensity	I	S	S	S	I	I	S	N
Social interactions	S	N	N	I	N	N	I	I
Medical concerns	I	S	S	S	S	S	S	N
Regular parental support	I	S	I	I	I	I	I	S

Note: These are general focus areas that are not necessarily an issue for each child; this is a checklist to use to begin gathering information critical for the IEP process and successful integration experiences.

I = Important consideration that needs to be addressed for many children with this condition.

S = In some cases, this issue may warrant consideration for successful inclusion.

N = No more of a concern than for any child without a disability.

References

American Cancer Society. (2014). *Physical activity and the cancer patient.* Retrieved January 1, 2020, from www.cancer.org/treatment/survivorship-during-and-after-treatment/staying-active/physical-activity-and-the-cancer-patient.html

American College of Sports Medicine. (2014). *Sickle cell trait: ACSM current comment.* www.acsm.org/docs/current-comments/sicklecelltrait.pdf

American Red Cross. (2020). *SafetyNet: Staying safe at home and at work.* Author.

Berardelli, A., Currà, A., Fabbrini, G., Gilio, F., & Manfredi, M. (2003). Pathophysiology of tics and Tourette syndrome. *Journal of Neurology, 250,* 781-787. https://link.springer.com/article/10.1007/s00415-003-1102-4

Brna, P.M., Gordon, K.E., Woodridge, E., Dooley, J.M., & Wood, E. (2017). Perceived need for restrictions on activity for children with epilepsy. *Epilepsy & Behavior, 73,* 236-239.

Centers for Disease Control and Prevention (2017). *National diabetes statistics report, 2017.* Centers for Disease Control and Prevention, U.S. Dept of Health and Human Services. Retrieved December 30, 2019, from www.diabetesresearch.org/file/2017-National-Diabetes-Statistics-Report-CDC.pdf

Centers for Disease Control and Prevention (CDC). (2019a). *Data and statistics on congenital heart disease.* Retrieved January 1, 2020, from www.cdc.gov/ncbddd/heartdefects/data.html

Centers for Disease Control and Prevention (CDC). (2019b). *Epilepsy data and statistics.* Retrieved January 22, 2020, from www.cdc.gov/epilepsy/data/index.html

Chow, D.C., Day, L.J., Souza, S.A., & Shikuma, C.M. (2006). Metabolic complications of HIV therapy. *IAPAC Monthly, 12*(9), 302-317. https://doi.org/10.1186/147-2334-6-67

Colberg, S.R., Sigal, R.J., Yardley, J.E., Riddell, M.C., Dunstan, D.W., Dempsey, P.C., Horton, E.S., Cstorino, K., & Tate, D.F. (2016). Physical activity/exercise and diabetes: A position statement of the American Diabetes Association. *Diabetes Care, 39,* 2065-2079. https://doi.org/10.2337/dc16-1728

Colson Bloomquist, L.E. (2003). Epilepsy. In J.L. Durstine & G.E. Moore (Eds.), *ACSM's exercise management for persons with chronic diseases and disabilities* (pp. 262-280). Human Kinetics.

Copur, M., Arpaci, B., Demir, T., & Narin, H. (2007). Clinical effectiveness of quetiapine in children and adolescents with Tourette's syndrome. *Clinical Drug Investigation, 27,* 123-130. https//doi.org/10.2165/00044011-200727020-00005

Doja, A., Bookwala, A., Pohl, D., Rossi-Ricci, Al, Barrowman, N., Chan, J., & Longmuir, P. (2018). Relationship between physical activity, tic severity and quality of life in children with Tourette syndrome. *Journal of the Canadian Academy of Child and Adolescent Psychiatry, 27,* 222-227. www.cacap-acpea.org/wp-content/uploads/Relationship-between-Physical-Activity-Tic-Severity.pdf

Freeman, R.D., Fast, D.K., Burd, L., Kerbeshian, J., Robertson, M.M., & Sandor, P. (2000). An international perspective on Tourette syndrome: Selected findings from 3,500 individuals in 22 countries. *Developmental Medicine & Child Neurology, 42,* 436-447. https://onlinelibrary-wiley-com.brockport.idm.oclc.org/doi/pdf/10.1111/j.1469-8749.2000.tb00346.x

Gaspard, K.J. (2009). Disorders of red blood cells. In C.M. Porth (Ed.), *Pathophysiology: Concepts of altered health states* (8th ed., pp. 301-318). Lippincott Williams & Wilkins.

Grenier, M., Miller, N., & Black, K. (2017). Applying universal design for learning and the inclusion spectrum for students with severe disabilities in general physical education. *Journal of Physical Education, Recreation, and Dance, 88*(6), 51-56. https://doi.org/10.1123/apaq.2018-0145

Hendren, G. (2002). Tourette syndrome: A new look at an old condition. *The Journal of Rehabilitation, 68*(2), 22-26.

Kann, L., McManus, T., Harris, W.A., Shanklin, S.L., Flint, K.H., Queen, B., Lowry, R., Chyen, D., Whittle, L., Thornton, J., Lim, C., Bradford, D., Yamakawa, Y., Leon, M., Brener, N., & Ethier, K.A. (2018). Youth risk behavior surveillance—United States, 2017. *MMWR, 67*(SS-8), 1-114. http://doi.org/10.15585/mmwr.ss6708a1

Kaplan, E.L. (2004). *Rheumatic fever and rheumatic heart disease.* World Health Organization.

Maas, D.M., Horton, L.A., & Chase, P. (2010). The use of insulin pumps in youth with Type 1 diabetes. *Diabetes Technology & Therapeutics, 12,* 59-65. https://doi.org/10.1089/dia.2009.0161

Melrose, D., Dawes, J., Kersterson, M., & Reuter, B. (2018). Immunologic and hematologic disorders. In P.L. Jacobs (Ed.), *NSCA's essentials of training special populations* (pp. 215-265). Human Kinetics.

Mitchell, E.A., Beasley, R., Björkstén, B., Crane, J., García-Marcos, L., & Keil, U. (2013). The association between BMI, vigorous physical activity and television viewing and the risk symptoms of asthma, rhinoconjunctivitis and eczema in children and adolescents: ISAAC Phase Three. *Clinical Experimental Allergy, 43,* 73-84. https://doi.org/10.1111/cea.12024

Moheeb, H., Wali, Y.A., & El-Sayed, M.S. (2007). Physical fitness indices and anthropometrics profiles in schoolchildren with sickle cell trait/disease. *American Journal of Hematology, 82,* 91-97. https://onlinelibrary.wiley.com/doi/pdf/10.1002/ajh.20755

National Dissemination Center for Children with Disabilities. (2012). *Other health impairment (FS15).* www.isbe.net/Documents/other-health-impairment.pdf

National Institutes of Health. (2019). *Sickle cell disease.* Retrieved March 18, 2020, from www.nhlbi.nih.gov/health-topics/sickle-cell-disease

Pan, B., Ge, L, Xun, Y., Chen, Y. Gao, C., Han, X., Zuo, L. Shan, H., Yang, K., Ding, G., & Tian, J. (2018). Exercise training modalities in patients with type 2 diabetes mellitus: A systematic review and network meta-analysis. *International Journal of Behavioral Nutrition and Physical Activity, 15,* 72-87. https://doi.org/10.1186/s12966-018-0703-3

San Juan, A.F., Fleck, S.J., Chamorro-Vina, C., Mate-Munoz, J.L., Moral, S., Garcia-Castro, J., Ramirez, M., Madero, L., & Lucia, A. (2007). Early-phase adaptations to intrahospital training in strength and functional mobility of children with leukemia. *Journal of Strength and Conditioning Research, 21,* 173-177.

Siegel, R.L., Miller, K.D., & Jemal, A. (2018). Cancer statistics, 2018. *A Cancer Journal for Clinicians, 68*(1), 7-30. www.ncbi.nlm.nih.gov/pubmed/29313949 doi: 10.3322/caac.21442

Souza, M.A., Oliveira, M.S., Furian, A.F., Rambo, L.M., Ribeiro, L.R., Lima, F.D., Dalla Corte, L.C., Silva, L.F.A., Retamosco, L.T., Dalla Corte, C.L., Puntel, G.O., de Avila, D.S., Soares, F.A.A., Fghera, M.R., de Mello, C.F., & Royes, L.F.F. Swimming training prevents pentylenetetrazol-induced inhibition of Na+, K+ATPase activity, seizures, and oxidative stress. *Epilepsia, 50*(40), 811-823. https://onlinelibrary-wiley-com.brockport.idm.oclc.org/doi/pdf/10.1111/j.1528-1167.2008.01908.x

Swank, A.M., & Sharp, C. (2018). Cardiovascular conditions and disorders. In P.L. Jacobs (Ed.), *NSCA's Essentials of Training Special Populations* (pp. 181-213). Human Kinetics.

Tran, B.D., & Galassetti, P. (2014). Exercise in pediatric Type 1 diabetes. *Pediatric Exercise Science, 26,* 375-383. http://dx.doi.org/10.1123/pes.2014-0066

U.S. Department of Education Institute of Educational Sciences. (2018). *40th Annual Report to Congress on the Implementation of the Individuals with Disabilities Education Act, 2018.* www2.ed.gov/about/reports/annual/osep/2018/parts-b-c/40th-arc-for-idea.pdf

U.S. Food & Drug Administration. (2016). *FDA expands indication for continuous glucose monitoring system, first to replace fingerstick testing for diabetes treatment decisions.* www.fda.gov/news-events/press-announcements/fda-expands-indication-continuous-glucose-monitoring-system-first-replace-fingerstick-testing

Wang, L., Mark, W., & DeWan, A.T. (2015). Genome-wide gene by environment interaction analysis identifies common SNPs at 17q21.2 that are associated with increased body mass index only among asthmatics. *Plos ONE, 10*(12), 1-14. https://doi.org/10.1371/journal.pone.0144114

Warner, J.T. (2008). Body composition, exercise and energy expenditure in survivors of acute lymphoblastic leukemia. *Pediatric Blood Cancer, 50,* 456-461. https://doi.org/10.1002/pbc.21411

Williams, M.A., Haskell, W.L., Ades, P.A., Amsterdam, E.A., Bittner, V., Franklin, B.A., Gulanick, M., Laing, S.T., & Stewart, K.J. (2007). Resistance exercise in individuals with and without cardiovascular disease. *Circulation, 116,* 572-584. https://doi.org/10.1161/CIRCULATIONAHA.107.185214

Print Resources

Barfield, J.P., & Michael, T.J. (2002). Responses to physical activity among children and youths with exercise-induced asthma. *Palaestra, 18*(2), 26-32.

Misconceptions about exercise and children with EIA are discussed and recommendations for educators are provided in this article.

Jacobs, P.L. (2018). *NSCA's essentials of training special populations.* Human Kinetics.

This text provides training recommendations and contraindications for a host of conditions that potentially fall under the category of other health impairment. The reader will also gain the information necessary to become certified to work with special populations in strength and conditioning contexts.

Moore, G.E., Durstine, J.L., & Painter, P.L. (2016). *ACSM's exercise management for persons with chronic diseases and disabilities* (4th ed.). Human Kinetics.

This is an excellent source of current medical implications for children with the disabilities covered in this chapter. Specifically, it provides activity recommendations and tables to help determine appropriate frequencies and intensities.

Video Resources

Diabetes: Why Many Teens Are at Risk [DVD]. (2008). Human Relations Media, 41 Kensico Dr., Mount Kisco, NY 10549.

This DVD contains interviews of children and teens with type 1 and 2 diabetes. The video explores the daily routines associated with living successfully with diabetes.

Tattoo Tom Mitchell. (2015, April 3). *Stillbrave: One father's journey to accept the unacceptable* [Video]. www.youtube.com/watch?v=5wyXEDuau14

This 14-minute video provides educators with a family perspective on working with children who have cancer and the parents' perspectives on their child's condition.

Online Resources

American Cancer Society: www.cancer.org

This site contains information on cancer that is geared to all audiences. Educators, parents, and children can access this site and gain valuable information about treatment and other medical aspects of cancer.

American Diabetes Association: www.diabetes.org

This site provides information about symptoms preceding diabetic coma that will help educators understand the early warning signs of this medical emergency.

18

Activity and Sports Injuries, Longer-Term Disabilities, and Obesity

G. Monique Mokha

Jessica, a wheelchair user, really enjoyed the tennis unit in her 10th-grade physical education class and would like to further develop her skills and join a competitive team. Jessica's parents are excited for their daughter's interest, but also want to know what injuries or conditions are common in wheelchair tennis players and if anything can be done to reduce the risk. The physical education teacher's advice to Jessica and her parents begins with scheduling an appointment with the family physician for a preparticipation physical examination. Her teacher might also tell them that common wheelchair tennis injuries are primarily overuse injuries like strains, tendinopathies, and abrasions to the upper extremities. Once on a team, Jessica's coach may suggest a progressive strength training program with specific exercises for the rotator cuff, scapula stabilizers, and elbow and wrist muscles. Other considerations are proper wheelchair ergonomics and racket fit. Finally, as for any athlete, it is important that Jessica stay hydrated and wear appropriate athletic attire fit for the weather conditions.

The author is grateful to Christine B. Stopka for her outstanding contributions to the previous editions of this chapter.

This chapter addresses care and prevention, recognition, and treatment strategies for injuries and longer-term conditions in physical education and sport settings, including obesity. The content is applicable to students both with and without disabilities. As noted in chapter 5, students without a designated disability but with unique physical education needs should have an individualized physical education program (IPEP). Students with long-term disorders, such as Osgood-Schlatter disease, benefit from physical education programs modified to meet their unique needs. Similarly, a student with a sprained ankle or concussion will be temporarily limited in the physical education setting and require accommodation (figure 18.1); some of the information offered in this chapter to help students with temporary injuries may also apply to students with longer-term disabilities. Finally, the physical educator and coach are in unique positions to prevent many injuries common in adolescents and should find the suggestions in this chapter helpful.

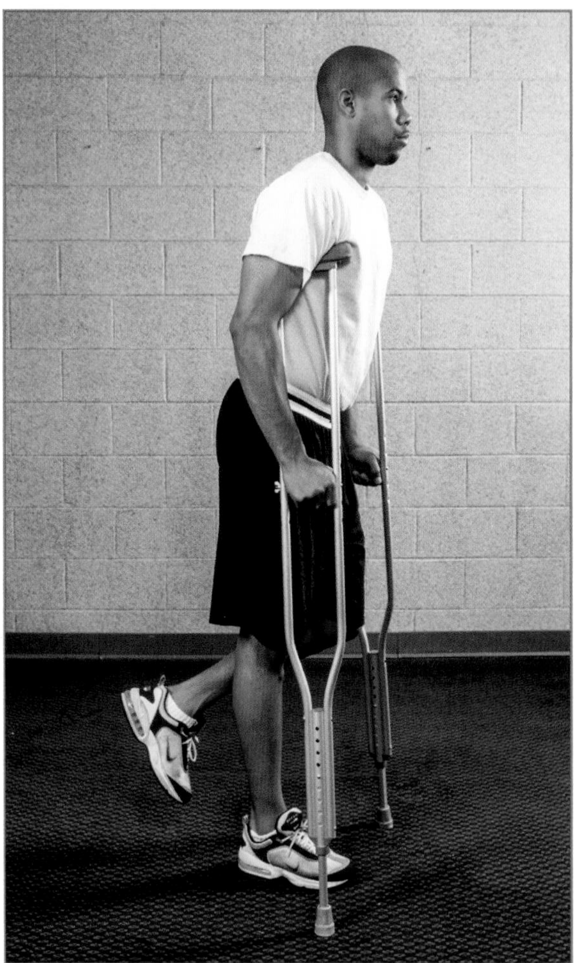

FIGURE 18.1 A student with a sprained ankle might only be temporarily limited in the physical education setting.

Care and Prevention of Activity and Sports Injuries

Students might sustain activity or sport injuries in various settings. Although some injuries might originate in a physical education class, more occur during free time or recreational pursuits. Injuries may be caused by acute (sudden specific) or overuse (prolonged repetitive) trauma and be mild, moderate, or severe in nature.

If an injury occurs in physical education or sport, immediate care should be provided in the **POLICE** sequence: protection, optimal loading, ice, compression, and elevation (table 18.1). This replaces the older RICE (rest, ice, compression, elevation) model (Bleakley, 2012). The focus of these initial management techniques is to limit swelling and minimize pain.

Although physical educators cannot act in the capacity of athletic trainers, they might be able to provide valuable first aid assistance. The physical educator also might recommend that the student see a medical professional if the injury is lingering or worsening. Many hospitals provide sports medicine services; these clinics or departments are staffed by sport physical therapists or athletic trainers.

If the injured student is progressing normally toward recovery, the physical education teacher, in consultation with the student's physician, might provide activities and exercises that ameliorate the condition. Following recovery from activity or sport injury, the Brockport Physical Fitness Test (BPFT) (Winnick & Short, 2014) may be used to assess aerobic functioning, body composition, and musculoskeletal functioning.

Prevention

Physical educators and coaches can help prevent activity- and sports-related injuries in students with and without disabilities. Management tactics such as defining perimeters with cones or tape and getting students accustomed to starting an activity session with a dynamic warm-up aid in preventing acute injuries (Merrie et al., 2016). Physical educators and coaches should be certified in cardiopulmonary resuscitation and first aid, know how to use an automated external defibrillator (AED), and have an emergency action plan (EAP) for their facilities. An EAP is a blueprint for handling

TABLE 18.1 Administering POLICE Sequence

Treatment technique	Rationale	Examples
Protection	To safeguard from further injury	Splint, brace, athlete transport, sling, crutches
Optimal loading	To facilitate healing by progressively mechanically loading the injured tissues	Curling and splaying the toes with an ankle sprain, isometric quad sets with a knee sprain
Ice	To decrease pain and lower the local metabolism at the injury site	Ice packs or ice massage for no longer than 30 minutes per application; may be reapplied in 60 to 90 minutes, depending on the extent of the injury
Compression	To decrease swelling by mechanically reducing the available space	Elastic wraps, elastic tape, and commercial pneumatic compression devices; may be maintained throughout the day and night, but may need loosening at night
Elevation	To reduce swelling	Prop or raise affected body part as high as possible, especially in the first 72 hours

emergencies that identifies specific components such as personnel involved, equipment needed to respond to the emergency, and a communication system to summon care. For more on planning for emergencies in sports and physical activity, consult the position statement from the National Athletic Trainers' Association (Anderson et al., 2002).

The following best practices may be used in most physical education and sports settings to prevent activity injuries:

- Ensure all facilities and equipment are safe and in good condition by routinely inspecting them.
- Fit personal equipment (e.g., helmets, rackets, sport wheelchairs) to students using appropriate guidelines.
- Supervise all activity.
- Understand and teach proper skill techniques (e.g., standing and seated throwing biomechanics).
- Monitor environmental factors (e.g., heat and humidity) and adapt physical activity accordingly.
- Identify common risks for the specific sport, group, or activity and take appropriate action to reduce risk.

The latter of these important actions will be presented in more detail. Additionally, in a sports setting, the coach must ensure that athletes have been medically cleared to participate by a physician.

Injuries such as strains, sprains, and contusions to the lower limb are common in youth. In fact, children and adolescents have higher rates of ankle sprains than adults (Doherty et al., 2014). These sprains tend to recur and lead to chronic instability when not addressed (Donovan et al., 2020). Sprains to the knee's anterior cruciate ligament (ACL) are concerning in youth activity and sports, especially for girls (Bonazza et al., 2019). Lower limb injuries are also common in ambulatory athletes with disabilities (Fagher & Lexell, 2014), especially track and field athletes with visual impairments (Athanasopoulos et al., 2009; Magno e Silva, Winckler, et al., 2013), amputations, and cerebral palsy (Ferrara & Peterson, 2000). Therefore, physical educators and coaches play vital roles in injury prevention.

Upper limb injuries are more common in sports and activities that include repetitive throwing motions (e.g., baseball, softball, swimming, tennis). Overuse injuries are common to the shoulder (rotator cuff impingement, tendinitis, bursitis), elbow (epicondylitis, sprains), and wrist and fingers (strains, sprains, and dislocations). Researchers found that although these overuse injuries are prevalent in adolescents and children, they often don't reach a pain threshold that causes them to seek medical attention (Fuglkjær et al., 2017) and therefore may linger, making injury prevention in physical education and youth sports even more important. It is especially important to identify and correct errors in technique.

Many wheelchair athletes are particularly prone to shoulder pain. The root of this pain is likely multifactorial, with training, activities of daily living, muscle imbalances, age, posture, and strength all playing a role. The nature of wheelchair propulsion combined with sport maneuvers tend to overdevelop the anterior musculature and cause the posterior musculature to be relatively weak; therefore, coaches should stretch the anterior musculature and strengthen the posterior musculature, especially the external rotators and scapula retractors. The rowing ergometer may be beneficial for this exercise. In a small training study of quad rugby players, researchers were able to improve muscle imbalances by increasing shoulder external rotation motion and scapula retraction strength over six weeks (Wilroy & Hibberd, 2018). Coaches should address dynamic stretching and strengthening exercises for the shoulders and scapulae by incorporating them into formal strength and conditioning sessions, warm-ups, or home programs.

Research shows neuromuscular training (NMT) is effective in preventing injuries (Barber Foss et al., 2018). NMT focuses on training the nerves and muscles to react and communicate—in other words, to create "readiness" in the muscles (Risberg et al., 2001)—so there is better dynamic joint stability, muscle firing, and body control. NMT also develops proprioception (e.g., the body's sense of motion and position in space); protocols often include proprioceptive neuromuscular facilitation (PNF) stretching (Prentice, 2017), as well as exercises such as moving the arm into functional positions without the benefit of sight. Deficits in proprioception are common after injury. For more information on PNF, consult Stopka (2008) and Surburg (1999). PNF stretching can be carried out in both physical education classes and sport settings as warm-ups to stretch any muscle group (Stopka, 2010). Most commonly, stretches include the hamstrings and gluteal muscles, calves, hip flexors, quadriceps, hip adductors, pectorals, and especially the triceps and deltoids.

NMT usually involves both open and closed kinetic chain exercises. Open kinetic chain exercises are non–weight-bearing exercises in which the distal end (foot or hand) is free to move; they generally involve motion in one joint. Seated knee extensions and dumbbell front raises are good examples of open kinetic chain exercises. Closed kinetic chain exercises are weight bearing, with the distal segment in contact with a supporting surface and several joints involved in the execution of movement. Squats and push-ups are good examples of closed kinetic chain exercises. Both open and closed kinetic chain exercises should be part of an injury prevention program (Jewiss et al., 2017). If one thinks of a basic movement, such as walking, there are both open (swing phase) and closed (stance phase) components to this motor skill.

Table 18.2 provides an NMT exercise protocol to prevent injuries that might occur from a variety of movement patterns, rather than from a single activity or sport. Many sports and physical activities have similar movement patterns that predispose students to injury (e.g., changing direction, acceleration/deceleration, jumping/landing, pushing/pulling, throwing/catching), making it easier for the physical educator to apply these injury prevention

TABLE 18.2 Neuromuscular Training Exercises for Injury Prevention

Exercise	Sets and repetitions
Forward jump and hold	1 set of 5-8 repetitions
Lateral jump and hold	1 set of 5-8 repetitions each direction
Forward hop and hold	1 set of 5-8 repetitions each leg
Lateral hop and hold	1 set of 5-8 repetitions each leg/direction
Tuck jump with soft landing	1-2 sets of 8-10 repetitions in a row
Front lunge	1 set of 8-10 repetitions
Single-legged Romanian deadlift	1 set of 5-8 repetitions each leg
Grid hop and hold	1 set of 3 repetitions each leg
Dynamic plank variations	1 set of 5-8 repetitions each arm/leg
Pelvic bridge	2 sets of 8-10 repetitions
Swiss ball back extension	2 sets of 12-15 repetitions

exercises. NMT could prevent acute injuries like inversion (rolling the foot inward) and eversion (rolling the foot outward) ankle sprains, anterior cruciate ligament sprains, calf muscle strains, thigh muscle strains (hamstrings, quadriceps, groin), and even upper limb fractures and dislocations resulting from falls (see figure 18.2*a-f*). These may be adapted given a student's abilities.

The reader is also invited to explore the Fédération Internationale de Football Association's (FIFA) 11+ injury prevention program when working specifically with soccer athletes (FIFA, 2019). The

Photos courtesy of Georgia Monique Mokha.

(continued)

FIGURE 18.2 *(a)* Lateral jump and hold, *(b)* lateral hop and hold, *(continued)*

(continued)

FIGURE 18.2 *(c)* front lunge, *(d)* single-legged Romanian deadlift, *(continued)*

FIFA 11+ is for participants age 14 and older and consists of 15 exercises divided into three components: (1) running, including change of direction, cutting, and landing; (2) strength, plyometric, and balance exercises; and (3) high-speed running, including change of direction. There is also a FIFA 11+ Kids program for soccer players younger than 14 that incorporates exercises for spatial orientation and attention, body stability and movement coordination, and learning appropriate fall techniques. Interestingly, the FIFA 11+ program has also been shown to be effective in preventing injuries in adolescent basketball players (Longo et al., 2012).

Acute injuries like growth plate (physeal) fractures are common in the elbow and wrist because they are caused by falling on an outstretched hand (FOOSH). A FOOSH mechanism may also cause elbow and shoulder dislocations (separation of the bones at a joint) as well as clavicle fractures. The NMT exercises in table 18.2 may help prevent these

Photos courtesy of Georgia Monique Mokha.

FIGURE 18.2 *(continued) (e)* grid hop and hold, and *(f)* dynamic plank variation.

acute injuries by improving balance, coordination and motor control. Physical educators and coaches must recognize that previous injury, growth, activity biomechanics, early sport specialization, and sleep can all affect the student's risk of injury (Stracciolini et al., 2017).

Sports Injuries Common to Athletes With Disabilities

More than 3 million athletes with disabilities are involved in organized sports in the United States, and many more participate in recreational sports (Patel & Greydanus, 2010). Although playing sports benefits all aspects of health and wellness, there is an accompanying risk of injury—however, this risk is no greater for athletes with disabilities than it is for able-bodied athletes (Ferrara & Peterson, 2000; Ramirez et al., 2009). Involvement in organized sports begins with medical clearance through a preparticipation physical evaluation (PPE). The PPE is multifaceted and is used to determine injury and illness risk based on the athlete's family history, personal medical history, and a physical examination. Coaches are responsible for ensuring all athletes have documented medical clearance and should familiarize themselves with pertinent health information like allergies, history of seizures, and medication use. Evidence of injuries specific to school-aged athletes with disabilities is limited; this section will include what is known from studying sports over a broad age range.

Team Sport Injuries

Injuries are more prevalent in team sports than in individual or dual sports. Team sport athletes have a higher risk for both traumatic and overuse injuries (Theisen et al., 2013), likely due to the more frequent contact between players and teammates. By identifying and understanding the common injuries in team sports, coaches and physical education teachers can institute team-based injury prevention programs that can be incorporated into warm-ups and strength and conditioning sessions.

Baseball and Softball

Baseball and softball are popular sports in the United States and are played both scholastically and recreationally. However, catastrophic injuries can occur from contact with a ball or bat. Commotio cordis may occur when the chest area over the heart is struck at a critical time during the heartbeat's cycle, causing cardiac arrest and possible sudden death. Coaches and physical education teachers should be prepared to provide chest compressions and use an AED as quickly as possible to improve survival. Prevention of impact injuries in baseball and softball includes the use of batting helmets and face protectors while at bat or on base, the use of special equipment for the catcher (mask, helmet, chest and neck protectors), the elimination of the on-deck circle, and protective screening around dugouts and benches.

The shoulder and elbow are susceptible to overuse injuries, especially in baseball pitchers. Youth baseball pitchers are especially at risk for Little Leaguer's shoulder and Little Leaguer's elbow, which are growth plate fractures to the upper and lower humerus, respectively. These injuries are discussed in more detail in the Adapted Physical Activities for Longer-Term Disorders section of this chapter.

Although beep baseball players will not be susceptible to overuse injuries from throwing, they may be prone to contact injuries during fielding when they use their bodies to block and trap hit balls on the ground. Coaches must emphasize correct fielding technique to minimize those injuries.

Wheelchair softball players must master overhead throwing, underhand pitching, and batting from a seated position, which puts additional stress on the shoulder, elbow, and wrist. Although data are lacking on injuries to these athletes, they may be prone to rotator cuff strains and overuse injuries like shoulder impingement, elbow sprains, and carpal tunnel syndrome. Coaches should ensure proper skill biomechanics and incorporate upper limb strengthening and stretching exercises to reduce the risk of injury. The softer ball is less likely to injure someone during errant contact; however, athletes may sustain collision injuries with one another or the ground that could result in concussions, fractures, contusions, and abrasions. Wheelchair softball is an area where additional research is needed, given its growth.

Basketball

Basketball is a contact sport with complex movements involving decelerations, abrupt changes in direction, and repetitive jumping and running. These movements cause frequent injuries, especially to the ankles and knees. Children and adolescents also sustain more head and neck injuries during basketball than older age groups (Andreoli et al., 2018). Players benefit from injury prevention exercises like the ones shown in table 18.2.

Wheelchair basketball predisposes the fingers, wrists, arms, and shoulders to acute and chronic injuries (Molik et al., 2011). Upper limb abrasions, contusions, and strains are common, as are finger dislocations and fractures. Hands and fingers can become smashed between wheelchairs during play just as in quad rugby. During the 2018 Wheelchair Basketball World Championship, the most frequent player injury was muscle spasms to the neck, upper back, and shoulders (Hollander et al., 2020). Shoulder pain from impingement syndrome is very common. In addition to shooting, blocking, passing, and dribbling, players must quickly push and change directions in their chairs. Players benefit from injury prevention programs that include strengthening, proprioceptive techniques, and flexibility exercises of the shoulder and upper back.

Hockey

Most injuries in field hockey, ice hockey, and sled hockey are contact related and involve being struck by a stick or the puck (or ball); players may also collide with one another. Common injuries include fractures, contusions, strains, sprains, and head injuries (Webborn & Van de Vliet, 2012). Dental injuries are common in ice hockey, though not in field or sled hockey. Lower limb fractures were frequent in sled hockey players in the 2002 Paralympics; however, these have dwindled since the International Paralympic Committee made regulation changes to protective equipment and sled height (Webborn & Emery, 2014). Athletes with spinal cord injury are particularly prone to fractures because overall bone density is lower and fractures can result from minor trauma. These athletes may benefit from vitamin D and other micronutrient supplements related to bone health (Figel et al., 2018; Krempien & Barr, 2011). Particular attention for all hockey players should be given to thoroughly warming up, wearing appropriate and well-fitting protective equipment, and undergoing a fitness test prior to competitive training.

Soccer

Soccer is one of the most popular team sports in the world—however, with widespread participation comes many injuries. Players younger than 15 are at greater risk for injuries and sustain more injuries than older players (Koutures et al., 2010). Young females in particular tend to sustain more knee injuries, whereas young males sustain more ankle injuries. Concussions are also prevalent. Players are also prone to acute injuries like hamstring and groin strains, thigh and shoulder contusions, and face lacerations.

Five-a-side soccer and seven-a-side soccer are adaptations played by athletes with visual impairments and athletes with cerebral palsy or other neurological disorders, respectively. At the 2012 Paralympics, five-a-side soccer had the highest injury rate of all sports (Willick et al., 2013). Most injuries to five-a-side soccer are to the knee, lower leg, head, and face and result from contact with another player, making them difficult to prevent (Magno e Silva et al., 2012; Willick et al., 2013). However, 60 percent of game-related injuries to the head and face in five-a-side soccer have been associated with foul play, highlighting the importance of referee behavior in preventing injuries (Webborn et al., 2016). Seven-a-side soccer was removed from the Paralympic Games after 2016, but is still in the Parapan American Games. Coaches may consider using the FIFA 11+ or FIFA 11+ Kids program to prevent injury in their soccer athletes.

Volleyball

Players of all ages and skill levels play scholastic and recreational volleyball on indoor and outdoor courts. Most injuries are related to blocking or spiking, both of which involve vertical jumps for standing volleyball players. Common acute injuries include ankle and thumb sprains. Repetitive jumping or shoulder motions can also lead to patellar and shoulder tendonitis, respectively. Teaching proper technique, enforcing game rules, and using the exercises in table 18.2 may reduce injuries. Coaches should know that patellar tendonitis is more common in those who play on concrete or linoleum than in those who play on softer wood courts (Briner & Benjamin, 1999).

The lower back and upper limbs are susceptible to injury in sitting volleyball players (Mustafins et al., 2009), especially when blocking and spiking the ball. Sprains and dislocations of the joints and bruising can also happen. One study found that the fingers were the most commonly injured body part (Nuhu et al., 2020). Concussions may be likely as well, and coaches should be trained to recognize signs and symptoms. Coaches should also be mindful that athletes with dysfunction of one limb may be susceptible to overtraining in the unaffected limb.

Goalball

After five-a-side soccer, goalball accrued the second highest rate of injury at the 2012 Paralympics (Willick et al., 2013). Goalball players are susceptible to contusions and skin abrasions when blocking and diving to prevent a goal, especially to the arms, hands, and fingers. This can also cause more serious injuries, including sprains and dislocations to the upper limbs (Gajardo et al., 2019; Zwierzchowska et al., 2020). It is important to teach students and athletes how to block and dive correctly and safely to avoid a FOOSH injury. For more information on teaching goalball skills, see Laughlin and Happel (2016).

Quad Rugby

Quad rugby is a contact sport in which athletes' fingers, wrists, arms, and shoulders are easily injured. Overuse injuries like tendonitis or impingement are common in the shoulder, whereas dislocations and lacerations are frequent in the fingers and hands. Abrasions and contusions are also common to the sides of the trunk, arms, and hands (Bauerfeind et al., 2015). The fingers and hands can become smashed between the player's and their opponent's wheelchairs. Players wear gloves to protect the hands and fingers during play, as well as to help with grip while maneuvering the chair and make catching, throwing and handling the ball easier. The front guards on the quad rugby chair also help protect the feet from impact injuries. Other injuries may be prevented by properly progressed training that incorporates aerobic activities, weight training, pushing, and game skills. The International Wheelchair Rugby Federation provides guidance for injury management, match preparation, and physical conditioning at www.wheelchairrugbyready.com.

Individual and Dual Sport Injuries

Injuries are less prevalent in individual and dual sports compared to team sports. However, coaches and physical education teachers must consider that these athletes generally have higher training-to-competition ratios than team sport players (Theisen et al., 2013) and may require greater emphasis on overuse injury prevention.

Athletics

Athletics refers to track and field events, including throwing (shot put, discus throw, hammer throw, and javelin throw), jumping (high jump, long jump, pole vault, and triple jump), running (race walking, sprints, middle distance, long distance, relays, and hurdles), and combined events (heptathlon, decathlon). In general, lower limb injuries such as hamstring strains, ankle sprains, and knee tendonitis are common in track and field (Pierpoint et al., 2016). However, injury patterns tend to be slightly different for each event or even subevent because of different movement patterns and stressors. For example, hamstring muscle strains are common in sprinters, whereas tibial stress fractures are more frequently seen in long distance runners. Rotator cuff strains are seen in throwers, whereas Achilles strains are common in jumpers. Shoulder injuries are also common in Paralympic athletes who use a wheelchair for throwing or track events (Blauwet et al., 2016). Paralympians who are ambulatory sustain a large proportion of their injuries to the thigh in the form of strains and spasms. The knee and ankle have been identified as the most common joints injured in Special Olympians (Platt, 2001).

Tennis

Tennis is a popular sport played recreationally and competitively by players of all levels. Unlike other sports, there are no time limits to how long a match can last, and matches can often last several hours. Therefore, competitive players must be highly fit both aerobically and anaerobically to avoid fatigue, which can lead to injury. Tennis also involves repetitive stresses through a variety of strokes and movement patterns. These factors put players at risk for overuse and acute injuries. Overuse injuries are common in the shoulder (impingement syndrome), elbow (tennis elbow), and wrist (extensor tendonitis). Ambulatory players are susceptible to low back strains and disc degenerative pathologies (Fu et al., 2018). The lower extremities are more prone to acute injuries such as groin muscle strains, ankle sprains, and meniscal tears and knee tendinopathies. Stability is an important contributor to performance in tennis players who use wheelchairs. Therefore, coaches should help these players determine optimal seat positioning, rear wheel camber, and wheel size. All players will benefit from NMT and aerobic fitness programs, appropriate racket selection and grip, and proper technique instruction. Depending on the strength and coordination of the player, coaches may encourage a two-handed backhand over a one-handed backhand stroke to not only maximize power but to help prevent tennis elbow (lateral epicondylitis).

Snow Skiing

Knee injuries are common in snow skiing, particularly to the ACL. Injuries to the shoulder are common when skiers put their arms out to break a fall (FOOSH injuries). The 2014 Sochi Paralympic Games saw a six-fold increase in acute alpine ski injuries from the 2010 Vancouver Paralympic Games (Derman et al., 2020), with the downhill event and steeper upper course setting particularly concerning. The high speed and technical aspects of alpine skiing put athletes at increased risk for injuries such as concussions, upper limb fractures, and ACL ruptures. Further, sitting class alpine skiers have been reported to have a higher injury rate than those with visual impairments and standing class athletes (Webborn & Van de Vliet, 2012). Although collision injuries may not be directly mitigated by injury prevention programs, coaches should institute sport-specific strength and conditioning programs to enhance aerobic capacity, reaction time, core stability, and overall working muscle strength. Logging the type, nature, and anatomical location of injuries as well as environmental conditions is important in providing information that can be used to prevent sports injuries. Using 2014 data, organizers made changes around course design, training run rules, and the communication structure between the technical and medical staff before the 2018 PyeongChang Games that brought the injury rates back down (Derman et al., 2020).

Swimming

Competitive swimmers are predisposed to injuries to the upper extremities, knees, and spine. The volume of swimming contributes to overuse injuries and muscle fatigue of the rotator cuff, upper back, and pectoral muscles. The shoulder is particularly vulnerable, with 40 to 91 percent of swimmers with and without disabilities incurring a shoulder injury (Magno e Silva, Bilzon, et al., 2013; Wanivenhaus et al., 2012). Poor stroke mechanics and overuse contribute to shoulder impingement, or "swimmer's shoulder." Training load should be carefully considered for swimmers who use wheelchairs and assistive devices outside the pool that put additional stress on the shoulder. Knee pain is the second most reported source of pain in swimmers, particularly in breaststroke swimmers due to the valgus (i.e., inward directed) loads on the knee during the kick. Abnormal kicking mechanics are often present in swimmers with knee pain, and coaches might want to invest in an underwater camera to view and correct improper body mechanics. Low back pain is common in both breaststrokers and butterfly swimmers due to the hyperextended low back position, which is believed to be a risk factor for pain, as is the use of training devices such as fins, kickboards, or pull buoys that also place the back in hyperextension (Wanivenhaus et al., 2012).

Head injuries appear to be minimal for swimmers with visual impairments due to the assistance of a support staff person who indicates the approach of the end of the pool by touching the athlete (Magno e Silva, Bilzon, et al., 2013).

Boccia

Boccia is played by athletes with neurological conditions (e.g., cerebral palsy, stroke or traumatic brain injury) that affect their motor function. Boccia players are known to sustain more acute injuries than chronic injuries (Willick et al., 2013). Athletes with brain injuries are more susceptible to muscle spasms in both upper and lower limbs. Acute spasms are common following high-intensity competition, and the upper trapezius muscle is specifically prone to fatigue (Fong et al., 2012; Tuakli-Wosornu & Derman, 2018). At the Rio 2016 Summer Paralympic Games, athletes with brain injury made up 16.1 percent of all athletes who sustained injuries at the Games. Athletes will benefit from muscle fatigue and endurance training exercises such as shoulder shrugs, neck extensions, and Ys, Ts, and Ws (see figure 18.3). Hypertonia, or too much muscle tone, is also linked to pain and injuries. Older athletes with brain injury are particularly prone to patellofemoral pain that is believed to be brought on by hypertonia of the quadriceps muscles.

Adapted Physical Activities for Longer-Term Disorders

In addition to acute injuries, some students may present with longer-term disorders, defined as a condition or a problem that lasts longer than 30 days. Fractures, common knee and foot anomalies, adolescent hip diseases, and obesity are the primary focus here, but the principles and procedures relevant to these conditions may also be applied to the integration of students with virtually any long-term disorder or condition into general physical education classes, including acute injuries that may not be fully rehabilitated within 30 days.

Fractures

Bones in the upper and lower extremities are often fractured in activity-related accidents, such as when landing on an outstretched arm. Although the focus of this chapter is activity, fractures might also result from other situations, such as child abuse

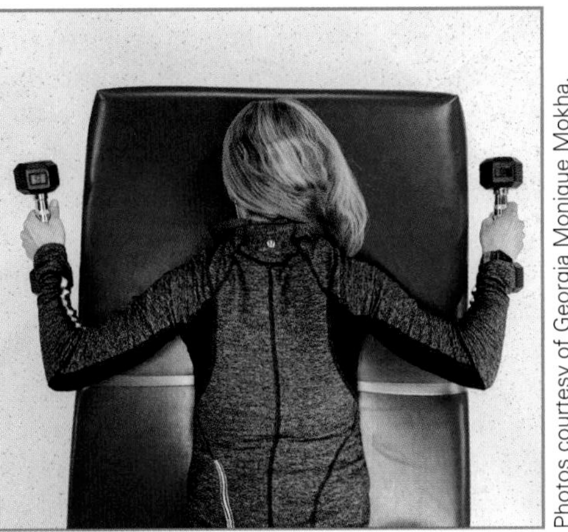

Photos courtesy of Georgia Monique Mokha.

FIGURE 18.3 Upper body Y, T, and W exercises. These can also be performed standing with small or no hand weight, or seated using light resistance elastic bands or cables.

and pathologic bone-weakening conditions (e.g., cancer, osteopenia, osteoporosis, osteogenesis imperfecta). For physical educators, a student with a fracture presents two challenges: (1) developing a program for a student immobilized in a cast, and (2) reintegrating the student into the general physical education program after cast removal.

Participation in physical education is based on the nature of the activities in the curricular unit. For example, although a track unit might mean little restriction for the student with a broken arm, a unit on gymnastics activities might entail considerable restriction. For the student with a broken radius of the nondominant arm, a badminton unit will need little modification, whereas an archery unit, although less vigorous, would require use of both upper extremities. However, the student could use a crossbow mounted on a camera tripod, which requires dexterity of one arm. When unit activities preclude participation because of a fracture, physical fitness of the remaining three extremities might be the focus of the student's involvement in physical education.

A student with a broken arm has no problem with ambulation and can easily maintain a high level of cardiorespiratory fitness; therefore strength development can be pursued with only minimal modification or adaptation. With a broken arm, certain lifts such as the bench press would have to be eliminated, but triceps development of the nonaffected arm could be accomplished through other exercises, such as elbow extension exercises. Involvement of the affected arm should be predicated on recommendations from the physician and on good judgment. For example, any type of isometric exercise involving muscles immobilized in a cast should be approved by the physician. Any exercises involving joints above or below the cast area should also have physician approval; however, this does not mean that exercises are contraindicated for these joints. Some fractures may not warrant a cast, but activity modifications still must be made. Two fractures common in growing athletes as a result of too much pitching or throwing are growth plate fractures to the shoulder and or elbow. Students may have an arm sling or not be immobilized at all. Successful return to activity should involve a biomechanical throwing assessment to identify technique flaws that are contributing to bone stress. Additionally, coaches should follow pitch count guidelines from Major League Baseball (2020) in conjunction with USA Baseball to prevent overuse.

Once the cast is removed, the curricular focus should be on reintegrating the student into general class activities. Part of this integration process might be to help develop range of motion, flexibility, strength, and muscular endurance in the affected limb. This assistance might be critical for students from low socioeconomic levels who do not have the benefit of appropriate medical services. Activities and exercises described earlier in the section Care and Prevention of Activity and Sports Injuries can be incorporated into this program, but may need to be modified. If activities need to be substituted altogether, table 18.3 provides guidance. The student's total inclusion into the general physical education program depends on the nature of the fracture, the extent of immobilization, the duration of the reconditioning period, the physician's recommendations, and the nature of activities involved in the unit.

Common Knee and Foot Conditions

Because they experience growth spurts, adolescents are predisposed to two growth-related conditions in the lower limb that cause a long-term dilemma for the physical educator and coach. The first is Osgood-Schlatter condition, often known as Osgood-Schlatter disease. The condition is not actually a disease, but instead involves incomplete separation of the epiphysis of the tibial tubercle from the tibia. The second is Sever's disease and involves the same type of separation, but at the calcaneus. Both conditions are painful and are aggravated by explosive movements like running, jumping, and hopping. Treatment involves the elements of POLICE and may include elastic wraps or neoprene sleeves, rest from explosive movements, and exercises to maintain range of motion (ROM) and strength (Prentice, 2017). Heel inserts might help ease pain in the student with Sever's. Treatment depends on the severity of the condition and the philosophy of the attending physician concerning its management.

The physical educator could help the student during both the acute stage of involvement and the recovery stage of these conditions. Because most cases are unilateral, affected students might have normal status for three-fourths of their extremities, in which case the approach discussed in the earlier section on fractures might be applied here.

Involvement of the affected limb in activity must be based on a physician's recommendation. For example, certain physicians might approve isometric contractions of the quadriceps and stretching of the hamstrings in the affected extremity. Ankle exercises might also be considered appropriate for the affected limb. When all symptoms have disappeared and the physician has approved full participation, the student should begin a general mobilizing program in physical education class. Development of quadriceps strength using exercises such as straight-leg raises, short-arc extension exercises, and wall-slide arcs, as well as quadriceps and hamstring stretches, should be part of the student's fitness program (Prentice, 2017). The physical educator should evaluate the student's gait pattern following the occurrence of Osgood-Schlat-

TABLE 18.3 Exercises During Injury Recovery

Conditions	Focus areas	Example exercises
Patellofemoral problems	• Strengthen quad, particularly vastus medialis oblique muscle, without putting additional stress on patellofemoral surface • Maintain full ROM, strength, and core power, including nonaffected side • Maintain thigh and lower leg muscle strength • Gradually return to squatting, lunging, jumping, and hopping	• Quad sets, straight-leg raises, short arc extensions • ROM and strengthening of thigh and lower leg muscles (may be done conventionally)
Knee ligament sprains, after casting or immobilization	• Maintain ROM, strength, and core power, including nonaffected side • Maintain thigh and lower leg muscle strength, especially hamstrings with anterior cruciate ligament injuries • Gradually return to squatting, lunging, jumping, and hopping	• Quad sets, straight-leg raises, quarter-squats, hamstring curls, and other tolerated conventional strength training exercises
Ankle ligament sprains, after casting or immobilization, and strains	• Maintain ROM, strength, and core power, including nonaffected side • Maintain lower leg and foot muscle strength • Maintain proprioception • Gradually return to squatting, lunging, jumping, and hopping	• Alphabet ROM exercises, open and closed chain Achilles tendon stretching • Flexion, extension, and spreading of toes • Heel raises, elastic band and other strengthening exercises of basic ankle motions • Single-leg balance exercises to include tilt board
Shoulder ligament sprains, after immobilization, clavicle fractures	• Maintain ROM, strength, and core power, including nonaffected side • Continue lower body training • Maintain shoulder and upper back strength • Maintain proprioception	• Wall climbing, cross-arm stretch, Codman's exercise*, and other ROM exercises • Elastic band, isometrics, and tolerated weights and push-up variations to enhance strength of basic shoulder motions • Y, T, W, and other scapula stabilization exercises • PNF exercises, replicating arm positions with and without the use of sight

(continued)

TABLE 18.3 *(continued)*

Conditions	Focus areas	Example exercises
Shoulder impingement, tendinopathies, rotator cuff strains, Little Leaguer's shoulder	• Improve skill biomechanics • Maintain ROM, strength, and core power, including nonaffected side • Continue lower body training • Maintain shoulder and upper back strength • Gradually return to throwing motions	• Technique analysis to identify and correct faulty biomechanics • Wall climbing, cross-arm stretch, Codman's exercise*, and other ROM exercises • Elastic band and low weights to enhance strength and endurance of rotator cuff and basic shoulder motions • Y, T, W, and other scapula stabilization exercises
Elbow, hand, wrist, and finger injuries	• Maintain ROM, strength, and core power, including nonaffected side • Continue lower body training • Maintain shoulder, elbow, wrist, and finger strength • Increase active ROM of affected joint	• Open (weights, bands, isometrics) and closed (push-up variations) chain exercises as tolerated
Trunk and back strains, curvature abnormalities	• Maintain stability • Correct strength imbalances • Increase full ROM to tolerance and capacity • May need to avoid heavy resistance and explosive activities	• Knee to chest, rotation, and other ROM exercises • Quadruped, dead bug, plank variations, and other stability exercises • Swiss ball back extensions

**Note:* Not to be used with glenohumeral dislocations.

ter condition. Consider the Application Example sidebar concerning weight training for a student with Osgood-Schlatter condition.

Knock-knees, or **genu valgum**, refers to an alignment problem in which the tibia bows outward from the midline and the knees are too close to midline, often touching. Genu valgum is a common postural deviation in children who are obese. Poor alignment of the knee results in a disproportionate amount of weight being borne by the medial aspect of the knee and predisposes the joint to strain and injury. Physical educators should carefully consider this point when selecting physical activity for students with this condition. Activities that increase the possibility of trauma to the knees (e.g., jumping from heights, running on hard or uneven surfaces, playing games or sports in which the knees could be hit laterally) should be avoided.

Bowlegs, or **genu varum**, refers to an alignment problem in which the tibia bows inward from the midline, resulting in the ankles touching; the knees are too separated, far apart from the midline. The bowing, usually bilateral, can occur in either the femur or the tibia but is most common in the tibia. This structural deformity is frequently accompanied by compensatory deformities in the feet. When the condition is suspected, the physical educator's major responsibility is to refer the child to a physician for possible treatment.

Although many foot deformities can be caused by skeletal and neuromuscular abnormalities, most are caused by compensatory postures required to offset other postural misalignments in the legs, hips, and spine. Physical educators should be aware of any students who have foot deformities. In most cases, the students will be able to participate in the general physical education setting; however, the physical educator might need to monitor specific students to ensure they are wearing any needed braces or orthotics and that they are performing exercises as prescribed by their physicians.

Talipes deformities, which involve deformities of the foot and ankle, refer to a number of conditions, such as **talipes equinus**, a result of a plantar-flexed ankle caused by tight tendoAchilles structures, and **talipes calcaneus**, the opposite condition,

Application Example

Weight Training for a Student With Osgood-Schlatter Condition

SETTING

Middle school physical education class

STUDENT

A 13-year-old student with Osgood-Schlatter condition

ISSUE

Develop a suitable strength program for a weight training unit

APPLICATION

The physical educator might include the following modifications:

- Use progressive resistance exercises for the upper body and the uninvolved leg.
- For the leg with Osgood-Schlatter condition, work on strength exercises for the ankle and hip.
- Do flexion and extension range of motion exercises for the knee with Osgood-Schlatter condition.

usually caused only as a result of overzealous TAL (tendoAchilles lengthening) surgery. Two other conditions are not uncommon: **talipes varus**, in which the foot and ankle are inverted (the toes and sole of the foot are turned inward, or supinated, so the person walks on the outside edge of the feet), and **talipes valgus**, in which the foot and ankle are everted (the toes and soles of the feet are turned outward, or pronated, so the person walks on the inside edge of the feet). Mild forms of the conditions are treated with special orthotic shoes. More severe forms might require braces, surgery, or a combination of the two.

Pronation is a foot deformity in which the person walks on the medial (inside) edge of the feet. The condition is frequently accompanied by the toes facing laterally (outward). The use of corrective shoes (or surgery in severe cases) can help minimize the deformity and relieve any associated pain. **Pes planus**, or flatfoot, is a congenital condition that results in a lowered, or flattened, longitudinal arch. Pain is a common symptom, and obesity exacerbates the condition. Students might need to be referred to a physician for evaluation for surgery, orthotics, or exercises to relieve the pain and, in severe cases, correct the alignment.

Hollow foot, or **pes cavus**, the opposite of flatfoot, is characterized by an extremely high longitudinal arch that results in a clawlike flexion of the toes that reduces the ability of the foot to absorb and distribute force. This condition is usually congenital. Although surgery might be indicated in severe situations, the use of orthotics is often sufficient to relieve pain and prevent further deformities.

Adolescent Hip Diseases

Legg-Calvé-Perthes disease (LCPD) and **slipped capital femoral epiphysis** (SCFE) are two common hip diseases affecting children and adolescents, mostly males. Legg-Calvé-Perthes disease is characterized by the degeneration of the femoral head. It occurs in children 3 to 12 years old and runs a definitive course of pain, necrosis, and regeneration, often with some degree of residual deformity (Stopka & Todorovich, 2011). Slipped capital femoral epiphysis involves the subluxation, or slippage, of the head of the femur at the epiphyseal plate. It usually affects children during their periods of rapid growth from 10 to 16 years of age (Stopka & Todorovich, 2011). Slipped capital femoral epiphysis is similar to Osgood-Schlatter condition n that they both involve a degeneration of a physis (growth plate). Rather than a degeneration of an apophysis (growth plate of a tubercle), as in Osgood-Schlatter condition, SCFE involves the degeneration of the growth plate through the entire femoral head.

In both LCPD and SCFE, early diagnosis is essential to minimize the damage. However, early diagnosis can be a challenge because both conditions involve pathologies of the femoral head, in which pain is not easily perceived; this relatively internal pain is referred to the knee region. Thus, a child or adolescent complaining of nonspecific, generalized knee pain should always be evaluated (at least radiographically) to rule out LCPD or SCFE. If these conditions are left untreated until the student can no longer bear weight on the hip, the damage is so severe that, in most cases, only surgery can provide hope for a full recovery.

The physical educator's job is clear: When students complain of diffuse, nonspecific hip or knee pain for no apparent reason, they should be referred to medical authorities. After diagnosis, the treatment will be directed at prevention of further involvement; avoidance of weight bearing through crutches, casting, or bracing; and possibly surgery. Although these directives must be observed, safe, appropriate physical education activities are essential at this time. Activities that aggravate the hip are contraindicated; the hip must heal by removal of pressure on the femoral head and the acetabulum. However, all activities are indicated in which the child can participate successfully and safely in the brace. Strength, endurance, flexibility, coordination, and balance must be trained and maintained as much as possible. To improve self-confidence and overall health, acceptance of the full treatment program of bed rest, wheelchair use, or brace wearing while continuing to participate in safe, motivating activities is essential (Stopka & Todorovich, 2011).

Obesity

Obesity is defined as an excessively high amount of body fat or adipose tissue in relation to lean body mass. The body mass index (BMI) is a mathematical formula that is commonly used for determining whether someone is overweight or obese. Body mass index is calculated by determining body weight in kilograms and dividing the result by the square of the height in meters (i.e., weight divided by height squared). Although BMI is imperfect because it lacks precision for mesomorphic (heavily muscled) and ectomorphic (very lean) people, producing artificially high or low scores, it remains a popular method because of its convenience and overall validity and reliability among populations. Because body composition changes with age and varies between girls and boys, a student's weight status is determined using an age- and sex-specific percentile for BMI rather than the BMI categories used for adults.

According to the Centers for Disease Control and Prevention (CDC, 2020), the term *overweight* is defined by having a BMI between the 85th and the 94th percentile for children and teens of the same age and sex. Students with a BMI at or above the 95th percentile for their height and age are considered obese. Although BMI does not measure body fat directly, it is highly correlated to more direct measures of body fat like skinfold thickness measures, bioelectrical impedance analysis (BIA), dual energy X-ray absorptiometry (DEXA), or magnetic resonance imaging (MRI).

Prevalence

A major public health concern today is the large number of students who are overweight and obese. For the years 2013 to 2016, the CDC reported the prevalence of obesity for children and teens aged 2 to 19 at 17.8 percent, affecting about 13 million school-aged persons (ODPHP, 2020).

Demographic variables related to obesity include sex, age, and socioeconomic level. Although women, especially those of Hispanic and non-Hispanic black populations, have higher percentages of obesity, this epidemic is pervasive and affects all ages, ethnicities, disabilities, and sexes. Results from the 2016 National Survey on Children's Health (Haegele et al., 2020) showed being overweight was more prevalent in youth with disabilities than those without disabilities.

Causes

The causes of obesity are multifaceted. At least three factors seem to play a significant role: (1) behavior (eating too many calories teamed with not getting enough physical activity); (2) environment (home, work, school, and community significantly influence opportunities for an active lifestyle); and (3) genetics (heredity plays a large role in determining how susceptible people are to obesity). Genes also influence how the body burns calories for energy or stores fat. The behavioral and environmental factors are the two principal contributors to overweight problems and obesity; fortunately, they provide the greatest opportunities for prevention and treatment. In addition, emotional factors can play a significant role. For example, some people eat as a means of emotional compensation or to reduce feelings of anxiety; others eat excessively when content and happy.

An increase in the number (hyperplastic obesity) or size (hypertrophic obesity) of the fat cells that make up adipose tissue may lead to obesity. Rapid increases in fat cell production (hyperplasia) occur during the third trimester of fetal development through the first year of life and again during the adolescent growth spurt. Thus, the need to educate adolescents about appropriate nutritional choices and physical activity programs is enormous.

Health Consequences of Being Obese

- High blood pressure and hypertension
- High "bad cholesterol" (low-density lipoprotein [LDL]) and low "good cholesterol" (high-density lipoprotein [HDL]) levels
- Type 2 (non–insulin-dependent) diabetes
- Insulin resistance (decreased insulin sensitivity) and glucose intolerance
- Coronary heart disease and stroke
- Atherosclerosis, peripheral vascular disease, and intermittent claudication
- Congestive heart failure
- Certain types of cancer (such as endometrial, breast, prostate, and colon)
- Gallstones and gout
- Diabetic retinopathy, angiopathy, nephropathy, and neuropathy
- Osteoarthritis
- Obstructive sleep apnea and respiratory problems
- Pregnancy complications and poor female reproductive health (such as menstrual irregularities, infertility, and irregular ovulation)
- Bladder control problems (such as stress incontinence)
- Psychological disorders (such as depression, eating disorders, distorted body image, and low self-esteem)

Centers for Disease Control and Prevention (2020).

Characteristics and Associated Problems and Health Consequences

People who are overweight are more likely to develop health problems such as heart disease, stroke, diabetes, cancer, gallbladder disease, sleep apnea, and osteoarthritis. The more overweight the person is, the more likely it is that these health problems will occur. The American Academy of Pediatrics (AAP) and CDC provide exhaustive lists of health consequences related to these health problems, which people with high BMIs are at increased risk to experience (AAP, 2020; CDC, 2020). These unfortunately common physical ailments are numerous and severe (see the Health Consequences of Being Obese sidebar). Without question, quality strategies for weight control, including excellent teaching content and methods, motivating activities, opportunities for athletic participation, and the skills to implement a safe, active way of life through adulthood and beyond, are crucial to combat the obesity epidemic (AAP, 2020; CDC, 2020).

Strategies for Controlling Weight

The physical educator is one member of a team who may help a student with obesity. However, just as exercise alone cannot remediate a weight problem, the physical educator alone cannot solve this problem. A team effort is needed, with the physician overseeing medical and dietary matters, the parents providing appropriate diet and psychological support, and the physical educator selecting the best exercises and activities for the student (Bandini et al., 2015).

There are three main ways to lose weight: diet, exercise, and a combination of the two. Diet alone is the most common method used by adults and is often the most abused method. The criterion frequently used to judge success with this approach is how quickly the maximum number of pounds can be lost. A crash diet may even trigger a starvation reaction, in which the basal metabolic rate diminishes, thus triggering the body to use fewer calories throughout the day, both at rest and during physical activity. In this way, the body counteracts certain effects of the crash diet and does not lose the desired weight. A far more effective method is to use a gradual approach with a reduction of 500 calories a day, which equals 3,500 calories per week—the number of calories needed to lose a pound (0.5 kilograms) of fat. Under the direction of a physician, a student with obesity may be on a diet that reduces intake by more than 500 calories per day.

MyPlate (MyPlate.gov) from the United States Department of Agriculture is a valuable resource for the physical educator to help students with weight control. MyPlate is based on the 2015-2020 Dietary Guidelines for Americans (U.S. Depart-

Dietary Considerations to Promote Weight Loss

- Restrict calories to 10 calories per pound (0.5 kilograms) of body weight (e.g., 1,600 calories per day for a 160-pound [73 kilogram] person).
- Reduce intake of saturated fats (daily intake should not exceed 30 percent of total calories, and saturated fats, including trans fatty acids, should not exceed 10 percent of total caloric intake).
- Increase intake of dietary fiber and complex carbohydrate (starches).
- Reduce intake of simple carbohydrate (sugars).
- Use lean meats and trim excess fat.
- Reduce or eliminate use of cooking oils and fats in the preparation of foods (e.g., substitute canola or olive oil; again, minimize saturated fat and avoid trans fat as much as possible).
- Avoid fried foods; broil or bake instead.
- Reduce sugar and fat in all recipes.
- Seek out fat-free and cholesterol-free alternatives.
- Feature fruits and vegetables at snack time.
- Avoid ordering nonnutritious foods at fast food restaurants.

ment of Health and Human Services, 2015) and provides tips and solutions about what and how much to eat within a calorie allowance that takes into account an individual's personal preferences, budget, culture, and traditions. Physical educators can offer other practical tips, such as trying to avoid foods that come in plastic packaging (e.g., candy, potato chips). Lunch should include fruits and vegetables, and fried and fast food should be avoided. Finally, students should be cautioned about what they drink. Diet sodas are preferable to sugared sodas, and water is better still. Necessary nutrients are plentiful in reduced-calorie fruit juices and fat-free milk.

In spite of the fact that there seems to be a genetic component to some forms of obesity, a healthy diet, combined with the proper type, duration, frequency, and intensity of physical activities, can successfully improve body weight and body composition for the long term. Participation in physical activity affects body composition and weight by facilitating fat loss while preserving or even increasing lean body mass. The rate of weight loss is related to the frequency and duration of the physical activity session, as well as to the duration (e.g., months, years) of the physical activity program. Also, the rate of weight loss resulting from increased physical activity along with dieting is enhanced compared to physical activity alone or dieting alone. Specific examples of diet guidelines are presented in the Dietary Considerations to Promote Weight Loss sidebar. Physical activity guidelines related to body composition are presented in chapter 23.

Finally, it is important to select the appropriate type, or mode, of exercise. To accomplish this, the FITT principle (frequency, intensity, time, and type) is often employed. Activities that facilitate the acquisition of more lean body mass, such as resistance exercises, have a positive effect on the basal metabolic rate by increasing it throughout the day. This is possible because muscle mass requires more calories for maintenance than does adipose tissue.

Also of critical importance is the pursuit of cardiorespiratory endurance, which burns calories while activity is being performed and for several hours after the exercise session has ceased. The types of activities selected should engage large-muscle groups and should be rhythmic and continuous. Such activities can include swimming, jogging, cycling, rowing, dancing, hiking, cross-country skiing, in-line skating, and walking. Additional characteristics of a desirable exercise training program for students who are obese are shown in the accompanying sidebar.

Physical Education and Students Who Are Obese

A well-designed physical education program for students who are obese may contribute to increased caloric expenditure. There are, however, certain limitations the physical educator must acknowledge when developing such a program. These barriers include lack of motivation, time, facilities, and equipment; anxiety and previous negative experiences; and poor balance, discomfort, or pain related to the weight problem. However, the physical education teacher is in an excellent position to deal with these barriers. Physical education provides access to both facilities and equipment to enhance a weight loss program. An atmosphere of commitment to students' goals and positive feedback from the teacher and peers can counter previous negative experiences.

Characteristics of a Desirable Training Program for Students Who Are Obese

- Low-impact aerobic activities should emphasize the use of large-muscle groups.
- Intensity should be deemphasized and duration should be stressed.
- The frequency of activities should be daily (or almost daily), thus raising the total daily energy expenditure.
- There should be a gradual increase in frequency, time, and intensity.
- Daily activity duration can be cumulative; thus, intermittent activities as well as participation in daily activities such as household chores should be encouraged, especially for younger children and those beginning an exercise program.
- The activities chosen should be enjoyable and should not cause pain.
- The participation of others such as partners, small groups, and especially family members is helpful for program maintenance, motivation, and enjoyment.

The physical educator should ease a student into a physical activity program and provide activities that are enjoyable. This is the best antidote for anxiety. Appropriate activities that reduce intensity, duration, and weight-bearing situations will minimize or eliminate discomfort and pain associated with exercise; activities that require lifting or excessively moving body weight will not result in positive experiences. Gymnastics activities, distance running, rope climbing, and field events such as the long jump might need extensive modification for students who are overweight or obese. Gradual enhancement of endurance capabilities should be part of the program. Fast walking, bicycle riding, and certain swimming activities might help develop aerobic endurance. Students can wear pedometers to measure distances covered or accelerometers to measure activity intensity throughout the day. The physical education teacher may work on balance and proprioception and provide activities such as water aerobics that minimize weight on joints and reduce reliance on balance skills. The President's Youth Fitness Program provides the educator with a variety of activities and personal and class-based incentives to fulfill activity objectives (U.S. Department of Health and Human Services, 2015). Additionally, the reader is encouraged to consult *The Brockport Physical Fitness Training Guide* (Winnick & Short, 1999), which provides specific information on enhancing weight loss and much more. Items from the BPFT manual (Winnick & Short, 2014) may also be used to evaluate health-related components of fitness. Awards can be given for progress through The President's Youth Fitness Program, individualized Physical Best programs (from SHAPE America), or the teacher's own programs.

Aquatic activities, in particular, are well worth the extra effort to include in a physical education program. They are appropriate for nearly all special populations because buoyancy allows those with physical limitations to experience more freedom of movement and thus an improvement in flexibility, strength, and endurance (Dunn & Leitschuh, 2020). For students who are obese, activities such as water calisthenics might reduce stress on joints such as the knees, ankles, and feet. As the students gain fitness, they can gradually work out in shallower water. Students who lag behind in coordination and motor skills often find the water to be a more forgiving and positive learning environment as well. For example, learning locomotor skills in the water eliminates the fear of falling or looking uncoordinated in front of peers and is terrific for skill learning, balance, fitness, and positive social interactions.

Adapted physical education, sports, and recreation opportunities for children and adolescents with disabilities are particularly vital because students with conditions such as diabetes, vision limitations, intellectual or developmental disabilities, and hearing impairments are at greater risk of being overweight or obese (Bandini et al., 2015). When students with disabilities (who might have less mobility than others and thus are at higher risk for becoming obese) grow older, it is important that they have the desire and skills to engage in an active adult lifestyle that maintains their physical fitness, health, and well-being while avoiding the dangers of a sedentary lifestyle. Research shows children with disabilities can adhere to short-term structured exercise and fitness programs and that family-centered lifestyle obesity interventions may be beneficial (Bandini et al., 2015).

It is critical for schools to offer quality physical education experiences to meet the needs of students with obesity. These may occur in general education, self-contained, small-group, or individualized settings. Opportunities may be provided informally or as a part of differentiated instruction. Unique needs related to obesity may also be addressed through (1) individualized education programs (IEPs) for students with disabilities, (2) individualized physical education programs (IPEPs) for students with or without disabilities, or (3) 504 plans for students with physical or mental impairments that substantially limit major life activities. Chapter 5 presents information related to the development of these plans. Students who are obese need to have physical education services, and their health is dependent on receiving appropriate instruction.

It is critical that instructors planning weight loss programs carefully consider the factors that motivate participants to engage in the activities and continue the program. Students must understand how to incorporate physical activity into their personal lifestyles (AAP, 2020; U.S. Department of Health and Human Services, 2015; WHO, 2020). For most children and adolescents, participation in games and sports that have a lifetime emphasis is especially desirable to make the activity both enjoyable and inviting to family and friends.

Developmentally appropriate activities are also essential. Children cannot be expected to experience success on a basketball or soccer team when they have not yet mastered basic locomotor and manipulative skills such as running, skipping, sliding, dribbling, and kicking. Well-planned obstacle courses and climbing activities are excellent for younger children for motivating enjoyment and the development of motor skills. Slightly older children might benefit significantly by participating in creative dance and music games as well as lead-up games that encourage teamwork and allow the practice of motor skills. Once these skills are learned, older children can successfully participate in team sport and sport-related conditioning and training activities. Other types of activities that downplay team competition but encourage the learning of skills on a more individual basis are walking, hiking, swimming, jogging, running, skiing, cycling, skating, and rowing. Group activities such as aerobic dance, aqua aerobics, and spinning encourage socialization without requiring participation with a specific team. See the sidebar Suggestions to Enhance and Maintain Participation in Physical Activities.

Many of the typical units covered in physical education may need considerable modification for students who are obese. A basketball or American football unit may focus on developing certain fundamental skills such as passing, catching, kicking, and shooting. Softball may include the development of fundamental skills and may involve modification of some rules, such as allowing for courtesy or pinch runners. Dual and individual sports with modifications such as boundary or rule changes (e.g., the ball may bounce twice in handball) are appropriate activities. Golf, archery, and bowling likely need no modification, whereas tennis and racquetball may be more successful in doubles play.

All curricular experiences should be oriented toward helping students with obesity develop a positive attitude toward themselves and toward physical activity. Physical education experiences—whether doing a caloric analysis of energy expenditures, learning to drive a golf ball, or being permitted to wear sport clothing other than the typical gym uniform—should contribute directly or indirectly to improving self-image and solving the weight control problem. Likewise, any strategy that changes the other students' attitudes toward their peers with weight problems will facilitate integration of students who are overweight or obese into the social environment. In the final analysis, the focus of a physical education class must be suitable physical activity. Short and colleagues (1999) provide helpful information to enhance weight loss in chapter 2 of *The Brockport Physical Fitness Training Guide*.

Summary

This chapter has addressed conditions that students both with and without disabilities may experience during physical education and sport programs. Although activity injuries and longer-term disorders may occur among all students, these conditions should not preclude participation in physical education or physical activity outside the school setting. Suggestions for appropriate physical activity and physical fitness experiences have been provided for students with activity injuries, longer-term disorders, and obesity.

Suggestions to Enhance and Maintain Participation in Physical Activities

- Select activities that are developmentally appropriate.
- Ensure that students have the necessary skills to participate successfully and safely.
- Select well-liked activities in pleasant surroundings.
- Emphasize that accumulated physical activity is beneficial.
- Give guidance regarding the amount, intensity, and duration of physical activity.
- Start easy and progress gradually; avoid doing too much, too fast, too soon.
- Teach skills for lifetime activities and those that invite the involvement of others.
- Provide individualized guidance, reinforcement, and personal attention.
- Empower participants by encouraging self-assessment and self-monitoring.
- Provide feedback regarding physiological and other skill improvements.
- Develop knowledge, understanding, and values regarding health-related fitness.
- Develop and implement award systems and other incentives for participation.

References

American Academy of Pediatrics (AAP). (2020). *Losing weight safely, sensibly, and successfully.* Retrieved from www.healthychildren.org/english/health-issues/conditions/obesity/Pages/default.aspx

Anderson, J.C., Courson, R.W., Kleiner, D.M., & McLoda, T.A. (2002). National Athletic Trainers' Association position statement: Emergency planning in athletics. *Journal of Athletic Training, 37*(1), 99-104.

Andreoli, C.V., Chiaramonti, B.C., Biruel, E., Pochini, A., Ejnisman, B., & Cohen, M. (2018). Epidemiology of sports injuries in basketball: Integrative systematic review. *BMJ Open Sports & Exercise Medicine*, 4, e000468. http://dx.doi.org/10.1136/ bmjsem-2018-000468

Athanasopoulos, S., Mandalidis, D., Tsakoniti, A., Athanasopoulos, I., Strimpakos, N., Papadopoulos, E., Pyrros, D.G., Parisis, C., & Kapreli, E. (2009). The 2004 Paralympic Games: Physiotherapy services in the Paralympic village polyclinic. *Open Sports Medicine Journal,* 3, 1-8. https://doi.org/10.2174/1874387000903010001

Bandini, L., Danielson, M., Esposito, L.E., Foley, J.T., Fox, M.H., Frey, G.C., Fleming, R.K., Krahn, G., Must, A., Porretta, D.L., Rodgers, A.B., Stanish, H., Urv, T., Vogel, L., & Humphries, K. (2015). Obesity in children with developmental and/or physical disabilities. *Disability and Health Journal*, *8*(3), 309-316. http://doi.org/10.1016/j.dhjo.2015.04.005

Barber Foss, K.D., Thomas, S., Khoury, J.C., Myer, G.D., & Hewett, T.E. (2018). A school-based neuromuscular training program and sport-related injury incidence: A prospective randomized controlled clinical trial. *Journal of Athletic Training, 53*(1), 20-28. https://doi.org/10.4085/1062-6050-173-16

Bauerfeind, J., Koper, M., Wieczorek, J., Urba?ski, P., & Tasiemski, T. (2015). Sports injuries in wheelchair rugby—a pilot study. *Journal of Human Kinetics,* 48, 123-132. https://doi.org/10.1515/hukin-2015-0098

Blauwet, C.A., Cushman, D., Emery, C., Willick, S.E., Webborn, N., Derman, W., Schwellnus, M., Stomphorst, J., & Van de Vliet, P. (2016). Risk of injuries in Paralympic track and field differs by impairment and event discipline: A prospective cohort study at the London 2012 Paralympic Games. *American Journal of Sports Medicine, 44*(6), 1455-1462. https://doi.org/10.1177/0363546516629949

Bleakley, C. (2012). Price needs updating, should we call the POLICE? *British Journal of Sports Medicine, 46*(4), 220-221. https://doi.org/10.1136/bjsports-2011-090297

Bonazza, N., Smuin, D.M., Sterling, N., Ba, D., Liu, G., Leslie, D.L., Hennrikus, W., & Dhawan, A. (2019). Epidemiology of surgical treatment of youth sports injuries in the United States: Analysis of marketscan commercial claims and encounters database. *Arthroscopy, Sports Medicine, and Rehabilitation, 1*(1), e59-e65. https://doi.org/10.1016/j.asmr.2019.07.004

Briner, W.W., & Benjamin, H.J. (1999). Volleyball injuries. Managing acute and overuse disorders. *Physician and Sportsmedicine, 27*(3), 48-60. https://doi.org/10.3810/psm.1999.03.720

Centers for Disease Control and Prevention (CDC). (2020). *Childhood obesity facts.* Retrieved from www.cdc.gov/obesity/data/childhood.html

Cooper Institute. (2017). *FitnessGram administration manual: The journey to MyHealthyZone* (5th ed.). Human Kinetics.

Derman, W., Runciman, P., Jordaan, E., Schwellnus, M., Blauwet, C. Webborn, N., Lexell, J., Van de Vliet, P., Kissick, J., Stomphorst, J., Lee, Y., & Kim, K. (2020). High incidence of injuries at the PyeongChang 2018 Paralympic Winter Games: A prospective cohort study of 6804 athlete days. *British Journal of Sports Medicine, 54,* 38-43. https://doi.org/10.1136/bjsports-2018-100170

Doherty, C., Delahunt, E., Caulfield, B., Hertel, J., Ryan, J., & Bleakley, C. (2014). The incidence and prevalence of ankle sprain injury: A systematic review and meta-analysis of prospective epidemiological studies. *Sports Medicine, 44*(1), 123-140. https://doi.org/10.1007/s40279-013-0102-5

Donovan, L., Hetzel, S., Laufenberg, C.R., & McGuine, T.A. (2020). Prevalence and impact of chronic ankle instability in adolescent athletes. *Orthopaedic Journal of Sports Medicine, 8*(2), 1-10. https://doi.org/10.1177/2325967119900962

Dunn, J.M., & Leitschuh, C.A. (2020). *Special physical education* (10th ed.). Kendall/Hunt.

Fagher, K., & Lexell, J. (2014). Sports-related injuries in athletes with disabilities. *Scandinavian Journal of Medicine and Science in Sports, 24,* 320-331. https://doi.org/10.1111/sms.12175

Fédération Internationale de Football Association (FIFA). (2019). FIFA 11+. Retrieved from www.fifamedicalnetwork.com/lessons/prevention-fifa-11/

Ferrara, M.S., & Peterson, C.L. (2000). Injuries to athletes with disabilities: Identifying injury patterns. *Sports Medicine, 30*(2), 137-143. https://doi.org/10.2165/00007256-200030020-00006

Figel, K., Pritchett, K., Pritchett, R., & Broad, E. (2018). Energy and nutrient issues in athletes with spinal cord injury: Are they at risk for low energy availability. *Nutrients, 10*(8), 1078. https://doi.org/10.3390/nu10081078

Fong, D.T., Yam, K., Chu, V.W., Cheung, R.T., & Chan, K. (2012). Upper limb muscle fatigue during prolonged boccia games with underarm throwing technique. *Sports Biomechanics, 11*(4), 441-451. https://doi.org/10.1080/14763141.2012.699977

Fu, M.E., Ellenbecker, T.S., Renstrom, P.A., Windler, G.S., & Dines, D.M. (2018). Epidemiology of injuries in tennis players. *Current Reviews in Musculoskeletal Medicine, 11*(1), 1-5. https://doi.org/10.1007/s12178-018-9452-9

Fuglkjær, S., Dissing, K.B., & Hestbæk, L. (2017). Prevalence and incidence of musculoskeletal extremity complaints in children and adolescents. A systematic review. *BioMed Central Musculoskeletal Disorders,* 18(1), 418. https://doi.org/10.1186/s12891-017-1771-2

Gajardo, R., Aravena, C., Fontanilla, M., Barría, M., & Saavedra, C. (2019). Injuries and illness prevalence prior to competition in goalball players. *Journal of Visual Impairments and Blindness, 113*(5), 443-451. https://doi.org/10.1177/0145482x19876478

Haegele, J.A., Foley, J.T., Healy, S., & Paller, A. (2020). Prevalence of overweight among youth with chronic conditions in the United States: An update from the 2016 national survey of children's health. *Pediatric Obesity, 15*(4), e12595. https://doi.org/10.1111/ijpo.12595

Hollander, K., Kluge, S., Glöer, F., Ripenhof, H., Zech, A., & Junge, A. (2020). Epidemiology of injuries during the wheelchair basketball world championships 2018: A prospective cohort study. *Scandinavian Journal of Medicine and Science in Sports, 30*(1), 199-207. https://doi.org/10.1111/sms.13558

Jewiss, D., Ostman, C., & Smart, N. (2017). Open versus closed kinetic chain exercises following an anterior cruciate ligament reconstruction: A systematic review and meta-analysis. *Journal of Sports Medicine, 2017,* 4721548. https://doi.org/10.1155/2017/4721548

Koutures, C.G., Gregory, A.J.M, & The Council on Sports Medicine and Fitness. (2010). *Pediatrics, 125,* 410-414. https://doi.org/10.1542/peds.2009-3009

Krempien, J.L., & Barr, S.I. (2011). Risk of nutrient inadequacies in elite Canadian athletes with spinal cord injury. *International Journal of Sports Nutrition, Exercise and Metabolism, 21*(5), 417-425. https://doi.org/10.1123/ijsnem.21.5.417

Laughlin, K., & Happel, K. (2016). Developing an appropriate goalball unit for secondary physical education. *Strategies, 29*(1), 16-23. https://doi.org/10.1080/08924562.2015.1111784

Longo, U.M., Loppini, M., Berton, A., Marinzonni, A., Maffulli, N., & Denaro, V. (2012). The FIFA11+ program is effective in preventing injuries in elite male basketball players: A cluster randomized controlled trial. *The American Journal of Sports Medicine, 40*(5), 996-1005. https://doi.org/10.1177/0363546512438761

Magno e Silva, M.P., Bilzon, J., Duarte, E., Gorla, J., & Vital, R. (2013). Sports injuries in elite Paralympic swimmers with visual impairment. *Journal of Athletic Training, 48*(4), 493-498. https://doi.org/10.4085/1062-6050-48.4.07

Magno e Silva, M.P., Morato, M.P., Bilzon, J.L.J., & Duarte, E. (2012). Sports injuries in Brazilian blind footballers. *International Journal of Sports Medicine, 34*(3), 239-243. https://doi.org/10.1055/s-0032-1316358

Magno e Silva, M.P., Winckler, C., Costa e Silva, A.A., Bilzon, J., & Duarte, E. (2013). Sports injuries in Paralympic track and field athletes with visual impairment. *Medicine and Science in Sports and Exercise, 45*(5), 908-913. https://doi.org/10.1249/mss.0b013e31827f06f3

Major League Baseball. (2020). *Guidelines for youth and adolescent pitchers.* Retrieved from www.mlb.com/pitch-smart/pitching-guidelines

Merrie, M.D., Shewmake, C., & Calleja, P. (2016). Injury prevention in physical education: Scenarios and solutions. *Strategies,* 29(4), 15-18. https://doi.org/10.1080/08924562.2016.1181590

Molik, B., Mędasik, A., Łuczak, E., Kaźmierska, K., & Gołębiewski, S. (2011). Characteristic of sport injuries in team games for persons with disabilities. *Journal of Orthopaedics Trauma Surgery and Related Research, 6*(26), 22-26.

Mustafins, P., Vetra, A., & Scibrja, I. (2009). The sport participation limiting injuries, musculoskeletal complaints and the SF-36v2 health survey data in Paralympic volleyball players. *International Journal of Rehabilitation Research, 32,* S11. https://doi.org/10.1097/00004356-200908001-00151

Nuhu, A., Nishimwe, B.H., Nteziryayo, J.B., Nyirahabimana, A.F., Stareehe, J., Kumurenzi, A., & Sagahutu, J.B. (2020). Profile of injuries among sitting volleyball players with disabilities in Rwanda. *Rwanda Journal of Medicine and Health Sciences, 2*(3), 250-264. https://doi.org/10.4314/rjmhs.v2i3.8

Office of Disease Prevention and Health Promotion (ODPHP). (2020). *Obesity in children and adolescents (NWS-10.4)*. Retrieved from https://www.healthypeople.gov/2020/leading-health-indicators/2020-lhi-topics/Nutrition-Physical-Activity-and-Obesity/data#NWS-10

Patel, D.R., & Greydanus, D.E. (2010). Sport participation by physically and cognitively challenged young athletes. *Pediatric Clinics of North America, 57*(3), 795-817. https://doi.org/10.1016/j.pcl.2010.03.002

Pierpoint, L.A., Williams, C.M., Fields, S.K., & Comstock, R.D. (2016). Epidemiology of injuries in United States high school track and field. *American Journal of Sports Medicine, 44*(6), 1463-1468. https://doi.org/10.1177/0363546516629950

Platt, L.S. (2001). Medical and orthopaedic conditions in Special Olympics athletes. *Journal of Athletic Training, 36*(1), 74-80.

Prentice, W. (2017). *Principles of athletic training: A competency-based approach* (16th ed.). McGraw-Hill.

Ramirez, M., Yang, J., Bourque, L., Javien, J., Kashani, S., Limbos, M.A., & Peek-Asa, C. (2009). Sports injuries to high school athletes with disabilities. *Pediatrics, 123*, 690-696.

Risberg, M.A., Mørk, M., Jenssen, H.K., & Holm, I. (2001). Design and implementation of a neuromuscular training program following anterior cruciate ligament reconstruction. *Journal of Orthopaedic & Sports Physical Therapy, 31*(11), 620-631. https://doi.org/10.2519/jospt.2001.31.11.620

Short, F., McCubbin, J., & Frey, G. (1999). Cardiorespiratory endurance and body composition. In J. Winnick & F. Short (Eds.), *The Brockport physical fitness training guide*. Human Kinetics.

Stopka, C. (2008). *Maximize your stretching potential: Use the "ultra-stretch" for safe and effective results!* PE Central.

Stopka, C. (2010). Increasing student flexibility—the ultra-stretch way! *Palaestra, 24*(4), 31-35.

Stopka, C., & Todorovich, J. (2011). *Applied special physical education and exercise therapy* (6th ed.). Pearson.

Stracciolini, A., Sugimoto, D., & Howell, D.R. (2017). Injury prevention in youth sports. *Pediatric Annals, 46*(3): e99-e105. https://doi.org/10.3928/19382359-20170223-01

Surburg, P. (1999). Flexibility/range of motion. In J. Winnick & F. Short (Eds.), *The Brockport physical fitness training guide*. Human Kinetics.

Theisen, D., Frisch, A., Malisoux, L., Urhaussen, A., Croisier, J., & Seil, R. (2013). Injury risk is different in team and individual youth sports. *Journal of Science and Medicine in Sport, 16*(3), 200-204.

Tuakli-Wosornu, Y.A., & Derman, W. (2018). Para and adapted sports medicine. In *Physical Medicine and Rehabilitation Clinics of North America*. Elsevier.

U.S. Department of Health and Human Services. (2015). *United States dietary and physical activity guidelines for Americans*. https://health.gov/our-work/food-nutrition/2015-2020-dietary-guidelines/guidelines/executive-summary/

Wanivenhaus, F., Fox, A.J.S., Chaudhury, S., & Rodeo, S.A. (2012). Epidemiology of injuries and prevention strategies in competitive swimmers. *Sports Health, 4*(3), 246-251. https://doi.org/10.1177/1941738112442132

Webborn, N., Cushman, D., Blauwet, C.A., Emery, C., Derman, W., Schwellnus, M., Stomphorst, J., Van de Vliet, P., & Willick, S.E. (2016). The epidemiology of injuries in football at the London 2012 Paralympic Games. *Physical Medicine and Rehabilitation, 8*(6), 545-552. https://doi.org/10.1016/j.pmrj.2015.09.025

Webborn, N., & Emery, C. (2014). Descriptive epidemiology of Paralympic sports injuries. *Physical Medicine and Rehabilitation, 6*(Suppl. 8), S18-S22. https://doi.org/10.1016/j.pmrj.2014.06.003

Webborn, N., & Van de Vliet, P. (2012). Paralympic medicine. *Lancet, 380*(9836), 65-71. https://doi.org/10.1016/s0140-6736(12)60831-9

Willick, S.E., Webborn, N., Emery, C., Blauwet, C.A., Pit-Grosheide, P., Stomphorst, J., Van de Vliet, P., Marques, N.A.P., Martinez-Ferrer, J.O., Jordaan, E., Derman, W., & Schwellnus, M. (2013). The epidemiology of injuries at the London 2012 Paralympic Games. *British Journal of Sports Medicine, 47*, 426-432. doi: 10.1136/bjsports-2013-092374

Wilroy, J., & Hibberd, E. (2018). Evaluation of a shoulder injury prevention program in wheelchair basketball. *Journal of Sport Rehabilitation, 1*(27), 554-559. https://doi.org/10.1123/jsr.2017-0011

Winnick, J., & Short, F.X. (1999). (Eds.). *The Brockport physical fitness training guide*. Human Kinetics.

Winnick, J.P., & Short, F.X. (2014). *The Brockport physical fitness test manual*. Human Kinetics.

World Health Organization (WHO). (2020). *Physical activity and young people*. Retrieved from www.who.int/dietphysicalactivity/factsheet_young_people/en/

Zwierzchowska, A., Rosolek, B., Celebańska, D., Gawlik, K., & Wójcik, M. (2020). The prevalence of injuries and traumas in elite goalball players. *International Journal of Environmental Research and Public Health, 17*(7), e2496. https://doi.org/10.3390/ijerph17072496

Print Resources

Smedes, F., Heidmann, M., Schäfer, C., Fischer, N., & Stępień, A. (2016). The proprioceptive neuromuscular facilitation-concept; the state of the evidence, a narrative review. *Physical Therapy Reviews, 21*(1), 17-31.

This article explains the basis of PNF, the types of techniques, and the use of these techniques by practitioners.

It reviews the uses of PNF techniques and provides ideas regarding practical applications.

Online Resources

American Academy of Pediatrics. (2020). *Losing weight safely, sensibly, and successfully.* www.healthychildren.org/english/health-issues/conditions/obesity/Pages/default.aspx

The American Academy of Pediatrics is the principal professional body of pediatricians dedicated to the health and well-being of infants, children, adolescents, and young adults. The information in this chapter comes from its findings on issues and conditions related to obesity.

State of Childhood Obesity: http://stateofobesity.org

This website comes from the Centers for Disease Control and Prevention (CDC) and provides multiple links to issues on health, dietary advice, physical activity advice, family life, and other topics and current articles.

United States Dietary and Physical Activity Guidelines for Americans: https://health.gov/our-work/food-nutrition/2015-2020-dietary-guidelines/guidelines/executive-summary

This website provides the latest U.S. Department of Agriculture (USDA) Dietary Guidelines and provides links to resources, public comments, questions and answers, and more.

Special Olympics Sports Sciences: Sports Injury Guide for Coaches: https://media.specialolympics.org/resources/sports-essentials/sport-sciences/SpecialOlympics_SportsSciences-Injury_Prevention.pdf

This resource from the Special Olympics website provides coaches with specific methods to manage sports injuries and conditions in Special Olympics athletes when an injury occurs and medical personnel are not immediately available.

Part III

Developmental Considerations

Part III focuses on early childhood development and services for children with disabilities at the youngest ages. These chapters discuss motor development (chapter 19), perceptual–motor development (chapter 20), adapted physical education services for infants and toddlers (chapter 21), and early childhood adapted physical education (chapter 22).

The information presented in chapters 19 and 20 is intended to review and build on foundational knowledge related to motor development and the perceptual–motor process. Chapter 21 covers the role physical education teachers play in program delivery for infants and toddlers, including assessment, goals, and objectives for programs, along with recommendations for interacting with children and their families. Chapter 22 provides information related to program objectives, developmentally appropriate teaching approaches and activities, and assessment for the early childhood years (ages 3 to 5).

19

Motor Development

John C. Ozmun, Byungmo Ku,
and David L. Gallahue

Kwan and Joon are cousins. Although only a month apart in age, they vary significantly in development, because Joon was born with Down syndrome. As they grew older, Kwan's motor development aligned with the typical early milestones, such as grasping, rolling, sitting, standing, and walking. Joon, however, was slower to reach these milestones. Joon's parents recognized these concerns and paid extra attention to his motor development, engaging him almost every day in activities such as walking, balancing, and throwing and catching a ball. As Joon was exposed to these activities, he developed greater interest in them, especially in playing with a ball. Unlike Joon, Kwan was not interested in playing with balls as he grew older; instead, he enjoyed more sedentary activities such as playing video games.

When Kwan and Joon were in elementary school, Joon regularly participated in a variety of youth sport programs, including soccer, basketball, and floor hockey, but Kwan preferred reading and watching videos. Although Kwan sometimes wanted to play sports with his friends, he hesitated to join because he was not a competent player. By that time, Joon's motor skills were clearly more advanced than Kwan's. Although Joon experienced early developmental deficits, he mastered the fundamental motor skills with his parents' support. This led him to regular participation in physical activities, which provided additional opportunities to learn and practice motor skills and maintain a healthy active lifestyle. Disability factors such as Down syndrome may delay motor development, but they do not entirely determine outcome. In this scenario, Joon received appropriate support from his parents and became interested in doing physical activities throughout his childhood. His motor skills were maximized through teaching, practice, and continual reinforcement.

For years the topic of motor development has been of considerable interest to physical educators in general and adapted physical educators in particular. Without knowledge of the development process, teachers can only guess at appropriate educational techniques and intervention strategies to maximize students' learning potential. Educators who use developmentally based instruction incorporate learning experiences geared to the needs of their students. They reject the all-too-frequent textbook ideal of all students being at the same level of development at given chronological age markers. In fact, one of the most valuable outcomes of studying human development has been less reliance on the concept of age appropriateness and more attention paid to the concept of individual appropriateness.

In a very real sense, adapted physical education is developmental education. Program content and instructional strategies are designed to meet individual developmental needs. Unfortunately, human development is frequently studied from a compartmentalized viewpoint—that is, the cognitive, affective, and motor domains are viewed as unrelated entities. Although perhaps valid from the standpoint of basic research, such a perspective is of little value when it comes to understanding the learning process and devising appropriate interventions. It is essential for teachers of students with developmental disabilities to be knowledgeable about the typical process of development so that they have a baseline for comparing the students with whom they are working. The totality and integrated nature of the student must be recognized, respected, and accommodated in the educational process.

This chapter discusses how humans gain motor skills across their development, the factors that influence motor development, and the differences between those with and without disabilities. The focus is on defining motor development and describing the categories of human movement. Developmental theory is briefly examined from the viewpoints of two popular theoretical frameworks: dynamic systems theory and the phases of motor development. Applications and variations as they relate to adapted physical educators and students with disabilities are discussed throughout the text.

Motor Development Defined

Development is a continuous process of change over time, beginning at conception and ceasing only at death. **Motor development**, therefore, is the progressive (and in some cases regressive) change in movement behavior throughout the life cycle, involving continuous adaptation in a person's movement capabilities in a never-ending effort to achieve and maintain motor control and movement competence. Such a perspective does not view development as domain specific, nor does it view development as stage-like or age dependent. Instead, a life span perspective suggests that *some* aspects of a person's development can be conceptualized into stage-like and age-related domains, whereas others cannot. Further, the concept of achieving and maintaining competence encompasses all developmental change, both positive and negative.

Motor development can be studied as both a **process** and a **product**. The process standpoint considers underlying factors that influence motor performance and movement capabilities from infancy through old age. The product standpoint typically views motor development in broad time frames, phases, and stages. **Dynamic systems theory** (Haywood et al., 2012; Hollenstein, 2011; van Geert, 2011) is popular among developmentalists as a means of better understanding the *process* of development, whereas the **phases of motor development** (Goodway et al., 2021) serve as a descriptive means for better understanding and conceptualizing the *product* of development. Both concepts are briefly discussed after an initial overview of the categories of human movement.

Categories of Movement

Both the processes and products of motor development are revealed through changes in a person's movement behavior across the life span. During all developmental stages—infancy, childhood, adolescence, and adulthood—humans learn how to move with control and competence in response to the daily movement challenges they face. Educators can observe developmental differences in motor behavior by observing these changes in body mechanics and motor performance.

Observable movement takes many forms and may be grouped into categories. One technique involves three categories—stability, locomotion, and manipulation—and combinations of the three (Cleland-Donnelly et al., 2017; Goodway et al., 2021). **Stability** is the most basic form of movement and is present to a greater or lesser extent in all movement. A stability movement is any movement that places a premium on gaining and maintaining equilibrium in relation to gravity. Gaining control of the muscles of the head, neck, and trunk is the first stability task of the newborn. Sitting with support, sitting unaided, and pulling oneself to standing are important stability tasks for most developing infants. Standing without support, balancing momentarily on one foot, and being able to bend and stretch, twist and turn, and reach and lift are all important stability tasks of childhood through old age.

Many disabling conditions are associated with deficits in stability and can result in the delay of some movement tasks. Central nervous system disorders such as cerebral palsy can delay the onset of independent sitting, standing, and walking in infants. Muscular strength deficits associated with conditions such as Down syndrome can inhibit children from developing key stability skills often mastered during childhood. Because of various orthopedic conditions or sensory impairments, an older adult might lack the necessary stability to prevent falls.

The **locomotion** movement category refers to movements that involve a change in location of the body relative to a fixed point: walking, running, jumping, hopping, skipping, or leaping. In this use of the term, activities such as a forward or backward roll might be considered to be both locomotive and stability movements—locomotive because the body is moving from point to point, and stability because of the premium placed on maintaining equilibrium in an unusual balancing situation.

The development of locomotor skills for those using a wheelchair might involve moving the chair forward, backward, or in a zigzag pattern. More advanced locomotor skills include moving the chair forward or backward while riding on two wheels in a wheelie position. People with lower limb amputations might also need to modify their locomotor patterns to compensate for the use of a prosthesis.

The **manipulation**, or object control, category refers to both gross and fine motor manipulation. The tasks of throwing, catching, kicking, and striking objects are all gross motor manipulative movements. Activities such as sewing, cutting with scissors, and typing are fine motor manipulative movements. The development of basic manipulative movements, such as grasping and releasing a fork or raising a spoon to the mouth with control and accuracy, is of significant importance for the person who is severely disabled. A person with tetraplegia might strive for the development of these manipulative skills in an effort to decrease dependence on others. A person missing an upper body limb may modify a prosthetic device for better manipulation.

Many movements involve a combination of stability, locomotive, and manipulative movements. In essence, all voluntary movements involve an element of stability. This is why stability is the most basic category of movement—and why it is absolutely essential for progressive development in the other two categories. For people with disabilities, supportive assistance such as balance bars, walkers, or peer assistance might be necessary to compensate for a lack of stability and facilitate the performance of more advanced movement skills.

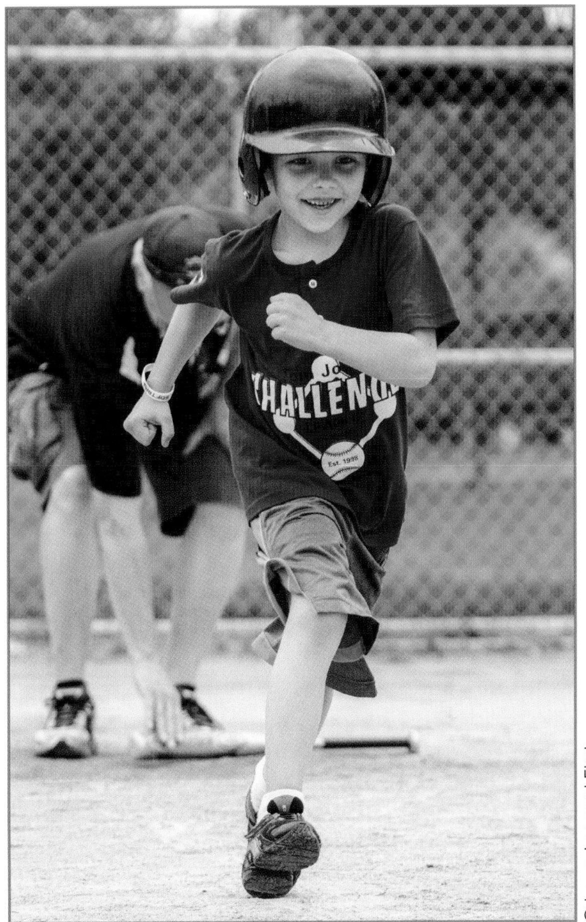

© Laura Leonard Fitch

Enhancing running through participation in Challenger baseball.

Motor Development as a Dynamic System

Theory should undergird all research and science, and the study of motor development is no exception. Motor development theory is based on the acquisition and refinement of motor skills in people without disabilities. This information provides insight into the influence of developmental disabilities on the learning of new movement skills, thereby permitting adoption of appropriate instructional strategies.

To be of practical benefit, developmental theory must be both **descriptive** and **explanatory**. It is important to understand what people are typically like during particular ages (description). It is equally important, however, to know what causes these changes (explanation). Many motor developmentalists use explanatory models in an attempt to understand more about the underlying processes that govern development. Dynamic systems theory is one such popular model (Haywood et al., 2012; Hollenstein, 2011; van Geert, 2011).

The term *dynamic* conveys the concept that developmental change is **nonlinear** and **discontinuous**—that is, individual change over time is not necessarily smooth and hierarchical, and it does not necessarily involve moving toward ever higher levels of complexity and competence in the motor system. Individual impairments can impede motor development, especially disabling conditions. For example, children with cerebral palsy are frequently delayed in learning to walk independently. When independent walking is achieved, at a point in time appropriate for each child, the gait pattern will be individualized. The dynamics of change occur over time, but in a highly individual manner influenced by critical factors within the system.

The term *systems* conveys the concept that the human organism is self-organizing and composed of several subsystems. A human is self-organizing in that it is natural for humans to strive for motor control and movement competence. It is the subsystems—namely, the task, the individual, and the environment—operating separately and in concert that determine the rate, sequence, and extent of development. In other words, a person's development does not follow a preprogrammed universal plan that unfolds on an inflexible schedule.

Dynamic systems theory attempts to answer the *why* questions—that is, the process questions that result in the observable product of motor development. For instance, what are those enabling factors (affordances) that allow or promote developmental change, and what are those inhibiting factors (rate limiters) that restrict or impede development? For children with cerebral palsy, for example, rate limiters are neurological and biomechanical, whereas affordances might include assisted support, handholds, encouragement, and guided instruction.

For years, developmentalists have recognized the interactive role of two primary systems on the developmental process—individual (i.e., heredity and biological factors) and environmental (i.e., experience or learning factors). Interestingly, many have now taken this view one step further by recognizing that the demands of a movement task itself also interact with the individual and the environment in the development of stability, locomotor, and manipulative movement abilities. This transactional model recognizes that factors

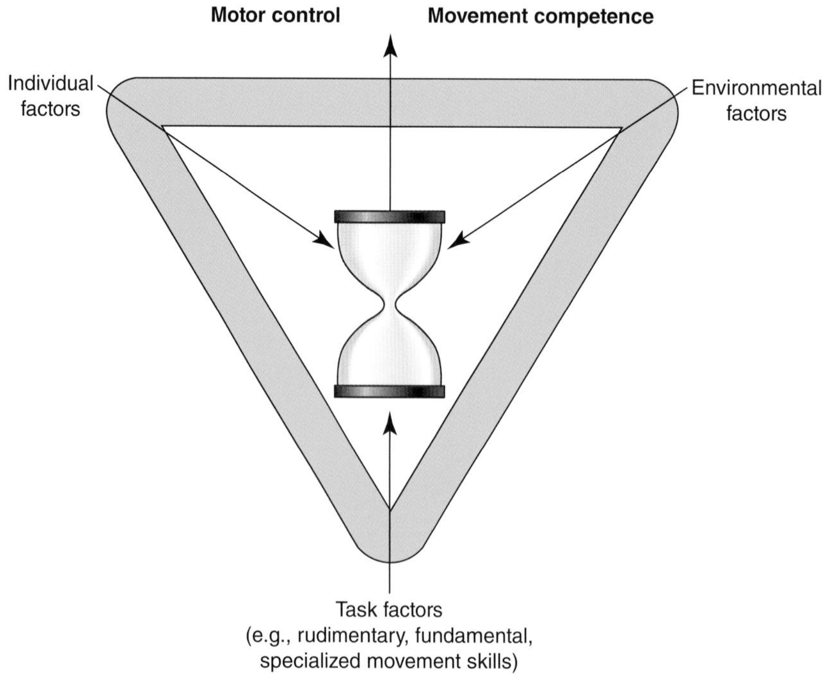

FIGURE 19.1 A transactional model of causality in motor development and movement skill acquisition.

within various subsystems of the task, individual, and environment interact with and modify one another as a person strives to gain motor control and movement competence. These factors serve as variables on which task analyses and ecological task analyses (ETA) of skills should be founded. The adapted physical educator should be prepared to manipulate these variables to stimulate optimal teaching and learning (figure 19.1).

Both the processes and the products of motor development should constantly remind us of the individuality of the learner. Although our biological clocks are rather specific when it comes to the **sequence** of movement skill acquisition, the **rate** and **extent** of development are individually determined and dramatically influenced by the specific performance demands of the task itself. Typical ages of development are just that, typical—and nothing more. Age periods merely represent approximate time ranges during which certain behaviors might be observed for the so-called average person. Overreliance on these typical ranges negates the concepts of continuity, specificity, and individuality in the developmental process, and are of little practical value when working with people with developmental disabilities.

Phases of Motor Development

If observing movement serves as the window for understanding motor development, then one way of studying development is by examining the typical sequential progression in the acquisition of movement abilities. The phase of motor development (figure 19.2) and the developmental stages within each phase (table 19.1) serve as a useful descriptive model for this study (Goodway et al., 2021).

Reflexive Movement Phase

The first movements noted in humans are reflexive and can be observed as early as the fourth month of fetal life. **Reflexes** are involuntary, subcortically controlled movements through which the infant gains information about the immediate environment. Touch, light, sounds, and pressure changes all trigger involuntary movements. These reflexes, coupled with increasing cortical sophistication in the early months of life, play an important role in helping children learn more about their body and the outside world. Involuntary movements are typically referred to as **primitive reflexes** or **postural reflexes**. Primitive reflexes are information-gathering, nourishment-seeking, and protective responses. Postural reflexes resemble later voluntary movements and are used to support the body against gravity or to permit movement. See tables 19.2 and 19.3 for a summary of common primitive and postural reflexes. The reflexive movement phase may be divided into the two overlapping stages of information encoding and decoding.

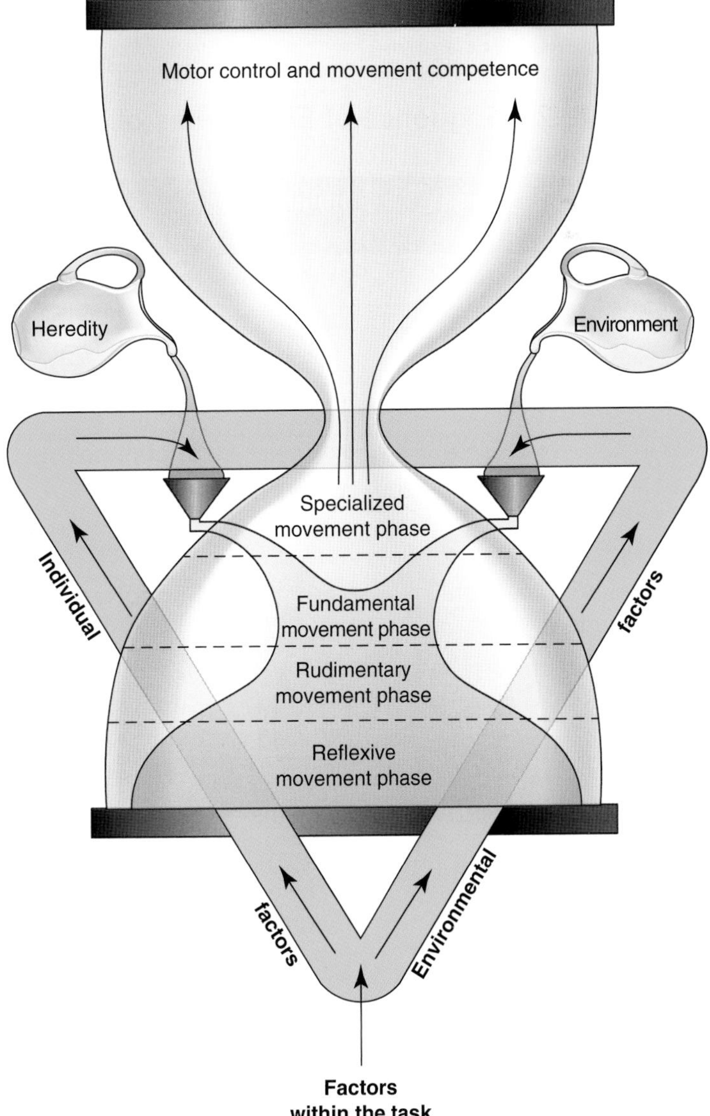

FIGURE 19.2 The hourglass: Gallahue's life span model of motor development.

Reprinted from J.D. Goodway, D. Gallahue and J. Ozmun, *Understanding Motor Development: Infants, Children, Adolescents, Adults*, 6th ed. (Burlington, MA: Jones & Bartlett Learning, 2021), 553. Reprinted with permission.

TABLE 19.1 Phases and Stages of Motor Development

Phases of motor development	Approximate periods of development	Stages of motor development
Reflexive movement phase	In utero to 4 months 4 months to 1 year	Information-encoding stage Information-decoding stage
Rudimentary movement phase	Birth to 1 year 1-2 years	Reflex inhibition stage Precontrol stage
Fundamental movement phase	2-3 years 3-5 years 5-7 years	Initial stage Emerging stage Proficient stage
Specialized movement phase	7-10 years 11-13 years 14 years+	Transition stage Application stage Lifelong utilization stage

Adapted from J.D. Goodway, D. Gallahue and J. Ozmun, *Understanding Motor Development: Infants, Children, Adolescents, Adults*, 6th ed. (Burlington, MA: Jones & Bartlett Learning, 2021), 133.

TABLE 19.2 Sequence of Emergence of Selected Primitive Reflexes of the Newborn

Reflex	Onset (age)	Inhibition (age)	Stimulus	Behavior
Moro	Birth	3 months	**Supine position** Rapid or sudden movement of infant's head caused by sudden loud noise	Stimulation will result in extension of the infant's extremities, followed by a return to a flexed position against the body.
Tonic neck (asymmetrical)	Birth*	6 months	**Supine position** Neck turned so head faces left or right	Extremities on side of body facing head position extend; those on side opposite flex.
Tonic neck (symmetrical)	Birth*	6 months	**Supported sitting** Flexion or extension of infant's neck	Extension or flexion of neck will result in extension of arms and flexion of legs.
Grasping	Birth	4-6 months	**Supine position** Stimulation of palm of the hand or ball of the foot	Stimulation will result in a grasping action of the fingers or toes.
Babinski	Birth	6 months	**Supine position** Stimulation by stroking the sole of the foot	Stimulation will result in extension of the toes.
Sucking	Birth	3 months	**Supine or supported sitting** Stimulus applied directly above or below the lips	Touching area of mouth will result in a sucking action of the lips.

*Not seen in all children.

Information-Encoding Stage

The information-encoding (gathering) stage of the reflexive movement phase is characterized by observable involuntary movement during the fetal period until about the fourth month of infancy. During this stage, lower brain centers are more highly developed than the motor cortex and are in command of fetal and neonatal movement.

TABLE 19.3 Sequence of Emergence of Selected Postural Reflexes of the Newborn

Reflex	Onset (age)	Inhibition (age)	Stimulus	Behavior
Labyrinthine righting	2 months	12 months	**Supported upright position** Tilting trunk forward, rearward, or to side	Infant will attempt to keep head in an upright position by moving head in opposite direction from tilt.
Supportive reactions	4 months (arms) 9 months (legs)	12 months	**Prone or upright supported** Movement of the child's extremities toward a surface	Extension of the extremities to a position of support.
Pull-up	3 months	4 months	**Upright sitting supported by hands** Tilting of child from side to side and front and back	Infant will flex arms in an attempt to maintain equilibrium.
Stepping	2 weeks	5 months	**Supported upright position** Holding child in upright position with soles of feet touching a surface	Lower extremities perform definite stepping action.
Crawling	Birth	4 months	**Prone unsupported position** Stimulus is applied to sole of one foot	Crawling action exhibited by both the upper and lower extremities.
Swimming	Birth	5 months	**Prone held over water** Holding child over or in water	Swimming movements elicited in both the upper and lower extremities.

These brain centers are capable of causing involuntary reactions to stimuli of varying intensity and duration. During this stage, reflexes serve as the primary means through which the infant is able to gather information, seek nourishment, and seek protection.

Information-Decoding Stage

The information-decoding (processing) stage begins around the fourth month of postnatal life. There is a gradual inhibition of many reflexes as higher brain centers continue to develop. Lower brain centers gradually relinquish control over skeletal movements and are replaced by voluntary movement mediated by the motor area of the cerebral cortex. The decoding stage replaces sensorimotor activity with perceptual–motor behavior—that is, the infant's development of voluntary motor control involves processing sensory stimuli with stored information, not merely reacting to stimuli.

Developmental Divergence

The evaluation of an infant's reflexes is a much-used method of screening for developmental problems and serves as a primary means of diagnosing central nervous system integrity in full-term, premature, and at-risk infants. The complete absence of a reflex is usually less significant than a reflex that remains too long. Other evidence of possible neurological problems might be found in a reflex that is too strong or too weak. In addition, a reflex that elicits a stronger response on one side of the body than on the other might indicate dysfunction of the central nervous system. For example, an asymmetrical tonic neck reflex that shows full arm extension on one side of the body and only weak extensor tone when the other side is stimulated might provide evidence of developmental complications. The following list summarizes the reflexive behaviors that might indicate neurological dysfunction:

- Nonexistence of reflex response
- Weakness of reflex response
- Asymmetrical reflex response
- Persistence of reflex response

This evaluation serves as a basis for intervention by the physical and occupational therapists and the adapted physical education specialist working with students displaying pathological reflexive behavior. One such intervention is represented by the use of a small treadmill to elicit the stepping reflex in developmentally delayed infants. Research demonstrates that when supported in an upright position with feet placed on the treadmill, an infant will begin stepping reflexively once the treadmill belt begins to move (Angulo-Barroso et al., 2013; Ulrich et al., 2008; Wu et al., 2007). Results from these investigations have demonstrated that treadmill-trained infants with Down syndrome tend to walk independently much sooner than infants with the same condition who did not train, suggesting that the treadmill training plays a role in muscular strength development as well as promoting practice of the movement pattern of walking. In addition to Down syndrome, similar investigations have been initiated with conditions such as spina bifida and cerebral palsy.

Another common type of early motor intervention is referred to as *neurodevelopmental therapy* (Morgan et al., 2016). The basic concept of the therapeutic approach is to provide stimulation to the infant's tactile, vestibular, and somatosensory receptors. The therapist scaffolds fundamental movements of infants with disabilities (sitting, cruising, and walking) using different types of toys and equipment. In addition, parents are educated to maximize opportunities for the infants to repeat and practice the movements in their daily routine (providing motor skill–related toys such as various sized balls and mats).

Rudimentary Movement Phase

The first forms of voluntary movement are rudimentary. **Rudimentary movements** are maturationally determined behaviors seen in the normally developing infant from birth to about age 2. Rudimentary movements are characterized by a highly predictable sequence that is resistant to change under normal conditions. The rate at which these abilities appear, however, varies from child to child and relies on biological, environmental, and task-specific factors. The rudimentary movement abilities of the infant represent the basic forms of voluntary movement required for survival. See table 19.4 for a descriptive profile of selected rudimentary stability, locomotor, and manipulative abilities.

The rudimentary movement phase can be subdivided into two stages: reflex inhibition and precontrol. These stages represent progressively higher orders of motor control and movement competence.

Reflex Inhibition Stage

The **reflex inhibition stage** of the rudimentary movement phase begins at birth. Although reflexes dominate the newborn's movement repertoire, movements are increasingly influenced by the developing cortex. Development of the cortex and the lessening of certain environmental constraints cause several reflexes to gradually disappear. Primitive and postural reflexes are replaced or suppressed by voluntary movement behaviors. At the level of reflex inhibition, voluntary movement is poorly differentiated and integrated because the neuromotor apparatus of the infant is still at a rudimentary stage of development. Movements, though purposeful, appear uncontrolled and unrefined. If, for example, the infant desires to make contact with an object, there will be global activity of the entire hand, wrist, arm, shoulder, and even trunk. In other words, the process of moving the hand into contact with the object, although voluntary, lacks control.

Precontrol Stage

Around one year of age, most developing children begin to bring greater precision and control to their movements. The process of differentiating between sensory and motor systems and integrating perceptual and motor information into a more meaningful and congruent whole takes place. The rapid development of higher cognitive processes as well as motor processes makes for rapid gains in rudimentary movement abilities during this stage. Children learn to gain and maintain their equilibrium, manipulate objects, and locomote throughout their environment. The maturational process might partially explain the rapidity and extent of development of movement control during this stage, but the growth of motor proficiency is no less amazing.

Developmental Divergence

A number of disabling conditions can place an infant or toddler at risk for delayed development of rudimentary movements. Central nervous system disorders, orthopedic conditions, and intellectual disabilities can hinder motor development during these early periods of voluntary movement. One study indicated that persistent head lag, a progressive aspect of motor development, may be one of

TABLE 19.4 Sequence of Emergence of Selected Rudimentary Movement Abilities

Movement pattern	Selected abilities	Approximate age of onset
Control of head and neck	Turns to one side Turns to both sides Held with support Chin off contact surface Good prone control Good supine control	Birth 1 week 1 month 2 months 3 months 5 months
Control of trunk	Lifts head and chest Attempts supine-to-prone position Success in supine-to-prone roll Prone-to-supine roll	2 months 3 months 6 months 8 months
Sitting	Sits with support Sits with self-support Sits alone	3 months 6 months 8 months
Standing	Stands with support Supports with handholds Pulls to supported stand Stands alone	6 months 10 months 11 months 12 months
Horizontal movements	Scooting Crawling Creeping Walking on all fours	3 months 6 months 9 months 11 months
Upright gait	Walks with support Walks with handholds Walks with lead Walks alone (hands high) Walks alone (hands low)	6 months 10 months 11 months 12 months 13 months
Reaching	Globular ineffective Definite corralling Controlled	1-3 months 4 months 6 months
Grasping	Reflexive Voluntary Two-hand palmar grasp One-hand palmar grasp Pincer grasp Controlled grasping Eating without assistance	Birth 3 months 3 months 5 months 9 months 14 months 18 months
Releasing	Basic Controlled	12-14 months 18 months

Reprinted from J.D. Goodway, D. Gallahue and J. Ozmun, *Understanding Motor Development: Infants, Children, Adolescents, Adults*, 6th ed. (Burlington, MA: Jones & Bartlett Learning, 2021), 135. Reprinted with permission.

the earliest defining features of autism spectrum disorder (ASD) (Flanagan et al., 2012). In the study, at-risk infants were measured by a pull-to-sit test, and the presence of persistent head lag at six months had a strong association with a confirmed ASD diagnosis at 36 months of age. Other common motor skill deficits of young children with ASD include delayed postural development during the early years (Nickel et al., 2013).

Rudimentary postural reactions (i.e., maturational motor skills) can also serve as important indicators for diagnosing central nervous system disorders in infants (Zafeiriou, 2004). Postural reactions typically develop during the first year following birth; however, infants with cerebral palsy often experience delay in the development of postural reactions, particularly as they relate to sitting and standing positions. Assessment of postural reactions, particularly in high-risk infants, may be beneficial in the early diagnosis of central nervous system disorders.

Sensory impairments can also represent hurdles in the developmental process. In particular, infants and toddlers with visual impairments often experience delays in motor development (Bakke et al., 2019). Intervention strategies, however, can help minimize such delays. Through incorporation of auditory cues where visual cues usually exist, infants with visual impairments can be stimulated to interact with their environment and smooth the progress of their motor development.

Fundamental Movement Phase

The fundamental movement abilities of early childhood are an outgrowth of the rudimentary movement phase of infancy. Fundamental movements are basic movement skills (e.g., walking, running, throwing, catching) that are building blocks for more developed and refined movement skills. This phase of motor development represents a time when young children are actively involved in exploring and experimenting with the movement capabilities of their bodies. It is a time for discovering how to perform many of the basic stabilizing, locomotor, and manipulative movements, first in isolation and then in combination with one another. Children who are developing fundamental patterns of movement are learning how to respond to a variety of stimuli with motor control and movement competence. Tables 19.5, 19.6, and 19.7 present an overview of the typical developmental sequence of fundamental stability, manipulative, and locomotor movements.

Several researchers and developers of assessment instruments have attempted to subdivide fundamental movements into a series of identifiable sequential stages (Goodway et al., 2021; Haywood & Getchell, 2020; Payne & Isaacs, 2016). Within this chapter, the entire fundamental movement

TABLE 19.5 Sequence of Emergence of Selected Fundamental Stability Abilities

Movement pattern	Selected abilities	Approximate age range of onset
Dynamic balance Dynamic balance involves maintaining one's equilibrium as the center of gravity shifts.	Walks 1 in. (2.5 cm) straight line. Walks 1 in. (2.5 cm) circular line. Stands on low balance beam. Walks on beam 4 in. (10 cm) wide for a short distance. Walks on same beam, alternating feet. Walks on 2-3 in. (5-8 cm) beam. Performs basic forward roll. Performs mature forward roll.*	2-4 years 3-5 years 2-3 years 2-4 years 3-5 years 2-5 years 5-7 years 6-7 years
Static balance Static balance involves maintaining one's equilibrium while the center of gravity remains stationary.	Pulls to standing position. Stands without handholds. Stands alone. Balances on one foot 3-5 s. Supports body in basic three-point inverted positions.	7-10 months 9-11 months 10-12 months 3-5 years 4-6 years
Axial movements Axial movements are static postures that involve bending, stretching, twisting, turning, and the like.	Axial movement abilities begin to develop early in infancy and are progressively refined to a point where they are included in the emerging manipulative patterns of throwing, catching, kicking, striking, trapping, and other activities.	2 months-6 years

*The child has the developmental potential to be at the mature stage. Actual attainment will depend on task, individual, and environmental factors.

Reprinted from J.D. Goodway, D. Gallahue and J. Ozmun, *Understanding Motor Development: Infants, Children, Adolescents, Adults*, 6th ed. (Burlington, MA: Jones & Bartlett Learning, 2021), 135. Reprinted with permission.

TABLE 19.6 Developmental Sequences of Five Manipulative Skills

Fundamental motor skill	Stage 1	Stage 2	Stage 3	Stage 4	Stage 5
	INITIAL STAGE	EMERGING STAGES			PROFICIENT STAGE
Throw	**Chop** Vertical windup "Chop" throw Feet stationary No spinal rotation	**Sling shot** Horizontal windup "Sling shot" throw Block rotation Follow-through across body	**Ipsilateral step** High windup Ipsilateral step Little spinal rotation Follow-through across body	**Contralateral step** High windup Contralateral step Little spinal rotation Follow-through across body	**Windup** Downward arc windup Contralateral step Segmented body rotation Arm–leg follow-through
Catch	**Delayed reaction** Delayed arm action Arms straight in front until ball contact, then scooping action to chest Feet stationary	**Hugging** Arms encircle ball as it approaches Ball is "hugged" to chest Feet are stationary or may take one step	**Scooping** "To chest" catch Arms "scoop" under ball to trap it to chest Single step may be used to approach the ball	**Hand catch** Catch with hands only Feet stationary or limited to one step	**Move to ball** Catch with hands only Whole body moves through space
	INITIAL STAGE	EMERGING STAGES		PROFICIENT STAGE	
Kick	**Stationary push** Little/no leg windup Stationary position Foot "pushes" ball Step backward after kick (usually)	**Stationary leg swing** Leg windup to the rear Stationary position Opposition of arms and legs	**Moving approach** Moving approach Foot travels in a low arc Arm/leg opposition Forward or sideward step on follow-through	**Leap-kick-hop** Rapid approach Backward trunk lean during windup Leap before kick Hop after kick	
Punt	**Yoking-push** No leg windup Ball toss erratic Body stationary Push ball/step back	**Stationary leg swing** Leg windup to the rear Ball toss still erratic Body stationary Forceful kick attempt	**Moving approach** Preparatory step(s) Some arm/leg yoking Ball toss or drop	**Leap-punt-hop** Rapid approach Controlled drop Leap before ball contact Hop after ball contact	

(continued)

TABLE 19.6 *(continued)*

Fundamental motor skill	Stage 1	Stage 2	Stage 3	Stage 4	Stage 5
	INITIAL STAGE	EMERGING STAGES		PROFICIENT STAGE	
Strike	**Chop strike** Chopping motion with bat Feet stationary	**Pushing** Horizontal push/swing Block rotation Feet stationary/stepping	**Ipsilateral step** Ipsilateral step (back foot steps across) Diagonal downward swing	**Contralateral step** Contralateral step Segmented body rotation Wrist roll-over on follow-through	

Reprinted from J.D. Goodway, D. Gallahue and J. Ozmun, *Understanding Motor Development: Infants, Children, Adolescents, Adults,* 6th ed. (Burlington, MA: Jones & Bartlett Learning, 2021), 183. Reprinted with permission.

phase is viewed as having three separate but often overlapping stages: the initial, emerging, and proficient stages.

Initial Stage

The **initial stage** of a fundamental movement phase represents the child's first goal-oriented attempts at performing a fundamental skill. Movement itself is characterized by missing or improperly sequenced parts, markedly restricted or exaggerated use of the body, and poor rhythmical flow and coordination. In other words, the spatial and temporal integration of movement is poor during this stage.

Emerging Stages

The **emerging stages** represent one or more intermediate steps that occur after the initial stage but before the proficient stage. Emerging movements involve greater control and better rhythmic coordination of fundamental motor skills. The temporal and spatial elements of movement are better coordinated, but patterns of movement are still generally restricted or exaggerated. Children without delays in intellectual or physical functioning tend to advance to the emerging stages primarily through the process of maturation. Many people, even adults, fail to get beyond the emerging stages in many fundamental patterns of movement.

Proficient Stage

The **proficient stage** of the fundamental movement phase is characterized by mechanically efficient, coordinated, and controlled performances. The majority of available data on the acquisition of fundamental movement skills suggests that most children can and should be at the proficient stage in most fundamental skills by five or six years of age. However, manipulative skills, which require tracking and intercepting moving objects (catching, striking, volleying), develop somewhat later because of the sophisticated visual–motor requirements of the tasks.

Developmental Divergence

As children advance through the early childhood and elementary years, their movement requirements become increasingly complex. As they grow older, children with disabilities might experience a widening of the gap between themselves and their peers without disabilities. This disparity might be due to a child's physical limitations, limited learning capabilities, inadequate instruction, or limited physical activity participation. Children with physical limitations might benefit from an instructional focus on the outcome of a task (i.e., how far, how fast, how many) rather than the mechanics of a particular skill. On the other hand, a child who has limited learning capabilities might possess the physical ability to complete a task but might not grasp the required movements. By breaking down a task into meaningful parts, the student might be able to experience success (see the Application Example sidebar). Inadequate instruction might require the intervention of parents or other advocates to discuss achievable strategies with school administrators.

Moreover, low levels of physical activity participation might be a contributing factor for delayed motor development. It has been demonstrated that children with disabilities have lower levels of

TABLE 19.7 Developmental Sequences of Five Locomotor Skills

Fundamental motor skill	Stage 1	Stage 2	Stage 3	Stage 4
	INITIAL STAGE	EMERGING STAGES		PROFICIENT STAGE
Run	**Run high guard** Arms—high guard Flat-footed contact Short stride Wide stride, shoulder width	**Run middle guard** Arms—middle guard Vertical component still great Legs near full extension	**Heel–toe arms extended** Arms—low guard Arm opposition—elbows nearly extended	**Pumping arms** Heel–toe contact (toe–heel when sprinting) Arm–leg opposition Elbow flexion
Gallop	**Choppy run** Resembles rhythmically uneven run Trail leg crosses in front of lead leg during airborne phase, remains in front at contact	**Stiff back leg** Slow–moderate tempo, choppy rhythm Trail leg stiff Hips often oriented sideways Vertical component exaggerated		**Smooth rhythmical** Arm action reduced/hands below shoulders Easy, rhythmical movement
Skip	**Broken skip** Broken skip pattern or irregular rhythm Slow, deliberate movement Ineffective arm action	**High arms and legs** Rhythmical skip pattern Arms provide body lift Excessive vertical component		**Rhythmical skip** Arm action reduced/hands below shoulders Easy, rhythmical movement Support foot near surface on hop
Hop	**Foot in front** Nonsupport foot in front with thigh parallel to floor Body erect Hands shoulder height	**Foot by support leg** Nonsupport knee flexed with knee in front and foot behind support leg Slight body lean forward Bilateral arm action	**Foot behind support leg** Nonsupport thigh vertical with foot behind support leg, knee flexed More body lean forward Bilateral arm action	**Pendular free leg** Nonsupport leg is bent, knee pumps forward and back in a pendular action Forward body lean Arm opposition with swing leg
Long jump	**Braking arms** Arms act as "brakes" Large vertical component Legs not extended	**Winging arms** Arms act as "wings" Vertical component still great Legs near full extension	**Arms swing to head** Arms move forward, elbows in front of trunk at takeoff Hands to head height Takeoff angle still above 45 degrees Legs often fully extended	**Full body extension** Complete arm and leg extension at takeoff Takeoff near 45-degree angle Thighs parallel to surface when feet contact for landing

Reprinted from J.D. Goodway, D. Gallahue and J. Ozmun, *Understanding Motor Development: Infants, Children, Adolescents, Adults*, 6th ed. (Burlington, MA: Jones & Bartlett Learning, 2021), 221-222. Reprinted with permission.

physical activity participation when compared to their nondisabled peers, particularly as it relates to moderate to vigorous physical activity (Jung et al., 2018). Because physical activity provides an opportunity for children with and without disabilities to develop their motor skills (Stodden et al., 2008), low levels of physical activity participation may lead children with disabilities to develop their motor skills at a slower rate.

Specialized Movement Phase

The specialized movement phase of motor development is an outgrowth of the fundamental movement phase. Instead of learning to move for the sake of movement itself, movement now becomes a tool applied to specialized activities for daily living, recreation, and sport pursuits. This is a time when fundamental stability, locomotor, and manipulative skills are progressively refined, combined, and elaborated so that they can be used in increasingly demanding situations. The fundamental movements of hopping and jumping, for example, might now be applied to jumping rope, performing folk dances, and performing the triple jump in track and field.

The onset and extent of skill development within the specialized movement phase depend on a variety of task, individual, and environmental factors. Just a few of these factors are task complexity; physical, mental, and emotional limitations; and environmental factors such as opportunity for practice, encouragement, and instruction. There are three identifiable stages within the specialized movement phase: the transitional stage, application stage, and lifelong utilization stage.

Application Example

Improvement of Throwing and Catching Skills

SETTING

An adapted physical education class

STUDENTS

A group of students with intellectual disabilities

ISSUE

How to improve the students' throwing and catching skills in order to use these fundamental skills more effectively in play, game, and sport activities

APPLICATION

The adapted physical education teacher will assess the students' present skill levels in overhand throwing and catching and use this information when engaging students in individually appropriate skill development activities. The teacher will use the following four-step approach:

1. *Preplan* a partner throwing and catching activity in order to observe the students' present levels of developmental skills (e.g., initial, emerging, proficient).
2. *Assess* each student's present skill level from a location in which unobtrusive observation is possible. While the children are playing catch, she will do a total body configuration analysis by watching each student's entire throwing or catching pattern. After identifying students who are less than proficient, she will do a segmental analysis by breaking their movement pattern down and observing individual body segments.
3. *Plan and implement* a series of individually appropriate movement lessons designed to bring lagging body parts in line with more advanced ones, using a universal design for learning (UDL) framework that includes multiple means of representation (using various methods to provide information), multiple means of action and expression (allowing learners to express their knowledge in alternative ways), and multiple means of engagement (motivating learners by providing challenges matched to their interests and characteristics) (Rose, 2000).
4. Take time to *evaluate students* and revise lessons, use ongoing observation and evaluation to determine if they have made progress in throwing and catching, and make modifications in subsequent lessons as appropriate.

Transitional Stage

Somewhere around seven or eight years of age, children commonly enter a **transitional stage** in their movement skills. The fundamental movement skills that were developed and refined for their own sake during the previous phase now begin to be applied to play, game, and daily living situations, as well as combined and applied to the performance of specialized sport and recreation skills. Walking on a rope bridge, jumping rope, and playing kickball are examples of common transitional skills. These skills contain the same elements as fundamental movements, but greater form, accuracy, and control of movement are required. Transitional skills are simply an application of fundamental movement patterns in somewhat more complex and specific forms. As mentioned, children with disabilities participate in less physical activity than children without disabilities do (Jung et al., 2018). This means that children with disabilities may have fewer chances to integrate the learned fundamental motor skills into different contexts. Because this stage is considered a stepping stone for the following stages, it is important for children with and without disabilities to undergo this stage in an appropriate manner.

Application Stage

From about ages 10 to 13, interesting changes take place in skill development. During the previous (transitional) stage, children's limited cognitive abilities, affective abilities, and experiences, coupled with a natural eagerness to be active, caused the normal focus on movement (without adult interference) to be broad and generalized to all activity. During the **application stage**, increased cognitive sophistication and a broadened experience base enable children to make many learning and participation decisions based on a variety of factors. These decisions are based largely on their perceptions regarding the extent to which factors within the task, themselves, and the environment either enhance or inhibit chances for personal enjoyment and success. Research suggests that key barriers to physical activity participation of children with disabilities are lack of success, fear, and being teased by peers (Moran & Block, 2010; Shields et al., 2012). This highlights the important role of disability-knowledgeable coaches or teachers. If they are part of inclusive physical activity programs, children with disabilities are more likely to participate in and enjoy physical activity, which can be a building block for the future participation in the lifelong utilization stage.

Lifelong Utilization Stage

The **lifelong utilization stage** typically begins around age 13 and continues through adulthood. This stage represents the pinnacle of the motor development process and is characterized by the use of one's acquired movement repertoire throughout life. The interests, competencies, and choices made during the previous (application) stage are carried over to this stage, further refined, and applied to a lifetime of daily living, recreational, and sport-related activities.

Developmental Divergence

Continuing to develop motor skills through adolescence and adulthood is an extremely important endeavor for people with disabilities. The enhancement of movement skills plays a significant role in maintaining or increasing independence for those with disabilities. Certain locomotor and manipulative skills are needed to access opportunities in the community, be they occupational or recreational. Reynolds and colleagues (2015) found that a motor skill intervention improved bicycle riding skills in youth with ASD, which allowed them to ride independently, providing the opportunity for increased social interactions with others in their community. In addition, Baran and colleagues (2013) found that a Special Olympics Unified Sports Soccer training program positively influenced the development of dribbling, passing, and shooting skills in youth with intellectual disabilities, reinforcing the need for sport programming from childhood through adulthood. The development of movement skills also increases the options for physical activity, which in turn enhances the potential for health benefits and functional daily living throughout the lifespan.

Summary

The acquisition of motor control and movement competency is an extensive process beginning with the early reflexive movements of the newborn and continuing throughout life. Dynamic systems theory and the phases of motor development are helpful for conceptualizing both the process and the product of motor development. The process through which a person progresses from the reflexive movement phase, through the rudimentary and fundamental movement phases, and finally to the specialized movement skill phase is influenced by factors within the task, individual, and environment.

Reflexes and rudimentary movement abilities are largely maturational, forming an important base on which fundamental movement abilities are developed. They appear and disappear in a fairly rigid sequence, deviating only in the rate of their appearance. Fundamental movement abilities (locomotor, manipulative, and stability) are basic movement patterns that begin developing around the same time a child is able to walk independently, and they lead to freely moving through the environment. Three stages within this phase have been identified for a number of fundamental movements: the initial, emerging, and proficient stages. Attainment of the proficient stage is significantly influenced by opportunities for practice, encouragement, and instruction in an environment that fosters learning. These same fundamental skills will be elaborated on and refined to form the specialized movement abilities so highly valued for recreational, competitive, and daily living tasks.

The specialized movement phase of development is an elaboration of the fundamental phase. Specialized skills often involve a combination of fundamental movement abilities and require a greater degree of precision in performance. Specialized skills move through the transitional, application, and lifelong utilization stages. From the transition stage onward, children purposefully combine and apply fundamental movement skills in play, games, sport, and daily living tasks. If the fundamental abilities used in a particular activity are not at the mature stage, the person will have to use less mature patterns of movement.

People with disabilities might experience a delay in motor development; in some cases, development occurs that diverges somewhat from the usual course of progression. By examining the characteristics of the individual, task demands, and environmental factors, intervention strategies can be devised to increase the opportunity for successful motor performance across the life spans of all people.

References

Angulo-Barroso, R.M., Tiernan, C., Chen, L.C., Valentin-Gudiol, M., & Ulrich, D.A. (2013). Treadmill training in moderate risk preterm infants promotes stepping quality—Results of a small randomized controlled trial. *Research in Developmental Disabilities, 34,* 3629-3638. https://doi.org/10.1016/j.ridd.2013.07.037

Bakke, H.A., Cavalcante, W.A., Santos de Oliveira, I., Sarinho, S.W., & Cattuzzo, M.T. (2019). Assessment of motor skills in children with visual impairment: A systematic and integrative review. *Clinical Medicine Insights: Pediatrics, 13,* 1-10. https://doi.org/10.1177/1179556519838287

Baran, F., Aktop, A., Özer, D., Nalbant, S., A□lamı□, E., Barak, S., & Hutzler, Y. (2013). The effects of a Special Olympics Unified Sports Soccer training program on anthropometry, physical fitness and skilled performance in Special Olympics soccer athletes and non-disabled partners. *Research in Developmental Disabilities, 34*(1), 695-709. https://doi.org/10.1016/j.ridd.2012.10.003

Cleland-Donnelly, F., Mueller, S.S., & Gallahue, D.L. (2017). *Developmental physical education for all children* (5th ed.). Human Kinetics.

Flanagan, J.E., Landa, R., Bhat, A., & Bauman, M. (2012). Head lag in infants at risk for autism: A preliminary study. *American Journal of Occupational Therapy, 66*(5), 577-585. https://doi.org/10.5014/ajot.2012.004192

Goodway, J.D., Ozmun, J.C., & Gallahue, D.L. (2021). *Understanding motor development: Infants, children, adolescents, adults* (8th ed.). Jones & Bartlett.

Haywood, K.M., & Getchell, N. (2020). *Life span motor development* (7th ed.). Human Kinetics.

Haywood, K.M., Roberton, M.A., & Getchell, N. (2012). *Advanced analysis of motor development.* Human Kinetics.

Hollenstein, T. (2011). Twenty years of dynamic systems approaches to development: Significant contributions, challenges, and future directions. *Child Development Perspectives, 5,* 256-259. https://doi.org/10.1111/j.1750-8606.2011.00210.x

Jung, J., Leung, W., Schram, B.M., & Yun, J. (2018). Meta-analysis of physical activity levels in youth with and without disabilities. *Adapted Physical Activity Quarterly, 35*(4), 381-402. https://doi.org/10.1123/apaq.2017-0123

Moran, T.E., & Block, M.E. (2010). Barriers to participation of children with disabilities in youth sports. *TEACHING Exceptional Children Plus, 6*(3), n3.

Morgan, C., Darrah, J., Gordon, A.M., Harbourne, R., Spittle, A., Johnson, R., & Fetters, L. (2016). Effectiveness of motor interventions in infants with cerebral palsy: A systematic review. *Developmental Medicine & Child Neurology, 58*(9), 900-909. https://doi.org/10.1111/dmcn.13105

Nickel, L.R., Thatcher, A.R., Keller, F., Wozniak, R.H., & Iverson, J.M. (2013). Posture development in infants at heightened versus low risk for autism spectrum disorders. *Infancy, 18*(5), 639-661. https://doi.org/10.1111/infa.12025

Payne, V.G., & Isaacs, L.D. (2016). *Human motor development: A lifespan approach* (9th ed.). Routledge.

Reynolds, J.L., Pitchford, E.A., Hauck, J.L., Ketcheson, L.R., & Ulrich, D.A. (2015). Outcomes of home-support consultation on the maintenance of bicycle-riding skills for youth with autism spectrum disorder. *Journal of Educational and Psychological Consultation, 26,* 166-185. https://doi.org/10.1080/10474412.2015.1067147

Rose, D. (2000). Universal design for learning. *Journal of Special Education Technology, 15*(3), 45-49.

Shields, N., Synnot, A.J., & Barr, M. (2012). Perceived barriers and facilitators to physical activity for children with disability: A systematic review. *British Journal of Sports Medicine, 46*(14), 989-997. http://dx.doi.org/10.1136/bjsports-2011-090236

Stodden, D.F., Goodway, J.D., Langendorfer, S.J., Roberton, M.A., Rudisill, M.E., Garcia, C., & Garcia, L.E. (2008). A developmental perspective on the role of motor skill competence in physical activity: An emergent relationship. *Quest, 60*(2), 290-306. https://doi.org/10.1080/00336297.2008.10483582

Ulrich, D.A., Lloyd, M.C., Tiernan, C., Looper, J., & Angulo-Barroso, R.M. (2008). Effects of intensity of treadmill training on developmental outcomes and stepping in infants with Down syndrome. *Physical Therapy Journal, 88*(1), 114-122. https://doi.org/10.2522/ptj.20070139

van Geert, P.V. (2011). The contribution of complex dynamic systems to development. *Child Development Perspectives, 5,* 273-278. https://doi.org/10.1111/j.1750-8606.2011.00197.x

Wu, J., Looper, J., Ulrich, B.D., Ulrich, D.A., & Angulo-Barroso, R.M. (2007). Exploring effects of different treadmill interventions on walking onset and gait patterns in infants with Down syndrome. *Developmental Medicine & Child Neurology, 49,* 839-845. https://doi.org/10.1111/j.1469-8749.2007.00839.x

Zafeiriou, D.I. (2004). Primitive reflexes and postural reactions in the neurodevelopmental examination. *Pediatric Neurology, 31*(1), 1-8. https://doi.org/10.1016/j.pediatrneurol.2004.01.012

Print Resources

Block, M.E. (2016). *A teacher's guide to adapted physical education: Including students with disabilities in sports and recreation* (4th ed.). Paul H. Brookes.

This user-friendly, theoretically grounded text contains developmentally appropriate instructional strategies for teaching students with disabilities.

Pangrazi, R.P., & Beighle, A. (2019). *Dynamic physical education for elementary school children* (19th ed.). Human Kinetics.

This text provides guidance for creating developmentally appropriate adaptations for the teaching of movement skills to children with disabilities. Multiple ancillary materials are also available.

PHE Canada. (2018). *Fundamental movement skills: Active start and FUNdamentals stages card set.* Human Kinetics.

This set of cards serves as a quick and portable reference tool for teachers to create and assess activities for developing fundamental movement skills.

Sugden, D., & Wade, M. (2013). *Typical and atypical motor development.* Wiley.

This text provides an extensive examination of motor development and impairment using sources from developmental psychology, motor learning, and medical and health-related research.

Ulrich, D.A. (2019). *Test of gross motor development* (3rd ed.). Pro-Ed.

This is a multi-item test of selected fundamental locomotor and ball skills with norm-referenced and criterion-referenced interpretations.

Online Resources

Adapted Physical Education Resources for Teacher's Toolbox: www.shapeamerica.org/publications/resources/teachingtools/teachertoolbox/Teachers_Toolbox_adapted.aspx

Adapted Physical Education Information/Resources: http://pecentral.org/adapted/adaptedmenu.html

These sites from SHAPE America and PE Central provide information on adapted physical education, including developmentally appropriate adaptations, research, books, assessment instruments, and national standards.

BlazeSports America: www.blazesports.org

BlazeSports America provides a variety of movement skill development resources for various sports for individuals with disabilities.

Center on Physical Activity and Health in Pediatric Disabilities, Division of Kinesiology, University of Michigan: www.kines.umich.edu/research/cpah

This site describes cutting-edge research in the area of motor development with infants and children who have various disabilities.

20

Perceptual–Motor Development

Barry W. Lavay and Melissa D. Bittner

Sean is a 12-year-old boy with autism spectrum disorder (ASD) who loves playing soccer. He especially looks forward to kicking the soccer ball back and forth with his older sister Quin, who plays on the varsity high school soccer team. When he is passing the soccer ball at home or at the park with his sister, it always goes well. However, Sean, who plays on an American Youth Soccer Organization team, struggles during practice and games—it seems the ball moves too fast for him to follow and he is easily distracted by background noise such as students yelling. He often accidentally bumps into opponents during games and even his own teammates during practice and becomes frustrated. What perceptual–motor processing and sensory challenges is Sean exhibiting? How can his sister and coach help him better follow the ball, not bump into other players, and not be distracted by the background noise during practice and games?

As you read this chapter, think about children with perceptual–motor deficits and sensory issues like Sean and the challenges they face. The ability to learn and function effectively is affected by perceptual–motor development, which permits an individual to receive, transmit, organize, integrate, and attach meaning to sensory information and formulate appropriate responses. These responses are important for the individual to learn while moving in a variety of environments. Thus, they have a direct impact in physical education and sport.

Ordinarily, perceptual–motor development occurs without the need for formal intervention. Sometimes, however, perceptual–motor abilities need attention because they have not developed satisfactorily. For example, deficits related to perceptual–motor ability are commonly seen in certain conditions such as learning disabilities or autism spectrum disorder. These deficits might include poor spatial orientation, difficulty with body awareness, immature body image, clumsiness or awkwardness, coordination deficits, and poor balance. The higher incidence of perceptual–motor deficits among people with cerebral palsy or intellectual disability is also well known (Sherrill, 2004). Perceptual–motor experiences are particularly important in situations in which sensory systems are generally affected but residual abilities might be enhanced, and in cases in which perceptual–motor abilities must be developed to a greater degree to compensate for loss of sensory abilities (e.g., visual or auditory disabilities).

In this introductory section, it is important to comment on the influences of perceptual–motor programs. In the 1960s and early 1970s, such programs were strongly advocated and supported because of the belief that they led to a direct and significant improvement in academic and intellectual abilities; however, the literature has not supported this notion (Goodway et al., 2020; Kavale & Mattison, 1983; Payne & Isaacs, 2016). On the other hand, the literature indicates clearly that perceptual–motor abilities, as measured by various tests, may be attained through carefully sequenced programs (Cheatum & Hammond, 2000; Johnstone & Ramon, 2011; Roth et al., 2016; Sherrill, 2004). For example, it is clear that balance, a perceptual–motor ability basic to movement skill, might be enhanced through systematic training. Because perceptual–motor abilities are fundamental to many motor and academic skills, as well as the ability to focus and perform functional daily living skills, their nurturing or remediation is vital to physical educators (Nielson et al., 2018; Ratey & Hagerman, 2008).

After reading this chapter, it should be clear that all the movement activities experienced in physical education are perceptual–motor experiences. When perceptual–motor abilities require nurturing or when they have developed inadequately, there may be a need to plan programs to enhance their attainment. This chapter is designed to serve as a resource for planning and program implementation.

Terminology of the Perceptual–Motor Process

Terms associated with the perceptual–motor process are used in many ways. The following are definitions of some terms used in this chapter.

Perception is the monitoring and interpretation of sensory information or knowledge resulting from the interaction between sensory and central nervous system processes. Perception occurs in the brain and enables an individual to derive meaning from sensory information. **Perceptual–motor development** is the process of enhancing the ability to integrate sensory stimuli arising from or relating to observable movement responses. It involves the ability to combine kinesthetic and tactual perceptions with and for the development of other perceptions, the use of movement to explore the environment and develop perceptual–motor abilities, and the ability to perceive both tactually and kinesthetically (Gabbard, 2018). Perception occurs as sensory information is interpreted or given meaning. Because the perceptual–motor process includes both an interpretation of and a response to sensory stimulation, it requires cognitive ability. On the other hand, **sensorimotor activity**, characterized by motor responses to sensory input, occurs at a subcortical level and does not involve meaning, interpretation, or cortical-level functioning (Payne & Isaacs, 2016; Sherrill, 2004). Sensory integration results in perception and other types of sensory data synthesis. Thus, perception is one aspect of sensory integration.

During the 1980s and continuing today, the physical education literature has developed a view on perception that has implications for perceptual–motor development. This view, known as the direct or **ecological approach** to perception, is based on the classic work of Gibson (1979) and emphasizes that perception is specific to each person and that the environment is perceived directly in terms of its usefulness for the perceiver. (For more on Gibson's work, see Online Resources at the end of this chapter.) Humans perceive the environment in terms of the actions they can exert on it—that is, the **affordances** provided by the environment. For example, children might perceive a chair predominantly in terms of their ability to crawl under it, whereas adults perceive it as an object to sit on (although they might also recognize its other possibilities). Advocates of this orientation feel that perceptual deficits might be defined in terms of inadequate perception of affordance, or the function an environmental object provides the individual. Thus, perception might become a prime candidate in the search for potential rate limiters or individual constraints in children with movement deficits (Burton, 1990; Colombo-Dougovito & Block, 2016; Davis & Broadhead, 2007; Davis & Burton, 1991; Haywood & Getchell, 2020).

Overview of the Perceptual–Motor Process

To implement perceptual–motor programs effectively, it is helpful to have an understanding of how the process works. A simplified four-step schematic of perceptual–motor functioning is presented in figure 20.1.

- *Sensory input.* The first step in the perceptual–motor process, **sensory input**, involves receiving stimuli from the environment and from within the body itself and processing this information for integration by the central nervous system. Tactile (touch), kinesthetic (movement), vestibular (balance), visual (sight), and auditory (hearing) sensory systems gain information that is transmitted toward the central nervous system through these sensory (afferent) pathways.

- *Sensory integration.* The second step in the perceptual–motor process is **sensory integration**, which can involve one or more sensory systems and appears to increase with age as the individual gains valuable experiences (Gabbard, 2018). Present and past sensory information is integrated, compared, and stored in short- or long-term memory. An important phase occurs as the person selects and organizes an appropriate motor output based on the integration. The resultant decision becomes part of long-term memory, which is transmitted through the motor (efferent) system or away from the central nervous system toward the muscles to cause movement.

- *Motor–behavioral output.* The third major step in the perceptual–motor process is **motor–behavioral output**. Overt movements or observable behaviors occur as a result of decisions from the central nervous system. This is the actual movement response, such as running, jumping, and throwing. As output occurs, information is also continually fed back as sensory input about the ongoing response by the human organism.

- *Feedback.* Sensory information received via **feedback** continues the process. Similar to sensory input, feedback in movement settings is usually kinesthetic, tactile, visual, or auditory.

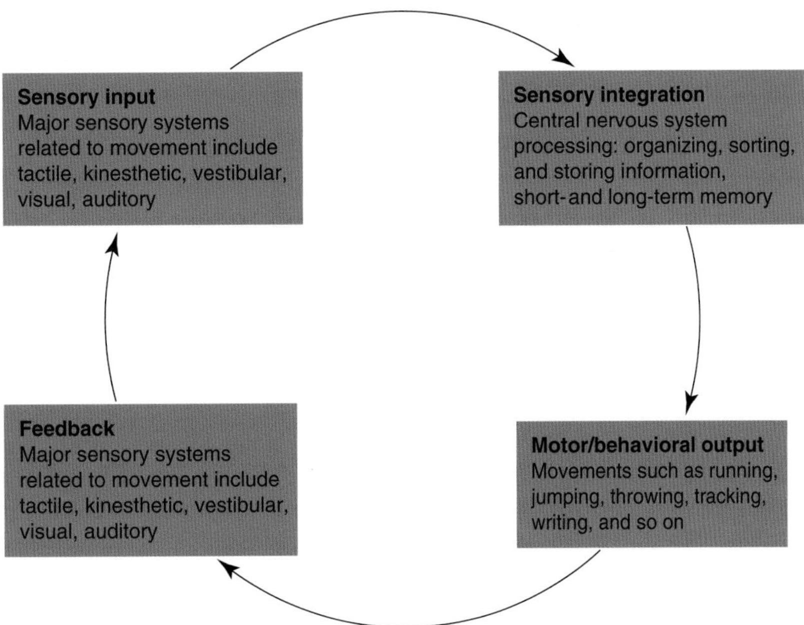

FIGURE 20.1 A simplified model of the perceptual–motor process.

During feedback, the adequacy or nature of the movement response is evaluated or judged. If it is judged inadequate, adjustments are made; if it is successful, adjustments are not required.

Example of a Perceptual–Motor Skill

Batting a pitched softball can be used to illustrate the introductory concepts of the perceptual–motor process described in figure 20.1. As the pitched ball comes toward the plate, the batter focuses on the ball and tracks it. Information about speed, direction, spin, and other flight characteristics is picked up (stimulus reception) by the visual system (sensory input) for further processing. The information is transmitted via sensory neurons to the central nervous system, where it undergoes sensory integration. Because of the characteristics of the environment, the nature of the sensory information, and past experience, the incoming object is perceived as a softball (perception) to be hit (perceptual–motor or observable movement response). The batter's past experience will influence the ability to track the softball and process information about how to hit it. How to hit it involves comparative evaluations—for example, the arc and speed of the ball is compared with that from previous instances when the act was performed (feedback). Information and examples of the sensory systems in the perceptual–motor process are discussed in detail later in this chapter.

The batter decides on the appropriate swing (decision about motor behavior) on the basis of earlier steps in the process. This decision becomes part of the long-term memory to be used for future reference. During the pitch, the brain is constantly kept informed about the position of the bat and the body (kinesthetic) and will use this information to enhance the overt behavior or movement response of swinging the bat. Once the motor behavior or movement response has been determined, messages are sent to appropriate parts of the body to initiate the response (motor output). As the batter moves and completes the task, information is provided on which to judge whether the response is successful or inadequate (feedback). If the pitch was missed, the batter might decide that adjustments such as moving closer to home plate or moving the hands higher on the bat handle are necessary in similar future instances; this information is stored in long-term memory and serves as a basis for learning.

If the ecological perspective on perception is applied to this example, the ball will be perceived by each observer in terms of ability to hit the ball, or to hit the ball to a particular place on the field given one's body size and skill, rather than in terms of ball velocity, spin, and so on. Thus, people perceive the ball in terms of their individual ability to hit it, and based on this perception, they decide what to do and respond accordingly (Davis & Broadhead, 2007; Haywood & Getchell, 2020).

Perceptual–Motor Deficit

Because figure 20.1 depicts perceptual–motor processing, it is a useful reference for determining breakdowns in the process, including at the input, integration, output, and feedback sites. A breakdown at the input site might occur for a variety of reasons. For example, people with sensory impairments such as blindness or deafness might not be able to adequately take in visual or auditory information from the environment, and the result is that this information does not reach the central nervous system. Students with intellectual disabilities, learning disabilities, attention deficit/hyperactivity disorder (ADHD), or autism spectrum disorder (ASD) might not attend to, and thus not receive, relevant information or may take in too much sensory information (Healey et al., 2013). People with neuromuscular impairments might be inhibited by the lack of appropriate kinesthetic, vestibular, or tactual information basic to quality input. For example, a young child with cerebral palsy and faulty kinesthetic perception may demonstrate difficulty with balance during playground climbing activities and therefore need physical assistance to keep up with peers, whereas a child with ASD participating in physical education may be overwhelmed by too much noise in the gymnasium.

Sensory integration may be affected by factors such as intellectual disability or neurological conditions that impair the functioning of the central nervous system. Also, sensory integration may be influenced by the quality of information received and the ability to process sensory input. For example, a student with a learning disability might have difficulty with the motor planning steps needed to dribble, shoot, and pass a ball during a basketball game.

Motor–behavioral output can be affected by inappropriate functioning during previous steps, as well as conditions influencing movement, such as cerebral palsy, muscular dystrophy, and other neurological or orthopedic impairments such as a spinal cord injury. Breakdowns at the feedback site can result from factors that affect earlier steps and any additional factors that bear on the ability to modify or correct behavior. The child with developmental coordination disorder (DCD), for example, might lack body awareness because of faulty kinesthetic perception, which would impair the reception of adequate and appropriate feedback in order to make proper movement adjustments.

Based on the ecological approach, perception should be examined more closely when movement challenges occur (Burton, 1987, 1990; Davis & Broadhead, 2007; Gabbard, 2018; Hutzler, 2007). Consistent with this view, actual performance may be used as a criterion to determine if the motor outcomes are due to faulty perception. For example, a golf club is selected for a particular shot based on distance, height desired, and so on. If the golfer makes a shot short of the target, it is possible that this inadequate performance resulted from faulty perception of shot requirements—the golfer might have selected the wrong club or underestimated the wind resistance—rather than from poor skill. Although the shortness of the shot might have been caused by other factors, the possibility for faulty perception exists and needs to be assessed.

Many factors causing perceptual–motor deficits are associated with student disabilities seen in the school environment; therefore, physical educators might need to develop programs to nurture development or remediate performance. The nature of an individualized program depends on the cause of the perceptual–motor breakdown, the student's perception and abilities, and the purpose of the program. In the case of a student with total blindness, for example, it might be necessary to focus on heightening auditory perceptual–motor components to improve orientation to school grounds and focus on kinesthetic perception to enhance movement in the environment. A student with an intellectual disability and delayed reaction time, on the other hand, might need simplified teacher instructions and more time to take in or process information. Table 20.1 presents an analysis of prominent perceptual–motor need and deficit areas as a function of specific disabilities, as well as examples an instructor can use to help students offset the given specific deficit area.

Sensorimotor Stimulation

As stated earlier, perceptual–motor deficits can occur as a result of sensory input and processing problems. Physical educators who have reviewed and analyzed research and literature on the value of sensory stimulation (Cheatum & Hammond, 2000; Johnstone & Ramon, 2011; Roth et al., 2016;

TABLE 20.1 Analysis of Prominent Perceptual–Motor Need and Deficit Areas

Disability	Prominent need and deficit areas
Visual disability (visual impairments)	Need to focus on the development of residual visual perceptual abilities and help the child compensate for visual perceptual–motor deficits by enhancing auditory, vestibular, tactual, and kinesthetic perception. Give particular attention to **input** and **feedback** steps in the perceptual–motor process. For example, provide immediate feedback such as a beeping sound when a goal is scored.
Auditory disability (hard of hearing, Deaf)	Need to focus on the development of residual hearing and vestibular abilities (if affected) and help the child compensate by enhancing development associated with sensory systems that are intact. Give particular attention to **input**, **integration**, and **feedback** steps in the perceptual–motor process. For example, provide visual directions or pictures at stations.
Haptic disabilities that include vestibular, kinesthetic, and tactual perception (primarily children with orthopedic, neuromuscular, or neurological impairments)	Need to focus on the development of vestibular, kinesthetic, and tactual perception and to integrate motor experiences with visual and auditory perception. There may be a particular need to focus on **input**, **motor response**, and **feedback** steps in the perceptual–motor process. For example, use physical guidance or prompting techniques as part of instructions.
Cognitive or affective disabilities (children with intellectual disabilities, emotional disturbance, and the like)	Need to focus on needs as determined through assessment of perceptual–motor abilities. Involvement throughout the perceptual–motor process might exist. For example, provide positive specific feedback (kinesthetic, auditory) for a skill performed correctly.

Seaman et al., 2007; Sherrill, 2004) believe that sensorimotor stimulation enhances development and learning. Acceptable levels of sensorimotor development generally occur without the need for special intervention by professionals (Gabbard, 2018; Haywood & Getchell, 2020); however, programs including sensorimotor activity are sometimes recommended for people with disabilities, especially those exhibiting severe disabilities. This stimulation is designed to overcome developmental delays or deficits caused by such factors as distorted, weakened, or inadequate central nervous system development or functioning, diseases, disabilities, and limited opportunities for development. Programs designed to nurture sensory systems may be conducted by educators as part of early childhood or physical education, movement therapists as part of movement education programs, or occupational therapists as part of sensory integration programs. The specific goals of the program will influence program approaches.

Programs designed for sensorimotor nurturing emphasizing movement have several identifiable commonalities. First, they are closely associated with the major sensory modalities related to movement (e.g., tactile, kinesthetic, vestibular, visual, auditory). Second, they focus on subcortical activity—that is, activity not dependent on cerebral cortex and cortical tracts. A key distinction between sensorimotor activity and perceptual–motor activity is that the former is subcortical and the latter includes cognition; however, there is considerable overlap. Perceptual–motor functioning depends on sensorimotor functioning because sensory information is processed, integrated, and organized in the cerebral cortex. For example, if a child is blindfolded and given a wet sponge and it feels squishy to the child, this is sensorimotor functioning. When the child says it is a wet sponge—giving meaning to what is felt—this is perceptual–motor functioning. Perceptual–motor functioning occurs when meaning is given to sensorimotor information.

Factors that affect sensorimotor function include muscle and postural tone, reflexes and postural reactions, and sensory input systems (Cowden & Torrey, 2007; Roth et al., 2016; Sherrill, 2004). Sample activities to begin developing a sensorimotor stimulation program are shown in table 20.2. Although the activities are grouped by component—tactile, kinesthetic, vestibular, visual, or auditory—most activities involve two or more of these components. These components correspond closely to the perceptual–motor components to be discussed subsequently in the chapter.

Facilitating Development

The teacher has an important role in the nurturing or remediation of perceptual–motor abilities. The exact role and teaching styles need to vary with the characteristics of the learner. Because perceptual–motor abilities appear to develop optimally between ages 2 and 7, indirect teaching styles such as movement exploration, guided discovery, and open-ended tasks that allow more than one response are generally appropriate in the early years. As children reach ages 6 and 7, more direct teaching styles requiring a specific movement response are developmentally appropriate and thus more effective.

Burton (1987) describes two implications for teaching that might be important for enhancing perceptual–motor development. First, teachers should provide **purposeful movement** because it is motivating and encourages attention to the information in the environment. Movements are purposeful when they are performed in natural settings as a means to an end rather than as the end itself. Key to purposeful movement is to select an activity involving an objective beyond the actual movement itself. For example, if the lesson objective is to improve the accuracy of kicking, purposeful movement would be to kick the ball into a goal in a soccer lead-up activity. This is more motivating and fun than a drill of kicking a ball for the sake of kicking a ball.

A second teaching implication is for students to become more accurately attuned to **affordances in the environment** (Davis & Broadhead, 2007; Haywood & Getchell, 2020). One way this is accomplished is by encouraging students to make perceptual judgments and to assess the accuracy of their judgments. Applied to a golf example, the question posed might be "Can I hit the ball to the green using the nine iron?" In another example, the question might be "Can I pass the ball to a teammate without it being intercepted by a defensive player?" In these situations, the congruency between perception and movement is evaluated. The accuracy of one's perception of the environment or the affordances available is evaluated. The influence of perception on motor performance might be evaluated to determine if poor performance results from faulty perception.

Sensory Systems

Many sensory systems are associated with perceptual–motor development. The remainder of

TABLE 20.2 Components and Activities Associated With Sensorimotor Development

Components	Typical activities
Tactile integration	Activities involving water, sand, mud, and clay; massage; stroking; partner touching activities; barefoot activities; movement education activities; activities performed on various surfaces; handling objects of various textures such as a sponge; crawling through tunnels, rolling on a mat, or sitting on a carpet square; tactual discrimination between familiar and unfamiliar objects, including identifying objects, textures, or shapes in a bag while blindfolded
Kinesthetic integration	Activities involving touching body parts (e.g., Simon Says); moving body parts for purposeful movement such as bending to the right or left, up or down; push or pull activities (e.g., pulling a scooter board with a rope or pushing a weighted ball); active movements that develop a knowledge of body parts and their position in self- and general space; the ability to move to different time, space, force, and flow of movement
Vestibular integration	Activities involving equilibrium, posture, and balance, including rocking and cradling on boards, cribs, or chairs; simple bouncing activities on spring-type or trampoline equipment; simple spinning and swinging activities using hammocks or other swings; sliding down an incline; therapy ball activities; riding a scooter board; sitting and standing postures; nonlocomotor movements
Visual integration	Activities involving object manipulation, including ball handling in which speed, distance, size, color, and mass are modified; recognition and tracking of objects, including following a swinging or moving ball or beam of light; looking; sorting; fundamental visual motor activities including eye–hand coordination, such as catching and striking, and eye–foot activities, such as kicking; finding objects
Auditory integration	Activities involving sound recognition, including finding a hidden beep ball; auditory discrimination, including differentiating between finding a loud and soft sound; sound localization, including pointing in the direction of a whistle; auditory figure–ground, including recognizing spoken words or a tambourine over music; listening and responding to auditory stimuli, including following spoken directions; making sounds and talking activities, including auditory memory

this chapter discusses tactual, kinesthetic, visual, and auditory perception, including examples of physical education and sport activities. The Application Example sidebar suggests perceptual–motor activity stations designed to promote the sensory systems in fun, educational, and challenging ways.

During a movement response, the sensory systems work collectively and simultaneously. For example, visual–motor coordination combines the use of the visual, kinesthetic, and tactual sensory systems. A multisensory approach is among the more widely accepted instructional practices used to teach children with disabilities. Chapter 11 includes further discussion of the multisensory approach.

One tool that uses a multisensory approach is the Sensory Processing Assessment of Responses (SPAR) (Weiner & Davis, 2019). This informal screening tool is designed to gather information that will support active and successful engagement in structured physical activity environments. SPAR assesses individual responses to stimuli through seven sensory systems (auditory, interoception, olfactory, proprioception, tactile, vestibular, and visual) as well as oral processing (a combination of tactile and proprioception). The tool includes sensory system definitions, a glossary of terms, and instructions for administering the SPAR screening form.

Other assessments such as the Test of Gross Motor Development (Ulrich, 2019) allow for accommodations to assist individuals with perceptual–motor development challenges. In addition, equipment accommodations can include a beep baseball, basketball with bells, or a metronome to determine target areas.

Application Example

Fun Activity Stations to Promote the Sensory Systems

SETTING

A third- and fourth-grade adapted physical education class

STUDENTS

A group of 12 children with various neurological and developmental disabilities (e.g., ASD, mild intellectual disabilities), plus a fifth-grade peer tutor to assist at each station

ISSUE

Promote the sensory systems for children in fun and challenging ways

APPLICATION

Ms. Sayers, the adapted physical education teacher, has created four stations throughout the gymnasium, as follows:

- Station 1, Spiderweb, is a web made out of yarn intertwined between two volleyball poles. To promote spatial awareness, the children move individually and then cooperate as a group holding hands, with each child moving through the openings without touching the web (Kress & Lavay, 2006).
- At station 2, Walk the Pirate's Plank, the children move up, across, and down the five sets of bleachers in the gymnasium to promote functional dynamic balance. To challenge students to climb to the top, each student must touch a picture of a pirate located on the highest bleacher.
- Directionality and spatial awareness are reinforced at station 3, Drive Your Car, where each child performs different locomotor movements (e.g., walk, slide, run) at different speeds while holding a small hula hoop as a steering wheel, following arrows on the gym floor and moving around large pylon cones without bumping into classmates' cars.
- Station 4, Surprise Bag, promotes tactual awareness; children sit in chairs while blindfolded, place their hands in four bags, and tell the peer student the contents of each bag (e.g., sand, clay, a wet sponge, steel wool scouring pad, gummy worms).

Tactile Perception

Tactile perception, the ability to interpret external sensations from the layers of the skin throughout the body, responds to touch, feel, and manipulation. Through tactile perception, the student experiences sensations that contribute to a better understanding of the environment. For example, tactile perception enables one to distinguish wet from dry, hot from cold, soft from hard, and rough from smooth. For students with a learning disability, instruction is enhanced and made more concrete when they touch, feel, hold, and manipulate objects. The term *soft* becomes more meaningful and tangible when students feel something soft and distinguish it from something hard.

Some students have a disorganized tactile system and consequently exhibit **tactile dysfunction**. A lack of tactile perception or the inability to localize touch might occur with children with learning problems related to a lack of body awareness (discussed later in the Proprioception section of this chapter). Other children with conditions such as serious emotional disturbance or ASD might be **tactile defensive** (i.e., hypersensitive) or have a low tolerance for normal touch. For example, the feeling of clothes or a touch on the body may cause a negative or painful reaction. They perceive touch as irritating and avoid contact with objects and people. They dislike touching others (e.g., getting a hug, giving high fives), tag games, tumbling, and contact sports such as football, wrestling, and soccer. Other children who have not received necessary amounts of stimulation might be tactile deprived and crave touch (i.e., hyposensitive) (Cheatum & Hammond, 2000). For example, a child with ASD who is hyposensitive may wear a weighted vest or take a sensory break to squeeze a rubber ball for a few minutes before rejoining the class.

Gross motor activities in physical education and sport offer many opportunities to use tactile perception. Relevant activities include those

Mayte Torres/Moment/Getty Images

For young children, climbing on equipment is a fun activity to promote the tactile system.

involving contact with a variety of surfaces and textures, such as touching body parts with a wet sponge or a nylon net used to collect equipment. Tactile perception combines with kinesthetic sensations as children crawl through a tunnel, walk along a balance beam, jump on a minitrampoline, climb a ladder, wrestle, or tumble. Students might walk barefoot on floors, lawns, beaches, balance beams, mats, or in swimming pools, or they might climb cargo nets, ladders, playground equipment, or a low-ropes adventure course (Kress & Lavay, 2006). Swimming activities are particularly important because of the unique sensations that water provides.

Proprioception

Proprioception consists of perceptual–motor abilities that respond to stimuli arising within the body. These include sensory stimuli arising from skin, muscles, tendons, joints, and vestibular sense receptors. Such abilities emphasize movement and are discussed within the categories of kinesthetic perception and balance.

Kinesthetic Perception

It is apparent even to the casual observer that we use information gained through auditory and visual receptors to move within and learn from the environment. Just as we know a sight or sound, we also have the ability to know a movement or body position. We can know an action before executing it, and we can feel the correctness or discriminate the positions of a movement. The awareness and memory of a planned movement and position is **kinesthetic perception** and is related to internal sensations. It develops from impulses that originate throughout the body's proprioceptors located in the muscles, tendons, and joints. Because kinesthetic perception is basic to all movement, it is associated with other sensory systems such as visual–motor and auditory–motor abilities (Gabbard, 2018; Roth et al., 2016). Overall, kinesthetic perception is "body sense," which is needed to position and move the body in space and helps with understanding the use of effort and force (Haywood & Getchell, 2020).

Similar to all perceptions, kinesthetic perceptions depend on sensory input (including kinesthetic acuity) provided to the central nervous system. The central nervous system processes this information in accordance with the perceptual–motor process. Certain conditions might cause kinesthetic perception to be impaired. For example, in the case of a person who has had an amputation, all sensory information that normally would be processed by that extremity would be missing. Cerebral palsy, muscular dystrophy, and other disabilities or conditions affecting the motor system might result in a pattern of input or output that is not fluid and is different from that of a person without disabilities. A student with a learning disability and DCD might have difficulty selecting appropriate information from the many sources in the body to successfully complete a planned movement. Inadequate kinesthetic perception might manifest itself in clumsiness due to lack of opportunity for participation in movement experiences. Abilities closely associated with kinesthetic perception are body awareness and directionality.

BODY AWARENESS One of the most fundamental aspects of kinesthetic perception is *body awareness*, an elusive term that has been used in many ways to represent different but related constructs. Used here, **body awareness** is a comprehensive term referring to the ability to derive meaning from the body and includes body schema, body image, and body concept or knowledge.

Body schema is the most basic component of body awareness and is sometimes called the *sensorimotor component* because it depends on information supplied through activity of the body itself. It involves awareness of the body's movement capabilities and limitations, including the ability to create appropriate muscular tension during movement and awareness of the position of the body and its parts in space. Body schema helps people know where the body ends and external space begins. Thus, an infant uses feedback from body action to become aware of the dimensions and limitations of the physical being and begins to establish separateness of the body from external surroundings. As body schema evolves, higher levels of motor development and control appear and follow a continuous process of change throughout life.

Body image refers to the feelings one has about one's body. Body image is affected by biological, intellectual, psychological, and social experiences. It includes the internal awareness of body parts and how they function. For example, people learn that they have two arms and two legs or two sides of the body that sometimes work in combination and other times function independently.

Body concept, or body knowledge, is the verbalized knowledge one has about one's body. It includes the intellectual operation of naming body parts and the understanding of how the body and its parts move in space. Body concept builds on body schema and body image.

The importance of movement experiences for the stimulation and nurturing of body awareness,

FIGURE 20.2 Scooter-board activities enhance body awareness during the developmental years.

and the importance of body awareness for movement proficiency, are obvious. Virtually all gross motor activities involve body awareness at some level. Movement experiences that might enhance body awareness in the developmental years include those in which parts of the body are identified, named, pointed to, and stimulated (e.g., Simon Says). Imitation of body part movements, balance activities, rhythmic or dance activities, scooter-board activities, mimetic activities, movement exploration, swimming games, activities conducted in front of a mirror, and stunts and tumbling are all examples of helpful movement experiences (figure 20.2). Thus, instructors who desire to enhance body awareness must provide children with many positive movement opportunities in a variety of fun, challenging, and safe settings.

DIRECTIONALITY Directionality is an important aspect of kinesthetic perception that is an extension of body awareness and moving in space. Directionality includes understanding the location of movement, such as left and right (laterality), up and down (verticality), in and out, and forward and backward (Gabbard, 2018; Sherrill, 2004). Obstacle courses such as moving through a spiderweb (see previous Application Example sidebar) are good examples of promoting directionality.

Laterality is the **internal awareness** of both sides of the body and their relations as well as differences. With good laterality, a child can catch a ball on the right side with the right hand, the left side with the left hand, or toward the center of the body with both hands. He can also use the two limbs of the body to perform opposite tasks, such as using one hand to hold a paper and the other hand to write (Cheatum & Hammond, 2000). Children who have issues with laterality often avoid using one side of their body. For example, they slide well in one direction, usually their dominant side, but avoid sliding in the other direction. **Verticality** refers to an internal awareness of up and down and includes the ability to raise the body from a horizontal to upright position (Sherrill, 2004). Development of verticality is also believed to be enhanced through experimentation in upper and lower parts of the body. Laterality and verticality are included in many physical education activities, and nurturing these abilities enhances their successful development and performance. Examples include most balance activities such as walking up steps, locomotor activities such as jumping and leaping, and object-control activities such as moving the body up, down (e.g., jumping jacks), and to both sides to catch a ball.

Balance

As mentioned previously, proprioception includes sensation pertaining to vestibular sense reception. The vestibular system provides information about the relation of the body to gravitational pull and thus serves as the basis for balance or equilibrium. Vestibular sense perception combines with visual, auditory, kinesthetic, and tactual information to enhance the attainment of **postural** (unconscious reflexes to keep the body erect), **static** (stationary or held), and **dynamic** (moving) forms of balance.

Balance is a key element in the performance of most movement activities. Examples of everyday functional activities that require balance are stepping off a sidewalk curb to get on a bus or walking up bleachers to view a game. Many activities may be used to nurture or remediate balance during the perceptual–motor developmental years (Haywood & Getchell, 2020). These include activities conducted on tilt boards, balance boards, stepping stones, low-ropes courses, and balance beams. Mimetic activities, stunts and tumbling, and a variety of games can also be used to develop balance.

Visual Perceptual–Motor Development

As the dominant perceptual modality, vision is crucial to successfully moving in the environment, determining reference points, and judging the movement of objects. It has been estimated that approximately 80 percent of all sensory information outside the body is derived from vision (Gabbard, 2018). **Visual perceptual–motor abilities** are important in academic, physical education, and sport settings. In the academic setting, visual perceptual abilities are used in writing, drawing, reading, spelling, and mathematics. In physical education and sport, they are important for performing such fundamental movements as running, catching, throwing, kicking objects, playing tag, and balancing. Age-appropriate visual perceptual–motor abilities are built on visual acuity, which affects the ability to see, fixate, and track (input). On the basis of input, people develop the components of the visual perceptual–motor process associated with central nervous system processing and output. Components closely associated with this process that affect movement include visual figure–ground perception, spatial relationships, visual perceptual constancy, and visual–motor coordination.

Figure–Ground Perception

Figure–ground perception involves the ability to distinguish the main figure or target from its surrounding background and give meaning to the forms or the combination of forms or elements that constitute the figure. It requires the ability to give selective attention, differentiate, and integrate parts of objects to form meaningful wholes and to appropriately shift attention and ignore irrelevant stimuli. Visual figure–ground perception is needed, for example, when students are asked to pick out a specific letter of the alphabet from a field of extraneous items. Students with inadequate perception might exhibit difficulties in differentiating letters, numbers, and other geometric forms; combining parts of words to form an entire word; or sorting objects. For instance, a student who has difficulty with figure–ground perception might hold her paper closer to her face to block out background information (Cheatum & Hammond, 2000).

In physical education, figure–ground perception is required in games that depend on tracking moving objects, observing lines and boundaries, and concentrating on relevant stimuli. These include activities in which children move under, over, through, and around tires, hoops, or playground equipment, as well as activities in which they follow or avoid the lines and shapes associated with obstacle courses, geometric figures, maps, mazes, hopscotch diagrams, or footprints. In sport, figure–ground perception is clearly demonstrated in baseball—a batter must distinguish the figure, a white ball, from the actual background of the sky or outfield fence when attempting to hit or catch the ball.

Spatial Relationships

The perception of **spatial relationships** means locating objects in space relative to oneself, or self-space (egocentric localization), as well as locating objects relative to one another, or general space (objective localization). **Egocentric localization** is demonstrated as students attempt to move through hoops without touching them. **Objective localization** is seen as a player attempts to complete a pass to a guarded teammate.

Spatial relationships, which affect virtually all aspects of academic learning, involve direction, distance, and depth. Position in space is basic to the solution of reversal or directional problems (such as the ability to distinguish *d*, *p*, and *q*; *36* and *63*; *saw* and *was*; and *no* and *on*). Perception of spatial relationships also encompasses temporal ordering and sequencing. Students who have difficulty placing objects in order will have difficulty in various academic areas, including arithmetic sequencing problems (performing operations in correct order). In physical education, students who have difficulty with spatial relationships seem to be lost in space and often bump into others, and may need to be oriented to their position on the court or field. Some authors contend that spatial awareness is preceded by body awareness and that the awareness of relationships in space grows out of an awareness of relationships among the parts of one's own body.

Visual Perceptual Constancy

Perceptual constancy is the ability to recognize objects despite variations in their presentation. It entails recognizing the sameness of an object even though the object might in actuality vary in appearance, size, color, texture, brightness, shape, and so on. For example, an American football is the same size even when seen at a distance, it has the same color in daylight as in twilight, and it maintains its shape even when only its tip is visible during a spiral pass. Development of perceptual constancy involves seeing, feeling, manipulating, smelling, tasting, hearing, naming, classifying, and analyzing objects. Inadequate perceptual constancy affects the recognition of letters, numbers, shapes, and other symbols in various contexts. Physical education and sport provide a unique opportunity for nurturing perceptual constancy because objects are used and manipulated in many ways and are viewed from many perspectives, such as different distances and angles.

Visual–Motor Coordination

Visual–motor coordination, the ability to coordinate vision with body movements, combines visual with tactual and kinesthetic perception. Although coordination of vision and movement might involve many parts of the body, eye–hand and eye–foot coordination are usually most important in physical education and sport activities. Effective eye–hand coordination is also important in such pursuits as cutting, pasting, finger painting, drawing, tracing, coloring, scribbling, using the chalkboard, and manipulating clay and toys, and is particularly important in writing. Eye–limb coordination is also necessary for such functional activities of daily living as putting on and tying shoes, dressing, eating and drinking, and using simple tools. In physical education, eye–limb coordination is needed for object-control skills used in games and sport, such as throwing, catching, kicking, dribbling, and striking. As shown in figure 20.3, the teacher can assist children with visual–motor challenges by using larger equipment during striking activities.

David Nelson CSULB.

FIGURE 20.3 A child finds success with striking by using a large foam hockey stick to hit a large beach ball.

Development of Visual Perceptual–Motor Abilities

Many experiences in physical education and sport call on visual perceptual–motor abilities. Although motor activities are not generally limited to the development of one ability, some activities are especially well suited for figure–ground development. These include rolling, throwing, catching, kicking, striking, and dodging; chasing a variety of objects in a variety of ways; moving under, over, through, and around tires, hoops, geometric shapes, ropes, playground equipment, and other apparatus; following or avoiding lines associated with obstacle courses, geometric shapes, maps, mazes, hopscotch games, or grids; and stepping on or avoiding footprints, stones, animals, or shapes painted or placed on outdoor hard surfaces or floors, such as poly spots. Additional activities include imitating movements, as in leapfrog, follow the leader, or Simon Says; and doing simple rope activities, such as moving under and over ropes and jumping rope.

Spatial relationships are involved in tumbling, swimming, jumping rope, rhythms and dance, and obstacle courses. Activities particularly useful in helping to develop spatial abilities include moving through tunnels, tires, hoops, mazes, and perception boxes. Activities in which one must locate objects in space relative to oneself (egocentric localization or self-space) or relative to one another (objective localization or general space) also promote perception of spatial relations.

Visual–motor coordination is extremely important in physical education and sport. Exhibiting difficulty moving around other players and objects, not tracking an object, and turning the head or blinking when attempting to catch a ball are all examples of potential visual problems. Games and sports that include throwing, catching, kicking, and striking balls and other objects are among the activities requiring such coordination. Age-appropriate games and sports are highly recommended because they enhance the purposefulness of movement, motivate the learner, and promote socialization.

Auditory Perceptual–Motor Development

Although auditory development may not be as critical as vision to movement success, its vital role in physical education and sport should not be overlooked. Age-appropriate **auditory perceptual–motor abilities** are built on auditory acuity and perception. The ability to receive and transmit auditory stimuli as sensory input is the foundation of auditory figure–ground perception, auditory discrimination, sound localization, temporal auditory perception, and auditory–motor coordination.

Auditory Figure–Ground Perception

Auditory figure–ground perception is the ability to distinguish and attend to relevant auditory stimuli against a background of general auditory stimuli. It includes ignoring unimportant auditory sensations or irrelevant stimuli (e.g., a noisy gym) to attend to relevant stimuli (e.g., the teacher's directions). In situations in which irrelevant auditory stimuli are present, people with inadequate auditory figure–ground perception might have difficulty concentrating on the task at hand, responding to directions, and discriminating spoken information from other sounds received in a noisy setting. They might not attend to a honking horn, a shout, or a signaling whistle and might have difficulties in physical education and sport when transitions are signaled through sound. Visual signals to ensure smooth transitions for students with auditory difficulties can include an actual picture of the child moving to transition, tossing a scarf in the air, or using a hand signal. Other examples of transition signals are discussed in chapter 11.

Auditory Discrimination

Auditory discrimination is the capacity to recognize and distinguish among variations of auditory stimuli, including different pitches, volumes, frequencies, qualities, and amplitudes of sound. It also involves auditory–perceptual constancy, or the ability to recognize the same auditory stimulus under varying presentations. People with inadequate auditory discrimination might exhibit problems in games, dances, and other rhythmic activities that depend on this ability—for example, a player who cannot distinguish the official's whistle from the noise of the crowd.

Sound Localization

Sound localization—the ability to determine the source or direction of sounds in the environment—is used, for example, during a basketball game to find an open player calling for the ball. Sound localization is basic to goalball, which is played blindfolded with a sound-emitting ball. Another fun and challenging way to reinforce sound localization is to hide an object in the gym that emits a sound, such as a beep ball, and have the students find the object.

Temporal Auditory Perception

Temporal auditory perception involves the ability to recognize and discriminate among variations of auditory stimuli, such as rate, emphasis, tempo, and order of auditory stimuli. Students with inadequate temporal auditory perception might exhibit difficulties in rhythmic movement and dance, singing games, and other physical education activities.

Auditory–Motor Coordination

Auditory–motor coordination is the ability to coordinate auditory stimuli with body movements. This coordination is readily apparent when a student responds to a beat in music (ear–foot coordination) or to a particular cadence when football signals are called out. Auditory–motor coordination is evident as a dancer, skater, or gymnast performs a routine to musical accompaniment.

Development of Auditory Perceptual–Motor Abilities

Physical education and sport offer many opportunities to develop auditory perception. Participants might follow verbal directions or perform activities in response to music, and the activities might be suggested by the music itself. For example, children might walk, run, skip, or gallop to a musical beat, or they might imitate trains, airplanes, cars, or animals as suggested by music. Dances and rhythmic activities with variations in the rate and beat are useful, as are games and activities in which movements are begun, changed, or stopped in response to various sounds. Triangles, drums, tambourines, bells, sticks, or whistles might direct children in movement or serve as play equipment. A teacher conducting such activities should minimize distracting stimuli and vary the tempo and loudness of sound. It might be necessary to speak softly at times so that students must concentrate on listening.

Summary

This chapter discussed sensorimotor stimulation and perceptual–motor development, or the process of enhancing the ability to integrate sensory stimuli arising from or relating to observable movement experiences. It focused on how systematically implemented movement activities can be used for sensorimotor stimulation and perceptual–motor development, as well as how they contribute to students' development and consequent movement experiences.

References

Burton, A.W. (1987). Confronting the interaction between perception and movement in adapted physical education. *Adapted Physical Activity Quarterly, 4,* 257-267.

Burton, A.W. (1990). Assessing the perceptual–motor interaction in developmentally disabled and handicapped children. *Adapted Physical Activity Quarterly, 7,* 325-337. https://doi.org/10.1123/apaq.7.4.325

Cheatum, B.A., & Hammond, A.A. (2000). *Physical activity for improving children's learning and behavior.* Human Kinetics.

Colombo-Dougovito, A.M., & Block, M. (2016). Make task restraints work for you: Teaching object control skills to students with autism spectrum disorder. *Journal of Physical Education, Recreation and Dance, 87*(1), 32-37. http://doi.org/10.1080/07303084.2015.1109492

Cowden, J.E., & Torrey, C. C. (2007). *Motor development and movement activities for preschoolers and infants with delays: A multisensory approach for professionals and families* (2nd ed.). Charles C Thomas.

Davis, W.E., & Broadhead, G.D. (Eds.). (2007). *Ecological task analysis and movement.* Human Kinetics.

Davis, W.E., & Burton, A.W. (1991). Ecological task analysis: Translating movement behavior theory into practice. *Adapted Physical Activity Quarterly, 8,* 154-177. https://doi.org/10.1123/apaq.8.2.154

Gabbard, C.P. (2018). *Lifelong motor development* (7th ed.). Wolters Kluwer.

Gibson, J.J. (1979). *The ecological approach to visual perception*. Houghton Mifflin.

Goodway, J.D., Ozmun, J.C., & Gallahue, D.L. (2020). *Understanding motor development: Infants, children, adolescents and adults* (8th ed.). Jones & Bartlett Learning.

Haywood, K.M., & Getchell, N. (2020). *Lifespan motor development* (7th ed.). Human Kinetics.

Healey, S., Msetfi, R., & Gallagher, N. (2013). "Happy and a bit nervous": The experiences of children with autism in physical education. *British Journal of Learning Disabilities, 41,* 222-228. https://doi.org/10.1111/bld.12053

Hutzler, Y. (2007). A systematic ecological model for adapting physical activities: Theoretical foundations and practical examples. *Adapted Physical Activity Quarterly, 24,* 287-304. https://doi.org/10.1123/apaq.24.4287

Johnstone, J.A., & Ramon, M. (2011). *Perceptual-motor activities for children: An evidence-based guide to building physical and cognitive skills*. Human Kinetics.

Kavale, K.A., & Mattison, P.D. (1983). One jumped off the balance beam: A meta-analysis of perceptual motor training programs. *Journal of Learning Disabilities, 16,* 165-173. https://doi.org/10.1177/002221948301600307

Kress, J., & Lavay, B. (2006). Traveling on the OutBAC: Challenging children with disabilities on a low ropes course. *Palaestra, 22*(2), 20-26.

Nielson, K., Henderson, S., Barnett, A.L., Abott, R.D., & Berninger, V. (2018). Movement issues identified in Movement ABC2 checklist parent ratings for students with persisting dysgraphia, dyslexia, and OWL LD and typical literacy learners. *Learning Disabilities, 23*(1), 10-23. https://doi.org/10.18666/LDMJ-2018-V23-I1-8449.

Payne, V.P., & Isaacs, L.D. (2016). *Human motor development: A lifespan approach* (9th ed.). McGraw-Hill.

Ratey, J.J., & Hagerman, E. (2008). *Spark: The revolutionary new science of exercise and the brain*. Little Brown.

Roth, K., Zittel, L., Pyfer, J., & Auxter, D. (2016). *Principles and methods of adapted physical education and recreation* (12th ed.). Jones & Bartlett Learning.

Seaman, J.A., DePauw, K.P., Morton, K.B., & Omoto, K. (2007). *Making connections: From theory to practice in adapted physical education* (2nd ed.). Holcomb Hathaway.

Sherrill, C. (2004). *Adapted physical activity, recreation, and sport: Crossdisciplinary and lifespan* (6th ed.). McGraw-Hill.

Ulrich, D. (2019). *Test of gross motor development* (3rd ed.). Pro-Ed.

Weiner, B., & Davis, T. (2019, December). *Sensory processing assessment of responses (SPAR)*. www.myphysicaleducator.com/resources/assessment

Print Resources

Cheatum, B.A., & Hammond, A.A. (2000). *Physical activity for improving children's learning and behavior*. Human Kinetics.

This resource provides a comprehensive, easy-to-read approach to neurological development and the sensory systems. Part II of the text devotes a chapter to each of the sensory systems.

Cowden, J.E., & Torrey, C.C. (2007). *Motor development and movement activities for preschoolers and infants with delays: A multisensory approach for professionals and families* (2nd ed.). Charles C Thomas.

This book emphasizes organizing and conducting movement intervention programs for infants, toddlers, and preschoolers with delays or disabilities. It includes exercises and activities for increased muscle tone and strength, decreased muscle tone and reflex integration, and sensory motor development (postural reactions and vestibular stimulation, visual–motor control, auditory discrimination, tactile stimulation, and kinesthetic and spatial awareness).

Davis, W.E., & Broadhead, G.D. (Eds.). (2007). *Ecological task analysis and movement*. Human Kinetics.

This resource shows instructors how to apply the ecological task analysis (ETA) model to the dynamics of movement behavior by examining the interacting constraints of the performer, environment, and task in coaching, teaching, and therapy.

Gabbard, C.P. (2018). *Lifelong motor development* (7th ed.). Wolters Kluwer.

This comprehensive research-based book on motor development includes a section on special populations and an excellent overview of the various sensory systems.

Johnstone, J. A., & Ramon, M. (2011). *Perceptual-motor activities for children: An evidence-based guide to building physical and cognitive skills*. Human Kinetics.

The text provides a blueprint for improving perceptual–motor skills that includes a 32-week program of sequential station lesson activities with over 200 activities. Included is a section on how to design a perceptual–motor learning laboratory for students.

Kranowitz, C. (2006). *The out-of-sync child has fun: Activities for kids with sensory integration dysfunction*. Perigee.

This revised edition includes updated information and new activities with more than 100 enjoyable activities that reinforce the sensory systems for young children.

Ratey, J.J., & Hagerman, E. (2008). *Spark: The revolutionary new science of exercise and the brain*. Little Brown.

In the first book to comprehensively explore the connection between exercise and the brain, John Ratey, MD, explains the mind–body connection, illustrating that exercise is truly our best defense against everything from depression to ADD to addiction to menopause to Alzheimer's.

Weiner, B., & Davis, T. (December, 2019). *Sensory processing assessment of responses (SPAR)* [PDF file]. www.myphysicaleducator.com/resources/assessment

SPAR is a screening tool that assesses individual responses to stimuli through seven sensory systems and oral processing (a combination of tactile and proprioception), including auditory, interoception, olfactory, proprioception, tactile, vestibular, and visual systems.

Online Resources

Center for the Ecological Study of Perception and Action (CESPA): http://ione.psy.uconn.edu

This site features a discussion on the ecological approach to perception and action in the tradition of the late James J. Gibson. CESPA's organizational structure allows unparalleled integration of research across specialties, with extensive collaboration among faculty and students.

Educational Activities, Inc.: www.edact.com

This website is the publisher of educational music CDs, DVDs, software, and children's books by bestselling authors Hap Palmer and others, and is an excellent source for perceptual–motor development materials.

Kimbo Educational: www.kimboed.com

The Kimbo Educational website provides educational tips for teaching perceptual–motor activities and includes such resources as music, books, and activity tips for special needs and young children.

School Specialty Sportime: www.sportime.com

This online catalog includes products designed to assist professionals who implement physical education and sport programs. The Abilitations catalog and link have sensory equipment and many ideas and activity sheets for movement, positioning, sensorimotor, and perceptual–motor activities for students with special needs.

Vestibular Disorders Association (VEDA): www.vestibular.org

This organization is dedicated to helping people better understand vestibular disorder as well as providing relevant resources and support. Their website includes links to specific resources for balance, hearing, vision, and exercise.

21

Infants and Toddlers

Cathy Houston-Wilson

Ms. Quinn, an early childhood adapted physical educator at the Center for Discovery, prepares for a motor session with several young children ages 8 to 24 months and their caregivers. There is Kelly, who was born with a congenital heart defect, and her mom Sara; Oliver, who was born exposed to drugs, and his Uncle Luke; and Kiera, who was born blind, and her nanny Camille. This diverse group of individuals represents the many children born every day with potential long-term needs and the importance of providing early intervention services as soon as possible. Ms. Quinn facilitates a program that allows children and their caregivers an opportunity to engage in a variety of activities that promote early motor development. Using equipment such as incline mats, soft balls, scarves, pull toys, toys that make noise when activated, slides, and tunnels, she structures her room in a way that encourages the children and their caregivers to act on the equipment in a natural, free-flowing manner. Ms. Quinn greets the children individually as they enter and talks with their caregivers about the progress the children are making and what objectives have been developed for the day with the equipment that has been set up. She has specific objectives for each child: weight bearing and walking with a pull toy for Kelly, play skills for Oliver, and sound tracking for Kiera. Ms. Quinn and the caregivers follow the young children's lead as they begin to play with the equipment and engage in reciprocal interactions throughout the session. Throughout the session, Ms. Quinn facilitates the interactions between the children and their caregivers, shares tips on activities that can be done at home, and notes the progress the children are making on their daily assessment sheets.

This chapter presents an overview of adapted physical education as it relates to infants and toddlers with unique needs. This includes legislative mandates and implications for early intervention services and the role of teachers in the identification and assessment of infants and toddlers with unique needs. Program planning is described, including goals, objectives, and activities of early childhood motor programs for young children with and without unique needs; the need for sensory stimulation and play-based experiences; appropriate ways to interact with infants and toddlers; and the importance of families in the development of infants and toddlers.

Legislation and Implications for Intervention Services

The Individuals with Disabilities Education Act (IDEA, 2004) mandates that infants and toddlers with developmental delays or at risk for developmental delays are to be provided with early intervention services. According to IDEA, infants and toddlers who are eligible for early intervention are defined as children under three years of age who are experiencing developmental delays in one or more of the following **functional areas**, as measured by appropriate diagnostic instruments and procedures: cognitive development (learning and thinking), physical development (growth or gross and fine motor abilities), communication development (understanding and using words), social or emotional development (relating to others), or adaptive development (self-help skills such as feeding).

In addition, those who have a diagnosed physical or mental condition that has a high probability of resulting in developmental delay are eligible. Infants and toddlers with disabilities might also include, at the state's discretion, **at-risk** infants and toddlers, defined as a child under three years of age who would be at risk of experiencing a substantial developmental delay if early intervention services were not provided (IDEA, 2004).

States are given flexibility in determining additional criteria for eligibility. For example, in New York State, a child would qualify for early intervention services if any of the following conditions are met (New York State Department of Health, 2005):

- A child is experiencing a 12-month delay in one or more functional areas.
- A child is experiencing a 33 percent delay in one functional area.
- A child is experiencing a 25 percent delay in two functional areas.
- A child scores two standard deviations below the mean in one functional area.
- A child scores one and a half standard deviations below the mean in two or more functional areas.

Early childhood experts agree that determining eligibility for children who are so young is a complex process. A variety of methods for determining eligibility are recommended, including direct observation, play-based assessment, standardized tests or developmental inventories, clinical professional opinion, and, most important, reports by parents or caregivers. Young children do not typically respond on cue, so the importance of information from parents or caregivers should not be underestimated. Given the complexity of assessing such young children, authentic assessments are used widely in the evaluation process. Rubrics, checklists, and rating scales can be helpful in determining if the child has reached certain milestones or desired levels of functioning; this data can also be used to determine progress (known as **formative assessment**). A family may also choose to be involved in what is known as a **family assessment**. With this process, family members meet with the early intervention team to identify their concerns, priorities, and resources in relation to their child's development (McLean et al., 2004).

To determine if the child is experiencing a developmental delay in one or more of the functional areas listed previously, a comprehensive **multidisciplinary assessment** must be conducted. *Multidisciplinary* means that the child will be evaluated by more than one professional. Members of the multidisciplinary team include parents, a service coordinator, advocates, professionals from at least two disciplines, and any other person with an interest in the child (Koralek et al., 2019). Although not explicitly identified as a professional service provider, adapted physical educators may serve as "other professionals" who can assess the child in the motor domain. Team members engage in various forms of data collection to determine the strengths and needs of the child. Tests used to determine unique needs must be valid and administered by trained professionals. Once a developmental delay has been established, an **individualized family service plan** (IFSP) is developed by the team members. IDEA (2004) specifies that the IFSP contains the following information:

- A statement of the child's present level of functioning

- A statement of the family's resources, priorities, and concerns related to their child's development
- A statement of the major outcomes expected from early intervention services
- A statement of the early intervention services, including transportation, needed to meet the child's and family's needs
- A statement of the natural environments where early intervention services will be provided ("natural environments" means settings where infants and toddlers are typically found in the community)
- A plan for when the child is in daycare, and when needed, for early intervention service providers to train the daycare staff to meet the needs of the child
- A physician's or nurse practitioner's order for early intervention services that require an order from specific medical professionals
- A statement about other services, including medical services needed for the child and family that are not provided by the early intervention program
- The projected dates that services will begin (as soon as possible after the IFSP meeting) and the period of time during which the services will be delivered
- The name of the service coordinator
- If the child is turning three years of age, the steps to help the child and family transition to other services, including preschool special education services

Teachers of Early Childhood Adapted Physical Education

Infants and toddlers with developmental delays, whether cognitive, physical, or emotional, might also demonstrate psychomotor delays. Psychomotor delays are a major disadvantage because movement serves as an important basis from which children initially learn. For example, if children lack the ability to maintain an upright position or move across a room, they are unable to interact with their environments in a meaningful way. Teachers of early childhood adapted physical education are in a unique position to develop and implement motor programs for infants and toddlers with special needs. These teachers may serve as valuable members of the multidisciplinary team by conducting motor assessments or observing motor behavior, thereby helping select relevant goals and objectives to enhance the child's development. They may provide direct teaching services or serve as consultants to early intervention providers and parents. As resource consultants, they can provide appropriate activities that stimulate development in areas beyond the motor domain, including cognitive, social, emotional, communication, and adaptive development.

Assessment

Well-prepared teachers of adapted physical education should be able and willing to serve as members of the multidisciplinary team responsible for direct screening and assessment of motor behaviors for infants and toddlers with disabilities. This assessment serves as the primary means of determining eligibility for and implementing early intervention services. Various techniques and examples of assessment are described in the following sections.

Screening

Before a comprehensive assessment is conducted, infants and toddlers might first be screened to determine if there is a probable delay. On completion of the screening procedure, recommendations are made regarding the need for further evaluation. Screening can be either informal or formal. Informal screening includes observations, checklists, rating scales, and rubrics of developmental milestones. Formal screenings are commercially available and are often done at medical offices or at early intervention centers.

One example of a formal motor screening test is the Alberta Infant Motor Scales (Piper & Darrah, 2004), which was developed for infants from birth through independent walking. The test is observatory in nature and relatively easy to administer, taking approximately 20 minutes. The 58 test items are grouped into four categories: prone, supine, sitting, and standing. Each test item is scored as either "observed" or "not observed." Another popular screening test is the Ages & Stages Questionnaires (ASQ-3) (Squires & Bricker, 2009). This screening instrument provides parents or caregivers with easy-to-follow instructions and pictures to determine if their child is able to complete a task. Parents check off what the child is able to do based on the five developmental areas of communication, gross motor skills, fine motor skills, problem solving, and personal–social behaviors. Professionals score the parent responses and determine if delays are evident and if early intervention is warranted. These are just two of the many commercially available screening tools that can be used to determine if needs exist and if further testing is warranted.

Standardized Assessment

If it is determined that a child might have a delay after initial screening, a more extensive formal assessment may be conducted. One way to determine the unique needs of infants and toddlers is through the use of standardized assessments. Standardized assessments are often used because they lend themselves to the determination of developmental status, are technically sound, and are relatively easy to administer. Standardized assessment instruments might be norm referenced, criterion referenced, or both. **Norm-referenced assessments** allow testers to compare the child against others of similar age and characteristics, whereas **criterion-referenced assessments** compare the child's performance against preestablished criteria. Tests that are both norm and criterion referenced help with identification of unique needs as well as program planning and implementation.

One example of a motor assessment instrument that is both norm and criterion referenced is the Peabody Developmental Motor Scales (PDMS-2) (Folio & Fewell, 2000). This test provides in-depth assessment and training of gross and fine motor skills for children from birth through age 5. The test is broken down into six subtests that measure reflexes, stationary positions, locomotion, object manipulation, grasping, and visual–motor integration. The test yields fine motor and gross motor quotient scores as well as a total motor quotient score. The total motor quotient is the best estimate of the child's overall motor abilities. The PDMS-2 also provides a motor activity program with units of instruction organized developmentally by skill area to aid in the development and implementation of appropriate goals and objectives to meet the unique needs of the child.

Another example of a standardized test that is both norm and criterion referenced is the Brigance Inventory of Early Development III (IED-III) (Brigance, 2013). This test is unique in that it contains both a screening test and a formal assessment. Once the child has been screened and a delay is suspected, the child is further evaluated with the formal assessment. The Brigance system provides tools for assessing children from birth to age 7. Areas assessed include motor skills, self-help skills, speech and language, general knowledge and comprehension, and early academic skills. The Brigance IED-III is one of the most widely used comprehensive assessments because it targets all areas of functional development, generating a valid picture of the child's current level of performance.

Curriculum-Based Assessment

Curriculum-based assessment has become a popular means by which to generate data about a child's present level of performance. It takes place in natural environments and is based on a predetermined set of curriculum objectives. The Carolina Curriculum for infants and toddlers with special needs (Johnson-Martin et al., 2004) and the Hawaii Early Learning Profile (HELP) Strands (Parks, 2013) are both examples of curriculum-based assessment. The Carolina Curriculum was developed for infants and toddlers from birth to 24 months, whereas the HELP Strands was developed for infants and toddlers from birth to 36 months. Both tests assess the child in five functional areas of development—cognitive skills, communication and language, social–emotional adaptation, fine motor skills, and gross motor skills—that are embedded in naturally occurring activities. Based on the assessment data, a profile of the child is developed. Because these assessments are linked to a curriculum, there is a smooth transition from the assessment phase to the intervention phase. Both the Carolina Curriculum and the HELP Strands include activities to develop skills.

Transdisciplinary Play-Based Assessment

Another form of assessment that is appropriate for use with infants and toddlers is transdisciplinary assessment, which differs from traditional forms of assessment in several ways. Traditional forms of assessment typically involve experts in various domains determining the strengths and needs of the child for a particular domain, then coming together to report their findings and generate a comprehensive picture of the child's current level of performance. **Transdisciplinary assessment**, or arena assessment, calls for a play facilitator to interact with the child, their parents, and a peer. The interactions are based on a set of criteria observed unobtrusively in both structured and unstructured play environments by representatives from various disciplines who are knowledgeable about all areas of development.

Linder (2008) is credited with the development of the Transdisciplinary Play-Based Assessment

(TPBA2) and Transdisciplinary Play-Based Intervention (TPBI2). Throughout the testing, professionals observe cognitive, social–emotional, communication and language, and sensorimotor development. Based on the observations, developmental level, learning style, interaction patterns, and other relevant behaviors are analyzed and recorded onto observation sheets, which are later transferred to summary sheets during postobservation sessions (Linder, 2008). If the TPBA2 indicates delays are evident, then the TPBI2 program can be implemented to help remediate these delays.

The role of the parents in the TPBA2 cannot be overemphasized. Parents are involved in the process from start to finish by completing a developmental checklist, directly interacting with the child during the assessment, and developing the IFSP. This form of assessment has many benefits; most notably, it helps provide an accurate picture of the child's present level of performance. Because data are collected in natural environments with caregivers directly involved in the assessment process, children are typically more at ease and perform more naturally than they normally would with this type of assessment. In addition, with the use of a play facilitator, the child is exposed to only one professional, rather than the traditional three to five members of an assessment team. Teachers of early childhood adapted physical education can easily serve as play facilitators, because their primary means of developing motor abilities is through the use of play.

Authentic Assessment

The final form of assessment used to evaluate young children is **authentic assessment**, which is conducted in authentic or real-life situations. Although the tests described previously can be useful in determining eligibility for services, they have their limitations. For example, some children will not respond on cue or may act differently with strangers than they would in a typical setting. In addition, the previous assessments tend to be summative; that is, the information gained presents a picture of the child's present level of performance but does not monitor ongoing performance or track formative data. Authentic assessment, then, can be used as a mechanism to screen and evaluate infants and toddlers and can provide both formative and summative assessment data. The assessment is often created based on the outcome, or the overall goal to be achieved (e.g., sliding down a slide), and the skills needed to be mastered in order to reach this outcome (e.g., climbing stairs).

The most common form of authentic assessment is a rubric. A rubric is a rating method that uses a fixed scale describing characteristics of each point of the scale—for example, criteria may reflect the ability of the child to always, sometimes, rarely, or never accomplish a task. Rubrics often provide a detailed guideline for making scoring decisions. Scoring is qualitative rather than quantitative, and the scoring criteria are used to evaluate student performance and progress (Lieberman & Houston-Wilson, 2018).

Another form of authentic assessment is the checklist. A checklist identifies a list of tasks the child should be able to accomplish, and performance is measured against the list. Checklists in early childhood are related primarily to developmental tasks such as reaching certain milestones in the five areas of development.

Finally, rating scales can be used to determine the quality of performance (e.g., excellent, very good, good, fair, and poor). Rating scales can be especially helpful when assessing children who require physical assistance to perform tasks. The assessor can determine the level of assistance needed to perform a given task (e.g., total physical assistance, partial physical assistance, or no physical assistance) and use that as the basis for present level of performance. As the child is able to accomplish more tasks independently, the scale can be updated and progress can be continually monitored.

Goals, Objectives, and Activities of Motor Programs for Typically Developing Infants and Toddlers

Infants and toddlers learn by experiencing their environments in several ways: through their senses (seeing, hearing, tasting, smelling, and feeling), through reciprocal adult–child interactions, and through movement actions and reactions (Bredekamp & Copple, 2009). For example, when an infant cries, a natural reaction on the part of the parent or caregiver is to interact with the child to determine his needs. Similarly, if a child swats at a mobile (i.e., movement action), the natural reaction is for the mobile to move. These constant interactions among the child, the environment, and those within the environment serve as the basis for cognitive, affective, and psychomotor development. Because children learn by moving, creating environments that facilitate movement aids in the total development of the child. Thus, the primary goal of motor programs for infants and toddlers is the development of motor milestones and the acquisition of motor skills.

Figure 19.2 in chapter 19 depicts Gallahue's life span model of motor development. Within the model, four phases of motor development are noted: reflexive movement, rudimentary movement, fundamental movement, and specialized movement. Infants and toddlers operate within the reflexive, rudimentary, and fundamental movement phases.

The reflexive movement phase is characterized by involuntary movements elicited by external stimuli. Reflexes are either primitive (used for survival or precursors to voluntary movement) or postural (the body's attempt to keep itself in an upright position). Most reflexes are inhibited or integrated between 4 months and 12 months of life (Goodway et al., 2021). The rudimentary movement phase is the first form of voluntary movement. Rudimentary movements are purposeful, although they may not be as precise as later forms of movement. During the rudimentary phase of development, stability, locomotion, and manipulative skills begin to emerge. Stability—the ability to maintain control of the head, neck, and trunk—serves as the basis for locomotion and manipulation. The enhanced motor ability that comes with rudimentary movement, such as crawling, creeping, and walking, allows infants and toddlers to move freely within their environments, and the ability to reach, grasp, and release allows infants and toddlers to make meaningful contact with objects within the environment.

Together, these movement interactions help to shape the overall development of infants and toddlers and lead to more refined movement forms, known as *fundamental movement*. Fundamental movement includes both locomotor and object-control skills that become more fully refined over time and through a variety of experiences. Other forms of active movement, such as rhythm and dance, gymnastics, aquatics, and games, can also enhance the motor skills of children.

The need for active movement cannot be overstated. SHAPE America (2009) has identified the following guidelines related to physical activity for infants and toddlers. Note that young children are not miniature adults, and the methods for increasing physical activity in adolescents and adults differ significantly from the methods used for infants and toddlers. The intent is to provide infants and toddlers with opportunities for movement to foster active lifestyles over time.

Infant Guidelines

- *Guideline 1.* Infants should interact with caregivers in daily physical activities that are dedicated to exploring movement and the environment.
- *Guideline 2.* Caregivers should place infants in settings that encourage and stimulate movement experiences and active play for short periods of time several times a day.
- *Guideline 3.* Infants' physical activity should promote skill development in movement.
- *Guideline 4.* Infants should be placed in an environment that meets or exceeds recommended safety standards for performing large-muscle activities.
- *Guideline 5.* Those in charge of infants' well-being are responsible for understanding the importance of physical activity and should promote movement skills by providing opportunities for structured and unstructured physical activity.

These guidelines can be realized a variety of ways. Infants need opportunities to practice their newly developed skills, such as sitting up, rolling over, and crawling, and caregivers and instructors are responsible for creating safe environments that encourage this practice. If an infant is kept in a playpen or infant seat for extended periods of time, delays in motor milestones will occur. Additionally, research suggests that inactivity in childhood leads to inactivity in adulthood (SHAPE America, 2009). Baby games such as peekaboo and patty-cake are ideal, as is placing children on their stomachs with objects nearby for them to reach for and interact with. "Tummy time" is especially important because the only safe sleeping position for infants is on the back (American Academy of Pediatrics, 2016). As a result, many babies don't get the time they need to stretch and strengthen the back and neck muscles, which can lead to early motor delays. Equipment that the baby interacts with should be easy to grasp, brightly colored, and varied in texture. Blocks, stacking toys, nesting cups, squeeze toys, and baby gyms are all ideal, as is providing adequate space in which to play. For example, SHAPE America (2009) recommends a minimum of a five- by seven-foot (1.5- by 2-meter) rug or blanket for playing, rolling, and other large-muscle activities. Providing the environment, however, is not enough. Caregivers must also take an active role in interacting with the child and showing interest in and approval of the baby's discoveries. These adult–child interactions not only enhance motor development but also help children in their social–emotional and cognitive development.

Toddler Guidelines

- *Guideline 1.* Toddlers should engage in a total of at least 30 minutes of structured physical activity each day.
- *Guideline 2.* Toddlers should engage in at least 60 minutes—and up to several hours—per day of unstructured physical activity and should not be sedentary for more than 60 minutes at a time, except when sleeping.
- *Guideline 3.* Toddlers should be given ample opportunities to develop movement skills that will serve as the building blocks for future motor skillfulness and physical activity.
- *Guideline 4.* Toddlers should have access to indoor and outdoor areas that meet or exceed recommended safety standards for performing large-muscle activities.
- *Guideline 5.* Those in charge of toddlers' well-being are responsible for understanding the importance of physical activity and promoting movement skills by providing opportunities for structured and unstructured physical activity and movement experiences.

These guidelines can be realized through a variety of strategies. As the toddler moves from an awkward walking gait to running in the blink of an eye, other skills such as kicking and throwing will also emerge. Though maturation plays a part in this rapid development, environmental opportunities greatly influence these behaviors. Toddlers who are not provided with equipment or opportunities to engage in these behaviors often demonstrate motor delays (SHAPE America, 2009). These rudimentary manipulative movements also serve as a basis for more refined fundamental motor skills. Rhythms and musical instruments should be incorporated into the environment to stimulate movement and creative expression. In addition, toddlers may be capable of acting out stories, touching body parts, and playing chasing games.

The toddler needs ample time to move, discover, and interact in a play-based environment. The recommended time frame reinforces the need for the child to have both structured (activities with specific goals and objectives) and unstructured (free time to interact within the environment) motor time. To accommodate these newly developed motor skills, SHAPE America (2009) recommends that a minimum of 50 square feet (15 square meters) of accessible outdoor play space be available to toddlers. Additionally, a minimum of five by seven feet (1.5 by 2 meters) should be available per child for active movement. Finally, play spaces should be childproofed, accessible, and inviting. Caregivers create the environments for increased physical activity and set appropriate boundaries based on the toddler's physical capabilities. They provide activities for imitation as well as imagination. They engage with and reassure the toddler as she gains new skills.

Creating a movement environment in which infants and toddlers can thrive is another goal of the motor program. Environments should be child centered and should stimulate the child's interests in and abilities to act on the environment. Figure 21.1 is an example of a play-based motor environment for infants and toddlers.

Colorful walls and equipment are used to intrigue the child and elicit movement. Crawling and climbing areas are scaled appropriately. Open space, toys that elicit cause and effect, and toys with differing shapes, sizes, and textures should also be available. Similarly, adults who follow the child's lead playfully and who delight in the child's newfound discoveries help to foster the child's confidence and overall abilities.

A final goal of motor programs for infants and toddlers is to aid in the development of independence. Though infants might not be ready to function independently of their caregivers, they have opportunities to engage in isolated activities from time to time. Toddlers, however, will need guidance and support as they begin to release their total dependence on their parents or caregivers and learn to function more independently. This need for independence helps shape positive psychosocial behaviors later in life. Play is crucial to the development of autonomy because it allows children to function within their own boundaries, not the boundaries established by others.

As children attempt new skills, they need to feel successful so that they will continue to attempt to refine the skill as well as try out new skills. **Self-initiated repetition** is one way to foster this independence (Bredekamp & Copple, 2009). Teachers of early childhood adapted physical education are responsible for developing environments that allow for ample opportunities to practice both already learned skills and new skills. For example, if a toddler finds rolling a ball stimulating, balls of various shapes and sizes should be available to the

© Cathy Houston-Wilson

FIGURE 21.1 Example of a play-based environment at the Strong National Museum of Play, Rochester, New York.

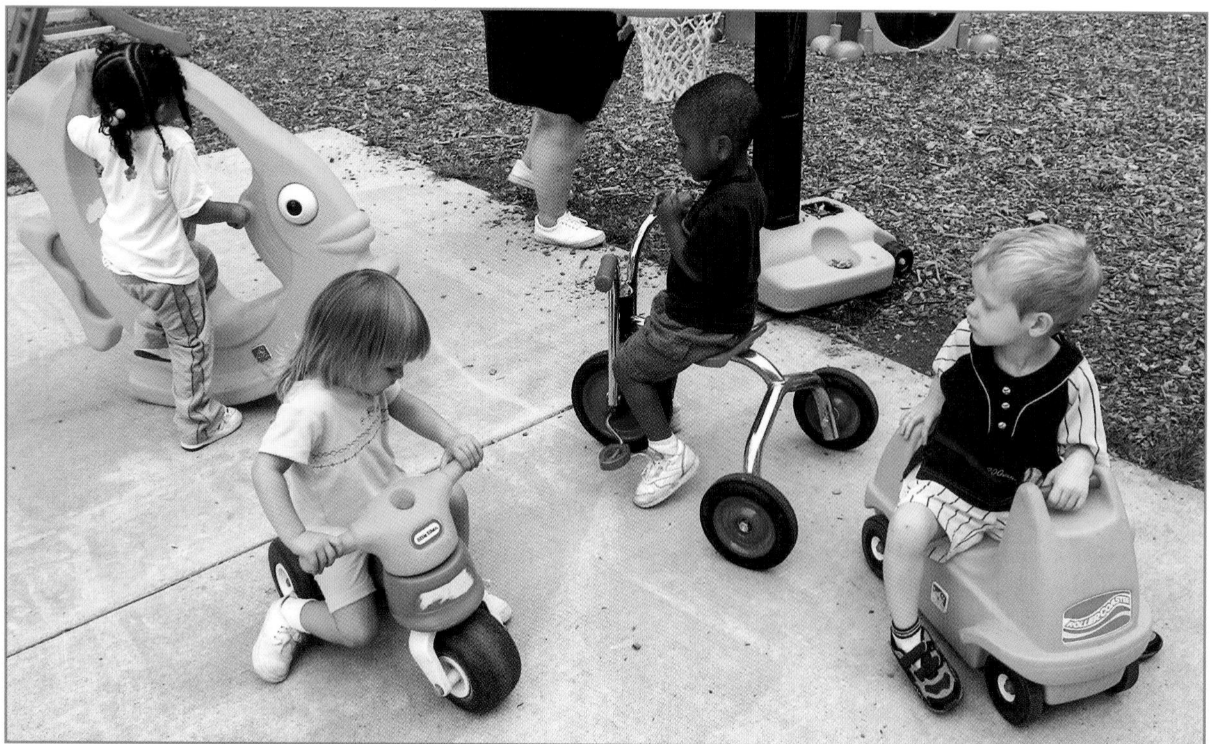

FIGURE 21.2 Plenty of similar toys should be readily available.

child. Because young children are egocentric, they should have ample equipment so that they do not have to wait for a turn or share. Figure 21.2 depicts a group of children who are provided with similar riding toys, allowing for maximum participation.

Goals, Objectives, and Activities of Motor Programs for Infants and Toddlers With Unique Needs

Motor programs for typically developing infants and toddlers provide opportunities for activities that help shape motor development, as well as cognitive and social development. Infants and toddlers with unique needs, however, may have motor delays that inhibit their abilities to move freely and interact with their environments. Whereas the goals and objectives previously discussed are applicable to all infants and toddlers, this section identifies unique motor needs that teachers of early childhood adapted physical education might encounter, as well as strategies to promote the development of children with these unique needs.

Although typically developing infants and toddlers move from the stage of reflexive movement to rudimentary movement in a smooth, integrated fashion, infants and toddlers with special needs might demonstrate unique motor problems that benefit through intervention. Cowden and Torrey (2007) identify several areas of emphasis in which motor programs for infants and toddlers with unique needs are developed. The first deals primarily with increasing muscle tone and strength. Infants and toddlers lacking in muscle tone are said to be **hypotonic**. Disabilities associated with hypotonicity include Down syndrome, muscular dystrophy, and metabolic disorders. Infants with low muscle tone often demonstrate delays in primitive reflex integration, especially with the tonic neck group of reflexes. Teachers of early childhood adapted physical education should provide physical assistance as needed to move the child through various strength enhancing activities.

Strength control activities should occur in four positions: prone, supine, side-lying, and upright (Cowden & Torrey, 2007). In the prone position, the child is developing greater control of the head and trunk. These prerequisite skills aid in the development of locomotor movements, such as crawling

FIGURE 21.3 Eliciting head lifting with a toy fosters the infant's control of the head.

and creeping. A typical prone position stimulus that elicits head control involves squeaking or rattling a favorite toy above the child's head (see figure 21.3). The child will attempt to reach for the toy and in so doing will lift his head from the floor.

Control of the trunk can be realized by encouraging and even helping the child to roll from stomach to back. Again, a favorite toy just out of reach will motivate the child to roll over. After the child has accomplished the task, it is important to allow her to interact with the toy. Once head and trunk control have been established, crawling and creeping positions should be maintained.

Activities in the supine and side-lying positions also stimulate muscle strength. However, for children with extremely high or low muscle tone, supine positions should be avoided and activities should be done in the side-lying position for greater control. A typical supine or side-lying activity involves offering the child a toy just slightly out of reach. The child will then reach for the toy (extend arms), obtain it, and bring the toy into midline (flex arms). These types of activities can be repeated in several ways using a variety of equipment to stimulate the child's interest.

Finally, activities that enhance strength can be attained in upright positions. Children can interact with caregivers and their environments in a sitting position. Repeating any activity that maintains the child's interest, such as peekaboo, may stimulate a child and foster an upright position. As the child gains additional strength, standing and finally walking will be achieved.

The second area of motor emphasis for infants and toddlers with special needs is to decrease muscle tone and enhance reflex integration (Cowden & Torrey, 2007). Increased muscle tone, also known as **hypertonicity**, results from delayed reflex integration. Infants and toddlers with spastic cerebral palsy exhibit hypertonicity. The lack of reflex integration interferes with typical movement skills, thus creating substantial motor delays. Activities that involve relaxation techniques, massage, therapy ball exercises, and appropriate positioning help to minimize and alleviate hypertonicity. Figure 21.4 illustrates a young child being placed in a prone position on a therapy ball with legs slightly separated and toes pointed outward. The child is gently rocked forward and backward. This position on the therapy ball helps to normalize muscle tone by relaxing the muscles.

FIGURE 21.4 A child using a therapy ball to help normalize muscle tone.

Stimulation and development of the sensorimotor system are also areas of emphasis for infants and toddlers with unique needs. Cowden and Torrey (2007) identify five components of the sensory system—vestibular integration, visual integration, auditory integration, tactile integration, and kinesthetic integration—and provide activities to enhance each (see also chapter 20). Vestibular integration activities are needed so that children can achieve or maintain an upright position. Infants and toddlers who lack the ability to right themselves can easily be injured and demonstrate delayed locomotion and balance abilities. Therapy balls are useful for enhancing postural reactions. With the child lying over the ball, the ball is rolled forward so that the child extends the arms in a protective fashion. Activities that use incline mats, balance boards, and scooters are all appropriate for enhancing postural reactions because they stimulate opportunities for movement in several positions and situations.

The abilities to track objects, discriminate among shapes and sizes, and distinguish objects from a background are all part of visual integration (figure 21.5). Activities that can enhance visual integration should be incorporated in early childhood motor programs. Simple tasks such as tracking a rolling ball, matching shapes, and walking on overlapping geometric shapes are all appropriate for enhancing visual integration.

Having children search for sounds in a room, move their bodies to music, and follow simple directions can enhance auditory integration. Allowing the child to interact with a variety of textured equipment such as scooters, mats, balance boards, and ropes, as well as physically stroking a child with various textures, is helpful for tactile integration. However, some children might be hyper- or hyposensitive to touch; in these instances, carefully sequenced tactile integration activities can be incorporated into the program. Finally, kinesthetic integration can be enhanced by providing activities that allow the child to move through space, such as obstacle courses with tunnels, mats, and scooters.

The ability to manipulate objects might also be a needed area of emphasis for infants and toddlers with unique needs. The ability to reach, grasp, hold, and release is crucial for acquiring self-help skills, such as eating, and for making meaningful contacts within the environment, such as swinging on a swing.

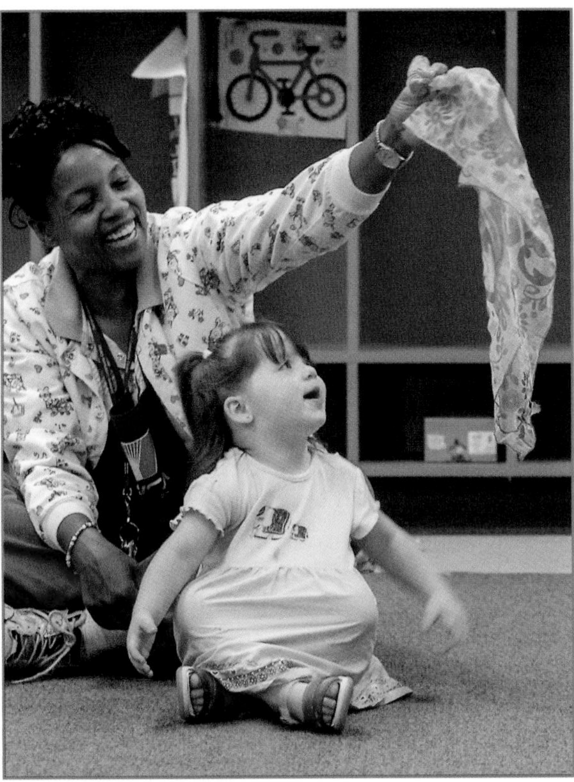

FIGURE 21.5 Tracking a slow-moving scarf is one way to enhance visual–motor control.

Developmentally Appropriate Interactions With Infants and Toddlers

Traditional formats for teaching physical education obviously do not apply to teaching infants and toddlers. Teachers of early childhood adapted physical education are primarily responsible for setting up an environment that is intriguing to children and their parents or caregivers. Infants and toddlers should be free to explore and engage in self-initiated repetition as much as desired.

Direct teaching is not recommended with such young children; rather, indirect approaches such as guided discovery and exploration are embedded within the learning environment. This method is **child directed** or **child initiated**; teachers and caregivers should follow the child's lead in activities and "teach from behind," meaning the adult responds to the child's interactions. One way of teaching from behind is by describing what the child is doing rather than telling the child what to do (McCall & Craft, 2000). For example, if a young child is interacting with blocks, the caregiver can label the blocks by their colors or shapes with statements such as, "Shannon is stacking the red block."

Adults play a role in providing choices for young children by creating the environment that the child acts upon. The environment allows for guided discovery in which children explore and interact with the equipment that has been set out for them. For example, a motor room might contain push toys, stacking toys, balls, and tunnels. Any of these activities would be suitable: Tunnels and balls allow children to enhance their gross motor abilities, whereas push toys and stacking toys enhance fine motor abilities. Activity participation also has naturally occurring consequences—that is, if a child climbs to the top of the slide, the natural consequence would be to slide down. These activities contribute to an understanding of the environment and enhance sensorimotor development. Refer to the Application Example sidebar for a description of a developmentally appropriate motor environment.

Interacting With Families

As noted, parents or caregivers will typically accompany the young child in the motor environment; thus, teachers of early childhood adapted physical education need to respect and embrace the role of parents and caregivers in their programming. Early

Application Example

Developing an Appropriate Motor Environment

SETTING

Motor room at a daycare facility

STUDENTS

Toddlers with and without unique needs

ISSUE

Setting up a developmentally appropriate motor environment that promotes the movement of the young children

APPLICATION

The environment contains the following areas:

- Push toys for fine motor development
- Stacking toys for fine motor development
- Balls for gross motor development
- Tunnels for gross motor development

The teacher allows the children to interact with the environment and follows their lead as they move from one piece of equipment to another. Choosing an area should be encouraged, though children with special needs might need to be brought to various areas if they are unable to ambulate independently.

childhood adapted physical education programs should be based on a **family-centered** philosophy (Raver & Childress, 2015), with goals and objectives developed not in isolation of the family but rather in conjunction with them. Although professionals can assist families in understanding their child's unique needs and facilitate the child's acquisition of appropriate skills, families have their own priorities and aspirations for their child. Learning about these priorities and collaboratively developing a plan of action is one way in which professionals can support families. Professionals can also support families by teaching them appropriate ways to facilitate movement, such as types of objects or equipment to use, pace at which to engage the child, proper positioning, and developmentally appropriate activities that young children would enjoy.

Finally, the most important family-centered principle is communication. Teachers of early childhood adapted physical education need to maintain constant open communication with parents or caregivers. The development of the young child is based on the combined efforts of parents and supportive professionals whose major role is to guide the family in the development of their child, not to direct the development of the child. With a strong collaborative partnership, infants and toddlers with special needs and their families can benefit from early intervention services.

Summary

This chapter has illustrated the role of teachers of early childhood adapted physical education as it relates to infants and toddlers with unique needs. As noted, teachers of early childhood adapted physical education might be involved in early intervention services for infants and toddlers by serving as members of the multidisciplinary team convened to determine areas of need, conduct valid assessments of motor abilities, develop appropriate motor goals and objectives for the IFSP, and implement motor programs. In some instances, teachers might also serve as consultants to caregivers or parents.

Teachers of early childhood adapted physical education are in a unique position to help minimize further delays by creating environments that allow infants and toddlers to discover, explore, and interact with their surroundings. These interactions enhance motor development and improve cognitive and social development. Although all infants and toddlers can benefit from developmentally appropriate motor programs, infants and toddlers with unique needs should have specific goals and objectives embedded in their activities. These goals might include increasing muscle tone and strength, decreasing muscle tone and enhancing reflex integration, stimulating the sensorimotor system, or enhancing manipulative abilities. A variety of activities were presented in this chapter to help teachers realize these goals; however, the reader is encouraged to seek out the Print, Video, and Online Resources to further develop motor programs for infants and toddlers with unique needs.

Finally, this chapter has highlighted the importance of family in the lives of infants and toddlers. It is suggested that teachers of early childhood adapted physical education embrace family-centered principles, including collaborating to create goals based on needs identified by the family, developing the family's repertoire of skills and competencies, and maintaining open communication.

References

American Academy of Pediatrics. (2016). *Back to Sleep, Tummy to Play.* Author.

Bredekamp, S., & Copple, C. (2009). *Developmentally appropriate practice in early childhood programs serving children from birth through age 8* (3rd ed.). National Association for the Education of Young Children.

Brigance, A. (2013). *Brigance inventory of early development II (IED-II).* Curriculum Associates.

Cowden, J.E., & Torrey, C.C. (2007). *Motor development and movement activities for preschoolers and infants with delays.* Charles C Thomas.

Folio, M.R., & Fewell, R. (2000). *Peabody developmental motor scales* (2nd ed.). Pro-Ed.

Goodway, J., Ozmun, J.C., & Gallahue, D.L. (2021). *Understanding motor development: Infants, children, adolescents, adults* (8th ed.). Jones & Barlett.

Individuals with Disabilities Education Improvement Act of 2004 (IDEA) PL 108-446, 20 U.S.C. 1400 (2004).

Johnson-Martin, N., Attermeier, S.M., & Hacker, B.J. (2004). *The Carolina curriculum for infants and toddlers with special needs* (3rd ed.). Brookes.

Koralek, D.G., Nemeth, K.N., & Ramsey, K. (2019). *Families and educators together: Building great relationships that support young children.* National Association for the Education of Young Children.

Lieberman, L., & Houston-Wilson, C. (2018). *Strategies for inclusion: Physical education for everyone* (3rd ed.). Human Kinetics.

Linder, T. (2008). *Transdisciplinary play-based assessment* (2nd ed.). Brookes.

McCall, R., & Craft, D.H. (2000). *Moving with a purpose: Developing programs for preschoolers of all abilities.* Human Kinetics.

McLean, M.E., Wolery, M., & Bailey, D.B. (2004). *Assessing infants and preschoolers with special needs.* Merrill.

New York State Department of Health. (2005). *Infants and toddlers: Eligibility criteria.* Author.

Parks, S. (Ed.). (2013). *HELP Strands: Curriculum-based developmental assessment birth to three years.* VORT.

Piper, M., & Darrah, J., (2004). *Alberta infant motor scales (AIMS).* Saunders.

Raver, S.A., & Childress, D.C. (2015). *Family-centered early intervention.* Brookes.

SHAPE America. (2009). *Active start: A statement of physical activity guidelines for children from birth to age five* (2nd ed.). Author.

Squires, J., & Bricker, D. (2009). *Ages & stages questionnaires, third edition (ASQ-3).* Brookes.

Print Resources

Bardige, B.S. (2009). *Talk to me, baby! How you can support young children's language development.* Brookes.

This resource uses movement-based activities to stimulate language development.

Chen, D. (Ed.). (2009). *Early intervention in action.* Brookes.

This resource uses a crossdisciplinary approach for providing early intervention services and provides video clips of children to demonstrate key concepts.

Cowden, J.E., & Torrey, C.C. (2007). *Motor development and movement activities for preschoolers and infants with delays.* Charles C Thomas.

This adapted physical education approach to enhance motor development of young children with special needs provides many hands-on activities that can easily be implemented by practitioners.

Crawford, M. (2014). *Early intervention every day.* Brookes.

This resource provides families with strategies for fostering goals and objectives in everyday activities.

Johnson, J.J., Rahn, N.L., & Bricker, D. (2015). *An activity-based approach to early intervention* (4th ed.). Brookes.

This resource details how activity-based assessment can be used to link goal development, intervention, and evaluation for children from birth to age 5. It is useful in developing IFSPs and individualized education programs (IEPs).

Noonan, M., & Linda, M. (2014). *Teaching young children with disabilities in natural environments* (2nd ed.). Brookes.

Designed for preservice professionals who will be working in the field of early intervention, this book uses a noncategorical approach to provide information on best practices for working with young children with a range of developmental disabilities.

Widerstrom, A.H. (2004). *Achieving learning goals through play* (2nd ed.). Brookes.

This practical guide uses play to help young children with and without special needs learn, with ready-to-use strategies and plans to achieve learning goals.

Video Resources

Growth: A study of Jimmy and Johnny [Video]. YouTube. https://youtu.be/UhrTNLdY-2Y

This video describes a growth and development study of twins, Jimmy and Johnny.

Pathways. (2018, December 11). *2 month old baby typical & atypical development side by side* [Video]. https://youtu.be/_0cErYu3A8Q

This seven-minute video describes both a typical and atypical infant side by side in eight different positions to identify differences in motor development.

Sunnybrook Hospital. (2011, June 23). *Tummy time exercises for your baby* [Video]. YouTube. https://youtu.be/UEnzqSK-j_s

This two-minute video describes shoulder and abdominal exercises as well as information on how to make eye contact with a baby.

Observing Kassandra: A Transdisciplinary Play-Based Assessment of a Child With Severe Disabilities, Revised Edition [DVD]. (2010). Brookes.

This DVD uses the TPBA to observe a child with severe disabilities and provides detailed instructions and application of this assessment approach, including an accompanying booklet. Running time is approximately 50 minutes.

Online Resources

Council for Exceptional Children: www.cec.sped.org

This website provides information on laws and best practices related to early intervention programs for children with disabilities.

National Association for the Education of Young Children (NAEYC): www.naeyc.org

This is the primary site for resources and best practices for the education of young children from birth to nine years.

Zero to Three: www.zerotothree.org

This organization is one of the leading resources in the United States on the first years of infancy.

22

Early Childhood Adapted Physical Education

So-Yeun Kim and Lauriece L. Zittel

Mr. Sanchez and Ms. Brooks are elementary physical education specialists at North Ridge Elementary School. Both teachers have experience modifying their instruction to successfully include children with disabilities in their K-3 program. Recently, their district instituted an inclusive early childhood program for preschoolers with disabilities or developmental delays who have been identified as needing special education services; this special education program has been combined with the existing preschool program housed in the elementary school.

Rather than just providing instruction to the children with developmental delays, the teachers have designed a preschool physical education program for all of the children within this new program. The teachers are aware that the majority of children in the new preschool program have communication delays in addition to their disability diagnosis or general developmental delay. They are eager to collaborate with the classroom teachers and speech therapist to develop a movement program that will provide opportunities for children to be physically active as well as enhance motor and communication skills. Additionally, the teachers are excited to incorporate the new, fully accessible playground, built last year with a universal design for learning (UDL) framework in mind. This provides another opportunity to incorporate motor development and physical activity during the school day for children with all abilities. The challenge is to design a preschool program that will build a skill foundation for the children as they prepare to enter their elementary physical education program.

These early childhood physical education instructors are not alone. It is not uncommon to find preschool classrooms for children with developmental delays and specific disabilities in an elementary school building. Many physical educators have had experience teaching children with disabilities in kindergarten through the third grade, but teaching a preschool population might be new to them. This chapter presents information about accurately assessing the abilities of young children, understanding the developmental differences between preschool children and those entering elementary school, incorporating UDL in motor development and physical activity settings, and planning for instruction and developmentally appropriate teaching practices for children aged 3 to 9.

Identifying Young Children With Developmental Delays

According to IDEA (2004), children aged 3 through 9 who have developmental delays qualify for early educational services if they are

> (1) . . . experiencing developmental delays, as defined by the State and as measured by appropriate diagnostic instruments and procedures, in one or more of the following areas: physical development, social or emotional development, or adaptive development; and
>
> (2) . . . by reason thereof, [need] special education and related services. (Assistance to States for the Education of Children with Disabilities, 2006, p. 46756)

In preschool and early childhood (ages 3-9), a noncategorical approach is used to classify students' eligibility to receive special education services. This approach allows for programming that is based on the child's functional areas of development rather than disability-specific. Federal legislation also requires that instruction be provided to these children in the least restrictive and most natural learning environment. Thus, inclusive programs designed to accommodate children with and without unique needs should be the norm rather than the exception. Teachers of physical education are thus faced with the challenge of determining if movement delays exist and then structuring movement programs to meet the needs of young children with varying levels of abilities.

Assessment of Performance

Appropriate assessment procedures are necessary to assist teachers of early childhood adapted physical education in determining the functional skill abilities and physical activity levels of the young children in their classrooms. Identifying a gross motor developmental delay through accurate assessment is essential in order to determine a child's eligibility for an individualized adapted physical education program and to plan and implement a developmentally appropriate individualized program.

Professional guidelines and federal legislation recommend that assessment information come from several measures and sources. Additionally, children at risk for developmental delay should be observed in a variety of settings. A complete picture of a young child's present level of performance in all areas of learning can be drawn from a group of people most familiar with the child's routines and behaviors. A multidisciplinary team should collect screening information while observing the child in structured settings as well as unstructured authentic play environments. Members of the multidisciplinary team should include classroom teachers, adapted or general physical educators, therapists, parents or guardians, and others who see the child on a regular basis. These team members will develop the child's individualized educational program (IEP) and participate in the IEP planning committee.

Assessment data may be collected using objective measures and formal testing procedures or using an informal, play-based approach (Linder & Linas, 2009). Federal guidelines encourage early childhood teachers to use data from multiple observations and measures for gathering information to make decisions about performance ability. Information collected in standardized settings should be combined with observations made in authentic play environments.

Objective Measures and Formal Testing

Before selecting an instrument to assess young children, the purpose of testing should be clear (Williams & Monsma, 2006). Will the results be used to document a developmental delay, or is information needed for planning and teaching? Norm-referenced standardized tests are administered to determine a child's gross motor developmental level and provide comparison information of same-age children without delays. Criterion-referenced instruments typically provide more information about delays in functional skill areas (e.g., locomotor, object control) to assist with teaching and program planning (Bagnato et al., 2014). Standardized test instruments that are both norm and criterion referenced will assist adapted physical education specialists in making eligibility decisions and provide instructional information. Instruments that incorporate flexible testing procedures (i.e., equipment selection and testing environments) are more sensitive to the testing characteristics of young children with disabilities and thus lead to more accurate results. Examples of norm- and criterion-referenced tools used to assess the gross motor skills of young children include the Brigance Inventory of Early Development III (IED-III) (Brigance, 2013), the Peabody Developmental Motor Scales (PDMS-2) (Folio & Fewell, 2000), and the Test of Gross Motor Development (TGMD-3) (Ulrich, 2019).

Each of these assessment instruments is designed to assist early childhood physical education specialists in determining a child's gross motor developmental level as well as to provide information for instructional programming. Additionally, each of these tools will assist specialists in developing goals and objectives for the child's IEP. The testing procedures outlined for the Brigance IED-III, the PDMS-2, and the TGMD-3 provide test administrators with flexibility in testing environment, equipment, and instruction procedures. For example, the PDMS-2 test manual suggests that a station testing format be used for evaluating several young children at a time, and the testing materials used are those commonly found in preschool or primary programs and familiar to most children. The Brigance IED-III and the PDMS-2 are also common formal assessment instruments for infants and toddlers (see chapter 21).

Accelerometers and pedometers are also commonly used to objectively measure physical activity levels in preschoolers (e.g., Bornstein et al., 2011; De Craemer et al., 2015; Dobell et al., 2019; Robinson & Wadsworth, 2010). Accelerometers measure the acceleration of the body in one or more dimensions, whereas pedometers record ambulatory movements. Preschool children typically wear the device on the right side of the hip using an elastic belt, but the device can also be worn on the wrist or ankle. Accelerometers can be used successfully with preschoolers with developmental disabilities when age-appropriate familiarization practices are followed (Park et al., 2017). Pedometers may need to be secured to prevent the device from being opened by preschoolers who want to open or reset the counter (Cardon & DeBourdeaudhuij, 2007). Advantages and disadvantages of using these devices are summarized in table 22.1.

TABLE 22.1 Advantages and Disadvantages of Physical Activity Measurements

Measure	Advantages	Disadvantages
Accelerometer	• Objective • Small and noninvasive • Measures intensity and duration of physical activity • Relatively easy data collection • Can collect data for extended periods • Waterproof	• Cost • No information on activity type or context • Limited accuracy of non–weight-bearing activities (e.g., upper body movement, biking) • Limited validity evidence for individuals with physical disabilities
Pedometer	• Objective • Noninvasive • Inexpensive, easy to administer to large group • Relatively easy data collection	• Possibility of participant reactivity • No information on activity type or context • Limited ability to measure nonambulatory activities • Limited validity evidence for individuals with physical disabilities
Direct observation	• Measures both type and intensity of physical activity • Provides various qualitative information (e.g., social and environmental factors)	• Burdensome and time consuming (e.g., training, observing time) • Necessary to check inter- and intraobserver reliability • Possibility of participant reactivity

Subjective Measures and Informal Testing

The authenticity of data collected in natural settings provides instructors with useful information about the child's preferences and functional abilities. The ability to write accurate instructional objectives and structure an effective teaching environment is maximized when teachers observe and record children's behaviors during typical games and activities and watch them interact with age-appropriate equipment. Criterion-referenced skill checklists can also yield information about the child's abilities in the context of a predetermined set of curriculum objectives (Bailey, 2017; McLean et al., 2004). For a child who may not find success performing some objectives within the curriculum, a functional motor development assessment (FMDA) should be completed. The FMDA provides information about what skills a child can do and how the child performs the skills.

In the area of early childhood adapted physical education, two curriculum-based tools are recommended to assist physical education teachers in securing performance assessment data. *Smart Start: Preschool Movement Curriculum Designed for Children of All Abilities* (Wessel & Zittel, 1995) includes useful skill checklists organized in a LOOP model: **l**ocomotor (e.g., jumping, hopping), **o**rientation (e.g., body awareness, imitative expressive movements), **o**bject-control (e.g., throwing, kicking), and **p**lay skills (e.g., parachute play, tricycle riding). *I CAN Primary Skills: K-3* (Wessel & Zittel, 1998) also uses LOOP checklists, but they have been updated to include personal–social participation skills (e.g., problem solving, self-control) in place of play skills. This reflects the need expressed by teachers to address goals and objectives related to social–emotional learning.

The LOOP organization in these early childhood programs allows instructors to assess children according to skill areas relevant for both the preschool and elementary years. Additionally, the model gives instructors the freedom to select skill objectives from different areas for different units of instruction. For example, a preschool adapted physical educator might choose to assess three locomotor skills (vertical jump, hop, gallop) and two play skills (parachute play, tricycle riding) to organize or "LOOP" one six-week unit of instruction. Similarly, an elementary adapted physical educator may select two locomotor skills and four object-control skills to "LOOP" a six-week unit.

The Carolina Curriculum for preschoolers (Johnson-Martin et al., 2004) and the Assessment, Evaluation, and Programming System (AEPS) for infants and children (Bricker et al., 2002) are multidomain, curriculum-based programs designed for preschool-aged children with disabilities or those who are at risk of developmental delays. The Carolina Curriculum assesses children in five learning domains and provides a curriculum sequence in each area. The gross motor domain assesses skills in locomotion, stair climbing, jumping, balance, balls, and outdoor equipment. The AEPS includes a functional skill assessment across six learning domains and a curriculum to provide programming and teaching suggestions for instructors. The gross motor domain includes two skill strands: Strand A, balance and mobility, focuses on stair climbing. Strand B, play skills, includes five goals in these areas: (1) jump forward; (2) run while avoiding obstacles; (3) bounce, catch, kick, and throw; (4) skip; and (5) ride and steer a bicycle.

Teacher-made checklists and rubrics can also be useful for assessing functional motor and play skill performance. Standards of performance can be written to address the unique movement abilities of children, and progress on those standards can be used to evaluate improvement on instructional objectives. These methods give teachers the freedom to collect performance information on skills or behaviors that might not be found in published checklists. Additionally, task analyzing skills for children with ambulatory difficulties or severe disabilities give early childhood teachers the opportunity to assess functional abilities by individualizing the critical elements in a checklist. For example, a teacher might be assessing the galloping abilities of preschool children while they pretend that yardsticks are their horses. One child in the class with cerebral palsy who uses a gait trainer (with the horse attached) is working on stepping. Another child who uses a wheelchair may "feed" the horses, working on upper trunk stability and overhand throwing. In this example, the teacher might use the Smart Start galloping and overhand throwing checklist for some of the children in the class and create his own stepping and upper trunk stability checklist to evaluate the ability of the children with ambulatory difficulties.

Portfolio assessment is a means of gathering information about a child in order to monitor progress on teaching objectives or to inform teaching practice (Lynch & Struewing, 2001). Information from the movement environment can be added to a child's portfolio in collaboration with the classroom teacher, or the adapted physical educator can begin a portfolio system for a child on her own. Because the purpose of a portfolio is to enhance teaching, collaboration is recommended. Ideally, movement skills are practiced not only in the physical education class but also at home and during movement times that the classroom teacher arranges. All who work with a child should add samples of the child's activity or practice on certain IEP objectives. Written comments from teachers, parents, or teaching assistants as well as videotapes, photos, and drawings related to movement skills and practice are examples of items to include in a movement portfolio. At the end of each evaluation period, the adapted physical educator should organize all of the material and provide an overview and reflection on the child's year. For children who will remain in a preschool program for multiple years, the portfolio can be used to document progress and then be shared with the elementary specialists during the transition to kindergarten.

Direct, systematic observation is widely used to measure physical activity behavior of young children. Information about physical activity intensity (e.g., sedentary, light, moderate, vigorous), type (e.g., running, sitting, throwing), and environmental (e.g., use of portable or fixed equipment) and social contexts (e.g., group composition) can be obtained using this method (Pate et al., 2010). An early childhood teacher typically observes one child at a time and codes behaviors based on observation procedures. Various systematic observation tools have been used extensively with preschoolers, including the Observational System for Recording Activity in Children—Preschool Version (OSRAC-P) (Brown et al., 2006), the System for Observing Children's Activity and Relationships During Play (SOCARP) (Ridgers et al., 2010), and the Physical Activity Level Screening (PALS) tool (Park et al., 2017). Advantages and disadvantages of using direct observation are listed in table 22.1.

Whether gathered formally or informally, performance data should provide a direct link to designing and evaluating an individualized intervention plan. The activities a teacher uses should minimize sedentary behaviors and address each child's gross motor strengths and challenges. Teachers of early childhood adapted physical education should become familiar with curriculum designs and instructional strategies that are both age and individually appropriate.

Early Childhood Program Standards and Learning Objectives

The development of early childhood physical education programs should be aligned with best practices in early childhood education and early childhood special education. Early childhood movement programs should provide children with the opportunity to explore and act on objects in their physical environment (Odom & Wolery, 2003). A well-designed movement curriculum for preschool through third grade should focus on fundamental movement abilities in the preschool years, specialized movement abilities in the early elementary years, and opportunities for all children to be physically active. Young children experiencing delays in their motor development should receive the same opportunities and instruction as their same-age peers, but modified to address individual challenges.

The preschool years give instructors the opportunity to guide children through games and activities in order to build a skill foundation and maintain appropriate activity levels. This fundamental movement phase should focus on stability, locomotor, and object-control skills. It follows, then, that the early elementary years (kindergarten through third grade) allow the teacher to integrate the knowledge and skills that children have acquired and begin to refine them for more advanced games and activities. The specialized movement phase gives children the opportunity to combine fundamental skills to complete a single specialized activity. (See chapter 19 for a review of the phases of motor development.)

The connection between the fundamental movement phase and specialized movement phase in the early childhood years is critical for physical education curriculum development. As a guide, national standards for physical education (SHAPE America, 2014) have been written for elementary children in the United States. These five physical education standards for students age 5 to 9 are written to reflect what children should be able to do after participation in a quality physical education program. PE Metrics-3 (SHAPE America, 2019) is a valid and reliable tool developed to assess the first national physical education standard, which reads "The physically literate individual demonstrates competency in a variety of motor skills and movement patterns" (SHAPE America, 2014, p. 12). A quality physical education program for elementary-aged children should follow national standards and build on the fundamental movement skill programs introduced in preschool.

However, early learning standards vary state by state for preschool-aged children. To assist early childhood educators, the National Institute for Early Education Research (NIEER) has organized a standards database on what states have identified as educational priorities for children of prekindergarten age (NIEER, 2014). Using learning standards to guide programming for children with and without disabilities through the early childhood years can be beneficial in all domains of learning, including physical health and development. Early childhood physical educators should be knowledgeable about learning standards, how to assess them, and how they contribute to program development. Mastering fundamental movements and skills and integrating them into games and activities are processes.

It has been recommended that preschool-aged children accumulate at least 60 minutes of structured physical activity and at least 60 minutes of unstructured physical activity per day, and should not be sedentary for more than 60 minutes except when sleeping (NASPE, 2009). The National Association for the Education of Young Children (NAEYC, 2009) also suggests that playing time (including large motor activities) can benefit young children in physical competence, social skills, self-control, and problem-solving abilities, as well as give them an opportunity to practice emerging skills.

Activity environments designed to provide instruction for young children with developmental delays and disabilities should be individualized according to assessment information. Arbitrarily selecting games and activities because they seem fun and the children appear to enjoy them is not necessarily in line with good practice. Specifically, learning environments should parallel the strengths and challenges identified during the assessment process and written in the IEP as instructional objectives. Instruction is based on a good understanding of each child's present level of performance. An activity setting should be carefully planned to build on what children already know and promote the acquisition of new skills.

Developmental theorists support instruction that encourages children to explore and manipulate their environment in order to construct meaning (Lefrancois, 2006). Individualizing instruction for each child is the challenge faced by teachers providing early childhood adapted physical education in an inclusive setting. Although using a differentiated instructional approach helps teachers address the diverse learning needs of several children in the same class (Sands & Barker, 2004), UDL addresses the learning needs of *all* children. Nonetheless, the child's developmental abilities (physical, social, and cognitive) and the effect that a certain disability might have on development must be considered.

Developmental Differences Between Preschoolers and Primary-Aged Children

As children develop cognitively and socially, they incorporate their movement strategies in new ways. As a result, the cognitive and social developmental status of a four-year-old differs from that of a six-year-old. Teachers providing adapted physical education must understand these age-related developmental differences in order to construct appropriate learning environments for children who exhibit delays in one or more areas of learning (Haywood & Getchell, 2014).

Developmentally appropriate movement environments designed for preschool-aged children (ages 3-5) differ from those planned for kindergarten and elementary school children (ages 6-8). A watered-down kindergarten curriculum presented to children in preschool is not appropriate. Games, activities, and equipment meaningful to a four-year-old might be of little interest to a seven-year-old and vice versa. Preschoolers love to experiment with speed, direction change, and space, and they are intrigued by new spaces and the opportunity to explore these seemingly simple environments. For example, a refrigerator box with holes cut for climbing and hiding might entice a preschooler to explore and move for a long time. With a little creativity and imagination, teachers of early childhood physical education can create stimulating and motivating learning environments (see figure 22.1). On the other hand, a seven-year-old might find these activities simplistic and boring. She would be much more interested and challenged by moving under and through a parachute lifted by classmates (an activity that might be frightening and unpredictable for a three- or four-year-old). Children at this age have greater ability to reason and logically integrate thoughts than younger children do and might be challenged by activities that encourage a higher level of problem solving.

The NAEYC (2009) provides guidelines for developmentally appropriate practice in early childhood and discusses the differences between preschool and primary-aged children in their physical, social, cognitive, and language development.

FIGURE 22.1 A young boy makes his way through a tunnel, a familiar play space for preschoolers.

Teachers providing adapted physical education should keep in mind that the cognitive and social development of young children cannot be ignored when developing goals and objectives in the psychomotor domain. The interplay between each of these functional areas of learning and an individual child's development within each area must be considered when planning movement environments and instruction.

Developmental Considerations for Young Children With Disabilities

The effect of a child's disability on communication, social, cognitive, or motor learning and performance is essential for the development of an appropriate physical education program. Young children with orthopedic impairments, for example, might begin independently exploring their physical environments by using a walker, wheelchair, or crutches but might also require accommodations in order to benefit from age-appropriate activities. Instructors should be aware of physical barriers that exist in the activity setting and design the environment in a way that encourages interactions with peers and equipment (see figure 22.2). Assistive devices that allow children with orthopedic impairments to initiate tasks that are both physically and intellectually challenging should be available to promote independence. Instructors can accomplish this goal by modifying physical and social environments with the principles of UDL in mind (Conn-Powers et al., 2006). For example, attention to the physical layout of space (e.g., wide pathways) will promote safety and access to equipment and peers (Mistrett, 2017).

Young children with delays in social interaction—for example, children with autism spectrum disorder (ASD)—may require modifications in the introduction and delivery of games and activities. Group activities may be difficult for children with ASD, and practicing motor skills might need to occur in social environments that offer options for solitary and parallel play. For young children with ASD, interaction with others might not be the best instructional approach or least restrictive environment for learning new skills. On the other hand, children with intellectual disabilities often benefit from age-appropriate peer interactions that are consistent and repetitive. As shown in figure 22.3, a predictable environment with familiar equipment

Realistic Reflections/Getty Images

FIGURE 22.2 Children of all abilities should be encouraged to interact.

Photo courtesy of NIU. Photographer: Molly Coleman.

FIGURE 22.3 Familiar environments promote learning among children with disabilities.

and routines will enhance opportunities for learning. Physical educators need to be aware of the characteristics of young children with disabilities and plan activities and environments accordingly.

Facilitating Communication in a Movement Lesson

Interacting with others requires some level of communication. Some young children with disabilities use speech and language to communicate, whereas those who are nonverbal might use alternative methods and strategies. Not only is speech or language impairment considered the most prevalent disability category among preschoolers, children with a variety of diagnoses might also have differing communication needs (U.S. Department of Education, 2013). The movement setting, typically motivating for young children, can be an ideal environment to enhance communication skills. Collaboration with classroom teachers and speech therapists assists the early childhood physical educator in determining what communication goals and objectives can be integrated within the physical education setting.

The movement setting is a natural place to incorporate concepts such as *under, over, more, through,* and *around*. To reinforce the meaning of movement concepts and model the use of speech, a physical educator should talk with children as they participate in each movement lesson. For example, as children are pretending to be in the jungle climbing over rocks (bolsters under mats) and jumping over cutout ants and snakes (taped to the floor), a teacher might say, "I like the way everyone is jumping *over* the creatures in the jungle. Everyone find a creature and say 'over' as we jump. Ready?" Prompting children to use the words to identify the concept (e.g., over) as they practice the skill (e.g., horizontal jump) reinforces the meaning of commonly taught concepts in early childhood and encourages children to use speech. Similarly, identifying shapes, colors, or equipment can become a natural part of an early childhood movement setting.

Children with speech and language delays or those who are nonverbal as a result of a disability might use augmentative and alternative systems to communicate (Millar et al., 2006). Sign language is a popular method of communicating with young children of all abilities; however, children with communication delays and those who are hard of hearing might benefit in particular. Physical educators not proficient in sign language should consult with classroom teachers, interpreters, or speech therapists to learn the signs used by young children in the classroom.

Picture systems can also be used to increase communication among a nonverbal child, his peers, and the teacher. Young children with autism often have sophisticated picture systems in place to assist with identifying activities, equipment, directions, and transitions. Helping a child with communication delays understand what to do and when to do it increases the opportunity to engage in movement activities to the maximum extent possible and often decreases the time spent managing unwanted behaviors. Pictures posted in the activity area or taped to pieces of equipment can also be a great communication strategy for all children, verbal or nonverbal. A visual schedule (sequence of pictures) is a functional method for communicating an activity, skill sequence, or transition that helps children manage their environment while often decreasing the amount of adult intervention needed. Figure 22.4 shows an example of a young boy removing a picture of a completed activity from his schedule. The pictures remaining on the schedule give him a clear indication of activities to follow. Depending on the learning style of the child, all pictures can be on the board at the beginning of the class, or pictures can be added as the activity is presented.

Voice output devices are another method used to communicate with children who are nonverbal. A voice output system makes use of pictures and symbols along with prerecorded words and phrases

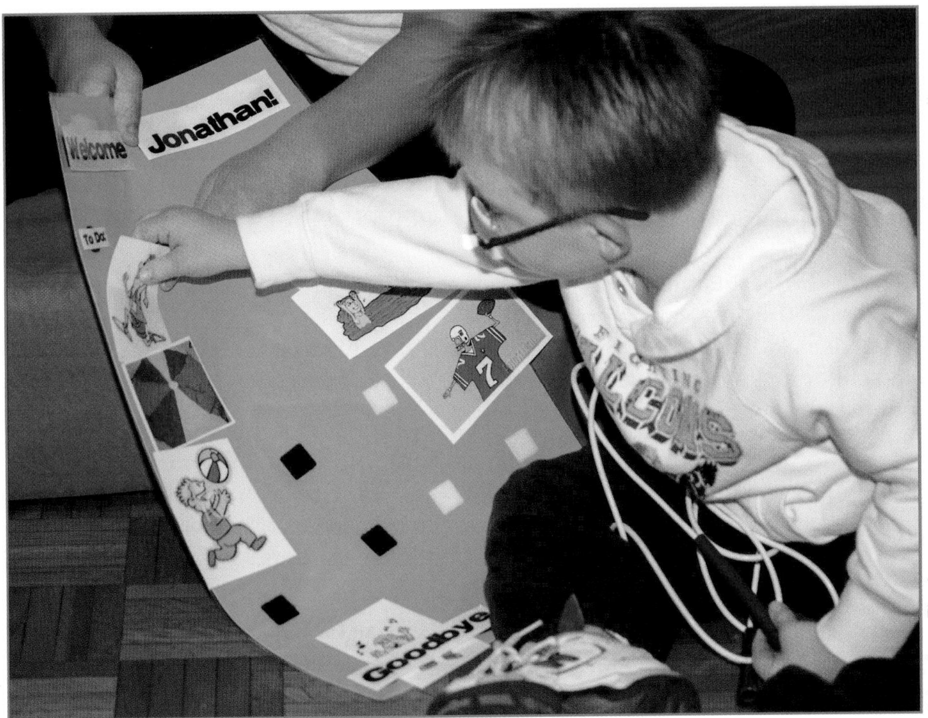

© Lauriece Zittel

FIGURE 22.4 Visual schedules help children manage their environments.

(Blischak et al., 2003). Programming movement concepts, names of equipment or activities, and general statements allows for functional communication during physical education. For young children, a movement setting might provide an opportunity to reinforce practice with a new voice output device.

Planning for Instruction

A curriculum, including assessment and instruction, should be designed according to what is known about how children learn (NAEYC, 2009). Intentional teaching strategies and supportive learning environments for all children will facilitate daily curriculum goals (Mistrett, 2017). Importantly, the physical education curriculum for young children with disabilities or developmental delays must be balanced to be both age and individually appropriate. The three Cs of curriculum design—content, construction, and contact (Wessel & Zittel, 1995, 1998)—can serve as a guide for adapted physical education teachers working toward attaining this balance.

First, the skills selected as instructional **content** must be considered. The instructional focus of a preschool physical education program might include community-based, neighborhood activities such as riding a tricycle or pulling a wagon, whereas it might be appropriate to teach primary-aged children how to jump rope. The selection of age-appropriate content depends on how well the teacher has examined assessment information and understands the developmental differences between children of the same or similar chronological age.

Second, **construction** of a teaching environment must be carefully planned. Because they differ developmentally, how the teacher of adapted physical education constructs the physical environment and introduces activities will differ for preschool and primary-aged children. Physical environments should be designed to promote interactions for the purpose of skill development. The organization of the physical environment, as well as how and when activities are introduced, must be considered.

Finally, a critical consideration in planning for instruction is adopting strategies that maximize the **contact** a young child has with equipment and peers versus with teachers. Regardless of developmental level, young children must be given the opportunity to explore their physical environment in order to develop impressions about their world. Young children with disabilities or developmental delays might require additional prompting during exploration so they are not denied opportunities to interact with equipment and peers. Instructors working with young children have the primary responsibility of promoting interactions within the movement environment as an alternative to direct instruction.

Organization of the curriculum may vary from program to program. Teachers of early childhood adapted physical education might choose to set up an instructional unit to focus on a certain fundamental skill area at a certain time of the year or to introduce skills in a particular sequence. For example, a specialist might design a unit that targets locomotor skills at the beginning of the school year, with all games and activities during that unit focused on the ongoing teaching and assessment of skills such as hopping, jumping, and galloping. Other instructors might choose to organize instructional material around themes, which may be used in collaboration with classroom teachers and their instructional concepts. For example, a physical education day at the zoo or circus provides children with the opportunity to practice fundamental and motor fitness skills while interacting within a familiar theme. The curricular vehicle used to organize instruction (units or themes) often depends on the instructor's style of teaching and comfort level with this age group. Regardless of the organization used, a primary goal in designing the movement environments should be to minimize sedentary behavior. The number of skill objectives taught and the time needed to learn each objective depend on the severity of the child's delay. However, what should never be compromised in any early childhood program is developmentally appropriate design and instruction.

Developmentally Appropriate Teaching Approaches

The following sections discuss developmentally appropriate teaching approaches for planning and delivering adapted physical education programs for preschool and primary-aged children. Attention to the principles of UDL will accommodate all learners in these settings.

Preschool-Aged Children

Preschool classrooms typically include 12 to 18 children with one teacher and an assistant. Classrooms for young children with severe developmental delays and disabilities often have fewer students.

One challenge in providing instruction for this age group is that many preschool programs have multiage classrooms, meaning that children aged 3 to 5 are taught in the same class. As stated earlier in this chapter, planning instruction requires teachers to consider early learning standards, assessment results, and the developmental status of each child in the class, regardless of chronological age or how a disability might affect development. Although ages and abilities might differ for children in the same class, the approach to intervention should remain similar for this age group.

Developmentally appropriate practice in preschool physical education emphasizes the role of the teacher as guide or facilitator. Teachers structure the environment with objectives in mind—for example, throwing and kicking—and guide students toward these movement objectives. Environments are adapted to allow for several choices to meet learning objectives and for maximum active participation (Mithaug & Mithaug, 2003). This child-directed style of teaching differs from the teacher-directed style of instruction in which the instructor focuses on one task at a time and students move as a group from one activity to the next on the teacher's signal. It would be developmentally inappropriate to expect preschool children to respond to a teacher-directed format.

One example of a child-directed approach to early childhood education is activity-based intervention (ABI) (Pretti-Frontczak et al., 2003). Activity-based intervention is designed to embed each child's IEP goals and objectives within activities that are naturally motivating to young children. Teachers can design activity areas that are motivating for children and that encourage skill practice within the environment (see the Application Example sidebar). Young children with disabilities or developmental delays benefit from structured movement environments that incorporate the following principles:

- Child-directed versus teacher-directed learning
- Opportunity for choice
- Self-initiated exploration
- Experience with novel and familiar equipment
- Exposure to peer models

The following scenario highlights how these principles of best practice can be seen within one preschool physical education setting.

Emma and her classmates are on their way to physical education class, where they will soon discover that today is an adventure with wheeled toys.

Application Example

How to Ensure a Child-Directed, Teacher-Facilitated Lesson

SETTING

Early childhood physical education classroom

STUDENTS

Children ages 3 to 5, some with developmental delays

ISSUE

What environmental construction would be appropriate to ensure child-directed learning?

APPLICATION

The teacher has selected the following content objectives: body and space awareness (under, over, through) and jumping down. The learning environment should contain multiple opportunities to practice these objectives. Children will choose equipment, and teachers will facilitate learning by providing verbal prompts, demonstrations, physical assistance, or redirection. The goal is to minimize teacher interaction and maximize each child's activity level and interaction with peers and equipment. The following equipment will prompt child-directed activity:

- Tunnels, cardboard boxes, and archways with scarves attached will prompt movement through and under.
- Bolsters covered with mats will prompt climbing over.
- Various platforms or steps with pictures of letters, numbers, smiley faces, or bugs will prompt stepping up and jumping down.

As they enter the activity area, they see tricycles, wagons, scooters, and other ride-on toys scattered throughout the area. They also notice that jump ropes have been laid down to create pathways, cardboard trees have been spaced throughout the activity area, and arches held up with orange cones have been scattered around as obstacles to move under and through. As Mr. Sanchez welcomes the children into the activity environment, he announces, "Let's take a ride through the park today."

As the children scurry into the activity area to select their mode of transportation, Mr. Sanchez takes notice of Emma. He knows that Emma has autism, and from reviewing her IEP he is aware that she has a gross motor objective focused on pulling an object around obstacles, a social skill objective focused on initiating social interactions, and a communication objective focused on making verbal requests. He notices that Emma gets on a ride-on toy and begins to maneuver through the park. As Emma crosses the room, she slows down to take notice of a teddy bear sitting in a wagon. Emma knows that she has been given a ride in a wagon before and decides that she will give the teddy bear a ride.

Mr. Sanchez sees that Emma has directed her attention toward the wagon. Knowing that pulling an object is one of her objectives, he begins to interact with Emma, telling her how nice it is that she is giving the teddy bear a ride. Emma continues to pull her wagon through the pathways and around the cardboard trees. Mr. Sanchez is able to promote communication (another of Emma's IEP objectives) by suggesting that Emma ask Misha, a classmate, if she would like to go for a ride. Once Misha is in the wagon, Mr. Sanchez suggests that Emma ask Misha where she would like to go. In this manner, Mr. Sanchez is facilitating work on Emma's IEP objective of initiating social interactions. Misha's request will encourage Emma to move through her physical environment, encountering various obstacles in the park as well as other children moving with wheeled toys.

A structured movement environment should allow children to direct the process through which they manipulate the physical environment. **Child-directed learning** is not synonymous with free play. Teachers of preschool adapted physical education are responsible for designing environments that motivate children to practice skills outlined in their individualized plans. Interaction with equipment and practice on IEP objectives will be far more likely and children will persist with the task much longer if they initiate the interaction themselves. The teacher then becomes a facilitator within the movement environment, following the child's lead and promoting challenges based on the choices the child has made.

The intensity with which children practice a skill or explore a new task depends on how interested they are in the task itself. The fact that Emma recognized the teddy bear sitting in the wagon and related that to her previous experiences was enough to interest her in the task and encourage further exploration. Mr. Sanchez was able to accommodate the interests and abilities of all the children in his class by using multiple pieces of equipment and structuring his activity environment around one theme. This activity design gives children the opportunity to view peer models and initiate social interactions. For example, Mr. Sanchez may now prompt Erik to follow Emma while riding his tricycle.

Primary-Aged Children

Primary school classes, including kindergarten through third grade, typically vary in size in accordance with school policies. One approach in primary education is multiage class groupings, which may include kindergarten and first-grade students in the same classroom. Designing developmentally appropriate instruction for this age group can follow only if a good assessment of individual abilities has been completed. As children grow and mature physically, discrepancies in movement abilities among children in the same age range may become more evident. However, primary-age children with disabilities or developmental delays will have an interest in participating in the same physical activities as their same-age, typically developing counterparts.

Planning instructional content for this age group should focus on fundamental movement skills (locomotion, object control) and perceptual–motor skills (body awareness, spatial relationships) and build on the rudimentary skills learned in preschool. For some children this means refining skills, and for others it will be a time to begin to integrate fundamental skills into organized games and activities. Integrating fitness concepts within the curriculum also becomes important. Regardless of the curricular focus, it is critical that children learn to move and enjoy movement at this age in order to increase the possibility that they will continue to be physically active as they mature. Following the guidelines and grade-level expectations set forth in the national standards for physical education

(SHAPE America, 2014) will provide teachers with the content that they need to develop an age-appropriate program.

Instructional settings for primary-aged students of differing abilities should combine movement exploration and guided discovery techniques with specific skill practice. With an **exploration** style of teaching, the teacher selects the instructional materials to be used and designates the area to be explored (Pangrazi & Beighle, 2010). Rather than having the environment already set up with embedded goals and objectives, students choose a piece of equipment and figure out ways to interact with the equipment. Teachers might offer directives such as, "Get a hoop and see how many ways you can make it spin." This teaching style takes advantage of children's desire to move and explore. It emphasizes self-discovery, which is a necessary part of learning, and allows children to note variations in movement forms and equipment usage. However, when using this teaching style, the instructor should avoid praising students for their creative movements too quickly because this might lead to imitative or noncreative behavior (Pangrazi & Beighle, 2010).

Guided discovery is used when there is a predetermined choice or result that the teacher wants students to discover (Pangrazi & Beighle, 2010). With this approach to teaching, students are presented with many methods to perform a task and then asked to choose the method that seems to be most efficient or that works best. Students with disabilities might find that their movement choice differs from what typically developing peers choose. This discovery reinforces the idea that just because a movement form is different does not mean it is incorrect.

Children should also have the opportunity to use fundamental skills in low-organization games. Equipment and instruction should be modified, if necessary, to accommodate the physical, sensory, behavioral, and cognitive abilities of each child in the class, and the environment should be organized to accommodate a variety of learning styles. This follows the tenets of universal design for learning, which include multiple means of engagement (various ways to engage student interest), multiple means of representation (various ways to acquire information), and multiple means of expression (various ways to demonstrate learning) (Lieberman et al., 2021).

Designing developmentally appropriate adapted physical education for primary students using these principles might include the following:

- Using different teaching styles to individualize instruction for the variety of learning styles (visual, auditory) present in one classroom
- Providing varied equipment (e.g., different-sized rackets) to allow for student choice
- Having rule flexibility in tasks to encourage creativity and problem solving
- Varying classroom designs (activity stations, small group, large group)
- Providing opportunities for peer observation and interaction

The following scenario provides an example of how UDL may be used to accommodate children in a first-grade classroom.

Louis is selected as the line leader by his classmates as they prepare to leave for physical education. Ms. Brooks greets the children outside of their classroom and walks with them to the gym. As they walk together, Ms. Brooks explains to the children that they will continue working on striking activities today. Once inside the gym, the children see a familiar sight. Ms. Brooks has set up five activity stations, each with a different task to complete. Ms. Brooks asks the children, "What do we use for striking?"

"We strike with bats," says Claire.

"We can use Styrofoam rackets," yells Mia.

"I like the hockey sticks," exclaims Jose.

Ms. Brooks explains that everyone will have an opportunity to use all of the implements today as they spend time at each activity station. She informs the children that they will select an implement out of the station bin and practice at one station until they hear the sound of the drum. At that time they will put their implements back into the bin and follow the floor arrows to the next station, select their new implement, and begin the next task.

Ms. Brooks has asked Louis to begin at the racket and balloon station. As Ms. Brooks designates other stations for children in the class, Louis turns to Sammy and whispers, "That's my favorite!" Louis has spina bifida and uses braces on his legs. He ambulates slowly but is proud of the fact that over the summer months before first grade began, he stopped using his walker for most activities. Ms. Brooks is familiar with Louis' IEP and has written his gross motor objectives. In addition to increasing his static and dynamic balance, striking is a focus for Louis. The activities that Louis will participate in today are functional for him. He will work on striking, just like the rest of his classmates, but this activity will also address his balance goals as he swings different implements and moves among stations.

Ms. Brooks has constructed enough activity stations to give this class of 28 children the opportunity to explore various movements with various striking implements. The equipment used to accomplish the skill objective in a few of the stations has been changed (e.g., some stations have rackets, whereas others have bats), but for the most part the students are familiar with the activity structure and have been practicing their striking for several classes now. This activity environment allows Ms. Brooks to individualize instruction, provide specific skill feedback, and modify equipment and tasks to accommodate the learning abilities of all the children in the class.

In Ms. Brooks' next first-grade class, she will see Micah. He has a severe intellectual disability, and Ms. Brooks will use a location–station approach for him. This means that she will use the same environmental structure to practice striking, but when the drum sounds for the rest of the class to rotate stations, Micah will remain in the same balloon-striking station, and his peer tutor will assist him in selecting another implement to strike the balloon. All of this has been planned by Ms. Brooks because she is familiar with her students and their ability levels.

For now, she admires Louis' stability as she watches him swing the racket to hit the suspended balloon to his classmate Bryce. As Bryce tracks the balloon and gets ready to hit it back, he exclaims, "Here it comes, Louis!"

Activities

Developmentally appropriate activities for preschool and primary-aged students are those selected, designed, sequenced, and modified to maximize learning and active participation. Fundamental motor skills and patterns form the basis for higher-level movement sequences and skills and should thus be emphasized in early childhood motor programs. Activities that promote body awareness, perceptual motor skills, communication, and academic abilities should also be incorporated into the program. Using the strategies presented in this chapter, physical educators can select games and activities to meet IEP goals and objectives that are both age and developmentally appropriate, presented in a way that fosters child-directed interactions, and maintains appropriate levels of physical activity.

Summary

Although physical educators might have experience working with older students with developmental delays or disabilities, the increase in early childhood motor programs has brought new challenges to physical educators. Children as young as three years old might be included in adapted physical education programs designed to meet their unique needs. This chapter has provided information to assist teachers of early childhood adapted physical education by suggesting strategies and tools necessary for the development of appropriate goals, objectives, and activities for young children with unique physical education needs, including information related to assessment, program planning, and program implementation. With an understanding of what constitutes developmentally appropriate intervention, teachers of adapted physical education should be able to challenge and reinforce children's motor learning and physical activity so they can experience success and enjoy movement.

References

Assistance to States for the Education of Children with Disabilities. 34 C.F.R. 300.530 (2006).

Bagnato, S.J., Deborah, D.G., Pretti-Frontczak, K., & Neisworth, J.T. (2014). Authentic assessment as "best practice" for early childhood intervention: National consumer social validity research. *Topics in Early Childhood Special Education*, 34(2), 116-127. https://doi.org/10.1177/0271121414523652

Bailey, A. (2017). Building quality early childhood assessment: What really matters? The University of Minnesota Digital Conservancy. http://hdl.handle.net/11299/191401

Blischak, D., Lombardino L., & Dyson A. (2003). Use of speech-generating devices: In support of natural speech. *Augmentative and Alternative Communication, 19,* 29-35. https:/doi.org/10.1080/0743461032000056478

Bornstein, D.B., Beets, M.W., Byun, W., & Mclver, K. (2011). Accelerometer-derived physical activity levels of preschoolers: A meta-analysis. *Journal of Science and Medicine in Sport, 14*(6), 504-511. https://doi.org/10.1016/j.jsams.2011.05.007

Bricker, D., Capt, B., & Pretti-Frontczak, K. (Eds.). (2002). *AEPS test for birth to three years and three to six years.* Brookes.

Brigance, A. (2013). *Brigance diagnostic inventory of early development III.* Curriculum Associates.

Brown, W.H., Pfeiffer, K.A., McIver, K.L., Dowda, M., Almeida, M.J.C.A., & Pate, R.R. (2006). Assessing preschool children's physical activity: The observational system for recording physical activity in children—preschool version. *Research Quarterly for Exercise and Sport, 77*(2), 167-176. https://doi.org/10.1080/02701367.2006.10599351

Cardon, G., & De Bourdeaudhuij, I. (2007). Comparison of pedometer and accelerometer measures of physical activity in preschool children. *Pediatric Exercise Science, 19*(2), 205-214. https://doi.org/10.1123/pes.19.2.205

Conn-Powers, M., Cross, A., Traub, E., & Hutter-Pishgahi, L. (2006). The universal design of early education: Moving forward for all children [PDF]. *Beyond the Journal.* The National Association for the Education of Young Children. https://fpg.unc.edu/sites/fpg.unc.edu/les/resources/presentations-and-webinars/Conn-PowersBTJ%281%29.pdf

De Craemer, M., De Decker, E., Santos-Lozano, A., Verloigne, M., De Bourdeaudhuij, I., Deforche, B., & Cardon, G. (2015). Validity of the Omron pedometer and the actigraph step count function in preschoolers. *Journal of Science and Medicine in Sport, 18*(3), 289-293. https://doi.org/10.1016/j.jsams.2014.06.001

Dobell, A., Eyre, E.L.J., Tallis J., Chinapaw, M.J.M., Altenburg, T.M., & Duncan, M.J. (2019). Examining accelerometer validity for estimating physical activity in pre-schoolers during free-living activity. *Scandinavian Journal of Medicine & Science in Sports, 29*(10), 1618-1628. https://doi.org/10.1111/sms.13496

Folio, M.R., & Fewell, R. (2000). *Peabody developmental motor scales-2.* Pro-Ed.

Haywood, K.M., & Getchell, N. (2014). *Life span motor development* (6th ed.). Human Kinetics.

Individuals with Disabilities Education Act Amendments of 2004 (IDEA), PL 108-446, 20 U.S.C. 1400 (2004).

Johnson-Martin, N., Hacker, B., & Attermeier, S. (2004). *The Carolina curriculum for preschoolers with special needs.* Brookes.

Lefrancois, G.R. (2006). *Theories of human learning.* Thomson Higher Education.

Lieberman, L., Greier, M., Brian, A., & Arndt, K. (2021). *Universal design for learning in physical education.* Human Kinetics.

Linder, T., & Linas, K. (2009). A functional, holistic approach to developmental assessment through play: The transdisciplinary play-based assessment, second edition. *Zero to Three, 30*(1), 28-33.

Lynch, E., & Struewing, N. (2001). Children in context: Portfolio assessment in the inclusive early childhood classroom. *Young Exceptional Children, 5*(1), 2-10. https://doi.org/10.1177/109625060100500101

McLean, M., Wolery, M., & Bailey, D. (2004). *Assessing infants, toddlers and preschoolers with special needs.* Pearson, Merrill, Prentice Hall.

Millar, D.C., Light, J.C., & Schlosser, R.W. (2006). The impact of augmentative and alternative communication intervention on the speech production of individuals with developmental disabilities: A research review. *Journal of Speech, Language, and Hearing Research, 49,* 248-264. https://doi.org/10.1044/1092-4388(2006/021)

Mistrett, S.G. (2017). *Universal design for learning: A checklist for early childhood environments.* Center on Technology and Disability. www.ctdinstitute.org/sites/default/files/file_attachments/UDL-Checklist-EC.pdf

Mithaug, D.K., & Mithaug, D.E. (2003). Effects of teacher-directed versus student-directed instruction of self-management of young children with disabilities. *Journal of Applied Behavior Analysis, 36,* 133-136. https://doi.org/10.1901/jaba.2003.36-133

National Association for the Education of Young Children (NAEYC). (2009). *Developmentally appropriate practice in early childhood programs serving children from birth through age 8: Position statement.* www.naeyc.org/positionstatements.

National Association for Sport and Physical Education (NASPE). (2009). *Active start: A statement of physical activity guidelines for children from birth to age 5* (2nd ed.). American Alliance for Health, Physical Education, Recreation, and Dance.

National Institute for Early Education Research (NIEER). (2014). *The state of preschool 2014: State preschool yearbook.* http://nieer.org/sites/nieer/files/Yearbook2014_full3.pdf

Odom, S.L., & Wolery, M. (2003). A unified theory of practice in early intervention/early childhood special education: Evidence-based practice. *Journal of Special Education, 37,* 164-173.

Pangrazi, R.P., & Beighle, A. (2010). *Dynamic physical education for elementary school children* (16th ed.). Pearson Higher Education.

Park, C., Kim, S.-Y., Zittel, L.L., & Looney, M. (2017). Validity and reliability evidence of the physical activity level screening (PALS) for preschoolers with developmental delay and/or a disability. *Journal of Exercise Rehabilitation, 13*(2), 210-213. https://doi.org/10.12965/jer.1732888.444

Pate, R.R., O'Neill, J.R., & Mitchell, J. (2010). Measurement of physical activity in preschool children. *Medicine and Science in Sports and Exercise, 42*(3), 508-512. https://doi.org/10.1249/MSS.0b013e3181cea116

Pretti-Frontczak, K.L., Barr, D.M., Macy, M., & Carter, A. (2003). Research and resources related to activity-based intervention, embedded learning opportunities, and routines-based instruction: An annotated bibliography. *Topics in Early Childhood Special Education, 23,* 29-39. https://doi.org/10.1177/027112140302300104

Ridgers, N.D., Stratton, G., & McKenzie, T.L. (2010). Reliability and validity of the system for observing children's activity and relationships during play (SOCARP). *Journal of Physical Activity & Health, 7,* 17-25. https://doi.org/10.1123/jpah.7.1.17

Robinson, L.E., & Wadsworth, D.D. (2010). Stepping toward physical activity requirements: Integrating pedometers into early childhood settings. *Early Childhood Education Journal, 38,* 95-102. https://doi.org/10.1007/s10643-010-0388-y

Sands, D.I., & Barker, H.B. (2004). Organized chaos: Modeling differentiated instruction for preservice teachers. *Teaching and Learning, 19,* 26-49.

SHAPE America. (2014). *National standards & grade-level outcomes for K-12 physical education.* Human Kinetics.

SHAPE America. (2019). *PE Metrics: Assessing student performance using the national standards and grade-level outcomes for K-12 physical education (3rd edition).* Author.

Ulrich, D.A. (2019). *Test of motor development* (3rd ed.). Pro-Ed.

U.S. Department of Education. (2013). *Thirty-fifth annual report to Congress on the implementation of the Individuals with Disabilities Education Act.* Author.

Wessel, J.A., & Zittel, L.L. (1995). *Smart start: Preschool movement curriculum designed for children of all abilities.* Pro-Ed.

Wessel, J.A., & Zittel, L.L. (1998). *I CAN primary skills: K-3.* Pro-Ed.

Williams, H., & Monsma, E.V. (2006). Assessment of gross motor development. In B.A. Bracken & R.J. Nagle (Eds), *Psychoeducational assessment of preschool children* (4th ed., pp. 397-433). Lawrence Erlbaum.

Print Resources

Bricker, D., & Waddell, M. (2002). *AEPS curriculum for three to six years.* Brookes.

Activities in this curriculum correspond with goals and objectives in the AEPS test.

Clements, R.L., & Schneider, S.L. (2005). Excerpts from movement-based learning: Academic concepts and physical activity for ages three through eight. *Strategies, 19,* 31-32.

Practical ready-to-use activities are presented for those teaching in childcare or school settings. Accommodations for children with disabilities are highlighted.

Cowden, J.E., & Torrey, C.C. (2007). *Motor development and movement activities for preschoolers and infants with delays: A multisensory approach for professionals and families.* Charles C Thomas.

Principles of motor development theory are linked to practical intervention for parents, caregivers, and teachers. The impact of specific disabilities or delays is outlined.

Cunconan-Lahr, R.L., & Stifel, S. (2007). *Building inclusive child care project (BICC).* Northampton Community College. www.miracosta.edu/instruction/childdevelopmentcenter/downloads/5.6UDLforPreschoolEnvironments.pdf

These questions and checklists can assist early childhood specialists in completing environmental observations to determine if universally designed learning practices are in place.

Landy, J., & Burridge, K. (2000). *Motor skills and movement station lesson plans for young children.* Center for Applied Research in Education.

This is a program for teachers, professionals, and parents teaching fundamental motor skills to children who have coordination difficulties.

Linder, T. (1999). *Storybook activities for young children: Read, play, and learn.* Brookes.

This play-based, storybook-oriented curriculum allows teachers to incorporate skills in all domains of learning while providing a motivating experience for the young learner.

Linder, T. (2008). *Transdisciplinary play-based intervention.* Brookes.

This resource offers play-based interventions for children across all domains and help for generalizing skills to new situations and settings.

McCall, R., & Craft, D. (2000). *Moving with a purpose: Developing programs for preschoolers of all abilities.* Human Kinetics.

This resource provides information to teachers responsible for structuring movement programs for preschool children, including games and activities. A section is also devoted to children with special needs.

National Association for Sport and Physical Education (NASPE). (2009). *Active start: A statement of guidelines for children birth to age 5* (2nd ed.). American Alliance for Health, Physical Education, Recreation, and Dance.

This book provides physical activity recommendations for children birth to 5 years old. It is written as a guide for teachers, caregivers, and parents.

National Association for Sport and Physical Education (NASPE). (2002). *Physical activity for children: A statement of guidelines for children ages 5-12* (2nd ed.). American Alliance for Health, Physical Education, Recreation, and Dance

These guidelines provide information regarding the amount and type of physical activity recommended for children ages 5 to 12. Concepts regarding appropriate physical activity and models of service delivery are presented.

Winders, P. (1997). *Gross motor skills in children with Down syndrome.* Woodbine House.

This resource addresses the physical development of children with Down syndrome and suggests guidelines for promoting gross motor development. Activities and strategies are provided.

Online Resources

Best Autism Apps for kids on iPad, iPhone and Android in 2020: www.autismparentingmagazine.com/best-autism-apps

This article highlights mobile apps to make communication more accessible and cost-effective.

Boardmaker: https://goboardmaker.com

Boardmaker is an online resource used to create symbol-based communication and educational materials.

National Association for the Education of Young Children: www.naeyc.org

This website serves as the primary site for resources and best practices for the education of young children.

Part IV

Activities for Individuals With Unique Needs

Part IV includes chapters on physical fitness (chapter 23), aquatics (chapter 24), team sports (chapter 25), individual and dual sports and activities (chapter 26), adventure sports and activities (chapter 27), winter sports and activities (chapter 28), and the enhancement of wheelchair sport performance (chapter 29). Although the content of each chapter is influenced by the nature of the activities discussed, there are several common threads. To the extent relevant and appropriate, the chapters identify skills, lead-up activities, modifications, and variations associated with each activity. In many instances, these include modifications and variations used in established sport programs. Some chapters provide information on sports organizations. All chapters provide helpful information for enhancing learning and performance in a variety of inclusive settings. Chapter 29 recognizes the importance of the use of wheelchairs in physical education and sport and recommends ways to enhance performance for wheelchair users.

Part IV applies much of the information presented earlier in the book to physical education and sport content, with a focus on how program content is adapted or modified to meet unique needs. It serves as a great resource to service providers because it provides answers on how activities can be modified to help individuals with unique needs to be active, be physically educated, and work toward self-actualization.

23

Health-Related Physical Fitness and Physical Activity

Stamatis Agiovlasitis

Mr. Barnett, a social studies teacher, and Ms. Novak, a physical education teacher, were in the teachers' lounge.

"What are you working on?" Mr. Barnett asked.

"I'm just planning some fitness activities for my third-period class."

"Isn't that the class with the students who use wheelchairs? How are they doing? Are the athletes in the class treating them okay?"

"Well," said Ms. Novak with a smile, "some of my students who use wheelchairs *are* athletes, but what I do in my class is more health related than sport related."

"Health related? Is that really necessary? I mean, I haven't heard of too many junior high school students dying of heart attacks lately."

"Well, that's right, but good fitness and physical activity habits should be established early, and besides, health-related fitness, especially for kids with disabilities, is not just about reducing the risk of disease. Having good health-related fitness also means having the independence to perform important day-to-day skills, like pushing a wheelchair uphill or even getting dressed. In fact, fitness might be more important for students with disabilities than it is for students without disabilities."

This chapter is largely based on a previous version authored by Francis X. Short in the sixth edition of this book. The present author and the editors would like to thank Francis Short for his contributions.

Physical fitness has long been viewed as a vehicle for improving both sport performance and health. From the ancient Greeks to the modern athlete, people have used physical activity to enhance their fitness and improve their athletic prowess. The relationships among activity levels, fitness development, and improved sport performance are often obvious, and sometimes dramatic. The relationships among physical activity, physical fitness, and *health*, however, usually are less obvious; we cannot observe, for instance, the reduced risk of acquiring coronary heart disease, diabetes, or some forms of cancer associated with good levels of fitness. However, research data accumulated over the years clearly indicate that being physically active and getting fit improves health.

The relationships among physical activity, health-related physical fitness, and health are complex. Researchers have proposed several models for describing this complexity. In the theoretical model shown in figure 23.1, each of these constructs (activity, fitness, and health) can influence and be influenced by each of the others (indicated by the double arrows). For example, higher physical activity can directly improve health, but someone with better health may have greater ability to increase physical activity levels than someone who is less healthy; a similar reciprocal relationship is shown between physical fitness and health. Apart from its direct effect, physical activity is also conceptualized as having an indirect impact on health through physical fitness; that is, increasing physical activity improves fitness, eventually leading to better health.

It is worth mentioning here that, due to its close relationship with health, physical fitness is often considered a health outcome (Physical Activity Guidelines [PAG] Advisory Committee, 2018). Physical activity, physical fitness, health, and their associations are also influenced by genetics, other personal attributes (e.g., sex, race, ethnicity, psychosocial profiles), and factors in the physical and social environment (e.g., accessibility, policy, attitudes toward disability) (Bouchard et al., 2012). Research data support the complexity of such models in adults and to a lesser extent in children (Rowland, 2012). Research data are also supportive of complex positive relationships between physical activity, fitness, and health in youth with disabilities (Johnson 2009; Lankhorst et al., 2019; O'Brien et al., 2016; Srinivasan et al., 2014), but more research is needed.

The relationships among physical fitness, physical activity, and health are explored further in this

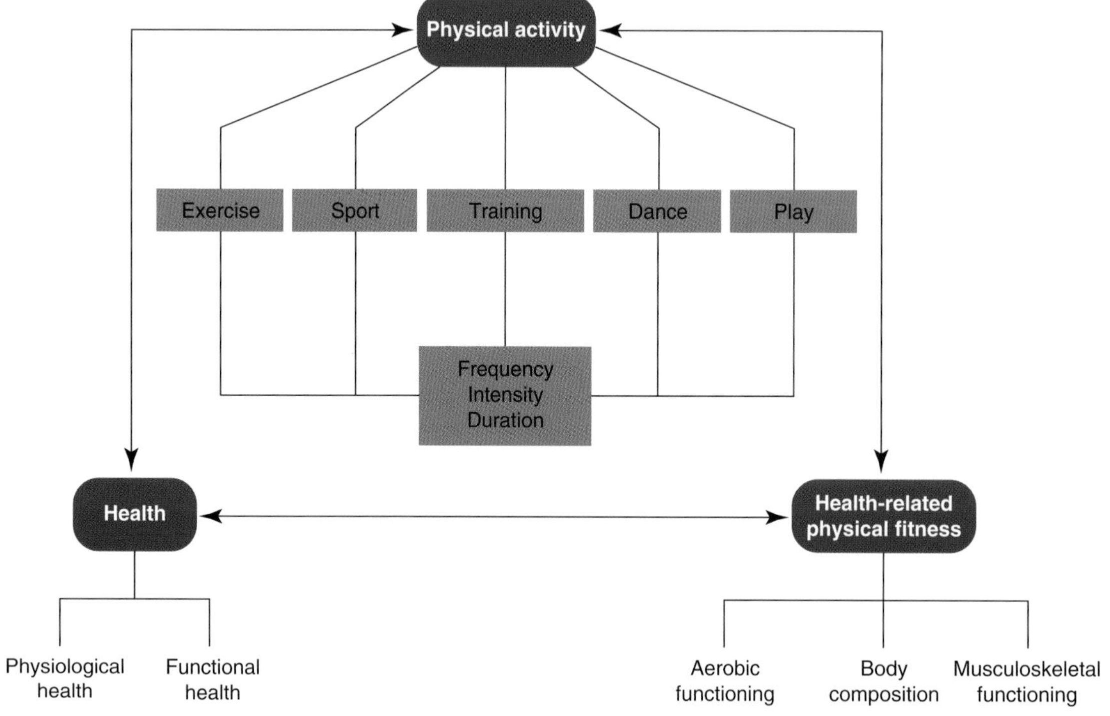

FIGURE 23.1 Relationships among physical activity, health-related physical fitness, and health.

Reprinted by permission from F.X. Short, J. McCubbin, and G. Frey, "Cardiorespiratory Endurance and Body Composition," in *The Brockport Physical Fitness Training Guide,* edited by J.P. Winnick and F.X. Short (Champaign, IL: Human Kinetics, 1999), 24.

chapter. Particular attention is paid to how physical activity can be used to promote health-related physical fitness, but readers should keep in mind that developing the skill-related components of fitness is also appropriate for students with disabilities and may be necessary to foster certain types of physical activity (e.g., sport). Although some examples of modifications for students with disabilities are provided, the chapter is written primarily from a noncategorical perspective—that is, most of the information is generic and not specific to any one category of disability. Disability-specific fitness information can be found in other chapters of this book.

Definitions of Health, Fitness, and Physical Activity

Health has been defined in many different ways, and the conceptualization of health is still evolving. In its constitution, the World Health Organization (WHO, 2006) defines health as "a state of complete physical, mental and social well-being and not merely the absence of disease or infirmity" (p. 1). However, this definition, originally developed in 1946, has been criticized because it describes an ideal condition not attainable by many people (Jambroes et al., 2015; Lancet Editorial, 2009). Kinesiology scholars have proposed variations of this definition, emphasizing that each dimension of health exists on a continuum. According to this viewpoint, health is "a human condition with physical, social, and psychological dimensions, each characterized on a continuum with positive and negative poles. Positive health is associated with a capacity to enjoy life and to withstand challenges; it is not merely the absence of disease. Negative health is associated with morbidity and, in the extreme, with premature mortality" (Bouchard & Shephard, 1994, p. 84). Winnick and Short (2014) suggested that in broad terms, health can be categorized by its physiological or functional aspects. **Physiological health** relates to the organic well-being of the person, including the absence of a disease or condition and low risk of developing a disease or condition. **Functional health** relates to physical capability, which includes the ability to perform important tasks independently and sustain the performance of those tasks (see figure 23.1).

Applying these definitions of health may suggest that individuals with disabilities do not have good health due to underlying impairments. Disability studies scholars, however, have argued that people with disabilities can still be healthy in the context of underlying impairments, and research findings support this notion (Albrecht & Devlieger, 1999; Drum et al., 2008). Some of the problems in defining health in people with disabilities can be overcome by emphasizing **wellness**, "a holistic concept, describing a state of positive health in the individual and comprising physical, social and psychological well-being" (Bouchard et al., 2012, p. 10). We may also consider a more recent definition of health as "a structural, functional and emotional state that is compatible with effective life as an individual and as a member of society" (McCartney et al., 2019, p. 28). Despite difficulties in defining health, it is important to note that, according to WHO (2006), "the enjoyment of the highest attainable standard of health is one of the fundamental rights of every human being" (p. 1).

It has been documented, however, that individuals with disabilities across the life span experience health disparities (Allerton et al., 2011; Krahn et al., 2015; Rimmer et al., 2007). **Health disparities** are "systematic, plausibly avoidable health differences adversely affecting socially disadvantaged groups" (Braveman et al., 2011, p. S151). Adapted physical educators can contribute to reducing the health disparities that youth with disabilities experience by delivering physical education programs geared towards improving aspects of health and physical fitness.

The U.S. Department of Health and Human Services (HHS, 1996) defined **physical fitness** as "the ability to carry out daily tasks with vigor and alertness, without undue fatigue, and with ample energy to enjoy leisure-time pursuits and to meet unforeseen emergencies" (p. 20). The components of physical fitness can be categorized as either health related or skill related. **Health-related physical fitness** refers to those components of fitness that are associated with health. Most experts agree that these components include aerobic functioning, body composition, muscular endurance, muscular strength, and flexibility (the latter three are sometimes referred to as *musculoskeletal functioning*). The components of **skill-related physical fitness**, or performance-related fitness, generally include agility, balance, coordination, speed, power, and reaction time. It is important to note that the conceptualization of health-related physical fitness has been evolving, and, as research data accumulate, several of the components of skill-related physical fitness (e.g., balance, speed of movement) are considered to also have health implications (Bouchard et al., 2012; PAG Advisory Committee, 2018).

Physical activity is defined as bodily movement produced by skeletal muscle resulting in an increase in metabolic rate over resting energy expenditure (Bouchard et al., 2012). Physical activity encompasses concepts such as leisure-time physical activity, exercise, sport, play, dance, transportation, occupational work, and chores. **Leisure-time physical activity** is activity that individuals choose to perform for leisure during discretionary time (Bouchard et al., 2012). **Exercise** is a type of leisure-time physical activity that is planned, structured, repetitive, and designed to improve or maintain physical fitness, physical performance, or health (American College of Sports Medicine [ACSM], 2018; Bouchard et al., 2012). **Sport** is another type of physical activity that involves competition in the context of rules defined by a regulatory agency (Bouchard et al., 2012).

Physical Fitness and Health

Since the 1980s, researchers have been working to improve our understanding of the relationships between physical fitness and health. It is known, for instance, that acceptable levels of aerobic capacity are associated with a reduced risk of hypertension, coronary heart disease, obesity, diabetes, some forms of cancer, and other health problems in adults. More recently, researchers have been examining the association between physical fitness and health in youth. In general, associations seem to be weaker in youth compared to adults (Rowland, 2012). Although this line of research is still relatively new, relationships between aerobic functioning and several cardiometabolic risk factors (body fat; blood pressure; blood levels of lipids, glucose, and insulin; and insulin sensitivity) have been identified in youth, especially those with cardiometabolic risk factors (Barker et al., 2018; Institute of Medicine [IOM], 2012; Rowland, 2012). The evidence, however, is inconclusive, and it is likely that the association between aerobic functioning and cardiovascular risk is accounted for by adiposity (Mintjens et al., 2018; Rowland, 2012). Indeed, a relationship has been shown to exist between body composition and physiological health. Body composition has been linked to risk factors for type 2 diabetes, hypertension, cardiovascular disease, and all-cause mortality in both youth and adults (IOM, 2012). In fact, the American Medical Association (2013) now recognizes obesity as a disease that requires treatment and prevention. It is therefore alarming that childhood obesity has been on the rise worldwide (NCD Risk Factor Collaboration, 2017), and prevalence is even higher for youth with disabilities (Bandini et al., 2015; Bertapelli et al., 2016; Maïano et al., 2016). Importantly, youth with disabilities are at high risk for obesity-related secondary conditions (Rimmer et al., 2007). (See chapter 18 for more on disability-related obesity.)

Researchers have had a more difficult time establishing associations between muscular strength and endurance and physiological health. Researchers have identified inverse relationships between muscle strength and cardiometabolic risk factors, frequency of cardiovascular disease events, risk of general morbidity, and all-cause mortality in adults (IOM, 2012). Some research also indicates that muscular strength is independently associated with adiposity and cardiovascular and metabolic risk in youth (Barker et al., 2018; Rowland, 2012; Smith et al., 2014). Although research is still emerging on the links between muscular strength and endurance and physiological health, there is a logical association between the two. Clearly, minimal levels of muscular strength and endurance are necessary to perform many activities of daily living and to participate in leisure activities. Indeed, research on adults has found positive relationships between muscle strength and personal independence and quality of life (IOM, 2012). Similarly, a logical relationship exists between flexibility and functional health—that is, having sufficient range of motion in the joints to perform daily activities. There is also some evidence that hamstring flexibility is linked to low back pain in some people, but there is no clear evidence linking flexibility and physiological health (IOM, 2012).

Over the years, several studies have compared the physical fitness performance of young people with disabilities against that of their peers without disabilities. With few exceptions, research in youth with intellectual disabilities, cerebral palsy, spinal cord injuries, visual impairments, and developmental coordination disorder (DCD) has documented that their fitness performance is below that of their peers without disabilities. It is therefore probable that students with disabilities are at greater risk for the health concerns mentioned previously than are students without disabilities.

Physical Activity for Health-Related Physical Fitness

This section of the chapter focuses on improving the health-related physical fitness of students with disabilities through physical activity, including the importance of personalizing physical fitness programs to achieve fitness objectives and the ways physical activity can be measured. It also addresses physical activity recommendations for promoting the components of health-related fitness, as well as a few general considerations for fitness development.

Because age, biological maturation, coordination, and other factors can affect children's fitness more than physical activity does, the relationship between activity and fitness is believed to be weaker for children than it is for adults (Pangrazi & Corbin, 2008; Rowland, 2012). Still, the physical fitness of children—both with and without disabilities—can be improved with physical activity (Eisenmann et al., 2013).

Personalizing Physical Fitness

When designing programs for students with disabilities, the physical educator must first determine the student's purpose for developing fitness. In an adapted physical education program, objectives can range from fitness for the execution of rudimentary movements (e.g., sitting, reaching, creeping) to fitness for the execution of specialized movements (e.g., sport skills, recreational activities, vocational tasks) to fitness for better health (e.g., better daily functioning and reduced risk of acquiring diseases or conditions) (see figure 23.2). Fitness objectives for a student with a disability can be influenced by several factors, including present level of physical fitness, functional motor abilities, physical maturity, age, nature of the disability, the student's interests or preferences, and availability of equipment and facilities.

With the help of the student as much as is appropriate, teachers should design personalized fitness programs tailored to individual needs. For instance, for a student with leg paralysis, the teacher might consider the following questions (with examples of possible answers):

- What are the top-priority fitness needs for this student, including any health-related concerns, and what would be the objectives of the program (or personalized profile)? *Example: Develop upper body fitness to promote the ability to lift and transfer the body independently and to self-propel a wheelchair.*
- Which components of health-related or skill-related physical fitness should be targeted for development given the identified needs and objectives? Which areas of the body will be trained? *Example: Focus on muscular strength and endurance for the shoulders, arms, and hands.*

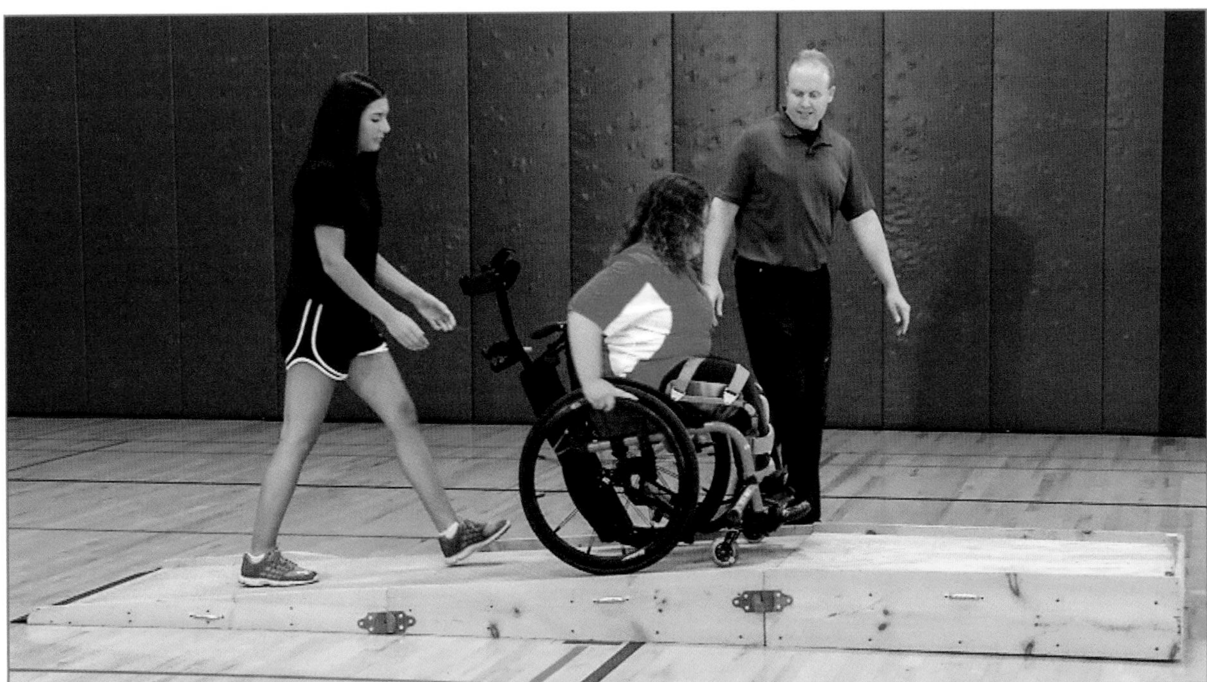

FIGURE 23.2 Propelling a wheelchair up a ramp is an index of functional health and a test item on the Brockport Physical Fitness Test.

- Which tests will be used to measure physical fitness for this student, and which standards will be adopted for evaluative purposes? *Example: Use test items (seated push-ups, dominant grip strength, and dominant dumbbell press) and standards provided by the Brockport Physical Fitness Test (BPFT) to assess progress. (The BPFT is a health-related, criterion-referenced test; see chapter 4 and appendix C for more information.)*

Designing Physical Activity Programs for Improving Fitness

Once the objectives of the personalized program have been established and baseline testing has been conducted, the teacher must develop a physical activity program that addresses the student's fitness objectives. As shown in figure 23.1, the physical activity program can be arranged by manipulating the variables of **frequency**, **intensity**, and **time** of various **types** of activity (e.g., cardio, strength training, flexibility); the acronym FITT is often used to emphasize these important variables of physical activity programming. Importantly, physical activity programs should follow the principle of **progression**—the notion that the frequency, intensity, time, and overall volume of the program should gradually increase (ACSM, 2018).

Monitoring appropriate levels of frequency and time is straightforward. Frequency generally is expressed in the number of times per day or days per week that activity is performed (e.g., three to five days per week; twice a day for five to seven days per week). Time is monitored by charting the length of the activity (e.g., 6-10 seconds, 20-40 minutes) or the number of repetitions of an exercise. It is important to mention here that physical education classes have natural frequency and time limitations; however, adapted physical educators can increase participation time and achieve progression by minimizing wait time among students with disabilities. Furthermore, teachers can make recommendations for physical activity outside of class time.

Tracking exercise intensity is somewhat more difficult. Different indices of intensity are used with different components of fitness. For instance, for muscular strength and endurance, intensity could be estimated from the degree of exertion or the amount of resistance (e.g., a certain percentage of the maximum weight that can be lifted one time). In the case of flexibility, intensity could be a function of perceived discomfort or length of a stretch (e.g., touching toes rather than ankles). The intensity of activity selected to improve either aerobic functioning or body composition might be measured by heart rate, rating of perceived exertion (RPE), or estimated metabolic equivalents (METs) (see table 23.1).

A heart rate monitor (or manual pulse rate measurement) provides an easily determined, objective measure of intensity. Maximal heart rate (HRmax) is usually estimated from the simple formula 220 – age (e.g., the estimated HRmax for a 10-year-old is 210). Physical educators, however, should be cautious when using this formula because it might not be valid for youth with conditions that alter the autonomic control of heart rate—for example, an adolescent with high-level thoracic spinal cord injury is likely to have significantly lower HRmax than that estimated with the formula.

Ratings of perceived exertion provide a subjective but valid measure of intensity in which participants gauge effort by sensations such as perceived changes in heart rate, breathlessness, sweating, and muscle fatigue. Participants then translate these sensations to a numerical scale, such as the one suggested by

TABLE 23.1 Three Methods of Estimating Activity Intensity

	METHOD		
Intensity	**Percent maximum heart rate**	**RPE**	**METs**
Very light	<57	<9	<2.0
Light	57-63	9-11	2.0-2.9
Moderate	64-76	12-13	3.0-5.9
Vigorous	77-95	14-17	6.0-8.7
Near maximal to maximal	≥96	≥18	≥8.8

Adapted by permission from American College of Sports Medicine (2018); U.S. Department of Health and Human Services (1996).

Borg (1998), which ranges from 6 (no exertion) to 20 (maximal exertion). Borg's RPE scale has good utility for adapted physical education programs and has been used successfully in research projects employing individuals with intellectual disabilities, asthma, spinal cord injuries, and cerebral palsy.

Metabolic equivalent (MET) values represent multiples of resting energy expenditure. For instance, when a person participates in an activity that is 4 METs, the body is using four times more oxygen than it does at rest. Estimated MET values, often published in charts in exercise physiology and fitness books, reflect the theoretical average person's energy expenditure for a given activity (e.g., running a 10-minute mile = 10.2 METs; playing basketball = 8.3 METs). Because physical impairments often alter exercise metabolism or biomechanics, the use of METs to estimate intensity has the most relevance for students without physical impairments (e.g., intellectual disabilities, visual impairments) and the least relevance for students who have physical impairments (e.g., cerebral palsy, spinal cord injuries, amputations).

Physical Activity Recommendations for Health-Related Physical Fitness

The following sections include recommendations for developing aerobic functioning, body composition, muscular strength and endurance, and flexibility and range of motion. Recommendations for adjustments for students with disabilities, as well as some suggested activities, are also included.

Aerobic Functioning

Aerobic functioning refers to the component of physical fitness that permits one to sustain large-muscle, dynamic, moderate- to high-intensity activity for prolonged periods of time. Aerobic functioning can be estimated by measuring aerobic capacity or aerobic behavior. **Aerobic capacity** refers to the highest rate of oxygen that can be consumed during exercise (known as $\dot{V}O_2$max) and ordinarily is the preferred measure of aerobic functioning. Aerobic capacity is most accurately measured in laboratory settings using expensive equipment for metabolic measurements. Aerobic capacity can also be estimated with field tests, including the 1-mile run and the PACER (a 15- or 20-meter multistage shuttle run). However, field tests are not always recommended for students with disabilities because the estimates of aerobic capacity are based on equations developed for people without disabilities. **Aerobic behavior** provides an alternative measure of aerobic functioning and refers to the ability to sustain physical activity of a specific intensity (e.g., >70 percent of HRmax) for a given duration (e.g., 15 minutes). Field tests of aerobic behavior include measuring the length of time one can exercise in a target heart rate zone (e.g., the BPFT's Target Aerobic Movement Test [TAMT]). Aerobic behavior can be measured in anyone who can sufficiently elevate the heart rate through physical activity.

Frequency, intensity, and time guidelines for improving aerobic functioning are summarized in table 23.2. Youth should participate in activities for improving aerobic functioning on all or most days

TABLE 23.2 Guidelines for Developing Aerobic Functioning and Enhancing Weight Loss

Training variable	Recommendation	Special considerations
Frequency	3-7 days/week	Gradually increase frequency; gradually include vigorous-intensity activity at least three days per week
Intensity	Moderate to vigorous 64%-95% HRmax 12-17 RPE 3.0-8.7 METs	Gradually increase intensity; some students may need to engage in light-intensity activity prior to advancing to moderate to vigorous intensity; adjust THRZ for arms-only activity and for students with quadriplegia
Time	20-60 min/day	May be continuous or intermittent; intermittent activity may be needed initially; increase time gradually
Type	Aerobic activities and sports	Activities should be enjoyable, developmentally appropriate, and adapted to the needs and abilities of students with disabilities

THRZ: Target heart rate zone

Based on American College of Sports Medicine (2018).

of the week for at least 20 to 60 minutes each day. The duration depends on the stage of progression; it may be shorter initially, but it should gradually increase (ACSM, 2018). The intensity of activity ranges from moderate to vigorous. Intensity may also begin at a lower level and then gradually increase; higher levels of intensity are usually necessary to improve aerobic capacity. When needed, youth may reduce their frequencies and times somewhat in exchange for higher levels of intensity.

Students with disabilities should be encouraged to participate regularly in aerobic activity, and many can meet these guidelines without modification. Some adjustments, however, are appropriate in certain situations. Ordinarily, frequency does not have to be adjusted; however, greater periods of recovery from physical activity might be necessary for students with neuromuscular diseases, arthritis, or other disabilities. When students with disabilities cannot maintain continuous activity for the recommended length of time, the first alternative would be to accumulate the target time with intermittent activity (i.e., several shorter bouts of activity followed by rest periods) before electing to reduce the time guidelines.

Adjustments to intensity will likely be necessary when students have a history of inactivity. For these students, activity might be more appropriately conducted at lighter intensities, particularly if the frequency and time guidelines can be achieved, then gradually increased over time. If intensity is being measured via heart rate, it will be necessary to adjust the target heart rate zone (THRZ) for students who engage in arms-only forms of activity or for those with spinal cord injuries. Subtracting 10 beats per minute from the THRZ values given in table 23.2 constitutes a reasonable adjustment in intensity for arms-only activity.

A range of activities can be used to meet the aerobic functioning guidelines in table 23.2. Teachers should select age-appropriate developmental activities for children (ages 6-12). Included in this group might be jump rope activities, relay races, obstacle courses, climbing activities (e.g., jungle gyms or monkey bars), active lead-up games, low-organization games, and rhythmic activities, including creative dance and moving to music.

Adolescents (ages 13-18) are generally ready for more sport-related activities and should be exposed to activities that have a lifetime emphasis. Appropriate activities might include fast walking, jogging, running, swimming, skiing, racket sports, basketball, soccer, skating, cycling, rowing, hiking, parcourse (fitness trail) activities, and aerobic dance or aquatics.

As with all good physical education instruction, teachers should start with the student and select, modify, or design appropriate activities rather than start with an activity and hope that it is somehow appropriate for the student. Many students with disabilities can participate in most of the activities previously listed, although some modifications might be necessary. Students who use wheelchairs or those with visual impairments may require alternative activities or modifications to meet the aerobic functioning guidelines. Ideas for students using wheelchairs might include slalom courses, freewheeling (i.e., jogging in a wheelchair), speedbag work (i.e., rhythmically striking an overhead punching bag), arm ergometry, seated aerobics, and active wheelchair sports (e.g., sled hockey, basketball, track, rugby, team handball). Students with visual impairments might participate in activities such as calisthenics, rowing, stationary or tandem cycling, wrestling, judo, step aerobics, aerobic dance, swimming, or track.

Body Composition

Body composition refers to the percentage of body weight that is fat versus the percentage that is muscle, bone, connective tissue, and fluids. Measurement of body composition can be done multiple ways, with varying degrees of accuracy. Laboratory-based methods such as hydrodensitometry and dual-energy X-ray absorptiometry (DEXA) are the most accurate methods, but they are cumbersome, expensive, and usually not available to teachers. However, percent body fat can be estimated with formulas based on anthropometric methods; these include the body mass index (BMI), skinfolds measured with calipers, and waist circumference measurements. Teachers may also use bioelectric impedance analyzers, which are portable and often inexpensive. These devices estimate percent body fat by measuring the conductivity of a low-level electric current; a body with more fat will have greater resistance to current flow.

It is important to mention that youth are most often classified as underweight, normal, overweight, or obese not based on percent body fat but based on BMI. This section of the chapter focuses on weight loss strategies for overweight or obese youth. However, some students might be underweight, and this is also a health-related concern. When physical educators believe that a student is underweight due to inadequate diet, an eating disorder, or a medical condition, the school's medical staff should be consulted.

Strategies for improving body composition (i.e., for weight loss) are similar to those for improving aerobic functioning and are summarized in table 23.2. Students who can meet the aerobic functioning guidelines likely will see improvements in both cardiorespiratory endurance and body composition. There may be circumstances, however, when weight loss is a more important goal than improved aerobic functioning. In such cases, the aerobic functioning guidelines could be adjusted by increasing frequency and duration while decreasing intensity. Greater weight loss will be achieved with moderate to vigorous activity, but those who are just beginning a weight loss program might need to start at a lighter intensity and progress to higher levels over time.

Another weight loss recommendation is to attain a minimal energy expenditure of at least 1,000 kilocalories (kcal) per week. If MET estimates are available, kilocalories can be calculated from the following equation:

kcal/min = METs × 3.5 × body weight (kg) / 200

As mentioned earlier, published MET estimates might not be particularly appropriate for students with physical disabilities because of differences in mechanical efficiency. However, estimating kilocalorie expenditure for students with physical disabilities is still possible.

Assume that Eddie is a 15-year-old boy with spastic paraplegia, and his weight is 150 pounds (68 kilograms). He uses forearm crutches to walk and run. He enjoys playing floor hockey, and his dad has devised a way to attach the blade of a floor hockey stick to the end of one of his crutches so that he can play in his general physical education class. Because there are no MET estimates for people with cerebral palsy playing floor hockey with forearm crutches and a modified stick, energy cost must be estimated in another way—for instance, Eddie's teacher could determine Eddie's average heart rate during the game. (This most easily could be done with a heart rate monitor but could also be done by taking manual pulse rates periodically.) If Eddie averaged 160 beats per minute over the course of the game, he would have been working at about 78 percent of his age-predicted maximal heart rate (220 − 15 = 205; 160 / 205 = 0.78%). By consulting table 23.1, the teacher can see that Eddie is at the lower end of vigorous activity, or 6 METs (the range for vigorous intensity is 6.0-10.0 METs). If 6.0 METs is used to estimate the energy cost of Eddie's activity, his energy expenditure in kilocalories per minute would be

kcal/min = 6.0 × 3.5 × 68 / 200 = 7.14.

To expend 1,000 kilocalories for the week, Eddie will need to participate in floor hockey (or some other 6-MET activity) for 140 minutes (1,000 / 7.14 = 140). If he plays twice a week, he could meet this goal if he played for 70 minutes each time (140 / 2 = 70), or he could play three times per week for 47 minutes each time. Activities that are less intense require greater frequencies or durations to meet the goal. If reaching the goal of 1,000 kilocalories per week during physical education classes is not realistic due to time restrictions, then teachers could advise students on performing additional physical activities outside of school time.

Muscular Strength and Endurance

Muscular strength is the ability of the muscles to produce a maximal level of force. Strength can be measured with dynamometers (e.g., grip strength) or by recording the maximum amount of weight that can be lifted in a single repetition (known as one-repetition maximum or 1RM). **Muscular endurance** refers to the ability to sustain submaximal levels of force over an extended length of time. Curl-ups and flexed arm hangs are examples of field-based tests of muscular endurance. Strength training is traditionally the type of physical activity selected to improve muscular strength and muscular endurance. Strength training exercises typically involve overcoming a resistance of some kind (e.g., gravity, body weight, free weights, exercise machines, elastic bands, medicine balls, weighted cuffs). Programs must be developed and supervised by physical activity professionals knowledgeable in designing strength training for youth. In general, children as young as 7 years of age can safely participate in such programs if they have received proper instruction in performing resistance exercise; students with medical conditions should receive medical clearance prior to participating in resistance exercise (American Academy of Pediatrics, 2008; Behm et al., 2008; Faigenbaum et al., 2009). For gains in strength and endurance to be made, muscles must be overloaded—that is, they must work at a greater level than normal. When resistance is used, a light load is recommended initially, followed by a progressive increase in resistance as exercise skill is mastered and muscles develop.

Several professional organizations and researchers offer recommendations for strength training in youth (American Academy of Pediatrics, 2008; ACSM, 2018; Behm et al., 2008; Faigenbaum et al., 2009). Recommendations generally call for a frequency of one to four sessions per week, preferably on nonconsecutive days, and for performing 1 to 4 sets of 8 to 10 dynamic (i.e., isotonic or isokinetic) exercises, with a rest period of 1 to 4 minutes between sets. Depending on training experience, the intensity may vary between 50 to 80 percent of the 1RM. Determining the 1RM, however, is not always practical. An alternative approach is to determine the maximum load that can be lifted for a given number of repetitions (e.g., 8RM or 10RM) and use this load for strength training (Faigenbaum et al., 2009). It is also recommended that 8RM to 15RM be performed when strength is the primary goal and 15RM to 25RM when endurance is being targeted. Youth should perform resistance exercises in a controlled manner at a moderate speed of movement. Each resistance training session should include warm-up and cool-down periods.

Guidelines for designing programs for improving muscular strength are shown in table 23.3. Consistent with the classification approach used by the National Strength and Conditioning Association (Faigenbaum et al., 2009), recommendations differ as a function of training experience; children are classified as novice (having no or less than 3 months of resistance training experience), intermediate (3-12 months experience), or advanced (more than 12 months of experience). These exercise recommendations are appropriate for most students with disabilities. Some students with disabilities might need to work at lighter intensities (lower resistance) but still be able to meet the frequency and repetition guidelines.

Apart from training experience, adapted physical educators should consider the cognitive and physical maturity of their students. Importantly, teachers should ensure that students have mastered proper technique for safely performing resistance exercises and that the training environment is free of hazards.

Although resistance training exercises may be the preferred type of activity for enhancing strength and endurance, children likely will benefit from a wide range of developmentally appropriate activities that are less structured (ACSM, 2018). Activities that require children to move their own weight or the weight of an object against gravity might be most appropriate. Examples include climbing on monkey bars, jungle gyms, ropes, or cargo nets; crawling through obstacle courses; pushing a wheelchair up a ramp; propelling scooter boards with legs or arms or by pulling on a rope; and emphasizing fundamental movements that require power, such as throwing, kicking, jumping, leaping, and hopping. Such activities offer variety, promote enjoyment, and may be especially relevant for younger children.

Flexibility and Range of Motion

Although many experts consider flexibility and range of motion to be synonymous, Winnick and Short (2014) have distinguished between the two

TABLE 23.3 Guidelines for Developing Muscular Strength

Training variable	Novice	Intermediate	Advanced
Frequency (days/week)	2-3	2-3	3-4
Exercises (number)	8-10	8-10	8-10
Repetitions	8-15	8-15	8-15
Sets	1-2	2-3	2-4
Intensity	50%-70% 1RM	50%-80% 1RM	50%-80% 1RM
Speed of movement	Moderate	Moderate	Moderate
Rest periods (min)	1-2	2-3	2-4
Special considerations	• Youth with medical conditions should receive medical clearance • Programs should be designed and supervised by knowledgeable professionals • Youth should receive proper instruction in exercise techniques • Multi-joint and single-joint exercises may be included • Early in the program, emphasize technique and not maximal performance • The program should progress gradually • Activities should be enjoyable and developmentally appropriate		

1RM: One-repetition maximum

Adapted from American Academy of Pediatrics (2008); American College of Sports Medicine (2018); Behm et al. (2008); Faigenbaum et al. (2009).

terms: **Flexibility** is conceptualized as the extent of motion possible in multiple joints during performance of a functional movement. The back-saver sit-and-reach test and the shoulder stretch are measures of flexibility. **Range of motion** (ROM) is defined as the extent of movement possible in a single joint. An objective measure of ROM can be obtained through goniometry; the BPFT Target Stretch Test provides a subjective alternative (see appendix C).

For improving flexibility and ROM, stretching exercises targeting major muscle groups are recommended. Several stretching techniques are available, including passive stretching, active–assisted stretching, and active stretching.

In **passive stretching**, the participant is not actively involved in the exercise; the muscle is stretched to a point of slight discomfort by an outside force (e.g., elastic band, weight, gravity, therapist). Passive stretching is generally used in rehabilitative settings when participants are weak, when muscles are paralyzed, or when exercise protocols require sustained stretches. Nevertheless, passive stretching can be used in educational settings as well. Physical educators who wish to employ passive stretching techniques should consult qualified professionals.

Active–assisted stretching combines the efforts of the participant and a partner assistant (e.g., teacher, therapist, aide). The participant stretches the muscle as far as possible, and then the partner assists the movement through the full (or functional) ROM.

Active stretching is characterized by the participant moving the joint through its full (or functional) ROM without outside assistance. Active stretching exercises have been categorized as static (slow stretches held for 10-30 seconds) and ballistic (brief bouncing or twisting movements) (Surburg, 1999). Although ballistic stretching might replicate certain sport-related movements, it has the potential to cause injury and generally is not recommended for improving health-related fitness.

Active static stretching exercise is usually the preferred mode for improving flexibility and ROM. In this method, properly selected exercises are used to isolate muscles or muscle groups, and intensity can be monitored or controlled. The intensity of a static stretching exercise is judged by a feeling of discomfort; muscles should be

Stretching exercises are important in physical education.

stretched to a point of tightness or slight discomfort and then held there for 10 to 30 seconds. Exercises for all major muscle groups should be selected. The American College of Sports Medicine (2018) recommends that individuals perform static stretching exercises several times until they complete a total of 60 seconds per exercise (e.g., four times for 15 seconds each). In most cases, it takes about 10 minutes to complete a flexibility training session. To improve flexibility and ROM, stretching exercises should be performed at least two to three days per week, but daily flexibility exercise is more effective (ACSM, 2018). Flexibility and ROM training is more successful when muscles are warm, as is the case after light warm-up aerobic activity or toward the end of the activity session (ACSM, 2018; Surburg, 1999). Students who use wheelchairs may perform flexibility exercises while sitting. Students with conditions that limit flexibility (e.g., cerebral palsy) should be performing flexibility exercises through the available ROM and gradually improve; these students may also benefit from performing flexibility training more often (e.g., two times daily). These recommendations for active static stretching are summarized in table 23.4.

General Considerations for Physical Fitness

When developing programs of physical fitness, the physical educator should be aware of students' initial fitness levels and select activities accordingly (see the Application Example sidebar). In all cases, the program should start at lower intensities and progress gradually. Students should be taught to warm up before a workout and cool down afterward. The physical educator should motivate students to pursue higher levels of fitness by keeping records, charting progress, and presenting awards.

FitnessGram (Cooper Institute, 2017) is an excellent tool for keeping fitness records and charting progress. Once a student's fitness test scores are entered, FitnessGram provides a report card that shows current and past performance, documents whether the "healthy fitness zone" (HFZ) was achieved for each test, and provides a series of messages to the student related to the current test performance. The BPFT (Winnick & Short, 2014) extends the FitnessGram approach to students with selected disabilities using HFZs and "adapted fitness zones" (AFZs) to assess fitness performance. Students who achieve the HFZ on five of six FitnessGram test items or achieve either the HFZ or AFZ on all, or almost all, of the BPFT test items are eligible to receive the Presidential Youth Fitness Award through the Presidential Youth Fitness Program.

Selecting enjoyable activities will also help maintain interest in physical fitness; for instance, charting all students' cumulative running distances on a map for a cross-country run is more interesting and motivating than simply telling students to run three laps. The physical educator should also be a good role model for students; this includes

TABLE 23.4 Guidelines for Developing Flexibility and Range of Motion With Active Static Stretching

Training variable	Recommendation
Frequency	At least 2-3 times a week; gradually progress to daily
Intensity	Perform stretches to a point of slight discomfort
Time	Each stretch should be held for 10-30 seconds Perform several repetitions of each stretch for a total of 60 seconds per exercise (e.g., 4 × 15 seconds) A typical training session takes approximately 10 minutes
Type	Select stretches for all major muscle groups
Special considerations	• Perform exercises after muscles are warm • Students with conditions that limit flexibility should perform exercises through the available range of motion and gradually improve • Exercises may be performed while sitting in a wheelchair • Some students may benefit from two training sessions daily

Adapted from American College of Sports Medicine (2018).

Application Example

Helping a Student With a Spinal Cord Injury Achieve Physical Fitness

SETTING

An inclusive high school physical education class

STUDENT

A 15-year-old girl with paraplegia due to spina bifida who uses a manual wheelchair for ambulation

ISSUE

One of the student's goals is to improve physical fitness. Present level of performance (i.e., baseline data) was established using the BPFT, and improvements in aerobic functioning and body composition (i.e., weight loss) were identified as the primary fitness objectives. What strategies should be used to help the student achieve these goals?

APPLICATION

The teacher might recommend or pursue the following strategies:

- Use ActivityGram (or some other self-report instrument) to monitor activity levels.
- Encourage the student to engage in at least moderate-level activity with a minimum heart rate of 121 beats per minute (220 − 15 = 205 × 0.64 = 131.2 − 10 for arm activity = 121.2) for at least 30 minutes per day, five days per week.
- If the student has difficulty achieving these guidelines, reduce criteria for intensity (i.e., heart rate) and, if necessary, add multiple bouts of shorter activity to achieve the 30-minute daily goal.
- If the student is able to achieve these guidelines on a regular basis, modify the activity pattern so that some of the activity is done within a THRZ of 148 to 185 (i.e., 77 to 95 percent of age-predicted HRmax with a 10-beat adjustment for arm-only activity) for at least 20 minutes a day on three days per week. Such a pattern will likely contribute to improved aerobic functioning.
- Recommend enjoyable aerobic-based activities to participate in outside of class, such as wheelchair slaloms, freewheeling, speed-bag work, swimming, arm ergometry, seated aerobics and dance, scooter-board activities, and wheelchair sports.
- Consult with the student's parents; encourage their support at home and include a dietary component with their help.

staying fit and participating in class activities whenever appropriate. Finally, the physical educator should view physical fitness as an ongoing part of the physical education program and not just one unit of instruction. Although several units will be taught throughout the year, activities within a unit (exercises, games, and drills) should be arranged to enhance or maintain physical fitness.

Physical Activity and Health

Although physical activity can enhance physical fitness and thus positively influence health, regular participation in physical activity in and of itself can enhance health status, regardless of fitness (see figure 23.1 earlier in the chapter). In 2018, the U.S. Department of Health and Human Services published the second edition of the Physical Activity Guidelines for Americans, asserting that being physically active is one of the most powerful actions for improving health (PAG Advisory Committee, 2018). Physical activity has beneficial effects on the risks of mortality and many chronic conditions, functional and mental health, sleep, weight status, bone health, and risk of falls, among other benefits (PAG Advisory Committee, 2018). The benefits of physical activity can be gained by all people, including men and women of all races and ethnicities, young children to older adults, women who are pregnant or postpartum, and people experiencing chronic conditions or disabilities (PAG Advisory Committee, 2018). Importantly, the benefits of physical activity outweigh any possible risks. In youth ages 6 to 17, regular physical activity improves cognitive function (memory, processing speed, attention, and academic performance), cardiorespiratory and muscular fitness, bone health, cardiovascular risk factor profiles, weight status, and adiposity, and reduces symptoms of depression (PAG Advisory Committee, 2018). Notably, the improvements in bone health and weight status extend to children as young as 3 to 5 years of age. In fact, one of the most important updates in the second edition of the guidelines was the addition of physical activity guidelines for children aged 3 to 5. For more information, readers are encouraged to visit https://health.gov.

In general, the guidelines for children and adolescents also apply to those with disabilities. Notably, the guidelines for children and adolescents require the inclusion of vigorous-intensity aerobic activity on at least three days per week, as well as muscle- and bone-strengthening activities. Improving aerobic functioning generally requires aerobic activity of progressively more vigorous levels of intensity. Furthermore, programs for musculoskeletal functioning can fulfill the need for muscle- and bone-strengthening activities. Therefore, if physical educators design and deliver physical activity programs geared toward improving their students' physical fitness, they may concurrently address the requirements for regular vigorous-intensity aerobic activity as well as muscle- and bone-strengthening activities.

Currently, individuals with disabilities across the life span have lower levels of physical activity and higher levels of sedentary behavior than individuals without disabilities, and most do not meet physical activity recommendations (Carroll et al., 2014; Ng et al., 2017; Ross et al., 2020). The available evidence indicates that this is due to both personal and environmental factors. Personal factors include associated and secondary conditions, functioning and mobility, and psychosocial factors such as attitudes toward physical activity, self-efficacy, knowledge about healthy lifestyles, and outcome expectations. Environmental factors include accessibility and transportation issues, social exclusion, negative attitudes toward people with disabilities, reduced availability of knowledgeable physical activity professionals, and low availability of inclusive physical activity programs (Agiovlasitis et al., 2018). There is certainly a need for intervention programs that can address the barriers to physical activity that youth with disabilities experience. Physical education settings offer a unique opportunity to promote lifelong physical activity habits among youth with disabilities, and knowledgeable adapted physical educators can have a significant positive impact on the lives of their students.

The physical activity recommendations discussed in this chapter generally do not need to be modified for most youngsters with disabilities, although they might employ different movement patterns to elevate heart rate and reach moderate to vigorous physical activity. When they cannot meet the recommendations, students should pursue physical activity within their tolerance level, and teachers should consider reducing the duration of the physical activity bout as a first modification. Teachers should initiate physical activity programs compatible with the student's present level of functioning and gradually progress to greater volumes of activity over time.

General Considerations for Physical Activity

Physical activity will improve the health status of the student only if it is sustained. A commitment to the physical activity guidelines presented in this chapter is really a commitment to a healthy lifestyle. One of the challenges facing physical educators who hope to encourage their students to adopt a physically active lifestyle is adherence. In schools, teachers can support activity adherence by tracking students' physical activity, by establishing award programs, and by selecting activities that are enjoyable to students (figure 23.3). Furthermore, teachers may apply theories of behavior change (e.g., social cognitive theory, self-determination theory) that increase motivation, self-efficacy, and acquisition of lifelong healthy lifestyles (Agiovlasitis et al., 2018). Finally, physical educators can use the principles and guidelines of universal design for learning (UDL) to enhance the physical activity levels of *all* students, including those with disabilities (see chapters 2 and 7). The UDL approach allows teachers to proactively design educational programs by (1) enhancing the interest of learners; (2) giving them options of how to obtain or acquire knowledge; and (3) providing them with alternative ways to express, demonstrate, or exhibit what they know (CAST, 2020). To assist physical educators in implementing UDL, Lieberman and colleagues (2021) provide several lesson plans for enhancing physical activity.

ActivityGram (a companion to FitnessGram) is a three-day physical activity assessment in which

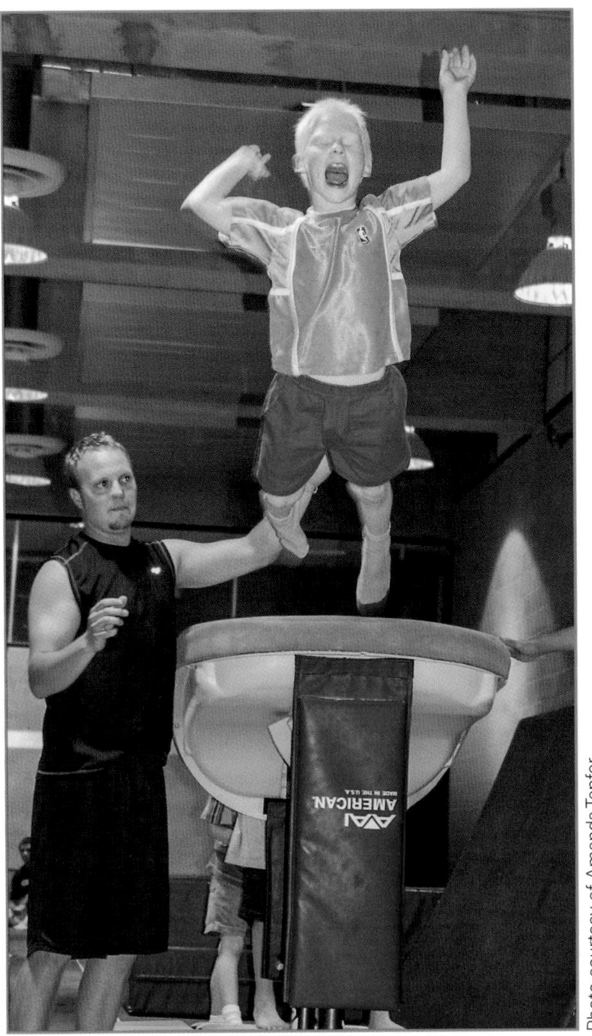

Photo courtesy of Amanda Tepfer.

FIGURE 23.3 Selecting activities that are fun will promote activity adherence and a healthier lifestyle.

students can record and monitor daily activity patterns. The ActivityGram report aggregates a student's activity time across four intensity categories (rest, light, moderate, and vigorous), generates messages summarizing the results, and offers congratulations or suggestions for improvement. Most students with disabilities can use ActivityGram without modification, although some may need help recalling their recent activity patterns or entering their activity data into the program. Students aged 6 to 17 with and without disabilities who are active for at least 60 minutes a day, at least five days a week, for at least six out of eight consecutive weeks and who meet healthy eating goals during that time qualify for the Presidential Active Lifestyle Award (PALA+) through the Presidential Youth Fitness Program.

Physical Activity or Physical Fitness?

Physical education teachers who work with students with disabilities may find that it is easier to follow the recommendations for physical activity than the exercise prescriptions for improving physical fitness discussed earlier in the chapter. First, it may be difficult or impossible to measure fitness in some students with disabilities, especially those with more severe disabilities. Second, because physical activity recommendations tend to be less intense, they may be more attainable by some students with disabilities. Finally, a wider range of possible activities is available to meet the activity guidelines than is usually recommended for fitness development. Consequently, pursuing the physical activity guidelines for some students with disabilities may be preferable over exercise programs for fitness.

Nevertheless, it is the recommendation here that whenever appropriate, teachers should afford students with disabilities with opportunities for improving health-related physical fitness through well-designed exercise programs. There are several reasons for this: (1) an exercise program for fitness could be more easily supported by a typical physical education class schedule (the physical activity guidelines cannot be achieved solely during school time); (2) exercise programs for fitness will contribute to meeting the physical activity guidelines (especially the requirement to perform vigorous-intensity physical activity at least three days per week); and, most importantly, (3) improved fitness levels may be associated with additional functional health-related benefits, including those that may contribute to a student's independence. As Rimmer (2008) suggested, low physical fitness in combination with functional impairments (such as spasticity) and secondary health conditions (such as obesity) may limit physical independence and performance of daily activities that require moderate to high levels of energy expenditure (such as community ambulation or pushing a wheelchair up a ramp).

Summary

Physical fitness is critical to the person with a disability. In addition to improved performance, health, and appearance, high levels of fitness can foster independence, particularly among people with physical disabilities. The goals of a fitness program for students with unique needs depend on the type and severity of the disability and current levels of physical fitness. Increasing fitness for developing physiological or functional health and for improving skill or performance are all reasonable goals in adapted physical education.

Fitness programs should be personalized to meet the goals of each student. Teachers must understand that, with few exceptions, students with disabilities will exhibit a favorable physiological response to increases in physical activity. Increased physical activity likely will result in improvements in both health status and physical fitness. In many cases, the recommendations for frequency and time do not differ significantly from those for students without disabilities; the type and intensity, however, frequently must be modified to provide an appropriate workout. Students with and without disabilities should pursue the recommended guidelines for physical activity: at least 60 minutes of moderate- to vigorous-intensity activity every day.

References

Agiovlasitis, S., Yun, J., Jin, J., McCubbin, J.A., & Motl, R.W. (2018). Physical activity promotion for persons experiencing disability: The importance of interdisciplinary research and practice. *Adapted Physical Activity Quarterly, 35*(4), 437-457. https://doi.org/10.1123/apaq.2017-0103

Albrecht, G.L., & Devlieger, P.J. (1999). The disability paradox: High quality of life against all odds. *Social Science & Medicine (1982), 48*(8), 977-988. https://doi.org/10.1016/s0277-9536(98)00411-0

Allerton, L.A., Welch, V., & Emerson, E. (2011). Health inequalities experienced by children and young people with intellectual disabilities: A review of literature from the United Kingdom. *Journal of Intellectual Disabilities, 15*(4), 269-278. https://doi.org/10.1177/1744629511430772

American Academy of Pediatrics, Council on Sports Medicine and Fitness (2008). Strength training by children and adolescents. *Pediatrics, 121*(4), 835-840. https://doi.org/10.1542/peds.2007-3790

American College of Sports Medicine (ACSM). (2018). *ACSM's guidelines for exercise testing and prescription* (10th ed.). Lippincott Williams & Wilkins.

American Medical Association. (2013). *Resolutions: 2013 annual meeting.* Retrieved from www.ama-assn.org/sites/ama-assn.org/files/corp/media-browser/public/hod/a13-resolutions_0.pdf

Bandini, L., Danielson, M., Esposito, L.E., Foley, J.T., Fox, M.H., Frey, G.C., Fleming, R.K., Krahn, G., Must, A., Porretta, D.L., Rodgers, A.B., Stanish, H., Urv, T., Vogel, L.C., & Humphries, K. (2015). Obesity in children with developmental and/or physical disabilities. *Disability and Health Journal, 8*(3), 309-316. https://doi.org/10.1016/j.dhjo.2015.04.005

Barker, A.R., Gracia-Marco, L., Ruiz, J.R., Castillo, M.J., Aparicio-Ugarriza, R., González-Gross, M., Kafatos, A., Androutsos, O., Polito, A., Molnar, D., Widhalm, K., & Moreno, L.A. (2018). Physical activity, sedentary time, TV viewing, physical fitness and cardiovascular disease risk in adolescents: The HELENA study. *International Journal of Cardiology, 254,* 303-309. https://doi.org/10.1016/j.ijcard.2017.11.080

Behm, D.G., Faigenbaum, A.D., Falk, B., & Klentrou, P. (2008). Canadian Society for Exercise Physiology position paper: Resistance training in children and adolescents. *Applied Physiology, Nutrition, and Metabolism, 33*(3), 547-561. https://doi.org/10.1139/h08-910

Bertapelli, F., Pitetti, K.H., Agiovlasitis, S., & Guerra-Junior, G. (2016). Overweight and obesity in children and adolescents with Down syndrome—prevalence, determinants, consequences, and interventions: A literature review. *Research in Developmental Disabilities, 57,* 181-192. https://doi.org/10.1016/j.ridd.2016.06.018

Borg, G.A. (1998). *Borg's perceived exertion and pain scales.* Human Kinetics.

Bouchard, C., Blair, S.N., & Haskell, W.L. (2012). Why study physical activity and health? In C. Bouchard, S.N. Blair, and W.L. Haskell (Eds.), *Physical activity and health* (pp. 3-20). Human Kinetics.

Bouchard, C., & Shephard, R.J. (1994). Physical activity, fitness, and health: The model and key concepts. In C. Bouchard, R.J. Shephard, & T. Stephens (Eds.), *Physical activity, fitness and health: International proceedings and consensus statement.* Human Kinetics.

Braveman, P.A., Kumanyika, S., Fielding, J., LaVeist, T., Borrell, L.N., Manderscheid, R., & Troutman, A. (2011). Health disparities and health equity: The issue is justice. *American Journal of Public Health, 101*(S1), S149-S155. https://doi.org/10.2105/ajph.2010.300062

Carroll, D.D., Courtney-Long, E.A., Stevens, A.C., Sloan, M.L., Lullo, C., Visser, S.N., Fox, M.H., Armour, B.S., Campbell, V.A., Brown, D.R., & Dorn, J.M. (2014). Vital signs: Disability and physical activity—United States, 2009-2012. *Morbidity and Mortality Weekly Report, 63*(18), 407-413.

Center for Applied Special Technology (CAST). (2020). *Universal design for learning.* www.cast.org

Cooper Institute. (2017). *FitnessGram administration manual: The journey to MyHealthyZone* (5th ed.). Human Kinetics.

Drum, C.E., Horner-Johnson, W., & Krahn, G.L. (2008). Self-rated health and healthy days: Examining the "disability paradox." *Disability and Health Journal, 1*(2), 71-78. https://doi.org/10.1016/j.dhjo.2008.01.002

Eisenmann, J.C., Welk, G.J., Morrow, J.R., & Corbin, C.B. (2013). Health benefits of physical activity and fitness in youth. In S.A. Plowman & M.D. Meredith (Eds.), *FitnessGram/ActivityGram reference guide* (4th ed., pp. 3-1-3-14). Cooper Institute.

Faigenbaum, A.D., Kreamer, W.J., Blimkie, C.J., Jeffreys, I., Micheli, L.J., Nitka, M., & Rowland, T.W. (2009). Youth resistance training: Updated position statement from the National Strength and Conditioning Association. *Journal of Strength and Conditioning Research, 23*(5 Suppl), S60-S79. https://doi.org/10.1519/JSC.0b013e31819df407

Institute of Medicine (IOM). (2012). *Fitness measures and health outcomes in youth.* National Academies Press.

Jambroes, M., Nederland, T., Kaljouw, M., van Vliet, K., Essink-Bot, M., & Ruwaard, D. (2015). Implications of health as 'the ability to adapt and self-manage' for public health policy: A qualitative study. *The European Journal of Public Health,* 26(3), 412-416. https://doi.org/10.1093/eurpub/ckv206

Johnson, C. (2009). Benefits of PA for youth with developmental disabilities: A systematic review. *The Science of Health Promotion, 23*(3), 157-167. https://doi.org/10.4278/ajhp.070930103

Krahn, G.L., Walker, D.K., & Correa-De-Araujo, R. (2015). Persons with disabilities as an unrecognized health disparity population. *American Journal of Public Health, 105*(S2), S198-S206. https://doi.org/10.2105/ajph.2014.302182

Lancet Editorial. (2009). What is health? The ability to adapt. *Lancet, 373,* 781. https://doi.org/10.1016/s0140-6736(09)60456-6

Lankhorst, K., Takken, T., Zwinkels, M., van Gaalen, L., Velde, S.T., Backx, F., Verschuren, O., Wittink, H., & de Groot, J. (2019). Sports participation, physical activity, and health-related fitness in youth with chronic diseases or physical disabilities: The health in adapted youth sports study. *Journal of Strength and Conditioning Research.* https://doi.org/10.1519/JSC.0000000000003098

Lieberman, L., Grenier, M., Brian, A., & Arndt, K. (2021). *Universal design for learning in physical education.* Human Kinetics.

Maïano, C., Hue, O., Morin, A.J., & Moullec, G. (2016). Prevalence of overweight and obesity among children and adolescents with intellectual disabilities: A systematic review and meta-analysis. *Obesity Reviews, 17*(7), 599-611. https://doi.org/10.1111/obr.12408

McCartney, G., Popham, F., McMaster, R., & Cumbers, A. (2019). Defining health and health inequalities. *Public Health, 172,* 22-30. https://doi.org/10.1016/j.puhe.2019.03.023

Mintjens, S., Menting, M.D., Daams, J.G., van Poppel, M.N.M., Roseboom, T.J., & Gemke, R.J.B.J. (2018). Cardiorespiratory fitness in childhood and adolescence affects future cardiovascular risk factors: A systematic review of longitudinal studies. *Sports Medicine, 48,* 2577-2605. https://doi.org/10.1007/s40279-018-0974-5

NCD Risk Factor Collaboration. (2017). Worldwide trends in body-mass index, underweight, overweight, and obesity from 1975 to 2016: A pooled analysis of 2416 population-based measurement studies in 128.9 million children, adolescents, and adults. *Lancet, 390,* 2627-2642. https://dx.doi.org/10.1016/S0140-6736(17)32129-3

Ng, K., Tynjälä, J., Sigmundová, D., Augustine, L., Sentenac, M., Rintala, P., & Inchley, J. (2017). Physical activity among adolescents with long-term illnesses or disabilities in 15 European countries. *Adapted Physical Activity Quarterly, 34,* 456-465. https://doi.org/10.1123/apaq.2016-0138

O'Brien, T.D., Noyes, J., Spencer, L.H., Kubis, H.P., Hastings, R.P., & Whitaker, R. (2016). Systematic review of physical activity and exercise interventions to improve health, fitness and well-being of children and young people who use wheelchairs. *BMJ Open Sport & Exercise Medicine, 2*(1), e000109. https://doi.org/10.1136/bmjsem-2016-000109

Pangrazi, R.P., & Corbin, C.B. (2008). Factors that influence physical fitness in children and adolescents. In G.J. Welk & M.D. Meredith (Eds.), *FitnessGram/ActivityGram reference guide* (3rd ed.). Cooper Institute.

Physical Activity Guidelines (PAG) Advisory Committee. (2018). *Physical activity guidelines advisory committee scientific report, 2018.* U.S. Department of Health and Human Services. https://health.gov/paguidelines/secondedition/report/

Rimmer, J.H. (2008). Promoting inclusive physical activity communities for people with disabilities. *Research Digest, President's Council on Physical Fitness and Sports, 9*(2), 1-8.

Rimmer, J.H., Rowland, J.L., & Yamaki, K. (2007). Obesity and secondary conditions in adolescents with disabilities: Addressing the needs of an underserved population. *Journal of Adolescent Health, 41*(3), 224-229. https://doi.org/10.1016/j.jadohealth.2007.05.005

Ross, S.M, Smit, E., Yun, J., Bogart, K., Hatfield, B., & Logan, S.W. (2020). Updated national estimates of disparities in physical activity and sports participation experienced by children and adolescents with disabilities: NSCH 2016-2017. *Journal of Physical Activity and Health, 14*(4), 443-455. https://doi.org/10.1123/jpah.2019-0421

Rowland, T. (2012). Physical activity, fitness, and children. In S. Bouchard, N. Blair, and W.L. Haskell (Eds.), *Physical activity and health* (pp. 273-286). Human Kinetics.

Short, F.X., McCubbin, J., & Frey, G. (1999). Cardiorespiratory endurance and body composition. In J.P. Winnick & F.X. Short (Eds.), *The Brockport physical fitness training guide.* Human Kinetics.

Smith, J.J., Eather, N., Morgan, P.J., Plotnikoff, R.C., Faigenbaum, A.D., & Lubans, D.R. (2014). The health benefits of muscular fitness for children and adolescents: A systematic review and meta-analysis. *Sports Medicine*

44(9), 1209-1223. https://doi.org/10.1007/s40279-014-0196-4

Srinivasan, S.M, Pesccatello, L.S., & Bhat, A.N. (2014). Current perspectives on physical activity and exercise recommendations for children and adolescents with autism spectrum disorders. *Physical Therapy, 94*(6), 875-889. https://doi.org/10.2522/ptj.20130157

Surburg, P. (1999). Flexibility/range of motion. In J.P. Winnick & F.X. Short (Eds.), *The Brockport physical fitness training guide.* Human Kinetics.

U.S. Department of Health and Human Services (HHS). (1996). *Physical activity and health: A report of the Surgeon General.* Author.

Winnick, J.P., & Short, F.X. (2014). *The Brockport physical fitness test manual* (2nd ed.). Human Kinetics.

World Health Organization. (2006). *Constitution of the World Health Organization.* www.who.int/governance/eb/who_constitution_en.pdf

Print Resources

Canales, L., & Lytle, R. (2011). *Physical activities for young people with severe disabilities.* Human Kinetics.

This resource presents ways to modify simple activities for meeting the needs and abilities of youth with severe disabilities.

Moore, G.E., Durstine, J.L., & Painter, P.L. (Eds) (2016). *ACSM's exercise management for persons with chronic diseases and disabilities* (4th ed.). Human Kinetics.

Written by people with research or clinical experience in exercise programming, this source provides information on how to effectively manage exercise for those with chronic disease or disability and includes 32 chapters, categorized by disability, disease, or condition. Prominent in the book are suggestions for exercise testing and exercise programming, as well as numerous case studies.

Murphy, N.A., Carbone, P.S., & Council on Children with Disabilities. (2008). Promoting the participation of children with disabilities in sports, recreation, and physical activities. *Pediatrics, 121*(5), 1057-1061. (Also available at http://pediatrics.aappublications.org/content/121/5/1057.)

This clinical report by the American Academy of Pediatrics summarizes the benefits of participation and the preparticipation considerations for children with disabilities. It includes advice for pediatricians and could be helpful to physical educators who consult with physicians on appropriate activity programs for students with disabilities.

Winnick, J.P., & Short, F.X. (Eds.). (1999). *The Brockport physical fitness training guide.* Human Kinetics.

Designed to be used in conjunction with the BPFT, this guide provides principles for fitness development in the areas of cardiorespiratory endurance, body composition, muscular strength and endurance, and flexibility and ROM. It incorporates CDC and ACSM physical activity guidelines and focuses on young people with intellectual disabilities, visual impairments, cerebral palsy, spinal cord injury, and amputations.

Online Resources

Exercise Buddy: www.exercisebuddy.com

This app that allows students with autism spectrum disorder and other disabilities to develop individualized fitness profiles and perform fitness activities using visual supports.

Centers for Disease Control and Prevention: www.cdc.gov/healthyschools/index.htm

This site from the CDC provides statistics and resources for managing nutrition, physical activity, and obesity in schools.

The Cooper Institute: www.cooperinstitute.org/youth

The Cooper Institute provides research and resources pertaining to physical fitness, physical activity, and health. It is also home to FitnessGram and ActivityGram and related documentation.

Fitstats: www.fitstatswellness.com

This software is designed to track and report fitness, motor skills, physical activity levels, nutrition, and more on a single platform.

National Center on Health, Physical Activity and Disability: www.nchpad.org

The mission of this information center is to promote the substantial health benefits of participation in regular physical activity for people with disabilities.

Presidential Youth Fitness Program: www.pyfp.org

This site supports fitness education by providing access to assessment (FitnessGram and the Brockport Physical Fitness Test), professional development for teachers, and student recognition (Presidential Active Lifestyle Award; Presidential Youth Fitness Award).

Welnet: www.focusedfitness.org

The Welnet software provides physical educators with a tool to gather fitness data and communicate results. It allows for fitness goal setting and includes behavior logs to track activity, nutrition, and other parameters.

24

Aquatics

David G. Lorenzi

Justin is a 15-year-old boy with Down syndrome. Swimming is Justin's favorite form of physical activity and he participates regularly in a Special Olympics swimming program outside of school. In school, Justin has an individualized education program (IEP) that includes instructional modifications and annual goals and objectives for physical education. Justin participates in the general physical education program with his same-age peers.

Although the school district has a small instructional swimming pool, aquatics is not currently part of the general physical education program in the high school curriculum. However, Justin's parents have informed the IEP team of Justin's interest and experience in aquatics. As a result, in addition to his inclusion in general physical education, Justin also regularly receives adapted aquatics instruction as part of an adapted physical education class.

The author would like to thank Pamela Arnhold and Monica Lepore for their significant contributions to previous editions of this chapter.

It is apparent from the preceding scenario that adapted aquatics instruction can be a needed complement to a general or adapted physical education program. This chapter identifies the benefits of aquatics, illustrates the best practices in adapted aquatics, and provides information for meeting the needs of students with disabilities in aquatics programs.

Benefits of Adapted Aquatics

Swimming and aquatic activities for individuals with disabilities can foster physical fitness and motor skill development within a physical education program and during recreational pursuits. Aquatics instruction for students with disabilities is neither a luxury nor a therapeutic (related) service. Aquatics is listed as a component of physical education under the Individuals with Disabilities Education Act (IDEA); therefore, in the opening scenario, Justin's parents are within their legal rights to request swimming as part of their son's IEP. **Adapted aquatics** means modifying the aquatic teaching environment, skills, facilities, equipment, and instructional strategies for people with disabilities. It can involve aquatic activities of all types, including instructional and competitive swimming, small-craft boating, water aerobics, and skin diving or scuba diving (AAHPERD-AAALF, 1996).

Physical educators, school administrators, parents, related service personnel, and special education teachers must be educated about the benefits of aquatics and its role in a child's physical education. The physical and psychosocial benefits of aquatics for students with disabilities are more pronounced and significant than for students without disabilities (Pan, 2011). Because of the buoyancy afforded by water, many people whose disabilities impair mobility on land can function in an aquatic environment without the assistance of braces, crutches, walkers, or wheelchairs. Although adapted aquatics does not focus on therapeutic water exercise, warm water facilitates muscle relaxation, joint range of motion (ROM), and improved muscle strength and endurance (Brody & Geigel, 2009). Swimming strengthens muscles that enhance the postural stability necessary for locomotor and object-control skills. Water supports the body, enabling a person to walk more easily (possibly for the first time), thus increasing strength for ambulation on land. Adapted aquatics also enhances breath control and cardiorespiratory fitness (Rogers et al., 2010). Blowing bubbles, holding one's breath, and inhalation and exhalation during the rhythmic breathing of swimming strokes improve respiratory function and oral motor control, aiding in speech development (Casey & Eames, 2011; see figure 24.1). In summary, because of the unique characteristics of water, individuals with disabilities have the ability to perform motor skills with variations that match their physical capabilities and fitness levels and in turn help them to become independent movers (Lee & Porretta, 2013).

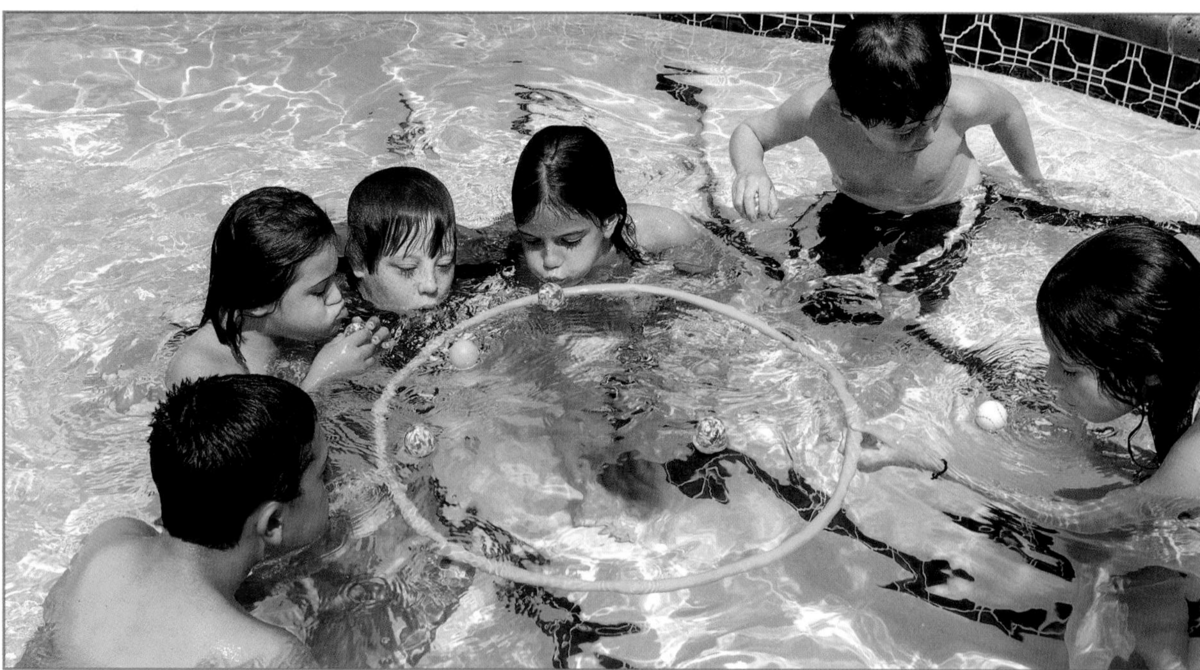

FIGURE 24.1 Breath-control exercises help improve oral motor control.

Water activities that are carefully planned and implemented to meet individual needs also contribute to psychosocial and cognitive development. As a student with a physical disability learns to move through the water without assistance, self-esteem and self-awareness improve. Moreover, the freedom of movement made possible by water boosts morale and provides an incentive to maximize potential in other aspects of rehabilitation (Koury, 1996).

The motivational and therapeutic properties of water provide a stimulating learning environment. Some instructors even reinforce academic learning by integrating math, spelling, reading, and other cognitive concepts during water games and activities. Participants might count laps, dive for submerged plastic letters, or read their workout instructions from a whiteboard. These types of activities also help participants improve judgment and orientation to the surrounding environment.

Finally, participation in an aquatics program can provide an individual with a disability an opportunity to learn and practice self-care skills such as dressing and undressing, showering, and personal grooming and hygiene. Practicing these skills will help students with disabilities gain a greater sense of independence and directly contribute to their autonomy (Arnhold & Lorenzi, 2018).

General Teaching Suggestions

Each person is unique; it should never be assumed that all characteristics associated with a disability are endemic to each person with that diagnosis. Generalizations merely present a wide scope of information that might pertain to swimmers with any particular disability. Each swimmer should be taught sufficient safety and swimming skills to become as safe and comfortable as possible during aquatic activities. Choice and presentation of skills should be tailored to meet the needs of each individual (Lepore et al., 2007). Individualization is the key to safe, effective, and relevant programming.

Before instruction begins, the teacher must gather information from written, oral, and observational sources. In addition to reading previous records and interviewing the swimmer and others, an aquatic assessment must be conducted to determine present level of functioning. General instructional suggestions include writing long-term goals and short-term performance objectives, task analyzing aquatic skills, determining proper lift and transfer methods, establishing communication signals, and developing holding and positioning techniques to facilitate instruction. Knowledge of typical growth and developmental patterns is helpful in understanding the difference between movements that are developmentally inappropriate and movements that have just not developed yet. For example, doing a bicycle kick is a developmentally appropriate sequence for most children who are learning to swim, but with more experience and decreased fear, this type of kick is inappropriate during freestyle movements.

Beginning with teaching basic safety skills, such as mouth closure, rolling over from front to back, changing directions, recovering from falling into the pool, vertical recovery from front and back positions, and holding on to the pool wall, will help alleviate fear of more difficult skills. A balanced body position in the water is also an important prerequisite. The instructor must experiment with horizontal and vertical rotation and appropriate placement of arms, legs, and head to teach the development of proper buoyancy, balance, and water comfort in relation to the student's unique physical characteristics. One method of teaching balance and body positions in adapted aquatics is the Halliwick method (Stanat & Lambeck, 2001).

Finally, presenting swimming cues in a concise manner and connected to something that the student already is familiar with strengthens learning (Yilmaz et al., 2010). Because swimming takes place in a unique setting, swimmers with disabilities need cues that refer to situations or movements they already know or know how to do (Rogers et al., 2010). An example is using the phrase, "Move your hands as if you are opening and closing curtains" to explain the movement of the hands while treading water or sculling.

Aquatic Assessment

Individualized instructional planning begins with defining which skills a participant needs to learn and assessing the present level of performance in those skills. Before performing the assessment, an instructor should determine the skills to be assessed. To help prioritize skills, questions such as these should be asked of the participant or caregiver:

- What is the participant interested in learning?
- What are important safety skills for the participant to acquire?
- Where will the participant use the skills outside of class?
- What are same-age peers performing in aquatics?

- What equipment does the family or facilities have available?
- What are the medical, therapeutic, educational, and recreational needs of the participant?

After looking at all the possible skills that are important for a student, the instructor should determine if there are any repeat skills. Skills common to many of the questions should become the priorities to be assessed and then taught, if they are lacking. Assessment items that determine the present level of performance in these skills should be developed (Block, 2016).

Swimming instructors typically use curriculum-based or ecologically based assessment checklists or rubrics to determine the extent of a student's aquatic skills (figure 24.2). Curriculum-based

WWW

Aquatic Skill Evaluation Chart

Student: ______________________________

Scoring codes:
O = cannot perform V = needs verbal cues to perform G = needs gesture cues to perform
I = independent PC = needs picture cues to perform P = needs physical cues to perform
* More than one code might describe a step (e.g., V, PC).

Target Steps and Skills	Date/Scoring
I. Entries	
Ladder	________
Ramp	________
Lift	________
Stomach slide-in	________
Jump: shallow	________
Jump: deep	________
Dive: kneel	________
Dive: compact	________
Dive: stride	________
Dive: standing	________
II. Exits	
Ladder	________
Ramp	________
Lift	________
Pull-up (side of pool)	________
III. Water Orientation	
Washes face	________
Puts chin in water	________
Puts mouth in water	________
Puts mouth and nose in water	________
Puts face in water	________
Puts whole body in water	________
Blows bubbles	________
Blows bubbles with face in water	________
Blows bubbles lying on front with face in water	________
Blows bubbles with full body underwater	________
Bobs 5 times in shallow water	________
Bobs 10 times in shallow water	________

Bobs 5 times in deep water	______
Bobs 10 times in deep water	______
IV. Safety Skills	
Prone float	______
Supine float	______
Tread water	______
Reach assist	______
V. Front Propulsion	
Pushes off side with face out of water	______
Pushes off side with face in water	______
Prone glide	______
Pushes off side with face in water and kicks	______
Arm stroke while walking	______
Arm stroke with underwater recovery (5 ft or 1.5 m)	______
Arm stroke with underwater recovery, face in water (5 ft or 1.5 m)	______
Arm stroke with underwater recovery, face in, kicking (10 ft or 3 m)	______
Arm stroke with over-water recovery (10 ft or 3 m)	______
Arm stroke with kick (20 ft or 6 m)	______
Front crawl with rhythmic breathing to front (20 ft or 6 m)	______
Front crawl with breathing to side (20 ft or 6 m)	______
VI. Breaststroke	
Push-off in streamlined position for beginning breaststroke	______
Breaststroke arms (on deck)	______
Breaststroke arms while standing in water	______
Breaststroke arms over a noodle (30 ft or 9 m)	______
Breaststroke kick correctly on deck (5 times)	______
Breaststroke kick over a noodle (30 ft or 9 m)	______
Breaststroke combined arms and kick (30 ft or 9 m)	______
VII. Back Propulsion	
Back glide off wall with a noodle	______
Back glide (10 ft or 3 m)	______
Back glide with kick (20 ft or 6 m)	______
Back glide with finning or sculling (10 ft or 3 m)	______
Back crawl arms (on deck)	______
Back crawl arms over a noodle	______
Back crawl arms with kick (20 ft or 6 m)	______
VIII. Side Propulsion	
Sidestroke glide	______
Sidestroke legs (on deck)	______
Sidestroke legs while holding a noodle (20 ft or 6 m)	______
Sidestroke arms (on deck)	______
Sidestroke arms with a noodle (20 ft or 6 m)	______
Sidestroke (30 ft or 9 m)	______

FIGURE 24.2 This checklist helps instructors determine a student's aquatic skills.

From J.P. Winnick and D.L. Porretta, *Adapted Physical Education and Sport*, 7th ed. (Champaign, IL: Human Kinetics, 2022).

assessment items include skills that the swimmer needs to function effectively within an integrated class. The American Red Cross progressive swim levels (American Red Cross, 2014), YMCA swim levels (YMCA, 1999b), and SwimAmerica programs (SwimAmerica, n.d.) are examples of curriculums from which a swim instructor would draw skills for a curriculum-based assessment checklist.

The Modified TWU Aquatics Assessment (Lepore et al., 2015) can be used to evaluate a student's readiness for swim lessons. This curriculum-based assessment instrument includes assessments for the following skills: water adjustment, flotation, basic propulsion, breathing, swim strokes, and entry and exit skills. Skills in each of these areas progress from simple to complex and the assessment results will provide the instructor with useful information that can be used for lesson planning.

Ecologically based assessments include skills needed for a person's current and future environment. Aquatic skill assessments of this kind might include components of the curriculum-based assessment but also include skills such as entering and exiting the facility and the pool area, using a locker, dressing and undressing, showering, using appropriate language in a swim group, performing stretching exercises before swimming, knowing how to swim in a lane, using a flotation device, or clearing the mouth of water. These are important prerequisite skills but would not usually appear within a general swim curriculum because they are typically acquired through incidental learning before formal swim lessons commence. Ecologically based assessments should be developed based on individual needs and assess all areas of the aquatic experience.

Adapted Swimming Skills

Before adapting skills to meet a student's needs, the instructor must first look at why the skill is needed and how and where the skill will be used. Some swimmers might want to pass the competencies for the American Red Cross swim levels, some might want to improve cardiorespiratory functioning, and yet others might want to enter a swim meet. These differing purposes for performing, for example, the front crawl might cause an instructor to take a different approach to adapting strokes and other aquatic skills. Important considerations in adapting strokes include the following:

- What are the physical constraints of the disability?
- What is the most efficient way to propel through the water, given the constraints?
- What movements will cause or diminish pain or injury?
- What adaptations can be used to make the stroke or skill as much like the nonadapted version as possible?
- What equipment is available to facilitate the skill?
- Why does the swimmer want to learn this skill (competition, relaxation)?

In order to address these considerations, the instructor might need to adjust the swimmer's body position by adding flotation devices or light weights, change the propulsive action of the arms or legs, or adapt the breathing pattern.

Adjusting the swimmer's body position is typical for people who have disabilities such as cerebral palsy (CP), stroke, traumatic brain injury, spina bifida, obesity, limb loss, muscular dystrophy, or traumatic spinal cord injury. Because of variations from the norm in regard to muscle mass and body fat in many people with physical disabilities, the center of gravity and center of buoyancy might be atypical. It is important to find an efficient body position and experiment with flotation devices and weights (e.g., scuba diving and ankle weights, inflatable arm floaties, foam swim noodles, rescue tubes, life jackets, or ski belts). A body position close to horizontal is the most streamlined and effective.

The swimmer's arm and leg actions might need to be adjusted as well. Typical propulsive action might not be feasible because of contractures, muscle atrophy, or missing limbs. Adaptations such as changing the ideal *S*-curve of the arms in the front crawl to a modified *C* or *J* should be considered. Lower body propulsive adaptations might include bending the knees more during flutter kicking, using the scissor kick while breathing in the front crawl, or using fins while doing the dolphin kick during any of the strokes.

Breathing patterns can be changed from one-side breathing to alternate-side breathing, front breathing, rolling over onto the back to breathe, or using a snorkel. Swimmers can be taught explosive breathing, breathing using the mouth only, or breathing using a closed-throat technique. Finally, nonphysical adaptations include developmentally appropriate progressions, frequent practice of skills, detailed traditional and ecological task analysis (ETA), verbal and visual cues, repeating of directions, and altered skill objectives.

Orientation to Water

Acquisition of aquatic skills is based on the learner's readiness to receive the skill, readiness to understand the goal, opportunities to practice at a challenging but manageable level, and ability to receive feedback. Orientation to water focuses on the readiness of the learner and other psychological and physiological factors. Physiological factors are anatomical and functional variations in the body that affect how and what the person learns, including disability and medication and their effects on each body system. A swimmer might not be neurologically ready to perform a skill because of brain damage, lack of central nervous system maturity, or developmental delays. When the instructor understands the effect of a disability on learning and provides developmentally appropriate skill progressions, learning increases (Dimitrijevi et al., 2012).

Emotionally, each person is unique and learns at an individual rate. People with disabilities might have characteristics that hinder the acquisition of aquatic skills. Psychological factors such as anxiety and cognitive readiness should be considered before developing instructional strategies. Most anxiety during swim instruction stems from fear and discomfort and inhibits mental adjustment to the aquatic environment. Although mental adjustment takes time for all new or frightened swimmers, it might be even more difficult for students with disabilities. Issues such as a limited ability to develop breath-holding and rhythmic breathing as a consequence of oral muscle dysfunction, asthma, or high or low muscle tone or inability to grasp and hold the pool gutter make it likely that some people with disabilities are at high risk of anxiety that affects their ability to learn.

Factors that might cause anxiousness include fear of drowning, past frightening water experiences, submerging unexpectedly and choking on water, fear reinforced by warnings (e.g., "Don't go near that water or you'll drown"), capsizing in a boat, being knocked down by a wave, or feelings of insecurity caused by poor physical ability or unfamiliar surroundings (Lepore et al., 2007). Fear stimulates physiological responses, such as heightened muscle tone, increased involuntary muscle movements, and inability to float. In short, insecurity prevents success in swimming. Helping participants get past fear and apprehension to practice aquatic skills that will make them safer in the water is an initial step in teaching swimming. When participants are free of fear, they are free to learn (Stillwell, 2007). The following tips, taken from the YMCA's *Parent/Child and Preschool Aquatic Program Manual* (1999a), will promote comfort and reduce fear. These suggestions can be used for participants of all ages:

- Allow reluctant participants extra time for water acclimation activities.
- Use patience without pampering.
- Gently guide; don't force.
- Explain everything in a calm, quiet, matter-of-fact voice.
- Teach in shallow water (e.g., on pool steps, water tables, or water docks) or on a gradually sloping ramp.
- Emphasize noncompetitive activities.
- Provide a mask or goggles if water in the eyes is an issue.
- Redirect crying or anxious behaviors by using a colorful piece of equipment or discussing the swimmer's favorite food.
- Use the swimmer's name frequently; smile and praise small steps in the progression of water adjustment.

Fear is diminished when the instructor and swimmer communicate easily. In addition to communication skills, a thorough understanding of participant positioning, guiding, and supporting is essential. Proper methods of transferring, touching, and supporting participants in the locker room, on the pool deck, and in the pool will also develop relationships based on trust. Knowing how to use the adapted equipment, wheelchairs, and flotation devices provides an atmosphere of efficiency and safety that makes everyone feel comfortable. Likewise, holding someone with a firm and balanced grip as close as safety and comfort allow communicates care and establishes trust and rapport (Lepore et al., 2007). In addition, an environment in which the instructor exhibits a consistent temperament, practices discipline methods that are flexible but stable, uses caring verbal assurances, and provides balanced, controlled physical handling promotes trust, security, and mental adjustment.

The instructor should use fun activities instead of drills to promote a more comfortable atmosphere. Games, music, and props help a fearful student become prepared to accept the aquatic setting. Activities such as a flower hunt with plastic flowers inserted into the gutters help acclimate the fearful student in a nonthreatening manner. Other activities include square dance and social dance; physical education games, such as cooperative musical chairs using hoops; land games; and activities such as basketball and sponge tossing to inflatable tubes. These activities build on familiar activities, and the instructor can progress from there.

Safety, Facility, and Equipment Considerations

For participants and instructors alike, facilities and equipment must be accessible and safe and lend themselves to successful, satisfying experiences. Familiarity with the Americans with Disabilities Act (ADA) accessibility guidelines (Architectural and Transportation Barriers Compliance Board [ATBCB], 2004), state and local health codes for aquatic facilities, and resources for equipment and supplies that promote aquatic participation (see the Video, Online, and Other Resources for this chapter) help provide quality swimming experiences.

Safety

Safety considerations need to be at the forefront of planning and service delivery in an aquatic setting. Teaching participants to be safe in and around water and educating parents and guardians on proper supervision and water safety is the responsibility of the instructor. Water safety concepts should be incorporated into each lesson and may need to be repeated and reinforced frequently, depending on the nature of an individual's disability. The National Drowning Prevention Alliance (NDPA) is a national organization devoted to the elimination of drowning deaths through increased awareness, education, and training. The NDPA website contains a wealth of information on drowning prevention and educational resources that can be used to teach water safety (see https://ndpa.org).

Teaching water safety to individuals with disabilities is especially important. Accidental drowning rates tend to be higher among individuals with disabilities, especially children with autism. High drowning rates among children diagnosed with autism spectrum disorder in particular have been attributed to wandering behaviors, a natural curiosity of water, and a lack of fear in and around water (Lorenzi & Taliaferro, 2018).

To ensure both success and safety in a swim class, a proper instructor-to-student ratio is required. Whereas students without disabilities may be successful in a 1-to-10 or 1-to-12 instructor-to-student ratio, students with disabilities, especially those with more severe disabilities, may require a 1-to-2 or even a 1-to-1 ratio (Lepore et al., 2015). Additionally, a teaching assistant or paraprofessional may be required to ensure a safe and successful environment.

Facilities

Facility characteristics should be discussed with the participant before the first session. This discussion should center on information about the locker room, path to the pool, pool deck, and pool itself. Locker rooms can cause frustration for people with disabilities. Factors such as shower handles and locker shelves too high for people with dwarfism, inadequate lighting for people with visual impairment, and combination-only lockers that impede people with arthritis do not motivate people to use a facility. Other factors inhibiting independence include benches cemented into the floor in front of lockers, shower area ledges or lips that limit access for participants who use wheelchairs, and lack of braille signs on lockers, entrances, and exits. Since the ATBCB published its final ruling on accessibility and recreation facilities, it is easier to determine exactly what facilities meet the standards (ATBCB, 2004).

Facility design must enable participants to move freely around the locker area, pool deck, and water. Newly designed, newly constructed, or significantly altered pools must have at least one primary means of access, plus a secondary means of access if the pool has over 300 linear feet (91 meters) of pool wall or if access is limited to one place (e.g., a lazy river pool at a water park) (Brown, 2003). A primary means of access may be a lift (figure 24.3*a*) or gradual-slope entry ramp (wet ramp) with handrails and a flat landing area at the bottom that connects the deck directly to the water (figure 24.3*b*). Secondary means can be a lift, a sloped entry, a transfer wall (see figure 24.3*c*), a transfer system (see figure 24.3*d*), or pool stairs that meet the ADA code (not the ladders built into the walls of the pool) (Gelbach, 2013). A transfer wall (sometimes called a *dry ramp* because it is outside the pool on the deck) is constructed such that the deck of the pool slopes down below the pool edge so it is flush with the wheelchair seat. This method of access is the least used because of its limitations for exiting the pool and the extensive strength and stability required to use it. Lifts and transfer systems are further described in the next section on equipment.

Facilities already in existence can use any or all of the access means mentioned here to make reasonable accommodations to remove existing architectural and service barriers. New guidelines will set a high standard for reasonable accommo-

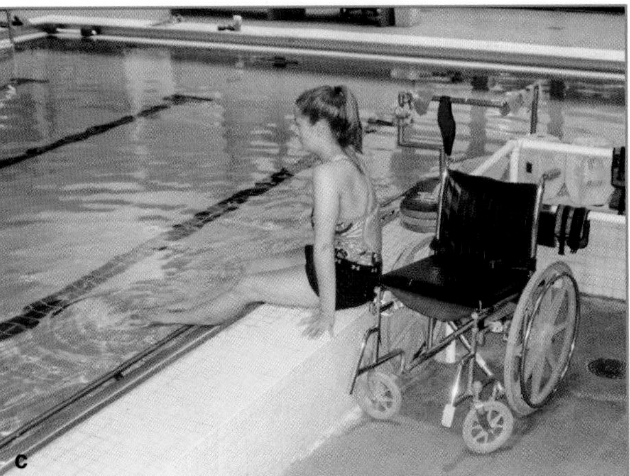

FIGURE 24.3 *(a)* Lifts are a primary means of access according to the ADA guidelines. *(b)* Gradual-slope entry is a primary means of access. *(c)* A dry ramp provides access to a transfer ledge. *(d)* A transfer system can be a secondary means of access.

dations (ATBCB, 2004), so facility managers would be prudent to develop a long-term barrier-removal plan to bring their pool up to code.

In addition to the structure and architecture, pool temperature and chemical composition must be compatible with the groups it serves. In general, children with disabilities perform better with water temperature between 86 and 90 degrees Fahrenheit (30 and 32 degrees C); air temperature should be about 4 degrees higher. Participants should be made aware of the type of water purification used because some people have chemical sensitivity to chlorine.

Equipment

Appropriate equipment and supplies are even more important for classes serving individuals with disabilities than for the general population. Adapted equipment is often necessary for entry and exit, safety, maintenance of a proper body position in the water, arm and leg propulsion, fitness purposes, and motivation. Of course, safety equipment is mandatory for an adapted aquatics program. It includes typical rescue equipment, a floor covering to decrease slipping, closed-cell foam mats for use during seizures, and transfer mats to cover pool gutters.

As mentioned in the previous section, safe entrances and exits are crucial to accessible swim instruction. In addition to the method of entry afforded by the facility design, lifts, portable ramps, stairs, and transfer systems are important items for entrance and exit when equipment is not built into the facility. Lifts often provide primary access to pools for people with severe orthopedic disabilities (see figure 24.3*a*). A lift is a pneumatic, water-powered, mechanical, or fully automated electrical assistive device that permits a user to transfer from a wheelchair to a seat or sling and move from deck to pool using little strength. According to the newest guidelines (ATBCB, 2004), the lift must be capable of unassisted operation from both deck and water levels and should have a hard plastic seat with a backrest rather than a sling (cloth) seat. Independent usage is best facilitated when hand controls are located at the front edge of the seat, are operational with one hand, do not require tight grasping, and require 5 pounds (2.25 kilograms) or less of force to operate.

Portable ramps and gradual steps have been used for many years to offer access to pools when the facility design does not provide any other means of access. However, these items take up extra room on the deck when they are removed and do not provide the most independent access (because users must rely on staff to place them in the water when needed). Portable equipment also breaks more frequently as a result of wear and tear from removal and storage.

For people who have good upper body function but cannot negotiate stairs or ladders because of lower body involvement, a transfer system often allows more independent pool access. A transfer system is a rectangular platform 19 by 24 inches (48 by 61 centimeters) rising 16 to 19 inches (41 to 48 centimeters) above the deck (see figure 24.3*d*). This platform is connected to a series of steps 14 to 17 inches (36 to 43 centimeters) deep by 24 inches (61 centimeters) wide that participants use to gradually lower themselves into the water from the chair to the platform to each step. The process is reversed for exiting.

Another useful piece of equipment is an aquatic chair with push rims, especially if the pool has a gradually sloped ramp as its primary means of access. Aquatic facilities should provide an aquatic wheelchair that can be used on the sloped entrance because personal wheelchairs are not appropriate for submersion.

Equipment used to maintain body position is the most common equipment typically seen in an adapted aquatics program. Support equipment useful in an adapted swim program might include personal flotation devices (PFDs) (see figure 24.4), foam noodles, sectional rafts, and flotation collars. A large variety of flotation devices, including PFDs, water wings, pull buoys, dumbbell floats, and sectional rafts, provide an extra hand when working with people who are dependent on others to stay above the water. Pool noodles are an example of an inexpensive piece of equipment that can be used in a variety of ways for support in prone, supine, and vertical floating positions (Stopka, 2008). If they are Coast Guard–approved, flotation devices can ensure safety and might also reduce or even eliminate fear. Because flotation devices help to support, stabilize, and facilitate movement, they open a new world to people with mobility impair-

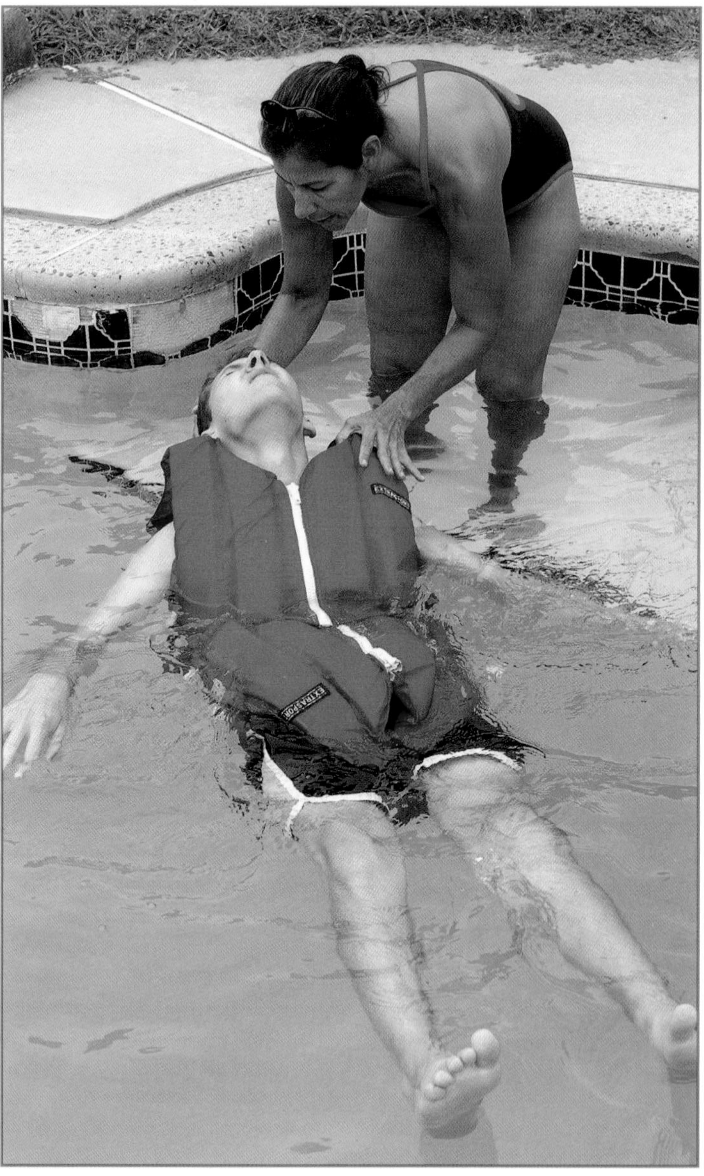

FIGURE 24.4 Learning to float on back with the use of a Personal Floatation Device (PFD).

ments, allowing freedom of movement not possible on land (Jackson & Bowerman, 2009).

Although flotation devices are useful, they may pose certain concerns. For example, they might impair independence if swimmers continue to rely on them after they should have progressed to independent, unaided swimming. Also, devices typically tested on people without disabilities are often not fully functional when used with swimmers who have atypical body postures, uneven muscle development or tone, or poor head control. Thus, if students use flotation devices for support, proper supervision must be provided even if the PFDs are Coast Guard approved. Generally speaking, each person with a disability has unique needs; thus it is difficult to make blanket statements or recommendations regarding safety and buoyancy. It is important to know each swimmer's abilities. In addition, an assessment should be performed to determine body control and horizontal balance through experimentation (under supervision) with buoyancy in various positions. Buoyancy can be used to resist or assist movement or to support the swimmer (Getz et al., 2012).

Propulsion equipment affords participants with a disability the ability to move in ways they might not be able to naturally. Propulsion is affected by variances in streamlined position, difficulty with horizontal and lateral body positions, inadequate strength, poor ROM, atypical buoyancy, and other factors, including poor coordination and disproportionate body shape contributing to drag (Prins & Murata, 2008). The first step to efficient propulsion is to put the body in the most streamlined and balanced position possible, using other support as necessary. If the participant is still having difficulty with propulsion, try other devices such as hand paddles and fins to increase surface area for propulsive efficiency. For ideas and possible uses for these devices, see Patterson and Grosse (2013) and Paciorek and Jones (2001). However, remember that in official competition, these devices are not allowed, although those who have a partial or full upper limb amputation might be able to use a swimming prosthesis.

An increased interest in water fitness has resulted in a greater diversity of fitness supplies. Underwater treadmills, aquacycles, water workout stations, and aqua exercise steps can be used for cardiorespiratory conditioning, muscle toning, and strength training. Water fitness participants also use supportive and resistive equipment and supplies in the water that are handheld, pushed, or pulled, including finger and hand paddles, balance-bar floats, upright flotation vests and wraps, aqua shoes, webbed gloves, waterproof ankle and wrist weights, workout fins, buoyancy cuffs, water ski belts, aqua collars, and water jogging belts.

Motivational equipment provides swimmers of all ages the push necessary to attempt and complete tasks that might be otherwise overwhelming or boring. The developmental levels, interests, and attention spans of participants in adapted aquatics require a unique approach to instruction and recreation. Instructional strategies that focus on fun are enhanced by attractive, brightly colored equipment; nontoxic, sturdy supplies; and entertaining toys, flotation devices, and balls. Other devices include swim belts, bubbles, and foam squares, many of which come with modules to increase or decrease flotation. Water logs (i.e., pool noodles) are hefty, flexible buoyant logs that encourage water exploration and kicking in a fun way.

Meeting Participants' Unique Needs

To provide safe, effective, and relevant aquatic opportunities while meeting a variety of needs, it is necessary to know the unique attributes of learners. However, it is important not to assume that these attributes apply to every person in an identified category. Suggestions for teaching people with specific disabilities are similar to land-based teaching tips; thus, readers can generalize the information in chapters 8 through 18 to an aquatic setting.

Participants With Cerebral Palsy

People with cerebral palsy (CP) exhibit a variety of skills depending on the type and severity and the body parts affected. The following are some suggestions for teaching swimming to participants with cerebral palsy:

- Many stroke adaptations are based on limited ROM; try having the person use an underwater versus out-of-water recovery of the arms, especially for the front crawl.
- Maintain water temperature between 86 and 90 degrees Fahrenheit (30 and 32 degrees C) and air temperature 4 degrees higher than the water temperature.
- Guard against sudden submersion of the face; people with CP often have a weak cough and cannot clear water from the throat effectively.
- Consider hand paddles for participants with wrist flexion contractures.

- Develop strokes executed in the back-lying position, eliminating the need for head control with rhythmic breathing.
- While in a prone position, have the participant wear a ski belt or rescue tube across the chest and under the armpits (with closing clip on back) to elevate the chest and face.

For people with primitive reflex retention, the following suggestions apply:

- Sudden noises, movements, or splashing may cause sudden reflex activity, possibly causing the participant to lose a safe position. Maintain a position at or near the participant's head to prevent sudden submersion.
- Consider allowing the participant to wear a flotation collar to hold the head above water.
- Neck hyperextension or turning of the head to the side may affect arm and leg control in swimmers with reflex retention. Encourage a full-body roll for breathing or the use of a snorkel.
- Avoid quick movements and sudden hands-on and hands-off movements. Slow movements and a steady touch are best with swimmers who have high muscle tone.
- Be aware of sudden spastic movements during transfers in and out of the pool. Have adequate personnel for transfers and use a mat under the transfer area.
- Encourage participants to flex their heads slightly while on their backs. When the head is in extension while lying on the back, the mouth tends to open and the arms tend to extend.
- Keep the participant stable; unstable positions in the water or a feeling of falling causes the body to stiffen, the arms and legs to involuntarily extend and flex, and the mouth to open.
- Use positions that inhibit reflexes, such as a neutral or slightly tucked chin and the head in midline of the shoulders. Hips and knees should be slightly flexed.
- Use symmetrical activities as much as possible (both sides of the body doing the same thing at the same time) such as the breaststroke, elementary backstroke, inverted breaststroke, finning, or sculling.
- Use caution with the scissors kick and the flutter kick because they promote the crossed extension reflex, causing scissoring of the legs. If scissoring occurs, place a comfortable piece of cushioning between the knees during swimming.

Participants With Orthopedic Disabilities

Although people with orthopedic disabilities have a wide range of characteristics, certain similarities can be considered within the aquatic environment. Balance, buoyancy, body position, and ROM might be affected. People with arthrogryposis, amputations, dwarfism, spina bifida, spinal cord injuries, osteogenesis imperfecta, traumatic brain injury, stroke, spinal cord injury, orthopedic disabilities, multiple sclerosis, muscular dystrophy, or myasthenia gravis might benefit from the following teaching tips:

- Use in-water benches or docks for people with fatigue or those who have short stature and cannot stand on the bottom of the pool.
- Look for ways to streamline the body, such as changing head position or attaching flotation devices or weights to lower or raise body position. Achieve a balanced body position by experimenting within proper safety limits.
- Check skin for abrasions before and after swimming if the person has decreased sensation.
- Encourage use of aqua shoes to decrease lesions caused by transferring and by scraping the feet when swimming.
- Be aware that muscle spasms and strange sensations may sometimes interrupt the aquatic session.
- Become knowledgeable about proper assistance in taking off and putting on braces and other orthotic devices.
- Alter stroke mechanics as necessary for uneven muscle strength and abnormal centers of gravity and buoyancy. Change strokes as little as possible from normal efficiency. If necessary, use smaller ROM or sculling arm movements.
- If upper body impairment causes difficulty in lifting the head to breathe, a participant should use a mask and snorkel or roll over onto the back to breathe. Initially, teach the back crawl or elementary backstroke.
- Ensure that all excretion collection bags are emptied before swimming.

- Allow the participant to wear a neoprene vest or wetsuit to keep warm in cooler pools.
- Provide assistance for balance problems while participants are on deck.

Participants Who Have Seizures

Participants with seizure disorders need instructors who have a plan of action in case of a seizure incident. Current practice suggests that steps be taken to ensure that the person having the seizure has an open airway and is protected from physical injury caused by contact with other people or objects and water ingestion or aspiration. When in doubt, always activate the emergency medical system (EMS). This section describes how to manage a seizure effectively.

The first aid objectives for assisting a person having a seizure in the pool are to keep the face above the water, to maintain an open airway, and to prevent injury by providing support with a minimal amount of restraint. One position that meets these objectives is standing low in the water behind the person's head and placing the body in a supine position, then supporting the person under the armpits, shoulders, and head. Provide only the support needed to keep the participant's face out of the water; unnecessary restraint might cause injury to the participant or instructor. Remove the person from the water as soon as it is safe to do so. Do not allow the person to remain in the pool if the seizure lasts for more than several minutes, if seizures continue in rapid succession, or if injury or hypothermia is imminent. The Epilepsy Foundation of America (2020) offers the following suggestions: If a seizure occurs in water, support the person's head and keep her face out of the water. Bring her to the shore or side of the pool and place her on her side. Check her airway. If water has been ingested or breathing is labored, get medical treatment.

The following teaching tips will help ensure swimming safety for people who have seizures:

- Obtain medical clearance and a list of any contraindicated activities.
- Maintain supervision during aquatic activities.
- Factors provoking onset of seizure include playing games of holding the breath as long as possible; hyperventilation before underwater swimming; excessive drinking of pool water, which can lead to hyperhydration or hyponatremia; hyperthermia; and excessive looking into the sun.
- Discuss scuba diving with participants and their physicians before attempting deep dives.
- Be aware that some seizure medications increase photosensitivity. When outdoors, it may be important to swim in the early evening. The swimmer should use sunscreen or wear a T-shirt or rash guard over a swimsuit.
- Fill out an appropriate incident report following a seizure.

Swimming as a Competitive Sport

Including athletes with disabilities into competitive sport experiences has long been a goal of disability advocates. USA Swimming, the national governing body for all U.S. swimming competition, has done an exemplary job of advocating for vertical integration, or the inclusion of people with disabilities in aquatic meets and teams. The mission statement for the USA Swimming Disability Committee states, "USA Swimming encourages people with disabilities to participate in the sport of swimming and facilitates their inclusion in USA Swimming programs through education and collaboration. We seek to involve people with disabilities in existing competitions and programs for all swimmers, rather than provide unique disability-only opportunities." The committee has written several resources for coaches, local swim committees, officials, meet directors, parents, and swimmers with disabilities (USA Swimming, n.d.). *USA Swimming Rules and Regulations* (2013) has guidelines for officiating meets that include swimmers with a disability.

The goal of USA Swimming is for swimmers with disabilities to train with their local swim clubs and participate in swim meets that integrate swimmers with and without disabilities. USA Swimming encourages this integration by providing reasonable accommodations to barriers that might otherwise preclude the participation of swimmers with disabilities. According to USA Swimming (n.d.), local swim committees are encouraged to develop administrative procedures and circumstances that encourage swimmers with disabilities to participate, such as the following:

- Include a statement inviting swimmers with disabilities to provide notice of needed accommodations.
- Develop standards for seeding swimmers that do not interfere with the time line and

flow of the meet and do not place an undue spotlight on the athlete with a disability. (For example, swimmers who have CP might be placed in a 100-meter event but swim 50 meters if their 50-meter time is similar to the 100-meter times of peers without disabilities.)

- Waive qualifying time standards.

Additional guidelines for officiating swimmers with disabilities meets might include some of the following accommodations from the 2013 *USA Swimming Rules and Regulations*:

- Allow the swimmer to start in the water.
- Allow the swimmer's assistant on the deck to assist the start.
- Use a visual starting system (e.g., a strobe light or hand signals) for Deaf and hard of hearing participants.
- Be lenient regarding the time it takes to get into starting positions.
- Modify starting positions on blocks, deck, or gutter (see figure 24.5).
- Use tappers (assistants who hold a pole with a soft tip to tap the swimmer at turns and finishes) for swimmers with vision impairments.
- Use physical touch to signal relay swimmers when their teammates have touched the wall.
- Do not judge a part of the body that is absent or not used as part of a stroke technique.

Photo courtesy of Joe Kusumoto.

FIGURE 24.5 One reasonable accommodation in competitive swimming for athletes with disabilities might be to allow modified starting positions.

In addition to integrated swim meets, the US Paralympics Swimming Championships are held once a year. This multidisability swim championship is conducted for elite disabled swimmers who have met qualifying times for their events. USA Swimming rules and regulations apply during these meets; however, swimmers are classified into categories according to their functional ability (rather than merely separated by gender and swim stroke) so that swimmers can compete against others of similar functioning.

Although most competitive training in the United States takes place in USA Swimming clubs, the YMCA and other organizations conduct integrated club teams as well. For those who prefer training only with other swimmers who have disabilities, disability-specific organizations such as Special Olympics (for athletes with intellectual disabilities) can provide segregated competitive opportunities (although Special Olympics offers some Unified swimming events that provide reverse inclusion of athletes without disabilities). Deaf or hard of hearing swimmers may participate in the Deaflympics through the USA Deaf Sports Federation (USADSF); people with dwarfism may participate as members of the Dwarf Athletic Association of America (DAAA) in the organization's regional and national games; and swimmers who are blind or visually impaired may participate in United States Association of Blind Athletes (USABA) competitions. However, these competitions are limited in number and may be far from a swimmer's home pool.

Although swimming is the most common sport in aquatic competition, competitive diving (Special Olympics) and water polo (USADSF) are other options. However, these will generally need to be pursued through inclusive team settings.

Other Aquatic Activities

People with disabilities of all ages enjoy water sport as much as their counterparts without disabilities. Aquatic activities such as waterskiing, scuba diving, and boating can help increase independence and empowerment, as well as provide recreational opportunities with peers, families, and community members. With more legal mandates for accessibility, including boat docks and fishing piers, more chances exist for participation in instructional, recreational, and competitive water sport (ATBCB, 2004).

Waterskiing

Prerequisites to waterskiing include consultation with a swimmer's physician, acquisition of basic swim skills, and knowledge about using a PFD. All skiers should practice using PFDs for support and buoyancy in a controlled environment before using them in open water. The driver of the boat, the observer, and the skier should agree beforehand on communication techniques (e.g., hand or head movement signals) to make the activity safe for all.

To make waterskiing easier for the beginner and for those with disabilities, equipment modifications must be made, especially for those with lower extremity involvement. Ski tip connectors (STC) can keep the skis together for those with leg weakness or paralysis. A kneeboard, ski biscuit (inflatable inner tube with a cover), or specially designed sit ski can accommodate the skier who cannot stand up. LiquidAccess is one provider dedicated to the design and manufacture of adapted equipment for waterskiing in the United States (www.liquidaccess.org).

In addition, several adaptations to ski progressions might be combined with equipment modifications, as evidenced by UCanSki2, a USA Water Ski–affiliated ski club in Winter Haven, Florida (www.ucanski2.com). The staff conducts dry land instruction followed by the use of a boom off the side of the boat as a first step to waterskiing. A triple bar in back of the boat with one instructor on either side of a student allows another progression.

USA Adaptive Water Ski & Wake Sports (USA-AWSWS), an official sport division of USA Water Ski, offers an adaptive waterskiing certification program in addition to an adaptive coach's certification. This group also puts together the national championship each August and sponsors the 14-member USA Adaptive Water Ski team to represent the United States at the world championships. Events include slalom, audio slalom, tricks, and jumps. There are eight classification groupings for skiers with physical disabilities and three for skiers with visual impairments (www.usaadaptivewaterski.org).

Scuba Diving

Traditionally, scuba diving was not a sport open to people with disabilities, but scuba and snorkeling have become a core part of adapted adventure-based activities. Before beginning training, the instructor and diver need to discuss water access and entry from the poolside, beach, or boat as well as medical issues that affect breathing, mobility, and vision. Once in the water, no architectural barriers prevent interaction with nature, and mobility is enhanced by a minimal amount of gravity. Modifications to equipment might include pressure gauges that have braille numbers or that emit auditory signals, divers tethered together, hand paddles or swim mitts, diving boots, low-volume masks, octopus regulators, jacket-type buoyancy compensators, flexible vented fins, Velcro on wetsuits, and diver propulsion vehicles for those who cannot propel themselves (Paciorek & Jones, 2001).

Handicapped Scuba Association (HSA) has programs to train people with disabilities to scuba dive and also trains scuba instructors to meet the needs of divers with disabilities. Founded in 1981 by Jim Gatacre, HSA certifies divers according to physical performance standards, regardless of disability type. Level A demonstrates that the diver can care for themselves and others, level B includes students who need partial support and must dive with two buddies, and level C includes students who need full support (two dive buddies, one of whom who is trained in dive rescue). Another international scuba diving organization is the International Association for Handicapped Divers (IAHD), founded in 1993 and based in The Netherlands. Similar to HSA, the IAHD certifies three levels of divers and conducts instructor training programs. The IAHD publishes a newsletter for its members and conducts seminars, symposiums, and dive conventions.

Although all agree that certified divers should possess requisite knowledge and skills for a safe and successful experience, controversy surrounds the subject of medical clearance. Scuba diving has been generally accepted for most people with orthopedic, vision, and auditory disabilities. However, secondary disabilities such as limited breathing capacity, osteoporosis, poor circulation, temperature regulation disorders, psychological conditions, and medical conditions such as seizure disorders, insulin-dependent diabetes, and asthma present a real concern for physicians and dive instructors

(Wang & Hung, 2009). Presently, the only sound advice for the prospective diver with a disability is to consult a physician experienced in hyperbaric medicine and to use caution when diving.

Boating

Boating activities can be enjoyed by all but are especially good for people with disabilities that affect the lower body, because paddling, rowing, and sailing emphasize upper body strength. Adaptations to equipment are the primary concern, along with embarking, disembarking, seating, and balance. People with cognitive disabilities have similar needs for instructional modifications in boating as they do in swimming: simplify, demonstrate, and repeat. People with vision impairments should have land-based training and a chance to practice their skills in shallow water or a pool. This practice is important because it is difficult for people who need to use tactile modeling (putting hands on the person demonstrating to feel movements) to be out in a boat and unable to move around because of safety or capsizing concerns. Two-person tandem kayaks are ideal for paddlers with visual impairments to use with a sighted partner.

Paddlers with mobility disabilities often need modifications to the access points of paddle sports. Hard-surface runways on beachfronts—including routes to accessible launch ramps, slips, and boarding piers—are needed for those who use wheelchairs, crutches, or canes and those who have balance problems. When runways are not available, a beach wheelchair could be used. Once a person with a mobility disability reaches the boat, it is recommended that a mat or cushion be placed over the gunwale, the boat steadied, and a plan of action for embarking established. Entry and exit procedures can be modified in several ways. For example, a modification might be as simple as the instructor standing or swimming in the water and stabilizing the boat, or two assistants helping to lift a boater onto a transfer mat from the dock. If the riverbed or lakebed is firm enough, it might be possible to push a water wheelchair into shallow water for water entries, with assistants to help lift and transfer, if necessary.

Commercial equipment for seating is available, such as sling-back seats, rubber materials to prevent slipping on the seat, and cushioning to protect people with sensitive skin. Instructors should analyze the movements, stability, cognitive ability, and strength of the participant to determine what type of canoe or kayak would be best. Several models of canoes and kayaks lend themselves to various needs. Open-decked or sit-on-top kayaks are advisable for warm water and for people who have difficulty in transferring. These vessels are easy to enter and exit but have a high center of gravity and don't lend themselves to seating adaptations (Adaptive Adventures, 2020). People who need adaptive seating systems or have poor balance would do best in an inflatable kayak (duckie). Sea kayaks are helpful for those who need seating systems because they have deep wells and come in many shapes.

Propulsion in paddle sports can be adapted using mitts or tubing to secure a paddler's hands to the paddle shaft. Further equipment modifications to enhance propulsion include printing the words *right* and *left* on the opposite paddle blades on a double-blade paddle or on the inside of the boat to help a paddler with an intellectual impairment, painting the inside of the boat with nonslip paint, using suction-cup bath mats on the bottom or seats of the boat, keeping a variety of paddle lengths available, and having participants use rubber or leather-palm gloves for a better grip.

In the United States, the primary organization for paddle sports is the American Canoe Association (ACA). The ACA sponsors the Adaptive Paddling Program (APP), which promotes canoeing, kayaking, and rafting as lifetime recreational activities for people with disabilities. In addition, its mission includes full integration of paddlers with varying abilities in all aspects of paddle sports. The APP is a clearinghouse on adaptations to equipment and accessibility to instruction, as well as a resource for instructors who want to include paddlers with disabilities. Adaptive paddling workshops are conducted nationally and provide certified paddling instructors with the information needed to integrate paddlers with disabilities into their programs (ACA, 2004). On completion of the four-day workshop, which includes classroom instruction, hands-on learning, and pool and open-water sessions, the adaptive paddling endorsement is achieved by certified paddling instructors. Because of new accessibility regulations for marinas, advancements in technology, and creative designs of adapted seating and paddles, more people with disabilities can now experience boating.

In addition to canoeing and kayaking, sailing opportunities have expanded rapidly through new programs and adapted boats for people with disabilities. Worldwide, the International Association for Disabled Sailing (IFDS, formerly the International Foundation for Disabled Sailing) makes positive contributions to the sport and is the governing body of Paralympic sailing (IFDS, 2007). The IFDS promotes sailing through the publication of reports of worldwide events and articles pertinent to the sport on its website. The IFDS publishes *IFDS Bulletin*, which contains information related to current and future trends in adapted sailing, upcoming races, and race results. The World Sailing Organization has a Para World Sailing committee that is responsible for sailing for individuals with disabilities throughout the world.

US Sailing has an adaptive sailing section on their website that provides information, resources, and opportunities for connections for sailors with disabilities. On the website, you will find an adaptive sailing events calendar, the *Adaptive Sailing Resource Manual*, and information on various awards associated with adaptive sailing.

Sailors with intellectual disabilities may participate in international competition through Special Olympics, which has included sailing in its World Games since 1995. Special Olympics individual, team, and Unified Sports categories exist at the local, national, and international levels. Athletes are placed in divisions according to age, sex, and ability.

One of the first adapted sailing programs in the United States, the Lake Merritt Adapted Boating Program of the Office of Parks and Recreation in Oakland, California, began in 1981. Glo Webel, boating programs coordinator, pioneered the development of sailing facilities for people with disabilities. Another pioneer and innovator in sailing is Harry Horgan, founder of Shake-A-Leg of Newport, Rhode Island. His boat design with adapted seating proved successful, and participants consider it to be the benchmark of modified sailing vessels.

People with disabilities may also pursue rowing for recreation or competition. At the international level, adaptive rowing is a commission within the World Rowing Federation (FISA), an advocate for inclusion of rowers with disabilities in races such as the World Rowing Championships. The goals of the commission are to oversee all areas of international adaptive rowing, increase participation in adaptive rowing on all levels, promote and monitor trends, and provide advice on adaptive rowing. The commission has been instrumental in the development of a classification and ranking system for racing. It successfully applied to the International Paralympic Committee (IPC) to make adaptive rowing a Paralympic sport for the first time in the 2008 Games. At present, there are three sport classes in para rowing:

PR1: For rowers with minimal or no trunk function who primarily propel the boat through arm and shoulder function. These rowers have poor sitting balance, which requires them to be strapped to the boat/seat.

PR2: For rowers that have functional use of arms and trunk but have weakness/absence of leg function to slide the seat.

PR3: For rowers with residual function in the legs which allows them to slide the seat. This class also includes athletes with a visual impairment.

USRowing is the national governing body for rowing in the United States and is a member of FISA. Its adaptive rowing committee has been active in recruiting members for the national team since its inception in 2002. One of the most active programs is the Philadelphia Rowing Program for the Disabled, held in the prestigious boathouse-row section of the Schuylkill River.

Safety and risk management are concerns for everyone in boating, but some people with disabilities need to take extra precautions. Those who are interested can become certified as instructors through the ACA or through USRowing. Zeller (2009) suggests that safety planning of any boating class should include a swim skills assessment, considerations for accessibility to the boating site, review of medical information, and considerations of the specific medical condition. In addition, it is crucial to assess what the participant can do on land and determine what medical information needs to be shared with others in the group in relation to an emergency action plan. Other safety issues include stumbling over unseen items on the boat or dock for boaters with vision impairments, failure to hear a shouted warning for Deaf boaters, bowel and bladder management issues for participants who are incontinent, change of weather conditions for those with temperature regulation disorders, and balance or grip problems on rough seas.

The amount of responsibility a paddler, sailor, or rower should have depends on functional ability. It is important to test the balance, stability, and buoyancy of the boat with the person in it while in shallow, calm water and to test equipment before undertaking a river or a lake trip. Other elements of safety include planning for embarkation and disembarkation, instructor-to-student ratio, and—as with all water sports—an emergency action plan. To determine which boat, method, and paddle are most appropriate, consider the participant's balance, grip strength and endurance, coordination, and upper extremity ROM. Consider, too, how much sight and hearing the person possesses, the ability to make decisions, and knowledge of cause and effect.

Water orientation should include instruction in safety, personal rescue, and proper PFD use. After the water orientation, boat orientation may begin on land, move into a pool and then calm outdoor water, and finally progress to moving and open water. Boat orientation should take into account terminology that is understandable to the participants, exploration of the boat by participants who are blind, entry and exit procedures, and propulsion and steering techniques. Participants and instructors must work together to modify equipment through trial and error based on knowledge of available commercial equipment.

Strategies for Inclusion

Including a student with a disability in an aquatic activity with peers without disabilities requires the teacher to review the results of the individual skill assessment and to look at the goals of the program, class, or activity in which the student will be placed. Even if a student is included in a general physical education environment on land, several questions must be answered by the IEP team before the student begins an inclusive aquatics program. Typical questions might include the following:

- How many of the participant's targeted goals and objectives match those that are possible within the general aquatics program?
- Can the participant follow rules and guidelines within the general program so as not to compromise the safety of all?
- Is an age-appropriate class available?
- Does the placement provide an emotionally and physically safe environment?
- Is the ultimate goal of the placement to be able to participate in aquatic activities in an integrated setting?
- Does the placement meet other goals in addition to instructional goals (e.g., recreational or therapeutic goals)?

Refer to the Application Example sidebar for a practical situation involving the inclusion of a student with disabilities.

Application Example

Including a Student With Cerebral Palsy in a General Education Diving Class

SETTING

A sixth-grade general physical education aquatics class

STUDENT

A 12-year-old girl with spastic CP who uses a power wheelchair

ISSUE

The class is learning how to dive, but the student does not have the prerequisite skills to participate—how can this student be accommodated?

APPLICATION

The student has head control and can close her mouth in response to splashing water. She can also hold on to the pool gutter and use her arms to do a modified elementary backstroke. Based on this information, the adapted aquatics instructor suggests the following modifications:

- An additional instructor trained in adapted aquatics should be available.
- While the rest of the class is practicing kneeling or standing dives, the student practices sitting on the pool edge with maximal support while wearing a life jacket. Assistants in the water and on deck help the student to fall into the pool and recover on her back.
- While the others are practicing diving, the student can work on surface dives in the deep end with an aide to assist her in plunging under the water and then recovering onto her back.
- The student can work on diving prerequisites, such as streamlined body position and pike or tuck position.
- The student can work on her IEP aquatic goals in the shallow end.

A critical factor in the successful inclusion of students with disabilities in the general aquatics program is the instructor. Instructors should work with swimmers and their caregivers to provide the most appropriate placement and curriculum for teaching aquatic skills (Chu & Pan, 2012). Studies show that aquatics instructors have positive attitudes toward including students with mild disabilities and that they have expressed perceived needs in the areas of adapted aquatics training, equipment, and class management in order to feel more successful with inclusion programs (Conatser et al., 2000). Currently, there is one formal adapted aquatics training program in the United States: the YMCA Swim Lessons for Individuals with Disabilities Instructor Certification.

Another critical factor for successful aquatics inclusion programs is matching the participants' prerequisite skills with the programs or classes they are put into. Participants should have a minimal level of skill competencies and possess several prerequisite skills for safe and successful experiences in an integrated class, regardless of whether the tasks are as simple as holding the pool gutter, closing the mouth when someone splashes, or not drinking pool water. Other prerequisites might include such factors as social, cognitive, and aquatic readiness skills vital to inclusive group integrity and learning. Support services are often needed to assist with skill prerequisites.

Unlike land-based physical activities, some students with disabilities cannot safely participate in aquatics with same-age peers without disabilities because of lack of ability. For example, if an entire instructional unit is taking place in a diving well and the student with a disability is overly fearful, the caregiver and the student must communicate with the instructor about what is needed, desired, and feasible.

Medical and health conditions are also concerns. Lepore and colleagues (2007) contend that some medical and health conditions, such as the following, might warrant a segregated setting, such as a hospital or therapy-oriented facility, or even a suspension of aquatic activities:

- Open sores, such as decubitus ulcers
- Uncontrolled seizures requiring emergency removal and clearing of the pool
- Tracheotomy tubes or ventilator dependency that might require shallow water, qualified health care professionals, heavily grounded electrical cords, and calm water with no splashing
- Neuromuscular conditions, arthritic conditions, cardiovascular diseases, or other conditions such as multiple sclerosis that require modified water temperatures
- Neurological conditions that require gradual change from water to air temperature because of inadequate thermoregulation systems
- High susceptibility to infection, requiring more sterile environments
- Allergies to chlorine, requiring pools with alternative chemical, UV, or ozone disinfection
- Behavior disorders, such as uncontrolled aggression, that may compromise the safety of others
- Hemophilia, possibly requiring calm water and limited bumping into other participants and equipment
- Detached retinas, requiring the need to avoid projectiles and any bumping of the head and face

Ways to enhance inclusion include modifications to equipment, rules, instruction, and the environment. Many suggestions have been integrated into the information in this chapter. Here are other strategies to try:

- Provide an alternative swimming activity (e.g., participants can complete a cannonball jump instead of a dive).
- Use an aide to provide physical support within an inclusive aquatics class.
- Provide a temporary segregated program in a small group or one on one when the skills in the inclusion group do not match the goals or abilities of the swimmer.
- Have the swimmer work with an adapted aquatics instructor in another area of the pool.
- Use peers trained as water safety aides or adapted aquatics teaching assistants who can provide assistance (e.g., repeating directions or providing constructive feedback).

An approach now receiving considerable attention for the education of all students is universal design for learning (UDL). As discussed in previous chapters, UDL involves a set of principles that teachers can use when planning for instruction, which include considerations for physical as well as curricular barriers that can affect student learning (Lieberman et al., 2021).

In an aquatics setting, planning for instruction using the principles of UDL can help to guide instructors in making appropriate modifications for all students. These may include modifications to instructional strategies and techniques, equipment, or the environment. Environmental modifications might include reducing background noise in the pool area, modifying the area of the pool used for the lesson, reducing the number of students in the class, or altering the instructor-to-student ratio. By implementing UDL principles when planning for instruction in an aquatics setting, all students can benefit. To assist teachers with implementing UDL principles in aquatic settings, Stribing (2021) and Gilbert and Stribing (2021) provide a number of lesson plans on units such as water exploration, basic strokes, and water safety, as well as canoeing and kayaking.

Summary

Aquatics can be an important part of a physical education program for students with disabilities. This chapter summarized the benefits of adapted aquatics, the importance of assessment, issues related to facilities and equipment, and general teaching tips for adapted aquatics. Physical educators should be familiar with the many possibilities afforded by water and advocate for aquatic experiences within the physical education program for students with disabilities, as well as after-school recreational and competitive opportunities, including swim team, boating, waterskiing, and scuba.

References

Adaptive Adventures. (2020). *Adaptive dragon boat racing, kayaking, paddleboarding, water skiing, wake boarding, and whitewater rafting.* Retrieved July 16, 2020, from https://adaptiveadventures.org/programs/

American Alliance for Health, Physical Education, Recreation and Dance (AAHPERD), & American Association for Active Lifestyles and Fitness (AAALF). (1996). *Adapted aquatics: Position paper.* Author.

American Red Cross. (2014). *Water safety instructor's manual.* StayWell.

Architectural and Transportation Barriers Compliance Board (ATBCB). (2004). Americans with Disabilities Act accessibility guidelines for buildings and facilities; final rule. *Federal Register,* 36 CFR Parts 1190 and 1191, July 23, 2004.

Arnhold, P., & Lorenzi, D.G. (2018). Aquatics for students with disabilities. In M. Grenier & L.J. Lieberman (Eds.), *Physical education for children with moderate to severe disabilities* (pp. 97-108). Human Kinetics.

Block, M.E. (2016). *A teacher's guide to adapted physical education: Including students with disabilities in sports and recreation* (4th ed.). Brookes.

Brody, L.T., & Geigel, P.R. (Eds.). (2009). *Aquatic exercise for rehabilitation and training.* Human Kinetics.

Brown, A. (2003). Access points: Ground rules. *Aquatics International, 15*(2), 14-16.

Casey, A.F., & Eames, C. (2011). The effects of swim training on respiratory aspects of speech production in adolescents with Down syndrome. *Adapted Physical Activity Quarterly, 28,* 326-341. https://doi.org/10.1123/apaq.28.4.326

Chu, C.H., & Pan, C.Y. (2012). The effect of peer- and sibling-assisted aquatic program on interaction behaviors and aquatic skills of children with autism spectrum disorders and their peers/siblings. *Research in Autism Spectrum Disorders, 6*(3), 1211-1223. https://doi.org/10.1016/j.rasd.2012.02.003

Conatser, P., Block, M.E., & Lepore, M. (2000). Aquatic instructors' attitudes toward teaching students with disabilities. *Adapted Physical Activity Quarterly, 17,* 197-207. https://doi.org/10.1123/apaq.17.2.197

Dimitrijevi, L., Aleksandrovic, M., Madic, D., Okicic, T., Radovanovic, D., & Daly, D. (2012). The effect of aquatic intervention on gross motor function and aquatic skills in children with cerebral palsy. *Journal of Human Kinetics, 32,* 167-174. https://doi.org/10.2478/v10078-012-0033-5

Epilepsy Foundation of America. (2020). *Seizure first aid resources.* Retrieved July 16, 2020, from www.epilepsy.com/living-epilepsy/toolbox/seizure-first-aid-resources

FISA Adaptive Rowing Commission. (2011). *FISA adaptive classifiers instruction manual.* www.worldrowing.com/mm/Document/General/General/11/35/13//FISA_Manual_2010hyperlinked_English.pdf

Gelbach, C. (2013, January). Aquatics and accessibility: Beyond ADA compliance. *Recreation Management,* 22-28.

Getz, M., Hutzler, Y., Vermeer, A., Yarom, Y., & Unnithan, V. (2012). The effect of aquatic and land-based training on the metabolic cost of walking and motor performance in children with cerebral palsy: A pilot study. *ISRN Rehabilitation, 2012,* Article ID 657979. https://doi.org/10.5402/2012/657979

Gilbert, E., & Stribing, A. (2021). Universal designed lesson plans for aquatics. In L. Lieberman, M. Grenier, A. Brian, & K. Arndt, *Universal design for learning in physical education* (pp. 171-185). Human Kinetics.

International Association for Disabled Sailing (IFDS). (2020). *Para world sailing.* Retrieved July 16, 2020, from www.sailing.org/new-to-sailing/disabled-sailing.php#.XxB0gihKjD4

Jackson, D.J., & Bowerman, S.J. (2009). Development of low cost functional adaptive aquatic equipment. *Texas Association HPERD Journal, 78*(1), 8.

Koury, J.M. (1996). *Aquatic therapy programming.* Human Kinetics.

Lee, J., & Porretta, D.L. (2013). Enhancing the motor skills of children with autism spectrum disorders: A pool-based approach. *Journal of Physical Education, Recreation and Dance, 84*(1), 41-45.

Lepore, M., Columna, L., & Friedlander Litzner, L. (2015). *Assessments and activities for teaching swimming.* Human Kinetics.

Lepore, M., Gayle, G.W., & Stevens, S.F. (2007). *Adapted aquatics programming: A professional guide* (2nd ed.). Human Kinetics.

Lieberman, L., Grenier, M., Brian, A., & Arndt, K. (2021). *Universal design for learning in physical education.* Human Kinetics.

Lorenzi, D., & Taliaferro, A. (2018). Swimming and water safety for children with autism. *Pennsylvania State Association for Health, Physical Education, Recreation, and Dance Journal, 88*(2), 31-33.

Paciorek, M.J., & Jones, J.A. (2001). *Disability sport and recreation resources* (3rd ed.). Cooper.

Pan, C.Y. (2011). The efficacy of an aquatic program on physical fitness and aquatic skills in children with and without autism spectrum disorders. *Research in Autism Spectrum Disorders, 5*(1), 657-665. https://doi.org/10.1016/j.rasd.2010.08.001

Patterson, C., & Grosse, S. (2013). Swimming for individuals with severe multiple impairments: A fitness imperative. *Palaestra, 27*(1), 30-35.

Prins, J., & Murata, N. (2008). Kinematic analysis of swimmers with permanent physical disabilities. *Journal of Aquatic Research and Education, 2*(4), 330-345. https://doi.org/10.25035/ijare.02.04.06

Rogers, L., Hemmeter, M., & Worley, M. (2010). Using a constant time delay procedure to teach foundational swimming skills to children with autism. *Topics in Early Childhood Special Education, 30*(2), 102-111. https://doi.org/10.1177/0271121410369708

Stanat, F., & Lambeck, J. (2001). The Halliwick method. *AKWA, 15*(1), 39-41.

Stillwell, B. (2007). Swimming instruction for those fearful of water. *Palaestra, 23*(1), 36-42.

Stopka, C. (2008). *Adapted equipment ideas to facilitate aquatics skills learning.* PE Central.

Stribing, A. (2021). Universal design lesson plans for recreation. In L. Lieberman, M. Grenier, A. Brian, & K. Arndt, *Universal design for learning in physical education* (pp. 155-169). Human Kinetics.

SwimAmerica. (n.d.). Organizational documents provided by SwimAmerica. 2101 N. Andrews Ave., Ste. 107, Fort Lauderdale, FL 33311.

USA Swimming. (n.d.). *Including swimmers with a disability.* Author.

USA Swimming. (2013). *USA Swimming rules and regulations.* Author.

Wang, J.S., & Hung, W.P. (2009). The effects of a swimming intervention for children with asthma. *Respirology, 14*(6), 838-842. https://doi.org/10.1111/j.1440-1843.2009.01567.x

Yilmaz, I., Konukman, F., Birkan, B., & Yanardag, M. (2010). The effects of most to least prompting on teaching simple progression swimming skills for children with autism. *Education and Training in Autism & Developmental Disabilities, 45*(3), 440-448.

YMCA of the USA. (1999a). *The parent/child and preschool aquatic program manual.* Human Kinetics.

YMCA of the USA. (1999b). *The youth and adult aquatics program manual.* Human Kinetics.

Zeller, J. (2009). *Canoeing and kayaking for people with disabilities.* Human Kinetics.

Video Resources

The Halliwick Method [PowerPoint and Video Clips]. International Halliwick Therapy Network (IHTN). www.halliwick.net/en/video/videos-water-specific-therapy

These videos present critical factors to consider when working with individuals with disabilities in the water using the Halliwick method.

Introduction to Adapted Aquatics [DVD]. (2009). Rothhammer International in conjunction with Human Kinetics.

This best practices DVD includes segments on aquatic assessment, inclusive groups, and a variety of commonly seen disabilities in children's adapted aquatics programs.

Online Resources

Adaptive Water Skiing: www.usaadaptivewaterski.org/adaptive-aquatics

This nonprofit organization is dedicated to the introduction, teaching, and advancement of adapted waterskiing for children and adults with physical disabilities.

American Red Cross: www.redcross.org

The American Red Cross provides water safety instructor certifications.

Aquatic Access: www.aquaticaccess.com

This site includes information related to aquatic lifts and ADA pool access.

Aquatic Physical Therapy: https://aquaticpt.org/

This site provides opportunities for physical therapists who would like to use the water for career opportunities.

Aquatic Therapy and Rehab Institute: www.atri.org

This resource provides continuing education opportunities for aquatic therapy.

International Paralympic Committee (IPC): www.paralympic.org

This organization conducts the Paralympics and creates classification procedures for athletes, including swimmers and boaters with disabilities.

National Center on Accessibility: www.ncaonline.org

This site contains information on all types of accessible recreation, including the swimming pool access project. It also includes an extensive bibliography on accessibility and pools.

National Drowning Prevention Alliance: www.ndpa.org

This site contains information and resources related to water safety and drowning prevention.

Swim Angelfish: www.swimangelfish.com

Specializing in adapted aquatics, this website includes resources and certifications.

USA Swimming: www.usaswimming.org/home/disability

USA Swimming has published a series of brochures, video resources, and articles, including guides for coaches, officials, swimmers and parents, meet directors, and local swimming committees. These are excellent resources that cover in-depth issues related to inclusion of swimmers with a variety of disabilities in general swim competitions and teams.

USRowing: www.usrowing.org

This site presents information about rowing programs, including the adaptive rowing committee.

Other Resources

Access to Recreation. 8 Sandra Ct., Newbury Park, CA 91320; phone: 800-634-4351. www.accesstr.com

This business offers adapted products designed to put people with disabilities into recreation and physical activities, including pool lifts and ramps, bath and shower chairs, pool floats, beach access chairs, and adapted water skis.

25

Team Sports

Amaury Samalot-Rivera

Juliana, a 15-year-old wheelchair user, will be included in a general physical education class as she transitions from middle to high school. Juliana is functioning at grade level academically; however, she has difficulty interacting with peers and becomes very frustrated when things don't go her way (e.g., losing a game). Mr. Thomas, the physical educator, was consulted about whether Juliana could safely and effectively participate in general physical education without her behavior affecting other students. Mr. Thomas believes that it will be challenging, especially because the curriculum has many sport units—however, he believes in inclusion and is willing to make the necessary accommodations to include Juliana.

The author thanks David Porretta for his significant contributions to this chapter and in all earlier editions of this book.

Team sports participation can promote community integration and social inclusion for individuals with disabilities. Further, sport participation has physical, emotional, and social benefits (Diaz et al., 2019). People with disabilities have excelled and continue to excel in amateur as well as professional team sports in elite and inclusive settings. Even though interscholastic sport opportunities have grown since the 1990s (Kozub & Ozturk, 2003; Kozub & Porretta, 1996), the lack of sufficient opportunities still exists (Kozub & Samalot-Rivera, 2020). For this reason, it is important to continue promoting sport opportunities in school and recreation settings, especially those of an inclusive nature. This chapter presents variations and modifications for popular team sports designed to promote inclusion and to help teachers such as Mr. Thomas provide the best possible physical education programs for students with disabilities.

Fully integrated sport is especially encouraged for people with auditory impairments. As early as the late 19th century, athletes with auditory impairments were excelling in sport alongside teammates without disabilities. For example, William Ellsworth "Dummy" Hoy, inducted into the Cincinnati Reds Hall of Fame in 2003, played Major League Baseball from 1886 to 1902 and was the first person with profound deafness to become a superstar in the game. He is also regarded as the first person to use hand signals typically used today by umpires and coaches. Kenny Walker (professional football) and Curtis Pride (professional baseball) are other examples of Deaf athletes who have excelled in sport. Both received signals from managers, coaches, and teammates while on the field. In sports that are played in a relatively small area (e.g., basketball and volleyball), few modifications might be needed. In volleyball, an official pulling the net might signal the beginning or ending of play. On the other hand, sports played on a large field might require more modification. For instance, in American football, flags and hand gestures can supplement whistles as signals. For Deaf players, a bass drum on the sideline might signal the snap of the ball instead of the quarterback's verbal cadence. However, it is now common for play to begin with Deaf players visually responding to the snap of the ball.

The USA Deaf Sports Federation (USADSF) and its international counterpart, the International Committee of Sports for the Deaf (ICSD), offer competition solely for those with hearing impairments. The USADSF and ICSD are independent of both the U.S. Olympic and Paralympic Committee (USOPC) and the International Paralympic Committee (IPC). USADSF team events include basketball, ice hockey, soccer, softball, team handball, and volleyball, in which athletes are classified according to sex and degree of hearing loss. These sports are regularly featured at the Deaflympics and follow international sport federation rules, with some minor adjustments. Because few modifications are needed for people with hearing impairments to participate in team sport, the focus in the remainder of this chapter is people with other types of disabilities.

Many organizations are now dedicated to providing sport programs for athletes with disabilities, such as the National Beep Baseball Association (NBBA), Special Olympics, and Move United. Beep baseball, goalball, quad rugby, and wheelchair softball, among others, are relatively new team sports designed for players with disabilities. Although still insufficient, sport opportunities for students with disabilities continue to grow, with new support for the development of club teams, intramurals, and interscholastic competition. This can be attributed, in part, to a 2013 position statement from the Office of Civil Rights emphasizing the need to support both the physical and competitive needs of athletes with disabilities in inclusive interscholastic programs (Kozub & Samalot-Rivera, 2020).

Basketball

Basketball is a popular activity in both physical education and sport programs. Most ambulatory people can participate in basketball with few or no modifications. However, those with severe mental disabilities or mobility problems might need greater modifications—for example, wheelchair basketball. Modifying skills, rules, or equipment can allow students with disabilities to effectively participate in the game.

Sport Skills

Important basketball skills include shooting, passing, and dribbling. Selected modifications are provided for each skill.

- *Shooting and passing.* Bounce passing is advised for partially sighted players because the sound of the bounce lets them know from which direction the ball is coming. Bounce passing also provides more time for players with unilateral upper limb impairments to catch the ball. One-hand shots and passes should be encouraged for players who have upper limb impairments. Players who use wheelchairs find the one-hand pass useful for long passes; when shooting at the basket, however, they often prefer the two-hand set shot (especially for longer shots) because both arms can put more force behind the ball. Hook passes are useful for those who use wheelchairs, especially when they are being closely guarded by an opponent. For people with ambulation difficulties, a net placed directly beneath the basket during shooting practice facilitates return of the ball. Players with upper limb impairments might find it helpful to trap or cradle the ball against the upper body when trying to catch a pass.

- *Dribbling*. For players with poor eye–hand coordination or poor vision, dribbling can be performed with a larger ball. For those with poor body coordination, it might be necessary to permit periodic bouncing during running or walking, although they can dribble the ball continually when standing still. Players who use wheelchairs will need to dribble to the left or the right of the chair and carry the ball in the lap when wheeling.

Lead-Up Games and Activities

Lead-up games and activities are important prerequisites to learning the game of basketball. Selected lead-up games and activities are discussed next.

- *Pig*. Two or more players play this shooting game, competing against each other from varying distances from the goal. To begin the game, a player takes a shot from anywhere on the court. If the shot is made, the next player must duplicate the shot (e.g., type of shot, distance). Failure to make the shot earns that player the letter *P*. If, however, the second player makes the shot, an additional shot may be attempted from anywhere on the court for the opponent to match. Players attempt shots that they feel their opponents might have difficulty making. The first person to acquire all of the letters (*P-I-G*) loses.
- *Circle shot*. This activity involves shooting a playground ball in any manner to a large basket about 45 inches (1.2 meters) high from six spots ranging from about 2 feet (0.5 meters) to 5 feet (1.5 meters) away from the basket. Two shots are attempted from each spot for a total of 12 shots. The player's score is the number of successful shots.
- *Other activities*. Other basketball lead-up activities might include bouncing a beach ball over a specified distance and shooting or dropping a playground ball into a large barrel or container.

Sport Variations and Modifications

Basketball is an official sport of the Dwarf Athletic Association of America (DAAA). The only modification to the game is that players use a slightly smaller ball (the size used by women in international play) for better dribbling and shooting control.

In Special Olympics competition, the game follows rules developed by the International Basketball Federation (FIBA) for all multinational and international competition (Special Olympics, 2016). Both full-court (5-on-5) and half-court basketball (3-on-3) are offered by Special Olympics. The only significant modifications are as follows:

- A smaller (size 6) basketball, 28.5 inches (72.5 centimeters) in circumference and 18 to 20 ounces (510-567 grams) in weight, might be used for women's and junior division play.
- A shorter basket of 8 feet (2.4 meters) might be used for junior division play.
- Players may take two steps beyond what is normally allowable while dribbling. In regulation basketball, the player can take no more than two steps while dribbling. So, for Special Olympics, players can take a total of four steps between dribbles. (However, if the player scores or escapes the defense, a violation is called.)

The National Wheelchair Basketball Association (NWBA, 2019) has also modified the game for wheelchair users (see figure 25.1). Examples of some major rule modifications include the following:

- The wheelchair is considered part of the player.
- Players must stay firmly seated in the chair at all times.
- An offensive player shall not remain in the key for more than four seconds.
- Dribbling consists of simultaneously wheeling the chair and dribbling the ball (a player cannot take more than two consecutive pushes without bouncing the ball). Taking more than two consecutive pushes results in a traveling violation.
- No player on the team with a throw-in into the front court shall enter the free throw lane until the throw-in starts.
- Personal fouls are charged to players who intentionally block, push, charge, or impede the progress of other players with either the body or the wheelchair.

FIGURE 25.1 Wheelchair basketball play.

Skill Event Variations and Modifications

Special Olympics offers two levels of individual basketball skills competition. Level 1 consists of shooting, dribbling, and passing. Scores for all three events are added to obtain a final score. The shooting competition is called *spot shot* and measures the athlete's skill in shooting a basketball. Six spots are marked on the basketball floor—three spots to the left of the basket and three spots to the right of the basket. The athlete attempts two shots from each of the six spots. The first six shots are taken from the right of the basket, and the second six shots are taken from the left. Points are awarded for every field goal made. The farther the spot is from the basket, the higher the point value. For any shot that hits the backboard or rim and does not go into the basket, 1 point is scored. The athlete's score is the sum of all 12 shots.

The 10-meter event requires the athlete to dribble with one hand as fast as possible for a distance of 10 meters. If control of the ball is lost, the athlete can recover the ball. If, however, the ball goes outside of the designated 1.5-meter lane, the ball may be retrieved, or a backup ball placed 5 meters outside of the lane at the start of the event might be picked up. Points are awarded depending on how long it takes to dribble the entire 10 meters. A 1-second penalty is added for each illegal (e.g., two-handed) dribble. Two trials for this event are allowed. The athlete's score is the better of the two trials.

In the target pass event, the athlete must pass the ball from a distance of 2.4 meters to a 1-meter-square target on the wall that is 1 meter off the floor. Five attempts are allowed. The athlete receives 3 points for hitting the inside of the target, 2 points for hitting the lines of the target, 1 point for hitting the wall but no part of the target, and 1 point for catching the ball on the return from the wall. The final score is the sum of all five passes.

Level 2 individual skills competition consists of a 12-meter dribble, a catch and pass event, and perimeter shooting. Complete descriptions of these skills can be found in the Special Olympics basketball rules (Special Olympics, 2016).

Other Variations and Modifications

Game rules might be simplified by reducing the types of fouls players are allowed to commit. The basket can be lowered, enlarged, or both. The game area might be restricted to half-court for players with mobility impairments, such as those using lower limb prostheses. Shorter play periods and frequent substitutions might be incorporated into the game for players with cardiac or asthmatic conditions. Those with poor arm strength, coordination, or range of motion can be allowed to tap the ball at least once rather than dribbling it before it can be shot or passed. Lightweight or playground balls might also be used.

American Football

People with mild impairments who are in good physical condition can play the regulation game of tackle football. A small number of players possessing partial sight participate on high school and collegiate teams, and people who are legally blind can be successful placekickers or play offensive line, depending on the degree of vision loss. For example, Jake Olson, who lost his sight, played long snapper on his high school American football team. People with unilateral amputations either below the knee or above or below the elbow are able to participate in regulation American football as long as their prostheses do not pose a safety risk. For safety purposes, flag or touch football is more commonly offered in physical education and recreation programs. Most people with intellectual disabilities, except those with severe impairment, can be safely included with other players. Players with significant physical impairments may prefer modified or less integrated participation.

Sport Skills

Important American football skills include passing, catching, and kicking. Selected modifications are provided for each skill.

- *Passing.* Players possessing partial sight are able to pass the ball as long as distances are short and receivers wear bright-colored clothing. For players with poor grip strength or pronounced hand or wrist contracture, or for those on crutches, a softer, smaller ball may be used to promote holding and gripping. Wheelchair users are able to pass the ball if they have sufficient arm and shoulder strength; however, they will find it almost impossible to perform an underhand lateral pass while facing the line of scrimmage, so this type of pass must be performed facing the receiver.
- *Catching.* Players with partial sight and those who are wheelchair users should face the passer when attempting to catch the ball. Instead of trying to catch with the hands only, they should cradle the ball with both hands or trap the ball in the midsection. The ball should be passed from short distances without great speed; a foam ball should be used for safety purposes. Players who have unilateral arm deformities should catch the ball by stopping it with the palm of the nonimpaired hand and trapping it against the body. Wheelchair users are able to catch effectively if the ball is thrown accurately (using a chair limits catching range).
- *Kicking.* Players with partial or no available sight might be encouraged to practice punting without shoes so they can feel the ball contacting the foot. In learning the punt, players should be instructed to point the toes (plantar flex the foot) while kicking. A player with unilateral arm amputation can punt the ball by having it rest in the palm of the nonimpaired hand. A punting play might begin with the player already holding the ball instead of with a snap from center.

Lead-Up Games and Activities

Lead-up games and activities are important prerequisites to learning the game of American football. Selected lead-up games and activities are recommended here.

- *Kickoff football.* The game is played on a playground 30 yards (27.5 meters) by 60 yards (55 meters) by two teams of six to eight players each. The football is kicked off from the center of the field; the object of the game is to return the kickoff as far as possible before being touched by an opponent (two-handed). The team returning the ball may use a series of lateral passes to advance it; forward passes are not permitted. Play stops when the ball carrier is touched. The other team then kicks off from the middle of the field. The team advancing farthest up the field is the winner.
- *Football-throw activity.* A player attempts to pass a football from a distance of 20 feet (9 meters) through the hole of a large rubber tire suspended 4 feet (1.2 meters) from the ground on a rope. Ten attempts are given, and the player's score is the number of successful passes out of 10.
- *Other activities.* Other lead-up activities include placekicking or punting the ball for distance,

centering the ball to a target for accuracy, performing relays in which players hand the ball off to each other, and guessing the number of throws or kicks it will take to cover a predetermined distance.

Sport Variations and Modifications

Wheelchair football is one variation that is gaining in popularity. It can be played on any hard, flat surface—the boundaries for a standard basketball court work well. With few exceptions, the game is similar to touch football. Teams are composed of six players to a side and a standard youth football is used; power, standard, or sport chairs are acceptable. Because most contact occurs wheelchair to wheelchair, protective equipment is optional, but could include a bike helmet, gloves, seat belt, and eyewear. The American Association of Adapted Sports Programs (AAASP) publishes a wheelchair football rulebook (2019a). Some of the more common rule modifications are as follows:

- Two first-down markers divide the field of play (court) into three equal sections.
- Throwing the ball down the field simulates a kickoff or punt.
- Contact behind the opponent's rear axle is considered clipping; grabbing an opponent or the opponent's chair is considered holding.
- Players cannot raise both hips simultaneously off the wheelchair to gain advantage. Raising one hip such as in reaching out to catch a pass is acceptable.
- Point-after attempts are initiated from either the court's three-point line or free throw line, depending on whether one-point or two-point attempts are initiated.

Skill Event Variations and Modifications

Various skill events are possible. A catching event might require a player to run a specified pattern (e.g., down and out) and catch the ball. Five attempts are given, with the total number of catches constituting the player's score.

In a field goal event, players attempt to placekick a football over a rope suspended 8 feet (2.4 meters) from the ground between two poles 40 feet (12.2 meters) apart. Kicks might be attempted from 5 yards (4.6 meters), 10 yards (9.1 meters), 15 yards (13.7 meters), 20 yards (18.3 meters), or 25 yards (22.9 meters) from the rope. Ten kicks are given; players might kick from any or all of the five distances. Points are awarded from 1 to 5 according to the distance kicked. The total number of points after 10 successful kicks is the player's score.

Other Variations and Modifications

Game situations can be simplified by restricting them to include only specific skills—for example, only passing plays might be allowed. The field can be shortened and narrowed, and the number of players on each team can be reduced. In addition, first-down yardage can be reduced to less than 10 yards (9.1 meters). Players who are unable to throw with one hand due to lack of arm strength, coordination, or range of motion can be allowed to perform a two-handed chest pass or a two-hand overhead throw.

Soccer

Soccer is included in many physical education and sport programs. Because of the large playing area and continuous play, soccer requires stamina. However, the game can be varied or modified so that people with disabilities can participate. For those with minimal impairments (e.g., mild learning disability), no modifications in the game are necessary. When regulation sport competition is not possible, the United States Power Soccer Association (USPSA), the Cerebral Palsy International Sports and Recreation Association (CPISRA), the USADSF, and Special Olympics provide competition opportunities for players with disabilities.

Sport Skills

Important soccer skills include kicking, trapping, heading, and goalkeeping. Selected modifications are provided for each skill.

- *Kicking*. Whether dribbling, passing, or shooting, kicking is of paramount importance in soccer. People with upper limb amputations can learn to kick the ball effectively, but they might have difficulty with longer kicks because the arms are normally used to maintain balance. People with unilateral lower limb amputations might use a prosthesis for support or might prefer to play in a wheelchair. Wheelchair users dribble the ball by using the footrests of the chair to contact the ball and push it forward; they are also permitted to throw the ball.

• *Trapping.* Most players can learn to trap the ball effectively. Foam balls are good for players who are hesitant to have the ball hit the body or whose medical conditions limit rougher play. Players in wheelchairs might have some difficulty trapping because the sitting position impedes the reception of the ball on the chest and abdomen. However, some players learn to trap the ball in their laps.

• *Heading.* Most players can learn to head the ball successfully, although heading should not be encouraged for players with conditions such as brain injury or atlantoaxial instability. Players with mental or visual impairments might find using a balloon or beach ball helpful for learning to head because they are soft and give players time to make body adjustments before ball contact. Players with upper limb amputations can be very effective in heading the ball. Players who use wheelchairs are able to head the ball as long as it comes directly to them; however, the distance the player can head the ball will be limited because the backrest of the chair and sitting position limit the player's ability to exert force on the ball.

• *Goalkeeping.* Goalkeeping requires that the goalie be able to catch or trap the ball with the hands, as well as kick. It also requires that the goalie be able to react quickly. Because playing this position requires little cardiorespiratory endurance, many players with limited endurance can successfully play goalie. Wheelchair users can catch effectively as long as upper limb involvement is minimal. Most players with one arm find it difficult to catch in the goalie position. In this case, they should be encouraged to slap, trap, or strike the ball. For some players with limited mobility, reducing the size of the goal can help.

Lead-Up Games and Activities

Lead-up games and activities are important prerequisites to learning the game of soccer. This section presents selected lead-up games and activities.

• *Line soccer.* The game might be played on a playground with two teams, preferably of 8 to 10 players each. The teams stand in two lines facing each other from a distance of about 8 meters, with players spaced about 0.5 meters apart. Players on each team try to kick a soccer ball below shoulder level past their opponents. After each score, players rotate one position to the right. A team scores 1 point each time the ball passes the opponents' line, and 1 point is scored against a team that uses hands to stop the ball.

• *Accuracy kick.* This activity involves kicking a playground ball into a goal area 1.5 meters wide from a distance of 3 meters. A player is allowed three kicks from either a standing or sitting position. The player receives 3 points each time a ball is kicked into the goal, 2 points each time the ball hits a flagstick (placed at either side of the goal) but does not pass through the goal, and 1 point each time the ball is kicked in the direction of the goal but does not reach the goal. Following three kicks, players' scores are compared.

• *Other activities.* Additional activities include heading a beach ball into a large goal area from a short distance, dribbling a soccer ball in a circle around stationary players as fast as possible, throwing a soccer ball inbounds for distance, keeping a balloon in the air by kicking it, punting a soccer ball for distance, and playing scooter soccer.

Sport Variations and Modifications

Modifications in the sport of soccer have been introduced by several organizations. The American Association of Adapted Sports Programs (AAASP) and the European Handball Federation offer information and competition for wheelchair handball (also known as indoor wheelchair soccer). In wheelchair handball, players are classified into four groups by trunk movement and stability; then the degree of upper limb ability is taken into consideration. For example, class I players use a motorized wheelchair, whereas class IV players use manual wheelchairs and have near-normal function of the upper extremities and good-to-normal trunk control. Teams are composed of four to six on-court players, including the goalie. The game is composed of two 25-minute halves. A 10-minute sudden death overtime is played if the score is tied after regulation play. AAASP publishes a wheelchair handball rulebook (2019b). The following are modifications for wheelchair handball:

- The game is played on a gym floor with boundaries 50 feet (15.2 meters) wide and 84 feet to 94 feet (25.6-28.6 meters) long.
- A yellow number 10 rubber playground ball with a bladder is used.
- The goal measures 5 feet, 6 inches (1.7 meters) high, 5 feet (1.5 meters) wide, and 4 feet (1.2 meters) deep.
- Penalty boxes are located at midcourt on the opposite side of team benches.

- Penalty shots and power plays are used.
- The hands, feet, chair, or any part of the body can be used to move the ball.
- Dribbling the ball with one or both hands simultaneously is permitted.
- Players are not permitted to rise from the wheelchair to gain an advantage.
- A maximum of 3 seconds is permitted for a player to hold or maintain possession of the ball before attempting a pass, dribble, or shot.
- Unnecessary roughness, holding, hooking, or ramming into another wheelchair results in penalties.

Players who can ambulate are eligible to play seven-a-side soccer. Rules generally follow Fédération Internationale de Football Association (FIFA) standards (IFCPF, 2020) and players adhere to a three-level classification (level 1: severe impairment; level 2: moderate impairment; level 3: minimal impairment). Along with the seven-player limit, some modifications are as follows:

- At least one level 1 player must be on the field at all times, whereas no more than one level 3 player is on the field at any one time.
- Players are not allowed to use crutches.
- No offside rule is applied.
- An underhand throw-in is permitted.
- Teams may consist of male and female players.
- The field dimensions are 82 yards (75 meters) by 60 yards (55 meters); standard junior-size goals are 19 feet (5.8 meters) by 7 feet (2.1 meters).

In Special Olympics, soccer is played as five-a-side, seven-a-side, and 11-a-side, and FIFA rules are followed (Special Olympics, 2018a). There are no major modifications for 11-a-side soccer. However, the standard length of the game (two 45-minute periods) can be shortened to account for players' ability levels and physical condition. The following modifications, among others, are applied for five-a-side soccer:

- The field dimensions must be a minimum of 40 by 30 meters and a maximum of 50 by 35 meters. The smaller field is recommended for lower-ability teams.
- The goal must be between a minimum of 3 by 2 meters and a maximum of 4 by 2 meters.
- A ball over the sideline results in a kick-in.
- There are two 15-minute periods.

The following modifications, among others, are applied to seven-a-side soccer:

- The field dimensions must be a minimum of 50 by 35 meters and a maximum of 70 by 50 meters. The smaller field is recommended for lower-ability teams.
- The goal must be 5 by 2 meters.
- A ball over the sideline results in a kick-in.
- There are two 20-minute periods.

The game of soccer is also modified for players using motorized wheelchairs (figure 25.2). Known as *power soccer*, it originated in France in the early 1970s and was introduced in the United States in the 1980s. Because many countries developed their own versions of the sport, an international meeting held in Paris in 2005 created the Fédération Internationale de Powerchair Football Association (FIPFA), and in 2006 the USPSA was formed. The USPSA promotes both national and international play and sponsors a training program for officials. The organization is currently working toward getting power soccer recognized as a Paralympic sport. Power soccer is also offered through Move United.

USPSA (2012) has published a power soccer rules manual. It is played on an indoor court (regulation basketball court) with a 33-centimeter soccer ball. Teams are mixed-gender and composed of four players each. The strategy is similar to that in rugby. Bumpers on footrests (to maneuver the ball and protect the chair and player) and anti-tip bars on chairs are mandatory for safety and ball control. To score, the ball must travel through a goal at the end of the court, designated by two cones 7.6 meters apart. According to Jeffress and Brown (2017), power soccer provides participants with an increased sense of empowerment, social capital, and independence.

Both the American Youth Soccer Organization (AYSO) and the United States Youth Soccer Association (USYSA) offer modified programs for young people with disabilities. The AYSO sponsors a VIP (Very Important Player) program in which children with physical and intellectual disabilities are matched with volunteer buddies to play a modified game. Teams are organized according to ability, size, and gender when numbers allow. For more information on the VIP soccer program, visit the AYSO website (www.ayso.org). The USYSA sponsors a similar modified program for young people with disabilities called TOPSoccer and offers grants

FIGURE 25.2 Power soccer is a relatively new sport for those who have quadriplegia.

to communities interested in starting a TOPSoccer program. TOPSoccer players are placed on teams according to ability, not age. Each community program is unique in that it is created around the needs of its participants. For more information on TOPSoccer, visit the USYSA website (www.usyouthsoccer.org).

Skill Event Variations and Modifications

Special Olympics offers individual soccer skills competitions in dribbling, shooting, and running and kicking. Athletes perform each event twice, and all scores are then added for a total score. In the dribbling event, the player dribbles the ball 15 meters down a 5-meter lane into a 5-meter finish zone marked with cones. The clock stops when both the player and the ball are stopped inside the finish zone. If players overdribble the finish zone, they must dribble the ball back into the zone to finish. If the ball runs over the sideline, the referee places another ball in the center of the lane opposite the point at which the ball went out. The elapsed time it takes to do this is converted into points. The maximum number of points that can be obtained is 60, and the minimum is 10, minus a 5-point deduction each time the ball runs over the sideline or a player touches the ball with her hands.

In the shooting event, the player runs forward a distance of 2 meters and then kicks a stationary ball into a goal 4 meters wide by 2 meters deep from a distance of 6 meters. Once the kick is made, the player returns to the starting line. A total of five kicks are allowed, and each successful kick is worth 10 points.

In the run-and-kick event, the player stands 4 meters from four balls (one to the left, one to the right, one in front, and one in back). The player begins by running to any ball and kicking it 2 meters through a target gate that is 2 meters wide and formed by cones. Play continues until all four balls have been kicked. From when the player starts to when the last ball is kicked, total time is recorded in seconds. The time is then converted into points. The maximum number of points is 50; the minimum number is 5. In addition, a bonus of 5 points is added for each ball kicked successfully through the target.

Other Variations and Modifications

For a simplified game, the number of players and field dimensions can be reduced. For players with low stamina, a partially deflated ball (which does not travel as fast as a fully inflated ball) can be used, and frequent rest breaks, substitutions, or time-outs can be incorporated into the game. A soft foam soccer ball or a cage ball can be used. Players with upper limb deficiencies might be allowed to kick the ball inbounds on a throw-in. Additional players may be situated along the sidelines to take throw-ins for their teams. Penalty kicks can be employed for penalties occurring outside of goal areas. To avoid mass convergence on the ball, players can be required to play in specific areas on the field.

Softball

With certain modifications, softball can be played in an inclusive setting by most people with disabilities, although players with visual or mobility impairments might find competing in disability-specific leagues more appropriate. Some organizations that sponsor these competitions include the National Wheelchair Softball Association (NWSA), the NBBA, Special Olympics, and the DAAA. The DAAA follows Amateur Softball Association of America (ASA) rules with no modifications.

Sport Skills

Important softball skills include throwing, catching, fielding, and batting. Selected modifications are offered for each skill.

- *Throwing.* People with visual impairments throw with better accuracy if the catcher communicates verbally with the thrower. For players with small hands or hand impairments, the use of a smaller or foam ball is recommended. Because of control problems, people with cerebral palsy might prefer using a slightly heavier ball. People with lower limb disabilities can learn to throw the ball quite well; however, they may have difficulty throwing for distance because body rotation might be limited. A player with a unilateral upper limb amputation is able to throw the ball without much difficulty.
- *Catching and fielding.* Players with visual impairments learn to catch more easily if a large, brightly colored ball is initially rolled or bounced. A beep baseball, described in the Sport Variations and Modifications section, will be most helpful. People using wheelchairs and those with crutches or with braces might wish to use a large glove. Players with upper limb deficiencies are able to catch with one hand as long as eye–hand coordination is well developed. (After the catch, the player removes the glove with the ball by placing it under the armpit of the limb segment; the hand is then quickly drawn from the glove to grasp the ball for the throw. Jim Abbott, a former major league pitcher, used this technique.)

  An oversized glove can facilitate fielding for players with poor eye–hand coordination. Fielders should face the direction from which the ball is being hit, and players with visual impairments should be encouraged to listen for a ground ball moving along the ground. Players with assistive devices or in wheelchairs can be paired with sighted players without disabilities for assistance in fielding. Although a fielder using a wheelchair should be able to intercept a ball independently, the assisting player can retrieve it from the ground after interception and hand it to the player with a disability for the throw.
- *Batting.* Players with upper limb deficiencies are able to bat as long as the nonimpaired limb possesses enough strength to swing the bat. To promote hitting, the player might use a lighter bat grasped close to the middle. Wheelchair users or those using crutches must rely more on arm and shoulder strength for batting because they lack lower body power for the swing. Plastic bats with large barrels are helpful for people with poor arm and grip strength or poor eye–hand coordination. In this case, a large Wiffle ball should be used.

Lead-Up Games and Activities

Lead-up games and activities are important prerequisites to learning the game of softball. Selected lead-up games and activities are discussed here.

- *Roundtrip softball.* The game is played on a softball field with a pitcher and catcher, a batter, and one fielder. The object of the game is for the batter to hit a pitched softball into fair territory, then run to first base and return home before the fielder or pitcher can get the ball to the catcher. The batter is out when three strikes are made, a fly ball is caught, or the ball reaches the catcher before the batter returns home.
- *Rotation team softball.* The game is played in any open area with six players. Players position themselves in any manner about 3.5 meters from each other. To begin play, the first player throws the ball to the second player. Each player attempts to catch the softball and throw it (in any manner) to the next one. When the sixth player catches the ball, he attempts to throw it to a 1-meter-square target from a distance of 4 meters. Following that throw, players rotate positions until each player has had an opportunity to throw the ball to the target.

• *Other activities.* Additional activities include throwing beanbags in an underarm manner through a hoop suspended from the floor, hitting balls for distance from a batting tee, punching a volleyball pitched underarm, keeping a balloon in the air by hitting it with a plastic stick, and batting a ball suspended from the ceiling or a tetherball pole.

Sport Variations and Modifications

Beep baseball, designed for athletes with visual impairments, is sanctioned by the NBBA. The object of the game is for the batter to hit a regulation 16-inch (40.6-centimeter) softball equipped with a special sound-emitting device and to reach base before an opposing player fields the ball. To obtain beep ball equipment, visit the NBBA website at www.nbba.org. The Telecom Pioneers, a volunteer organization, has been largely responsible for the success of beep baseball.

Teams are composed of six players. Each team may have two additional teammates on the roster; they play blindfolded only when no other player with visual impairment is available to play. All players, even those with visual impairment, must wear blindfolds. In addition to the two teammates who might be on the roster, two sighted players function as the pitcher and catcher. The pitcher throws the ball from a distance of 20 feet (6.1 meters) in an underarm motion to the batter. The pitcher must give two verbal cues to the batter before the pitch: "ready" and "pitch" (or "ball"). The sighted catcher not only retrieves pitched balls but also assists batters by positioning them in the batter's box. See figure 25.3 for a diagram of the beep baseball field.

On defense, both sighted players (spotters) stand in the field and assist their six teammates in fielding the ball by calling out the number of the defensive player closest to the ball. The spotters cannot field balls themselves. If a hit ball presents a chance of injury to a player, the spotter might yell a warning. Also, a spotter might knock down an unusually hard-hit ball headed directly toward a player; however, a run will be awarded to the offensive team. To assist players and spotters, position markers can be spray painted on the field to identify defensive positions. A batter gets four strikes—one ball may go by without penalty, and any additional pitched balls that are not swung at are strikes. Bunting is not allowed. Each side has three outs per inning, and there are six innings to an official game (unless more are needed to break a tie).

On hitting the ball beyond the foul line (see figure 25.3), the batter runs to one of two bases (one located down the third-base line and one located down the first-base line) that are at least 122 centimeters high. Bases are padded cylinders that contain battery-powered, remotely controlled buzzers that emit a steady buzz when activated (figure 25.4); the umpire predetermines which buzzer is to be activated by giving a hand signal to the base operator before the ball is hit. The bases are located off the foul line to prevent a defensive player from colliding with a base runner. To score a run, the batter must touch the appropriate base before an opposing player cleanly fields the ball.

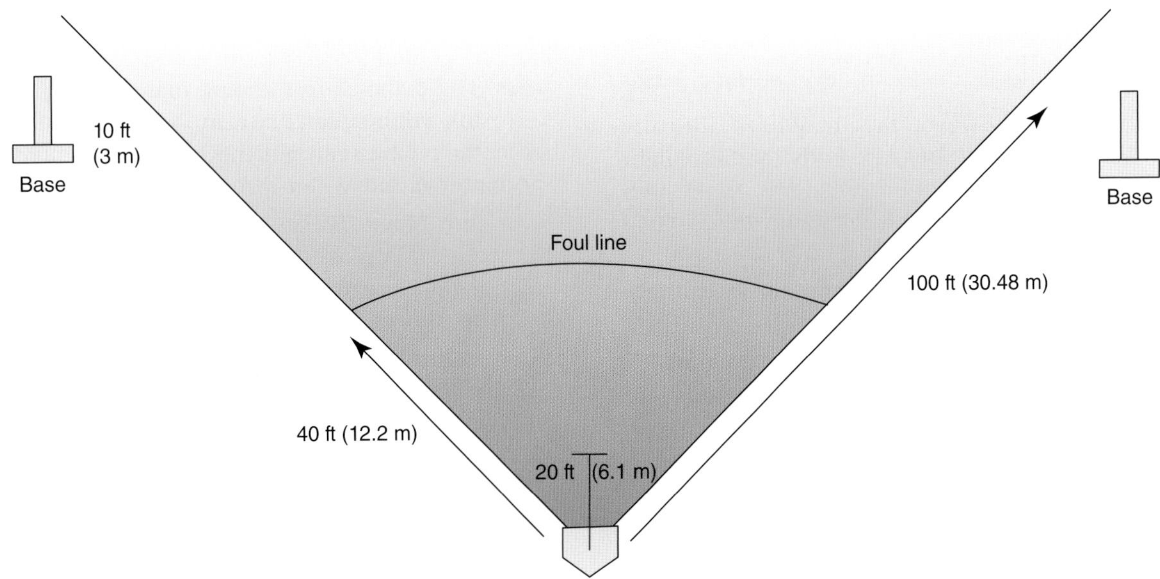

FIGURE 25.3 Beep baseball field.

© David L. Porretta

FIGURE 25.4 Batter running to touch the base, which buzzes to help the batter locate it, after hitting the ball.

However, if the opposing player fields the ball before the batter reaches base, the batter is out.

The game of softball has also been modified for players using wheelchairs by the NWSA (see figure 25.5). The game is played under official rules for 16-inch (40.6-centimeter) slow-pitch softball as approved by the ASA with the following major modifications:

- Manual wheelchairs with foot platforms must be used.
- The field is a smooth, level surface; bases are painted onto the surface.
- Bases are 50 feet (15.2 meters) in length from each other; home plate to second base is a distance of 70 feet, 8 inches (21.5 meters).
- The pitching stripe is located 28 feet (8.5 meters) from home plate.
- Second base is composed of a circle with a 4-foot (1.2-meter) diameter; first and third bases are composed of 4-foot (1.2-meter) semicircles.
- Teams are balanced by a point system.
- Neither a hitter nor a fielder (when playing the ball) can have any lower extremity in contact with the ground.
- Each team is composed of 10 players. Teams must have a player with quadriplegia on the team and in active play.

The game of softball is also modified for Special Olympics (2018b). Official events include slow-pitch, coach pitch, and tee ball competitions. All events follow International Softball Federation (ISF) and national governing body rules for slow-pitch softball. The following are some modifications used for the slow-pitch game:

- The distance from home plate to the pitching rubber can vary in distance from 40 feet (12.2 meters) to 50 feet (15.3 meters) as needed.
- Ten players play defense at any one time. An extra player may also be used; if so, all 11 players must bat, and any 10 are allowed to play defense.
- If the batter has two strikes and fouls off the third pitch, the batter is out.
- The catcher must wear a face mask and batter's helmet.

For young people with disabilities, additional modified programs are available. The Little League Challenger division is open to boys and girls with physical or intellectual disabilities who are

© David L. Porretta

FIGURE 25.5 Softball can also be modified for players who use wheelchairs.

5 to 18 years of age or who remain in school; a senior Challenger division is also offered. Players are assigned teams based on size, skill, and age. A buddy system may be used but is not mandatory. The Challenger division has three levels: tee ball, coach pitch, and player pitch. For additional information, visit the Little League website (see the Online Resources). For communities where Little League is not available, community organizers can offer a similar modified program through the Miracle League, in which children with various physical or intellectual disabilities participate with community children who serve as buddies. What makes the Miracle League unique is that games are played on a specially designed field with a rubber surface similar to that used in wheelchair softball. For more information on the program, visit the Miracle League website (www.miracleleague.com).

Skill Event Variations and Modifications

Special Olympics offers individual skills competition in four events: base running, throwing, fielding, and hitting. The scores for each event are added to obtain the athlete's final score. In the base running event, the player must start at home plate, run the bases positioned 65 feet (19.8 meters) apart, and return home as fast as possible. The completed time, in seconds, is subtracted from 60 to determine the point score; a 5-second penalty is given for each base missed or touched in improper order. The better of two trials is counted.

In the throwing event, the object is to throw a softball as far and as accurately as possible. Two attempts are given, and the player's score is the distance of the longest throw (measured from the restraining line to the point where the ball first touches the ground). The score reflects the throwing distance in meters minus the error distance (the number of meters the ball landed to the left or right of a perpendicular throwing line marked from the restraining line).

The fielding event requires the player to catch a total of 10 ground balls (five attempts per trial for a total of two trials) thrown by an official. The throw from the official must hit the ground before traveling 20 feet (6.1 meters). Catching the ball in the glove or trapping it against the body but off the ground earns 5 points, and blocking the ball scores 2 points. The athlete can move aggressively to the thrown ball as needed.

The hitting event requires the player to bat for distance by hitting a softball off a batting tee. Three attempts are allowed, and the longest hit is the player's score. The distance is measured in meters from the tee to the point at which the ball first touches the ground. If the score falls between meters, the score is rounded down to the lower meter.

Other Variations and Modifications

To accommodate players' varying ability levels, the number of strikes a batter is allowed can be increased. In some cases, fewer bases can be used, and distances between bases can be shortened. Half-innings might end when three outs have been made, six runs have been scored, or 10 batters have come to bat. In addition, lightweight and large-barreled bats might be used. A larger ball or restricted-flight softball, which travels a limited distance when hit, might also be used. For players with poor eye–hand coordination, such as those with cerebral palsy or traumatic brain injury, the ball might be hit from a batting tee. For players with more severe impairments, the ball might be rolled down a groove or tube-like channel when they are at bat. A walled or fenced area is recommended for players with mobility impairments so that distances can be shortened. In addition, a greater number of players on defense may be allowed, especially if players have mobility problems. The game can also be modified so that it is played in a gym with a Wiffle ball and bat. Finally, for those with amputations or severe arm deformities, the game of kickball may be substituted for the game of softball.

Volleyball

Volleyball is a popular game that can be played by most people with disabilities. However, for players with severe intellectual disabilities or those with significant visual or mobility impairments, the game might require modifications.

Sport Skills

Important volleyball skills include serving and striking. The following are selected modifications for each skill.

- *Serving.* Players with disabilities can learn to serve quite effectively. Very young players or those with insufficient arm and shoulder strength can move closer to the net. It is helpful to begin with an underhand serve, using the nondominant hand to support the ball and the dominant hand (fisted) to strike the ball in an underhand motion. As players develop coordination, they can progress to the overhand serve. Players with one functional arm can serve overhand by tossing the ball into the air with the nonimpaired arm and then hitting it with the same arm. Wheelchair users are able to perform both the underhand and overhand serves, though for the underhand serve, it is important to be in a chair without armrests.
- *Striking.* Players with visual impairments can competently hit the ball with two hands if the ball is first allowed to bounce to give the player more time to visually and aurally track the ball. Because of limited mobility, players on crutches need to learn to return the ball with one hand. However, players using wheelchairs can use both hands to return the ball within their immediate area. As these players become more adept in predicting the flight of the ball, they will be able to make a greater percentage of returns.

Lead-Up Games and Activities

Lead-up games and activities are important prerequisites to learning the game of volleyball. Selected lead-up games and activities are provided here.

- *Keep It Up.* This game is played by teams that form circles about 15 to 20 feet (4.6-6.1 meters) in diameter. Any number of teams of six to eight members each may play. To begin the game, a team member tosses the volleyball into the air within the circle. Teammates use both hands to keep hitting the ball into the air without letting it hit the ground. A player may not strike the ball twice in succession. The team that keeps the ball in the air the longest scores 1 point; the team with the most points (e.g., 5 points) wins the game.
- *Serving Accuracy.* A player hits a total of 10 volleyballs, either underhand or overhand, over a net and into the opposite court. Point values are assigned to various areas within the opposite court, with areas farther away from the net having higher values. The player's score is the point total for all 10 serves.
- *Other activities.* Additional activities might include setting a beach ball or large balloon to oneself as many times as possible in succession, serving in the direction of a wall and catching the ball as it returns, or spiking the ball over a net about 1 foot (30 centimeters) higher than the player.

Sport Variations and Modifications

Volleyball competition is governed in the United States by USA Volleyball and the USOPC and internationally by the IPC. Paralympic competition includes both standing and sitting volleyball events, with players classified into one of two categories, minimally disabled or disabled. *Minimally disabled* refers to some loss of muscular strength, flexibility, or a combination in a joint that hinders performance. *Disabled* refers to complete loss of muscular strength, flexibility, or a significant combination of the two in a joint that hinders performance. In 1980, sitting volleyball became an official

Paralympic sport. The following are modifications for sitting volleyball:

- The net is 3 feet, 9.3 inches (1.15 meters) for men and 3 feet, 3.5 inches (1.05 meters) for women.
- The court is 32 feet, 9.7 inches (10 meters) by 19 feet, 8 inches (6 meters).
- An attack line is located 6 feet, 6 inches (2 meters) from the center line and marks the front zone of play.
- Players are not allowed to lift their buttocks from the floor when carrying out any type of attack hit.
- Front row players are allowed to block serves, but at least one part of the buttocks must remain in contact with the floor.
- Player positions are determined by location of the buttocks to the floor. One or both hands and one or both legs may cross the service, attack, or center lines as long as they do not interfere with an opposing player.

Move United, DAAA, and Special Olympics also offer team sport competition in volleyball.

Two modifications of the sport under the DAAA consist of a lowered net of 6 feet (1.8 meters) and smaller court dimensions. Special Olympics volleyball competition is based on Fédération Internationale de Volleyball (FIVB) rules and the rules of each country's national governing board. Modifications of the game (Special Olympics, 2018c) include the following:

- The ball may be hit with any part of the body on or above the waist.
- The serving area is moved closer to the net (no closer than 4.5 meters).
- A lightweight ball is used (no heavier than 226 grams and no larger than 81 centimeters in circumference).
- The net is 7 feet, 11 inches (2.43 meters) for men and 7 feet, 4 inches (2.24 meters) for women.

Skill Event Variations and Modifications

Special Olympics competition includes three skill events: overhead passing (volleying), serving, and passing (forearm). Scores obtained in each event are added to obtain a final score. For the overhead passing event, the player stands 2 meters from the net and 4.5 meters from the sideline on a regulation-size court. A thrower provides the player with 10 two-handed underhand balls from the backcourt 4 meters from the baseline and 4.5 meters from the sideline in the left back position. The player sets the tossed ball to a target (a player standing 2 meters from the net and 2 meters from the front left sideline position). If any toss is not high enough for the player to set, it is repeated. The peak of the arc of each set should be above net height. The height of each set is measured. Participants earn 1 point for setting the ball 1 meter above the athlete's head, 3 points for setting the ball above net height, and 0 points for illegal contact (a ball that goes lower than head height or goes over the net outside the court). The final score is the sum of all points awarded for the 10 attempts.

Serving competition requires the athlete to serve a ball into the opponent's side of the court. That court is divided into three areas of equal size. One point is awarded for a serve landing in the area of the opponent's court closest to the net, 3 points are awarded for a serve landing in the middle third area, and 5 points are awarded for a serve landing in the area closest to the opponent's end line. For serves that land on a line, the athlete receives the higher point value. The final score is the total number of points made in 10 serves.

In the forearm passing event, the athlete stands on a regulation court at the right back position 3 meters from the right sideline and 1 meter from the baseline. A thrower standing on the same side of the net in front center court 2 meters from the net makes a two-hand overhead toss. The athlete returns the toss with a forearm pass to a target (person standing on the same side of and 2 meters from the net and 4 meters from the side away from the thrower). Varying point values are marked on the front court. This is repeated with the athlete at the left back position. To receive the maximum number of points, the peak of the arc of the pass must be at least net height. A ball landing on a line is assigned the higher point value. One point is received if the ball passes below net height. The final score is determined by adding the five attempts from both the left and right sides.

Other Variations and Modifications

Volleyball is easily modified for most players with disabilities. Most often, court dimensions are reduced, the net is lowered, and the serving line is brought closer to the net to accommodate varying abilities of players, especially for wheelchair users.

The number of players on each team might also be increased. Balls might be permitted one bounce before players attempt to return them over the net, or an unlimited number of hits by the same team might be allowed before the ball is returned. Players with arm or hand deformities can be allowed to carry or catch the ball on a hit or return. To serve, players might throw the ball over the net rather than hitting it. Players might have greater success by using a large, colored beach ball or a foam ball. Players who have mobility problems, such as those using crutches or walkers, might play the game from a seated position.

Goalball

Goalball, a sport invented almost 70 years ago in Europe, was created primarily for World War II veterans with visual impairments and was first introduced to world competition at the 1976 Paralympics in Toronto. The game is played in a silent arena in which blindfolded players attempt to score goals by rolling a ball across an opponent's goal line. Each ball contains bells that allow players to track it during play. To remove any advantages for players possessing partial sight, all players are blindfolded, even those who are totally blind, using blacked-out swim or ski goggles. Goalball requires players to use auditory tracking, agility, coordination, and teamwork. Goalball follows rules established by the International Blind Sports Association (IBSA). Information on purchasing goalballs can be obtained from the United States Association of Blind Athletes (USABA) (www.usaba.org).

Many players wear protective padding covering the knees, elbows, and hips, similar to the padding worn in volleyball or ice hockey. Some players prefer to wear American football pants and pads or soccer goalie pads combined with other pants for protection. Coaches are not permitted to communicate with their players outside of halftime or official time-outs. Spectators must also remain silent so that players can hear the ball. However, the rules permit communication between players in the form of talking, finger snapping, or tapping on the floor.

The game consists of two 12-minute periods, and halftime lasts 3 minutes. Running time is not used; rather, the clock is stopped at various points in the game (e.g., a scored goal). Four 45-second team time-outs are allowed during regulation play. Whistles are used to communicate clock times to players. Each team is allowed a total of six players, with three players on the court at any one time. Each team is allowed four substitutions per game.

Players must remain within their respective play zones. Boundaries are marked with textured tape about 5 centimeters wide. To assist players in remaining in their zones, a heavy string covered by tape can line the boundaries (figure 25.6). Play begins with a throw by the designated team. During the game, the ball must touch the floor at least once between the two overthrow lines (neutral area). If it does not touch the floor, the throw counts but cannot result in a score. The ball might be passed twice before each throw on goal.

All three players also play defense. Defensive players might assume a kneeling, crouching, or lying position to contact the ball, but they cannot assume a lying position on the playing surface until an opponent has thrown the ball. Defenders might move laterally within their team area. However, they cannot rush forward into the throwing area to intercept the ball except to follow a deflection. A player must throw the ball within 10 seconds after defensive control has been gained.

Should a personal or team penalty be assessed, the offending team must defend a penalty throw. In the case of a personal penalty, the player com-

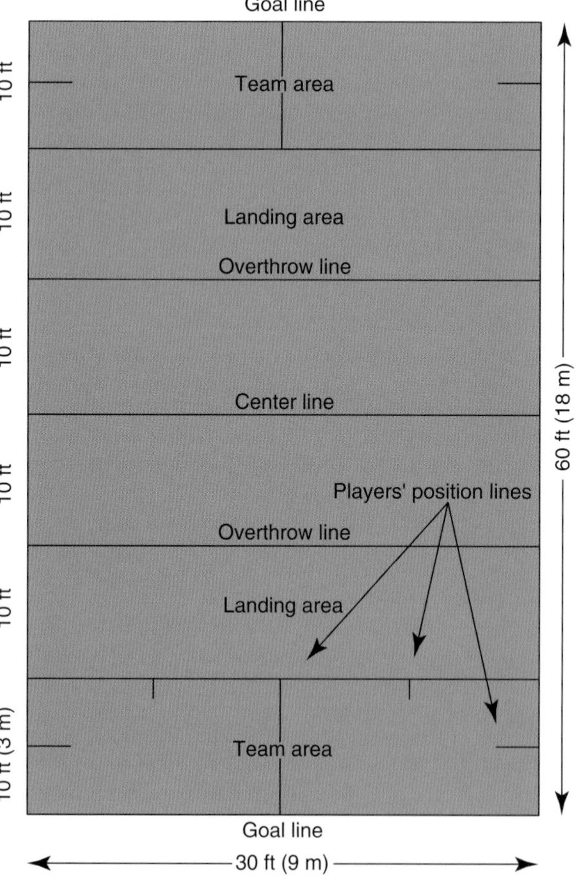

FIGURE 25.6 Goalball arena.

mitting the penalty is the only player to defend against the throw. In the case of a team penalty, the player who made the last throw before the penalty was awarded will defend the throw. If a team penalty is awarded before a throw has been taken, the player to defend the throw will be at the coach's discretion. Should the game end in a tie, two additional 3-minute periods are played. The team scoring the first overtime goal is the winner.

The USABA encourages and promotes goalball development camps across the country and provides technical assistance and professional support to members who are interested in offering these camps. The camps are designed to assist new players in learning the game.

Sport Skills

Important goalball skills include throwing, blocking, and ball control. Selected modifications are offered for each skill.

- *Throwing.* Most players can easily accomplish throwing. The ball is thrown in an underhand manner so that it rolls along the ground. People with poor upper body strength or poor motor control might need to use a lighter ball; players with orthopedic impairments who use scooters might need to push the ball with both hands along the ground rather than throwing it underhand. In other cases, players on scooters can throw the ball by striking it with a sidearm motion when it is located at their side.
- *Blocking and ball control.* Blocking and ball control are essential skills because defensive players must stop the ball from entering the goal area. Once the ball is blocked, it is brought under control with the hands so that a throw can be made. It might be helpful to have players with intellectual disabilities see the ball when learning to block so that they can more effectively coordinate body movement with the sound of the ball. Players with amputations can wear prosthetic devices to assist in blocking, as long as the ball does not damage the device or vice versa.

Lead-Up Games and Activities

Lead-up games and activities are important prerequisites to learning the game of goalball. Selected lead-up games and activities are provided next.

- *Heads-Up.* This game involves one-on-one competition with players positioning themselves in their half of the arena. A player is given possession of the ball with the object of scoring a goal. The ball must be continuously rolled as the offensive player moves about; the player cannot carry the ball. The defensive player can take control of the ball from the offensive player by deflecting or trapping a shot on goal. The first player to score three goals wins the game.
- *On-the-Spot.* This game involves two teams of three players. Each team forms a triangle with a distance of 12 feet (3.7 meters) between players. Players assume a crouching or kneeling position on a personal floor mat or small area rug, facing the middle of the triangle. On command, a designated player rolls a goalball as quickly as possible to the player on the immediate right, who controls the ball and rolls it to the next player on the right, and so on. If the player to whom it was rolled does not control the ball, that player must retrieve the ball and return to the area rug before rolling to the next player. Each time the ball completes a round, a point is scored. The team scoring the most points in 1 minute wins the game. Teams compete one at a time so that players can hear the ball.
- *Other activities.* Other activities include throwing for accuracy to the goal and passing the ball as quickly as possible between two players for a set amount of time.

Sport Variations and Modifications

Goalball has quickly gained popularity in the United States and is an official USABA competitive sport. People with other types of disabilities as well as people without disabilities can participate in the game as long as blindfolds are worn.

Other Variations and Modifications

Ways to modify the game include increasing or decreasing the size of the play arena and the number of players on a side. People with mobility challenges might play on scooter boards, and a lighter ball might be used for players with poor upper arm and shoulder strength.

Quad Rugby

Quad rugby (internationally known as wheelchair rugby), originally called *murderball*, was developed in 1977 by wheelchair users from Manitoba, Canada. In 1981, the game was introduced in the United States and quickly gained popularity, with the United States Quad Rugby Association (USQRA) forming in 1988. Stoke Mandeville in England was the site of the first international competition in 1990, and in 1996, the game was played at the Paralympics as an exhibition sport. By 2000, the sport had attained full medal status at the Paralympics. The International Wheelchair Rugby Federation (IWRF), the sport's governing body, also holds a world championship every four years. Today, quad rugby is the fastest-growing wheelchair sport in the world. To further advance the sport, the USQRA sponsors a number of instructional clinics each year around the country.

Quad rugby is designed for players who have quadriplegia that prevents them from participating in other sports, such as wheelchair basketball. People who exhibit upper and lower extremity limitations caused by spinal cord injuries, cerebral palsy, spina bifida, and les autres conditions are eligible to compete. Quad rugby is a combination of American football, hockey, and wheelchair basketball. Teams are composed of four on-court players. To equalize competition, players are classified by a point system according to functional ability. Players are provided a classification number from one of seven classifications ranging from .5 (most impaired) to 3.5 (least impaired). The player classified as .5 has function comparable to that with C5 quadriplegia, whereas a player classified as 3.5 has function comparable to that with C7 to C8 incomplete quadriplegia. The combined classification points cannot exceed 8 for the four on-court players. Because of the classification process, males and females can compete on the same team. A complete copy of quad rugby rules and regulations as well as information on how to become a referee or classifier can be obtained from the IWRF website (www.iwrf.com).

Quad rugby is played on a regulation basketball court. Cones placed at the end of each line identify the goal lines at each end of the court. In front of each goal line is a key area 8 meters by 1.75 meters. The object of the game is to carry the ball (regulation volleyball) over the opponent's goal line. Players try to gain possession of the ball by forcing a bad pass or a violation. The team with the most goals at the end of the game wins. At no time can all four defensive players be in the restricted area. Full chair contact is allowed (figure 25.7), and any form of hand protection may be used as long as it is not harmful to other players (e.g., hard or rough material). The game is composed of four 8-minute periods. Should the game end in a tie, 3-minute overtime periods are played. The team scoring the first overtime goal is the winner.

Photo courtesy of Chelsea L. Jerome.

FIGURE 25.7 Play illustrates the contact nature of the sport of quad rugby.

The ball handler can make an unlimited number of pushes, but the ball must be either passed or bounced within 10 seconds or else a turnover is assessed. A player has 15 seconds to advance the ball into the opponent's half of the court. Although only three defensive players can be in the key area at any one time, all four offensive players are allowed in the key area for 10 seconds at a time. Players committing personal fouls must serve time in a penalty box, which gives the opposing team a power play.

Sport Skills

Important quad rugby skills include wheelchair mobility, throwing, and catching. A brief description of each skill is provided here.

- *Wheelchair mobility.* Chair mobility is essential and skills consist of maneuvering the chair with the ball, picking, and sprinting. To maneuver effectively, the player must place the ball securely in the lap. Maneuverability consists of being able to move forward and backward as well as turn the chair as quickly as possible. Players who have the ability to quickly start from a stopped position have an advantage over other players, especially when sprinting the court, which places the offensive player in a better position to score and places the defensive player in an advantageous position to defend against a score. Players also must be able to bounce and pass the ball while the chair is in motion, as well as set picks to gain an offensive advantage by maneuvering to the side or behind a defensive player guarding an offensive teammate.
- *Throwing and catching.* Throwing for accuracy and distance is an essential game skill because it is the quickest way to advance the ball. Depending on ability level or impairment, a one-hand or two-hand throw can be used. The skill of catching needs to be mastered while the chair is either moving or stationary. Of course, the ability to catch while the chair is in motion is an advantage. For players who do not have full control of the hands, catching (trapping) the ball can be done with closed fists, wrists, or forearms.

Lead-Up Games and Activities

Lead-up games and activities are important prerequisites to learning the game of quad rugby. The following are selected lead-up games and activities.

- *Mobility relay.* Relay teams are composed of three or more players. Three cones are placed at 4-meter intervals from a starting line. The object of the relay is to wheel as fast as possible in a figure eight around each of the three cones. Rounding the third cone, the player returns to the starting line by wheeling backward. The first team to successfully complete the relay wins.
- *Precision passing.* A passing line is marked on the floor 5 meters from a stationary wheelchair situated on the court. The start line is marked 3 meters behind the passing line. On command, the player begins moving forward and passes the ball to the stationary wheelchair before crossing the passing line. The thrown ball cannot bounce prior to hitting the wheelchair. The player gets a total of five throws. The final score is the number of times the thrown ball hits the wheelchair. Should the player go over the passing line before the ball is thrown, a fault is called and the pass does not count.
- *Other activities.* A battery of quad rugby skill tests consisting of sprinting, passing, picking, and maneuvering has been validated (Yilla & Sherrill, 1998). These skills can be used in practice for the competitive sport or can be used as lead-up activities in physical education classes.

Strategies for Inclusion

During physical education, and at times in athletics, players with disabilities can be included in the regulation sports of basketball, football, soccer, softball, and volleyball. Even though the games of goalball and quad rugby have been designed for people with specific disabilities, those with other disabilities as well as individuals without disabilities may play them. As long as certain techniques are applied, most individuals with disabilities can successfully and safely be included into the sports identified in this chapter.

Many variations and modifications to these sports have already been presented (see Application Example sidebar). Another technique is to match abilities and positions; teachers and coaches should attempt to assign positions based on players' ability levels. In football, for example, players with mild intellectual disability possessing good catching skills could play end positions, whereas others with good speed could play the backfield. Players with upper limb impairments can be placekickers in football. In specific instances, a physical disability can be used to advantage. An example is Tom Dempsey, a successful placekicker in the

Application Example

Inclusion Strategies for Coaches

SETTING

Interscholastic freshman football

STUDENTS

Players with mild intellectual disabilities or specific learning disabilities

ISSUE

How can the learning needs of these players be accommodated?

APPLICATION

The coach could implement the following strategies:

- Require players to play only on special teams (e.g., kickoff, punt return) so that they will not need to know multiple play assignments
- Use task analysis for the learning of complex skills and assignments
- Allow players to wear a wristband to remind them of their play assignments
- Have teammates remind players of their play assignments in the huddle
- Teach new plays and new skills at the beginning of practice and then review them at the end of practice

National Football League during the 1970s, whose partial amputation of the kicking foot allowed for a broader surface with which to kick the ball. He has been credited with making a 63-yard field goal.

Teaching to players' abilities can also enhance inclusion. When teaching or coaching players with intellectual disabilities, emphasize concrete demonstrations over verbal instructions. Any verbal instructions should be short, simple, and direct. In football and basketball, a few simple plays that have been overlearned can promote success.

Equipment modifications can also foster inclusion. For players with visual impairments, the teacher or coach can place audible goal locators in goal areas for sports such as basketball, soccer, and floor hockey, or goals can be brightly painted or covered with colored tape. In games played on an indoor court, such as floor hockey or basketball, mats might be placed along the sidelines to differentiate the playing surface from the out-of-bounds area.

Finally, physical educators can implement the principles of universal design for learning (UDL), which maximizes sport participation and sport skill instruction in inclusive environments (see chapter 7 for more information regarding UDL). To assist teachers with implementing UDL within a sport context, Gilbert and Pennell (2021) provide lesson plans for team sport skills such as soccer and basketball. Lieberman and colleagues (2021) also provide detailed information on how physical educators can use UDL within inclusive environments to maximize the learning for all students. Given the importance of team sports in the transition of students with unique needs into inclusive community recreational sport programs (Samalot-Rivera, 2018), using UDL concepts in physical education programs can be beneficial.

Summary

This chapter described a number of popular team sports included in physical education and sport programs. Competition in these sports are sponsored by organizations such as the USADSF, DAAA, NBBA, Move United, NWBA, NWSA, Special Olympics, USABA, and international sport organizations (e.g., CPISRA, IWRF). Game skills, variations, and modifications specific to each sport were identified. Also presented were lead-up games and activities, as well as rules and strategies for modified sports. Finally, suggestions for maximizing inclusive participation were offered.

References

American Association of Adapted Sports Programs (AAASP). (2019a). *Wheelchair football rulebook 2019-2020* (3rd ed.). http://adaptedsports.org/wordpress/wp-content/uploads/2019/05/WF_Rule_Book-Rev.-3-6-16.pdf

American Association of Adapted Sports Programs (AAASP). (2019b). *Wheelchair handball rulebook 2019-2020* (5th ed). Retrieved from http://adaptedsports.org/wordpress/wp-content/uploads/2019/05/2017_WH_Rule_Book-Full-Page.pdf

Diaz, R., Miller, E., Kraus, E., & Fredericson, M. (2019). Impact of adaptive sports participation on quality of life. *Sports Medicine, 27*(2), 73-82. https://doi.org/10.1097/jsa.0000000000000242

Gilbert, E., & Pennell, A. (2021). Universally designed lesson plans for sports. In L.J. Lieberman, M. Grenier, A. Brian, & K. Arndt, *Universal design for learning in physical education* (pp. 109-133). Human Kinetics.

International Federation of CP Football. (2020). *IFCPF competition rules—2020.* Retrieved from www.ifcpf.com/rules

Jeffress, M., & Brown, W. (2017). Opportunities and benefits for powerchair users through power soccer. *Adapted Physical Activity Quarterly, 34*(3), 235-255. https://doi.org/10.1123/apaq.2016-0022

Kozub, F.M., & Ozturk, M.A. (2003). A reexamination of participation for individuals with disabilities in interscholastic sports programs. *Journal of Physical Education, Recreation & Dance, 74*(2), 32-35; 51. https://doi.org/10.1080/07303084.2003.10608376

Kozub, F.M., & Porretta, D.L. (1996). Including athletes with disabilities: Interscholastic athletic benefits for all. *Journal of Physical Education, Recreation & Dance, 67*(3), 19-24. https://doi.org/10.1080/07303084.1996.10607216

Kozub, F.M., & Samalot-Rivera, A. (2020). Interscholastic participation for athletes with disabilities revisited: Are today's programs doing enough? *Journal of Physical Education, Recreation & Dance, 91*(2), 42-51. https://doi.org/10.1080/07303084.2019.1693453

Lieberman, J., Grenier, M., Brian, A., & Arndt, K. (2021). *Universal design for learning in physical education.* Human Kinetics.

National Wheelchair Basketball Association. (2019). *2015-2016 NWBA official rules.* https://cdn3.sportngin.com/attachments/document/6c24-2006723/2019-2020_NWBA_Rule_Book_revised_1.21.20.pdf#_ga=2.212052180.1725571411.1586788407-1451220591.1586788407

Samalot-Rivera, A. (2018). Transition planning. In L.J. Lieberman & C. Houston-Wilson, *Strategies for inclusion: Physical education for everyone* (3rd ed., pp. 111-121). Human Kinetics.

Special Olympics. (2016). *Special Olympics summer sports rules: Basketball.* Retrieved from https://media.specialolympics.org/resources/sports-essentials/sport-rules/Sports-Essentials-Basketball-Rules-2018-v2.pdf?_ga=2.238615683.26534798.1586742676-1571688372.1586742676

Special Olympics. (2018a). *Special Olympics summer sports rules: Football (soccer).* Retrieved from https://media.specialolympics.org/resources/sports-essentials/sport-rules/Sports-Essentials-Football-Rules-2018-v2.pdf?_ga=2.266902669.26534798.1586742676-1571688372.1586742676

Special Olympics. (2018b). *Special Olympics summer sports rules: Softball.* Retrieved from https://media.specialolympics.org/resources/sports-essentials/sport-rules/Sports-Essentials-Softball-Rules-2018.pdf?_ga=2.194024494.26534798.1586742676-1571688372.1586742676

Special Olympics. (2018c). *Special Olympics summer sports rules: Volleyball.* Retrieved from https://media.specialolympics.org/resources/sports-essentials/sport-rules/Sports-Essentials-Volleyball-Indoor-Rules-2018.pdf?_ga=2.195203375.26534798.1586742676-1571688372.1586742676

United States Power Soccer Association (USPSA). (2012). *Power soccer: Laws of the game.* Retrieved from https://assets.website-files.com/59a2febe054ed30001e52784/5a382b57284c460001a09c14_2011_USPSA_Laws_of_the_Game.pdf

Yilla, A.B., & Sherrill, C. (1998). Validating the Beck battery of quad rugby skill tests. *Adapted Physical Activity Quarterly, 15,* 55-67. https://doi.org/10.1123/apaq.15.2.155

Print Resources

Orr, K., & Malone, L. (2010). Wheelchair rugby. In V. Goosey-Tolfrey (Ed.), *Wheelchair sport* (pp. 152-166). Human Kinetics.

This chapter focuses on the rules and skills used to play the game. It also covers topics such as classification and equipment selection and maintenance.

Spirit: The magazine of Special Olympics. Special Olympics, Inc., 1325 G St. NW, Ste. 500, Washington, DC 20005.

This is a quarterly publication focusing on such topics as sports, athletes, families, volunteers, world games, celebrities, and fundraising.

Video Resources

ESPN. (2015). *Jake Olson fights on* [Video]. http://espn.go.com/video/clip?id=10091429

This video chronicles the life of Jake Olson, who lost his sight to cancer, and how he found his way back to football by being his high school team's long snapper.

United States Power Soccer Association (USPSA). (n.d.). *Power soccer training* [DVD]. www.powersoccerusa.org/media/video

This website provides instructional videos showing a variety of training drills.

American Association of Adapted Sports Programs (AAASP). (n.d.) *Coach & play AAASP wheelchair football* [Video]. YouTube. www.youtube.com/watch?v=l5wSLMYAvp4&feature=youtu.be

This video from AAASP features offensive running and passing plays, defensive lineups, and blitzing, as well as interviews of athletes describing the skills needed to play the game.

Online Resources

Little League Baseball Challenger Division: www.littleleague.org/play-little-league/challenger/

This site provides information on the Challenger division designed for Little League players with disabilities. It includes the history of the division, its grant program to foster local development, and a series of brochures detailing various aspects of the program.

26

Individual and Dual Sports and Activities

E. Michael Loovis

Rodney is a 13-year-old student who wants to run the 100-yard dash for his middle school track team. He is an industrious youngster who does well in school and is involved in many leisure and recreational activities in his community. He also delivers advertising circulars for neighborhood businesses at 5:30 every morning before school. When the announcement was made that tryouts were being held for the track team, Rodney appeared at the designated time. However, Rodney was informed by the coach that he would not be permitted to try out—because he is legally blind. The coach said Rodney's presence would be a danger to himself and the rest of the team. If you were the adapted physical educator in the school district, what conversation you would have with this coach? What points regarding IDEA, reasonable accommodation, and inclusion would you highlight? What steps would you recommend to the principal, the coach, and perhaps more importantly, Rodney's parents to guarantee his equal opportunity to earn a spot on the team?

This chapter examines individual and dual sports and activities in which people with unique needs can participate inclusively and successfully. Skills, lead-up games, and activities taught as part of physical education programs are discussed, as are rules, procedural modifications, and adaptations for events sponsored by official sport organizations. The chapter includes a compendium of modifications for several activities and sports as well as dance.

Tennis

Tennis can be played in one form or another by almost all people except those with the most severe disabilities. It can be played as a singles or doubles activity, so the skill requirements (both psychomotor and cognitive) can be modified in many ways to encourage participation. Regardless of the variations and modifications, the objective remains the same: to return the ball legally across the net and prevent the opponent from doing the same.

Sport Skills

Most people can play tennis using only the forehand and backhand strokes and the serve. For the ground strokes, good footwork or effective wheelchair mobility along with good racket preparation—moving the racket into the backswing well in advance of the ball—is fundamental to execution. Under normal circumstances, racket preparation and movement into position to return the ball are performed simultaneously.

Lead-Up Games and Activities

Adams and McCubbin (1991) describe an elementary lead-up game, Target Tennis, that can be played indoors with limited space and is appropriate for both students in wheelchairs and ambulatory students. Players position themselves behind the end-zone line, which is 10 feet (3 meters) from a target screen. The screen has five openings, each 10 inches (25.4 centimeters) in diameter, which are the targets. The player tosses a tennis ball into the air and uses an overhand swing to bounce the ball midway between the end-zone line and the target so that the ball goes through one of the five openings. A bonus serve is permitted for every point scored. No points are awarded if the ball bounces twice.

Special Olympics pioneered four developmental events that can serve as lead-up activities for individuals with low ability: target stroke, target bounce, racket bounce, and return shot. In the target stroke, the athlete gets 10 attempts to drop-hit the ball within the boundaries of the opponent's singles court; 1 point is awarded for each successful hit. In the target bounce, the athlete bounces a tennis ball on the playing surface using one hand; the score is the highest number of consecutive bounces in two trials. In the racket bounce, the athlete bounces the ball off the racket face as many times consecutively as possible; the score is the most consecutive bounces in two trials. In the return shot, the athlete waits for the ball to bounce once and then attempts to return it over the net and into the opponent's singles court. One point is awarded for each successful hit, and the greatest number of successful consecutive attempts in two rounds is counted.

Sport Variations and Modifications

In 1980, the National Foundation of Wheelchair Tennis (NFWT) was founded to develop and sponsor competition. In 1981, the Wheelchair Tennis Players Association (WTPA) was formed under the aegis of the NFWT with the purpose of administering the rules and regulations of the sport. The United States Tennis Association (USTA) approved the formation of the Wheelchair Tennis Committee in 1996, and in 1998, it merged with the WTPA, making the USTA the governing body for wheelchair tennis.

Starting in 2021, USTA transitioned to a mixed-gender division system to replace the former men's and women's divisions. Divisions competing for national ranking include A, B, C, and D; 18 and under; and open (men, women, and quad); other divisions such as senior may also be offered but will not earn points toward national ranking. The quad division was established for players with limited power, mobility, and strength in at least three limbs as a result of accidents, spinal cord injuries, or other conditions. Also included in this division are players with quadriplegia who have the ability to walk, players who use power wheelchairs, and players with three amputations.

The rules for wheelchair tennis are the same as for regular tennis except that the ball is allowed to bounce twice before being returned (International Tennis Federation [ITF], 2020). The first bounce must land inbounds; the second bounce can land either inbounds or out of bounds. Before serving, the player must be stationary and in the legal service position. The player can then take one push before striking the ball. At no time can any wheel of the player's chair exceed the baseline or cross the center mark or sideline. Players with quadriplegia who cannot serve in the conventional manner may drop the ball or have someone drop the ball for them. Once this type of serve is chosen, it must be used consistently throughout the match. Players who are unable to propel their chairs with the wheel may use one foot; however, that foot may not be in contact with the court during the forward swing of the racket, including when contact is made with the ball.

Special Olympics (2020) offers the following events for tennis: singles, doubles, mixed doubles, Unified Sports doubles, Unified Sports mixed doubles, Unified team tennis, and individual skills competition. The latter consists of the forehand volley, backhand volley, forehand ground stroke, backhand ground stroke, serve into deuce court, serve into advantage (ad) court, and alternating ground strokes with movement. A player's final score is the cumulative score of all seven events. International Tennis Federation (ITF) rules are in effect except when there is a discrepancy with the rules of Special Olympics, in which case Special Olympics rules apply.

Other Variations and Modifications

If mobility is a problem, players without disabilities might defend their entire regulation court while players with disabilities defend half of their court. If the player with a disability has extremely limited mobility, the court could be divided into designated scoring areas, with those closest to that player receiving higher point values. Accommodation could also be accomplished by permitting players to strike the ball on the second bounce. Variations in the scoring system can promote participation, such as counting the number of consecutive hits, which structures the game as cooperative rather than competitive.

Racket control might also be a concern for some students. If a standard tennis racket is too heavy, consider shortening the grip on the racket, using a junior-size racket, or substituting a racquetball racket. In the case of a player with an amputation, the racket can be strapped to the stump (if one remains) to allow for effective leverage and racket use.

If mobility or racket preparation is a problem, reducing the court size, at least initially, assists in learning proper racket positioning and stroking (because footwork is minimal). If players are still unsuccessful, they can be placed in the appropriate stroking position with the shoulder of the nonswinging arm perpendicular to the net. This way, they only have to move into and swing at the ball (see figure 26.1).

FIGURE 26.1 Two-hand forehand in wheelchair tennis.

For people who lack either the coordination or strength to perform a traditional tennis serve, an appropriate variation is to bring the racket straight up in front of the face so that the hand holding the racket is even with the forehead or slightly higher. Although serving in this manner reduces speed and produces an arc that is considerably higher than normal, it allows players to serve who might otherwise not learn to serve correctly. To accomplish the toss, a player with a single-arm amputation might grip the ball in the racket hand by extending the thumb and first finger beyond the racket handle and hold the ball against the racket. The ball is then tossed in the air and hit in the usual way. A player with a double-arm amputation and the racket strapped to a stump uses a different approach. The ball lies on the racket strings, and, with a quick upward movement, the ball is thrust into the air and then struck either in the air or after it bounces.

Table Tennis

As is true of tennis, almost anyone can play table tennis or a version of it. Table tennis can be played in singles or doubles competition, and although the requisite skills are less adjustable than in tennis, modifications can make this sport suitable for people with disabilities. Regardless of the variations and modifications, the objective of the game remains the same: to return the ball legally onto the opponent's side of the table in such a way as to prevent the opponent from making a legal return.

Sport Skills

As in tennis, the basic strokes are the forehand and backhand. In contrast to tennis, the service is not a separate stroke. A serving player puts the ball in play with either a forehand or backhand stroke. The ball must strike the table on the server's side before striking the table on the receiver's side. In addition, servers must strike the ball outside the boundary at their end of the court.

Lead-Up Games and Activities

Appropriate for use in physical education programs is surface table tennis, an adapted table tennis game created at the Kluge Children's Rehabilitation Center at the University of Virginia Hospital. Two or four people can play this game, which involves hitting a regulation table tennis ball so that it moves on the surface of the table and passes through a modified net. The net is constructed from two pieces of parallel string attached a half-inch (1.25 centimeters) apart at the top of official standards, and two or three pieces of parallel string attached three-quarters of an inch (2 centimeters) apart at the bottom of the standards, with a 2-inch (5-centimeter) opening in the middle (Adams & McCubbin, 1991). At the start of play, the ball is placed on the table, and the player strikes it so that it rolls through the opening in the net into the opponent's court. Points are awarded to the player who last made a legal hit through the net. Points are lost when a player hits the ball over the net either on a bounce or in the air, when the ball fails to pass through the net, or when a player hits the ball twice in succession.

Another lead-up game, Corner Ping-Pong, was developed at the University of Connecticut (Dunn & Leitschuh, 2014). It is played in a corner in an area 6 feet (2 meters) high and 6 feet wide on each side of the corner. One player stands on either side of the center line. The server drops the ball and strokes it against the floor to the forward wall. The ball must rebound to the adjacent wall and then bounce onto the floor of the opponent's area. If the server fails to deliver a good serve, 1 point goes to the opponent. The ball may bounce only once on the floor before the opponent returns it. The ball must be hit against the forward wall within the opponent's section of the playing area so that it rebounds to the adjacent wall and onto the floor in the server's area. Failure to return the ball is 1 point for the server. Scoring is similar to that for table tennis. Each player gets five consecutive serves. A ball that is hit out of bounds is scored as 1 point for the other player. The winning score is 21 points, and the player must win by 2.

Special Olympics provides three developmental events that can serve as lead-up activities: the target serve, racket bounce, and return shot (Special Olympics, 2020). In the target serve, the athlete serves five balls from the right side and five balls from the left side of the table; 1 point is awarded for each ball that lands in the correct service area. In the racket bounce, the athlete bounces the ball off the racket face as many times as possible in 30 seconds; the score is the most consecutive bounces in two trials. The return shot involves returning a tossed ball to the feeder's side of the table; 1 point is awarded if the ball is successfully returned, and 5 points are earned if the ball lands in one of the service boxes. The athlete attempts to return five balls, with a maximum of 25 points possible.

Sport Variations and Modifications

Competitive table tennis is offered by Move United (www.moveunitedsport.org); the Dwarf Athletic Association of America (DAAA); the USA Deaf Sports Federation (USADSF) through its affiliate, the U.S. Deaf Table Tennis Association; and Special Olympics. For the most part, competition is based on the rules established by the International Table Tennis Federation (ITTF) (2019) and International Paralympic Table Tennis Committee. Some modifications are permitted. For example, using the International Dwarf Sports Federation (IDSF) rules, DAAA (2020) permits the use of a riser or an elevated platform. In Move United competition, the following rules apply to individuals who use wheelchairs:

- Competitors' feet and footrests may not touch the floor.
- Service shall be called a let if the ball leaves the table by either of the receiver's sides, if on bouncing on the receiver's side the ball returns in the direction of the net, or if the ball comes to rest on the receiver's side of the playing surface.
- The playing surface shall not be used as a support with the free hand as the ball is played.
- While striking the ball, players must maintain minimum contact with their seat or seat cushion with the back of the thigh.
- There are no exceptions to the playing rules for players who stand.

Special Olympics (2020) sanctions the following events: singles, doubles, mixed doubles, wheelchair competition, individual skills competition, Unified Sports doubles, and Unified Sports mixed doubles (see figure 26.2). In wheelchair competition, players who are serving may project the ball upward in any manner; they are not required to deliver the ball from the palm of the free hand. The individual skills competition is composed of five events: the hand toss, racket bounce, forehand volley, backhand volley, and serve. Scores from all five events are added for a final score.

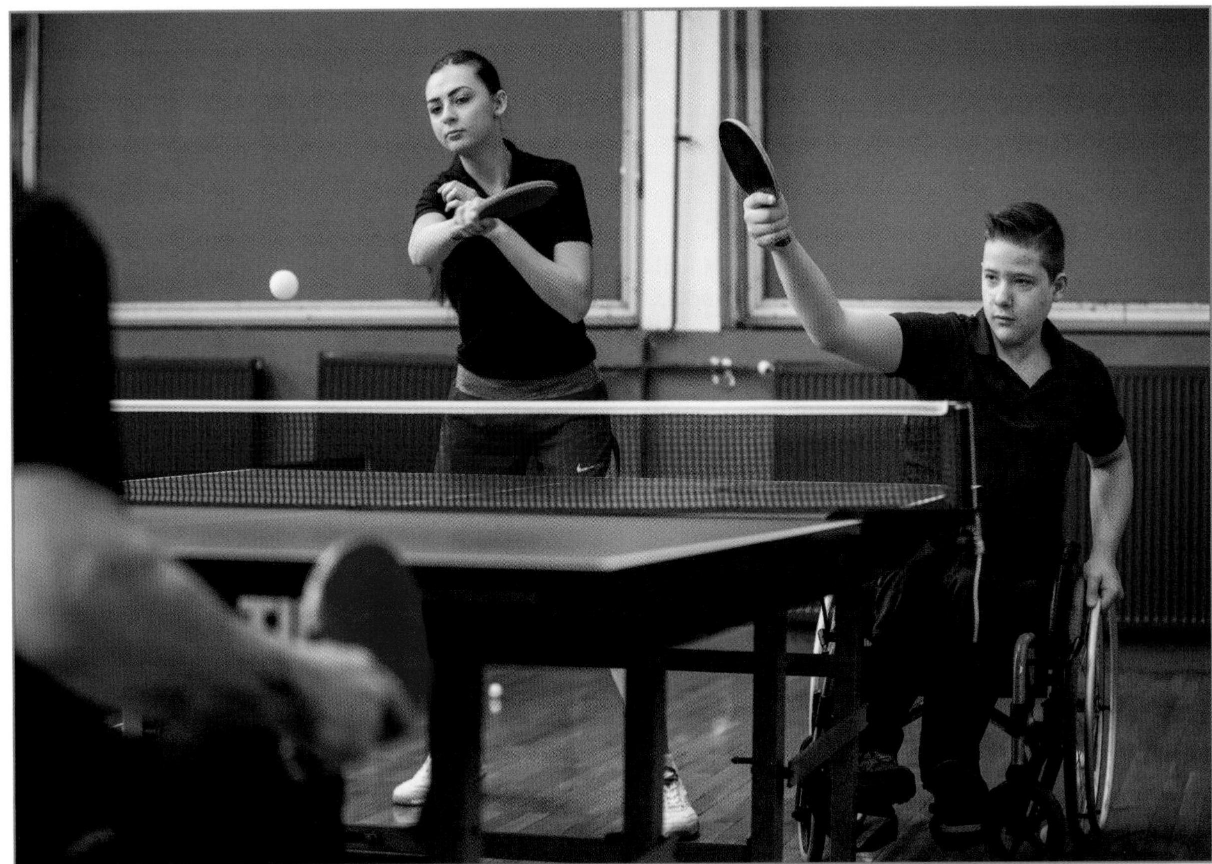

miodrag ignjatovic/E+/Getty Images

FIGURE 26.2 Unified Sports table tennis mixed doubles.

Other Variations and Modifications

Several assistive devices are available for players with severe disabilities (e.g., muscular dystrophy and other disorders that weaken or affect the shoulder). A ball-bearing feeder provides assistance for shoulder and elbow motion by using gravity to gain a mechanical advantage and makes up for loss of power resulting from weakened muscles. The bihandle paddle, which consists of a single paddle with handles on each side, is designed to encourage larger range of motion for participants. Its greatest asset is increased joint movement resulting from the bilateral nature of hand and finger positioning. A strap-on paddle that attaches to the back of the hand with Velcro has been designed for players with little or no functional finger flexion or grasp; however, it precludes use of a forehand stroking action. A table tennis cuff is also useful for players with limited finger movement and grip strength. The cuff consists of a clip that attaches to a metal clamp on the paddle handle and a Velcro strap that holds the cuff securely to the hand (Adams & McCubbin, 1991).

Another device, the space ball net, can replace the paddle for players who are blind (Dunn & Leitschuh, 2014). This device consists of a lightweight metal frame that supports a nylon lattice or webbing and is held in two hands. The net is large and provides an adequate rebounding surface to make participation feasible for players who are blind. Additionally, a special all-white table combined with an orange ball containing metal beads can accommodate players who have visual impairments. Individuals with visual impairments may also play Showdown, a game that in many respects mirrors the more familiar game of air hockey. Using a small paddle, players hit an audible ball back and forth across a table that is 12 feet long (366 centimeters) and 4 feet wide (122 centimeters). The object is to strike the ball into the opponent's goal pocket, which is a 10-inch (30-centimeter) by 4-inch (10-centimeter) hole in the end of the table. The first player to score 11 points (win by 2 points) wins the game.

Badminton

Badminton is ideally suited for people with disabilities and is played routinely in physical education classes. Special Olympics (2020) sponsors competition in badminton, as does the DAAA. The International Committee of Sports for the Deaf (ICSD) (2020) sponsors competition in badminton at the Deaflympics, where men's singles and doubles, women's singles and doubles, and mixed doubles are contested. Hearing aids and external cochlear implants are forbidden. Competition is based on the rules of the Badminton World Federation (BWF). Currently, badminton is an uncontested sport under the USADSF.

Sport Skills

Badminton can be played using only the forehand and backhand strokes and the underhand service. Beyond these strokes, development of the clear, smash, drop shot, and drive will depend on the participant's ability.

Lead-Up Games and Activities

There are two lead-up games that deserve mention. Loop badminton (Dunn & Leitschuh, 2014) is played with a standard shuttlecock, table tennis paddles, and a 24-inch (61-centimeter) loop placed on top of a 46-inch (1.2-meter) standard. The object of the game is to hit the shuttlecock through the loop, which is positioned in the center of a rectangular court 10 feet (3 meters) long and 5 feet (1.5 meters) wide. Scoring is the same as in the standard game of badminton. Loop badminton is well adapted for people with restricted movement who wish to participate in an active game that requires extreme accuracy. A second modified game is balloon badminton (Adams & McCubbin, 1991), in which a balloon is substituted for the shuttlecock and table tennis paddles are used instead of badminton rackets. People with visual impairments can play this game if a bell is placed inside the balloon to aid in directional cueing.

The developmental activities offered by Special Olympics that can also serve as lead-up activities are the target serve, return volley, and return serve (Special Olympics, 2020). In the target serve, the participant has 10 chances to hit the shuttlecock within the boundaries of the opponent's singles court; 1 point is awarded for each successful hit. In the return volley, the athlete has 10 chances to return the shuttlecock fed from the opponent's midcourt area to the opponent's single court; 1 point is awarded for each successful hit. The return serve involves attempting to return a serve to anywhere in the opponent's court; 1 point is awarded for each successful return up to a maximum of 10 points.

Sport Variations and Modifications

Special Olympics sanctions the following events: singles, doubles, mixed doubles, Unified Sports doubles, and Unified Sports mixed doubles. In Special Olympics competition (2020), the following rules apply to athletes who use wheelchairs:

- Athletes may serve an overhand serve from either the right or left serving area.
- The serving area is shortened to half the distance.

The DAAA (2020) permits the following rules modifications as per IDSF (2019):

- Sidearm serving is allowed if a combination of height, limited range of motion, and length of the racket makes underhand serving impossible.
- If sidearm service is permitted, the racket head may not exceed chest height.

Other Variations and Modifications

Some standard modifications are routinely used: reducing the court size (www.badmintonengland.co.uk), using racket straps for those with amputations or poor grip strength, and using Velcro on the butt end of the racket and the base of the shuttlecock to aid in shuttlecock retrieval. The extension-handle racket can also be helpful for a player who uses a wheelchair or a player with limited movement. Another useful device is the amputee serving tray, which attaches to the terminal end of the prosthesis to permit easier service and promote active use of the prosthesis. See also the Application Example sidebar.

Angling

The American Casting Association (ACA) is the governing body for tournament fly and bait casting in the United States. It sets the rules by which eligible casters can earn awards in registered tournaments. None of the sport organizations for people with disabilities sponsor competition in angling, and the activity is rarely seen in physical education programs. It is most commonly engaged in as a recreational sport. Ice fishing is popular in countries in northern latitudes. Individuals who are wheelchair users can be easily accommodated in this activity (see figure 26.3).

Lead-Up Games and Activities

Angling requires the mastery of casting and other fishing skills. In terms of lead-up activities, at least two casting games deserve mention. The game of skish involves accuracy in target casting at various distances. Each participant casts 20 times at each target, and 1 point is awarded for each direct hit (plug landing inside target or similar goal). Three targets can be used simultaneously to speed up the game, with players changing position after each has cast 20 times at a target. The player with the greatest number of hits at the end of 60 casts is the winner. The second game, speed casting, is a

Application Example

Modifying the Badminton Serve for a Student With Muscular Dystrophy

SETTING

Middle school physical education class

STUDENT

A seventh-grade student with muscular dystrophy who uses a wheelchair and is able to push himself

ISSUE

How to make modifications so the student can learn to serve during the badminton unit

APPLICATION

The physical educator might make reasonable accommodations in the following ways:

- Modify regular equipment to make it lighter or more manageable
- Permit serving into a larger court area
- Lower the net
- Shorten the distance of the serve

Photo courtesy of Jaana Huovinen.

FIGURE 26.3 Ice fishing is a recreational sport that can easily accommodate individuals who are wheelchair users.

variation of skish. Each player casts for 5 minutes at each target, and the player with the high score at the end of 15 minutes is the winner (Shivers, 2011).

Variations and Modifications

Major assistive devices for use in angling have become popular in recent years. For example, the Strong Arm rod holder is a 6-ounce (170-gram) sleeve into which the rod fits, enabling people with quadriplegia to cast. Other devices include the Ampo Fisher 1, Van's EZ Cast, Batick Bracket, and Handi-Gear. Several lines of electronic fishing reels are also available through Access to Recreation, Inc. (https://accesstr.com/).

Archery

Shooting the longbow is usually a six-step procedure: (1) assuming the correct stance, (2) nocking the arrow, (3) drawing the bowstring, (4) aiming at the target, (5) releasing the bowstring, and (6) following through until the arrow makes contact with the target. However, one or more of these steps may require some modification for those with disabilities.

Sport Variations and Modifications

Target archery is an athletic event sponsored nationally by Move United and internationally by the International Paralympic Committee (IPC). These groups observe the rules established by World Archery, with certain modifications. There are three classes for para archery: W1 is a wheelchair user with both arms and legs impaired, W2 is a wheelchair user with primarily leg impairment, and ST is an archer who stands or shoots from a stool or chair. Archers with a visual impairment are classified as either V11 or V12-13 combined. This corresponds to having a B2 or B3 classification, respectively. The International Dwarf Sports Federation (2019) offers competition in 18-meter crossbow and 9- and 18-meter recurve bow target archery. There are no classifications; men and women compete separately, and there are junior (12-15 years), open, and masters divisions. The following are adjustments that might encourage participation by students in wheelchairs, including les autres athletes (IPC, 2020; Move United, 2020):

- An adjustable arrow rest and arrow plate and any movable pressure button or pressure point on the bow may be used, provided they are not electric or electronic and do not offer any additional aid in aiming; a draw-check indicator that is audible or visible but not electric or electronic may be used.

- Archers in classes W1 and W2 may use strapping and body support.
- Only archers with bow-arm disability may have the bow bandaged or strapped into the hand. Archers with bow-arm disability may use an elbow or wrist splint; they may also have someone load their arrows into the bow for them.
- Archers in class W1 may use a mechanical release aid with recurve and compound bows; they cannot use any leveling device, nor can they use peep sights or scopes.
- A prosthetic arm, including a "hand," can be attached to the bow as long as it is not a rigid or permanent attachment.
- Archers with functional use of only one side of their body can use a bow stand that holds the bow vertical to the target (only in junior divisions at Move United events).
- Release aids attached to the wrist, elbow, or shoulder are permitted; only mouth tabs are permitted in the Recurve Open class.

Other Variations and Modifications

Several assistive devices are available to aid the archer who has a disability. These include the bow sling, commercially available from most sport shops, which helps stabilize the wrist and hand for bow control; the below-elbow amputee adapter device (see figure 26.4), which is held by the terminal end of the prosthesis and requires a slight rotation of the prosthesis to release the string and the arrow; the wheelchair bow stringer, which consists of an in-ground post with two appropriately spaced bolts around which the archer places the bow in order to produce enough leverage to string it independently; and the elbow brace, which is used to maintain extension in the bow arm when the archer has normal strength in the shoulder but minimal strength in the arm, possibly because of contractures. Other program adjustments include the use of a tripod assistive device or vertical bow set to accommodate people with bilateral upper extremity involvement (Paciorek & Jones, 2001).

Several modifications can promote participation by people with visual impairments in physical education and recreation settings (Paciorek & Jones, 2001):

- Using foot blocks to ensure proper orientation with the target
- Placing an audible goal locator behind the target to aid in directional cueing
- Using a brightly colored target for people with partial sight
- Placing balloons on the target as a means of auditory feedback

Various telescopic sights are also commercially available for the archer with partial sight.

Bowling

Both people who are ambulatory and people who use wheelchairs can participate in bowling with a high degree of success. Bowling is usually characterized by the approach, delivery (including the swinging of the ball), and release; however,

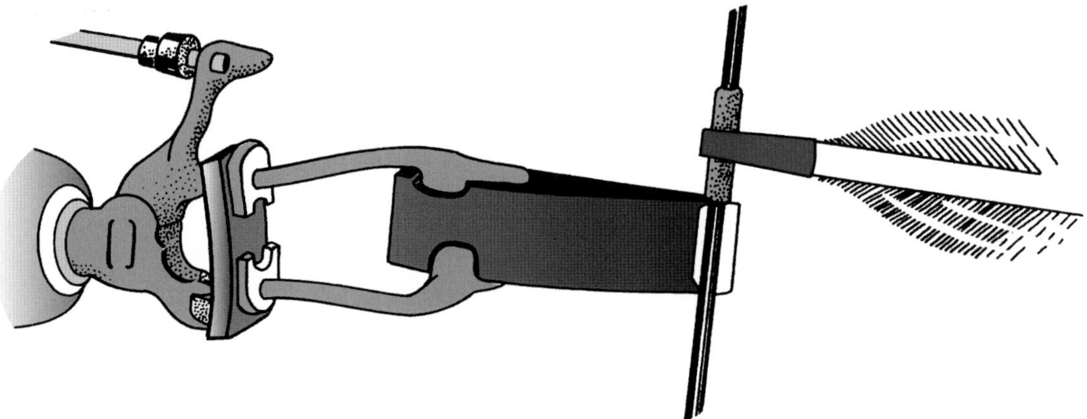

FIGURE 26.4 Amputee adapter device for archery.

a bowler with limited mobility or who uses a wheelchair may eliminate the approach and either perform the swing and release independently or use a piece of adapted equipment to assist this part of the procedure. Two organizations that have significantly influenced the lives of bowlers with disabilities are the American Blind Bowling Association (ABBA) and the American Wheelchair Bowling Association (AWBA).

Lead-Up Games and Activities

Special Olympics has traditionally sponsored two developmental events that can be used as lead-up activities: target bowl and frame bowl.

- *Target bowl.* In this activity, participants roll two 2-pound (1-kilogram) bowling balls in the direction of two regulation bowling pins positioned on a half-length bowling lane. Participants bowl five frames using the standard scoring systems of the United States Bowling Congress (USBC).
- *Frame bowl.* In this activity, the bowler rolls two frames (two rolls per frame) using plastic playground balls 30 centimeters in diameter. The object is to knock down the greatest number of plastic bowling pins from a traditional 10-pin triangular formation. The lead pin is set 5 meters from a restraining line. Bowlers either sit or stand and may use either one or both hands to roll the ball; the ball must be released behind the restraining line. Pins that are knocked down are cleared between the first and second rolls, and pins are reset for each new frame. A bowler's score equals the number of pins knocked down in two frames. Five bonus points are awarded when all pins are knocked down on the first roll of a frame; 2 bonus points are awarded when all remaining pins are knocked down on the second roll of the frame.

Sport Variations and Modifications

Special Olympics (2020) sponsors competition in bowling and follows the rules of the USBC. It sponsors singles (ramp unassisted and ramp assisted) competitions, as well as both doubles and team competitions in male; female; mixed gender; and Unified male, female, and mixed gender divisions. Modified rules for use in Special Olympics are as follows:

- Ramps (see figure 26.5) and other assistive devices are permitted for singles competition only.
- Bowlers using ramps shall compete in separate divisions. There are two classifications of ramp bowling: unassisted (in which athletes aim the ramp by themselves, place the ball on the ramp, and push the ball down the ramp toward the target) and assisted (in which an assistant aims the target based on verbal or visual cues from the athlete).
- Special equipment can be used to assist in gripping and releasing the ball if the hand or a portion of the hand is missing due to amputation.

The ICSD and USADSF also sponsor bowling, with the use of hearing aids and external cochlear implants prohibited during competition.

Other Variations and Modifications

Ambulatory bowlers use several types of assistive devices. The handle-grip bowling ball, which snaps back instantly on release, is ideal for bowlers with upper extremity disabilities and for people with spastic cerebral palsy, especially those who have difficulties with digital control. The USBC has approved the handle-grip ball for competitive play. People with upper extremity amputations who use a hook can use an attachable neoprene sleeve to hold and deliver a bowling ball. The sleeve can compress using a spring and expand for release with the same action used to open the conventional hook. Stick bowling, which is similar to the use of a shuffleboard cue, was designed for people with upper extremity impairments, primarily grip problems. The AWBA permits stick bowling in its national competitions, provided that the bowlers apply their own power and direction to the ball.

Several assistive devices can facilitate participation for bowlers who are wheelchair users. The recently approved chute/ramp division within AWBA permits bowlers with severe disabilities to compete at national competitions. The counterpart of stick bowling for people who use wheelchairs is the adapter–pusher device, originally designed for bowlers lacking sufficient upper arm strength to lift the ball. The handlebar-extension accessory, used in conjunction with the adapter–pusher device, assists ambulatory bowlers who do not have enough strength to lift the ball. Also available is the bowling ball–holder ring (third arm), a device that attaches to the wheelchair arm and holds a ball while the bowler wheels down the approach lane.

FIGURE 26.5 Assisted bowling with ramp.

The International Blind Sports Federation (IBSA) (2020) sponsors both 9-pin (skittles) and 10-pin bowling. There are several modifications that can enhance participation in the sport for people with visual impairments. These modifications include the following:

- Use of a bowling rail for guidance, which is the standard method employed by most bowlers in the ABBA National Tournament
- Use of an auditory goal locator placed above or behind the pins
- A scoring board system that tactually indicates the pins that remain standing after the ball is rolled

Boccia

Boccia, the Italian version of bowling, is generally played on a sand or soil alley 75 feet (23 meters) long and 8 feet (2.4 meters) wide. The playing area is normally enclosed at the ends and sides by boards 18 inches (46 centimeters) and 12 inches (30 centimeters) high, respectively.

Boccia made its initial appearance in the Paralympics at the 1992 Barcelona Games. Boccia is the only Paralympic sport in which men and women compete together in all events.

Sport Skills

The game requires that players roll or throw wooden balls (see figure 26.6) in the direction of a smaller wooden ball, or jack. The object is to have the ball come to rest closer to the jack than any of the opponent's balls. To do this, players try to roll balls in order to protect their own well-placed shots while knocking aside their opponent's balls.

Lead-Up Games and Activities

The Empire State Games for the Physically Challenged pioneered Crazy Bocce, a game that consists of throwing two sets of four wooden balls alternately into rings of various sizes for specified point

Shariff Che'Lah/fotolia.com

FIGURE 26.6 The game of boccia requires that players roll or throw wooden balls.

totals. Three smaller rings sit inside one large ring that is 13 feet (4 meters) in circumference. Points are awarded only if the ball remains inside the large ring. If the ball lands inside the large ring (but not in any of the smaller rings), 1 point is awarded. If the ball lands inside the small blue or red ring, 2 points are earned. Landing inside the small yellow ring nets 3 points. The game is usually played with the large ring in a small wading pool. The large ring can also be attached to swimming pool sides using a suction-cup attachment. The game can be played in the snow, on the beach, on the lawn, and on carpet. Crazy Bocce is enjoyed by people of all ages.

Sport Variations and Modifications

Both individual and team boccia are sanctioned events in the national competition of the the DAAA and Special Olympics. In the Paralympic Games, athletes eligible for individual competition are classified as BC1, BC2, BC3, and BC4 according to the Boccia International Sports Federation (BISF). There are also pairs events for BC3 and BC4, as well as team competition for BC1 and BC2. Special Olympics (2020) offers singles, doubles, and team competitions, Unified Sports doubles and team competitions, and a single ramp competition. Events in BISF (2018), DAAA (2020), and IDSF (2019) competition include standing, seated, combined standing and seated, and ramp boccia for athletes using wheelchairs or scooters. Major rule modifications to these events include the following:

- If a physical or medical condition exists that requires either the use of a mechanical aid to spot the jack or a bell or bright-colored cone (in the case of a participant with a visual impairment), then it is up to the discretion of the event manager whether to grant this accommodation.
- A sport assistant (SA) is allowed to adjust ramps or chutes and the player's chair position within the throwing box; however, all directions for adjustments must be initiated by the player. Assistive devices should not contain any mechanical device that aids in propulsion, such as a spring-loaded device.
- BC1 and BC3 players who have difficulty holding or placing the balls can receive assistance from one SA; however, they must

throw, kick, strike, push, or roll the ball independently. Players may use more than one assistive device during a match only after the referee has indicated it is their turn to throw.

- All balls must be thrown, rolled, pushed, struck, or kicked into the court; use of a head pointer, chin lever, or pull lever is acceptable; the athlete must have direct physical contact with the ball when it is released.

Other Variations and Modifications

There are several ways to modify boccia for participation by people with disabilities. If participants lack sufficient strength to propel the ball toward the jack, substitution of a lighter object, such as a foam ball or balloon, or reduction of the legal court size would facilitate participation. The player may also be permitted to kick the ball into the target area or use a bowling cue or stick if upper extremity involvement prohibits rolling or throwing the ball.

Fencing

Sir Ludwig Guttmann introduced fencing as a competitive event for people with disabilities in 1953 as part of the Stoke Mandeville Games in Stoke Mandeville, England, and it was included in the Paralympic Games in Rome in 1960. The objective in fencing is to score by touching the opponent's target while avoiding being touched. If fencing is included in physical education, several possible variations and modifications can make achievement of the primary objective feasible for people with disabilities.

Sport Variations and Modifications

Competition in fencing for people who use wheelchairs is normally conducted according to the rules of the International Wheelchair and Amputee Sports Federation (IWASF) (see figure 26.7). Competitors are classified into A, B, or C functional categories, representing good sitting balance and a functional fencing arm all the way to no sitting balance and a severely affected fencing arm. When appropriate, fencers in these classes with significant loss of grip or control of the sword hand may bind the sword to the hand with a bandage or similar device (IWASF, 2020). Participants eligible to compete in wheelchair fencing include people with cerebral palsy, spinal cord injuries, amputations, and les autres. Among the modified rules to ensure equal opportunity for all participants in wheelchair fencing, the following are important:

- A fencing frame must be used; the fencer with the shortest arms determines the length of the playing area.
- Fencers with significant loss of grip strength that makes it difficult to control their weapon may bind the weapon with the preapproval of two IWF officials.
- Fencers cannot purposely lose their balance, leave their chairs, rise from their seats, or use their legs to score a hit or to avoid being hit. The first offense is a warning, with subsequent offenses penalized by awarding one hit for each occurrence. Accidental loss of balance is not penalized.

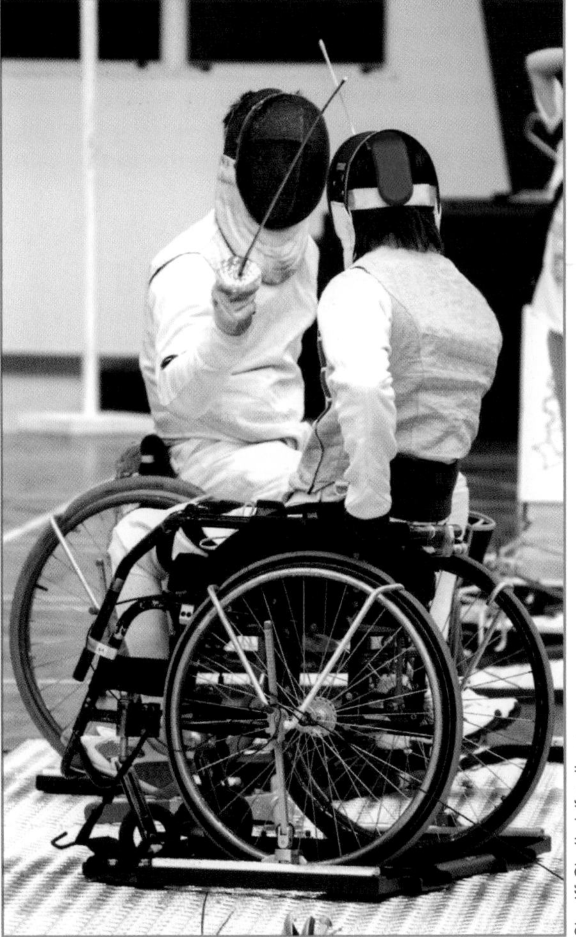

Shariff Che'Lah/fotolia.com

FIGURE 26.7 In wheelchair fencing, the wheelchairs are fixed in place to the floor by metal frames to keep the chairs from tipping.

- The legs and trunk below the waist are not valid targets for any weapon; the target area for the épée and sabre is exactly the same (i.e., any part of the body above the waist); and the target area for the foil is the torso above the waist, excluding the arms and head.

Other Variations and Modifications

Fencing is ordinarily conducted on a court measuring 6 by 40 feet (1.8 by 12.2 meters); however, to accommodate participants using wheelchairs, the dimensions of the standard court may be changed to 8 by 20 feet (2.5 by 6 meters), or a circular court 15 to 20 feet (4.6-6 meters) in diameter may be used (Paciorek & Jones, 2001). Fencers who are blind will require a smaller, narrower court, which may conceivably be equipped with a guide rail (Dunn & Leitschuh, 2014).

The only piece of adaptive equipment is the lightweight sword, which permits independent participation, especially for people with upper extremity disabilities. In cases in which no modification is necessary, the épée is recommended for ease of handling rather than the foil or sabre (Paciorek & Jones, 2001).

Horseback Riding

The Professional Association of Therapeutic Horsemanship (PATH) International (formerly North American Riding for the Handicapped Association, founded in 1969) is the primary advisory group to riders with disabilities in the United States and Canada. PATH International does not sponsor competition; however, it advises therapeutic, recreational, and competitive riding programs. PATH International also certifies riding instructors, accredits therapeutic riding facilities, and provides guidelines for operating safe programs of equine-assisted activities and therapies for individuals with special needs. Similar programs include the Cheff Therapeutic Riding Center in Michigan and Equest Therapeutic Horsemanship in Texas, two of the largest instructor training programs for therapeutic riding in the United States.

Sport Skills

Horseback riding involves, among other skills, mounting, maintaining correct positioning on the mount, and dismounting. Most therapeutic riding programs engage their students in lessons that emphasize mounting, warm-up exercises, riding instruction, games, and dismounting. Special consideration should be given to the selection and training of horses used for therapeutic riding programs. The horses should be small because children are less likely to be fearful of smaller animals and they also permit helpers to be in a better position for assisting unbalanced riders (the shoulder of the helper should be level with the middle of the rider's back).

Lead-Up Games and Activities

Several possibilities exist for using games in the context of horseback riding. The origin of some of these games is pole bending, which is common in Western riding. It is used to teach horses how to bend and riders how to compensate during the bending movement. One game that encourages stretching of the arms involves placing quoits over the poles; this activity is conducted in relay fashion, with two- or three-member teams competing. Another game consists of throwing balls into buckets placed on a wall or pole. This activity has benefits similar to those of quoits. The traditional game Red Light, Green Light can be played to reinforce certain maneuvers, such as halts, that are taught to riders.

Sport Variations and Modifications

Currently, Special Olympics is the only national governing body that offers equestrian competition or show for individuals with disabilities. Special Olympics (2020) offers English- and Western-style events, including dressage, English equitation, stock seat equitation, Western riding, working trails, gymkhana events, drill teams of two or four, prix caprilli, showmanship at halter and bridle classes, and Unified Sports team relays and drill teams. Riders are assigned to one of five divisions based on a rider profile completed by the coach: CS, CI, BS, BI, and A. Levels of support range from division CS, which requires a leader (horse handler) and one or two side walkers to act as spotters (figure 26.8), to division A, in which a rider is expected to compete with no modifications to national governing body rules. Special Olympics (2020) has designated the following rules for riding:

- Riders who must wear footwear other than heeled boots as the result of a physical disability must submit a physician's statement with their entry.

- English tack–style riders must use Peacock safety stirrups, *S*-shaped stirrups, or Devonshire boots; Western tack–style riders must use safety stirrups.
- All riders must wear protective helmets with full chin harness approved by the Safety Equipment Institute-American Society for Testing and Materials (SEI-ASTM) or British Horse Society (BHS).
- Riders may use adaptive equipment without penalty but may in no way be attached to the horse or saddle.
- An athlete with Down syndrome who has been determined to have atlantoaxial instability is prohibited from competing in equestrian competition.

Through its affiliate, US Equestrian Federation, the IPC offers competition in five classes for dressage (I, II, III, IV, and V) and two classes for para-driving, formerly known as carriage driving. Relative to dressage, the lower designated classes are intended for individuals with more significant impairments. Class I of para-driving is for drivers who use wheelchairs; whereas Class II is designed for lesser impaired drivers. For further details about the individual dressage test, consult the International Equestrian Federation website (www.fei.org). The IPC adheres to the International Para-Equestrian Committee (IPEC) rules, as follows:

- The rider may use Velcro to stay attached to the saddle and elastic rubber bands to keep feet in the stirrups; no other equipment is permitted that would affix a rider to a horse or saddle.
- Readers or callers (called *commanders*) are permitted for riders with intellectual impairments, visual impairments, or head injury in all events including freestyle; commanders may use radio communication if supervised by a steward.

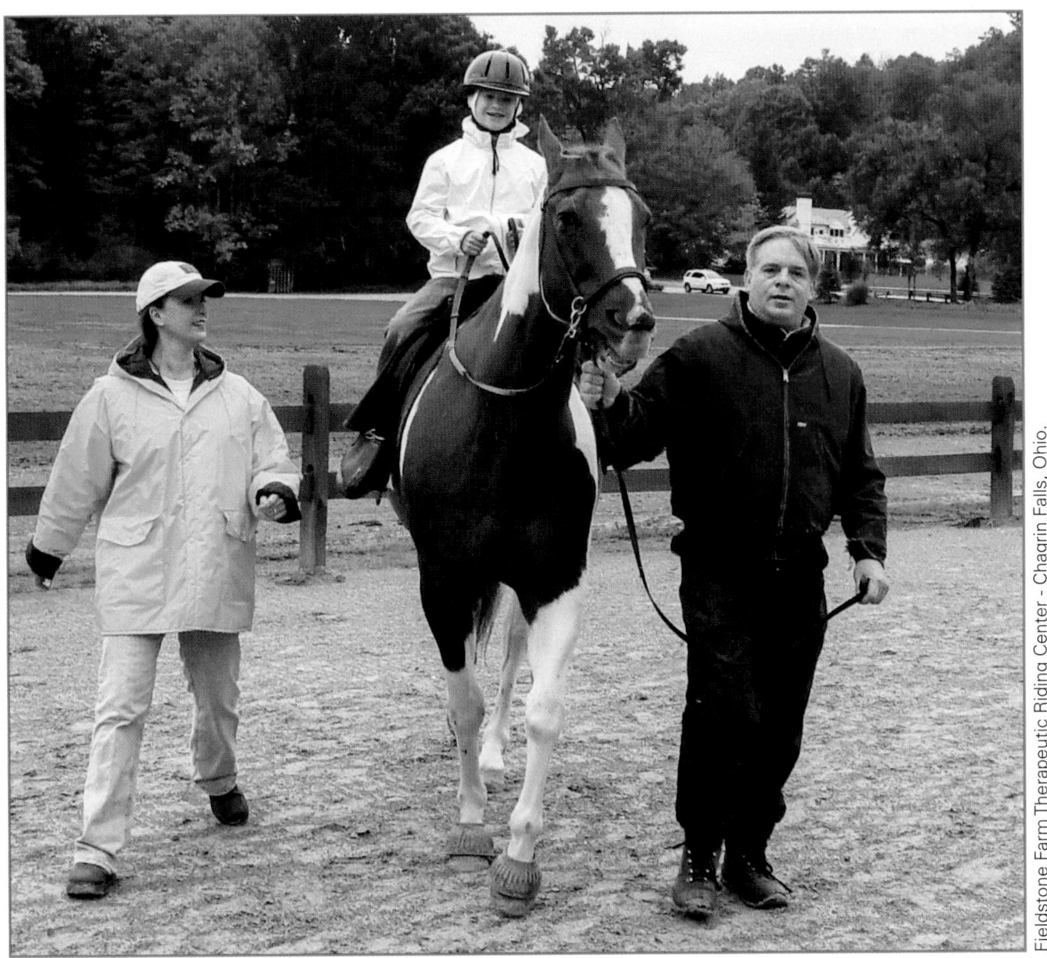

Fieldstone Farm Therapeutic Riding Center - Chagrin Falls, Ohio.

FIGURE 26.8 Division CS of Special Olympics requires that the rider have one or two side walkers and a leader.

- For dressage tests, riders with visual impairments may either have callers or use beepers for purposes of location.

Other Variations and Modifications

Mounting is the single most important phase of a riding program for people with disabilities. Because the typical method of mounting (placing the left foot in the stirrup, holding onto the cantle, and springing into the saddle) is impossible for some people, alternatives are available. Several mounting procedures are used by riders with disabilities, ranging from totally assisted mounts, either from the top of a ramp or at ground level, to normal mounting from the ground.

Once the rider is mounted, many options for adapted equipment can make riding an enjoyable learning experience. One commonly used item is an **adapted rein bar**, which permits riders with a disability in one arm to apply sufficient leverage on the reins with the unaffected arm to successfully guide the horse; use of this bar is faded as soon as the rider learns to apply pressure with the knees. Another adaptation is the **Humes rein**, consisting of large oval handholds fitted on the rein; this allows riders with impairment of the hands to direct the horse with wrist and arm movement.

Body harnesses are used extensively in programs for riders with disabilities. They consist of web belts about 4 inches (10 centimeters) wide with a leather handhold in the back, which a leader can hold on to to help maintain a rider's balance. Most riders who have disabilities also use the **Peacock stirrup**, which is shaped like a regular stirrup with a rubber belt attached to the top and bottom of one side to release quickly in case of a fall, reducing the chance of catching a foot. The **Devonshire boot** is used frequently if a rider has tight heel cords (Achilles tendons) or weak ankles. Designed much like the front portion of a boot, it prevents the foot from running through the stirrup, and consequently it promotes keeping the toes up and heels down, which can be invaluable if heel-cord stretching is desirable.

Gymnastics

Gymnastics has enjoyed considerable popularity because of its visibility in the Olympic Games. As a result, people with disabilities have begun to participate in gymnastics programs when opportunities are available.

Sport Skills

Beyond possessing the physical attributes necessary to participate in gymnastics (e.g., strength, agility, endurance, flexibility, coordination, and balance), participants must learn to compete in one or more artistic gymnastic events: pommel horse, rings, horizontal bar, parallel bars, vault, and floor exercise for men; and balance beam, uneven parallel bars, vault, and floor exercise for women. In both men's and women's competitions, participation in all events qualifies athletes for a chance to win the all-around title.

Lead-Up Games and Activities

The closest thing to lead-up activities in gymnastics can be found in the Special Olympics sport skills program. In its sport skills program manuals, *Artistic Gymnastics Coaching Guide* and *Rhythmic Gymnastics Coaching Guide* (Special Olympics, 2020), general conditioning exercises with emphasis on flexibility and strength are recommended. Doubles tumbling and balance stunts are also suggested. As an introductory experience, educational gymnastics, which uses a creative, problem solving approach, can be used to teach basic movement concepts. This could eventually allow participants to compete in more advanced forms of gymnastics competition.

Sport Variations and Modifications

Special Olympics offers gymnastics competition in standard men's and women's events, as well as mixed-gender events in vaulting, wide beam, floor exercise, and tumbling as well as the all-around. Rhythmic gymnastics consists of rope, ribbon, ball, hoop, and all-around competition. Level A, which is mixed gender, also competes in rhythmic gymnastics individual compulsory routines either sitting or standing. There are also Unified Sports events and group routines performed by groups of four to six athletes. Each individual competition (i.e., men's, women's, and mixed gender) has a Unified Sports event for each of the events that make up the specific category. No significant rule modifications are required, and each participant's performance is judged according to the rules established for that event by the International Gymnastics Federation (FIG) and the national governing body (Special Olympics, 2020).

Special Olympics rules to ensure equitable competition include the following:

- Gymnasts with visual impairments have the option of performing the vault with no run, one step, two steps, a multiple bounce on the board (with hands starting on the horse), or using a guide rope strung parallel to the runway; audible cues may be used in all routines.
- In the floor exercise, the coach may signal gymnasts with hearing impairments to begin the routine.
- Gymnasts using canes or walkers may have a coach walk onto the floor and remove (and replace) walkers and other aids as needed without any deduction of points.
- Gymnasts with visual impairments may use audible cues during all routines; during the floor exercise, music may be played at any close point off the mat, or the coach may carry the music source around the perimeter of the mat.
- Gymnasts in level A perform their rhythmic gymnastics routines while seated in either a wheelchair or a sturdy chair. Gymnasts who are blind can have audible cues during competition, and Deaf athletes can have a visual cue to start with music.

Other Variations and Modifications

Few modifications are used in gymnastics competition. If gymnastics is included in physical education programs, all of the modifications observed by the sport organizations in the conduct of their competitions would be valid.

Wrestling and Judo

The sports of wrestling and judo require strength, balance, flexibility, and coordination. If people with disabilities possess these characteristics and if they can combine knowledge of techniques with an ability to demonstrate them in competitive situations, then there is no reason why they cannot experience success in wrestling and judo.

Sport Skills

Wrestling consists of several techniques that are essential for success. These include takedowns, escapes and reversals, breakdowns and controls, and pin holds. Judo, on the other hand, consists of three primary branches: throws, groundwork (i.e., strangles, joint locks, and chokes), and striking techniques, including kicks and punches.

Lead-Up Games and Activities

Certain elementary physical education self-testing activities could potentially be used as lead-up activities for wrestling. Two such activities are listed here:

- *Hand wrestling.* Standing, two people face each other and grasp right hands; each person lifts one foot off the ground. On a signal, each participant attempts to cause their opponent to lose balance, thereby touching either the free foot or hand to the ground.
- *Indian leg wrestling.* Two people lie side-by-side, facing in opposite directions. Hips are adjacent to the partner's waist, and inside arms are hooked. Each person raises the inside leg to a count of three; on the third count, they bend knees, hook them, and attempt to force the other person into a backward roll.

Sport Variations and Modifications

Greco-Roman wrestling (which prohibits holds below the waist and use of the legs in attempting to take opponents to the mat) and freestyle wrestling, as well as judo, are sanctioned events in competitions governed by the USADSF. These events are conducted according to the rules established by the International Federation of Associated Wrestling Styles (FILA) and the International Judo Federation (IJF), respectively. Hearing aids and external cochlear implants are forbidden during competition.

The USABA previously sponsored competition in wrestling in an open division using international freestyle rules as interpreted by IBSA; however, USABA is currently not offering wrestling competition due to a lack of interest. IBSA has completely eliminated wrestling and now offers competition in judo exclusively, using the rules of the IJF (as interpreted by IBSA). In the Paralympic Games, world championships, and regional championships, competition for all weight classifications is combined for classes B1, B2, and B3. There are individual and team competitions for men and women. The basic sport adaptation for judo (for B1 and B2 competitors) is to have opponents start with a grip on each other's judogi (the traditional judo garment).

Special Olympics also offers competition in judo using divisions based on the participant's age, sex, weight class, ability level, and concept of strategy. Special Olympics has designated the following rules:

- Athletes with Down syndrome cannot participate in judo.
- Matches can be started in either a standing, sitting, or kneeling position at the discretion of the official.
- Athletes starting from a kneeling position may not push their opponent straight backward.

Other Variations and Modifications

Wrestling and judo are not for everyone. For people with disabilities who want to attempt these sports, several modifications can be used. For those with lower extremity difficulties that prevent ambulation, all maneuvers should be taught from the mat with emphasis on arm technique. Bilateral upper extremity impairment will probably restrict participation in all but leg wrestling maneuvers. After removal of prostheses, single-arm amputees can participate with emphasis placed on leg maneuvers.

Golf

Golf has been an event in the Special Olympics since 1995. It is also an activity that can be effectively included in physical education programs for students with disabilities. Professional golf achieved a milestone for athletes with disabilities in 1998, when Casey Martin, a golfer with a chronic and debilitating circulatory disorder in his leg, sued the Professional Golfers' Association (PGA) under the provisions of the Americans with Disabilities Act (ADA) and won the right to use a cart in PGA events.

Sport Skills

Golf typically requires a person to grasp the club and address the ball using an appropriate stance. Being able to swing the golf club backward and then forward through a large arc, including a follow-through, is also a requisite.

Lead-Up Games and Activities

An appropriate lead-up activity is miniature golf. This popular version of golf is quite suited to people with disabilities, and for many it might represent the extent to which the golf experience is explored. Holes should range from 8 to 14 feet (2.4-4.3 meters) from tee mat to cup with a width of 3 feet (1 meter), which accommodates reaching a ball lying in the center of the course from a wheelchair.

Sport Variations and Modifications

Special Olympics has created rules based on the rules of golf as written by the Royal and Ancient Golf Club of St. Andrews and the United States Golf Association (USGA). Official events include an individual skills contest (level 1), Unified Sports alternate-shot team play competition of 9 holes (level 2), Unified Sports alternate-shot team play competition of 18 holes (level 3), individual stroke play competition of 9 holes (level 4), and individual stroke play competition of 18 holes (level 5). Individual skills contests are designed to train athletes to compete in basic golf skills. Competition is held in short putting, long putting, and chipping, as well as the pitch shot, bunker shot, iron shot, and wood shot. The alternate-shot team play competition involves pairing one Special Olympics athlete with one golfer without disabilities, who serves as a coach and mentor. The format is a 9-hole tournament played as a modified four-person scramble. Level 3 is Unified Sports team play that is designed to provide the opportunity to play in a team format with a partner without intellectual disabilities but with similar ability. Level 4 enables athletes to play in regulation 9-hole golf competition, whereas level 5 is suitable for play in 18-hole competitions.

The U.S. Deaf Golf Association, an affiliate of the International Committee of Sports for the Deaf (2020), sponsors competition for Deaf and hard of hearing golfers. It offers events for youth and seniors, including individual events for men and women.

Other Variations and Modifications

Because of limitations experienced by people with disabilities, the essential skills of golf are often problematic. Dunn and Leitschuh (2014) have detailed many practical considerations necessary for successful participation by golfers with disabilities. These include using powered and adaptable carts for those who lack stamina to walk the golf course or for those who have significant mobility issues (see figure 26.9); providing a chair for players who cannot balance on one crutch or who are unable to stand; and eliminating the preliminary movement of the club (waggle) for blind golfers because this could produce an initial malalignment of the club with the ball. Additionally, players can gain information about distance by tapping on the cup or by asking others how far they are positioned from the cup; some wheelchair players also use extra-long clubs to clear the footplates.

The Putter Finger is an assistive device used to retrieve the ball from the hole that consists of a molded rubber suction cup designed to fit on the grip end of any putter (Adams & McCubbin, 1991). J.H. Huber (personal communication, January 1971) developed another adaptation that enables golfers who are blind to practice independently. Three pieces of material, all of which produce a different sound when struck, are hung in different positions 15 to 20 feet (4.6-6 meters) in front of golfers as they practice, allowing them to determine whether the ball went straight, hooked, or sliced based on the sound. Audio goal locators can also be used to develop independent putting skills. Finally, an amputee golf grip developed by TRS, Inc., fits any standard prosthetic wrist. It permits full rotation during backswing, squared clubface at impact, and complete follow-through. Additionally, it has an energy-storing capacity during backswing that promotes more powerful strokes.

Powerlifting

Powerlifting has developed over the years as an extremely popular sport for people with disabilities. In this chapter, powerlifting as a sport is distinguished from routine weight training.

Sport Skills

The IPC restricts powerlifting competition to the bench press only. Participants are classified by weight; however, braces and other devices are not counted in the total weight. In Move United competition, adjustments to recorded weight are made relative to the site of an amputation.

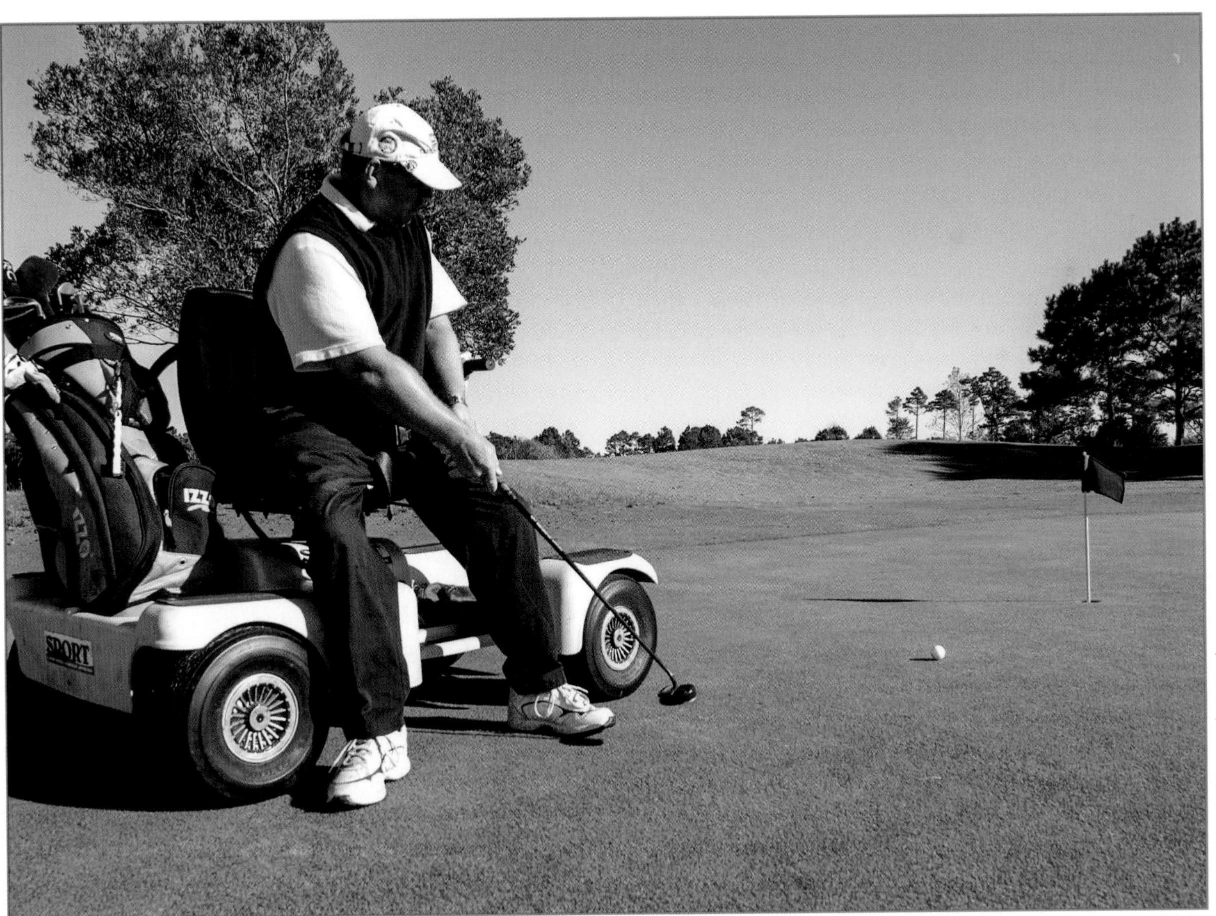

FIGURE 26.9 Practical considerations, such as an adapted golf cart, allow for successful participation by golfers with disabilities.

Sport Variations and Modifications

Move United, DAAA, Special Olympics, and USABA offer competitive powerlifting programs. IBSA sanctions three events: the bench press, squat, and deadlift. Special Olympics offers the bench press, deadlift, and squat, as well as two combination events: deadlift and bench press, and the deadlift, bench press, and squat. Special Olympics also offers Unified powerlifting. Move United provides competition in the powerlift press and bench press. The IPC offers powerlifting under the aegis of the World Para Powerlifting. Each organization has specific rules that accommodate its athletes. Some of the more significant modifications include the following:

- Strapping the legs to the bench either just above the knees or at the ankles is permissible as long as it is done with the strap provided by the organizing committee; for above-the-knee amputees, strapping is permitted between the hip and the remainder of the amputated limb (Move United).
- A lifter who has a physical disability may be strapped to the bench between the ankles and the hips with a strapping not to exceed 10 centimeters in width (Special Olympics).
- An athlete with Down syndrome with recognized atlantoaxial instability cannot compete in the squat lift (Special Olympics).
- In DAAA competition, lifters unable to fully extend at the elbow must have their range of motion tested by a classifier or official under the aegis of IDSF.

Cycling

Cycling, whether bicycle, tricycle, or handcycle, is a useful skill for lifelong leisure pursuit. It can also be a strenuous sport pursued for its competitiveness. To compete, participants must develop a high level of fitness and learn effective race strategy. For example, Challenge Alaska sponsors the Sadler's Alaska Challenge, which is the longest handcycle race in the world. In 2009 the race covered 267 miles (430 kilometers) in seven days with a total of approximately 16,000 feet (4,877 meters) of ascent during the race.

Sport Skills

Under most circumstances, cycling requires the ability to maintain balance on a cycle and to execute a reciprocal movement of the legs to turn the pedals. However, technological advances have opened cycling to people who would never have thought previously about cycling as a leisure pursuit or as a competitive event.

Sport Variations and Modifications

The USADSF through the United States Deaf Cycling Association (USDCA) sponsors three events: the 1,000-meter sprint, a road race, and a time-trial race on the road. At the international level, ICSD sponsors the following competitions for men: a 1,000-meter sprint, an individual time trial, an individual road race, and a 50K points race. For women, it sponsors a 1,000-meter sprint, an individual time trial, and an individual road race. The IPC sponsors four cycling events with one or more classifications per event using the regulations proffered by the Union Cycliste Internationale (UCI) (2019). These include handbike (H1-H5), tricycle (T1-T2), cycling (C1-C5), and tandem events (B). There are events for men and women as well as for cyclists who are blind and visually impaired. There are road races from 5 to 125 kilometers, including road race circuits of 7 and 15 kilometers for men and women in classes T1 and T2, C1 to C5, and tandem (B). There are individual time trials from 20 to 35 kilometers. Team relays are conducted for sport classes H1 to H5 for both men and women. Track races are contested at 500 meters for men and women C1 to C5 and tandem. Individual pursuit races are run at 3,000 meters for women C1 to C5 and tandem; at 3,000 meters for men C1 to C3; and 4,000 meters for men C4 and C5 and men's tandem.

Both USABA and IBSA (2020) offer four event categories: road races, track races, individual pursuit, and sprints. Within each category are races for men, women, and mixed tandems. Road races are 100 to 135 kilometers for men, 60 to 70 kilometers for women, and 65 to 80 kilometers for mixed teams. Track races are 1,000 meters for men and mixed teams and 500 meters for women. Individual pursuit events are 4 kilometers for men and 3 kilometers for women and mixed teams. Sprint competitions are contested over a distance of 1,000 meters for men, women, and mixed teams. With few exceptions, the rules for IBSA cycling are the same as those for the United States Cycling Federation (USCF). The primary exception is that the pilot (front rider) in tandem riding events must be sighted and have a group 1 permit; the stoker (back rider) can be from any vision class and must have a group 2 permit.

Special Olympics offers the following events: 250- and 500-meter time trial; 1K, 2K, 5K, and 10K time trials; 5K, 10K, 15K, 25K, and 40K road races; and 5K and 10K Unified Sports tandem time trials. All events are governed by the rules established by the UCI. Some specific modifications are as follows:

- Visual cues can be used to indicate the start of the race for riders with hearing impairment.
- Modified bicycles for use in time-trial events are permissible.

Other Variations and Modifications

People with impaired balance or coordination might require some adaptation to cycle successfully. Three- and four-wheeled cycles with or without hand cranks can facilitate cycling for people with disabilities. If riding a two-wheeled bicycle is the desirable approach, then training wheels suitable for full-size adult bikes can be constructed. Additionally, tandem cycling can be used when total control of the bicycle is beyond the ability of the person with a disability (e.g., visual impairment). Handcycling (figure 26.10) is now a Paralympic sport, with athletes competing in three divisions. Events include road races and individual time trials.

Track and Field

Because all major sport organizations for people with disabilities offer competitive opportunities in track and field, this section focuses on rule modifications that maximize participation. For each organization, the track portion is discussed first, followed by the field events. No attempt is made to examine sport skills, variations and modifications, or lead-up activities except as related to Special Olympics.

Move United

Track and field competitions are governed by the rules of USA Track & Field (USATF). Move United sponsors a classed division in track and field events. Seated classes include T31, T32, T33, T34, T51, T52, T53, and T54 for track events and F31, F32, F33, F34, F51, F52, F53, F54, F55, F56, and F57 for field events. Standing athletes compete in track as T35, T36, T37, T38, T42, T43, T44, T45, T46,

FIGURE 26.10 Handcycling is now a Paralympic sport with athletes competing in three divisions.

and T47 and in field events as F35, F36, F37, F38, F40, F42, F43, F44, F45, and F46. There is also a new sport class, T/F 61-64, for athletes with lower extremity deficiencies requiring use of a prosthetic device. The prothesis is optional in field events. There are three classes for athletes with visual impairments: T/F11, T/F12, and T/F13. There is also a T/F20 class for individuals with intellectual impairments. In addition, there are six junior divisions for children 7 to 22 years of age, as well as a futures category for children up to age 6.

Classes T11-13, T35, T38, T42, T46, T51, and T54 compete in 100-, 200-, 400-, 800-, 1,500-, 5,000-, and 10,000-meter races. T11-13 through T38 compete in a 4 × 100-meter circular relay, whereas T42 through T54 compete in both 4 × 100-meter and 4 × 400-meter circular relays. Classes T32, T33, and T34 compete in 100-, 200-, 400-, 800-, and 1,500-meter races. T31 competes in 100-, 200-, 400-, and 800-meter events. T40, T41, and T47 contest 100-, 200-, and 400-meter races only. T11-13 and T46 compete in 10-kilometer, half-, and full marathons. T32, T38, T51, and T54 also run 5-, 15-, and 20-kilometer road races. There are also two Frame Running classes (less impaired and more impaired). Athletes in these classes run with their feet while pushing a three-wheeled running frame that is used for body support. In field events, all classes compete in the discus, shot put, and javelin, with the following exceptions: Class F31 competes only in club throw; F32 substitutes club throw for javelin; and F51 competes in discus and club throw only. In jumping events, T11, T12-13, T45, T46, and T47 contest high jump, long jump, and triple jump. T42 and T44 compete in high jump and long jump. T20, T40-41, and T43 engage in long jump only. Additionally, all classes compete in pentathlon, which consists of five individual events (long jump, shot put, javelin, discus, club throw); 100- to 400-meter sprints; and 200- to 1,500-meter runs. These events are combined in a way that serves the athlete's functional ability best.

Move United has designated the following rules for track and field events:

- Wheelchairs shall have at least two large wheels and one small wheel with only one round hand rim for each large wheel; no mechanical gears or levers shall be allowed in any sanctioned Move United competition, and only hand-operated mechanical steering devices are permitted.
- Batons are not exchanged in relay races; the takeover shall be a touch on any part of the body of the outgoing competitor within the takeover zone.
- Athletes must ensure that no part of their lower limbs can fall to the ground or track during an event; if used, strapping must be of a nonelastic material.
- Approved hold-down devices can be used to stabilize competitors' chairs in field events. Classes F32 to F34 must have both legs off the ground and the entire femur in contact with the seat; F7 and F8 competitors are permitted lifting as long as one foot is in contact with the ground inside the throwing circle; lifting is prohibited from initiation of throw until implement is marked by an official.
- Competitors cannot use any device (e.g., taping two or more fingers together) to assist in making throws; gloves are not allowed. F51 through F53 may use strapping on the nonthrowing hand to anchor it to the chair.

United States Association of Blind Athletes (USABA)

World Athletics rules are employed in USABA track and field competitions. Within the USABA structure, there are three visual classifications: B1, B2, and B3. Events in 100-, 200-, 400-, 800-, 1,500-, 5,000-, and 10,000-meter races, as well as the marathon, are provided for men and women across all three classes. There are two relays for men and women: a 4 × 100 meter and a 4 × 400 meter with combined visual classes. Both men and women in all three classes compete in the following individual events: long jump, high jump, triple jump, discus, javelin, and shot put. Men in all three classes throw the hammer. Pentathlons are contested by all classes and both sexes. Men throw the javelin while women put the shot. Men run a 1,500-meter event, and women run an 800-meter race. Two divisions of youth events, junior and intermediate, are also contested. IBSA has determined that the following rule modifications are necessary to provide more suitable competition for athletes with visual impairments:

- Class B1 sprinters may run the 100-meter with the help of not more than two callers, one of whom must remain behind the finish line; the second caller has no restriction on position but may not cross the finish line ahead of the athlete.

- Guides are allowed for B1 and B2 in the 200-meter through marathon events. When guides are used in events between 200 and 800 meters, there is an allowance of two lanes per competitor.
- Competitors may also decide what form guidance will take. They may choose an elbow lead, a tether, or to run freely. At no time will the guide push or pull the competitor, nor will the guide ever precede the athlete. The runner may receive verbal instructions from the guide.
- Acoustic signals (a caller) are permitted for B1 and B2 athletes in field events.
- Class B1 high jumpers may touch the bar as an orientation before jumping; B2 jumpers are permitted to place a visual aid on the bar (e.g., hanging strips of 2-inch [5-centimeter] black or bright orange tape from the crossbar).
- Class B1 and B2 shot put, discus, and javelin throwers may enter the throwing circle or runway (run-up track) only with the assistance of a helper, who must leave the area before the first attempt.

USA Deaf Sports Federation (USADSF)

Competition for Deaf athletes conforms to World Athletics rules and regulations. Therefore, events sponsored by the USADSF parallel the 44 International Committee of Sports for the Deaf events. Track competition for men includes races at standard distances from 100 through 10,000 meters. It also includes the 110- and 400-meter hurdles, 3,000-meter steeplechase, 4 × 100-meter relay, 4 × 400-meter relay, and marathon. Women's competition in track and field parallels that described for men, with the exception of the 100-meter hurdle instead of 110-meter hurdle. Along with the standard field events, such as shot put, discus, javelin, high jump, long jump, and triple jump, the USADSF also provides competition in pole vaulting and the hammer throw. Additionally, there is a decathlon for men and a heptathlon for women.

Special Olympics

Special Olympics offers more track and field events than any other sport organization for people with disabilities. Included in the list of possible events that can be offered at a sanctioned competition are 25-, 50-, 100-, 200-, 400-, 800-, 1,500-, 3,000-, 5,000-, and 10,000-meter races as well as race walking events of 25, 50, 100, 400, 800, and 1500 meters. There are also assisted walking events at 10, 25, and 50 meters. Women compete in 100-meter hurdles, whereas men compete in 110-meter hurdles. Additionally, there are 4 × 100-, 4 × 200-, and 4 × 400-meter relays; each of these events has a Unified Sports counterpart. In field competition, the following events are contested: long jump, standing long jump, high jump, shot put (including wheelchair), softball throw, tennis ball throw, mini-javelin, and pentathlon (100-meter, long jump, shot put, high jump, and 800-meter). There is also a half-marathon and a full marathon. Wheelchair events consist of 10-, 25-, and 30-meter races, a 4 × 25-meter shuttle relay, 30- and 50-meter slalom, 25-meter motorized obstacle race, and 100-, 200-, and 400-meter wheelchair races. World Athletics rules are employed in competitions sanctioned by Special Olympics. Modifications to those rules include the following:

- In running events, a rope or sighted guide can be used to assist athletes with visual impairments; a tap start can be used only with an athlete who is deafblind.
- In walking races, athletes are not required to maintain a straight advancing leg while competing.
- In the softball throw, athletes can use any type of throw.
- In all races 400 meters and shorter, including hurdles and the 4 × 100-meter relay, athletes have the option of using starting blocks.
- Athletes with Down syndrome who have recognized atlantoaxial instability may not participate in either the high jump or the pentathlon.
- To participate in the long jump, athletes must qualify with a 1-meter jump minimum.

Special Olympics offers a full menu of track and field events for athletes using wheelchairs, including the 25- and 50-meter dashes or walks; 100-meter walk; 10-, 25-, and 50-meter assisted walks; softball throw; 10- and 25-meter wheelchair races; 30-meter wheelchair slalom; 4 × 25-meter wheelchair shuttle relay; 30- and 50-meter motorized wheelchair slaloms; and 25-meter motorized wheelchair obstacle race.

Cerebral Palsy International Sports and Recreation Association

Cerebral Palsy International Sports and Recreation Association (CPISRA, 2020) also uses the rules, regulations, and classification system established by the IPC. Events consist of races as short as 60 meters (weave) for athletes in electric wheelchairs up to 3,000 meters and cross-country running. There are 4 × 100-meter and 4 × 400-meter open relays, including wheelchair and ambulatory events. The field events include shot put, discus, javelin, club throw, and long jump. Additional events include the precision throw, soft shot, distance kick, high toss, and medicine ball thrust. There is also a pentathlon. Modifications of rules used to ensure equitable competition include the following:

- Athletes who use canes or crutches must use their assistive devices in a manner such that they make contact with the surface of the track a minimum of one time approximately every 10 meters.
- Athletes in wheelchair relays must make personal contact with their teammate to complete a successful changeover. This contact can be on any part of the outgoing teammate; either the incoming or outgoing competitor may initiate the tag within the change zone.

CPISRA incorporates the following additional modifications in its field events:

- An attendant or approved holding device may secure the chair in place; however, neither an attendant nor the apparatus may be inside the throwing area.
- The soft shot, precision throw, high toss, and soft discus are contested by athletes with significant impairment.
- The distance kick and medicine ball thrust are offered for athletes who cannot engage in routine throwing events. In the distance kick, a 13-inch (33-centimeter) playground ball is placed on a foul line; the competitors initiate a backswing and then kick the ball forward as far as possible while remaining seated. In the medicine ball thrust, a 6-pound (2.7-kilogram) medicine ball is used. Competitors may not kick the ball; rather, the foot must remain in contact with the ball throughout the entire movement until release.

Dwarf Athletic Association of America (DAAA)

The DAAA, in accordance with IDSF, sanctions the following track events: 15- and 20-meter runs for children under 6 years of age (futures), 20- and 40-meter runs for juniors aged 7 to 9, 40- and 60-meter runs for juniors aged 7 to 9 and 10 to 12, and 60-meter runs for juniors aged 10 to 12 and 13 to 15 and athletes over 35 years of age (masters). There is also a 100-meter race for juniors (13-15), open, and masters athletes. The open division competes in 60-meter, 100-meter, and 200-meter races. The masters class also competes in the 4 × 100-meter relay and 4 × 60-meter shuttle relay. All classes can contest wheelchair slalom. The rules of USATF and wheelchair competition are typically followed.

Field events contested in DAAA competition include the shot put, discus, and javelin in juniors 10 to 12, juniors 13 to 15, open classes, and masters. Other juniors and futures events include the softball throw or cricket ball throw, flippy flyer (soft discus), Frisbee throw, and tennis ball throw. In IDSF competition, athletes with short stature compete in sport class T40/41 and F40/41.

Dance

Dance can be as rudimentary as ring-around-the-rosy or as highly technical as ballet or ballroom dance. Many studies have addressed the potential benefits of dance, whether for children or adults or for individuals with or without disabilities (Prieto et al., 2020). Paramount among these are physical, psychological, and social benefits with anecdotal or quasi-experimental evidence being the primary sources of confirmation.

In a previous edition of this textbook, Boswell (2017) described three categories of rhythms and dance that serve as the basis for teaching in physical education. These categories include (1) rhythmic movement, (2) creative educational dance, and (3) structured dance. Each of these categories are discussed briefly here.

- *Rhythmic movement.* All children should engage in rhythmic experiences that help them develop the attributes essential to enjoying movement generally and dance specifically. In order to engage effectively in early forms of rhythmic activity, ultimately leading to participation in more highly skilled forms of dance, children must develop specific skills and refine certain innate abilities. These include "movement principles that relate to balance, transfer of weight, rhythm, and alignment as well as movement concepts such as time, space, and force" (Boswell, 2017, p. 456).

• *Creative educational dance.* As children get older, the breadth of their dance experiences expands and they have an opportunity to develop the aesthetic side of dance. In the elementary grades, creative educational dance (CED) provides an inclusive opportunity to refine the specific movement concepts of space, time, and force (Boswell, 2017; Carline, 2011; Gilbert, 2015). Each theme can be further broken down: for example, body and space can examine motion and stillness, spatial relationships, and body shapes. Time explores internal and external rhythms, changing tempo, and accents and patterns. Force involves movement qualities such as bending, twisting, and reaching; strong and light movements; and flow (Boswell, 2017).

• *Structured dance.* The final category is structured dance. In a physical education curriculum, this category typically includes social dance and folk dance. In elementary physical education curricula, teachers can integrate folk dance with history and geography lessons being taught in students' classrooms (e.g., when studying Serbia or Israel, students learn the kolo or hora, respectively). This category builds on the knowledge of basic steps and maneuvers required to execute particular dances such as swing and salsa. Basic steps are also recognized in performances of well-known dances of popular social and ballroom dances such as the waltz, foxtrot, cha-cha, and rumba. Many of the well-known ballroom dances are now contested as dancesport.

Competitive Dance (Dancesport)

Dance is a highly valued and competitive sport in the lives of individuals with disabilities. The IPC has provided competition in dancesport since 2010, and Special Olympics recognized dancesport in the 2019 World Summer Games. In this section we will analyze the types of dance competition provided by these organizations with emphasis on the categories of dance, the classification system employed by IPC, and certain rules and regulations that govern participation in the various dance forms.

Special Olympics provides competition in all types of dance styles under the main categories of ballroom, streetdance, performing arts (see figure 26.11), and specialty dance. Competition is divided into solos (only Special Olympics athletes), duos (two dancers side-by-side; either two Special Olympics athletes or one Special Olympics and one Unified Sports athlete), couples (two dancers together; either two Special Olympics athletes or one Special Olympics and one Unified Sports athlete), and teams (4 to 12 dancers; either all Special Olympics athletes or a combination of Special Olympics and Unified Sports athletes).

Special Olympics has a number of specific elements that govern dance competition in all disciplines and dance forms.

- In ballroom dance, all solos must perform a 360-degree rotation on one leg; couples, duos, and teams must also include a side-by-side piece for six seconds.
- In streetdance, solos and duos must perform the 360-degree rotation on one leg and add a floor element; duos and teams must also include isolations during the piece.
- In performing arts, solos, duos, couples, and teams must do a 360-degree rotation on one leg, have a jumping section, and add a floor element during the piece.
- In specialty dance, the chosen dance is inherent to the country of origin and it must be easily and visually recognizable; dancers must do a 360-degree rotation on one leg and add a jumping section during the piece.
- In all duos, couples, and team competitions, every dancer must execute each required element of the dance.

Competition in dancesport has a much longer tenure in the IPC, where championships have been staged since 2010. At the highest levels of international competition, IPC provides competition via six sport classes (SC 1 and 2, SD 1 and 2, and L&F 1 and 2) and four competition classes (duo standard 1 and 2 and duo Latin 1 and 2). Classification 1 is for individuals who present more impairment and 2 represents less impairment. When the event is single it implies the athlete is a wheelchair user, combined means one male and one female athlete with one athlete in a wheelchair, and duo events implies one male and one female athlete with both athletes in wheelchairs. In order to qualify for IPC competition an individual must possess minimally one of the following seven impairments: (1) impaired muscle power, (2) impaired passive range of movement, (3) limb deficiency, (4) leg length difference, (5) athetosis, (6) hypertonia, or (7) ataxia.

IPC has specific rules and regulations that govern dancesport. Most, if not all, of these rules and regulations reflect concerns about the size of the dance floor and athlete dress code. Additionally,

Andreea Campeanu/Moment/Getty Images

FIGURE 26.11 Special Olympics dancer rehearsing her performance.

there are regulations regarding the use of props and the selection of music, including duration and tempo. Other rules center on technical classifications for competition (e.g., an SC 1 designation implies that both athletes are assessed at the same level or their combined score is less than 50 points, whereas SC 2 denotes that both athletes are assessed at the same level or their combined score is greater than 50 points).

Other Variations and Modifications

There will always exist a need to provide for inclusive activities in order to promote the development of basic rhythmic skills and abilities for all students (Cone & Cone, 2012). Therefore, it is incumbent on physical educators to adapt or modify their approach and teaching techniques to accommodate students with a variety of learning styles. The following variations and modifications for teaching dance are highlighted without emphasis on a particular disability (Cone & Cone, 2011):

- Use color-coded wrist or ankle bracelets to promote directional intent.
- Use highly colorful props to enhance motivation.
- Link the rhythm or dance experience to learners' favorite cartoon characters or computer games.
- Use floor textures to promote understanding of space.
- Encourage nonambulatory individuals to use their upper bodies to explore their movement potential.
- Make the music a physical experience through the use of instruments and props (e.g., ribbons).
- Keep movement noncompetitive and nonthreatening.
- Use a multisensory approach (e.g., scarves, lummi sticks, balloons).

Strategies for Inclusion

The variations and modifications highlighted in this chapter reflect good practice in physical education as well as in sanctioned sport programs. Individual and dual sports and activities provide a unique opportunity for inclusion of people with disabilities with their peers without disabilities. From elementary school through high school, variations and modifications can be used to alter sports and activities to allow students with disabilities to participate in general physical education classes, including rhythm and dance programs. Not only will they derive the benefits of instruction in activities that are themselves inclusive, but also receive that instruction in the least restrictive environment.

Additionally, the use of universal design for learning (UDL) provides teachers with strategies that anticipate students' needs prior to instruction. Teachers can use alternate forms of presentation to accommodate students' unique learning styles. Students can also exercise alternative means for physically engaging in activity and expressing their learning (e.g., the innovative use of technology). Lieberman and colleagues (2021) offer useful information for practitioners that include examples of universally designed lesson plans for individual and dual sports and activities such as archery, bowling, tennis, golf, and track and field. Because of the reduced temporal and spatial demands of most individual, dual, and dance activities highlighted in this chapter, there is every reason to believe that success in these activities will be readily attainable within accessible programs in inclusive settings.

Summary

This chapter presented individual and dual sports and activities currently available in the competitive offerings of the major sport organizations serving athletes with disabilities. Lead-up activities were suggested, as were variations and modifications for use in competitive sport or in physical education programs. It is worth noting that the rules governing sport for people with disabilities continue to undergo modifications; national governing bodies and international federations continue to change rules and regulations, as well as add and subtract sports from their competitive offerings. For example, Special Olympics has added sports such as cricket, roller skating, short track speed skating, and even triathlon. Space limitations prevented discussion of other activities such as shooting, roller skating, blowdarts, and racquetball; information on these activities can be found in Paciorek and Jones (2001).

References

Adams, R.C., & McCubbin, J.A. (1991). *Games, sports, and exercise for the physically handicapped* (4th ed.). Lea & Febiger.

Boccia International Sports Federation. (2018). *BISFed international rules, vol. 3: Rules.* Retrieved from https://www.worldboccia.com/wp-content/uploads/2020/11/V.3_with_markup.pdf

Boswell, B.B. (2017). Rhythmic movement and dance. In J.P. Winnick & D.L. Porretta (Eds.), *Adapted Physical Education and Sport* (6th ed., pp. 455-475). Human Kinetics.

Carline, S. (2011). *Lesson plans for creative dance.* Human Kinetics.

Cerebral Palsy International Sports and Recreation Association (CPISRA). (2020). *Sports.* Retrieved August 20, 2020, from www.cpisra.org/sports

Cone, T.P., & Cone, S. (2011). Strategies for teaching dancers of all abilities. *Journal of Physical Education, Recreation and Dance, 82*(2), 24-31. https://doi.org/10.1080/07303084.2011.10598578

Cone, T.P., & Cone, S. (2012). *Teaching children dance* (3rd ed.). Human Kinetics.

Dunn, J.M., & Leitschuh, C. (2014). *Special physical education* (10th ed.). Kendall/Hunt.

Dwarf Athletic Association of America (DAAA). (2020). *Sport rules.* Retrieved from www.daaa.org/sport-rules.html

Federation Equestrian International (FEI). (2020). *Para dressage rules* (3rd ed.). Author.

Gilbert, A.G. (2015). *Creative dance for all ages* (2nd ed.). Human Kinetics.

International Blind Sports Federation (IBSA). (2020). *IBSA rules.* Retrieved from www.ibsasport.org/sports

International Committee of Sports for the Deaf (ICSD). (2020). *Deaflympics.* Retrieved October 27, 2020, from www.ciss.org/sports

International Dwarf Sports Federation. (2019). *2018 IDSF Rule Book.* Retrieved from www.internationaldwarfsportsfederation.com

International Paralympic Committee (IPC). (2020). *IPC home page.* Retrieved August 24, 2020, from www.paralympic.org

International Table Tennis Federation (ITTF). (2019). *ITTF PTT rules and regulations.* Retrieved from www.ipttc.org/rules/

International Tennis Federation (ITF). (2020). *ITF wheelchair tennis regulations.* Retrieved from www.itftennis.com/en/about-us/governance/rules-and-regulations

International Wheelchair and Amputee Sports Federation (IWASF). (2020). *IWAS wheelchair fencing rules for competition: Book 1—technical rules.* Retrieved from www.wheelchairfencing.iwasf.com/about/rules-and-regulations

Lieberman, L.J., Grenier, M., Brian, A., & Arndt, K. (2021). *Universal design for learning in physical education.* Human Kinetics.

Move United. (2020). *Home page.* Retrieved September 1, 2020, from www.moveunitedsport.org

Paciorek, M.J., & Jones, J.A. (2001). *Disability sport and recreation resources* (3rd ed.). Cooper.

Prieto, L.A., Haegele, J.A., & Columna, L. (2020). Dance programs for school-age individuals with disabilities: A systematic review. *Adapted Physical Activity Quarterly, 37,* 349-375. https://doi/10.1123/apaq.2019-0117

Shivers, J.S. (2011). *Programming recreational services.* Jones and Bartlett.

Special Olympics. (2020). *Sports.* Retrieved August 24, 2020, from www.specialolympics.org/our-work/sports/sports-offered

Union Cycliste Internationale. (2019). *Inside UCI: Regulations.* Retrieved August 19, 2020, from www.uci.org/inside-uci/constitutions-regulations

United States Association of Blind Athletes (USABA). (2020). *Home page.* Retrieved August 20, 2020, from www.usaba.org

United States Tennis Association (USTA). *Wheelchair.* Retrieved August 27, 2020, from www.usta.com/en/home/play/adult-tennis/programs.html#Wheelchair

Print Resources

Chatziefstathion, D., Garcia, B., & Sequin, B. (Eds.). (2021). *Routledge handbook of the Olympic and Paralympic games.* Routledge.

This new text discusses a host of governmental, social, cultural, and economic issues governing the continuous development and growth of both the Olympic and Paralympic movements.

Ladies Professional Golf Association (LPGA). (2005). *Accessible golf: Making it a game for all.* Human Kinetics.

This how-to manual provides all the essential tools for implementing a comprehensive golf program for individuals with disabilities, including modifications to equipment and instructional techniques.

United States Tennis Association (USTA). (2006). *Manual for teaching adaptive tennis.* Author.

This manual is designed to assist those interested in teaching tennis to people with a variety of disabilities, as well as those with differing abilities or circumstances.

Video Resources

United in Stride (2017, Oct 11). *Sighted guide tutorial with audio description* [Video]. YouTube. https://youtu.be/kOnKauvk2oI

This video provides specific suggestions about becoming a running guide for individuals with blindness and visual impairments. It discusses a variety of techniques necessary to perform effectively in the role of a guide.

Paralympic Games. (2016, July 23). *Paralympic sports A-Z: Wheelchair fencing* [Video]. YouTube. https://youtu.be/wGETrQ9ZU5M

This concise introduction to wheelchair fencing includes an emphasis on the rules, classification, equipment, and history of the sport.

BCAN Arts. (2018, March 23). *Adaptive Dance Toledo Ballet* [Video]. YouTube. www.youtube.com/watch?v=Wjgxte-Fuew

This is a video segment of the adaptive dance program provided for children and young adults with special needs sponsored by the Toledo, Ohio, Ballet.

Online Resources

Videos for Coaching High School Para-Athletes: www.nfhslearn.com/library/videos

This set of 15 videos, produced by the U.S. Federation of High Schools, demonstrate coaching techniques across a variety of adapted sports.

Kicking Up a Racket!: www.yumpu.com/en/document/read/43717629/kicking-up-a-racket-parabadminton-sports-coach-uk

This is a comprehensive resource for teaching and coaching parabadminton. It contains adaptations for a variety of disabilities as well as drills and instructional strategies.

Physical Education Abilities Tennis (PEAT): www.atanc.org/abilities-tennis-curriculum

PEAT is a standalone curriculum consisting of warm-up activities, specific drills, and equipment needed to facilitate inclusive instruction for players with differing abilities.

27

Adventure Sports and Activities

Sue Sutherland

"Today is the day," Jamal thought to himself. This was the day that he would finally get his chance to climb on a real rock face. Jamal first tried climbing two years ago, when his local parks and recreation department offered a climbing event that was open to everyone. His parents took Jamal and his sister to the event, and both got to try the indoor climbing wall. Despite only being able to climb about a third of the way up the wall, Jamal was hooked. He looked down on his wheelchair with the biggest smile on his face, and his parents knew this wouldn't be the last time he climbed. Jamal found a nonprofit organization about an hour from where he lived that offered adapted climbing classes. Now, two years later, after finding the right equipment for his needs and improving his skills, Jamal was venturing to a local national park with his group for a day of climbing. Excited but nervous, Jamal had been looking forward to this day for a while. He couldn't wait for the chance to challenge himself and enjoy the day with the friends he had made through climbing.

Adventure and extreme sports have grown in popularity and accessibility over the last two decades. Advances in technology, equipment, instruction, and adaptive sports organizations have especially facilitated the growth in popularity of adapted adventure sports. This chapter will present a variety of adventure sports that are available for individuals with disabilities. It is not within the scope of the chapter to provide a detailed discussion of each of these sports. Rather, this chapter will highlight seven of the most popular sports, discuss common equipment modifications and adaptations, and provide insight into the classifications and rules for competition.

Climbing

Climbing is a popular recreational activity and competitive sport for people of all abilities. Climbing can take place both outside on natural rock face and indoors on artificial walls, which makes it available in all areas of the United States.

Variations and Modifications

Ever since Mark Wellman's groundbreaking climb of El Capitan in 1989, climbing has become increasingly more accessible for individuals with disabilities. Wellman, a paraplegic, completed the climb with his climbing partner, Mike Corbett, while using an adapted ascending device that allowed him to climb the 3,000-foot rock face one pull-up at a time—a total of 7,000 pull-ups over eight days. In 2013, another advance in adaptive equipment occurred when Sean O'Neill used a tentacle pulley system to lead climb in Yosemite Valley, the first known lead climb by a paraplegic climber (Campbell, 2013). Today, adapted climbing can be enjoyed by people with disabilities on both artificial rock walls and natural rock faces. Adapted climbing is also an activity that can be successfully included within physical education classes using the principles of universal design (see Grenier et al., 2018). Refer to the Application Example sidebar describing inclusion strategies in climbing for elementary physical education.

Advances in adapted equipment have made climbing accessible to more people. A combination of a standard climbing harness or a seated harness (with larger leg loops and waist belts) with a chest harness allows individuals with spinal cord injuries to maintain a position to climb. An ascending device, which can be modified to allow for functional arm or hand grip, provides the person with a means of climbing the rope. Other adapted equipment includes prosthetic climbing feet (see figure 27.1), climbing knees, and specialized hand grips for climbers who are amputees. Sighted guides can be used for individuals with visual impairments or who are blind.

Paraclimbing

The International Federation of Sport Climbing has been holding competitions for paraclimbing since 2006 (Vettoretti, n.d.). The first World Championship for paraclimbing took place in 2011, with 35 athletes (men and women) competing (Gripped, 2019); it now takes place every two years. In 2017, paraclimbing became a recognized sport by the International Paralympic Committee, setting the stage for paraclimbing to become a Paralympic event in the future. Within the sport of paraclimbing, athletes compete in four different categories based on the nature of their impairments (USA Climbing, 2019), resulting in 20 different classifications overall (including male and female categories). Within the visual category there are three classifications:

- B1: Completely or almost completely blind (all B1 athletes must wear a blindfold during competition)
- B2: Visual acuity up to 20/600 and/or a visual field of less than 5 percent
- B3: Visual acuity between 20/600 and 20/200 and/or a visual field of 5 to 20 percent

For athletes with limited range, power, and stability there are three classifications:

- RP1: Disability severely affects all body parts
- RP2: Disability moderately affects all body parts
- RP3: Impaired passive range of movement, noticeable hypertonia, noticeably impaired muscle power, and athetosis creating asymmetry

The amputee category includes athletes who compete in one of the following classifications:

- AU1: Upper limb amputee (two arms or one full arm to shoulder; no prosthetics in competition)
- AU2: Upper limb amputee (at least one arm up to elbow; no prosthetics in competition)
- AL2: Lower limb amputee (prosthetics allowed)

The category for athletes who are paraplegic includes only one classification:

- AL1: No usable muscle function below waist, climbs using arms only

South_agency/E+/Getty Images

FIGURE 27.1 Advances in adapted equipment, such as prosthetic climbing feet, has allowed access to individuals with a variety of disabilities.

Application Example

Inclusion Strategies for Indoor Climbing

SETTING

Elementary physical education class

STUDENTS

Students with developmental disabilities

APPLICATION

To accommodate the needs of the students with developmental disabilities, the following strategies may be used:

- Use traverse climbing, in which the objective is to cross the wall laterally rather than scale the wall
- Use large climbing holds
- Design a route using clearly marked holds, such as holds of all one color
- Use peer partners who can provide simple guidance during the climb
- Break the traverse route into smaller sections

Mountain Biking

Mountain biking is a great way to exercise and enjoy nature. This popular sport involves riding off-road on a variety of terrains, including bike trails, back country roads, and single-track trails. Mountains are not a necessity, but certainly add to the thrill and challenge of the sport. With appropriate modifications, mountain biking can be enjoyed by individuals with a range of disabilities.

Variations and Modifications

Individuals who cannot ride a standard mountain bike can use adapted equipment or trails appropriate for their abilities (Break the Boundary, 2019). New technology and an awareness of universal trail design have increased the sport's popularity over the last two decades. Adapted mountain biking encompasses both downhill and cross-country or off-road versions of the sport. Downhill mountain biking is an extreme sport that involves hurtling down a mountain trail in a specially designed four-wheel bike. According to Move United (n.d.-a), downhill mountain biking can accommodate a range of physical ability levels but requires participants to be cognitively aware. Downhill trails can range from easy to difficult and, as such, participants can choose to challenge themselves on steep, technical trails, or take a more leisurely ride on easy trails. Cross-country or off-road mountain biking involves riding on a wide variety of trails that range in technical difficulty and pitch. This style of mountain biking can cater to a wide range of physical and developmental ability levels.

There are a number of different styles of bikes that can be used for both downhill and cross-country or off-road mountain biking, depending on the functioning level and preference of the participant. Adapted mountain bikes fall into one of five categories (Move United, n.d.-a):

1. A **4-cross downhill bike** is a ruggedly built, high-performing, gravity-powered bike that can withstand the demands of technical downhill trails. These bikes have a full suspension system, a bucket seat, and can be ridden by participants with good upper body strength (see figure 27.2). Helmets, gloves, and pads are essential when using these bikes.

Thomas Barwick/DigitalVision/GettyImages

FIGURE 27.2 Mountain biking.

2. **Delta-style recumbent bikes** are used for cross-country or off-road mountain biking. The rider sits in the seat with legs out in front, strapped onto foot rests on either side of the front wheel. A hand crank is attached to the steering column, typically set at chest height, to propel the bike (Break the Boundary, 2019). One drawback of this style, however, is that the front-wheel drive can lead to traction issues on steep climbs.

3. **Recumbent upright bikes** are similar in seating style to the delta-style recumbent bikes but with two wheels at the front and one at the back. This type of bike has rear-wheel drive and the hand crank is separate from the steering and braking arms, which allows for better control on technical descents. Adaptations can be made to the positioning of brakes and gear-shifting levers to adjust to differences in hand and arm strength or function.

4. **Tadpole prone bikes** also have two wheels in the front and one behind. The rider uses a bucket seat and is in a kneeling, prone position, which requires higher functioning and core strength. Large mountain bike tires, full suspension, rear-wheel drive, gears, and different riding positions for pedaling and riding downhill are features of this bike. The rider uses the hand crank system for pedaling but switches to the handlebars for more technical steering and braking.

5. **Recumbent leg trikes** are a tadpole-style bike with two wheels at the front and one behind. The rear-wheel drive bike is propelled by foot pedals and steered with handles that are connected to the two front wheels that also contain the brakes and gear shifting (Break the Boundary, 2019). The recumbent seated position allows for the use of torso straps to add stability for the rider if needed. Further adaptations for mountain bikes include power-assist devices, which provide assistance to the rider when pedaling.

Sailing

The freedom of being under sail on the water is a feeling that attracts many people to sailing. This popular sport can be enjoyed individually or with others, in boats of different sizes, and on small lakes, seas, or oceans. Sailing can also be experienced by individuals with a wide range of disabilities using a variety of modifications.

Variations and Modifications

Sailing can be enjoyed by individuals with physical, neurological, developmental, cognitive, and sensory disabilities through adaptations to seating, controls, and rigging (Marsh, 2014). The wealth of adapted sailing programs that have been established in the past two decades is a testament to the popularity of sailing for people with a wide range of disabilities. Sailing can also be a solo, tandem, or team activity, depending on the class of boat and individual functioning level. With an abundance of different sizes and styles of sailboats, there is invariably something for everyone.

The class of sailboat often determines the types of adaptations that can be made. Marsh (2014) highlights a number of different boats for adapted sailing, many of which follow the principles of universal design (Lieberman et al., 2021). **Access dinghies** are exceptionally stable, use a joystick system for steering, include a sling seat to fit all body shapes and sizes, and can be adapted for a variety of ability levels. The **Martin 16** is a high-performance, unsinkable two-person racing sailboat that can accommodate individuals with significant functional impairments, making it ideal for adapted sailing. The **Freedom 20** is a very accessible boat due to the broad, flat decks with two counterweighted, pivoting seats. A heavy keel makes this boat stable and the configuration of the sails, lines, and tiller system make it easy to sail from the pivoting seats. The **SKUD-18** is a Paralympic-class, high-performance, two-person boat that can be sailed by people with all levels of physical ability with adaptations to seating and steering. The **Sonar** is a Paralympic-class, high-performance, three-person keelboat that can be sailed by those with a wide range of levels of strength and skill. The **2.4mR** is a Paralympic-class, high-performance, single-handed boat that can be sailed by individuals with a wide range of physical functioning because the lines and steering are configured to avoid the need to move about the boat.

For all boats, the adaptations to accommodate a range of ability levels will center on transferring into the boat, seating configurations, steering, and sail trimming. Transferring onto the boat depends on the functioning level of the participant and the type of boat being sailed. Seating can be adapted using a variety of methods, including ridged backs, torso or leg straps, padding, and handles. Specially designed four-way joysticks that can be hand-, foot-, or chin-operated allow the sailor to steer and trim the sails (Marsh, 2014). A sip-and-puff system was designed for individuals with quadriplegia to steer and trim sails via bites, sips, or puffs of the controls (Marsh, 2014) (figure 27.3). Using sighted guides as crew members can also accommodate sailors who are visually impaired.

Competitive Sailing

Paralympic sailing made its debut as a demonstration sport at the 1996 Paralympic Games before becoming a medal sport at the 2000 Paralympic Games (see figure 27.3). Athletes are classified from 1 to 7 (7 being least impairment) on four factors: stability, hand function, mobility, and vision. There are three sailing events, which are mixed-gender: single-person keelboat, two-person keelboat, and three-person keelboat. However, sailing was dropped as a Paralympic sport after the 2016 Games and the future of the sport in the Paralympics is currently unknown.

Sailing was established as a Special Olympic sport in 1995. There are currently five skill levels of competition (Special Olympics, 2020):

- Level I Unified Sports Team: Special Olympic athletes will be responsible for main sail trim
- Level II Unified Sports Team: A Special Olympic athlete will be responsible for control of the helm for the entire race
- Level III Unified Sports Team: Special Olympic athletes will have complete control of the boat, with an onboard coach
- Level IV: The whole crew is Special Olympic athletes, with no coach
- Level V: A Special Olympic athlete competes single-handedly

Scuba Diving

Scuba diving is a popular sport worldwide that enables divers to explore a variety of underwater environments. Scuba diving has become increasingly popular for individuals with disabilities (see figure 27.4) in part because the buoyancy of the water aids the participation of individuals with physical disabilities (Cheng & Diamond, 2005). Before participating, however, individuals should undergo a physical examination to ensure they are medically fit to dive. This is especially important for individuals with disabilities considering the comorbidities that may occur with certain diagnoses.

Variations and Modifications

Adapted scuba diving is a sport that can be enjoyed by individuals with a wide range of disabilities, including physical, developmental, emotional, sensory, and neurological. Void of any medical reason not to dive, scuba diving can be adapted in a number of ways to meet the needs and abilities of all divers. The benefits of scuba diving for participants with disabilities can include feelings of weightlessness and independence, enhanced social experience, and improved self-concept (Carin-Levy & Jones, 2007; Yarwasky & Furst, 1996).

The Handicapped Scuba Association (HSA) was formed in 1981 and began diver training and

EMPICS Sport - PA Images via Getty Images

FIGURE 27.3 Athlete competing in the single-person keelboat event at the London 2012 Paralympic Games.

FIGURE 27.4 Athlete becoming acclimatized to the adapted scuba equipment.

certification in 1986. HSA offers diver education and courses to be a dive buddy and a certified instructor (HSA, n.d.). HSA offers three levels of adapted scuba certification (HSA, n.d.). Level A demonstrates that the diver can meet the physical performance requirements for divers, can perform the skills to be a buddy diver, and can dive with one other certified scuba diver. Level B demonstrates that the diver is certified to dive with two dive buddies who are certified Open Water Level A or above. Level C demonstrates that a diver is certified to dive with two dive buddies (one certified Level A or above) and an HSA dive buddy or certified Professional Association of Diving Instructors rescue diver. Although HSA was the first organization in the USA to offer adapted scuba diving, there are now numerous organizations that fit this bill.

Adapted scuba diving can accommodate individuals with a range of disabilities through the use of a variety of equipment (HSA, n.d.). **Fins** that give thrust on the downward kick but little resistance on the upward kick can be used for individuals who have leg weakness. **Webbed gloves** can also be used for increased propulsion by individuals who have limited use of their legs—these gloves come in a variety of different sizes, materials, and functions. **Adapted SCUBA prostheses** that are made of noncorrosive material and drain easily can be used to attach a fin or webbed glove to a residual limb.

Scuba tanks come in different shapes, sizes, and weights, which can all affect the diver's buoyancy and need to be considered when choosing equipment. A **buoyancy control device (BCD)** gives participants the ability to float both at the surface and underwater and is an important piece of equipment. Finding a BCD that works for individual functioning level is necessary for comfort and safety reasons. **Exposure suits** come in three different types (wet, semidry, and dry) based on functioning level, temperature of the water, and preference. Wetsuits are the most common and can be custom fitted with different zip locations to allow for ease of use and pockets for weight distribution or extra padding if needed. In addition, gloves and diving boots can protect individuals with loss of sensation on their extremities. **Scooters** can aid in propulsion in the water for individuals with lower limb impairments. **Dive boat platforms** are an important adaptation for individuals with limited mobility to allow for ease of entering and exiting the water.

Surfing

Polynesian culture is accredited with the creation of modern-day surfing through their use of olo boards (long boards created from wood) for their ruling class to explore the ocean (Cancelmo, 2019). Longboards today range in length from

8 to 12 feet (2.4-3.7 meters) and are made of a variety of materials and widths, making this type of board suitable for surfers with a wide range of disabilities. The long, light construction is ideal for beginners, though carrying the board to the water is more difficult due to the length. As the name suggests, short boards are seven feet or less in length and have multiple fins (or skegs) on the bottom to prevent drift and help with steering. This type of board is more difficult to master initially, but is perfect for fast, maneuverable, high-performance surfing and is synonymous with professional surfing. Surfing can be adapted for individuals with disabilities to allow them to enjoy the thrill of riding the waves.

Variations and Modifications

Originally used as a rehabilitation method for injured veterans, adapted surfing is recognized by the International Surfing Association (ISA), which has aided with the development and advancement of the sport across the globe (ISA, n.d.; Lopes et al., 2018). The benefits of surfing for individuals with disabilities include promoting physical well-being, building confidence, and combating discrimination (Lopes et al., 2018). Surfing is also a means for individuals to interact with the natural environment in a way that may not have been possible prior to adapted surfing. Advancements in board technology, prosthetics, and even wetsuit material have made surfing accessible to more people with disabilities.

Choice of surfboard is an important decision that can influence successful participation in the sport. Move United (n.d.-b) recommends a light, durable, buoyant board for beginners over a more traditional fiberglass model. The additional buoyancy and width of a soft board helps the surfer as they learn. There are now a number of different shapes of surfboard such as long, short, fish, egg, and hybrid (Lindsey, 2020).

Adaptations to surfboards to accommodate a range of functioning levels can help make the sport accessible to more individuals with disabilities. The addition of handles or a rail system on longboards allows for surfing in a prone position for individuals who are unable or do not want to ride in an upright kneeling or standing position. Seats can also be added to longboards to allow for a surfer to ride in a seated position facing forwards, much like the mono- or bi-ski for alpine skiing. Wave Jet propulsion motors can also be added into the bottom of longboards over nine feet in length, which allows adapted surfers to be more independent in the water and catch waves with less effort (Park, 2016). Other adaptations for surfing include waterproof prostheses, tandem riding, and sighted guides.

Waveski is a combination between a kayak and a surfboard that allows the rider to combine paddle power and maneuverability into an exciting experience. Waveskis come in many different shapes and designs and it is important to choose one that combines the surfer's functioning level with stability. Waveskis are also available in tandem models to allow surfers to learn with the assistance of an experienced partner.

Competitive Surfing

The first ISA World Adaptive Surfing Championships were held in 2015 and helped set the standard for rules and classifications in adapted surfing (Richards, 2017). Recently, adapted surfing has been renamed parasurfing, in part as a strategy for future designation as a Paralympic sport given the recent inclusion of surfing in the Olympics (Surfer Today, n.d.). The ISA currently recognizes nine eligible impairments for participation in competitions: (1) impaired muscle power, (2) impaired passive range of movement, (3) limb deficiency, (4) leg length difference, (5) short stature, (6) hypertonia, (7) ataxia, (8) athetosis, and (9) visual impairment (further broken down into B1, B2, and B3).

For competitions, athletes compete in one of eight parasurfing classes (ISA, 2019; Surfer Today, n.d.):

- Para Surf Stand 1 (PS-S1) is for athletes with upper body impairments who ride in a standing position (see figure 27.5).
- Para Surf Stand 2 (PS-S2) is for athletes with below-the-knee lower body impairments or short stature who ride in a standing position.
- Para Surf Stand 3 (PS-S3) is for athletes with above-the-knee lower body impairments or impairments to both lower extremities who ride in a standing position.
- Para Surf Kneel (PS-K) is for athletes who ride in a kneeling or sitting position.
- Para Surf Prone 1 (PS-P1) is for athletes who ride in a prone position; adaptations to help the athlete remain on the board are permitted if it does not increase their ability to surf.
- Para Surf Prone 2 (PS-S2) is for athletes who ride in a prone position; adaptations to help the athlete remain on the board are permitted if it does not increase their ability to surf.

JGalione/E+/Getty Images

FIGURE 27.5 Athletes with an upper body impairment would compete in the Para Surf Stand 1 class.

- Para Surf VI1 is for athletes who have a visual impairment (IBSA classification level B1) and surf in a standing position.
- Para Surf VI2 is for athletes who have a visual impairment (IBSA classification levels B2 and B3) and surf in a standing position.

For Para Surf Prone 2, athletes can receive support for accessing the water and getting onto their boards, as well as for paddling out to and being pushed into the wave, but the athlete must be independent when riding a wave and it is only scored if the athlete rides in a prone position. For all other classes, athletes can receive support for accessing the water and getting onto their boards, but the athlete must paddle into the wave with no assistance and a wave is only scored when the athlete is in the correct position.

Waterskiing

Waterskiing involves riding through the water on one or two skis while being pulled behind a boat. This popular sport began in the 1920s and has continued to develop and grow in popularity. Individuals with a range of disabilities can enjoy waterskiing with a variety of modifications.

Variations and Modifications

Adapted waterskiing first began with skiers who were amputees and visually impaired making accommodations to traditional stand-up skiing (USA Adaptive Water Ski and Wake Sports, n.d.). By the mid-1960s a new design was developed so the participant could sit directly on a large, flat-bottomed ski with a steel tube frame (USA Adaptive Water Ski and Wake Sports, n.d.). In 1983 the Kan Ski was invented and was the impetus for further development of the sport for athletes with disabilities. Adapted waterskiing— including slalom, jumping, and tricks—is a popular sport for individuals with visual, mobility, and other impairments at both a recreational and competitive level.

Beginner skis are usually at least 15 inches (38.1 centimeters) wide, flat bottomed, and have a notch or a starting block to hold the tow rope at the tip of the ski. This adaptation provides the skier with assistance during a deep-water start. Once a skier is up and balanced on the water, the handle can be pulled from the notch or starting block to allow more control of the ski. A skier can also choose to leave the tow rope in the notch or starting block, but a spotter and quick-release device for the tow rope is required in the case of a fall.

Intermediate or advanced skis are narrower than beginner skis—usually between 10 and 13 inches (25.4 and 33.0 centimeters) in width—and are easier to turn and edge due to the design and added fins. These skis generally don't have a starting block and the skier holds the tow rope for the deep-water start.

Following a universal design approach, a range of adapted equipment is available for skiers with differing functioning and skill levels.

- **Sit-skis** are used by skiers whose functioning level prohibits stand-up skiing, or by skiers who choose to ski in a sitting position (figure 27.6). These skis use a cage, or raised seat, for the skier.
- **Trick skis** are very maneuverable, allowing the skier to perform a variety of tricks. Some adapted skiers use kneeboards or wakeboards as trick skis, although mounting the cage to these boards requires special clamps or brackets.
- **Jump skis** can provide a wider base for increased stability and balance for stand-up skiers. Jump skis are flatter and wider than typical sit-skis.
- **Ski tip connectors (STC)** for stand-up skiers can hold the front of the skis together about shoulder-width apart for those who have difficulty performing this action. These can be attached at both the front and rear of the skis if more stability is needed.
- A **boom** attaches to the ski boat and helps beginners by adding more stability.
- A **triple bar handle** is a six-foot handle that contains three separate handles attached to individual tow ropes. This equipment enables an instructor to ski on either side of the skier to provide assistance if needed. The instructor tow lines can be separated smoothly when the skier gains confidence.
- **Arm slings** are used for skiers with upper limb impairments. There are a variety of different slings that use a shoulder, torso, or residual limb harnesses to provide shared pull on the tow rope handle. For safety, the sling device releases automatically when the handle is released.
- **Outriggers** can be attached to the sides of sit-skis to help skiers who may not have the functional ability or balance to stabilize the ski.
- **Back supports** provide balance for skiers who need it and also prevent a skier from falling out the back of the cage.
- **Audible buoys** are used by skiers with visual impairments for both competitive and recreational slalom skiing.

Competitive Waterskiing

Athletes with disabilities can compete in waterskiing slalom, trick, and jump events. World-level

FIGURE 27.6 The sit ski allows individuals with a variety of disabilities to enjoy waterskiing.

competitions for adapted skiing began in 1987, with the World Trophy event held in London, England, for 40 participants from 7 different countries (USA Water Ski and Wake Sports, n.d.). These competitions have continued on a biannual basis, with the first World Championship being held in 1993. The International Waterski and Wakeboard Federation (2020) holds competitions in standing, seated, and vision-impaired divisions for athletes in multiple disability categories:

- A1: Athletes with a hand or arm disability that prevents using the limb while skiing; the limb cannot come into contact with the tow rope or handle while skiing
- A2: Athletes with a hand or arm disability that prevents using the limb while skiing, but the limb may come into contact with the tow rope or handle while skiing
- L: Athletes with a leg amputation (without the use of a prosthetic)
- LP: Athletes with a leg amputation (with the use of a prosthetic)
- MP1: Athletes whose balance and movement are significantly impaired (no trunk control, little or no balance) and who are unable to hold the tow handle with hands
- MP2: Athletes with little or no trunk control, no active trunk rotation, and balance is significantly impaired
- MP3: Athletes who have partial trunk control in forward movements, little or no control for sideways movement, and poor lower trunk rotation
- MP4: Athletes with good forward trunk movement who can return to upright position without the use of arms, have limited controlled sideways movement, and have good trunk rotation
- MP5: Athletes who have normal trunk movement in all directions, can reach side to side, and can move hips normally
- V1: Athletes with no light perception, or who have light perception but cannot recognize shapes in any direction or at any distance
- V2/V3: Athletes who have up to 20/600 visual acuity and/or visual field of less than five degrees (V2), or from 20/600 to 20/200 visual acuity and/or visual field between 5 and 20 degrees (V3)
- A/L1 and A/L2: Athletes with arm and leg disabilities, including significant arm and leg impairments, arm and leg amputations, and hemiplegia

Wheelchair Motocross

In 2006 Aaron "Wheelz" Fotheringham performed the first wheelchair backflip and the sport of wheelchair motocross (WCMX) was born (Goad, 2014). A combination of skateboarding and BMX riding, WCMX is now one of the fastest growing extreme wheelchair sports. Athletes can participate in recreational WCMX at local skateboard parks and competitive WCMX events also take place around the globe, with the first World Championship taking place in 2015 in Texas. The popularity of the sport can be attributed in part to Wheelz and other WCMX athletes who have continued to push the boundaries of the sport. The first wheelchair double backflip and wheelchair front flip were both performed by Wheelz, in 2010 and 2011, respectively. He was also the only person to ride the Nitrus Circuit's Giganta ramp in a wheelchair. In 2015 Katherine Beattie performed the first wheelchair backflip by a woman.

Variations and Modifications

Performing high-level tricks and stunts required rethinking the design of the chair. A WCMX wheelchair is customized with lightweight materials, a full suspension frame, and racing shocks and wheels (Pridemobility, 2020). In addition to a wheelchair with a suspension and shock system, WCMX riders need to use protective equipment such as helmets, gloves, elbow and knee pads, and body armor. WCMX is a fun and exciting sport, but falling and crashes are an inevitable part of the sport and, as such, riders need to take precautions and wear protective equipment.

Competitive WCMX

There are currently five divisions in WCMX (Action Sports Foundation, 2018):

1. Open: Riders have advanced WCMX skills beyond divisions 1 and 2; should ride rails, perform flips, spins, and handplants, and hit each element of the course at least once; may not receive assistance during the ride
2. Women: Riders have advanced WCMX skills beyond divisions 1 and 2; should ride rails, perform flips, spins, and handplants, and hit each element of the course at least once; may have a pusher to get up ramps or out

of bowls and use a spotter, but points may be deducted if the spotter touches the rider or assists in a substantive manner

3. Division 1: Riders over 16 years of age who do not compete at the professional level and show command in a variety of intermediate wheelchair skills; may have a pusher to get up ramps or out of bowls and use a spotter, but points may be deducted if the spotter touches the rider or assists in a substantive manner
4. Division 2: Riders under 16 years of age who do not compete at the professional level and show command in a variety of intermediate wheelchair skills; may have a pusher to get up ramps or out of bowls and use a spotter, but points may be deducted if the spotter touches the rider or assists in a substantive manner
5. Division 3: Riders under 16 years of age with less than two years of experience who show command of beginner wheelchair skills; may have a pusher to get up ramps or out of bowls and have a coach on the course to help guide the run; cannot have assistance for the trick but point deductions will be more lenient if spotters assist the rider

WCMX events are judged on one run for Division 3 and on two runs for Open, Women, and Divisions 1 and 2, with the lowest score being discarded. The judging criteria are based on major and deciding factors as well as falls and instabilities, with major factors more heavily weighted (Action Sports Foundation, 2018). The major factor criteria are amplitude (how high and far a rider travels), execution (performing tricks cleanly and with control), difficulty (performing more difficult skills cleanly), and variety (not repeating the same trick). The deciding factor criteria are progression (performing new or more advanced tricks), risk (performing tricks with increased risk), combinations (linking tricks together) and course use (using the entire course). Point deductions are determined by the judges based on an athlete's falls or instabilities.

Other Adventure Sports

Adventure sports for individuals with disabilities is an ever-expanding area. Although this chapter has highlighted a number of adventure sports, this list continues to grow. A quick Internet search on the topic will provide a wealth of adapted adventure sports or activities not included in this chapter, such as dragon boat racing, paragliding, skydiving, stand-up paddleboarding, and whitewater rafting. Winter sports and paddle sports are discussed in other chapters of this book, many of which would fall under the umbrella of adventure sports as well.

Strategies for Inclusion

Adventure sports can provide an inclusive environment for individuals with a range of disabilities in both K-12 and community settings and are the perfect way to be active with peers, friends, and family. The activities discussed in the chapter require equipment modifications ranging from minor to more complex, with many of the modifications following the principles of universal design (Lieberman et al., 2021). Many of these activities also require specialized instruction for the athlete to gain the knowledge and skills to participate. Although it may seem daunting to think about the time and costs of equipment modification and specialized instruction, there are an increasing number of nonprofit organizations throughout the United States that offer equipment and instruction for a wide range of adapted sports at a reasonable cost. Many also have scholarships available to help offset this cost. In addition, these organizations offer the opportunity for friends and family members to learn about the activities and support the athletes. In addition to nonprofit organizations, parks and recreation departments may provide programming in adapted adventure sports or work with local schools to provide inclusive opportunities within physical education.

Summary

Although this chapter highlights seven adventure sports that are popular at both recreational and competitive levels, they are by no means the only adventure sports available for individuals with disabilities. Adventure sports are accessible to all with the right knowledge, modifications, and instruction. The number of organizations that offer adventure activities for individuals with disabilities has increased exponentially over the last two decades. There is an adventure sport for everyone—it's just a matter of finding the desire to try, the equipment to safely participate, and the instruction to learn.

References

Action Sports Foundation. (2018). *WCMX contest rules.* Retrieved from https://asfadaptivesports.org/all-events/wcmx-competition-rules

Break the Boundary. (2019). *What is adaptive MTB?* Retrieved from https://breaktheboundary.com.au/resources/what-is-adaptive-mountain-biking/

Campbell, D. (2013). *From a wheelchair to the sharp end: Story of the first ever paraplegic lead climb.* Patagonia. Retrieved from www.patagonia.com/stories/from-a-wheelchair-to-the-sharp-end-the-first-paraplegic-lead-climb/story-18099.html

Cancelmo, S. (2019, July 13). *The history of the longboard surfboard.* Center for Surf Research. Retrieved from https://centerforsurfresearch.org/best-longboard-surfboard/history/

Carin-Levy, G., & Jones, D. (2007). Psychological aspects of scuba diving for people with physical disabilities: An occupational science perspective. *Canadian Journal of Occupational Therapy, 74*(1), 6-14.

Cheng, J.F., & Diamond, M. (2005). SCUBA diving for individuals with disabilities. *American Journal of Physical Medicine and Rehabilitation, 84*(5), 369-375. https://doi.org/10.1097/01.phm.0000159974.01251.e2

Goad, C. (2014). Extreme wheelers. *Sports 'N Spokes, 40*(4), 30-36.

Grenier, M., Fitch, N., & Young, J. (2018). Using the climbing wall to promote full access through universal design. *Palaestra, 32*(4), 41-46.

Gripped. (2019, July 15). *A history of climbing competitions since 1985.* Retrieved from https://gripped.com/events/a-history-of-climbing-competitions-since-1985/

Handicapped Scuba Association. (n.d.). *Handicapped Scuba Association history.* Retrieved August 10, 2020, from www.hsascuba.com/body/history.php

International Surfing Association (ISA). (n.d.). *Para surfing.* Retrieved August 10, 2020, from www.isasurf.org/development-programs/adaptive-surfing/

International Surfing Association (ISA). (2019). *ISA para-surfing classification.* Retrieved from www.isasurf.org/development-programs/adaptive-surfing/isa-para-surfing-classification/

International Waterski and Wakeboard Federation. (2020). *Technical rules for water ski for the disabled.* Retrieved from https://iwwfwaterskidisabled.webnode.com

Lieberman, L., Grenier, M., Brian, A., & Arndt, K. (2021). *Universal design for learning in physical education.* Human Kinetics.

Lindsey, I. (2020). *Surfboard shapes.* Center for Surf Research. Retrieved from https://centerforsurfresearch.org/surfboard-shapes/

Lopes, J.T., Curz, G., & Masdemont, M. (2018). Adaptive surfing: Leisure, competition or therapy? *Brazilian Journal of Education, Technology, and Society, 11*(1), 148-159.

Marsh, C. (2014). Riding with the wind. *Challenge Magazine, 191*(1), 14-20.

Move United. (n.d.-a). *Mountain biking.* Retrieved May 13, 2020, from www.moveunitedsport.org/sport/mountain-biking/

Move United. (n.d.-b). *Surfing.* Retrieved August 9, 2020 from www.moveunitedsport.org/sport/surfing/

Park, D. (2016, November 3). *Surfing with disabilities.* Sunset Surf. Retrieved from http://sunsetsurfdominical.com/surfing-with-disabilities/

Pridemobility. (2020). *A beginner's guide to wheelchair motocross.* Pride Mobility Experience. https://experience.pridemobility.com/lifestyle/a-beginners-guide-to-wheelchair-motocross/

Richards, J. (2017). Rise of adaptive surfing. *Adaptive Surfing Magazine, 2,* 26-29.

Special Olympics. (2020). *Sports essentials sailing rules.* Retrieved from https://media.specialolympics.org/resources/sports-essentials/sport-rules/Sports-Essentials-Sailing-Rules-2020.pdf?_ga=2.268212806.933326520.1609177094-2046926889.1609177094

Surfer Today. (n.d.). *What is para surfing?* Retrieved August 19, 2020, from www.surfertoday.com/surfing/what-is-para-surfing

USA Climbing. (2019). *Classification rules for USA paraclimbing.* USA Climbing. Retrieved from www.usaclimbing.org/Assets/2020_Paraclimbing_Classifications_Doc.pdf

USA Adaptive Water Ski and Wake Sports. (n.d.). *History.* Retrieved August, 15, 2020, from https://www.usaadaptivewaterski.org/history

Vettoretti, M. (n.d.). *Paraclimbing.* International Federation of Sport Climbing. Retrieved August 20, 2020, from www.ifsc-climbing.org/index.php/paraclimbing

Yarwasky, L., & Furst, D.M. (1996). Motivation to participate of divers with and without disabilities. *Perceptual & Motor Skills, 82*(3), 1096-1098. https://doi.org/10.2466/pms.1996.82.3c.1096

Print Resources

Elliott, J., & Kauffman, M. (2014). *Diveheart adaptive scuba instructor and dive buddy.* Diveheart Publishing.

This resource provides information for instructors and dive buddies working with individuals with disabilities.

Fotheringham, S.C. (2015). *Wheelz.* WheelzBook. www.aaronfotheringham.com

This book tells the story of Aaron "Wheelz" Fotheringham from childhood to athlete and all the bumps, challenges, and achievements along the way.

Macdonald, D. (2015). *Adaptive climbing manual: A manual for instructors and climbers.* Paradox Sports.

This book provides a wealth of information on adaptive climbing, including systems, equipment, and techniques for both climbers and instructors.

United States Sailing Association. (2018). *Adaptive sailing resource manual.* United States Sailing Association.

This manual provides information about adaptive sailing, including rules and regulations, equipment modifications, instructional techniques, program development and safety, and risk management.

Video Resources

Taking the dis out of disability [DVD] (2014). www.superchairing.org/SC%202014%20DVD.html

This DVD covers a wide variety of adventure sports and activities as well as individual athlete profiles and stories.

Perlman, E., & Wellman, M. (Directors) (1998). *Beyond the barriers* [DVD]. www.nolimitstahoe.com/videos/beyond.htm

This video presents Mark Wellman and other athletes participating in a variety of adapted adventure sports, including climbing, sailing, scuba diving, surfing, and hang gliding.

Stream Factory Media. (2011, September 17). *Jake O'Connor—One Track Productions* [Video]. YouTube. www.youtube.com/watch?v=tVCQjXtqXho&feature=emb_title

This resource highlights trail riding using a prone mountain bike.

Paradox Sports. (2019, November 19). *Paradox Sports—An inside look at adaptive rock climbing* [Video]. YouTube. www.youtube.com/watch?v=IvzZs_bwx2E

This resource highlights an adaptive climbing program through Paradox Sports and incorporates athlete's stories.

Judd Goldman Adaptive Sailing Foundation. (2015, August 6). *Judd Goldman Adaptive Sailing Foundation—2015 video* [Video]. YouTube. www.youtube.com/watch?v=9aybr7vSS30

This resource highlights the Judd Goldman adaptive sailing program.

Diveheart Foundation. (2020, July 10). *The power of scuba diving for people with disabilities* [Video]. YouTube. www.youtube.com/watch?v=OgHECzaqJhw

This resource highlights the benefits of adapted scuba diving.

ShawTVSSM. (2012, August 11). *Sault Accessible Sports—Adaptive water skiing* [Video]. YouTube. www.youtube.com/watch?v=YIT4kdS5IVQ

This resource highlights a variety of different methods of adaptive waterskiing.

ISAsurfing. (2017, December 2). *What is adaptive surfing?* [Video]. YouTube. www.youtube.com/watch?v=IEP5VqlkkGQ

This resource highlights the sport of adaptive surfing for people with physical disabilities.

Aaron Fotheringham. (2020, October 3). *Aaron Wheelz—2020 WCMX edit* [Video]. YouTube. www.youtube.com/watch?v=ex0g_b2HPrQ

This resource highlights Aaron "Wheelz" Fotheringham performing WCMX.

Online Resources

Action Sports Foundation: https://asfadaptivesports.org

This organization provides information about WCMX and other action sports. It also includes event calendars, videos, grant resources and other information.

Diveheart: www.diveheart.org

This organization covers information about adapted scuba including programs within and beyond the United States, including an event calendar, instructor training, instructor directory, videos, and other resources.

Move United Adaptive Sports: www.moveunitedsport.org/sports/adaptive-sports/

This website provides a wealth of information on adapted adventure sports and beyond. It includes event calendars, equipment information, locations of programs within the United States, trainings, videos, and other resources.

Special Olympics Sailing: www.specialolympics.org/our-work/sports/sailing

This webpage provides information about sailing for Special Olympic athletes, including coaching guidelines, rules, and fact sheets.

USA Climbing, Paraclimbing: www.usaclimbing.org/Paraclimbing.htm

This website provides information about paraclimbing, including rules, competition, event calendar, and other resources.

28

Winter Sports and Activities

Wesley J. Wilson and Luke E. Kelly

On a frosty morning, 16-year-old Kason sat in the car, impatiently waiting for his mother to drive him to the local park. As an avid cross-country skier, Kason was excited to break in his new skis on the park's trail.

"Did you remember your poles?" his mother asks as she enters the car.

"Yes, Mom, let's go!" Kason exclaims.

As soon as the car is parked at the trail's entrance, Kason grabs his equipment from the trunk. As he starts putting on his skis, his mother says, "You remember that your teacher told you to work on—"

"Pushing and gliding!" Kason interrupts. He moves slowly and deliberately as he starts pushing forward through the snow. Kason adjusts his pace so that he is moving a bit faster and gliding further. He enjoys how he moves on his skis, sometimes finding it an easier way to locomote than his shuffle gait would typically allow.

Kason has cerebral palsy that primarily affects his lower limbs. Although he feels that his gait and balance may make participation in other recreational activities more challenging, he believes that he is successful in cross-country skiing. Living in a city with an abundance of parks and a cold climate make this winter sport activity a natural choice for Kason.

This chapter introduces winter activities that can be included in physical education and sport programs for people with disabilities. It is not within the scope of the chapter to cover in detail how each winter sport should be taught—instead, general guidelines are provided, along with a brief description of each activity and suggested adaptations for participants with various disabilities.

Value of Winter Sport

A major goal of physical education is for students both with and without disabilities to gain the knowledge, skills, and experiences they need to live healthy and productive lives. At the completion of their school physical education programs, students should have the basic physical fitness and motor skills required to sustain lifelong physical activity. Therefore, emphasis on sport skills in the school curriculum should reflect students' needs in terms of carryover value and the likelihood of continuing participation after the school years.

However, one area—winter sport skills—is frequently underrepresented in the physical education and sport curriculum. This is a serious omission for all students, especially students with disabilities. In many parts of the United States, the winter season is the longest season during the school year. Winter sport activities provide opportunities for people with disabilities to maintain or improve physical fitness levels, participate in community recreation activities, and pursue athletic competition. Failure to teach winter sport skills to students with disabilities limits their recreational options during the winter months, which in turn might affect their fitness and isolate them from many social activities and settings.

Given proper instruction and practice, people with disabilities can pursue and successfully participate in many winter sports, including alpine (downhill) skiing, snowboarding, cross-country (Nordic) skiing, ice-skating, ice picking, sledding, curling, and hockey. Instructional programs for people with disabilities should be guided by equal attention to safety, fun, and skill development. Safety concerns should encompass the areas of physical and motor readiness, appropriate clothing and equipment, and instructor qualifications (National Ski Patrol, 2020a). Particular attention should be given to properly fitting all participants with an appropriate helmet and requiring that a helmet be worn during participation in all winter sport activities (National Ski Patrol, 2020b).

Alpine Skiing

Alpine (downhill) skiing is a winter sport in which most people with disabilities can participate with little or no modification. Skiing frees many people from limitations that ordinarily hinder their mobility and allows them to move with great agility and at great speeds (figure 28.1). For many people with physical, mental, and sensory impairments, skiing offers a unique opportunity to challenge their environment.

The key to learning to ski is controlling weight distribution and directing where the weight is applied on the surface (edges) of the skis. The goal of any introductory ski program is to provide students with the basic skills needed to enjoy and safely participate in the sport. The basic skills of downhill skiing can be grouped into six categories:

- Putting on and taking off equipment independently
- Using rope and chairlifts independently
- Falling and standing
- Walking (side-stepping, herringbone)
- Stopping (wedge, parallel)
- Turning (wedge, parallel)

Instruction

Ski instruction should be preceded by a conditioning program and the development of basic skills such as falling and standing. When actual ski instruction begins, the skill sequence must be matched to the needs and abilities of the learners to ensure safety and maximize enjoyment. Although recovery (standing back up on the skis) is a required skill for independent skiing, it might not be appropriate to concentrate on this skill during early learning. For many people with disabilities, learning to stand up on skis after falling is strenuous and often frustrating. Students who are made to master this skill first are likely not to experience much success or fun and will soon become disenchanted with the idea of skiing. Initial instruction should focus on actual skiing skills, such as a wedge stop, and the instructor should provide assistance to compensate for the lack of other skills, such as the ability to independently recover from falls. This form of instruction provides students with confidence and some of the thrills of moving on skis. As skill and enjoyment increase, students become more motivated to work on mastering the other essential skills, such as independent recovery.

Lintao Zhang/Getty Images

FIGURE 28.1 A skier maneuvers down the slope using a monoski and outriggers.

Assistive Devices

Assistive devices for skiing have been developed to offset some of the limitations imposed by disabilities and to compensate for the general low fitness and poor motor coordination common to many people with disabilities. The most commonly used device is the **ski bra**, which is mounted to the tip of the skis and serves two primary functions. First, it stabilizes the skis while allowing them to move independently. Second, it assists the skier in positioning the skis in a wedge position, which improves balance and makes for easier stopping and turning. The ski bra can be used as a temporary learning device for any skier during the early stages of learning to assist with balance and control, or may be used as a permanent assistive device for people with lower extremity orthopedic impairments who lack sufficient strength or control of their lower limbs to ski independently.

Another common modification used to assist skiers with disabilities are **canting wedges,** or small, thin wedges placed between the sole of the ski boot and the ski. The wedges adjust the lateral tilt of the boot and subsequently affect the distribution of weight over the edges of the skis. Canting wedges are commonly used to assist skiers who have trouble turning to one side or the other.

Outriggers (see figure 28.2) are common assistive devices used by skiers with amputations and other orthopedic impairments who require additional support primarily in the area of balance. The outriggers are made from a Lofstrand crutch with a short ski attached to the bottom. The ski on the end of the crutch can be placed in a vertical (up) position and used as a crutch or positioned in a horizontal position for use as an outrigger. *Three-track* and *four-track skiing* are common terms used to describe skiing with outriggers. Three-track skiing is performed by people who use only one ski and two outriggers—for example, those with a unilateral lower limb amputation. Three-track skiing requires good strength and motor control in both arms and the one leg on the ski. Four-track skiing is performed by those who use two skis and two outriggers. Generally, individuals who can stand and ambulate independently using crutches, such as those with spina bifida, bilateral lower

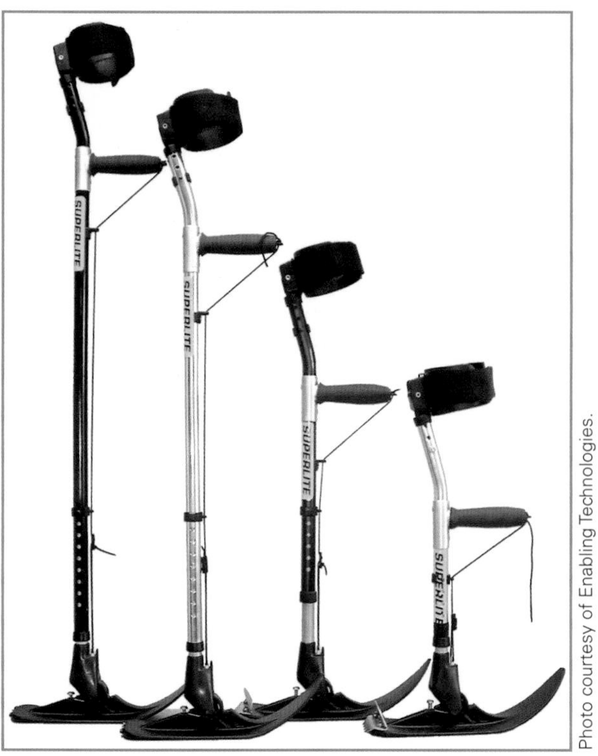

Photo courtesy of Enabling Technologies.

FIGURE 28.2 Outriggers come in a range of sizes: from left to right, tall, medium, monoski adult, and sit-ski adult.

limb amputations, and traumatic brain injuries, can four-track ski.

Sit-skiing is the method used by skiers with paraplegia and quadriplegia and involves the use of a special sled. The skier is strapped into the sled or bucket, which contains appropriate padding and support to hold the skier in an upright sitting position. The top of the bucket is covered by a water-repellent nylon skirt to keep the skier dry. The bottom of the bucket is connected to either one ski (monoskiing) or two skis (bi-skiing). Skiers control the sled by shifting their weight over the edge in the direction they want to go. A single kayak-type pole or two short poles can assist in balancing and controlling the sit-ski. Special mittens are available to allow people with limited grip strength to hold on to the poles. For the protection of both the sit-skier and other skiers on the slope, the beginner sit-skier should always be tethered to an experienced ski instructor (figure 28.3). Modified sit-skis are also available and can be used by people with paraplegia for cross-country skiing. Consult the Online Resources at the end of this chapter to find the latest advances in sit-skiing equipment.

Photo courtesy of Jaana Huovinen.

FIGURE 28.3 A student learning to sit-ski while tethered to the instructor.

Ski instructors must be able to provide enough physical assistance during early learning to ensure safety and success. Providing physical assistance to a moving beginner requires skills that must be learned and perfected. As the skills of a skier with a disability increase, the instructor must also know how to gradually fade out the physical assistance to verbal cues and eventually to independence.

In addition to the more universal assistive devices described so far, many other devices have been created to address the needs of skiers with disabilities. Special prosthetic limbs, for example, have been developed to allow single- and double-leg amputees to ski. Many of these devices are custom made. Watching a national ski competition for people with disabilities may provide an idea of the range of devices that can be created to assist skiers with various disabilities.

Snowboarding

The latest winter sport to evolve for athletes with disabilities is **snowboarding**. Snowboarding is comparable to skateboarding on snow but using a slightly longer and wider board. The snowboarder's feet are attached to the length of the board by bindings that require special boots (see figure 28.4). Snowboarding can be done at any facility that offers alpine skiing. With modified equipment, most people with disabilities can learn and participate in snowboarding. Skiers with disabilities should consult an adapted snowboard instructor when selecting and adapting snowboard equipment and should be individually fitted for their boards based on their height, weight, and ability. Most ski resorts that offer adapted ski instruction also offer snowboard instruction for people with disabilities.

The United States of America Snowboard Association (USASA) is the governing body for snowboarding competition. The USASA has a division for adaptive snowboarders at its regional and national competitions and offers events in alpine, freestyle, and boardercross (USASA, 2019). Special Olympics (2020) initiated snowboarding as an official event in the 2001 World Winter Games in Anchorage, Alaska. Athletes compete in three divisions (novice, intermediate, and advanced) in three events: super giant slalom (super G), giant slalom, and slalom.

In 1998, the U.S. Deaf Skiers Association was renamed the U.S. Deaf Ski and Snowboard Association (USDSSA). The USDSSA offers regional competitions in snowboarding that culminate

FIGURE 28.4 Snowboarding is one of the latest winter sports to evolve for athletes with disabilities.

in competition at the Winter Deaflympics. The instructional recommendations provided for alpine skiing also apply to teaching snowboarding. Many of the assistive devices used in teaching downhill skiing, such as outriggers and tethers, are also used when teaching snowboarding. The Professional Ski Instructors of America (PSIA) and the American Association of Snowboard Instructors (AASI) produce three helpful manuals for snowboarding instructors: *Adaptive Snowboard Guide* (2013), *AASI Snowboard Manual* (1998), and *AASI Snowboard Movement Analysis Handbook* (2003).

Cross-Country Skiing

Cross-country skiing has become a popular winter sport in recent years. It is an excellent physical fitness and recreational activity that can be done almost anywhere (e.g., golf courses, parks, open fields) and costs nothing after the initial equipment has been purchased. Because both the arms and the legs are used in cross-country skiing, it develops total body fitness—however, this means the skier must create the momentum to move. This difference precludes participation of many people with more severe orthopedic impairments who lack either the strength or the control to generate the momentum needed to cross-country ski. However, because the activity is performed on snow and does not require that the feet actually be lifted off the ground, many people with cerebral palsy who have difficulty walking (shuffle gait) can successfully cross-country ski.

A complete cross-country skiing outfit (skis, poles, gaiters, and shoes) is relatively inexpensive. For beginners, waxless (fish scale or step pattern) skis are recommended over wax skis. Waxless skis require no maintenance or preparation before use, and they provide more than enough resistance and glide for learning and enjoying cross-country skiing. Initial instruction should take place in a relatively flat area with prepared tracks (figure 28.5). Most beginning cross-country skiers tend to simply walk wearing their skis, using their poles for balance. This, unfortunately, is incorrect and very fatiguing. The key in learning to cross-country ski is getting the feel of pushing back on one ski while transferring the weight to the front foot and

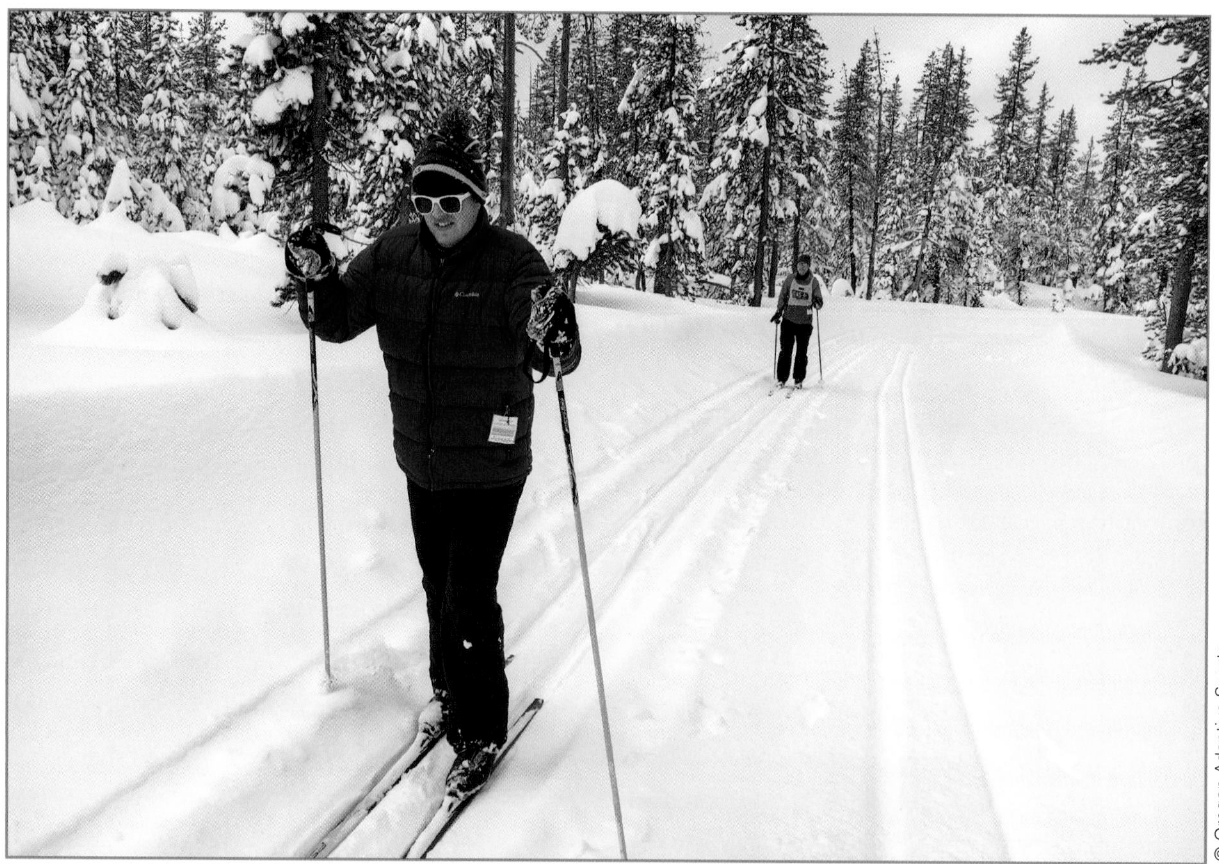

FIGURE 28.5 A young man participating in adapted cross-country skiing on a prepared track.

sliding the front ski forward. Instructors should focus on demonstrating this pattern and contrasting it with walking. An effective technique is to physically assist the beginning skier through this pattern so that the learner can feel what it is like (a method that works particularly well with skiers with intellectual disabilities or visual impairments). Cross-country skiers with visual impairments must be accompanied by sighted partners to inform them of upcoming conditions (turns, dips, changes in grade). The forward push-and-glide technique is the preferred pattern for most skiers with disabilities, as opposed to the more strenuous and skill-demanding skating or freestyle technique used by world-class Nordic skiers.

Competitive Skiing for People With Disabilities

Skiing for people with disabilities is sponsored by several sport associations that conduct local, state, and national skiing competitions. Three of the largest and most prominent sponsors of ski competitions are Move United, which sponsors skiing competitions for people with disabilities; the United States Association of Blind Athletes (USABA), which sponsors competition for skiers with visual impairments; and Special Olympics, which sponsors competitions for skiers with intellectual disabilities.

International Paralympic Committee Classification of Skiers

Move United promotes developmental and competitive sport programs through a grassroots community-based network for nearly 40 different sports, including alpine skiing, Nordic skiing, snowboarding, and snowshoeing (Move United, 2020). Skiing competition is contested in three categories: alpine (downhill, slalom, giant slalom), Nordic (5K, 10K, 15K, 20K, 30K, biathlon, relays), and sit-skiing (as listed for alpine and Nordic). Athletes are classified by the site and severity of their disabilities and the type of adapted equipment used in skiing according to International Paralympic Committee classes (IPC, 2020), as shown next.

Sport Classes LW 1-9: Standing Skiers

Sport Class LW 1: This sport class is allocated to athletes with an impairment that strongly affects both legs—for example, an above-knee amputation of both legs or significant muscle weakness in both legs.

Sport Class LW 2: Skiers have a significant impairment in one leg (e.g., congenital); they use one ski only.

Sport Class LW 3: This sport class is for athletes who have a moderate impairment in both legs. Some LW 3 skiers have mild coordination problems or muscle weakness in both legs, or a below-knee amputation in both legs. They ski with two skis and prosthesis.

Sport Class LW 4: Similar to skiers in Sport Class LW 2, LW 4 skiers have an impairment in one leg only, but with less activity limitation. A typical example is a below-knee amputation in one leg. They use two skis during a race.

Sport Class LW 5/7: Athletes in this sport class ski with an impairment in both arms. Some athletes have amputations, and others have limited muscle power or coordination problems. They race down the slopes without ski poles.

Sport Class LW 6/8: Skiers have an impairment in one arm. They compete with one ski pole only.

Sport Class LW 9: Skiers in this sport class have an impairment that affects arms and legs. Some skiers in this class have coordination problems, such as spasticity or some loss of control over one side of their body. Depending on their abilities, they ski with one or two skis and one or two poles.

Sport Classes LW 10-12: Sit-Skiers

All sit-skiers have an impairment affecting their legs. They are allocated to different sport classes depending on their sitting balance, which is very important for acceleration and balancing during the races.

Sport Class LW 10: Skiers in this sport class have no or minimal trunk stability (e.g., spinal cord injuries, spina bifida). They therefore rely mainly on their arms to maneuver the sit-ski.

Sport Class LW 11: Skiers have good abilities in their upper trunk, but very limited control in their lower trunk and hips, as would be the case for skiers with lower spinal cord injuries.

Sport Class LW 12: This sport class includes skiers with normal or only slightly decreased trunk function and leg impairments. Skiers with leg impairments in Sport Classes LW 1 through 4 often also fit this sport class, so they can choose if they want to ski sitting or standing in the beginning of their career.

Para Snowboard

Para snowboard currently offers three sport classes, one for athletes with a significant impairment in one or both legs, one for athletes with less severe activity limitation in their lower limbs, and one for athletes with arm impairments. The sport is under development, and with its growth, the classification system will be refined gradually.

Sport Class SB LL-1: Snowboarders in Sport Class SB LL-1 have a significant impairment in one leg (e.g., an above-the-knee amputation) or a significant combined impairment in two legs (e.g., significant muscle weakness or spasticity in both legs). This affects their ability to balance, control the board, and absorb the terrain. Athletes with amputations use prostheses during the races.

Sport Class SB LL-2: Snowboarders in Sport Class SB LL-2 have an impairment in one or two legs with less activity limitation. A typical example is a below-knee amputation or mild spasticity.

Sport Class SB UL: Snowboarders in the SB UL have impairments of the upper limbs, which affects the ability to balance when racing down the slopes.

IPC Sport Classifications for Skiers With Visual Impairment

The USABA (2020) has played a significant role in developing and promoting sport opportunities for individuals who are blind and visually impaired in sports such as Nordic and alpine skiing. Skiers with visual impairments compete in the standard IPC events: downhill, slalom, giant slalom, and super G. Separate men's and women's competitions are offered for each classification; there are no age divisions. Sighted guides ski in front of athletes with visual impairments and provide verbal instructions to assist them in all events. Skiers are divided into three classes on the basis of visual acuity with maximum correction, as determined by the IPC (2020):

Sport Class B1: Skiers in this sport class either are blind or have very low visual acuity, meaning that their level of visual acuity is such that they cannot recognize the letter *E* (15 × 15 centimeters in size) from a distance of 25 centimeters. During the race they are required to wear eyeshades.

Sport Class B2: This sport class profile includes athletes with a higher visual acuity than athletes competing in the B1 class, but they are unable to recognize the letter *E* from a distance of 4 meters. Moreover, athletes with a visual field less than 10 degrees in diameter are eligible for this sport class.

Sport Class B3: The B3 sport class profile describes the least severe visual impairment eligible for alpine skiing. Eligible athletes have either a restricted visual field less than 40 degrees in diameter or a low visual acuity.

Special Olympics

Special Olympics sponsors local, state, and national ski competitions for people with intellectual disabilities in both alpine and Nordic events (Special Olympics, 2020). The alpine events include super G, giant slalom, and slalom races. The Nordic events include the 500-meter, 1K, 2.5K, 5K, 7.5K, and 10K races as well as a 4 × 1K relay race and a 4 × 1K Unified relay race. Athletes are classified for competition into one of three classes—novice, intermediate, or advanced—on the basis of preliminary time trials in each event. There are no age or gender divisions. Special Olympics also offers developmental (noncompetitive) alpine and Nordic events. The developmental alpine events include a 10-meter walk, glide event, and super glide. The Nordic developmental events include 10-, 25-, 50-, and 100-meter cross-country skiing races.

Ice-Skating

Ice-skating is an inexpensive winter sport easily accessible in many regions. Most people with disabilities who can stand and walk independently can learn to ice-skate successfully. For those who cannot, a modified form of ice-skating called ice picking is available. Although skating is common in many areas on frozen lakes and ponds or water-covered tennis courts, the preferred environment for teaching ice-skating is an indoor ice rink. An indoor rink offers a more moderate temperature and a surface free from the cracks and bumps commonly found in natural ice. Ice rinks frequently can be used by physical education programs during off times, such as daytime hours on weekdays.

Properly fitting skates are essential for learning and ultimately enjoying ice-skating. Ice skates should be fitted by a professional experienced in working with and fitting people with disabilities. Either figure or hockey skates can be used. The important consideration is that the skates provide good ankle and arch support so that the skater's weight is centered over the ankles and the blades of the skates are perpendicular to the ice when the skater is standing.

As discussed previously, instruction should be guided by safety and success. The greatest obstacle in learning to ice-skate is often the fear of falling. Although falling while first learning to skate is inevitable, steps can be taken to minimize the frequency and severity of the falls and, consequently, the apprehension. At the same time, the early stages of learning must be associated with success, which gives learners confidence that they will be able to learn to skate. It is recommended that padding be used around the major joints most likely to hit the ice during a fall. Knee and elbow pads reduce the physical trauma of taking a fall and also provide psychological security that alleviates the fear of falling. Elbow pads and American football pants with knee, hip, and sacral pads can also be beneficial during the early stages. See the Application Example sidebar on overcoming fear.

The locomotor skill of ice-skating is similar to walking. Weight, the center of gravity, is transferred in front of the base of support and from side to side as the legs are lifted and swung forward to catch the weight. The back skate is usually rotated outward about 30 degrees to provide resistance to sliding backward as the weight transfers to the forward skate. Because success during the early lessons is essential, one-on-one instruction from an experienced instructor is highly recommended. Special Olympics (2020) has excellent coaching guides available for both figure skating and speed skating.

The primary aid used in teaching ice-skating is physical assistance. Some people with orthopedic and neuromuscular impairments might benefit from the use of polypropylene orthoses to stabilize their ankles. Ankle–foot orthoses can be custom made to be worn inside the skates. Skating walkers, such as the Skate Coach Early Skating Trainer, are devices that do not interfere with the skating action of the legs and provide the beginning skater with a stable means of support independent from the instructor. This can be used for temporary assistance for students who need a little additional support or confidence during the early stages of learning; it can also be a more permanent assistive device for skaters with more severe orthopedic impairments. It is beneficial to add some foam padding to the

Application Example

Helping a Student Overcome Fear in an Ice Hockey Unit

SETTING

A physical education class is starting an ice hockey skills unit. Most of the students can skate forward well and are working on increasing speed, changing direction, and skating backward.

STUDENT

John is an 11-year-old with a mild intellectual disability who recently moved to Michigan from Florida. He has slightly below-average coordination for his age but is generally willing to try new skills. John has recently become a big Michigan State hockey fan.

ISSUE

John had a negative experience with ice-skating the first time he tried it and now is extremely fearful and unwilling to put skates on.

APPLICATION

Based on the information available and a meeting with John's parents, the physical educator decides on the following strategies:

- Meet individually with John to discuss his fears of ice-skating and explain how these fears will be addressed.
- Contact the local university and borrow some official Michigan State hockey pads and a helmet of appropriate size.
- John will start using a padded skate walker to give him confidence. He will then transition to using a hockey stick as a balance aid.
- Prepare an aide to work with John during the initial lessons to ensure he is successful and to prevent any new negative experiences.

top support bar in the front of the skate aid to further reduce the chance of injury from falls. If skate aids are not available, chairs can be used in a similar fashion.

Ice picking is a modified form of ice-skating in which the participant sits on a **sledge** (a small sled with blades on the bottom) and uses small poles (picks) to propel the sledge on the ice. Ice picking can be performed by almost anyone and is particularly appropriate for people who have only upper limb control (e.g., people with paraplegia or spina bifida). Ice picking is an excellent activity for developing upper body strength and endurance. All skating activities and events (speed skating and skate dancing) can be modified and performed in sledges. Because people with and without disabilities can use the equipment, ice picking offers a unique way to equalize participation and competition in integrated settings.

Special Olympics sponsors competition in both figure skating and speed skating (Special Olympics, 2020). The figure skating events include singles, pairs, and ice dancing as well as Unified Sports pairs and Unified Sports ice dancing. The speed-skating events include the 111-, 222-, 333-, 500-, 777-, 1,000-, and 1,500-meter races, 3,000-meter relay, and 3,000-meter Unified Sports relay. For each event, athletes are divided into three classifications—novice, intermediate, and advanced—on the basis of preliminary performance and time trials. Developmental (noncompetitive) ice-skating events are also offered. These include the skills competition figure skating event and the 25- and 55-meter races.

Sledding and Tobogganing

In snowy regions, sledding and tobogganing are two common recreational activities universally enjoyed by children and adults. Many people with disabilities, however, avoid these activities because they lack the simple skills and confidence needed to successfully take part in them. This can easily be addressed in a physical education program. Given proper attention to safety and clothing, almost all children with disabilities can participate in sledding and tobogganing. Sleds and toboggans can be purchased or rented at minimal cost. Straps and padding can be added to sleds and toboggans to accommodate the specific needs presented by people with disabilities. Even students with the most severe disabilities can experience the thrill of sledding or tobogganing when paired with an aide who can control and steer the sled.

Snowshoeing

Another low-cost and popular recreational activity in snowy regions is snowshoeing. Most individuals with disabilities who can walk either independently or with an assistive device (e.g., a cane) can enjoy snowshoeing. Careful attention should be given to proper clothing for the weather conditions and outfitting students with appropriate snowshoes and poles. In most areas, snowshoe equipment can be rented for a minimal cost or purchased for around $150. Once appropriately dressed and equipped, participants can enjoy hiking and exploring the great outdoors in the winter. Although not an international Paralympic event, snowshoeing is a Special Olympics winter sport event, with competitions held in the 25-, 50-, 100-, 200-, 400-, 800-, and 1,600-meter; 5K, 10K; 4 × 100-meter relay, 4 × 400-meter relay, 4 × 100-meter Unified Sports relay, and 4 × 400-meter Unified Sports relay.

Hockey

Ice hockey is a popular winter sport in the northern areas of the United States and is the national sport of Canada. Because hockey is a continuous and highly active sport, many modifications and adaptations have been made to accommodate players with disabilities. Some common modifications are as follows:

- Use soft plastic balls, plastic pucks, or doughnut-shaped pucks instead of the traditional ice hockey pucks.
- Use shorter and lighter sticks made of plastic, which are more durable, easier to handle, and less harmful to other players.
- Change the size of the goals.
- Change the boundaries, number of players per team, or length of playing periods to accommodate players' abilities.

Modifications can easily be made with tape and Velcro to enable players with physical impairments to hold sticks or use sticks from wheelchairs. A wide range of abilities can be accommodated in a game if the teams are balanced and the players' abilities are matched to the various positions.

Sled hockey is a modified form of ice hockey played on sleds. The puck is struck with a modified stick about 30 inches (76 centimeters) long, called a pick. One end has metal points that grip the ice and allow the athlete to propel the sled. The other end, the blade, is rubber coated and used to strike the puck.

Sled hockey is an excellent recreational and fitness activity. Using sleds is also an ideal way to allow students with and without orthopedic disabilities to participate in the same activity. The United States won the gold medal in sled hockey in the 2002 and the 2010 Paralympics (figure 28.6). For more information on sled hockey, consult the Video Resources for this chapter.

Hockey can also be played on a gym floor or tennis court (i.e., floor hockey). A stick similar to a broomstick with a vinyl coating on the end is used in conjunction with a doughnut-shaped puck. The goalkeeper uses a regular hockey goalie stick. The playing area is 30 meters by 15 meters, or the size of a typical basketball court, and the goals are 1.8 meters wide and 1.2 meters high. Special Olympics sponsors local, state, and national floor hockey competition in team competition, Unified Sports team competition, and individual skills events.

Logical modifications should be made to the regulation game of floor hockey to accommodate beginners, such as reducing the playing area, increasing the number of players on each team, increasing the size of the goal, playing without goalkeepers, or changing the size or type of puck (e.g., substituting a playground ball). The goal of all modifications should be to maximize participation and success in basic skills while gradually progressing toward the regulation game.

Curling

Curling is a popular sport in Europe and Canada. The playing area is an ice court 46 yards (42 meters) long and 14 feet (4.3 meters) wide, with a 6-foot (1.8-meter) circular target, called a *house*, marked on the ice at each end. The game is played by two teams of four players, using kettle-shaped weights with a gooseneck handle on top called *stones*. Each stone is 36 inches (1 meter) in circumference and weighs about 40 pounds (18 kilograms). A game is composed of 10 or 12 rounds called *heads*, which consist of each player delivering (sliding) two stones. Players on each team alternate delivering stones until all have been delivered. After each stone is delivered, teammates can use brooms to sweep frost and moisture from the ice in front of the moving stone to keep it straight and allow it to slide farther. At the end of a round, a team scores a point for each stone they have closer to the center

Photo courtesy of Stephanie Wippert.

FIGURE 28.6 In this sled hockey game, the United States is taking a shot on the Canadian goal.

of the target than the other team. The team with the most points at the end of 10 or 12 rounds is the winner. If the score is tied, an additional round is played to break the tie.

Curling can easily be modified to accommodate people with just about any disability. The distance between the houses and the weight of stones can be reduced to facilitate reaching the targets. The size of the targets can also easily be increased to maximize success. Audible goal locators can be placed on the houses to assist players with visual impairments. Because the sweeping component of the game might be difficult to modify, mixed teams could be formed of players with and without disabilities or with various disabilities so that each team has a few members who could do the sweeping. Finally, assistive devices similar to those used in bowling, such as ramps and guide rails, could be used to help players with more severe disabilities deliver the stones. For the latest information on curling, check the Online Resources for this chapter.

Strategies for Inclusion

Although competition is available for most winter sports, most students participate in them as recreational activities. As such, it is especially important for winter sports to be taught as inclusive activities, using a universal design for learning (UDL) approach to meet the instructional needs of *all* students. Although UDL is discussed in more detail in chapters 2 and 7, its primary feature is "to make it possible for everyone to participate in an inclusive setting without being singled out" (Burgstahler, 2015, p. 14). Inclusive education—conceptualized by Stainback and Stainback (1996) as eliciting feelings of value, belonging, and acceptance from the perspectives of the students with disabilities themselves—includes intentionally designing instruction that meets the needs of a diverse range of learners from the outset. This proactive, rather than reactive, approach involves providing modifications upfront so that all students, even those with severe disabilities, are able to participate. For example, in winter activities such as skiing, snowboarding, cross-country skiing, ice-skating, and sledding, modifications to the equipment to increase stability and control and to the terrain to slow the activity down should be made available to all students to ensure success. These modifications may not only be beneficial to students with disabilities, but also to those who may be beginners or low-skilled, thus promoting a more inclusive education for all without singling out any one student. The goal of these modifications should be to capitalize on students' abilities and maximize participation while promoting value, belonging, and acceptance.

Simple modifications can also be broadly applied to make team events such as floor hockey, sled hockey, and curling more likely to elicit feelings of inclusion among participants. These typically involve modifying how the equipment is held to increase control, reducing the distances and boundaries to minimize the limitations imposed by reduced mobility, and defining safe areas if the students must be protected from physical contact or require a little more time to react during the game. Again, the goal should be to build on all students' strengths and maximize participation. Given the physical fitness and social benefits associated with winter activities, every effort should be made to ensure that all students have functional competency in these activities so that they can participate in them throughout their lives.

Summary

Winter sports are excellent all-around activities. They help participants develop motor skills, strength, and physical fitness, and at the same time they provide participants with functional recreational skills they can use for the rest of their lives. For many people with disabilities, winter sports performed on snow and ice allow them to move with agility and speed not possible under their own power on land. Thus, winter sports should be an essential component in physical education and sport programs, especially for students with disabilities. For this reason, activities have been discussed in this chapter with particular focus on ways to modify them for people with unique needs.

References

Burgstahler, S.E. (2015). *Universal design in higher education: From principles to practice* (2nd ed.). Harvard Education Press.

International Paralympic Committee (IPC). (2020). *Classification explained.* Retrieved from www.paralympic.org/classification

Move United. (2020). *Adaptive sports.* Retrieved from www.moveunitedsport.org/sports/adaptive-sports

National Ski Patrol. (2020a). *Before you go.* Retrieved from https://nspserves.org/before-you-go/

National Ski Patrol. (2020b). *On the mountain.* Retrieved from https://nspserves.org/on-the-mountain/

Professional Ski Instructors of America (PSIA) and American Association of Snowboard Instructors (AASI). (1998). *AASI snowboard manual.* Author.

Professional Ski Instructors of America (PSIA) and American Association of Snowboard Instructors (AASI). (2003). *AASI snowboard movement analysis handbook.* Author.

Professional Ski Instructors of America (PSIA) and American Association of Snowboard Instructors (AASI). (2013). *Adaptive snowboard guide.* Author.

Special Olympics. (2020). *Sports.* Retrieved from www.specialolympics.org/Sections/Sports-and-Games/Sports_and_Games.aspx?source=QL

Stainback, W., & Stainback, S. (1996). Collaboration, support network and community construction. In S. Stainback & W. Stainback (Eds.), *Inclusion: A guide for educators* (pp. 223-232). Paul H. Brookes Publishing Co.

United States Association of Blind Athletes (USABA). (2020). *Skiing.* Retrieved from www.usaba.org/sports/ski/

United States of America Snowboard Association (USASA). (2019). *Official rulebook 2019-2020.* https://drive.google.com/file/d/1EKJWu4SM2tk1FHjjZj9MkW-Seei923FLK/view

Print Resources

American Association of Snowboard Instructors. (2013). *Adaptive snowboard guide.* Author.

This in-depth manual covers teaching techniques, adaptive equipment, and profiles for skiers with visual, auditory, cognitive, neurological, structural, anatomical, and combination disabilities.

O'Leary, H. (1994). *Bold tracks: Teaching adaptive skiing.* Johnson Books.

This book is a must for anyone who teaches skiing to people with disabilities.

Special Olympics. (2007). *The Special Olympics alpine skiing coaching guide.* Author.

This manual provides a how-to approach for teaching the basic skills involved in alpine skiing, including teaching suggestions, sample drills, and activities.

Special Olympics. (2007). *The Special Olympics floor hockey coaching guide.* Author.

This manual provides a how-to approach for teaching the basic skills involved in floor hockey. Teaching suggestions, sample drills, and activities are provided for each skill.

Video Resources

International Paralympic Committee (IPC). *Video archive.* www.paralympic.org/videos

This website provides direct links to videos on alpine skiing, sled hockey, past Paralympic Games, and past world and regional championships.

Move United. *Videos.* www.moveunitedsport.org/about/news/videos/

This site provides videos showing athletes with disabilities competing in a variety of sports, including alpine and Nordic skiing.

Special Olympics. *All downloadable videos.* http://resources.specialolympics.org/Video-Resources2.aspx

This site provides an extensive list of videos on Special Olympics stories as well as past Special Olympics competitions, including winter sports.

Online Resources

AbleData Database of Assistive Technology for Winter Sports: https://abledata.acl.gov

This website provides information and links to the latest assistive devices to help people with disabilities participate in a variety of sport and recreational activities, including winter sports.

International Paralympic Committee: www.paralympic.org

The IPC website describes IPC-sponsored events, competitions, results, and classification system.

Move United: www.moveunitedsport.org

This website includes the official rule books and classifications for many adaptive sports, including archery, cross-country skiing, snowboarding, downhill skiing, handcycling, powerlifting, shooting, swimming, tennis, and track and field.

Oregon Adaptive Sports: https://oregonadaptivesports.org/sports/equipment/

This site provides information on various types of adaptive alpine skiing equipment and cross discipline equipment.

Sitski.com: www.sitski.com

This site provides information and pictures of the latest advances in sit-skiing equipment.

Skatebuys: www.skate-buys.com

This site provides online access to all types of skates and skating accessories. It also provides information on how to buy and match skates to different ability levels.

Special Olympics: www.specialolympics.org/Sections/Sports-and-Games/Sports_and_Games.aspx?source=QL

This page contains links to the rules and coaching guides for all Special Olympic sports. Many of these documents can also be downloaded as PDF files.

United States of America Snowboard Association (USASA): www.usasa.org

USASA is the national governing body for all snowboarding competition. This site contains the official rules and events, as well as information on regional and national competitions.

USA Curling: www.usacurl.org

This site provides information on curling history, rules, and strategies.

29

Enhancing Wheelchair Sport Performance

Victoria L. Goosey-Tolfrey and Barry S. Mason

This was my first wheelchair basketball fun-day session at school, where I was introduced to my first sport wheelchair.
It's wheeled out for my first view.
"What is it?" I ask.
"Your new wheelchair, of course," someone says.
"But that isn't a wheelchair."

And it isn't. I know because I am sitting on one. Chairs are heavy, wide, and comfortable. Chairs are for sitting on and for getting from point A to point B. No, this wasn't a chair; chairs are a necessity, and this was a luxury. Its bright white titanium frame glistened under the sports hall lights, wheels angled out towards the parquet floor like wings. It wasn't a chair; it was a weapon. And I loved her.

We took time to bond, but now when I move, she moves. If I push, lean, sway, she pushes, leans, sways. We sprint, we shoot, we score, we win.
She doesn't belong to me—she is part of me.
She isn't a chair; she's a weapon. A weapon with which I will win.
Narrative provided by Dr. Anthony Papathomas, 2020.

Since 1948, when Dr. Ludwig Guttmann organized the first competition for wheelchair athletes (called the Stoke Mandeville Games), the Paralympic Games have evolved to unprecedented new levels, and as always, at the heart of the Games remain the wheelchair events. Wheelchair racers have continued to break records, and wheelchair basketball, rugby, and tennis competitions have thrilled crowds. Athletes who compete in wheelchair sport combine themselves, their chairs, and their skills into performance systems to achieve levels of excellence far from that envisioned by early pioneers and unheard of in the days of medically driven attitudes and regulations. There is now a functional perspective in wheelchair sport that places disability second to the demands of the specific sport. This transition has been spearheaded by the athletes themselves, and they have been instrumental in developing many of the innovations in equipment and technique.

Sport for athletes with disabilities now parallels the world of athletes without disabilities; and to reach the highest levels, athletes must find the sport (and often the event or position) for which they are best suited. Suitability for specific sports is most commonly determined by the athlete's interests, disability type, body size and shape, and psychological makeup. In order to maximize wheelchair sport performance, event selection should be based on a systems approach that takes into consideration both the athlete and the wheelchair. Some training principles for wheelchair athletes are transferable from practice used with able-bodied athletes; that said, this chapter highlights the considerations needed to select both a sport and an appropriate wheelchair and to optimize the athlete–wheelchair interaction. Although many sports and activities could be considered (e.g., wheelchair dance, wheelchair fencing, wheelchair table tennis, seated skiing) this chapter will focus on track athletics and wheelchair court sports to describe the systems approach and factors that enhance wheelchair sport performance.

Athlete and Wheelchair: A Systems Approach

The athlete and the wheelchair, when combined, can be viewed as a performance system. This reflects the functional model of wheelchair sport now prevalent in both the design of wheelchairs and the functional classification systems employed in elite sport competition. Much of the early research on wheelchair sport examined either the athlete or the wheelchair. Many of these studies also examined wheelchair users outside of their preferred environment—that is, their competitive wheelchair. These approaches employed instruments such as ergometers that had scientific but not ecological validity. To appreciate the functional development in wheelchair sport, it is necessary to understand the importance of an approach that combines athlete and wheelchair into a system that is defined by the needs of the specific sport and the role of the players on court. This chapter examines performance enhancements for athletes using wheelchairs, provides a brief description of the equipment, and then examines the combination of the athlete and the wheelchair into a performance system (see figure 29.1).

Athletes

Success in wheelchair sport requires that an athlete be suited to meet the performance considerations of that sport (Goosey-Tolfrey, 2010b). For example, success in basketball requires height for the forward and center positions and speed and agility in the guard positions. In general, athletes with predominantly fast-twitch muscle fibers should focus on sprint events; those with slow-twitch, the endurance events. Those who enjoy cooperation and teamwork should, of course, focus on team events; those with an individual orientation should focus on the appropriate individual sport. Though this approach is something of a truism in sport for athletes without disabilities, in the past, athletes using wheelchairs have not always been able to match their personal goals to the appropriate athletic challenge. After identifying the appropriate event, the athlete needs to focus on meeting the demands of the particular sport by identifying an effective training regimen.

Training

Wheelchair users respond to physical training in a similar manner to the population of persons without disability (Jacobs & Nash, 2004; Paulson & Goosey-Tolfrey, 2016). In addition to developing a foundation of health-related physical fitness (see chapter 23), the athlete should develop levels of fitness associated with performance for the specific sport. The athlete should also consider factors such as individual orientation to specific sports and body anthropometry. As with the athlete without disability, performance-related fitness components, which include coordination, agility,

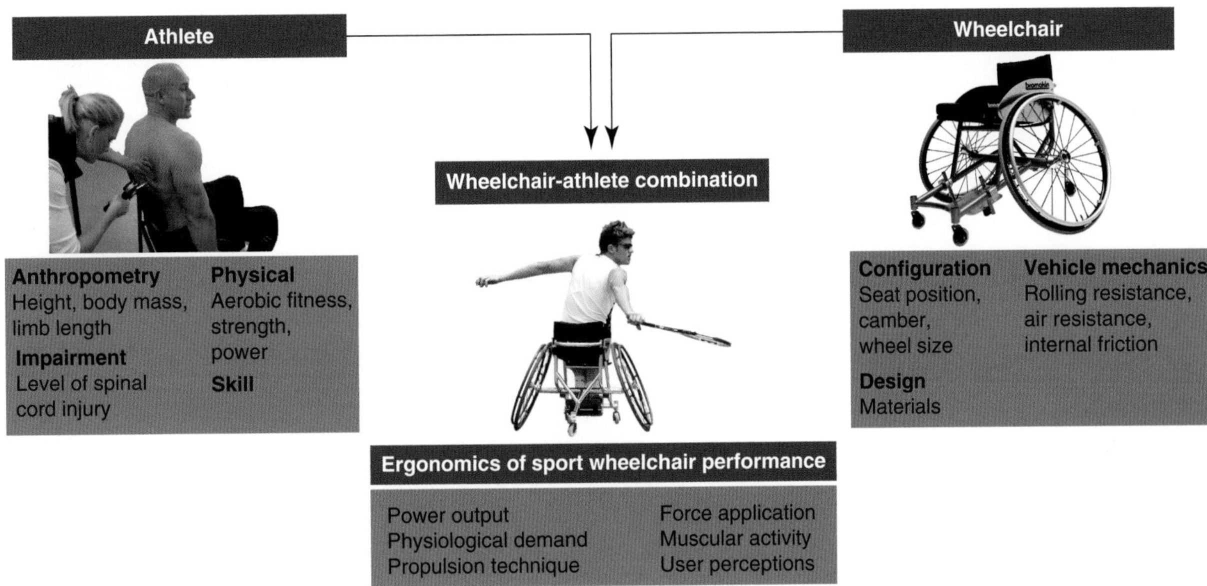

FIGURE 29.1 The wheelchair–user system: illustrating the factors that influence sport wheelchair performance.
Athlete photo © Vicky Tolfrey; wheelchair and wheelchair–athlete combination photos © Bromakin Wheelchairs.

power, speed, and balance, must be considered in a sport-specific manner (Tweedy & Diaper, 2010). Ultimately, the trained athlete may demonstrate improved performance in the sport under examination (Goosey-Tolfrey, 2010a; Goosey-Tolfrey et al., 2013), but improvements will be seen only if the training meets demands of the sport. Emerging technologies such as video analysis, wheelchair data loggers, global positioning systems (GPS), and indoor tracking systems are currently being used to get a true understanding of the sporting requirements in wheelchair sports (Rhodes et al., 2015; Sarro et al., 2010; Sindall et al., 2013); however, this is a topic on which the literature is still sparse.

Although they may involve the same training principles, training regimens for athletes without disabilities are not directly transferrable to athletes with disabilities, and in many cases require subtle yet significant modifications. For example, underpinning most athletic performances is the development of a sound cardiorespiratory base, which presents unique problems for the wheelchair athlete. Cardiorespiratory endurance is produced by stressing the heart and respiratory system through the use of major muscle groups, which expend large amounts of energy over prolonged periods of time. For athletes without disabilities, running, cycling, and swimming use the large muscles of the trunk and lower limbs and are excellent modes of exercise. The athlete using a wheelchair, however, is limited to using the relatively small muscles of the arms and, in some cases, the muscles of the trunk. This smaller working muscle mass places lower demands on the heart and lungs and makes cardiorespiratory training more difficult. Athletes who use wheelchairs usually train with Thera-Band resistance work (figure 29.2*a*), strength and conditioning training, pushing their chairs (figure 29.2*b*), handcycling, or arm cranking. This makes repetitive overuse injuries a concern, particularly of the wrist, elbow, and shoulder (Fagher & Lexell, 2014; Willick et al., 2013), although handcycling or arm crank exercise may result in less physical strain in the upper extremities and reduce this risk (Arnet et al., 2012).

The intensity of training can best be gauged using rate of perceived exertion (RPE) scales (Borg, 1998), which allow the trainer to account for the uniqueness of the athlete independent of standard measures. That said, recent work has suggested that the trainer must not only take into consideration the overall RPE but also use the differentiated scale to help with training quantification; this involves asking athletes to rate the perceived exertion in their arms as well (Paulson et al., 2013). The use of RPE is preferable to heart rate (HR) methods, because athletes with a high lesion may have a blunted HR response. There is some merit in using standardized field exercise tests to monitor training and quantify the standard of the athlete (Goosey-Tolfrey & Leicht, 2013); laboratory testing (van der Woude et al., 2002) showed that elite athletes

Photos courtesy of Dr. Steve Faulkner.

FIGURE 29.2 A wheelchair user training *(a)* with a Thera-Band and *(b)* by pushing his wheelchair with an athlete running beside him.

can be evaluated using standardized aerobic and anaerobic exercise tests provided that classification and current training status are taken into account.

Though a cardiorespiratory base is essential, power more directly relates to the performance demands made in the anaerobic sports exemplified on the court (e.g., tennis, basketball, quad rugby). Because of the small muscle mass involved in wheelchair propulsion and the asymmetry of the propulsion movements, systematic strength and flexibility training is critical. Stretching, both before and after exercise, may be more important for athletes with disabilities than for athletes without disabilities. Strength and conditioning training will develop strength and indirectly power.

The athlete propels the wheelchair using a relatively small range of motion at the shoulder and elbow, which often leads to muscle imbalance around the shoulder joint and postural problems due to the lack of attention to strengthening the opposing antagonist muscle groups (Ambrosio et al., 2005). An important component of the strength and conditioning program for wheelchair users should therefore be development of the posterior (back) muscles. A simple rule of thumb is to pair muscles in the training program (i.e., biceps and triceps) and to include free weight exercises that require the athlete to be facedown (prone) on the work bench. The latissimus dorsi and the trapezius muscles of the back are examples of muscles that should be targeted in a weight program, if such exercises are not contraindicated. Attention to appropriate stretching practices will also improve strength and conditioning training regimens, and where there is a strength imbalance in the muscles due to the disability, stretching can reduce problems such as contractures. Moreover, a carefully planned training program for persons who demonstrate asymmetries with their wheelchair propulsion technique (left vs. right sides) as a result of the nature of the physical impairment (such as stroke or cerebral palsy) is also an important consideration (Goosey-Tolfrey et al., 2018). The next section examines other disability-specific medical concerns.

Medical Concerns

Athletes using wheelchairs face several disability-specific medical concerns, of which the most important are those associated with thermal regulation. Because impairment of sensory nerves resulting from spinal cord damage means that athletes are often unable to feel heat, cold, or pain, both high and low ambient temperatures can present dangers. In cold weather, athletes receive no sensory warning that body extremities (usually the feet) are becoming frozen, which, coupled with reduced blood flow to the inactive feet, can result in frostbite if not monitored.

At high ambient temperatures, the problem is damage to the nerves that initiate and control sweat production. The problem is particularly severe in athletes with quadriplegia, especially those who play quad rugby, as many have little or no body sweat production and thus no way of reducing their core temperature compared to those with a non-spinal injury (Griggs et al., 2017). Quad rugby players who compete indoors also have thermoregulatory problems at mild temperatures, so it is very important to watch out for signs of heat-related illness such as fatigue, nausea, headaches, dizziness, bad decision making, and impaired coordination in all wheelchair users. The provision of shade, adequate drinking fluids, and wet towels for the reduction of surface temperature can help alleviate this problem (within the sporting rules). There is now growing evidence to encourage proper hydration strategies and use of pre- and postevent cooling strategies (e.g., wearing ice vests, employing hand-cooling techniques or fans and water sprays [see figure 29.3]). For further information the reader is directed to Goosey-Tolfrey and colleagues (2015) and Griggs and colleagues (2015).

A particularly pernicious medical problem that has surfaced in wheelchair sport is the life-threatening but deliberate precipitation of autonomic dysreflexia by athletes with quadriplegia, a process referred to as *boosting*. Autonomic dysreflexia is a medical condition characterized by hypertension, piloerection, headaches, bradycardia, and very high levels of catecholamine. Some athletes with quadriplegia believe that boosting increases their athletic performance by increasing blood pressure and thus cardiac output; experimental evidence supports this view (Krassioukov & West, 2014; Schmid et al., 2001). National and international sport groups are aware of the use of boosting and its dangers, and the practice is banned in Paralympic competition (Blauwet et al., 2013).

Wheelchairs

Developments in wheelchair design that match the chair to the demands of the sport have led to multiple choices for both the athletes and coaches wishing to enhance performance (Bundon et al., 2017; Mason et al., 2013). It is no longer feasible to expect a daily-life wheelchair to cope with the competitive demands of a sport at the elite level. Just as the athlete without a disability wears different shoes for different sports, the elite athlete uses different wheelchairs for different sports.

a

b

FIGURE 29.3 Athletes using cooling techniques during *(a)* sport competition (ice vest) and *(b)* training (water spray).

Nevertheless, there are some commonalties in wheelchair design that generalize across the spectrum of competitive wheelchairs.

Wheelchair Frame

The wheelchair frame performs one major function: It holds the other components—the seat, the main wheels, and the front wheels—in their proper positions (see figure 29.4). In addition, the frame must be matched to the body size and shape of the athlete and will vary depending on the performance considerations of the sport. Typically, the most important design consideration in building a wheelchair frame is to make it as light and as rigid as possible. These objectives have been achieved predominantly through advances in the materials

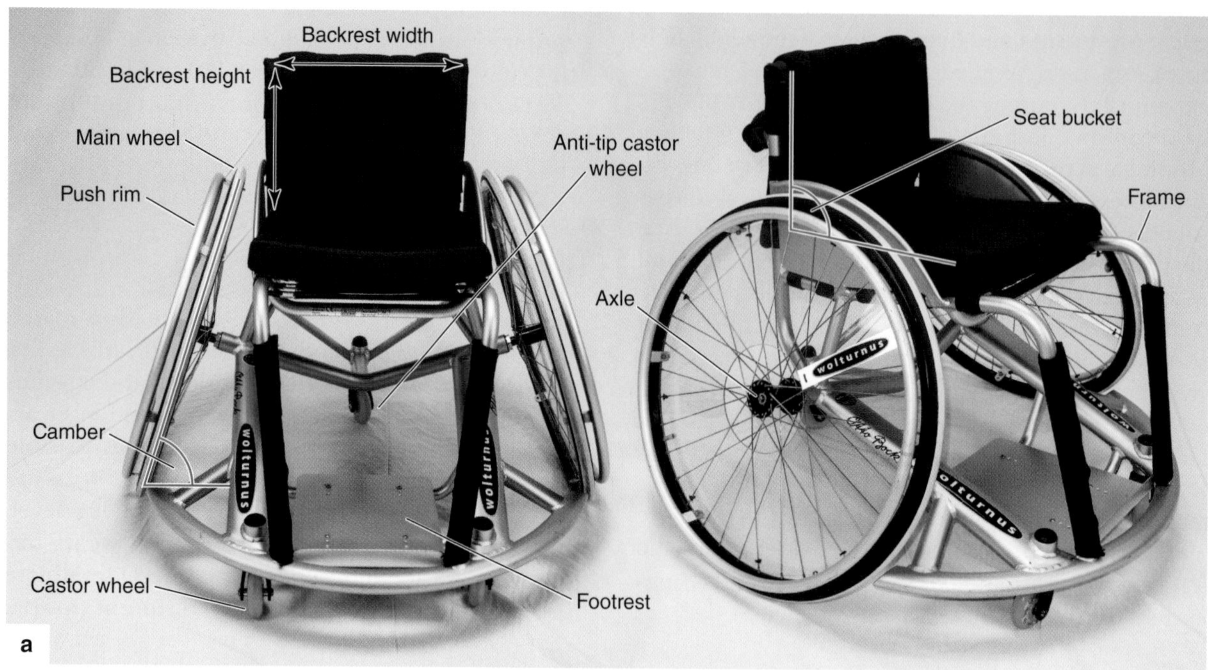

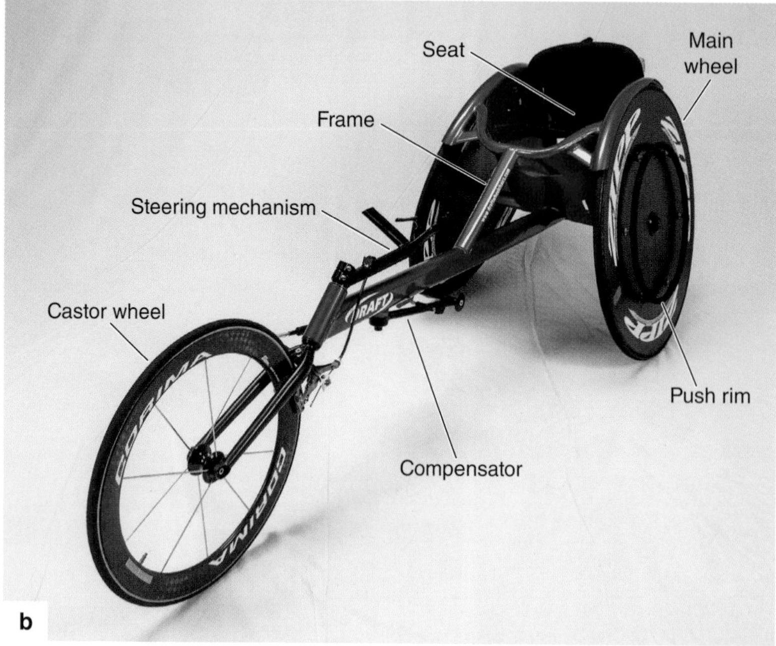

FIGURE 29.4 Schematic of *(a)* court sport (basketball) and *(b)* racing wheelchairs.
Photos courtesy of Draft Wheelchairs Ltd.

used to manufacture the chairs, which have seen a shift from steel to aluminum and titanium frames. Frames need to be lightweight so that the athlete has to propel as little weight as possible in order to minimize the strain on the upper body and improve the economy of propulsion. They also need to be rigid so that the energy the athlete applies to the wheelchair is used to drive the chair rather than to bend and deform the frame. Rigidity is also a key feature of chairs specific to wheelchair basketball and rugby in order to withstand heavy collisions with other wheelchairs.

Wheels

The rear wheels of racing wheelchairs are larger in diameter and narrower in cross section than those used in other sport chairs because of the differing demands of the activity. Unless the athlete is of very small stature, the main wheels are usually high-quality racing bicycle wheels 28 inches (71 centimeters) in size. Because additional weight in the wheels slows the athlete down twice as much as additional weight in the frame, racing wheels should be as light, strong, and rigid as possible. A smaller wheel increases rolling resistance; therefore the trend for front wheels is to use as large a wheel as the rules allow (usually around 20 inches [51 centimeters] in diameter).

For court chairs such as those used in wheelchair basketball, the size of the main wheels commonly ranges from 24 inches (61 centimeters) to 27 inches (69 centimeters), depending on the position played (Yilla et al., 1998). Wheels for court chairs have to be able to withstand rotational torque and, as mentioned earlier, contact with other wheelchairs. Therefore, some athletes in contact sports such as wheelchair basketball and quad rugby forgo lightness for additional robustness in the main wheel. This has been achieved by selecting wheels with a cross-spoked orientation or by reinforcing the wheels with spoke guards for added protection, as seen in quad rugby. The preferred castor wheels now tend to be the skateboard type available at regular hobby shops. However, the important factors associated with castor wheel selection center around the diameter of the wheel and the type of bearing within to minimize resistance and maximize maneuverability.

Number of Wheels

A wheelchair remains stable as long as the center of gravity of the wheelchair–athlete combination remains inside the wheelchair's base of support. The base of support is the area of ground marked by the points at which the wheels contact the surface. In wheelchair racing, three-wheel designs use a single castor wheel positioned at the front of the wheelchair to create a triangular base of support (figure 29.5*a*). This design minimizes rolling resistance because fewer wheels are in contact with the ground compared to other designs. However, if the center of gravity of the wheelchair–athlete combination moves farther forward (in an attempt to reduce air resistance) or laterally, athletes can encounter issues with stability. Because lateral movements are more common in the court sports, additional wheels have been introduced to improve stability. All modern wheelchairs used in wheelchair court sports contain a rear castor positioned at the back of the wheelchair to prevent athletes from tipping too far backward. In wheelchair tennis, some four-wheel designs do still exist (figure 29.5*b*); with these, the chair is equipped with a single front and rear castor wheel. However, given the need to perform sharp turns in tennis and the aforementioned issues with stability associated with a single front castor, these four-wheel designs are increasingly rare at an elite level. Alternatively, five- and six-wheel designs have become the most popular choice for court sport wheelchairs. The five-wheel design incorporates two front castors and a single rear castor wheel (figure 29.5*c*), whereas the six-wheel design features two castor wheels at the front and back of the wheelchair (figure 29.5*d*). Both of these designs offer far greater stability at the front of the wheelchair.

Main-Wheel Alignment

To allow the wheelchair to roll with the least resistance, it is critical that the main wheels point straight ahead. If the main wheels point slightly inward (toe-in) or slightly outward (toe-out), this can slow the wheelchair down significantly. Because the front wheels are essentially castors to allow turning, they are not subject to the same toe-in and toe-out problems as main wheels. They do, however, increase rolling resistance greatly when their bearings become worn.

Camber Angle

In order to allow for superior turning and ease of pushing, sport chairs are cambered, meaning the wheels are fixed at an angle so that the top of the wheel is closer to the frame and the bottom is farther away. With the wheels cambered, the hands fall naturally to the push rim to allow for maximum application of force while at the same time protecting athletes' arms from rubbing against the wheels. With court chairs, the camber also significantly enhances maneuverability. Camber can also affect

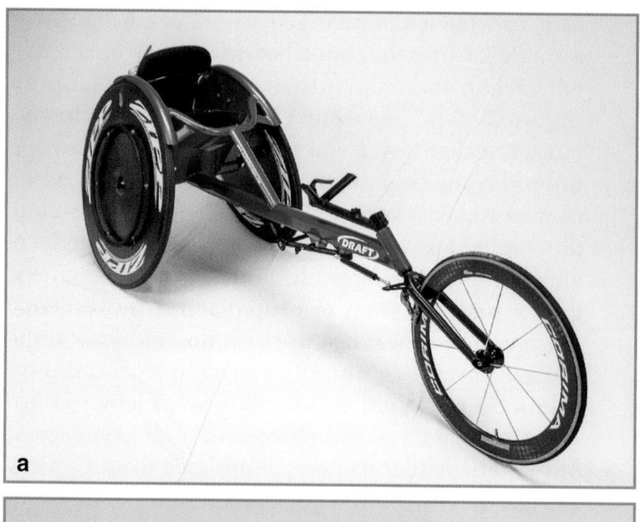

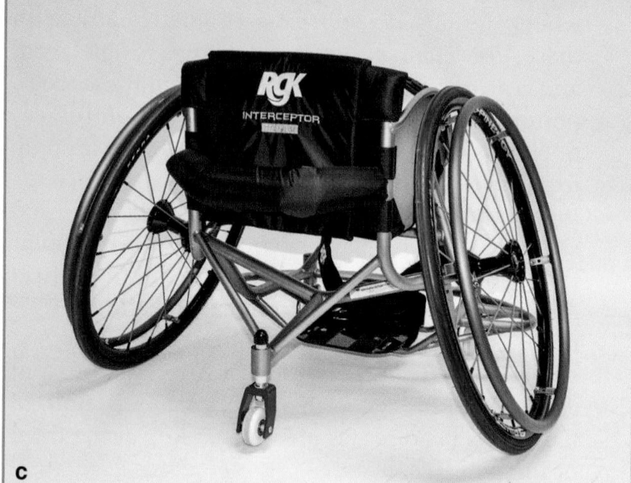

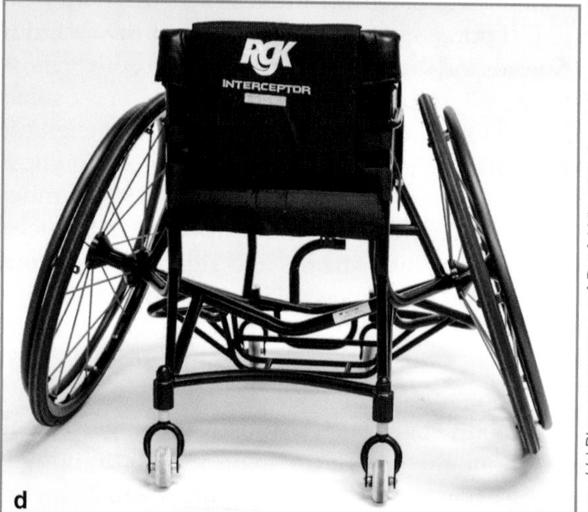

FIGURE 29.5 Examples of *(a)* three-wheel, *(b)* four-wheel, *(c)* five-wheel, and *(d)* six-wheel designs.

(a and b) Photos courtesy of Draft Wheelchairs Ltd. *(c and d)* Photos courtesy of RGK Wheelchairs.

the width of the wheelbase, which has an influence on stability and can have tactical implications in sports such as quad rugby—for example, offensive players like to remain as narrow as possible to penetrate through small gaps, whereas defensive players seek the opposite. The majority of athletes competing in court sports tend to select camber angles between 15 and 24 degrees, with 18 degrees proving the most popular.

Seat Height

All other factors being equal, the most effective seat height is a function of the athlete's trunk and arm length and of the push-rim size selected. Higgs (1983) reported that at the 1980 Paralympic Games, superior performances in racing events were recorded by athletes with lower seats. Experimental work by van der Woude and colleagues (1990) showed a relationship between the elbow angle (when the athlete was sitting upright with hands placed on top dead center of the push rim) and propulsion efficiency. Their results showed that efficiency was greatest when the elbow angle was 80 degrees and that the energy cost of sitting too high in the chair was greater than the penalty paid for sitting too low. However, performance considerations (height in basketball or the post position in quad rugby) offset some propulsion considerations and need to be taken into account when configuring a sport wheelchair. Additional sport-specific considerations for wheelchairs follow. Note, however, that there is a fundamental difference between the configurations of the racing wheelchair relative to court chairs.

Specific Considerations for Racing Wheelchairs

Specific considerations for racing wheelchairs involve the type of seat; weight distribution of the athlete in the wheelchair, which can be modified by the anterior–posterior seat position; the size of the push rims; and the use of accessories. Detailed explanations of these considerations follow.

Type of Seat

Two common seating positions are adopted in wheelchair racing: the seated position and more recently the kneeling position (figure 29.6). In the past, all athletes adopted a seated position; however, to maximize performance, modifications to the design of the seat were made to create a kneeling position whereby athletes' legs are tucked underneath them. The seated position affords the athlete greater stability because the raised knee position helps support the trunk, which is particularly important to those with limited function. However, athletes with sufficient trunk function can benefit from the kneeling position because it thrusts the body weight farther forward, so that the athlete is in an optimal position to drive the wheels forward and downward. The kneeling position also improves the aerodynamics of the wheelchair–athlete combination; because the athlete is constantly leaning forward, the surface area of the system is reduced.

Anterior–Posterior Seat Position

Little is known about the optimal anterior–posterior position of the wheelchair seat, although this position affects both stability and the effectiveness of force application to the push rim. If the athlete is too far toward the rear of the wheelchair, there is a tendency for the chair to become unstable (particularly when going uphill) and for the front wheel to lift off. A rear seat position makes it difficult for the athlete to apply force to the front of the push rim, where the most effective application of driving force can be made. Masse and colleagues (1992) identified the impact of different fore–aft positions on the biomechanics of propulsion. However, the effects on performance were minimal; hence, little evidence exists to help athletes identify their optimal anterior–posterior seating position.

Push Rims

The push rims are the point at which the athlete's energy is transmitted to the wheelchair, and as such, coupling between the athlete and the rims is critical to producing optimal performance. The three most important aspects of the push rim are diameter, thickness, and covering material.

PUSH-RIM DIAMETER The push rim acts as the gearing for the wheelchair. A small-diameter push rim acts as a high gear that produces poor acceleration but improved sprinting performance; a larger-diameter push rim of 14.5 inches (37 centimeters) can negatively affect physiological demand of racing propulsion compared to 13- to 14-inch (around 34- to 36-centimeter) rims (Costa et al., 2009). In general, stronger athletes are able

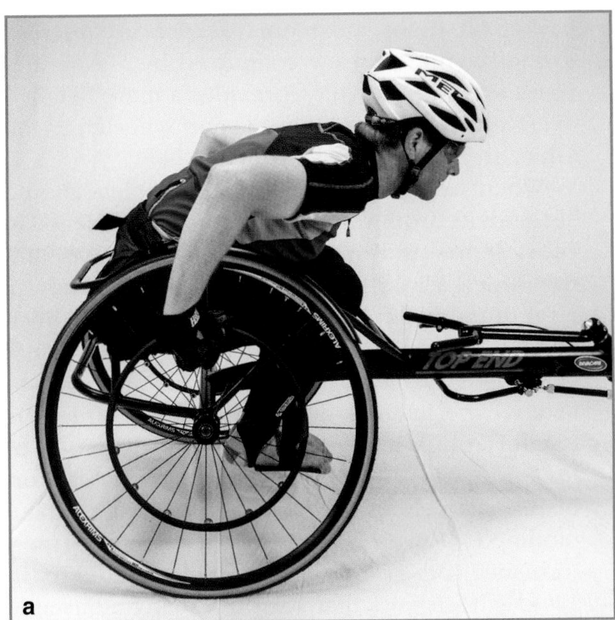

Photos courtesy of Draft Wheelchairs Ltd.

FIGURE 29.6 Racing performance system illustrating the two commonly adopted positions depending on the level of physical impairment: *(a)* seated and *(b)* kneeling.

to effectively push smaller-diameter push rims; thus the optimal push-rim diameter is a function of the size and physical characteristics of the athlete and the relative importance of acceleration and top speed. Most push rims are between 14 and 15 inches (35 and 38 centimeters) in diameter, and athletes should experiment to determine what works best for them. Paralympic rules require that there be only one push rim on each main wheel.

PUSH-RIM THICKNESS If the push rim is made of relatively thick tubing, it can be easier to grasp, which makes starts and uphill climbing easier. Alternatively, thinner tubing might encourage higher wheeling speeds because the athlete is more likely to strike the push rim rather than grasp and push it. In the absence of research studies specific to wheelchair racing, athletes determine their optimal push-rim width by trial and error.

PUSH-RIM MATERIAL The push-rim covering is of great importance because it is this material that the hand strikes during propulsion. If it is too smooth or slick, the hand will slip when power is applied. For this reason, a number of materials have been used for push-rim covers and many racers also apply adhesives to increase push-rim traction. Although the frictional grip of the push rim is important, the hand covering used by the athlete is of equal or greater importance. Most athletes wear gloves that have been sculpted to their exact requirements by the application of hundreds of layers of adhesive tape (Grey-Thompson & Thompson, 2010). This glove-and-tape combination provides protective cushioning and instant grip between the hand and the push rim. Some athletes are moving toward customized blocks, or plastic-and-rubber devices that rest on the knuckles to provide traction. Again, athletes are encouraged to experiment with materials to find the combination that meets their needs.

Accessories

There are numerous options for racing wheelchair accessories, but almost all racing wheelchairs incorporate at least a steering device, a compensator, and a computer. With downhill racing speeds reaching more than 40 miles per hour (64 kilometers per hour), a steering mechanism is necessary to help the athlete negotiate corners. The usual steering device is a small handle attached directly to the front wheel mounting that can be moved left or right to steer the wheelchair, although steering occurs only when the lever is held in place. Once released, the front wheel returns (under spring action) to a neutral, straight-ahead position. This process is called *active steering*, because turning occurs only when steering input is applied by the racer.

In addition to this active-steering mechanism, the wheelchair also incorporates a compensator, which permits small, long-term adjustments to the direction in which the chair moves and is most important in road racing. Most road races are held on public roads that are designed with a high crown along the midline, with the road sloped away on either side for drainage toward the curb. Unless propelled only in the center of the road, the wheelchair would be moving forward on a sideways-sloping surface and would tend to steer into the curb. A compensator applies a small offset to the front wheel to allow the chair to move straight ahead without the athlete needing to make constant small corrective steering adjustments. The rigidity provided by a compensator system (as opposed to rotating casters) also stabilizes the wheelchair in the event of surface irregularities.

Bicycle computers are now relatively inexpensive and are almost universally found on racing wheelchairs. These computers provide essential information on distance traveled, cadence, and top and average speeds. This feedback is essential for developing and maintaining accurate training and racing logs that enhance performance.

Specific Considerations for Court Chairs

The following general guidelines should help when selecting a wheelchair for court sports such as basketball, rugby, and tennis. Readers are referred to the scientific review conducted by Mason and coauthors (2013), which provides a more detailed overview of how modifying a sport wheelchair can affect an athlete's performance.

When selecting a wheelchair, an athlete should seek advice from someone who has experience in court sports and understands function level and the athlete's role on the court. There are now a large number of options in performance wheelchair designs, many of which are experimental (Bundon et al., 2017); however, it is advisable to avoid experimental designs until the athlete is comfortable with the performance demands of the sport. The athlete's first sport-specific performance chair should be adjustable so that it can be modified. However, because of weight and performance considerations, the athlete should try to avoid wheelchairs that have too many adjustable mechanisms, which tend to add weight to the chair. Adjustment mechanisms can also increase internal friction (greater resistance) and cannot provide the same rigidity as a weld, resulting in decreased life expectancy of adjustable chairs. Adjustments also require a level of expertise for the frame alignment to remain true. When purchasing any further sport chairs, it is advisable that athletes make as few modifications as possible—when making multiple changes at once it becomes difficult to isolate which modifications are affecting performance (either positively or negatively).

Combining the Athlete and the Wheelchair

The process of combining the athlete and the wheelchair into a unified system varies depending on the specific sport; however, some general principles can be applied. Additionally, there are some specific performance considerations for racing wheelchairs and court chairs.

Fitting the Wheelchair to the Athlete

Proper fitting of the wheelchair to the athlete is critical for high levels of athletic performance. Most manufacturers provide retail experts who are experienced in measuring athletes for performance wheelchairs.

In fitting the frame, the two most critical considerations are the dimensions of the seat (width, length, and backrest height) and the position of the seat in relation to the main wheels. Both of these considerations ensure that the athlete fits perfectly in an optimal position to apply force and maneuver the wheelchair. Refer to the Application Example sidebar for a list of considerations to keep in mind while helping athletes find the chair that is best for them.

System Considerations for Racing Wheelchairs

A number of system considerations apply to racing wheelchairs. The following section identifies **propulsion techniques** and how to overcome negative forces as important considerations in developing an athlete's wheelchair racing system.

Propulsion Techniques in Track and Road Racing

Coupled with the evolution of the racing wheelchair has been the development of ever more efficient propulsion techniques. A six-phase technique (see figure 29.7) is most frequently used, although not all athletes use each phase with the same degree of effectiveness. An analysis by O'Connor and colleagues (1998) led the authors to conclude

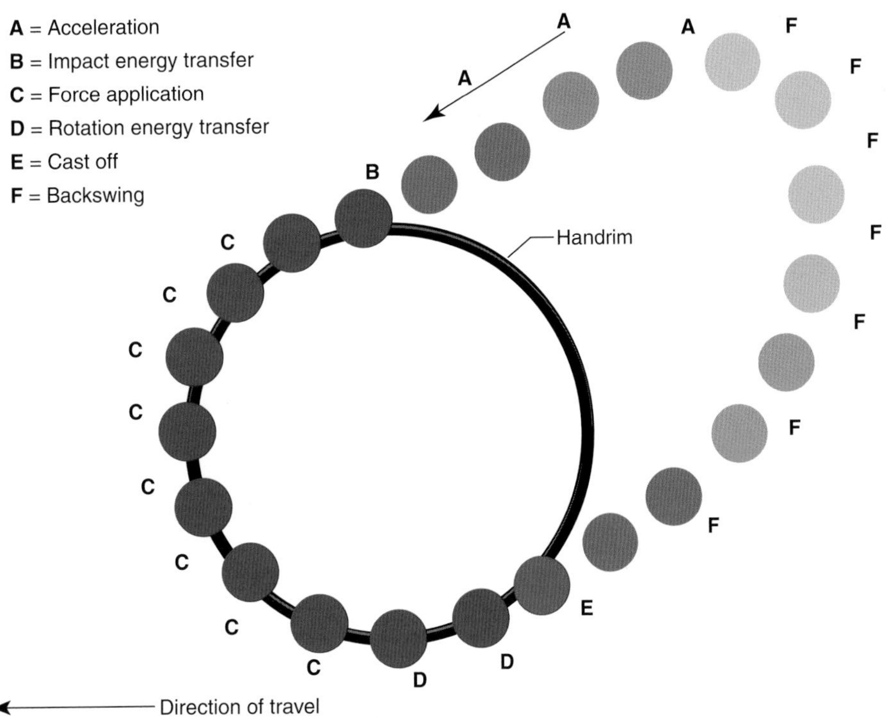

FIGURE 29.7 Six-phase propulsion cycle.

Application Example

Helping a Wheelchair Athlete Find the Right Sport and Chair

SETTING

A community-based junior wheelchair sport program

STUDENT

A 16-year-old junior wheelchair basketball player with a spinal cord injury needs recommendations to refine his individualized transition program to incorporate adult wheelchair sports. The player is tall, has played the center and forward positions, and wishes to purchase his own wheelchair.

ISSUE

What considerations should be taken into account when making recommendations to this athlete?

APPLICATION

Considerations for this athlete center on equipment, physical fitness, and individual skills.

Equipment Considerations

- Athlete's height
- Athlete's preference to play a certain position
- Athlete's physical impairment, sport classification level, and trunk stability when seated
- Adjustability for height and point of balance (being able to maximize the seat height to about 21 inches [53 centimeters] for the center and forward positions)
- System considerations, such as strapping and mobility in the wheelchair
- Reputable manufacturer

Individual Physical Fitness

- Strength training program that targets the upper body muscles in paired groups (e.g., biceps and triceps)
- Cardiorespiratory conditioning program that uses an arm crank ergometer or, preferably, a training roller

Individual Skills Targeted

- Wheelchair mobility skills both with and without the basketball
- Shooting skills both stationary and moving
- Passing skills both stationary and moving
- Studying the sophisticated strategies involved in the adult game

that there is a need for coaches to become more knowledgeable concerning appropriate wheelchair propulsion techniques.

BASIC STROKE The propulsion cycle starts with the hands drawn up as far above and behind the push rim as possible given the seating position and flexibility of the athlete. The hands are then accelerated as rapidly and forcefully as possible (acceleration phase) until they strike the push rim (see point A on figure 29.7). The moment of contact is the impact energy transfer phase (point B on figure 29.7), during which the kinetic energy stored in the fast-moving hand is transferred to the slower-moving push rim. With the hand in contact with the push rim, there is a force application, or push, phase (point C on figure 29.7), which continues until the hands reach almost to the bottom of the push rim. During the force application phase, most of the propulsion comes from the muscles acting around the elbow and shoulder.

As the hands reach the bottom of the push rim, the powerful muscles of the forearm are used to pronate the hand, which allows the thumb to be used to give a last, powerful flick to the push rim. This last flicking action is reversed by a few athletes who use supination in the rotational energy transfer phase (point D on figure 29.7) to flick the push rim with the fingers rather than the thumb; research indicates that this type of backhand technique may be more efficient in endurance races (Chow et al., 2001).

Immediately following the rotational energy transfer, the hands leave the push rim during the castoff phase (see point E on figure 29.7). Here it is important that the hand be moving faster than the push rim as it pulls away, because a slower hand will act as a brake on the wheelchair. Often the athlete will use the pronation or supination of the rotational energy transfer phase to accelerate the hands and arms and thus allow them to be carried up and back under ballistic motion, called the *backswing phase* (point F on figure 29.7). This phase is used to get the hands far enough away from the push rim to allow them to accelerate forward to strike the push rim at high speed at the start of the next stroke. Goosey-Tolfrey and colleagues (2000) reported that no single identifiable stroke frequency could be recommended as best for wheelchair racing, but the athlete's own freely chosen frequency was the most economical in laboratory conditions.

This basic propulsion stroke is modified by the terrain over which the athlete is wheeling, by the tactics of the race, and by the athlete's level of disability. On uphill parts of a course, the athlete shortens the backswing and acceleration phases so as to minimize the time during which force is not applied to the push rim and during which the chair could roll backward. Tactically, the athlete is either wheeling at constant speed or is making an attack and needs to accelerate. The basic stroke described previously is used at steady speed; during bursts of acceleration, the major change in stroke takes place during the backswing. At steady speeds, the backswing is a relatively relaxed ballistic movement in which the velocity at castoff is used to raise the hand to its highest and most rearward position. This relaxed backswing is efficient and allows a brief moment of rest during each stroke. During acceleration, however, the major change in stroke dynamics is to increase the number of strokes from approximately 80 per minute to more than 120 per minute. This is achieved by a rapid reduction in the time taken for a more restricted backswing.

RACE START The stroke is modified during the start of a race. Because the wheelchair is stationary, the hands should grip the push rim (rather than striking it), and for the first few strokes the arc of pushing will be more restricted with as rapid a recovery as possible. Some athletes attempt to make longer, more forceful pushes to get the wheels going, whereas others make shorter, sharper pushes to get the hands moving fast as early as possible; the approach is dependent on the athlete's preference.

Retarding Forces and Overcoming Them

While the athlete provides the energy to drive the wheelchair forward, the twin retarding forces of rolling resistance and aerodynamic drag act to slow it down. When propulsive forces are greater than resistance, the wheelchair accelerates, and when the retarding forces are greater, the chair is slowed. Obviously, reductions in rolling resistance and aerodynamic drag translate directly into higher wheeling speeds and improved athletic performance.

ROLLING RESISTANCE On a hard, smooth surface, the majority of the rolling resistance of the wheel occurs at the point where the tire is in contact with the ground. As the tire rotates, each part is compressed as it passes under the hub and is in contact with the surface; then it rebounds as it begins to rise again and contact with the surface is broken. Not all the energy used to compress the tire is recovered on the rebound, and the energy loss (called *hysteresis*) is the major determinant of rolling resistance.

Rolling resistance of racing wheelchairs is also affected by the camber angle of the main wheel, which increases with camber (Faupin et al., 2004; Mason et al., 2011) and wheel alignment, referred to as toe-in or toe-out. Because wheels that are not toed correctly dramatically increase the rolling resistance of a wheelchair, athletes should check and adjust alignment before every important race.

AERODYNAMIC DRAG The problem of aerodynamic drag of racing wheelchairs and athletes is unique because of the relatively low speeds at which events take place. Races on the track (10,000 meters) take place at average speeds between 6.84 and 8.40 meters per second (women and men, respectively). Although the race times of wheelchairs have dramatically improved over the last decade, the times are still considerably slower than the speeds found in cycling. This creates special low-speed aerodynamic conditions.

Aerodynamic drag is caused by two separate but interrelated forces called **surface drag** and **form drag**. Surface drag is caused by the adhesion of air molecules to the surface of an object passing through it, and it is very powerful at low speeds. Form drag, on the other hand, is caused by the difference in air pressure between the front and the back of an object, which in turn is created by the swirls and eddy currents formed as the wheelchair and athlete pass through the air. For wheelchair racers, the problem is that smooth surfaces increase surface drag while decreasing form drag. It is therefore important to reduce both surface and form drag by minimizing the drag-producing areas of the wheelchair and the athlete's clothing.

DRAFTING Because aerodynamic drag represents approximately 40 percent of the force acting to slow down a wheelchair racer, methods of minimizing drag can pay considerable dividends. The single most effective way in which drag can be reduced is the process of drafting. Drafting occurs when one wheelchair follows closely behind another wheelchair that acts as a wind deflector. At the end of long races, the energy saved by drafting can be a critical determinant of race outcome. Frequently teams work together, taking turns at both leading and drafting so that overall performance will be increased.

System Considerations for Court Wheelchairs

This section does not include information on propulsion techniques in court sports. Because of the wide variability in the propulsion techniques in court sports as compared to those in racing, there is less research in this area; however, Vanlandewijck and colleagues (2001) conducted a review of propulsion biomechanics that included not only wheelchair racing but also basketball and rugby. For those interested in increasing wheelchair sport performance, it is recommended reading.

As mentioned previously, the two fundamental features of a sport wheelchair are the dimensions of the seat and its positioning in relation to the wheels, although these features may differ in relation to racing wheelchairs. In wheelchair racing, the key performance indicator is speed or endurance (or both) in a predominantly linear direction; therefore, wheelchair racers require a perfectly fitting seat so that no energy is lost during propulsion. However, in court sports, maneuverability is also a key area of performance, which requires a seat customized to the athlete's personal anthropometrics to facilitate agility. If a seat is too wide, the athlete can slide around in the chair, which equates to a loss of energy during turning; the body has to then catch up before being in a position whereby force can be applied to the wheels. When the seat is the correct width, the wheelchair should be able to respond more effectively to the athlete. This enables those athletes with sufficient trunk function to be able to maneuver their chair without necessarily having to touch their wheels. This feature of performance can also be facilitated by strapping around the knees or lap, which further secures the athlete to the chair, making movements such as tilting in wheelchair basketball possible.

The backrest is another dimension of the seat that warrants consideration. The backrest is essentially designed to improve the athlete's stability, which can be impaired if the backrest is too low for the functional capacity of the athlete. Alternatively, a backrest that is too high can restrict movement when the athlete is trying to move backward to reach or hit a ball. Strapping around the trunk can be applied to facilitate stability, although similar precautions must be taken to ensure that strapping is used only if the functional capacity of the athlete requires it. If too much strapping is applied too tightly, the athlete's ability to move can be unnecessarily sacrificed at the expense of stability.

To further facilitate the fitting of the athlete to the sport wheelchair and subsequently maximize maneuverability performance, molded seats have recently emerged in wheelchair tennis and wheelchair basketball (figure 29.8). Because a molded seat will mimic the exact dimensions of each individual athlete, previous limitations associated with a conventional seat, such as energy loss during propulsion and impaired maneuverability, should be eradicated.

Once the seat is successfully designed for the specific athlete, the next thing to consider is where the seat fits in relation to the main wheels in both a horizontal (anterior–posterior) and vertical position (see figure 29.9).

Anterior–Posterior Seat Position

Horizontal positioning of the main wheels affects the mobility of the chair. The farther forward the main wheel from a hypothesized neutral position (see figure 29.9*a*, position A), the more maneuverable the chair (see figure 29.9*a*, position B). Unfortunately, the farther forward the main wheel relative to the center of gravity, the more likely it is that the chair will tilt up. Although the introduction of the anti-tip castor wheel prevents the athlete from falling backward, it does place a large percentage of body mass over the rear castors. Consequently, athletes need to reposition their body weight forward in order

Photos courtesy of Dr. John Lenton.

FIGURE 29.8 Example of *(a)* a conventional sport wheelchair seat and *(b)* a molded seat to facilitate maneuverability performance.

to drive the wheels forward, which may be limited by trunk function. However, this is a position that many low-point quad rugby players are forced to adopt because they do not have the triceps function or stability to sit above the wheel and drive it down. Alternatively, they may choose to sit farther back so that they can make the most of their biceps function and "pull" the wheel up and forward.

Vertical Seat Position

Vertical positioning of the main wheel affects the height at which the athlete sits and the system's center of gravity, which fundamentally affects the handling properties of the chair. The lower the athlete sits relative to a hypothetical neutral position (figure 29.9*b*, position A), the more maneuverable the wheelchair. This has been verified in a recent

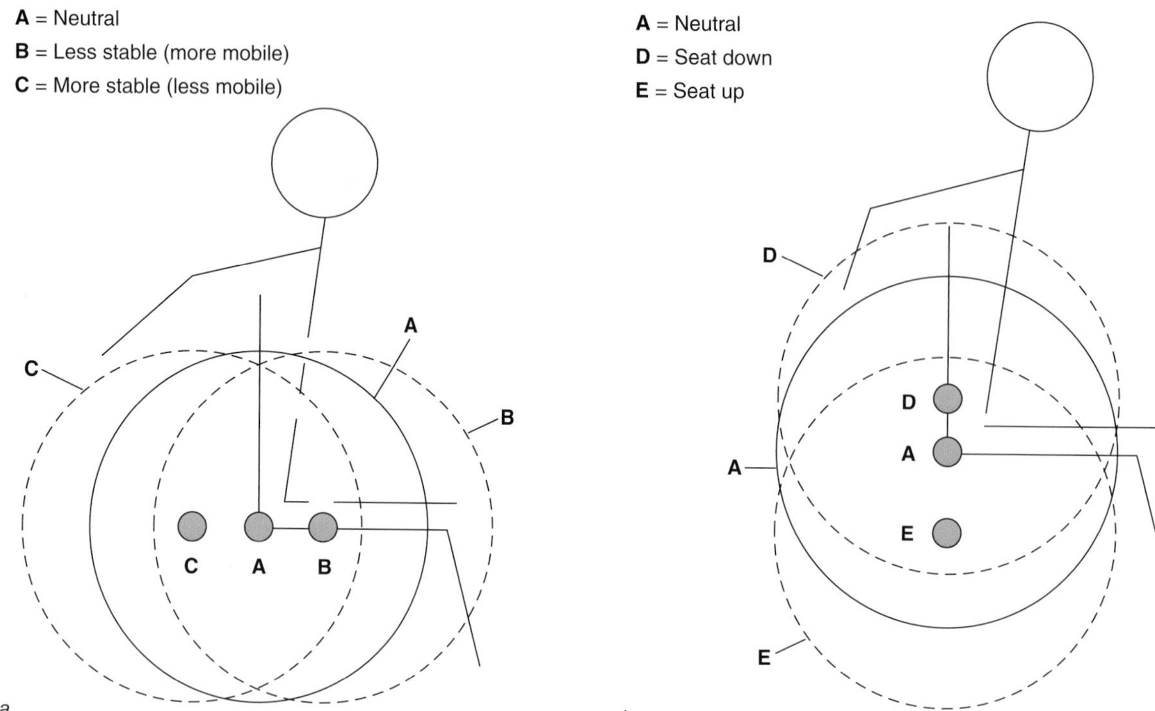

FIGURE 29.9 *(a)* Anterior–posterior and *(b)* vertical main-wheel adjustments.

study with wheelchair basketball players, whereby a lower seat position (figure 29.9*b*, position D) improved rotational aspects of performance and a higher seat position (figure 29.9*b*, position E) impaired rotational and linear performance compared to a neutral seat position (van der Slikke et al., 2018). Therefore, all other things being equal, the athlete should sit as low as possible. However, performance considerations place a premium on height in all sports. Shooting a basketball, receiving a rugby pass, and making a tennis serve are all made easier when the athlete sits higher in the chair. Given the advantages associated with sitting high, athletes often forsake the optimal position for pushing the wheelchair, putting their mobility performance at risk. As the height of the seat increases, the athlete effectively moves farther away from the wheels. In order to access enough of the wheels to effectively apply force, the athlete (depending on trunk function) will have to lean forward. Many have countered this by selecting a larger wheel size to make the wheels more accessible in a higher seat position; however, this can potentially introduce alternative detriments to performance, with a larger wheel thought to impair acceleration and maneuverability performance. Mason and colleagues (2012a, 2012b) have provided a more in-depth evaluation of the effects of wheel size on mobility performance in wheelchair basketball players.

In summary, when enhancing wheelchair sport performance on the court, athletes should identify the functional aspects of the game and their roles or positions coupled with their strengths and weaknesses. This will depend in part on the disability level of the athlete. After identifying these factors, athletes should select the wheelchair setup that will best address them, bearing in mind that the positioning of the main wheel will fundamentally affect the performance characteristics of the chair. After the athlete has identified the appropriate wheelchair setup, consideration needs to be given to combining the athlete and the wheelchair into a performance system through the use of appropriate strapping techniques. With respect to wheelchair configuration, further research is clearly required; however, applied case studies with individual athletes are recommended given the differences in on-court requirements and impairment types and severities among athletes. Such an approach has recently been adopted by Haydon and colleagues (2019) with quad rugby players.

Skill Development

Sport-specific skills are critical to the elite athlete's program. Common to skills in court sports are acceleration, speed (including power and strength), and maneuverability with both the wheelchair and the target object (ball, racket, etc.). Goosey-Tolfrey (2010b) reports other sport-specific skills as described by key sport coaches. Skills tests have been developed for wheelchair basketball, quad rugby, and tennis (Newbery et al., 2010; Yilla & Sherrill, 1998), and field-based fitness testing is described in detail in the review article by Goosey-Tolfrey and Leicht (2013). Task analysis of skill performance is also suggested by Davis (2002, 2011).

Instructional materials that focus on the skills and strategies involved in many wheelchair sports are also available (Goosey-Tolfrey, 2010b). Again, the systems approach should be incorporated, with athletes practicing their skills in their sport-specific wheelchair and strapping.

Future Directions

Technological advances and improved training techniques have changed the look of wheelchair sport dramatically and opened up many opportunities. Professionalism is now part of many wheelchair sports, with elite athletes traveling around the world to compete, and there is reason to believe this trend will become even more prevalent.

Whenever possible, we need to encourage students and practitioners to develop valid, objective, and reliable skill and fitness assessments for wheelchair athletes. This will help with talent identification and also with the evaluation of physical conditioning programs. The demands of each sport and the needs of its athletes must be systematically assessed, and suitable equipment must then be designed and built.

Elite wheelchair athletics combines the athlete and the wheelchair into a sport-specific, functional performance system, with even greater equipment and technique specialization anticipated as the wave of the future. That said, while focusing on enhancing wheelchair performance we must not neglect injury management and must work to minimize risk of injury through innovative equipment design and safe training methods.

Summary

This chapter has dealt with information on enhancing performance in wheelchair sport. It discussed the appropriate selection of a sport by the athlete, the athlete's individual training regimen, and sports-related medical issues faced by athletes with disabilities. Basic types of sport wheelchairs were identified (racing and court), as were specific performance considerations that influence selection of the appropriate chair. The chapter also examined the combination of the athlete and the chair to create a performance system. Racing performance considerations (stroke analysis, starting techniques, overcoming rolling resistance, and drafting) were separated from court performance considerations (adjusting the chair and individual skill development).

References

Ambrosio, F., Boninger, M.L., Souza, A.L., Fitzgerald, S.G., Koontz, A.M., & Cooper, R.A. (2005). Biomechanics and strength of manual wheelchair users. *Journal of Spinal Cord Medicine, 28*(5), 407-414. https://doi.org/10.1080/10790268.2005.11753840

Arnet, U., van Drongelen, S., Scheel-Sailer, A., van der Woude, L.H., & Veeger, D.H. (2012). Shoulder load during synchronous handcycling and handrim wheelchair propulsion in persons with paraplegia. *Journal of Rehabilitation Medicine, 44*(3), 222-228. https://doi.org/10.2340/16501977-0929

Blauwet, C.A., Benjamin-Laing, H., Stomphorst, J., Van der Vliet, P., Pit-Grosheide, P., & Willick, S.E. (2013). Testing for boosting at the Paralympic games: Policies, results and future directions. *British Journal of Sports Medicine, 47*(13), 832-837. https://doi.org/10.1136/bjsports-2012-092103

Borg, G. (1998). *Borg's perceived exertion and pain scales.* Human Kinetics.

Bundon, A., Mason, B., & Goosey-Tolfrey, V.L. (2017). Expert users' perceptions of racing wheelchair design and set up: The knowns, unknowns and next steps. *Adapted Physical Activity Quarterly, 34*(2), 141-161. https://doi.org/10.1123/apaq.2016-0073

Chow, J.W., Millikan, T.A., Carlton, L.G., Morse, M.I., & Chae, W.S. (2001). Biomechanical comparison of two racing wheelchair propulsion techniques. *Medicine and Science in Sports and Exercise, 33*(3), 476-484. https://doi.org/10.1097/00005768-200103000-00022

Costa, G.B., Rubio, M.P., Belloch, S.L., & Soriano, P.P. (2009). Case study: Effect of handrim diameter on performance in a Paralympic wheelchair athlete. *Adapted Physical Activity Quarterly, 26,* 352-363. https://doi.org/10.1123/apaq.26.4.352

Davis, R. (2002). *Inclusion through sport.* Human Kinetics.

Davis, R.W. (2011). *Teaching disability sport: A guide for physical educators* (2nd ed.). Human Kinetics.

Fagher, K., & Lexell, J. (2014). Sports-related injuries in athletes with disabilities. *Scandinavian Journal of*

Medicine and Science in Sports, 24, e320-e331. https://doi.org/10.1111/sms.12175

Faupin, A., Campillo, P., Weissland, T., Gorce, P., & Thevenon, A. (2004). The effects of rear-wheel camber on the mechanical parameters produced during the wheelchair sprinting of handibasketball athletes. *Journal of Rehabilitation Research and Development, 41,* 421-428. https://doi.org/10.1682/jrrd.2003.04.0050

Goosey-Tolfrey, V.L. (2010a). Supporting the Paralympic athlete: Focus on wheeled sports. *Disability and Rehabilitation, 32*(26), 2237-2243. https://doi.org/10.3109/09638288.2010.491577

Goosey-Tolfrey, V.L. (Ed.). (2010b). *Wheelchair sport.* Human Kinetics.

Goosey-Tolfrey, V.L., Campbell, I.G., & Fowler, N.E. (2000). Effect of push frequency on the economy of wheelchair racers. *Medicine and Science in Sports and Exercise, 32*(1), 174-181. https://doi.org/10.1097/00005768-200001000-00026

Goosey-Tolfrey, V.L., & Leicht, C. (2013). Field based testing of wheelchair athletes. *Sports Medicine, 43*(2), 77-91. https://doi.org/10.1007/s40279-012-0009-6

Goosey-Tolfrey, V.L., Mason, B., & Burkett, B. (2013). How athletes excel. In V. Girginov (Ed.), *Handbook of the 2012 London Olympic and Paralympic Games* (vol. 2, pp. 169-183). Routledge.

Goosey-Tolfrey, V.L., Paulson, T., & Graham, T. (2015). Practical considerations for fluid replacement for athletes with a spinal cord injury. In F. Meyer, Z. Szygula, and B. Wilk (Eds.), *Fluid balance, hydration, and athletic performance* (pp. 333-355). Taylor and Francis.

Goosey-Tolfrey, V.L., Vegter, R.J.K., Mason, B.S., Paulson, T.A.W., Lenton, J.P., van der Scheer, J.W., & van der Woude, L.H.V. (2018). Sprint performance and propulsion asymmetries on an ergometer in trained high- and low-point wheelchair rugby players. *Scandinavian Journal of Medicine and Science in Sports, 28*(5), 1586-1593. https://doi.org/10.1111/sms.13056

Grey-Thompson, T., & Thompson, I. (2010). Wheelchair racing. In V. Goosey-Tolfrey (Ed.), *Wheelchair sport* (pp. 133-150). Human Kinetics.

Griggs, K., Havenith, G., Price, M., Mason, B.S., & Goosey-Tolfrey, V.L. (2017). Thermoregulatory responses during competitive wheelchair rugby match play. *International Journal of Sports Medicine, 38,* 177-183. https://doi.org/10.1055/s-0042-121263

Griggs, K., Price, M.J., & Goosey-Tolfrey, V.L. (2015). Cooling athletes with a spinal cord injury. *Sports Medicine, 45*(1), 9-21. https://doi.org/10.1007/s40279-014-0241-3

Haydon, D.S., Pinder, R.A., Grimshaw, P.N., & Robertson, S.P. (2019). Wheelchair rugby chair configurations: An individual, robust design approach. *Sports Biomechanics*, Sept 19. [Epub ahead of print]. https://doi.org/10.1080/14763141.2019.1649451

Higgs, C. (1983). An analysis of racing wheelchairs used at the 1980 Olympic Games for the disabled. *Research Quarterly for Exercise and Sport, 54*(3), 229-233. https://doi.org/10.1080/02701367.1983.10605300

Jacobs, P.L., & Nash, M.S. (2004). Exercise recommendations for individuals with spinal cord injury. *Sports Medicine, 34*(11), 727-751. https://doi.org/10.2165/00007256-200434110-00003

Krassioukov, A., & West, C. (2014). The role of autonomic function on sport performance in athletes with spinal cord injury. *Physical Medicine & Rehabilitation, 6*(8 Suppl), S58-S65. https://doi.org/10.1016/j.pmrj.2014.05.023

Mason, B., van der Woude, L., de Groot, S., & Goosey-Tolfrey, V. (2011). Effects of camber on the ergonomics of propulsion in wheelchair athletes. *Medicine and Science in Sports and Exercise, 43*(2), 319-326. https://doi.org/10.1249/MSS.0b013e3181edf973

Mason, B.S., van der Woude, L.H.V., & Goosey-Tolfrey, V.L. (2013). The ergonomics of wheelchair configuration for optimal performance in the wheelchair court sports. *Sports Medicine, 43,* 23-38. https://doi.org/10.1007/s40279-012-0005-x

Mason, B.S., van der Woude, L.H.V., Lenton, J.P., & Goosey-Tolfrey, V.L. (2012a). The effect of wheel size on mobility performance in wheelchair athletes. *International Journal of Sports Medicine, 33*(10), 807-812. https://doi.org/10.1055/s-0032-1311591

Mason, B.S., van der Woude, L.H.V., Tolfrey, K., Lenton, J.P., & Goosey-Tolfrey, V.L. (2012b). Effects of wheel and hand-rim size on submaximal propulsion in wheelchair athletes. *Medicine and Science in Sports and Exercise, 44*(1), 126-134. https://doi.org/10.1249/MSS.0b013e31822a2df0

Masse, L.C., Lamontagne, M., & O'Riain, M.D. (1992). Biomechanical analysis of wheelchair propulsion for various seating positions. *Journal of Rehabilitation Research and Development, 29,* 12-28. https://doi.org/10.1682/jrrd.1992.07.0012

Newbery, D., Richards, G., Trill, S., & Whait, M. (2010). Wheelchair tennis. In V. Goosey-Tolfrey (Ed.), *Wheelchair sport* (pp. 167-186). Human Kinetics.

O'Connor, T.J., Robertson, R.N., & Cooper, R.A. (1998). Three-dimensional kinematic analysis and physiological assessment of racing wheelchair propulsion. *Adapted Physical Activity Quarterly, 15*(1), 1-14. https://doi.org/10.1123/ijspp.20140203

Paulson, T., Bishop, N., Eston, R., & Goosey-Tolfrey, V.L. (2013). Differentiated perceived exertion and wheelchair exercise in novice able-bodied users. *Archives of Physical Medicine and Rehabilitation, 94*(11), 2269-2276. https://doi.org/10.1016/j.apmr.2013.03.018

Paulson, T.A., & Goosey-Tolfrey, V.L. (2016). Current perspectives on profiling and enhancing wheelchair court sport performance. *International Journal of Sports Physiology and Performance, 12*(3), 275-286. https://doi.org/10.1123/ijspp.2016-0231

Rhodes, J.M., Mason, B.S., Perrat, B., Smith, M.J., Malone, L.A., & Goosey-Tolfrey, V.L. (2015). Activity profiles in elite wheelchair rugby players during competition. *International Journal of Sports Physiology and Performance, 10,* 318-324. https://doi.org/10.1123/ijspp.2014-0203

Sarro, K.J., Misuta, M.S., Burkett, B., Malone, L.A., & Barros, R.M.L. (2010). Tracking of wheelchair rugby players in the 2008 demolition derby final. *Journal of Sports Sciences, 28,* 193-200. https://doi.org/10.1080/02640410903428541

Schmid, A., Schmidt-Trucksaess, A., Huonker, M., Koenig, D., Eisenbarth, I., Sauerwein, H., Brunner, C., Storch, M.J., Lehmann, M., & Keul, J. (2001). Catecholamines response of high performance wheelchair athletes at rest and during exercise with autonomic dysreflexia. *International Journal of Sports Medicine, 22,* 2-7. https://doi.org/10.1055/s-2001-11330

Sindall, P., Whytock, K., Lenton, J.P., Tolfrey, K., Oyster, M., Cooper, R.A., & Goosey-Tolfrey, V.L. (2013). Criterion validity and accuracy of global positioning satellite and data logging devices for wheelchair tennis court movement. *Journal of Spinal Cord Medicine, 36*(4), 383-393. https://doi.org/10.1179/2045772312Y.0000000068

Tweedy, S., & Diaper, N. (2010). Introduction to wheelchair sport. In V. Goosey-Tolfrey (Ed.), *Wheelchair sport* (pp. 3-28). Human Kinetics.

van der Slikke, R.M.A., de Witte, A.M.H., Berger, M.A.M., Bregman, D.J.J., & Veeger, H.E.J. (2018). Wheelchair mobility performance enhancement by changing wheelchair properties: What is the effect of grip, seat height and mass? *International Journal of Sports Physiology and Performance, 13,* 1050-1058. https://doi.org/10.1123/ijspp.2017-0641

van der Woude, L.H.V., Bouten, C., Veeger, H.E.J., & Gwinn, T. (2002). Aerobic work capacity in elite wheelchair athletes: A cross-sectional analysis. *American Journal of Physical Medicine and Rehabilitation, 81*(4), 261-271. https://doi.org/10.1097/00002060-200204000-00004

van der Woude, L.H.V., Veeger, H.E.J., & Rozendal, R.H. (1990). Seat height in hand rim wheelchair propulsion: A follow up study. *Journal of Rehabilitation Science, 3,* 79-83.

Vanlandewijck, Y., Theisen, D., & Daly, D. (2001). Wheelchair propulsion biomechanics: Implications for wheelchair sports. *Sports Medicine, 31*(5), 339-367. https://doi.org/10.2165/00007256-200131050-00005

Willick, S.E., Webborn, N., Emery, C., Blauwet, C.A., Pit-Grosheide, P., Stomphorst, J., Van de Vliet, P., Patino Marques, N.A., Martinez-Ferrer, J.O., Jordaan, E., Derman, W., & Schwellnus, M. (2013). The epidemiology of injuries at the London 2012 Paralympic Games. *British Journal of Sports Medicine, 47*(7), 426-432. https://doi.org/10.1136/bjsports-2013-092374

Yilla, A.B., La Bar, R.H., & Dangelmaier, B.S. (1998). Setting up a wheelchair for basketball. *Sports 'N Spokes, 24*(2), 63-65.

Yilla, A.B., & Sherrill, C. (1998). Validating the Beck Battery of quad rugby skill tests. *Adapted Physical Activity Quarterly, 15*(2), 155-167.

Print Resources

Davis, R.W. (2011). *Teaching disability sport: A guide for physical educators* (2nd ed.). Human Kinetics.

This book identifies methodologies for integrating a variety of disability sports, including wheelchair basketball and tennis, into the physical education curriculum. It includes descriptions of the skills to be taught and modification strategies.

Goosey-Tolfrey, V.L. (Ed.). (2010). *Wheelchair sport.* Human Kinetics.

This book provides fundamental and practical information about wheelchair sports. The first part provides a general overview of and details about classification; psychological, mechanical, biomechanical, and physiological factors; strength and conditioning; nutrition and body composition; and the travel concerns that athletes may experience when participating in wheelchair sport. The second part comprises sport-specific information (background, tactics, and training drills and advice) on the sports of wheelchair basketball, racing, rugby, tennis, and handcycling.

Video Resources

Illinois Wheelchair Basketball Instructional Series [3-DVD set]. Wheelchair Basketball Office, University of Illinois, 1207 South Oak St., Champaign, IL 61820.

The DVD teaches the University of Illinois wheelchair basketball system from individual skills up to and including team offense, team defense, and transition.

Shapiro, D.A. (2005). *Murderball* [DVD]. Thinkfilm.

This Oscar-nominated documentary provides a powerful insight into the lives of wheelchair rugby players and the competitive environment that drives them.

Online Resources

International Paralympic Committee (IPC): www.paralympic.org

This is the home of the official governing body of the Paralympic Games. It includes extensive resources regarding rules, eligibility, and classification for international competition.

International Tennis Federation (ITF): www.itftennis.com/wheelchair/home.aspx

This is the wheelchair tennis site of the ITF. It provides information, including schedules and results, from the world of wheelchair tennis. There are a number of positive images of well-known tennis celebrities interacting with wheelchair tennis athletes and beginners.

International Wheelchair Basketball Federation (IWBF): www.iwbf.org

This site is the home of International Wheelchair Basketball.

International Wheelchair Rugby Federation (IWRF): www.iwrf.com

The official site of the international governing body of wheelchair rugby includes news, events, sport information, video, photos, downloads, and more.

Wheelchair & Ambulatory Sports, USA (WASUSA): www.wasusa.org

This is the home of the official governing body for wheelchair sport in general, and racing in particular, in the United States. The site includes extensive resources regarding rules, eligibility, and classification for competition in the United States.

The Peter Harrison Centre for Disability Sport, Loughborough University: www.lboro.ac.uk/research/phc/

This is the home of an internationally recognized research group in the United Kingdom specializing in research that aims to optimize wheelchair performance. The site includes extensive resources regarding wheelchair setup, training guidance in the form of infographics and fact sheets, and more.

Appendix A

WWW Definitions Associated With the Individuals With Disabilities Education Act (IDEA)

Several definitions are associated with infants, toddlers, and children with disabilities. To a great extent, the definitions used in this book are based on those from IDEA. Those definitions are summarized here.

Infant or Toddler With a Disability

The term "infant or toddler with a disability" means an individual under three years of age who needs early intervention services because the individual

1. is experiencing developmental delays, as measured by appropriate diagnostic instruments and procedures in one or more of the areas of cognitive development, physical development, communication development, social or emotional development, and adaptive development; or
2. has a diagnosed physical or mental condition that has a high probability of resulting in developmental delay; and
3. may also include, at a State's discretion, at-risk infants and toddlers. (Office of Special Education and Rehabilitative Services [OSE/RS] 34 CFR 303.16, 2006)

The term "at-risk infant or toddler" means an individual under two years of age who would be at risk of experiencing a substantial developmental delay if early intervention services were not provided.

Children With Disabilities

The term "children with disabilities" means those children having mental retardation [intellectual disability]; a hearing impairment including deafness, speech, or language impairment; visual impairments including blindness; serious emotional disturbance; orthopedic impairments; autism; traumatic brain injury; another health impairment; a specific learning disability; deafblindness; or multiple disabilities—and who, because of these disabilities and differences, need special education and related services. The term "children with disabilities," for children aged three through nine, may, at a State's discretion, include children

1. who are experiencing developmental delays, as defined by the state and as measured by appropriate diagnostic instruments and procedures, in one or more of the following areas: physical development, cognitive development, communication development, social or emotional development, or adaptive development; and
2. who, for that reason, need special education and related services. (Office of Special Education and Rehabilitative Services [OSE/RS] 34 CFR 300, 2006)

The terms are defined as follows:

1. "Autism" means a developmental disability significantly affecting verbal and nonverbal communication and social interaction, generally evident before age three, that adversely affects a child's educational performance. Other characteristics often associated with autism are engagement in repetitive activities and stereotyped movements, resistance to environmental change or change in daily routines, and unusual responses to sensory experiences. The term does not apply if a child's educational performance is adversely affected primarily because the child has a serious emotional disturbance.

2. "Deafblindness" means concomitant hearing and visual impairments, the combination of which causes such severe communication and other developmental and educational needs that they cannot be accommodated in special education programs solely for children with deafness or children with blindness.

3. "Deafness" means a hearing impairment that is so severe that the child is impaired in processing linguistic information through hearing, with or without amplification, that adversely affects educational performance.

4. "Hearing impairment" means an impairment in hearing, whether permanent or fluctuating, that adversely affects a child's educational performance but that is not included under the definition of deafness.

5. "Mental retardation" [intellectual disability] means significantly subaverage general intellectual functioning existing concurrently with deficits in adaptive behavior and manifested during the developmental period that adversely affects a child's educational performance.

6. "Multiple disabilities" means concomitant impairments (such as mental retardation [intellectual disability] and blindness, or mental retardation [intellectual disability] and orthopedic impairment), the combination of which causes such severe educational problems that they cannot be accommodated in special education programs solely for one of the impairments. The term does not include deafblindness.

7. "Orthopedic impairment" means a severe orthopedic impairment that adversely affects a child's educational performance. The term includes impairments caused by congenital anomaly (e.g., clubfoot or absence of some member), impairments caused by disease (e.g., poliomyelitis or bone tuberculosis), and impairments from other causes (e.g., cerebral palsy, amputations, or fractures or burns that cause contractures).

8. "Other health impairment" means having limited strength, vitality, or alertness as a result of chronic or acute health problems, such as a heart condition, attention deficit disorder, attention deficit/hyperactivity disorder, rheumatic fever, nephritis, asthma, sickle cell anemia, hemophilia, epilepsy, lead poisoning, leukemia, or diabetes that adversely affects a child's educational performance.

9. "Serious emotional disturbance" is defined as follows:

   a. A condition exhibiting one or more of the following characteristics over a long period of time and to a marked degree that adversely affects a child's educational performance.
      i. An inability to learn that cannot be explained by intellectual, sensory, or health factors.
      ii. An inability to build or maintain satisfactory interpersonal relationships with peers and teachers.
      iii. Inappropriate types of behavior or feelings under normal circumstances.
      iv. A general pervasive mood of unhappiness or depression.
      v. A tendency to develop physical symptoms or fears associated with personal or school problems.
   b. The term includes schizophrenia. The term does not necessarily apply to children who are socially maladjusted, unless it is determined that they have a serious emotional disturbance.

10. "Specific learning disability" means a disorder in one or more of the basic psychological processes involved in understanding or in using language, spoken or written, that may manifest itself in an imperfect ability to listen, think, speak, read, write, spell, or do mathematical calculations. The term includes such conditions as perceptual disabilities, brain injury, minimal brain dysfunction, dyslexia, and developmental aphasia. The term does not apply to children who have learning problems that are primarily the result of visual, hearing, or motor disabilities, intellectual disability, emotional disturbance, or environmental, cultural, or economic disadvantage.

11. "Speech or language impairment" means a communication disorder such as stuttering, impaired articulation, or a voice impairment that adversely affects a child's educational performance.

12. "Traumatic brain injury" means an acquired injury to the brain caused by an external physical force, resulting in total or partial functional disability or psychosocial impairment (or both) that adversely affects a child's educational performance. The term applies to open or closed head injuries resulting in impairments in one or more areas, including cognition; language; memory; attention; reasoning; abstract thinking; judgment; problem solving; sensory, perceptual, and motor abilities; psychosocial behavior; physical functions; information processing; and speech. The term does not apply to brain injuries that are congenital or degenerative or to brain injuries induced by birth trauma.

13. "Visual impairment including blindness" means an impairment in vision that, even with correction, adversely affects a child's educational performance. The term includes both partial sight and blindness.

Appendix B

Adapted Physical Education and Sport Contact Information

Multisport Organizations

Adaptive Sports Center
Kelsey Wright Building
19 Emmons Rd.
Mt. Crested Butte, CO 81225
866-349-2296 (phone)
Email: info@adaptivesports.org
Website: www.adaptivesports.org

American Association of Adapted Sports Programs (AAASP)
P.O. Box 451047
Atlanta, GA 31145
404-294-0070 (phone)
Email: sports@adaptedsports.edu
Website: http://adaptedsports.org

BlazeSports America
1670 Oakbrook Drive, Suite 331
Norcross, GA 30093
404-270-2000 (phone)
Email: info@blazesports.org
Website: www.blazesports.org

Canadian Blind Sports Association (CBSA)
#175-5055 Joyce St.
Vancouver, BC V5R 6B2
Canada
604-419-0480 (phone)
Email: info@canadiansports.ca
Website: www.canadianblindsports.ca

Canadian Cerebral Palsy Sports Association (CCPSA)
c/o House of Sport
RH Centre
2451 Riverside Dr.
Ottawa, Ontario K1H 7X7
Canada
613-748-1430 (phone)
Email: info@ccpsa.ca
Website: www.ccpsa.ca

Canadian Deaf Sports Association (CDSA)
CP 41035, CSP Centre Duvernay
3100 Blvd., Concorde East
Laval, QC H7E 5H1
Canada
Email: info@assc-cdsa.com
Website: www.assc-cdsa.com

Dwarf Athletic Association of America (DAAA)
P.O. Box 2
Kentfield, CA 94914-0002
415-915-9572 (phone)
Email: info@daaa.org
Website: www.daaa.org

Move United
451 Hungerford Dr., Suite 608
Rockville, MD 20850
301-217-0960 (phone)
Email: info@moveunitedsport.org
Website: www.moveunitedsport.org

National Sports Center for the Disabled (NSCD)
1801 Mile High Stadium Circle, #1500
Denver, CO 80204
303-293-5448 (phone)
Email: info@nscd.org
Website: www.nscd.org

Special Olympics
1133 19th St., NW
Washington, DC 20036
202-628-3630 (phone)
Email: jteitler@specialolympics.org
Website: www.specialolympics.org

United States Association of Blind Athletes (USABA)
1 Olympic Plaza
Colorado Springs, CO 80909
719-866-3224 (phone)
Email: mlucas@usaba.org
Website: www.usaba.org

United States Olympic and Paralympic Committee (USOPC)
1 Olympic Plaza
Colorado Springs, CO 80909
719-632-5551 (phone)
Email: communications@usoc.org
Website: www.teamusa.org

USA Deaf Sports Federation (USADSF)
P.O. Box 22011
Santa Fe, NM 87502
Email: homeoffice@usadsf.org
Website: www.usdeafsports.org

Wheelchair Sports Federation
6454 82nd Street, Suite 2
Middle Village, NY 11379-2329
917-519-2622 (phone)
Email: info@wheelchairsportsfederation.org
Website: www.wheelchairsportsfederation.org

Unisport Organizations

Aquatics

American Canoe Association (ACA)
503 Sophia St., Ste. 100
Fredericksburg, VA 22401
540-907-4460 (phone)
Website: www.americancanoe.org

USA Swimming
1 Olympic Plaza
Colorado Springs, CO 80909
719-866-4578 (phone)
Website: www.usaswimming.org

USRowing
2 Wall St.
Princeton, NJ 08540
800-314-4769 (phone)
Email: members@usrowing.org
Website: www.usrowing.org

Baseball

Little League Baseball and Softball
539 US Route 15 Hwy
P.O. Box 3485
Williamsport, PA 17701-0485
570-326-1921 (phone)
Website: www.littleleague.org/play-little-league/challenger/

National Beep Baseball Association (NBBA)
866-400-4551 (phone)
Email: president@nbba.org
Website: www.nbba.org

Basketball

National Wheelchair Basketball Association (NWBA)
1130 Elkton St., Ste. A
Colorado Springs, CO 80907
719-266-4082 (phone)
Email: info@nwba.org
Website: www.nwba.org

Wheelchair Basketball Canada
6 Antares Dr., Phase 1, Unit 8
Ottawa, ON K2E 8A9
Canada
613-260-1296 (phone)
Email: info@wheelchairbasketball.ca
Website: www.wheelchairbasketball.ca

Golf

American Disabled Golfers Association (ADGA)
200 S. Indian River Dr., Suite 206
Fort Pierce, FL 34950
888-346-3290 (phone)
Email: info@usgtf.com
Website: www.usgtf.com

United States Disabled Golf Association (USDGA)
598 Dixie Rd.
Clinton, NC 28328
910-214-5983 (phone)
Email: info@usdga.net
Website: www.usdga.net

National Amputee Golf Association (NAGA)
901 10th St.
Plano, TX 75074
888-868-0992 (phone)
Website: www.nagagolf.org

National Alliance for Accessible Golf
11718 SE Federal Highway, #324
Hobe Sound, FL 33455
772-233-1970 (phone)
Email: info@accessgolf.org
Website: www.accessgolf.org

Hockey

USA Hockey (Sled Hockey)
1775 Bob Johnson Dr.
Colorado Springs, CO 80906
719-576-8724 (phone)
Email: usah@usahockey.org
Website: www.usahockey.com/sledhockey

U.S. Electric Wheelchair Hockey Association
U.S. EWHA PowerHockey
7216 39th Ave. N.
Minneapolis, MN 55427
763-535-4736 (phone)
Email: info@powerhockey.com
Website: www.powerhockey.com

Horsemanship

Professional Association of Therapeutic Horsemanship International (PATH International)
P.O. Box 33150
Denver, CO 80233
800-369-7433 (phone)
Email: abratt@pathintl.org
Website: www.pathintl.org

Quad Rugby

United States Quad Rugby Association (USQRA)
248-607-3425 (phone)
Website: www.quadrugby.com

Running

Achilles International
42 West 38th St., 4th Floor
New York, NY 10018
212-354-0300 (phone)
Email: info@achillesinternational.org
Website: www.achillesinternational.org

Scuba Diving

Handicapped Scuba Association International (HSA International)
1104 El Prado
San Clemente, CA 92672-4637
949-498-4540 (phone)
Website: www.hsascuba.com

Shooting

Adaptive Shooting
11250 Waples Mill Rd.
Fairfax, VA 22030
703-267-1450 (phone)
Email: adaptiveshooting@nrahq.org
Website: www.adaptiveshooting.nra.org

USA Paralympic Shooting
1 Olympic Plaza
Colorado Springs, CO 80909
719-866-4670 (phone)
Website: www.usashooting.org/about/paralympic shooting

Skating

Skating Association for the Blind and Handicapped (SABAH)
2607 Niagara St.
Buffalo, NY 14207
716-362-9600 (phone)
Email: sabah@aabahinc.org
Website: www.sabahinc.org

Skiing

Ski for Light, Inc.
1455 West Lake St.
Minneapolis, MN 55408
612-827-3232 (phone)
Website: www.sfl.org

Soccer

American Amputee Soccer Association (AASA)
Website: www.ampsoccer.org

International Paralympic Committee (IPC)
IPC Headquarters
Adenauerallee 212-214
53113 Bonn
Germany
+49 (228) 2097-200 (phone)
+49 (228) 2097-209 (fax)
Email: info@paralympic.org
Website: www.paralympic.org

Softball

National Wheelchair Softball Association (NWSA)
13414 Paul St.
Omaha, NE 68154
402-305-5020 (phone)
Email: bfroendt@cox.net
Website: www.wheelchairsoftball.org

Tennis

United States Tennis Association (USTA)
70 W. Red Oak Ln.
White Plains, NY 10604
914-696-7000 (phone)
Website (wheelchair): www.usta.com/en/home/play/adult-tennis/programs.html#/Wheelchair
Website (adapted): www.usta.com/en/home/about-usta/who-we-are/national/about-adaptive-tennis.html

Water Skiing

USA Water Ski
Adaptive Skiing
1251 Holy Cow Rd.
Polk City, FL 33868-8200
863-324-4341 (phone)
Email: satkinson@usawaterski.org
Website: www.usawaterski.org

International Organizations

Cerebral Palsy International Sports and Recreation Association (CPISRA)
+44 1586 550026 (phone)
Email: infor@cpisra.org
Website: www.cpisra.org

International Blind Sports Federation (IBSA)
Email: ibsa@ibsasport.org
Website: www.ibsasport.org

International Committee of Sports for the Deaf (ICSD)
Av. de Rhodanie 54
Lausanne
CH-1007
Switzerland
Email: office@ciss.org
Website: www.deaflympics.com

International Paralympic Committee (IPC) Sledge Hockey
Adenaverallee 212-214
53113 Bonn
Germany
+49-228-2097-200 (phone)
Email: info@WorldParaIceHockey.org
Website: www.paralympic.org/ice-hockey

International Quad Rugby Federation
779-323-9470 (phone)
Email: info@iqrf.com
Website: www.iqrf.com

Virtus: World Intellectual Impairment Sport
13 Alison Business Centre
39 Alison Crescent
Sheffield S2 1AS
Great Britain
+44 845 600 9890 (phone)
Email: enquiries@virtus.sport
Website: www.virtus.sport

International Tennis Federation (ITF)
Bank Lane
Roehampton
London SW15 5XZ
United Kingdom
+44 208 878 6464 (phone)
Email: wheelchair@itftennis.com
Website: www.itftennis.com

International Wheelchair & Amputee Sports Federation (IWASF)
IWAS HQ, Aylesbury College
Oxford Rd.
Aylesbury, Buckinghamshire HP21 8PD
United Kingdom
+44 (0) 1296 780212 (phone)
Email: office@iwasf.com
Website: www.iwasf.com

International Wheelchair Basketball Federation (IWBF)
c/o FIBA
5 Route Suisse
1295 Mies
Switzerland
41 22 545 00 00 (phone)
Email: info@iwbf.org
Website: www.iwbf.org

General and Other Online Resources

National Center on Health, Physical Activity and Disability (NCHPAD)
NCHPAD provides information and resources to enable people with disabilities to become as physically active as possible.
4000 Ridgeway Dr.
Birmingham, AL 35209
1-800-900-8086 (phone)
Email: email@nchpad.org
Website: www.nchpad.org

PE Central
PE Central provides up-to-date information on developmentally appropriate programs for school-aged children, including resources and lesson ideas for general and adapted physical education classes.
75 Mill St.
Colchester, CT 06415
687-764-2536 (phone)
Email: pec@pecentral.org
Website: www.pecentral.org

Physical and Health Education America
This organization provides information related to health, physical education, and adapted physical education, including links and suggestions for programming.
Email: pwvanmullem@lcsc.edu
Website: www.pheamerica.org

Appendix C

Brockport Physical Fitness Test

This appendix contains a brief description of the test items included in the Brockport Physical Fitness Test (BPFT), which provides tests and standards for youngsters with selected disabilities. The BPFT is modeled after, and can be used in conjunction with, FitnessGram. It has been adopted by the Presidential Youth Fitness Program (PYFP) as the assessment of choice for youth with disabilities, and many of the BPFT materials can be accessed through the PYFP website. The BPFT includes 26 test items, described here, but a test battery for a particular individual generally includes just four to six items. Online videos of each test are available in HK*Propel*. See the card at the front of the print book for your unique HK*Propel* access code. For ebook users, reference the HK*Propel* access code instructions on the page immediately following the book cover. Test selection guidelines are included in the test manual. For a full description of the test, please see Winnick and Short, *The Brockport Physical Fitness Test*, Human Kinetics, 2014.

Aerobic Functioning

- *PACER Test (20 meters and modified 15 meters).* At the sound of a tape-recorded beep, participants run from one line to another, either 20 meters or 15 meters away. They must arrive at the second line before the next beep (initially a nine-second interval). The time between beeps gradually decreases over the length of the test, so students find it increasingly difficult to keep up with the pace the longer the test goes on. The test score is the number of laps completed on pace (scoring stops when two consecutive beeps are missed; one trial is given).
- *Target Aerobic Movement Test.* Participants engage in any type of activity to elevate their heart rates into a target heart rate zone (70 to 85 percent of predicted maximum heart rate). They then attempt to maintain their elevated heart rates for 15 continuous minutes (one trial).
- *One-Mile Run-Walk.* Participants have one trial to complete a one-mile distance as quickly as possible.

Body Composition

- *Skinfold Measures.* Skinfold calipers are used to determine skinfold thickness to estimate body fat percentage. Measures are taken at one of the following site options: triceps (only), triceps plus calf, or triceps plus subscapular. Three measures are taken at each site, and the middle score serves as the criterion.
- *Body Mass Index.* Height and weight ratios are used to determine if individuals are overweight or underweight for their height.

Musculoskeletal Functioning

Muscular Strength and Endurance

- *Trunk Lift.* From a prone position with hands under thighs, participants attempt to lift their chins up to 12 inches (30.5 centimeters) from the mat by arching the back. Allow two trials and count the better score.
- *Dominant Grip Strength.* Participants squeeze a grip dynamometer as hard as possible with their preferred hand. Three trials are given; the middle score is the criterion.
- *Bench Press.* From a supine position on a bench, participants are given one attempt to repeatedly lift a 35-pound (15.8-kilogram) barbell from the chest to a straight-arm position above the chest. Boys are limited to 50 repetitions and girls to 30 repetitions.

- *Push-Up.* Initially, participants lie prone on a mat with hands placed under the shoulders (palms flat on the mat), elbows at 90 degrees, legs straight, and toes tucked. The participant then pushes up so that the arms (and back) are straight and the body weight is supported completely by the hands and toes. Participants perform one push-up every three seconds, attempting to complete as many as possible using proper form until they are unable to do so. One attempt (trial) is given to complete this test item.
- *Isometric Push-Up.* Participants are given one trial to hold the up position for the push-up for up to 40 seconds.
- *Seated Push-Up.* Participants who are wheelchair users (paraplegic) attempt to lift their buttocks and posterior thighs off the seats of their wheelchairs by pushing up from the armrests or tires of the chairs with their hands and arms. The push-up is held up to 20 seconds. An alternative is to lift the buttocks off a mat using seated push-up blocks. One trial is provided.
- *Dumbbell Press.* From a seated position, participants are given one attempt to repeatedly lift a 15-pound (6.8-kilogram) dumbbell from shoulder height to a straight-arm position directly above the shoulder. Participants are limited to 50 repetitions.
- *Reverse Curl.* Participants with quadriplegia are given one attempt to lift a 1-pound (0.45-kilogram) weight from lap level to shoulder level, using a pronated grip, primarily extending the wrist and flexing the elbow at least 45 degrees.
- *40-Meter Push-Walk.* Participants with certain mobility problems are given one attempt to cover at least 40 meters in 60 seconds while maintaining a low heart rate (i.e., 10-second heart rate is generally below 19 beats).
- *Wheelchair Ramp Test.* Participants in wheelchairs are given one try to negotiate a standard ANSI ramp (12 inches [30.5 cm] of run for every inch [2.5 cm] of rise) up to a maximum of 30 feet (9 meters).
- *Curl-Up.* Participants lie in a supine position with knees bent and feet flat on the mat; arms are straight at the side with palms down and fingers at the edge of a 4.5-inch-wide (11.4-centimeter) cardboard strip. Participants lift their upper backs off the mat until the fingers slide to the far edge of the strip and then return to the starting position, performing as many curl-ups as possible (up to 75) by doing one curl-up every 3 seconds. One trial is given.
- *Curl-Up (modified).* This test is identical to the curl-up, except participants place their hands on the top of their thighs and slide them to the kneecaps during the curl-up.
- *Flexed Arm Hang.* Using a pronated grip, participants grasp an overhead bar with elbows bent and chin above the bar and attempt to hold that position for as long as possible. One trial is given.
- *Extended Arm Hang.* Using a pronated grip, participants grasp an overhead bar with elbows straight and attempt to hold that position for up to 40 seconds. One trial is given.
- *Pull-Up.* Using a pronated grip, participants grasp an overhead bar with elbows straight and repeatedly lift the body with the arms until the chin is above the bar. Participants complete as many pull-ups as possible using proper form. One attempt (trial) at this test item is given.
- *Pull-Up (modified).* Using a special apparatus, participants lie in a supine position and grasp a bar an arm's length above their chests. Keeping heels on the ground and their backs straight, they pull their bodies toward the bar until the chin passes an elastic band placed 7 to 8 inches (18-20 centimeters) below the bar. Participants perform as many modified pull-ups using correct form as possible. One attempt (trial) is given to complete this test item.

Flexibility

- *Back-Saver Sit-and-Reach.* The participant places one foot against a sit-and-reach box with a straight leg while the other leg is bent at the knee with the foot flat on the floor. With one hand placed on top of the other, the participant attempts to reach as far across the top of the box as possible while maintaining the straight leg. One trial is given for each leg.
- *Shoulder Stretch.* Reaching the right hand over the right shoulder between the scapulae while the left hand is brought up the back from the waist by bending the elbow, participants attempt to touch the fingertips of their two hands behind their backs. The

test is then repeated with the opposite arms; do one trial each.

- *Apley Test (modified).* Participants attempt to touch three landmarks with one hand, in descending order of difficulty: superior angle of the opposite scapula, top of the head, and the mouth. The test is repeated with the opposite hand; one trial each is performed.
- *Thomas Test (modified).* Participants lie supine on a table and pull one knee to their chests while the tester evaluates the length of the opposite hip flexors by observing the extent of "lift" present in the opposite leg. The test is repeated with the other leg. One trial is performed on each leg.
- *Target Stretch Test.* In one attempt, participants demonstrate their maximum movement extent for a variety of single-joint actions (e.g., wrist extension, shoulder abduction, elbow extension, forearm supination), and testers estimate the extent of movement from pictorial criteria.

The Brockport Physical Fitness Test Manual

The Brockport Physical Fitness Test Manual: A Health-Related Assessment for Youngsters With Disabilities comes with an online resource with reproducible charts such as forms for collecting and interpreting individual test results, copies of the fitness zone tables, and materials for administering the Target Stretch Test as well as video clips that demonstrate assessment protocols for the tests. The text provides teachers with all the information and tools they need for assessing students with disabilities, evaluating their readiness for inclusion in general physical education classes, and generating and assessing IEPs. The text also supplies a glossary and many appendixes, including a body mass index chart, guidelines on purchasing and constructing unique testing supplies, conversion charts for body composition and PACER, data forms, and frequently asked questions. All materials are available from Human Kinetics at www.HumanKinetics.com.

Appendix D

WWW School District Rating Scale for Adapted Physical Education

Name of school: ______________________________

Address: ______________________________

Level: __________ Number of students enrolled in adapted physical education: __________

Principal: ______________________________

Director of physical education: ______________________________

Reviewed by: ______________________________ Date: __________

Introduction

The rating scale assists school personnel in evaluating and improving adapted physical education services.

When properly guided and developed, physical education becomes a vital part of a student's learning. It aids in the realization of those objectives concerned with the development of favorable self-image, creative expression, motor skills, physical fitness, knowledge, and understanding of human movement. To promote self-actualization, individuals need many opportunities to participate in well-conceived, well-taught learning experiences in physical education. To have the best program in place, the essentials of a high-quality physical education program need to be identified.

This rating scale helps schools evaluate their programs as related to adapted physical education.

Use and Interpretation of the Scores

The rating scale comprises a series of ratings on the major areas that should concern school personnel relative to adapted physical education. There are six sections to the rating scale: curriculum, required instruction, attendance, personnel, facilities, and administrative procedures.

The persons making the assessment should consider the criterion statement in terms of the degree of achievement that exists for the program. Criteria for all sections reflect concern for an optimal adapted physical education program. The rating score is on a scale from 0 to 4, 0 meaning inadequate achievement and 4 meaning fully achieved with excellence. Each section can be rated by the total section score, or a program overall rating can be obtained by totaling all sections of the scale.

A careful analysis should be made of each statement, section, and overall rating to determine the areas in need of improvement. The interpretation of the score for each statement is as follows:

0 **Inadequate:** Extremely limited

1 **Poor:** Exists but needs a great deal of improvement

2 **Fair:** Adequate but needs some improvement

3 **Good:** Well done and needs only periodic review

4 **Excellent:** Has achieved outstanding results

Rating Scale for Adapted Physical Education

	Inadequate (0)	Poor (1)	Fair (2)	Good (3)	Excellent (4)
SECTION I: CURRICULUM					
1. The goals and objectives of the school district plan for physical education include adapted physical education.					
2. Provision is explicitly made for adapted physical education in the school district physical education plan.					
3. The school district has a written definition of adapted physical education, which is in accord with state, federal, and professional laws, regulations, or practices.					
4. Adapted physical education designed to meet unique needs may include students with as well as students without disabilities.					
5. There exists a variety of activities to meet unique student needs.					
6. Instruction in adapted physical education is based upon a curriculum guide that includes adapted physical education content.					
7. Instruction for all students is distributed among the following areas in accord with their needs and abilities:					
a. Basic movement experiences					
b. Adventure and risk challenge activities					
c. Rhythm and dance					
d. Games and sports					
e. Gymnastics					
f. Outdoor education					
g. Motor movement skills					
h. Physical fitness					
i. Aquatics					
8. Appropriate literature and other resource materials regarding adapted physical education are made available to professional staff.					
9. Students with disabilities are provided equivalent opportunities in intramural, extramural, or extra-class activities.					
10. Guidelines pertaining to adapted physical education are evaluated at least every five years.					
11. There is a procedure for reporting student status and progress.					

	Inadequate (0)	Poor (1)	Fair (2)	Good (3)	Excellent (4)
SECTION I: CURRICULUM *(continued)*					
12. Student progress is continuously measured.					
13. Cumulative records pertaining to the physical education of each student are maintained.					
14. Indicators of performance related to program standards may be modified for students with unique needs.					
15. Transition programs for students with disabilities are considered with regard to the physical education curriculum.					
16. Accommodations are provided, as appropriate, to enhance participation in physical education.					
17. Activities within the curriculum may be adapted to enhance participation and success.					
18. The individual education program of a student with a disability may consider the individual's strengths as well as weaknesses.					
19. The school district plan includes criteria for eligibility for adapted physical education.					
SECTION II: REQUIRED INSTRUCTION					
1. All students not receiving general physical education have an adapted physical education program.					
2. No student is excused from physical activity or from physical education because of participation in extra-class programs unless approved by the school's adapted physical education committee (or similar committee) or approved in a student's individualized education program.					
3. Instruction in adapted physical education is conducted with a time allotment, which is in accord with state regulations and in a frequency and duration comparable to that for chronological-aged peers in the school district.					
4. Class periods are scheduled in time lengths that are appropriate to student needs and achievement of instructional objectives.					
5. Physical education instruction is made available to every student with a disability.					

(continued)

(continued)

	Inadequate (0)	Poor (1)	Fair (2)	Good (3)	Excellent (4)
SECTION III: ATTENDANCE					
1. Physical education is required of all students, ages 3-21, and adapted physical education is provided for those who exhibit unique physical education needs.					
2. All students with disabilities ages 0-2 and/or ages 3-5 will be provided physical education consistent with physical education offerings in the general program for students in their age groups.					
3. Students with disabilities ages 0-2 and/or ages 3-5 are provided physical education if they exhibit unique physical education needs.					
4. Credit is provided for adapted physical education in accord with general physical education credit.					
SECTION IV: PERSONNEL					
1. Instruction in adapted physical education for students ages 3-21 is provided by a certified physical education teacher.					
2. Adapted physical education for infants and toddlers is provided by an adapted physical educator.					
3. Physical educators teaching adapted physical education who have not completed at least 12 semester hours of formal higher education in adapted physical education have access to appropriate resource personnel.					
4. Extra-class activities are provided under the supervision of personnel meeting state requirements and approved by the board of education.					
5. Physical educators teaching adapted physical education for 50% or more of their teaching load have completed at least 12 semester hours of formal study in adapted physical education, have a concentration or certification in adapted physical education from an accredited college or university, have a state credential or endorsement in adapted physical education, or have APENS certification.					
6. Supervision and coordination of all phases of adapted physical education (instruction, intramurals, extra-class programs, interscholastic athletics) are provided by a director certified in physical education and administrative and supervisory services.					

	Inadequate (0)	Poor (1)	Fair (2)	Good (3)	Excellent (4)
SECTION IV: PERSONNEL *(continued)*					
7. Paraeducators are provided and prepared for instructional classes in physical education.					
8. The qualifications of paraeducators are in accord with appropriate state and/or local regulations.					
9. A physician delegated by a district submits to appropriate committees/personnel medical limitations and areas of the program in which a student may participate when medical reasons are given to limit participation.					
10. Adapted physical education teachers are involved in individualized education programming and placement decisions.					
11. Teachers of students requiring adapted physical education are involved in assessment, setting objectives and goals, and determining unique needs of those students.					
SECTION V: FACILITIES					
1. Students receiving adapted physical education have equal access to facilities required to provide equal opportunity for programmatic benefits.					
2. Indoor facilities for adapted physical education:					
a. Have adequate and clear activity space					
b. Provide a safe environment for activity					
c. Have appropriate flooring and satisfactory finish					
d. Have adequate lighting					
e. Have adequate acoustical treatment					
f. Have protective wall padding					
g. Have sufficient ceiling clearance					
h. Have adequate ventilation					
3. Equipment and supplies required for reasonable accommodations are provided.					

(continued)

(continued)

	Inadequate (0)	Poor (1)	Fair (2)	Good (3)	Excellent (4)
SECTION V: FACILITIES *(continued)*					
4. For students receiving adapted physical education, the dressing, showering, and drying areas include:					
a. Adequate space for peak load periods					
b. Floors constructed to facilitate ambulation and maintenance of safe and clean conditions					
c. Lockers of proper type and sufficient quantity					
d. Sufficient number of showerheads					
e. Adequate ventilation					
f. Adequate lighting					
g. Adequate heating					
h. Adequate benches, mirrors, and toilets					
i. Facilities that are clean, sanitary, and in operable condition					
5. The outdoor adapted physical education facilities are designed for effective instruction and safety. They are:					
a. Readily accessible					
b. Free from safety hazards (glass, holes, stones)					
c. Properly fenced or enclosed for safety and efficient usage					
d. Properly surfaced, graded, and drained					
e. Laid out and marked for a variety of activities					
f. Properly equipped (playground structures, backstops, physical fitness equipment, etc.)					
6. Qualified supervision of areas and facilities is provided during use.					
SECTION VI: ADMINISTRATIVE PROCEDURES					
1. Class sizes for adapted physical education are equitable to those specified for special education classroom teaching.					
2. Teaching loads for adapted physical educators are equitable to that of special educators.					
3. Adapted physical education teachers receive support staff on the same student–teacher ratio as special education teachers.					
4. Appropriate committees use qualified physical educators to assess physical education status for IEP development when unique physical education needs are suspected.					

	Inadequate (0)	Poor (1)	Fair (2)	Good (3)	Excellent (4)
SECTION VI: ADMINISTRATIVE PROCEDURES *(continued)*					
5. Students with disabilities participate in general physical education classes to the maximum extent appropriate.					
6. Students with disabilities are provided reasonable accommodations in physical education classes.					
7. Provisions are made for physical educators to refer to appropriate committees all students suspected of having unique physical education needs.					
8. The physical education teacher is involved with individualized program development of all students who participate in physical education outside of general physical education classes.					
9. Physical education is included in the IEP of every student with a disability.					
10. Students are referred to appropriate planning committees and receive adapted physical education on the basis of objective criteria.					
11. The physical education abilities of all students not participating in general physical education are assessed by a physical educator.					
12. Staff implementing adapted physical education are provided relevant in-service education on at least an annual basis.					
13. School districts provide placement settings, which permit personalized attention in the most appropriate environment.					
14. The annual budget request for adapted physical education is prepared on the basis of an inventory of program needs, including needs specified in individualized education programs.					
15. The adapted physical education budget includes state and federal monies earmarked for instruction and extracurricular activity of students with disabilities if they are receiving an adapted physical education program.					
16. A variety of up-to-date reference materials are provided for adapted physical education teachers.					
17. The school library contains materials on adapted physical education, which are sufficient and appropriate.					

(continued)

(continued)

	Inadequate (0)	Poor (1)	Fair (2)	Good (3)	Excellent (4)
SECTION VI: ADMINISTRATIVE PROCEDURES *(continued)*					
18. Budgets for instructional, intramural, extramural, and athletic programs for students with disabilities are equitable to those for students without disabilities.					
19. The school district plan includes provisions for general extra-class programs for qualified students with disabilities.					

From J.P. Winnick and D.L. Porretta, *Adapted Physical Education and Sport,* 7th ed. (Champaign, IL: Human Kinetics, 2022).

Author Index

Subject Index

Note: Page references followed by an italicized *f* or *t* indicate information contained in figures and tables, respectively.

About the Editors

Joseph P. Winnick, EdD, passed away in 2019. He was a distinguished service professor in the department of kinesiology, sport studies, and physical education at State University of New York at Brockport. He received his bachelor's degree from Ithaca College and his master's and doctoral degrees from Temple University. For more than 50 years, Winnick taught undergraduate and graduate courses in adapted physical education at Brockport in addition to developing and coordinating programs for adapted physical education. He also directed nationwide research projects related to the physical fitness of people with disabilities and was involved in the publication of the Brockport Physical Fitness Test and support materials.

Winnick had been president and a board member of the National Consortium for Physical Education for Individuals With Disabilities and a consultant for the U.S. Department of Education since 1969. He also served as a reviewer for several professional journals, had more than 70 publications to his credit, and was a member of SHAPE America. His previous editions of *Adapted Physical Education and Sport* have been translated into five languages.

David L. Porretta, PhD, is an emeritus professor at Ohio State University and has taught undergraduate and graduate courses in adapted physical education for over 35 years. He earned his BS from Niagara University, his MS from Ithaca College, and his PhD from Temple University. Porretta has numerous major scholarly publications and a continuous record of external funding. He has served as editor of, and on the editorial board of, *Adapted Physical Activity Quarterly* (APAQ). He is a fellow of the National Academy of Kinesiology, the International Federation of Adapted Physical Activity, and the Research Council of SHAPE America. Porretta is the recipient of the Julian U. Stein Lifetime Achievement Award from SHAPE America as well as the recipient of the Hollis Fait Scholarly Contribution Award and G. Lawrence Rarick Research Award, both from the National Consortium for Physical Education for Individuals with Disabilities (NCPEID). He also served as NCPEID's president. Porretta has been a contributing author to all previous editions of *Adapted Physical Education and Sport*. He enjoys golf, traveling, and attending Ohio State sporting events.

About the Contributors

Stamatis Agiovlasitis is a professor in the department of kinesiology at Mississippi State University, where he teaches courses in exercise physiology and adapted physical activity. Dr. Agiovlasitis is a past president of the North American Federation of Adapted Physical Activity. Dr. Agiovlasitis holds degrees from Queens College of the City University of New York and Oregon State University.

Lindsay Ball is a doctoral student studying adapted physical education at Old Dominion University. She is a 2014 Paralympian in alpine skiing and now marathon runner. Currently, she is the president of the board of directors of the Maine Organization for Blind Athletic and Leadership Education, as well as cofacilitator of the organization's summer and winter sports education camps. She is a researcher in adapted physical education, concentrating on individuals with visual impairments.

Melissa D. Bittner, PhD, is an assistant professor in the Department of Kinesiology at California State University, Long Beach. Her primary responsibility is to prepare university students to teach physical education to individuals with disabilities. She assists with the After School Adapted Physical-activity Program (ASAPP) and Camp Nugget, designed to offer positive physical activity experiences to children with disabilities from ages 5 to 12. Dr. Bittner's scholarly interest is primarily focused on physical activity evidence-based teaching practices and technology for children/youth with autism spectrum disorder (ASD).

Lauren K. Cavanaugh is an APE specialist in the Decatur Independent School District in Decatur, Texas. She is also an adjunct professor for Indiana Tech as well as the University of Nebraska–Kearney, specializing in APE and motor development. She earned her PhD from Texas Woman's University, Denton, Texas. Dr. Cavanaugh is a codirector and social skills curriculum coordinator for Camp WAVES, a surf camp for students with autism spectrum disorder in Texas.

Douglas H. Collier received his bachelor's and master's degrees, along with a diploma in special education, from McGill University and his doctorate from Indiana University. He is an associate professor in the department of kinesiology, sport studies, and physical education at State University of New York at Brockport, where he teaches undergraduate courses in motor behavior, pedagogy, and adapted physical education and graduate courses in adapted physical education. His research, presentations, and writing focus on positive and proactive approaches to behavior management and urban physical education.

Ronald W. Davis has been involved in disability and Paralympic sport for over 35 years. He has served as a coach, official, training camp administrator, and classification director for the 1996 Atlanta Paralympics. Dr. Davis has authored two textbooks to help coaches and general physical education teachers teach, coach, and prepare professionals to use adapted sports for improving quality of life, entitled *Inclusion Through Sports: A Guide to Enhancing Sport Experiences,* and *Teaching Disability Sport: A Guide for General Physical Educators* (2nd ed.), both published by Human Kinetics. Following two years at the University of Wisconsin-La Crosse and 20 years at Ball State University, Dr. Davis took a new position at Texas Woman's University (TWU) in Denton, TX. He completed his 14th year at TWU as a professor in Kinesiology with emphasis in adapted physical activity earning the rank of Professor Emeritus. His research and instructional interests center on sport for individuals with disabilities, with an emphasis on injured veterans. In 2014, Davis developed Project INVEST (Injured Veterans Engaging in Sport Together), which sponsored several community-based events such as Run-Bike-Roll and Battle of the Backboards. It also hosted the Southwest Military Wheelchair Basketball Conference Tournament, which included 15 teams from Texas, Oklahoma, and Arkansas. His research interests have focused on assessing bone mineral density of persons with spinal cord injury, improving self-efficacy and quality of life, and helping wounded veterans organize and lead community events and fun runs.

Manny Felix is a professor in the department of physical education and sport science at Winona

State University, where he teaches in the physical education teaching program and coordinates the developmental and adapted physical education program. He received his bachelor's degree from University of California at Davis, master's degree from Northern Illinois University, and PhD from Oregon State University. He has had more than 25 years of experience directing physical activity and health programs and preparing adapted physical education specialists through funding from the U.S. Department of Education Office of Special Education and Rehabilitation Services.

David L. Gallahue is dean emeritus of the School of Public Health at Indiana University at Bloomington. He holds degrees from Indiana University (BS), Purdue University (MS), and Temple University (EdD). He is the author of several textbooks, journal articles, and edited book chapters. Dr. Gallahue is a past president of the National Association for Sport and Physical Education (NASPE) and former chair of the Motor Development Academy and the Council on Physical Education for Children (COPEC).

Victoria L. Goosey-Tolfrey is a professor in applied disability sport at Loughborough University in the United Kingdom and is responsible for the directorship of the Peter Harrison Centre for Disability Sport. Her research focuses on the physiology and biomechanics of wheelchair sport. Dr. Goosey-Tolfrey is a fellow of the British Association of Sport and Exercise Sciences (BASES) and, as a reaccredited BASES sport scientist, has provided applied sport science support to Paralympic athletes since 1994. She is the recipient of the BASES Award for Good Practice in Applied Sport Science. Moreover, in 2017, Dr. Goosey-Tolfrey received the prestigious IPC Paralympic Scientific Award and was named one of Loughborough University's Inspirational Women in Sport.

Justin A. Haegele is an associate professor in the department of human movement sciences at Old Dominion University. He earned his bachelor's and master's degrees from State University of New York at Brockport, and his doctorate from Ohio State University in 2015. Broadly defined, Justin's research centers on examining how individuals with disabilities, mostly those with visual impairments, experience physical activity participation. This line of inquiry has included (1) exploring the meaning individuals with disabilities ascribe to their school-based physical education experiences, (2) examining determinants and outcomes of physical activity participation among adults with disabilities, and (3) utilizing nationally represented data to understand trends in physical activity and other health behaviors among those with various disabilities. He is the lead editor as well as editorial board member of a number of professional journals. In 2020, he received the National Consortium for Physical Education for Individuals with Disabilities (NCPEID) G. Lawrence Rarick Research Award.

Linda C. Hilgenbrinck is an APE specialist in the Denton Independent School District in Texas. She earned her PhD from Texas Woman's University, Denton, Texas. Dr. Hilgenbrinck was recognized for her teaching as the National Adapted Physical Education Teacher of the Year in 2012. In 2013, she was invited to NASA's Johnson Space Center in Houston, Texas, as a part of the Mission X: Train Like an Astronaut project. She was recognized as a Distinguished Alumni of 2015 by Texas Woman's University and received the Texas AHPERD Honor Award in 2019.

Cathy Houston-Wilson is a professor and the chair of the department of kinesiology, sport studies, and physical education at State University of New York at Brockport. Cathy holds numerous leadership roles on her campus, including College Senate president. Her research and writing focus on inclusion and fitness education for students with disabilities. Cathy is also active in numerous organizations that support and enhance the lives of individuals with disabilities.

Luke E. Kelly is a professor emeritus of kinesiology at the University of Virginia, where he directed the master's and doctoral programs in adapted physical education. He received his doctorate from Texas Woman's University and his bachelor's and master's degrees from State University of New York at Brockport. Dr. Kelly worked extensively with public schools to develop functional physical education curriculums based on the achievement-based curriculum (ABC) model. Dr. Kelly is a fellow in the National Academy of Kinesiology, a past president of the National Consortium for Physical Education for Individuals with Disabilities (NCPEID), and the director of a United States Department of Education (USDE) grant that created the Adapted Physical Education National Standards and the Adapted Physical Education National Standards Exam.

So-Yeun Kim is a professor at Ewha Womans University, Seoul, Korea, where she teaches undergraduate and graduate course work in exercise science and adapted physical activity. She earned her doctorate at Oregon State University. Her research focuses on accurate measurements of physical activity and health promotion for children with and without disabilities. She conducted interdisciplinary research projects to develop early childhood intervention programs to promote healthy behaviors in preschool-age children at risk for a developmental delay.

Francis M. Kozub has been a professor in the department of kinesiology, sport studies, and physical education at State University of New York at Brockport since 2008. Dr. Kozub received his PhD at Ohio State University in 1997. He earned bachelor's and master's degrees from State University of New York at Brockport in 1995 and 1996. Dr. Kozub taught and coached in the public schools of New York as a general and adapted physical educator from 1986 until 1994.

Byungmo Ku is an assistant professor in physical education and sports science at Nanyang Technological University. He holds degrees from University of Seoul (BS), University of Texas at Austin (MS), and Oregon State University (PhD). His research focuses on promoting motor behaviors and physical activity of children with disabilities within the context of family. More specifically, he has been investigating the effects of parents on the motor behaviors and physical activity of children with disabilities.

Barry W. Lavay is a professor emeritus in the department of kinesiology at California State University at Long Beach. From 1988 to 2020, his primary responsibility was to prepare university students to teach physical education to individuals with disabilities. He obtained his PhD in special physical education from the University of New Mexico in 1984. His scholarship includes the areas of positive behavior support, effective teaching practices, and students with disabilities. He has authored or coauthored over 15 textbooks, textbook chapters, and manuals and has published over 75 juried articles in over a dozen different physical education and special education journals. He is the first author of the coauthored text *Positive Behavior Management in Physical Activity Settings* (3rd ed.). He has given many scholarly presentations on the international, national, regional, and state levels and provided many in-service training seminars and workshops in APE on the state and local levels. In 2020, he received the SHAPE America Julian Stein Lifetime Achievement Award.

Lauren J. Lieberman is a distinguished service professor of adapted physical education at State University of New York at Brockport. She currently teaches undergraduate and graduate classes in adapted physical education. She is codirector of the Institute of Movement Studies for Individuals with Visual Impairments. She has taught physical education and aquatics at the Perkins School for the Blind in Watertown, Massachusetts, in the deafblind program. She received her PhD from Oregon State University in the movement studies in disabilities program. In addition to teaching, she runs Camp Abilities, an educational sport camp for children with visual impairments and deafblindness in various places around the United States and abroad. Most recently she was awarded a Global Fulbright Scholarship to start new Camp Abilities programs in Ghana, Ireland, and Brazil.

E. Michael Loovis received his PhD from Ohio State University in 1975. He is professor emeritus at Cleveland State University and recently completed a four-year tenure as interim chairperson of the Department of Health and Human Performance. He is a fellow of the International Federation of Adapted Physical Activity. He was a Fulbright Scholar in 2011, teaching and doing research at the University of Jyväskylä in Finland. He was the Mark R. Shibles Distinguished Visiting Professor at the University of Maine, Orono, in 2015. The development of fundamental motor skills and patterns in children with and without disabilities is a primary research interest. An equally important area of inquiry is the development of motor proficiency in children and youth with intellectual disabilities with and without Down syndrome.

David G. Lorenzi is a professor in the department of kinesiology, health, and sport science at Indiana University of Pennsylvania (IUP). At IUP, Dr. Lorenzi is the founder and director of the special needs activity program and has served as the coordinator for the undergraduate teacher education program. Dr. Lorenzi regularly teaches undergraduate and graduate courses in adapted physical activity, adapted physical education, motor learning, and aquatics. Dr. Lorenzi is a Certified Adapted Physical Educator (CAPE), a Professional Ski Instructors of America Adaptive Instructor Level I teacher, a Master Teacher of Adapted Aquatics, and a member of the Starfish Aquatics Institute (SAI) Adapted Aquatics Faculty and Adapted Aquatics Advisory Committee. Previously, Dr. Lorenzi has worked with Special Olympics in Georgia and Pennsylvania as a coach and management team member.

Barry S. Mason is a senior research associate at the Peter Harrison Centre for Disability Sport at Loughborough University. He earned his doctoral degree from Loughborough University in 2011. Dr. Mason has provided applied sport science support to Paralympic athletes since 2007 with research focused on ergonomic aspects of wheelchair sports performance.

Brock McMullen is an assistant professor in the exercise and sport science department at the University of Wisconsin-La Crosse. His primary professional work focuses on the preparation of PK-12 adapted physical education teachers. He received his bachelor's degree from UW-La Crosse and his master's degree and PhD from the University of Utah. He teaches undergraduate and graduate APE courses and has directed adapted physical education personnel development grants funded by the U.S. Department of Education Office of Special Education and Rehabilitation Services. He coordinates the UW-La Crosse APE teacher preparation programs and serves as director of the campus-based Center on Disability Health and Adapted Physical Activity, which offers numerous preservice teacher development opportunities through community-sponsored programs.

G. Monique Mokha is a certified athletic trainer who earned her PhD in biomechanics along with a related cognate in adapted physical education from Texas Woman's University. She has directed undergraduate programs in both exercise and sport Science and graduate programs in biomechanics. She has a long history of teaching across adapted physical education, athletic training, and sport science. She has taught both undergraduate and doctoral level students about providing sport health care for individuals with disabilities. Her scholarship includes the study of pathomechanics during sport skills for athletes with and without disabilities. She has served on executive boards for various organizations such as the National Council on Athletic Training within the National Association of Sport and Physical Education, the Biomechanics Interest Group within the American College of Sports Medicine, and the Research and Education Committee for the Southeast Athletic Trainers' Association. Dr. Mokha has authored several chapters in sports medicine textbooks aimed at teaching athletic trainers how to provide sports health care for athletes with disabilities.

John C. Ozmun is a professor of physical education in the health and human performance division at Indiana Wesleyan University. He holds degrees from Taylor University (BS) and Indiana University (MS, PED). He is the coauthor with David Gallahue and Jackie Goodway of *Understanding Motor Development: Infants, Children, Adolescents, Adults* (8th ed.), one of the most widely used motor development textbooks nationally and internationally. His scholarly focus relates to physical activity characteristics of young children with and without disabilities.

Amaury Samalot-Rivera received his bachelor's degree from the University of Puerto Rico at Mayaguez and his master's and doctorate from Ohio State University in sport and exercise education with a concentration in adapted physical education. He is an associate professor in the department of kinesiology, sport studies, and physical education at State University of New York at Brockport, where he teaches undergraduate courses in assessment, diversity, and adapted physical education, as well as graduate courses in curriculum design and research. His scholarship areas are the affective domain in physical education, strategies to teach diverse learners, and transition in adapted physical education.

Sue Sutherland is a professor of physical education teacher education and associate department chair in the department of human sciences at Ohio State University. She teaches undergraduate and graduate courses in adventure-based learning, social justice, disability sport, elementary physical education methods, qualitative research, and teaching in higher education. Sue received her bachelor's degree in physical education from Bedford College of Higher Education in the UK, her master's degree in physical education from Ohio University, and her doctoral degree in adapted physical activity from Ohio State University. Dr. Sutherland's research focuses on the use of social justice education in physical education and physical education teacher education, adventure-based learning in K-12 and higher education, and social and emotional learning.

Wesley J. Wilson is an assistant professor of special education at the University of Utah, where he directs the adapted physical education master's and doctoral programs. Dr. Wilson received his doctorate from the University of Virginia and his bachelor's and master's degrees from Purdue University and Oregon State University, respectively. He studies adapted physical educators' beliefs and behaviors toward inclusion, their experiences with special education law implementation, and their experiences in teacher education and the workplace. Dr. Wilson directs a United States Department of Education (USDE) grant to train adapted physical educators and the U-FIT service-learning program for youth with disabilities.

Lauriece L. Zittel is a professor in kinesiology and physical education at Northern Illinois University, where she teaches undergraduate and graduate-level course work in the area of adapted physical activity and motor development. She co-coordinates the master's degree in adapted physical education and established a certificate of graduate study in adapted physical education. She is coauthor of the second edition of *I CAN K-3* and the 12th edition of *Principles and Methods in Adapted Physical Education and Recreation*. She received her PhD from Oregon State University in movement studies in disability. Her writing and research focus on assessment, curriculum development, and environmental variables influencing the motor development of preschool-age children with developmental delays and those at risk for developmental delay.

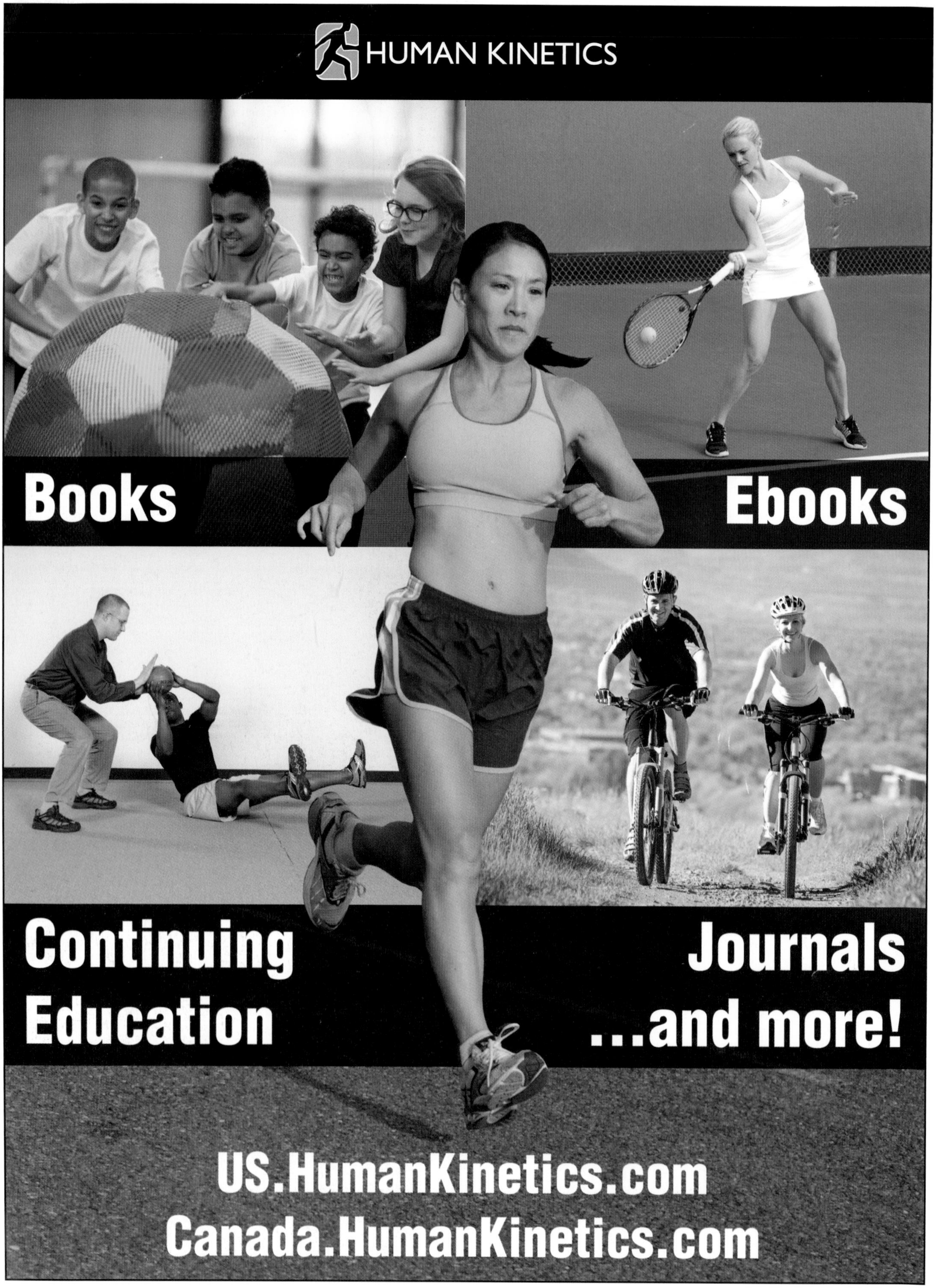